Third Edition
Revised

Employee
Benefits IN CANADA

**Third Edition
Revised**

Employee Benefits IN CANADA

*Editors and
Principal Contributors*

**RAYMOND KOSKIE

MARK ZIGLER

MURRAY GOLD

ROBERTO TOMASSINI**

International Foundation of Employee Benefit Plans

The opinions expressed in this book are those of the authors. The International Foundation of Employee Benefit Plans disclaims responsibility for views expressed and statements made in books published by the Foundation.

Copies of this book may be obtained from:
 Publications Department
 International Foundation of Employee Benefit Plans
 18700 West Bluemound Road
 P.O. Box 69
 Brookfield, Wisconsin 53008-0069
 (262) 786-6710, ext. 8240
 books@ifebp.org

Payment must accompany order.

Call (888) 334-3327, option 4, for price information.

Published in 2004 by the International Foundation of Employee Benefit Plans, Inc.
©2004 International Foundation of Employee Benefit Plans, Inc.
All rights reserved.
Library of Congress Catalog Card Number 03-109864
ISBN 0-89154-579-4
Printed in the United States of America

1M-8.03

Table of Contents

SECTION I—GENERAL PRINCIPLES

SECTION IV—PENSION AND RETIREMENT INCOME PLANS

SECTION V—PUBLIC SECTOR PENSION PLANS: JOINT GOVERNANCE

SECTION VI—DEFINED CONTRIBUTION EMPLOYEE-DIRECTED PENSION PLANS

SECTION VII—OTHER BENEFIT FUNDS

SECTION VIII—DELINQUENCY

SECTION IX—HUMAN RIGHTS ISSUES AND EMPLOYEE BENEFIT PLANS

SECTION X—A SELECTED EMPLOYEE BENEFITS GLOSSARY

Foreword

This is the second printing of the third edition of *Employee Benefits in Canada*. We are extremely pleased that many in the employee benefits industry and educators continue to find this work a valuable resource. We greatly appreciate the positive response and recognition received since the first printing in August 2000.

In the second printing, we have taken the opportunity to update parts of the book to reflect some important legislative and judicial developments. Unfortunately, things change quickly in the industry, and a more complete update will have to wait until the fourth edition. In particular, we have substantially revised and updated the chapters dealing with government-sponsored benefits, for which we wish to acknowledge and express our appreciation to Melanie Hess who was employed by Human Resources Development Canada. Ms. Hess took the time to thoroughly review these sections and offered extensive and helpful comments, many of which were adopted in the revisions. Unfortunately, we cannot seem to track her down these days to send her the Koskie Minsky yo-yo, which all contributors received in lieu of compensation.

Other revisions include the recent income tax changes applicable to pension benefits resulting from the federal 2003 budget and an update on the *Monsanto* pension case from Ontario, which deals with the controversial issue of surplus entitlement on the partial wind-up of a pension plan. The case continues to make its way through the courts and will soon be heard by the Supreme Court of Canada for a final disposition.

Of course, there have been many other legal and legislative changes since the first printing. However, because they affect so many parts of the book, in order to properly deal with them, it will be necessary to publish a new edition.

As we caution in the Introduction, parts of the text may have been subject to legislative or regulatory change or rendered obsolete due to case law development. While we believe the book continues to be a useful guide and educational tool, particularly for benefit fund trustees and administrators, it is not a substitute for proper advice.

We lastly wish to again acknowledge and extend our gratitude to the International Foundation, and in particular to Dee Birschel and Mary Jo Brzezinski for their continuing support and assistance.

The Editors

Toronto, Canada

Acknowledgments

The Third Edition of *Employee Benefits in Canada* draws largely on the work of the editors and principal contributors of the first two editions. As such, we wish to give special acknowledgment to two of the previous editors. **Guy Jobin** has now retired from the employee benefits field after a lengthy and distinguished career in the industry. We are grateful to Guy for his past contribution to this project and wish him the best in his retirement. The second is **Patrick Longhurst** of Watson Wyatt Worldwide. While Patrick was relieved of overall editing duties in this edition, he co-ordinated the research and writing of no less than 11 chapters. We are most appreciative of the work done by Patrick and his team at Watson Wyatt.

At Koskie Minsky, we wish to acknowledge the efforts and contributions of all our colleagues and our excellent support staff, without whom this book would not have been possible. Deserving of special mention for her extraordinary and dedicated effort is **Karen DeBortoli** who came to Koskie Minsky through the IFEBP I.F. Interns program. She served expertly as an assistant to the editors and a contributor, while juggling her responsibilities as an articling student with our firm.

We are most grateful to all the contributors to this book who took on the task of writing and rewriting chapters without compensation (Koskie Minsky yo-yos aside), despite their already heavy workloads and responsibilities. The quality of the materials is indicative of their dedication and enthusiasm for the employee benefits field. Also, we are pleased to include, for the first time, the identity of the author(s) with each chapter, along with their biographies, so that each contributor can receive individual acknowledgment for his or her work.

Once again, we owe a debt of gratitude (and probably a yo-yo) to **Mary Brennan** in particular, and all the staff of IFEBP for the ongoing support, guidance and patience.

Finally, the "benefit" of the Third Edition of *Employee Benefits in Canada* would not be available to our readers if not for the funding and other support of the IFEBP's Canadian and U.S. Boards of Directors.

The Editors

August 2000
Toronto, Canada

About the Editors

Raymond Koskie, Q.C., is a partner in the law firm of Koskie Minsky, Toronto, practising primarily in the field of domestic and international pensions and other employee benefits. He has been officer and chairman of the Labour Relations Subsection of the Ontario branch of the Canadian Bar Association, chairman of the board of directors of the Research and Resource Program for Prepaid Legal Services, and chairman of the Ontario branch of the Canadian Bar Association's Special Committee on Prepaid Legal Services. In addition, he was co-chairman of the Labour Relations Continuing Education Program for the Law Society of Upper Canada. Mr. Koskie earned his law degree from Osgoode Hall Law School in Toronto. He was a member of the National Council of the Canadian Bar Association and a member of the Advisory Committee of the Attorney General of Ontario on the Draft Construction Lien Act of Ontario. He was appointed by the Prime Minister of Canada as member of the Economic Council of Canada and served on the Council from 1986-1989. Mr. Koskie has been actively involved in IFEBP activities for the past 20 years. He is a past member of the IFEBP Attorneys Committee, currently serves as chair of the Canadian Government/Industry Relations Committee, and is a member of its Canadian Education and Educational Program Committees. Further, he was the first chairman of the IFEBP's Canadian CEBS Committee. He is a director of the Multi-Employer Benefit Plan Council of Canada and is presently the chair of its Government Relations Committee. Mr. Koskie has spoken on benefit and legal issues at numerous IFEBP conferences. He is presently the editor-in-chief of IFEBP's *Canadian Legal & Legislative Benefits Reporter,* and is an editor and principal contributor of the third edition of *Employee Benefits in Canada.*

Mark Zigler is head of Koskie Minsky's Pension and Employee Benefits Group. He advises trade unions, pension and benefit funds, plan administrators and groups of salaried employees and pensioners. Mr. Zigler has acted in many of the leading pension cases in Ontario. He led Koskie Minsky's team in a successful court action by seven former National Hockey League (NHL) players to obtain the return of more than $40 million in pension surpluses and interest. He has also appeared before the courts and Pension Commission to represent employee interests in cases involving Dominion Stores, Massey Ferguson, the Ontario Hospitals Association Pension Plan, Imperial Oil, Confederation Life and Molson Breweries. In addition, Mr. Zigler provides specialized counsel to trustees of pension funds. He is a member of the Pension Commission of Ontario Legal Advisory Committee, which advises the Commission's staff on proposed legislative and regulatory changes. Mr. Zigler is an editor and principal contributor to *Employee Benefits in Canada,* third edition. He is also editor of the IFEBP *Canadian Legal & Legislative Benefits Reporter* and is a frequent speaker.

Murray Gold is a partner at Koskie Minsky specializing in pension and employee benefits law. He provides specialized counsel in regard to public and broader public sector pension and benefits plans in Canada. Mr. Gold has been at the forefront of the advancement of multi-employer benefit plans for public sector employees. He has advised in regard to the development of jointly trusteed plans in Ontario, Manitoba, Saskatchewan, Alberta, and British Columbia and provides ongoing counsel to several of these plans, including the OPSEU Pension Trust. Mr. Gold chairs the Legal Advisory Committee to the Financial Services Commission of Ontario and is past chair of the Canadian Pension and Benefits Section of the Canadian Bar Association–Ontario, and the Canadian and Pensions Benefits Institute–Ontario Region. He is also a former director of the Employee Stock Ownership Plan Association of Canada. Currently, he is also a member of the editorial advisory board of *Benefits Canada*. Mr. Gold lectures regularly at the Pension Investment Management School, co-sponsored by the Schulich School of Business. He has lectured at the University of Toronto School of Continuing Education for the Certified Employee Benefit Specialist (CEBS) course and has spoken at numerous industry conferences sponsored by the Law Society of Upper Canada, Insight, the Canadian Institute, Infonex and IFEBP. Mr. Gold received an A.B. from Harvard University and an LL.B. from the University of Toronto.

Roberto Tomassini obtained his law degree from the University of Toronto. He worked as an associate lawyer in Pension and Benefits Department at Koskie Minsky advising and representing employees, unions, trustees and administrators on all aspects of benefit plan administration, as well as employment and labour law issues. He has represented pension plan members in hearings before the Financial Services Tribunal and in proceedings with the Superintendent of Financial Services. He served on Koskie Minksy's team in the successful court action by seven former National Hockey League (NHL) employees to obtain the return of more than $40 million in pension surpluses and interest from the NHL and the NHL Pension Society. Mr. Tomassini worked on the writing and editing of the third edition of *Employee Benefits in Canada*. He is a member of the Canadian Pension and Benefits Institute, IFEBP and the Canadian Bar Association—Pension and Employee Benefits Section. Mr. Tomassini is now a legal consultant and continues to provide legal advice to unions, plan administrators and trustees on pension and benefits issues. He also advises corporate clients on a variety of corporate, commercial and employment law matters.

About the Contributors

Frank Aiello, CIMA, is a specialist in Canada in the field of investment management consulting. He exclusively consults a limited number of clients, including pension plans, private families, institutions, corporations and international government agencies throughout Canada, the Caribbean, Asia and Latin America. Mr. Aiello joined ScotiaMcLeod in 1989 and has been awarded the J. Gordon Weir and Austin Taylor Awards in recognition for outstanding service to his clients. He is a standing member of Scotia McLeod's Presidents Counsel. Mr. Aiello, who holds a bachelor of arts degree from the University of Toronto, is a founding member of the Canadian Advisory Board of the Investment Management Consultants Association.

William D. Anderson is president of Benefits Counsel (Canada) Inc. Toronto, a division of the B.P.A. Consulting Group Limited. His accumulated experience over 25 years is specialized in trust fund management, member assistance programs and pre-retirement counselling. Mr. Anderson, who speaks frequently, holds an economics degree received with honours from the University of Western Ontario and has written frequently for IFEBP. He is a member of many pension and benefit organizations and is a founding member of the De Novo Drug and Alcohol Treatment Centre for the Building Trades in Ontario and of the Multi-Employer Benefit Plan Council of Canada, where he presently serves as president.

Michel Benoit is a partner with the firm Desjardins Ducharme Stein Monast in Montréal. He received his bachelor of arts degree from the University of Montréal and his bachelor of civil law degree from McGill University. He serves as lawyer and counsel to employers, pension funds and financial institutions. Mr. Benoit has been active in the employee benefits field for 23 years, and his experience and expertise lie in the areas of pension and employee benefits, trust law, corporate law and financing. He has lectured and written extensively. For the last five years he has been a member of the editorial board of *Pension Planning,* and he currently serves on the editorial board of *Estates, Trusts and Pensions Journal.*

Kent A. Botham, B.Math., C.A., is a senior manager at the Toronto North BDO Dunwoody LLP office. As a member of the Institute of Chartered Accountants of Ontario (ICAO), he has over 15 years experience in providing accounting, audit and related services to public, private and not-for-profit organizations with a primary focus on pension funds, benefit funds and unions.

Fiona Campbell obtained her LL.B. from Queen's University. Since 1990, she has practised primarily in the areas of human rights and employees benefits. She was with the law firm of Koskie Minsky in Toronto from 1990 until 1999, when she moved to Ottawa to join the law firm of Caroline Engelmann Gottheil. In 1992, during a leave of absence from her law firm, Ms. Campbell spent one year as counsel to the Ontario Human Rights Commission. She provides advice to employees, unions, pension and benefits plans and government organizations and has argued a variety of human rights and employee benefits cases before administrative tribunals and the courts. She has also spoken at a number of continuing education seminars on human rights and employee benefits-related topics.

Pui-Ying Chan is a senior vice president of the Segal Company, Ltd. and head of the firm's Toronto office. Her responsibilities include providing consulting services to many large multi-employer pension, health and welfare plans. Before joining the Segal Company, Ltd., Ms. Chan was employed with a major insurance company in the pension, group actuarial and systems departments. She received a B.S. in mathematics from the University of Guelph (Ontario).

Mary DaRosa is a law clerk with Koskie Minsky. She specializes in the area of disability benefits and assists union and non-union workers with workers' compensation, disability insurance and Canada Pension Plan matters. Ms. DaRosa has taken specialized training with the Ontario Federation of Labour. She is fluent in the Portuguese language and utilizes this skill in providing assistance to Koskie Minsky's labour, pension and benefits clientele.

Ron Davis was a member of the Koskie Minsky team in the successful court action by seven former National Hockey League (NHL) players to obtain the return of more than $40 million in pension surpluses and interest from the NHL and the NHL Pension Society. He has also represented pension plan members in hearings before the Financial Services Tribunal and in proceedings with the Superintendent of Financial Services. Mr. Davis provides advice to pension and benefit plan trustees and administrators as well as plan members and their unions. His previous experience as a business representative for a large construction union enables him to communicate easily with unions and their members concerning the issues that arise in pension and benefits plans.

Karen M. DeBortoli is a lawyer with Watson Wyatt's Canadian Research & Information Centre. She advises Watson Wyatt associates and clients on a wide range of pension and benefits, privacy and employment law matters, and also prepares internal and external articles, memoranda and submissions on a variety of topics. Prior to joining Watson Wyatt in January 2001, Karen worked with the law firm of Koskie Minsky, focusing primarily on pension and benefits law. Karen has a bachelor of arts degree in political science and English literature from the University of Toronto, and received her bachelor of laws degree from Dalhousie University in Halifax, Nova Scotia. She was called to the Ontario Bar in 2001.

George P. Dzuro practises corporate/commercial and securities law at Koskie Minsky. Mr. Dzuro has over 15 years of private practice legal experience acting for clients such as private companies and business entrepreneurs, charitable and professional organizations, pension and other employee benefit plans and funds, labour-sponsored venture funds and other pooled and mutual funds, trade unions, employee associations, and employee share ownership plans. He received his bachelor of commerce degree and a law degree at Windsor and has completed the Canadian Securities Course. Mr. Dzuro is a director and vice president of The ESOP Association (Canada).

Craig Flood practises with Koskie Minsky in the area of labour law, representing unions and workers in a wide variety of matters. He has developed a special expertise in the area of workers' compensation. Mr. Flood has represented clients in proceedings involving the acquisition and preservation of bargaining rights, unfair labour practice complaints, discipline and discharge, and grievances arising under collective agreements. He has appeared before a number of specialized tribunals. In addition, he has represented workers at all appeal levels of the workers' compensation system of Ontario. Mr. Flood writes and speaks frequently and is the current chair of the Administrative Law Section of the Canadian Bar Association – Ontario.

Judy Gerwing is a consultant with Watson Wyatt's Toronto office. Prior to joining Watson Wyatt, she was with Foster Higgins for eight years, where she was responsible for the firm's defined contribution practice. Ms. Gerwing provides advice on the design and implementation of defined contribution plans and the selection of trustee and recordkeeping services, and she reviews administration requirements and conducts employee communication seminars. She implements programs to test and monitor plan administration. Ms. Gerwing has extensive experience in plan conversions, helping clients and their employees move from defined benefit plans to new defined contribution plans.

Andrew J. Hatnay is an associate with Koskie Minsky's Pension and Employee Benefits Group, where he provides legal advice on all aspects of pension and benefit plans, executive supplemental retirement arrangements, employment and human rights issues, and a wide range of other human resource-related matters. His practice also includes representing clients at hearings before regulatory tribunals and the Ontario Superior Court of Justice. He has spoken on pension topics at numerous industry conferences. Mr. Hatnay has a B.Sc.from York, an LL.B. from Ottawa and an LL.M. from McGill.

Arleen Huggins' expertise lies in employment law, professional negligence claims, commercial, mortgage and real estate litigation. As a partner with Koskie Minsky, she has acted on behalf of both employers and employees. Her commercial, mortgage and real estate litigation practice includes the resolution of disputes as well as litigating at various court levels, with a particular emphasis on beneficial ownership interests. A member of the Canadian Association of Black Lawyers and a board member of the African Canadian Legal Clinic, Ms. Huggins has also worked with the Legal Education and Action Fund (LEAF) both as sub-committee member and co-counsel. She has co-authored various articles and papers in her areas of expertise.

Brian Jeffrey is the chairman of The Hub Group (Ontario) Inc. and is a fellow of the Insurance Institute of Canada and a registered insurance broker of Ontario. Mr. Jeffrey combines a focus on developing specialized new insurance products with other eclectic interests. He developed the "Trust Fund Protection Plan" and the "Labour Organization Protection Plan," two unique insurance products developed specifically for the Canadian marketplace.

Guy A. Jobin, who was a co-editor of the first and second editions of *Employee Benefits in Canada,* is retired. Prior to his retirement he was a principal and member of the executive committee of A. Foster Higgins & Co., Canada where he acted as a consultant to major corporations on strategic issues relating to employee benefit plan design, financing and administration. He is a past board member of the Canada Pension Conference and the Canadian Board and Canadian Government/Industry Relations Committee of IFEBP.

Ari N. Kaplan is an associate in Koskie Minsky's Pensions and Employee Benefits practice group. He provides advice on a wide variety of issues and represents clients before various levels of court and tribunals in pensions, benefits and individual employment matters. His clients include pension plan trustees and administrators, private and public sector trade unions, employee groups and individuals. He also specializes in workplace safety and insurance and other labour and employment-related matters, including employment standards, wrongful dismissal and grievance arbitration. Mr. Kaplan regularly contributes to legal publications related to his areas of expertise.

Daniel Kingwell is a student-at-law at the law firm of Koskie Minsky, working primarily in the areas of labour, employment, and pension and benefits law. He received his B.A. from Queen's University and his LL.B. from Osgoode Hall Law School. Mr. Kingwell has been a legal caseworker at Osgoode Hall's Community Legal Aid and Services Programme, appearing before a variety of administrative boards and tribunals, and at Parkdale Community Legal Services, representing tenants in court and organizing tenant associations. He has written numerous published articles and conference materials on current issues in employment law, including workers' compensation, human rights, and pension and benefits.

Peter Landry is vice president of Public Perspectives Inc. (PPI). Mr. Landry has extensive personal experience in the delivery of regulated training in the province of Ontario. He was the senior official responsible for regulated and unregulated apprenticeable occupations, and he led the development and maintenance of the legal and administrative framework to ensure delivery and certification of high-quality training. Mr. Landry has been a member of the Toronto Board of Trade's Education and Training Committee, which advises industry and governments on important policy matters. He has also served as a member of the Toronto Training Boards' Tax Disincentive and Fiscal Policy Working Group.

Gloria Lau is a business analyst, sales with Trimark Investment Management Inc. Her main tasks include building sales relationships with the head offices of the key accounts and disseminating investment and portfolio information to the sales department. Ms. Lau holds a B.Sc. (biology) from the University Western Ontario and an M.B.A. from Rochester Institute of Technology, Rochester, New York and is currently a CFA level II candidate.

Patrick Longhurst is a senior consulting actuary with Watson Wyatt in Toronto, with national responsibility for quality. He is a past chair of the Association of Canadian Pension Management (ACPM), co-author of *Your Pension* and was an editor and principal contributor for the second edition of *Employee Benefits in Canada*. Mr. Longhurst speaks frequently on pension issues.

Christopher May is a consultant with Public Perspectives Inc. (PPI). He has provided strategic advice in a variety of public policy areas including: education, health care, justice, labour, resource industries and economic development. As Canada's Employment Insurance program and labour market development activities have undergone dramatic changes, Mr. May has assisted clients to address the impact of these changes on their core business. He has also assisted clients in the development of innovative training and skills development proposals.

Michael Mazzuca is a partner in Koskie Minsky's Pensions and Employee Benefits Group, advising jointly trusteed pension plans, unions, plan administrators and non-unionized employee groups. Mr. Mazzuca has been involved in several cases involving pension surpluses and has represented clients before regulatory boards and the courts. His practice includes providing legal advice to pension plan administrators and boards of trustees concerning plan administration. In addition, he has experience in employment law, particularly wrongful dismissal actions and employment insurance issues and has represented clients in numerous administrative hearings. Mr. Mazzuca is an executive member of the Canadian Bar Association—Pension and Employee Benefits Section and a former member of the Ontario Council of the Canadian Pension and Benefits Institute.

Peter Miodonski is a senior library technician with Watson Wyatt's Canadian Research and Information Centre. As part of the library team, he provides information and research assistance to associates across Canada.

Peter O'Hara is an account manager with Prudent Benefits Administration Services Inc. and a consultant with Benchmark Decisions Ltd. Mr. O'Hara provides account management and consulting services to multi-employer benefit trust clients across Canada and has been doing so for over 13 years. He is currently working towards a CEBS designation and has contributed to past IFEBP publications. Mr. O'Hara served on two recent IFEBP educational planning committees and has spoken at, and moderated, a number of sessions at various IFEBP educational seminars and conferences.

Susan Philpott practises exclusively in Koskie Minsky's employee Pension and Benefits and Labour Groups. She has an extensive background representing trade unions, employees, retirees and pension funds from both the public and private sectors in all aspects of their labour relations and employee benefit needs. Ms. Philpott has appeared extensively before a wide variety of administrative tribunals including the Ontario Labour Relations Board, the Pension Commission, and public and private arbitration panels. She also appears in court, primarily on judicial review applications. Ms. Philpott is on the executive council of the Canadian Association of Labour Lawyers. She speaks and writes frequently.

Susan Rowland's practice centres on pension and benefits law and employment rights in insolvencies. She is also retained by actuaries to provide advice on their own and their clients' professional concerns. Ms. Rowland held several positions in the Ontario Ministry of Labour: counsel to the Employment Standards Branch; prosecutor of Occupational Health and Safety Act violations; Deputy Minister's designate, hearing discipline cases under the Public Service Act. In 1987, she served as head of the Legal Department at the Pension Commission of Ontario. Ms. Rowland regularly speaks to professional and lay groups and writes frequently.

Michael Sandell is a Chartered Financial Analyst and a founding principal of Lancaster Investment Counsel. His responsibilities include corporate management, fixed income investments and asset mix management. Mr. Sandell has 25 years' experience in all aspects of securities management, including bonds, mortgages, money market, active and passive strategies, and balanced fund asset mix decision making. He is a member of the Canadian Education Committee of IFEBP.

Leslie Steeves is a research lawyer with Watson Wyatt's Canadian Research and Information Centre. He is responsible for tracking, analyzing and reporting on legal developments affecting pensions and benefits to associates on a national basis.

Stephen Tatrallyay is a partner in Koskie Minsky's Civil Litigation Group. His practice includes all aspects of construction and real estate disputes. He represents trade unions, subcontractors, suppliers, general contractors, developers, mortgagees and owners. Mr. Tatrallyay also practises alternative dispute resolution as a cost-efficient and time-saving alternative to litigation. He is a founding fellow and a member of the executive of the Canadian College of Construction Lawyers and speaks frequently.

Catherine Vibien is now an associate in the Pensions and Employee Benefits Department of the United Kingdom law firm of Linklaters. Prior to joining Linklaters this year, she worked as an associate in the Pension and Benefits Department of Koskie Minsky, providing legal advice to plan administrators, employees and trustees. In addition to her knowledge of pension law, Ms. Vibien is experienced with freedom of information and protection of privacy rights, administrative, bankruptcy and insolvency laws, forensic accounting, taxation and contract law. She also worked as legal counsel with the Ministry General of Ontario at the Financial Services Commission of Ontario, where she provided advice on a wide variety of pension and broader government issues.

Sidney J. Wise, C.A., C.F.E., is a senior partner in the Toronto North office of BDO Dunwoody LLP, Chartered Accountants. His responsibilities relate to the servicing and supervision of the firm's extensive practice in the field of pension funds, health and welfare funds, local unions and other related funds. He is a member of the Institute of Chartered Accountants of Ontario (ICAO), has a Certified Fraud Examiner designation, and has over 30 years' related experience in both private and public sectors.

Introduction

When we updated the First Edition of *Employee Benefits in Canada* in 1995, we noted how dramatically this industry had changed since the first writing of the book (now almost a decade ago). Continuing changes and developments in the last five years prompted the writing of this Third Edition. During the early and mid-1990s we experienced almost unprecedented cutbacks in funding of government-sponsored and universal benefit plans. This eroded the social safety net that Canadians expect and rely on to fulfill a diverse range of needs, from health care to education and training. While government budgets and deficits are, relatively speaking, in good shape, there has been scant evidence of rebuilding these programs. As a result of the "off loading" of many benefit programs and the reduction in the size and availability of government-sponsored benefits, pressure continues to build on the private sector and the employee benefits industry to fill these gaps, particularly in the health care and retirement income security areas.

With increased reliance and expectations on private benefit plans, the complexity of these plans and the demands on their administrators and advisors continue to broaden. The book is primarily written for trustees, administrators, their staff and their advisors, who face the daunting task of ensuring the social and economic well-being of Canadian participants. As such, the book is primarily an easy reference guide for those in the industry entrusted with these responsibilities, and is modelled after a similar work published by IFEBP (the *Trustees Handbook*) for U.S. benefit fund trustees and administrators. The primer section is intended to provide the new trustee or industry practitioner with an overview of the issues that are discussed in detail throughout the book.

Pursuant to our commitment to keep our readers abreast of the latest developments and emerging issues in the industry, we have extensively updated the chapters as they appeared in the Second Edition and have added the following:

- A new chapter discussing trustee fiduciary liability insurance
- A chapter addressing member communication issues from a legal perspective.

Several new chapters dealing with some old and some emerging issues have been added to the pension benefits section. They include the following:

- The controversial issue of pension plan surplus
- Pension plan wind-ups and deficits
- A general guide to pension fund investments
- An in-depth exploration of the rights and obligations of pension funds as shareholders
- The issue of pension funds engaging in socially responsible or economically targeted investments
- Flexible benefit plans.

A new section has been added looking at public sector pension plans, with particular emphasis on jointly trusteed models. Another section has been added addressing the growth of employee-directed defined contribution plans and the liability issues faced by plan sponsors and consultants of these types of plans.

While every effort has been made to ensure the materials in the book are current, given the speed at which changes occur and new initiatives are introduced in the employee benefits area, some parts of the text, as you read it, may have been subject to legislative or regulatory change. Some parts of the book may become obsolete as legislation and case law develop in the upcoming months and years.

While the book provides a detailed guide for the benefit fund trustee or administrator, it is not a substitute for proper advice on any particular issue.

It has been a real pleasure bringing together the excellent contributors to this book who share our enthusiasm for the employee benefits field. We hope that you as the reader find the Third Edition to be a useful guide and educational tool.

August 2000
Toronto, Canada

Table of Contents
for
Introduction and Background of Employee Benefit Plans

Introduction and Background
of Employee Benefit Plans

1. GENERAL INTRODUCTION

In any society we would expect that a responsible individual would be prepared for most eventualities that may have a significant financial consequence. These eventualities might be of a catastrophic nature such as disability, severe illness or the death of a spouse. Alternatively, they may be events that can be anticipated with a fair degree of certainty, such as retirement or regular dental care. In general, we would expect that all of these eventualities will be met from one of three sources:

- ◆ Government programs
- ◆ Employee benefit plans
- ◆ Personal arrangements.

In this section we will briefly examine the main reasons why employee benefit plans have been introduced in Canada to meet these eventualities. We will then identify the major classes of existing programs. In the following section we will review how these programs interact with government-sponsored benefits.

Major reasons for providing employee benefit programs are discussed in Chapter 1. They include:

- ◆ The paternalism of employers—the concern that any employer will feel for the well-being of its employees
- ◆ Economics of scale—the extent to which benefits can be provided at a lower cost through "bulk purchase"
- ◆ Competitive pressures—the need to provide benefits as part of the compensation package in order to attract and retain key employees
- ◆ Income tax incentives—the extent to which it is

preferable to provide employee benefit programs rather than to pay direct compensation and to have employees purchase their own protection
- ◆ Collective bargaining and the role of unions—the use of the union's collective bargaining power to negotiate benefit programs
- ◆ Reinforcement of personnel policies—the need to provide particular benefits in order to make it easier to introduce certain corporate policies; for example, the use of a pension plan to reinforce an "open window" early retirement program.

As a result, the major types of programs that have emerged, and with which this primer will be concerned, include:

- ◆ Pension plans and savings plans
- ◆ Health and dental plans
- ◆ Short- and long-term disability plans
- ◆ Group life and accidental death and dismemberment plans
- ◆ Vacation pay trust funds
- ◆ Supplemental unemployment benefit funds
- ◆ Prepaid legal service plans
- ◆ Training and education plans
- ◆ Substance abuse funds.

2. HOW PRIVATE PLANS INTERACT WITH GOVERNMENT-SPONSORED PLANS

It was David Lloyd George who first said, "four specters haunt the poor—old age, accident, sickness and unemployment," but this statement is equally true today. It is not surprising that the major federal and provincial government programs are directed at meeting these needs.

Pensions are provided through a combination of:
- Canada/Quebec Pension Plan (C/QPP)
- Old Age Security (OAS)
- Guaranteed Income Supplement (GIS)
- Guaranteed Annual Income Supplement (GAINS).

Other needs are covered by:
- Workers' compensation (WC)
- Provincial health care
- Employment insurance (EI).

When designing an employee benefit plan, the sponsor will normally bear in mind the features of any government program providing parallel benefits. The two major reasons are to avoid duplication of coverage and to ensure that the two levels of plans combined meet the goals of the sponsor.

Duplication of coverage would result if a sponsor provided a health plan that included standard ward accommodation in a hospital. Since such coverage is already provided by provincial health care, this would clearly be poor plan design. However, it may be quite appropriate to provide semi-private or private accommodation and to thus complement the provincial program.

If a private pension plan provides benefits that are independent of the C/QPP, then the resulting combination will provide a higher level of income replacement in retirement for lower paid employees. If this is not the sponsor's intention, then an integrated plan design can be developed that will provide a level percentage of income replacement regardless of earnings level.

Many examples of the interaction of benefits exist:
- Long-term disability and C/QPP/WC
- Short-term disability and EI/WC
- Health and dental plans and provincial health care
- Supplementary unemployment benefits and EI.

3. THE GENERAL TAX SYSTEM PERTAINING TO EMPLOYEE BENEFITS

Tax legislation in Canada (both federal and provincial) plays an important role in the development and growth of employee benefits. Salary or earnings are taxed at both the federal and provincial levels. Employee benefits may be taxed in full, in part, or not at all.

In fact, the tax system impacts on employee benefits in the following ways.

Employer Contributions

- The question is whether or not they are a *deductible expense for the employer.* Most benefits are, in fact, deductible.
- The question is whether or not the *employer con-*

tributions create a taxable benefit to the employee. Often, they do not.

Employee Contributions

- The question is whether or not they are *tax-sheltered.* Retirement savings contributions generally are, while group insurance contributions are not.

Taxation of the Benefits Received

- The question is whether or not the amount received by the participant must be declared as taxable income.

Taxation of Investment Income

- The question is whether or not the interest or investment income generated by the funds accumulated to pay benefits is taxable. In many cases, investment income is excepted from income tax; in some cases it is fully exempted while, for retirement savings, it is only deferred.

Premium Taxes

- The question is whether or not the costs are subject to the provincial premium taxes that are generally levied on insurance premiums.

Sales Tax

- The question is whether or not the costs of insurance premiums or contributions to self-insured arrangements are subject to retail sales taxes, which are levied by some provinces (currently Ontario and Quebec only).

Tax Penalties

- The question is whether or not these are payable. Some penalties are payable, for example, if monies are not invested in accordance with the legislation.

The taxes payable vary significantly by benefit, and they also vary by province. Generally, the governments have increased the range of benefits that are taxed and the tax rate itself. However, many benefits still represent a very effective method of providing compensation to employees, notwithstanding the fact that the "benefit plan" may have a greater value than the cost itself, due to the protection and security it provides to employees.

Below we review a number of the traditional benefits provided to employees and consider the tax position that currently applies.

Group Life Insurance

- Employer premiums are fully deductible.
- Employee contributions are paid with "after tax income."
- Benefits paid are fully exempt from tax.
- Premiums include the provincial premium tax.

- The cost of insurance is taxed in the hands of employees by the federal and provincial governments.
- Provincial sales taxes apply in Ontario and Quebec.

Group Accidental Death and Dismemberment

- Employer premiums are deductible.
- Employee contributions are paid with "after tax income."
- Benefits paid are taxable as of 1994.
- The cost of this insurance, if paid by the employer, is not taxable in the hands of employees (except Quebec for provincial income tax).
- Provincial sales taxes apply in Ontario and Quebec.

Short-Term Disability (Self-Insured)

- Employer costs are fully deductible.
- Employees do not generally contribute to this type of plan.
- Benefits paid are subject to income tax, as salary.
- Provincial premium taxes do not apply.
- The cost of the benefit is not a taxable benefit per se for participants; only those who receive benefits will be taxed on the amount they receive, as salary or earnings.
- Provincial premium taxes do not apply.
- Provincial sales taxes do not apply in Ontario or Quebec.

Thus, the impact of taxation is neutral on this benefit.

Weekly Indemnity Benefit (Insured)

- Employer premiums are fully deductible.
- Employee contributions are paid with after tax income.
- Benefits are exempt from tax if fully paid by employee contributions. If paid by employer contributions in full, benefits are taxable in full.
- If the cost is shared, employees pay tax on benefits received, less the contributions made to the plan.
- Premiums include the provincial premium tax.
- The premiums are subject to provincial sales taxes in Ontario and Quebec.
- The cost of this insurance is not taxable in the hands of employees, when the employer pays the premiums. This also applies to Quebec employees.

Thus, the taxation of this benefit is neutral, if employer-paid. It is, however, an effective use of employee monies as benefits are not taxable if the cost is paid by the employee.

Long-Term Disability Benefits

- Employer premiums are fully deductible.
- Employee contributions are paid with after tax income.

- Benefits are exempt from tax if fully paid by employee contributions. If paid by employer contributions in full, benefits are taxable in full.
- If the cost is shared, employees pay tax on benefits received, less the contributions made to the plan.
- Premiums include the provincial premium tax.
- The premiums are subject to the retail sales tax in Ontario and Quebec.
- The cost of this insurance is not taxable in the hands of employees, when the employer pays the premiums. This also applies to Quebec employees.

Thus, the taxation of this benefit is neutral. It is, however, an effective use of employee monies as benefits are not taxable.

Health and Dental Benefits

- Employer premiums are fully deductible.
- Employee contributions are paid with after tax income (except to the extent that they can be used as part of the credit for tax purposes).
- Benefits paid are fully exempt from tax.
- Costs include the provincial premium tax, whether insured or uninsured, for Ontario and Quebec; only for insured plans elsewhere.
- The costs of this insurance are not taxable in the hands of employees (except Quebec for provincial income tax).

Thus, this benefit is very tax effective, except to a lesser degree in Quebec.

Registered Pension Plans

- Employer contributions or costs are fully deductible, up to *Income Tax Act* limits.
- Employee contributions are paid with pretax income as contributions are fully deductible from income for tax purposes (up to *Income Tax Act* limits).
- Benefits received in the form of an annuity at retirement or as a lump-sum in the event of termination or death are subject to income tax in the hands of the employee or beneficiary, except where deferred by a "tax-free rollover" or to the extent not offset by the $1,000 pension credit.
- Premium taxes and sales taxes on benefits do not apply.
- Investment income is fully sheltered from income tax.

This benefit is quite tax effective, and its effectiveness increases with the length of the accumulation.

Registered Retirement Savings Plans

- Employers cannot contribute directly, but they can increase an employee's earnings to allow the employee to make contributions.
- Employee contributions are fully deductible from

earnings, for tax purposes, up to *Income Tax Act* limits.

◆ Benefits paid are subject to tax when received, either as an annuity at retirement or in the form of a death benefit, except where taxes are deferred by a "tax-free rollover" or to the extent not offset by the $1,000 pension credit.

◆ Contributions are not subject to the provincial premium taxes nor to the provincial sales taxes.

◆ Investment income is fully sheltered from income tax, unless foreign content rules are exceeded.

As with registered pension plans, this arrangement is very tax effective, particularly for long periods of accumulation.

Deferred Profit-Sharing Plans

◆ Employer contributions are fully deductible, up to *Income Tax Act* limits.

◆ Employee contributions are not permitted for 1991 and subsequent years (nondeductible pre-1991 employee contributions are returned free of tax).

◆ Benefits paid are subject to income tax when received, either as an annuity at retirement or in the form of a death benefit, except where taxes are deferred by a "tax-free rollover" or to the extent not offset by the $1,000 pension credit.

◆ Provincial premium taxes and sales taxes do not apply.

◆ Investment income is fully sheltered from income tax, during the period of accumulation.

Now, looking at the historical development of tax legislation, it may be important to note that in the group insurance area:

◆ Health, dental and accidental death and dismemberment premiums were not taxable in the hands of employees until the Quebec 1993 budget, which contained proposals to tax the value of the employer-provided benefit from May 20, 1993.

◆ Premium taxes (4% Newfoundland, 2.35% Quebec, 3% Nova Scotia, 3.5% P.E.I. and 2% elsewhere) have historically been limited to insured group benefits (life, health, dental, disability, accident). Such taxes did not apply to self-insured or administrative services only (ASO) arrangements until 1992 in Quebec and 1993 in Ontario. The premium tax is now applicable to self-insured plans in Newfoundland, but has not been introduced in the other provinces, as of yet.

Thus, we find that group insurance has grown rapidly in the last 30 years. Many plans were designed to take full advantage of the tax legislation. For example, an employer-paid health and dental plan was more "tax efficient" than the corresponding cash compensation. However, with the introduction of provincial sales taxes in Ontario and Quebec, the (administration) cost has in-

creased, making the benefit less attractive. The introduction of the "taxable benefit" treatment in Quebec has taken the "tax advantage" away with respect to Quebec taxes. If the federal government and the other provinces were to follow suit, the design of plans would be greatly affected. The only reason for the continuation of a health and dental plan would be the financial security provided. One would expect that deductibles will be established, or increased if already in place. Reimbursement levels will decline from 100% or 90% to 80% or less so that group insurance costs would be reduced substantially.

Turning to registered pension plans, registered retirement savings plans and deferred profit-sharing plans, we find that legislation has had a significant impact. Until 1990, Revenue Canada had different rules for defined benefit plans (DBPs) and defined contribution plans (DCPs). The value of permissible benefits under DBPs was much higher than under DCPs. After many years of study—and several deferrals—the new legislation was passed on June 27, 1990, generally with effect from 1989. This law now attempts to equate the value of defined benefits to a contribution value. This relationship is represented by the pension adjustment (PA), which is calculated as follows:

◆ Annual Pension Benefit $\times$ 9 $-$ $600.

The formula says that a pension of $500 per year is worth $4,500. The $600 credit is the allowance for ancillary benefits that are not recognized by the formula. The PA for a DCP is the total of the contributions made by the employee and the employer.

In short, this legislation has made DCPs more attractive than before, and many employers have converted their DBPs to DCPs. Large employers with long-established DBPs will probably not convert these plans, although further enhancements will likely be of the DCP type.

4. WHAT ARE MULTI-EMPLOYER PLANS AND HOW DO THEY OPERATE?

Background: Collective Agreement, Employee and Employer Contributions

Multi-employer plans (MEPs) are typically established as a result of the collective bargaining process. They may apply to a specific industry group in a region or for a defined sector for the whole country. Generally speaking, the collective agreement will specify the rate of the contributions that will be made by participating employees and participating employers. The collective agreement may also specify in general terms the kinds of benefits that are to be provided. Also, the agreement typically calls for the establishment of a board of trustees that will be responsible for the overall administration of the multi-employer plan establishment in accordance with the collective agreement.

Once established, the MEP will exist and may continue to exist beyond the duration of the collective agreement. For example, a MEP covering a retirement pension plan will continue to exist to provide for the payment of benefits, even if the collective agreement ceases to exist and contributions to the plan cease. The board of trustees has the responsibility and duty to administer the plan and funds, until such time as the responsibilities of the plan have been fully met. For example, in the case of a retirement pension plan, this responsibility will continue until the last surviving pensioner has received his or her benefits or until the promised benefits have been purchased from an insurance company.

Structure and Design

Employee benefits are a form of compensation. Benefits are provided in lieu of direct cash earnings. The level of benefits provided reflects the needs of the participants, their willingness to receive benefits instead of direct cash compensation and the employer's ability to pay.

The employee benefit program, whether a MEP or a single employer plan, thus reflects an arrangement that meets the objectives of the employees and those of the employers.

The factors that make employee benefits more attractive than direct cash compensation include:

◆ *Advantages of group purchasing.* Benefits obtained through a group arrangement can be secured at a lower cost than on an individual basis. Also, some benefits are simply not available on an individual basis.

◆ *Financial security.* Benefits provide employees with financial security in the event of retirement, disability or where medical or dental expenses are incurred.

◆ *Tax effectiveness.* As reviewed in the previous section, some benefits are particularly tax effective, so that the same dollars spent on benefits have more impact for the employee on an after tax benefit than the same level of money spent on salary.

The type and level of benefits that will be provided under a MEP or in a single employer plan will depend on a host of factors, including the following:

◆ *Competitiveness.* That is, the level of benefits that is provided in the industry, by other comparable employers

◆ *Employee needs.* The level of benefits provided by the government and the change of this benefit either by increasing or reducing it has a direct impact on the need for benefits under a MEP or single employer plan.

◆ *Government benefits.* The level of benefits pro-

vided by the government and the change of this benefit either by increasing or reducing it has a direct impact on the need for benefits under a MEP or single employer plan.

◆ *Employer contributions.* The level of employer contributions and the ability of the employer or participating employers in a multi-employer situation to make contributions or to increase contributions is key to the determination of the level of benefits that may be provided. An employer that is in a fast-growing industry can probably more easily pass on increasing costs and can, therefore, more easily afford an increase in benefit cost structure. On the other hand, an employer in a declining industry with a large population of retired participants will be hit with the double impact of increasing costs and declining ability to raise contributions.

◆ *Employee contributions.* The willingness of employees to make contributions as a method of funding part of the benefits to be provided

◆ *Equity among participants.* Some benefits represent the accumulation of employees' funds at interest such as employee or employer contributions in a savings plan. This is fully equitable among participants. On the other hand, some plans are more in the nature of an insurance arrangement, and contributions from many participants or from the employer are used to provide benefits to a few only—for example, long-term disability benefits. The willingness of employees to receive benefits of one or the other type, their views with respect to equity compared to their need for insurance protection, is a key consideration.

◆ *Communications.* The ability of the MEP to communicate with employees to obtain their views and to provide details of plan options and benefits. The more complex the plan and the more options available, the more difficult the communication process. For example, a plan that provides a uniform level of $5,000 of life insurance to all participants prior to retirement and $1,000 after retirement would be very easy to communicate.

In summary, the plan that is accepted should reflect the best compromise between the position of employees and employers; it is a plan that will provide more satisfaction to all participants than any other plan or no plan at all.

Funding and Dealing With Surpluses/Deficits

In many employee benefit plans it will be necessary to accumulate assets over a period of time to meet the expected obligation for future benefit payments. This process is known as *funding.*

As an obvious example, an individual may join a pension plan at age 20 with an expectation of retiring over

40 years into the future. It would clearly be irresponsible to wait until retirement to start to contribute on this individual's behalf. Instead, an actuary will calculate the annual value of benefits being earned by the members of a pension plan (the current service cost), and this will be met by a combination of employer and employee contributions, as negotiated.

At the same time that the actuary calculates the required rate of contribution, he or she will also compare the value of all benefits (the liabilities) earned to date against the value of the investments (the assets) in the fund. If assets exceed liabilities there is a funding *surplus*; if liabilities exceed assets there is a funding *deficit*.

If there is a surplus, then the potential exists to improve benefits. However, the trustees should remember that the need for some margin of safety is important. If a deficit exists, then there are three possibilities available:

1. Ensuring that the negotiated rate of contribution is sufficient to pay both the current service cost and an additional contribution to eliminate the deficit over a period of years
2. Increasing contributions to meet this requirement
3. Reducing benefits in order to bring assets and liabilities back into balance. This is a very serious step and underlines the need for some conservatism in the funding process.

Similar considerations apply to programs such as long-term disability and postretirement life and health.

Administration, Auditing, Recordkeeping and Benefit Payments

Benefit administration is properly described as the business of employee benefits. The functions are the same whether the benefits provided are health and welfare, pension, vacation pay, supplementary unemployment benefits, education and training, or other types of plans.

The board of trustees retains the overall responsibility for the administration of the trust and plan. The board may retain an administrative agent to handle the day-to-day activities of the trust and plan.

Some of the functions of the administrator will include:

◆ Maintaining a database on participating employees and contributing employers
◆ Taking the necessary steps to ensure that contributions due are properly made to the fund
◆ Creating and modifying the rules relating to the administration of the trust
◆ Maintaining the trustees' documents
◆ Receiving and depositing all contributions to the trust fund
◆ Pursuing and collecting delinquent contributions

◆ Recording and receiving contributions and, where applicable, updating members' credits
◆ Receiving and verifying the acceptability of claims for benefits, as provided by the plan.

The administrator may also have the responsibility of keeping the individual records of all participants. Such files are key to the proper administration of the plan and will include all relevant information so that benefits can be paid quickly and accurately. Typically, all such records are computerized and provide the administrator with online access to the record of each individual participant to determine his or her eligibility for the benefits provided or claimed.

Similarly, benefit payments can be made by an insurance company or directly by the administrator, as the case may be. Some benefits may also be paid by an outside trustee, such as, for example, retirement benefits. In all cases, proper records have to be maintained by the party making the payments, and such information must be provided to the administrator regularly.

As far as the auditing process is concerned, this has to be performed to ensure that the plan is properly administered and that all aspects of the plan are respected. As a matter of common law, beneficiaries of the trust are entitled to an accounting of how trust monies are being spent. Thus, prudence dictates that trustees of any sizable trust fund engage the services of a firm of reputable chartered accountants to provide annual audits.

In addition, statutory requirements regarding pension plans may also require audits. For example, Section 76 of Ontario's Pension Benefit Regulations requires any fund with $3 million or more in assets to file an auditor's report annually.

The financial statement prepared by the auditor usually contains the following information:

◆ Description of the fund coverage
◆ Amount contributed by each employer
◆ Amounts contributed by members and the trade union, if any
◆ Statement of assets, specifying the total amount of each type of asset
◆ Statement of liabilities, receipts and disbursements
◆ Statement of salaries, fees and commission charged to the fund or plan, to whom they are paid and in what amount and for what purposes.

It should also be noted that the provisions of labour relations statutes, such as Section 93 of the Ontario *Labour Relations Act,* specify that audited financial statements are required for plans such as vacation pay funds, welfare funds or any pension fund for members of a unionized group and must be filed annually with the Minister of Labour. Notwithstanding these requirements, it is always good, prudent practice to have an auditor's report for plans covering a significant number of employees.

Plan Participant Communication

It is clear that if employee benefit plans exist but are not communicated to plan participants, then they are of very little value. A clear program of communication will acquaint the participant with:

- The rules of the plan
- The administrative procedures
- Any risks involved (for example, if the sponsor becomes bankrupt).

In some cases, minimum disclosure requirements will be established through legislation, for example, by the various provincial pension statutes. Otherwise, the level of communication is at the discretion of the trustees. Mechanisms for communicating benefit plan information to members include:

- Employee booklets
- Meetings of the participants
- Regular newsletters
- Personalized benefit statements
- Audio or video presentations
- Availability of documents for inspection
- Online benefit information.

Research has shown that the perception of the benefit programs provided is based more upon the communications received than on the actual quality of the programs. For this reason, the importance of communications must not be overlooked.

Investments

In plans that require prefunding, the assets that are accumulating must be invested. In some cases, the nature of the liabilities will suggest a certain type of investment. If the assets will be paid out in the current year, then short-term investments are indicated. If the liabilities are fixed, but not payable for some years, then bonds may be appropriate. If the liabilities are variable and long-term in nature, then a higher component of equities may be required.

Outside of these considerations, the normal rules of investment apply. The rate of investment return should be maximized subject to the level of risk that is acceptable. In some cases there are restrictions on certain types of investment, and the trustees are responsible for documenting the investment policies and goals.

5. TRUSTEES' DUTIES AND RESPONSIBILITIES

What Is a Trust and How Is It Established?

A trust is an arrangement under which one person or a group of people (the trustees) hold the property (the trust assets) for the benefit of others (the beneficiaries). The reason it is called a *trust* is that the trustee is trusted by the person who sets up the trust (the settlor) to ad-minister the trust assets for the benefit of the beneficiaries, rather than for the trustee's own benefit.

Employee benefit plans are one type of scheme that can usefully benefit by being set up as a trust. Of course, not all employee benefit schemes are set up as trusts. But there are many advantages to setting up a plan in this manner, especially in the case of MEPs, where there can be and often are many employers contributing. Further, because many people other than the plan member may have rights that are enforceable against the plan, a trust rather than a contract is often a useful vehicle to enable them to enforce these rights.

Except in certain circumstances, it is not necessary to establish a trust in writing. As a matter of practice, however, employee benefit trusts are always created by a written document known as a *trust agreement*. The trust agreement sets out such matters as:

- The number of trustees and their method of appointment
- The explicit powers conferred upon the trustees to administer the fund
- The responsibilities of the trustees and protection by way of indemnities for acts as trustees, provided all actions are in good faith
- Requirements for annual meetings, audits and periodic trustee meetings
- The basis for accepting contributions to the fund and delinquency procedures that may be available to the trustees, independent of the grievance procedures in the collective agreement
- Provisions for amendment and termination of the fund.

The trust agreement is just one of the documents detailing the manner in which an employee benefit plan operates. In their administration of a trust, benefit plan trustees and their professional advisors are also governed by the provisions of the plan text, the collective agreement and applicable legislation. This legislation may include pension benefits, trustees, labour relations and income tax legislation, among others. In addition, employee benefit trustees are, like all trustees, bound by common law standards of fiduciary conduct.

Fiduciary Responsibilities of Trustees Imposed by Statute or at Common Law

The role of a trustee gives rise to onerous responsibilities. Trustees stand in a *fiduciary* capacity to the beneficiaries of the trust and owe duties of care and prudence in the administration of a trust of a very high standard. The duty owed by a fiduciary really consists of four distinct duties:

- To act scrupulously for the benefit of the trust and never for himself or herself while carrying out his or her duties (*the conflict-of-interest rule*)
- To be active in carrying out those duties and per-

form them with complete integrity (*the standard-of-care rule*)

◆ To carry out those duties personally as a result of the trust and confidence reposed in him or her (*the no-delegation rule*)

◆ To act impartially between the beneficiaries unless the trust instrument authorizes favouritism (*the evenhanded rule*).

These duties apply to all trustees at common law, including employee benefit plan trustees. Breach of any of these duties can result in very serious liability.

Specific Duties of Trustees of Employee Benefit Trust Funds

In the case of pension plans, the common law fiduciary duties have been codified, in part at least, under many of the various provincial pension benefits statutes. Many of these statutes make it clear that other persons dealing with the pension fund, such as plan administrators and agents, will also be held to the standard of a fiduciary. Even where these statutes exist or where a different type of employee benefit fund is involved, the common law standards remain applicable to all employee benefit plan trustees.

In order to meet the challenge of being a fiduciary, the new trustee must, at a minimum, acquaint himself or herself with the terms of the trust, with the state of the trust property and with the contents of all documents affecting the trust property. At all times thereafter, the trustee must always be cognizant of his or her responsibilities as a fiduciary and act strictly in accordance with the terms of the trust. The following details some of the ongoing responsibilities of an employee benefit trustee.

Administering the Trust Fund and Communications

Employee benefit funds will have an administrator to deal with much of the day-to-day operation of the fund. It is the administrator who will likely have regular contact with the plan beneficiaries and who will be called upon to keep records of the day-to-day business of the fund. The administrative function can be performed by an independent person, firm or organization with whom the trustees contract (third-party administration) or by a person, organization or firm that is related, through ownership or other control, to the benefit trust (self-administration).

Since the administrator deals with the day-to-day business of the fund, many of the trustees' duties are actually performed by the administrator. The ultimate responsibility for the operation of the fund, however, remains with the trustees. This means that the trustees must always ensure that they have the right administrator doing the job. This in turn means that the trustees must be aware of:

◆ What an administrator does and does not do

◆ The kind of administration organization that should be employed

◆ The types and extent of the administrative functions to be delegated to the administrator

◆ The method, timing and quality expected in the delivery of the administrative functions

◆ The appropriate price to be paid for the administration service and the form the payment should take

◆ The procedure for assessing the acceptability of the ongoing administration work.

If, for example, there is a problem in communicating information related to the plan to its beneficiaries, the responsibility lies not only with the administrator but with the trustees themselves.

Collecting Employer Contributions

Contributions are the main source of income to a trust fund. Contributions to a multi-employer benefit plan are usually made by employers at the rate or amount set by the collective agreement. It is important to note that the contributions are made to the trust fund, not to the union. This means that it is the responsibility of the trustees to see that the trust receives the correct amounts at the correct time. This is one of the functions usually delegated to the administrator, but it still remains the ultimate responsibility of the trustees.

Collecting contributions can be a difficult task since there can be many small employers. Some employers may lack the sophisticated recordkeeping systems necessary to keep track of employee contributions as well as they ought to.

Trustees can help by providing as much information as possible to both employers and employees. Knowledgeable employers filling out their employer report form and knowledgeable employees who can understand their pay slips and employment records are the best insurance against incorrectly submitted contributions.

Investing Fund Assets

It is the responsibility of the trustees to invest the funds of the trust.

Trustees have four investment responsibilities:

1. To invest the funds according to legislative and trust agreement requirements
2. To establish a statement of investment policy and guidelines for the trust fund (the "Statement")
3. To decide whether an investment manager needs to be hired to meet the requirements of the Statement and, if so, to hire the manager
4. To periodically review both the Statement and the investment manager to ensure they are meeting the needs of the fund.

Investment Guidelines

Trust documents usually include wording that covers basic investment guidelines such as eligible investments. In the case of pension funds, pension benefits standards legislation details investment requirements. In the case of other employee benefit trusts, investments are governed by provincial trustee legislation.

Statement of Investment Policy and Guidelines

The Statement is crucial to a plan's successful investment strategy because it sets out clear guidelines for trustees, the investment manager and the investment consultant as to the background, operating procedures and goals of the trust. It expands greatly on the requirements detailed in the trust agreement. In some provinces, pension trusts are legally required to have a Statement. At a minimum, the Statement should cover the following.

Liability Structure

The fund should start off with the assumption that plan assets should be similar to plan liabilities in the way they are affected by economic events such as changes in interest rates, inflation and economic activity. For example, if a fall in interest rates will cause an increase in liabilities (as in a pension plan), then the plan's investments should be such that a fall in interest rates will also cause an increase in assets (such as long-term bonds).

Liquidity Requirements

A vacation pay trust needs to liquidate its assets at least once a year. Consequently, its investments need to be highly liquid, such as high-quality commercial paper. On the other hand, a growing pension trust may not need to liquidate any assets for many years. Consequently, its investments need little liquidity and can be in stocks, bonds and real estate.

Taxation

Although pension trusts are not taxable, many other trusts are, at least in theory, taxable. Investment strategy may change markedly depending on whether the trust pays taxes or not. The fund's auditors can best advise the trustees as to the fund's taxability. The investment counsellor can then devise an investment strategy to minimize those taxes.

Eligible Investments

The Statement should specifically mention what are eligible investments and, in some cases, what are not eligible investments. Eligible investments for a health and welfare trust are generally straightforward and might be Treasury Bills, bankers acceptances and commercial paper with a sufficiently high credit rating (perhaps at least R1 Low). Eligible investments for pension funds can be much more involved since pension funds can accept much higher risk investments and might include such diverse investments as small capitalization stocks, commercial real estate, Eurobonds and derivatives.

Benchmark

A benchmark is a very useful way of evaluating a fund's investment strategy and an investment counsellor's rate of return. A benchmark should reflect a normal or average portfolio. It should contain the entire range of eligible securities. A typical benchmark for a health and welfare trust is 30-day Canada Treasury bills. A typical pension fund benchmark might be 30% of the TSE 100 Index plus 15% of the S&P 500 Index plus 45% of the Scotia McLeod Bond Universe Index, plus 10% of 91-day Canada Treasury bills. The rate of return on the benchmark can then be compared to the actual return earned by the investment counsellor.

Investment Manager Responsibilities

If an investment manager is used, a clear listing of the manager's responsibilities should be part of the Statement. Responsibilities might include investing the portfolio within Statement guidelines, providing quarterly written reviews of activities and attendance at semiannual meetings.

Review Schedule

The trustees should set out a schedule for periodic reviews of the investment manager as well as the Statement itself. Although investment managers should be continually monitored, a formal review evaluating the manager's performance against preset objectives should be conducted at least annually. Likewise the Statement should be reviewed at least annually to confirm that it is still appropriate.

Investment Manager

Many trust funds hire an investment manager in order to help the fund meet its investment goals. Almost any investment, other than leaving small amounts in a bank account, requires a competent investment manager to earn a high income while reducing risk.

The following are some considerations when hiring an investment manager:

1. Obtain as much information as possible from at least three candidates. This information should include: history of company, number and size of similarly managed funds, investment philosophy

and style, experience, employee turnover, investment track record, reporting capabilities and fees.

2. Interview the candidates. Ask questions until you feel comfortable that the candidate understands your needs and can deliver your requirements. Do not allow the investment manager to use terminology you do not understand. If you do not trust the candidate, hire someone else.

3. Ask for references from other multi-employer trustees. Check the references.

Review

Investment needs can change. The Statement should be reviewed once a year. The investment manager should be reviewed at least once a year; however, some funds hold an investment review quarterly.

All three of these responsibilities may require the advice of a qualified investment advisor.

There are many advisors who specialize in multi-employer trusts. Again, ask other trustees for references.

Probably the best source of information on investing multi-employer trust funds comes from International Foundation conferences. Both the Annual Canadian Employee Benefits Conference and the Canadian Investments Institute offer several sessions covering investments.

Minimizing Expenses

Cost control is a difficult subject since it is very difficult to quantify what is a correct level of expenses. The question to ask of any expense is: Will this expense help meet the fund's stated objective? For example, sending a trustee to an IFEBP conference incurs an expense. However, the education gained from attending sessions and exchanging information with other trustees should result in considerably greater benefit being brought to the fund. Likewise, if a fund is having contribution delinquency problems, the financial benefit derived from setting up a delinquency committee could outweigh the cost incurred in chasing those delinquencies.

Liability for Breach of Trust

If trustees do anything that is wrong, it is called a *breach of trust.* Not only are they responsible for their own breaches of trust, they are liable for the breaches of trust committed by their fellow trustees.

Trustees may be indemnified and insured for their own negligence or actions undertaken in good faith under the provisions of a trust agreement. Trustees should therefore ensure that they have errors and omissions insurance to cover any losses that might result. There are limits to these insurance policies, however, and trustees remain personally exposed to a substantial amount of risk. It is clear, then, that those contemplating appointment as trustees of an employee benefit fund must be fully aware of the substantial obligations they may be acquiring as a result of such an appointment.

Conduct at Trustees Meetings

The trust agreement, the formal legal document that establishes the trust, will usually detail many matters dealing with how a trustees meeting will run. This will encompass such matters as the need for notice, the number required for a quorum, the manner in which voting will be conducted and the like. Trustees can prepare themselves for their first trustees meeting by familiarizing themselves with the trust agreement.

Many matters will not be detailed in the trust agreement. All the business conducted at a trustees meeting is very serious However, different boards will conduct their meetings with varying degrees of formality. New trustees can speak with more experienced trustees.

The Role of Professional Advisors

What They Do and Don't Do

Employee benefit plans can and usually do involve very complex matters with which the new trustee may have no prior experience. Trustees have an obligation to obtain and consider proper expert advice in areas where the trustees themselves are not expert. Typically, trustees will need to consult actuaries, accountants, lawyers and investment professionals. The *actuary* will perform pension plan costings and valuations, handle the related filings to government regulators, secure approvals from the government regulators and determine reserve requirements if health and welfare plans are self-funded. The *accountant* will prepare and file income tax returns and the special disclosure reports that flow from the trust fund audit. Both *investment* and *legal counsel* will be called upon to offer advice related to their respective areas of expertise.

Interaction With Trustees

While trustees are obliged to obtain and consider expert advice, they should not merely rubber-stamp it. That would be as bad as not taking the advice in the first place. This is because the trustees are still ultimately responsible for the actions of the trust even where they are relying on professional advice.

Trustees must therefore exercise the appropriate care and attention in selecting professional advisors. Even when this is done initially, each individual piece of advice must also be considered and scrutinized in just as careful a manner.

6. THE NEW TRUSTEE: WHAT TO DO FIRST?

Acting as a trustee of an employee benefit plan trust is an onerous task that should not be taken lightly.

Trustees are typically required to handle the day-to-day administration of the fund, ensure contributions are made, oversee the investment of fund assets, appoint and supervise agents and employees to carry out the trust funds responsibilities, and comply with legal requirements. Moreover, they are required to do all these tasks with a degree of competence and diligence so as not to run astray of fiduciary standards imposed upon them by the common law and applicable statutes.

In an attempt to assist trustees of various employee benefit plans, several benefit professionals have prepared checklists to guide trustees in the performance of their responsibilities. We have distilled from these sources a summary checklist for the new trustee and recommend the trustees consult the original sources for a more complete checklist.[1]

Checklist

Trustees should obtain a copy of the following documents:
- ✔ The trust agreement with all amendments
- ✔ Plan documents with all amendments
- ✔ Collective agreements where applicable
- ✔ Employee booklets that summarize the plan provisions
- ✔ Investment guidelines for investing the trust assets where they exist
- ✔ Trustee meeting minutes for at least the last two years
- ✔ Trustee insurance policies and fidelity bonds
- ✔ A copy of periodic benefit statements, if any, sent to plan members.

Reports That Should Be Obtained

Trustees should obtain a list of all of the plan's professional advisors and the organizations that provide services to the trust. Any reports submitted by each of these advisors should be reviewed. The reports include the following:
- ✔ Actuarial reports
- ✔ Auditors reports
- ✔ Reports from an investment manager, preferably covering the past quarter, year and five-year period
- ✔ Reports from the investment monitor if the plan has one
- ✔ The financial report(s) from the plan administrator covering the past reporting period, the plan year to date and the past plan year
- ✔ The custodian's report where a custodial trustee, bank or insurance company is used, for the most current reporting period
- ✔ A copy of the pension plan's enrolment card and/or application form
- ✔ Advisory memos or opinions from the plan's legal

counsel submitted to the trustees over the past three years.

In addition to the above reports, the trustees of a health and welfare fund should also obtain the following:
- ✔ If the plan is fully insured, a copy of the insurance contract(s)
- ✔ If the plan is fully insured, the insurance broker's or insurance advisor's report on how the carrier contract was negotiated for the current plan year
- ✔ If the plan is self-funded, copies of the insurance contract with the insurance carriers that provide stop-loss coverage
- ✔ If the plan is self-insured, a copy of the report from the professional who advises the trustees on underwriting
- ✔ The summary or report(s) on claims experience from the insurance broker or claims paying organization
- ✔ The report(s) should cover the most recent quarter, the plan or contract year to date and the past plan year.
- ✔ Any reports from any of the professional advisors to the trustees that pertain to retiree medical coverage
- ✔ The report on participant eligibility for the most recent reporting period. This may include hours of eligibility, vacation and holiday eligibility, hours banked, etc.

As individual trustees do not normally have all the expertise necessary to perform the responsibilities of the office, consulting with professional advisors is essential for carrying out the trustees' tasks competently. Therefore, in addition to obtaining the reports from professional advisors as discussed in the above checklist, the new trustee should also meet with each of the plan's professional advisors to become familiar with the role each advisor plays and have the advisor's report explained where necessary.

The new trustee should review the trust documents with both the plan's legal counsel and the administrator. The trustees should discuss the following points:
- ✔ The purpose of the trust
- ✔ The duties and powers of the trustees
- ✔ Procedures for conducting trust meetings; who can call meetings; what are the voting and quorum requirements; who keeps minutes; number of required meetings per year
- ✔ The powers and limitations of the trustees to delegate responsibility and the trustees' duty to monitor the performance of the person to whom function is delegated
- ✔ Limitation on liability for the trustees and provisions that protect the trustees
- ✔ The payment of costs and expenses

- ✔ The use of plan assets for legal assistance and educational expenses of the trustees
- ✔ The dispute resolution procedures for the trust and how they are applied
- ✔ The network that is used to communicate with participants
- ✔ Review the report(s) that each respective plan advisor has provided
- ✔ New trustees should ask the advisor to explain the scope of the service that the advisor provides to the trust. The trustee should also enquire as to the advisor's experience and qualifications.
- ✔ The new trustee should ask the advisor to discuss the reports he or she has prepared.
- ✔ The new trustee should identify problems or concerns that he or she has about the trust and what corrective steps are recommended.
- ✔ The trustee should ask the advisor to identify the strong points and positive aspects about the trust and the steps necessary to ensure these continue.
- ✔ The trustee should ask the advisor to explain what he or she needs from the trustees or other professional advisors to make the trust more efficient.
- ✔ The new trustee should ask the advisor to point out the procedures, rules or policies that are unique to this trust.
- ✔ The new trustee should discuss cost escalation trends with all the advisors, and in particular with respect to a health and welfare plan.
- ✔ The new trustee should inquire as to how the trust's experience compares with the norm.
- ✔ The trustee should ask the advisor what cost-containment procedures have been initiated and whether they are effective.
- ✔ If the plan provides retiree coverage, the trustee should ascertain what effect that coverage is having on the plan.
- ✔ The trustee should ask what cost-containment procedures the advisors recommend and the reasons for their recommendations.

The day-to-day operations of the plan are usually governed by well-defined administrative procedures. The plan administrator is charged with the responsibility to oversee these day-to-day operations. The new trustee should become familiar with the administrative procedures for the plan.

When meeting with the administrator, the new trustee should raise the following issues with regard to administrative procedures used to collect employer contributions:

- ✔ When does the administrator send out the billings to employers?
- ✔ A typical billing, including the employer census report form, should be reviewed.
- ✔ The new trustee should understand what information the employer must complete on such a form.
- ✔ If codes are used on these forms, the new trustee should be apprised of their significance.
- ✔ When are the form and payment due back to the administrator?

The new trustee should also become familiar with the administrative procedures upon receipt of the employer's contributions. The following items should be discussed:

- ✔ Who receives the contribution?
- ✔ How is the money deposited and when does interest start accruing?
- ✔ How is the employer's report processed?
- ✔ How long does it take to process the report?

With regard to the delinquency procedure, the new trustees need to be aware of the remedies available to them when employer participants do not comply with the terms of the trust. The following issues should be addressed:

- ✔ What happens when an employer is late or does not make the payment?
- ✔ Who processes the delinquency and what are the steps?
- ✔ When does legal counsel get involved?
- ✔ What happens to participant eligibility in a delinquency situation?
- ✔ What are the penalties? Who determines the penalties? Are the penalties ever waived?
- ✔ How are trustees kept informed of delinquency matters?
- ✔ Is the local union informed? Can the local union take action under the applicable collective agreement?

With regard to other plan income, the new trustee should address these issues:

- ✔ Does the plan receive income from sources other than employer contributions (i.e., investment income, employee contributions, etc.)?
- ✔ How is the additional income received and reported?

With regard to participant eligibility, the new trustee needs to know:

- ✔ How is participant eligibility determined? Are there different types of eligibility? What are the eligibility requirements?
- ✔ Is there a lag month(s) system and, if so, how does it work?
- ✔ How does the participant know if he or she is eligible?
- ✔ Is there an hours bank or other continued eligibility system and, if so, how does it work?
- ✔ What happens when a participant's eligibility ends? How are the participants notified?
- ✔ Are there coverage continuation and self-pay

procedures for employees and dependants who lose their eligibility? If so, how does this procedure work?

✔ How is participant eligibility reported to the trustees?

The new trustee should also review the plan's participation statistics for the past month, quarter and year. The following information should be considered:

✔ The number of participants in each coverage category

✔ If applicable, the number of active employees reported compared to the number actually eligible

✔ For a pension plan, the number of participants who meet the minimum service of requirements for vesting each year and the number who do not

✔ For a pension plan, the average number of retirees each month in each retirement category and the average benefit for retirees

✔ The statistical data on hour banks or continued eligibility system.

The new trustee must also immediately become familiar with the plan's expenses.

✔ What are the typical expenses of the plan?

✔ The new trustee should review the plan's expenses for the past several months.

✔ How are expenses paid? Is it necessary for the trustee to approve payment of bills and expenses? If so, by whom and when and what is the procedure?

The new trustee must also become immediately aware of the assets in the benefit plan and the sources for paying out the benefits under the plan. For a pension plan the trustee needs to know the following:

✔ What resources are used to pay pension benefits and plan expenses?

✔ If contribution cash flow exceeds benefit and expense payments, how are the excess contributions allocated to the investment managers?

✔ If contribution cash flow is less than benefit and expense payments, what plan assets are used to pay the shortfall?

✔ What are the investment guidelines for the plan assets? Who establishes the guidelines? Who makes the investment decisions? How is the investment performance monitored?

✔ What has been the investment performance for the past quarter, year and three-year period?

✔ Who monitors the investment counsellors' transaction fees? How are they accounted for?

✔ How is investment return accounted for? Who is responsible for payment of interest and dividends? Who suffers the loss for late dividend or interest payments?

✔ For a defined contribution pension plan, how is investment return posted to the individual's account? How often? What is done upon retirement to close the individual's account?

For a health and welfare plan, the trustee is concerned with the following additional issues regarding the plan's assets:

✔ What type of reserve account(s) does the plan have?

✔ What is the purpose of each reserve account?

✔ How is the amount of the reserve determined?

✔ What is the current amount in each reserve account?

✔ If a payment is made out of a reserve, how are funds replaced?

✔ What are the investment guidelines for the reserves? Who establishes the guidelines? Who makes the investment decisions? Who monitors investment performance? What is the history of investment performance? Who suffers the loss for late dividend payments?

✔ If contribution cash flow does not meet the expenses, what funding source is used to make up the shortfall?

The new trustee should become familiar with the procedure for applying for and obtaining benefits pursuant to the plan. Normally a professional is responsible for the payment of benefits, and the trustee should meet with such professional and discuss the following issues:

✔ The enrolment process

✔ How are the enrolment cards distributed to new plan participants? Who is responsible?

✔ How is the completed enrolment card returned to the administrator?

✔ What does the administrator do with the completed enrolment card?

✔ What are the checks to assure the accuracy of the data on the enrolment card?

✔ What is done to verify that the dependants claimed are really dependants?

✔ What do the checks do to eliminate benefit fraud?

✔ What are the strengths and weaknesses of the enrolment process and what can be done to improve it?

With regard to benefit application, the new trustee needs to know:

✔ What does the participant have to do to apply for benefits?

✔ Are there any conditions or limitations?

✔ What happens if the participant does not follow the proper application procedure? Are there penalties?

✔ For pension benefits, what documents must a participant submit in addition to the application form?

✔ For health and welfare benefits, how long after receiving treatment may a participant submit a claim and have it paid?

✔ For life insurance benefits, what documents have to be filed?

With regard to benefit payment, the new trustee needs to know:

✔ For the health and welfare plan, who receives the payment? Is it the participant or the provider? How is the participant informed if the payment is made directly to the provider?

✔ For pension benefits, what are the benefit payment options and how does the participant select an option?

✔ For pension and life insurance benefits, who receives payment after the death of the participant? How is the right of payment determined? What if there is a dispute? Is there a plan rule that determines payment in the event that the participant does not have a designated beneficiary?

✔ What are the administrative procedures to notify a participant about required income taxes on benefits and assist in payment?

✔ What is the benefit appeal procedure and how does it work?

The new trustee must also become familiar with any specific legislated duties and responsibilities. In particular the trustees should consider:

✔ Registration requirements for benefit plans and any amendments to such plans

✔ Requirements to file valuation reports with provincial pension regulators and Revenue Canada where a new plan is established

✔ Periodic statements that are to be issued to plan members setting out information prescribed by provincial benefit statutes

✔ Filing requirements for annual income tax returns, information returns and financial statements on behalf of the plan and trust fund as are required by the *Income Tax Act*

✔ Statements to be provided to members for income tax purposes.

ENDNOTE

1. Adopted from: Joseph Brislin, "A Checklist for New Trustees of Health and Welfare and Pension Plans," *Employee Benefits Digest,* November 1991; and Thane Woodside, "Demonstrating Prudence: Practical Steps Trustees Can Take to Protect Themselves From Liability," presented at the 27th Annual Canadian Employee Benefits Conference sponsored by the International Foundation of Employee Benefit Plans, November 1994.

CHAPTER 1

Why Employee Benefits?

by Patrick Longhurst

NEEDS OF EMPLOYEES AND THEIR DEPENDENTS

Employee benefits are one element in the total compensation system that employers establish for their employees. This compensation system consists of *direct compensation,* such as salaries and bonuses; *indirect compensation,* such as employee benefits; and *noncompensation rewards,* such as job satisfaction and personal development. To be effective, benefits must satisfy the needs of employees and their dependents. Employee benefits generally satisfy employees' basic needs of security and satisfaction.

Events That Can Be Anticipated

Benefits are designed to meet employee needs in the event of death, disability, illness and retirement. Some of these events can be anticipated and budgeted for by both employees and employers, while others cannot.

When designing a benefit plan, trustees or employers determine first what government plans and individual employee sources are available. Then they can fill in any gaps and provide benefits to supplement these other sources.

The expenses that occur most frequently are medical and dental costs. In Canada, every province and territory has a government-sponsored medical plan that covers basic hospital and medical expenses and doctor fees. Some also pay for dental care for children. Beyond this basic coverage, if there is no employer medical or dental plan, employees must pay their own health care costs. With a plan, employees can budget for most of these expenses, since such events as trips to the dentist or pharmacy bills are generally expected. Retirement can also be readily anticipated. Employees know they will probably be entitled to a minimum level of government benefits. They may develop a personal savings plan to supplement those benefits, but often they either begin one too late in life or find it difficult to set up such a plan. Consequently, pension plans meet their retirement needs by providing another source of income and financial security.

Catastrophes

Some medical expenses cannot be predicted, so they are more difficult to budget for. Not only is illness or accident often unpredictable, but the costs associated with it can be substantial. For instance, one might suffer a prolonged illness requiring either 24-hour nursing care or a chronic care facility, neither of which may be covered by provincial health care plans.

Death and disability can also be expensive. In addition to funeral and medical expenses for an employee or his or her dependents, a wage earner's death or disability may result in serious loss of income and be a severe financial drain on family resources. An employee benefit plan can meet these expenses.

PATERNALISM OF EMPLOYERS

Basic Employer Responsibility

Most employers feel a basic responsibility to employees, especially long-term employees, and their dependents in the event of death, disability, illness or retirement. Benefit plans, whether basic, enhanced or very rich, provide for these events over and above government plans and employee sources.

Additional Employer Considerations

However, there is also an element of self-interest in providing benefit plans. Employers do not want to see employees distracted from work by financial problems. They also do not want to see at their doorstep widows and orphans or retired employees who cannot make ends meet.

In addition, an organized fund for employee benefits eliminates the need to take up a collection each time something goes wrong. And, of course, a sound benefit program helps the employer attract and retain good employees.

ECONOMIES OF SCALE

Lower Cost

Benefits purchased for a group are almost always less expensive than if bought for individuals. This is because buying for a group spreads the costs and risks over a large number of people. It is desirable to have most, if not all, employees covered by the benefit plan to keep the cost per employee low.

Availability

Many group benefits are available to employees after an eligibility or waiting period but, in many cases, there is no waiting period and employees are covered from date of employment. Also, because risk is spread over a large group, most plans do not require medical evidence of insurability from employees, except for unusually high amounts of coverage.

By contrast, individual plans almost always require medical evidence, so a group plan not only saves employees from shopping around for their own plan, but insures them even when they might otherwise be denied coverage or find the costs prohibitive.

Payroll Deduction

Benefits can be made even more accessible to employees if the employee portion of the costs is paid by payroll deduction. Employees will not suddenly be faced with a discouragingly large expense. Payroll deduction spreads payments over a year and, with deductions made at the source, employees find the costs much more manageable.

COMPETITIVE PRESSURES

One objective of compensation policy is to attract and retain qualified employees. To achieve this, employers must offer a competitive and internally equitable compensation program. In addition, employees should clearly understand the compensation policy, what they must do to win increases or bonuses, and be rewarded on the basis of their performance. Competitive pressures on staff arise across industry, geography and profession or trade boundaries.

Industry

Employees in comparable jobs in the same industry often will be aware of the compensation practices throughout the industry. Direct compensation is readily comparable, but a basis for comparing indirect compensation is much harder to determine. Employee benefits generally are not easily costed and, even when they are, the costs are not always made known to employees. Besides, costs of a plan vary over time. Because direct compensation for similar jobs across an industry may be nearly the same, indirect compensation through employee benefits is often the deciding factor in attracting and retaining employees.

Geography

Although organizations in a particular region may represent different industries, there can be competitive pressures on employers to offer similar compensation and benefits for jobs with similar skill requirements across several industry groups. For example, in a city with a large industrial base, firms in different industries may compete for the same employees because employees can readily move to other jobs requiring similar skills. Employers may have to pay the going rate and offer very similar benefit packages. For employers with branches or plants across the country, such competitive pressure can force them to provide different levels of benefits at each location.

Profession or Trade

Professionals and tradespeople are often the most aware of compensation practices in their industry. Professionals, who may recognize and place a high value on employee benefit programs, will be concerned if their firm's program is not competitive. Tradespeople, who are often members of a multi-employer plan, may turn down jobs or projects of organizations that do not belong to such a plan.

INCOME TAX INCENTIVES

Employee Contributions

Generally, employee contributions to employer-sponsored group benefit plans are not tax deductible. However, under current tax legislation, medical expenses (including contributions to group benefit plans) above 3% of net income are eligible as a tax credit. Because the contributions are not deductible, many employee benefit plans do not require employee contributions. An exception to this may be disability plans, where the benefit paid to a disabled employee is not taxable if the employee pays the entire premium cost.

Employee contributions to registered pension plans and registered retirement savings plans are tax deductible up to limits set by the *Income Tax Act*.

Employee contributions to the Canada/Quebec Pension Plan and employment insurance are tax deductible, while provincial medicare premiums are not.

Employer Contributions

Employers' costs for their group benefit plans are tax deductible. Employer contributions to registered money purchase pension plans and deferred profit-sharing plans are also deductible up to the limit allowed under the *Income Tax Act*. In addition, *all* employer costs associated with a registered defined benefit pension plan are tax deductible.

Employer contributions to the Canada/Quebec Pension Plan, employment insurance and workers compensation are tax deductible, as are all premiums paid to provincial medicare plans.

Investment Income

Employee benefit plans can be set up as a *trust*. While trusts are taxed on investment earnings, they are allowed to deduct normal operating expenses and certain premiums and benefits when computing their taxable income. In this way, investment income of many employee benefit plans is not taxable.

Investment income earned on a pension fund is not included in either the employee's or the employer's income for tax purposes. However, accumulations are taxed when paid to employees in the form of a pension, death benefit or withdrawal of funds. In addition, the trust will be subject to tax if the limit on foreign investment is exceeded.

Payments to Employees

Most payments to employees from employer-sponsored group benefit plans are not taxable income. Short-term and long-term disability (LTD) plans are an exception to this rule: Disability benefits are taxed in the hands of the employee unless the entire premium is paid by the employee.

Pension death benefits and withdrawals from the pension fund are subject to income tax. Pension payments to retired employees or surviving spouses are taxed as income.

Benefits payable from the Canada/Quebec Pension Plan, Old Age Security and employment insurance are considered taxable income. Workers' compensation, provincial medicare, spouse's allowance, Guaranteed Income Supplement and provincial pension supplements are not taxable income.

COLLECTIVE BARGAINING AND THE ROLE OF UNIONS

Single Employer

The collective bargaining process has contributed to the introduction and spread of employee benefit plans. Unions negotiate for employee benefit improvements and new benefits, particularly when wage increases are minimal. A union's collective bargaining power tends to ensure a more favourable deal for its members than a single employee could negotiate alone.

It is generally recognized that the concept of *total compensation* was developed in union negotiations. Often in negotiations the cost or value of indirect compensation, such as employee benefits, is converted to an equivalent direct compensation value. This enables both sides to plan and cost new benefits and improvements. Collective bargaining will persuade employers to implement new or improved benefits. Even in nonunion firms there may be a great deal of pressure to implement new benefits to remain competitive and attract good employees.

Multi-Employer

Multi-employer plans usually are set up in industries with very mobile workforces. For instance, in construction, workers travel from job to job during the year. These plans enable small employers, which cannot provide group benefits economically, to participate in an industrywide plan. While employers are free to set up associations to provide group benefits, most multi-employer plans have resulted from union demands.

The negotiation process for multi-employer plans is similar to the process for single employers. Collective bargaining between union representatives and employers results in a collective agreement that governs the plan. The agreement may specify the level of contributions to be made into a trust fund, or it may establish the type of benefit available under the plan. The trustees of the fund are responsible for the administration of the plan.

REINFORCEMENT OF PERSONNEL POLICIES

An organization will design and implement direct and indirect compensation systems to reinforce its corporate culture and motivate employees to contribute to the firm's objectives.

Similarly, employee benefit programs can be used to reinforce specific personnel policies. For example, a profit-sharing plan can attract good employees and reward exceptional performance. A well-structured sick leave plan can combat absenteeism problems. Early retirement features in the pension plan, plus enhanced benefits, can help reduce an older workforce and make way for younger employees.

Benefit packages can also be used to reinforce a firm's reputation and culture. Well-established, paternalistic organizations will most likely provide a sound benefit package with many features for employees and their dependents. Newly established companies, such as high-tech firms, may decide to provide a limited benefit program in favour of direct compensation to motivate and attract employees.

ALTERNATIVES TO COMPANY-SPONSORED EMPLOYEE BENEFITS

Personal Arrangements

In the event of death, disability, illness or retirement, employees could meet their financial needs through personal savings. Alternatively, they could choose individual life, disability, medical and dental insurance. Often, however, they may be unable or unwilling to set up a savings or investment plan. Besides, individual insurance coverage may not be available to them, for either financial or medical reasons. Finally, employees may simply choose not to purchase one or all of the coverages. In that case, large or prolonged expenses could cause financial disaster for employees.

Government Programs

Most government programs are available to all employees, but the level of coverage may be inadequate for their needs. The Canada/Quebec Pension Plan provides lump-sum death and survivor benefits, disability benefits and retirement income. But the retirement income may not be adequate, particularly if an employee has not worked many years in Canada. The universally available Old Age Security and the means-tested Guaranteed Income Supplement, spouse's allowance and provincial pension supplements also provide a minimum level of retirement income.

Provincial health plans cover basic hospital and medical expenses. However, many expensive services, such as 24-hour nursing care, ambulance services and out-of-country expenses in excess of the provincial plan, are not covered. Dental expenses, unless accidental, are not covered by provincial health plans, although some provinces do provide limited dental benefits to children.

Workers' compensation provides death and disability benefits, and employment insurance provides limited disability and maternity benefits.

CHAPTER 2

Historical Development

by Pui-Ying Chan

In the mid-19th century, society was forever changed by the Industrial Revolution. Work in factories and offices began to replace traditional work on family farms. The lone craftsman was replaced by employees working in mills and mines, on assembly lines and behind rows of desks. Canadians began to leave farms and small towns to share in the economic rewards offered in urban centers.

A new employer-employee relationship emerged. Employees traded their labour and time for payment in cash from their employers. More often than not, in the early stages of the Industrial Revolution, hours were long, work was hard and the payment was small. As industrialization progressed, the large, tightly knit family began to break down, replaced by the smaller, often scattered, industrial family. Those who were ill, infirm or old could no longer depend on family members for care and support.

Undoubtedly, there were some enlightened employers that cared about their employees. But, unfortunately, there were just as many that took advantage of them. In fact, the horrors of the early Industrial Revolution spawned a liberal/socialist movement. More and more, workers turned to unions and government to protect their rights and force employers to provide better working conditions.

One result of such employee pressure was the *fringe benefit*—pensions for long-service employees, disability pensions for those who became ill or were injured for a long time and could not find work, health plans to help employees pay for doctor and hospital bills, and group life insurance to ease the burden on a family when the wage earner died.

The history of employee benefit programs can be seen in these stages:

1. 19th century: Governments of industrialized countries in Europe and North America begin to pass legislation to require employers to look after the welfare of employees. Legislation includes employment standards and accident compensation.
2. Turn of the century: This is an era of paternalism. Employers begin to provide such things as company stores and housing.
3. The Depression: Fewer paternalistic benefits are offered because of increasing government legislation and the rise of unions.
4. The 1940s: Modern benefit programs begin to develop due to wartime controls on wages and the increasing bargaining power of unions.
5. The 1950s: Growth in employee benefit programs accelerates as the economy booms and employers add benefits to compete for and retain workers.
6. 1960 to 1975: Growth of benefit programs begins to level off as inflation and costs soar.
7. 1975 to 1978: Federal government battles soaring prices, and the Anti-Inflation Board is put in place. Employers are forced to calculate the precise cost of all compensation items. The cost of benefits to employers becomes obvious.
8. 1975 to 1990: Cost becomes a more important consideration, and flexible benefits start to be offered from the early 1980s. Flexible benefits allow employees to choose the benefits that are most important to them, while allowing the employer more control over cost. Benefit programs begin to reflect changes in society—the increasing role of women in the workforce, the

increasing number of part-time workers and the aging of the population.

9. 1985 to the 1990s: The impact of rising costs of government programs (medicare, workers' compensation, Old Age Security and Canada and Quebec Pension Plan) causes governments to review plan provisions. Provinces implement restrictions in medicare plans such as Ontario's changes regarding out-of-country coverage, and then to full drug benefits for seniors. Also, commencing in 1989, the Old Age Security pension became subject to a "claw back," which required pensioners with an annual taxable income of more than $50,000 to repay part or all of their pension. The unemployment benefit level is reduced. Subsequently, governments express the need to fully review the "social security" net for all Canadians.

At the same time, extensive pension studies of the late 1970s and the 1980s result in the introduction of full-scale changes to the Income Tax Act Regulations and to pension legislation in some provinces.

Following this change, defined contribution plans grow rapidly, with some of this growth at the expense of defined benefit plans.

Registered retirement savings plans (RRSPs) are allowed much higher limits that are permitted to be carried forward if not used. Their popularity continues to grow.

10. 1990s: The tax advantage of benefits is threatened. Quebec and Ontario extend the provincial sales tax to group insurance benefits (1991 for Quebec, 1993 for Ontario). In 1993 the Quebec Government takes a further step and makes all group life and health benefit coverage paid by the employer taxable. The federal government also begins taxing all group life insurance benefits beginning in 1994. On the pension front, governments in need of funds to cover rising deficits look at tax-sheltered capital accumulations in pension plans and RRSPs. The maximum annual RRSP contribution limit is frozen at the 1994 level until 2004. Similarly, the maximum registered pension plan benefit accrual ceiling is frozen at the 1995 level until 2005. Also, the benefit commencement age for registered pension plans, deferred profit-sharing plans and RRSPs is lowered from 71 to 69.

The federal government also begins a public consultation process on the future of the CPP. Through that process, various changes are made to the CPP, including higher contributions, fuller funding and implementation of a new investment policy.

In summary, employee benefits have been very much influenced by government programs, legislation regulating benefits, demographics and general economic conditions. Changes are taking place at an increasing rate, and guarantees that all of us counted on in planning our future and retirement are being questioned more and more. All of us involved in the benefits field need to take steps to bring to the forefront the needs and rights of contributors, retirees and beneficiaries of employee benefit plans.

CHAPTER 3

Structure and Design of Employee Benefit Programs

by Patrick Longhurst

Employee benefit plans are, by nature, a compromise between what an employer considers reasonable and what employees consider desirable. In this chapter, we will discuss these two positions in detail and see how benefit programs are designed in practice.

CORPORATE NEEDS—MEETING THE EMPLOYER'S OBJECTIVES

An employer's objectives arise directly from the corporate strategy of the organization. Benefits are structured to reinforce this strategy and provide a strong message to employees about the corporate culture. For example, a company with no benefit programs hires employees who are less concerned with future financial security than with maximizing their current incomes. Such employees are likely to have no dependents and be young and fit enough to know they can qualify for individual insurance if they require it.

At the other end of the scale, a company that provides "Cadillac" benefits to all employees at the expense of direct pay is likely to attract employees who value security and may not be particularly aggressive.

Most organizations will be on a spectrum somewhere between these two extremes. Following are some typical issues that an employer might consider when preparing a statement of objectives for employee benefits.

Adequacy

Adequacy of a benefit that provides income is typically expressed as one of two kinds of replacement ratio. The most common is the *gross replacement ratio*.

It is the ratio of the benefit to be provided to the employee's total income. Consider a pension plan in which the pension benefit is $20 a month per year of service. For an employee retiring with 30 years of service and earning $2,000 a month, the gross replacement ratio is 30%, calculated as the pension benefit of $600 a month ($20 multiplied by 30 years of service) divided by pre-retirement earnings ($2,000 a month). There is another measure of adequacy called the *net replacement ratio*. This takes both the individual's tax situation and the level of government benefits into account. In the above example, if the individual also receives $700 a month in government pension and pays $100 a month in tax while retired (compared with $400 a month while working), then the net replacement ratio is 75%. This is calculated as $1,200 (after tax income in retirement of $600 + $700 − $100) divided by $1,600 (after tax income of $2,000 − $400 before retirement).

Many employers consider the net replacement ratio a more meaningful indicator than the gross replacement ratio since it compares anticipated disposable retirement income from all sources with the net take-home pay while working. In practice, the net replacement ratio will vary, depending on assumptions about future tax rules, levels of income and government benefits, the employee's tax position, years of service at retirement and level of income.

An employer assesses the adequacy of a plan by examining a number of representative situations. Replacement ratios provide a good indicator for retirement and disability benefits. However, another measure of adequacy must be applied to health and dental benefits. In this case, the ratio should represent the difference between the expense incurred and the amount reimbursed.

Competitiveness

Most employers make a point of learning what the competition is doing, so they can establish total compensation levels. Sometimes a tradeoff is made. A company may provide above-average direct pay and below-average benefits, resulting in average compensation.

Comparisons are critical for the employer. A large employer may compare the benefit program for general salaried employees with other similar size employers in the same province and the same industry. For executives and specialized professionals, the comparison may have to be made nationally, or even internationally.

Comparisons can be difficult. To compare a contributory pension plan with a noncontributory plan, for instance, the value of employee contributions must be factored in. Care must be taken to compare apples with apples.

Flexibility

It is becoming increasingly difficult for employers to anticipate the needs of their employees. Gone are the days when a "typical" employee was a male with a wife and two children at home. Today, employees are looking for a choice in their benefit programs. This choice can be built in by a series of options or by a full flexible benefits program.

Simplicity

An effective benefit program must be clearly understandable to both the sponsor and beneficiaries. Simplicity is the key. There has always been a tendency for people to think that benefit plans, particularly pension plans, are terribly complex. There is no need for this. Any program that is so complicated that it defies description is not successful.

Tax Effectiveness

One of the prime justifications for benefit plans is that they are a tax-effective way of compensating employees. If the plan bestows a large taxable benefit on employees, it immediately loses some of that effectiveness, although it may still be a good benefit for other reasons.

Sometimes the tax status of a particular program will change as tax rules change. Some employers respond by redesigning their programs. Others believe that to do so would amount to "the tail wagging the dog," since the prime purpose of the program is to provide a benefit in accordance with corporate objectives.

Cost Control

Most employers do not have limitless funds available, and most introduce controls to protect themselves against runaway costs. The two main forms of control are:

1. To place an upper limit on the financial exposure of the employer
2. To share some of the cost with employees. This gives employees built-in incentive to control their claims against the program.

An employer will also control costs by regularly auditing the claims experience and making sure the administration system is not paying claims that fall outside the scope of the program.

Reinforcement of Personnel Policies

Frequently, companies will use their benefit programs to reinforce a personnel decision. For instance, pension plans may be used to provide enhanced benefits to people eligible for early retirement. Alternatively, postretirement life, health and dental programs may be set up to make early retirement more attractive. Or a fitness program may be established to help reduce chronic absenteeism.

Employee Participation

For some employers, it is critical to have employees share the cost of benefits. It is commonly said that individuals do not appreciate something unless they help pay for it. On a practical level, some employers cannot afford a full package of benefits unless employees help pay for it. Finally, using employee contributions may be a logical extension of a fully tax-effective benefit program.

Integration

When determining whether their benefit program is "adequate," many employers will set income replacement targets that include expected government benefits. In this case, it is only logical that the ultimate plan design be integrated with government programs.

Integration is achieved in one of two ways:

1. *Direct offset.* This means that benefits are reduced by the expected government benefits.
2. *Step-rate.* In this method, benefits are calculated using one formula on earnings up to the Canada Pension Plan's year's maximum pensionable earnings (YMPE) and a different formula on earnings in excess of the YMPE.

Inflation Protection

Although concern has been reduced recently because of lower inflation rates in the 1990s, inflation protection was one of the most contentious issues in the 1980s. The critical question is whether the promise made by an employer to provide a particular level of income following a certain event—typically retirement, death or disability—implies the additional commitment to update such payments in line with inflation. Clearly, the principle of adequacy breaks down if such adjustments are not made. But the principle of cost-containment may break down if employers take on an open-ended commitment to index benefits.

Optional or Compulsory

Having decided, or negotiated with a union, which benefit programs to provide, the level of benefits payable and the cost sharing to be applied, it must be determined or negotiated whether the plans are to be optional or compulsory and what rules of eligibility will apply. Often employees are not eligible to join all benefit plans on the date of hire. They frequently are required to meet some minimum eligibility standards before they are enrolled.

If all benefit plans are compulsory, employees may resent having to contribute to programs that may have little or no value for them. At the same time, if employees are allowed to opt out of certain benefit plans, employers face the moral dilemma of not knowing what to do when an employee dies, becomes disabled or retires with no benefit entitlement.

Internal Equity

Employers will decide, or negotiate with a union, what benefits policy to apply to different classes of employees, such as hourly, salaried, management and executive; unionized and nonunionized. Some firms have a clear policy or agreement of the same benefits for all; others have a structured system that gives executives benefits superior to those of other employees. The decision reflects the sponsor's corporate strategy and the type of environment the employer wishes to create.

Mergers and Acquisitions

After a merger or acquisition, the plan sponsor will have to decide how to administer the benefits of the new unit. Should present benefits be continued to new employees? Should the new employer share in the existing benefits program? This decision can only be made following a review of both the present and new benefits. Sometimes changes will be phased in over a period of years.

A similar question arises for a multidivisional company. If the divisions operate in different industries, it may be quite inappropriate to have the same benefits at each division. But there should be some similarity so that management can move employees from one divi-

sion to another without causing them to lose any benefits. In cases where a collective agreement exists, there may be no choice but to continue the same benefit program.

Meeting Legislated Requirements

Of course, all benefit plans must satisfy all existing legislation. This includes provincial and federal pension legislation, insurance laws, human rights and family law acts. Whatever the source, plan sponsors spend a good deal of time ensuring that, as rules change, their plans continue to meet all legal requirements.

Employee Needs

Once employees understand the benefits payable under their employer's plan and government programs, they can still use their personal savings to augment their income. The employer should stress this ability through a clear communications program.

Employees require many of the same things that employers require, and we have already mentioned most of them:
- Adequacy
- Flexibility
- Simplicity
- Tax effectiveness
- Inflation protection
- Equity.

EMPLOYEES' VIEW OF BENEFITS

For employees, some other issues are also important.

Advantages of Group Benefits

Even when employees pay for a benefit, they should still obtain an advantage from the use of payroll deductions and from the bulk purchasing power of the employer.

Financial Security

As long as employees depend on a benefit program, they will be concerned about the program's security, regardless of whether or not they contribute to the plan.

Union Negotiation

The structure and design of employee benefit plans subject to union negotiation follow the same general principles described earlier in this chapter, except that the resulting benefit programs and/or contributions to the same are usually negotiated by the union and employer and not unilaterally imposed.

CHAPTER 4

Funding Employee Benefit Programs

by Patrick Longhurst

BASIC PRINCIPLES

Nature of Risk

In this chapter, we will discuss how employee benefit programs are paid for. We will see that annual funding requirements may be different from actual claims costs for the year, and we will see why this might make sense in certain circumstances.

First, what risks are we talking about? There are many risks attached to employee benefit programs:

- An employee might die and a lump-sum or income benefit may have to be paid to a spouse or estate.
- An employee may become disabled and, therefore, eligible for short- or long-term disability payments.
- An employee or a family member may make a health or dental claim.
- An employee may retire.

Sharing of Risk

Risk can be spread either between several employers or from year to year. In this way, an employer can be protected from a catastrophic year in which claims are so significant they affect the financial results of the company.

Such sharing of risk is not without cost. The employer has to find a balance between fluctuating annual claims costs and an ability to assume risk.

The most appropriate funding method for an employee benefit plan will depend on three major criteria:

- Frequency of occurrence
- Predictability of the event
- Average claim per occurrence.

Frequency of Occurrence

Life and disability benefits protect employees and their dependents against infrequent occurrences. Table I—4-I shows the likely average number of deaths or long-term disability claims in a year.

Table I—4-I

Size of Group	Deaths	LTD Claim
100 employees	0.3	0.4
1,000 employees	3	4
10,000 employees	30	40

Predictability

Frequency is relatively easy to establish; predictability is much more difficult. For instance, life insurance tables tell us that the probability of death increases with age; they also tell us that a typical female at a certain age is less likely to die than a typical male of the same age. But it is almost impossible to predict when an individual will die.

On the other hand, retirement is much easier to predict, since it normally depends on an employee's informed choice. Sixty-five is still a very common age for retirement. However, early retirement formulas tend to encourage a younger retirement age, and this has led to the development of many of the funding techniques used in pension plans.

Some health and dental benefits are extremely predictable. The routine dental checkups every six months and normal prescription usage are obvious examples. Other events, like the heavy costs associated with a severe heart attack, clearly are far more difficult to predict. Nevertheless, for a large group, aggregate health and dental claims are not subject to great fluctuations from year to year, so they are relatively easy to budget in advance (with reasonable safeguards in plan design).

Average Claims

How sophisticated a funding approach may be will rest, to a great extent, on the size of the average individual claim. If a program provides a death benefit of $5,000 on the death of an employee's spouse, the event may be rare and hard to predict but, when it happens, it will not have a significant impact on the company's bottom line. On the other hand, a $1 million travel accident benefit, even rarer and harder to predict, could severely affect the company's profit picture.

The Savings Element

Generally, in retirement plans, other postretirement benefits and individual whole life products, the annual funding requirement consists of an insurance and a savings element. The insurance element is to pay for unexpected occurrences, such as someone's death. The savings element accumulates toward some future predictable date, such as retirement, when a lump sum or income flow is required.

The Importance of Stability of Cost

It is important for the employer to maintain benefit costs within a certain budgeted range. Normally, an employer or a multi-employer trust fund wants to be protected from a series of chance occurrences that suddenly increase the number of major claims or a rising trend in the number of predictable claims.

An employer's size and nature of business will dictate the level of risk a company is prepared to tolerate. An exploration company expecting wide swings in annual earnings may be prepared to accept more risk than, say, a regulated utility whose annual results should be in line with projections.

Security for Employees

An important element of funding is the security it provides employees. In some cases, the government establishes minimum funding levels to ensure that sufficient assets are available to cover expected claims. In other cases, the contract negotiated with an insurer will guarantee full benefits even if the employer runs into financial difficulties.

Tax and Accounting

If the amount needed to fund a benefit is different from the amount of actual claims in a year, which amount is to be used (funding or actual claims) to calculate such items as a taxable benefit earned by an employee—the tax deduction taken by the employer or expenses for accounting purposes? For that matter, should an entirely different amount be used?

There are many answers, depending on the benefit in question. For a self-insured short-term disability plan, actual claims will dictate both the accounting and the tax treatment. For an insured life or disability insurance program, the premium is the critical factor. For a pension plan, the Canadian Institute of Chartered Accountants has developed an accounting treatment quite independent of the funding method. Finally, the tax treatment depends on the actual amount funded.

Financial Strength of the Sponsor

The range of funding approaches is dictated by the financial strength of the sponsor. The federal government can run the Old Age Security program on a pay-as-you-go basis because it has the power to collect sufficient tax revenues to pay for the benefits promised. A private sector employer does not have that luxury. If the pension plan were not funded (as it, in fact, must be), the employee would lose everything if the sponsor went bankrupt.

The Role of the Actuary

What does the actuary have to do with all this? Professional training enables the actuary to use probabilities and discounted cash flow techniques to calculate premium rates and funding requirements. Not only is this helpful to the plan sponsor, it is a legal requirement. As a fellow of the Canadian Institute of Actuaries, the actuary must certify for the regulatory authorities the funded status and contribution requirements for certain employee benefit plans.

Ownership of Possible Surplus

When the value of funding for a benefit increases faster than the benefit plan's liabilities, a surplus is created. One of the thorniest issues to have arisen in the last 15 years is the disposition of this surplus, especially in pension plans. A key question in the debate is whether money allocated to fund a particular plan is irrevocably attached to the plan members. A number of subsidiary questions arise:

- Can we be sure a surplus exists?
- Who paid the amounts in the first place?
- What is the wording of the trust document, insurance contract or plan booklet?

As the money tied up in pension plans grows, this debate will continue to be a major issue and will influence the pace and method of funding chosen for each plan.

Employee Participation

There are several ways an employee can help pay for a particular benefit:

- By paying part of the required premium
- By *co-insurance,* which means that only a percentage of the expense can be claimed
- By a deductible, under which only benefits in excess of a certain amount are payable.

Funding

When we use some form of group insurance mechanism, three things are really happening:

1. Risk is being *shared* among a large number of people, ensuring a more stable incidence of claim. For example, most people go to the dentist regularly, so dental insurance is essentially prepayment of a predictable cost. (For tax reasons, it is also cost-effective—compared to the alternative of paying each employee more salary to pay the dentist out of taxed income.) There are many examples of risk sharing of frequent and predictable events. For instance, a group of ten people, each with a deductible of $500 on auto insurance claims, might decide to put $50 each into a common pool. If they are all reasonably careful drivers, there will be enough in the pool to pay the deductible when one of them needs to claim. The pool will have to be replenished each time there is a claim. The idea is to make budgeting easier for an expense that is bound to occur to at least one person in the group sooner or later. Sharing, or pooling, risk does not *require* funding, although a fund may be established.

2. Risk is being spread forward in time. A pension or disability plan's promise to pay extends a long way into the future, so funds are set aside and invested to prepare for the future pension or a possible claim. This is known as *funding.* It would be unfair to burden future generations with the cost of today's promises, so we set aside enough money today to pay the claims when they fall due. For a large group of people, most of the costs can be predicted, and funding becomes an important feature of the plan. Millions (or billions) of dollars can be built up in such funds, so proper handling and investment of the cash becomes a major consideration.

3. Risk can also be *insured;* some risks are simply too large for one group to take or for a few groups to share. They must be spread among the huge numbers of groups in an insurance portfolio. Typically, such risks are rare, unpredictable events that require a large dollar payment when they occur. For instance, we have all heard of the bizarre risks insured by Lloyd's of London—Betty Grable's legs or a concert pianist's hands insured for $10 million. Besides those, there are also normal risks that should be insured rather than shared. An accidental death benefit, for example, is paid only under *accidental* circumstances. By definition, we do not expect it to happen—although we know it can—and the benefit usually is large. This sort of risk is better insured. In practice, most risks are a combination of all these elements.

The skill of the risk manager is to identify what should be shared, what should be funded and what should be insured. After this kind of analysis, the targets and strategy for funding can be developed.

FUNDING METHODS

Pay-as-You-Go

The most rudimentary form of funding is called *pay-as-you-go.* It is as simple as it sounds. As claims or benefits become due, they are paid by the plan sponsor. No reserves are set up for either possible unexpected current claims or likely future claims.

The main advantage of this approach is its simplicity. The main disadvantage is that it can lull the plan sponsor into a false sense of security. Early cash costs can be low, but promises that are made currently can prove expensive later on. If no funds have been set aside for future expenditures, budgets of the future will have to pay for *past* promises, which were, perhaps, more than could be afforded.

Prefunding

The advantage of *prefunding* is the opposite of pay-as-you-go. Funds will be available when they are needed, and future expenses will be properly accrued in today's accounts. There also may be an advantage in the profitable investment of the funds: The extra return on investments will reduce the cost of the plan, and the economy will gain from the active deployment of savings in useful long-term projects.

It is also possible to overfund. Overfunding would create a surplus, and it could be argued that opportunities to spend the money wisely had been sacrificed in favour of excessive saving. Normally, this is not a problem, since the surplus can be used up in various ways. Currently, however, these ways are being restricted, and most employers try not to generate a surplus—that is, they will underfund the plan as far as is permissible.

Self-Insurance

With the help of an actuary, future cash flows can be estimated, and a rate of funding (usually, a percentage of payroll) is established. The idea is to provide a smooth, easily budgeted series of payments to build up the required fund. If the plan is large enough, it is simpler and cheaper to pay the premiums to a benefit trust rather than to an insurance company. This is known as *self-insurance*.

Insurance

Risks the employer does not wish to assume can be handled by an insurance company. This clearly offers some convenience and peace of mind; however, everything has its price. The insurance company requires a return on its capital, so it will retain an investment margin and may also collect a "risk charge." Finally, there are additional taxes, including federal sales tax and provincial sales taxes in some provinces, levied on the insurance premiums.

VARIATIONS IN INSURANCE COVERAGE

Pooling

This is pure insurance. For an accidental death benefit, for example, the claim is high in relation to the premium. But the insurance company takes the entire risk; if there are no claims, it keeps the premium as its due reward. Since there is a large pool of hundreds or thousands of similar groups insured, the statistical law of large numbers will tend to even out the fluctuations in claims experience for any one group. Thus, the pooling mechanism produces a fair insurance price for the risk.

Experience Rating

In some situations, an employer may feel fluctuations in the plan's claims experience are not wide and, therefore, wants to participate in any surplus generated by the plan. For example, typical group life insurance is a multiple of each individual's salary (two or three times salary, for instance), and the number of death claims for a large, stable employee group does not vary much. Assuming the premiums are sufficient to allow at least minimal fluctuations in claims, the plan will tend to generate a surplus over time.

Such a group will commonly have an experience rating arrangement with the insurer. The cost of the plan over time will reflect actual claims—plus an expense allowance formula (called the *retention formula*). For very large groups generating millions of dollars of premium each year, the arrangement may be quite sophisticated, with various allowances for interest earned from day to day on cash flow, or from year to year on specific reserves. Life, disability, health care and dental plans can be experience rated.

Large Amount Pooling and Stop-Loss Insurance

Sometimes claims may be frequent but consistently small. If this is the case, there is a risk the normal experience rating arrangement would be plunged into deficit by a single unexpected and very heavy claim.

Suppose a group of 3,000 employees has an average death claim of $40,000 and there are about ten claims a year, giving aggregate claims of $400,000. But suppose the president and one or two senior executives are insured for $400,000 each, and one of them dies. Suddenly, claims that year have doubled.

To guard against this eventuality, a company may buy separate insurance. Then, the rest of the risk—the stable part of the experience—continues to be experience rated.

There are two major methods of limiting risk:

1. *Large amount pooling.* In this method, a *pooling level* is set per claim. Claims under this level are charged to the company's experience; claims above the level are insured and paid by the insurance company. In effect, no experience-rated claim can exceed the pooling level. For this risk, the insurance company levies a *pooling charge* that it retains, regardless of the actual claims experience.

2. *Stop-loss.* Large amount pooling limits individual claims to the pooling level. However, the company's concern may not be individual claims, but with total claims in a year. With a stop-loss, total claims charged to the experience in a year are limited to the stop-loss level—usually whatever claims are normally expected to be. If a company is insured at 125% of expected claims, the insurance company pays claims in excess. The insurance company levies a stop-loss charge, which it retains whatever the actual claims are.

Both these methods limit risk and reduce fluctuations in the experience. They may also be combined: Individual claims can be limited by large amount pooling, and the aggregate of these claims can be limited by a stop-loss arrangement.

Without stop-loss insurance, *catastrophe* insurance is often necessary. If a number of employees (say, three or more) are killed simultaneously in an accident, claims could be very large. Large amount pooling will not necessarily be sufficient to limit this risk.

Reinsurance

Sometimes an insurer takes on a risk it would find too large to handle on its own. In this case, it spreads the risk by reinsuring with other insurance companies or reinsurance companies—specialists in this type of business.

In group life or disability insurance, for instance, coverage is usually related to salary. A top executive's salary may be as much as $1 million, so it could be difficult for an insurer to offer meaningful insurance. However, with reinsurance, satisfactory coverage can be arranged. By pooling many similar risks, reinsurance companies can operate a reasonably stable business.

The so-called liability insurance crisis of 1986 was actually a reinsurance crisis. Because of unpredictable and, in some cases, extremely expensive court decisions affecting liability insurance, reinsurers withdrew from the market. This forced primary carriers to reduce the amount of risk they could insure, by either refusing to renew insurance contracts or substantially increasing premiums and deductibles.

That crisis illustrated the importance of reinsurance in maintaining a stable and orderly insurance market that can satisfy customers' needs at an affordable price.

Health and Welfare Trust

When companies self-insure—that is, take all the risk on themselves instead of using an insurance company—they usually establish a *health and welfare trust*. The trust provides some security for employees by separating the employer's benefit plan funds from its day-to-day business requirements.

A trust arrangement offers tax advantages to the employer and employee. The employer's contributions are generally deductible in that tax year. And, as with other employer-paid premiums, they are not deemed to be a taxable benefit for employees. Finally, the trust's investment income is generally not taxable as long as it does not exceed expenses incurred to earn the investment income, administration costs or taxable benefit payments.

MULTI-EMPLOYER TRUSTS

When employees work for different employers in the same industry or belong to one bargaining unit in the industry, they may have group insurance benefits that are agreed to by all employers in the group. Or the employers and union may agree to the amount of contributions to a plan, leaving it to the trustees thereof to agree on the benefits to be provided. These multi-employer arrangements are more common for skilled tradespersons, such as construction workers, who are hired on a project basis by various employers and who move from site to site throughout the year. They also exist in industries such as clothing, food and service, trucking, hotels and entertainment.

Sharing Risk

The advantages of setting up a multi-employer trust are economy of scale and sharing risk. By having one plan for everyone in a trade or industry, additional security and stability of experience is obtained.

Administration

There are also administrative savings. In selecting an administrator, trustees of these plans may choose from among the following:

- A salaried administrator—someone hired and paid by the fund to maintain an administrative office for the trustees
- A contract administrator—company that administers services to several trusts simultaneously
- An insurance company.

A salaried administrator will be able to give personal service to trust beneficiaries, but the cost of maintaining the office may outweigh the advantages of such service. Both a professional contract administration company and an insurance company can offer sophisticated office equipment and systems that few single trusts could afford. As well, since contract administrators and insurance companies work with many different trusts covering various occupations, their experience is bound to be broader than the salaried administrator's. Administrative costs are a prime concern to trustees, but so is effective administration.

In some cases, it might make sense to use both a fund administrator and an insurance company. For example, collecting premiums, accounting and recordkeeping might be carried out by a salaried administrator, and claims processing and control by an insurance carrier. Whichever administration system is chosen, trustees must see that the trust property is administered as efficiently and prudently as possible. Trustees are entitled to delegate administrative responsibilities, but they bear the ultimate responsibility.

Equity Among Employers

By sharing risk and administrative costs, all employers, large and small, are charged the same basic rate for insurance benefits. Also, a fairer and probably cheaper premium rate is assured because the risk has been spread and more sophisticated administration techniques are available to a large group.

In the interest of fairness, trustees should set up effective collection procedures that include audit controls, timely accounting for contributions received and follow-up of delinquent employers for nonpayment of contributions.

Tax and Accounting for Cost

Multi-employer trusts face the same basic tax and accounting questions as single employer funds (see earlier discussion). They, too, must determine how to calculate the value of taxable benefits earned by each employee, the deduction taken by the trust and the expenses used by the trust for accounting purposes.

Basically, the trust must keep sufficient documentation for each covered employee and each participating employer in order to satisfy accounting requirements.

If employees are not fully aware of all rules governing a benefit plan, some trusts find it difficult to maintain an up-to-date list of eligible employees. Determining eligibility is made easier if the rules are clearly stated and communicated to the employees. Verifying an employee's eligibility can be delayed, partly by the time employers take to prepare contribution records, and partly by the time needed by the fund administrator to update records.

Recordkeeping is more complicated if the fund participates in *a reciprocal agreement,* if some employers are persistently late making contributions or if it is a contributory plan.

Administration is also complicated if eligibility requirements vary among benefit plans. For example, the minimum number of hours worked to qualify for supplementary medical and hospital benefits may be different from the number of hours needed to qualify for vacation, disability or dental programs. Variable eligibility requirements may help control benefit costs, but the more diverse the formulas, the more time-consuming and expensive will be the administration of the fund—and the greater the difficulty of communicating the plan to employees.

Participation Agreement

A written participation agreement between the trustees and each employer is essential. It is the document that establishes the employer's contractual obligation to contribute to the trust fund.

Financial difficulty alone is not sufficient reason for an employer to avoid contributing to a pension or welfare fund. Indeed, in certain bankruptcy cases, contributions owing to the fund have been considered to be *wages* and have priority over other general claims against the employer. Nor will an employer's defense that the union has not lived up to the collective bargaining agreement usually provide sufficient grounds for the employer to discontinue contributions to the trust fund.

The extent to which trustees are personally liable for failure to collect unpaid contributions is one of those questions falling into a gray area of legal uncertainty.

Despite this uncertainty, the trustees bear a strong moral and legal obligation to see that every employer lives up to the terms of both the trust agreement and the collective bargaining agreement, including the commitment to contribute to the trust fund.

Trustees have an ongoing obligation to verify an employer's contributions and ensure that the contributions are in accordance with the collective bargaining agreement. Trustees must judge for themselves when to try to collect delinquent payments and how to do it. If they think an attempt to enforce a claim would make it impossible for the employer to pay it, and if a reasonable extension is likely to result in payment, trustees may delay enforcement and seek a compromise, provided they always act prudently, in good faith and in the best interests of the beneficiaries.

Fluctuations in Contribution Flow

Because of the seasonal nature of certain occupations, fluctuations in contribution income can be anticipated. With some experience, these fluctuations become predictable.

A fund manager, aware of these fluctuations, can seek the advice of an investment specialist when investing cash flow. If outgo from a fund is expected to exceed income at certain times of the year, fund assets should not be tied up in long-term or nonliquid investments. Matching investments to anticipated cash flow is part of the fund management process.

Ownership of Funds

Funds in a multi-employer trust do not belong to any one employer or even to all employers; rather, they belong to the trust beneficiaries. They arise as a result of a collective agreement; any surplus must be dealt with under terms of that agreement or, more commonly, under the trust agreement. When a deficit arises, the trustees have to consider the possible steps to take in order to put assets and liabilities back into balance.

Because of the nature of a multi-employer trust, pension benefits are usually expressed as a fixed dollar amount or as an accumulation of defined contributions. Therefore, complications of ownership of surplus that arise in defined benefit pension plans do not arise as frequently, if at all.

Trust agreements must specify the conditions governing the funds when the plan is wound up or terminated. Normally, all remaining funds must be used for the benefit of existing members and former members.

CHAPTER 5

Benefit Trust Administration

by Peter O'Hara

Benefit trust administration, which here is simply referred to as *administration,* is properly described as the business of the trust. That description is appropriate for any type of benefit trust, whether it be health and welfare, pension, vacation pay, supplementary unemployment benefit (SUB), education and training, or any of the other variations on the theme. As well, it is appropriate regardless of the combination of agencies performing the services—and regardless of the extent to which the governing board of trustees involves itself in the administration process.

This chapter examines the process of administration from the standpoint of the trustees. It concentrates attention on the part of the process performed by the so-called administrator, thereby ignoring the activities of the actuary, the auditor, the consultant, the custodian, the investment manager and the other service agencies that contribute to the overall administration of most benefit trusts. They are explored in other sections of this book.

A series of topics is presented in a manner that should serve as a ready reference for trustees. But, first, it may be helpful to set the stage by identifying the functions that should be performed by the administrator.

THE FUNCTIONS OF THE ADMINISTRATOR

While natural differences among benefit trusts sometimes dictate otherwise, the administrator will generally perform all of the functions listed below.

1. Create, maintain and secure the database from which the benefit trust operates. This should include all the identifying information, past and present, about:

   - Contributing employers
   - Reciprocal payers
   - Participating members of the trust and their dependents
   - Records on the amount and the timeliness of contributions to the trust fund
   - Where applicable, the members' credits in the trust fund.

2. Update the information in the database continuously, so that the quality of the records, as assessed by the trust fund's auditor, always exceeds the standard established by the trustees.

3. Assist with the creation and modification of the rules and guidelines that form the operating framework for the benefit trust. The related documentation should cover such diverse matters as:

   - The steps to be taken when contributions are delinquent (the collection control program)
   - The rules governing members' eligibility to participate in the trust fund
   - The circumstances under which trustees' expenses are reimbursed and the amounts of such reimbursements
   - Members' options to make personal payments to the trust fund
   - Reciprocal and transfer agreements with other benefit trusts
   - The reallocation of excess members' credit
   - Dozens of other provisions aimed at the elimination of guesswork and at the assurance of evenhanded treatment for all.

4. Maintain and protect the trustees' document files. Such files will include, among other things:

- The related collective agreements
- The trust agreement
- The participation agreements executed by the contributing employers
- The acceptances of trusteeship signed by the trustees
- The text for the contribution control program
- Reciprocal and transfer agreements with other benefit trusts
- Insurance policies
- Service agreements with the actuary, the administrator, the banking facility, the consultant, the custodian, the investment manager and the legal counsel
- The benefit plan text
- Audit reports and financial statements
- Actuarial costings and valuations
- Legal opinions
- Consulting reports
- PST registration forms
- Copies of reports made to government regulators
- Minutes of trustees' meetings.

5. Receive, bank and verify the accuracy and timeliness of all contributions to the trust fund.
6. Record the receipt of contributions and, where applicable, update members' credits accordingly.
7. Pursue the collection of delinquent contributions and, when appropriate, participate with others to resolve the consequences of non-payments or partial payments resulting from employers' insolvencies or bankruptcies.
8. Calculate and redirect contributions to other benefit trusts with which the trustees have reciprocal and/or transfer agreements.
9. Calculate and redirect contributions to other trust funds with which the trustees have collection agreements. Typically, a health and welfare or pension trust may agree to collect contributions for:
   - An education and training fund
   - The remission of tax reports to appropriate government agencies
   - Membership fees due to the employers association
   - Promotion and field dues owing to the union.
10. Answer appropriate questions from beneficiaries, doctors, hospitals and other health care providers, contributing employers, government regulators and the other agencies that serve or otherwise interact with the trustees.
11. Receive and verify the acceptability of claims for benefits. In this sense, claims may be for:
    - Health and welfare benefits
    - Death benefits

- Retirement income
- Termination allowances
- SUB
- Vacation pay
- Various other benefits that may accrue to the member.

12. Pay claims and record the payment or redirect the claim for payment from another agency. (Health and welfare claims may be paid by the administrator, an insurance company or a prepaid service provider like Blue Cross. Life insurance is invariably paid by the insurance company. Retirement income, death and termination benefits, derived from a pension trust, may be dispersed by the administrator but, more often, they are paid by a trust company or insurance company. Virtually all vacation pay and SUB pay is issued by the administrator.)
13. Perform all banking transactions.
14. Transfer funds to custodians.
15. Keep a complete general ledger for each trust fund and issue financial reports at such frequency as the trustees stipulate.
16. Accommodate the auditor in the periodic review of the trust fund's records.
17. Provide such information as is required by the actuary, the auditor, the consultant, the insurance company and the legal counsel in the performance of their duties.
18. Direct the investment of such funds as the trustees may specify. (Almost without exception, the administrator's investment assistance is limited to the short-term investment of small amounts of health and welfare, vacation pay and SUB money, it being understood that larger blocks of money should be handled by firms specializing in investment management.)
19. Pay insurance premiums, service fees and the other expenses incurred by the benefit trust.
20. Prepare and distribute annually (or more frequently if specified by the trustees) statements revealing to the members their personal recorded data, their trust fund credits and such other information as is required by the trustees and by government regulators.
21. Distribute to the members benefit descriptions and such other information as the trustees direct.
22. Distribute notices of, and agenda and other documentation for, all meetings of the trustees.
23. Attend such meetings of the trustees as the trustees require. Record, transcribe and distribute the minutes of such meetings.
24. File annual information returns with the pension regulators.
25. Hold the trust fund and the trustees harmless

against third-party action or diminution of the trust fund assets resulting from the error, omission or misconduct of the administrator. Insure such undertakings in the favour of the trust fund.

26. Guarantee the prompt transfer of all documentation held for the trustees, including the database, which should be guaranteed to be transferred, in machine-readable form, to the trustees or to their designated agent at such time as the trustees specify. (Generally, such action will occur only if the administrator's services are terminated.)

27. In relation to the administrator's service to a particular trust fund, the administrator should accept, as complete remuneration, only those fees that are specified in the administration service agreement.

The foregoing functions of administration exclude certain activities that are sometimes mistakenly attributed to the administrator but that, in fact, should be performed by other service agencies. They are noted below.

- The consultant, not the administrator, should be responsible for the design and modification of the benefit plan, the marketing and the renewal of insurance, the drafting of plan texts and descriptive literature on the benefits, the selection of funding arrangements, and the development of a formal investment policy.

- The actuary, not the administrator, should perform pension plan costings and valuations, and should handle the related filings with, and secure approvals from, the government regulators, and should determine the reserve requirements if health and welfare programs are self-funded.

- The auditor, not the administrator, should prepare and file income tax returns and, where applicable, the auditor should submit the special disclosure reports that flow from the trust fund audit.

WHAT TRUSTEES SHOULD KNOW ABOUT ADMINISTRATION

Ordinary self-interest dictates that trustees should have, or should acquire, a basic knowledge of administration. Since the administrator is the focal point for most of the benefit trust's business, many of the trustees' responsibilities are fulfilled by the administrator but, in the final analysis, the legal obligation remains with the trustees. Therefore, the trustees must, at all times, be comfortable in the fact that they have the right administrator doing the right job. That warrants a level of knowledge at least sufficient to decide the issues noted below.

- The kind of administration organization that should be employed

- The types and extent of the administration functions to be delegated to the administrator
- The method, timing and quality expected in the delivery of the administration functions
- The appropriate price to be paid for the administration service and the form the payment should take
- The procedure for assessing the acceptability of the ongoing administration work.

THE DIFFERENT KINDS OF ADMINISTRATION

There are two basic kinds of administration: contract administration (sometimes called *third-party administration*) and self-administration.

Contract Administration

Contract administration is performed by a person, organization or firm that is entirely unrelated, through ownership or other control, to the benefit trust, the trustees, the contributing employer(s) or the sponsoring union(s).

The contract administrator is hired by the trustees to perform a set of functions specified in a service agreement or contract. (This was the first kind of benefit trust administration to develop in Canada. Beginning in the mid-1950s, the concept of *contract administration* was imported from the United States. Transplanted in Canada by the international transportation and construction unions, contract administration—the natural companion of benefit trusts—grew and spread in concert with the proliferation of benefit trusts. Today, it is the predominant kind of benefit trust administration across the country.)

Self-Administration

Self-administration was developed as an alternative to address certain interests that were perceived not to be satisfied by the contract administration approach. It is performed by a person, organization or firm that is related, through ownership or other control, to the benefit trust in one of the following forms.

Salaried Self-Administration

Salaried self-administration (SSA) is an arrangement whereby the administration staff is employed by a benefit trust and works under the direction of the trustees.

In most cases, SSA has been chosen because trustees located outside the major business centers believe their primary interests are not served adequately by the contract administrators that, in turn, are generally based in the bigger cities. Such trustees tend to represent smaller benefit trusts in circumstances where the trustee-member relationships are quite personal. Those relationships are perceived as needing more tailored and intimate service than the contract administrator may be accustomed to providing.

Cooperative Self-Administration

Cooperative self-administration (CSA) involves an organization that serves several unrelated benefit trusts that share the operating expenses for the service and dictate the operating policy.

CSA originated in western Canada, where the average benefit trust tends to be smaller than in certain other parts of the country. It follows that the desire for local, more personalized service is strongly felt, but the solution manifested itself, not in the basic SSA approach, but in the form of the co-op, a concept that is well founded in the West.

It may be argued that the CSA, by serving several masters, surrenders some of the tailor-made intimacy of the SSA approach. However, CSA has advantages that flow from economies of scale.

Employer-Performed Self-Administration

Employer-performed self-administration (EPSA) is peculiar to single employer benefit trusts wherein the employer does the administration work for the trustees.

EPSA has advocates in various parts of Canada but, generally, within those industries that have turned most recently to the trust-sponsored form of benefit funding. In many cases, the employer had previously operated and controlled the benefit plans for the bargaining unit employees. Subsequently, the union negotiated the transfer of that control to a benefit trust, but the administration services have been left with the employer.

Some people look upon EPSA as a transitional adjustment toward one of the other forms of administration, either contract or self-administration. The speed with which the transition occurs depends upon the will of the bargaining parties to recognize, and react to, the dangers of EPSA. In terms of philosophical bias, conflict of interest, and the inadequate protection and enhancement of the beneficiaries' interests, the potential liabilities are magnified for the employer and the trustees alike when EPSA is used.

Client-Owned Self-Administration

Client-owned self-administration (COSA) involves a corporation that is owned by one or more of the benefit trusts it serves.

COSA was developed primarily by former users of contract administration. Generally, a number of boards of trustees came together, regionally or nationally, to create a large block of administration work that is judged to be big enough to support a full-blown and technically advanced administration firm.

The trustees may or may not come from the same industry. Their benefit trusts may or may not be merged. The commonality of interest is, simply, better and less expensive service than they perceive to be available on the open market.

THE TYPES AND EXTENT OF THE ADMINISTRATION FUNCTION TO BE PERFORMED

Some administration functions are required by law or government regulations. Most are made necessary by prudence and good common sense. Consider, for instance, that all pension statutes require the issuance of annual statements for the members, whereas similar statements are not legally required for the other kinds of benefit trusts.

The need for the member to know about, and be equipped to question, his or her fund status is arguably just as important under health and welfare or SUB as it is under pension. Therefore, many trustees have arranged for members' statements to be issued—sometimes more often than annually—from all kinds of benefit funds. In fact, some health and welfare trustees began the practice of issuing such statements before the parallel pension regulations ever existed. Obviously, the incentive for such farsightedness came from thoughtful analysis and good planning—the prerequisites for prudent action.

The list of mandatory administration functions varies somewhat from province to province and is affected by federal regulations. Therefore, each board of trustees should work with its professional advisors to understand and fulfill the legal requirements first. Then the trustees should compare the expectations of the members they serve with the current standards of the marketplace, to establish a desired package of functions.

After balancing the desired functions with the ability of the trust fund to pay, they should reach an optimum whereby the functions they come to employ are reasonable and affordable. Thereafter, the administration functions must be reassessed, continuously, and adjusted to maintain that balance.

THE METHODS, TIMING AND QUALITIES THAT SHOULD BE EXPECTED IN THE DELIVERY OF ADMINISTRATION SERVICE

After they have chosen an optimum set of administration functions, trustees must again take stock of the members' expectations and the trust fund's ability to pay. But, this time, the administration functions must be coordinated with the methods by which the functions are performed, the timing of that performance, and the principles and philosophies that should temper performance.

In many ways, members' expectations vary less from one benefit trust to the next than anything else. The members are, after all, just people who bring to the benefit trust relationship the attitudes of society at large regarding things monetary. They demonstrate the public's heightened awareness of good service: the common inclination to demand a full measure of personal entitlements and a large dose of cynicism for administrations, public and private. The trustees cannot alter those expectations. They must understand them and, in doing so, they must try to ensure that every administration function is delivered in ways and by means that are as compatible with the members' expectations as good judgment will allow.

Having anticipated methods, timing and qualities of administration that reflect the members' expectations, the trustees may have difficulty in making compatible arrangements. Not only is the translation from *expected* to *actual* a tedious task but, sometimes, it requires standards of service that are not readily available. That is because the organizations that perform administration (whether contract or self-administrators) possess a natural and understandable tendency to standardize their procedures and systems in order to control cost.

Cost control is, after all, a primary component of competition. It is also a condition that must concern the trustees. In the final analysis, the trustees may have to temper the members' expectations to arrive at realistic functional objectives. Then they must communicate those objectives in a clear and consistent manner to the members and to the agencies that serve their needs.

THE SELECTION, MONITORING, RETENTION OR TERMINATION OF AN ADMINISTRATOR

The final compromise, between the members' expectations and all the other conditions surrounding administration functions, is the basis for a formal specification from which competitive quotations may be secured. To complete the job, the trustees must define the scope and dimensions of the trust operations, such as the numbers of contributing employers, members, trustees meetings and general information mailings, and any other conditions that may have an impact on the cost of the administration service. That done, the specifications may be circulated to potential administrators from whom compliance, commitment and cost quotations will be received.

Analysis of the quotations on compliance and cost will tell the trustees whether any of the competing organizations are prepared to meet their requirements. If so, at what price? Armed with that information, the trustees can direct their attention to choosing between self-administration and contract administration and, if the latter, to choosing from among the competing firms.

Whatever the trustees' final decision on the kind of administration they want to employ (contract or self-administration), the specifications used to secure the quotations should form the contractual foundation for the administration service agreement. After enlargement by the trust fund's legal counsel to cover such matters as the purchase of insurance against administrative errors and omissions, the bonding of administrative staff, the consequences of nonfulfillment of the administrator's duties, the procedures for renewal of the agreement and the conditions of termination—and after the agreement has been executed by the administrator and the trustees—the trustees will have a benchmark from which to monitor the administrator's work.

The monitoring process warrants clear, precise definition. Who will develop and document the testing procedures? Who will carry them out? How frequently will the testing be done? How will the findings be acted upon? The answers to those questions should constitute a program for monitoring the administration services.

One of the more effective approaches to service monitoring involves the formation of a subcommittee of the board of trustees. For the sake of economy, such a subcommittee may be composed entirely of trustees, with the authority to call upon professionals, as they are required. Otherwise, the subcommittee's guidelines may be as described below.

1. It should be vested with authority and responsibility for the development and documentation of the monitoring program, to take effect after final approval by the board of trustees. Following board approval, the committee should operate the program.

2. The monitoring program should encompass at least the following conditions, to be judged against preset standards.
   - The quality of the database of member and employer records should be checked at least quarterly for accuracy, completeness and improvement.
   - The level of the members' satisfaction with the administration service should be sampled at least yearly in terms of clarity of communications, courtesy, response time and general helpfulness.
   - The trust fund's auditor should be directed to review (twice each year) and report on the administrator's work with regard to collection control, banking, investment, bookkeeping and related recordkeeping.
   - The overall quality and the cost of the administration services should be tested competitively, at least once every three years, by going to the open market for compliance and cost quotations. (The procedures for testing the

competitive market are explained in a subsequent part of this chapter.)

3. The subcommittee should establish a grading system against which the administration service may be scored. The grade levels should be interpretive, and each should require specific action. For example:
   - *A* means *above expectations* (related action: extend service agreement)
   - *B* means *meeting expectations* (related action: extend service agreement with caution)
   - *C* means *below expectations* (related action: issue warning and retest)
   - *D* means *nonfulfillment* (related action: terminate service agreement).

4. If the administrator is found to be performing above expectations or meeting expectations, then the service agreement may be extended. However, in the latter case, caution should apply because good administrators generally outperform the basic requirements of their agreements.

5. If the administrator is found to be performing below expectations, a formal warning should be issued. The warning should specify the nature of the performance deficiency, as well as the time limits for rectification. Appropriate testing must follow to determine whether the deficiency has been overcome within the prescribed time frame. If so, the administration service may be continued with appropriate qualification. If the deficiency is not overcome to the trustees' satisfaction, then the administration service must be terminated.

6. If the administrator is found not to have fulfilled the terms of the service agreement, then the related contract should be terminated forthwith.

7. The subcommittee should report at least semiannually to the full board of trustees on the results of the monitoring process. If remedial action, particularly termination, is required, then interim reporting may be necessary.

PROCEDURES FOR TERMINATING THE ADMINISTRATION SERVICE

Within reason, the trustees must have the absolute right to terminate the administration service, short of exhausting the full term of the current administration agreement. This right must, of course, cover breach or nonfulfillment of the agreement, as well as that nebulous condition wherein the trustees have lost faith in the administrator. (The legal terms *with cause* and *without cause* serve well, in this instance, to describe these two general conditions.)

The administration agreement must be precise in its dealing with service termination. It must express—precisely—the methods for giving notice of termination, the time constraints on such notice, and the responsibilities of both parties after notice has been given. The following illustration may be helpful.

1. Either party to the administration agreement may terminate the agreement without cause by giving 90 days' written notice to the other party.

2. The trustees may terminate the administration agreement with cause at such time as they, in their sole discretion, deem necessary. Written notice will be given. For this purpose, cause is constituted by:
   - Nonfulfillment or substantial breach of any term of the administration agreement
   - The administrator ceasing or threatening to cease to carry on its business, committing an act of bankruptcy, becoming insolvent, making an assignment in bankruptcy or making a bulk sale of its assets, or proposing a compromise or arrangement to its creditors
   - Proceedings being taken to have the administrator declared bankrupt or wound up, or to have a receiver appointed over any part of the administrator's property, or to allow an encumbrancer to take possession of any part of the administrator's property
   - The benefit trust ceasing to exist.

3. In the event the administration agreement is terminated, then the trustees and the administrator will proceed in the following ways.
   - The administrator will perform all the services that are normal for the period up to the termination date specified by the notice from the trustees.
   - The administrator will provide to the trustees (or their designated agent), within seven days of receiving the notice of termination, a machine-readable copy of the master record file (on members and contributing employers) as at the end of the last month prior to notice of termination being given.
   - The administrator will cease all administration services on the termination date, except for the post-termination actions described below.
   - During the 30 days immediately following the termination date, the trustees and the administrator will take and/or accommodate the following post-termination actions: The trustees will order, and the administrator will accommodate, a final audit of the trust fund; the administrator will deliver to the trustees, or their designated agent, all records (including a machine-readable copy of the master file on members and contributing employers as at the

termination date), all supporting documentation, all correspondence (old and new), all work in progress, all banking and investment records and materials, all assets, any computer programs and related documentation developed exclusively for the trust fund, and any other material or supplies purchased (directly or indirectly) by the trust fund. The trustees will provide to the administrator a detailed receipt for all of the items delivered in accordance with the foregoing provision. The administrator will present to the trustees an invoice for the services performed after the termination date to the extent that such services are not part of the administrator's routine responsibilities and, thereby, financed by other compensation; and, in the absence of dispute over the invoice described in the foregoing provision, the trustees will cause payment of the invoice to be made.

TESTING THE COMPETITIVE MARKET

Most businesses find it necessary to test the competitive position of their suppliers from time to time. The ways in which it is done and the frequency of doing it are peculiar to each enterprise. Trust funds are no different. Prudence dictates that trustees buy wisely; in other words, the cost and the quality of administration must be in line with the open market. That means that competitive testing must occur, but how and when?

Going to market with any service means preparing and distributing specifications and then analyzing the quotation results. Those three steps may be accomplished in various ways.

- If the trustees employ a benefit consulting firm unrelated to the administrator, then the consultant may do the work.
- If the administrator and the consultant are from the same organization, then an independent analyst may be required, especially when the trustees do not have the necessary expertise within their own group.
- If the trustees must go beyond themselves for consulting assistance, they may use their auditor, their legal counsel or both. If that fails, they may have to hire an outside consulting firm on a one-time basis.

Regardless of the trustees' final resolution of their need for technical assistance, there is a shortcut available to all trusts: Have the administrator describe the work. The administrator knows it best. And the administrator has a natural incentive to prepare the description. That incentive is fear: fear that someone else will misstate or understate the scope of the administration work through lack of familiarity with it; fear that a mis-

stated or understated set of specifications may produce inappropriately low quotations; fear that the administrator may lose the business as a result.

Assuage the incumbent's concerns. Tell the administrator that, as a matter of policy, not discontent, the market must be tested. Tell the administrator that the trustees want an apples and apples comparison. Express an understanding that the administrator can best describe the administration work, which is to everyone's advantage. The administrator will likely prepare the description faster, less expensively and much more accurately than anyone else.

The incumbent administrator's description of the current administration work should need little dressing up before distribution. That is the consultant's job. Then, it is the consultant's job to receive, analyze and report on the resulting quotations. Thereafter, the decision to change, or not to change, administrators rests solely with the trustees.

The frequency with which a given board of trustees tests the administration market will depend largely on the following factors.

1. Their satisfaction with the current services
2. Their understanding of the relationship between the service charges imposed and the administrator's costs to do business
3. The effectiveness of the current administration agreement in accommodating service charges reasonably and with controls satisfactory to both parties
4. The ability of the administrator to minimize the costs for service charges through technological advancement.

GOVERNMENT SCRUTINY: A GROWING TREND

The significance of thorough, accurate, benefit trust administration has recently taken several giant steps forward. In large measure the impetus for change has come from a new, more aggressive, form of government intervention. Whereas, in the past, Ottawa and the provinces legislated and communicated with plan sponsors from afar, they are now joining the operating grounds. They are sending representatives to administrative workshops, demanding direct access to documents and records, and evaluating trustees' governance, largely on the basis of their findings.

This new approach has sprung from the confluence of several regulatory streams. But, whether funding deficits or erratically applied provincial taxes or senatorial inquiries about the quality of trustees' governance was the main cause, the intrusions are here and likely to stay. Adherence to sound administrative practice is, unquestionably, a necessary defence.

CHAPTER 6

Fiduciary Responsibilities

by Roberto Tomassini

WHAT IS A FIDUCIARY?

The term *fiduciary* comes from the Latin *fiducia,* meaning trust or confidence.[1] In law, a person in whom trust or confidence is reposed is termed a *fiduciary* and is impressed with a duty of loyalty to those placing their trust in him or her.[2] This definition raises a further question: What kind of behaviour *in law* constitutes the reposing of trust or confidence in an individual?

The answer is not easily determined. As a noted Ontario justice said:

> In my opinion the category of cases in which fiduciary duties and obligations arise from the circumstances of the case and the relationship of the parties is no more closed than the categories of negligence at common law.[3]

The classic example of a fiduciary relationship is that of a trustee vis-á-vis the trust. The trust deed or agreement vests legal title to the trust property in the trustee and requires him or her to apply that property to a certain purpose in the best interest of the beneficiary of the trust. The concept of the fiduciary has been substantially expanded beyond the traditional doctrine rooted in trust law. A fiduciary relationship may be found to exist:

> . . . whenever any person acquires a power of any type on condition that he also receive with it a duty to utilize that power in the best interests of another, and the recipient of the power uses that power.[4]
>
> . . . where one party has placed "trust and confidence" in another and the latter has accepted expressly or by operation of law to act in a manner consistent with the reposing of such "trust and confidence."[5]

Therefore, on this expanded definition, anyone who has the authority to act with respect to an employee benefit plan in a way that can vitally affect the interests of a plan beneficiary, where the beneficiary reposes his or her trust and confidence in that person—for example, by making investment or benefit entitlement decisions or through a power to amend the plan—is likely to be labelled as a fiduciary. Accordingly, at common law, employers, administrators, corporate trustees and boards of trustees of such plans may be impressed with fiduciary status.

SOURCE OF FIDUCIARIES' DUTIES AND RESPONSIBILITIES

In their administration of a trust, benefit plan trustees and their professional advisors are governed by:

- The provisions of the plan and trust agreement
- Common law standards of fiduciary conduct
- Applicable legislation, which may include pension benefits, trustees, labour relations and income tax legislation, among others.

THE COMMON LAW DUTY OF CARE

What Are the Common Law Fiduciary Duties?

It is common to speak of a trustee's fiduciary responsibility at common law by saying that he or she owes a duty of care to the beneficiaries of the trust. Generally speaking, the duty owed to a beneficiary by a fiduciary is one of utmost good faith, requiring a "heightened sense of loyalty and fidelity."[6]

The fiduciaries' duty of care encompasses at least four distinct specific duties:

1. To act scrupulously for the benefit of the trust or the beneficiaries and never for himself or herself while carrying out his or her duties (the conflict-of-interest rule)
2. To be active in carrying out those duties and perform them with complete integrity (the standard-of-care rule)
3. To carry out those duties personally as a result of the trust and confidence reposed in him or her (the no-delegation rule)
4. To act impartially between the beneficiaries unless the trust instrument authorizes favouritism (the even-handed rule).

These duties apply to all trustees at common law, including employee benefit plan trustees.[7]

Conflict-of-Interest Rule

Still one of the leading cases on trustees and conflicts of interest is the English decision decided over 200 years ago. *Keech v. Sandford*[8] involved a trustee who held trust property consisting of a lease. When the lease expired, the owner refused to renew it with Sandford in his capacity as trustee but offered it to Sandford in his personal capacity. Sandford accepted and, in so doing, was found to have placed himself in a conflict-of-interest position despite the fact that the lease was no longer available to the trust.

In other words, a trustee will be in breach of the conflict-of-interest rule where he or she secures a benefit as a result of his or her status as trustee. It makes no difference whatsoever that his or her benefit was not secured at the expense of the trust or that it was a benefit that the trust was incapable of obtaining.

In fact, in a subsequent case, *Regal (Hastings) Limited v. Gulliver,*[9] trustees who acted in order to benefit the trust and incidentally made a personal profit were required to disgorge that profit. The court concluded:

The rule of equity which insists on those, who by use of a fiduciary position make a profit, being liable to account for that profit, in no way depends on fraud, or absence of bona fides; or upon such questions or considerations as whether the profit would or should otherwise have gone to the plaintiff, or whether the profiteer was under a duty to obtain the source of the profit for the plaintiff, or whether he took a risk or acted as he did for the benefit of the plaintiff, or whether the plaintiff has in fact been damaged or benefitted by his action. The liability arises from the mere fact of a profit having, in the stated circumstances, been made.[10]

Generally, trustees and other fiduciaries are required to avoid not only *actual* conflicts of interest but also *potential* conflicts of interest. Those aspects of benefit plan administration that may potentially give rise to conflict-of-interest situations are described later.

Common Law Standard of Care

The classic formulation of the standard of care owed by a trustee to the beneficiaries of a trust is over 100 years old now:

. . . the law requires of a trustee no higher degree of diligence in the execution of his office than a man of ordinary prudence would exercise *in the management of his own affairs.*[11] [Emphasis added.]

At a minimum, the standard of care requires that the trustee acquaint himself or herself with the terms of the trust, with the state of the trust property and with the contents of all documents affecting the trust property.[12] In a relatively recent decision, the Ontario Court (General Division) quoted from *Halsbury's Laws of England,* as follows:

The first duty of a trustee is to acquaint himself with the terms of the trust under which he acts, with the state of the trust property, and with the contents of all the deeds, notices and other documents and papers relating to or affecting the trust property which come into his possession or under his control.[13]

The court also noted that:

[n]ew trustees should further ascertain that the trust fund is properly invested, and that their predecessors have not committed breaches of trust which ought to be set right.[14]

The court, in its decision, held that:

[t]here can be no relief available to [the trustee] for its failure to be intimately familiar with the terms of the Plans.

Accordingly, [the trustee] cannot be excused from liability as a result of its failure to read the terms of the Plans. In addition, [the trustee] cannot and should not be excused from all of the consequences which were the direct result of its failure to read and understand the terms of the Plans and trust documents.[15]

The trustee is required to act strictly in accordance with the terms of the trust and, if he or she does so, he or she will not be liable if a loss subsequently occurs to some beneficiaries.[16] This standard of care also requires the trustee to bring proceedings to protect trust property and to defend against such proceedings where there is a reasonable prospect of success.[17] A failure to perform any one of these duties could place the trustee in breach of the standard of care owed by him or her to the trust and the beneficiaries.

The standard is not one of absolute correctness, but one that will excuse mistakes or errors of judgment. Thus, trustees who sold trust property for its appraised value were not found to have breached the standard of care even though the market value of the property was much higher.[18]

Although traditionally the common law in Canada established the same standard of care for all trustees, regardless of whether they are lay or professional trustees, courts are beginning to hold professional trustees to a higher standard of care.[19] In many instances, this standard of care has been elevated by statute for professional trustees or advisors with special skills, as well as for benefit plan trustees in general.

In the case of an agent who is paid for his services, a higher standard is exacted than in a case of an agent acting without reward. The care, skill or diligence required is not merely that which the agent in fact possesses, but rather is such as is reasonably necessary for the due performance of his undertaking. If he is an agent following a particular trade or profession, and holding himself out to the world for employment as such, he represents himself as reasonably competent to carry out the business which he undertakes in the course of such trade or profession. He must then show such care and diligence as are exercised in the ordinary and proper course, and such skill as is usual and requisite, in the business for which he receives payment....[20]

No-Delegation Rule

The general rule is that an administrator must personally perform all of the duties of the office requiring the exercise of his discretion. However, as an exception to this rule, an administrator is permitted to select agents to perform certain tasks where it would be regarded as prudent for a person in the ordinary course of business to delegate the performance of these duties....[21]

The no-delegation rule requires trustees to oversee all aspects of trust administration personally and prohibits them from delegating any tasks requiring the exercise of discretion to others. Unlike the conflict-of-interest rule and the standard-of-care rule, it is possible for a trust instrument to abrogate from this rule. Most employee benefit plans and trust agreements providing for the establishment of those plans will empower the trustee to retain professional advisors to assist in the administration of the trust. Even where the trustee is permitted to employ agents or to otherwise delegate functions, there is an obligation on him or her to:

- Select and supervise the agent or employee personally
- Employ him or her only so far as the matter lies within his or her professional competence.

Where these prerequisites are satisfied, the trustee will not be liable for any loss occasioned to the trust by the delegate's dishonesty, unless the trustee assists the delegate in his or her perfidy by failing to supervise him or her properly.[22]

In a case dealing with the administrator of an estate, it was noted that:

An administrator who puts the assets of an estate in the hands of an agent and takes no steps to ensure that the assets are properly dealt with, has breached the duty to supervise.[23]

The pension benefits legislation in several Canadian jurisdictions also authorizes the delegation of tasks to employees or agents.

The ultimate restriction on a trustee's ability to delegate trust matters is the principle that a *trustee may not divest himself or herself of the trust by employing an agent.* In other words, certain tasks are so central to the administration of the trust that they are nondelegable. Such decisions cannot be delegated to advisors or to the beneficiaries of the plan.[24] The determination of what tasks are of the nondelegable variety will depend on the nature of the duty and the settlor's intent as revealed in the trust instrument.

The rule which emerges from the authorities seems to be this: whenever the power, discretion or duty assigned to the trustee requires that a policy decision be made, the trustee must make it himself. A policy decision is one which, if dispositive, determines how much and at what time a beneficiary takes; if administrative, it directly affects the likelihood of the trust's object or purpose being achieved.[25]

For example, where a particular trust fund was for the purpose of providing academic scholarships, then a determination of who from among the designated class of beneficiaries ought to be the recipients of those scholarships was a policy decision required to be made by the trustee personally.[26] Where a trust was created by will and the trust property consisted in part of real estate that the trustee was expressly empowered to retain, the decision whether or not to retain the property was an administrative policy decision and, again, the trustee was required to make it personally.[27]

It must be emphasized that the common law requirement that a trustee act personally does not preclude a trustee from seeking professional advice; it merely precludes him or her from divorcing himself or herself completely from the decision making process.[28] An Ontario court dealt with the issue of delegation of responsibilities in a pension setting in a criminal law context. In *R. v. Blair*[29] a pension committee that the court deemed to be the administrator of the plan had purported to delegate the supervisory function over the investment manager to a trust company. The investment manager used half of the trust funds to purchase the sponsoring employer's shares to stave off a hostile takeover. The subsequent devaluation of the shares caused a major loss to the master trust. The committee was charged criminally under the Ontario *Pension Ben-*

efits Act for, inter alia, breaching the regulation that restricts a pension plan's investment in the sponsoring employer's corporation to 10%. The court held that:

> The P.B.A. requires, obligates, or mandates an administrator who by virtue of S.23(1) of the P.B.A. is a fiduciary, to perform certain responsibilities pursuant to the wording of S. 23(1); (2); and (7). The purpose or scheme of the Act requires a . . . pro-active approach as opposed to the approach engaged in and relied upon by the accused who urge me to find that by contractual agreement with Montreal Trust, the supervisory function over [the investment manager] in effect has been transferred to and assumed by Montreal Trust. This amounts to the administrator delegating its statutory supervision responsibility in S.23 (7) of the P.B.A. . . . I find that the statutory duty of the administrator to supervise under S. 23(7) of the P.B.A. in relation to the facts of this charge, is one that the administrator is obliged to discharge and is unable to delegate to another person or body.[30]

This decision was, however, overturned on appeal by the Ontario Court General Division. The primary basis upon which the conviction was reversed was that the pension committee was not held to be the administrator of the plan within the meaning of the PBA, and therefore its members could not be convicted for breaching the legal obligations imposed on the administrator by the statute. Moreover, the court also emphasized the lower court's failure to consider the role of the custodial trustee in monitoring fund investments when it determined that the committee did not prudently delegate and supervise the investment manager.

The decision on appeal in this case does not alter the fundamental principles of the nondelegation rule relied on by the lower court. Where trustees delegate certain of their responsibilities, the trustees must prudently select and supervise the agents or advisors selected.[31]

Even-Handed Rule

This duty generally requires fiduciaries to treat different beneficiaries and classes of beneficiaries equitably. However, as in the case with the above duties, the even-handed rule is subject to modification in the trust agreement. For example, a rich industrialist dies, leaving a will that provides for the distribution of his money among all his children in unequal proportions. The executor of his will is a trustee for the children who are the beneficiaries. The even-handed rule does not require the executor to give all the children an equal share of the money. Instead, provisions of the will requiring him to distribute it unequally prevail.

In a similar fashion, it is likely that many employee benefit plans will provide for the unequal allocation of benefits. For example, in a pension plan, participants who retire before a certain date may be entitled to benefits in accordance with a specified rate. Those who retire subsequently will be entitled to benefits at a different and sometimes higher rate. To the extent that the plan provisions permit the trustees to favour one group of beneficiaries, the even-handed rule will not be breached.

There are certain instances, however, when the trustees will be required to make discretionary decisions that are not contemplated by the plan or trust agreement. For example, money in excess of that required to fund the benefits promised under the plan may accumulate, and the trustees may wish to use it to increase benefits. At that point, they will have to determine the extent to which those benefit increases ought to be made retrospective, so that persons currently in receipt of benefits also enjoy the advantage of the increases.

Similarly, should the fund's solvency become threatened, the trustees may have to consider reducing benefits. Again, they will have to assess the extent to which certain classes of beneficiaries ought to bear more or less of the burden of the decision.

To Whom Do the Common Law Duties Apply?

Until now, reference has been made to the common law fiduciary standards as if they apply only to trustees. Certainly, trustees are the preeminent example of fiduciaries but, increasingly, the common law has extended the concept of *fiduciary* to impress these duties on all manner of persons. Almost anyone who exercises a discretionary power that he or she is required to exercise in the best interests of another may be considered a *fiduciary*.[32]

As the Supreme Court of Canada has stated:

> It is sometimes said that the nature of fiduciary relationships is both established and exhausted by the standard of categories of agent, trustee, partner, director, and the like. I do not agree. It is the nature of the relationship, not the specific category of actor involved that gives rise to the fiduciary duty. The categories of fiduciary, like those of negligence, should not be considered closed. . . .[33]

When the court is dealing with one of the traditional relationships, the characteristics or criteria for a fiduciary relationship are assumed to exist. Conversley, when confronted with a relationship that does not fall within one of the traditional categories, it is essential that the Court consider: what are the essential ingredients of a fiduciary relationship and are they present?[34]

While no "ironclad" formula has been formulated by the courts, the key ingredients of a fiduciary relationship are:

- The fiduciary has discretionary power.

- The fiduciary can unilaterally exercise the power so as to affect the beneficiaries' interests.
- The beneficiary is vulnerable to the fiduciaries' discretionary power.
- The beneficiary reasonably relies on the fiduciary to exercise the power in his or her best interest.[35]

Although the jurisprudence is not extensive, Canadian courts have imposed the fiduciary label on benefit plan administrators, advisors and agents based on the common law principle.

Re Collins and Pension Commission of Ontario[36] was a case in which a regulatory agency, the Pension Commission of Ontario, was held to owe a fiduciary duty to the members of a pension plan. Although there has been considerably less litigation in Canada concerning this issue, it has been held that financial advisors may be fiduciaries.[37]

In the British Columbia case of *Wynne v. William M. Mercer Ltd.,*[38] the actuarial firm was found liable for damages suffered by the plan when the actuaries prepared an erroneous valuation. However, the court held that the actuaries were not acting in a fiduciary capacity. Liability in this case was based on negligence.

In the *Aetna* case, the court held the fund manager accountable for losses suffered by the Metropolitan Toronto Pension Plan on the basis of a breach of fiduciary duty.

In *Froese v. Montreal Trust*[39] the British Columbia Court of Appeal imposed liability on the custodial trustee of a pension plan when it failed to recognize and disclose to participants the fact that the fund was in financial troubles. The court reached this conclusion notwithstanding that the trust agreement limited the trustee's responsibility excluding any duty with respect to pension fund investments. The court stated that the custodial trustee owes a common law duty to plan participants to warn or inform the beneficiaries that the employer has failed to make contributions when due. Where danger signals exist, the trustee has a duty to the beneficiaries to make adequate inquiries concerning the health of the plan fund.

In *Anova Inc. Employee Retirement Pension Plan v. Manufacturers Life Insurance Co.*[40] the court imposed the fiduciary label on the employer-sponsor of the pension plan with respect to its power to make amendments to the plan dealing with the use of surplus funds. The court held that the employer, as an administrator of the plan, owed a fiduciary duty to plan beneficiaries when making amendments regarding plan surplus. The court concluded that amendments introducing early retirement incentives for some plan members using surplus funds is consistent with the administrator's fiduciary duty. The rationale of the court is that such early retirement inducements benefit the company and are, therefore, of benefit to the employees. This rationale is clearly questionable in light of the voluminous litigation regarding the issue of surplus ownership where clearly the company's interest and employee interests are in conflict. The court did hold, however, that Anova's amendment, to the extent that it was a covert attempt to divert surplus to the employees who were shareholders of the company, was a violation of Anova's fiduciary duties.

Aside from these cases, there has been little litigation in Canada dealing with the issue of who, in addition to the trustees, might be the fiduciaries of a plan (although the courts have been steadily expanding the common law ambit of fiduciary duties).[41]

In the United States, the following categories of persons have been found to be fiduciaries:
- Those with the power to unilaterally amend the plan or propose amendments to it
- Those who act as plan administrators
- Those with the power to appoint the plan administrator or trustees
- Those supplying investment advice or services
- Persons assuming the pivotal role in plan administration through the operation of law rather than under the plan agreement, such as interest arbitrators or trustees in bankruptcy.

HOW EACH OF THE PROVINCES AND THE FEDERAL GOVERNMENT DEAL LEGISLATIVELY (IF AT ALL) WITH TRUSTEES' DUTIES AND RESPONSIBILITIES

The federal jurisdiction and each of the ten provinces have pension benefits legislation,[42] although Prince Edward Island's legislation has yet to be proclaimed.

Pension benefits legislation governs the administration of plans, providing for what is probably rightfully considered to be the single most important employee benefit: retirement income. It does not, however, govern the administration of plans established to provide other employee benefits independent of retirement benefits such as health and welfare benefits, vacation pay trust funds, training trust funds or supplementary unemployment insurance benefits. The administration of these plans will be governed primarily by the common law, but also by any applicable legislation respecting trustees generally. Because such legislation will govern trustees of estates for minors, executors appointed under a will and any other trustees, it obviously will not deal with the administration of employee benefit plans in the same detailed way that the pension benefits legislation does with respect to pension plans. Nevertheless, it is important to be aware of the provisions of those acts.

In some jurisdictions, the administration of employee benefit plans may be affected by provisions in the labour relations legislation. For example, the Alberta *Labour Relations Code*[43] limits the personal liability of trustees and the joint board of trustees of an employee benefit plan, except where the trustees failed to act honestly or in accordance with the intent and purpose of the trust instrument.[44] This provision is expressly stated to be paramount over any provision in the *Trustees Act.*

Finally, all employee benefit plans in Canada are affected by the provisions of the *Income Tax Act.* For example, this legislation places a ceiling on the amount of pension benefit payable to a retiree annually without tax consequences to the sponsor. Trustees of any pension plan will have to keep these provisions in mind in determining, for example, how to allocate surplus for benefit increases in order to minimize tax consequences.

A LOOK AT CERTAIN SPECIFIC AREAS OF IMPORTANCE FOR TRUSTEES

Duty of Care

Since 1985, new pension benefits legislation has been introduced in the following Canadian jurisdictions: Alberta, British Columbia, Manitoba, New Brunswick, Nova Scotia, Ontario, Prince Edward Island (not yet proclaimed) and the federal jurisdiction. The legislators in each of these jurisdictions consciously attempt to achieve a degree of uniformity in the statutes.

One area in which considerable uniformity was achieved was the articulation of the duties of care imposed on plan administrators (i.e., trustees). With the exception of Alberta, all these jurisdictions provide that the standard of care imposed on a trustee is that of "*a person of ordinary prudence dealing with the property of another.*" However, in the British Columbia *Pension Benefits Standards Act,*[45] the wording is "under comparable circumstances" rather than "dealing with the property of another." The standard of care appears to be somewhat higher than the one that would be imposed on the trustees at common law, where they would be required to exercise the care that a person of ordinary prudence would in dealing with "his or her own property."

Additionally, the as yet unproclaimed legislation in Prince Edward Island and the legislation in Manitoba, New Brunswick, Nova Scotia, Ontario, Quebec and the federal jurisdiction impose on the trustee possessing any special professional or business skill the obligation to utilize that skill in the operation of the fund. This standard coincides with the higher standard of care that courts are beginning to impose on professional trustees.

The legislation in these provinces also contains an express prohibition on trustees placing themselves in conflict-of-interest positions. The approach to trustees' duties and responsibilities under the Alberta legislation is completely different. Instead of articulating the specific duties imposed on a trustee, the *Employment Pension Plans Act*[46] merely provides that the administrator of the plan stands in a fiduciary capacity in relation to plan beneficiaries. Arguably, this provision incorporates the common law standards.

Although Newfoundland and Saskatchewan also have pension benefits legislation in effect, these statutes do not contain a general articulation of the standard of care imposed on the plan administrator (i.e., trustees) in the administration of the trust. In the case of Saskatchewan, the legislation does stipulate that a fiduciary relationship exists between the plan administrator and the beneficiaries, and that a trustee relationship exists in relation to the fund.[47] These provisions therefore incorporate the common law fiduciary duties. Where the fiduciary duties imposed on trustees are not specified in legislation, presumably, the common law standards apply (except in the case of Quebec).

In New Brunswick, this standard will be identical for all employee benefit plans, at least with respect to investments, because the *Trustees Act* in that province specifies that the standard of care in connection with investments is that of a person of prudence, discretion and intelligence dealing with the property of others.

Some assistance respecting the application of the standard of care to the administration of employee benefit plans may be derived from the American jurisprudence under the *Employee Retirement Income Security Act of 1974* (ERISA). ERISA is helpful in Canada as it is based to a large extent on the common law. The following examples illustrate situations in which benefit plan trustees have been found to have violated the prudence standard:

- Where the trustees entered into a real estate deal that they had not properly investigated by obtaining evaluation reports, surveys and so on[48]
- Where the trustees purchased whole life insurance rather than group term insurance without knowledge of the differences between the two plans, without the advice of professionals and without securing a competitive bid, and where the cost of the whole life insurance was three times that of the group life insurance[49]
- Where the trustees failed to seek outside advice concerning the soundness of a loan[50]
- Where the trustees failed to create a system to ascertain the amounts owed to the plan under a reciprocal agreement with another fund and to verify that those amounts were actually remitted[51]
- Where the plan administrator failed to notify plan members of financial problems arising from insufficient employer contributions when such information would have enabled the participants to arrange for other health and welfare coverage.[52]

From these examples, trustees are most likely to get

themselves into a situation where they are in violation of the prudence standard when they fail to adequately investigate and assess the risks associated with a proposed investment or transaction. When they do take such investigative steps, however, they will not necessarily violate the prudence standard even though they enter into investments that are apparently disadvantageous to the fund, as illustrated by the following example.

The trustees of a fund consulted with lawyers, actuaries and other professional advisors before deciding to charge plan participants an interest rate below the prevailing market rate for mortgages. They did not violate the prudence standard, since the experts' advice revealed that this sort of rate would have to be offered by a noninstitutional lender in order to attract borrowers.[53]

Although benefit plan trustees can act imprudently even while acting honestly,[54] the question of whether they have observed the prudence standard frequently arises in cases that also involve an element of self-dealing. The following cases are illustrative of how closely connected these two fiduciary duties are:

- Trustees who did not demand a fair building rental from the plan sponsors violated both the prudence standard and ERISA's prohibition on transacting with parties in interest.[55]
- Similarly, trustees who inadequately investigated plan loans that they then offered to the union sponsoring a building project violated both duties.[56]
- Trustees who hired a consultant at an exorbitant price without inquiring into his qualifications or following the accepted standards for hiring him violated the prudence standard. They also violated the conflict-of-interest rule by loaning plan dollars from one plan to another at below-market interest rates.[57]
- Trustees who invested all of the plan's assets in loans to companies affiliated with the sponsor in exchange for unsecured promissory notes violated the prohibition on transacting with a party in interest and also violated the prudence standard since the high interest rates paid on the loans did not adequately compensate the fund for the magnitude of the risk involved.[58]
- Trustees who loaned trust assets to a former trustee on the basis of inadequate security also violated both duties.[59]
- Trustees who purchased an enormous amount of employer stock at an inflated price in order to thwart a corporate takeover also violated both duties.[60]
- The administrator of a trust fund may violate the standard of prudence in failing to establish an adequate supervision system over the investment manager of the fund.[61]

In the above situations, it is sometimes difficult to tell whether the fact that the trustees entered into a transaction with the employer or someone closely identified with the employer would in itself have constituted a violation of ERISA because the party is obviously in a conflict-of-interest position, or whether it was a combination of an imprudent investment benefiting the party in interest that grounded the finding that ERISA had been violated.

However, there is authority for the proposition that the fund and one of the constituting parties to the trust can enter into a transaction where the transaction is beneficial to the participants and is otherwise prudent. Thus, in *Donovan v. Walton,*[62] it was held to be permissible for the fund to lease a building to the union as a tenant since both the fund and the union benefited from the transaction, a reasonable rent was charged, and it was a prudent transaction for the fund to enter into. This is an important case for multi-employer plan trustees since they often enter into cost-sharing agreements with the union or an employer association.

ENDNOTES

1. J.C. Traupman, *The Bantam New College Latin and English Dictionary* (Toronto: Bantam Books, 1995), at p. 180.

2. Waters, D., *Law of Trusts in Canada,* second edition (Toronto: Carswell, 1984), at p. 33.

3. Per Arnup, J. A., in *Laskin v. Bache and Company Inc.,* [1972] 1 O.R. 465 (C.A.), at p. 472. See also *Guerin v. The Queen* (1984), 13 D.L.R. (4th) 321 (SCC) per Dickson C.J.C. at p. 341.

4. J.C. Shepherd, *The Law of Fiduciaries,* (Toronto: Carswell, 1981) at p. 96.

5. M.V. Ellis, *Fiduciary Duties in Canada* (Toronto: Carswell, 1993), at pp. 1-2.

6. *Ibid.,* at pp. 1-2.

7. *Cowan v. Scargill,* [1984] 2 All E.R. 750 (Ch. D.).

8. *Keech v. Sandford,* [1726] All E.R. Rep. 230.

9. *Regal (Hastings) Limited v. Gulliver,* [1941] 1 All E.R. 378 (H. L.).

10. *Ibid.,* at p. 386.

11. *Learoyd v. Whiteley* (1887), 12 App. Cas. 727 (H. L.) at p. 733.

12. 48 Hals. 4th, para. 817; *Hallows v. Lloyd* (1988), 39 Ch. D. 686; *Harvey v. Olliver* (1887), 567 L.T. 239; *Ford v. Laidlaw Carriers Inc.* (1993), 1 C.C.P.B. 97 (O.C. (G.D.)) rev'd in part (1994), 12 C.C.P.B. 179 (Ont. C.A.), leave to appeal to the S.C.C. refused (1995), 191 N.R. 400 (note).

13. *Ibid.,* 48 Hals. 4th, para. 817 as quoted in *Ford v. Laidlaw* (1993) 1 C.C.P.B. 97 (O.C. (G.D.)) at p. 166, rev'd in part (1994), 12 C.C.P.B. 179 (Ont. C.A.), leave to appeal to the S.C.C. refused (1995), 191 N.R. 400 (note).

14. *Ford v. Laidlaw Carriers Inc., supra* note 13 at p. 168, quoting from *Underhill's Law of Trusts and Trustees,* 13th ed., art. 48.

15. *Ford v. Laidlaw Carriers Inc., supra* note 13 at p. 169.

16. 48 Hals. 4th, para. 818. *Ford v. Laidlaw Carriers Inc., supra* note 13.

17. 48 Hals. 4th, para. 820; *Re Brogden, Billing v. Brogden* (1888), 38 Ch.D. 546 (C.A.), [1886-90] All E.R. Rep. 927.

18. *Davies v. Nelson*, [1928] 1 D.L.R. 254 (Ont. C.A.).

19. *Bartlett v. Barclays Bank Trust Co. Ltd.*, [1980] 1 All E.R. 139; *Ford v. Laidlaw Carriers Inc., supra* note 13; *Metropolitan Toronto Pension Plan v. Aetna Life Assurance Co. of Canada* (1992), 98 D.L.R. (4th) 582 (O.C. (G.D.)).

20. *Metropolitan Toronto Pension Plan v. Aetna Life Assurance Co. of Canada, supra* note 19 at p. 597.

21. *Wagner v. Van Cleeff* (1991), 5 O.R. (3d) 477 at 484 (Div. Ct.).

22. Waters, *supra* note 2 at p. 698.

23. *Wagner v. Van Cleeff, supra* note 21 at p. 485.

24. *Metropolitan Toronto Police Services Board v. Ontario Municipal Employees Retirement Board* (1994), 20 O.R. (3d) 210 (Div. Ct.).

25. Waters, *supra* note 2 at p. 707.

26. *Re Partanen* (1944), O.W.N. 130, [1944] 2 D.L.R. 473 (C.A.).

27. *Re Wilson*, [1937] 3 D.L.R. 178 (C.A.).

28. See, for example, *Wagner v. Van Cleeff, supra* note 21.

29. *R. v. Blair* (1993), 106 D.L.R. (4th) 1 (Ont. Prov. Div.), rev'd on appeal (1995), 9 C.C.P.B. 1 (G.D.).

30. *Ibid.*, at p. 80.

31. Eileen E. Gillese, *The Law of Trusts,* (Concord, Ontario: Irwin, 1997), at p. 136.

32. Shepherd, *supra* note 4 at p. 35.

33. *Guerin v. The Queen, supra* note 3 at p. 341.

34. *Lac Minerals Ltd. v. International Corona Resources Ltd.*, [1989] 2 S.C.R. 574 at p. 598.

35. *Hodgkinson v. Simms* (1994), 117 D.L.R. (4th) 161 (S.C.C.).

36. *Re Collins and Pension Commission of Ontario* (1986), 56 O.R. (2d) 274 (Div. Ct.).

37. *Hodgkinson v. Simms, supra* note 35.

38. *Wynne v. William M. Mercer Ltd.* (1993), 1 C.C.P.B. 301 (B.C. S.C.), aff'd (1995), 11 C.C.P.B. 1 (B.C.C.A.).

39. *Froese v. Montreal Trust Co. of Canada* (1996), 11 C.C.P.B. 233 (B.C. C.A.).

40. *Anova Inc. Employee Retirement Pension Plan v. Manufacturers Life Insurance Co.* (1994), 121 D.L.R. (4th) 162 (O.C. (G.D.)).

41. *Lac Minerals Limited v. International Corona Resources Limited, supra* note 34.

42. *Employment Pension Plans Act*, S.A. 1986, c.E.-10.05; *Pension Benefits Standards Act*, R.S.B.C. 1996, c. 352; *Pension Benefits Standards Act*, 1985, R.S.C. 1985, c. 32; *Pension Benefits Act*, R.S.M. 1987, c. P32; *Pension Benefits Act*, S.N.B. 1987, c. P-5.1; *Pension Benefits Act*, S.N. 1996, 1997, P-4.01; *Pension Benefits Act*, R.S.N.S. 1989, c. 340; *Pension Benefits Act*, R.S.O. 1990, c. P.8; *Pension Benefits Act*, S.P.E.I. 1990, c. 41, not proclaimed; *Supplemental Pension Plans Act*, R.S.Q. 1990, R-15.1; *Pension Benefits Act*, 1992 S.S. 1992, c. P-6.001.

43. Alberta *Labour Relations Code*, S.A. 1988, c. L-12.

44. *Ibid.*, s. 24.

45. British Columbia *Pension Benefits Standards Act, supra* note 42.

46. Alberta *Employment Pension Plans Act, supra* note 42, s. 6(5).

47. Saskatchewan *Pension Benefits Act*, 1992, *supra* note 42, s. 11(2).

48. *Brock v. Wells Fargo Bank*, N.A., 7 EBC 1221 (N.D.Cal. 1986).

49. *Donovan v. Tricario*, 5 EBC 2057 (S.D.Fla. 1984).

50. *Katsaros v. Cody*, 5 EBC 1777 (2d Cir. 1984).

51. *Nichols v. Trustees of Asbestos Workers Pension Plan*, 3 EBC 1726 (D.C.Cir. 1982).

52. *McNeese v. Health Plan Marketing Inc.*, 8 EBC 1154 (N.D.Ala.).

53. *Brock v. Walton*, 7 EBC 1769 (11th Cir. 1986).

54. *Brock v. Robbins*, 8 EBC 2489 (7th Cir. 1987).

55. *Brock v. Self*, EBC 1512 (W.D.La. 1986).

56. *Davidson v. Cook*, 4 EBC 1816 (E.D.Va. 1983).

57. *Donovan v. Mazzola*, 4 EBC 1865 (9th Cir. 1983).

58. *Freund v. Marshall & Ilsley Bank*, 1 EBC 1898 (W.D.Wis. 1979).

59. *Dooley Associates Employees Retirement Plan v. Reynolds*, 8 EBC 1785 (E.D.Mo. 1987).

60. *Donovan v. Bierwirth*, 3 EBC 1417 (2d Cir. 1982).

61. *R. v. Blair, supra* note 29.

62. *Donovan v. Walton*, 6 EBC 1677 (S.D.Fla. 1985).

CHAPTER 7

Trustees and Their Professional Advisors

by Susan Philpott

WHO ARE THE ADVISORS?

Generally, employee benefit trust funds, and pension funds in particular, permit the trustees to seek the opinion and advice of professionals such as actuaries, lawyers and accountants. The right to do that must be specifically provided for in the trust agreement creating the fund, as trustees at common law cannot delegate any of their responsibilities. Given the complexity of modern day trust funds, the large number of beneficiaries involved and the legal framework under which trustees and trust funds must operate, professional advice is increasingly critical to trustees.

As we have already examined the role of the administrator, we review the role of various other advisors in this chapter. Specifically, we will now turn our attention to the role of the actuary, the auditor, consultants, legal counsel and investment counsel.

SELECTING PROFESSIONAL ADVISORS

Although trustees are dependent on professional advisors and have the power to engage and rely on them, it must always be remembered that the buck stops with the board of trustees. Ultimately, the trustees are responsible for the actions of the trust, even though they are relying on ostensibly valid professional advice.

It is for this reason that the trustees must be particularly careful in the selection of their advisors, ensuring that they obtain competent and professional service. This is consistent with the fiduciary obligation of trustees at common law, as the exercise of the duty of prudence requires that appropriate care and attention be given to the selection of professional advisors.

In the case of pension funds, this concept has been codified in pension benefits legislation. For example, in the Ontario *Pension Benefits Act* (the "Ontario Act"), Subsection 22(5) provides that:

> 22(5) Where it is reasonable and prudent in the circumstances so to do, the administrator of a pension plan [i.e. the board of trustees] may employ one or more agents to carry out any act required to be done in the administration of the pension plan and in the administration and investment of the pension fund.[1]

If they do retain an agent, the trustees of the pension fund must personally select the agent and supervise his or her performance, as required by Subsection 22(7) of the Ontario Act:

> An administrator [the trustees] of a pension plan who employs an agent shall personally select the agent and be satisfied of the agent's suitability to perform the act for which the agent is employed, and the administrator shall carry out such supervision of the agent as is prudent and reasonable.[2]

As trustees are generally laypeople, it is not expected that they exercise the same skill and ability as the professionals they retain. They must, however, satisfy themselves of the suitability of the professional advisors they select. Moreover, they have an obligation to *supervise* the agents to the extent that it is prudent and reasonable to do so.

Personal Selection

In order to best ensure that this requirement is met, there are some basic steps that a trustee should follow in selecting and reviewing the performance of professional advisors. In selecting advisors, it is critical that trustees entertain proposals from a number of firms and interview potential auditors, actuaries, legal counsel, investment managers or other professionals, before making a selection. References should be sought and investigated, and attention should be paid to whether the individual or firm has experience in handling trust fund work. One method used by some funds to judge candidates is to ask them to provide advice based on a fictional fact situation, and thereby measure how the candidate will perform. Although there is not a fail-safe method of selecting the best candidate for any position, inquiries of other clients and use of experienced experts, particularly for large funds, are useful guidelines.

Supervision

In addition to taking appropriate steps in selecting advisors, it is also critical that trustees monitor the performance of their advisors and periodically review them. Performance reviews should be conducted at regularly scheduled intervals, and the trustees should establish standards against which the performance of professionals is judged. This is particularly so with respect to investment counsellors, whose performance can be measured against that of others in the field. Most sizable pension funds compare their investment performance with other funds annually and engage the services of performance measurement consultants for this purpose.

Further, it is incumbent on trustees to question any area of the performance of their professional advisors where they have some concerns. It will not always be sufficient for the trustees to reply to complaints of beneficiaries regarding the administration or investment of a fund by saying that they are only following the advice of the actuary or the investment manager.

Agents' Fiduciary Obligations

In addition to the trustees' obligations of prudence in selecting and monitoring their agents and professional advisors, those agents may have an independent duty to act in accordance with fiduciary standards. Section 22(8) of the Ontario *Pension Benefits Act* imposes upon the professional advisors the same standards of prudence and obligation to avoid conflicts of interest that apply to the trustees themselves. It provides:

An employee or agent of an administrator is also subject to the standards that apply to the administrator under subsections (1), (2) and (4).

Additionally, the Supreme Court of Canada has ruled that advisors may be in a fiduciary relationship with those whom they advise and thus will be required to meet the standards of a fiduciary, as set out in the previous chapter, while executing their advisory functions.[3]

The frequency with which courts have enforced fiduciary duties and professional advisory relationships is not surprising. The very existence of many professional advisory relationships, particularly in specialized areas such as law, taxation and investments, is premised upon full disclosure by the client of vital personal and financial information that inevitably results in a "power-dependency" dynamic.[4]

The following judicial statement was made in relation to investment brokers but is equally applicable to other types of advisors:

The relationship of the broker and client is elevated to a fiduciary level when the client reposes trust and confidence in the broker and relies on the broker's advice in making business decisions. When the broker seeks or accepts the client's trust and confidence and undertakes to advise, the broker must do so fully, honestly and in good faith. . . . It is the trust and reliance placed by the client which gives to the broker the power and in some cases, discretion, to make a business decision for the client. Because the client has reposed that trust and confidence and has given over that power to the broker, the law imposes a duty on the broker to honour that trust and respond accordingly.[5]

This requirement that advisors behave as fiduciaries does not mean that trustees should be any less vigilant. They are still ultimately responsible and, in the event of a major financial loss to the fund, the professional advisor may not be solvent or have sufficient insurance to cover any liabilities. Then the injured parties may look to the trustees for their remedies.

ACTUARIES

The CIA

Actuaries are a recognized professional group with a level of technical expertise that is necessary to the operation of pension plans and useful in many other contexts. They are governed by professional regulatory body called the Canadian Institute of Actuaries (the "CIA"), which is responsible for ensuring that the appropriate level of education, skill and expertise exists among its membership, and requires that actuaries, to be recognized and practise as such, comply with the CIA's prescribed criteria for qualification and Rules of Professional Conduct. The role of the CIA has been formally recognized in pension benefits legislation that defines *actuary* in reference to the CIA.[6]

The Role of the Actuary

Actuaries are most active in the context of pension trust funds, though they frequently consult on health and welfare funds, particularly when group risk arrangements are undertaken in areas such as life insurance or long-term disability. The role of an actuary in a pension plan, however, is crucial in respect of all sorts of matters including pension plan design, funding and efficient reporting and administration. This role is, of course, recognized under pension benefits legislation in the various provinces and under the federal *Pension Benefits Standards Act,* which requires that defined benefit plans use an actuary to provide:

- A triennial actuarial report
- Calculation of commuted values for purposes of portability, marriage breakdown and pre- and post-retirement death benefits
- Actuarial certificates on plan wind-up
- In the case of a multi-employer pension plan (MEPP), particularly under Ontario's regulations, certificates regarding the solvency of the plan and benefits being provided in relation to the contributions being received.

In the case of multi-employer plans, the role of an actuary is even more important because there is a defined contribution component in addition to the usual defined benefit. In single employer plans, by way of contrast, the employer generally underwrites the costs of the defined benefit and does not have a specific fixed rate of contribution. In the case of a MEPP, however, the advice of the actuary is necessary to ensure that an appropriate benefit package can be provided. In addition, certificates for plans other than defined contribution plans and insured plans must be made by an actuary as required by the regulations under the Ontario Act.[7]

Professional Standards of Care

As pension law has developed, numerous actuarial practices have been standardized and adopted by the Canadian Institute of Actuaries, such as the method for calculating commuted values. Those standards have in turn been adopted into the regulations under pension benefits legislation, and thus the CIA plays an increasingly larger role in the standardization of pension administration and in the standards to which actuaries will be held.

The Supreme Court of Canada has recently stated:
[T]he rules set by the relevant professional body are of guiding importance in determining the nature of the duties flowing from a particular professional relationship. . . . [I]t would be surprising indeed if the courts held the professional advisor to a lower standard of responsibility than that deemed necessary by the self regulating body of the profession itself.[8]

As indicated above, the CIA, as a professional regulatory body to which all actuaries belong, has in place a set of Rules of Professional Conduct. Those rules require actuaries to perform their duties with "integrity,

skill and care" and prohibit them from accepting work where it places them in a position of conflict of interest.

Because of their special expertise and the extensive dependence of pension clients on their services, the courts will likely continue to hold actuaries to a high standard in providing advice. In fact, the British Columbia Supreme Court has held actuaries responsible for all losses incurred by the trustees of a pension plan where the actuaries made an error in their valuation of the pension plan on which the trustees relied.[9]

Fiduciary Obligations?

At the time of writing, the issue of whether the fiduciary obligations enshrined in pension legislation, and at common law, apply to actuaries vis-á-vis plan members, when providing advice and services to a pension plan administrator, has not been legally tested in Canada. However, in a recent Ontario case,[10] an actuarial firm has been named a defendant in an action based on an alleged breach of fiduciary duties. The actuarial firm argued, on a preliminary motion, that the claim ought to be dismissed, as no Canadian decision has ever held that a pension plan actuary owes a fiduciary duty to plan beneficiaries.

The judge rejected the arguments of the actuaries, noting that the fact that the legal claim is a novel one does not bar an action from proceeding. Moreover, the mere fact that the defendants were actuaries could not conclusively determine the issue of whether or not they are fiduciaries. The court stated:
. . . fiduciary relationships do not depend on the identity of the individuals or entities involved, but rather arise from the nature of the relationship itself.

Selecting an Actuary

Certainly the professional obligations of actuaries extend to the plan beneficiaries to the extent that their role in ensuring the solvency of the plan is critical in protecting the interests of the beneficiaries. In choosing an actuary, it is important to ensure that he or she is a member of the Canadian Institute of Actuaries. Beyond this basic requirement, trustees should also consider the following criteria:

- What is the capability of the actuary/firm?
- Is local service important?
- What experience does the firm have in serving similar funds?
- What is the reputation of the firm?
- What services does the actuary need to provide to the plan?
- Is the firm large enough to provide services needed by the plan? Does the firm have the resources?
- What are the fees? Are they competitive?

AUDITORS

As a matter of common law, beneficiaries of the trust are always entitled to an accounting of how trust fund monies are being expended. Accordingly, prudence dictates that trustees of any sizable trust fund engage the services of a firm of reputable chartered accountants to provide annual audits. It is important to ensure that the accountants hired are licensed under the applicable provincial legislation regulating the accounting profession, such as the *Public Accountancy Act.*[11] In fact, many trust agreements require that the trustees retain an auditor and perform annual audits.

Pension Plans

Statutory requirements regarding pension plans may also require audits. For example, Section 76 of the regulations under the Ontario *Pension Benefits Act* requires any fund with at least $3 million in assets to file an auditor's report annually respecting the financial statements. Such report must be prepared by an accountant licensed under the *Public Accountancy Act* and must be filed within six months of the fiscal year-end. The regulations provide a detailed checklist with which the audit report must comply.

Further, Subsection 76(8) of Ontario's regulations adopts the requirement that audits for pension funds must be performed in accordance with the principles and standards set out in the handbook of the Canadian Institute of Chartered Accountants. Much like the standards of actuarial practise, the rules established by the professional bodies for accountants are also expressly approved and adopted by legislation.

The regulations in the Ontario Act also require an accountant, by virtue of Section 76(15), to report to the plan administrator (or board of trustees) any irregularity that may indicate a contravention of the audit requirements set out in the regulation. If such irregularity is significant and has not been corrected within 30 days of it first being reported, the auditor has an "obligation" to notify the Superintendent of Financial Institutions. Accordingly, there are statutory obligations in Ontario, in addition to professional ones, imposed upon auditors involved with pension funds. British Columbia, New Brunswick, Quebec and federal pension legislation now also contain auditing requirements for some, but not all, pension plans.

Other Trust Funds

An additional requirement pertaining to auditors is contained in Section 93 of the Ontario *Labour Relations Act.*[12] This provision requires the administrator of any vacation pay fund, welfare fund or pension fund for the members of a trade union to file an annual audited financial statement with the Minister of Labour, certified by a person licensed under the *Public Accountancy Act.* This financial statement must contain such information as:

- Description of fund coverage
- Amount contributed by each employer
- Amounts contributed by members and the trade union, if any
- Statement of assets, specifying the total amount of each type of asset
- Statement of liabilities, receipts and disbursements
- Statement of salaries, fees and commission charges to the fund or plan, to whom they are paid, in what amount and for what purposes.

Apart from such statutory provisions as Section 93 of the Ontario *Labour Relations Act,* beneficiaries of trusts are entitled at common law to an accounting that details how the trust fund monies are being spent. Trust funds should always maintain proper audited financial statements.

CONSULTANTS

There is no statutory recognition of a "benefit plan consultant." Under pension legislation, such consultants would, of course, be agents, as contemplated by Section 22 of the Ontario legislation and the counterparts of this provision in other jurisdictions.

In the United States, consultants have been found liable to the trustees and found in breach of their fiduciary obligations where they advised the trustees to enter into prohibited lease transactions and the trustees relied heavily upon the consultant to answer any and all questions regarding administration and management of the plan.[13] The Supreme Court of Canada has also indicated that advisors such as consultants will be held to the standard of a fiduciary in carrying out their advisory functions.[14]

LEGAL COUNSEL

Lawyers have historically been found by the courts to owe a fiduciary duty to their clients in respect of any matter in which their advice is sought. Given the special confidence involved in the lawyer-client relationship and the heavy reliance on legal advice, the duty that a lawyer owes to his or her client is very high, even without the fiduciary standards that are imposed under pension benefits legislation.

In selecting a lawyer for the trust fund, it is important to ensure that the lawyer who is hired to represent a trust has sufficient errors and omissions insurance coverage, which they are required to purchase. Additionally, it is important to ensure that any legal counsel hired is a member in good standing of the professional body that regulates the legal profession.

Although many trustees generally deal with legal

counsel in the context of outstanding litigation, there is a great deal of *preventive* work that legal counsel can perform in a proactive way to put the trust fund in the best possible position to avoid future litigation and avoid running afoul of the legal requirements trustees must adhere to. In addition to drafting legal documents, such as trust agreements, counsel are often called upon to review plan texts, particularly in view of the more complex legal requirements under pension legislation.

Legal counsel also often draft such documents as investment counsel agreements, custodian agreements, cost sharing agreements and other formal agreements entered into by the trustees, as well as providing legal opinions to the trustees on various matters arising in the course of the exercise of their administrative duties.

It is not generally necessary for legal counsel to attend all trustees meetings, although some trust funds prefer this. The most efficient use of legal resources would require counsel to come and report at trustees meetings at a fixed time and deal solely with legal issues. In respect of other matters discussed at trustees meetings, many trust funds follow the practice of forwarding their minutes to legal counsel for review, in the event that other matters have arisen that may give rise to legal concerns.

INVESTMENT COUNSEL

Employee benefit funds, and pension funds in particular, are heavily dependent on investment counsel to produce investment returns. Given the liberalization of investment rules applicable to such funds and the broad discretion trustees have in making investments, it is important that trustees act very carefully in choosing investment advisors. An essential step in this process is to ensure that the investment advisor is duly registered under the appropriate provincial securities legislation governing such persons, such as the *Securities Act* in Ontario.[15]

Further, it is important that the trustees develop an investment policy setting out goals and objectives. In Ontario (s. 67), British Columbia (s. 38(3)), New Brunswick (s. 44(3)) and in the federal jurisdiction (s. 7.1), the creation of such an investment policy is mandatory.[16] Given the large sums of money investment counsellors must invest, prudence dictates that the trustees be very careful to ensure that such persons have experience in the investment field and are indeed licensed under the applicable securities legislation in the provinces where the pension fund operates.

In the United States, the Department of Labor has promoted a number of factors that ought to be considered by trustees in selecting investment managers. These factors have been highlighted in a number of consent judgments and include:

- The business structure and affiliations of the candidate
- The financial condition and capitalization of the candidate
- A description of the investment style proposed by the candidate
- A description of the investment process to be followed by the candidate
- The identity, experience and qualifications of the professionals who will be handling the plan's portfolio
- Whether any relevant litigation or enforcement actions have been initiated within a reasonably relevant time against the candidate, the candidate's officers or directors, or the candidate's investment professionals who have responsibility for the plan's portfolio
- A description of the experience and performance record, over an appropriate time period, of the candidate and its investment professionals, including experience managing other tax-exempt and employee benefit plan assets
- Whether the candidate has and would propose to utilize the services of an affiliated broker/dealer and, if so, the types of transactions for which such affiliates would be used and the financial arrangement with the broker/dealer.[17]

Many large funds take the further prudence step of diversifying their assets among a number of investment managers so as to spread the risk of poor performance.

In determining the goals and objectives of a pension fund and the list of permissible investments, trustees must often rely on their investment managers for advice as to which types of investments are most appropriate for the fund. Accordingly, the setting of investment goals and objectives should not be done without the advice and assistance of investment managers.

Once goals and objectives have been set, the next critical step is entering into a signed investment counsel agreement with the investment manager, setting out the rules under which the investments are made, and establishing the fee schedules and the powers and duties of investment counsel. Many investment counsel agreements further require the *personal* services of certain named officers of the investment managing company, as it is their investment skill and expertise that has led the fund to retain their services.

In *Hodgkinson v. Simms,*[18] an investment counsellor was held to be a fiduciary to those he advised due to the specialization of knowledge involved in the area of investments. The Supreme Court of Canada endorsed the following characterization of a fiduciary in the context of independent professional advisory relationships:

Where the elements of trust and confidence and reliance on skill and knowledge and advice are present, the relationship is fiduciary and the obligations that attach are fiduciary.[19]

Another court in Ontario noted that:

[T]he standards for choosing the people who invest the funds . . . are quite high.[20]

The court in *R. v. Blair* suggested that in the very least, the investment counsel must fulfill the qualification parameters as an investment advisor under the provincial securities legislation.[21]

Of course, the investment counsellor may not have sufficient funds to cover any liabilities that are generated through his or her negligent actions. For that reason it is important that investment managers, and indeed all professionals, carry *errors and omissions insurance* so that the trustees are protected in the event of any losses due to the negligence of investment counsel. Those handling trust fund monies should further be *bonded* to avoid losses due to thefts or other acts of dishonesty. Trustees should insist on proof of the investment manager carrying the necessary errors and omissions insurance and bonding as part of the investment counsel agreement. Although this insurance will not protect against investment losses that are made in the ordinary course of business, they will protect the trustees in the event of gross negligence or misconduct.

ENDNOTES

1. *Pension Benefits Act,* R.S.O. 1990, c. P.8, s. 22(5).
2. *Ibid.,* s. 22(7).
3. *Hodgkinson v. Simms* (1994), 117 D.L.R. (4th) 161 (S.C.C.).
4. *Ibid.,* at p. 188.
5. *Ibid.,* at p. 184.
6. See, for example, Ontario Regulation 909, R.R.O. 1990, as amended, Section 1, which provides: "actuary" means a Fellow of the Canadian Institute of Actuaries.
7. *Pension Benefits Regulation,* R.R.O. 1990, Reg. 909, s. 15.
8. *Hodgkinson v. Simms, supra* note 3, at p. 188.
9. *Wynne v. William M. Mercer Ltd.* (1993), 1 C.C.P.B. 301 (B.C.S.C.) aff'd (1995), 11 C.C.P.B. 1 (B.C.C.A.).
10. *McLaughlin v. Falconbridge Ltd.* (1999), 21 C.C.P.B. 133 (O.S.C.J.), leave to appeal denied (unreported decision of MacFarland J., September 13, 1999).
11. *Public Accountancy Act,* R.S.O. 1990, c. P.37.
12. Ontario *Labour Relations Act,* 1995, S.O. 1995, c. 1, s. 93.
13. *Brock v. Self* (1986), 632 F.Supp. 1509 (U.S.D.C.L.A.).
14. *Hodgkinson v. Simms, supra* note 3.
15. *Securities Act,* R.S.O. 1990, c. 5.
16. *Pension Benefits Standards Regulation,* R.B.C. 1993, Reg. 443/93, as amended as Reg. 337/94, s. 38(3); *Pension Benefits Act Regulation,* R.R.O. 1990, Reg. 908, s. 67; General Regulations; *Pension Benefits Act,* R.N.B. 1991, Reg. 91-195, as amended by N.B. Reg. 93-144 and N.B. Reg. 94-78; *Pension Benefits Standards Regulations,* R.R.C. 1985, SOR/87-19, as amended.
17. E. Burroughs, *Trustees and Their Professional Advisors,* (Brookfield, Wisconsin: International Foundation of Employee Benefit Plans, Inc., 1996).
18. *Hodgkinson v. Simms, supra* note 3.
19. *Hodgkinson v. Simms, supra* note 3, at p. 184 quoting *Varcoe v. Sterling* (1992), 7 O.R. (3d) 204 (G.D.).
20. *Varcoe v. Sterling, supra* note 19 at p. 234.
21. *R. v. Blair* (1993), 106 D.L.R. (4th) 1 at p. 64 (Ont. Prov. Ct.), rev'd on appeal (1995), 9 C.C.P.B. 1 (G. D.).

CHAPTER 8

The General Tax System Pertaining to Employee Benefits

by Catherine Vibien

GOVERNMENT POLICY ON TAXATION OF EMPLOYEE BENEFITS

Employee remuneration is generally taxed under Section 5 of the *Income Tax Act* (the "Act"), which includes all of the taxpayer's income for a taxation year from an office or employment, including "salary, wages and other remuneration."

Section 6(1)(a) of the act deals with employee benefits and specifies that there shall be included in computing the income of a taxpayer for a taxation year "the value of board, lodging and other benefits of any kind," subject to certain exceptions.

The exceptions listed in Section 6(1)(a) include contributions to registered pension funds, private health service plans, group term life and group sickness or accident insurance. These exceptions have been in place since 1948. Section 6 also goes on to deal with certain taxable benefits payable to employees under employee benefit plans or employee trusts (we deal with this later in the chapter).

The benefits exempted from taxation under Section 6(1)(a) represent some of the very few tax exemptions accorded to ordinary working people. Parliament, for policy reasons, has determined that it is in the public interest to encourage employers to provide certain benefits to employees. This has created a private sector pension and supplementary benefit system that provides benefits to persons who ordinarily might not be able to afford the actual cost of, for example, supplementary health or dental care, and provides greater retirement income security.

Multi-employer benefit trust funds have arisen as a mechanism for delivering those benefits that are tax-exempt under Section 6(1)(a).

The trust mechanism has also been used to provide taxable benefits, such as vacation pay and prepaid legal service plans. It must be remembered that these trust funds are created essentially to assist bargaining unit employees under collective agreements and are not a common method of executive compensation. The trust acts as a conduit whereby employer contributions are paid to a third-party trustee who then delivers the benefits to the employees. Accordingly, the trust mechanism is simply an efficient administrative arrangement that permits the delivery of benefits to large groups of employees covered under numerous collective agreements with different employers.

As a matter of tax policy, trusts established to provide employee benefits have not been viewed as a source of tax revenue by Revenue Canada. Certain types of trust funds that provide part of an employee benefit package—such as registered pension plans, group registered retirement savings plans (RRSPs), registered supplementary unemployment benefit plans and certain qualifying vacation pay trust funds—are exempt from taxation on their income pursuant to Section 149 of the Act.

This is consistent with the policy position that an employee benefit trust fund is not the type of "taxpayer" that has traditionally provided revenue to the public coffers. Any investment income is usually used for providing the benefits or paying for the administration costs of the fund. The 1979 introduction of the concepts of the *employee benefit plan* and the *employee trust* into the Act was intended to deal with tax avoidance mechanisms whereby tax deferrals or expanded pension benefits could be obtained, primarily for "executive employees." However, these concepts are applicable in respect of any plans developed to deliver new benefits that are not otherwise tax-exempt (e.g., prepaid legal service plans).

The introduction of these provisions in 1979, and the subsequent introduction in 1986 of the *retirement compensation arrangement,* demonstrated a trend in tax policy to limit the scope of tax-free employee benefits to those currently in existence, and to tax any new benefits. The rationale provided for this policy was the equitable tax treatment of all employees, which required that no tax preferences be given to those who were fortunate enough to obtain certain fringe benefits from their employers. The *employee benefit plan* provisions also ensure that employers deduct their contributions in the same year as the benefits are taxed in the hands of the employee, so that the trust vehicle is not used as a means of deferring taxes.

This expansion of the tax base into the field of employment benefits has occurred at different levels. Provincially, in April of 1985 Quebec started a trend when it assessed retail sales tax (RST) on group insurance premiums. Quebec further broadened the tax base in 1990 by extending RST to self-insured benefit arrangements, regardless of the funded status of the benefit plan. Administratively, a pay-as-you-go plan attracted RST at the time of benefit payment, whereas a funded plan was subject to RST at the time of the contribution into the plan.

Then in its 1993 budget, Quebec effected the most dramatic change to the taxation of benefit plans to date, introducing RST on employer contributions to *private health insurance plans* (defined as including plans covering medical, hospitalization and dental expenses). It also eliminated the employer's tax exemption for the first $25,000 of group life insurance, subjecting all employer contributions to RST. This eliminated any tax preferential treatment for group term life insurance in Quebec.

In 1993, the Ontario government followed the Quebec model. It extended its RST to insured and self-insured benefits plans, applied equally to funded and unfunded plans. Notably, however, Ontario continues to exempt all contributions to individual life and health plan premiums from RST.

Also in 1993, Ontario expanded its insurance premium tax, a tax on the insurer calculated on the basis of the amount of premiums. Traditionally applied only to insured plans, the premium tax was extended to cover self-insured arrangements.

The federal government in 1994 introduced amendments eliminating the $25,000 income tax exemption on group term life insurance, mirroring the Quebec approach. However, group private health and dental benefits remained exempt from income taxation.

There has clearly been a shift in the taxation of employee benefits. The need for additional revenue to reduce federal and provincial deficits has induced governments to remove the tax sheltering that has historically been provided to traditional employee benefit plans.

THE SCHEME OF THE INCOME TAX ACT EMPLOYEE BENEFIT PLAN TAXATION

Who Is Taxed?

The three parties concerned with the tax consequences of benefits resulting from employment, including benefits negotiated under collective agreements, are:

1. The employee—who is primarily concerned with whether the benefit or the contribution for the benefit is taxable to him or her or exempt from tax and, in contributory plans, whether employee contributions are deductible from income

2. The employer—who is primarily concerned with the deductibility of any contributions toward employee benefits from its income and the timing of such deduction

3. The trust fund—subject to certain exceptions, a trust is a taxable entity to the extent that it earns any investment income, subject to deductions from income pertaining to expenditures required to earn such income, to administer the trust and certain taxable payments to beneficiaries. Accordingly, interest or dividend income earned by a trust fund, as a result of trustees' obligation to make the trust assets productive, may result in some income tax consequences unless proper tax planning measures are undertaken.

What Is Taxed?

The *Income Tax Act* purports to tax income. This concept of *income* has historically proven to be very difficult to define and has generated much debate among experts in the field. Problems as to what is deductible from income have compounded the issues even further.

In the case of employee benefits, determining what is income is not particularly difficult. Employee income is the remuneration paid to an employee over the course of a taxation year in money or its equivalent arising from the employment of such employee, subject to certain deductions, exemptions and tax credits.

An employer's income is its net income as a result of carrying on business, subject to the deductibility of costs of doing business, including benefit costs.

As for the trust fund itself, its income is generally

derived from interest, dividends and capital gains, less certain deductions that are reviewed below.

It is important to note that there are a number of employee benefits that, although they would otherwise constitute income, are exempt from taxation pursuant to specific provisions of the *Income Tax Act,* which we review below. Further, certain types of trust funds are exempt from taxation on their income.

Taxation of Employee Income

Section 5 of the *Income Tax Act* is the general taxing provision regarding income from office or employment. It states that:

Subject to this Part, a taxpayer's income for a taxation year from an office or employment is the salary, wages and other remuneration, including gratuities, received by him in the year.

Section 5 takes a broad view of income and remuneration and seeks to include virtually any benefit. To the extent that Section 5 is not explicit, Section 6(1)(a) of the Act specifies that there shall be included in computing the income of a taxpayer for a taxation year as income from an office or employment, ". . . the value of board, lodging and other benefits of any kind whatever received or enjoyed by him in the year in respect of, in the course of, or by virtue of an office or employment," subject to certain exceptions. Accordingly, the Act specifies that any remuneration from employment or any benefits whatsoever is *taxable unless one can find a specific exemption for the benefit in the Act.*

Section 6(1)(a)(i) of the Act specifically exempts from tax the value of benefits derived from an employer's contributions to or under a registered pension plan, group sickness or accident insurance plan, private health services plan, supplementary unemployment benefit plan, deferred profit-sharing plan or group term life insurance policy. As a consequence, an employer's contributions to a fund in respect of any of these plans do not trigger any tax consequences for employee beneficiaries of that fund unless other provisions of the *Income Tax Act* bring the contributions back into taxable income.

The receipt of certain benefits by an employee from a fund or from the insurer with which that fund contracts may, however, trigger tax consequences for the employee. For example, Section 6(1)(f) of the Act provides that the following amounts are included in an employee's income:

6(1)(f) the aggregate of amounts received by him in the year that were payable to him on a periodic basis in respect of the loss of all or any part of his income from an office or employment, pursuant to:

(i) sickness or accident insurance plan, or

(ii) disability insurance plan, or

(iii) an income maintenance insurance plan to or under which his employer has made a contribution. . . .

On the other hand, an employee's receipt of benefits exempt from tax pursuant to Section 6(1)(a) and not taxable pursuant to other sections of the act remain nontaxable. Thus, benefits provided to an employee under a private health services plan, such as drug, medical and supplementary health benefits, are not subject to tax. As well, lump-sum payments to an employee's estate or a named beneficiary as a result of a group term life insurance policy are not taxable in the recipient's hands.

Section 6 renders taxable any benefits provided under an employee benefit plan or an employee trust, concepts we deal with later in this chapter. The tax treatment of employee contributions toward various benefit plans that are contributory is discussed in greater detail in those sections dealing with taxation of life and health insurance benefits (Section III, Chapter 3), the taxation of pension funds (Section IV, Chapter 7) and the chapter dealing with savings plans (Section VII, Chapter 1).

Employer Deductibility

The act requires, under Section 18(1), that no taxpayer make deductions from income from a business or property, unless such outlay or expense "was made or incurred by the taxpayer for the purpose of gaining or producing income from the business or property."

Payments mandated under a collective agreement are payments of labour costs for purposes of gaining or producing income and are deductible by the employer. There are, of course, limitations on such deductions, to the extent that contributions for certain types of benefits are involved. There are special limitations for:

1. Supplementary unemployment benefit plans
2. Registered pension plan contributions
3. Employee benefit plan contributions
4. Contributions to employee trusts
5. Contributions to retirement compensation arrangements.

In discussing the taxation of the specific benefits below, we will deal with the concept of *employer deductibility* in each case (with the exception of retirement compensation arrangements, which are described in Section IV, Chapter 7). Expenses for benefit costs are generally deductible from employer income in the year in which they are incurred. However, in respect of contributions to an employee benefit plan, there is no employer deduction until the year in which the employee receives the benefits, subject to certain adjustments set out in Sections 18 and 32.1 of the Act.

Taxation of Trusts

Trusts are separate legal entities and are taxable on

their income. The trust is the most common method of holding plan assets for multi-employer plans established under collective agreements. Certain individuals are generally named as trustees, and they are responsible for the obligations of the fund, including the payment of any taxes. The taxation of trusts is a complex and difficult area, particularly when dealing with testamentary and charitable trusts. Trusts established for the purpose of providing employee benefits are subject to the general rules for the taxation of trusts, with certain exceptions set out in the Act itself or in Revenue Canada Interpretation Bulletins. In general, there are three categories of trusts:

1. Trusts that are totally tax exempt on their income, such as registered pension plans, group retirement savings plans, supplementary unemployment benefit plans and certain qualifying vacation pay trust funds

2. Trust funds subject to special rules, such as health and welfare trusts covered by Interpretation Bulletin IT-85R2[1] or employee benefit plans and employee trusts covered by Interpretation Bulletin IT-502[2]

3. All other trusts that are subject to the general rules for taxation of trusts.

We will review the special cases and tax-exempt trusts individually.

With respect to the general rules of taxation of trusts, Section 104(2) of the Act taxes a trust as if it were an individual. Generally, trusts are taxed at the highest personal rate in Canada and, accordingly, it is important to attempt to avoid taxation of any income of a trust, if at all possible.

Trusts can deduct certain expenses from their gross income, namely:

• Expenses incurred in earning the income
• Certain administrative expenses of operating the trust
• Money paid or payable directly to beneficiaries of the trust during any tax year (subject to certain limitations set out in Section 104(6) of the Act for employee benefit plans and employee trusts), which is then taxed in the hands of the beneficiary.

As a general proposition, the costs of providing non-taxable premiums and benefits payable to employees out of the trust fund are not deductible from the income of the trust. Revenue Canada has also adopted a policy in respect of taxable multi-employer plan trusts, to the effect that any trust with gross income in excess of $500 must file a T3 income tax return (see IT-85R2 and IT-502).

Employee Benefit Plans and Employee Trusts

Employee benefits not paid directly by the employer to its employees may be delivered in three different ways, each of which has distinct tax implications. One vehicle for delivering benefits is the health and welfare trust, which may provide those health and welfare benefits set out in Section 6(1)(a)(i) of the *Income Tax Act.* (Health and welfare trusts are considered in Section III.) The second and third vehicles are the employee benefit plan and the employee trust. Each of these arrangements involves a third-party custodian in the administration of the benefit plan.

Employee Benefit Plans

An *employee benefit plan* is generally defined in Section 248 of the *Income Tax Act* as any arrangement under which an employer makes contributions to another person (the custodian) and under which payments are made to or for the benefit of employees or former employees. An arrangement that provides only for benefits that are expressly excluded from income by reason of Subparagraph 6(1)(a)(i) of the Act is not an employee benefit plan, but may be a health and welfare trust. As well, Section 248 specifically excludes certain other plans such as employee trusts, vacation pay trusts, education and training arrangements, retirement compensation arrangements, and prescribed plans from employee benefit plan status.

The tax treatment of employees, employers and custodians involved in an employee benefit plan is somewhat complex. Under Subsection 6(1)(g) of the *Income Tax Act,* an employee is required to take into his or her income the value of taxable benefits received from the employee benefit plan in the year in which such benefits are received. It is noteworthy that all amounts taxable under Subsection 6(1)(g) are fully taxable as income from employment, regardless of how the plan received its income (as employer contributions, capital gains, dividends, etc.) and regardless of the fact that such income previously may have been taxed in the custodian's hands.

If it is organized as a trust, the employee benefit plan is taxable as a trust on its income determined under Part 1 of the *Income Tax Act.* Contributions are not included in gross income, and payments out of those contributions or prior year's accumulated income are not deductible by the trust. The trust may deduct expenses incurred by it in earning investment income, normal operating expenses, or amounts paid to beneficiaries out of the trust's current income and taxable to the beneficiaries. Where the plan is not a trust, the custodian is taxable on the plan's net income at the custodian's applicable tax rate.

The taxation rules applicable to an employer that contributes to an employee benefit plan are particularly complex. The thrust of the act's employee benefit plan provisions is to synchronize the employer's deduction of contributions with the taxation of employees who receive benefits from the plan. The mechanical complexity of this matching is most evident in the calculation of the contributing employer's tax position. Since the deductibility of the employer's contributions to an employee benefit plan is contingent on the taxation of the corresponding benefit, a contributing employer may not deduct its contribution in the year it is made but may only deduct its contribution pursuant to Section 32.1 in the year it is paid out as a benefit.

The amount of the employer's deduction for a taxation year is the amount allocated under Subsection 32.1(2) to the employer for that year by the plan custodian. Under Subsection 32.1(2), benefits paid out of the plan are considered to come from:

1. The plan beneficiary contributions
2. The income of the plan for the year
3. Employer contributions
4. The plan's prior year's income, if any.

Employee Trusts

An *employee trust* is defined in Section 248 of the *Income Tax Act* as an arrangement whereby an employer makes contributions to a trust for the sole benefit of its employees. The employee's right to benefits must vest when the contribution is made, and the amount of the employee's benefit cannot be contingent on the employee's position, performance or compensation as an employee.

The definition of an *employee trust* requires that the trustee must elect that the trust be treated as an employee trust within 90 days of the end of the trust's first taxation year.

The Act permits employers to deduct their contributions to employee trusts in the year in which such contributions are made. Thus, unlike employee benefit plans, the employer can deduct its contribution to the employee trust immediately and need not wait for its contribution to be paid out to the trust's beneficiaries as a benefit.

The employee trust must then allocate to its beneficiaries all employer contributions and investment income in the year in which it receives such contributions and income. The employee trust is not taxable on the income it allocates. Such allocation need not correspond with the actual payment of benefits.

Beneficiaries are taxable on such amounts as are allocated to them by the trustee in the year. The amount that is taxable to the employee in the year is not the amount of benefits actually received by the employee but, rather, the amount allocated to the employee. As well, all amounts allocated by the trust to the employee are included in the employee's income, regardless of whether the trust earned any amount as capital gains or dividends.

An employee trust arrangement allows a plan to distribute the tax burden of its benefits across the entire class of its beneficiaries. Employees each pay tax on their allocated amounts, not on the value of the benefit that they may actually receive in any particular year. This type of arrangement may be particularly convenient in the case of a prepaid legal plan, for instance, where an employee's receipt of benefits could otherwise trigger a large tax liability.

ENDNOTES

1. Revenue Canada, Interpretation Bulletin IT-85R2, "Health and Welfare Trusts for Employees" (31 July 1986).

2. Revenue Canada, Interpretation Bulletin IT-502, "Employee Benefit Plans and Employee Trusts" (28 March 1985).

CHAPTER 9

Legal Aspects of Trustee Expenses and Attendance at Educational Programs

by Raymond Koskie

INTRODUCTION

The starting point is the duty of trustees to exercise their powers in the best interests of the present and future beneficiaries of the trusts. This duty of the trustees toward their beneficiaries is paramount.[1]

Trustees of employee benefit funds, like any other class of trustees recognized by the law, are subject to very close scrutiny by the trust beneficiaries, the public and the courts when it comes to spending and accounting for trust fund money.

As the law develops in Canada and the United States on the subject of trustee expenses at educational conferences, control over such expenditures becomes increasingly important. On the one hand, there are advantages of educating trustees in all aspects of fund administration so that they may perform their duties more prudently and efficiently. On the other hand, the great degree of discretion often exercised by trustees in expending trust fund money leaves open possibilities for abuse when dealing with such matters as attendance at educational conferences. It is necessary to consider the civil, criminal and tax liability that trustees may be subject to for abuses with respect to conference expenses. It will also be helpful to briefly examine the treatment of this area in the U.S. law, which, in the main, is a codification of the common law, which applies to all provincial jurisdictions except Quebec.

POTENTIAL ABUSES BY TRUSTEES

Noel Arnold Levin in his article "Trustee Expenses and Attendance at Educational Programs"[2] notes a number of areas of concern with respect to expenditures incurred by trustees at educational conferences and proposes "six measures of prudence" to which trustees should address themselves, as follows:

1. *The reasonableness of expenses.* One must examine the amount spent by the trustee in light of the locale of the conference and the amount that a trustee may be reasonably expected to expend. In addition, there is a need to itemize all expenses so that individuals receive the lesser of the per diem rate or the actual expenses incurred.

2. *The number of meetings attended per year and who attends.* Some advisors recommend limiting trustees to one conference per year. Although it may not be advisable to maintain such an absolute limit, the position of a trustee should not be used as a means of attending numerous meetings at widespread locations. More importantly, lay trustees should not attend conferences for professional advisors from which they cannot reasonably derive any knowledge because, for example, they are not involved in the particular issues discussed at the meeting.

3. *The location of the meeting.* The concern here is that a trustee should attend the meeting nearest to his or her home if similar meetings are held in different locations.

4. *The number of persons from the particular board of trustees attending.* It is clearly not prudent to send a large number of trustees to any one conference. Trustees who attend confer-

ences are expected to report back to their respective boards, and little can be gained by having all or most trustees attend.

5. *Attendance at all sessions of the conference.* It is clear that trustees should not engage in recreational activity or other diversions during the hours that sessions are in progress. Failure to adhere to this rule may result in conviction for fraud or embezzlement.

6. *Charging more than actual expenses incurred.* This raises difficult questions with respect to the personal, civil, criminal and tax liabilities of trustees.

The above concerns are as applicable to trustees in Canada as they are in the United States. The major difference is the *Employee Retirement Income Security Act of 1974* (ERISA) and the regulations promulgated thereunder that provide definitive guidelines for the conduct of trustees in the United States, including the incurring of expenses by trustees.

Although there is no Canadian counterpart to ERISA in this respect, Canada does not lack statutory guidance regarding conduct of trustees, most of which is found in the trustee acts of the various provinces.[3] Although these statutes were drafted with a view to regulating testamentary or family trusts rather than major employee benefit plans, they are, nevertheless, applicable. In addition, one must consider the provisions of the *Criminal Code* where fraud or criminal breach of trust might be involved. There is also some assistance to be derived from the basic common law of trusts.

Further assistance is provided by the Office of the Superintendent of Financial Institutions Canada (OSFI), which is responsible for regulating all pension plans in the federal jurisdiction. In May of 1998, OSFI published a Guideline for the Governance of Federally Regulated Pension Plans[4] that addressed the issue of plan expenses and trustee compensation.

With respect to compensation of trustees, OSFI advises:

If, for example, the plan wishes to update the knowledge of its administrator and staff by sending them to conferences, documented guidelines could specify for instance what conferences are considered appropriate, what is to be gained from the attendance, what reporting of findings is expected of the attendees, who should attend, what accounting of expenses is expected, and what are reasonable expenses.[5]

Regarding plan expenses, the OSFI Guidelines remind trustees that the standards of prudent care imposed on them require the establishment of "clear written rules and guidelines regarding the use of plan assets for purposes other than benefit payments." The rules should set out the issues the trustees ought to consider

before an expense payment is authorized and guidelines regarding what expenses are appropriate. As an example, the OSFI Guidelines address attendance at educational conferences:

The board of trustees should establish a policy for compensating its members for their time and earnings lost while they work as trustees. In doing so, they should seek the opinion of independent advisors with expertise in compensation. The policy should be reviewed by legal counsel to ensure that it is consistent with trust law and the specifics of the plan. The board should consider disclosing to members the actual compensation and any honourium or repayment of expenses to trustees as well as the plan's policy in this regard.[6]

What follows is a summary of the current status of Canadian law with respect to trustee education expenses as compared with United States law.

CAN TRUSTEES ATTEND CONFERENCES AT ALL?

In the absence of an express provision in the trust agreement permitting expenditure for trustee expenses, there is some question as to whether such expenses may be properly incurred. For example, Section 32 of the Ontario *Trustee Act* in describing the extent of trustee liability states that a trustee:

may reimburse himself or discharge out of the trust property all expenses incurred in or about the execution of his trust or powers.[7]

As Donovan Waters notes in the *Law of Trusts in Canada*:

It would be an extraordinary system of law which did not permit trustees to recover their out-of-pocket expenses incurred in the discharge of their duties and powers under the trust, and in fact, Courts of Chancery were never in any doubt that the trustee was entitled to such indemnification.[8]

The issue arises as to whether trustee expenses at a conference are expenses that are "properly incurred in the discharge of trust duties." An expenditure on educating trustees would provide something in the nature of an indirect benefit to the trust beneficiaries rather than a more tangible financial gain. Nevertheless, the importance of educating trustees, given the complexity of modern day employee benefit plans and the ongoing nature of the trusts, cannot be overstated. Trustees will be attending conferences that enable them to properly discharge their trust obligations. Canadian regulators have recognized that adequate knowledge and skills on the part of pension plan administrators is an underlying principle of good governance.[9]

As it is difficult to establish a direct connection between expenses for conferences and the benefits to the trusts, it is crucial that these expenses be reasonable in amount and be incurred in the honest belief that the trust will benefit. Obviously, this places some constraints on the extent to which these expenditures may be made.

REGULATION OF EXPENSES INCURRED AT EDUCATIONAL CONFERENCES

As the issues and concerns with respect to trustee expenditures at educational conferences are fairly new to Canada, the common law of trusts is the primary source of general guidelines and principles from which a code of behaviour might be developed for trustees attending such conferences. There are three guiding common law principles with respect to trustee expenses:

1. Trustee expenses must be *properly incurred.*
2. Trustees are under an obligation to account for all expenses.
3. Trustees must meet the standard of care that a person of ordinary prudence would exercise in the management of his or her own affairs.

Trustee Expenses Must Be Properly Incurred

It is a basic principle of common law that trustees are entitled to be indemnified for all charges and expenses "properly incurred." Although this criterion can be vague and nebulous, the courts and legal scholars have offered some assistance in providing a more precise definition of what constitutes a "properly incurred" expense. Waters provides a threefold test as follows:

. . . in allowing or refusing claims made by trustees, the test is whether the expense incurred arose out of an act within the scope of the trusteeship duties and powers, whether in the circumstances it was reasonable, and whether it was something that his duty as a trustee required him to do.[10]

Is Expense Within Scope of Trustee's Duties and Powers?

This question has been dealt with above with respect to the issue of whether expenditures on educational conferences can be made in the first place. Such expenditures are readily justifiable when there is an express provision in the trust agreement permitting them, although the importance of educating the trustees of an employee benefit trust can be viewed as a matter within the scope of the trusteeship duties in most circumstances.

Reasonableness of Expenditure

There is very little guidance from the courts when dealing with the question of whether certain expenditures are *reasonable.* The facts of each case often dictate the reasonableness of the expenditure. For example, it may be reasonable for one trustee to attend a conference on a specialized subject relating to fund administration (such as data processing), but it may not be reasonable for several trustees of the same fund to attend. The *reasonableness* test often manifests itself in the form of trustees choosing the more reasonably priced of various alternative expenditures, such as economy air travel over first-class travel or accommodation at lower priced hotels over luxury suites. Although it may be impossible to compile an exhaustive list of reasonable expenditures, the list of Trustees' Do's and Don'ts in the appendix to this chapter can be of some assistance in outlining what expenditures are generally viewed as reasonable in the context of trustees' attendance at conferences.

In any event, it is clear that a trustee may not recover expenses where they arose out of his or her own misconduct.[11] This includes situations where the trustee has falsified his or her accounts or unjustifiably run up expenses.[12] Examples of this type of activity include cashing first-class airline tickets provided by the trust fund and traveling economy class, payments for travel and accommodation of spouses at the expense of the trust fund, or simply being absent from part or all of the conference. Conduct of this nature often gives rise to serious criminal and civil liabilities.

Does Duty of the Trustee Require This Activity?

A crucial aspect of conference expenditures is the practicable relevance to the trustee's duties. Accordingly, a trustee not involved in fund delinquencies should not attend a conference on this topic. Expenditures may be justified for trustees with considerable time commitments to trust fund work who exercise a degree of skill and ability and have had some success in trust administration. Justifying such expenditures for trustees with few or no commitments and responsibilities may be extremely difficult.

Duty of Trustees to Account

The second key area of the law of trusts to be considered is the duty of trustees to account and disclose information.

The law requires trustees to keep clear and distinct accounts. In the old English case of *Chisholm v. Barnard,*[13] this obligation was held to mean that trustees must give full explanations of all their dealings and of the causes why outstanding assets were not collected or property of the estate has disappeared. Beneficiaries of the trust fund are entitled to an accounting for all expenditures as a matter of common law and may bring legal proceedings for such accounting at any time. Accordingly, it is crucial for trustees to account fully for conference expenditures. Trustees receiving a per diem allowance while attending conferences must account for all amounts actually spent to avoid the suspicion that they might be profiting from this allowance by, for example, "doubling up" in hotel rooms and having meals paid by others. Trustees are legally obliged to return the unused balance of any allowance. On the other hand, if reasonable additional expenses were incurred, the trustees should be reimbursed.

Standard of Care of Trustees

A final matter to be considered is the general standard of care expected of trustees in conducting the affairs of the trust. Apart from maintaining the highest standards of honesty and good faith, the law requires of a trustee no higher degree of diligence in the exercise of his or her office than a person of ordinary prudence would exercise in the management of his or her own affairs.[14] Accordingly, if a trust fund is in a precarious financial position or has a large number of trustees, attendance at conferences by any or all of the trustees should be carefully considered in light of the circumstances. Additionally, charging illegitimate expenses to pension funds is a breach of this standard.[15]

LIABILITY OF TRUSTEES

Trustees who abuse their trust position and transgress the guidelines noted above or actually fall prey to the temptations of improperly benefiting from trust monies may be subject to serious liability in civil courts, criminal courts and under the *Income Tax Act*.

Civil Liability

Trustees need not be found to have acted fraudulently, negligently, incompetently or in an otherwise blameworthy manner in order to incur civil liability. The operating principle is:

If the letter of the trustee's obligation has not been adhered to for whatever reason, he is liable to the beneficiaries for any loss which has occurred as a result.[16]

Trustees are jointly and severally liable to the trust beneficiaries for a loss arising out of a breach of trust, meaning that each trustee is personally liable for his or her own part in the loss and also for the loss caused by all the other trustees. However, this common law position has been modified by the trustee legislation in most provinces, which provides that a trustee is not accountable for the acts of any trustee "unless the loss happens through his own wilful default."[17] Thus, a trustee who condones abuses by other trustees with respect to attendance at educational conferences and is fully aware of such abuses may share liability.

The specific remedies available to beneficiaries and the trustees of the fund are twofold. The first, where expenses are improperly incurred regardless of any dishonesty on the part of the trustee, consists of reinstatement of the funds improperly advanced and possibly payment of any damages arising from the loss of the use of the funds to the trust. A more stringent civil remedy, where it can be proven that the trustee was actually dishonest, is "the gravest breach of trust."[18] Furthermore, most of the trustee acts permit nomination of a new trustee in replacement of a trustee who is found, among other things, "unfit to act" or is "convicted of an indictable offence."[19]

Criminal Liability

There are various criminal charges to which a trustee suspected of abuses of trust may be subject, including criminal breach of trust, theft, theft by a person required to account and fraud. All of these offences relate to the misappropriation of money or property that does not belong to the trustee and can result in prison terms on conviction.

The offence of criminal breach of trust is set out in Section 336 of the *Criminal Code* as follows:

Every one who, being a trustee of anything for the use or benefit, whether in whole or in part, of another person, or for a public or charitable purpose, converts, with intent to defraud and in contravention of his trust, that thing or any part of it to a use that is not authorized by the trust is guilty of an indictable offence and liable to imprisonment for a term not exceeding fourteen years.[20]

With respect to criminal breach of trust, the courts have determined that even if the trustee is given an unfettered discretion to look after the trust property, he or she is not entitled to use it as to make a personal gain and, if the trustee does so, he or she will be found guilty under this section.[21] Furthermore, the necessary fraudulent intent may be deduced from the accused's conduct and, where the natural consequences of the accused's acts would be to defraud his or her beneficiaries, the onus is on the accused to rebut the presumption that he or she intended these consequences.[22] Finally, the courts have determined that it is not at all inconsistent to charge a trustee with criminal breach of trust and theft for the same offence, as it is possible to be convicted of one and not the other.[23]

Under Section 322 of the *Criminal Code,* one commits theft when, among other things, one:

. . . fraudulently and without colour of right takes, or fraudulently and without colour of right converts to his use or to the use of another person, anything either animate or inanimate with intent to deprive...temporarily or absolutely, the owner of it, or a person who has a special property or interest in it, of the things or of his property or interest in it. . . .[24]

Section 330 of the *Criminal Code* further creates an offence of theft by a person required to account, as follows:

Everyone commits theft who, having received anything from any person on terms that require him to account for or pay it or the proceeds of it or a part of the proceeds to that person or another person, fraudulently fails to account for or pay it or the proceeds of it or the part of the proceeds of it accordingly.[25]

Under Section 330 of the *Criminal Code*, it might be possible to obtain a conviction against a trustee who refuses to account for expenditures while attending an educational conference or simply cannot account for how the money was spent. Conviction for theft under Section 322 or Section 330 of the *Criminal Code* may result in a jail term of up to ten years where the stolen property exceeds $1,000 in value. Theft under $1,000 may still result in a jail term of up to two years or a fine.

Section 380 of the *Criminal Code* sets out the offence of fraud that is committed by:

. . . one who, by deceit, falsehood or other fraudulent means, whether or not it is a false pretence within the meaning of this Act, defrauds the public or any person, whether ascertained or not, of any property, money or valuable security. . . .[26]

The penalties for fraud are the same as those for theft and are dependent on whether the amount in question exceeds $1,000. There has, in recent years, been an upsurge of theft and fraud cases against politicians and civil servants who misappropriate public funds given to them for express public purposes. For example, there is a case of a British Columbia cabinet minister who cashed in first-class airline tickets and traveled economy, pocketing the difference in price. This activity resulted in a conviction under the fraud provisions of the *Criminal Code*. As well, a member of Parliament in Newfoundland was convicted of fraud in excess of $200 under the then-Section 338 of the *Criminal Code* for claiming the mileage allowance available to members of Parliament for trips to his constituency that he did not make. He was convicted despite the evidence that many members of Parliament believe that the mileage expenses were an allowance to be used regardless of whether the trip was taken or not. Similarly, trustees may fall victim to the same types of charges where they seek reimbursement for expenses not actually incurred.

Income Tax Liability

A final matter to be considered is the income tax consequences that may result from attending educational conferences and conventions. Generally, trustees are not taxable for their expenses when being reimbursed by the trust fund, just as employees are not taxable to the extent that they are reimbursed by employers for attending conventions as part of the duties of employment. However, Revenue Canada Interpretation Bulletin IT-131R2 provides that:

. . . if the employer gives an employee a nonaccountable allowance to cover the cost of attendance at convention, as a rule, the employee is taxable on that allowance.[27]

Similarly, it may be argued that trustees receiving a nonaccountable allowance are receiving remuneration for their work as trustees and will, accordingly, be taxable on such an allowance. Accordingly, a nonaccountable per diem allowance given to a trustee for purposes of attending a conference may be a taxable receipt.

Finally, if the trustee is convicted of a criminal offence or engages in criminal activity whereby he or she illegally misappropriates trust funds, such illegally obtained income is, nevertheless, taxable to the trustee under the *Income Tax Act.*[28]

CONCLUSIONS

It is generally possible under the terms of most employee benefit plans and pursuant to the relevant provisions of the trustee acts of Canada's provinces, for trustees to incur expenses for attending educational conferences, provided such expenditures are closely controlled. It would be prudent to establish controls to ensure that expenses charged to pension funds are reasonable and adhere to the standards set out in the pension benefits legislation and the common law.

In determining the principles governing controls over such expenditures, one should have to account for all expenses and the reasonableness thereof. The trustee's duty is to fully account for his or her expenditures, and to observe the standard of care expected of trustees.

Failure to operate within these controls may result in adverse civil, criminal and tax liability to the trustee.

ENDNOTES

1. *Cowan v. Scargill,* [1984] 2 All E.R. 750 (Ch.D.) at p. 760.
2. N.A. Levin, "Trustees Expenses and Attendance at Educational Programs," *Employee Benefits Digest,* June 1979.
3. R.S.A. 1980, c. T-10, s. 14, 25, 26; R.S.B. 1979, c. 414, s. 27, 35, 97; R.S.M. 1987, c. T-160, s. 8, 9, 78; R.S.N.B. 1987, c. T-15, s. 13, 29; R.S.Nfld. 1990, c. T-10, s. 1, 30; R.S.N.S. 1989, s. 16, 29; R.S.O. 1990, c. T-23, s. 3, 33; R.S.P.E.I. 1988, c. T-8, s. 4; R.S.N.W.T. 1988, c. T-8, s. 6, 7, 8; R.S.Y.T. 1986, c. 173, s. 8, 9, 10; R.S.S. 1978, c. T-23, s. 13, 14, 15; R.S.C. 1985, c. P-7.
4. Memorandum to Administrators of Federally Regulated Pension Plans Under the Pension Benefits Standards Act, 1985, May 1, 1998, Guidelines for Governance of Federally Regulated Pension Plans.
5. *Ibid.,* at p. 21.
6. *Ibid.,* at p. 13.

7. R.S.A. 1980, c. T-10, s. 26; R.S.B.C. 1979, c. 414, s. 97; R.S.N. 1987, c. T-160, s. 78; R.S.N.B. 1987, c. T-15, s. 13; R.S.Nfld. 1990, c. T-10, s. 30; R.S.N.S. 1989, c. 479, s. 29; R.S.O. 1990, c. T-23, s. 3; R.S.N.W.T. 1988, c. T-8, s. 6; R.S.Y.T. 1986, c. 173, s. 8; R.S.S. 1978, c. T-23, s. 13.

8. Waters, *Law of Trusts in Canada,* 2d ed. (Toronto: Carswell, 1984) at p. 943.

9. Standing Senate Committee on Banking, Trade and Commerce, "Report on the Governance Practices of Institutional Investors," November 1998; OSFI, "Guidelines for the Governance of Federally Regulated Pension Plans," *supra* note 4.

10. Waters, *supra* note 8, at p. 944.

11. *Ibid.,* at p. 945.

12. *Ibid.,* at p. 945.

13. *Chisholm v. Barnard* (1864), 10 Fr. 479 (Ch.).

14. *Learoyd v. Whitely* (1887), 12 Cas. 727 (H.L.).

15. OSFI, "Guidelines for Federally Regulated Pension Plans," *supra* note 4 at p. 13.

16. Waters, *supra* note 8 at p. 988.

17. R.S.A. 1980, c. T-10, s. 25; R.S.B.C. 1979, c. 414, s. 97; R.S.M. 1987, c. T-160, s. 78; R.S.N.B. 1987, c. T-15, s. 13; R.S.Nfld. 1990, c. T-10, s. 30; R.S.N.S. 1989, c. 478, s. 29; R.S.O. 1990, c. T-23,

s. 33; R.S.N.W.T. 1974, c. T-8, s. 6; R.S.Y.T. 1986, c. 173, s. 8; R.S.S. 1978, c. T-23, s. 13.

18. Waters, *supra* note 8 at p. 684.

19. R.S.A. 1980, c. T-10, s. 14; R.S.B.C. 1979, c. 414, s. 27, 35; R.S.M. 1987, c. T-160, s. 8, 9; R.S.N.B. 1987, c. T-15, s. 29; R.S.Nfld. 1990, c. T-10, s. 1; R.S.N.S. 1989, c. 479, s. 16, 31; R.S.O. 1990, c. T-23, s. 3; R.S.Y.T. 1986, c. 173, s. 9, 10; R.S.S. 1978, c. T-23, s. 14, 15.

20. *Criminal Code,* R.S.C., 1985, c. C-46, s. 336.

21. *R. v. Belanger* (1925), 44 C.C.C. 129 (Que. K.B.).

22. *Ibid.*

23. *R. v. Petricia* (1974), 17 C.C.C. (2d) 27 (B.C.C.A.); *R. v. Nakonechny* (1980), 3 Sask. R. 209 (Sask. C.A.); *R. v. Lowden* (1981), 59 C.C.C. (2d) 1 (Alta. C.A.), aff'd (1982), 68 C.C.C. (2d) 531 (S.C.C.).

24. *Criminal Code, supra* note 20, s. 322.

25. *Ibid.,* s. 330.

26. *Ibid.,* s. 380.

27. Revenue Canada, Interpretation Bulletin IT-131R2, "Convention Expenses" (24 November 1989) at para. 7.

28. *R. v. Poynton* (1972), 72 D.T.C. 6329 (Ont. C.A.); *Lennox Industries Ltd. v. The Queen* (1987), 87 D.T.C. 5041 (F.C.T.D.).

APPENDIX 9-A

TRUSTEES' DO'S AND DON'TS

DO'S

1. Report to the board of trustees with respect to attendance at all educational conventions, including subject matter of sessions and what was learned.

2. Substantiate all expenditures while attending an educational conference, including full accounting for all trust fund monies spent. Keep receipts whenever possible.

3. Attend all sessions relevant to the duties of the trustee while at the conference.

4. Keep all expenses with respect to travel, meals and accommodations at reasonable levels, taking less expensive options wherever practically possible.

5. Attend educational conferences closest to home where the same conference is being offered at more than one location.

DON'TS

1. Attend conferences that are devoid of content that is relevant to Canadian trustees.

2. Attend conferences when the financial position of the trust fund would not reasonably justify such attendance.

3. Travel first class when economy transportation is available.

4. Attend more than one or two conferences per year.

5. Accept a per diem allowance without accounting for all amounts actually spent.

6. Receive payment from two sources (e.g., two different trust funds) for the same expenses.

7. Charge to the trust fund expenses incurred by friends, spouses or children attending a conference.

8. Charge for expenses for days other than those actually spent in attendance at conferences or traveling to or from a conference.

9. Permit an unreasonable number of trustees of the same fund to attend the same conference.

CHAPTER 10

Understanding Accounting, Actuarial and Investment Reports

by Sidney J. Wise, Kent A. Botham, Patrick Longhurst and Michael Sandell

ACCOUNTING REPORTS

Overview

The culmination of the year's financial and accounting activities is the preparation and presentation to the board of trustees of the audited financial statements. At this time, it is the auditor's function to report and comment on the efforts of all of the individuals responsible for the operations of the fund and the results that have been achieved for the benefit of the beneficiaries. This team effort between the fund's trustees and their professional advisors is reported in the financial statements as a summary of what has occurred within the fund over the preceding year and as a snapshot of the status of the fund at a given point in time, usually December 31, being the legally mandated year-end for trust funds.

As the financial transactions are audited and the resulting financial statements prepared after the year has been completed and the events have taken place, the auditor is acting like a historian would in reporting what has already happened. This should not minimize the relevance of these statements but should emphasize the importance of having them completed on a timely basis.

The financial statements consist of the auditors' report and various other statements depending upon the type of fund being reported on. Also, the accompanying notes are an integral part of the statements as they explain various items in the statements and the figures found therein. These statements will be explained in more detail later on, but they usually consist of a balance sheet or statement of financial position (your snapshot of the fund's assets at a point in time), statement of operations (your summary of the year's activity) and a statement of changes in net assets (the change in the year of fund balances).

These financial statements should provide the reader with much needed information, confirm or reject the results of decisions previously made and be a useful tool, along with the statements supplied by the fund's other professional advisors, in making decisions for the future. In order to achieve these results, one must review, analyze and understand the financial statements. To understand them, you cannot read them in isolation. You must know what makes up the figures reported in them and how they are arrived at.

The remainder of this chapter deals with two specific types of multi-employer financial statements, pension plan statements and health and welfare (benefit) plan statements and will explain the importance of the different financial statement numbers, how they interact and the importance of fluctuations in the different numbers.

Responsibility for Financial Statements and Accounting Records

The trustees of any fund have the ultimate legal and fiduciary responsibility for the security of the plan's assets and providing the agreed-upon benefits. While the trustees will hire a number of different professionals to assist them in fulfilling their duties—for example, an administrator, an actuary, an investment counselor, a lawyer, etc.—the trustees will be held responsible for the actions of all such agents. The audited financial statements prepared by the fund's auditors are no exception.

The auditors prepare the statements from the information provided by the trustees or, more commonly, from their agent, the administrator, and give an opinion as to their fairness. But, as pointed out in the first paragraph of all audit reports: *These financial statements are the responsibility of the fund's management (the trustees).* The trustees must not lose sight of that important fact; these are your financial statements.

Chapter 7 in this section of the book discusses in greater detail to what extent trustees can rely on the services performed on their behalf by others. It is safe to say that accepting the reports prepared by others blindly and without due care and diligence can expose the trustees to grave risks.

Auditors' Report

The auditors' report tells the reader what the auditor has done to arrive at an opinion as to the fund's financial position at the year-end and the results of its operations for the year. It emphasizes that there is normally a limit on the amount of work performed and indicates that the records of the fund were checked only on a test basis. The amount of testing carried out depends upon the internal controls maintained by the fund's administrator and other professionals to ensure that the records and operations of the fund are accurate and properly safeguarded. Based upon the auditors' assessment of the fund's internal controls and the risk associated with any particular aspect of the audit, they carry out sufficient tests *to obtain reasonable assurance (but not absolute assurance) whether the financial statements are free of material misstatement.*

What is *material*? The concept of a *material* item is that it is probable that, if the item or piece of information were missing or misstated, it would influence or change a decision. Materiality is subject to professional judgment and depends upon the size of the particular fund and is, therefore, something that should be discussed with the auditor in each separate case.

Scope Limitation

The third paragraph of most audit reports for multi-employer trust funds contains what is referred to as a *scope limitation,* which reads as follows:

> The scope of our audit did not extend to an examination of the payroll records of the contributing employers. Our verification of contribution revenue was limited to the amounts recorded in the records of the organization and we were not able to determine whether any adjustments might be necessary to contribution revenue and net assets.

What this is saying is that the auditor did not audit the payroll records of the contributing employers to ensure that the contribution reports were accurately submitted. Instead, the auditor compared and test checked that the contribution reports as submitted by the employers were recorded properly and accurately in the books and records of the pension plan trust fund.

Some plans are formed by collective agreements that provide the trustees with the authority to carry out payroll audits. In these instances, payroll audits are often carried out where the trustees have reason to believe that the contributions received by the fund are inaccurate or the fund's administrator reports some unusual activity with a particular contributing employer. The trustees should consider the amount of the potential misstatement versus the cost of having the fund's auditors carry out a payroll audit.

It is difficult to estimate the cost of such an audit, but it will likely run somewhere between $2,000 and $10,000, depending upon the size of the fund and the extent of the problems. Some collective agreements provide that the contributing employer will pay the cost of all payroll audits, while others provide for such payment only if a discrepancy in excess of an agreed-upon amount is determined.

Qualified Auditors' Report

Most trustees would like to see an unqualified audit report that indicates the auditor has found no problems and is able to attest to the fairness of the financial statements without reservation. Where the above noted scope limitation is present, the auditors' opinion must be qualified to the extent of this limitation. While not perfect, this is an acceptable qualification in most instances and one that most trustees of multi-employer plans are used to seeing and having explained by their auditors.

Other problems may be encountered during the course of an audit and, as long as they are not serious, they are usually reported to the trustees verbally or by way of a management letter. Where a problem is uncovered that is not properly resolved and it is material enough to affect the fairness of the financial statements, the auditor will be required to add another qualification to the opinion paragraph. While this is quite rare, the reader must read the auditors' report in its entirety to understand everything that is being said and must be prepared to ask questions when something unusual appears.

Date of Report

The last item on the bottom of the report is usually the date of the auditors' report. This is generally the date on which the final audit tests were carried out at the administrator's office. The importance of this date deals with the time delay between this date and the year-end date and the date on which the statements are presented to the trustees. If either of these differences is too long, it may be indicative of some problems with the fund's operations and should be questioned.

Balance Sheet or Statement of Financial Position

The next page is the balance sheet, for most trust funds, or the statement of financial position or net assets available for benefits when you are dealing with a pension fund. This statement sets out the assets owned by the fund and the liabilities owed by the fund. The difference between the two indicates the fund's net assets. We will describe the most common accounts found on a fund's balance sheet and how they interact with one another. The actual order in which they are shown is not that important, but they are usually shown in descending order based on their liquidity, which means how quickly they can be turned into cash. All financial statements should show the current year's figures alongside comparative figures for the previous year. This enables the reader to see whether any significant changes have occurred between the two years and to question all relevant or material changes. A review and analysis of these changes is one of the most important steps that the reader can take in trying to understand the financial statements and what has happened during the past year.

Cash

All cash held by a fund should be maintained in interest bearing accounts where possible. If there is a large cash balance at the end of the year, one should ask why and whether it is being held in an interest bearing account. If it is not, why not? As noted above, any large changes between the current and previous years should be questioned. The administrator should ensure that any surplus cash is turned over to the fund's money managers, or put into interest bearing investments, as quickly and as often as is practical in order to attain the best investment return available.

Contributions Receivable

This account represents employer/employee contributions for the December or prior work months that were due to the fund but not received until after December 31, but before the date of the audit report. A large increase or decrease from the prior year should be questioned. A large increase might be indicative of poor delinquency control procedures, poor follow-up of delinquent accounts by the administrator, one or more large delinquent employers or something as simple and less concerning as an increase in the number of reported hours or in the contribution rate during or near the end of the year. But the reader will not know whether there is a potential problem without first asking why there was a change.

Investments

The balance sheet will usually show only a single total of the investments, which will be detailed in one of the accompanying notes to the statements. It is important to review this note and to analyze the different investment categories for large changes that may need to be questioned. The type of investments held will be determined by the type of fund and its liquidity requirements. For example, a health and welfare or vacation pay fund will usually keep most of its investments in short-term vehicles, while a pension fund will maintain most of its investments in longer term vehicles. Where more than one money manager is employed by the fund, the notes should provide details of the investments held by each such manager. These details will likely indicate that each money manager has invested different amounts of money in the different investment categories based upon different investment philosophies. These different investment philosophies provide the fund with a diversified portfolio that is a hedge against any one segment of the market crashing and taking the fund with it.

The prevailing accounting bodies and provincial legislation require that all investments in a pension plan be reported in the financial statements at their current market values rather than at their historical cost.

Accrued Interest/Dividends Receivable

This account represents the amount of interest or dividends due at December 31 but not yet received by the fund. This information is either provided by the investment managers on their year-end statements or calculated by the administrator's accounting staff or the auditor. Any significant change from the prior year should be questioned.

Prepaid Expenses

This account is composed of expenses that have been paid during the year but as at December 31 have not been utilized. An example would be a deposit for the last month's rent or the payment of an annual insurance premium on July 1, which would leave half of the premium unused at December 31.

Accounts Payable and Accrued Liabilities

The first liability listed is usually this account, and it represents amounts owing to third parties for expenses incurred prior to December 31 that were not paid until some time after that date. As well as the normal monthly operating expenses that are paid in arrears once the invoice is received, this balance often contains the fourth quarter fees from the fund's professional advisors. Where there is a particularly large amount payable with respect to a particular expense, it may be reported separately at the request of the trustees. An example of this type of expense would be for insurance premiums or benefits payable.

Hour/Dollar Bank

The hour/dollar bank account is probably the most misunderstood item on a benefit trust fund financial statement. The hour/dollar bank can best be explained by comparing it to your own bank account. There are deposits and withdrawals. Each month, hours worked by an employee as shown by the employer contribution reports are deposited into this account either in the form of actual hours reported or as actual dollars received by the fund. Each month, the number of hours or dollars required to qualify and pay premiums for full benefits is withdrawn from the bank. The balance that remains at the end of the year after monthly deposits and withdrawals is used to calculate the hour/dollar bank liability.

To arrive at the dollar value of the hour bank liability, one of two methods can be used depending on the decision of the trustees as to the best estimate of the liability for the fund. In the first method, we multiply the hour bank hours at the end of the year by the employer contribution rate. For the second method, we divide the hour bank hours by the monthly drawdown and multiply by the premium rate in effect at the end of the year. What we are trying to do is quantify and set money aside in order to be able to pay benefits in the future to qualified beneficiaries as evidenced in the hour bank even if we do not receive future contributions on their behalf.

It is important to question the auditor as to whether there was a change in the contribution rate, the monthly drawdown rate, the monthly premium rate or any other parameter that affected the determination of the hour/dollar bank account. Some changes require that the balance in the bank be recalculated, and the trustees should confirm that any such change was checked by the auditor. The trustees should also confirm the last time the hour/dollar bank was purged of deceased, retired or other inactive participants. This should be done at least every two or three years, as a large reduction in this liability account could allow the trustees to consider improving the plan's benefits.

Restricted and Unrestricted Net Assets

Restricted net assets are amounts set aside for a specific purpose, while *unrestricted* amounts are for general use by the trustees in accordance with the trust agreement. Funds with restricted net assets will need to show these separately from unrestricted amounts.

Restrictions dictate how, where and when the money in the fund can be spent, and these guidelines are not subject to a change by the trustees. Unrestricted net assets are the amounts remaining in the fund to pay the benefits to the members. A type of unrestricted net asset is an internally restricted net asset. Net assets can be internally restricted by the trustees for a specific purpose, for example, a strike fund, but may be redirected to other funds by a majority vote by the trustees. The internally restricted net assets and the unrestricted net assets are shown separately in the financial statements.

A description of the restricted net assets should be found in the notes to the financial statements. Trustees are responsible for ensuring the contributions are being properly allocated and spent for the purpose for which they were received.

Incurred but Not Reported Claims

This account appears in benefit fund statements where one or more benefits are being self-insured by the plan and is designed to allocate a portion of a fund's net assets to cover the potential liability for unknown claims that are outstanding and are the responsibility of the fund. Such internally restricted net assets are important to ensure that the trustees do not think they have more net assets available than they actually do.

The trustees should not hesitate to ask how this amount was determined and whether the auditor checked the calculations for reasonableness. The trustees should also question their insurer as to the existence of any reserves or deficits the insurance company is carrying on its books that may be considered an asset or the responsibility of the fund.

Statement of Operations

The next statement that we come to is the statement of operations, or the statement of changes in net assets available for benefits if you are dealing with a pension fund. These statements used to be referred to as the *statement of income* in the past. These statements provide a summary of the transactions that have taken place during the past year. As noted above, it is important to review the revenue and expense items and question any accounts that show large changes from the previous year. All figures reported on this statement should be on the accrual basis. This means that all contributions received within a reasonable period from the year-end and investment income that was earned and should have been received are reported here with the unreceived and outstanding amounts being reported on the balance sheet as outstanding receivables, as explained earlier. Likewise, all expenses that were incurred but remained unpaid at the year-end are reported on this statement with the offsetting outstanding payables being reported on the balance sheet, as discussed above.

This accrual method of accounting allows for income and expense items for the year to be properly matched.

Contribution Revenue

Contributions consist of the employer/employee payments received as the result of a collective bargaining agreement. This figure will fluctuate depending upon the number of hours earned during the year and reported by the contributing employers and the contribution rate in effect throughout the year.

Investment Revenue

This figure represents the actual investment income received by the fund during the year and will usually consist of interest, dividends and gains or losses on investments when they are actually sold. An analysis of the types of income should normally be detailed in one of the notes to the statements. Where more than one money manager is employed by the fund, the details should be available by manager. The auditor relies upon the accuracy of the custodian's year-end statement and, as part of the audit, test checks it against those received from the investment managers and reconciles any differences.

As most funds are now required to report their investments at their current market value, this approach has resulted in the reporting of a notional or unrealized gain or loss from investments annually on the income statement as *unrealized fair value adjustment* or *unrealized appreciation on investments*. This figure is based on the increase or decrease in the current year's market value as compared to that of the prior year. This figure is an unrealized or *paper* entry, as the actual gain or loss on any investment is not realized until the investment is actually sold. This approach is supposed to result in a more even income flow and a better allocation of income to the year when it actually occurred. While this may be the case over a long period of time, it can result in large annual fluctuations in the short term when the stock or bond market becomes volatile.

Expenditures

The expenses incurred by most funds are fairly consistent and not of an unusual nature. As noted previously, a comparison of each expense between the current and prior year is essential and should reveal any unusual occurrences. The trustees should expect the auditor to highlight and explain any significant changes between the years. Some funds prepare annual budgets, and this will provide another means of comparison with resulting explanations. These expenditures will vary by the type of fund but will usually consist of such items as insurance premiums, self-insured claims, benefit payments, administration costs and professional fees.

Statement of Changes in Net Assets

This statement shows the opening net assets and reconciles the change in the year to the ending balance of the net assets as reported on the balance sheet. Trustees should look for unusual transfers between restricted and unrestricted net assets and inquire to ensure the amounts have been properly allocated.

Notes to the Financial Statements

The last several pages of the statements contain the notes that form a very important and integral part of the financial statements. The notes contain backup detail to the numbers reported on the balance sheet, statement of operations and statement of changes in net assets or explanations of things that happened during the year that affected the fund. The notes provide a brief description of the plan benefits, the recipients of professional fees and possibly a list of the contributions by employers that may be reported with comparative contributions for the prior year. As noted previously, these are the trustees' financial statements, and they can contain whatever and as much information as the trustees wish.

Conclusion

The year-end audited financial statements can be a source of valuable information. The trustees' meeting is not the place for your first look at them, and you should insist upon receiving them well in advance of any meeting. This will enable you to examine them more thoroughly and prepare any questions you may have. Remember that these are your financial statements, and you are going to be asked to approve them as a trustee on behalf of all the beneficiaries of the trust. All trustees are expected to review the financial statements in light of the information that they have available to them as a result of their position as a trustee and as a management or union representative. Understanding these statements will allow you to participate more fully in the trustees' meetings, be better prepared to make knowledgeable decisions and be seen as a desired and valuable trustee on any board of trustees that you serve.

ACTUARIAL REPORTS

Although the work of the actuary is complex, plan sponsors and trustees should feel that they understand the general issues involved and that they can select the most appropriate of the alternatives provided.

The work of the actuary will be discussed in the later sections of this book. Generally, it involves making assumptions about the future in order to comment on the security of benefits provided by a particular plan and the contributions required in the current year to maintain that security.

It is important that you believe that the assumptions and methods being used are broadly suitable for the particular situation involved. The actuary should be prepared to explain why he or she has proposed the actuarial basis being used and to describe in general terms the impact of changes to that basis on the financial forecasts being presented.

The actuary's report should begin with the purpose for which the calculations have been carried out. The assumptions may vary depending on whether the intent is to consider:

• Ongoing funding of the plan
• The solvency position on a particular date
• The expense to be charged for accounting purposes.

Next there should be reference to the source of both the employee data and the asset data. Normally you should expect to see a reconciliation for both these items from the most recent valuation to the current one. These reconciliations will give you confidence that the data to be used is accurate. In addition, you will be able to see items, such as high employee turnover or low rates of return, that may explain why the valuation results are not what would have been expected. The actuarial assumptions and methods should be summarized together with an explanation of any changes that have been made since the previous valuation.

These changes should be justified by reference to the funding strategy of the sponsor/trustees or because of the experience under the plan. It is important that, in addition to each assumption being individually reasonable, the actuarial basis should also be internally consistent.

The focus of the report will be the actuarial balance sheet that compares the value of the liabilities under the plan with the value of the assets available to meet them. The liabilities are normally split between active, deferred vested and retired members. They should be reasonably consistent with the results shown at the previous valuation. The assets may be adjusted to reflect contributions and benefits due but not paid as of the valuation date.

If there is a surplus, then the actuary should recommend how this surplus should be utilized. If there is a deficit, then the actuary should recommend a plan for eliminating the deficit over a period of years through the payment of additional contributions. For those wishing to really understand the actuary's report, the key item may well be *the gain and loss analysis*. This analysis reconciles the expected financial position of the plan, based on the previous valuation, with the actual position revealed. You will be able to see which areas contributed to more favourable results than expected (gains) and which to less favourable (losses). If a partic-

ular item consistently gives rise to a gain or loss, then it may be appropriate to ask the actuary why the assumption for this item has not been changed.

Finally, the report should contain a recommendation for the contributions to be made between now and the next valuation. Once again, this contribution rate should be consistent with the previous report unless there has been a significant change in the composition of the membership.

Various appendixes to the report may contain additional details and an actuary's certificate suitable for the regulatory authorities.

INVESTMENT REPORTS

Overview

There are two types of investment reports: *financial statements* and *investment analysis*. Financial statements are usually produced by the fund's custodian, though pooled funds sometimes have financial statements prepared by the pooled fund investment manager. Investment analysis can be prepared by the investment counsellor, the performance measurement service, the investment advisor or all three.

Financial Statements

Financial statements take the same form as corporate financial statements. However, they look different because they are dominated by the assets and the trading of those assets.

Balance Sheet

The assets of an investment fund usually consist only of cash and securities. Consequently, the fund's portfolio listing is the main part of the balance sheet. This portfolio listing should contain the par value, book value, market value and percentage of total market value for each security that is owned. (These and other terms are defined in the glossary of this handbook.) Accrued interest can be shown either individually or for the entire portfolio. The listing of securities is usually separated between money market, bonds, stocks and foreign securities. Foreign securities should have their values converted into Canadian dollars.

The portfolio listing and the cash transaction statement we will discuss later are the two best and most objective sources of information about what your investment manager is doing. The trustees should review them carefully. In particular, with regard to the portfolio listing:

• Make sure the fund is invested according to the investment policy the trustees have set for the manager.
• Look for investments you do not understand and ask your manager about them.

Cash Transaction Statement

This statement shows the beginning cash balance in the fund and then all deposits, withdrawals, dividends, interest, purchases, sales, other transactions and ending cash balance.

This statement will show you exactly what the investment manager did during the period. It should also be reviewed carefully. In particular:

- Check the amount of turnover (purchases plus sales as a percent of total assets). There is a cost involved in purchases and sales. Make sure the manager's turnover is not higher than he or she originally said would occur. If it is, question why.
- Make sure there are no overdrafts.
- Make sure all expenses have been authorized.

Other Statements

Often there is a *statement of realized gains and losses.* Realized losses, by themselves, don't necessarily mean much; they may be offset by unrealized gains. However, persistent realized losses should be questioned.

Commission statements show the amount of commissions paid by the investment manager to various brokers to execute trades. These should be reviewed carefully by the trustees. If a large portion of commissions are going to one or two brokers, this should be questioned. If a soft dollar commission arrangement is being employed, it is imperative that the trustees check the amounts of commissions paid against the contractual arrangement. Unfortunately, commission statements are not always provided. In this case, the trustees must ask their custodian that one be included regularly.

Investment Manager Reports

The investment manager should provide a written report to the trustees at least annually. This report should present first a review of the economic and financial markets for the period. This should be done in non-technical, easy-to-understand language. Do not allow your manager to use buzzwords, technical jargon or words and phrases you do not understand. Investments are difficult enough to comprehend without the additional barrier of techno-speak.

This background information should then form the basis for your manager to discuss the fund's rate of return. Which rates of return are presented should be decided by the trustees, not the manager. We suggest that the manager give time-weighted returns for at least the period under review, the year to date and since inception (annualized). The manager might also present the most recent 12 months and five years (annualized).

The fund's rate of return shows how much the fund has earned but can only be evaluated when compared to the rate of return for the fund's benchmark. Setting an appropriate benchmark (and evaluation period) is covered in the chapters on investments in Sections III and VII. The manager's actual return should be compared to the return earned by the benchmark. Any difference, whether positive or negative, should be explained by the manager.

The manager's report should also contain a discussion of the current portfolio as well as any significant trading that occurred during the period.

Finally, the manager's report should include an outlook and strategy section in which the manager indicates his or her views regarding what economic and financial events are expected to take place and how the fund is positioned to take advantage of those events.

Performance Measurement Report

A *performance measurement report* usually shows how your fund's rate of return compares to rates of return on other funds that are similar to yours. It is important that the funds have similar asset mix and eligible security guidelines. For example, do not compare a balanced fund with a 20% equity maximum to balanced funds with 60% in equities.

Figure I—10-1 on page 56 shows a typical report page.

The vertical rectangles in the figure show the range of returns for 90% of all funds included in the survey. The highest 5% and lowest 5% of returns are not included. Number 1 is for the most recent one-year period ending December 31, 1999. Number 5 shows the five years ending December 31, 1999. Each rectangle is broken into four areas. The top area shows the range of returns for the highest returning 20% of funds. This is called the *first quartile of returns* or *first quartile*. The second highest area of each rectangle includes the next highest returning 25% of funds and is called the *second quartile* for each period. Then come the third and fourth quartiles. It is the aim of most investment managers to be in the first or second quartile, since that indicates returns that are "above average." The numbers at the bottom of the page show the actual breaks between quartiles as well as your own fund's return and percentile rank. Your fund is plotted on the chart as an asterisk. Other returns, such as appropriate indexes and inflation, can also be shown.

Figure I—10-1

BALANCED FUNDS TOTAL FUND ANNUALIZED RATE OF RETURN

For Periods Ending December 31, 1999

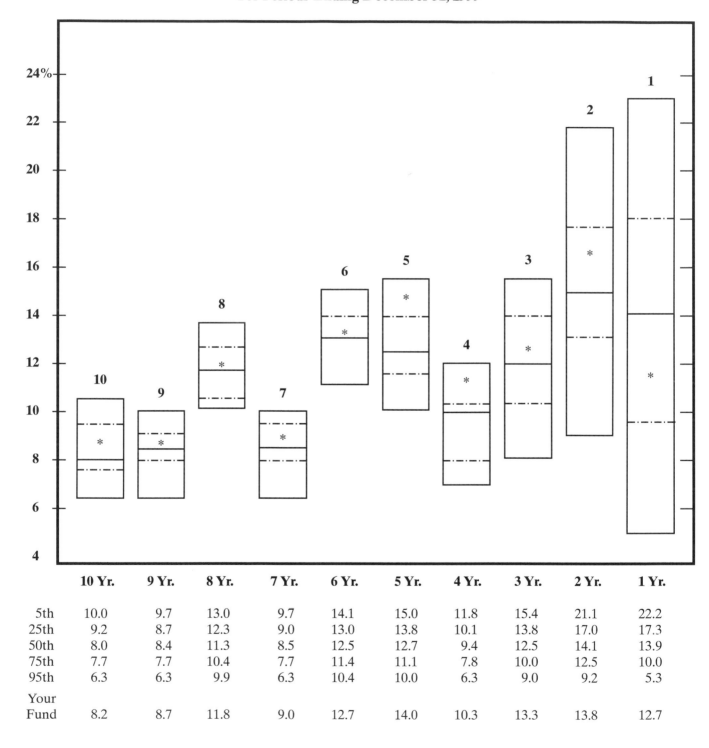

	10 Yr.	9 Yr.	8 Yr.	7 Yr.	6 Yr.	5 Yr.	4 Yr.	3 Yr.	2 Yr.	1 Yr.
5th	10.0	9.7	13.0	9.7	14.1	15.0	11.8	15.4	21.1	22.2
25th	9.2	8.7	12.3	9.0	13.0	13.8	10.1	13.8	17.0	17.3
50th	8.0	8.4	11.3	8.5	12.5	12.7	9.4	12.5	14.1	13.9
75th	7.7	7.7	10.4	7.7	11.4	11.1	7.8	10.0	12.5	10.0
95th	6.3	6.3	9.9	6.3	10.4	10.0	6.3	9.0	9.2	5.3
Your Fund	8.2	8.7	11.8	9.0	12.7	14.0	10.3	13.3	13.8	12.7

CHAPTER 11

Trustee Fiduciary Liability Insurance

by Brian Jeffrey

LEGAL CONTEXT

Much has been written about the responsibility of trustees. When a trustee acts in a fiduciary capacity, the trustee owes the beneficiary a duty of loyalty. Aside from the moral implications arising from fiduciary duty, the trustee (as is everyone) is subject to the "law of the land" (i.e., the common law (except for Quebec)). In addition, provinces also impose statutory duties on trustees (e.g., Quebec *Supplemental Pension Plans Act*).[1]

The legal responsibilities and liabilities of trustees are discussed in detail in other chapters of this book. Trustees also have available to them many excellent publications detailing their legal responsibility. The trustee also has access to the fund's legal counsel who should provide advice on this subject. For the purposes of this chapter, it is a given that trustees have legal liability and that the legal liability imposed on trustees is meaningful.

CANADA/UNITED STATES

Because of the closeness between the two countries, the many business, labour and travel links, there are a lot of similarities in the growth of fiduciary "practice" and "law" between the United States and Canada; however, there are many important differences. Key differences will be discussed later.

THE NEED FOR INSURANCE

As indicated above, the primary need for insurance arises out of the legal obligations imposed upon trustees, but also because, in most cases, the purchase of adequate insurance is the prudent course to take. While the focus of this chapter is trustee fiduciary liability insurance, it is important for the trustee to know that this is not the only exposure the trustee and the fund have to potential loss. Most trustees are aware of fiduciary liability insurance and fidelity bonding, but there are many other potential exposures. The whole question of risk and insurance should be discussed with the fund's advisors, including the fund's insurance brokers. To give trustees some "food for thought," attached as Appendix I-11-A[2] is an exposure checklist.

RISK MANAGEMENT AS A FIRST LINE OF DEFENCE

There are many excellent articles on risk management.[3] The informed trustee should know what steps to take to prevent (as much as is possible) losses. The old saw "an ounce of prevention is worth a pound of cure" certainly applies. Again, discussion with the fund's advisors is essential.

THE RIGHT TO PURCHASE FIDUCIARY LIABILITY INSURANCE

The *Employee Retirement Income Security Act of 1974* (ERISA) in the United States is very specific about the ability of trustees to buy insurance with plan assets. Canadian legislation is mainly silent on the subject. The main issue is whether or not it is proper for trustees to use plan assets to purchase insurance to protect the trustees from liabilities associated with their personal responsibilities. To date, there are no known circumstances where this has been a problem in Canada (although there has been discussion regarding similarities with directors and officers liability insurance). Legal advice should be sought on this topic. If, after discussion with legal counsel, there is still concern, the fund's insurance broker should approach the insurer(s) to arrange a premium split between the fund and the trustees and have each trustee pay his or her own premium allocation. It would be expected that the premium allocation for trustees would be nominal.

THE CANADIAN INSURANCE MARKET FOR TRUSTEE FIDUCIARY LIABILITY

Historically, coverage was provided either by Lloyd's of London or the Canadian subsidiaries of U.S. companies. Because the marketplace was limited and the demand not great, policies tended to be either U.K. or U.S. policies nominally amended to reflect the Canadian context. In the late 1970s, Canadian wording was developed after discussion with, and input from, Canadian trustees, lawyers and administrators. In terms of policy coverage, the policy forms offered are relatively unchanged today. There are four insurers[4] that write meaningful amounts of trustee fiduciary insurance and approximately four or five others that offer the coverage. It is important for the trustee to know that an insurer has a meaningful amount of similar business (thus is committed to providing the coverage on a long-term basis)[5] and is not trying to just "buy" premiums in a soft market. In terms of credibility of statistics, there are few insurers that have a sufficient portfolio of Canadian fiduciary insurance premiums to produce stand-alone viable loss results. This can mean that their portfolios are subject to shock (large) losses or are lumped in with other "similar" insurances that may not inure to the benefit of Canadian trustees/trust funds.

WHO CAN BE/SHOULD BE AN INSURED?

The policy should cover all trustees, i.e., past, present and future. The fund itself should be named and should be insured against loss arising from the actions of the trustees. *It is important that the policy cover the trust fund regardless of any hold harmless or exculpatory clauses contained within the trust document.* It is common, where allowed by law, for trustees to be held harmless for their inadvertent actions. While this protects the trustees, there may still be financial loss to the fund, and it is essential that any insurance purchased picks up this type of loss. If the fund has its own employees, they should also be named insureds. "Outside" administrators can also be added in certain circumstances; however, by so doing there is an impact on limits of liability, which is discussed later in this chapter.

FIDUCIARY LIABILITY COVERAGE ANALYSIS HIGHLIGHTS

1. The "insuring agreement" should "pay on behalf of" and not "reimburse." *Pay on behalf of* means the insurer pays first and thus trust funds are not expended. Usually, the policies cover all sums for which the insured may become legally obligated to pay for any wrongful act. One definition of *wrongful act* means "any error, or omission, misstatement, misleading statement, breach of any responsibility, obligation, duty or negligent act performed by or required to be performed by or on behalf of an insured.

2. All policies include "defence costs." It is important to know whether or not the defence costs are included within the policy limits or are in addition to the policy limits. Obviously, it is better to have defence costs in addition to the limits. If defence costs are included within the limit, then higher limits should be considered.

3. Most, if not all, fiduciary liability policies are on a "claims made" basis. With claims made policies, it is important to know how the policy will respond to "prior acts." Most, if not all, known situations would be excluded. *It is important that "unknown" situations, at the time of inception of the policy, are included.*

4. *Sometimes an insurer will offer a retroactive effective date.* What this means is simply that any "unknown" claims that arise out of circumstances that occurred prior to the retroactive effective date would not be covered. *This is an important area that requires discussion with your insurance broker and legal advisors.*

5. *It is important also to know under a claims made policy what the "extension" rights are. Once a policy is cancelled or lapsed, there is no further coverage. As it can take sometimes many years for an actual claim to manifest itself, it is important first that coverage remain in effect.* Where, for whatever reason, coverage is not available, the longest possible extension period for claims to manifest themselves is the best coverage to have. Most policies incorporate such an extension, which usually requires the payment of an additional premium when the extension is exercised. Again, it is important that this coverage granted is fully understood and consultation with the insurance broker and legal counsel is essential.

6. What limit should be purchased? This is asking the trustees to answer the question, "How high is up?" This, however, is a subjective decision that has to be made by the trustees.

A business decision must ultimately be made based on a review of as many factors as possible. To assist trustees to make prudent, reasoned decisions, consideration should be given to at least the following factors (in no particular order of importance).

A. Advice of professionals
   i. Accountants
   ii. Lawyers
   iii. Insurance brokers
   iv. Insurers
   v. Insurance consultants
   As many professional opinions should be obtained as possible and should be weighted based on the particular professional's expertise in the insurance field.
B. What limits do other like insureds purchase?
   i. See attached Appendix I-11-B[6]
   ii. See attached Appendix I-11-C[7]
C. Policy coverage
   i. Are defence costs included in the limit? If so, then higher limits should be considered than for a policy with defence costs in addition to the limit.
   ii. Most policies contain an annual aggregate limit for all claims arising in the policy year. Funds should consider the possibility of having more than one claim in a policy year.
D. Prior claims history
   A review should be made of:
   i. The fund's own loss history (if any)
   ii. Loss history for other "like" Canadian insureds[8]
   iii. Loss history for other "like" U.S. insureds.
E. What limits are available in the marketplace?
   For certain risks, very little limit is available, and thus the issue can be moot (the client may have to look to alternative risk financing vehicles, e.g., reciprocals, spread loss, etc.). At the present time, limits of $25 million or more are available for well-managed Canadian trust funds.
F. Future trends
   i. Although not to the level of our neighbours to the south, we are becoming a more litigious society. At the extreme end, parts of our society seem unwilling to suffer the least inconvenience or injury without seeking compensation from someone—anyone! Professionals are being held to a higher standard of accountability. The original object of the tort system was to allow redress against others who, through carelessness, cause harm to third parties. Insurers are concerned that in a number of cases the need to show negligence is being replaced by simply showing involvement. The "deep pocket" syndrome—"Who can pay"?
   ii. There seems to be a swing toward having professionals and those in fiduciary capacities be more and more accountable for their actions.
   iii. Continuing changing legislation. In particular, pension plan management is becoming increasingly complicated, and the laws governing such management have placed a higher duty of care on plan trustees, dictating that they assume more and more responsibility for the plan's administration and investment.
G. Financial statement reporting requirements
   If a suit is received that exceeds the limits purchased, this can have a detrimental impact on the annual financial statements. The likely impact of such a claim should be discussed with the fund's auditors and legal counsel. It should be remembered that it is not uncommon for liability claims to take up to ten years to settle.
H. Number of insureds involved/exposure to loss
   It is not uncommon for more than one insured to be covered by the same policy. In deciding upon adequate limits, trustees must, as best as possible, assess their exposure, particularly if more than one insured is involved. The annual aggregate limit normally applies to all insureds on an inclusive basis.
I. Most policies are subject to a deductible. This can be two-layered, i.e., a higher deductible for the trust fund and a lower deductible for the trustees. In most cases, the deductible is negotiable and often times can be a vehicle for reducing the premium. Again, it is important to know whether or not the deductible applies to legal costs.
J. What are reasonable premiums? At the present time, the Canadian insurance marketplace is "soft," and thus most premiums are negotiable. There is obviously a direct relativity among the exposure (size of fund, number of trustees, employees, etc.), the deductible level and the limits selected. If a decision has to be made with respect to an absolute amount of premium to be paid, strong consideration should be given to protecting the catastrophic risk rather than the first dollar. E.g., if the choice is between the same premium for:
   i. $10 million limit with a $25,000 deductible
   ii. $5 million limit with a $1,000 deductible
   provided there is a $10 million exposure, then the purchase of the $10 million limit is likely the more prudent option.
K. In the United States, insurers have a "right of recourse, being the right to subrogate against an

insured. This can be negated by payment of an additional premium. This has not been an issue in Canada (see comments above under "Right to Purchase Insurance" heading).

L. What is not covered? Exclusions—There are two types of exclusions:

  i. Absolute: Uninsurable in the conventional market (there are more and more "financial insurance" products available; however, these tend to be very specific and are unlikely to have application except for the largest trust funds)

  ii. Insurable elsewhere: Most fiduciary liability policies contain similar exclusions. The main exclusions are:

    1. War, insurrection: Can be insured, if needed.

    2. Bodily injury and property damage: Should be insured separately.

    3. Nuclear energy hazard: Can be insured, if needed.

    4. Automobile: Can be insured, if needed.

    5. Watercraft: Can be insured, if needed.

    6. Workers' Compensation: Can be insured, if needed.

    7. Pollution: Can be insured, if needed.

    8. Dishonesty: Should be insured separately.

    9. The failure of any investment plan to perform as represented by an insured: Uninsurable in the conventional marketplace.

    10. Discrimination, libel, slander, defamation of character: Should be insured separately.

    11. Fines, penalties, punitive and exemplary damages: Can be insured, if needed and *not* against "public policy."

M. Time period—Policies can usually be purchased for a one- or a three-year term. Longer periods may be required in the case of a fund ceasing to exist to cover the "run-off" period. "Run-off" policies of seven years or more have been offered. The most common term (other than run-off) is annual.

Final Thoughts

Accepting the principle that the purchase of insurance is prudent, trustees should recognize that not all insurers are equal and, while price is important, it is not the only factor. The insurer's reputation, financial strength and claims payment record should also be considered. The breadth of coverage and limits available and the insurer's track record providing trustee fiduciary liability insurance should also have a bearing.

The selection of an insurance broker also requires care (trustees have a fiduciary responsibility to select advisors and continue to monitor those advisors, including their insurance broker). A good broker should help trustees assess their exposure to "risk" and design an insurance program to meet those exposures and assist in the selection of a suitable insurer.[9]

ENDNOTES

1. *Supplemental Pension Plans Act,* R.S.Q. 1990, R-15.1, s. 151.

2. Appendix I-11-A—Exposure Checklist provided by Knox Vicars McLean Insurance Brokers.

3. D. Bailey, *ERISA Fiduciary Liability Loss Prevention* (New Jersey: Chubb & Sons. Inc., 1989), applicable to Canadian Trustees; "Non-Profit Governance: The Executive's Guide," an American-oriented recent publication of The American Bar Association and The American Society of Corporate Secretaries (Chicago, 1997).

4. Commercial Union Assurance Company (now CGU Canada Ltd.) and Axa Insurance Canada; Chubb Insurance Company of Canada; American Home Assurance Company; London Guarantee Insurance Company.

5. M. Larsen and P. Sinott, "Our Latest D&O Survey Shows . . . , " Watson Wyatt's D&O Newsletter, 1989 Winter, pp. 1-2. Although related to directors and officers, the comments contained in Watson Wyatt's D&O Newsletter (Winter 1998) are appropriate to this circumstance: *"Current premium, loss, and coverage trends suggest that we could be only a few years away from some fairly adverse loss ratios and shrinking profit margins. Corporate insurance purchasers should therefore take a longer term during 1998 or 1999 D&O policy renewal negotiations. While looking to identify the best D&O insurance value for their particular circumstances, they should also be prepared to:*

  • *Negotiate a fair price*
  • *Establish a long-term strategy to maintain appropriate coverage*
  • *Assess the strength and reputation of the D&O liability insurers with whom they negotiate.*

In addition, multiyear policies may merit consideration for many companies, particularly if the organization has some comfort level with its current insurer.

6. Excerpt from the 1991 Watson Wyatt *Canadian Directors and Officers Liability Survey Report* (page 18).

7. Excerpt from the 1993 Watson Wyatt *Directors and Officers Liability Survey Report* (United States, pp. 13 and 17).

8. Knox Vicars McLean advised that in their *"18+ years' experience with trust funds, the largest claim encountered was for $20,000,000 (this claim is still ongoing and it is unlikely (but not impossible) that the final settlement will ever reach the amount claimed. It is interesting to note that the particular fund in question had limits of $2,000.00)."*

9. The author recognizes the use of general information contained in Jeffrey D. Mamorsky's article contained in the *Trustees Handbook,* 5th edition, "Trustee Fiduciary Liability Insurance" (Brookfield, Wisconsin: International Foundation of Employee Benefit Plans, Inc., 1998).

APPENDIX I—11-A

TRUST FUND/TRUSTEES ASSESSMENT OF POTENTIAL EXPOSURE TO LOSS/INSURANCE NEEDS

	COMMENTS
I. Fiduciary/General Errors & Omission	
Protects the Trustees and the Trust Fund against depletion of its assets through Errors and Omissions on the part of Trustees in carrying out their duties and responsibilities as Trustees. Coverage should apply even if the Trustees are not held to be legally liable for the particular nature of the Error or Omission by Exculpatory Clauses.	Limits usually start at $500,000 for a small Fund; average limit purchased is $5,000,000, with limits of $25,000,000 or more not being uncommon for very large Funds.
The definition of Insured should include the Trust Fund, all Trustees and any person acting on behalf of the Trust Fund within the organization of the Trust Fund, including employees of the Trust Fund if any.	
NOTE: 1) Independent Administrators, Actuaries, Auditors, Investment Managers, Investment Management Services, Consultants, Lawyers or Accountants while acting in their capacities as such are excluded.	If the Trust uses the services of an Independent Administrator, then consideration should be given to adding them as an Additional Insured, or if not added, proof of adequate Administrators Errors or Omissions Insurance should be verified.
2) Consideration may be given to adding an Independent Administrator as an Additional Insured, if requested by the Trust.	The Trust should verify that all Professionals utilized carry Professional Liability Insurance of sufficient limits (Certificates of Insurance).
II. Dishonesty	
Protects the Trust from Dishonest Acts of Trustees and Employees, if any (acting alone or in collusion with others) which cause loss to the Trust Fund.	Limit range from $500,000 to $25,000,000 or more, depending on size of Fund.

	COMMENTS
III. Legal Liability (General)	
Commercial General Liability insures against Legal Liability for Bodily Injury and Property Damage arising out of the Trust Fund's premises, operations and products. It may be extended to include: ☐ Premises and Operations ☐ Products and Completed Operations ☐ Personal Injury ☐ Non-Owned Automobile ☐ Non-Owned Watercraft ☐ Owners and Contractors Protective ☐ Contractual Liability ☐ Contingent Employers Liability ☐ Employers Liability ☐ Employee Benefits Errors and Omissions ☐ Advertising Liability ☐ Liquor Liability ☐ Incidental Medical Malpractice ☐ Medical Expenses ☐ Elevator Collision ☐ Employees as Insureds ☐ Trustees as Insureds ☐ Occurrence Property Damage ☐ Broad Form Property Damage ☐ Hostile Fire Extension ☐ Intentional Injury Amendment ☐ Tenants Legal Liability **NOTE:** **General Liability Policies exclude Owned Aviation, Owned Automobile, Owned Watercraft, Environmental, Nuclear, Professional and Employment Practices Liability**	Limits range from $1,000,000 to $25,000,000 or more. A $5,000,000 limit can usually be purchased at a reasonable price. Most, if not all of the possible Extensions should be included. A number of these Extensions can be included at little or no cost. A combination of Commercial General Liability Coverage and Umbrella Liability Coverage may be a desirable way to achieve appropriate limits of liability.
IV. Automobile (Owned or Operated)	
A) Direct Damage All Perils or Collision and Comprehensive B) Loss of Use C) Third Party Liability	This coverage is required **if** any motor vehicles are owned by, leased to or registered in the name of the Trust Fund.
V. Watercraft (Owned or Operated)	
A) Direct Damage B) Loss of Use C) Third Party Liability	This coverage is only required **if** the Trust Fund owns, leases, operates or has assumed responsibility for any watercraft.

	COMMENTS
VI. Aircraft (Owned or Operated)	
A) Direct Damage B) Loss of Use C) Third Party Liability	This coverage is only required **if** the Trust Fund owns, leases, operates or has assumed responsibility for any aircraft.
VII. Property (Owned, leased or for which the Insured has agreed to be responsible)	
A. Direct Damage	
1. Building(s) 2. Boiler & Machinery 3. Exterior Glass 4. Signs 5. Growing Trees, Plants & Shrubs 6. Office/Plant Equipment & Stock 7. Computers (Hardware, Software, Extra Expense) 8. Fine Arts 9. Customers Goods 10. Employee Property 11. Tenants Improvements 12. Property in Storage (Off Premises) 13. Property in Transit 14. Property in Custody of Sales Reps 15. Accounts Receivable Records 16. Valuable Papers Records	Coverage should be written on a "Blanket" "All Risks" except as excluded basis. It should include Replacement Cost and Stated Amount Clauses and be extended to include Earthquake, Flood, Sewer Back-up; Full By-Laws Coverage. Interruption by Civil Authority—30 days; 60 days notice of cancellation; Mechanical Breakdown and Transit on Computers. Sufficient sub-limits should be established for Valuable Papers, Accounts Receivables Records, Professional Fees and other Extensions as appropriate. If required, Boiler and Machinery coverage should be on a Comprehensive Form, Repair and Replacement, covering all objects. Appropriate Limits for Extensions i.e. Extra Expense, Expediting Expense, Ammonia Contamination etc. Sufficient limits should be established for Extra Expense Coverage with 100% of Limit available 1st month. Separate coverage for Computers, as well as General Extra Expense.
NOTE: **Property Policies exclude Money and Securities.**	**NOTE:** **Your lease should be reviewed to determine any special insurance requirements or obligations.**
B. Loss of Use	
1. Loss of Income	
2. Increased Expenses ☐ Auditors/Professional Fees ☐ Other	

	COMMENTS
VIII. Money & Securities	
A. Loss Inside the Premises B. Loss Outside the Premises C. Depositors Forgery D. Computer Theft and Funds Transfer E. Employee Dishonesty	Employee Dishonesty addressed under II. above. Other coverages may be appropriate, depending on the Funds handling of Money and Securities etc.
IX. Environmental Liability	Coverage may be required if the Trust Fund owns properties from which there may be the possibility of Environmental Damage.
X. Professional Liability	
A. Trustees/Directors & Officers Liability B. Errors & Omissions Liability	Items A and B addressed under Item 1, Directors and Officers Liability, above. (If, as for some larger Funds an owned corporation has been set up to handle a specific(s) need, e.g. Real Estate).
C. Employment Practices Liability	Employment Practices Liability relates to Sexual Harassment, Wrongful Dismissal, etc.
D. Outside Directors Liability	(E.G., If a Trustee is asked to sit on the board of a company in which the Fund has substantial investments).
XI. Accidental Death or Dismemberment	Coverage can be purchased to provide A.D. &D. Coverage for Trustees and Employees.
XII. Key Person Insurance	Coverage can be purchased on the lives of Key Persons to the Trust Fund whose death would result in possible financial loss to the Trust Fund.
XIII. Ransom/Kidnap	Coverage can be purchased against the possibility of Trustees or Key Employees being kidnapped and held for ransom.

	COMMENTS
XIV. Credit Insurance	Not likely to be appropriate to the Fund.
XV. Ocean Marine	Not likely to be appropriate to the Fund.
XVI. Employee Benefits Insurance	Coverage can be arranged to provide a "package" of Employee Benefits i.e. Group Life, Dental etc.
XVII. Package of Insurance Products for Sale to Members (i.e. AD&D; Medical Coverage, Home, Auto Insurance).	Trustees might want to consider offering to members a package of Insurance Products for sale to members i.e. Auto, Home, Life etc. Can provide considerable benefits to members.

APPENDIX I—11-B

FINANCIAL SERVICES: LIMITS, DEDUCTIBLES, PREMIUMS BY ASSET SIZE

Asset Size	Average Limit	Average Corporate Reimbursement Deductible	Average Premium
$15 million-$50 million	$ 3,000,000	n/a	$ 14,150
$50 million-$150 million	13,400,000	$ 40,000	47,769
$150 million-$600 million	7,050,000	1,750,000	24,917
$600 million-$1.5 billion	7,400,000	133,000	79,342
$1.5 billion-$5 billion	11,000,000	175,000	100,622
Over $5 billion	33,750,000	1,036,139	390,286
Low	250,000	250	300
Median	10,000,000	100,000	80,000
High	125,000,000	5,000,000	1,016,004
Average	17,607,143	663,552	170,849

APPENDIX I—11-C

AVERAGE COVERAGE LIMITS BY ASSET SIZE
(in millions)

	1993	1992
<$100 ML	$ 6.2	$ 6.7
$100-400 ML	11.5	11.7
$400 ML-$1 BL	22.4	22.2
$1-2 BL	35.8	30.1
Over $2 BL	55.0	51.8
All Asset Sizes	*$30.7*	*$28.4*

TOTAL COVERAGE LIMITS BY BUSINESS TYPE
(in millions)

	No. of Participants	First Quartile	Median	Third Quartile	Average
Petroleum, Mining & Agricultural	54	$10.00	$20.00	$40.00	$33.26
Electronics & Computers	114	5.00	20.00	50.00	32.01
Durable Goods Manufacturing	86	7.00	20.00	40.00	29.20
Non-durable Goods Manufacturing	130	15.00	25.00	50.00	40.17
Transportation & Communications	71	10.00	25.00	65.00	40.20
Utilities	111	25.00	50.00	75.00	54.33
Merchandising	87	5.00	15.00	35.00	23.27
Large Banking	96	10.00	20.00	32.50	25.97
Non-Banking Financial Services	99	10.00	15.00	30.00	25.84
Construction & Real Estate	30	7.00	10.00	25.00	15.47
Personal & Business Services	66	5.00	10.00	20.00	16.17
Middle Market Banking	63	2.00	3.00	5.00	3.89
All Business Types	*1,007*	*$10.00*	*$20.00*	*$45.00*	*$30.74*

CHAPTER 12

Plan Member Communications Legal Implications

by Mark Zigler

WHAT WE HAVE HERE IS A FAILURE TO COMMUNICATE

The essence of virtually any claim or litigation involving loss of employee benefits or pensions usually involves a failure to communicate. Although liability arises under a series of legal theories, these are only the methods by which the courts can determine that serious miscommunication of some kind has occurred. Liability generally falls upon the "deep pockets" of the plan administrator, be it an employer, insurance carrier or the trustees of a multi-employer pension plan (MEPP).

Most communications to employees are written by professionals with some expertise in benefits communication, or by the benefits staff of larger employers or trust funds. However, there is generally a tension between benefit communication experts, who urge "clear, crisp and concise" language in literature and prefer to deliver "good news," and lawyers, who tend to be overly technical and urge their clients to advise of risks as well as benefits. No doubt there is a fine balance to be struck, but the balance can only be understood when one looks at some of the worst cases and determines where the source of the problem lies.

One thing is certain: Plaintiffs in benefit communication cases generally tend to be of the most sympathetic kind, the infirm, the elderly or widows and survivors of workers who did not understand their entitlements because of a failure of a "deep pocket" organization to adequately communicate. While one can probably blame findings of legal liability for communication failures on the "deep pocket" theory, this would be a foolish approach, as it ignores the sources of the problem.

While there is an overall obligation on an employer, sponsor or board of trustees to provide detailed and on-going information regarding benefit plans and retirement benefits, not every situation will lead to legal liability. However, an understanding of the legal framework is essential.

THE LANGUAGE OF LEGAL LIABILITY

Legal liability must be based on what is known as a *cause of action.* In cases involving benefits, this essentially involves a breach of contract, a breach of a fiduciary duty or a tort. The basis for liability will depend very much on the relationship between the parties: Usually it is the relationship between a plan member and the person responsible for providing benefits. Sometimes the provider is the employer, while other times it will be a multi-employer trust fund, an administrator or an insurance company, depending on the situation.

The *causes of action* analysed below are *common law* causes of action, arising from the unwritten common law that has evolved in the United Kingdom, the United States and Canada, with the exception of Quebec, which employs a civil law system. In addition to common law liability, there is also *statutory liability,* which can exist under legislation that is passed by federal or provincial governments. There are many obligations to provide documentation to, and to communicate with, plan members under pension benefit legislation. These obligations are reviewed in Chapter 2 of Section IV, which deals with disclosure obligations to members. In addition, the federal pension regulator has developed a guideline for disclosure to plan members.[1] Failure to provide the disclosure required by provincial legislation, or by federal statute for federally regulated pension plans, can result in intervention (i.e., in the form of making an order) by superintendents of pensions or other regulatory bodies.

However, the emphasis in this chapter is with respect to common law liability that can arise out of legal proceedings in a court or through a labour arbitration. While it is beyond the scope of this chapter to deal with all possible legal grounds for liability, understanding the vocabulary of legal liability and the types of situations that arise in the context of employee benefit communications is important. Key concepts are outlined below.

Breach of Contract

Employee benefits generally arise out of the employment contract. Every employee has such a contract with his or her employer, be it a written individual contract, a collective agreement or an unwritten arrangement. All that is required to form a contract is "consideration" given as part of an exchange between parties. Even in the case of an unwritten employment contract, the employee provides his or her labour in exchange for a promise of remuneration. Often there are other implied promises in the unwritten contract, and these may give rise to liability when employee benefits are part of that arrangement. There is, for example, the implied promise to give an employee sufficient notice of the termination of the agreement. During that notice period, benefits as well as remuneration are lost, and the employee's "damages for breach of contract" would include the value of such benefits.

In recent years, the common law of contract has expanded to cover implied promises or other obligations arising out of employment contracts that are "quasi-contractual," rather than an explicit part of the written agreement. It is this type of situation, some examples of which are outlined below, that gives rise to some of the potential areas of liability.

Detrimental Reliance

While detrimental reliance is not in itself a "cause of action" that results in liability, the idea of an employee relying to his or her detriment on a promise or representation made by an employer, and thus "changing his or her position" as a result of the representation, has given rise to many theories of legal liability. The "detrimental reliance" can be related to a representation, a promise or a "misrepresentation" made in a negligent manner. What is critical is that the employee has taken a step, or deliberately failed to act, in reliance on some kind of assurance from his or her employer. Where such assurance can be tied to some other aspect of legal liability, the employee usually succeeds in his or her claim. The theories of promissory estoppel, negligent misrepresentation and unjust enrichment outlined below have

breach of fiduciary duty, or have some element of "reliance," attached to them.

Promissory Estoppel

This cause of action is defined as the principle that:
. . . a promise made without consideration may nonetheless be enforced to prevent injustice if the promisor should have reasonably expected the promisee to rely on the promise and if the promisee did actually rely on the promise to his or her detriment.[2]

Negligent Misrepresentation

The Supreme Court of Canada has set out the elements of this cause of action in the following passage from a leading case on the issue:
Five general requirements that must from now on be met before liability will be imposed for negligent misrepresentation:
(1) there must be a duty of care based on a "special relationship" between the representor and the representee;
(2) the representation in question must be untrue, inaccurate, or misleading;
(3) the representor must have acted negligently in making said representation;
(4) the representee must have relied, in a reasonable manner, on said negligent misrepresentation; and
(5) the reliance must have been detrimental to the representee in the sense that damages resulted.[3]

Unjust Enrichment

This cause of action was characterised by an Ontario court as follows:
The principles which give rise to the imposition of a constructive trust, based upon unjust enrichment, require the finding of a benefit to or enrichment of one party, a corresponding detriment to or deprivation suffered by the other party, and an absence of any juristic reason for the benefit or enrichment.[4]

Breach of Fiduciary Duty

This type of claim arises in cases where a special duty of loyalty is owed. Trustees typically hold such duties, as do professional advisors. In the pension context, these duties have been codified in various provincial statutes. For example, the Ontario *Pension Benefits Act* (PBA) codifies the common law of trusts (at the highest level for trustees) in respect of fiduciary duty. Section 23 of PBA states:
(1) The administrator of a pension plan shall exercise the care, diligence and skill in the

administration and investment of the pension fund that a person of ordinary prudence would exercise in dealing with the property of another person.

(2) The administrator of a pension plan shall use in the administration and investment of the pension plan and in the administration and investment of the pension fund all relevant knowledge and skill that the administrator possesses or, by reasons of the administrator's profession, business or calling, ought to possess.[5]

The types of claims described above represent the tools lawyers will often use to endeavour to establish liability on the part of an administrator, insurer or employer for their communications to employees. In virtually all cases, these communications, whether written or verbal, will either form a contractual basis for the agreement, if there are no other documents to rely on, or will be used to prevent the administrator or employer from relying on formal, legal, written documentation where the communications to the employees appear to be contradictory. In a way, this is an extension of the well-known *contra proferentum* rule, which is commonplace in the vocabulary of insurance lawyers. This rule stipulates that anyone who unilaterally drafts contract documentation that is ambiguous will have it interpreted contrary to their position, or *contra proferentum,* if there is any litigation regarding the meaning of the words. As noted by one American commentator:

Attorneys who represent plan participants will use various legal theories, including breach of fiduciary duty, ERISA notice requirements, breach of contract, promissory estoppel, detrimental reliance, misrepresentation of facts and breach of good faith in fair dealings.[6]

The rest of this chapter will focus on examples of how lawyers and judges use these tools to determine legal liability in employee communication cases.

EXAMPLES OF LIABILITY

Having determined the causes of action that are most popular in the Canadian jurisdictions, it is important to see some of the examples of cases in Canada and a few in the United States where these concepts have been put to use. Sometimes there are written misrepresentations, oral misrepresentations or even failures to disclose matters or to inquire about pertinent issues. Often when trustees and administrators rely upon other parties, such as union officials or company personnel managers, to communicate with plan participants, the plan administrator can be held liable for errors.[7] However, if trustees are able to establish that written plan documents and rules are well-communicated to the partici-

pants, these communications may prevail. Having the necessary staff and procedures in place to adequately communicate the information is critical.

Other examples of situations involving communication errors are outlined below.

Pension Surplus Cases

The role of employee booklets has been canvassed in a number of decisions involving ownership of pension surplus on the wind-up of a plan. The effect of statements made in booklets was best summarized by the Supreme Court of Canada in *Schmidt v. Air Products of Canada Ltd,*[8] the leading case on pension surpluses:

Documents not normally considered to have legal effect may none the less form part of the legal matrix within which the rights of employers and employees participating in a pension plan must be determined. Whether they do so will depend upon the wording of the documents, the circumstances in which they were produced, and the effect which they had on the parties, particularly the employees.[9]

Schmidt considered other cases such as the earlier *Dominion Stores* case, where it was found that constant references to the pension plan assets belonging to the employees were factors that the court might have considered with respect to surplus ownership on pension plan wind-up.[10] The Pension Commission of Ontario has also touched upon the issue in the case of *Tie Communications Canada.* In this case, the Commission upheld the reasoning in *Schmidt* with respect to statements in booklets where no additional evidence was led as to the reliance, if any, placed by the employees on the statements in question.[11] In *Schmidt,* there was only one vague statement in a booklet regarding surplus that was made 16 years before the plan was wound up. This distinguished the case from the situation in *Dominion Stores* in the opinion of the Court. However, the door has not been closed to finding a legal liability in surplus cases where the booklet contradicts the plan text. The Supreme Court's statements on the booklet issue are sufficiently flexible to ensure that the issue will depend on the facts of the case and the evidence about the impact the statements in booklets had on the employees. It is clear that merely producing booklets before a trial court without providing evidence from employees or others as to the impact of the booklets will not necessarily assist in advancing the case of the employees.

Contractual liability can arise in surplus cases where an employer seeks to offer surplus to employees as part of a pension plan wind-up, a surplus sharing agreement or a promise of certain levels of surplus as part of an early retirement package. For example, in a recent decision, an Ontario judge found that an employee had relied on certain representations and estimates of surplus made by an employer in accepting an early retirement package that included such a surplus payout.[12]

Terminating or Reducing Retiree Health and Insurance Benefits

This has been a major source of litigation in the United States and is now becoming a common occurrence in Canada. Many employers promise retirees certain benefits after retirement that are not likely to be funded and are not part of a pension plan. These benefits are usually in the form of supplementary health and life insurance. As can be seen from the decision of the Supreme Court of Canada in *Dayco Canada v. Canadian Auto Workers*,[13] the court has determined that these types of benefits can "vest" and there may be a contractual prohibition against terminating them. While the *Dayco* case involved a collective agreement and its interpretation, many situations involving retiree benefits will be based entirely on communications made to employees during their employment, upon retirement and after retirement. In this respect the leading case in Ontario thus far, *Attorney General v. Confederation Life*,[14] has determined that these benefits are usually contractual in nature. However, in *Confederation Life*, the court rejected the argument that assets should be set aside to form a trust within the insolvency of Confederation Life,[15] given the nature of the arrangements with the employees in question and the competing claims of Confederation Life policyholders.

The *Confederation Life* case contains an in-depth analysis of both the contractual obligations that may arise in respect of retiree health benefit and supplementary pension promises and whether such obligations can be elevated to a "fiduciary" level.

In the United States, where there has been extensive litigation in this area, much of the case law turns on "disclaimers" that are contained in employee booklets. A typical disclaimer will provide:

This booklet is for information only and does not constitute a contract. If there is any inconsistency between this booklet and the insurance policies governing the plan, the insurance policies will govern. If you wish a copy of the insurance policies, please contact the personnel department.

The effectiveness of these types of disclaimers contained in booklets is often questioned, particularly if the employees are not given access to the real insurance policies or contractual documents but only provided with the booklets. As noted by one U.S. court:

Although Southern Life submits that both the plan and summary are consistent, Southern Life asserts that if a conflict arose between the plan and the summary, the plan should prevail. Such an assertion defeats the purpose of the summary. It is of no effect to publish and distribute a plan sum-

mary booklet designed to simplify and explain a voluminous and complex document, and then proclaim that any inconsistencies will be governed by the plan. Unfairness will flow to the employee for reasonably relying on the summary booklet.[16]

It is very risky to rely on disclaimers where the actual documents have never been provided to the employees and where the disclaimers are, themselves, vague. Many times those drafting employee communication material tend to downplay the negative issues and adverse consequences, to the point where it is unclear what these consequences are. While it may often be a good communications strategy to accentuate the positive, totally eliminating or misstating the negative is of no assistance in any ultimate legal dispute.

Often simple contract theory provides the basis for liability in the United States. In the case of *Sprague v. General Motors Corporation*, a class action brought by 50,000 former employees (early retirees) was successful on the basis that GM contracted with the former employees to provide unreduced health care benefits in exchange for early retirement. This precluded the company from reducing the health care benefits for these individuals.[17]

Entitlement to Profit-Sharing Plans, Bonuses and Other Benefits Based on "Secret Documents"

A series of cases have developed in Canada where the eligibility rules for a profit-sharing entitlement or supplementary pension arrangement have not been made clear to the employee because the communications to these employees are vague and dependent on contractual documents that are kept secret from the employees. In such situations courts will generally preclude an employer from relying on such secret documents.[18]

Misleading and Poor Communications Regarding Pension and Benefit Entitlements

This is by far the area where there will be more and more cases in the future. A poorly drafted booklet with respect to qualifications for entitlement to certain benefits; a letter that suggests entitlement to a benefit where there is none in the actual documents; even a telephone confirmation of a benefit entitlement that does not really exist can be known to give rise to liability. Most recently, failure to communicate effectively by telephone so that an employee thought he would be collecting a cost-of-living allowance earlier rather than later gave rise to liability in the case of *Campbell v. Alberta Teachers Retirement Fund*.[19]

There is no doubt that errors by employees of benefit plans and written communications such as letters and even telephone calls, if relied on by the employee, will give rise to negligent misrepresentation claims. While it is not possible to avoid all claims, special care must be taken in such communications, given the consequences of making a serious error. This is particularly true when dealing with such matters as pension and long-term disability benefits, where the liability may be significant.

Failure to Disclose Relevant Information and Options

It is not only the giving of inaccurate or misleading information that can give rise to liability. Failure to disclose relevant information based on an employee inquiry also gives rise to liability. Most recently in the case of *Spinks v. The Queen,*[20] an employee succeeded on a claim against a federal public service plan on the basis that the plan administrator failed to disclose to him the ability to "buy back" benefits for certain foreign service prior to his joining a federal government agency.

Not every case will result in a finding of liability. For example, in one case the court found that despite the employee in question taking retirement based on erroneous information as to a lump-sum option, this did not result in liability to the employer. The court found that the employee would have terminated his employment contract in any event and, accordingly, there was no detrimental reliance.[21]

In another case, a plaintiff sued an employer seeking damages for breach of contract and negligent misrepresentation where erroneous information as to a lump-sum option did not produce the expected amount. The court found that there was no breach of contract in that the information received together with the plan documentation revealed that the final amount of the employee's entitlement was subject to formal calculation and was only an estimate.[22]

The area of failure to communicate material information is also unclear in terms of providing advice to employees regarding pension options. In a recent British case, the court found that there is no obligation to indicate to an employee that he would be better off retiring one month later because of a pension offer that would be made available to him at that time.[23] On the other hand, in a 1994 British Columbia case a trial judge found that an employee and his wife relied on erroneous advice that was negligently given regarding the conversion of a group life insurance policy to a personal policy. The labour relations officer of the company advised that the life insurance could not be converted and, even if it could, it would be very costly. This was incorrect, and the employee died uninsured a few months later. The court agreed that the employer was liable in negligent misrepresentation because the employee and his wife relied on the erroneous advice and suffered damages as a result.[24]

Recently, the Ontario Court of Appeal upheld a lower trial court decision that determined that the administrator and trustees of a MEPP were liable to a plan member's widow in connection with the widow's waiver of her spousal pension.[25]

Prior to receiving his pension entitlement from the plan, the member and his wife met with a union pension counsellor to discuss payment options. With respect to the spousal pension waiver, the counsellor advised:

> If you leave a pension for your wife, this is how much you would get. **If you don't leave a pension for your wife**, this is how much you would get.[26]

Notwithstanding this statement, the court noted that nowhere on the page containing pension calculations prepared by the counsellor was there an indication that the result of the widow signing a spousal waiver would be that she received no benefits when her husband died.

The court concluded that the pension counsellor failed in her duty to inform the union member and his wife in "express terms" that, if the wife signed a spousal waiver, she would receive "zero" benefits when her husband died.

In a unanimous decision of the Ontario Court of Appeal, the court found that the pension counsellor had "specialized knowledge and skill" in her position as agent of the union that administered the pension plan. As such, she owed a duty of care pursuant to Section 23 of the Ontario *Pension Benefits Act*. The counsellor's failure to advise the widow that she would receive nothing if she signed the waiver was, in the court's opinion, misleading and a misrepresentation that deprived the widow of the opportunity to make an informed decision.

There are several important implications arising from this decision. First, the court set a very high threshold test on plan administrators, trustees and pension advisors in discharging their obligations when communicating to plan members. The court broadened the scope of the duty characterized by the court in *Spinks*, which said that the duty of a pension advisor is to advise competently, accurately and fully.

Secondly, the court was very critical of the spousal pension waiver form, which it called "highly confusing." The form is prescribed by the *Pension Benefits Act Regulations*. The decision warns advisors that they cannot completely rely on statutorily mandated forms to adequately communicate plan information to members and may serve as a wake-up call for the Ontario legislature to revise the form, which has been unchanged for a decade.

Inaccurate Calculation of Benefits and Reclaiming Overpayments

A further area where there has been litigation is that of attempting to reclaim overpayments due to errors made in calculating benefits. There is always a risk that employees may claim, quite legitimately, that they accepted an early retirement based on a calculation of anticipated benefits. An attempt by the plan sponsor to later reduce those benefits after retirement can give rise to a cause of action. While there are not many cases yet on this issue, it is one that is certainly of great concern and may be the subject of future litigation.

Corporate Communications in Pension Plan Wind-Up Cases[27]

In recent decisions of the Pension Commission of Ontario involving Stelco, Imperial Oil and McDonnell Douglas, corporate communications to plan members contained in employee bulletins, shareholder reports and videos to employees were determinative factors in finding that a reorganization of a business had taken place.[28]

AREAS OF VULNERABILITY FOR FUTURE CASES AND CONCLUSION

While no one can ever predict where future cases in the area of benefits communication may arise, the following areas are some where we have previously seen threatened litigation or litigation that is settled and where attention should be given to any communications. Specifically these areas are:

1. Failure to disclose exclusions and other terms of insurance policies
2. Offsets in disability claim situations
3. Descriptions of investment options in group RRSP and defined contribution plans[29]
4. Special benefits for retirees such as employee discounts, social club privileges, etc.
5. Employee buybacks and early retirement options
6. Government withdrawal from areas of benefit coverage.

In conclusion, there is no magic formula to ensuring that benefit communications will be perfect and not give rise to any legal claims. However, benefits communication professionals in search of some preventive medicine should consider the following points:

1. There is no substitute for clear, crisp, concise communication.
2. There is nothing more dangerous than vague, evasive or misleading communication.
3. Do not let lawyers write your communication material, but a legal review for potential liabilities does not hurt.
4. Use disclaimers wisely and communicate them effectively.
5. Get advice and buy errors and omissions insurance.

Editor's note: Excerpts from this chapter were originally published in an article by the author, "Employee Communications and Legal Liability," *Pension Planning* (1996) 3:4. The material was revised in a paper entitled "Communications to Employees: Employee Rights, Obligations of Administrators and Employees," published by Osgoode Hall Law School, October 1997.

ENDNOTES

1. Office of the Superintendent of Financial Institutions, "Guidelines for Governance of Federally Regulated Pension Plans," May 1, 1998.
2. B.A. Garner, ed., *Black's Law Dictionary,* 7th ed. (St. Paul: West Group, 1999) at p. 571.
3. *The Queen v. Cognos Inc.* (1993), 99 D.L.R. (4th) 626 (S.C.C.) at p. 643.
4. *Canada (Attorney General) v. Confederation Life Insurance Co.* (1995), 24 O.R. (3d) 717 (Gen. Div.) at p. 768; aff'd (1997), 32 O.R. (3d) 102 (C.A.).
5. *Pension Benefits Act,* R.S.O. 1990, c. P.8.
6. See J. A. Brislin, "Legal Requirements of the Communication Program" in *Trustees Handbook,* 4th ed. (Brookfield, Wisconsin: International Foundation of Employee Benefit Plans, Inc., 1990) at p. 314.
7. *Deraps v. Labourers' Pension Fund of Central and Eastern Canada(Trustees of)* (1999), 21 C.C.P.B. 304 (O.C.A.); *Galvez v. Local 804 Welfare Trust Fund,* 3 EBC 1857 (E.D.N.Y. 1982).
8. *Schmidt v. Air Products of Canada* (1994), 115 D.L.R. (4th) 631 (S.C.C.).
9. *Ibid.,* at p. 676.
10. *Collins et al. v. Pension Commission of Ontario* (1986), 31 D.L.R. (4th) 86 (Ont. Div. Ct.).
11. *Re: Tie Communications Inc.(1994),* 5:3 PCO Bulletin at p. 55 (P.C.O.).
12. *Caie v. Caterpillar of Canada Ltd.* (1998), 20 C.C.P.B. 141 (O.C.(G.D.)).
13. *Dayco (Canada) v. Canadian Auto Workers,* [1993] 2 S.C.R. 230.
14. *Supra* note 5.
15. *Supra* note 5, at p. 768.
16. *McKnight v. Southern Life Insurance Company* 6 EBC 1707 (11th Cir. 1985) at pp.1710-11.
17. *Sprague v. General Motors Corporation,* 17 EBC 2457 (E.D.Mich 1994).
18. See *Madott v. Chrysler Canada,* [1989] O.J. No. 912 (G. D.) and *Daniels v. Canadian Tire Corporation* (1991), 5 O.R. (3d) 773 at p. 777 (G. D.).
19. *Campbell v. Alberta Teachers Retirement Fund* (1993), 110 D.L.R. (4th) 400 (Alta. Q.B.).
20. *Spinks v. The Queen* (1996), 134 D.L.R. (4th) 223 (F.C.A.).
21. *Manuge v. Prudential Assurance Co. Ltd.* (1977), 81 D.L.R. (3d) 360 (N.S.S.C.).
22. *Greenley v. Xerox Canada Limited* (1997), 199 A.R. 248 (Q.B.).
23. *University of Nottingham v. Eyett and Another* (No. 1), [1999] 2 All E.R. 437 (Ch. D.).
24. *Lehune v. Kelowna (City)* (1994), 5 C.C.P.B. 111 (B.C.C.A.).

25. *Deraps v. Labourers' Pension Fund of Central and Eastern Canada, supra* note 7.

26. *Supra* note 7 at p. 308.

27. See D. McFarlane, "Employer Communications," *International Pension Lawyer* 20 (6) (1997), for an earlier discussion of this topic.

28. See *Stelco Inc. v. Superintendent of Pensions* (1993), 4:1 PCO Bulletin, p. 40, aff'd (1994), 115 D.L.R. (4th) 437 (Ont. Div. Ct.), aff'd (1995), 126 D.L.R. (4th) 767 (C.A.), leave to appeal to S.C.C. denied (1996), 131 D.L.R. (4th) vii (S.C.C.), *Imperial Oil v. Superintendent of Pensions* (1996), 6:4 PCO Bulletin, at p. 90 (P.C.O.), aff'd, (1996), 15 C.C.P.B. 31 (O.C.(G. D.)), and *Maynard v. Ontario (Superintendent of Pensions)* (1999), 19 C.C.P.B. 91 (P.C.O.); aff'd, [2000] O.J. No. 881 (S.C.J.).

29. For example, the recent settlement between Bell Canada and some of its pensioners with respect to losses in a group RRSP plan arising from the demise of Confederation Life, based in part on representations made to such employees about investment options.

CHAPTER 1

Canada Pension Plan and Quebec Pension Plan: An Overview

by Ari N. Kaplan

INTRODUCTION

The Canada Pension Plan[1] (CPP) is a mandatory coverage national social insurance program that provides financial protection to eligible contributors and their families for loss of income due to retirement, disability and death. Substantive benefits are earnings related and take the form of retirement pensions, disability and survivor benefits. A similar, but not identical, plan in Quebec, the Quebec Pension Plan (QPP),[2] provides comparable benefits for eligible persons employed in that province. Reciprocity agreements allow CPP/QPP to be harmonized with similar public pension schemes in other countries. Questions regarding eligibility, coverage, entitlement to benefits and assessment of contributions in connection with decisions of the plan administrator are procedurally addressed by a quasi-judicial administrative adjudicative regime.

History of CPP

The idea of a national public pension plan has existed for many years; however, the concept of CPP was actively pursued in the early 1960s. The objective was to establish an income-related plan that would provide retirement benefits to all working Canadians.[3] At the same time that the CPP was being developed, at least two provinces (Ontario and Quebec) were considering mandating minimum levels of pension coverage for all employees in each province. This would have required employers to sponsor a pension plan with benefits of at least defined minimums.

The CPP became law[4] on April 3, 1965, was proclaimed into force on May 5, 1965 and came into effect on January 1, 1966. Following a ten-year transitional period, CPP became fully effective in 1976.

When it was first introduced in 1966, CPP covered only retirement benefits. After consultation with the provinces, however, it was expanded in scope to provide a wider range of benefits, such as disability benefits; widows', widowers', orphans' and death benefits.

It is important to understand that the CPP was not set up to provide a total retirement income. Rather, it was viewed as the second level of a three-level retirement income system, namely, Old Age Security, CPP/QPP and, lastly, benefits arising from private pension schemes and insurance annuities, savings and other sources of ongoing income. The first two levels comprise the public portion of Canada's retirement income system, and they are intended to provide a modest base for people to build upon with additional private sources of retirement income. As discussed in Chapter 8, the Old Age Security Program was founded prior to the CPP and provides retirement pensions on a more universal scale than does the CPP.

Important Developments in CPP

The CPP legislation has been amended several times since it was enacted in 1965. Some of the more important amendments have included:

- The introduction of full annual cost-of-living indexation
- The availability of the same benefits to male and female contributors as well as to their surviving spouses or common law partners and dependent children
- The elimination of the retirement and employment earnings test for retirement pensions at age 65

- The exclusion of periods of zero or low earnings while caring for a child under the age of seven
- The division of pension credits (credit splitting) between spouses or common law partners on marriage breakdown.

In January 1987, several major new provisions came into effect. These included:
- Flexible retirement benefits payable as early as age 60
- Increased disability pension
- Continuation of survivor's benefits if the spouse remarries
- Sharing of retirement pensions between spouses or common law partners
- Expansion of credit splitting to cover the separation of married or common law partners.

In 1992, three major amendments came into effect:
- A new 25-year schedule for employer-employee contribution rates was established.
- Children's benefits were increased and provision was made for individuals who were denied disability benefits because of late application.

Significant changes were also introduced in 1998, which included:
- A move away from a pay-as-you-go system to a fuller funding regime by establishing a five-year reserve fund (previously at two years)
- Contribution rates increased from 5.85% of contributory earnings to 9.9% over six years
- A new investment policy was introduced that includes the establishment of an independent investment board (CPP Investment Board), with investment professionals, with a mandate to invest the reserve fund in accordance with prudent portfolio standards applicable to all other pension fund administrators.

Prior to April 2000, the CPP legislation defined *spouse* as including persons who are married as well as unmarried persons of the opposite sex who are in a spousal relationship. However, as a result of the Supreme Court of Canada decision in *M v. H*,[5] federal and provincial governments were required to amend all legislation that contained a definition of *spouse* that discriminated against same-sex partners. As such, Bill C-23[6] was introduced to repeal the definition of *spouse* in the CPP legislation and replace the term with *common law partner,* defined as:

> common law partner, in relation to a contributor, means a person who is cohabiting with the contributor in a conjugal relationship at the relevant time, having so cohabited with the contributor for a continuous period of at least one year. For greater certainty, in the case of a contributor's death, the "relevant time" means the time of the contributor's death.[7]

ADMINISTRATION AND STRUCTURE

The CPP is governed by the *Canada Pension Plan Act,* (the "CPP Act").[8] It is nationwide in scope; however, each province has the right to opt out of the plan and set up a comparable provincial plan covering employees in that province. Quebec is the only province to have exercised its constitutional right to opt out of participation in the scheme and set up the comparable QPP in 1966.

CPP

The CPP Act provides the text of the CPP and contains three distinct parts:
- Part I: Contributions
- Part II: Pensions and Supplementary Benefits
- Part III: Administration.

The CPP is administered jointly by Revenue Canada and Human Resources Development Canada (HRDC). The former is responsible for the "control and direction" of those aspects of the plan dealing with the coverage, assessment or collection of contributions under Part I,[9] while HRDC is responsible for administering those aspects of the plan dealing with benefit features under Parts II and III.[10] The Minister of National Revenue is required to report each year to the Minister of HRDC on information obtained under the CPP Act with respect to earnings and contributions of any persons for purposes of calculating entries in the record of earnings or for determination of the amount of any benefit payable under the CPP Act, and statistical and other general information as is necessary for the administration of the CPP, such as conducting actuarial studies relating to the operation of the act.[11]

In addition, if so directed by the Governor in Council, the Department of Public Works and Government Services, as well as the Canada Employment Insurance Commission, are required to assist HRDC in the administration of the act.[12]

QPP

The Régie des Rentes du Québec (the "Régie") is constituted by the QPP and is responsible, among other things, for the plan's administration. The Régie is administered by a board of directors composed of 12 members appointed by the Quebec government. The 12 members consist of the president of the board and 11 others. There are no restrictions on the appointment of the president. However, the QPP does specify some requirements on the appointments for the other 11 members, namely:
- Two members shall be appointed after consultation with representative bodies from business.
- Two members shall be appointed after consultation with representative bodies from labour.
- Two members shall be appointed after consultation with representative socioeconomic groups.

- One member shall be appointed after consultation with bodies working in the field of social benefits for employees.
- Two members shall be appointed from among the beneficiaries of benefits paid by the board.
- Two members shall be appointed from among the officers of the government or its bodies.

The president is appointed for a term of not more than ten years, and the other members are appointed for not more than three years.

The Régie is also responsible for the administration of Quebec's *Supplemental Pension Plans Act,* which is the act that regulates private sector pension plans. Thus, the Regie has not been established solely for the purpose of administering the QPP. Rather, it is the instrument of the government of Quebec that deals with the regulation of all of the province's pension laws. This arrangement is different from that under the CPP, where HRDC is responsible only for the plan's administration.

Federal-Provincial Cooperation

The operation of the two plans is coordinated through a series of agreements between the federal and Quebec governments. Benefits from either plan are based on pension credits accumulated under both, as if only one plan existed. People making valid contributions to the CPP and QPP are considered "dual contributors." Dual contributors, who, at the time of application, live outside Quebec receive benefits from the CPP. The reverse also occurs. Dual contributors who, when applying, live in Quebec or who lived in Quebec just before leaving Canada to live elsewhere, receive benefits from the QPP.

Reciprocal Agreements With Other Countries

The Minister of HRDC may enter into reciprocal international social security arrangements with other countries in respect of CPP coverage, contributions and benefits. To qualify, the other country must have a program similar to CPP to provide old age, survivor or disability benefits. Such reciprocal agreements are made on behalf of the government of Canada, and must be approved by the Governor in Council. The terms of these agreements relate to the administration and operation of the two programs and deal with subjects such as:

- The exchange of such information as is needed to give effect to the agreement
- The administration of benefits payable under CPP to persons resident in the other country, or benefits payable under the other country's program to persons resident in Canada.

Basically, these agreements enable periods of contributions made by an individual to the other country's social security system to be added to the periods of contribution to the CPP in order to meet the minimum qualifying conditions for a pension. Once eligibility for a benefit is established through the adding together of periods, each country pays a benefit in proportion to the actual periods of contributions made under its own social security system. To date, Canada has entered into such agreements with over 40 other countries. (See Appendix II-1-A.)

Reciprocal agreements on behalf of either CPP or QPP are negotiated separately. More detailed provisions respecting reciprocal agreements are located at Section 107 of CPP and Section 215 of QPP.

COVERAGE

As mentioned earlier, CPP is an earnings-related plan; therefore, virtually every person between the ages of 18 and 70 who earns more than a minimum level of earnings in the participating provinces is eligible to be covered by CPP. Excepted employment is discussed below. Coverage is mandatory for eligible individuals, who are called *contributors,* since there is a requirement for each individual to contribute a portion of his or her earnings to fund the benefits paid under the plan. The use of the term *contributor* reinforces the concept that both CPP and QPP are insurance arrangements.

In order for an individual to be covered under QPP, he or she must be *employed* in Quebec (rather than reside). In other words, the individual must report to work at an employer's establishment situated in Quebec in order for that employee to be covered by QPP rather than under CPP.

Contributions

Contribution amounts are earnings related, based on taxable income from employment or business. In other words, for employees, contributions are based on wages and salary; for the self-employed, contributions are based on net, after-expenses business income. No contributions to CPP/QPP are required for income from investment sources.

Since self-employed persons are both an employer and employee, such persons must contribute 9.9% of earnings to the fund, namely, the sum of what would otherwise be contributed by a contributor-employee and his employer. The combined employee-employer contribution rate has increased from 7% in 1999 to 9.9% in 2003 and is expected to remain at 9.9% thereafter.

In addition, under QPP, contributions are required for every retired person who continues to be employed. Retirement benefits for such individuals are revised when that person stops working. In the case of phased-in retirement, contributions may be made based on a full salary.

Excepted Employment

As stated, CPP/QPP covers virtually all employed and self-employed individuals in the participating provinces. However, coverage excludes certain kinds of employment, which include, but are not limited to:

- Casual employment other than for the purpose of the employer's trade or business
- Employment in agriculture, fishing, hunting, forestry, logging, lumbering, trapping or horticulture, by an employer who either pays the employee less than $250 in a year or employs the employee for fewer than 25 working days in a year
- Provincial employees, unless a province agrees to cover them and pays the required contributions
- Miscellaneous employment, such as exchange teachers from another country and members of religious orders and
- In Quebec, members of the judiciary.

Since individuals in such "excepted" groups are usually employees, they may elect to be covered under CPP/QPP as deemed self-employed persons, if they pay the required contributions.

Social Insurance Number

Each contributor is required to have a social insurance number (SIN) so that his or her entitlement under the plan may be administered. Without a SIN, persons cannot claim benefits under the plan. This requirement is enforced by the administration of the plan. There has been at least one case when an individual did not obtain a SIN but made contributions to the plan. Benefits were applied for in respect of the individual contributions; however, no benefits were allowed due to the failure of the individual to obtain a SIN.

BENEFITS

There are three types of benefits available under CPP/QPP:

- *Retirement benefits* (pensions)
- *Disability benefits* (including pensions for disabled contributors and benefits for their dependent children)
- *Survivor benefits* (which include a death benefit, a pension for a surviving spouse or common law partner and an orphan's benefit).

All CPP/QPP benefits, with the exception of the lump-sum death benefit (discussed below), are adjusted each year for cost-of-living increases in accordance with the Consumer Price Index.

Application for and Assignment of CPP/QPP Benefits

No benefit is payable under CPP unless an application is made in writing to HRDC. Conversely, while under a private pension plan an employee might expect the employer to automatically direct the pension to commence at retirement age, under CPP the onus is on the employee to apply for benefits when he or she becomes eligible to receive them. Similarly, application for benefits under QPP must be made in writing to the Régie.

Benefits generally may not be assigned, attached, seized or given as security. Any transaction or agreement purporting to do so is void. The exception to this rule under CPP is in the case where any provincial or municipal authority pays a person any advance or social assistance or welfare payment for a month that would not be paid if a benefit under CPP had been paid for that period. Where subsequently a benefit becomes payable under CPP to that person for that period, HRDC may deduct from the CPP benefits payable for that period and pay to the government of the province an amount not exceeding the amount of the advance for that period. This deduction from CPP benefits may only be made if a person had, before receiving the advance, consented in writing to such deduction and payment by HRDC. The reason for this is so that the intended beneficiaries will be the actual beneficiaries of the plan payments.

This requirement is not unique to CPP/QPP. All private pension plans coming under the jurisdiction of federal or provincial pension legislation are also required to have a similar provision regarding assignment, seizure or attachment of benefits.

Another exception to the prohibition of assigning CPP/QPP benefits is with respect to spousal pension sharing, discussed below.

Retirement Benefits

A contributor is eligible to receive a retirement pension under CPP commencing at age 65, provided that at least one valid contribution has been made on that person's behalf. An early retirement pension is available at age 60 if the contributor has "substantially ceased working." Under QPP, since contributions are required for every retired person who continues to be employed, retirement benefits for such individuals are revised when that person stops working. In the case of phased-in retirement, contributions may be made based on a full salary. Retirement benefits are adjusted annually to the Consumer Price Index and terminate upon the pensioner's death.

Early/Late Retirement Bridging

A CPP/QPP pension is reduced permanently by 6% per year (0.5% per month) for each year below 65 (to age 60) that a contributor elects to apply for a pension; conversely, the pension is increased by 6% per year (0.5% per month) for each year above 65 (to age 70) that the contributor applies for the pension.

CPP Spousal Assignment or "Pension Sharing"

Spouses in a continuing marriage and partners in a common law relationship may apply to receive an equal share of the retirement pension earned by both parties during their life together. Pension sharing redistributes a couple's pension or pensions but does not increase or decrease the overall pension(s) paid. The advantage of pension sharing is in allowing a higher-income pensioner to reduce his or her annual taxable income by transferring part of his or her CPP retirement pension to a lower-income spouse or partner.

Only one of the parties can apply. Both spouses and common law partners must be at least 60 years old and have applied for their retirement pensions. The assignment of pensions may be cancelled and reinstated at a later date. No pension sharing can occur if there has been an agreement between the parties that this cannot happen.

A pension-sharing agreement will end:
- The 12th month after separation from a legal marriage
- The month after common law partners separate
- The month that the noncontributor becomes a contributor
- The month of divorce
- The month of the death of either person in the relationship. At this time, the surviving spouse or partner receives the full amount of his or her own retirement pension.
- If both parties ask CPP to end the assignment of pensions.[13]

A similar pension-sharing scheme is also available under QPP.

CPP/QPP Credit Splitting

In the event that spouses or common law partners divorce or separate, CPP and QPP recognize that both spouses or partners may contribute to the plan during the time that they live together. Consequently, CPP and QPP allow for the equal splitting of these CPP/QPP "credits" between such separating spouses or common law partners, regardless of who contributed the most to the CPP/QPP.

CPP/QPP pension credits are split by adding together all credits of both spouses or common law partners during the time they lived together and dividing the credits equally between them. The credits are not actually paid to the individuals upon separation. Rather, credits are used to determine the amount of CPP or QPP benefits to which they may be entitled upon retirement. The Income Security Office of HRDC and the Quebec Pension Board provide assistance to persons in credit splitting situations.

Given the evolution of CPP over the years, spouses'

date of separation is important in determining access to credit splitting. For example, spousal credit splitting was not available before January 1, 1978; accordingly, if spouses separated prior to that date, the arrangement is not available. For common law partners, credit splitting was not available if they separated prior to January 1987. Same-sex former common law partners may be eligible for credit splitting if the separation occurred after July 31, 2000.

Disability Benefits

CPP pays a monthly pension to eligible contributors who are disabled, according to CPP legislation. A person is "disabled" if he or she has a disabling condition that is "severe," i.e., an inability to regularly perform any substantially gainful occupation. While a disabling condition can be either physical or mental, it must also be "prolonged." In other words, the disability must be of indefinite duration or likely to result in death.

A disabled person is eligible for a disability pension if he or she is between the ages of 18 and 65, and sufficient contributions have been made on that person's behalf. Under CPP, if a person becomes disabled after December 31, 1997, he or she must have contributed for at least four of the preceding six years and earned at least 10% of the Year's Maximum Pensionable Earnings for each year. Under QPP, contributions must have been made for at least two of the preceding three years, or at least five of the preceding ten years, or for one-half of the total number of years that contributions have been made (with a two-year minimum).

Benefits commence from the fourth consecutive month of the month of disability. The disability benefit is paid until the client recovers from the disability, receives a CPP early retirement pension, turns 65 or dies. When the contributor reaches age 65, the disability benefit converts to a retirement pension.

Since the disability pension scheme is designed as a temporary benefit, a person's level and state of disability is periodically reviewed and reassessed. In this regard, CPP assists in a return-to-work program and provides vocational rehabilitation, where appropriate.

Benefits for Children of Disabled Contributors

The dependent child of a person receiving a CPP/QPP disability pension is eligible to receive a fixed monthly children's benefit. Generally, a person is a *dependent child* if he or she is under the age of 18 and is the natural or adopted child, or is a child in the care and control, of the contributor in receipt of the disability pension. Under the CPP, a *dependent child* also includes a child if he or she is between the ages of 18 and 25 and is in full-time attendance at a recognized educational institution.

The benefit for children of disabled contributors terminates when:

- The contributor is no longer disabled.
- The child no longer meets the eligibility requirements.
- The child dies.
- The contributor's disability benefit converts to a retirement pension.

Under the CPP only, children may receive up to two benefits as children of disabled contributors if both parents are disabled. To be eligible, both parents must have made the required contributions to the CPP.

Survivor Benefits

There are three types of CPP/QPP benefits paid in the event a contributor to the plan dies:

- The *death benefit*
- The *survivor benefit*
- The *orphan's benefit*.

In order for a survivor of a contributor to be eligible for a death benefit, the deceased must have contributed to the plan for at least three years. In addition, if the deceased's contributory period is greater than nine years then, to be eligible for the death benefit, contributions must have been made for the *lesser* of one-third of all calendar years during the contributory period, or ten years.

Death Benefit

If eligible, the estate or beneficiary of a contributor is entitled to a one-time lump-sum payment equal to the *lesser* of six months of what the deceased's retirement pension would have been had the deceased been 65 years old when he or she died, and $2,500. For contributors to the QPP whose death occurs after January 1, 1998, the benefit is fixed at $2,500.

Survivor Benefit

A person who is the spouse or common law partner of a deceased contributor at the time the contributor dies may be entitled to a monthly survivor's pension (referred to in the QPP as the surviving spouse's pension), provided that the minimum contribution eligibility period is met. Under the CPP, to qualify for the survivor's benefit, the surviving spouse or common law partner must be at least 45 years of age or older, or at least 35 years of age when the contributor died, and must be disabled and have dependent children. Under the QPP, there is no minimum age requirement for eligibility for the surviving spouse's pension.

The amount of the monthly survivor pension depends on a number of variables, including:

- The period of time the deceased contributed to the plan

- The amount of contributions the deceased made to the plan
- The survivor's age at the time of the contributor's death
- Whether the survivor is or becomes disabled
- Whether the survivor has dependent children
- Whether the survivor is receiving a disability or retirement pension.

However, under the CPP, for a survivor who is a common law partner, unless that person meets the old definition of *spouse,* the common law partner does not qualify for a survivor pension unless he or she became a survivor on or after January 1, 1998.[14]

In the Supreme Court of Canada decision *Law v. Canada (Minister of Employment and Immigration)*[15] the court unanimously decided that determining the eligibility of a spouse to CPP survivor benefits solely on the basis of the spouse's age does not infringe the antidiscrimination provisions in Section 15 of the Canadian Charter of Rights and Freedoms.

Orphan Benefit

The child of a deceased contributor who met the minimum contribution eligibility requirements is entitled to monthly orphan benefits under CPP/QPP. The benefit is referred to as the *benefit for children of a deceased contributor* under the CPP. The orphan's benefit under the CPP/QPP is a flat rate monthly amount that is identical to the benefit for children of disabled contributors, described above. Under CPP only, a child may receive double benefits if both parents are deceased, or if one parent is deceased and the other is disabled.

Like the benefit for the child of a disabled contributor, the orphan's benefit is paid until the child reaches the age of 18 or, alternatively, for purposes of CPP only, if the person is between the ages of 18 and 25, so long as he or she is in full-time attendance at a recognized educational institution.

APPEALS

As may be expected, neither the CPP text nor the underlying legislation and regulations is detailed enough to eliminate questions of interpretation respecting eligibility, contributions, coverage and benefits. Therefore, administrative appeal procedures have been set up to allow employers, employees and other contributors and individuals to question rulings made by either of the departments in the course of performing their administrative duties. There are several levels of appeal:

- Reconsideration
- CPP Review Tribunal
- Pension Appeals Board.

Reconsideration

Initial recourse from a decision of the administrator is to request a reconsideration from the Minister of HRDC within 90 days of receiving the decision. The request must be in writing, and all supporting documentation and necessary information to substantiate the grounds for reconsideration must be submitted at that time. An officer who was not the decision maker at first instance then reviews the claim and provides its decision.

CPP Review Tribunal

Any person who is dissatisfied with the decision on reconsideration may appeal the decision in writing within 90 days to the Commission of the Canada Pension Plan Review Tribunal (the "Review Tribunal"). The Review Tribunal is an independently appointed administrative adjudication tribunal, composed of three members selected by the Commission. The chairperson is always a member of the legal profession.

An appeal to the Review Tribunal proceeds by way of an oral hearing de novo on the merits of the subject matter of the appeal. Parties to the hearing include the appellant, the Minister of HRDC and, in certain types of appeals, any other person that in the Minister's opinion is directly affected by the decision.

A decision of the Review Tribunal is based on the majority opinion of the members, and the Tribunal may either confirm or vary the original decision of the Minister. The Review Tribunal is required to provide written reasons for its decision.

Pension Appeals Board

A party dissatisfied with the decision of the Review Tribunal (including the Minister, the appellant, the appellant's spouse, former spouse, beneficiary, beneficiary's spouse or estate) may, within 90 days of the Tribunal's decision, apply in writing to the independent Pension Appeals Board (PAB) for leave to appeal. It is important to note that, while an appeal to the Review Tribunal is an automatic one by right, an appeal to the PAB can only proceed once the PAB grants the applicant *leave* to appeal the Tribunal's decision.

The PAB is appointed by the Governor in Council and is composed of the following members:

- A chair and vice chair, each of whom is a judge of the Federal Court of Canada or of a superior court of a province and
- At least one, but not more than ten, other judges of the Federal Court of Canada or a superior, district or county court of a province.

Leave to appeal is considered by the chair or vice chair, or his or her designate. If leave is refused, then reasons in writing must be provided to the parties. If leave is granted, the application for leave to appeal becomes a notice of appeal and a panel of the PAB is composed of either one, three or five members to hear the appeal, again as a hearing de novo. Either the chair or vice chair must be present at a hearing where a decision on an appeal is made. Where the panel consists of more than one person, decisions are made on the basis of the opinion of the majority of the members present at the hearing.

Like the Review Tribunal, the PAB may reverse, affirm or vary the determination made by the Minister, and reasons for decision to that effect must be delivered in writing. The decision of the PAB is final and binding for all purposes of the *CPP Act*.

Finality of the Pension Appeals Board

Since a decision of the PAB is final, the only recourse from such decision is by way of judicial review. Judicial review of a decision of the PAB proceeds directly to the Federal Court of Appeal.

Appeals Under QPP

The appeal process under QPP is similar to that under CPP. Appeals on contributions are made first to the Minister of Revenue and then to the Review Tribunal. Appeals on benefits are made first to the Régie des Rentes du Québec and then to the Commission des affaires sociales. The time requirements are exactly the same under QPP as under CPP.

PUBLIC ACCOUNTABILITY OF CPP

Given that CPP is a public pension scheme, the principle of public accountability is manifest. Accordingly, mechanisms have always been in place to consistently review the CPP and its continued economic and social viability. In 1967, a committee known as the Canada Pension Plan Advisory Committee (the "Advisory Committee") was established as a statutory body appointed to represent employees, employers, self-employed persons and the public. The duties of the Advisory Committee were to review the operation of the CPP, its adequacy of coverage and benefits payable under the plan, and the state of the Canada Pension Plan Investment Fund (the "Investment Fund"). The Advisory Committee published annual reports for the Minister of HRDC.

The Advisory Committee was repealed in 1997. However, other review procedures, both previously existing as well as new bodies created to replace the Advisory Committee, continue to provide accountability to the public.

Canada Pension Plan Investment Board

In 1998, the Canada Pension Plan Investment Board (the "Investment Board") was established to create investment policy for the CPP. The Investment Board operates at arm's length from both the federal and provincial governments and hires qualified professionals to invest CPP assets in financial markets. The Investment Board is required to publish its reports regularly.

Actuarial Review

Like private pension plans, the CPP undergoes triennial actuarial review. Actuarial examinations are published by the Chief Actuary of the Office of the Superintendent of Financial Institutions and are based on the state of the CPP account and the investments of the Investment Board. The Chief Actuary's report is tendered to the Minister of Finance who, in turn, tables it in Parliament.

Financial Review

The Minister of HRDC is required to prepare annual financial statements of the CPP in respect of that year, setting out consolidated statements of accounts and the financial positions of the CPP account, the CPP Investment Fund and the CPP Investment Board. The Minister of HRDC then delivers the annual financial statements to the Auditor General of Canada for his own audit of the report.

Ministerial Review

The Ministers of Finance and HRDC are required to annually review the administration of the CPP and the CPP Act, including a review of the annual financial statements and to report on the number of contributors and persons to whom benefits were paid.

Other Review Procedures

Lastly, commencing in the year 2000, the Minister of Finance, together with the ministers of the respective provinces who participate in CPP, are required every three years to review the financial state of the CPP and make recommendations as to whether benefits and/or contribution rates should be changed.

FUTURE OF THE CPP

In 1998, CPP moved from pay-as-you-go financing to more fuller funding. This reflects the policy desire to more closely conform to funding obligations required by plan sponsors in the private sector pension regulatory regimes. Due to the demographic situation in Canada created by baby boomers, the number of retirees and other beneficiaries is expected to increase in the coming years disproportionately to the number of active contributors. Simply increasing contributions to meet rising costs may not be acceptable, and other alternatives will need to be considered, such as deferring

the normal retirement age from 65 to 66 or 67, as other countries have done.

ENDNOTES

1. R.S.C.1985, c.C-8, as amended.
2. QPP is governed by *An Act Respecting the Quebec Pension Plan,* R.S.Q. 1977, C.R. 9, as amended.
3. Objectives of the Canada Pension Plan were not stated in the *Canada Pension Plan Act* enacted in 1965, nor was a specific list of objectives presented during the preliminary discussions prior to the passage of the act. However, initial objectives can be deduced from the white paper tabled in the House of Commons by the Honourable Judy LaMarsh at the time she introduced a resolution respecting an act to establish the *Canada Pension Plan* (Bill C-75 in July 1963). As a result of subsequent discussions with the provincial governments, a revised bill (C-136) was introduced in March 1964, also accompanied by a white paper. While the variations from the objectives stated in 1963 were not numerous, they were significant and reflected changes necessitated by the decision of the Province of Quebec to establish its own pension plan. The objectives that are identified below are taken from the March 1964 white paper as reported in Hansard, March 17, 1964, on pages 1197-8 and 1200-1.E.

   - In conjunction with Old Age Security (OAS) and private pension plans, to assure a fair and practical way for Canadians to retire in security and dignity
   - To provide a program of coverage for Canadian income earners
   - To make reasonable minimum levels of income available at retirement and at the same time to allow scope for the continuation and extension of private pension plans and personal savings over these minimum levels
   - To provide such retirement income at normal retirement ages
   - To achieve realistic minimum levels of pension income by relating benefits and contributions to earnings
   - To be entirely self-financing
   - Initially to provide a fund for use by the provinces
   - To provide parallelism with the Quebec Pension Plan
   - To provide survivor and disability benefits.

4. S.C.1964-1965, c.51.
5. *M. v. H.* (1999), 171 D.L.R. (4th) 577 (S.C.C.).
6. Bill C-23, *An Act to Modernize the Statutes of Canada in Relation to Benefits and Obligations,* 2d Sess. 36th Parl., 1999-2000.
7. *Ibid.,* Section 42.
8. *Supra* note 1.
9. *Ibid.,* Subsection 92(2).
10. *Ibid.,* Subsection 92(1).
11. *Ibid.,* Subsection 92(2).
12. *Ibid.,* Sections 93 and 94.
13. *Ibid.,* Section 65.1.
14. *Ibid.,* Section 44.
15. *Law v. Canada (Minister of Employment and Immigration),* [1991] 1 S.C.R. 497 (S.C.C.).

APPENDIX II-1-A

COUNTRIES WITH WHICH CANADA HAS RECIPROCAL AGREEMENTS

Country	Effective Date
Antigua and Barbuda	January 1, 1994
Australia	January 1, 2003
Austria	November 1, 1987
Barbados	January 1, 1986
Belgium	January 1, 1987
Chile	June 1, 1998
Croatia	May 1, 1999
Cyprus	May 1, 1991
Czech Republic	January 1, 2003
Denmark	January 1, 1986
Dominica	January 1, 1989
Finland	February 1, 1988
France	March 1, 1981
Germany	April 1, 1988
Greece	December 1, 1997
Grenada	February 1, 1999
Iceland	October 1, 1989
Ireland	January 1, 1992
Italy	January 1, 1979
Jamaica	January 1, 1984
Jersey, Guernsey	January 1, 1994
Korea	May 1, 1999
Luxembourg	April 1, 1990
Malta	March 1, 1992
Mexico	May 1, 1996
Netherlands	October 1, 1990
New Zealand	May 1, 1997
Norway	January 1, 1987
Philippines	March 1, 1997
Portugal	May 1, 1981
St. Kitts and Nevis	January 1, 1994
Saint Lucia	January 1, 1988
Saint Vincent and the Grenadines	November 1, 1998
Slovakia	January 1, 2003
Slovenia	January 1, 2001
Spain	January 1, 1988
Sweden	January 1, 1986
Switzerland	October 1, 1995
Trinidad and Tobago	July 1, 1999
United Kingdom of Great Britain and Northern Ireland	April 1, 1998
United States	August 1, 1984
Uruguay	January 1, 2002

CHAPTER 2

Canada Pension Plan and Quebec Pension Plan Benefits

by Leslie Steeves, Karen DeBortoli and Peter Miodonski

OVERVIEW

The Canada Pension Plan (CPP) and the Quebec Pension Plan (QPP) are designed to provide some income replacement for contributors and their families as a result of retirement, disability or death.

The CPP/QPP is a contributory, earnings-related program, covering virtually all employed and self-employed workers in Canada who earn more than a prescribed minimum amount each calendar year. The operation of the CPP and QPP is coordinated through agreements between the federal and Quebec governments. Benefits from either plan are based on pension credits accumulated under both plans, as if only one plan existed.

The following benefits are provided under both the CPP and the QPP, while some benefit rates and eligibility requirements may differ between programs:
- Retirement benefits
- Disability benefits
- Benefits payable to dependent children of disabled contributors
- Orphans' benefits
- Surviving spouse benefits
- Lump-sum death benefits.

In 1998, the CPP and QPP were amended to ensure the sustainability of the plans by moving from a pay-as-you-go system to fuller funding. Contribution rates have risen in steps to the current level of 9.9% of payroll for 2003 and subsequent years. This increase, in combination with a reduction in certain benefits and a prudent investment strategy, will result in a fuller funding system with a reserve fund from which to pay benefits.

Table II-2-I shows the maximum monthly benefits that contributors and their families are entitled to in 2003. The benefits are fully indexed to the Consumer Price Index.

CONTRIBUTIONS AND GENERAL INFLATION PROTECTION

Benefits under the CPP/QPP are funded by compulsory employer and employee contributions and the contributions of self-employed individuals. The contributory period for a contributor for the purpose of retirement benefits is defined to be the years from January 1, 1966, or attainment of age 18 if later, to the earlier of (a) the month before the month that the retirement pension starts; (b) the month before the month of the contributor's 70th birthday; or (c) the month of the contributor's death, less any years during which a disability pension is payable under the CPP.

The CPP is what is known as a *unit* or *defined benefit* plan. For each year that an individual contributes to the plan, he or she accrues more credits toward a benefit. Generally speaking, the amount of benefit is dependent upon the number of years an individual makes contributions and the level of those contributions.

For example, if two individuals retired on the same day and the first individual had earned the Year's Maximum Pensionable Earnings (YMPE) each year, while the second had earned half that amount, then the first individual could expect to receive more retirement benefit from the CPP than the second individual.

The reader will notice that it was not stated how much more the first individual would receive in the above example. As will be seen, not all benefit accruals are directly prorated as a ratio of the number of years

Table II-2-I

MAXIMUM MONTHLY BENEFITS PAYABLE UNDER THE CPP AND QPP, 2003

	Maximum CPP Benefits	Maximum QPP Benefits
Retirement Pension (for contributors retiring at age 65)	$ 801.25	$ 801.25
Disability Pension	971.26	971.23
Orphans and Children of Disabled Parents	186.71	59.28
Surviving Spouse Age 65 and Over	480.75	480.75
Surviving Spouse Age 55 to 64	444.96	700.06
Surviving Spouse Age 45 to 54	444.96	670.76
Death Benefits (lump-sum)	2,500.00	2,500.00

actually worked to the number of years possible, or as a ratio of actual earnings to the YMPE. However, it is important to keep in mind that to varying degrees, these ratios affect the amount of benefit payable.

The CPP is also what is known as a *career average* plan, with inflation protection related to changes in the YMPE. That means that the amount of benefit payable is dependent upon the average level of the YMPE (and other things) at the time of retirement. Thus, during the accrual period, one does not accrue a specific amount of benefit each year, but rather a certain amount of credit. When a benefit becomes payable, the credits are added up to see how much of the current maximum benefit will be paid. Thus, no one will know the exact amount of a benefit until it actually becomes payable.

The reason for using the *career average* approach is that it provides inflation protection for benefit accruals during the period of accrual.

The *basic amount* of any benefit is defined as the amount that is calculated to be payable at the time the benefit becomes payable. It should be noted that adjustments to benefits except the death benefit in course of payment are made annually on a calendar year basis. Every January after a benefit commences there is an adjustment made to the monthly amount paid. These adjustments are made in accordance with the Pension Index, which is tied to the Consumer Price Index. The Pension Index is not allowed to decrease; therefore, there will not be any negative adjustments to benefits paid under the CPP.

The use of the Pension Index to make adjustments to benefits in course of payment provides additional inflation protection after the benefit becomes payable (that is, during the payout stage). Thus, the CPP provides inflation protection during both the accrual and payout stages.

CPP RETIREMENT PENSION

The retirement pension is the basic benefit of the CPP.

To be eligible for a CPP retirement pension, a contributor must:

- Have made at least one valid contribution to the CPP;
- Be between the ages of 60 and 65 and have wholly or substantially stopped pensionable employment or have annual employment earnings below the monthly maximum retirement pension payable at age 65 for the year in which the pension is claimed ($801.25 in 2003) and
- Must be age 65 or over, whether or not the contributor has stopped working.

The retirement pension is payable the month after the applicant's 65th birthday and is equal to 25% of the contributor's average monthly pensionable earnings during the individual's contributory period. At age 65 or over, the applicant does not have to cease employment in order to receive the benefit; however, once the pension payment begins, no further contributions can be made to the plan.

Changes to the CPP retirement benefit, effective January 1, 1987, allow for payment to begin as early as age 60 and as late as age 70. Between ages 60 and 64, the basic pension is decreased by 0.5% for each month between the month the pension begins and the month after the applicant's 65th birthday. Applicants must wholly or substantially cease employment or self-employment; i.e., their annual earnings will be less than the current maximum annual CPP retirement pension payable at age 65. In 2003 this was $9,615. Once the pension payment begins, while the contributor can continue to work, no further contributions can be made to the plan. The pension amount will not be readjusted at age 65.

Between ages 65 and 70 the basic pension is increased by 0.5% for each month between the date the pension begins and the month after the applicant's 65th birthday. Applicants between ages 65 and 70 do not have to cease employment.

After age 70 the basic pension is increased by 30% (up to the contributor's 70th birthday). Applicants over age 70 do not have to cease employment. Contributions to the plan cease at age 70 regardless of whether or not an application for the retirement benefit has been made. Retroactive payments can only be made for a maximum of 12 months, including the month in which the application is received.

The decision of when to begin receiving the CPP retirement benefit will be determined by the contributor based on his or her individual circumstances. The choice may depend on the length of time and the level of contributions made to the plan, whether or not employment has at least substantially ceased, the amount of income from other sources and the individual's retirement plans.

If an applicant should die after an application has been made but not yet approved, the pension can be paid from the later of the month of application or the month specified on the application, to the month the death occurred. If the contributor was at least age 70 at the time of death and had not yet applied for the pension, the retroactive payments can be made for a maximum of 12 months from the month after the 70th birthday up to the month the death occurred.

The retirement benefit is paid as a life annuity with no guaranteed period. That is, payments cease on the death of a contributor regardless of how soon or long after the date of commencement of payments the death occurs. There are survivorship benefits for the spouse or common law partner and children of a deceased contributor.

The basic amount of the annual retirement benefit is 25% of $\frac{1}{12}$ of the average of the YMPE for the last five years.

In order to prevent low- or zero-income periods from affecting the pension amount, up to 15% of an individual's contributory period is excluded from the calculation of average monthly pensionable earnings. This adjustment compensates for periods of unemployment, illness, schooling, etc. In addition, months of low or no earnings in which the contributor was caring for children under 7 are excluded.

For example, suppose an individual worked each year since the inception of the CPP and retired in January 1999 at the age of 65. He or she would be able to drop out three years from the 20 years in his or her contributory period.

The average of the annual earnings ratio for the years in the adjusted contributory period is now calculated. This will be called the *average earnings ratio*.

QPP RETIREMENT BENEFIT

The contributory period for retirement benefits under the QPP is basically the same as under the CPP with a slight difference involving the years when the contributor was disabled. This difference has to do with receipt of benefits payable by the Commission de la santé et de la securite du travail.

Application for the retirement benefit may be made up to 12 months prior to the benefit becoming payable. The earliest age at which a retirement benefit may become payable is age 60. In order for a contributor between the ages of 60 and 64 to receive a retirement benefit, he or she must have ceased working.

As with the CPP, ending employment is not a requirement for collection of retirement benefits at age 65 or older.

Similarly, the basic amount of retirement benefit is 25% of the average of the YMPE for the year that the benefit becomes payable and the four previous years, times the average earnings ratio for the years during the contributory period.

Under the QPP, there is also a reduction in the amount of retirement benefit if it becomes payable prior to age 65. The reduction is .5% for each month the contributor is younger than 65, to a maximum of 30%.

Similarly, there is an increase in benefits for retirement that is delayed past age 65. The benefit is increased by .5% for each month that the contributor is older than 65, to a maximum of 30%.

CPP DISABILITY BENEFIT

The CPP provides for the payment of disability pensions to eligible CPP contributors and for the payment of benefits to their dependent children.

The definition of *disability* under the CPP is quite stringent. The disability must be a physical or mental impairment that is both severe and prolonged. *Severe* means that the contributor is not able to regularly pursue any substantially gainful employment. *Prolonged* means that such disability is likely to be of indefinite duration or is likely to result in death. Medical adjudicators from Human Resources Development Canada (HRDC) determine eligibility for CPP disability benefits. They also review cases to ensure that claimants continue to satisfy the definition of *disability*.

The determination of whether a contributor is disabled has probably generated more appeals than any other question. Applicants who are not satisfied with the adjudicator's decision have three stages of appeal. First, they can request reconsideration by the Minister of HRDC. Second, appeal is possible to a three-member Review Tribunal. Finally, an appeal can be made to the Pension Appeal Board.

As mentioned above, the definition of *disability* is far more stringent than under private long-term disability insurance plans. Comparison with private plans is probably inaccurate since they are designed to provide protection against loss of income from an individual's specific job. That is, if an individual is not capable of performing his or her job, then the employer may not have another job for that individual. Therefore, private plans usually have a disability definition that covers inability to perform an individual's own occupation, at least for the first two to five years.

Because the CPP is not tied to a specific employer, the concern regarding income replacement protection is with being able to have an income regardless of the occupation.

In order to be eligible to receive a disability benefit, a contributor must have made sufficient CPP contributions, be disabled according to CPP legislation, be under age 65 and not receiving a CPP retirement pension, and apply in writing for the benefit. Individuals who become disabled after December 31, 1997 must have contributed to the CPP in four of the last six years and earned at least 10% of each year's YMPE during that period. In 2003, the YMPE is $39,900. There are provisions that may help late applicants qualify for the benefit.

The reason for requiring a portion of the contributory period is that the disability benefit is an income replacement benefit. If no contributions have been made recently, then it is questionable whether there is any income to replace.

The basic amount of the disability benefit is the flat rate benefit ($370.32 per month in 2003) plus 75% of the contributor's retirement pension calculated as if the contributor turned 65 in the month the disability benefit started. The maximum monthly disability benefit for 2003 is $971.26. The disability benefit may not commence until the fourth month after the month of disablement unless the contributor had received a disability benefit within the last five years. In that case, the benefit becomes payable following disability onset.

Disability benefits cease on the earliest of:

- The month the contributor recovers from the disability
- Attainment of age 65 (when the retirement pension automatically begins)
- The receipt of a CPP early retirement pension
- The death of the contributor.

RETIREMENT AND DISABILITY PENSIONS

A contributor cannot receive a disability pension and a retirement pension at the same time. If the contributor is between the ages of 60 and 65, either pension could be payable. If at age 65 the contributor is in receipt of a disability pension, the pension will automatically be converted to a retirement pension without application.

QPP DISABILITY BENEFIT

Eligibility for the disability benefit is somewhat more liberal under the QPP than under the CPP. For contributors under 60 years of age, the definition of *disability* is the same. However, for contributors ages 60 to 65, the definition of *disability* has been relaxed from any occupation to the contributor's own occupation at the time he or she ceased working because of the disability.

To qualify for a disability benefit, contributions are required in at least two of the last three years, or in at least five of the last ten years, or in at least half of the total years in the contributor's contributory period, with a minimum of two years.

Since a contributor under the QPP between the ages of 60 and 64 may be eligible for either a disability benefit or a retirement benefit, a provision has been added that a contributor may not be in receipt of both benefits at the same time.

The disability benefit ceases to be payable on (1) death, (2) recovery from the disability or (3) age 65 or any earlier age when a retirement pension becomes payable.

The disability benefit formula is similar under the two plans, namely, a flat rate benefit plus 75% of the retirement pension available to the disabled contributor. The flat rate benefit under the QPP is generally the same as under the CPP. For 2003, the monthly flat rate QPP disability component is $370.29 to a maximum monthly disability pension of $971.23.

CPP BENEFITS FOR CHILDREN OF DISABLED CONTRIBUTORS

CPP may provide benefits to dependent children of a contributor receiving disability benefits. The definition of a *dependent child* is any unmarried child of the contributor who is:

- Less than 18 years of age
- 18 or more years of age but less than 25 years of age and is in full-time attendance at an educational institution.

Upon application, payments begin in the same month that a disability benefit becomes payable to the contributor, or the month after the month the child was born or adopted. Payments will stop if:

- The contributor is no longer eligible for a disability benefit
- The contributor's disability benefit is converted to a retirement pension
- The child no longer meets the eligibility criteria
- The child dies.

In 2003, the monthly benefit for children of disabled contributors is $186.71.

CPP BENEFITS FOR CHILDREN OF DECEASED CONTRIBUTORS

A CPP benefit may also be paid to the child of a deceased contributor if:

- An application is made in writing
- Contributions have been made by the contributor for the minimum qualifying period and
- The child is under 18, or between 18 and 25 and in full-time attendance at a recognized educational institution.

A child may receive up to two benefits if both parents were CPP contributors and are either deceased or disabled. Payments begin the month after the month when the contributor died and stop when the child no longer meets the criteria or dies. In 2003, the monthly benefit is $186.71.

QPP DEPENDENT CHILDREN'S BENEFIT

The monthly benefit for the children of disabled contributors under the QPP is $59.28 for 2003. The monthly QPP orphan's benefit is also $59.28 for 2003.

The definition of a *dependent child* is slightly different under the QPP and does not include a child over 18 who is a full-time student, as is the case under the CPP.

CPP SURVIVOR'S BENEFIT

A spouse, common law partner or, for contributors who die on or after January 1, 1998, the same-sex partner of a deceased contributor, may be eligible for a survivor's benefit if the deceased contributed to the CPP during at least one-third of the number of calendar years in his/her contributory period. If the contributory period was less than nine years, at least three years of contributions are required. If the contributor dies before reaching age 65, his/her contributory period ends in the month of death.

It should also be pointed out that the term *surviving spouse* (now referred to as a *survivor*) includes widows and widowers. Prior to 1975 this benefit was a surviving widow's benefit. The effect of this change was made retroactive, but no payments would be made for periods prior to 1975. Thus, a widower whose wife died in 1973 could claim a benefit in 1975 or later, but no benefits would be allowed for the periods prior to 1975.

In order to be eligible for a survivor benefit, the surviving spouse/partner must:

- Be 45 or older; or
- If under age 45, must be at least 35 at the time of the contributor's death, have been a surviving spouse or partner with dependent children, or disabled.

Please note that, if the deceased contributed to both CPP and QPP and the surviving spouse/partner lives in Quebec, survivor benefits are payable even if the spouse/partner is under age 35.

It does not matter that the contributor may not have been eligible to receive a retirement pension. What does matter is the benefit the retirement formula produces. For example, if a deceased contributor had pensionable earnings greater than the YMPE every year since turning 18 years of age, then the retirement formula applied to those years prior to death would yield the maximum benefit. The flat rate amount is adjusted each year to reflect changes in the Consumer Price Index.

The actual benefit depends upon the age of the survivor. If the survivor is under age 65, then the basic benefit formula is a flat amount ($144.49 per month in 2003), plus 37.5% of the actual or calculated retirement pension of the deceased contributor.

For survivors under age 65, there are further complications. If the survivor is under 35 years of age, is not disabled, has no dependent children, there is no benefit payable.

If the survivor is between ages 35 and 45 and is not disabled and has no dependent children, then the basic benefit amount is reduced by 1/120 for each month that the survivor is younger than 45. The maximum monthly survivor's benefit payable to a surviving spouse/partner under age 65 is $444.96 in 2003.

If the survivor is age 65 or older, then the basic benefit is 60% of the retirement the deceased contributor could have received at age 65. If the contributor died before reaching age 65, the retirement pension is calculated as if he/she turned 65 in the month of death. The maximum monthly survivor's benefit payable to surviving spouses/partners age 65 and over is $480.75 in 2003. If the survivor is eligible to receive both a survivor pension and a retirement pension, the entitlement is to receive the larger of the two benefits plus 60% of the smaller benefit to a prescribed maximum.

There are similar integration rules for disabled survivors receiving disability pensions. In 2003, the maximum monthly rate for the combined survivor/retirement benefit is $801.25 and $971.26 for the survivor/disability benefit.

As of January 1, 1987, CPP survivor's benefits do not terminate on remarriage.

CREDIT SPLITTING

The CPP allows for the division of unadjusted pensionable earnings. Provisions governing the circumstances under which such a division can take place became effective January 1, 1987. The provisions:

- Extend the coverage to the separation of legal spouses.
- Extend the coverage to the breakdown of common law relationships.
- More clearly specify the implications of spousal agreements.
- Alter the requirements for application.

As a result of Bill C-23, credit splitting is also available to same-sex partners who meet the definition of *common law partner.*

QPP SURVIVING SPOUSE'S BENEFIT

The contributor's qualifying period for the surviving spouse's benefit is the same under the QPP as under the CPP. The benefit formula is also the same, namely, a flat rate benefit plus 37.5% of the deceased contributor's available retirement benefit. However, despite this similarity, the benefit rates differ between CPP and QPP. In 2003, the monthly benefit for spouses between the ages of 45 and 54 is $670.76. The monthly benefit is $700.06 for spouses ages 55 to 64 and $480.75 for spouses aged 65 and over.

When a retirement pension becomes payable to a surviving spouse, there is a maximum on total benefits received under the QPP as there is under the CPP. However, the formula is different in that the QPP has different rules depending on the age of the surviving spouse, when he or she becomes eligible for the retirement benefit, and when he or she became eligible for the surviving spouse's benefit.

Specifically, if an individual becomes eligible for both benefits (retirement and surviving spouse's) before reaching age 65, that is, between ages 60 and 65, then the new amount of the surviving spouse's benefit is the sum of a and b where:
a. Is the flat amount portion of the surviving spouse's benefit ($399.59 in 2003); and
b. Is the minimum of 37.5% of the deceased contributor's retirement pension available and the difference between the maximum retirement pension benefit and the surviving spouse's benefit.

If an individual becomes eligible for both benefits after reaching age 65, then the new amount of the surviving spouse's benefit is the lesser of a and b where:
a. Is the maximum of 60% of the deceased contributor's retirement pension less 40% of the surviving spouse's retirement; and 37.5% of the deceased contributor's retirement pension and
b. Is the difference between the maximum retirement pension benefit and the surviving spouse's retirement pension.

For an individual who became eligible for both benefits prior to reaching age 65, the surviving spouse's pension benefit amount is recalculated upon reaching age 65. The formula used is the one above, as though the individual had just become eligible for both benefits.

As with the CPP, there are also rules under the QPP for integrating disability benefits and surviving spouse's benefits when both are payable to an individual. Basically, under the QPP, the combined amount of the two benefits may not be less than the amount of the surviving spouse's benefit payable had there been no disability. The combined amount also may not be greater than the maximum retirement benefit.

As of January 1, 1984, QPP surviving spouse's benefits do not terminate on remarriage.

The QPP has a slightly different (more restrictive) definition of *surviving spouse* in a common law situation. The QPP requires that neither party was married and that a child was or is to be born of the union before lowering its three-year cohabitation requirement to one year. However, the QPP was amended effective June 16, 1999 to extend surviving spousal benefits to same-sex partners.

CPP/QPP LUMP-SUM DEATH BENEFIT

There is also a lump-sum death benefit payable under the CPP/QPP if contributions were made for the minimum qualifying period. This benefit is equal to six times the monthly retirement pension of the deceased contributor to a maximum of $2,500 in 2003.

The death benefit is payable to the estate of the contributor. Where there is no will or estate, the death benefit will be paid to the person responsible for funeral expenses.

Table II-2-II[1] shows the maximum monthly retirement pension, monthly flat rate component and maximum death benefit for the CPP in the years 1966 to 2003.

Table II-2-III[2] shows the maximum monthly retirement pensions, monthly flat rate component and maximum death benefit for the QPP in the years 1966 to 2003.

TAXATION AND CPP/QPP BENEFITS

All benefit payments are included in income for income tax purposes. This treatment is similar to treatment of benefit payments from private registered pension plans. Retirement benefits are eligible for the pension income deduction, however.

The rationale for this is that all premium payments into the plan are deductible for income tax purposes. Therefore, in order for the monies to be eventually taxed, the benefits must be taxable.

ENDNOTES

1. *CCH Canadian Employment and Pension Guide,* (Toronto: CCH Canadian Limited, 1997), p. 839.
2. *Ibid.*

Table II-2-II

MAXIMUM MONTHLY RETIREMENT PENSION, DISABILITY MONTHLY FLAT RATE COMPONENT AND MAXIMUM DEATH BENEFIT UNDER THE CPP

Year	Maximum Monthly Retirement Pension	Disability Monthly Flat Rate Component	Maximum Death Benefit
1966	—	$ 25.00	—
1967	$104.17	25.00	—
1968	104.86	25.50	$ 510
1969	106.25	26.01	520
1970	108.33	26.53	530
1971	110.42	27.06	540
1972	112.50	27.60	550
1973	114.58	28.15	560
1974	122.92	33.76	660
1975	136.11	37.27	740
1976	154.86	41.44	830
1977	173.61	44.84	930
1978	194.44	48.19	1,040
1979	218.06	52.51	1,170
1980	244.44	57.25	1,310
1981	274.31	62.91	1,470
1982	307.65	70.68	1,650
1983	345.15	78.60	1,850
1984	387.50	83.87	2,080
1985	435.42	87.56	2,340
1986	486.11	91.06	2,580
1987	521.52	94.79	2,590
1988	543.06	98.96	2,650
1989	556.25	264.04	2,770
1990	577.08	276.71	2,090
1991	604.86	289.99	3,050
1992	636.11	306.81	3,220
1993	667.36	312.33	3,340
1994	694.44	318.26	3,440
1995	713.19	319.85	3,490
1996	727.08	325.61	3,540
1997	736.81	330.49	3,580
1998	744.79	336.77	2,500
1999	751.67	339.80	2,500
2000	762.92	345.24	2,500
2001	775.00	353.87	2,500
2002	788.75	364.49	2,500
2003	801.25	370.32	2,500

Table II-2-III

MAXIMUM MONTHLY RETIREMENT PENSION, DISABILITY MONTHLY FLAT RATE COMPONENT AND MAXIMUM DEATH BENEFIT UNDER THE QPP

Year	Maximum Monthly Retirement Pension	Disability Monthly Flat Rate Component	Maximum Death Benefit
1966	—	$ 25.00	—
1967	$104.17	25.00	—
1968	104.86	25.50	$ 510
1969	106.25	26.01	520
1970	108.33	26.53	530
1971	110.42	27.06	540
1972	112.50	27.60	550
1973	114.58	80.00	560
1974	122.92	86.56	660
1975	136.11	95.56	740
1976	154.86	106.26	830
1977	173.61	114.97	930
1978	194.44	123.59	1,040
1979	218.06	134.64	1,170
1980	244.44	146.78	1,310
1981	274.31	161.31	1,470
1982	307.65	181.18	1,650
1983	345.15	201.44	1,850
1984	387.50	214.94	2,080
1985	435.42	224.40	2,340
1986	486.11	233.38	2,580
1987	521.52	242.95	2,590
1988	543.06	253.64	2,650
1989	556.25	264.04	2,770
1990	577.08	276.71	2,090
1991	604.86	289.99	3,050
1992	636.11	306.81	3,220
1993	667.36	312.33	3,340
1994	694.44	318.26	3,440
1995	713.19	318.26	3,490
1996	727.08	325.58	3,540
1997	736.81	330.46	3,580
1998	750.69	336.74	2,500
1999	751.67	339.77	2,500
2000	775.00	345.21	2,500
2001	762.92	353.84	2,500
2002	788.75	364.46	2,500
2003	801.25	370.29	2,500

CHAPTER 3

Workers' Compensation

by Craig Flood and Mary DaRosa

OVERVIEW

The establishment of workers' compensation schemes can be traced to the dual influences of appalling rates of industrial accidents in the late 19th and early 20th centuries and the inability of large numbers of workers to be compensated for their injuries under traditional common law principles.

By the end of the 19th century, it was clearly established that, although the common law recognized an employer could be held liable to an employee for injury suffered by an employee during the course of employment, the possibility of the employee establishing liability or recovering damages was remote.

The first workers' compensation board in Canada was established in Ontario in 1914, with similar agencies subsequently created in every province and territory in this country. The principles of the regime were clearly stated in *Re Workers' Compensation Act, 1983 (Nfld.)*:

Workers' compensation law is founded upon five principles. These are that there should be:

(1) compensation without fault;
(2) security of payment;
(3) collective liability on the part of employers;
(4) an administrative body to collect assessments and disburse benefits;
(5) an adjudicative body to assess quantum.[1]

In part, the Canadian schemes are pure no-fault, because the legislation replaces the right of legal action against the employer or fellow employees with compensation made available under the statutes instead. In limited circumstances, a worker may have the option of claiming workers' compensation benefits or maintaining an action against third parties other than employers or employees for negligence. In certain circumstances, the respective board may be subrogated to the employee's cause of action and maintain an action against the negligent third parties. In those cases, if the board recovers more in the civil action than has been paid in compensation benefits, the difference less legal and administrative costs is paid to the injured worker.

For specified employer and employee groups, participation in the scheme, including its obligation to remit premiums, is compulsory. For others, coverage is optional.

In each province, a board is established to carry out the provisions of the statutes and adjudicate claims for injury or disease. This typically involves the development of a comprehensive set of policies, internal review and appeal schemes and formal appeals to an independent, impartial tribunal. In Ontario, as in most jurisdictions, workers are required to file their claim for compensation as soon as possible after the accident, but no later than six months after the accident. If workers suffer from an occupational disease, they must file their claim after learning that they suffer from such disease.[2] As well, recent amendments to the Ontario statute have brought in formal time limits in which decisions must be appealed. Workers will have six months following the decision to inform the board that they wish to appeal the decision. In the Yukon and British Columbia, for example, workers have 90 days in which to request an appeal.

The general idea is that an accident or disease will be seen as compensable if it arose "out of and in the course of employment." If one of those elements is present in a claim, the board will presume the other is present as well and the worker will be compensated.[3]

In the adjudication of a claim, it must also be considered whether the injured person was a worker and, medically, whether the worker's condition is causally connected to the employment or the injury. The Quebec statute presumes that an injury in the workplace while the worker is at work is an employment injury. In Ontario a disability with a gradual onset does not have the benefit of such a presumption.

Most of the jurisdictions also have a "merits and justice" provision in their policy or statute, that makes it clear that the board is not bound by legal precedent but must make its decision "based upon the merits and justice of a case."[4] Further, in cases where the evidence weighs equally in favour of upholding the claim and in favour of disallowing it, the case is to be resolved in favour of the worker.[5]

Some of the statutes also have a presumption regarding workers found dead in the workplace. If a worker is found dead, it is presumed the death was due to a compensable workplace accident, if the worker was found in a place where the worker had a right to be, during the course of his or her employment. This presumption is not part of the British Columbia, Manitoba, New Brunswick, Newfoundland, Ontario or Prince Edward Island statutes.

Finally, it is not just employment injuries or accidents that invoke entitlement to compensation. Some cases of industrial or occupational disease can be compensated as well. Ontario was the first jurisdiction to specifically include a schedule of occupational diseases in its 1915 act. Occupational disease can present problems in the determination of causation, as it may have been caused by nonoccupational factors. A presumption of work-relatedness will arise in many jurisdictions if specific statutory requirements are met. Some statutes state that proof of work exposure automatically entitles a worker to compensation, while other statutes do not. In some areas, nonwork exposure will be considered when determining entitlement, and in others it will not.

When an accident occurs in the course of employment, the employer is required to notify the board within a specified period (usually three days) if the accident disables the worker or necessitates medical or dental aid. The employer is responsible for the initial costs of transporting an injured worker to a hospital or medical facility. The employer must complete an accident report, outlining the details of the injury. If a report is not filed, financial penalties may be assessed against the employer.

Effective January 1, 1998 a major overhaul of the compensation system in Ontario occurred with the passage of the *Workplace Safety and Insurance Act*. The changes demonstrate a movement to a compensation for loss of earnings as opposed to compensation based solely on the existence of a disability. The board eliminated entitlements to benefits for chronic stress and limited benefits for chronic pain. Also, the responsibility for dealing with return to work has been shifted to the employer and employee and away from the board. The influence of these changes is already reflected or is expected to be felt throughout the country, as other provinces have been or will be influenced by this shift in emphasis.

ADMINISTRATION

Each province has its own workers' compensation legislation that, along with the various regulations and policies, defines and describes the rules and benefits available to eligible employee groups.[6] There is also federal legislation whereby provincial boards adjudicate and pay compensation on behalf of federal employees and the government of Canada.[7]

COVERAGE FOR FEDERALLY REGULATED EMPLOYEES

Although the federally regulated sphere is covered by the *Government Employees Compensation Act,* it is provincial workers' compensation boards that look after the treatment of injured employees. The provincial board adjudicates the claim and pays compensation on behalf of the government of Canada to be reimbursed by Human Resources Development Canada.

The particular workers covered are employees of the public service of Canada, including those of Crown corporations and agencies. The nature and extent of the benefits provided will be the same as those provided in the particular provincial compensation statute.

PREMIUMS/FUNDING

The main funding principle from the point of view of most employers covered by the legislation is that compensation for industrial accidents is premised on a mutual or collective accident scheme.

For those employers that are so covered, workers' compensation schemes are funded by employer contributions to an accident fund. In contrast to other income protection schemes, such as unemployment insurance, employees do not contribute to the fund; contributions are the financial responsibility of employers. Furthermore, governments generally do not make revenue contributions to the accident fund.

The amount of the employer's contribution is determined by a payroll assessment rate, which reflects the accident risk of similar firms within the industry. Records are maintained, and the assessment rate is determined based on the experience of individual industrial classes in relation to payrolls. The boards may adjust the assessment rates to ensure the sufficiency of funds to provide for future payments.

Among the various provinces there are several ways of computing the assessment that the employer is required to pay. Most frequently, the assessment is done on the basis of an estimated payroll at the beginning of the year and adjusted at year-end based on the actual payroll and the claims experience of the class. For example:

ABC Company
Assessable payroll $100,000
Assessment rate .60 per $100
Employer's assessment is
    ($100,000 ÷ 100) × .60   = $600

Assessments are normally due and payable on an annual basis, and there are various penalties imposed for late payment. If an employer thinks it has been incorrectly classified or unfairly assessed, an appeal may be made to the board for reclassification or for a review of the assessment.

Penalties are also imposed where actual payroll figures exceed the estimated payroll upon which the assessment is based. An example of this would be where the actual payroll exceeds the estimated payroll by more than 150%, a 10% penalty is imposed on the difference.

Some forms of income are not included in the assessable payroll in some provinces. Examples of such non-assessable income are:
- Separation pay
- Tuition expenses
- Maternity benefits
- Stock benefits
- Medical/dental benefits.

In a departure from the basic principle of employer funding, Ontario amended its *Workers' Compensation Act,* effective January 2, 1990, with respect to employee benefit contributions for the first year after an employee's injury. For injuries from and after 1990, employers are required to continue making employee benefit contributions on behalf of their injured workers for the first year after a compensable injury.

However, employers participating in a multi-employer plan (MEP) do not have to contribute for employee benefit contributions on behalf of their injured workers. Rather, MEPs are required to provide benefits and benefit accruals for injured workers from their own resources.

COVERAGE

Each province, in its respective statute and regulations, designates the industries where workers must be covered under the workers' compensation plan.

Industries normally covered by workers' compensation are:

- Mining and quarrying
- Forestry
- Manufacturing
- Transportation
- Construction
- Fishing, dredging and stevedoring
- Sales industries
- Operation of theatres
- Light, power, gas and waterworks systems
- Retail stores.

Each provincial statute should be consulted to determine whether specific industries or occupations are required to be covered for compensation benefits. In situations where legislation is unclear, it is advisable to contact the respective board specifically to determine the conditions of coverage.

As well as listing the categories of industries where workers *must* be covered, each statute will specify industries or occupations that are exempt from its provisions. The following are occupations that may have compensation exempt status:

- Artists, entertainers and performers
- Circus operations, travelling shows and trade shows
- Clergy
- Workers employed in respect of a function in a private residence
- Newsboys employed in delivering papers
- Door-to-door salespersons
- Salespersons whose employers do not have a place of business in the province
- Street sellers
- Sports professionals, instructors, players and coaches
- Outworkers
- Farm labourers
- Barber shops, taxidermy shops and taxicab operators
- Gardeners
- Surgical, medical, dental or veterinary work.

Since the list of exempt industries and occupations varies from province to province, each particular statute should be consulted when determining an employer's status.

Employers engaged in industries where the legislation does *not require* the workers to be covered may nonetheless apply to the board to have their employees covered under special application rules for *optional coverage.*

Finally, persons who are self-employed or involved in a partnership may also apply for personal coverage.

EMPLOYERS

With allowance for minor variances among the provincial statutes, the following represents a sample definition of an *employer* for the purposes of determining coverage.

Employer includes every person having in his or her service, under a contract of hire or apprenticeship, any person engaged in work in or about an industry and includes:

a. Principals, contractors and subcontractors
b. Receivers, liquidators and executors appointed by a court with authority to carry on an industry
c. Municipalities and school boards
d. Provincial governments
e. Federal governments
f. Fishing bank managers or operators in the fishing, whaling and scaling industries.

EMPLOYEES

The definition of *eligible employees* will vary from province to province. The following is provided as a sample definition of *employee*.

Employee includes a person who has entered into or is employed under a contract of service or apprenticeship whether by way of manual labour or otherwise and includes:

a. A learner or apprentice
b. A member of a municipal volunteer fire or ambulance brigade
c. An auxiliary member of a police force
d. An independent operator
e. People called upon to assist in controlling forest fires or participating in search and rescue operations.

COMPREHENSIVE SCHEME OF PRESCRIBED BENEFITS

When discussing workers' compensation most people automatically think of disability benefits for someone injured on the job.

However, the scheme generally covers all injuries caused by accidents arising out of and in the course of employment. This includes *disablement* injuries that may gradually develop over time without specific trauma and *occupational diseases*.

The benefits available go far beyond weekly income replacement to include medical expenses, hospital expenses, dental expenses, rehabilitation services, survivor benefits and dismemberment awards.

The benefits payable under workers' compensation schemes are *not* designed to provide full compensation for all financial or personal consequences arising from a work-related accident. Recovery of losses is limited by the statutorily prescribed percentage of pre-accident earnings, by maximum insured earnings limits and by the elimination of certain types of compensation from the calculation of compensable earnings. For example, unlike the general measure of damages potentially recoverable in an action founded in tort, there is no provision in any of the Canadian provinces for the direct recovery for pain and suffering or loss of amenities of life.

Generally speaking, the benefits awarded reflect varying degrees of disability and resultant impairment of earnings capacity over time such as temporary total disability, temporary partial disability, permanent total disability and permanent partial disability.

MAXIMUM EARNINGS AND TAXATION OF BENEFITS

Each province sets a ceiling on the level of earnings that are compensable. In some provinces there are annual escalations provided.

Workers will only receive benefits for the prescribed portion of their pre-accident wages or for their loss of earnings up to the maximum amount.

Table II-3-I illustrates the various maximums within provinces, the effective date of these set maximums and any escalation provision.

Benefits received under workers' compensation are generally considered "not taxable." When the particular scheme provides for payment based on the worker's net earnings, the benefits, although reported to Revenue Canada, are not taxed at that point. However, this net amount of compensation will reflect the worker's wages minus an amount for the likely income tax deduction. In those few jurisdictions where compensation is based on the employee's gross pay, the payments from the board are neither taxed nor reduced to reflect the likely tax consequences. However, benefits must be reported to Revenue Canada.

TEMPORARY TOTAL DISABILITY BENEFITS

If a worker is temporarily totally disabled due to an injury at work, the respective board will, upon receiving and approving a claim, pay a weekly benefit to replace a prescribed portion of the workers' pre-accident earnings. The percentage of wage replacement varies among the provinces but is usually between 75% of net earnings and 90% of gross earnings. It should be noted that pursuant to a major overhaul of Ontario's legislation effective in January 1998, temporary benefits are now calculated on a loss-of-earnings basis—i.e., 85% of the difference between the pre-accident earnings and the amount a worker can earn in suitable and available employment.

The worker's claim must be supported by a physician's report outlining the worker's physical impairment and an estimate of the time required for recovery. In

Table II-3-I

MAXIMUM EARNINGS COVERED

Province	Maximum Earnings	Effective Date	Escalation
NFLD	$45,500	1-1-83	May be adjusted by regulations.
PEI	36,200	1-1-98	Automatic annual increase is provided.
NS	39,700	1-1-99	May be set by Order in Council.
NB	44,600	1-1-99	Automatic annual increase is provided.
QUE	50,500	1-1-99	Automatic annual increase is provided.
ONT	59,200	1-1-99	Automatic annual increase is provided.
MAN	51,460	1-1-99	Automatic annual increase is provided.
SASK	48,000	1-1-99	Automatic annual increase is provided.
ALTA	45,600	1-1-99	By order of the Board of Directors.
BC	57,500	1-1-99	Automatic annual increase is provided.
NWT	60,000	1-1-99	May be set by Legislative Assembly.
YUKON	57,500	1-1-99	Automatic annual increase is provided.

certain jurisdictions, the worker must also provide consent to the board and accident employer for the release of information concerning functional abilities.

Table II-3-II is a comparison of the various provincial levels for temporary disability benefits. Values shown in the Percentage of Earnings column of Table II-3-II are those in effect as of January 1999. The "90% of net" approach as opposed to, for example, the "75% of gross" is now law in five jurisdictions and permits compensation to be more closely related to pre-injury take-home pay, with less likelihood of over- or under-compensation related to differences in tax impact based on level of income and personal exemption. In some provinces benefits are increased after specified period of payment, based in some cases on the Consumer Price Index (CPI) or a percentage thereof. As well, in some instances, benefits are reduced proportionately by any Canada Pension Plan (CPP) disability benefits that the worker may receive.

TEMPORARY PARTIAL DISABILITY

Temporary partial disability benefits become payable when a worker suffers an injury or disease that may prevent him or her from returning to regular work but allows the worker to resume another type of employment or engage in medical or vocational rehabilitation. If the worker suffers a loss of earnings as the result of this partial disability, the board will pay a proportionate benefit based on an estimate of the impairment of earning capacity.

As noted above, there has been a major shift in Ontario regarding the premise of temporary benefits toward a loss-of-earnings model. In some sense, this has eliminated the historical distinction between temporary total and temporary partial benefits.

PERMANENT PARTIAL DISABILITY

In cases where a compensable injury or disease is of a permanent nature, there is provision under the various provincial statutes for payment of a permanent disability benefit. In exceptional cases of severe disability, the worker may be entitled to permanent total disability benefits. In other cases, the worker will receive a permanent partial disability benefit.

This benefit is normally payable monthly, and the benefit percentage is the same as for the weekly temporary benefit. The maximums vary from province to province. Such payments may be made for the employee's lifetime or until age 65, when an annuity or retirement pension may become payable. In certain circumstances, the amount of the permanent benefit is payable as a lump-sum, reflecting the commutation of the lifetime award, either at the option of the worker or as mandatorily required by the relevant legislation.

Table II-3-II

TEMPORARY DISABILITY BENEFITS

Province	Percentage of Earnings	Effective Date	Weekly Minimum/Maximum
PEI	80% of net*	1-1-99	None/$392.62 (80%) $417.15 (85%)
NB	85% of net	1-1-99	None/$526.23 (Married)
QUE	90% of net	1-1-99	$244.31/$614.42 (With dependants)
ONT	85% of net	1-1-99	$184.38/$580.20
MAN	90% of net**	1-1-99	$184.41/$568.63 (With dependants)
SASK	90% of net	1-1-99	$271.11***/$573.04
ALTA	90% of net	1-1-99	$237.04***/$566.05
BC	75% of gross	1-1-99	$284.03***/$827.05
NWT	90% of net	1-1-99	$380.77***/$766.83 (With a spouse)
YUKON	75% of gross	1-1-99	None*****/$829.33
NFLD	80% of net	1-1-99	$200.00***/$490.74 (With a spouse)
NS	75% of net****	1-1-99	None/$422.73

*or first 39 weeks, 85% of net thereafter
**for first 26 weeks, 80% of net thereafter
***or 100% of earnings if less
****for first 26 weeks, 85% of net thereafter
*****unless earnings less than $16,000, then worker is paid 100% of gross

Table II-3-III is a comparison of the provincial permanent total disability benefits (effective January 1999). Increases based on the CPI, or some percentage thereof, are a common feature of these benefits, as are full or partial offsets for CPP disability awards.

A monthly benefit will be payable based on a proportion of average earnings. Typically, the amount of the benefit is at least partially dependent upon the extent and nature of the permanent injury. Such disabilities are normally rated as a percentage impairment of the "whole person" after maximum medical recovery and compensation is payable at this percentage.

Several provinces (including, for example, Ontario and Nova Scotia) now use a "dual" pension approach for the calculation of the permanent award. A *future economic loss* award depends on the extent to which future earning capacity is impaired by the injury measured against the availability and suitability of employment. There may also be a lump-sum payment for *noneconomic loss* based on a medically determined impairment rating multiplied by a prescribed monetary amount, varying by the age of the worker.

In various provinces, the injured worker may also have the right to a retirement pension that is funded by monies set aside by the board.

WAITING PERIODS

There may be a waiting period between the onset of the disability and the date compensation benefits begin. In some provinces, benefits are backdated to the date of the injury, while in others benefits begin the day following the day of the injury, with no compensation paid by the board for the day of the injury. However, in those cases the accident employer may be required to pay normal wages for the day of the accident.

Medical and dental benefits become payable as of the date the expenses are incurred with no working period requirement.

Table II-3-IV outlines the various provincial waiting periods (effective January 1999).

DEATH AND SURVIVOR BENEFITS

In the event of a worker's compensable death, lump-

Table II-3-III

PERMANENT DISABILITY BENEFITS
(As of January 1, 1999)

Province	Maximum Period	Lump-Sum Awards	Monthly Benefits
NFLD	Benefits to age 65; annuity for those who reach age 65	Min.—$1,000 Max.—$45,500	80% of net
PEI	Life	Min.—$500 Max.—$36,200	85% of net
NS	Life	Lump-sum paid if less than 30%	30% × permanent impairment × 85% of net
NB	Benefits to age 65; annuity for those who reach age 65	Min.—$500 Max.—$44,100	80% for 1st 39 weeks, 85% thereafter, $2,226.51 maximum
QUE	Life	Min.—$757 Max.—$75,715 at age 18 or less, decreasing by age	$2,343.97 to $2,637.10
ONT	Life	$51,535.37, plus or minus $1,145.63 for each year under/over age 45 up to $22,912.60	$2,942.28 maximum
MAN	Life	Min.—$342 Max.—$102,830	$2,514.01 (with dependants)
SASK	Benefits to age 65; annuity for those who reach age 65	Min.—$100 Max.—$22,600	$2,466.95 maximum (with depandents)
ALTA	Life	Min.—$1,274 Max.—$63,685	$2,459.64
BC	Life	N/A	$3,593.75 maximum
NWT	Life	N/A	$3,322.93 maximum (with a spouse)
YUKON	Benefits to age 65; annuity for those who reach age 65	Permanent impairment × $80,000 × average wage, depending on age	$3,387.50 maximum

sum and/or monthly benefits accrue to the spouse and dependent children of the worker. This may include rehabilitation services to lessen the impact of the loss of the worker.

As well, there are benefits provided for funeral expenses at the time of a worker's death and for transportation of the worker's body.

Table II-3-V illustrates the maximum lump-sum

Table II-3-IV

WAITING PERIODS

Province	Day Benefits Begin	Backdated to Date of Injury
NFLD	2nd	No—Employer is required to pay worker for the full day of the injury.
ONT	2nd	No—Employer is required to pay worker for the full day of the injury.
ALTA	2nd	No—Employer is required to pay worker for the full day of the injury.
PEI	2nd	Yes—if disabled more than one day.
NB	2nd	Yes—if disabled more than one day.
NS	4th	Yes
QUE	2nd*	No
MAN	2nd	No
BC	2nd	No
SASK	2nd	No
NWT	2nd	No
YUKON	2nd	No—Employer required to pay worker for the full day of injury.

*In Quebec, the employer must pay the worker normal net pay for the day of injury at the time it would normally have been had the injury not occurred. The employer is also required to pay the workers 90% of net pay for the first 14 days of disability following the date of injury. If the compensation claim is approved, the board refunds this amount to the employer. If the claim is not approved, the board will request a refund from the worker.

benefits payable in each province in the event of a worker's death (effective January 1999).

The monthly benefit payable to a surviving spouse normally includes a specific amount for each dependent child. The child's benefit may be payable to a specified age or until his or her education is complete. The spouse's benefit is normally payable to age 65 unless the spouse remarries, when a lump-sum benefit may be paid.

REHABILITATIVE SERVICES/ RETURN TO WORK

The early and safe return to work is an important goal of every compensation board. The purpose of a return-to-work program is to ensure that the worker's job is consistent with the worker's functional abilities and that the worker suffers none or as little as possible in the way of loss of earnings due to workplace injury.

In Ontario, the recent amendments to the statute have changed the way rehabilitation is dealt with by the board. The board has a lesser role to play in the employee's return to work. Workers, in fact, have a duty to cooperate in their own return to work. The board, however, still must provide a labour market re-entry assessment if it is unlikely that the worker will be able to

return to work. If necessary, a labour market re-entry plan will be prepared in consultation with the worker, the worker's employer and health practitioners. Modifications to the workplace or assistive devices may be provided if they are determined to be necessary by the board decision maker. A number of programs may be provided under the plan, including English as a second language, academic upgrading, skills training, formal training, counselling and creative job search techniques. Where a worker dies as a result of a workplace injury, the board may even provide services to the widowed spouse in the form of training to enable the spouse to enter the labour market. There is no fixed duration for labour market re-entry plans, but duration can be agreed to, by the decision maker and the worker during the preparation of the plan. The board will pay for incidental expenses associated with the plan, if they are documented in detail.

In general, compensation boards generally initiate some type of physical rehabilitation program, when necessary. The object is to eliminate, or at least reduce, any handicap resulting from the workplace injury. In Alberta and Quebec, the boards go so far as to include social rehabilitation in their statutes as well. Other jurisdictions may provide for such a program in their

Table II-3-V

MAXIMUM LUMP-SUM BENEFITS PAYABLE IN THE EVENT OF DEATH
Fatal Benefits Other Than Pensions

Province	Immediate Lump-Sum	Funeral Cost	Transportaion Expense
British Columbia	$1,893.73	$2,272.34 plus $752.60 for incidentals	$752.60
Alberta	$1,300	Up to $8,150	$550 within Alberta, maximum of $1,000 outside province
Saskatchewan	Nil	$5,575	Actual costs in Canada
Manitoba	Minimum—$31,100 Maximum—$51,460	$5,660 maximum	Necessary costs
Ontario	$28,476.37 (min.) to $84,429.13 (max.)	$8,650 maximum	Necessary costs
Quebec	$1,515	$2,271	Necessary costs
New Brunswick	Nil	20% of N.B. $5,778 less CPP	Necessary expenses within Canada
Prince Edward Island	$10,000	$4,000 maximum	Necessary costs
Nova Scotia	$15,000	$5,000 maximum	Actual costs
Newfoundland and Labrador	26 times the worker's avg. net (weekly) or $15,000, whichever is greater	$4,500 maximum where worker dies leaving no dependants	Necessary costs
Northwest Territories	$2,400	$2,400 maximum	Necessary costs within NWT
Yukon Territory	Nil	Actual cost to max. of $4,000 plus $2,000 for incidentals	Reasonable and actual costs within Canada

policy statements. This type of rehabilitation can include such things as psychological treatment and academic assistance.

SPECIAL BENEFITS FOR THE HANDICAPPED

In cases where a worker has been deemed to be permanently disabled, each province provides specified benefits for individuals who require assistance with their personal care or require some type of nursing assistance. In some cases, the board will provide for housing renovation to deal with needs arising from the injury.

These additional benefits are usually expressed as an additional monthly benefit subject to specified maximum amounts.

As well, a clothing allowance may be provided to workers who are fitted with a prosthetic device to assist the worker with additional clothing expenses. It is normally stated as a specified amount per year and varies from province to province.

ENDNOTES

1. *Re Workers' Compensation Act, 1983 (Nfld.),* ss. 32,34 (1987), 44 D.L.R. (4th) 501 (Nfld. C.A.) at p. 509, aff'd (1989), 56 D.L.R. (4th) 765 (S.C.C.).

2. *Workplace Safety and Insurance Board Act,* S.O. 1997, c.16.

3. *Ibid.,* s.13(2).

4. *Ibid.,* s.119(1).

5. *Ibid.,* s.119(2).

6. Newfoundland *Workers' Compensation Act,* R.S.N. 1990, c.W-11; Nova Scotia *Workers' Compensation Act,* R.S.N.S. 1989, c.508; Prince Edward Island *Workers' Compensation Act,* R.S.P.E.I. 1995, c.W-7.1; New Brunswick *Workplace Health, Safety and Compensation Commission Act,* S.N.B. 1994, c.W-14; Quebec *Accidents du travail et les maladies professionnelles, Loi sur les,* L.R.Q., c.A-3; Ontario *Workplace Safety and Insurance Act,* S.O. 1997, c.16; Manitoba *Workers' Compensation Act,* R.S.M. 1987, c.W200; Saskatchewan *Workers' Compensation Act,* S.S.1979, c.W-17.1; Alberta *Workers' Compensation Act,* S.A.1981, c. W-16; British Columbia *Workers' Compensation Act,* R.S.B.C. 1996, c.492; Northwest Territories *Workers' Compensation Act,* R.S.N.W.T. 1988, c.W-4; Yukon *Workers' Compensation Act,* S.Y. 1992, c.16.

7. *Government Employees Compensation Act,* R.S.C. 1985, c.G-5.

CHAPTER 4

Government Health Services Plans

by Peter O'Hara

OVERVIEW

Prior to the establishment of public health insurance, Canadians were responsible for paying for their own health services. The level and quality of care received was influenced by income levels.

"Free wards" in hospitals, public clinics, sanatoriums and charitable hospitals supplemented by private agencies such as the Victorian Order of Nurses, the Red Cross and churches served the health needs of those who could not afford to pay. There was some provincial and federal reimbursement paid to physicians for these services; however, generally, these physicians were expected to donate their services.

The majority of Canadians paid for the health services they received. Fees were usually set by the physician based on the physician's assessment of the recipient's ability to pay. This approach had serious implications for the fee structure, the physician's role and the ability of Canadians to secure health care.

After World War II, a variety of medical and hospital insurance schemes were developed. These insurance plans, which varied in coverage, cost and quality, did not, however, serve the needs of the entire population and were least likely to serve the poor, the old and the chronically ill.

The need for a public health insurance system that would address some of the drawbacks of the existing system was recognized most notably by the medical profession. In 1934, the Canadian Medical Association's Committee on Economics proposed a national health insurance plan "to make available for every Canadian the full benefits of curative and preventive medicine, irrespective of individual ability to pay." Insured health services would be comprehensive in scope, delivered by the provinces with federal financial assistance and funded by the Canadian people as a whole through taxes. Patients would not pay fees for their health care "because the main objective is to remove any economic barrier, which now keeps doctor and patient apart."[1]

The concept of a national health insurance plan was endorsed by the Canadian Hospital Council, the Trades and Labour Congress, the Canadian Congress of Labour, the Canadian Federation of Agriculture and the insurance industry.

The federal government proposed a comprehensive health insurance plan, but the idea was dropped in 1945 because the provinces would not agree to increased taxation. However, by 1955 Saskatchewan, British Columbia, Alberta, Ontario and Newfoundland had responded to citizen demands for financial assistance by offering some form of public hospital insurance. The provinces, in turn, pressured Ottawa for financial assistance for these programs. In 1958, an agreement, the *Hospital Insurance and Diagnostic Services Act,* was reached whereby the federal government would share the cost of administering these plans. This act will be discussed in more detail later in this chapter.

The success of national hospital insurance increased public demand for a comparable system for all Canadians. In 1961, a Royal Commission on Health Services was given the mandate of proposing reforms to the varied medical insurance schemes in effect at that time.

The Canadian Medical Association, in a move away

from its earlier position, several provincial governments and the insurance industry favoured a two-tier system of medical insurance—private insurance for the majority of Canadians and government subsidies for those who couldn't pay the private premiums.

The Commission, however, formulated a universal medical insurance plan for the following reasons:

- Private health insurance was not designed to provide a comprehensive health service dedicated to prevention and treatment.
- There was some question as to the insurance industry's ability to improve the quality of the benefits offered or to extend coverage to the unprotected groups.
- The percentage of Canadians requiring government premium subsidization was substantial.
- A two-tier system would be expensive and operationally cumbersome compared to a single system.
- Health care and the relationship between patient and doctor should not be dependent on price.

The conclusions reached by the Royal Commission and largely implemented by the *Medical Care Act of 1966* are best stated as follows:

. . . the trauma of illness, the pain of surgery, the slow decline to death, are burdens enough for the human being to bear without the added burden of medical or hospital bills penalizing the patient at the moment of vulnerability. The Canadian people determined that they should band together to pay medical bills and hospital bills when they were well and income earning. Health services were no longer items to be bought off the shelf and paid for at the checkout stand. Nor was their price to be bargained for at the time they are sought. They were a fundamental need, like education, which Canadians could meet collectively and pay for through taxes.[2]

ADMINISTRATION

Unlike many of the benefits discussed thus far, medical and hospital services come under provincial rather than federal control. The administration of these plans is left to the provincial governments, and each province has its own legislation and regulations that set out the level of services that are covered. As a result, there are great variations among the provinces with regard to hospital and medical procedures, plan eligibility, plan financing and plan cost.

However, the plan must be administered on a non-profit basis by a public authority appointed by the government. In some provinces, the operations of the hospital and medical services plans are governed by separate legislation. In others, the two plans are combined for purposes of legislation and regulations.

CANADA HEALTH ACT

The *Canada Health Act*, effective 1984, replaced both the *Hospital Insurance and Diagnostic Services Act* and the *Medical Care Act*. This act set out the criteria and conditions to be met by provincial health programs in order to be eligible for the full cash federal contribution. They are as follows:

- Public administration: The program must be administered on a non-profit basis by a public authority appointed by and accountable to the provincial government.
- Comprehensiveness: The program must cover all necessary hospital and medical services and surgical-dental services rendered in hospitals. In addition to these insured health services the provinces are encouraged to provide certain extended health care services as defined in the act.
- Universality: 100% of the province's residents must be entitled to insured health services.
- Portability: Coverage must be portable from one province to another. The waiting period for new residents must not exceed three months. Insured health services must be made available to Canadians temporarily out of their own province. In such cases, payment for services within Canada is to be made by the home province at the host province's rates; payment for services out of Canada can be made at the home province's rates.
- Accessibility: Insured services must be provided on uniform terms and conditions for all residents. Reasonable access to insured services must not be precluded or impeded, either directly or indirectly, by charges or other mechanisms. Reasonable compensation must be made to physicians and dentists, and adequate payments made to hospitals, in respect of insured health services.[3]

In addition to these criteria, the act states that extra billing and user charges, other than user charges allowed by regulations, must not be permitted. The federal government can impose financial penalties on provinces that do not abide by the "rules." To eliminate these user charges, the act provides for a reduction in the federal government's cash contribution to a province equal to the amount collected through such charges. The federal government can withhold one dollar in federal grants to a province for every dollar collected in that province through extra billing by physicians. For the first three years the act is in force, funds withheld from a province because of extra billing or user charges will be held in the public accounts and will be returned to the province if these practices are eliminated during those three years. This is intended to encourage provinces to prohibit extra billing.

DENTAL AND PHARMACARE PROGRAMS

In some provinces the medicare program has been extended to include coverage for specific individuals for certain dental services. Such coverage is not to be confused with the oral surgery coverage provided by all provincial plans when rendered in-hospital. The type of dental services covered under the dental programs are those routine services rendered in a dentist's office.

Pharmacare programs are also administered by the provincial authority having responsibility for the administration of the medicare program.

BENEFITS

The benefits provided under the various provincial programs are almost uniform across Canada. The common definition of *insured services* is those services rendered by physicians, surgeons or qualified health professionals that are medically required. The expression *medically required* is included in the definition to ensure wise and effective use of the available programs by both patients and practitioners.

EXCLUDED SERVICES

Services excluded are:
• Services that a person is entitled to receive under another statute or certain other federal or provincial statutes
•Services not medically required, for example:
  1. Medical examinations required for employment, life insurance, schools, camps, passports, visa or similar purposes
  2. Cosmetic surgery for purely aesthetic purposes
  3. Advice by telephone
  4. Medico-legal services
  5. Hospital charges for private or semi-private accommodation.

RESIDENCE REQUIREMENTS

In all provinces and territories participating in the medicare program, residence in the particular province or territory is a prerequisite to obtaining benefits. The definition of *resident* is uniform since the general tenor of the legislation is the same in all provinces or territories. *Resident* means a person lawfully entitled to be or to remain in Canada who makes his or her home and is ordinarily present in the particular province or territory. The definition excludes tourists, transients and visitors. Persons not falling within the above definition are excluded from the benefits of insured services and must pay out of their own pockets the full cost of any medical or hospital services obtained.

CONCLUSION

In this chapter, we have examined the development of and logic behind Canada's national health insurance system. The system is intended to provide universal coverage. Health services must be made available to all residents on the same terms and conditions. The services must be delivered in a manner "that does not impede or preclude, either directly or indirectly whether by charges made to insured persons or otherwise, reasonable access."[4] The provinces must provide a comprehensive range of health services as specified in the hospital and medical insurance acts. A province must cover the cost of insured services for its residents visiting another province as well as those who have moved and are waiting to be insured under their new province's medicare plan. Finally, health insurance must be administered and operated on a non-profit basis by a public agency of the provincial government.

ENDNOTES

1. Canadian Medical Association, Committee on Economics, *A Plan for Health Insurance in Canada* (Calgary: Report to the Annual Meeting, June 18-22, 1934), at pp. 31, 36.
2. The Honourable Emmet M. Hall, *Canada's National Provincial Health Program for the 1980s* (Ottawa), at p. 6.
3. *Canada Health Act,* R.S.C. 1985, c. C-6, Sections 7-12.
4. *Ibid.,* s. 12(1)(a).

CHAPTER 5

Hospital Services

by Peter O'Hara

OVERVIEW

In 1958 an agreement was reached between various provinces and the federal government wherein each province would provide a hospital plan that satisfied the requirements of the federal *Hospital Insurance and Diagnostic Services Act.* The agreement specified that the federal government would share in the cost of such a plan by approximately 50%. Yukon and the Northwest Territories joined the agreement in 1960. The administration of these plans is left to the provincial governments, and each province has its own legislation and regulations that set out the level of services that are covered. The plan must be administered on a non-profit basis by a public authority appointed by the government. In some provinces the operations of the hospital and medical services plans are governed by separate legislation. In others, the two plans are combined for purposes of legislation and regulations.

During the latter part of the 1970s the federal government's concern with abuses, such as the collection of user fees for hospital beds, led to the enactment of the *Canada Health Act.* This act replaced the *Hospital Insurance and Diagnostic Services Act* and came into force in April 1984.

PREMIUMS/FUNDING

In some provinces, premiums must be paid by residents to cover the cost of hospital services. This may be done by requiring that all employers deduct premiums from their employees' salaries and remit these premiums to the provincial authority.

Some provinces levy a payroll tax and require employers to fund the plan. In other provinces, and in both territories, no direct premium payment is made, and the funds to support the plans come from general operating revenue.

Table II-5-I shows a comparison of the premium/funding arrangements in each province and territory (as at January 2000).

In Alberta, there are certain residents who may be considered exempt from premium paying status or pay a reduced premium, such as:
- Persons over age 65 and their dependants
- Persons unable to pay due to financial hardship who get a waiver of premium by the province
- Persons whose income is below a specified dollar amount
- Persons receiving social assistance.

In Alberta, employers with five or more employees are designated as an *employer group,* and all employees must be enrolled or properly exempted. Smaller groups may make application to be considered as an employer group.

The employer is responsible for the collection and remittance of premiums to the health plan.

TAX CONSIDERATIONS

The *Income Tax Act* (ITA) allows for the deduction of certain medical expenses. However, the premiums paid by individuals for provincial hospital/medical services plans are not deductible. Where an employer pays all or part of the individual's cost for the provincial plan, the employer's contribution is added to the employee's income for tax purposes.

Table II-5-I

PROVINCE/TERRITORY	PREMIUM/FUNDING ARRANGEMENTS
NFLD	No premium payable. Funded by general revenues.
PEI	No premium payable. Funded by general revenues.
NS	No premium payable. Funded by general revenues.
NB	No premium payable. Funded by general revenues.
QUE	Employers pay 4.26% of payroll to help fund the plan (For employers with a gross annual payroll in excess of $5 million). In addition, taxpayers contribute at a rate of 1% of all nonsalary sources of income, excluding alimony. For employers with a gross annual payroll under $5 million the tax rate is as follows: • $1 million total payroll: 3.75% as of July 1, 1999; 2.70% as of July 1, 2000. • $2 million total payroll: 3.88% as of July 1, 1999; 3.09% as of July 1, 2000. • $3 million total payroll: 4.01% as of July 1, 1999; 3.48% as of July 1, 2000.[1]
ONT	Employers pay 1.95% of payroll to help fund the plan. The balance is funded from general revenues. Effective January 1999, the first $400,000 of payroll is exempt from the Employer Health Tax.
MAN	Employers pay 2.15% of payroll to fund the plan.
SASK	No premiums payable. Funded by general revenues.
ALTA	Composite premium for hospital/medical plan is payable by residents.
BC	No premium is payable for hospital services.
NWT	No premium payable. Funded by general revenues.
YUK	No premium payable. Funded by general revenues.

It should also be noted, here, that where an employer makes a contribution to a trust fund and the trust then pays the hospital insurance premium on behalf of an employee, the payment should be included in the employee's income and is, therefore, subject to tax.[2]

COVERAGE—INSURED RESIDENTS

There is uniformity among the provinces in defining who is eligible to be covered under the provincial hospital services plan. This is a prerequisite under the agreement between the federal and provincial governments. *Resident* means a person lawfully allowed to be or to remain in Canada who is ordinarily present in the particular province or territory and makes his or her home there.

By definition, this would exclude tourists, visitors and transients.

EFFECTIVE DATES OF COVERAGE

The normal residency period that must be established in each province is three months for persons moving from province to province in Canada. If the person leaves one province to establish residence in another province, he or she is usually covered for the three-month period by the plan in the prior province of residence.

Application for coverage must be made in writing and, if this is delayed, coverage may be postponed until the first day of the second calendar month following the month in which the application is received.

Individuals in a given province attending school outside the province are generally considered to be residents of their own province for purposes of the hospital services plan.

Persons establishing residence in a province who were previously residents outside Canada are normally considered residents on the date of their arrival.

Included as such insured residents are the spouse and dependent children of a resident as a family unit. The head of the family is required to register all members of the family.

The following are examples of the age limits used by some provinces in determining the eligibility of dependent children:

• Quebec—dependent children under age 18 are eligible under family coverage. Handicapped dependants are eligible with no age limit.

- Manitoba—dependent children under age 19 are eligible. Dependent children under age 21 who are attending school are eligible. Handicapped dependants are eligible with no age limit.

EXTENSION OF COVERAGE

In most cases, when a person moves from his or her province of residence and the move is permanent, coverage under the hospital plan of the originating province will cease three months after departure or when the new province's hospital plan takes effect.

In the case of a temporary absence, coverage may be extended beyond the usual three months and up to 12 months provided application is made for such extension of coverage.

INSURED SERVICES

The basic hospital services provided by all provinces to insured residents are:
- Accommodation and meals at the standard public ward level
- Necessary in-hospital nursing services
- Laboratory, x-ray and other diagnostic procedures
- Drugs, biological and related preparations administered in a hospital
- Use of operating room, case room and anaesthetic facilities, including necessary equipment and supplies
- Routine surgical supplies
- Use of radiotherapy and physiotherapy facilities
- Services rendered by persons employed by the hospital.

Other types of hospital services are offered by various provinces in addition to these basic services, such as:
- Ambulance transportation
- Occupational and speech therapy
- Prosthetic limbs and orthopedic devices
- Psychiatric counselling
- Renal dialysis services
- Rehabilitation services.

EXCLUDED SERVICES

Each province has specified certain services that are excluded from the list of their insured hospital services. Some examples of excluded services are:
- The cost of private or semi-private hospital accommodation
- The cost of special duty nurses
- Treatment for which the Workers' Compensation Board is responsible
- Treatment for which provision is made under any

other provincial or federal act (i.e., RCMP, National Defence, etc.)
- Services that a patient is declared not to be in need of
- Cosmetic surgery other than as approved by each province
- Drugs to be taken home from hospital.

OUT-OF-PROVINCE BENEFITS

Generally, all provinces provide hospital benefits to residents who are hospitalized outside their province of residence.

The benefits provided may differ where the illness or injury occurs in the province of residence and treatment is not available within the province or where the illness or injury occurs outside the province while the resident is travelling, on vacation, business, etc.

As well, benefits may also differ where hospitalization occurs in another province as opposed to outside Canada. Generally, where hospitalization is in another province, the resident province will provide benefits up to the usual level of charges made by the province where hospitalization occurs under reciprocal agreements.

Where hospitalization occurs outside Canada, benefits vary from province to province depending upon whether the hospitalization is required for emergency reasons while an individual is travelling during a temporary absence or whether he or she is on referral because the services are unavailable in Canada. In most cases of referral, prior approval is required by the *Hospital Act.* In recent years, coverage levels have been severely restricted under provincial medicare plans.

In most provinces, there is a limit of three months on the period of hospitalization that will be considered eligible for coverage out of province. Special coverage is also provided in some provinces in the case of mental illness or tuberculosis.

USER FEES

Some provinces have instituted a system of user fees for some hospital services. The insured resident is required to pay this fee when receiving such services from hospitals.

PAYMENT OF CLAIMS

In each province a public, non-profit authority is appointed to handle the administration of claims. Insured residents are required to pay charges for preferred accommodations, such as semi-private or private rooms as well as user fees in the provinces that levy them. All other hospital services in Canada are payable by the provincial plan.

In the case of out-of-Canada hospitalization, insured

residents must support their claim with receipts from the facility where the services are rendered in order to receive reimbursement. Many hospitals, particularly in the United States, will not require payment from Canadian residents if proof of provincial coverage is provided and benefits assigned. In these cases, the provincial plan will reimburse the hospital directly.

CONCLUSION

Although each province has its own hospital plan, a person in Canada will basically receive similar care any-where in Canada. An insured person is virtually guaranteed that he or she will receive care regardless of income and is thus released from the worry of crippling hospital bills.

ENDNOTES

1. *CCH Canadian Employment and Pension Guide*, (Toronto: CCH Canadian Limited, 1997).

2. See Revenue Canada, Interpretation Bulletin IT-85R2, "Health and Welfare Trusts for Employees" (31 July 1986).

CHAPTER 6

Pharmacare and Dental Programs

by Peter O'Hara

OVERVIEW

Pharmacare programs are administered by the provincial and territorial authority having responsibility for the administration of the medicare program.

In most cases, there is agreement between the authority and the province's/territory's pharmacists as to the drugs and medicines that are supplied, the ingredient cost for these substances and a stated dispensing fee that is charged by the pharmacist for dispensing the medications.

Each province/territory has a list of drugs that is covered under its Pharmacare program. This is done by way of the Drug Identification Number that each drug is assigned. Not all drugs require a prescription in order to be dispensed (for instance, over-the-counter drugs). Generally, however, the provincial/territorial drug pro-grams require that a drug be prescribed before it is eligible for coverage under the program. Some governments require that the drug only be available with a physician's prescription (prescription drug), and some require only that it be prescribed by a physician (prescribed drug).

COSTS AND FUNDING OF PHARMACARE

The costs for Pharmacare programs are normally included in the total cost of operating the province's/territory's medical services insurance plan. Therefore, where premiums are charged to residents, a portion of the premium applies to the funding of Pharmacare programs.

In some cases, there are deductible amounts that must be paid by the resident and certain co-payment features, such as the 80%/20% split in British Columbia.

PHARMACARE COVERAGE— SENIOR CITIZENS

In certain jurisdictions, residents over age 65 and sometimes their dependants are eligible for coverage whereby all or a portion of the cost of prescription drugs is reimbursed by the provincial/territorial medical plan.

PHARMACARE BENEFITS

Pharmacare benefits vary for each province and territory, some covering only the cost of prescribed drugs, others extending to other types of medical supplies.

Also, in some cases there are deductible amounts and co-payment features where residents bear responsibility for a portion of their drug costs.

The following is a summary of the benefits available under the existing Pharmacare programs, universal as well as those for senior citizens.

British Columbia (BC)

For residents under age 65, there is an $800 deductible per calendar year, which a single resident or family must satisfy before Pharmacare begins reimbursement. After a resident or family has reached the $800 limit, the Pharmacare program reimburses 70% of the cost of the drug or medication. The resident is responsible for paying the 30% co-payment after the deductible is satisfied. The maximum annual payment, per family, is $2,000.

For residents over age 65, the program reimburses 100% of the ingredient cost and dispensing fees in excess of $200 per year. A deductible of $200 applies from January 1, 2000 forward.

The program covers, in addition to prescribed drugs and medicines:

- Certain ostomy supplies
- Diabetic syringes
- Blood glucose monitoring strips
- Designated permanent prosthetic appliances and children's orthotic devices (braces).

Alberta (ALTA)

Senior citizens and residents in receipt of a widow's pension under the *Widow's Pension Act* are sent a Blue Cross drug card, which entitles them to receive prescribed drugs and medicines for 30% of their cost. The remaining 70% is reimbursed to the pharmacist by the program.

Saskatchewan (SASK)

All residents are covered for the cost of prescribed drugs and medicines (unless covered by another government program), as listed in the Saskatchewan drug formulary, which includes over 2,000 drug products.

If an individual or family spends in excess of $850 on prescription drugs in either of two calendar year deductible periods (January to June or July to December), the plan pays 65% of the cost of further prescription drug-related expenses incurred in the same period.

If a resident or his or her spouse is in receipt of the Guaranteed Income Supplement (GIS), the semi-annual deductible is reduced to $200. Thereafter, the plan pays 65% of incurred prescription drug charges.

For residents of special care homes in receipt of GIS, residents or their spouses in receipt of the Saskatchewan Income Plan (SIP) or residents or their spouses in receipt of Family Income Plan (FIP) supplements, the deductible is reduced to $100 semi-annually. Thereafter, the plan pays 65% of incurred prescription drug charges.

Manitoba (MAN)

All residents are covered under this program, which reimburses for the cost of most prescribed drugs and medicines. Each person or family unit is required to satisfy a deductible, based on a calculation to determine an adjusted family income. Where the adjusted family income is less than $15,000, the income is multiplied by 3% to determine the deductible. Where the adjusted family income is in excess of $15,000, the income is multiplied by 2% to determine the deductible.

Residents must submit their claims to the Pharmacare program with official Pharmacare receipts in order to receive reimbursement.

Ontario (ONT)

Residents over age 65 or recipient's of social assistance through the Ministry of Community and Social Services are eligible for coverage under the Ontario Drug Benefit (ODB) program.

Residents in receipt of the ODB are required to pay a $2 co-payment for each prescription filled. Single senior citizens with a net income of more than $16,018 and senior couples earning more than $24,175 will be required to pay their first $100 in prescription drug costs. Thereafter, they will be required to pay the maximum ODB dispensing fee of $6.11 per prescription.

In 1995, the Ontario government introduced a second program, the Trillium Drug Program (TDP), for residents not in receipt of the ODB or Special Drugs program. The TDP provides reimbursement for each year where a resident or family incurs prescription drug-related costs in excess of a certain proportion of their earnings. Benefits under the TDP are not payable to residents covered by private insurance plans. Each person or family must satisfy a fiscal year deductible, based on a sliding scale of net income, that is adjusted for families of two, three and families in excess of three.

Beneficiaries of the TDP are also responsible for a $2 co-payment for each prescription filled.

Quebec (QUE)

Effective January 1, 1997 the government of Quebec implemented a universal prescription drug plan through the Régie d'assurance-maladie du Québec (RAMQ). (The program went into effect for seniors and residents in receipt of social assistance on August 1, 1996.)

All residents of Quebec are legally required to be covered under the RAMQ plan or through a private group insurance plan. The basic RAMQ plan pays 75% of the cost of prescription drug costs and limits members' annual out-of-pocket expense, for prescription drugs, to $750 per family, per year. Annual premiums in respect of the RAMQ plan are $175 for single coverage and $350 for family coverage. In exchange, members receive reimbursement for any prescription drug listed in the Quebec RAMQ formulary (after satisfying the deductible), which is updated twice every year. A $25 quarterly deductible also applies.

Private group insurance plans with members resident in the province of Quebec must match the RAMQ basic plan as a minimum requirement. However, private plans are entitled to provide richer programs and can include all drugs for ease of administration.

When plan members turn age 65, they may elect to have their private coverage continue (if the plan offers retiree benefits) or move to the RAMQ plan.

New Brunswick (NB)

The Prescription Drug Program in New Brunswick consists of several individual drug plans, for specific beneficiary groups. The beneficiary groups include seniors, age 65 or over; residents living in licensed nursing homes; persons suffering from cystic fibrosis, HIV or multiple sclerosis; organ transplant recipients; persons in need of human growth hormone; children in care; and recipients of family and social services benefits.

The Seniors Beneficiary Group (Plan A) is available to all residents of New Brunswick, 65 years of age or over and who are in receipt of Old Age Security (OAS) or Guaranteed Income Supplement (GIS) or who qualify by virtue of an annual income ceiling. Eligibility based on income is determined in the following manner:

- Single residents over age 65, with an annual income of $17,198 per year or less, are eligible.
- Seniors age 65 or older, with a spouse over age 65, and a combined annual income of $26,955 per year or less are eligible.
- Seniors age 65, with a spouse under age 65, and a combined income of $32,390 or less are eligible.

Beneficiaries of Plan A are responsible for a co-payment of $9.05 per prescription, with an annual ceiling of $250.

Each of the other drug programs have similar co-payment features and annual maximums, except the Nursing Home Beneficiary Group and the Children in Care Beneficiary Group.

Nova Scotia (NS)

Residents age 65 and over are eligible under the Seniors Pharmacare, which reimburses pharmacies directly for the cost of drugs, medications and other supplies requiring a prescription. Families in receipt of income assistance in relation to disabilities are also eligible.

Seniors are required to pay an annual premium of $215, as well as a co-payment of 20% of the total cost of the prescription, to an annual maximum of $200.

In addition to prescription drugs, the program reimburses for the cost of ostomy and diabetic supplies.

Yukon Territory (YUK)

Residents age 65 or over, or residents age 60 or over whose spouse is a Yukon resident who is 65 years of age or over and is enrolled in the Health Care Insurance Plan, are eligible for coverage.

The plan covers the total cost of prescription drugs and certain nonprescription drugs and products, including compounds used in the treatment of heart disease, anti-inflammatory drugs and insulin syringes.

Newfoundland (NFLD)

All residents of Newfoundland and Labrador who are 65 years of age and over and registered with National Health and Welfare for OAS and are in receipt of the GIS are eligible under this plan.

The plan pays the entire cost of the drug ingredients of approved benefits while the recipient is responsible for payment of any dispensing fee.

Prince Edward Island (PEI)

Residents age 65 and over who are registered with the Health Services Commission for benefits under the Health Service Plan (medicare) are eligible for benefits. The purpose of this plan is to provide financial assistance to seniors for drug costs, particularly those costs associated with long-term drug use for chronic conditions. Users pay $8 toward the total cost of the drug ingredient and the total cost of the dispensing fee for each prescription. The plan pays the remainder of the cost of the ingredient.

ADMINISTRATION— DENTAL PROGRAMS

In some jurisdictions, the medicare program has been extended to include coverage for routine dental services rendered in a dental office.

This coverage should not be confused with the oral surgery coverage provided by all provincial/territorial plans when rendered in a hospital.

These dental programs are extensions of the provincial/territorial health care programs. Claims for such services are submitted directly by the dentists to the provincial/territorial plan for reimbursement. There are no specific premium charges for this coverage except in PEI, where there is a $4 annual registration fee per child up to a maximum of $12 per family.

The amounts reimbursed to the dentist for services performed are a matter of negotiation between the dental association and the province/territory.

The dental associations produce their own suggested fee guide. It is not intended to set maximum fees, but rather allows the dental association to state what a reasonable charge would be for a given procedure. In private practice, dentists can charge lower, equal or higher fees than those suggested in the fee guide.

DENTAL COVERAGE— INSURED PERSONS

In some jurisdictions, the in-office dental plans are intended to cover residents over age 65; in others, children under specified ages.

Table II-6-I shows the various jurisdictions offering an in-office dental care program and the residents covered.

Table II-6-I

ALTA	Under the Extended Health Services program, residents age 65 or over and dependents are covered for specific dental services.
SASK	Families and children of families (age 18 and under) in receipt of social assistance are covered under the provincial dental services program.
QUE	Children are covered under the dental program to age 10 for specified services. Social aid recipients are also covered for some specified dental services.
NS	Children are covered until the last day of the month in which they become 10 years of age.
NFLD	All children up to and including 12 years of age are covered for specific services with a payment of $5 required for each service or treatment. Children of social aid recipients are covered from age 13 to age 17 for basic services only.
PEI	Children between the ages of 3 and 17 are eligible for registration in the program.
YUK	Residents age 65 and over and spouses age 60 married to a 65-year-old resident are covered under the Yukon dental program.

BENEFITS—COVERED DENTAL SERVICES AND LIMITATIONS

The range of dental services provided to eligible residents varies for each province and territory. In those jurisdictions where senior citizens are the beneficiaries of the program, the in-office dental plan provides for coverage of major restorative services, such as dentures. In those jurisdictions where children are the beneficiaries, the emphasis is on preventive and basic restorative services.

Table II-6-II shows the types of dental services provided under each program along with any limits imposed.

ORAL SURGERY IN HOSPITAL

As previously discussed, certain oral surgical procedures are covered by the provincial medicare plans when rendered in a hospital. The following is a list of some of the types of oral surgery that are usually covered as a medical service:

- Surgical removal of teeth including anaesthesia
- Alveoplasty and gingivoplasty
- Sulcus deepening and ridge construction
- Treatment of traumatic injuries to soft tissue within the mouth
- Incision and draining of dental abscesses
- Excision of cysts and tumours
- Open reduction of fractures of the mandible and maxilla

- Excision of ronula
- Condylectomy
- Surgical correction of prognathism.

CONCLUSION

The Pharmacare programs are to some degree extensions of the provincial/territorial health care plans. There are variations by province and territory as to who is covered and whether or by what means there is cost sharing by the covered individual. The fact that they may not be "universal" or that they may require or allow the charging of a dispensing fee differentiates the Pharmacare programs from the regular provincial/territorial health care plans and, since each province and territory is responsible for its own dental service plan, there is wide variation as to the benefits offered and persons insured. The expense of providing universal dental care is almost prohibitive. In fact, British Columbia and Manitoba actually dropped the limited plans they had. While the existing plans do offer financial relief for children and some seniors, we are a long way from having a comprehensive, universal dental care system in Canada.

The cost of drugs has increased rapidly in the recent past so that the cost of Pharmacare programs has increased as well. This factor may influence the adoption of these programs by provinces and territories that currently do not have universal programs.

Table II-6-II

ALTA Eligible residents are covered for goods and services provided by a dental surgeon or dental mechanic, as follows:
- Two examinations per calendar year
- X-rays
- Restorations (fillings)
- Extractions
- Root canals
- Two units of planning per calendar year
- Two units of scaling per calendar year
- Denture relining every two calendar years
- Installation of a complete denture or reset of a complete denture in a given arch every five years
- Installation of a partial denture in a given arch every five years.

In addition to the limitations noted above, the program has reimbursement limits for each category of service.

SASK Eligible families and children of families (ages 18 and under) are covered for the following services when rendered by a dentist:
- Examinations and diagnostic services, including x-rays
- Fillings
- Periodontal services
- Extraction of teeth
- The provision of certain prosthetics and orthodontic appliances as approved by the program
- Necessary drugs and medicines required for a dental condition.

QUE Eligible children are covered for the following services, as specified dependent upon their age:
- Preventive prophylaxis, fluoride
- Diagnostic exams and x-rays
- Restorative fillings and stainless steel crowns
- Endodontics—root canals, pulpotomies
- Extractions and oral surgery.

Children ages 13 to 15 years are covered for the following services:
- Preventive
- Diagnostic
- Oral surgery.

NS Eligible children are covered for the following services up to the indicated limits:
- Oral exams and bitewing x-rays once every 12 months
- Prophylaxis, fluoride and counselling once every 12 months
- Space maintainers, retainers and cross bite correction
- Fillings and crowns (excluding gold crowns)
- Root canal therapy and other endodontic services
- Periodontal services; periodontic surgery is covered only if done in a hospital
- Oral surgery
- Lab services in connection with the above dental services.

PEI Most dental services are covered for children as follows:
- Exams, x-rays
- Prophylaxis, fluoride treatment
- Fillings
- Endodontics.

NFLD Eligible children are covered under the program for the following services:
- Examinations every six months
- X-rays every two years
- Prophylaxis and fluoride treatment every 12 months
- Cross bite correction
- Amalgam and composite fillings
- Replacement of missing anterior teeth
- Extractions
- Endodontics such as root canals, pulpotomies.

Prior approval from the program is required for extensive restorations and replacement of anterior teeth.

YUK Eligible residents are covered for the following services subject to a maximum of $1,400 for any two consecutive years:
- Diagnostic exams and x-rays
- Fillings and other restorations
- Dentures
- Preventive services.

CHAPTER 7

Interaction Between Private and Public Plans

by Guy A. Jobin[1]

OVERVIEW

Canada is a country that is noted for its tendency to approach benefits through government-sponsored benefit programs. For example, in the United States, health care is a matter of private business. In Canada, health care is a high-profile government-funded program. The United States has a true potpourri of unemployment insurance and workers' compensation programs. In Canada these are well-coordinated, tightly structured government-sponsored benefit programs.

As has been noted in previous chapters, many of the government-sponsored programs are universal in nature. They are designed to provide a uniform minimum level of coverage to the widest possible cross section of eligible claimants. This is often not what all eligible claimants necessarily want, perhaps even need. Many desire a level of coverage that is more in keeping with their preferred standard, which may be above that provided by the universal program or benefit.

Consequently, many of the government-sponsored benefits are thought of as providing a base level of support. There is often room, and indeed government encouragement, for individuals to build in their own preferred level of coverage over and above the government program.

HEALTH CARE

Medicare in Canada is a government-sponsored benefit program that provides coverage of a universal nature. It is a hybrid system of one national health statute that is complemented by distinct provincial health care legislation. Historically, the system was funded on an approximately equal basis by both the provincial and federal governments. However, in recent years the federal government has reduced its share of funding significantly. Currently, the federal government estimates its percentage of health care funding at 34%. Provincial governments, which are lobbying the federal government to restore its health care funding to pre-1994 levels, have stated that federal funding is actually only 11%, excluding tax credits granted to the provincial governments since 1977 in respect of health care funding. The *Canada Health Act* sets out the conditions the provincial health care programs must meet to be eligible for federal funding.

Government health insurance provides for mandatory coverage. A person or group cannot contract out of it or contract around it with a private insurer. But the system does allow for persons or groups to utilize services at a level over and above the government-sponsored level. These services are provided by health care institutions as an adjunct to the government plan at a price designed to at least recover all costs. This price is not inexpensive.

As a result, people who desire additional or extended care coverage usually obtain it on a group coverage basis. This is normally done through employer-sponsored extended care group health care plans.

Extended health care plans are operated by private insurance companies. As such, proper design and administration of a plan that provides for cost-effective service is critical.

The private group plans usually emphasize two types of coverage. First, they offer extra coverage over and above a standard already provided by medicare. For example, medicare pays for standard ward accommodation in hospitals. Most private plans will pay the additional funds above the medicare rate for a semi-private or private room. Second, private group plans offer certain types of coverage that do not meet the definition of *insurable coverage* under medicare. Medicare does not cover all potential health problems. For example, it may not cover preventive dental care. Private insurers therefore provide group dental plans to cover treatment costs in this area. These services, excluded from government health care programs, are more fully discussed in Section III. There are some areas that private insurers are not allowed to cover.

The private plans co-exist quite nicely within the framework of government-sponsored plans. Governments encourage such plans by allowing employers to deduct their contributions to the plans from taxable income. Within fairly wide guidelines, claimants receive benefits from the plans tax-free. The plans can, therefore, serve as an attractive employee perquisite. In fact, many employees are attracted, at least in part, to some organizations because they have good group health care plans.

WORKERS' COMPENSATION

Workers' compensation (discussed in detail in Chapter 3) is a government-controlled and -administered social insurance program. It provides care for injured workers. It differs from government health care in two important respects. First, in its coverage of injuries suffered by employees, it provides compensation for lost wages as well as health care. This gives it an income benefit component. Second, it has a base of well-defined targeted interest group funding from the contributions of employers that benefit from the system.

Workers' compensation is not voluntary. Provincial legislation as a rule obligates most employers, particularly industrial and lower wage service ones, to join the system. Some professions are exempted, as are self-employed persons. Assessments and coverage are as prescribed by the legislation and regulations. It is a serious quasi-criminal offense not to cover an eligible employee or to attempt to deny a person access to the system in the case of a work-related injury. In fact, employers are normally required by law to notify a workers' compensation board forthwith of a claim.

There are still well-prescribed limitations to comprehensive workers' compensation coverage. For one thing, an injury must be ruled by a board to be work related to qualify for benefits. This can often be a matter of some dispute, particularly in cases of long-term chronic illness or industrial disease. For another, workers' compensation only provides compensation on a scale determined by way of board policy. It is not intended to compensate completely for all income losses due to injury at work. It is intended primarily to prevent a real hardship accruing from the loss of all wages.

There is obviously room for additional coverage to be provided to individuals or groups not wanting to depend on government-determined levels of coverage and government administration of their claim. Governments recognize and accept this. They allow for employer-sponsored disability insurance programs to be provided by private insurers.

Private group disability insurance plans usually provide for disability coverage for any injury or sickness, whether work related or not. They are thus considerably wider in scope than workers' compensation. They usually provide for payment of lost wages and benefits that are more closely related to a disabled person's actual wage and salary loss. In addition to wage and salary losses, many disability benefit programs also provide some sort of income protection to keep other employee benefit programs in place. The ultimate payment of benefits is almost always structured to complement workers' compensation benefits. This avoids duplication and any possible inference that private plans are controverting the mandatory coverage.

Private plans are usually structured to provide for two distinct types of benefits. These are labeled as *short-term disability (STD)* and *long-term disability (LTD)*. STD typically covers disabilities from one day to 26 weeks. It is geared to providing immediate income support for a substantial portion of, but not all, lost wages. LTD is concerned with providing rehabilitation, if necessary, as well as long-term compensation for lost wages, benefits and other employment considerations for disabilities that last from 26 weeks to normal retirement age.

Many private short- and long-term disability plans provide benefits that are coordinated (or integrated) with government wage loss programs such as workers' compensation or the Canada/Quebec Pension Plans (CPP/QPP). The rationale for this integration is that an individual who is paid as much or more while disabled than he or she could earn while employed has little economic incentive to go back to work. Normally, the insurance company would require that the individual apply for benefits under the government program. Then, if the application is approved, the benefit amount paid by the insurance company would be reduced by the amount of benefit (or a portion thereof) received under the government program.

EMPLOYMENT INSURANCE

Employment insurance (EI) (previously called *unemployment insurance*) is universal in its application to all employees (refer to Chapter 10 for a more detailed discussion of EI). An employer cannot contract out of the plan, nor can an employee. Indeed, it is a quasi-criminal offense to attempt in any way to avoid contributing to the plan unless clearly exempted by regulation.

The EI program does have its limitations. This is particularly the case with respect to its upper limits of coverage for wages lost due to lack of employment. There are a number of industries, particularly those in the unionized sectors, where workers earn wages considerably in excess of compensation limits covered by EI.

There are also industries that in some cases have highly trained workers who are subject to cyclical layoffs. Employers do not want to lose the services of such highly skilled workers. One way of insuring against such a situation is to provide some sort of cushion over and above eligible EI benefits in cases of short-term unemployment. This is in fact done and strongly supported by the government, in sectors such as the automotive industry.

It is possible for employers to supplement benefits available under the *Employment Insurance Act* through the provision of a supplemental unemployment benefit (SUB). Such a plan must be registered with Human Resources Development Canada and must be registered with Revenue Canada if amounts are paid out of a trust fund. When that is done, benefits payable to a claimant are not deducted from unemployment insurance benefits as employment income. They are recognized as supplementary income to help cover the present employment loss.

There are currently approximately 3,000 SUB plans in effect in Canada. To date, most SUB plans are included in collective agreements in unionized industries.

SUB plans provide an interesting illustration of how the government achieves a macroeconomic policy objective through a government-supported private sector benefit program. The government is committed to making Canada a world-class producer and exporter of commodities like autos. It recognizes that this goal requires a committed work force of highly skilled people. However, the government EI program, because of its universal application, is not capable of supporting the type of income requirements common to an industry that is subject to short-term cyclical layoffs. Thus, the employer-sponsored SUB plan provides the required income insurance and support that is in the interest of both the employer and the work force.

SUB plans must be registered with Revenue Canada if amounts are paid out of a trust fund. Once the plans are registered, the employer contributions and interest earnings are tax-exempt. The income (contributions and interest) from the plans is only taxed when it is received by the employee in the form of a benefit. To provide for

orderly administration, the plans must be administered through a trusteeship arrangement.

An eligible employee builds up credits. These entitle that person to SUB benefits in the event of a layoff. The benefits can be flat weekly dollar amounts that, when combined with EI payments, can bring benefits up to 95% of lost wages.

SUB plans are also available for training and illness. Supplements paid of maternity and paternity benefits can also be exempted even though this is subject to different legislation.

SUB funds are self-funded, much like private pension plans.

LIFE INSURANCE

Most people are aware that government-sponsored benefit programs like workers' compensation and the CPP/QPP pay benefits to those who are disabled. Many are not aware that they also provide a combination of life insurance and survivor benefit to the surviving spouse of a deceased eligible claimant.

Workers' compensation legislation provides for death benefits to a surviving spouse when death has been caused as a direct result of an employment injury. In Ontario, there is a provision for a variable lump-sum cash payment as well.

CPP/QPP also provides for a lump-sum death benefit that is similar to a life insurance payment. To be eligible, the surviving spouse must have had a partner who contributed to CPP for at least ten years. Upon death of a partner, the surviving spouse receives a lump-sum payment that is equal to six times the monthly retirement pension of the deceased contributor, or 10% of the year's maximum pensionable earnings (YMPE) for the year in which the contributor died, whichever is less.

The CPP/QPP lump-sum death benefit is quite clearly of a minimal nature. In many instances it may hardly cover burial expenses. This is just one more example of how current government-sponsored programs can and do leave sole surviving elderly spouses, the majority of whom are women, as the most needy of Canada's elderly.

The governments are therefore most interested in encouraging individuals to come up with supporting mechanisms to fill the gap, so to speak, in this area. That gap has been filled for many years by group life insurance. It is the original and traditional group benefit provided by employers. It operates in all provinces in conjunction with the public system of lump-sum death payments mentioned above.

The group life concept is based upon a life insurance company entering into a master group life contract with an employer. That contract provides basic yearly term insurance for all employees in the workplace, without any qualification other than their being bona fide employees at the time of coverage. A cash lump-sum life insurance benefit is paid to a deceased employee's beneficiary if death results from any normal insurable cause. That cause does not have to be in any way employment related.

The choice of beneficiary is usually much more open to the preference of the policyholder in private group life insurance than is the case with the government-sponsored programs. In private plans, the employee can usually designate a person of his or her choice to be the beneficiary. In the government plans, the spouse or immediate family members are usually automatically the beneficiaries. This is explainable in that the two sectors have different purposes. The private insurer is interested in offering an employee an option to engage in estate planning. Government-sponsored benefit programs are primarily interested in bringing about income distribution among immediate family members in an effort to eliminate or alleviate poverty.

PENSIONS

Chapters 1 and 2 document in considerable detail the role of the government of Canada, and the provinces, in the field of pensions and related income benefits for elderly Canadians. The federal government sees its primary objective in public pension benefits as the necessity to redistribute income to elderly Canadians in an effort to keep them within reasonable range of a poverty line.

Private pension plans are of two basic varieties. The first is the formal, structured group plan. These are the company pensions. The second is the personal registered retirement savings plan (RRSP). The federal and provincial governments are highly supportive of both types. Indeed, the RRSP was created by federal statute. Tax deferrals are provided to strongly encourage Canadians to invest in one or the other, or both of these two basic pension plans.

It is widely recognized that the main reason for government-sponsored benefit programs for the elderly is that many have little or no savings with which to look after themselves. Because they are no longer capable of doing so in their retirement years, the government must step in at considerable public expense. The government does recognize that, if more people were able to save during their working years, the burden on government would be reduced in the future. Therefore, it is to the government's advantage, as much as to the public's, to encourage savings through pensions during a person's income earning years.

The most common form of private pension arrangement is the plan provided through employment. These plans are referred to as *registered pension plans (RPPs)*.

Unfortunately, only about a third of the work force as of 1997 was covered by such plans. Approximately 41% of the paid work force is covered by RPPs.[2]

Most private plans are structured on the basis of prescribed core elements. These are usually:
- Eligibility
- Normal and early retirement
- Postponed retirement
- Retirement pensions
- Form of pension
- Rates of contribution
- Termination of employment
- Death before retirement
- Death after retirement
- Disability benefits.

There are an almost endless number of methods in which these elements can be defined and utilized in plan design and administration. While this is in marked contrast to the relative simplicity and uniform structure of government-sponsored plans, it should not be surprising. The goals and objectives of these plans are considerably different. The government plans are concerned with distributing income to help claimants meet a common standard. The private pension plans are designed to meet the preferences of a select group on the basis of proven income potential and projected standard-of-living requirements. Sections IV, V and VI are devoted entirely to pension plans for those interested in learning more about the design and funding of private pension plans.

Contributions to properly registered plans are strongly encouraged by the federal government. Generous tax deferrals are provided to employees and to employers on behalf of employees. All reasonable contributions to a pension fund by an employer and contributions by employees to prescribed limits are deductible from income for income tax purposes in the year the contributions were made. Earnings of the fund are not taxable. Payments from the pension fund are only taxed as they are received.

The government provides additional ongoing support by helping to ensure the continuing viability of plans through government supervision under provincial pension benefits legislation. Although some may feel that the provincial regulation of private pension plans is more interference than support, the purpose is to ensure that promises made by pension plans are kept. Provincial regulations also act to define minimum requirements that a private plan must meet if it is to receive preferential tax treatment.

There are some private pension plans that integrate or coordinate the benefit paid from the private plan with benefits paid by government-sponsored programs such as Old Age Security (OAS) and CPP/QPP. The justification for such integration is that the employer is contributing to the government program and, therefore, the total retirement income of these plans can be considered in determining what is a reasonable retirement benefit. Since the OAS benefit is paid out of the federal Consolidated Revenue Account and there is no specific tax for this program, others feel that integration of private plans with OAS should not be allowed. Many provinces (and the federal government) have changed their legislation to disallow future integration of private pension plans with OAS.

Many provinces (and the federal government) have amended their legislation to allow integration of private plans with CPP/QPP only to the extent that those CPP/QPP benefits earned by the employee while a member of the pension plan be taken into account. Previously it was possible for an individual to belong to two or three pension plans with different employers and have each one integrate benefits with the employee's entire CPP/QPP benefit.

For individuals who are not members of pension plans, or who have not exceeded the tax-assisted savings level as a result of their membership in an RPP and/or a deferred profit-sharing plan, the government provides an additional retirement saving vehicle. The RRSP is a personal savings plan into which an individual can deposit money and defer taxes until withdrawn during retirement years when taxes are lower. Tax treatment of contributions and earnings of an RRSP is similar to that for RPPs.

Recognizing that some taxpayers benefit from greater tax assistance because of the type of their pension and retirement savings plan, the federal government revised the *Income Tax Act* by setting a uniform limit on tax-assisted savings of 18% of earnings to an annual dollar limit.

RRSP funds must be held by a third party capable of carrying out a trust or fiduciary responsibility. Most Canadian insurance companies, trust companies and banks are eligible to issue RRSP certificates of deposit. How the taxpayer directs or uses the money in an RRSP account is left open to individual choice. However, it generally cannot be withdrawn for personal or family use without incurring tax.

Government support of RRSPs is accomplishing two objectives. It is, first, encouraging savings for retirement.

Second, it is encouraging Canadian taxpayers with sufficient disposable income to distribute a portion of their incomes into investment-oriented vehicles. These funds in turn can be loaned to investors, thus increasing general economic activity.

For those with access to more disposable income than the average Canadian, the government has created more specialized plans. These tend to be linked with executive compensation from company sources. The most common are those under the classification of profit-sharing plans.

The deferred profit-sharing plan (DPSP) is the most popular. The plan is somewhat similar to the normal RPP from a tax deferment perspective. The employer makes contributions to a designated account. The contributions are tax-deductible to the employer and tax-exempt to the employee while in the account, or more appropriately, trust fund. Unlike normal pension plans, the employer's contribution varies on the basis of profits. In addition, there are oftentimes a number of small, or even individual, trust accounts to hold and manage the funds for employees. These allow for greater flexibility and investment control by the individual.

CONCLUSION

There is considerable interaction between government-sponsored and private benefit programs. Consistently, the government benefits have the primary objective of providing uniform levels of coverage sufficient to protect the widest possible selection of eligible participants against real loss or hardship. Private benefit programs have the primary objective of starting where the government-sponsored benefit stops. There is a well-defined role for each kind of program, and each in most instances has tacit government recognition and support.

ENDNOTES

1. Guy A. Jobin wrote the original chapter for the first and second editions of the book. Parts of this version of the chapter were edited by Roberto Tomassini to provide updated information and data.
2. Statistics Canada, *Pension Plans in Canada* (1 January 1998), Catalogue no. 74-401-XPB, at p. 18.

CHAPTER 8

Old Age Security

by Leslie Steeves, Karen DeBortoli and Peter Miodonski

OVERVIEW

The Canada Pension Plan (CPP) or, in Quebec, the Quebec Pension Plan (QPP), as discussed in previous chapters, is separate and apart from the Old Age Security program. Old Age Security (OAS) is viewed as the first tier of the three-level system (OAS, CPP and private pension benefits and annuities) set up to help provide income replacement following retirement. While the CPP/QPP retirement pensions are earnings related, the basic OAS pension is universal. It is a flat rate benefit that, effective July 1, 1977, may be prorated according to the number of years of residence in Canada. Depending on their income, pensioners may also be eligible for a Guaranteed Income Supplement; and pensioners' spouses, common law or same-sex partners ages 60 to 64 may qualify for the Allowance for the Survivor. The only requirements are age and residency.

The current OAS program, established in 1952, is not the first of its kind—even for Canada. However, it is significantly different from the immediately preceding federal plan, which was the 1927 *Old Age Pension Act*. Under this act, the federal government reimbursed a province one-half of the amount paid by the province under its old age pension legislation. Old age pensions under these statutes were comparable to the current welfare system. Recipients were subject to:

- Citizenship requirements
- Stringent residence requirements
- A financial means test
- The assumption that they were receiving financial help from children and income from owned property (whether or not it was true).

These requirements became unacceptable for a retirement pension plan in a society where withdrawing from the labour force due to age was becoming more acceptable.

The OAS program was improved in a number of important ways on July 1, 1977 by Bill C-35.[1] The new provisions authorize the inclusion of the OAS program in international social security agreements, established partial OAS pensions based on residence, and provided for the use of a single eligibility criterion instead of the three previous ones.

OLD AGE SECURITY ACT

The governing legislation is known as the *Old Age Security Act*.[2] Regulations made pursuant to this act are known as the *Old Age Security Regulations*.[3] As is the case with most benefit legislation, the act allows regulations to be developed that give specific details as to how OAS is to be administered.

ADMINISTRATION

The *Old Age Security Act* is administered by the Minister of Human Resources Development Canada (HRDC). The Income Security Programs Branch[4] of HRDC administers OAS through regional offices, while the International Operations Division[5] administers the benefits included in Canada's international social security agreements.

FINANCING

Currently, all benefit payments under the *Old Age Security Act* are made out of the Consolidated Revenue

Fund of Canada. That is, they are general operating expenses of the government (just as the salaries of civil servants are) and are financed out of general tax revenue to the government of Canada. Prior to 1972 there was an Old Age Security Tax, but this was repealed effective January 1, 1972.

ELIGIBILITY

Full OAS Pension

The OAS basic pension is a monthly benefit available to virtually all persons 65 years of age and over who apply for the benefit and meet certain basic eligibility requirements. These requirements are:
- Proof of age
- Residence status
- Residence requirements.

Proof of age must be made at time of application by either a birth or baptismal certificate, if available. If these documents are not available, at least two of any other documents showing age or date of birth can be substituted.

To meet the residence status requirements, one must be a Canadian citizen, must be a legal resident in Canada when the application is approved, or must have been a Canadian citizen or a legal resident in Canada immediately prior to the date that one ceased to reside in Canada.

Residence requirements are somewhat more complicated. The amount of an applicant's pension is determined by how long he or she has lived in Canada, according to the following rules:
- A person who has lived in Canada for periods totaling at least 40 years after age 18 may qualify for a full pension.
- A person who has not lived in Canada for a total period of at least 40 years may still qualify for a full pension if he or she was 25 or over on July 1, 1977 and
  a. Lived in Canada on July 1, 1977 or
  b. Had lived in Canada before July 1, 1977 after reaching age 18 or
  c. Possessed a valid immigration visa on July 1, 1977.

In the situations listed above, the applicant must have lived in Canada for the ten years immediately prior to the approval of his or her application for an OAS pension. If the applicant was absent from Canada during part of this ten-year period, the absences may be offset if the applicant previously lived in Canada for a period of time that was at least three times the length of the absence after reaching 18 but before the commencement of the period. Even if the applicant qualifies to have any absences offset, he or she must still

have lived in Canada for at least one year before the date his or her application for an OAS pension was approved.

For example, a 65-year-old applicant who was absent from Canada for two years between the ages of 61 and 63 will have this absence offset if he or she resided in Canada for at least six years between the ages of 18 and 55.

Canadians who work outside of Canada for Canadian employers, such as the armed forces, may have the time spent working abroad counted toward their Canadian residence requirement. To qualify, applicants must have either returned to Canada within six months of ending their employment, or have turned 65 while still working outside Canada. Applicants must provide both proof of employment and proof that they physically returned to Canada. Spouses, partners or dependents of Canadians working for international organizations abroad may also apply for this treatment in certain circumstances.

If an individual makes a late application for an OAS pension, he or she may receive retroactive payments for up to one year before the application was made. The applicant must still meet all eligibility requirements in order to receive retroactive payments.

Partial OAS Pension

Anyone who does not satisfy the residence requirements for the full OAS pension may possibly qualify for a partial pension. A partial OAS pension is earned at the rate of 1/40th of the full monthly pension for each full year the applicant lived in Canada after turning 18.

Once a partial pension is approved, that pension may not be increased as a result of additional years of residence in Canada.[6]

Under the rules for a partial pension, a former resident of Canada with at least 20 years of prior residence in Canada after age 18 would be entitled to receive a partial pension abroad at age 65, without returning to Canada.

Proving Residency

The question of how an individual proves a period of residence needs to be addressed. The *Old Age Security Act* allows the regulations to spell out how this is done. The regulations state that ". . . there shall be furnished by the applicant or on his behalf a statement giving full particulars of all periods of residence in Canada and of all absences therefrom relevant to such eligibility."[7] For most people this would not be a problem as they file income tax returns that state they have resided in a given province. It is for the few exceptions that there is a problem, and it is up to these individuals to prove residency. Where an individual's statement is not accepted, there are appeal procedures. These will be discussed later.

According to the regulations, "a person resides in

Canada if he makes his home and ordinarily lives in any part of Canada."[8] This is generally applied to any Canadian citizen or permanent resident. However, the regulations exclude periods of residence for certain individuals, such as:

a. Diplomats or consular officers or representatives of foreign governments
b. Members of military forces (non-Canadian) present in Canada
c. Spouses or dependants of individuals in a. or b.[9]

Periods of absence from Canada are also dealt with by the regulations. Basically, any interval of absence will not be deemed to have interrupted the individual's residence if:

- The absence was of a temporary nature and did not exceed one year.
- The absence is for the purpose of attending a school or university.
- The absence is required due to employment by:
  - The government of Canada
  - NATO
  - The Canadian Armed Forces
  - A religious group or organization or
  - A Canadian firm or corporation

and the individual maintains a permanent residence in Canada and returns within six months after the end of his or her employment outside of Canada.[10]

As has been discussed, the eligibility requirements for the flat amount benefit (or retirement benefit) under the *Old Age Security Act* are based on two things: age and residency. There are no income requirements either during the period of benefit accrual (i.e., prior to age 65) or during the period of benefit payment. The residence requirements during the benefit accrual period have been discussed extensively in this section. The residence requirements during the payment period will be discussed in the section dealing with the payment of benefits.

Residence Requirements Under Social Security International Agreements

Persons who are unable to satisfy the residence requirement for a full or partial pension as outlined in the preceding paragraphs may use the provisions of an international social security agreement to qualify for a pension. Thus, if an applicant has not resided in Canada for the necessary minimum period, but has periods of residence and/or social security contributions in a country with which Canada has concluded an international agreement, such periods may be taken into consideration for the purpose of satisfying the minimum residence requirement.[11]

The amount of pension payable by virtue of an international agreement is calculated at the rate of $\frac{1}{40}$th of the full pension for each complete year of residence in Canada after age 18.

As noted above, the act provides for payment of a partial pension, the amount of which is determined by the number of years' residence in Canada. The partial pension is prorated on years of residence so that a person with 17 full years of residence in Canada will receive 42.5% ($\frac{17}{40}$) of the full pension.

It should be noted that the number of years of residence used is the whole number of years without regard for any additional months.[12] For example, if an individual had 17 years and 11 months of eligible residence, then he or she would receive 42.5% (or $\frac{17}{40}$) of the maximum for his or her monthly benefit.

It is clear the new rules allow some individuals to receive benefits when they would not have under the original rules (for example, an individual with 29 years' residence between ages 25 and 55). Also, the new rules do not eliminate any individuals from receiving benefits that would have qualified under the original rules. However, the amount of benefit could be affected when using the new rules. For example, an individual who has resided in Canada from age 45 to age 65 would receive a full benefit under the original rules but only 50% of that amount under the new rules.

APPLICATION FOR BENEFITS

Application for pension benefits must be made in writing to HRDC. Application should be made approximately six months before becoming eligible for the pension (i.e., at age 65) to allow for proof of age to be obtained and history of residence confirmed. The application form is made available by the regional directors. Application for benefit is deemed to have been made only when the completed form is received by HRDC. Application may be approved on the date on which both the age and residence requirements are met. Where an individual is incapable of making an application for any reason, such application may be made for him or her by a responsible person or agency.

BENEFITS

The original benefit payable under the *Old Age Security Act* was a flat monthly pension or universal old age pension based only on age and residence. The term *flat* is used because, under the old rules, everyone qualifying for a pension received the same amount. Now, however, as stated earlier, it is possible to qualify for a partial pension.

The monthly pension originally was $40 per month. This amount was increased on an ad hoc basis until 1972 when formal escalation was introduced. This escalation was annual in accordance with the change in the Consumer Price Index (CPI) to a maximum of 2% per year. This formula for escalation was continued until 1971, when it was abolished. In 1973 escalation resumed in its current form, namely, in accordance with the CPI with no limitation and with changes being made quarterly. The only exceptions to this new escalation method were in 1983 and 1984, when the total increases over the years were 6% and 5%, respectively.

The method for determining the amount of escalation is detailed in the *Old Age Security Act* and Regulations. It should be noted that the benefit amount may not be reduced in the case of a decreasing CPI. However, the act does specify that when the CPI does decrease, no benefit increases will be allowed until the CPI exceeds its value at the point where it first started to decline.

The amount of the (maximum) monthly benefit payable for January 1 to March 31, 2003 is $453.36. As previously discussed, the amount of partial pension is calculated by dividing the number of years of eligible residence (between ten years and 40 years) by 40.

Payment of the pension is made monthly in arrears. That is, the payment for a given month is made at the end of that month. Commencement of the benefit will always be at the end of the month following the month that the application is approved. However, the effective date of the benefit approval may be earlier or later than the commencement date. In fact, the regulations provide for the allowance of up to one year of retroactive benefit payments.

The OAS pension is paid as a life annuity with no number of guaranteed payments and no benefit is payable to the surviving spouse or partner. The rationale for having no survivor benefits is that the spouse will generally receive his or her own benefits under the program. The final benefit payment is for the month in which the pensioner dies; thus, in many cases there will be a benefit payment cheque received after the death of the pensioner that rightfully belongs to the estate of the pensioner.

Residence Requirements During Receipt of Benefits

As mentioned earlier, there are residence requirements for the pensioner to receive the benefit payments. If a pensioner has had 20 or more years of residence in Canada after attaining the age of 18, then benefit payments will continue indefinitely outside Canada. If a pensioner has less than 20 years of residence in Canada after age 18, payments will be made only for the month the pensioner leaves Canada and for an additional six months before being suspended. Benefit payments may be reinstated if the pensioner resumes residence in Canada and meets eligibility requirements.

TAX TREATMENT OF BENEFIT PAYMENTS

OAS benefits are considered taxable income when received, both federally and provincially. Higher-income pensioners may also have to repay all or part of their benefits through the tax system. In addition, the benefits are not eligible for the pension income credit.

APPEALS AND REVIEWS

Where an applicant is dissatisfied with a decision or determination that no benefit is payable, or with the amount of benefit that is payable, he or she may make a written request for a reconsideration of the decision. Such written request is to be made to the Minister of HRDC. The request should be made within 90 days from the date a copy of the decision was mailed to the applicant. The Minister has the authority to allow a longer period if he or she feels it is warranted under the circumstances.[13] The act does not specify a time limit for the Minister to act upon this request but requires the Minister to reconsider the decision without delay and make a decision. The Minister is also required to notify the applicant without delay of his or her decision.[14]

A dissatisfied applicant has 90 days to appeal a decision of the Minister to a Review Tribunal under Subsection 82(1) of the CPP Act.[15]

Where the issue under appeal to the Review Tribunal relates to the income or income from a particular source, the appeal is to be referred to the Tax Court of Canada for determination.[16]

A decision of the Review Tribunal may be subject to a judicial review, commenced by either the applicant or the government. The judicial review would proceed before the Federal Court of Canada.[17]

SOCIAL SECURITY AGREEMENTS

The Minister of HRDC may, on behalf of the government of Canada, enter into an agreement with the government of another country that would integrate the OAS program with a similar plan in that country. Such agreements allow for:
- The exchange of information
- Administration of benefit payments under both plans that are payable to residents of Canada or the other country and
- Combining periods of residence or contributions in that country with periods of residence in Canada.[18]

The advantage of these agreements is that they allow one country to make the total benefit payments (while collecting the other country's share). Probably more important, they allow someone with between ten and 20 years' residence in Canada to receive a partial pension while residing outside of Canada, as long as the years of residence or contribution in the other country make up the amount by which years of residence in Canada are less than 20.

Table II-8-I shows the countries with which there is a social security agreement in force and the effective date of the agreement.[19]

ENDNOTES

1. Bill C-35, S.C. 1976-77, c.9.
2. *Old Age Security Act*, R.S.C. 1985, c.0-9.
3. *Old Age Security Regulations*, C.R.C., c. 1246.
4. http://www.hrdc-drhc.gc.ca/isp/common/home.shtml.
5. http://www.hrdc-drhc.gc.ca/isp/common/intind_e.shtml.
6. *Old Age Security Act, supra*, s. 3(5).
7. *Old Age Security Regulations, supra*, s. 20.
8. *Ibid.*, s. 21.
9. *Ibid.*, s. 21(2.1).
10. *Ibid.*, s. 21(4)(5).
11. *Old Age Security Regulations, supra*, s. 21(5.1).
12. *Old Age Security Act, supra*, s. 3(4).
13. *Old Age Security Act, supra*, s. 27.1.
14. *Ibid.*, s. 27.1(2).
15. *Ibid.*, s. 28(1).
16. *Ibid.*, s. 28(2).
17. *Ibid.*, s. 28(3).
18. *Ibid.*, s. 40(1).
19. A current summary of the status of Canada's international social security agreements can be found at http://www.hrdc-drhc.gc.ca/isp/internat/sum_e.shtml.

Table II-8-I

Country	Effective Date
Antigua and Barbuda	January 1, 1994
Australia	January 1, 2003
Austria	November 1, 1987
Barbados	January 1, 1986
Belgium	January 1, 1987
Chile	June 1, 1998
Croatia	May 1, 1999
Cyprus	May 1, 1991
Czech Republic	January 1, 2003
Denmark	January 1, 1986
Dominica	January 1, 1989
Finland	February 1, 1988
France	March 1, 1981
Germany	April 1, 1988
Greece	December 1, 1997
Grenada	February 1, 1999
Iceland	October 1, 1989
Ireland	January 1, 1992
Italy	January 1, 1979
Jamaica	January 1, 1984
Jersey, Guernsey	January 1, 1994
Korea	May 1, 1999
Luxembourg	April 1, 1990
Malta	March 1, 1992
Mexico	May 1, 1996
Netherlands	October 1, 1990
New Zealand	May 1, 1997
Norway	January 1, 1987
Philippines	March 1, 1997
Portugal	May 1, 1981
St. Kitts and Nevis	January 1, 1994
St. Lucia	January 1, 1988
Saint Vincent and the Grenadines	November 1, 1998
Slovakia	January 1, 2003
Slovenia	January 1, 2001
Spain	January 1, 1988
Sweden	January 1, 1986
Switzerland	October 1, 1995
Trinidad and Tobago	July 1, 1999
United Kingdom of Great Britain and Northern Ireland	April 1, 1998
United States	August 1, 1984
Uruguay	January 1, 2002

CHAPTER 9

Guaranteed Income Supplement

by Leslie Steeves, Karen DeBortoli and Peter Miodonski

OVERVIEW

Canada has a three-level retirement income system. The foundation of that system is the Old Age Security (OAS) program, which was discussed in Chapter 8 of this section. The Canada Pension Plan (CPP)/Quebec Pension Plan (QPP) constitute the second tier or level. They are discussed in Chapters 1 and 2 of this section. The third level consists of private pension plans and retirement savings schemes. These are strongly supported by the federal and provincial governments through special incentives incorporated into the income tax system. Private pensions are discussed in detail in Sections IV, V and VI.

It is of fundamental importance to understand the notion of Canada's three-level retirement income system when examining the scope and nature of the Guaranteed Income Supplement (GIS) and the Allowance.[1] The GIS was initially introduced in 1967 as a temporary support component of OAS. It was intended to assist a small projected percentage of the population whose basic OAS income would not be augmented by the universal CPP/QPP plan during its first five to ten years of existence.

GIS is a nontaxable, monthly benefit payable to residents who receive a basic OAS pension and have little or no other income. GIS payments begin in the same month as OAS payments. GIS benefits are not payable to individuals outside Canada for a period beyond six months. The amount of GIS payable depends on the income and marital status of the applicant.

GIS was originally intended to be an interim measure. It was to provide a basic minimum level of income for those who had access to no other retirement income outside of OAS. Since the date of its inception in January 1967, the entitlement has been subject to an income test. Benefits are nontaxable in view of their being almost in the category of public welfare and are indexed quarterly. GIS recipients must renew their benefit annually, which is typically done through the income tax system.

GIS is, however, no longer realistically thought of as a temporary interim measure for a small portion of low-income senior citizens. It is now recognized as a main-line permanent benefit. It must be maintained and, in the opinion of some advocates, improved upon to satisfy basic retirement income needs of a growing elderly poor segment of society.

GIS INCOME TEST QUALIFICATIONS

GIS benefits are available only to individuals whose yearly income[2] (yearly combined income if married or a common law partner) falls below certain limits, and are based upon attempts to help recipients meet a poverty line.[3] Poverty lines are subjective and heavily influenced by political and public policy considerations. One method of establishing a poverty line, for GIS purposes, is to determine what is required to maintain a minimum, adequate standard of living on the basis of food, clothing and housing. That is often called the *budget method.* It is often measured in conjunction with the Consumer Price Index (CPI). Another method is to establish what is deemed to be a minimum required income. Those with an income below the minimum are below the poverty line.

Government retirement income benefit programs directed toward the poor are ostensibly intended to bring the recipient within a reasonable range of a poverty line. In the case of GIS, the federal government has not clearly defined by way of public policy what the poverty line is. But there is a qualification procedure that is directly tied into the level of total income an applicant is receiving based on an income test. The qualification and benefit entitlement amount are dependent on a formula designed to match the total OAS and GIS benefit with well-defined total income amounts. One can therefore use this formula as a way of determining the federal government's policy decisions on what constitutes poverty among the elderly.

In effect, the basic poverty line threshold that GIS attempts to meet is the total of the basic OAS benefit plus the maximum GIS benefit amount. The poverty line is subdivided into the single pensioner and married pensioner category. For illustrative purposes, the period April 1, 2003 is used to show how this "poverty line" is calculated. For a single pensioner, the poverty line was determined to be the basic OAS benefit of $456.08 per month, plus a maximum of $542.03 per month of GIS benefits, if no other income was available. This generates a maximum yearly pension of $11,977.32 for the single qualified pensioner.

In the case of a married or common law couple (both of whom are pensioners), the starting point is twice the basic one-person OAS amount, or $912.16, plus twice the maximum monthly benefit for retired spouses/partners under the GIS,[4] which equals $706.12 per month, if no other income was available. The maximum yearly public pension for retired couples is $19,419.36.

The amount of GIS benefit payable[5] depends on the applicant's marital status and income. While income such as earnings-related retirement pension payments, foreign pension payments, interest or dividend is considered income, the following items are excluded from the income calculation:

- The amount of any pension, supplement or spouse's allowance paid under the *Old Age Security Act* or similar provincial law
- The amount of any allowance under the *Family Allowance Act*
- The amount of any social assistance payment made on the basis of a means, needs or income test
- The amount of any death benefit under the Canada Pension Plan; and
- The amount of any grant under government of Canada programs relating to home insulation or energy conversion.

There are two basic GIS payment rates. The first applies to single pensioners (including survivors and divorced or separated persons) and to married or common law pensioners whose partner does not receive either the OAS benefit or the Allowance. The second rate applies to married and common law couples where both are pensioners. For a single GIS recipient, the maximum monthly payment ($542.03 for the second quarter of 2003) is reduced by one dollar for every two dollars of other monthly income. If both partners are receiving either the OAS benefit or the Allowance, the maximum monthly payment ($353.06 for the second quarter of 2003) is reduced by one dollar for every four dollars of the couple's combined monthly income. For the second quarter of 2003, the income cut-off is $13,032 for a single person, $16,992 for the spouse/partner of a pensioner and $31,584 for the spouse/partner of an Allowance recipient.

There is an exception to the basic rates described above for a couple in which only one person is a pensioner and the other is not eligible for either the basic OAS pension or the Allowance. In this case, the maximum monthly GIS payment, which is $542.03 for the second quarter of 2003, is reduced by one dollar for every four dollars of combined monthly income, excluding the pensioner's OAS benefit.

As mentioned above, maximum benefits from OAS and GIS for the second quarter of 2003 were $11,977.32 for a single person and $19,419.36 for a retired couple. As of January 1, 2002 (i.e., for 2001), Statistics Canada estimated the poverty line for one person living in an urban centre to be $18,841. For two individuals in an urban centre the poverty line was estimated at $23,551.

ALLOWANCE PROGRAM

The federal government has tacitly recognized the problem of GIS failing to bring all Canadians up to the poverty line threshold. A serious problem occurs when one spouse is over 65 and receiving OAS and GIS as a sole source of support, while the other spouse or common law partner is under 65 and receiving no income or benefits. That couple is classified as single for normal government income benefit program purposes. They are relegated to a standard of living well below the poverty line, regardless of how one defines it.

In 1975, the federal government introduced the Allowance in an attempt to meet this problem.

To qualify for the Allowance, an individual must:

- Be between the ages of 60 and 64
- Be the spouse or partner of a person receiving OAS and GIS benefits
- Be a Canadian citizen or legal resident of Canada on the day preceding the approval of the Allowance application.

In addition, the combined yearly income of the applicant and the spouse or partner, or the annual income of the surviving spouse/partner, cannot exceed certain limits. Please note OAS and GIS payments are not included when calculating annual income.

The maximum Allowance payable to a spouse or partner is equal to the combined full OAS pension and the maximum married/common law GIS benefit. The maximum monthly Allowance, which is increased quarterly, was $809.14 for the second quarter of 2003. The Allowance is reduced at the rate of three dollars for every four dollars of other family income until the OAS equivalent decreases to zero. Then, for a couple, both the GIS equivalent portion of the Allowance and the pensioner's GIS are reduced by one dollar for every additional four dollars of the couple's combined monthly income. *Other income* is as defined for the GIS benefit. The Allowance stops when the recipient becomes eligible for OAS benefits at age 65,[6] leaves Canada for more than six months or dies.

Prior to 1984, the payment of the Allowance to the spouse of a GIS recipient aged 60 to 64 would be continued even if the older spouse died. However, if the GIS recipient died prior to this spouse attaining age 60, there would be no Allowance payable. In 1984, the *Old Age Security Act* was changed to allow any surviving spouse or partner who has been a resident of Canada for at least ten years to apply for the Allowance. However, the Allowance paid to a survivor will cease if the survivor remarries or enters into a common law relationship for more than 12 months. For survivors, the GIS equivalent portion of the Allowance is reduced by one dollar for every additional two dollars of monthly income.

Even in the case of the nonworking surviving spouse/partner receiving the Allowance, there is some question as to how well off he or she is with just this benefit. The Allowance benefit paid to a survivor ($893.31 for the second quarter of 2003) is just over 81% of the maximum OAS and GIS benefits payable to a single pensioner, which would still leave that person well below the poverty line for individuals.

PROVINCIAL INCOME SUPPLEMENTS

A number of provinces have recognized the inadequate living conditions of those whose sole or primary means of support is OAS, or GIS and the Allowance. They have put in place provincial income supplement programs to provide an additional cushion for these people. These programs vary widely by province. Generally, minimum acceptable monthly income thresholds for the elderly were established based upon province-by-province policy considerations. These thresholds are then supplemented with an annual stipend where required. This supplement is both means-tested against other income and subject to an annual contribution ceiling. Alberta, British Columbia, Manitoba, Ontario and Saskatchewan each provide a variable supplemental benefit. Nova Scotia, New Brunswick, Newfoundland and Labrador, the Northwest Territories, the Yukon and Nunavut all pay a flat benefit amount.

The provincial income supplements are desirable programs in that they provide additional benefits to those eligible. However, they are criticized for favouring couples when in fact elderly singles have more demonstrable need. Unlike the federal programs, the provincial supplements are not indexed to the cost of living in any way. They remain in place as set amounts until changed through a provincial public policy decision. Such decisions, unfortunately, tend to be heavily dependent upon political developments.

ADMINISTRATION

The basic GIS and complementary Allowance programs are run as adjuncts to the OAS program. The previous chapter's comments with respect to the administration of OAS through Human Resources Development Canada apply to both GIS and the Allowance.

One difference between the OAS benefit and GIS or Allowance benefits is that they are only payable to residents of Canada. Once an individual stops residing in Canada for a period of more than six months, the GIS or Allowance benefit ceases to be payable.[7] This differs from the OAS benefit where in some cases the benefit is payable to former residents. Individuals or couples may reapply for GIS or Allowance benefits after returning to Canada, however. Another important difference that is peculiar to GIS and the Allowance, as mentioned previously, is the necessity to comply with an income test to qualify for the benefits.

At the time of initial application, the spouse must also fill out an accompanying income qualification statement. It is comparable to the one illustrated above for the single applicant. These income qualification statements must be revised and updated yearly.

The income qualification statement is all-inclusive. It indicates that, in the vast majority of cases, people who do qualify for the GIS or Allowance really have no other income from any source. This, in turn, indicates that, in view of the fact these people have no pension income or any sort of savings, there are large numbers of Canadians reaching old age who are not in a position to lead a comfortable life.

ENDNOTES

1. As a result of Bill C-23, the *Old Age Security Act* was amended to extend spousal benefits to same-sex partners who qualify as *common law partners*. As such, what was previously defined as the *Spousal Allowance* is now the Allowance.
2. An individual's income, for the purposes of determining GIS eligibility, includes income such as earnings-related retirement pension payments, foreign pension payments, interest, dividends, rents or wages.
3. Please note that, while the terms *poverty line* and *poverty*

are used by the authors, the Canadian government uses the terms *low income cut-off* and *low income,* respectively.

4. Under the GIS, there are different maximum monthly benefits for the following three categories of individuals who are not single (monthly maximum benefits reflect second quarter 2003 values):

   a. The spouse/partner of a nonpensioner: $542.03

   b. The spouse/partner of a pensioner: $353.06

   c. The spouse/partner of an Allowance recipient: $353.06.

5. The provisions establishing the GIS, and the calculation of benefits payable are set out in Part II of the *Old Age Security Act,* R.S., c. 0-9, s.10-18.

6. The SA provisions are found in Part III of the *Social Security Act, supra,* s.19-26.

7. *Old Age Security Act, supra,* ss. 11(7) for GIS and ss. 19(6) for SA.

Table II-9-I

MAXIMUM ANNUAL GOVERNMENT BENEFITS—APRIL 1, 2003

SINGLE PERSONS

Province	Federal OAS/GIS	Prov. Supp.	Total
Alberta	11,977.32	2,820.00	14,797.32
British Columbia	11,977.32	239.16	12,216.48
Manitoba	11,977.32	446.40	12,423.72
Ontario	11,977.32	996.00	12,973.32
Saskatchewan	11,977.32	1,080.00	13,057.32

COUPLES

Province	Federal OAS/GIS	Prov. Supp.	Total
Alberta	19,419.36	4,200.00	23,619.36
British Columbia	19,419.36	874.56	20,293.92
Manitoba	19,419.36	479.60	19,898.96
Ontario	19,419.36	1,992.00	21,411.36
Saskatchewan	19,419.36	1,740.00	21,159.36

CHAPTER 10

Employment Insurance

by Michael Mazzuca and Christopher May

OVERVIEW

The stated objective of the employment insurance (EI) system is: to assist workers suffering unemployment due to work shortage, sickness, non-occupational accident, maternity, adoption, quarantine and retirement; to upgrade their skills; and to get them back to work. A key component of this is to facilitate the best possible match between unemployed workers and available jobs.

The concept of unemployment insurance dates back to the late 19th century, with its roots in Germany. In Canada, as far back as 1919, the Royal Commission on Industrial Relations recommended a national program of unemployment insurance. The initial federal attempt in 1935 to introduce a national unemployment insurance program was found to be unconstitutional by the Supreme Court of Canada and the Privy Council of Great Britain. The courts reasoned that the division of legislative power as made principally under Sections 91 and 92 of the *British North America Act* conferred responsibility for unemployment insurance on each of the provincial legislatures. Resolution of this problem was achieved in 1940 by amending the *British North America Act* to confer on the federal government exclusive jurisdiction in matters relating to unemployment insurance legislation. Unlike most social welfare measures, unemployment insurance thereby became a federal rather than a provincial government responsibility.

The *Unemployment Insurance Act,* 1971, represented the first major overhaul of the legislation and, since that time, the act has undergone a number of major amendments. In 1977, the *Employment and Immigration Reorganization Act* came into effect. In addition to program changes, it provided for the integration of the Department of Manpower and Immigration and the Unemployment Insurance Commission by creating the Department of Employment and Immigration and the Canada Employment and Immigration Commission.

On January 1, 1996 Canada's new *Employment Insurance (EI) Act* came into force, replacing its forerunners the *Unemployment Insurance Act* and the *National Training Act.* The new EI Act represents a fundamental restructuring of the old unemployment insurance system, including a renewed role for provinces and territories in labour market development. EI now consists of a two-part re-employment system: redesigned income benefits and active re-employment benefits and support measures.

The reorganization of the unemployment system followed the creation of the new Department of Human Resources Development Canada (HRDC) in 1993, the stated purpose of which was to provide a more integrated approach to Canada's national investment in people. HRDC administers programs supporting the income of Canadians and human resources programs linked to the requirements of the national economy and labour market. HRDC's stated mission is to enable Canadians to participate fully in the workplace and in the community.

COVERAGE

Insurable Employment

One of the criteria for coverage under the act is that a person must be employed in insurable employment. *Insurable employment* is defined as:

(a) employment in Canada by one or more employers, under any express or implied contract of service or apprenticeship, written or oral, whether the earnings of the employed person are received from the employer or some other person and whether the earnings are calculated by time or by the piece, or partly by time and partly by the piece, or otherwise;

(b) employment in Canada as described in paragraph (a) by the federal government;

(c) service in the Canadian Forces or in a police force;

(d) employment included by regulations made under subsection (4) or (5); and

(e) employment in Canada of an individual as the sponsor or co-ordinator of an employment benefits project.[1]

Excluded Employment

Employment that is excluded is:

(a) employment of a casual nature other than for the purpose of the employer's trade or business;

(b) employment of a person by a corporation if the person controls more than 40% of the voting shares of the corporation;

(c) employment in Canada by a provincial government;

(d) employment in Canada by the government of a country other than Canada or of any political subdivision of the other country;

(e) employment in Canada by an international organization;

(f) employment in Canada under an exchange program if the employment is not remunerated by an employer that is resident in Canada;

(g) employment that constitutes an exchange of work or services;

(h) employment excluded by regulations made under subsection (6); and

(i) employment if the employer and employee are not dealing with each other at arm's length.[2]

The areas dealing with insurable employment included by regulation and excepted by regulation require expansion. The Canada Employment and Immigration Commission may, with the approval of the Governor in Council, regulate the following for inclusion under insurable employment:

(a) Employment outside Canada or partly outside Canada that would be insurable employment if it were in Canada;

(b) the entire employment of a person who is engaged by one employer partly in insurable employment and partly in other employment;

(c) employment that is not employment under a contract of service if it appears to the Commission that the terms and conditions of service of, and the nature of the work performed by, persons employed in that employment are similar to the terms and conditions of service of, and the nature of the work performed by, persons employed under a contract of service;

(d) employment in Canada by a provincial government if that government waives exclusion and agrees to insure all its employees engaged in that employment;

(e) employment in Canada by the government of a country other than Canada or of any political subdivision of the other country if the employing government consents;

(f) employment in Canada by an international organization if the organization consents; and

(g) the tenure of an office as defined in subsection 2(1) of the Canada Pension Plan.[3]

In addition, the Commission may (subject to certain statutory approvals) include any person who is employed within the definition of *business* in the *Income Tax Act*.

Under the same provision stated for insurable employment, the Commission may exclude the following from insurable employment:

(a) Any employment if it appears to the Commission that because of the laws of a country other than Canada a duplication of contributions or benefits will result;

(b) the entire employment of a person who is engaged by one employer partly in insurable employment and partly in other employment;

(c) any employment if it appears to the Commission that the nature of the work performed by persons employed in that employment is similar to the nature of the work performed by persons employed in employment that is not insurable employment;

(d) the employment of a member of a religious order who has taken a vow of poverty and whose remuneration is paid directly or by the member to the order;

(e) any employment in which persons are employed hardly at all or for nominal remuneration; and

(f) any employment provided under regulations made under section 24 or under employment benefits.[4]

It should be noted that within the act there is a separate set of regulations dealing solely with persons engaged in fishing. It concerns such areas as coverage, determination of the employer, determination and allocation of earnings, payment of premiums, declaration to the buyer, fishing insured weeks and year-round fishermen.

Approximately 95% of all workers in Canada are employed under a contract of service in insurable employment and therefore are protected by employment insurance.

Every person employed in insurable employment must be registered with the Commission. This is administered by assigning a number to all registered persons, and this number becomes their social insurance number (SIN). The Commission also maintains a social register that contains the names of the registered individuals, the names of individuals who have been assigned a SIN under the Canada Pension Plan (CPP) and the names of individuals who have applied for a SIN.

ELIGIBILITY FOR BENEFITS

Prior to 1997, eligibility for income benefits was determined by the number of weeks worked, based on weekly minimum and maximum insured earnings. However, as of January 1997, under the EI system, eligibility for income benefits is based on the number of hours worked rather than weeks. Insurability now counts all hours of work and all earnings, thus, allowing the earnings of those who are only able to locate irregular short-term employment, such as part-time or contract workers, to be counted for EI eligibility. In addition to being employed in insurable employment, a claimant must also have participated in the labour force for a certain number of hours.

As of January 1997, individuals require at least 420 to 700 hours of insured work in the past 52 weeks, or since the start of their last claim—whichever is shorter—to qualify for EI income benefits. The number of hours required depends on the regional rate of unemployment. Claimants from a region where unemployment is 13% and over require 420 hours of work to qualify for benefits. As the rate of unemployment decreases, the required number of hours worked increases, to the point where claimants in a region with an unemployment rate of 6% and under require 700 hours of work before they qualify. These requirements are illustrated in Table II-10-I.

New Entrant and Re-Entrant Eligibility Requirements

New entrants are individuals who have no attachment to the labour force. *Re-entrants* are individuals who have less than 490 hours of insurable employment, benefits, prescribed employment in the labour force or a combination of these during the previous 52 weeks. Both classes of claimants must work a minimum of 910 hours, regardless of the unemployment rate, during their

Table II-10-I

Unemployment Rate in Claimant's Region	Minimum Number of Hours of Work Needed to Qualify
6% and under	700
Over 6% to 7%	665
Over 7% to 8%	630
Over 8% to 9%	595
Over 9% to 10%	560
Over 10% to 11%	525
Over 11% to 12%	490
Over 12% to 13%	455
Over 13%	420

first year of entering or re-entering the labour force before they qualify for income benefits. If they work at least 490 hours in their first year, in the second year they will not be considered new entrants or re-entrants and will qualify for benefits based on the variable entrance rates of 420 to 700 hours. Re-entrants can qualify for *re-active employment benefits* and *support measures* if they were recipients of EI benefits in the past three years, or if they were recipients of maternity or parental benefits in the past five years.

There is an allowance for the extension of the qualifying period where a person proves he or she was not employed in insurable employment because for any week he or she was:

(a) incapable of work because of a prescribed illness, injury, quarantine or pregnancy;
(b) confined in any jail, penitentiary or other similar institution;
(c) receiving assistance under employment benefits; or
(d) receiving payments under provincial law on the basis of having ceased to work because continuing to work would have resulted in danger to the person, her unborn child or a child whom she is breast feeding.[5]

The qualifying period may also be extended as a result of severance payments preventing the person from establishing an interruption of earnings. Under any of these conditions, the qualifying period shall be extended by the sum of any such weeks. In addition, a further extension of the qualifying period may occur. This may happen when a person proves that for any week during any extension of a qualifying period referred to above, he or she was not employed in insurable employment for any of the above reasons; the qualifying period will be extended further by the sum of those weeks. A week during which a person received benefits does not count, and the maximum allowable qualifying period is 104 weeks.

The second criterion needed to qualify for benefits is the more obvious one; the insured person must have had an interruption of earnings from employment.

An interruption of earnings occurs when, following a period of employment, an insured person has a layoff or separation from that employment for a period of seven or more consecutive days during which no work is performed and no earnings (other than statutory holiday pay) are payable.

An interruption of earnings also occurs in the case of a person who stops work by reason of an illness, an injury, or quarantine or the placement with that person of one or more children for adoption purposes. There must also be a reduction of more than 40% in that person's normal weekly insurable earnings.

The EI Regulations include additional information regarding the definition of interruption of earnings in specific instances. These include the special cases of real estate agents and people who work more hours in a workweek than normally worked.

When an insured person who qualifies for benefits makes an initial claim, a benefit period is established. It begins on Sunday of the week in which (a) the interruption of earnings occurs or (b) the initial claim for benefit is made, whichever is later. It is therefore important to make a claim as soon as possible.

As with the qualifying period, the benefit period can be extended where the claimant proves that for any week during the benefit period he or she was not entitled to initial or extended benefit because he or she was:

(a) confined in any jail, penitentiary or other similar institution; or
(b) in receipt of severance or termination pay; or
(c) in receipt of workers' compensation benefits; or
(d) in receipt of payments under a provincial law on the basis of having ceased to work for the reason that continuing to work would have entailed danger to the claimant, the claimant's unborn child or a child whom the claimant is breast feeding.[6]

In these instances, the benefit period shall be extended by the sum of any such weeks. A further extension can occur where a claimant proves that during any extension of a benefit period as described above, he or she was not entitled to initial or extended benefits for the reasons stated above; then the benefit period will be further extended by the sum of any such weeks. The benefit period shall not exceed 104 weeks. However, all claimants must serve a two-week waiting period that begins with a week of unemployment for which benefits would otherwise be payable.

There are instances, however, where a claimant is either disqualified completely from receiving benefits, or disqualified for a temporary period. If a claimant has lost his or her employment by reason of a labour dispute (strike or lockout), he or she is not entitled to receive benefits until (a) the work stoppage ends or (b) he or she becomes engaged elsewhere in insurable employment.

A claimant may be disqualified for a period of between seven and 12 weeks following his or her waiting period for the following reasons.

(a) He or she has refused or has failed to apply for a position in suitable employment that is vacant after becoming aware that situation is vacant or becoming vacant, or if he or she fails to accept such a position offered to him or her;
(b) he or she has failed to carry out any written direction (if reasonable) by an officer of the Commission;
(c) he or she has failed to attend an interview that the Commission directed him or her to attend;
(d) he or she has failed to attend a course of instruction or training to which he or she was referred by the Commission;
(e) he or she has neglected to avail himself or herself of an opportunity for suitable employment.[7]

However, a claimant does not have to accept employment that is deemed by the Commission as unsuitable. This includes employment arising from a labour dispute, employment at his or her usual occupation at a lower rate of earnings, or less favourable conditions, or employment other than his or her usual occupation until a reasonable interval has elapsed. After that, the employment becomes suitable.

As of April 1993, a claimant is completely disqualified from receiving any benefits if the claimant has lost his or her employment by reason of his or her own "misconduct" or if the claimant has voluntarily left his or her employment without just cause. Just cause for leaving one's employment will be found, where having regard to all the circumstances, the claimant had no reasonable alternative to leaving the employment. Specific examples of just cause for leaving one's employment include:

(a) sexual or other harassment;
(b) obligation to accompany a spouse or dependent child to another residence;
(c) discrimination on a prohibited ground of discrimination within the meaning of the *Canadian Human Rights Act;*
(d) working conditions that constitute a danger to health and safety;

(e) obligation to care for a child or a member of the immediate family;

(f) reasonable assurance of another employment in the immediate future;

(g) significant modification of terms and conditions respecting wages or salary;

(h) excessive overtime work or refusal to pay for overtime work;

(i) significant changes in work duties;

(j) antagonistic relations between an employee and a supervisor for which the employee is not primarily responsible;

(k) practices of an employer that are contrary to law;

(l) discrimination with regard to employment because of membership in any association, organization or union of workers; and

(m) undue pressure by an employer on employee to leave their employment.[8]

Employees who voluntarily accept an employer's separation package offered as part of an employer work force reduction process that preserves the employment of co-workers will not have their benefit eligibility penalized. When facing a downsizing, both employers and employees should consult with HRDC to make certain of all conditions that may affect employees.

To recap, EI benefits are payable to an insured person who qualifies to receive such benefits. These benefits are payable when a person is unemployed and available for work. This applies to both income and re-active employment benefits and support measures.

INCOME BENEFITS

Prior to April 1993, the rate of benefit payable to a claimant for a week of unemployment that fell in his or her benefit period was an amount equal to 60% of his or her average weekly insurable earnings in his or her qualifying weeks. Between April 1993 and January 1997, the federal government began reducing the benefit rate and providing supplemental assistance to claimants with low family incomes and dependants. As of January 1997, the benefits rate was set at 55% of a claimant's weekly insurable earnings, up to a maximum of 80% for low-income families eligible for the new *Family Income Supplement*.

The amount of a claimant's weekly benefit cheque will depend on his or her earnings in the last 26 continuous weeks.

A claimant's weekly benefit will be calculated in the following manner:

• HRDC looks at the total earnings a claimant has been paid in the last 26 continuous weeks ending with his or her last day of work.

• HRDC takes into consideration the number of weeks in which a claimant has worked in the last 26 continuous weeks.

• HRDC determines the unemployment rate in the claimant's area and the minimum divisor that applies at that unemployment rate (see Table II-10-II).

• To determine a claimant's average weekly insured earnings, HRDC divides the total earnings in the last 26 continuous weeks by the greater of:

• The number of weeks the claimant has worked in the last 26 continuous weeks or

• The minimum divisor number.

• HRDC then multiplies the result by 55% (or the benefit rate that applies to the claimant) to obtain the weekly benefit to a maximum of $413 per week.

The EI Act permits regular claimants to earn $50 or up to 25% of their weekly benefit rate without those earnings affecting the benefits paid in any week of unemployment. Earnings above this 25% limit are deducted dollar for dollar from the weekly benefit rate. All such earnings must be reported to the EI office.

In the two-week waiting period and currently for illness, maternity or adoption benefits, all earnings are deducted dollar for dollar; that is, the 25% limit does not apply. The 2000 federal budget proposes to change this and allow parents to earn up to 25% of their maternity or parental benefits or $50 before the dollar-for-dollar deduction from weekly benefits applies.

The earnings to be taken into account for the purposes of determining whether an interruption of earnings has occurred and the amount to be deducted from the benefits payable are:

(a) the entire income of a claimant arising out of any employment;

(b) workers' compensation payments other than permanent settlement workers' compensation payments;

(c) the amount of payments a claimant has received or is entitled to receive under a group sickness or disability wage-loss indemnity plan or a paid sick, maternity, adoption leave plan or a specified child care leave plan;

(d) the amount of payments a claimant has received or is entitled to receive from motor vehicle accident insurance provided under a provincial law in respect of the actual or presumed loss of income from employment due to injury if the benefits payable under the EI Act are not taken into account in determining the amount that the claimant receives from such insurance;

(e) the amount of payments a claimant receives or is entitled to receive pursuant to a provincial law in respect of an actual or presumed loss of income from employment, if the benefits payable under the EI Act are not taken

Table II-10-II[11]

NUMBER OF WEEKS CLAIMANTS CAN RECEIVE BENEFITS

Unemployment Rate in Claimant's Region

Number of Hours of Insurable Employment	6% and Under	Over 6% to 7%	Over 7% to 8%	Over 8% to 9%	Over 9% to 10%	Over 10% to 11%	Over 11% to 12%	Over 12% to 13%	Over 13% to 14%	Over 14% to 15%	Over 15% to 16%	Over 16%
420-454									26	28	30	32
455-489								24	26	28	30	32
490-524							23	25	27	29	31	33
525-559						21	23	25	27	29	31	33
560-594					20	22	24	26	28	30	32	34
595-629				18	20	22	24	26	28	30	32	34
630-664			17	19	21	23	25	27	29	31	33	35
665-699		15	17	19	21	23	25	27	29	31	33	35
700-734	14	16	18	20	22	24	26	28	30	32	34	36
735-769	14	16	18	20	22	24	26	28	30	32	34	36
770-804	15	17	19	21	23	25	27	29	31	33	35	37
805-839	15	17	19	21	23	25	27	29	31	33	35	37
840-874	16	18	20	22	24	26	28	30	32	34	36	38
875-909	16	18	20	22	24	26	28	30	32	34	36	38
910-944	17	19	21	23	25	27	29	31	33	35	37	39
945-979	17	19	21	23	25	27	29	31	33	35	37	39
980-1,014	18	20	22	24	26	28	30	32	34	36	38	40
1,015-1,049	18	20	22	24	26	28	30	32	34	36	38	40
1,050-1,084	19	21	23	25	27	29	31	33	35	37	39	41
1,085-1,119	19	21	23	25	27	29	31	33	35	37	39	41
1,120-1,154	20	22	24	26	28	30	32	34	36	38	40	42
1,155-1,189	20	22	24	26	28	30	32	34	36	38	40	42
1,190-1,224	21	23	25	27	29	31	33	35	37	39	41	43
1,225-1,259	21	23	25	27	29	31	33	35	37	39	41	43
1,260-1,294	22	24	26	28	30	32	34	36	38	40	42	44
1,295-1,329	22	24	26	28	30	32	34	36	38	40	42	44
1,330-1,364	23	25	27	29	31	33	35	37	39	41	43	45
1,365-1,399	23	25	27	29	31	33	35	37	39	41	43	45
1,400-1,434	24	26	28	30	32	34	36	38	40	42	44	45
1,435-1,469	25	27	29	31	33	35	37	39	41	43	45	45
1,470-1,504	26	28	30	32	34	36	38	40	42	44	45	45
1,505-1,539	27	29	31	33	35	37	39	41	43	45	45	45
1,540-1,574	28	30	32	34	36	38	40	42	44	45	45	45
1,575-1,609	29	31	33	35	37	39	41	43	45	45	45	45
1,610-1,644	30	32	34	36	38	40	42	44	45	45	45	45
1,645-1,679	31	33	35	37	39	41	43	45	45	45	45	45
1,680-1,714	32	34	36	38	40	42	44	45	45	45	45	45
1,715-1,749	33	35	37	39	41	43	45	45	45	45	45	45
1,750-1,784	34	36	38	40	42	44	45	45	45	45	45	45
1,785-1,819	35	37	39	41	43	45	45	45	45	45	45	45
1,820-	36	38	40	42	44	45	45	45	45	45	45	45

into account in determining the amount that the claimant receives from such insurance; and

(f) the monies paid or payable to a claimant on or after January 5, 1986, on a periodic basis or in a lump sum from a pension.[9]

This last type of earnings has caused much controversy as, prior to the above date, pension income had been excluded from earnings. Indeed, certain kinds of pension income are still excluded. These include the return or refund of a worker's own pension contributions upon separation and a transfer of pension fund contributions into another employer's fund until the worker becomes a pensioner.

The EI Regulation cites a number of specific types of income that are not included as earnings. These include:

- Disability pension or permanent settlement workers' compensation payments (effective January 5, 1986)
- Payments under a sickness or disability wage-loss indemnity plan that is not a group plan
- Relief grants in cash and
- Payments received under a private supplemental unemployment benefit plan where the plan has been approved by the Commission.[10]

The benefit period depends on two variables—the claimant's hours of insurable employment and the regional rate of unemployment applicable to the claimant. The EI Act sets out maximum hours of benefits in accordance with these two variables as set out in Table II-10-II.

Previous Claims History

The EI Act introduces two measures to discourage people from becoming overly reliant on EI. Frequent users of the EI system saw their income benefits rate drop based on a five-year claims history starting June 30, 1996, under the measure known as the "Intensity Rule." Any claims history prior to this date is not factored into the application of these new measures. Those with an annual taxable income over a threshold set under the EI Act are required to repay a portion of those benefits under a measure known as the "Clawback." All income benefits paid out, regardless of whether they have been repaid under the clawback provisions of the EI Act, are used to calculate a claimant's previous claims history. Special benefits (sickness, maternity, parental) are not included in the calculation of claimed benefit weeks, but may need to be repaid.

A repeat claimant who has more than 20 weeks of EI income benefits history during a five-year period will see his or her basic benefit rate decreased by 1%. The rate will be reduced by a further 1% for each additional 20 weeks of claims. The Intensity Rule can only reduce the benefit rate to 50%, maximum reduction of 5%. (See Table II-10-III.)

Table II-10-III

INTENSITY RULE

Weeks, for Which EI Was Paid, That Began As of June 30, 1996 (Over a Five-Year Claim History)	EI Benefit Rate for Duration of Next Claim (% of Average Insurable Earnings), As of January 1997
0 to 20	55%
21 to 40	54%
41 to 60	53%
61 to 80	52%
81 to 100	51%
More than 100	50%

Work Credits

Individuals who earn a partial income while they receive income benefits and earn enough to reduce their EI cheque can earn "work credits" to be applied against the Intensity Rule (a credit is the equivalent of one week or more of an EI claim). The total amount they earn while working during a claim will be converted into weeks of unpaid benefits. Those weeks are then credited against the application of the Intensity Rule for their next claim.

The Clawback of Income Benefits

Once a claimant's taxable income surpasses a certain amount, based on his or her claims history over five years, the benefits are taxed back. For example, if a person has claimed less than 21 weeks of either regular or special benefits in the last five years, up to 30% of the benefits will have to be repaid if the claimant's taxable income surpasses $48,750. If the number of weeks of benefits exceeds 21 weeks, the clawback begins on a taxable income over $39,000 up to 50% of benefits. Thereafter, the maximum percentage of benefits to be repaid increases by 10% for each additional 20 weeks of claimed benefits. Where benefits were paid out for more than 120 weeks over five years, the claimant is required to repay 100% of the benefits exceeding $39,000 in taxable income. Any benefits that are repaid as a result of the clawback are still considered as paid for purposes of applying the Intensity Rule.

SPECIAL BENEFITS

At present, special benefits are payable to claimants who suffer a loss of employment income by reason of sickness, pregnancy or parental responsibility, to care for a newborn or adopted child, if they have more than 700 or more hours (20 weeks) of insurable employment in their qualifying period. Unlike regular income benefits, any income earned while collecting special benefits is deducted dollar for dollar from the claimant's weekly cheque. A claimant cannot claim more than 30 weeks of combined sickness, maternity and parental benefits in a period. EI also provides a special income supplement, known as the Family Income Supplement, to claimants with a low family income. The 2000 federal budget has proposed lowering the entrance requirements from 700 to 600 insurable work hours for sickness, maternity and parental benefits. Claimants would be eligible for benefits with as little as 12 hours a week of work over the course of a year.

Maternity Benefits

Maternity benefits provide for a maximum of 15 weeks of benefits for a claimant who is pregnant. Benefits can be claimed between the earlier of eight weeks before expected confinement and actual confinement and 17 weeks after the later of actual or expected confinement. If the child is confined to the hospital, the 17-week limit can be extended for every week the child is hospitalized up to 52 weeks.

Parental Benefits

A claimant is eligible for ten weeks of parental benefits to care for a newborn or adopted child, commencing when the newborn child arrives at home, or the adopted child is placed in the claimant's home, and ending 52 weeks later. Parental benefits may be increased to 15 weeks if the claimant's child suffers from a physical, psychological or emotional condition that requires extended care. The weeks of parental benefit can be claimed by either parent or shared between them. If the parents choose to share the parental benefit, they both must serve the standard two-week benefit waiting period.

The 2000 federal budget has proposed increasing the number of weeks of parental leave by 25 weeks, from ten to 35 weeks, doubling the combined maternity and parental leave. Also, if the parents choose to share the parental leave, once one parent serves the two-week waiting period, it is waived for the other parent. The enriched benefits are proposed to take effect for claimants who have a child born or adopted on or after December 31, 2000.

Sickness Benefits

Claimants are eligible for 15 weeks of sickness benefits if they fall sick, are injured or are quarantined and unable to work, and the claim is supported by a medical certificate. Claimants may qualify for these benefits with less than the currently required 700 hours of work force attachment if they fall ill while on an EI claim unrelated to illness. Further, sickness benefits may be backdated to the beginning of the illness, injury or quarantine if claimants were unable to immediately register the claim due to the nature of the illness.

The Family Income Supplement

Beginning in January 1997, claimants with children whose family income is below $25,291 and who receive the Canada Child Tax Benefit (CCTB) began receiving a supplement to their EI income benefits of up to 65% of their benefit rate. The supplement was phased in over the period from 1997 to 2000 with yearly 5% increases in the maximum benefit rate. As of January 2000, the maximum rate will be as high as 80%.

The supplement is based on the family income, number and age of the children and is automatically added to the claimant's EI benefit cheque. The amount increases with the number of children up to the maximum rate. For families with incomes above $20,291, the amount of the supplement is proportionately reduced. Eligible claimants are exempted from the Intensity Rule. The Family Income Supplement benefit amounts are set out in Table II-10-IV.

PREMIUMS

Rates

Under EI, premiums payable by employees and employers are based on the annual insurable earnings of the employees. The premium rate is set by the EI Commission toward the end of each year. The employee premium for 2000 is $2.40 for each $100 of weekly insurable earnings. As set out in the legislation, employers pay 1.4% of the employee rate, or $3.36 per $100 of employee earnings. The annual Maximum Insurable Earnings has been set at $39,000 for the years 1997 to 2000; the amount for subsequent years will be set by the EI Commission on the advice of the Minister of Human Resources Development and the Minister of Finance.

Collecting Premiums

Premiums are now paid by all employees and all employers on every dollar that is earned up to the annual Maximum Insurable Earnings, currently set at $39,000, no matter whether the earnings are gained through part-time, full-time or contract work. It is the responsibility of the employer to deduct the employee's premium payable and remit it together with the employer's premium. With the move to an hours-based system,

TABLE II-10-IV

FAMILY INCOME SUPPLEMENT

Family Income Range

Number of Children	<$20,921	$20,921 to $21,250	$21,251 to $21,500	$21,501 to $21,750	$21,751 to $22,000	$22,001 to $22,250	$22,251 to $22,500	$22,501 to $22,750	$22,751 to $23,000	$23,001 to $23,250	$23,251 to $23,500
1	31.30	31.25	28.50	26.45	24.45	22.55	20.70	18.90	17.15	15.45	13.80
2	58.70	58.60	53.60	49.90	46.25	42.70	39.30	35.95	32.70	29.55	26.50
3	86.10	86.00	78.80	73.45	68.20	63.15	58.15	53.30	48.60	44.00	39.55
Top-Up for each additional child	27.45	27.40	25.60	24.25	22.85	21.50	20.15	18.75	17.40	16.00	14.65
Age supplement for each child under 7 years old	4.15	4.10	3.85	3.65	3.45	3.25	3.05	2.80	2.60	2.40	2.20

Family Income Range

Number of Children	$23,501 to $23,750	$23,751 to $24,000	$24,001 to $24,250	$24,251 to $24,500	$24,501 to $24,750	$24,751 to $25,000	$25,001 to $25,250	$25,251 to $25,500	$25,501 to $25,750	$25,751 to $25,920
1	12.25	10.70	9.25	7.85	6.55	5.25	4.00	2.85	1.75	0.70
2	23.55	20.70	17.95	15.30	12.75	10.25	7.90	5.65	3.45	1.40
3	35.25	31.05	26.95	23.05	19.20	15.55	12.00	8.55	5.25	2.10
Top-Up for each additional child	13.30	11.90	10.55	9.15	7.80	6.45	5.05	3.70	2.30	0.95
Age supplement for each child under 7 years old	2.00	1.80	1.60	1.40	1.20	1.00	0.75	0.55	0.35	0.15

there is no longer a weekly minimum or maximum deduction level. Deductions stop once a worker has reached $39,000 in earnings with one employer. If an employee leaves one employer to start work with another during the year, the new employer also has to deduct EI premiums. This is the case even if the employee has paid the maximum premium amount during the previous employment. Any overpayment of EI premiums by an employee is refunded via the income tax system. There is no refund for employers in such circumstances.

Employers that remit late are subject to penalties. These remittances must be sent to the Receiver General and be accompanied by the proper information return. An employer that fails to deduct and remit an amount is liable for the whole amount. Directors of the corporation may also be liable.

Premium Relief

Employers are also permitted to pay reduced premiums when employees are covered under a private employment insurance approved wage-loss indemnity plan for illness or maternity.

Individuals earning $2,000 or less in a given year are entitled to a refund of the entire amount of EI premiums that they paid during that year. The refund is provided via the income tax system. Also, the earnings of the individual remain insurable even if a refund is provided.

ACTIVE RE-EMPLOYMENT BENEFITS AND SUPPORT MEASURES

The stated purpose of the active re-employment benefits is to help those who are prepared to take an active part in securing or retaining employment and who are likely to find or keep a job. These benefits are designed to help people facing barriers to employment improve their skills and create new opportunities for returning to work.

Part II of the EI Act requires the federal government to work together with the provinces and territories in providing active re-employment benefits and support measures. In May 1996 the government began a process of transferring greater responsibility to the provinces in the area of labour market development. This would allow provinces to manage employment measures such as wage subsidies, income supplements, support for self-employment, partnerships for job creation, and the possibility of skills loans and grants. To date, the only province not to have signed a transfer agreement or to have at least entered into tentative transfer agreement is Ontario.

To be eligible for active re-employment benefits, you must:

- Be receiving income benefits or
- Have received income benefits that ended in the past three years or
- Have received maternity or parental benefits in a period that began within the past five years.[12]

Under the Federal-Provincial/Territorial Labour Market Development Agreements, the provinces and territories can implement the following active re-employment support measures.

- **Targeted Wage Subsidies:** HRDC will contribute part of a worker's wages to encourage an employer to hire and provide claimants with on-the-job experience that will assist them in return to the work force. Wage subsidies are designed to assist people who have been unemployed for a long time or face special barriers to employment.
- **Self-Employment:** Claimants may qualify for financial support, planning assistance and ongoing support to start their own business and get it up and running.
- **Job Creation Partnerships:** Claimants may qualify to work on special projects, developed in partnership with the provinces, the private sector, labour and community groups, which will help a claimant regain an attachment to the work force and also help to develop the local economy, improving future job prospects.
- **Targeted Earnings Supplements:** If a job is available but it pays less than the one a claimant lost before he or she began collecting income benefits, the claimant may qualify for a "top-up" of the wages at the new job for a short time. The earnings supplement is designed to draw claimants off income benefits and back to work, where they have a better chance of learning new skills and moving on to better paying jobs.

- **Skills Loans and Grants:** Claimants who require training to upgrade their skills may be eligible for loans or grants to help with course fees and living expenses.

National Employment Service

The EI Act also includes regulations dealing with the National Employment Service. This nonincome-related employment support incorporates the labour market as an integral part of a program for the achievement and maintenance of the highest possible level of employment. It is available free of charge to all employable workers whether insurable or not, or whether they are claiming benefits or not. Automated systems will provide labour market information and help match workers and employers. Individuals may also be referred to training opportunities or services available in the community.

PENALTIES FOR FRAUD

Measures to combat fraud in the employment insurance system have been increased under the new EI Act.

Fraud or intentional deception includes claimants knowingly failing to declare work-related earnings, and employers knowingly issuing false records of employment.

As of January 5, 1997 claimants who commit fraud will face stiffer eligibility rules on future claims based on their history of fraud since June 30, 1996.

For offences under $1,000, claimants will be required to work 25% more than the minimum entrance requirement to qualify, increasing from 420-700 hours to 525-875 hours.

For offences between $1,000-$4,999, entrance requirements will increase by 50%, rising to 630-1,050 hours.

For offences over $5,000, entrance requirements will increase by 75%, rising to 735-1,225 hours.

For repeat offenders, regardless of severity, entrance requirements will double, increasing to 840-1,400 hours.

Employers that engage in fraud also face higher fines. An employer may be penalized up to $12,000 for each offence. In the case of employer/employee collusion to commit fraud, the employer's penalty may equal the full value of the fraud. If for some reason a company cannot pay its fines, corporate directors may be held liable if they fail to exercise due diligence.

APPEALS

The EI Act establishes a three-tiered system to provide for reconsideration of decisions affecting application for employment insurance benefits.

The Employment Insurance Agent

Upon presentation of a claim for adjudication, the decision of whether or not a benefit is payable is made by insurance agents.

If a benefit is denied, the claimant is notified by the agent and advised that he or she is entitled to appeal to a Board of Referees within 30 days from receipt of the original decision. Notification of appeal requires the agent to review the case to determine whether the original decision should stand, be amended or be rescinded. If the agent does not alter the original decision or it is simply modified, the case is submitted to the local Board of Referees. If the agent reverses his or her original decision and allows the claim, no further action is required.

The Board of Referees

Boards of Referees are appointed bodies that exist and function independently of the Canada Employment and Immigration Commission. A Board is comprised of three members. The chairperson is appointed by the Governor in Council with the members being drawn from union and employer association recommendations and appointed by the Commission. Determination of the appeal is conducted in an orderly but informal manner.

The Umpire

Section 80 of the act provides any claimant, employer, association of which the claimant or employer is a member such as a trade union, or the Commission, a limited right of appeal to the umpire from a decision of the Board of Referees

The appeal is required to be filed within 60 days of receiving written notice of the Board of Referees' decision.

The umpire is a judge of the Trial Division of the Federal Court of Canada. The umpire may decide any questions of law or fact that are necessary for the disposition of the appeal. The umpire has the authority to dismiss the appeal, refer the matter back to the Board for rehearing or rescind or vary the decision of the Board in part or in whole.

The decision of the umpire is final and is not subject to appeal or review by any court except in accordance with the Federal Court Act, which does provide for limited review by the Federal Court of Appeal.

CONCLUSION

Employment insurance has become an increasingly significant and integral part of the Canadian income protection system. With the exception of Old Age Security, Employment Insurance has consistently paid out more in annual benefits at all levels of government than any other program.

Fifty years after its inception, a number of issues continue to affect the program. These include:

- The conflicts and implications arising from the interactions between insurance principles and considerations of need and income transfer
- The program's influence on the labour market and economy as a whole and
- Specific design issues like insurability, admission requirements, disqualification provisions, regionalization, seasonal coverage, and terms and conditions relating to illness, maternity and related matters.

ENDNOTES

1. *Employment Insurance Act,* S.C. 1996, c. 23, ss. 5(1).
2. *Ibid.,* ss. 5(2).
3. *Ibid.,* ss. 5(4).
4. *Ibid.,* ss. 5(6).
5. *Ibid.,* ss. 8(2).
6. *Ibid.,* ss. 10(10).
7. *Ibid.,* ss. 27(1).
8. *Ibid.,* ss. 29(c).
9. *Employment Insurance Regulation,* SOR/96-332, ss. 35(2).
10. *Ibid.,* ss. 35(7).
11. *Employment Insurance Act, supra,* ss. 12(2) and Schedule I.
12. *Ibid.,* s. 58.

APPENDIX II—10-A

A Quick Reference Summary
of Government Benefit Programs

by Leslie Steeves, Karen DeBortoli and Peter Miodonski

The Canada Pension Plan and the Quebec Pension Plan

The Canada and Quebec Pension Plans (CPP and QPP) are contributory, earnings-related social insurance programs that provide benefits to contributors and their families against loss of income due to retirement, disability and death. All benefit payments are taxable and adjusted yearly in response to changes in the Consumer Price Index (CPI), with the exception of the death benefit, which is not indexed.

Almost all workers in Canada, age 18 to 70, who earn more than the Year's Basic Exemption (YBE) are covered by one of the Plans. Contributions are required on the portion of a worker's annual earnings that are above the YBE and up to the Year's Maximum Pensionable Earnings (YMPE). The YBE is $3,500 and the YMPE is $39,900 for 2003, and both numbers are indexed annually. In 2003, employed workers earning more than the YBE make contributions at the rate of 4.95% of their maximum contributory earnings (the difference between the YBE and the YMPE) to a maximum of $1,801.80. Employers match this amount. For self-employed workers, the contribution rate is 9.90% of contributory earnings to a maximum of $3,603.60 in 2003.

Employees are eligible for a full retirement pension at age 65. While a worker can retire between the ages of 60 and 64, his or her pension will be reduced by 0.5% for each month prior to his or her 65th birthday. If a worker elects to postpone his or her retirement, the pension will be increased by 0.5% for each month after his or her 65th birthday, up to retirement or his or her 70th birthday. The maximum CPP/QPP pension equals 25% of his or her average monthly adjusted pensionable earnings (up to the YMPE) for the last five years of employment. In 2003, the maximum monthly CPP/QPP benefit is $801.25.

The Federal Old Age Security Program

The Old Age Security (OAS) pension is a monthly benefit payable regardless of income to persons who are age 65 and over and meet certain residency requirements. Low-income pensioners who qualify under an income test are eligible for an additional amount called the Guaranteed Income Supplement (GIS). The amount of GIS benefit depends on level of income. A pensioner's spouse or common law partner aged 60 to 65 who meets residency requirements is eligible for an Allowance if the combined income of the couple also meets an income test. Both the OAS and GIS benefits are indexed quarterly on the basis of changes in the CPI. The OAS program is funded from general tax revenue; it is not a contributory program.

For the first quarter of 2003, the basic OAS pension is $453.36. The requirement to repay part of the OAS pension begins when an individual's net income exceeds $57,879, and no OAS pension is payable to individuals earning $94,148 or above in 2003. The OAS basic pension, the GIS and the Allowance are indexed quarterly. The OAS pension is taxable, while the GIS and the Allowance are not.

Guaranteed Annual Income Plans

Eight provincial governments and the Yukon Territory, the Northwest Territories and Nunavut have established income-tested guaranteed annual income plans to provide basic income in addition to that available under the federal OAS program. They provide the difference between the maximum income under the federal OAS program and a somewhat higher income level set by each jurisdiction.

The Employment Insurance Program

The Employment Insurance Program is administered by Human Resources Development Canada. It provides unemployment, sickness and maternity benefits. Most of the labour force working between 420 and 700 hours per year will be covered by the program. Employers are required to deduct premiums on behalf of their employees who work in insurable employment. The annual rate of premium payable by an employee is calculated as a percentage of his or her insurable earnings for that year. The employer's annual contributions, unless he or she qualifies for a rate reduction, are calculated at 1.4 times the employee's contributions for that year.

Workers' Compensation Programs

Workers' compensation programs in each of the provinces and territories provide compensation for a worker in a covered industry or for his or her survivors when the worker has been injured or killed on the job. Wage loss, medical, hospital, rehabilitation costs, disability pensions, and survivor benefits are paid out of an accident or injury fund. Only employers pay into the fund, premiums being assessed on the basis of industrial (risk) classification and claims experience. While all industrial occupations are included under the provincial programs, many other occupations are also covered, if not automatically, then at an employer's request. A workers' compensation board administers the program in each province and territory, collecting premiums, assessing claims, paying compensation, and directing rehabilitation programs.

Provincial Hospital and Medical Plans

Hospital plans cover standard ward accommodation, the use of hospital facilities and the cost of drugs administered in hospital. Medical plans pay the cost of medically required services of approved practitioners. Eye examinations are covered for some segment of the population under certain conditions in all provinces as well as in the Yukon Territory. All the plans cover certain specified oral surgery procedures performed in approved institutions. Provisions for other dental care and for the cost of prescribed drugs vary from plan to plan.

There are no direct premiums or payroll tax for coverage in New Brunswick, Nova Scotia, Prince Edward Island, Saskatchewan, the Northwest Territories, the Yukon Territory and Nunavut. Provinces requiring premiums (that is, Alberta and British Columbia) reduce or waive them for low-income residents. In Quebec, Manitoba, Ontario, Newfoundland and Labrador, employers pay a payroll tax.

- In Quebec, the annual rate varies depending on the employer's total payroll. Since 2001, the rate ranges from 2.70%, for organizations with a total payroll of $1 million or less, to 4.26%, for organizations with a total payroll in excess of $5 million.
- In Manitoba, employers with gross annual payrolls of less than $1 million are exempt from payroll tax. Employers with gross annual payrolls of between $1 and $2 million are taxed at a rate of 4.3% for the amount exceeding $1 million. For gross annual payrolls in excess of $2 million, the rate is 2.15% of monthly remuneration.
- In Ontario, the first $400,000 of the payroll of "eligible employers" is exempt from Employer Health Tax (EHT). EHT is payable at 1.95% on payrolls of $400,000 or more.
- In Newfoundland and Labrador, employers with gross annual payrolls in excess of $500,000 pay a Health and Post-Secondary Education Tax of 2% on their payroll in excess of $500,000 per year (1% in the fishery, forestry and agriculture industries).

CHAPTER 1

Plan Design and Administration

by Pui-Ying Chan

The principle of insurance is simply the idea of sharing risk. There are many acknowledged risks in life that everyone faces. Being severely injured or killed accidentally is the most obvious; falling ill for a prolonged period is another. The cost of such a disaster to an individual is, at best, hard to handle and, at worst, can be ruinous.

However, though everyone faces the risk, not everyone endures the hardship. So, if the risk is shared, if everyone pays regular small amounts to a pool, there is enough in the pool to pay the costs of those who do have to cope with disaster.

This basic principle of insurance was first launched as a business enterprise in England, probably as early as 1563. About 200 years later (1757), a petition to the House of Commons at Westminster requested the creation of what is generally acknowledged to be the first modern life insurance company.

Today, in both group and individual insurance, people pay an institution to share a particular risk. For individuals, the arrangement is between them and the insurer; in group insurance, the risk is shared between members of the group and the insurer.

By far the majority of group insurance plans cover employees of a single employer. There are five fundamental principles applicable to such groups:

1. All insured employees must be working regularly.
2. Employees do not unilaterally set the amount of their coverage.
3. If employees contribute, it must be through payroll deduction.
4. Except in special circumstances, the employer must contribute.
5. The number of insured employees must be large enough to spread the risk satisfactorily. The number of people covered is less important to the insurer than the proportion of eligible employees who choose to participate.

Although group insurance plans provide coverage for individuals, the policy is issued to an employer or board of trustees of a multi-employer plan. Insured people are not named but defined as classes of eligible employees.

Group insurance plans help those in difficulty in two ways: usual insurance protection for specific events and general budgeting assistance to cope with expenses.

Common insurance protection programs include group life insurance, accidental death and dismemberment insurance, short-term disability insurance, long-term disability insurance, extended health care insurance, and dental insurance.

These plans are in addition to government-sponsored health and welfare plans. They include federally administered plans like employment insurance and the Canada/Quebec Pension Plans (CPP/QPP), and health care and workers' compensation plans, which are generally provincially administered. Federal and provincial government plans are described in detail in Section II.

An effective group benefits plan meets four essential needs:

1. It provides the best level of benefits suited to the needs of employees.
2. It requires contributions that are acceptable to employer and employees alike.
3. It offers benefits that are easily communicated and readily understood.
4. It is easy and inexpensive to administer.

In all group programs, administration involves the following major functions:

1. Collecting and monitoring contributions from both the employee and the employer
2. Regularly depositing contributions with a trustee (if a multi-employer plan)
3. Paying insurance premiums to the insurance company
4. For each participant, maintaining records of dates and amounts of premiums and benefits paid
5. Monitoring the eligibility of employees
6. Verifying claims and paying benefits.

TYPES OF GROUP PLANS

While plan sponsors do not need to include all benefits in their group plans, here is what should be considered in each one.

Group Life

Plan sponsors face four key administrative decisions:

1. Whether to offer all employees the same amount of coverage or vary the amounts according to job categories
2. Whether coverage will be defined as specific dollar amounts or as a multiple of salary
3. Whether to provide optional coverage in addition to basic coverage
4. Whether to contribute all required premiums or share the cost with employees.

In multi-employer programs, the benefit level is usually the same for all eligible employees, as a uniform contribution rate is used to finance the benefits.

Group Accidental Death and Dismemberment

Plan sponsors generally provide this benefit with the same terms and conditions they offer with group life. However, accidental death and dismemberment (AD&D) coverage, and in what amount, may be optional.

Group/Occupational/Travel Accident Coverage

In single employer plans, sponsors often provide additional accident coverage for employees who travel on company business. In certain instances, coverage is extended to 24 hours a day so that all accidents are covered.

Group Short-Term Disability

Plan sponsors must consider whether they want to provide a short-term insured disability plan, a self-administered sick leave program, or an insured or self-insured weekly indemnity plan. Plan sponsors must also decide how long an employee must wait before benefits

are payable, how long benefits will continue and how much the benefit will be. They must also decide whether to coordinate their plan with the government-run employment insurance (EI) program. If the plan provides benefits equal to or better than the EI program, the employer can register for EI premium reduction. If so, the employer's plan must conform to EI criteria.

Group Extended Health Care Benefits

Under this benefit, plan sponsors face three key decisions: what is to be covered, how much the benefit will be and the amount of the deductible, if any.

In determining the list of available services, most insurance companies are flexible, particularly for larger employee groups. Indeed, the larger the group, the greater the flexibility. The normal hospital benefit common to most insurers' lists is the difference between ward and semi-private room and board, often without deductible or co-insurance. Other coverages vary from plan to plan but will generally include the cost of prescription drugs and out-of-country medical expenses.

Group Vision Care Benefits

This is generally regarded as a "plan enrichment" that may not always be included in an initial benefit program. If it is included, the employer or board of trustees must decide what level of benefit to offer for eyeglasses and contact lenses and how often these can be replaced.

Group Dental Benefits

Dental costs can be expensive to employees, so this benefit is always well received and is becoming increasingly common.

Dental benefits generally cover three levels of treatment: basic, major restorative treatment and orthodontics. Plan sponsors must decide on the level of treatments, the amount of the deductible and the level of co-insurance (including whether to meet current or earlier dental association fee schedules), and the maximum benefit payable. These benefits are usually provided as an indemnity plan, which reimburses part or all of the expenses after they have been incurred.

Group Long-Term Disability

The elimination period before long-term disability insurance benefits start usually dovetails with coverage provided by a short-term disability plan, sick leave program or weekly indemnity plan. Plan sponsors without one of these plans will generally dovetail the elimination period with the employment insurance sickness benefit or simply set it at, say, six months.

Benefit levels usually range from 50-66⅔% of pre-disability earnings, but sometimes are as high as 75%.

Long-term disability benefits are usually payable

until recovery, age 65 or the normal retirement age in the pension plan. Although five- and ten-year benefit period plans are available, they are not traditional *long-term* plans.

Contributory or Not?

A key element in designing group insurance plans, particularly single employer plans, is deciding whether or not employees will contribute towards the cost of the plan. With employee contributions, a higher level of benefits may be made available than the employer could provide on its own. On the other hand, a noncontributory plan is usually simpler to administer because all employees are covered and there are no payroll deductions.

If employee contributions are to be made, how much the contributions will be, and on what basis, will need to be decided. Contributions could be a flat dollar amount, a percentage of the plan costs or a percentage of the employee's salary. The contribution basis can also be varied by benefit.

There are also tax considerations that may impact the contribution basis. Benefits may be taxed on the basis of premiums paid and on the basis of benefits paid. For example, federal income tax is payable by an employee on employer-paid life insurance premiums. Employer-paid premiums for disability benefits are not federally taxed, but benefit payments collected under these benefits are. Therefore, varying employee contributions by type of benefit can be used to maximize tax advantages.

Traditionally, regular employee contributions are not made under multi-employer benefit plans. For these plans, the employer's contribution level is often set at the bargaining table and is included in the collective agreement.

For both single employer and multi-employer plans, the premiums paid or contributions made for benefits are a deductible business expense to the employer.

In this chapter, we will deal with group life insurance, accidental death and dismemberment insurance, short-term disability insurance (often called *weekly indemnity*), long-term disability insurance, dental plans and extended health care.

GROUP LIFE INSURANCE

Group life insurance plans are almost always term insurance. In the past, insurers have tried to market group permanent (or *whole*) life policies with limited success. Their existence today is rare; they are not a significant factor in the marketplace.

Group term insurance is generally a yearly renewable policy that pays the beneficiary a lump-sum benefit in the event of the employee's death for any rea-

son while insured. Premium rates are lower than individual premiums for the same coverage at the same age, because of savings in marketing and administration. Rates are average rates, based on the average age of the group. In a growing company or industry, they generally remain stable throughout the life of the policy as new, younger members replace retiring members and offset the aging of continuing members.

Most group policies contain a *disability waiver* that provides a continuation of coverage, with no further premium payments, for employees who become totally disabled while insured. However, coverage will not increase beyond the level in force at the time of disability.

Some plans now include a living death benefit, which provides terminally ill employees with payments during the last period of their life (typically, one year). This is intended to help the employees pay for increased health expenses that may arise due to their terminal illness and that they may not otherwise be able to afford. This provision provides employees with income under these circumstances but it also reduces, and may eliminate, the death benefit.

All group term insurance policies must contain a conversion clause by virtue of guidelines administered by the Canadian Life and Health Insurance Association (CLHIA). This clause allows a terminating employee to convert the group coverage to individual coverage without proof of insurability provided it is done within 31 days of termination of insurance coverage. Although premiums for individual coverage may be substantially higher than group premiums, often it is a useful way for employees, who might otherwise not qualify for coverage, to buy insurance.

Amount of Coverage

The amount of coverage is generally determined based on the following five bases.

A *flat dollar amount.* All employees are covered for the same amount. This kind of coverage is most common in multi-employer plans, due in part to the fact that the covered employees' earnings levels can vary throughout the coverage period.

Earnings-related amounts. Many plans express the amount of coverage as a multiple of earnings, commonly equal to one year's earnings. Other plans provide two or three times annual earnings.

Classified amounts. Under some plans, amounts of coverage may vary by position or occupation. For instance, coverage levels may vary for executives, salaried and hourly employees.

Layered optional coverage. Plans that include additional optional coverage are now common, particularly for single employer plans. With this basis, the employer typically pays all or nearly all of the cost of basic coverage (such as one year's earnings), allowing employees to add further fixed amounts (or layers) at their own expense. They are usually rated according to age, sex and whether or not the insured is a smoker.

Flat dollar optional coverage. This basis is similar to the layered option coverage except that participants buy a flat dollar amount of additional coverage, unrelated to earnings levels.

GROUP LIFE FOR OTHER THAN ACTIVE EMPLOYEES

Retired Employees

For many years, group life insurance coverage ended when employees retired. But, at retirement, some employees cannot afford to buy individual life insurance because premiums are high and income is lower.

Recognizing this problem, many plans now continue some coverage into retirement. Compared with active employees, the coverage levels may seem low, as they often run between $5,000 and $10,000. Frequently, the employer or health and welfare trust fund assumes the full cost. If the employee is asked to contribute, it is only a small part of the full cost.

In some plans, coverage may be as much as 50% of pre-retirement coverage, with the amount decreasing in steps until it reaches some minimum amount. Continuation of coverage on this basis can substantially increase the overall cost of a group insurance plan.

Dependants

Some plans include dependent life coverage, in amounts ranging from $3,000/spouse, $1,000/child to $10,000/spouse, $5,000/child. Some plans include this coverage on an optional basis, where the employee would pay the premium costs. Under these circumstances, the coverage levels available are usually higher.

ACCIDENTAL DEATH AND DISMEMBERMENT

Accidental death and dismemberment (AD&D) benefits provide coverage only due to accidental circumstances. Traditionally, this benefit provided payments for losses such as accidental death, or accidental dismemberment of a limb, or accidental loss of vision.

In recent years, covered losses have been expanded and now commonly provide payments for paralysis due to an accident. They also often provide reimbursement of other expenses incurred due to an accident, such as paying to transport a body home when an accidental death occurred away from home or to provide some education expenses for dependent children of someone who was accidentally killed.

Most commonly, AD&D benefits now provide 24-hour coverage, including work-related injuries. Some plans may provide only non-occupational coverage to employees who are covered for work-related injuries by workers' compensation benefits.

Since coverage is provided for accidents only, the premiums charged for this benefit are generally not sensitive to the age and sex of the covered group. Typically, one flat rate per $1,000 of benefit is charged, although the rate can be affected by the occupations of the covered individuals when 24-hour coverage is provided.

SHORT-TERM DISABILITY

Short-term disability, or weekly indemnity, pays a weekly benefit when an employee is off either for a relatively short period of time or during the initial stages of a major illness or permanent disability. In a single employer plan, the benefit payment period is often governed by the employee's length of service. Recently hired employees may be provided payments for a shorter period than long-service employees. In any event, the period is capped, typically at six months, but sometimes up to a year.

The benefit to be paid is a proportion of salary, usually at a higher level than long-term disability benefits. It may range between 50% and 75% of salary. Employers that provide salary continuance plans or self-insure the short-term disability sometimes provide as much as 100% of salary for long-service employees.

In a multi-employer plan, the level of weekly indemnity benefit is generally uniform for all employees. It usually begins immediately if disability is due to an accident. If the absence is due to illness, the benefit begins three to seven days afterwards. Typical payment periods for these benefits range from 15 weeks to 52 weeks.

If disability benefits are paid while the employee is eligible to receive sickness and accident benefits from EI, the EI benefit payments will be reduced dollar for dollar by the amount received. For this reason, many disability plans may pay benefits for the first two weeks of disability, stop payments during the period covered by EI and then resume payments after EI has expired.

LONG-TERM DISABILITY

Long-term disability usually commences when short-term disability expires. Benefits may be in the form of a flat monthly benefit but most frequently are a proportion of salary. The proportion of salary is often lower than the proportion for short-term disability. This is because disabled employees are more able to make adjustments to their living expenses when they know it is for the long term than they can on a short-term basis. Some insurers also limit the percentage of income available to ensure that there is a greater incentive for the employee to return to work, when possible.

Long-term disability benefits are paid monthly rather than weekly, for as long as the employee is disabled and usually up until age 65. The definition of *totally disabled* may change after an initial benefit period, generally, two or five years. For example, in the first two years of disability, employees would be considered totally disabled if they could not perform their own occupation, and after two years they would need to be unable to perform any occupation to still be considered totally disabled.

Long-term disability plans are commonly integrated with benefits from the CPP/QPP, either by direct offset or by limiting the combined benefits to a set proportion of regular earnings—say, 75%. If it is a direct offset plan, then long-term disability payments are reduced dollar for dollar by the amount of CPP/QPP disability payments. If it is an all source limit plan, then long-term disability payments are only reduced once the combined benefit payments reach the set limit, such as 75% of pre-disability earnings.

Long-term disability plans may cover non-occupational disability or, more frequently, disability from any cause. In the latter case, workers' compensation will probably be paid, if the disability results from an occupational injury or illness. Under this circumstance, most long-term disability plans would reduce their payments by the amount of workers' compensation benefits received.

Another consideration with long-term disability benefit design is the financing basis, due to the tax implications. If the employer pays any portion of the long-term disability premium, then the benefit payments received by an employee are taxed. If the employee pays all of the premiums, then benefit payments received are non-taxable. (Although this is also true for short-term disability benefits, the implications are given more consideration with long-term disability because these benefits are paid for such a long period of time.)

This means that employees who receive non-taxable benefit payments actually retain a higher proportion of their pre-disability earnings than employees who will be subject to taxes. Therefore, the tax implications affect the replacement level of benefits provided.

All of the above factors are key considerations in long-term disability benefit design. Since this benefit is almost always provided through insurance, there are limitations and underwriting rules that are often required by insurance carriers and can vary between carriers.

SUPPLEMENTAL UNEMPLOYMENT BENEFIT PLANS

The *Employment Insurance Act* also provides benefits for employees who are laid off. Many collective agreements in industries such as automobile, construction or steel, include supplemental unemployment benefit plans (known as SUBs) to protect workers from seasonal layoffs. They pay a benefit, usually weekly, in addition to the regular EI benefits.

A SUB plan can also be used to supplement the EI maternity benefits. So long as the plan meets the federal regulations, any benefits paid will not offset the EI maternity benefits. (If the plan is not qualified, the payment will simply serve to reduce EI maternity benefits.)

HEALTH AND HOSPITAL PLANS

With the introduction of medicare during the 1960s, much of the regular hospital, surgical and medical coverage under private group insurance plans became irrelevant. However, the demand grew for coverage of expenditures for supplementary hospital, extended health care, prescription drugs, vision and hearing care.

Expenses covered under extended health care are those not covered by government plans. As a rule, most plans use deductibles and co-insurance for each benefit except supplementary hospital care.

Most supplementary hospital benefit plans cover the full cost for charges for semi-private hospital accommodation in Canada (in excess of ward accommodation that is provided by the provincial plan). Some plans also pay part or all of the difference between semi-private and private accommodation costs. In recent years, some hospitals began charging fees on the basis of "preferred accommodation" rather than for semi-private or private room accommodation. Where this is applicable, hospital benefit plan coverage has been adjusted accordingly.

Extended health care benefits can include coverage for such benefits as private duty nursing, physiotherapy, purchase or rental of artificial limbs, specialized treatment such as radium and radioisotopes, ambulance services, psychologists, masseurs, and speech therapy. These expenses are usually subject to limits, which range from liberal to severe. For example, the limit on coverage for emergency treatment outside Canada may vary from $50,000 to $1 million with little difference in premium. On the other hand, other coverage limits, such as, $10,000 per three years for private duty nursing or $500 per year for paramedical services, are more prone to premium rate changes for coverage level changes.

PRESCRIPTION DRUGS

Commonly included under extended health care plans, coverage of prescription drug costs is sometimes provided by a separate plan. Eligible expenses are most frequently limited to drugs that can only be obtained by a prescription. They must be medically necessary and have a drug identification number (DIN). Therefore, if a doctor writes a prescription for something that can be bought over the counter, it is not usually considered an eligible expense.

Some types of drugs that are generally not considered eligible are steroids, those that are considered experimental, vitamins, dietary supplements and sometimes birth control pills.

Arriving at the proper price to be paid for a drug is not always straightforward. Prices charged for a drug may vary widely among different pharmacies, and several manufacturers may produce their own version of a drug at varying prices. As a result, some plans pay claims only according to an established price list, called a *formulary plan.*

Substituting generic drugs for brand-name drugs is usually permitted in most provinces, unless the doctor specifies no substitution.

Plan sponsors may establish deductibles and co-insurance features to control the cost of these programs. Deductibles are usually expressed as a flat dollar amount that must be paid by the employee before he or she receives benefits from the plan. Up to two or three deductibles (or their dollar equivalent) may be applied to those with family coverage. The co-insurance is the amount paid by the employee. If co-insurance is used, the level is usually either 10% or 20%, so the plan payments are 80-100%.

Drug costs have been increasing at a faster pace than most other privately insured health costs. As a result, some managed care concepts have been applied to prescription drug plans. For example, on the ingredient front, specific formularies may be used, some based on government plans such as the Ontario Drug Benefit (ODB) or some specifically designed for an employer or employer group. Also, the reimbursement of the dispensing fee may be limited to a specified dollar amount. Conditions may also be applied to reimburse the drug expense on the basis of the cost of the generic drug (when a generic equivalent is available and is permitted by the doctor) even if a brand-name drug was purchased.

A prescription drug card program can be beneficial for managed care plans. With a drug card program, the pharmacist has immediate access to the plan's coverage basis and can confirm to the covered person the amount that will be paid by the plan and the amount or balance that must be paid by the covered person.

Mail-order drug facilities are also available and are encouraged under some drug plans. Mail-order facilities have been particularly successful for controlling costs of maintenance drugs. They often provide automatic generic substitution and charge a lower dispensing fee.

VISION AND HEARING CARE

Most vision and hearing care plans will limit the amount payable in any 12- or 24-month period for eyeglasses and contact lenses and in any five-year period for the purchase or repair of hearing aids. The dollar limit of coverage varies with common eyeglasses/contact lenses limits of $100 to $300 and hearing aid limits of $500.

It used to be that provincial medicare plans paid the professional fees for the diagnosis of vision and hearing problems. However, in more recent years, most provinces have withdrawn this coverage for eye examinations for persons between the ages of 18 and 64 years. Therefore, it is not uncommon for private insurance plans to now include coverage for eye examinations, typically one exam, limited to $40, every two years.

DENTAL CARE

The inclusion of dental coverage in a group plan was once considered very generous. This coverage has now become much more common and, although it is not included in all group plans, it would now be considered a norm, particularly for larger groups.

Many dental services are preventive rather than curative and, therefore, obtaining the treatment is often not as "medically necessary" or immediately required as the benefits provided by extended health coverage. Furthermore, some dental services can be elective, or there can be several different treatment options, such as a bridge versus a denture.

Because of this, dental plans may contain eligibility provisions and limits that are more restrictive than for extended health benefits. For example, eligibility for dental coverage may start later than for extended health, and dollar limits for treatment paid or services that are covered may be lower for the first year of coverage than in subsequent years. These types of limitations are intended to control a dental plan's expenses so that a large proportion of the cost is not provided to employees covered only for a short period of time or to minimize fluctuations in the plan's expenses from year to year.

The optional forms of treatment available also result in plans including a predetermination-of-benefits provision. Such a provision usually recommends (but sometimes requires) that an employee submit the dentist's proposed dental treatment plan for review by the claims adjudicator before the treatment is actually performed. This provides the opportunity to let the patient and the dentist know if the plan will not provide coverage for all of the proposed treatment because lower cost alternatives may be available. The employees can then decide (before they incur the expense) whether to have the alternative treatment done that would be more fully covered under the dental plan or to have the initial proposed treatment done, but be responsible for more of the associated expenses.

Most insured dental plans provide coverage on a

reimbursement basis, and the reimbursement level is tied to the schedule of fees recommended by each province's dental association. (Fee guides are recommended or suggested charges for dental procedures listed by procedure codes. Dentists are free to charge whatever they like and are not required to bill in accordance with the fee guides, but most do.) Typically, the fee guides are increased annually by the dental association, but the dental plan's reimbursement basis would not automatically increase unless the plan language used was "current fee guide" rather than specifying the year. For example, if the plan language specified the 1998 fee guide and expenses were incurred in 1999, the reimbursement of expenses would still be made on the 1998 fee guide level, even though the dentist may have charged using a 1999 fee guide. Had this same plan's language said "current fee guide" instead of 1998 fee guide, then the reimbursement of expenses would automatically have been adjusted to the 1999 level.

There are advantages and disadvantages to plan sponsors using the "current fee guide" language in their plan design. It is administratively more efficient as they do not need to change the plan language every year if their intent is to keep the reimbursement basis in line with the existing fee guide charges. On the other hand, it usually results in a corresponding automatic increase in the expenses to provide the coverage, which may or may not be acceptable to the plan sponsors. A "current fee guide" reimbursement basis also often results in employees being more aware of their out-of-pocket expenses when going to the dentist. For example, if dental services are reimbursed at 100% of the "current fee guide," then employees know they will not be out-of-pocket for any of these expenses (unless the dentist charges more than the fee guide). If, however, the fee guide specified in the plan is 1995, and employees go to the dentist in 1999, they often will not know what their out-of-pocket expenses are until they receive the reimbursement for their claim.

Some plans are designed to keep the fee guide reimbursement basis at a one- to two-year lag; that is, 1999 expenses are reimbursed using a 1998 fee guide basis. This can be done by changing the year specified on an annual basis, or the plan language could specify "the current year less one year fee guide." Quite often, if the plan's reimbursement basis is on a one-year fee guide lag, the dentist will charge on that basis.

Generally, there are three types or levels of dental coverage; basic and preventive, major restorative, and orthodontic. Not all plans provide coverage for all three levels, but the levels are usually available on a stepped basis. That is, an insurer will not usually provide major restorative coverage if the plan does not include basic and preventive coverage. Similarly, orthodontic cover-

age is only included if the other two levels are also included.

The plan is usually designed to provide a different reimbursement percentage for each level of coverage, with the highest reimbursement provided for basic and preventive services. This is done, not only because those are the services used most frequently, but also to encourage maintenance of good dental health, which can prevent other more expensive treatment from being required later on. For example, if an employee has cavities attended to at an early stage, it can eliminate the need for a bridge later on. In addition, some services, such as orthodontic treatment, can have an elective element associated with them. Therefore, if the employee bears a higher level of the financial responsibility, it helps to control expenses for services that may be obtained more because they are available than because they are needed.

Most typically, a dental plan would provide reimbursement of 80% of basic and preventive services, 50% of major restorative and 50% of orthodontic. However, it is not unusual for some large, well-established plans to provide reimbursement of 100%, 80% and 50%, respectively.

Dollar limits for expenses that will be reimbursed also typically vary by level of coverage. Currently, typical reimbursement limits are unlimited for basic and preventive, $1,500 to $2,000 per insured person per year for major restorative and $2,000 to $2,500 lifetime for orthodontic. Orthodontic coverage is also most often limited to dependent children under age 19, although some plans may include orthodontic coverage for adults as well.

As noted, most insured dental plans provide coverage on a reimbursement basis; however, electronic submission of claims directly from the dentist's office is becoming more and more common.

Some dental programs are provided through a dental clinic. This is most likely to be found in large companies or union locals where the majority of employees or members are found in one location. The plan sponsors can set up their own dental clinic and have the dentists on staff.

TAXATION

All provinces levy a premium tax on group insurance premiums, and the rates range by province from 2-4%. In addition, in the provinces of Quebec and Ontario, sales tax is applicable to group insurance premiums at 9% and 8%, respectively.

Life insurance premiums paid by or through employment are treated by the federal government as taxable income to the employee. Disability income payments received by an employee are also treated as taxable income, unless the employee paid the full cost of the premiums for the disability insurance.

In the province of Quebec, life, health and dental benefits paid by the employer are also treated as taxable income to the employee.

The expenses paid by an employer to provide employee benefit coverage (including associated taxes) can be deducted as a business expense.

FUTURE

The future evolution of all private plans will continue to be influenced by the level of taxation charged directly or indirectly, demographics, changes to our medicare plans, and our ability to pay for these and other services.

The increase in the costs to provide benefit plan coverages has resulted in some employers limiting or fixing their contribution levels for coverages. Changes to cost-sharing arrangements with employees have also resulted from this. These considerations, combined with the current tax implications of coverages and the more common occurrence of duplicate coverage through spousal benefits, have fostered the growth of flexible benefits plans. Flexible benefits plans provide employees with more choice concerning their coverages and can help to make the coverages available on a more tax-effective basis.

CHAPTER 2

Legal Issues in Respect of Health, Life and Disability Insurance Plans

by Susan Philpott

CONTEXT

There have traditionally been two structures for the provision of health and welfare benefits in the employment context as part of the wage package that includes extended health benefits, including vision and dental care, prescription drugs, paramedical services, life insurance, and disability insurance. One exists in the single employer context, and the other generally exists in the multi-employer context, though there is some overlap.

In the single employer context, the employer generally agrees with the bargaining agent to provide certain benefits, and then makes the necessary external arrangements to do so. The actual benefits are then provided through contracts with insurers, through a self-funded (uninsured) program, or a combination of the two. Usually, the collective agreement sets out the kind of benefit to be provided and the level or amount which the employer will pay for, and will sometimes prescribe the arrangement whereby the benefits are to be provided. The degree of detail in the collective agreement and the nature of the bargain provided for therein are the determining factors in any later benefits dispute, and parties ought to carefully address their minds to these issues at inception.

In the multi-employer context, the prevalent structure is the health and welfare trust fund—most commonly funded by a defined contribution set out in a collective agreement. The trustees of the health and welfare trust are then responsible to provide such benefits as can be purchased with the negotiated level of contributions. They do this either by contracting with an in-surer to provide benefits or by funding the benefits out of the trust. The trustees then administer the benefit plan through an internal administrative structure, or contract with a third-party administrator to manage the benefit plan. In this structure, the employer is usually responsible only to make the prescribed contributions, and any benefits decisions are made by the trustees, who are then responsible in the event of a dispute with the employee–beneficiaries.

Below we will be reviewing legal issues that arise in matters of health and other insured benefits that are provided in both the multi-employer and single employer plan contexts. Some issues are common to both, while others are unique to one system or the other. The most common concern for an aggrieved employee is what mechanism is available to him or her if the benefit promised is not provided. In the case of collectively bargained multi-employer plans, the remedy does not generally lie in the grievance and arbitration procedure because the trustees, not the employer, have determined what benefits and how to provide them. Further, the provisions of labour relations statutes pertaining to unfair representation generally do not apply in this context. The Ontario Labour Relations Board in the case of *Angelo Moro*[1] held that the duty of fair representation applies to representation of employees vis-à-vis an employer and precludes the board from undertaking an enquiry into irregularities involving a multi-employer pension fund. Accordingly, employees in this context will have recourse to the courts or regulatory authorities in cases involving pension plans. In the single employer context, there will be recourse under the collective agreement grievance procedure only in circumstances as set out below. In other situations, it will be necessary to proceed against an employer or insurer in the courts or before regulatory authorities.

ARBITRABILITY OF BENEFIT PLAN DISPUTES UNDER COLLECTIVE AGREEMENTS

As a general matter pertaining to all fringe benefits, the specific language of the collective agreement will determine the extent of the employer's liability in respect of benefits and the arbitrability of benefit disputes. Where a collective agreement provides for benefits, the arbitrator must determine in what manner the parties intended those benefits be provided, and whose responsibility it would ultimately be in the event of a dispute.[2]

Benefit Entitlement Disputes

Historically, there have been recognized categories of benefit provisions that help an arbitrator determine whether the employer must actually provide benefits or simply contract for their delivery. At the time of writing, this classification guide, called the "Four Brown & Beatty Categories,"[3] is in a state of legal uncertainty, which will be more fully described below. First, we set out the four-category system.

In some cases the employer is merely obligated to ensure that certain benefits are provided. In such cases the manner in which the employer chooses to deliver those benefits is its prerogative (and its contractual responsibility) so long as the benefits set out in the collective agreement are provided.[4] If the employer's obligation is simply to provide premium contributions to the insurance plan, disputes as to entitlement to specific benefits must be settled between the employee and the insurer, and such disputes will not be arbitrable because the terms of the plan will not be part of the agreement.[5] It is a well-established principle that parties to a collective agreement can negotiate benefit provisions in which the obligation of the employer is limited to the payment of premiums. In those circumstances, the enforcement of the benefits would require an action in the courts.

Where the agreement simply states that:

The Company will provide a welfare plan particulars of which are set out in the policies and other documents carrying such plans, and the details shall be summarized in the printed agreement following the signature page,

it was held that the employer's obligation is simply to provide coverage through an insurance policy and that it is not responsible for paying the benefit itself. In *Labatts Ontario Breweries Ltd.,*[6] Arbitrator Palmer found that:

The cases suggest that there must be extremely clear language in order to find an obligation on the part of an employer or company to pay the benefit itself rather than merely provide coverage.[7]

If the employer has agreed to provide certain benefits, disputes as to entitlement will usually be arbitrable. In *Green Valley Fertilizer*[8] it was noted that terms of a plan that are inconsistent with the terms of the collective agreement are unenforceable, but standard provisions that are not in conflict with the agreement are enforceable. In that case, the employer was found to have agreed in positive terms to provide wage loss benefits to disabled employees in a prescribed amount. References in the provision to a plan and an insurance carrier support the inference that it was within the contemplation of the parties that the employer would be free to meet its obligations by introducing a plan. The language falls far short of constituting an agreement between the parties that the only obligation of the employer is to provide a plan. There, it was admitted that the union had never been invited to negotiate the terms and provisions of the plan and never received a copy of it. The board's conclusion was that the parties agreed that the employer was required to apply the designated level of benefits. However, by necessary implication, the parties were presumed by the board to have intended that the employer could meet its obligation by providing a standard plan.

In *Pilon,*[9] an employee at a workplace governed by a collective agreement brought an action against his employer and the insurer when he was denied short- and long-term benefits under a group insurance plan. The only insured benefits were long-term disability benefits; the remainder were provided directly by the employer. The long-term disability benefits were administered by the employer and paid for by the employees through salary deduction. The collective agreement did not define the eligibility criteria for long-term disability benefits but did incorporate by reference the terms of the benefits handbook, which was distributed to employees. This was likely a "category 4" kind of case, though the court never discussed or determined that question.

At first instance, the court dismissed the employee's action on the basis that it arose out of a dispute concerning entitlements under a collective agreement. Pilon appealed that decision, but only as against the insurer, conceding that the dispute as against the employer would have to proceed by way of arbitration. The Court of Appeal relied upon the Supreme Court of Canada's rulings in *St. Anne-Nackawic*[10] and *Weber*[11] and concluded:

The appellant's attempt to frame the dispute as a contractual matter wholly independent from the collective agreement is without merit. In our view, it is clear that the dispute arises under the collective agreement, and that the grievance and arbitration mechanisms contained therein should govern the resolution of this conflict.[12]

The court reached this conclusion even though the employer was no longer an affected party. The decision related purely to Pilon's action against the insurer.

There have been numerous arbitration and court decisions since the Court of Appeal's ruling in *Pilon,* and the approach of arbitrators has been divided. On the one hand, there are arbitrators who take the view that the Ontario Court of Appeal meant to radically alter the jurisprudential landscape and ruled that insurers can be brought to arbitrations and forced to participate as third parties, with the results binding upon them.[13] Diametrically opposed to that approach is that of a number of other arbitrators who operate from the premise that the four Brown and Beatty categories remain good law, as does the dichotomy whereby category 1 or 3 disputes are actions against insurers to be pursued in the courts, and category 2 or 4 disputes are arbitrable matters under the collective agreement.[14]

For unions that wish to rely on grievance and arbitration provisions to resolve benefit disputes, care should be taken to incorporate by reference the benefit plan or insurance policy or to otherwise qualify benefit eligibility and coverage. The collective agreement provides the primary contractual commitment and will, therefore, govern in the event of conflict with the provisions of the insurance policy. If the insurance policy acquired by the employer does not provide the benefit specified in the collective agreement, the employer will be liable to pay dental benefits upon the bankruptcy of its dental plan carrier. In *Fleet Manufacturing,*[15] the employer was found liable for the amount by which the coverage proposed by the agreement exceeded the insurance coverage. In *Re Corporation of City of London (Dearness Home),*[16] the arbitrator confirmed *Fleet Manufacturing,* finding that the employer is liable for the amount of benefit provided by the collective agreement, irrespective of the carrier's understanding of the coverage.

If terms and conditions of the plan or policy are not incorporated by reference into the agreement, they may not be relied upon in order to interpret or qualify the terms of the agreement.[17] In *Union Gas,*[18] the board found that, where the provisions of the agreement dealing with sick pay made no reference to any booklet, benefit plan document or policy of insurance, the booklets and insurance policy could not be introduced into evidence by the company at a hearing concerning the extent of the employer's obligation to provide benefits. In a later *Union Gas*[19] decision, the board confirmed that regard may be had to the insurance policy itself only where the matter is not dealt with specifically or by necessary implication in the agreement. The board said

further that where the terms of the policy were inconsistent with the agreement, the agreement must govern. This position was also taken in *O.N.A. and O.N.A. Staff Union.*[20] Further, not only must the agreement govern, but also it cannot be read down. In *O.N.A.,* the eligibility for disability was held to include coverage for an employee despite the fact that the medical condition requiring her to be off work existed at the time she attained status as a full-time employee.

Where the benefit plan or insurance policy is incorporated by reference into the agreement, the conditions described in the policy become part of the agreement and are subject to challenge or enforcement at arbitration.[21] The courts have held that an employee pension plan agreement that is appended to a collective agreement forms part of the agreement so that a civil action thereunder is barred pursuant to the provisions of the *Rights of Labour Act* of Ontario.[22]

In *Re Heritage Nursing Homes,*[23] Arbitrator MacDowell held that where there is an obligation on an employer to make contributions to a health and welfare fund, the employer is liable to make such contributions even though it has provided alternative and equivalent benefits.

Finally, some collective agreements specifically provide that insured benefit disputes are outside of the collective agreement. Such agreements may provide that benefit disputes shall be adjudicated directly between the employee and the insurer and are not arbitrable under the collective agreement.

Arbitrability of Changes in Insurance Carriers

If particular plans and insurance carriers are named, the employer is generally bound to provide the named plan and cannot change to an equivalent or even superior plan with a different carrier unless the agreement so provides or the union consents.[24] Often the parties provide for substitution so long as equivalent benefits are maintained. In *North Central Plywoods*[25] it is emphasized that employers that change to another plan with a different carrier have a responsibility to inform the union and the employees of the changes. Generally, whether or not the employer can change the carrier of the insurance policy will be determined by the wording of a collective agreement. The employer has an obligation to inform the union and the employees of any changes to the plan or carrier.[26] Where the identity of the insurance carrier forms an essential part of a negotiated insurance plan and is a significant issue to the parties, an arbitration board found that a change in the insurance carrier represented a unilateral amendment to the insurance plan contrary to the collective agreement. Even where an employer is permitted to change insurance carriers, any lapse that exists during a change in carriers and results in unintentionally depriving an employee of his or her benefit provision may result in an arbitration board finding the employer liable for the benefit.[27]

Expiry of the Contract

Insurance coverage upon the expiry of a collective agreement can vary. In *Welland County Hospital*,[28] an employee was found to be entitled to benefits under the terms of the new collective agreement even though it had been signed following the employee's injury. However in *Gates Canada Inc.*,[29] the arbitrator concluded he did not have the jurisdiction to decide the matter because the prior agreement and the statutory freeze had expired and the new agreement did not contain a provision dealing with retroactivity. The arbitrator supported his decision by referring to *General Tire Limited*.[30]

Had the statutory freeze period been in effect, the result would have been different, given the employer's obligation during the freeze to maintain all terms and conditions of employment. This obligation may extend to those privileges that by reason of custom and practice have become part of the employment relationship.[31]

Retiree Claims

A more significant issue arises in respect of claims that may be made by retired employees, particularly for life and health and insurance benefits that are promised to retired employees after they leave the employment of the company. Where the employer seeks to terminate the collective agreement and shut down its operations, the Supreme Court of Canada has held in *Dayco (Canada) Limited v. C.A.W.*[32] that the rights that accrue to a party during the life of a collective agreement are in the nature of vested rights that are not automatically extinguished by the termination of the collective agreement. It was held that, as a general proposition, a promise of retirement benefits can survive expiry of the collective agreement in which it is found, if the terms of the collective agreement contemplate survival of those rights. In the discussion, Justice La Forest noted that upon retirement, a worker withdraws from the collective bargaining relationship and, at that point, his or her accrued employment rights may crystallize into the form of a vested retirement right. Presumably, the same crystallization also occurs upon the retirement of an employee who has a contractual relationship with his or her employer as an individual not covered by a collective agreement. Hence, there may be such rights for non-unionized employees who bring a court action asserting continuation of retiree health benefits where they have been terminated.[33]

Courts have refused to intervene on a summary basis where an employer continues to pay benefits to retirees but the employees are seeking security for their benefits where the employer is winding down its operations.[34] In one bankruptcy case, *Re St. Mary's Paper*,[35] a trustee in bankruptcy was held to be an "employer" for the purposes of the *Pension Benefits Act*. The court found that, although it was not necessary for the trustee to have become an "employer" within the meaning of the act, by making contributions to the pension plans, the trustee thus fell within the definition of *employer* within the act. Although it would have been possible for the trustee to re-engage the employees without making a contribution to the pension plans, it did not do so and, hence, became responsible for the pension fund liabilities.

Rights of a Grievor's Estate

The arbitrability of a grievance submitted by the union on behalf of the estate of a deceased employee was upheld in the case of *Erie Iron Works Ltd.*[36] The arbitrator held that the grievance was arbitrable notwithstanding the death of the grievor and that the union was entitled to grieve on behalf of persons having a claim under the deceased employee's insurance policy. In *Re Pacific Press*,[37] the widow of a deceased employee was entitled to life insurance benefits as set out in the collective agreement, notwithstanding the insurer's lower assessment.

Where there is no collective bargaining relationship, the deceased's estate may have a cause of action against the deceased's employer for benefits to which the deceased was entitled.[38]

SPECIFIC BENEFIT ISSUES ARISING UNDER COLLECTIVE AGREEMENTS

It is impossible to provide a complete review of all benefit issues that have arisen in arbitration proceedings. Benefit disputes arise virtually on a daily basis in collective bargaining relationships. However, some of the more common issues that have arisen in arbitration are set out below.

Disability: Total or Partial?

In an old arbitration case, *Steinberg's Limited*,[39] Arbitrator O'Shea defined the term *total disability* as follows:

Provisions for weekly indemnity benefits for sickness or accident, by their very terms are intended to provide indemnity or compensation for loss of earnings which may be sustained because of an inability to work for the employer for a specific period of time. Such benefits usually contemplate that an employee will eventually be able to return to his job. There is, therefore, no suggestion in Article 23.02(b) or in the weekly indemnity policy that an employee is required to seek alternative employment to mitigate his loss in order to be entitled to weekly indemnity benefits. However, even if an employee is not able to perform his regular job, he is not considered to be "totally disabled" if he is physically able to perform light duties or other work which the company may have available since the policy defines "totally disabled" as "preventing" one from work for remuneration or profit. We, accordingly find that the phrase "totally disabled" for the purposes of weekly indemnity benefits is intended by the parties to mean totally disabled from performing any work which the company has available for which it is prepared to pay remuneration.[40]

In *Wilpark Foods*,[41] the arbitrator held that when a plan or collective agreement refers to *disability*, it is to be understood in its ordinary meaning and there must be specific language to support any limitation to an employee's entitlement.

Although the individual terms of the plan in question will govern, a long-term disability (LTD) plan normally requires that an employee be "totally disabled" to be entitled to benefits. This is generally defined to mean that the employee is prevented from performing the duties of his or her "own occupation" for the first two years of disability and the duties of "any occupation for which he or she is reasonably suited" by virtue of education, training or experience, after the two-year period. This definition has proved reasonably appropriate for salaried white-collar groups, but has created difficulties where large groups of hourly paid employees are involved. As a result, some insurance companies are now requiring *total disability* to refer to a lack of ability to perform any job for which the employee is reasonably suited from the outset of the LTD claim.

So, for example, in applying the definition of *disability* found above, the arbitrator in *Steinberg's Limited* concluded as follows:

> For purposes of long term disability, it must be established that the disabled employee must be unfit for any work, for any employer, which the employee is reasonably fitted by education, training or experience. Since the grievor has claimed this benefit, the onus is on the grievor to establish this latter type of disability. As of the date of this hearing in this matter, the grievor made no attempt to find any form of alternate employment. Since the grievor is obviously not totally disabled for all purposes (e.g., she can move about and use her hands, provided she is not required to stand for prolonged periods), we must accordingly find that she has failed to establish her entitlement for long term disability benefits.[42]

In recent years, there has been a great deal of discussion as to what constitutes a "total" or "partial" disability. For example, in *TRW Canada*,[43] an obese employee who suffered injuries at work related to weight was held to be entitled to a disability pension but was required to participate in a weight control program. In this case, it was determined that the employee had the ability to control the disability. Similar issues arise with respect to substance abuse such as drug or alcohol dependency, which has been recognized in some cases as a disability.

In *Regional Municipality of Halton*,[44] a nurse had been off work for 16 months because of Epstein-Barr syndrome, which gave her severe environment sensitivity. While in the past this condition may have been seen as a total disability, the board of arbitration held that the employer had a duty to accommodate her by providing a rural work environment and ensuring that she worked in an environment free of cigarette smoke, perfume, chemicals, dust, etc.

Three court decisions indicate the factors that will be considered by the court in determining whether "total disability" exists. In *Crawford v. The Citadel General Assurance Corp.*,[45] the court found that an entrepreneur who had owned and operated two companies including a real estate firm was totally unable to undertake responsibility of being an entrepreneur because of his psychiatric illness, although he had started a "dance factory" where he had worked for some time in a limited capacity. The insurer argued that the work at the dance factory was a "gainful occupation," but the court found that *gainful occupation* meant "one which will bring him an income which will be reasonable in amount in relation to the income received from the occupation he was compelled to discontinue."[46] The court found that the plaintiff did not have any education or training to do any other job that would have provided income commensurate with what he was receiving prior to his illness and that, therefore, he was totally disabled.

In *Corr v. London Life*,[47] the same court found that the plaintiff, a certified nursing assistant who had suffered a massive heart attack, was totally disabled because she was required to take heavy dosages of potent medication (including a diuretic and valium) and because her heart was functioning at approximately 50% of normal capacity so that she tired easily. The court said that it could not contemplate that any employer in the circumstances would employ the plaintiff and held that the cumulative effect of the illness and medication rendered her functionally unemployable and, therefore, entitled to total and permanent disability benefits.

In *Paul Revere Life Insurance Company v. Sucharov*,[48] the Supreme Court of Canada found that a policy that defined *total disability* as the inability to engage in a person's regular occupation covered the plaintiff. He was able to perform a portion of his former duties as an insurance broker but was unable to perform them collectively as owner/manager. The court found that he was totally disabled because he was unable to perform "substantially all" of the duties of owner/manager.

In *Dominion Stores Ltd.,*[49] the grievor had worked as a bookkeeper for 19 years. She developed serious eye problems that resulted in her being unable to perform any work in the stores or offices of the employer. She was placed on disability benefits that were discontinued after two years. Certain doctors had reported that, although the grievor had little or no vision in one eye and could see only with the aid of an extremely thick cataract lens through her other eye (which resulted in tunnel vision), work as a bookkeeper was difficult but not impossible. The definition of *total disability* in the policy was "continuous inability of the insured to engage in each and every gainful occupation or employment for which he is reasonably qualified by virtue of education, training or experience." The board of arbitration reviewed the common law definition of *total disability* relying in particular on a decision of the Alberta Supreme Court wherein it was found that *total disability* does not mean that the person is not entitled to the benefit if he is so sick that he can take on only trivial or inconsequential work, or work for which he is overqualified, or work for which he is completely unsuited by background. The board stated:

> . . . to put it bluntly, the grievor does not need to be reduced to a vegetable to fall within the definition of "total disability" nor is she disqualified merely because she might be trained to weave baskets or work in some other cottage industry. In our view the question is whether the grievor could perform work reasonably comparable to the cashier and bookkeeper's work she had performed, having regard for her education, training or experience.[50]

The approach of adjudicators to the application of disability criteria is becoming more and more purposive—taking into account the sensitive nature of disability issues, and the need for compliance within human rights statutes.

Disability: Employment Status

The payment of benefit premiums and the entitlement to benefit payments during a temporary interruption of employment such as a strike, layoff or leave of absence is a source of continuing controversy. On one hand, employment status determines entitlement to benefits. On the other hand, the entitlement to benefits will in some cases be relied upon to determine employment status. The collective agreement should specify whether employees who are laid off or absent for other reasons will be entitled to receive benefits and for how long.

In *Burns Meats, Division of Burns Foods,*[51] a number of principles emerge. First of all, an employee already in receipt of sickness or accident benefits, either a weekly indemnity or LTD, under the terms of the collective agreement itself cannot be terminated for innocent absenteeism if to do so would be to deprive him or her of a "vested benefit" already being received. This is true especially where the employer assumes the "primary" responsibility for providing benefits.

Second, matters are less clear where the only obligation of the employer is to provide insurance coverage through a third-party insurer. Some of the authorities appear to suggest that the employer still cannot terminate for innocent absenteeism if the termination disentitles an employee from the right to apply for the benefit where it is dependent on "employment status." In these cases, the ultimate decision on eligibility will rest with the insurer, and the result of these arbitration cases is that the only right preserved is the ability to apply for benefits by preserving employment status. There is no certainty as to whether or not the benefit would be allowed.

One test that has been used in order to determine entitlement to benefits is "whether one may reasonably infer that this kind of employee was intended by the parties to enjoy the contract benefit in question."[52] The test has been summarized as follows:

> Recent cases . . . have focused on the nature of the benefit in question in light of the particular reason for the employee's absence . . . this latter reasoning has sanctioned the payment of health and other kinds of insurance premiums for grievors who are absent on Workers' Compensation; the payment of welfare benefits for an employee absent from work without pay for some time because of illness; the entitlement to holiday pay of employees who are absent on sick pay; entitlement to the payment of OHIP premiums for employees laid-off but who worked at least one day in the month for which the premium was to be paid; and the payment of both holiday pay and welfare plans premiums on behalf of regular employees on temporary lay-off. . . .[53]

In *Somerville Packaging,*[54] an employee who was laid off after being unable to exercise his seniority rights because of a work-related disability was held to still be entitled to his benefit premium payments.

On Vacation

The Ontario Court of Appeal in *Vouzas v. Lewis Motors et al.*[55] considered the phrases *active full-time employment for full pay* and *ceases to be employed by the employer.* The first definition was the condition of eligibility for the life and health insurance policies under a group plan, and the second was the eligibility requirement for disability coverage.

The plaintiff had left Canada for a vacation in Greece with an open return ticket at the end of January 1979 and suffered a stroke in Greece on February 14,

1979. The court found that the employment relationship continued to exist because the employee had a return ticket, had left his wife in Canada and had left his tools at his place of employment. The employee was, therefore, entitled to disability benefits. The majority of the court, however, found that "active full-time employment for full pay" contemplates an employee who is "ready and able to perform the work demanded of him (during) . . . the days and hours customary in that trade or Occupation." The court found that the employee was away for an indefinite period of time and his employer did not know if or when he would return. He was, therefore, not entitled to benefits under the life and health insurance policies.

On Layoff

One arbitrator has found that an employee on layoff is not entitled to continue to accumulate sick leave credits on the basis that sick pay benefits are meant to insulate an employee against loss of pay due to illness.[56] The same reasoning has been applied to a claim for a cash payment with respect to unused sick credits while on permanent layoff.[57]

Some arbitrators have required that the employee work some amount of time in the month in order to be entitled to payment of welfare premiums.[58] The result may be different if the layoff is characterized as an indefinite layoff from the outset.[59]

On Strike

At least one arbitrator has held that employees were entitled to benefits during a legal strike because they had been earned under the previous collective agreement.[60]

Under Section 86 of the Ontario *Labour Relations Act,* 1995,[61] it is an unfair labour practice for an employer to alter any term or condition of employment or any right, privilege or duty of the employer, the trade union or the employees during the strike process.

On Workers' Compensation

Workers' compensation payments are a form of income supplement and are paid only to "workers." The legal basis is a statutory entitlement, not current work or even work in the previous year. The payment, while measured as a function of time and the general wage rate set by provincial workers' compensation boards, is not dependent on the employer at all. The employing entity could be sold or could close its doors without affecting the continuance of benefits.[62] Nevertheless, an employee has a statutory right to require investigation of an injury and an assessment of a disability, especially when a collective agreement does not delegate exclusive responsibility for assessing fitness to the compensation board.[63]

In *Unity Hospital Board v. Metcalfe et al.,*[64] the collective agreement provided that workers' compensation benefits would be "topped up" by the employer for a period of one year. After the one year had expired, the employee sought to top up her compensation benefits by charging the difference against her own accumulated sick leave. The hospital argued that sick leave and workers' compensation leave were mutually exclusive and that an employee was not entitled to use accumulated sick leave to maintain his or her regular income. That argument was rejected by the arbitration board, which found that specific language would have been necessary to preclude the employee from utilizing the sick leave credit at any time. That finding was upheld by the court.

In *City of Trail,*[65] the board found that an employee off on workers' compensation was entitled to accumulate sick leave, statutory holiday pay and annual vacation entitlement. The board found that vacation entitlement depended on years of continuous service, which implied uninterrupted existence of the employment relationship rather than active service in the workplace. With respect to sick leave, the employee was receiving sick leave credits for the purpose of topping up his workers' compensation benefits to full salary. The board found that under the collective agreement, the only condition was that sick leave credits could not be accumulated and used at the same time. With respect to the statutory holiday benefit, the board found that it was a separate negotiated benefit to which the employee was not disentitled by reason of his absence.

The board in *Etobicoke General Hospital*[66] found that a provision in a collective agreement dealing with deemed termination, while not nullified with respect to disabled employees by Section 5 of the Ontario *Human Rights Code,* must nevertheless be interpreted and applied consistently with the *Code.* In order for employers to act consistently with the *Code,* they have a duty to accommodate a grievor's needs to the extent required by the legislation. Subsequent arbitrators have followed the decision in *Etobicoke General* and have recognized that employers may have an obligation to reasonably accommodate employees to the point of undue hardship in order to avoid human rights complaints.[67]

The duty to accommodate can stretch across bargaining unit lines in some circumstances.[68] Temporary employees are also entitled to the duty to accommodate, although the undue hardship threshold is lower given the nature of the employment relationship.[69] The reasonable accommodation obligation also extends to probationary employees.[70]

After a Lengthy Absence

There is an onus on employers to establish that there is no prospect of an employee attending work regularly in the future, before the employee can be discharged.

Furthermore, an employer cannot assume there are going to be further absences.[71] However, severe and ongoing health problems can give rise under certain circumstances to an inference that an absence by an employee will continue indefinitely. Under these circumstances, the onus shifts to the grievor to show there is a reasonable likelihood of improved future attendance.[72] In this case, a nurse was discharged after a 16-month absence due to Epstein-Barr syndrome and, though the evidence established that she was unable to return to her old job, she provided evidence that she would be able to work in a modified work environment.

Employers must be fair in their evaluation as to whether or not absenteeism has been excessive. In *Alberta v. A.U.P.E.*,[73] it was held that despite an employee's excessive absenteeism due to a variety of illnesses over a five-year period, any comparison to other employees must be done in an unbiased way using absenteeism averages for all employees for the same time period. Generally, the likelihood of absences being ongoing or indefinite can be established by medical evidence.

In *Ferranti-Packard Transformers Ltd.*,[74] the grievor had been receiving LTD payments for approximately three years with the company maintaining her fringe benefits in accordance with its existing policy. After three years, in accordance with her seniority, the grievor was laid off along with others. The collective agreement specified that LTD recipients could be laid off only "should eligibility for long-term disability cease." The arbitrator upheld the grievance and concluded that employees on disability leave were entitled to retain their status as employees even during periods when they would otherwise have been subject to layoff had they been at work. The arbitrator found further that the grievor was entitled to vacation pay and pension contributions as provided by the collective agreement but that, because group life insurance premiums were not guaranteed by the agreement, the company was not obliged to pay them.

In *Mississauga Transit*,[75] the company sought to discharge the grievor as a result of innocent absenteeism due to degenerative disc disease. The arbitrator found that the company was entitled to discharge the grievor on the basis of her record of excessive absenteeism and a prognosis of further intermittent absenteeism. However, the grievor had been terminated just as she completed the qualifying period for entitlement to LTD benefits. Therefore, the arbitrator found that the history of absenteeism could not justify termination where termination had the effect of denying the grievor access to the disability plan just as she completed the qualifying period.

In *Dehavilland Aircraft*,[76] the employer terminated the grievor, arguing that the contract of employment had been frustrated by the inability of the employee to attend at work. The arbitrator found that in negotiating and instituting sickness and disability benefits, the parties obviously contemplated the very situation that now formed the basis of the company's application of the doctrine of frustration. The board found that the company was not entitled to terminate the disabled employee.

The employer may be entitled to terminate an employee if termination does not affect his or her entitlement to disability benefits. In *Queensway General Hospital*,[77] the grievor suffered a back injury that led to prolonged absences from work. Her family doctor provided a medical certificate that indicated that the grievor might well become permanently disabled. The employer terminated the grievor's employment for innocent absenteeism. The grievor then applied for and was granted LTD benefits notwithstanding that she had lost her status as an employee. A majority of the board of arbitration concluded that an employer could terminate an employee on LTD only where the grievor's rights under the LTD plan were sufficiently established so that the employee's entitlement would not be affected by termination. The grievor was in fact reinstated because the medical opinion from the insurer's doctor indicated that she might return to work at some future date.

A similar decision was made in *Glideen Co.*[78] The employer attempted to require an employee on LTD to take an unpaid leave of absence. The employer argued that the management rights clause in the collective agreement gave it the unilateral right to grant a leave of absence, but the arbitrator found that a grant of a leave of absence was not the same as the unilateral imposition of a leave of absence.

In *Wolverine Tube*[79] a disabled employee on LTD was entitled to severance pay like other employees upon plant closure. However, this was based on entitlement being vested and not dependent on his status as an employee.

Proof of Disability

Clearly, employers will require medical certification of an employee's ability to return to work and/or entitlement to continued disability benefits. Arbitrators have normally upheld the right of the company to require a direct medical examination but, because of the personal nature of a medical examination, absent some specific provision in the collective agreement, the company is not entitled to select the doctor without the employee's consent.[80]

Employers also have a legitimate interest in knowing the nature of an employee's illness for the protection of both the employee and other employees. However, employers only need this information provided to them where an illness could have an impact on a work environment, and employee confidentiality interests must be protected.[81]

In *Air Canada*[82] the arbitrator went on to find that a company rule that required employees to undergo a periodic medical examination was unreasonable because it applied whether or not the employees had symptoms of illness or had been absent due to illness. An employer must have reasonable cause to insist on a medical or psychiatric examination.[83]

One employer, the City of London, Ontario, took a novel approach to verifying sick leave claims by instituting a program of home visitations by an occupational health nurse. The employees felt that the purpose of the visit was to confirm that they were home and that they were sick, that is, to find out whether they were telling the truth when they phoned in sick. The arbitrator found that this program did not serve a medical purpose but a policing function. The collective agreement already contained a clause requiring the production of evidence of sickness reasonably satisfactory to the personnel director and provided that employees could be requested to submit to a medical examination by a physician appointed by the employer. The arbitrator found that these provisions indicated that the union and the employer had turned their minds to the question of monitoring sick leave and that the employer was not entitled to augment the agreement midway through its term.[84]

In the *City of London*[85] case, one argument made by the employees was that the home visits were an invasion of privacy. The same argument was made in *Ontario Hydro*[86] in support of a grievance against the practice of requiring completion of a standard form required by the company as evidence of illness. The board found that:

> There may well be circumstances in which it would be a petty invasion of the real privacy interests of an employee to insist that a detailed diagnosis be set out by the attending physician. In the absence of any more specific requirement in the collective agreement or any statutory or regulatory provision expressly permissive, the employer is limited to the rights provided to it by the collective agreement in matters of personal privacy.[87]

The employer was entitled to insist upon medical certification of absence due to illness but not necessarily upon a full and exhaustive diagnosis. However, the board found that the medical certificate provided by the grievor is simply inadequate on its face and that more information was required in order to satisfy the requirements of the sick leave plan. The grievance was dismissed.

A doctor's opinion on a medical certificate is valid unless proven wrong. Once a medical opinion is tendered into evidence, it must stand until rebutted.[88]

Disability Plans: Offsets

A common provision in disability plans, particularly long-term disability plans, involves integration with other disability plans or government benefits. A typical plan will often provide from 50-70% of the employee's earnings subject to offsets from any source other than an employee's individual policy. Typical offsets are workers' compensation benefits and the Canada and Quebec Pension Plans (CPP/QPP), which pay disability benefits, as well as any other pension plans that pay disability pensions. However, there have been some recent court decisions dealing with these "offsets" that clarify some outstanding problems.

In *Trailo v. Allied Chemical Canada Ltd.*[89] Mr. Justice Richard Holland of the Ontario Supreme Court found that receipt of Social Security disability benefits as a result of a previous employment in the United States did not represent an offset. The insurer was entitled to deduct amounts payable under the "Canada Pension Plan, the Quebec Pension Plan or other federal, provincial or municipal government plans." The court held that the wording of the insurance policy as a whole dealt only with Canadian benefits or plans and that no deduction should be made for the U.S. Social Security benefits the plaintiff received. In the arbitration case of *Casimir Jennings and Appleby,*[90] the collective agreement provided that employees would receive LTD benefits of 75% of normal salary pursuant to a "sickness and accident insurance policy." The arbitrator held that this permitted offsets of Canada Pension Plan (CPP) disability payments from the 75% benefit because the wording of the insurance policy specifically made reference to the offset. The collective agreement did not refer to the offset but did indicate that the employer was to provide health and welfare benefits in accordance with the terms and conditions of the collective agreement "and any insurance policies issued in respect thereof or any successor policies thereof."[91]

Disability: Human Rights Issues

Whereas many of the benefit issues discussed above have emphasized the importance of the collective agreement in determining eligibility, it is important to note that, if the collective agreement provisions are found to be in conflict with human rights principles, these provisions must be set aside. Both employers and trade unions have a duty to interpret and apply collective agreement provisions in a manner consistent with human rights legislation. As noted by Constance Backhouse in *Dennis v. Family and Children Services of London and Middlesex:*[92]

> The labour relations grievance process is designed for private parties, employers and unions to enable them to resolve differences over the inter-

pretation of their privately bargained labour agreements. The problems of individual employees are filtered through the medium of a trade union. . . . Human Rights proceedings are designed to promote the broad public interest in the elimination of discrimination. . . . The goal is to compensate individuals or groups which have been treated unfairly and the focus of human rights jurisprudence is upon developing sensitivities to the forms and manifestations of discrimination.[93]

With respect to disability, in the past there was a two-pronged test for termination due to "innocent absenteeism."

1. Does the employee's medical record indicate a past record of unacceptable absences?
2. Does the future medical prognosis provide any assurance that the grievor's attendance record will improve?

More recently, however, if an absence for which an employee was discharged is supported by medical evidence, it may be found that the employer discharged the employee due to a handicap, which is contrary to the provincial and federal human rights legislation. Where an employee has a handicap, the employer is required to accommodate, not terminate. An employer's obligation to accommodate means that it must take reasonable measures short of undue hardship. In *Central Oakanogan School District No. 23 v. Renaud*[94] the Supreme Court of Canada emphasized that the duty to accommodate is limited only to the extent that it does not cause "undue hardship." Hence, accommodating an employee with a disability may be limited by the size of an employer's operation, whether or not safety is an issue, financial cost and whether or not the accommodation would mean a cost to the employer so substantial that it would alter the essential nature of the enterprise or its viability. The duty to accommodate will be discussed further in Section IX dealing specifically with human rights. Also in Section IX is a discussion of what is known as the "bona fide occupational requirement (BFOR)." A *bona fide occupational requirement* means a rule or a policy that can have the effect of discriminating against particular employees, but is justified for safety or efficiency reasons. Essentially, any BFOR or qualification must meet the following threshold:

... it must be imposed honestly, in good faith and in the sincerely held belief that such limitation is imposed in the interests of the adequate performance of the work . . . with all reasonable dispatch, safety and economy. . . .[95]

Second, a BFOR must be related in an objective sense to the performance of the job concerned, in that it is reasonably necessary to assure the efficient and economical performance on the job without endangering

either the employee, fellow workers and/or the general public. An important aspect of the definition of *disability* was canvassed in the Supreme Court of Canada dealing with the rights of pregnant women to apply for disability benefits. In *Brooks v. Canada Safeway Limited*[96] the Supreme Court of Canada determined that providing a disability benefit plan under which pregnant female employees were ineligible for benefits during a 17-week period surrounding the time of their expected confinement was unlawful discrimination contrary to the Manitoba *Human Rights Act.*

In *British Columbia v. B.C.G.S.E.U.*[97] a female applicant successfully argued that the minimum aerobic fitness standards that kept her from becoming a firefighter were discriminatory. In reaching its decision, the Supreme Court of Canada developed a new three-part test for determining whether something is a BFOR.

1. Is it rationally connected to the performance in question?
2. Was it adopted in the honest and good faith belief that it was necessary for the fulfilment of a legitimate work-related purpose?
3. Is it reasonably necessary to the reasonable accomplishment of that legitimate work-related purpose?

By adopting the new test, the court abandoned the previous distinction between direct and adverse effect discrimination in favour of a more unified approach. In assessing whether the elements of the test are met in an accommodation case, courts will take into consideration the procedures, if any, that were used to assess the issue of accommodation, the substantive content of a more accommodating standard and the employer's reason for not providing that standard.

The *Thornton*[98] case was a challenge to the provisions of a group contract of insurance for disability insurance that contained a pre-existing condition exclusion from coverage for long-term disability benefits. The exclusion was challenged under the Ontario *Human Rights Code* on the basis that it constituted discrimination on the basis of handicap. The exclusionary clause was defended on the basis that it fell within the permissible forms of discrimination under Subsection 25(3)(a) of the *Code*, which states:

The right under section 5 to equal treatment with respect to employment without discrimination because of handicap is not infringed,

(a) where a reasonable and "*bona fide*" distinction, exclusion or preference is made in an employee disability or life insurance plan or benefit because of a pre-existing handicap that substantially increases the risk.

(b) where reasonable and "*bona fide*" distinction, exclusion or handicap is made on the grounds of a pre-existing handicap in respect of an employee pay-all or participant pay-all benefit in an employee benefit, pension or superannuation plan or fund, or a contract of group insurance between an insurer and an employer, or in respect of a plan, fund or policy that is offered by an employer to employees if they are fewer than 25 in number.[99]

Specifically, the pre-existing condition clause was challenged and ultimately found to be reasonable and *bona fide,* and that clause was appropriately related to the concrete and substantial increase in risk that it must address in order to fall under the specific exemptions allowed.

Dental Plans

There is not a great deal of jurisprudence in respect of claims pertaining to dental plans. One common issue that arose in the context of the dental benefit but can arise in respect of other employee benefits contained in collective agreements is whether a benefit is mandatory or optional. In the case of *Re Toronto Transit Commission*[100] the employer argued that its agreement in the collective agreement to make a payment to a dental plan on the first of the month following completion of six months' service was optional rather than mandatory. The union and the arbitration board disagreed. Although the employer may have distributed a company booklet to new employees indicating that the coverage was optional, and the contract between the employer and the benefit plan administrator referred to "optional coverage," the wording in the collective agreement indicated that the dental plan coverage was mandatory and must prevail. The arbitration board further stated that any waiver of coverage signed by an individual employee was of no force or effect because an employer cannot, as a matter of private contract with its individual employees, deprive them of the rights secured to them under a collective agreement. Other issues involving dental plans often relate to matters such as "deductibles" and the appropriate dental association fee schedule on the basis of which employees are reimbursed for dental benefits. Most of these cases turn on the wording of the particular collective agreement.

Accidental Death and Dismemberment

An issue that has arisen in some court cases and may arise at arbitration pertains to claims for "accidental dismemberment benefits" where the employee suffers from a particular medical condition that may result in a relatively trivial incident ultimately leading to dismemberment. In such circumstances, courts have adopted a broad definition of what constitutes an *accident* and have indicated that a pre-existing condition, such as a disc protrusion that resulted in a spinal cord malfunction[101] or a diabetic condition that led to an amputation after stepping out of an automobile and slipping,[102] still amounts to an accidental dismemberment.

Changes Due to Legislation

One matter that arises in the context of benefits is whether an employer can unilaterally reduce or discontinue certain benefit contributions as a result of legislative changes. For example, in 1990, the Ontario government abolished health insurance premiums to the Ontario Health Insurance Plan. Numerous employers sought to reduce their contributions to the multi-employer health and welfare trust funds as a result. However, where collective agreements negotiated a fixed contribution to a trust fund that could provide a number of benefits, the Ontario Labour Relations Board has held that an employer could not arbitrarily reduce its contributions by relying on the legal doctrine of frustration of contract.[103]

MULTI-EMPLOYER PLANS TERMINATION

One issue that is unique to multi-employer plans is the ownership of plan assets where the trust in effect fails or is terminated for lack of beneficiaries. In *Re Provincial Plasterers' Benefit Trust Fund*[104] an Ontario high court judge ruled that where a trust fund ceased to have any beneficiaries because all of its members had left the union that created the trust fund as well as the employ of any of the employers, then it was appropriate to merge the trust fund with that of a successor union even though only a small number of the union members actually joined the successor union. The court rejected the argument that there should be a resulting trust in favour of the original members of the trust fund who left the trust, as the trust agreement in question required that any distribution of the fund on termination was to be used for such purposes as in the opinion of the trustees would best implement the trust.[105]

ENDNOTES

1. *Angelo Moro,* [1983] O.L.R.B. Reports August 1354.

2. *B.C. Rapid Transit* (1989), 6 L.A.C. (4th) 310 (McColl).

3. D. Brown and D. Beatty, *Canadian Labour Arbitration,* Third Edition (Aurora, Ontario: Canada Law Book Inc., 1988) topic 4:1400.

4. See: *Abitibi Consolidated Inc.* (1998), 75 L.A.C. (4th) 211 (Craven); *Green Valley Fertilizer* (1991), 22 L.A.C. (4th) 417 (Somjen); *Molson's Brewery (Ont.) Ltd.* (1978), 17 L.A.C. (2d) 354 (Curtis); *Bendix Automotive Canada* (1973), 3 L.A.C. (2d) 21 (Weatherill); *Rexall Drug Co.* (1953), 2 L.A.C. 1468 (Laskin); *Hydro Electric Power Commission of Ontario* (1966), 17 L.A.C. 244 (Thomas); *Globe and Mail Ltd.* (1978), 2 L.A.C. 112 (Fox), application for judicial review dismissed 23 L.A.C. (2d) 144 (Ont. Div. Ct.).

5. *B.C. Rapid Transit* (1989), 6 L.A.C. (4th) 310 (McColl).

6. *Labatts Ontario Breweries Ltd.* (unreported, September 21, 1981 (Palmer)).

7. *Ibid.*

8. *Green Valley Fertilizer* (1991), 22 L.A.C. (4th) 417 (Somjen).

9. *Pilon v. International Minerals and Chemical Corporation (Canada) Limited et al.* (1996), 31 O.R. (3d) 210 (C.A.).

10. *St. Anne-Nackawic Pulp and Paper Company v. Canadian Paper Workers Union, Local 219* (1986), 28 D.L.R. (4th) 1 (S.C.C.).

11. *Weber v. Ontario Hydro* (1995), 125 D.L.R. (4th) 583 (S.C.C.).

12. *St. Anne-Nackawic, supra* note 10 at p. 215.

13. See, in particular, the decisions of arbitrator Mitchnik in *Honeywell Ltd. and CAW-Canada (Moore)* (1997), 65 L.A.C. (4th) 37 and the decision of arbitrator Beck in *Hamilton (City) and C.U.P.E., Local 167* (Poole) (1998), 66 L.A.C. (4th) 129.

14. See, for example, *Walltec Components (Machining Plant) and U.S.W.A., Local 9143* (1998), 69 L.A.C. (4th) 144 (G.J. Brandt); *Abbott Laboratories Ltd. and Retail Wholesale Canada (Div. of U.S.W.A.)*, LOC. 440 (Goodberry)(1998), 74 L.A.C. (4th) 331 (R.Brown); *Oakville (Town) and C.U.P.E., Local 136* (Pillon) (1997), 68 L.A.C. (4th) 117 (O'Neil).

15. *Fleet Manufacturing* (1967), 18 L.A.C. 311 (O'Shea).

16. *Re Corporation of City of London (Dearness Home)* (1991), 19 L.A.C. (4th) 213 (Hunter).

17. *Shell Canada Products Ltd.* (1990), 10 L.A.C. (4th) 30 (Brandt).

18. *Union Gas* (unreported, April 12, 1976 (Weatherill)); application for judicial review dismissed, [1977] O.J. No. 47 (Div. Ct.).

19. *Union Gas* (unreported, October 23, 1981 (Palmer)).

20. *O.N.A. and O.N.A. Staff Union* (1989), 5 L.A.C. (4th) 181 (Burkett).

21. See: *Lever Pond's* (1998), 74 L.A.C. (4th) 81 (Briggs); *Parkwood Hospital & McCormick Home* (1992), 24 L.A.C. (4th) 149 (Haefling); *A.E. McKenzie Co. Ltd.* (1993), 37 L.A.C. (4th) 129 (Hamilton); *Steinberg's Ltd.* (1979), 23 L.A.C. (2d) 331 (O'Shea); *Lufkin Rule Co. of Canada Ltd.* (1973), 3 L.A.C. (2d) 295 (Brown); *Orenda Ltd.* (1969), 20 L.A.C. 337 (Christie); and see generally D. Brown and D. Beatty, *Canadian Labour Arbitration,* supra note 3, topics 3:1200, 4:1400 and 8:3222.

22. *Rights of Labour Act,* R.S.O. 1980, c. 456; see also *Drohan v. Sangamo* (1975), 65 D.L.R. (3d) 15 (Ont.H.C.J.).

23. *Re Heritage Nursing Homes* (unreported, January 9, 1984 (MacDowell)).

24. *Board of Trustees of Edmonton Roman Catholic Separate School District #7 and Alberta Teachers' Association* (1985), 22 L.A.C. (3d) 187 (A.V.M. Beattie).

25. *North Central Plywoods* (1990), 13 L.A.C. (4th) 264 (Somjen).

26. See *North Central Plywoods, supra* note 25; *A.E. McKenzie Co. Ltd., supra* note 21.

27. *Libbey St. Clair Inc.* (1988), 33 L.A.C. (3d) 228 (Brent).

28. *Welland County Hospital* (1986), 24 L.A.C. (3d) 421 (Jolliffe).

29. *Gates Canada Inc.* (unreported, (H.D. Brown)) cited in *Arbitration Review* (January 1985), p. 2.

30. *General Tire Limited* (1985), 15 L.A.C. (3d) 81 (Rayner).

31. *St. Mary's Hospital,* [1979] O.L.R.B. Report August 795 (MacDowell).

32. *Dayco (Canada) Limited v. C.A.W.* (1993), 102 D.L.R. (4th) 609 (S.C.C.).

33. *James v. Town of Richmond Hill* (1986), 54 O.R. (2d) 555 (H.C.); *Canada (Attorney General) v. Confederation Life Insurance Co.* (1995), 24 O.R. (3d) 717 (G.D.).

34. *Blair v. Dominion Stores Limited,* [1987] O.J. No. 420 (S.C.O.).

35. *Re St. Mary's Paper* (1993), 15 O.R. (3d) 359 (G.D.); aff'd (1994), 26 C.B.R. (3d) 273 (Ont. C.A.).

36. *Erie Iron Works Ltd.* (1970), 21 L.A.C. 320 (Weatherill).

37. *Re Pacific Press* (1991), 22 L.A.C. (4th) 241 (Fraser).

38. *Torcullo v. Allied Chemical Canada Ltd.* (1989), 26 C.C.E.L. 209 (Ont. H.C.).

39. *Steinberg's Limited* (1979), 23 L.A.C. (2d) 331 (J.D. O'Shea).

40. *Ibid.,* at p. 340.

41. *Wilpark Foods* (1991), 21 L.A.C. (4th) 441 (Ladner).

42. *Supra* note 21 at p. 341.

43. *TRW Canada* (1990), 19 L.A.C. (4th) 374 (O'Shea).

44. *Regional Municipality of Halton* (1991), 18 L.A.C. (4th) 428 (R.M. Brown).

45. *Crawford v. The Citadel General Assurance Corp.* (1982), 54 N.S.R. (2d) 407 (S.C.), supplementary reasons at (1982), 54 N.S.R (2d) 533.

46. *Ibid.,* supplementary reasons at p.534.

47. *Corr v. London Life* (1983), 63 N.S.R. (2d) 116 (S.C.).

48. *Paul Revere Life Insurance Company v. Sucharov* (1985), 5 D.L.R. (4th) 199 (S.C.C.).

49. *Dominion Stores Ltd.* (1983), 11 L.A.C. (3d) 221 (M.G. Picher).

50. *Ibid.,* at p. 235.

51. *Burns Meats, Division of Burns Foods* (1991), 23 L.A.C. (4th) 318 (Hamilton).

52. *Andres Wines (B.C.) Limited* (1977), 16 L.A.C. (2d) 422 (Weiler).

53. *In Automatic Electric (Canada) Ltd.* (1978), 18 L.A.C. (2d) 234 (Adams).

54. *Somerville Packaging* (1990), 11 L.A.C. (4th) 248 (Barton).

55. *Vouzas v. Lewis Motors et al.* (1983), 41 O.R. (2d) 538 (C.A.).

56. *Association Freezers of Canada Ltd.* (unreported, July 25, 1984 (Christie)).

57. *Aylmer Foods Warehousing Ltd.* (unreported, March 2, 1982 (Burkett)).

58. *Re Caland Ore Co. Ltd.* (1974), 4 L.A.C. (2d) 428 (Brown).

59. *Canada Carbon and Ribbon Co. Ltd.* (1977), 15 L.A.C. (2d) 133 (Dunn).

60. *York Region Board of Ed.* (1990), 11 L.A.C. (4th) 345 (Marszewski).

61. *Labour Relations Act,* 1995, S.O. 1995, c. 1, Sch. A.

62. *B.C. Transit* (1988), 3 L.A.C. (4th) 151 (MacIntyre).

63. *Canada Post Corporation v. C.U.P.W.* (Gugins) (1991), 25 C.L.A.S. 219 (M.G. Picher).

64. *Unity Hospital Board v. Metcalfe et al.* (1984), 34 Sask. R. 95 (Q.B.).

65. *City of Trail* (unreported, February 25, 1983 (Munroe)).

66. *Re Etobicoke General Hospital and ONA* (1992), 25 L.A.C. (4th) 376 (Craven).

67. See *Toronto District School Board* (1999), 56 C.L.A.S. 122 (Knopf); *Greater Victoria School District No. 61 (Board of School Trustees)* (1998), 78 L.A.C. (4th) 289 (Jackson); *West Park Hospital Toronto* (1996), 55 L.A.C. (4th) 78 (Emrich); and see generally Brown and Beatty, *supra* note 3, topic 7:3220.

68. See *Queen's Regional Authority* (1999), 78 L.A.C. (4th) 269 (Christie); *Greater Niagara General Hospital* (1995), 47 L.A.C. (4th) 366 (Brent).

69. *Canada Post Corp.* (1998), 73 L.A.C. (4th) 15 (Ponak).

70. *Treasury Board (Employment and Immigration Canada)* (1993), 33 L.A.C. (4th) 203 (P.S.S.R.B., Burke).

71. *Colonial Cookies* (1990), 17 L.A.C. (4th) 366 (Barton); *Hamilton Street Railway Co. & A.T.U., Loc. 107* (1994), 41 L.A.C. (4th) 1 (Levinson).

72. *Regional Municipality of Halton* (1991), 18 L.A.C. (4th) 428 (R.M. Brown).

73. *Alberta v. A.U.P.E.* (1992), 26 C.L.A.S. 70 (Munroe).

74. *Ferranti-Packard Transformers Ltd.* (unreported, July 16, 1984 (Devlin)).

75. *Mississauga Transit* (unreported, August 27, 1984 (Devlin)).

76. *Dehavilland Aircraft* (1982), L.A.C. (3d) 271 (Rayner).

77. *Queensway General Hospital* (1984), 17 L.A.C. (3d) 9 (Swan).

78. *Glideen Co.* (unreported, January 25, 1985 (Samuels)).

79. *Wolverine Tube* (1991), 22 L.A.C. (4th) 62 (Munroe).

80. See: *Dare Foods* (unreported, July 17, 1980 (O'Shea)); *Keeprite* (1982), 7 L.A.C. (3d) 112 (Brown).

81. *Dufferin County v. C.U.P.E.* (1990), 22 C.L.A.S. 103 (McLean); *Brinks Canada Ltd.* (1994), 41 L.A.C. (4th) 424 (Stewart).

82. *Air Canada* (unreported, November 22, 1983 (Simmons)).

83. *Thompson and Town of Oakville* (1964), 1 O.R. 122 (Ont. H.C.); *Brinks Canada Ltd., supra* note 81.

84. *City of London* (unreported, March 20, 1983 (Langille)).

85. *Ibid.*

86. *Ontario Hydro* (unreported, February 25, 1985 (Swan)).

87. *Ibid.*

88. *Parkridge Care Home* (1991), 23 C.L.A.S. 146 (Larson).

89. *Trailo v. Allied Chemical Canada Ltd.* (1989), 26 C.C.E.L. 209 (Ont. S.C.).

90. *Casimir Jennings and Appleby* (1989), 5 L.A.C. (4th) 443 (Joyce).

91. *Ibid.,* at p. 444.

92. *Dennis v. Family and Children Services of London and Middlesex* (1990), 12 C.H.H.R. D/285 (Backhouse).

93. *Ibid.,* at D/288.

94. *Central Okanogan School District No. 23 v. Renaud* (1992), 95 D.L.R. (4th) 577 (S.C.C.).

95. *Ontario Human Rights Commission v. Etobicoke (Borough of),* [1982] 1 S.C.R. 202 at p. 208, 132 D.L.R. (3d) 14 at 19-20 (S.C.C.).

96. *Brooks v. Canada Safeway Limited* (1989), 59 D.L.R. (4th) 321 (S.C.C.).

97. *British Columbia (Public Service Employee Relations Committee) v. British Columbia Government and Service Employees' Union (B.C.G.S.E.U.),* [1999] 3 S.C.R. 3.

98. *Thornton v. North American Life Assurance Co.* (1992), 93 C.L.L.C. ¶17,002 (Ont. Bd. of Inquiry); aff'd (1995), 123 D.L.R. (4th) 709 (Ont. Div. Ct.).

99. Ontario *Human Rights Code,* R.S.O. 1990, c. H.19.

100. *Re Toronto Transit Commission* (1989), 4 L.A.C. (4th) 129 (Springate).

101. *Voison v. Royal Insurance* (1988), 66 O.R. (2d) 45 (C.A.).

102. *Meyer v. Allstate Insurance,* [1981] I.L.R. 1-1334 (Man. C.A.).

103. See *Halton Forming,* [1990] O.L.R.B. Reports May 553 (Gray) and *Hamilton Harbour Commissioner's* (unreported, August 20, 1990 (Rayner)).

104. *Re Provincial Plasterers' Benefit Trust Fund* (1990), 71 O.R. (2d) 558 (H.C.J.).

105. Parts of this chapter are excerpted from A. Esson, D. Wakely and M. Zigler, *Negotiated Employee Benefits A Guide for the Labour Practitioner,* Chapter C of Law Society of Upper Canada Labour Law Update, 1985, "Pension and Other Negotiated Employee Benefit Plans."

CHAPTER 3

Taxation of Life and Health Insurance Benefits

by Roberto Tomassini

GENERAL TAXATION PRINCIPLES

General taxation principles for life and health insurance benefits are those set out in Section I, Chapter 8, dealing with government policy on taxation of employee benefits and the general system of taxation of income. However, with respect to life and health insurance benefits, recent political trends and legislative changes need to be highlighted. As well, there are particular provisions in the *Income Tax Act* (Canada) (ITA)[1] that should be considered.

The income tax status of employee life and health insurance benefits stems primarily from Section 6(1)(a) of ITA, which taxes the value of "board, lodging and other benefits of any kind whatever received or enjoyed" by a taxpayer in respect of "an office or employment." To this general rule of taxing all benefits, there are certain tax-free exceptions, particularly those set out in Section 6(1)(a)(i), which refers to those benefits:

> . . . derived from the contributions of the taxpayer's employer contributions to or under a registered pension plan, group sickness or accident insurance plan, private health services, supplementary unemployment benefit plan, deferred profit sharing plan or group term life insurance policy . . .

There is a further exemption for benefits derived from counselling services in respect of the mental or physical health of the taxpayer under Section 6(1)(a)(iv), or with respect to such counselling services for an individual related to the taxpayer.

Revenue Canada has issued a number of Interpretation Bulletins, and there have been a few cases pertaining to some of these benefits. Group life and health insurance benefits have generally been covered under the umbrella of "group sickness or accident insurance plans, private health services plans" or "group term life insurance policies." Revenue Canada's Interpretation Bulletins, although they do not have the force of law, are quite helpful in dealing with these issues. Further, the Revenue Canada Interpretation Bulletin on Health and Welfare Trusts, IT-85R2,[2] a copy of which is attached as Appendix III-3-A to this chapter, governs most of the transactions that a multi-employer health and welfare trust fund would engage in.

RECENT TRENDS

Against this legislative backdrop, one must bear in mind that the tax status of employment benefits is not static. Moreover, the policy reasons for having tax-based incentives for creating and maintaining employment benefits plans are not universally accepted. Although historically employer contributions to private health care benefit funds have enjoyed tax-exempt status and premiums paid to employer-provided group life insurance plans were tax-exempt up to the first $25,000 worth of benefits, both the economic realities of the '90s and emphasis on deficit reduction have forced governments in Canada to look for new sources of revenue. Life and health benefit funds have become one of several primary targets.

The federal government, in its 1994 budget, removed the tax-exempt status enjoyed by employer-funded life insurance benefits for periods after the June 1994 budget. The amendment was touted as part of the Liberal government's objective to promote tax equity rather than increase taxes. The stated rationale for taxing employer-funded life insurance benefits is that workers without employer-funded plans are forced to buy life insurance benefits, not publicly provided, with their after tax income, thereby creating inequity between those employees with the good fortune of working for employers that provide the benefits and those that did not. Therefore, employer contributions to group life insurance plans are now taxable benefits in the hands of employees.

While the federal government also considered taxing employer-funded health benefits in its pre-budget consultation in 1994 and 1995—primarily due to the lobbying efforts of multi-employer benefit funds, trade union groups, the health and life insurance industry and the Canadian Dental Association, among others—privately funded health insurance plans were spared, at least for now.

The Quebec government was not as reserved as its federal counterpart with respect to utilizing privately funded health benefit funds as a source of additional revenue. In its May 1993 budget, the previous tax exemption on employer contributions to private health insurance plans was revoked. In addition, the previous tax exemption on employer contributions for the first $25,000 of benefits under a private group life insurance plan was eliminated. These tax measures are discussed in greater detail below.

Apart from income tax measures, other means of taxation are now being utilized by governments to raise revenues at the expense of employee benefits. Provincial retail sales taxes and the federal Goods and Services Tax (GST) may not directly affect employees receiving benefits from employer-funded plans, but the indirect effect in terms of the increased costs in providing such benefits cannot be ignored. These non-income-based taxes are reviewed in greater detail below after we review the income tax status with respect to certain specific benefits.

GROUP SICKNESS OR ACCIDENT INSURANCE PLANS

Contributions to these plans are not taxable under Section 6(1)(a) of ITA. However, there must be a plan, and the plan must be one to which the employer contributes. The plan must be a *group* plan, not an individual plan of the employee to which the employer contributes. In *Meyer v. M.N.R.*,[3] the taxpayer was covered by a trust agreement but was held taxable on premiums paid by the employer because he was the only employee and the insurance could not be considered to be a group plan.

In dealing with group sickness or accident insurance plans, consideration should also be given to Section 6(1)(f) of ITA, under which payments eventually received by the employee to supplement lost income are taxable. Accordingly, short-term and long-term disability benefits under an insured plan are taxable to the employee as wage loss replacement plans even though the premiums are not taxable if paid by the employer. In some instances, employees prefer to pay their own premiums out of *after tax* income so as to obtain a tax-free insurance benefit.

PRIVATE HEALTH SERVICES BENEFITS

As noted above, Section 6(1)(a)(i) of ITA provides for specific exemptions to the general rule that all employee benefits are taxable. One such exception is for benefits derived from a "private health services plan."

A *private health services plan* is defined in ITA, Section 248, and essentially refers to:

(a) a contract of insurance in respect of hospital expenses, medical expenses or any combination of such expenses, or

(b) a medical care insurance plan or hospital care insurance plan or any combination of such plans . . .

Specifically *excluded* from the definition are government-operated plans such as provincial health insurance plans or plans created by federal legislation that authorizes provision of medical care insurance or hospital care insurance.

This exclusion for private health services benefits in Section 6(1)(a)(i) covers most employer contributions to any kind of plan or trust that provides typically "private" health benefits. Revenue Canada Interpretation Bulletin IT-339R2[4] attached as Appendix III- 3-B to this chapter sets out Revenue Canada's opinion on private health services plans. Its text is self-explanatory, and it is important to review it when establishing any trust fund or plan to provide private health insurance type benefits. These benefits typically include supplementary medical benefits, dental benefits, drug plans, eyeglass and hearing aid plans, plans involving medical equipment and prostheses, private hospital room coverage, out-of-province and out-of-country medical and hospital coverage, etc. For an extensive list of possible benefits, consideration should be given to any benefit for which the medical expense credit is available and that is listed in the section on medical expense credit in this chapter.

Revenue Canada has produced rulings to indicate that self-insured health and welfare trust funds come within the definition of *private health services plan* as long as there is some form of a pooled risk and a proper trust fund established. Most multi-employer health and welfare funds come within such definition. The statutory definition of *private health services plan* requires either an insurance contract or a "plan" that "is in the nature of insurance." This is defined in the Interpretation Bulletin to involve an undertaking by one person to indemnify another person for an agreed consideration from a loss or a liability in respect of an event, the happening of which is uncertain.

Where the premium under a private health services plan is paid by the employer in terms of contributions to a health and welfare trust, the contribution is a deductible expense to the employer and is not a taxable benefit to the employee. Employees who must pay their own premiums are permitted a tax deduction as a medical expense under Section 118.2(2)(q) of ITA.

QUEBEC

As indicated at the outset of this chapter, the Quebec government in May of 1993 eliminated the tax-exempt status for employer-funded health benefits. The legislation effecting these tax measures (Bill 112)[5] was assented to on December 17, 1993 but is effective from May 21, 1993.

The Bill 112 amendments provide two methods of calculating the amount of tax to be paid on employer health plan contributions, depending on whether the plan is an insured or self-insured one. A further provision was implemented to deal with the situation of multi-employer plans.

For insured plans, the value of the taxable benefit is the premium paid by the employer less the portion of the premium that can be reasonably attributed to coverage related to the cost that would be assumed by the Régie de l'assurance-maladie du Québec in respect of insured services under the *Health Insurance Act*. Where an employee has reimbursed his or her employer with respect to benefits received or where the employer receives a premium discount or dividend, the taxable benefit is reduced by the sums reimbursed and the portion of any return or dividend attributable to the benefits received by the employee.

The premium by an employer includes the 2.35% insurance premium tax and the 9% sales tax on group insurance premiums, payable in Quebec.

For self-insured plans, the value of the taxable benefit is the employees' pro-rata share of the plan's benefit payments based on the number of days they were covered under the plan during the calendar year. This includes any expenses incurred with a third party to administer or operate the plan as well as the above-mentioned insurance premium tax and sales tax on group insurance premiums. As in the case of insured plans, the taxable benefit does not include that portion of the benefit paid by the employer that can reasonably be related to the costs that would be assumed by the Quebec Public Health Insurance Plan under the *Health Insurance Act*.

In order to allocate the total taxable amount to each employee, the number of employees entitled to protection under the plan is first to be determined for each day of the year. Totaling the data for each day of the plan's existence during the year produces the number of employee days of coverage for this year. The benefit conferred on an employee is obtained by multiplying the ratio of the total amount of benefits to be allocated to the number of employee days of coverage by the number of days for which he or she benefited from the protection provided by the plan. The benefit calculated for any employee who contributed must be reduced by the value of his or her contributions during the year.

Administering the employee benefit tax with respect to multi-employer insurance schemes is somewhat more exacting for at least two reasons. First, many multi-employer plans provide coverage for items other than the insurance protection that is the object of the tax measure, i.e., wage loss protection. Secondly, the communal nature of the plan does not allow employers to know the value of the benefit conferred on any particular employee. Individual employers, therefore, may not have the necessary information for determining the taxable value of the benefits conferred.

Addressing the first issue, the legislation imposes tax on individual employees for the portion of contributions made on their behalf to the administrator of such plans, "which can reasonably be attributed to a plan for the insurance of persons otherwise other than in relation to coverage against the loss of all or part of income from an office of employment."[6]

With respect to the second issue, the Ministry of Revenue and Finance released an Information Bulletin on October 8, 1993, providing guidance to employers and plan administrators in determining the value of the taxable benefit with respect to benefits paid pursuant to a multi-employer plan.

The Bulletin imposes upon the plan administrator the obligation to determine for each employee, by actuarial methods, the portion of contributions made to the plan that can reasonably be attributed to insurance protection other than income replacement protection. This amount must be disclosed to each employer belonging to the plan. The plan administrator is also required to produce a statement for each employee indicating the value of the benefit he or she received during a given year, calculated according to the method prescribed in the Information Bulletin.

Each employer member of the multi-employer plan will be required, for the purposes of withholding tax deductions at source, to add the amount attributable to each employee, as determined by the administrator, to the salary or remuneration otherwise paid to the employee for each pay period. These totals are then recorded, in the normal manner, on each employee's Relevé 1 statement (T4 equivalent) for the year.

GROUP TERM LIFE INSURANCE

Payments to a group term life insurance policy by the employer were, prior to February 1994, deductible by the employer from its income and neither the benefit nor the contribution was taxable to the employee for the first $25,000 of the benefit. As noted above, in 1994, the federal government removed the partial tax exemption on life insurance benefits. Employee participants in group life insurance plans are required to include in their calculation of income from an office or employment an amount in respect of the value of the entire benefit as of July 1994.

Subsection 6(4) of the ITA, as amended to implement the 1994 budget changes, requires a taxpayer to include in income for the year from an office or employment the amount "prescribed for the year in respect of the insurance."

Regulation 2700 to 2704 of the ITA sets out the method by which the "prescribed amount" is to be calculated. The amount equals the amount of term insurance purchased for the year calculated on a daily basis, multiplied by the average daily cost of providing the insurance for the year. The taxpayer is also required to include in income all sales and excise tax payable on premiums by the taxpayer's employer.

The Regulations include a special transition provision for "paid-up insurance benefits." The legislation defines *paid-up insurance premiums* as payments made to secure insurance on the life of an individual where the insurance is for the remainder of the life of the individual and no further premiums are payable. The transition provision permits a taxpayer to spread over three taxation years any lump-sum premium payment made before 1997 that qualifies as paid-up insurance.

COUNSELLING SERVICES FOR HEALTH, RE-EMPLOYMENT OR RETIREMENT

Section 6(1)(a)(iv) of ITA provides an express exemption from tax for the value of any contributions made by the employer for counselling services in respect of mental or physical health or re-employment or retirement of a taxpayer. Accordingly, many health and welfare plans or pension plans may provide retirement counselling or "mental or physical health counselling" to assist employees. In December of 1989 the Department of Finance by Special Release[7] amended its Interpretation Bulletin IT-470R[8] dealing with "employee fringe benefits" to provide that "counselling benefits" that would be tax-free include benefits for such services as tobacco, drug or alcohol counselling, stress management counselling, and job placement and retirement counselling, among others.

OTHER BENEFITS

Interpretation Bulletin IT-470R deals generally with "employee fringe benefits." The Bulletin deals with many benefits, most of which are *not* related to life and health insurance and most of which are not traditionally provided under any multi-employer trust arrangement. However, there is a list of benefits that are to be *included* in income as opposed to those *excluded.* Below is a brief review of the benefits included in income, namely:

- Board and lodging subject to IT-91R4[9] dealing with employment at remote worksites where there are special exemptions
- Subsidized housing
- Travel benefits pertaining to business travel
- Use of automobiles
- Gifts in excess of $100
- Holiday trips, prizes and other incentive awards
- Frequent flyer program trips for non-business purposes
- Travelling expenses of an employee's spouse unless the spouse is engaged primarily in business activities on behalf of the employer
- Premiums under provincial hospitalization and medical care insurance plans
- Tuition fees, unless the course was undertaken on the employer's initiative and for the benefit of the employer rather than the employee
- Cost of tools
- Financial counselling and income tax preparation
- Interest-free and low-interest loans. These are dealt with specifically under Revenue Canada Interpretation Bulletin IT-421R2.[10]

The following amounts are generally *not* included in income:

- Discounts on merchandise
- Subsidized meals
- Uniforms and special clothing
- Free or subsidized school tuition provided by the employer in remote or unorganized areas, or where the employer is a school
- Transportation to the job, unless there is a reimbursement allowance
- Employer-provided recreational facilities
- Moving expenses
- Premiums under private health services plans
- Employer contributions required under provincial hospitalization or medical care plans or statutes
- Transportation passes provided to employees and retired employees of airlines, bus and rail companies.

As a general principle, benefits are taxable unless specifically excluded in ITA or by virtue of Revenue Canada's administrative practice as set out in Interpretation Bulletins.

MEDICAL EXPENSE CREDIT

An important factor to consider in the taxation of health benefits is the medical expense credit available to any taxpayer in terms of medical expenses actually incurred by him or her. Essentially, this credit, available under Section 118.2 of ITA, is the amount of medical expenses incurred subtracted from the *lesser* of $1,500 or 3% of the individual's income for the year. The definition of *medical expenses* is fairly extensive and is, in fact, quite helpful in determining the types of expenses that are deductible if provided through a group life and health insurance plan under Section 6(1)(a). Such expenses include:

1. Payments to medical practitioners, dentists, nurses, or public or licensed hospitals in respect of medical or dental services
2. Remuneration for one full-time attendant or full-time care in a nursing home
3. Remuneration paid to one full-time attendant in a self-contained domestic establishment in which the patient lives if a medical certification has been given that such attendant is required for a long, continued period of indefinite duration *and* the attendant is not under 18 years of age or a blood relative to the individual or his or her spouse
4. Care and training at a school or institution, or other place if the patient is handicapped
5. Ambulance transportation to or from a hospital
6. Transportation to medical services under certain circumstances
7. Artificial limbs, iron lungs or other medical devices
8. Eyeglasses or other devices to correct vision defects as prescribed by a medical practitioner or optometrist
9. Oxygen tent or other devices to administer oxygen
10. Seeing eye dog
11. Drugs prescribed by a medical practitioner or dentist and as recorded by a pharmacist
12. Reasonable expenses including legal fees and insurance premiums incurred to locate a compatible donor and arrange a transplant of bone marrow or an organ
13. Reasonable expenses relating to renovations or alterations to make a dwelling accessible or functional for patients who lack physical development or suffer from severe and prolonged mobility impairment
14. Reasonable expenses relating to rehabilitative therapy
15. Laboratory, radiological and other diagnostic procedures prescribed by medical practitioners or dentists
16. Denture repairs
17. Premiums, contributions or other consideration to a private health services plan in respect of a taxpayer, a taxpayer's spouse and any member of the taxpayer's household with whom the individual is connected by blood relationship, marriage or adoption.

In the February 1999 Federal Budget this list was expanded to include:[11]

1. Care and supervision of persons with severe and prolonged disabilities living in a group home
2. Therapy for persons with severe and prolonged disabilities
3. Tutoring for persons with learning disabilities (or other mental impairments)
4. An expansion of the list of eligible perceptual equipment for persons with disabilities to include talking textbooks prescribed in connection with an enrolment at an educational institution.

ITA Regulation 5700 contains an extensive list of medical devices and equipment for which tax deductions are available. Of course, a taxpayer cannot claim the medical expense credit for any medical expense for which he or she has been reimbursed through any group or individual insurance plan.

TAXATION OF HEALTH AND WELFARE TRUST FUNDS

Revenue Canada Bulletin IT-85R2[12] is attached as Appendix III-3-A to this chapter and is, for the most part, self-explanatory. It attempts to govern *health and welfare trust funds,* even though such trust funds are not explicitly referred to in ITA.

Health and welfare trust funds are generally taxable under the act as *inter vivos* trusts. The Interpretation Bulletin is an attempt to adapt the concept of the taxation of private health service plans and group life, sickness and disability benefits, and taxation of trusts, to trust funds that have been established to provide these benefits. However, there are difficulties in situations where the trust funds provide other benefits that are not tax-free or where payments of the income of the trusts are payable for purposes *other than* the provision of benefits or the administration of the fund. For example, IT-85R2 does not make reference to benefits such as group life insurance or payments for provincial health insurance premiums where applicable. Until such time as there is clear legislative recognition of health and welfare trust funds or clarification of Revenue Canada's administrative position in IT-85R2, many of the taxation issues that arise in taxing the income of a health and welfare trust or benefits to employees, and deductibility to employers, will remain unclear.

RETAIL SALES AND GOODS AND SERVICES TAXES

In May of 1993 the Ontario government announced, as part of its annual budget, an amendment to the *Retail Sales Tax Act*[13] that would impose an 8% tax on all premiums paid in respect of all contracts of insurance, subject to certain exceptions such as individually purchased life, health and disability insurance contracts. Therefore, all contracts of insurance for employment benefits will be subject to the Ontario sales tax of 8% where the contract was entered into on or after May 20, 1993, all renewals containing a substantial change in their terms and conditions with effect after May 20, 1993, and all renewals of individual contracts where the expiry date is after June 30, 1993.[14]

The tax measures were contained initially in Bill 30, *An Act to Amend the Retail Sales Tax Act,* introduced in the legislature on June 1, 1993. Although the government's intention was to impose the 8% sales tax on all group life insurance plans, the proposed legislation was ambiguous with respect to its application to multiemployer group life insurance plans. This ambiguity was subsequently corrected by the introduction of Bill 138, *An Act to Amend the Retail Sales Tax Act,* which replaced Bill 30.

Bill 138 imposes upon members of multi-employer group life insurance plans an obligation to remit an additional 8% on its contributions to the plan administrator or trustees. However, whether the sales tax is in fact remitted, the Ontario government's position is that the tax is deemed to have been paid to the fund when a contribution is made, and the plan administrator or trustees bear the risk of loss if the employer members fail to make required contributions or fail to remit the 8% tax on contributions made. This risk borne by the plan is of particular concern given that the legislation does not confer on plan administrators or trustees any powers to enforce or collect the additional 8% sales tax from delinquent employers.

Although the 1993 budget marked the first time in Ontario that group insurance contracts were made subject to provincial sales tax, insurance premiums paid in Quebec have been subject to a 9% provincial sales tax since 1985.

The 7% federal Goods and Services Tax (the GST) was introduced in 1990 and is levied on almost all goods and services with some exceptions as set out in Schedules V and VI of the *Excise Tax Act.*[15] Schedule V sets out the products or services that are "exempt supplies" and do not attract the GST for those who purchase the product or service. The exemption covers most financial services, including services provided by insurers to employee benefit plans with respect to life and health insurance coverage. Therefore, premiums paid by employees or their employers to group life and health benefit plans do not attract the 7% GST. Moreover, when the insurer or an employer purchases prescription drugs or medical devices pursuant to a benefit plan, no tax is paid with respect to these purchases as these products are *zero-rated supplies* as defined in Schedule VI of the *Excise Tax Act.*

Apart from the direct impact on employee benefits, the GST has an important indirect effect on employee benefits in terms of the costs of administering such plans.

The GST is intended to be a value-added consumption tax only. That is, vendors engaged in *commercial activities,* as defined by the *Excise Tax Act,* are only required to pay the GST on the difference between the value of goods and services that they purchase and the value of the product or services they produce. Therefore, vendors charge the GST on their products but are not required to remit the entire amount of GST they collect. Rather, they are permitted to deduct the amount of GST they have paid on goods and services purchased in order to make their product or provide their service.

These deductions are referred to as *input tax credits (ITCs).* They are available only to those who pay GST on services or products purchased in the course of "commercial activity." Final consumers are intended to bear the ultimate cost of the full tax, with no deduction or rebates, except for credits related to income levels. Arguably, employee benefit trust funds are really intermediaries or conduits providing an end product to consumers and should not have to bear the full cost of the GST. However, this is not the case.

The GST treats benefit plans as comprising of two elements; a "financial service" element and an "administrative service" element. In the case of a health and welfare plan, the "financial service" is the purchase of insurance policies providing health and welfare coverage. Under the GST, most "financial services" are exempt services. No GST is charged by a person providing exempt services to the recipient of them. However, the provider of "exempt services" is not eligible for any ITCs with respect to them. Accordingly, to the extent that life and health benefit plans purchase supplies to provide "financial services," they must pay the GST on those supplies and are not eligible for ITCs.

The *administrative element* in a health and welfare or group life insurance plan refers to services such as: the design of a health plan; the preparation of plan documents and information booklets for members; the design and publication of appropriate forms; the establishment of application procedures; the process of receiving, reviewing and adjudicating applications for benefits; amending the plans; and contracting with outside professionals to accomplish these ends. These supplies are "taxable supplies" and not GST exempted. In a single employer plan, these administrative services are considered to be undertaken by the employer in the course of its "commercial activities." Accordingly, the employer may claim ITCs with respect to the services it purchases to administer its plan.

Multi-employer plans, on the other hand, were treated quite differently. Since contributing employers have no role in the administration of the plan, the trustees of the plan must incur both administrative and investment expenses. However, when plan trustees incur GST for administrative services they purchase, they are not eligible for ITCs. In the single employer sector, the employer itself is able to incur these administrative expenses and to claim ITCs for GST amounts expended. For multi-employer plans, trustees must incur these expenses directly. Since trustees are not engaged in "commercial activity," they are not eligible for ITCs, even on the expenses incurred for the administration of the plan. Consequently, multi-employer plans have been at a serious disadvantage as compared to their single employer counterparts.

In 1999, the Department of Finance recognized this inequity. The Minister of Finance in a Release dated August 12, 1999 introduced a rebate to trust funds equal to 33% of the otherwise unrecoverable taxes incurred on expenses relating to the plans.[16] This measure is intended to put trusteed multi-employer plans on equal footing with single employer plans.

ENDNOTES

1. *Income Tax Act,* R.S.C. 1985 (5th Supp.).

2. Revenue Canada, Interpretation Bulletin IT-85R2, "Health and Welfare Trusts for Employees" (31 July 1986).

3. *Meyer v. M.N.R.,* [1977] CTC 2581 (Tax Review Board).

4. Revenue Canada, Interpretation Bulletin IT-339R2, "Meaning of Private Health Services Plan" (8 August 1989).

5. *An Act to Again Amend the Taxation Act and Various Legislative Provisions,* R.S.Q., 1993, C.64, Sections 37.01.1. to 37.0.1.6 and 43 and 43.1 of the Taxation Act, R.S.Q., I-3.

6. R.S.O., c.I-3, s.43.2, as amended.

7. Revenue Canada, Interpretation Bulletin Special Release IT-470RSR, "Employee Fringe Benefits" (11 December 1989).

8. Revenue Canada, Interpretation Bulletin IT-470R, "Employees' Fringe Benefits" (8 April 1988).

9. Revenue Canada, Interpretation Bulletin IT-91R4, "Employment at Special Work Sites or Remote Work Locations" (17 June 1996).

10. Revenue Canada, Interpretation Bulletin IT-421R2, "Benefits to Individuals, Corporations and Shareholders from Loan or Debt" (9 September 1992).

11. Notice of Ways and Means Motion, Federal Budget, February 16, 1999.

12. *Supra* note 1.

13. *Ontario Retail Sales Tax Act,* R.S.O. 1990, c.R.31.

14. *Ibid.,* Section 2.1.

15. *Excise Tax Act,* R.S.C. 1985, c. E-14.

16. Department of Finance, "Sales Tax Proposals Announced Relating to Passenger Transportation Services, Multi-Employer Pension Plans, and the Federal Sales Tax Rebate on Books" (News Release 99-072, August 12, 1999).

APPENDIX III-3-A

JULY 31, 1986

HEALTH AND WELFARE TRUSTS FOR EMPLOYEES

Paragraph 6(1)(a) and section 104 (also subsections 6(4), 12.2(3), (4), and (7), paragraphs 6(1)(f), 56(1)(d), and (d.1), 60(a), 110(8)(a) and subparagraphs 148(9)(c)(vii) and (ix); also section 19 of the Income Tax Application Rules, 1971 (ITAR)).

This bulletin replaces and cancels IT-85R, dated January 20, 1975. Proposals contained in the Notice of Ways and Means Motion of June 11, 1986 are not considered in this release.

1. The general thrust of paragraph 6(1)(a) is to include in employment income the value of all benefits received or enjoyed in respect of an employee's employment. However, there are a number of specific exceptions many of which can be described as benefits relating to the health and welfare of the employee. In some cases, the scope of the excepted benefits and applicable tax treatment are well established by other provisions of the Act, (e.g., registered pension funds or plans, deferred profit sharing plans, supplementary unemployment benefit plans, the standby charge for the use of an employer's automobile, employee benefit plans and employee trusts). The treatment to be accorded to the other exceptions can be less clear, particularly when the benefits form part of an omnibus health and welfare program administered by an employer. The purpose of this bulletin is to describe the tax treatment accorded to an employee health and welfare benefit program that is administered by an employer through a trust arrangement and that is restricted to

   (a) a group sickness or accident insurance plan (see 2 below),
   (b) a private health services plan,
   (c) a group term life insurance policy, or
   (d) any combination of (a) to (c).

2. Paragraph 6(1)(f) sets out the treatment of periodic receipts related to loss of income from employment under three types of insurance plans to which the employer had made a contribution. These types of plans are sickness or accident, disability and income maintenance (also known as salary continuation). In the absence of any statutory definition, the Department generally accepts that an employer's contribution to any of the three types of plans will be a contribution to a "group sickness or accident insurance plan" as described in subparagraph 6(1)(a)(i), provided that the particular plan is a "group" plan and an insured plan. This is based on the assumption that a "disability" resulting in loss of employment income would almost invariably arise from sickness or an accident and that an "income maintenance" payment would likely arise from loss of employment income due to sickness or an accident if not lay off (the latter reason justifying an exception under subparagraph 6(1)(a)(i) as a supplementary unemployment benefit plan). There may be situations where these assumptions will prove invalid but, subject to this caveat, 1(a) above may also be read as a "group disability insurance plan" or "a group income maintenance insurance plan that is not a supplementary unemployment benefit plan."

Employee Benefit Plans and Employee Trusts

3. Employee benefit plans are broadly defined in subsection 248(1) and can encompass health and welfare arrangements. However, funds or plans described in 1(a) to (d) above are specifically excluded in the definition and are thus accorded the tax treatment outlined in this bulletin. Health and welfare arrangements not described in 1(a) to (d) above (e.g., those not based on insurance) may be employee benefit plans or, less likely, employee trusts subject to the tax consequences outlined in IT-502.

4. Where part of a single plan could be regarded as a plan described in 1(a) to (d) above and another part as an employee benefit plan or an employee trust, the combined plan will be given employee benefit plan or employee trust treatment in respect of the timing and amounts of both the employer's expense deductions and the employees' receipt of benefits under the plan. However, if contributions, income and disbursements of the part of the plan that is described in 1(a) to (d) above are separately identified and accounted for, the tax treatment outlined in this bulletin will apply to that part of the plan.

Meaning of Health and Welfare Trust

5. Health and welfare benefits for employees are sometimes provided through a trust arrangement under which the trustees (usually with equal representation from the employer or employers' group and the employees or their union) receive the contributions from the employer(s), and in some cases from employees, to provide such health and welfare benefits as have been agreed to between the employer and the employees. If the benefit programs adopted are limited to those described in 1(a) to (d) above and the arrangement meets the conditions set out in 6 and 7 below, the trust arrangement is referred to in this bulletin as a health and welfare trust.

6. To qualify for treatment as a health and welfare trust the funds of the trust cannot revert to the employer or be used for any purpose other than providing health and welfare benefits for which the contributions are made. In addition, the employer's contributions to the fund must not exceed the amounts required to provide these benefits. Furthermore, the payments by the employer cannot be made on a voluntary or gratuitous basis. They must be enforceable by the trustees should the employer decide not to make the payments required. The type of trust arrangement envisaged is one where the trustee or trustees act independently of the employer as opposed to the type of arrangement initiated unilaterally by an employer who has control over the use of the funds whether or not there are employee contributions. Employer control over the use of funds of a trust (with or without an external trustee) would occur where the beneficiaries of the trust have no claim against the trustees or the fund except by or through the employer.

7. With the exception of a private health services plan, two or more employees must be covered by the plan. Where a partnership seeks to provide health and welfare benefits for both the employees and the partners by means of a trust, two distinctly separate health and welfare trusts (one for the partners and one for the employees) must be set up to ensure that the funds of each are at all times identifiable and that cross-subsidization between the plans will not occur. The exception in subparagraph 6(1)(a)(i) will of course not apply to such a trust established for the partners.

Tax Implications to Employer

8. To the extent that they are reasonable and laid out to earn income from business or property, contributions to a health and welfare trust by an employer using the accrual method of computing income are deductible in the taxation year in which the legal obligation to make the contributions arose.

Tax Implications to Employee

9. An employee does not receive or enjoy a benefit at the time the employer makes a contribution to a health and welfare trust. However, subject to 10 below, the tax consequences to an employee arising from benefits provided under such a trust are as follows:

Group Sickness or Accident Insurance Plans

(a) Where a group sickness or accident insurance plan provides that benefits are to be paid by the insurer directly to the employee, the premium paid by the trustees to the insurer for the employee's coverage will not result in a benefit to be included in the employee's income.

(b) Where this type of group sickness or accident insurance plan existed before June 19, 1971 and the requirements of section 19 of the ITAR are met (see IT-54, "Wage Loss Replacement Plans"), the benefits paid to an employee by the trustees or the insurers under such a plan in consequence of an event happening before 1974 will not result in a taxable benefit to the employee. Where these requirements are not met and in all cases of payments for events happening after 1973, the wage loss replacement benefits will be taxable under paragraph 6(1)(f) (see IT-428, "Wage Loss Replacement Plans").

Private Health Services Plans (defined in paragraph 110(8)(a))

(c) Payment by the trustees of all or part of the employee's premium to a private health services plan does not give rise to a taxable benefit to the employee. Benefits provided to an employee under a private health services plan are also not subject to tax.

(d) Payment by the trustees of a premium under a group term life insurance policy will not result in a taxable benefit to the employee unless the aggregate amount of the employee's coverage under one or more group term life insurance policies exceeds $25,000. (See IT-227R, "Group Term Life Insurance Premiums"). The provisions of section 12.2 which tax accrued amounts under a life insurance policy do not apply since a group term life insurance policy will be an exempt policy for that purpose.

(e) Where a group term life insurance policy provides for a lump sum payment to the employee's estate or a named beneficiary, the receipt of the payment directly from the insurer is not included in the recipient's income.

(f) Certain group term life insurance policies provide beneficiaries thereunder with an option to take periodic payments in lieu of the lump sum payment and others provide only for periodic payments to beneficiaries. Prior to the introduction of the accrual rules in section 12.2 for 1983 and subsequent taxation years, benefits thus paid by the insurer to a beneficiary, whether as a result of exercising the option or by the terms of the policy, were annuity payments that were income of the recipient (paragraph 56(1)(d)) who deducted the capital element of the annuity payment (paragraph 60(a) of the Act and Part III of the Regulations).

(g) For the 1983 and subsequent taxation years, paragraphs 56(1)(d) and 60(a) continue to apply to a beneficiary who is a holder and annuitant under an annuity contract if subsection 12.2(3) does not apply because of the exceptions in paragraphs 12.2(3)(c) to (e) or the application of subsection 12.2(7). Generally speaking, this will occur where the annuity contract

(i)   is a prescribed annuity contract as defined in Regulation 304,

(ii)   was acquired before December 2, 1982 under which annuity payments commenced before December 2, 1982,

(iii) is an annuity contract that was received as proceeds of a group term life insurance policy which was itself neither an annuity contract nor acquired after December 1, 1982, or

(iv)   was acquired before December 2, 1982, can never be surrendered and in respect of which the terms and conditions have not been changed

and is not the subject of an election under subsection 12.2(4).

(h) For annuity contracts other than ones described in (g) above, the annuitant is required by subsection 12.2(3) for the 1983 and subsequent taxation years to include in income accrued amounts on every "third anniversary" of the contract. In addition, in any year that does not include a "third anniversary," paragraph 56(1)(d.1) requires the inclusion of amounts in respect of annuity payments received during the year under the contract. As an alternative to the application of subsection 12.2(3) and paragraph 56(1)(d.1), the annuitant may elect under subsection 12.2(4) (before annuity payments commence) to include accrued amounts on an annual basis. In each instance, the issuer will provide the annuitant with a T-5 information slip indicating the amount of income to be reported respect of the annuity contract.

Shared Contributions

10. In 9 above the trustees are assumed to be receiving contributions only from the employer to pay for the cost of benefits under the trust plan. However, the trustees may also receive employee contributions to pay a part of the cost of the benefits being provided under the plan. If the plan does not clearly establish that the trustee must use the employee contributions to pay all or some part of the cost of a specific benefit, then it will be assumed that each benefit under the plan is being paid out of both the employer and the employee contributions. If the benefit in question is otherwise taxable to the employee, then in these circumstances a part of it is non-taxable. The non-taxable part is that proportion of the benefit received by the employee for the year that the total of employee contributions received by the trustees in the year is of the aggregate of the employer and employee contributions received by the trustees in the year. The above treatment will not apply if the benefit must be reported as income according to paragraph 6(1)(f) (see 9(b) above). However, the employee's contributions to plans referred to in 9(b) may be deductible for tax purposes from benefits received from the plan. See IT-428 for details.

Taxation of Trust

11. A trust which invests some of the contributions received and earns investment income, or has incidental income (other than contributions from employers and employees which are not included in computing income of the trust), is subject to tax under section 104 on the amount of such "trust income" remaining after the deductions discussed in 12 below. Where gross income (i.e., the aggregate of its income from all sources) exceeds $500 in the taxation year (and in certain other circumstances indicated on the form), the trustee is required to file form T3 (Trust Information Return and Income Tax Return).

12. In computing trust income subject to tax, the trust is allowed to deduct, to the extent of the gross trust income, the following expenses, premiums and benefits it paid, and in the following order:

(a) expenses incurred in earning the investment or other income of the trust,

(b) expenses related to the normal operation of the trust including those incurred in the collection of and accounting for contributions to the trust, in reviewing and acquiring insurance plans and other benefits and for fees paid to a management company to administer the trust, except to the extent that such expenses are expressly not allowed under the Act,

(c) premiums and benefits payable out of trust income of the current year pursuant to paragraph 104(6)(b). Benefits that are paid out of proceeds of an insurance policy do not qualify. Other benefits paid are normally regarded as having been paid first out of trust income of the year. However, premiums and benefits that would not otherwise be taxable in the hands of the employee by virtue of paragraph 6(1)(a) may be treated at the trustee's discretion as having been paid out of prior year's funds or current year's employer's contributions, to the extent that they are available, to avoid the application of subsection 104(13). The remainder of the income of the trust is subject to income tax under section 122 of the Act. As an inter vivos trust, the taxation year of the trust coincides with the calendar year.

13. For administrative simplicity, payments of taxable benefits by the trustee to or on behalf of employees are to be reported on Form T4A by the trustee and not on the T3 Supplementary. Information on the completion of Form T4A is contained in the "Employer's and Trustee's Guide." Although the trustee is required to withhold income tax from taxable benefits paid to employees, these amounts will not be subject to either Canada Pension Plan contributions or unemployment insurance premiums when paid by the trustee.

14. Although actuarial studies of the trust may recommend the establishment of "contingency reserves" to meet its future obligations, transfers to such reserves are not deductible for tax purposes by the trust.

Setting up a Plan

15. There is no formal registration procedure for a health and welfare trust and no requirement that the trust agreement be submitted to the Department for approval prior to the implementation of the plan. However, the advice of the District Taxation Office may be requested where there is any doubt as to the acceptability of the trust agreement as a health and welfare trust. Full particulars of the arrangement including a copy of all pertinent documents should accompany the request.

Last updated on 1986-07-31.

APPENDIX III-3-B

INTERPRETATION BULLETIN IT-339R2

AUGUST 8, 1989

MEANING OF "PRIVATE HEALTH SERVICES PLAN"

Subsection 248(1) (also paragraphs 6(1)(a), 18(1)(a), 118.2(2)(q) and 118.2(3)(b))

Application

The provisions discussed below are effective for the 1988 and subsequent taxation years. For taxation years prior to 1988, refer to Interpretation Bulletin IT-339R dated June 1, 1983.

Summary

This bulletin discusses the meaning of a "private health services plan" and describes some of the arrangements for covering the cost of medical and hospital care under such a plan. It also discusses the tax status of contributions made to such a plan by an employer on behalf of an employee and the circumstances under which the premium costs incurred by an employee qualify as medical expenses for purposes of the medical expense tax credit.

Discussion and Interpretation

1. Contributions made by an employer to or under a private health services plan on behalf of an employee are excluded from the employee's income from an office or employment by virtue of subparagraph 6(1)(a)(i). On the other hand, an amount paid by an employee as a premium, contribution or other consideration to a private health services plan qualifies as a medical expense for purposes of the medical expense tax credit by virtue of paragraph 118.2(2)(q). The amounts so paid must be for one or more of
   (a) the employee
   (b) the employee's spouse and
   (c) any member of the employee's household with whom the employee is connected by blood relationship, marriage or adoption.

For further comments on the medical expense tax credit see the current version of IT-519.

For purposes of the Act, a "private health services plan" is defined in subsection 248(1).

2. The contracts of insurance and medical or hospital care insurance plans referred to in paragraphs (a) and (b) of the definition in subsection 248(1) of "private health services plan" include contracts or plans that are either in whole or in part in respect of dental care and expenses.

3. A private health services plan qualifying under paragraphs (a) or (b) of the definition in subsection 248(1) is a plan in the nature of insurance. In this respect the plan must contain the following basic elements:
   (a) an undertaking by one person,
   (b) to indemnify another person,
   (c) for an agreed consideration,
   (d) from a loss or liability in respect of an event,
   (e) the happening of which is uncertain.

4. Coverage under a plan must be in respect of hospital care or expense or medical care or expense which normally would otherwise have qualified as a medical expense under the provisions of subsection 118.2(2) in the determination of the medical expense tax credit (see IT-519).

5. If the agreed consideration is in the form of cash premiums, they usually relate closely to the coverage provided by the plan and are based on computations involving actuarial or similar studies. Plans involving contracts of insurance in an arm's length situation normally contain the basic elements outlined in 3 above.

6. In a "cost plus" plan an employer contracts with a trusteed plan or insurance company for the provision of indemnification of employees' claims on defined risks under the plan. The employer promises to reimburse the cost of such claims plus an administration fee to the plan or insurance company. The employee's contract of employment requires the employer to reimburse the plan or insurance company for proper claims (filed by the employee) paid, and a contract exists between the employee and the trusteed plan or insurance company in which the latter agrees to indemnify the employee for claims on the defined risks so long as the employment contract is in good standing. Provided that the risks to be indemnified are those described in paragraphs (a) and (b) of the definition of "private health services plan" in subsection 248(1), such a plan qualifies as a private health services plan.

7. An arrangement where an employer reimburses its employees for the cost of medical or hospital care may come within the definition of private health services plan. This occurs where the employer is obligated under the employment contract to reimburse such expenses incurred by the employees or their dependants. The consideration given by the employee is considered to be the employee's covenants as found in the collective agreement or in the contract of service.

8. Medical and hospital insurance plans offered by Blue Cross and various life insurers, for example, are considered private health services plans within the meaning of subsection 248(1). In addition, the Group Surgical Medical Insurance Plan covering federal government employees qualifies as a private health services plan within the meaning of subsection 248(1). Therefore, payments made by an individual under any such plan qualify as medical expenses by virtue of paragraph 118.2(2)(q).

9. Private health services plan premiums, contributions or other consideration paid for by the employer are not included as medical expenses of the employee under paragraph 118.2(2)(q) by virtue of paragraph 118.2(3)(b) and are not employee benefits (see 1 above). They are however, business outlays or expenses of the employer for purposes of paragraph 18(1)(a). On the other hand, contributions or premiums qualify as medical expenses under paragraph 118.2(2)(q) where they are paid directly by the employee, or are paid by the employer out of deductions from the employee's pay. The amounts so paid must be for one or more of
   (a) the employee,
   (b) the employee's spouse and
   (c) any member of the employee's household with whom the employee is connected by blood relationship, marriage or adoption.

Last updated on 1989-08-08.

CHAPTER 4

Post-Retirement Benefit Issues

by William D. Anderson and Murray Gold

OVERVIEW

All Canadians, and retired Canadians in particular, must consider themselves extremely fortunate to have the health care system that exists in our country today. All retirees regardless of age are covered free of charge under the applicable provincial medicare system and, once age 65 is reached, are covered to one degree or another under a provincial drug program.

As well, many retirees participate in post-retirement benefit programs sponsored by their employer or union. These programs vary in coverage but could include small amounts of life insurance and accidental death and dismemberment, supplementary health care including vision care, private duty nursing, and out-of-country emergency coverage and dental coverage. It is only in the last few years that this area of health care has emerged. All of us are getting older, and it was probably a matter of evolution for those of us who have grown accustomed to a benefit plan during our working years that we should feel there is an entitlement to benefits in retirement. As a result, health care benefits for seniors have grown.

However, the costs of providing these benefits have also grown. This is true, not only for private benefit plans, but also for government-sponsored medicare. As governments reduce spending on health care, a greater financial responsibility is created for private benefit plans and the individual.

For several years the federal government has been reducing its share of health care funding, a process that has been accelerated since 1992 to a point where it now finances less than half of what the provinces do and less even than that of the private sector. The Liberal government promised to arrest this decline.

What makes all this even more alarming is, at the same time the federal government is seeking to cut back on health care funding, Canadian's health costs have continued to soar. In the 1980s costs grew from 7.5% of Canada's Gross Domestic Product to 10%, which in 1998 represented $70 billion. Another way of expressing this is that spending galloped ahead by 5% a year, twice the pace of economic growth. By 1998, public funding stood at $56 billion, a mere 8% higher than in 1992. In nominal dollars and in real dollars, spending in 1998 was $1 billion less than in 1992.

The consequences of an underfunded system, such as even longer waiting lists, growing pressure for user fees and more people seeking medical care out of the country, have potential to leave out the very old and powerless in society.

THE CANADA HEALTH ACT

The primary objectives of Canadian health care policy is to protect, promote and restore the physical and mental well-being of the residents of Canada and to facilitate reasonable access to health services without financial or other barriers. The following excerpts from the *Canada Health Act*[1] outline the five promises of medicare:

1. **Accessibility:** In order to satisfy the criteria respecting accessibility the Health Care Insurance Plan of a province:
   a. Must provide for insured health services on uniform terms and conditions and on a basis that does not impede insured persons
   b. Must provide for payment for insured health services in accordance with a system of payment

c. Must provide for reasonable compensation for all insured health services rendered

d. Must provide for the payment of amounts to hospitals.[2]

2. **Comprehensiveness:** The plan of a province must insure all insured health services provided by hospitals (medical practitioners or dentists).[3]

3. **Universality:** The health care insurance plan of a province must entitle 100% of the insured persons of the province to the insured health services provided.[4]

4. **Portability:** In order to satisfy the criteria respecting portability, the health care insurance plan of a province:

   a. Must not impose any minimum period of residence in the province, or waiting period, in excess of three months before residents of the province are eligible

   b. Must provide for and be administered and operated so as to provide for the payment of amounts for the cost of insured health services provided to insure persons while temporarily absent from the province.[5]

5. **Public Administration:** The health care insurance plan of a province must be administered and operated on a non-profit basis by a public authority appointed or designated by the government of the province.[6]

REDUCTION IN HEALTH CARE COVERAGE

After 1992, all provinces except Prince Edward Island reduced or eliminated coverage they had offered over and above the requirements of medicare. The following are some examples.

British Columbia

- Patient visit charge increased as have ambulance fees
- Deductibles for prescription drug program increased and reimbursement decreased
- Frequency allowance for eye exams changed.

Alberta

- Chiropractic services maximum reduced
- Out-of-country benefits reduced
- Health care premium increased
- Seniors drug program modified to provide only the least expensive products.

Saskatchewan

- Out-of-country benefits reduced
- Prescription drug program virtually eliminated

- Coverage of chiropractor services reduced
- Eye examinations for persons 18 or over excluded.

Manitoba

- Out-of-country benefits reduced.

Ontario

- Out-of-country benefits reduced
- Ontario drug benefit plan for seniors removed a total of 234 drugs and reduced to 100 days from 250 days the maximum number of day's supply.
- Government fees for optometrists, physiotherapists, dentists, chiropractors and podiatrists frozen
- Repatriation air ambulance coverage reduced
- Eye exams for persons ages 20 through 64 reduced to one exam every two years
- Exclusion of 22 cosmetic procedures that are generally performed by a physician.

Quebec

- Eye exams for persons ages 41 through 64 excluded
- Seniors drug program modified to provide only the least expensive products
- Deductible per prescription implemented for seniors drug program.

New Brunswick

- Optometrist services excluded
- Prescription drug program for seniors eliminated
- Prescription drug program modified to nominate private plan as primary carrier.

Nova Scotia

- Eye exams eliminated for adults and children.

This reduction in health care benefits started in the early 1990s and had a lot to do with provincial deficits. The health department in each province is a big spender and, if you are cutting, you will have to cut there. What the government is attempting to do is shift the burden from itself to the individual directly or to the individual through his or her benefit program, and this drastically affects post-retirement benefit programs.

The cost of these programs is escalating. The cutbacks in government provincial health care benefits discussed earlier, combined with increases in the unit costs of most health care services that have significantly outpaced inflation and an aging work force, have all contributed to the cost escalation.

But retiree plans will undergo extra pressures. Ballooning numbers of retirees and declining numbers in the active work force will cause unpleasant increases in the ratio of retirees to active employees for many groups, making retiree health care plans, which are by and large unfunded, more and more challenging to manage.

EMPLOYEE POST-RETIREMENT BENEFITS

Historically, members who retire are covered for benefits until their hour bank or dollar bank is exhausted. The fund may then allow the member to self-pay either the full cost or a subsidized portion for some period of time. The cost of providing retiree benefits in Canada can be substantial. Costs vary significantly, depending on plan design, location and characteristics of the retiree group. Current annual cash costs for an individual retiree ages 55 to 65 can range from $1,200 to $2,500 for insurance, including $10,000 of life insurance, drugs, semi-private hospital, supplemental medical, nursing home care and dental insurance. Cost ranges for most of these escalate rapidly with age. It is true that provincial medical plans will cover many prescription drugs at age 65, but even this is being chipped away by the use of deductibles, formularies, quantities dispensed, etc.

Trustees of trust funds offering retiree benefits on a wholly paid or subsidized basis must consider measuring the cost of retiree benefits over the long term rather than on a year-to-year cash basis. The cash basis of measurement, since it recognizes only the benefits currently being provided for those already retired, will almost always understate the long-term costs of a trust fund's non-pension benefit program for retirees. Costs are not accrued during the working years of the member but are deferred until after retirement. Benefit payments have been increasing rapidly and will increase in the future due to factors we have discussed earlier, such as medical care costs, inflation, government cost shifting, growth of the retiree group as current employees retire and increasing longevity. A recent study shows the annual cash cost of nursing home benefits for a retiree age 90 is approximately 30 times the cost for a retiree age 65.

None of these factors are anticipated under the cash basis of measurement. When they eventually occur, the resulting level of benefit payments could prove to be a significant and unexpected burden on the trust fund's cash flow.

If trustees are going to offer post-retirement benefits in whole or in part to their retirees, they should be aware of the long-term obligation. If more retiree benefits are to be provided because of the government cutbacks and retirees' limited sources of funds, consideration must also be given to what benefits should be made available and with what type of limits, i.e., deductibles and co-insurance.

Let us take a look at a retired member of a typical multi-employer plan. As a result of the collective agreement, he or she is participating in a pension plan and, thanks to the member's years of service, he or she is now receiving a pension. In the eyes of the member, the contribution to the pension plan is looked upon as deferred compensation. As soon as members go on pension, they are for the most part on their own; and the trustees of the plan have little contact with them other than periodic increases that some plans carry out by way of voluntary indexing. If we take this same pensioner and implement a health care plan, there are a number of issues that must be considered.

Who is responsible? What documents stipulate that benefits will or may be provided? Is it the collective agreement? Is it the trust agreement? Is it the text of the health and welfare plan or insurance contract, or is it the text of the pension plan? If it is contained in the collective agreement, who is responsible for implementation: The health and welfare trustees or the pension trustees, or a completely separate committee?

The configuration of a benefit plan will, of course, have a determination on this but, where possible, it is best not to establish another full committee. More than likely, the collective agreement is silent on the subject of benefits for pensioners. However, the trust document may permit provisions for retiree benefits or may be amended to permit this.

Who is eligible? Assuming that it is the board of trustees of the health and welfare plan that is responsible for the implementation and maintenance of a plan for retirees, exactly who will come under this category? Does the individual require some vesting time? If so, how long? Can a qualification period be justified, or should the door be wide open? If the cost is to be subsidized, this will definitely have some bearing on the decision arrived at. What happens in the case of a member who has taken early retirement and is working elsewhere?

When will benefits commence? Traditionally retirement age has been age 65, but more and more we are seeing a reduction in this, and age 55 to 60 is not at all uncommon. The Canada Pension Plan (CPP) changed regulations as of January 1, 1987 to allow payment to commence at age 60 with some reduction. This factor alone has had a bearing upon retirement age. Early retirement in many funds is now down between 50 and 55 years of age. The retirement formula of "30 and out" has been around for some time and is gaining popularity.

If benefits commence at time of retirement, whether early retirement, disability retirement or normal retirement, and assuming there is a premium charge to the retiree, should there be a different rate for early retirees? It could be argued that the lower age factor is to the benefit of the plan.

What benefits will be provided? Do the needs of retirees differ from those of active employees? I think so.

It can be assumed, with rare exception, that the retiree does not have dependent children and, therefore, we are talking in terms of a two-person family: retiree and spouse. As more retirees become available for coverage and as the government reduces its spending on medical care, it becomes imperative that plans should be weighted toward the insurance aspect of protection from large dollar amounts of claims, such as out-of-province emergency care and nursing care, as compared to maintenance drug or dental claims that tend to be relatively consistent year to year.

The increasing longevity of retirees and the financial constraints facing them and their benefit plans require that careful consideration be given to the benefits currently being provided and those that may be available in the future. Trustees should also review how current benefits are described in their booklets and insurance contracts to avoid the automatic increase in coverage being provided by the plan because of a reduction in government benefits.

How will benefits be funded? As mentioned earlier, many factors, such as an increase in retirees, a decrease in active members, an increase in longevity of retirees and a decrease in the coverage from government programs, will put tremendous cost restraints on trust funds in the future. Will the active employees be willing to pay for retiree coverage? Will they be able to? Simple numbers and economic reality may offer a negative response to these questions.

Another issue that will simply compound the problem is the provincial and federal governments' taxing of benefits and their intent to tax even further. At the present time Quebec and Ontario have retail sales tax in the amount of 9% and 8%, respectively, on all contributions to health and welfare trust funds, and life insurance premiums are subject to federal income tax. The intent of both levels of government is to introduce further personal income tax on health and welfare premiums.

If active members are taxed, both from the retail sales tax and personal income taxes on contributions into a health and welfare trust fund that provide for retiree benefits, it is unlikely they will continue to provide this benefit for retirees. This means that retiree coverage in the future for most trust funds will be self-paid and, even then, the premium will be subject to retail sales tax, if applicable.

If a retiree program becomes funded solely by the retiree participants within the program, there are a number of considerations worthy of attention. Will the program be self-standing or cross experience rated with the active employees? Will all the retirees be eligible for coverage? Will coverage be on a voluntary basis? If coverage is on a voluntary basis, will a medical examination of one form or another be required, and will there be minimum participation requirements?

There will be an increasing need in the future for retiree benefit programs. A rapid increase in the future costs burden, driven by growing numbers of aged retirees, medical care cost inflation and other factors, cries out for the consideration of alternative programs and the accurate assessment of the costs of each alternative.

POST-RETIREMENT BENEFITS: LEGAL ISSUES

Benefits constitute a significant portion of the compensation earned by active employees. But retired employees are especially affected by the reduction or elimination of any benefits they receive from former employers, because of their inability to replace their former employer's group health coverage. Retirees, already a vulnerable group, are particularly dependent on health benefits that supplement their limited pension incomes. Any decrease in retirement benefits provided to retirees in compensation for their years of service is unfair; the question that is being asked more and more frequently is whether such decreases are also a breach of contract. The following examination of post-retirement benefits includes a discussion of cases that determined when a benefit vests and whether it can be altered after vesting; retirees' options in enforcing the benefits promised to them; and the ability and obligations of unions to represent former members.

Although the status of retiree health benefits has also been subject to litigation in the insolvency area, we will not consider insolvency-related issues.

Changing Demographics

The current concern about post-retirement benefits is prompted in part by our changing demographics. Declining fertility rates and increased life expectancy have produced a population with an ever-increasing number of older people.[7] As the proportion of retired workers to active workers increases, the cost of retiree health coverage relative to current payroll increases.[8] The economic impact of higher private sector health costs is particularly difficult in light of the fact that, unlike pension plans, health plans are not pre-funded.[9] Pay-as-you-go financing means that future costs, even where they can easily be anticipated, are deferred to a future that is uncertain, and in which workers may be resentful of the burden left behind by their predecessors.

The strongest consequences of the directions in which we are headed are well illustrated by U.S. case law. In Canada, litigation over retiree health benefits has been limited and concerns, in the main, the effect of various forms of insolvency upon health benefits and the arbitrability of retiree health claims. Perhaps this is because the costs of private health coverage in Canada have been much less than in the United States, due to

Canada's public health care system. If public health care deteriorates, however, and some of the burden is shifted to private plans, it is not unreasonable to expect increased controversy over changes and reductions to costly but vital private health benefits. American case law has already considered such issues.

Vesting: The U.S. Jurisprudence

The question of whether employees, especially retirees, can be "vested" with respect to post-retirement health benefits is the threshold question in this area. If retirement health benefits do not vest, then the employer may unilaterally reduce or eliminate them and the employee is entirely at risk with respect to them. Where benefits do not vest, retirees would have little or no recourse against the elimination of employer-sponsored health care coverage.

On the other hand, if retiree benefits do vest, then the retiree has some certainty as to the level of employer-sponsored health coverage in retirement. In this case, the risk borne by the employee is a function of employer insolvency. The insolvency risk is, of course, higher with respect to health benefits than pension benefits, because pension funds are funded, whereas health and welfare arrangements are not.

The considerations relevant to vesting are similar to those that the courts considered some years ago in respect of pension benefits. Vesting with respect to pension plans was mandated and codified in the United States by the *Employee Retirement Income Security Act of 1974* (ERISA). Prior to that time, the question of vesting was determined in accordance with the common law. In 1960, the Supreme Court of Ohio in *Cantor v. Berkshire Life Ins. Co.* summarized the evolution of judicial thinking in regard to vesting as follows:

It is of course axiomatic that, although a contract may be terminated, vested rights which have arisen under such contract are not and cannot be destroyed by such termination.

The concept of employees' rights and of the place of the so-called fringe benefits in relationship to employees' remuneration has undergone a substantial change in recent years.

Due perhaps to the increased span of life, retirement benefits have assumed a more important role in the consideration of an employee when he accepts employment. Management has recognized this fact and, to encourage career service and to minimize labour turnover, which is so costly to industry, has inaugurated retirement programs in addition to Social Security. Some of these programs are supported by joint contributions of the employer and the employees, whereas others, as an inducement to career employment, are supported entirely by the employer.

When pension programs first came before the courts, pensions were construed primarily as mere gratuities by the employer, subject completely to the will of the employer. Later, as contributing pension systems arose, a distinction was drawn between the contributing and the non-contributing types of plan, the first being held to be a vested right, whereas the latter continued to be construed as a mere gratuity on the part of the employer which could be withdrawn at any time.

There has been, however, in recent years a gradual trend away from the gratuity theory of pensions. The courts, recognizing that a consideration flows to an employer as a result of such pension plans, in the form of a more stable and a more contented labour force, have determined that such arrangements will give rise to contractual rights enforceable by the employee who has complied with all the conditions of the plan, even though he has made no actual monetary contribution to the fund.[10]

Clearly, the court in *Cantor* was appalled by the possibility that an employee could spend his or her lifetime working for an employer and then retire on pension only to find the pension unilaterally terminated by the employer. In this regard, the court cited the earlier U.S. decision of *Bird v. Connecticut Power Co.*, as follows:

Even where an employer declares the Plan is within the absolute discretion of the directors, the court will interpret the Plan as a whole so as to give effect to its general purpose in securing the loyalty and continued service of the employees, and the employer may not defeat the employees' reasonable expectations in receiving the promised reward.[11]

Latter day courts in the United States have not adopted the same attitude towards vesting of retirement health benefits. In part, U.S. courts seem to have been moved by the argument that open-ended exposure to the high and unpredictable costs of AIDS and other experimental treatments imperiled the general viability of retiree health plans. Rather than require clear drafting to define the limits of coverage in vested situations, U.S. courts seem to accept that cost concerns are relevant to the question of vesting itself.

Retiree vulnerability to changes in an employer-sponsored health plan, or even its termination, is well illustrated by the U.S. Court of Appeals, 4th Circuit, 1994 decision in *Gable v. Sweetheart Cup Company, Incorporated.*[12] In *Gable,* retirees were covered by a comprehensive medical and life insurance benefit plan. Plan benefits were initially delivered through an insurance carrier. The insurance policy provided that it could be:

. . . amended or discontinued at any time by written agreement between the Company and the holder thereof without the consent of or notice to any employee or beneficiary or any other person having a beneficial interest in said policy. . . .[13]

Plan participants received individual certificates of insurance with a similar provision. Upon retirement, however, employees were provided with a document known as a *Schedule II,* which described the level of health care benefits to which retirees would be entitled. It stated that the employer would "continue this coverage for you during the remainder of your lifetime at company expense."[14]

On October 1, 1985, the plan was converted into a self-insured plan. The plan document continued to provide that it could be ". . . amended, modified or terminated at any time by action of the Employer. . . ." The Schedule II document was amended to advise retiring employees as follows:

> Whether or not medical coverage will be continuing for you as a retiree, and at what level of benefits, will depend upon the particular plan provisions and Company policy in effect at any specific time in the future.[15]

All employees, including retirees, were also provided with a summary plan description in 1986, which also advised the employees that the employer retained the ". . . right to modify, change or terminate medical coverage for retirees at any time in the future, just as it does for active employees."[16]

In 1989, the employer made significant reductions in the plan's benefits. Employees who retired before 1985 (when the plan was converted to a self-insured plan) and who continued to be covered by the plan on June 1, 1989 (when the benefits were reduced) were certified as a class of plaintiffs. The retirees argued that their benefits could not be reduced, because of the Schedule II promise made to them that coverage would continue during their lifetimes at company expense.

The court of appeals found against the retirees. The court wrote that the presumption in U.S. law is that health benefits are not vested, and that any promise to vest them must be "stated in clear and express language."[17] The burden of proof with respect to vesting, the court held, was upon the retirees. The court held that the employer had reserved its right to amend the plan, by virtue of the provision permitting it to do so in its contract with the insurer. About the company's representation that its retirees would have lifetime benefits at company expense, the court wrote as follows:

> In particular, the fact that Schedule II documents referred to retirees' benefits as "lifetime benefits" does not nullify the Company's right to modify, because the Schedule IIs are informal communications that do not govern the Company's obligations under an ERISA plan. ERISA prohibits informal written or oral amendments of employee benefit plans . . . and references to lifetime benefits contained in non-plan documents cannot override an explicit reservation of the right to modify contained in the plan documents themselves."[18]

Accordingly, the court upheld the employer's right to reduce the health benefits of pre-October 1, 1985 retirees, notwithstanding the employer's promise to continue coverage to retirees during the remainder of their lifetimes at company expense. The court was clearly moved by the potential costs and liabilities of lifetime health benefits, when it concluded as follows:

> There is a further reason why the explicit reservation of a right to amend an official plan document cannot be overridden by informal communications. Such communications often contain explanations of Plan benefits intended to sound promissory by their very nature. While these explanations may state the Company's current intentions with respect to the Plan, they cannot be expected to foreclose the possibility that changing financial conditions will require the Company to modify welfare benefit plan provisions at some point in the future.[19]

A Canadian court would likely not have decided *Gable* in the same way as the Fourth Circuit. Canadian employment law remains more paternalistic than its U.S. counterpart, and Canadian courts are more protective of vulnerable classes than their U.S. cousins. Most important, however, the statutory context for private benefits is very different in the two countries. In the United States, *ERISA* has been interpreted to not vest employees in health benefits, whereas the question of vesting in Canada is not governed by statute, but falls to be determined under the common law. No Canadian statute expressly or by implication considers vesting of health benefits. Moreover, no Canadian statute, directly or by implication, degrades the significance of company communications upon which employees reasonably rely for their retirement planning. Unlike the Fourth Circuit, a Canadian court would likely be reluctant to fully discount the company's promise of lifetime benefits in its Schedule IIs, on the basis that those documents were only "informal."[20]

Vesting: Canadian Jurisprudence

The Supreme Court of Canada's decision in *Dayco* is the leading Canadian case with respect to the vesting of health and welfare benefits.

Although it is the leading decision on this question, the *Dayco* case was not about whether benefits had or had not vested. Rather, the issue that went to the Supreme Court of Canada was whether retiree health benefits vest, or whether any such vesting was impossible such that the elimination of retiree health coverage after the expiry of a collective agreement was not grievable. Although the court ultimately determined that health benefits could vest and that their termination therefore could be grieved after a collective agreement's expiry, it made no determination on the merits of vesting. In this regard, it is important not to over-read *Dayco*.

The employer, Dayco, operated a factory in Hamilton until 1985, when its operations were transferred to Mexico and the Hamilton plant was closed. The plant's employees had been represented by the Canadian Auto Workers since 1965, when the first of a series of two-year collective agreements was made. The last such agreement was signed on April 27, 1983 and expired on April 21, 1985. Under the terms of this final collective agreement, as under the previous agreements, Dayco provided certain group insurance benefits to its employees:

60(ix) The Company agrees to provide all retirees with a paid-up $2,500.00 Life and Accidental Death and Dismemberment Policy, and other benefits negotiated, unless coverage is provided by the Government.[21]

These other benefits included OHIP premiums, semi-private hospital coverage, extended health care and dental insurance.

Prior to the final closing of the Hamilton factory in January 1985, the company and the union negotiated a shutdown agreement. It was provided that group insurance benefits for active employees would be discontinued six months after the closing of the plant. The agreement was silent on the status of retiree benefits.

The collective agreement was formally terminated on May 29, 1985. Two days later, all retirees were informed by the company that their benefits under Article 60(ix) would be terminated as of June 30, 1985, the same day that the benefits for active employees were to be discontinued. When the union lodged a grievance on behalf of the retirees, the company refused to acknowledge the grievance, because "there was no collective agreement in place at the time the said grievance was lodged, and the company had no obligations to these retirees on any other basis."[22]

In accordance with provisions in the collective agreement regarding grievances not settled by the grievance procedure, the union took the grievance to arbitration. The company raised an objection to the jurisdiction of the arbitrator on the basis that the collective agreement had expired. When the arbitrator determined that he did indeed have jurisdiction to decide the matter, the company applied for judicial review.

The arbitrator's decision in regard to his jurisdiction was rooted in his conclusion that Article 60(ix) was intended to vest benefits with the retirees.

I find this specific provision to have been intended and drawn as such by the parties as a retirement benefit and not an employment benefit, which would be extinguished at the end of the collective agreement in the circumstances set out in Article 60.[23]

In this regard, the arbitrator wrote that:

. . . these benefits are considered as earned benefits for service provided for the employer and are part of the retirement benefits to which the retiree is entitled.[24]

The benefits having been entirely earned, they therefore survived the expiry of the collective agreement.

The arbitrator's decision as to jurisdiction was appealed to the Supreme Court of Canada, which ultimately upheld the arbitrator's conclusion. Along the way, however, courts and judges reached different positions about the case, reflecting both its novelty and its difficulties.

In reviewing the arbitrator's decision, Mr. Justice Holland, writing for the majority of the divisional court, turned first to the standard of review for the application and concluded that "in determining the threshold question of arbitrability, the arbitrator was required to be correct."[25] The court concluded that, because the termination of the retirees' benefits arose after the collective agreement expired, the arbitrator did not have jurisdiction in the matter. The court held that the American case law in support of the arbitrator's award was distinguishable on the ground that it rested on a "concept of vested rights unknown to Canadian labour law."[26] The court held that the award should be quashed.

Writing in dissent, Mr. Justice White disagreed with both the majority's standard of review and its determination in regard to the vesting of rights. White J. found that the decision of the arbitrator was not patently unreasonable. He also concluded that Canadian case law supports the right of an arbitrator to hear a grievance in regard to benefits acquired under a collective agreement, even after the collective agreement has expired.

White J. was explicit about what he considers to be implicit in the employer's provision of retirement benefits to its retired employees.

There does not seem to be any escape from the likelihood that, unless the Company had promised to provide [the employees] with such retirement benefits, the rate of pay bargained for, while they were active members of the Union, in the collective agreements, would have been higher. A promise to provide for an employee in his retirement years is a promise which, of its very nature, anticipates that he will enjoy the benefit of the promise when he no longer belongs to the Union. It is also a promise which, of its very nature, is not dependent upon the Union (which negotiated that benefit for the employee) and the Company (which promised that benefit) necessarily being a continuing collective bargaining relationship. The promise of the Company, as expressed in Article 60(ix) of the last agreement and in predecessor agreements is not subject to the express condition subsequent that it shall no longer be effective if there is no longer extant a collective bargaining agreement between the Union and the Company.[27]

The decision of the Divisional Court was overturned by a unanimous decision from the Court of Appeal. The Court of Appeal held that Section 44(1) of the *Labour Relations Act* explicitly gave the arbitrator the jurisdiction to determine whether the question was arbitrable. The Court of Appeal held that the issue to be determined was "whether an *obligation had accrued* that could survive the termination of the agreement."[28] This is a rejection of the Divisional Court's focus on whether the alleged breach occurred during the lifetime of the collective agreement. The Court of Appeal's determination that the matter should be remitted to arbitration was appealed by the company.

Writing for the majority of the Supreme Court of Canada, Mr. Justice La Forest disagreed with the Court of Appeal's standard of review. He held that:

> . . . the arbitrator was not acting *within* his jurisdiction *stricto sensu.* Rather, he was deciding *upon* jurisdiction. As such, he was required to be correct.[29]

In order to determine whether or not the arbitrator decided correctly in regard to his jurisdiction, the court then turned to the question of whether "it is possible for a promise or retirement benefit to survive the expiry of the collective agreement in which it is found."[30]

In so doing, La Forest J. considered whether the expiry of a collective agreement was akin to the expiry of a fixed term contract or was more similar to the rescission of a contract. Under a fixed term contract, rights accrued under the contract continue to exist after the term expires. In contrast, where a contract is rescinded, it becomes null and void and leaves the parties with no obligations arising from it. In this regard, La Forest J. held that a collective agreement was analogous to a fixed term contract, and that rights acquired during its term were enforceable after its expiry.

> The analogy I would draw is to the common law notion of termination of a contract. A collective agreement is rather like a contract for a fixed term. At the end of the term, the contract or agreement is said to "expire" by mutual agreement. But the contract is not thereby rendered nullity. It ceases to have prospective application, but the rights that have accrued under it continue to subsist. This termination or expiration can be contrasted with the contractual notion of rescission, whereby the contract is rendered null and void, and the parties have no obligations thereunder. . . . Thus, it should not be seen as a novel concept that grievances can arise after the expiration of a collective agreement that relate to rights accruing under that agreement. It seems to me

that it would take very clear words to demonstrate that the parties intended to rescind their agreement by agreeing to enter into a succeeding agreement. Rather, the presumed intention is only that the prospective relationship between the parties is to be governed by the new agreement, and that the old agreement ceases to have any relevance to that ongoing relationship.[31]

In *Hémond and Coopérative Fédérée du Québec,*[32] the Supreme Court of Canada had held that a worker's seniority rights granted on the basis of a collective agreement do not vest in that worker, but can be derogated by a later collective agreement. La Forest J. distinguished *Hémond* on the basis that only the most current collective agreement can govern a prospective employment relationship. However, a retired worker has withdrawn from that relationship. At the point of termination, the worker's employment rights crystallized and vest into retirement rights. The fact that these rights may only be enforceable through collective action by the union on behalf of the retiree is due to other aspects of Canadian labour law and does not affect the basic contractual analysis.

La Forest J. also compared the Canadian and U.S. statutory contexts in regard to vested retiree benefits. He noted that ERISA provides for vesting of pension benefits and, although it regulates health plans, does not stipulate vesting standards for them. In *Dayco* he wrote about the statutory contexts of the two countries as follows:

> Canadian jurisdictions do not provide for an explicit dichotomy between pension and welfare benefits for retirees, but provincial pension legislation, to varying degrees, protects the vested nature of pension plans.
>
> . . .
>
> To my knowledge there is no equivalent legislative protection for welfare benefits, thus mirroring the American position.[33]

A Canadian court had another opportunity to consider the vesting of health benefits in *Emery v. Royal Oak Mines Inc.,*[34] a case of wrongful dismissal. The plaintiff, David Emery, was dismissed in 1989 after working for Giant Yellowknife Mines Limited ("Giant Yellowknife"), a subsidiary of Falconbridge Limited, for 29½ years.

In 1986, Pamour had acquired Falconbridge's interest in Giant Yellowknife. It agreed, at the time of acquisition, to honour all existing employee benefit plans.

In 1991, Pamour merged with several other companies to create Royal Oak Mines Inc. Mr. Emery was then advised that his benefit coverage would only continue until he reached the age of 65, as did the coverage for active Royal Oak employees, under the revised benefit plan. Previously, Mr. Emery's coverage had been for himself and his spouse for their respective lifetimes.

Royal Oak's explanation for curtailing Mr. Emery's benefits was that the company "was prepared to honour only those obligations known to and specifically assumed by Pamour at the time of the acquisition"[35] of control of Giant Yellowknife.

Counsel for the employer argued that it had the right to make changes to an employment contract unilaterally, provided that reasonable notice of the change is given. It was Royal Oak's position that the four years that had passed since it sent Mr. Emery the letter in 1991 was more than enough notice. Although Madam Justice Chapnick cited case law supporting the right of an employer to make such changes, in giving her reasons for judgment, she made note of the fact that, at the time of dismissal, there was no notice of any change to the plan, when the obligations of both parties were fixed.

The court held that Mr. Emery was contractually entitled to receive the benefits promised him at the time of his dismissal, and that the employer was not entitled to unilaterally terminate them. Chapnick J. found that Pamour was aware of these benefits at the time of acquisition, and Royal Oak was aware of them at the time of dismissal. The fact that Pamour's purchase agreement did not specifically undertake to continue the specific coverages that applied to Mr. Emery did not permit Royal Oak to avoid the obligations that were in place at the time of termination. However, the court declined to order specific performance in respect of the reinstatement of Mr. Emery's benefits and instead ordered damages in Mr. Emery's favour.

Emery supports the proposition that unqualified employer promises of lifetime health benefits cannot be rescinded after the employee retires. However, it is of no assistance to employees whose employers make such changes just before their retirement. *Baxter v. Abbey*[36] concerned an amendment to limit the definition of *credited service* and therefore reduce the value of accrued benefits under a pension plan. Although the case involves a pension plan, it is of interest in the benefits area generally because British Columbia had no *Pension Benefits Act* and no statutory vesting rules at the time.

At trial, the question to be determined was whether the amending agreement was binding upon all those with a beneficial interest in the pension plan. The trial judge held that the agreement is "not binding on those who have retired, or such others, whose interest had vested"[37] before the amendment was made. In defining when a member's interest vested in the plan, the trial judge wrote:

> . . . it is only at the time of retirement or termination that members' interests are determined according to the terms of the plan (including any amendments) as they exist at that time. It is those interests which are determined which then vest and are not altered by subsequent amendments.[38]

The trial judge's decision was upheld on appeal on the basis that no common law authority was cited for the proposition that an employee's rights in a pension plan become automatically vested once the employee accepts employment under the plan and complies with the conditions set out therein. Also, as a matter of contract, all parties to the plan agreed that the plan could be amended in accordance with the relevant provision. Special emphasis was placed on the fact that plan members were aware of the possibility of such changes. The Court of Appeal also concluded that "Canadian and Commonwealth cases do not support the principle of *immediate vesting,*"[39] which could only occur in accordance with the specific terms of a particular plan.

Some Canadian courts have also considered whether employers may be estopped from reducing or eliminating health benefits after retirement. In *Re: James et al. v. Town of Richmond Hill,*[40] four former municipal employees brought an application for declaration that their life insurance coverage was improperly terminated by the municipality of Richmond Hill. Before their retirements the town had taken out a group policy that covered them. The town agreed to pay the policy's premiums during employment and after the retirement of each employee, at which point the death benefit was reduced. When the employees retired, each of them was advised that the town would continue to pay the premiums on the policy for the rest of their lives. In fact, the respondent did continue to maintain the policies and pay the premiums until March 1983.

On March 1, 1983, each retired employee received a letter from the personnel administrator of the respondent advising that the provision of life insurance for retired employees was a contravention of the *Municipal Act* and would therefore be terminated as of March 31, 1983. The coverages could be continued at the expense of the retired employees.

Counsel for the employees argued that the town did in fact have authority to continue to pay the life insurance premiums for retired employees and also made an alternative argument of promissory estoppel. Three of the applicants stated that they had relied on the continuation of life insurance coverage after retirement and therefore did not make any other alternative arrangements. The fourth applicant, the widow of the fourth retiree, made a deposition to the effect that her late husband intended for her to be able to rely on his life insurance coverage, and therefore he had not made any other arrangements. In granting the application the court wrote:

> In this case all of the equities favour the applicants. They received the additional life insurance coverage as a term of their employment many years ago, and they relied on the representations of the municipality that this coverage would continue in force after their retirement.[41]

However, the court declined to decide the case on the basis of estoppel, since the:

> . . . doctrine of promissory estoppel is not available to the applicant. It is well established that a Municipal Corporation cannot be estopped from taking the position that it had no legal authority to enter into the agreement in the first place.[42]

Instead, the application was granted on the basis of the court's interpretation that the *Municipal Act* permitted the provision of retiree life insurance benefits.

The applicants' argument of promissory estoppel failed because the respondent was a municipal corporation, arguing lack of statutory authority. However, the court's emphasis on the applicants' reliance on the promise of life insurance coverage indicates that the doctrine of promissory estoppel may well be successful if applied to private sector employees.

Vesting: Summary Comments

Although vesting in respect of health benefits has important social implications, courts in Canada and the United States have approached the issue, as they must, on technical terms. Given its social significance, however, it may be more appropriate to deal with vesting legislatively. This would eliminate uncertainty about whether benefits are vested or not and would establish basic rules around which parties may knowingly arrange their affairs.

Under the law as it stands, whether a retiree is vested in health benefits depends upon the terms of the health plan and the representations made in connection with it. Vesting is clearly possible in both the United States and Canada. In both countries, unconditional promises of lifetime health benefits will crystallize vested rights in health plan members when they retire. Also in both countries, promises of lifetime benefits qualified by an express reservation by the employer of a power to amend or terminate may not create vested rights to plan benefits. In the United States, promises to employees of lifetime benefits made outside official plan documents are discounted, and it is difficult to found a claim to vested benefits upon them. Canadian law knows no distinction between official and unofficial representations and is likely more sympathetic to claims for vested health benefits based on employer promises upon which employees reasonably rely.

The Role of the Union

The right to an arbitration hearing is important because Canadian retirees whose rights to retirement benefits vested pursuant to a collective agreement may not have recourse to private litigation if the employer reduces or eliminates benefits. Instead, these retirees may have to rely on their former unions to grieve on their behalf.[43]

In *Canadian Paperworkers Union and Pulp and Paper Industrial Relations Bureau*,[44] the Canadian Paperworkers Union (CPU) filed a complaint, alleging that the employer was contravening the statutory requirement to bargain in good faith, when the employer refused to discuss an improved pension plan for retired workers with the CPU. The employer refused on the grounds that retirees are not part of the bargaining unit and, therefore, are not part of the CPU's certification. The CPU argued that it was established practice for the union to negotiate improved pension payments and other benefits for retirees. The British Columbia Labour Relations Board held that the CPU was entitled to bargain for an increase in the benefits of retired workers. The board stressed the connection between past and present workers and that there was a commonality of interest on the issue of pensions and retirement benefits, as active employees would one day be retirees.

Ultimately, the board ruled that the obligation to bargain in good faith does not "impose a binding obligation on a party to negotiate about *each* . . . subject of bargaining which is of interest to the other side."[45] The board stated that a refusal to discuss a particular issue might be circumstantial evidence that a party's overall conduct regarding the negotiation has been in bad faith. However, the CPU agreed that no such inference could be drawn under these circumstances, particularly in relation to "an item which, while not uncommon, is peripheral to the usual course of negotiations."[46] Therefore, while making the determination that the union should be able to represent retirees in negotiation, the board simultaneously undermined the position of retirees by viewing their issues as peripheral. The fact that a pension increase for retirees was not considered to be an issue central to the negotiation of a collective agreement was determinative in the finding that the employer's refusal was not a violation of its obligation to bargain in good faith.

The employer in *Canadian Paperworkers* argued that the rights of retirees vested in the individual at the time of retirement, and that the union does not have authority to negotiate on their behalf. In this case, the employer was not trying to decrease retiree benefits and it was therefore in the employer's interest to argue in favour of vesting at retirement as a way of displacing the union's right to represent retirees. The board compromised on the extent of the union's authority and concluded that the union could negotiate on behalf of retirees only to increase their benefits, but not to reduce them. Unless an agreement setting out the mutual authority of parties to alter the contract was built into the agreement from the beginning, the union did not have the right to negotiate a decrease.

The proposition that trade unions can only bargain increases in vested retiree benefits raises the question of what constitutes a *decrease* or *elimination* of a benefit.

In *Canadian Paperworkers,* for example, the board considered the example of a collective agreement that provides a prescription drug program for active and retired employees. If such a plan were made redundant by a government program to cover the costs of prescription drugs, the board assumed that the trade union could bargain to eliminate the benefit and put the money (including money previously spent on retirees) elsewhere. However, the retirees would no longer be members of the bargaining unit and, therefore, would have no say as to where the money would go. Possibly, the money would be expended in a way that does not benefit the retirees at all. It could be argued that the retirees have not lost anything, because they are still receiving prescription drugs free of charge. However, money earmarked for their use would be spent elsewhere.

One example of employees challenging an amendment that seemed to benefit them is the American case of *Schwartz v. Newsweek Inc.*[47] The plaintiffs were former employees of the defendant, Newsweek. Its original severance policy was to offer severed employees another position with the same employer or severance pay. Then, Newsweek added the fourth option of remaining in the employ of an employer that had purchased a part of Newsweek's business.

The employees' lawsuit was prompted by the fact that the new owner of the business did not last for very long. The employees who chose to work for the new owner chose not to take the severance package, as was their option. The court held that to allow the plaintiffs to recover for such a claim would be contrary to reasons of policy and that the provision of another option was something to be encouraged. Although the decision was based on an American statutory scheme, it indicates how benefits risks can be shifted to employees, and the value of benefits reduced, by extending new options to employees.

The most likely scenario for reduced health benefits is where an employer reduces certain elements of the health plan, but enhances others. The employer may, for example, reduce an expensive chronic care coverage for a small number of retirees, while providing a small enhancement to a widely used benefit. This change may be especially difficult to challenge, as it may have a number of retiree supporters. One basis for challenge, however, is on the ground of discrimination.

In *Haberern v. Kaupp Vascular Surgeons Ltd. Defined Benefit Plan,*[48] the plaintiff, Ruth Haberern, worked full-time as a secretary-bookkeeper for Lehigh Valley from 1974 until her retirement in 1985 and part-time for a year after that. Ms. Haberern and two surgeons were the only employees of Lehigh Valley. In October of 1980, Lehigh Valley amended its plan to eliminate life insurance for employees over the age of 56. Ms. Haberern was the only employee affected by the change. Meanwhile, the life insurance for the surgeons tripled.

The district court held that the elimination of life insurance for one employee, simultaneous with tripling the coverage for the other employees, violated *ERISA's* prohibition against discrimination for the purposes of interfering with the attainment of plan rights. The district court found the defendant's argument that there was not enough money for coverage of the plaintiff "beyond belief,"[49] in light of the significant increase in coverage for the surgeons.

This decision was reversed on appeal. The appeal court held that the purpose of *ERISA's* prohibition was to prevent an unscrupulous employer from firing or harassing employees in order to prevent them from attaining rights under the plan and did not, the court held, apply to changes in the terms of the plan itself. As a result, the employer was permitted to amend the plan to Ms. Haberern's substantial detriment without breaching *ERISA's* prohibition against discrimination.

In *McGann v. H & H Music Company,*[50] the court held that there was no genuine issue of fact to be decided at trial and granted the defendants' motion for summary judgment. The plaintiff, Mr. McGann, sued his employer, H & H Music, for discrimination and violation of *ERISA.* The plaintiff had been diagnosed with AIDS in late 1987. At that time, employees of H & H Music with AIDS were entitled to up to $1 million in benefits. In July 1988, that amount was reduced to $5,000. It was the employer's position that they were faced with the choice of making changes to the plan or dropping it entirely.

The court found that it was well within the rights of the employer to reduce the benefits, particularly as the employees had already been provided with the information that their health coverage could change from year to year. Under *ERISA,* the employer is not obligated to provide any particular benefits.

In his judgment, Black J. concluded that "the purpose of the changes in the group medical plan made by the defendants' jibe with the ultimate purpose of *ERISA*: protection of the plan."[51] He found that the alterations were not made to discriminate against the plaintiff or any other employee who has been diagnosed with AIDS. In this case, it was not only considered acceptable to deprive the few in order to continue to provide for the many, it was held to be the duty of the employer.

A Role for Retirees

The right of retired employees to be represented by their former union has been well established by *Dayco.* Nonetheless, representation by a trade union, which does not include retirees as members, may leave retirees with the feeling that they lack control over the issues that affect them. In *Cominco Pensioners Union, Sub-Local of the United Steelworkers of America, Local 651 and Cominco Ltd.,*[52] the union applied for certification for a unit of retired employees of Cominco. The union argued, based on *Canadian Paperworkers*,[53] that retirees were considered to be employees; and they should therefore be permitted to establish a bargaining unit, specifically to deal with any changes to pensions or benefits after retirement. The union relied on the concept of pensions and benefits as deferred compensation to argue that retirees are workers on extended leave, with pay.

The British Columbia Labour Relations Board held that almost all the characteristics of an employer/employee relationship were absent and that retired workers are not exposed to "the abuses and evils which labour relations statutes are designed to eradicate."[54] Any concerns retirees might have about an employer's violation of pension benefit provisions were held to be adequately addressed through representation by the trade union and proceeding to arbitration. The board concluded that "it is really only pension benefits, and a couple of other fringe areas, which are of continuing concern to the retired worker at Cominico."[55]

The tension between the social significance of retiree benefits, and the practical and legal obstacles to their effective enforcement through arbitration, remains unsatisfactory. Collective representation of retirees is essential, for practical reasons, to their ability to effectively defend their interests. Some trade unions include retirees in their membership and offer them effective representation. In other cases, however, retiree interests may conflict with the interests of active members, or the protection of retiree interest may be financially unbearable for the trade union. In these cases the interests of retired union members should be enforced in much the same ways as those of other retirees, through the civil courts.

ENDNOTES

1. *Canada Health Act*, R.S.C. 1985, c. C-6.
2. *Ibid.*, Section 12.
3. *Ibid.*, Section 9.
4. *Ibid.*, Section 10.
5. *Ibid.*, Section 11.
6. *Ibid.*, Section 8.
7. John A. Turner, "Demographic Change and Retirement Income," for the 1995 International Pension and Employee Benefits Lawyer Association, June 1995, p. 3.
8. *Ibid.*, at pp. 2-3.
9. Ian R. Winter, *Post Retirement Benefit Payouts* (Toronto: Insight Press, 1993) Part III, 1.
10. *Cantor v. Berkshire Life Ins. Co.*, 171 N.E. 2d 518 at pp. 520-521 (Ohio Sup.Ct. 1960).
11. *Ibid.*, at p. 521.
12. *Gable v. Sweetheart Cup Company, Incorporated*, 35 F.3d 851 (4th. Cir. 1994) at p. 851.

13. *Ibid.*, at p. 854.
14. *Ibid.*
15. *Ibid.*
16. *Ibid.*
17. *Ibid.*, at p. 855.
18. *Ibid.*, at p. 857.
19. *Ibid.*
20. *Gable* is a strong example of the U.S. approach to retirement health benefits, although it is not unusual. Contrary cases have, however, found that retiree health benefits do vest on the basis of applicable trust law principles (where the plan is a trust) or on the basis of "formal" employer communications (see, for example, *Houghton v. Sipco, Inc.*, 38 F.3d 953 (8th Cir. 1994).
21. *Dayco and C.A.W.—Canada* (1993), 102 D.L.R. (4th) 609 (S.C.C.).
22. *Ibid.*, at p. 613.
23. *Ibid.*, at p. 615.
24. *Ibid.*, at pp. 615-16.
25. *Ibid.*, at p. 616.
26. *Ibid.*
27. *Ibid.*, at p. 617.
28. *Ibid.*, at p. 618.
29. *Ibid.*, at p. 619.
30. *Ibid.*, at p. 634.
31. *Ibid.*, at p. 635.
32. *Hémond and Coopérative Fédérée du Québec*, [1989] 2 S.C.R. 692.
33. *Dayco, supra* note 21, at p. 646.
34. *Emery v. Royal Oak Mines Inc.* (1995), 24 O.R. (3d) 302 (G.D.).
35. *Ibid.*, at p. 308.
36. *Baxter v. Abbey* (1986), 33 D.L.R. (4th) 142 (B.C.C.A.).
37. *Ibid.*, at p. 146.
38. *Ibid.*, at p. 147.
39. *Ibid.*, at p. 148.
40. *Re: James et al. v. Town of Richmond Hill* (1986), 54 O.R. (2d) 555 (H.C.J.).
41. *Ibid.*, at p. 561.
42. *Ibid.*
43. *Dayco, supra* note 21, at pp. 658-9.
44. *Canadian Paperworkers Union and Pulp and Paper Industrial Relations Bureau* (1977), 77 C.L.L.C. 675 (B.C.L.R.B.).
45. *Ibid.*, at p. 689.
46. *Ibid.*, at p. 691.
47. *Schwartz v. Newsweek Inc.*, 653 F.Supp. 384 (S.D.N.Y. 1986).
48. *Haberern v. Kaupp Vascular Surgeons Ltd. Defined Benefit Plan*, 24 F.3d 1491 (3rd Cir. 1994).
49. *Ibid.*, at p. 1502.
50. *McGann v. H & H Music Company*, 742 F.Supp. 392 (S.D.Tex. 1990).
51. *Ibid.*, at p. 393.
52. *Cominco Pensioners Union, Sub-Local of the United Steelworkers of America, Local 651 and Cominco Ltd.*, [1979] 2 Can L.R.B.R. 321.
53. *Ibid.*
54. *Ibid.*, at p. 330.
55. *Ibid.*, at p. 332.

CHAPTER 5

Group Insurance Underwriting and Financing

by Pui-Ying Chan

The underwriting of group insurance benefits is an important part of any employee benefit plan. It is essentially the assessment of the future cost of the plan. The future cost of the plan is made up of three components:

- An estimate of the benefit that will be paid or the claims under the plan
- The expenses of administration of the plan and benefits, net of any investment income generated
- Risk sharing charges, profit or margin required by the underwriter.

The total of these three components is represented by the expected premium. How these factors are assessed and projected, as well as the analysis of the components that have an impact on claims and benefits, will be discussed in more detail below.

The financing alternatives, on the other hand, reflect the various approaches that have been developed by consultants and insurance companies to finance employee benefit plans of various types. These financing arrangements take into consideration the type of risk being underwritten, the size of the group, the prior experience and tax considerations relative to the various approaches. They are designed to reflect the needs of the employer or the groups of employers and their ability to assume risk relating to the administration and provision of employee benefits. The principal financing methods currently used to administer various types of employee benefits programs will be reviewed in the second part of this chapter.

Finally, in Appendix III-5-A, we provide some data on recent historical growth of various types of employee benefit plans, as compiled by the Canadian Life and Health Insurance Association.

UNDERWRITING

As mentioned above, underwriting is the process by which an insurance company will project future claims, expenses and required profit for a group benefit program. In its basic form, this will be reflected in the premium that has been set by the insurance company to underwrite the risk. Let us now examine each of those components in turn.

Assessment of Future Benefits or Claims

The projection of claims is a function of the plan design, the demographics of the group and the prior experience generated for the group of employees/dependants to be covered.

The plan design is obviously the key consideration. Quite simply, a group life insurance plan providing a death benefit of $10,000 will cost half as much as one that will provide a death benefit of $20,000. These relationships apply when it is assumed that the individual will have no incentive to increase utilization because of the level of coverage. This is the usual assumption made with respect to life insurance (except for the two-year typical suicide exclusion clause that applies to individual policies but not to group contracts), as individuals typically are not involved in making an election of the exact amount of coverage to be obtained under the group plan. For other benefits such as disability insurance, the higher the percentage of income that is replaced, the higher the expected average cost of claims. Statistics have shown, time and again, that a plan that provides a much higher replacement of income will pay more claims for longer durations, because individuals will have less incentive to return to work when they find that the difference in income is marginal or non-existent. This is especially the case with certain disabilities, such as lower back pain or mental or nervous conditions resulting from stress. With these types of disabilities, it is more difficult to medically "prove or disprove" the continuation of the disability; and the patient's statements have a more significant impact in the determination of eligibility and in the continuation of eligibility for benefits.

Demographics

Another factor that affects claims is the demographics of the participants. For certain benefits, such as life insurance, an examination of the demographics of the group has demonstrated a very strong correlation between age, gender, smoking status and occupation as factors having a strong impact on the level of claims incurred. By and large, experience with respect to life insurance has been improving during the last decades as life expectancy for both men and women has improved significantly. As an indication of the impact of age, gender and smoking status on the cost of life insurance, Table III-5-I shows the sample annual cost for a benefit of $10,000 for selected demographic characteristics. Thus, if a group is represented by young, non-smoking females with an average age of 25, one would expect the average cost of the plan to be very low. On the other hand, if the group is best represented by males with an average age of 45, most of whom are smokers, then the expected average cost would be substantially higher. Based on the table, the cost would be more than ten times as much.

For disability insurance, the impact of demographics is also significant. The demographic factors are similar to those for life insurance, except that the gender of the covered group tends to have the reverse impact on disability insurance. Generally, women have a lower mortality rate than men do, resulting in lower life insurance costs. However, women have a higher morbidity (sickness) rate than men, resulting in higher disability insurance rates.

Turning now to health benefits—including hospitalization, prescription drugs and so forth—it should be noted that the cost again could be very much influenced by the demographics of the group. In this instance, the difference in cost between employees with an average age of 25 compared to a group with an average age of 45 is not that dramatic, as the individual use of medical services does not vary greatly at those ages. (This could be different if the cost of providing coverage to dependants is also considered, because the age 45 group is likely to have more covered dependants than the age 25 group.)

As the group's average age increases, the use of prescription drugs and of hospital benefits increases, resulting in higher health benefits costs. This is most evident in plans that provide coverage to retired employees.

In Canada, provincial medicare plans bear a lot of these costs, but not all. For example, until recent years

Table III-5-I

ANNUAL COST OF $10,000
OF LIFE INSURANCE

Females		Age	Males	
Non-Smokers	**Smokers**		**Non-Smokers**	**Smokers**
$ 3.84	$ 5.40	25	$ 13.10	$ 16.71
6.72	12.00	35	14.16	22.56
14.76	34.44	45	21.36	45.36
33.00	81.24	55	53.40	142.08
94.32	195.36	65	154.08	394.56
298.08	467.52	75	480.84	929.28

Note: The above costs are based on the Canadian Institute of Actuaries Mortality Table: 1986-1992 experience, ultimate (published May 17, 1995) plus allowance for taxes, expenses and margin.

most drugs were provided to individuals ages 65 and over by the provincial plans. In recent years there have been, and continue to be, changes to the levels of coverage provided by some provinces.

In addition, new drugs are introduced into the marketplace at a faster pace and are not always covered, or immediately covered, by the provincial plans. This has had the impact of private health plans becoming even more susceptible to the effects of increased costs at these post-retirement ages.

The demographic influences are less significant for dental benefits than for health benefits. For most employees, routine checkups and services at least annually, but sometimes as frequently as every six months, are a significant factor in maintaining good dental health and in preventing further, more expensive, treatment. However, there are individuals who do require more use of the major restorative services in spite of regular attention to preventive and maintenance services. Age is sometimes a factor in this regard; for example, employees in their 40s and 50s typically require more periodontal treatment than younger employees. (As noted under health benefits, age can also be an overall benefit costs factor, with consideration of the number of dependants.)

Prior Experience

If the number of employees covered is significant, the experience that has developed in the past is key to the estimation of future costs. The number of employees required to have credibility for experience purposes varies with the frequency of the incidence of claims and the variability in the level of claims. Certain benefits have a low frequency (e.g., accidental death) and large variations in benefits (e.g., $10,000 to $500,000 for some accidental death and dismemberment (AD&D) plans). In this instance, a very large number of employees are required to have a credible impact on the projected level of future claims, probably 10,000 employees or more. For other benefits, such as dental coverage where claims are frequent (e.g., two-to-four claims per person per year) and the variability in claims is relatively low (e.g., $50 to $1,500), the experience is credible for a small group of 100 employees or more. In addition, the more years of experience available, the more relevant this factor becomes in projecting future claims. Naturally, in examining the prior claims information, the underwriter will take into consideration any benefit change that has been implemented during that time. Another factor that must be recognized is the fact that the group of employees covered may have changed. The employer may have had acquisitions or divestitures or may have implemented a reengineering plan with significant reductions of staff, perhaps among the older employees. The existence of coverage for retirees and the changes to

that retiree group is yet another factor that must be considered. Given the many factors that come into play, it is not unusual to find that different underwriters come up with varying levels of premiums for the same case.

Reserves

Reserves are established for the payment of future claims. An unrevealed claims reserve is used to pay claims that occur during a policy period but do not get paid until after the end of the policy period. For example, someone may go to the dentist on December 20, but the claim may not be submitted and paid until January of the next policy year. Had the benefit plan terminated with the insurance carrier at the end of the year, the carrier would still pay that claim in January, using the unrevealed claims reserves that it had established. The actual amount of reserves required varies by benefit line and also varies by insurance carrier based on the method or formula it uses.

Reserves are also established for actual claims occurrences such as waiver of premium for life insurance and future years' payments under long-term disability. In these situations, a reserve is calculated for each individual circumstance based on actuarial tables and factors. These reserves are used to continue claims payments even if coverage with the insurance carrier is terminated after the employee first becomes eligible for payments.

Expenses

The expenses of administration must be factored into the cost of benefits. These expenses include:
- Claims adjudication
- Employee and dependant recordkeeping
- Employee communication (booklets or leaflets, certificates, toll-free communication lines, etc.)
- Pooling charges (insurance of claims beyond a certain level)
- Credibility charges or credits (to smooth out claims for smaller groups)
- Contingency or risk charges by the carrier (a contribution to the insurance company for the risk they are taking)
- Profit
- Provincial premium taxes (2-4% of the net premiums) payable to the provincial governments
- Commissions (if any) paid to the broker or consultant.

The level of expenses will vary by insurance company, based on the level and extent of services provided, the insurer's cost structure and whether or not a particular group falls within the target market of that company. Another factor that affects the cost levels that will be quoted is the strategy of the carrier relative to business growth and its willingness to invest to generate this growth.

Margin

Most underwriters will want to factor in a margin for claims fluctuation. The level of the margin will vary with the size of the group and the type of benefits involved. Typically, the larger the group, the lower the margin and the more fluctuation in claims levels, the higher the margin.

Interest Adjustment

For large groups, it is common practice for the insurance company to credit interest earned on the reserves that are held by them.

Cash flow interest adjustments are also typical. A cash flow interest credit would be made when premiums exceed claims and expenses. A cash flow interest charge would be made when the claims and expenses exceed the premiums.

The net effect of the interest adjustments is usually reflected in the expense charges. That is, interest credits would be used to reduce the actual expenses charged.

Premiums

The billed premium rates represent the total of claims, expenses, margin and interest adjustments. Billed premiums may be subject to sales taxes. This is the case in Ontario (8%) and Quebec (9%). Premiums and the sales taxes (where applicable) are usually paid monthly.

In most cases, premiums are set and agreed on an annual basis. On occasion, premium rates may be guaranteed for a longer period. For health and dental benefits, the period will seldom exceed 12 months. For life, AD&D and long-term disability (LTD), the premium agreement period may often be for longer than one year.

FINANCING ARRANGEMENTS

Over the years, consultants and insurance companies have collaborated in the development of techniques to recognize the particular needs of employers and multi-employer groups and to maximize tax efficiency. The two extremes are *fully insured (or fully pooled)* and *administrative services only (ASO)*. In between, there are a whole range of options including:
- Partial pooling
- Retention accounting
- Retrospective arrangements
- Minimum premium
- Split funding.

Fully Insured or Fully Pooled

As the title implies, this is the situation where full insurance coverage is obtained for the associated risk. The employer/employees pay the premiums and the insurer is responsible for paying claims. The plan sponsor receives no adjustment, whether claims are incurred or not. If there are claims, the underwriter may lose and, if there are no claims, the underwriter will have made a profit on this policy but not necessarily on its book of business of similar coverages. This arrangement is ideal for smaller groups for most coverages and for large groups for specific coverages, such as AD&D. Future premiums are determined more on the basis of the carrier's pool than on the experience of any one particular group and the demographics of the covered persons.

Administrative Services Only (ASO)

As the name implies, insurance is not provided. Only the carrier's services are retained. Some carriers have set up separate corporate entities to handle the provision of these services. Typically, this approach is used for health and dental benefits for larger groups. This method has the advantage of eliminating the charges for contingencies and the requirement to advance the funds. ASO is often combined with direct bank transfer arrangements, allowing the ASO provider to charge the claims paid each day to the employer's bank account. The savings in cost can be worthwhile. It should be noted, however, that goods and services tax (GST) must be paid on the ASO provider's fees. This is different from insurance arrangements, all of which are excluded from GST.

Partial Pooling

Like the name implies, some pooling of insurance purchase takes place. In this instance, only part of the benefits is pooled or fully insured, and the balance is covered under an ASO or retention accounting arrangement. This arrangement is often used for life insurance, for large amounts of individual coverages (large amount pooling) or limiting the aggregate claims charges to a specified amount. There may also be a limitation on health claims of a particular type (stop-loss pooling), such as, $25,000 for any medical out-of-country claims. In this instance, a pooling charge is made to the group, and the carrier is fully responsible for the claims above the pooling limit.

Retention Accounting

Under this arrangement, the carrier provides a full analysis and report on the claims paid and expenses incurred. If a surplus is generated, it is refundable to the plan sponsor. If a deficit is incurred, it is normally carried forward (with interest charges) and offset by future surpluses.

Since policies are often terminated following a year in which there was a deficit, most insurance carriers have a rate stablization reserve (RSR) or premium stablization fund (PSF) requirement. The RSR is established by accumulating portions of surpluses in years in which they are generated. The RSR is then used to reduce or eliminate deficits in years in which they occur.

Retrospective Arrangements

There are many variables of this arrangement, but essentially it involves the elimination of the margin from the premiums paid, with the agreement that any losses up to that margin will be paid to the carrier after the end of the policy year, if required by claims and expenses. In this case, the employer has the advantage of holding funds that would otherwise be paid to the carrier. The value of these funds to the employer may well be much higher than the interest that would be credited by the carrier.

Minimum Premium or Split Funding

Minimum premium is a combination of ASO and retention accounting. With this arrangement, most of the cash flows through the ASO account—typically 90% of the expected total. The balance of 10% is paid as a premium to the carrier. This premium provides the guarantee that, if the level of claims and expenses exceeds 100% of the expected or agreed level, the carrier will advance the sums required, as provided under a regular retention accounting basis. This allows the plan sponsor to have many of the financial advantages of an ASO arrangement, while having some of the insurance guarantees of a retention accounting method.

SUMMARY

Underwriting and financing of employee benefits can be a sophisticated science involving actuarial principles as well as accounting and tax considerations. The success of an employee benefit plan is dependent upon the ability of the carrier to accurately adjudicate claims and the plan sponsor's ability to select the most appropriate financing arrangement. When these factors are properly considered, they help to manage the costs and maintain reasonable stability from year to year.

APPENDIX III- 5-A

SUMMARY OF SURVEY OF GROUP INSURANCE PREMIUMS IN CANADA

Benefit	Number of Employees Covered			Premiums Written or Benefits Payments If ASO ($)		
	1995	1996	1997	1995	1996	1997
Life insurance	N/A	N/A	N/A	2,065,000,000	2,180,000,000	2,273,000,000
AD&D	7,526,449	8,403,917	8,732,935	216,655,000	215,419,000	244,399,000
Loss of income						
STD	1,559,973	1,558,115	1,710,863	544,422,000	451,883,000	478,521,000
LTD	4,824,365	4,852,110	5,299,061	1,763,278,000	1,799,570,000	1,971,051,000
ASO	1,601,478	1,842,222	1,792,554	550,577,000	597,227,000	631,341,000
Extended health						
Insured*	4,935,559	5,247,651	5,517,294	1,810,107,000	1,890,590,000	2,071,051,000
ASO*	3,159,176	3,276,935	3,104,005	1,366,810,000	1,427,434,000	1,580,405,000
Drug expense**	77,925	68,021	147,992	32,327,000	27,779,000	46,701,000
Supplementary hospital**	204,805	152,266	168,582	11,666,000	10,559,000	11,380,000
Dental						
Insured	2,660,842	2,675,217	2,843,263	1,314,842,000	1,334,890,000	1,483,176,000
ASO	2,704,923	2,793,272	2,859,825	1,079,006,000	1,148,023,000	1,164,061,000
Total						
Insured	***	***	***	7,758,297,000	7,910,690,000	8,579,279,000
ASO	***	***	***	2,996,393,000	3,172,684,000	3,375,807,000
Total	***	***	***	10,754,690,000	11,083,374,000	11,955,086,000

*Coverage providing payments to encompass a wide range of health care expenses and frequently includes most health care expenses not paid by provincial government plans.

**Contracts provide only benefits indicated.

***Totals are not relevant, as most employees are covered under more than one type of benefit plan.

Source: Canadian Life and Health Insurance Survey of Health Insurance Benefits in Canada—1995, 1996 and 1997.

CHAPTER 6

Investments

by Michael Sandell

The assets of a health and welfare trust are the accumulated differences between the contributions into the trust and the payments and expenses coming out of the trust. For fully insured plans, this money can be used as a reserve to offset future rate increases or to increase benefits. For self-insured plans, the assets can be used to offset claim fluctuations or to increase benefits.

The assets of health and welfare trusts should be invested to generate additional income to the trust. This income is taxable. However, expenses of the fund are deductible against this income and, in most cases, completely eliminate any income taxes payable by the trust. Consequently, most trusts can be invested without taxes being a concern.

Health and welfare funds, like all trusts, are regulated by the trustee legislation in the province in which they are registered. The various provincial statutes all include a set of investment guidelines. Some provinces include a "legal list" of eligible investments. This list states what investments can be made by trust funds.

On July 1, 1999, the province of Ontario eliminated its legal list and adopted a prudent investor rule that includes a number of factors trustees must take into account in establishing investment guidelines.

If the particular trust document governing a health and welfare fund does not mention investment guidelines, then, by default, the fund's investments are regulated by the trustee legislation guidelines. However, these guidelines are not complete and fall short of what is required. For example, the guidelines say nothing about term of investments, credit quality or diversification. In addition, the statutory guidelines allow some equity investments, which may not be appropriate to the majority of health and welfare funds.

The various provincial trustee statutes do allow trustees to set investment guidelines that differ from the guidelines in the acts. Consequently, the trustees of a health and welfare fund should, in conjunction with their investment consultant, formulate a set of investment guidelines that are appropriate to that particular trust.

There are six areas to address. Most of these are shaped by the short-term nature of the trusts.

1. **Taxability.** If the fund may end up the year owing taxes, then the trustees may want to consider investing in tax-advantaged investments such as preferred shares. However, in this event great care must be taken that the fund does not end up taking on more credit or liquidity risk than it should.

2. **Eligible securities.** These would normally include bills, notes and short bonds issued or guaranteed by the federal and provincial governments, Schedule I and II banks and high-quality trust companies and corporations. Eligible securities could also include mortgage-backed securities and other asset-backed packages. Eligible securities would not normally include investments in longer term bonds and equities. This is because the short-term nature of health and welfare trusts means they cannot invest for a long enough term to recover from capital losses that these investments sometimes incur.

3. **Term of investments.** The maximum term for any one investment by the trust should be around one year. The average term of the entire portfolio should not normally exceed six months. If the trust has a large surplus, then it could perhaps go out to two or three years.

4. **Credit risk.** Most health and welfare trusts put

a minimum credit rating of R1 Low (as rated by Dominion Bond Rating Service) or Single A (as rated by Canadian Bond Rating Service) on their investments. Even with this minimum, investment managers will need to be alert to deteriorating credit quality in their investments.

5. **Liquidity.** Health and welfare trusts need the ability to liquidate their investments relatively quickly, at low cost. A rough rule of thumb would be ability to sell an investment in less than a month with a cost of less than .1% of the value of the investment.

6. **Diversity.** The best way to lower risk is through diversification, putting your eggs in more than one basket. One common rule is never put more than 10% of a fund into any one credit risk (other than the government of Canada) or any one maturity date.

Many health and welfare trusts find that investing in a money market pooled fund is the best way of meeting their investment guidelines, particularly for liquidity and diversification. In addition, money market pool fees tend to be lower than other funds' fees.

CHAPTER 1

Plan Design and Administration

by Patrick Longhurst

The design of pension plans in Canada is influenced by three main forces:

1. Minimum standards required by legislation, discussed in Chapter 2
2. Maximum benefit provisions permitted by Revenue Canada guidelines, discussed in Chapter 7
3. Objectives of plan sponsors and the impact of union negotiations or employee demands, discussed in the introductory section.

This chapter describes the points to consider when designing and administering a plan if there were no legislation. We will look at the general principles underlying the design of a pension plan anywhere in the world. Later chapters in this section will cover the restraints that apply to pension plans in Canada.

THE TYPE OF PLAN

The first question to decide is what type of plan to choose. There are two types of plan. One is called a *money purchase* or *defined contribution* plan. The level of contributions by employer and employee is decided in advance. The ultimate benefit to be paid from the plan is what can be purchased by those accumulated contributions.

The second type of plan is a *defined benefit plan.* Here, the ultimate level of benefit is based on some formula set out in the pension plan document. Sometimes, it may set employee contributions at a specific level. In certain situations, most commonly in multi-employer plans, the employer's contributions are also defined. The differences between *single employer* and *multi-employer* pension plans will be discussed in Chapters 3 and 6. For

now, it is sufficient to say that when both benefits and contributions are defined, the plan is treated as a defined benefit plan.

ELIGIBILITY RULES

Having decided on the type of pension plan, the next question to address is eligibility. Members may be eligible to join a pension plan as soon as they are hired, or they may have to satisfy some service requirements.

Eligibility may also depend on class of employment. For example, a plan may be solely for salaried employees and not open to unionized hourly employees. Eligibility rules must, however, comply with all human rights legislation. A rule that discriminates by sex, for example, is not acceptable.

Special eligibility rules may apply to part-time employees. Commonly, a plan may require a minimum number of hours worked per year or a minimum level of earnings for a part-timer to be eligible.

As a final point in plan eligibility, plans may be optional, compulsory or a combination of the two (optional up to, say, age 30 and mandatory thereafter). The choice between optional and compulsory plans is extremely important. Employers that provide optional plans are often confronted with the problem of dealing with older employees who, not having chosen to join the plan, retire after long service with no pension to look forward to. It is far from satisfactory for the employer to dismiss the problem, simply because it was the employee's choice.

Having settled the question of how soon employees are eligible to join the plan, the next one to settle is the source of contributions. Canada has a tradition of providing contributory pension plans—those to which both employees and employers contribute. In countries like the United States, where employee contributions are not tax-deductible, non-contributory plans—those to which only employers contribute—are more common.

Even so, many Canadian pension plans are non-contributory and, indeed, as we will see later, administration is much simpler if employee contributions are not required. However, employees may be allowed to contribute voluntarily. If so, the money may be used either to buy additional defined benefit pensions or to increase the ultimate pension through a money purchase arrangement. In a defined contribution plan, the employer's level of contribution is defined. In a defined benefit plan, the employer's contribution is recommended by an actuary and is normally what is required to provide the benefits promised by the plan.

DEFINED BENEFIT FORMULAS

In designing the rest of a pension plan, it is easiest to consider the benefits payable according to the major events in the life of a member. A logical starting point is the pension to be provided at the *normal retirement date* of an individual. This refers to the date defined in the pension plan document as the *standard retirement date*. In Canada, it is frequently one's 65th birthday.

The benefit payable at normal retirement date under a defined contribution plan is simply the amount that can be purchased by accumulated employee and employer contributions. In a defined benefit plan, the pension depends on the formula provided. There are three major categories of defined benefit formulas:

1. Final or best average
2. Career average
3. Flat benefit.

Final or Best Average Plan

A *final* or *best average* plan expresses the benefit as a percentage of average earnings near retirement, multiplied by years of service. A typical formula might be 1% of final average earnings per year of plan membership.

The final averaging period may be as short as three years and as long as ten years. It is intended to avoid the risk of recognizing only one year that may not be representative of the employee's earnings level.

A *best average* formula, slightly more sophisticated than a final average, copes with cases where the earnings level of long-service individuals declines as they near retirement and their capacity to work reduces. It bases the pension on the period when the employee was at peak earnings.

Career Average Plan

The second formula is *career average*. In this type of plan, the pension is based on earnings in each year of plan membership rather than the years closest to retirement. For example, an employee who retires with 30 years of service would receive a pension of, say, 2% of total earnings in those 30 years. Of course, the weakness of this type of formula is the risk that inflation will have significantly reduced the value of a pension earned in the early years of service.

Because of this, career average plans frequently update benefits so that the benefits earned early in a member's career are increased in line with either the actual earnings of the individual or some index that will help protect the individual from the effects of inflation, such as the Consumer Price Index (CPI).

Flat Benefit Plan

The third type of formula, the *flat benefit* formula, is the easiest to understand and communicate. Here, the employee receives a flat dollar amount per month per year of service or membership. For example, someone might receive $20 a month per year of service, which will provide a monthly pension of $600 for a person retiring after 30 years in the plan. Once again, the flat dollar amount will likely be increased from time to time in response to inflation. It is possible that only benefits in respect of future service will be updated. However, more frequently, all years of service, both past and future, are treated uniformly. Having considered the pension payable at normal retirement age, what happens if someone wants to retire before then?

EARLY RETIREMENT (DEFINED CONTRIBUTION PLANS)

In the first place, the plan will probably provide a minimum age before an employee can draw a pension from the plan. A common formula in Canada is age 55 and fully vested.

Since the size of pension under a defined contribution plan depends on the amount of accumulated contributions, the pension will clearly be less than if the individual had waited until normal retirement. There are two interrelated reasons: First, there are fewer years of contributions and, second, there are fewer years for the contributions to earn investment income.

EARLY RETIREMENT (DEFINED BENEFIT PLANS)

Under a defined benefit plan, the most common approach is to use the formula that would apply at normal retirement but reduce the pension by some factor to allow for the earlier retirement. The factor might be half a percent for each month early retirement occurs before normal retirement date.

Alternatively, the pension may be the *actuarial equivalent* of what would have been paid at age 65. That means the early retirement pension will have the same value as the pension at normal retirement.

Often, employer personnel policies will encourage early retirement, so the employer may subsidize the early retirement penalties in one of several ways. One approach is to waive the reduction, provided some additional age and service criteria are met, such as age 60 with 30 years of service. In that case, a retiring employee would receive a pension calculated with the formula used at normal retirement age.

The formula does not have to involve both age and service. Some plans provide *unreduced early retirement,* as it is known, after 30 years of service, or when an individual reaches, say, age 62. Another possibility is for the reduction to be subsidized so that, rather than a reduction of 6% a year (which is close to the actuarial equivalent value), it may be only 2% or 3% a year. This provides an additional incentive to members to retire early.

Another inducement to early retirement is known as an *open window policy.* In this situation, members are given a limited time in which to take advantage of special early retirement rules. For example, for three months members may be allowed to retire with no reduction in their pension if they are more than 55 years old and have 20 years of service. After three months, the window is closed and the plan reverts to its normal rules.

Revenue Canada also implemented downsizing rules, where for a limited period plan sponsors can offer incentives such as increased service, waived early retirement reductions or bridge benefits.

Employers may also encourage early retirement by offering what is known as a *bridging benefit.* Traditionally, both the Canada Pension Plan and Quebec Pension Plan (CPP/QPP) and Old Age Security (OAS) were only payable from age 65. So, someone retiring at 60, for example, would have to live for five years on a corporate pension benefit alone. Only at age 65 would he or she start to receive benefits from government programs as well.

To compensate for this, bridging benefits were introduced to provide an additional amount from the early retirement age to age 65. This bridging benefit is either a flat dollar amount for each year of service or a benefit related to the social security benefits not being paid.

Remember, whatever inducement is offered, it ends at age 65 when government benefits formally begin. Although the CPP/QPP will pay reduced pensions as early as age 60, this has not had a significant impact on the payment of bridging benefits.

POSTPONED RETIREMENT

Just as early retirement presents special challenges to a pension plan, so does late retirement. Most plans allow an individual to remain a member after normal retirement age, though the benefit provisions may differ.

In some instances, a member may continue to earn pension for years of service after normal retirement age. In other cases, no pension is earned after normal retirement age but, by the same token, no contributions are required from the member. However, the pension is increased, recognizing that the pension will be paid for a shorter period than if the member had retired at the age of 65. In some plans, there is an option to continue working and start receiving the pension at age 65.

DISABILITY PENSIONS

It is possible a plan member could become disabled before being entitled to an immediate pension. Once again, there are several ways of dealing with this situation.

Much depends on how the plan is integrated with group insurance programs. Where the employer has a long-term disability plan, it may not be necessary for the employee also to receive a pension benefit during the time leading up to normal retirement age. In this case, the employee will continue to be credited with years of service while disabled. Usually, these years of service will be based on earnings at the point of disability. So, when an employee reaches 65, insured long-term disability payments stop and the pension begins, based on years of membership plus years of disability.

Alternatively, if the employer does not have an insured long-term disability plan, the pension plan itself may pay a disability benefit to a member who becomes totally and permanently disabled. The level of benefit will likely be based on the plan formula and could either recognize service up to the date of disability or projected service up to normal retirement age.

DEATH BENEFITS

The next event we will consider is the death of the individual. This can occur while an individual is still an active member of the plan or in retirement.

Before retirement—For someone who dies while still a member of the plan, but not yet eligible for early retirement, there are several forms of death benefit. As a minimum, the individual's estate (or beneficiary) should receive the member's contributions with interest at some reasonable rate. But other forms of payment are possible. The actuarial value of the pension earned to the date of death could be paid as a lump-sum; a percentage of the pension earned to the date of death could be paid as an immediate pension to the spouse;

the employer could provide a benefit equal to the member's contributions with interest. Finally, of course, any combination of these options might also be paid.

By contrast, the standard death benefit from a money purchase plan is relatively straightforward: the accumulated contributions in the individual's account. As in the case of disability, the final benefit to be paid must, to some extent, recognize the value of any insured death benefit. In this way, the employer knows the combination of insured amount and pension amount provide adequately for members who die while still employed.

For someone who dies while still employed but is eligible for early retirement, the obvious approach is to treat individuals as if they had retired the day before they died, providing their spouses with the benefit they would have been entitled to under those circumstances.

After retirement—The third and final situation is when a person dies after retirement. Here, one needs to be familiar with the expression *normal form,* which is the standard way a plan provides the pension benefit.

A *normal form* might be a pension payable only for the life of the individual. It might provide a minimum guarantee period of, say, five or ten years, during which the pension continues whether the member is alive or not. As well, it may provide for automatic continuation of a percentage of the pension benefit to the spouse following the death of the member. This is known as a *joint and last survivor normal form.* The most common example is to continue the pension to the member's spouse at 60% of its previous level. Some plans are designed to reduce the pension if the employee stays alive but the spouse dies. This more unusual form is called a *pension reducing on first death.*

Typically, a plan document defines the normal form, allowing a member to select other optional forms of the same value. For example, the normal form might be a pension payable for life and guaranteed for five years. A retiring member might want a pension, 60% of which will continue to his or her spouse following the member's death. An actuary can calculate an equivalent value, and the member will receive a lower pension payable in the form he or she asked for.

The selection of optional forms has gained new importance in the early 1990s because of the new tax rules described in Chapter 7. If the normal form of pension is, say, 60% joint and survivor, but the option exists to take a greater pension payable for life only, then the pension adjustment (PA) will be based on the greater amount.

TERMINATION

The last major event to consider is terminating employment before becoming eligible for early retirement. This usually arises when an employee changes jobs.

In a defined contribution plan, the treatment is simple. The employee is entitled to his or her own contributions, with interest, plus a percentage of employer contributions. The percentage will depend on whether the member is *vested.*

Vesting is the process by which a member becomes fully entitled to a pension at his or her normal retirement age. When someone who is not vested terminates, that individual receives a refund only of his or her own contributions with interest. Someone who is vested will also receive a share of the employer's contribution. The share can vary from 1-100%, depending on years of service or plan membership.

Vesting is often linked with the *locking-in* rule. They generally occur at the same time, but they are different. The government has decreed that money set aside for retirement should be used only in retirement. So, after a few years as a member of a plan (the rules vary from province to province), participants are not allowed to spend the money accumulating for their retirement until they retire. It is *locked-in* to the plan, and the member must wait until a certain age to receive the benefits, which must take the form of a life annuity.

Vesting, locking-in and portability—transferring the value of a pension when moving to a new employer—have all been major issues in the pension debate that took place in Canada through the 1980s. As the rules governing all forms of retirement savings have been modified, the registered retirement savings plan (RRSP) has become one of the key vehicles in portability. The *commuted value*—roughly equivalent to the current cash value—of the pension earned to the date of termination is calculated and transferred to an RRSP. The RRSP itself is locked-in and is referred to as a Locked-In Retirement Account (LIRA) in many provinces, so employees may receive their pension only at some later date when the proceeds of the RRSP must be used to buy an annuity or a life income fund (LIF).

LIFE INCOME FUNDS

A LIF is an arrangement between an authorized financial institution and an individual who has locked-in pension monies. Upon termination, a pension plan may offer a new portability option allowing the purchase of a LIF, subject to an age limit and spousal requirements.

Spouses or former spouses of plan members who are entitled to a pension benefit may also purchase a LIF, if the plan member has a LIF option. Finally, individuals with locked-in RRSPs may choose a LIF option.

A LIF is a registered retirement income fund (RRIF) with a maximum annual withdrawal and a conversion requirement at age 80. This arrangement allows individuals to defer the purchase of a life annuity until the end of the year in which they turn 80. A LIF, which receives the locked-in pension monies, may be opened as soon as age 55. A life annuity must be acquired no later than March 31 of the year in which the individual turns 81.

Amounts in the LIF are subject to minimum and maximum withdrawals. The minimum annual withdrawal from a LIF is set by the new RRIF rules, since a LIF is, for income tax purposes, a RRIF. A minimum withdrawal is calculated by dividing the balance in the LIF as of January 1 of each year by 90 minus the planholder's age at that date. It is not necessary to withdraw an amount in the first year of the plan.

The maximum withdrawal formula has been designed to ensure that sufficient monies are left in the plan to purchase an annuity at age 80. The regulations prescribe actuarial rules limiting the annual withdrawal.

Ontario, Quebec, Alberta and Saskatchewan pension legislation offer this or a similar option to holders of locked-in RRSP funds. In Alberta the LIF is known as a life retirement income fund (LRIF).

MARRIAGE BREAKDOWN

One more event in life that can affect one's pension is when a marriage breaks down. When a marriage comes to an end, the spouse of a pension plan member is normally entitled to a share of the pension earned during the period of matrimony. As might be expected, this calculation is simple for a money purchase plan but can be extremely complicated for a defined benefit plan. It is the plan sponsor's responsibility to perform these calculations only for members subject to the Quebec pension legislation. For a more detailed discussion of this subject, please refer to Chapter 13.

INTEGRATION

An important and much debated issue is how pensions can be integrated with government benefits. Integration can take one of two forms: Either contributions to the company plan and government plans are integrated, or the benefits paid by each are integrated.

Contributions are *integrated* by reducing the employee's contribution by the amount of contribution required by the CPP or QPP. This approach has become more complex in recent years, as contributions to both CPP and QPP are now steadily increasing to 9.9% by 2003 (split between employer and employee). So, if the integration is applied directly, contributions to a corporate pension plan would slowly decline. As a compromise, it is possible to freeze the level of integration at some percentage such as 1.8% up to the year's maximum pensionable earnings (YMPE).

Integration of the benefit may also be done in one of two ways: either by a *step-rate* or a *direct offset* method.

In the step-rate approach, a lower level of benefit is paid on earnings up to the YMPE. This helps to compensate for the fact that earnings are not recognized under the CPP or QPP.

In the direct offset method, a percentage of the CPP/QPP benefit is offset against the company plan's benefit. In this way, the combined amount paid by a company pension plan and the CPP/QPP will meet certain preset objectives for long-service employees.

ADMINISTRATION

The administrative needs of the pension plan follow directly from the plan features we have discussed. A process will have to be established to enroll employees on their eligibility date or, if the plan is voluntary, to give them the choice of joining. Administrators will also need a clear record of those employees who have been informed of their right to join the plan and have opted not to do so.

If the plan requires employee contributions, a process must be established to receive and account for them. The administrator needs a means of calculating the amount of pension payable to any member, whether he or she is subject to early, normal or deferred retirement. Similarly, calculations must be prepared if an employee becomes disabled. All these processes will follow from the terms in the plan document.

When a member dies, whether before or after retirement, the administrator needs clear records on the employee's marital status and choice of beneficiary. At retirement, the individual must be given a clear description of the choices available, and these choices must be documented. Possibly the most complex calculations will take place at the time of termination, and routines must be established to calculate the commuted value of the pension that has been earned up to that date. Currently, there are formulas set up to do these calculations using actuarial bases specified by the Canadian Institute of Actuaries. One province, Saskatchewan, has also established its own tables. Similar calculations must be performed at the time of marriage breakdown, and great care must be taken in performing these calculations to ensure that all legal requirements are met.

There are additional administrative requirements that do not flow from the various events we have reviewed in this chapter but that are nevertheless important. One is to explain the plan and provide annual status reports to each member in the form of booklets and/or annual personalized statements. Another is to set up an administrative committee to oversee the relationship between members and the plan sponsor. In multi-employer plans, this relationship is handled through the board of trustees.

In summary, there is potential for tremendous complexity in pension plan design, particularly for defined benefit pension plans. In theory, to provide a defined level of pension benefit at retirement is relatively simple: In practice, early and late retirement, disability, death and termination, and integration with government plans make for a very complex system. This is what puts such heavy demands on the administrators of defined benefit plans.

CHAPTER 2

Basic Employee Protections
Under Pension Legislation

by Mark Zigler

MINIMUM EMPLOYEE PROTECTIONS

Pension benefits legislation in Canada, whether under the federal jurisdiction or that of most provinces, was initially enacted in the mid-1960s, as minimum standards legislation. These statutes dealt primarily with requirements for registering pension plans and with minimum vesting standards so that pensions could not be taken away from employees with at least ten years' service who had attained age 45. There were few protections beyond vesting. The initial legislation did not deal with many of the substantive and procedural pension benefit protections that we have today. For the most part, the early legislation was uniform across provincial lines, although British Columbia, Newfoundland, Prince Edward Island and New Brunswick had no legislation at all until much later. By 1990, all provinces, apart from Prince Edward Island and British Columbia, had enacted pension benefits legislation of some kind, although the uniformity of the 1960s is no longer to be found. On June 27, 1991, British Columbia gave Royal Assent to its *Pension Benefits Standards Act,* Bill 6, which took effect on January 1, 1993. While Prince Edward Island passed its *Pension Benefits Act* in 1990, it has not, as of yet, been proclaimed in force.

While there are periodic attempts at discussing uniform legislation, none of these have succeeded. Certainly most provinces will not be amenable to legislation that provides the lowest common denominator of protection, while other provinces may not wish to extend some of the more generous provisions that exist elsewhere in the country. **As a result, it is necessary to read this chapter very carefully because standards vary from province to province and they are constantly being changed. Any statutory references should be updated.**

The past four decades have seen a substantial growth in private sector pension plan assets and an increased awareness of the importance of pensions on the part of employees. The aging employee population and the desire for greater employee protection brought about a substantial movement for change to the minimal legislation of the 1960s. The private pension system lent itself to many potential abuses, particularly in employer-controlled plans where employees could render substantial service under the plan and still receive few or no pension benefits. Protection for surviving spouses and concerns with situations arising out of marriage breakdown, plan wind-ups and surplus withdrawals brought about a greater demand for change and more careful regulation of pension plans. Like the field of securities regulation, the regulation of pension fund assets and benefits has become a "growth area" for legislators in order to protect employees and the public from abuses and unfair dealings.

The pension reform legislation of the 1980s and 1990s, starting with the federal *Pension Benefits Standards Act, 1985* (PBSA)[1] and followed by initiatives in almost all provinces, has brought about a totally new regime in terms of pension protection for employees. The "minimum standards" have been enhanced to the point where there are substantial protections in a number of areas, in addition to the basic concerns over vesting periods. Even the minimum vesting periods have been reduced from the ten-year standard that was prevalent in the 1960s to the two-year vesting periods that are common in today's legislation (subject to Quebec's most recent proposal to grant immediate vesting).

The more conservative 1990s led to a slowing of the pace of reforms, with more emphasis on changes pertaining to individual rights issues such as unlocking access to locked-in funds in cases of terminal illness or complying with court-ordered changes such as providing survivor pension rights to same-sex spouses. Other provinces have updated their statutes and, most recently, at this writing, Quebec has proposed further reforms in its Bill 102 that may lead to further advancement of the minimum standard protections. Unfortunately there have not been too many new pension plans created in recent years, and this has been viewed by many as the reason not to enhance member protections under pension legislation. Further, many of the protections granted to plan members under legislation are only as good as the willingness and ability of government regulators to enforce them. As a result of cutbacks in government spending, the resources available to enforce many of these protections are not available, and feeble attempts at "self-regulation" can only lead to lesser enforcement, in the absence of vociferous complaints by members or their representatives.

The major employee protections under the current pension legislation can be divided into two categories, those that are structural or procedural in nature and those that provide improved substantive minimum standards.

STRUCTURAL AND PROCEDURAL PROVISIONS

Codifying the Common Law

Most pension plans are established as trusts, whereby the employer or its designated trustees administer pension fund assets in trust for the employee beneficiaries.

Most multi-employer pension plans, in fact, are established pursuant to formal trust agreements maintaining such a structure. Regardless of whether a written trust agreement is used to establish a pension plan or not, most plans create trust or, at the very least, *fiduciary* obligations on the part of the pension plan administrators in respect of pension plan assets. Such fiduciary obligations exist pursuant to the common law of trusts and have been part of our legal system for centuries. As noted in the well-known English case of *Cowan v. Scargill*,[2] the law of trusts applies to pension funds in the same manner as any other trusts. Accordingly, trustees owe the beneficiaries such common fiduciary duties as the duty to make the trust fund productive and obtain the best investment return for the beneficiaries. Further, the *Scargill* case deals with such basic trust law principles as the duties of trustees to avoid "conflicts of interest" and ensuring that their obligations to the beneficiaries are foremost in determining their actions as trustees.

The Ontario *Pension Benefits Act* (the "Ontario Act")[3] now codifies two of the basic principles of the law of trusts, namely:

1. The requirement that administrators exercise the care, diligence and skill in the administration and investment of the pension fund that a person of ordinary prudence would exercise in dealing with the property of another person[4]

2. The prohibition against an administrator of a pension plan knowingly permitting his or her interest to conflict with his or her duties and powers in respect of the pension fund.[5]

Like the United States' *Employee Retirement Income Security Act* (ERISA),[6] the Ontario Act enshrines in a statute concepts that already exist at common law. These broad legal principles, perhaps more than some of the specific employee protections contained in the legislation, can serve to ensure that the employee interests are first and foremost in the minds of those responsible for administering the pension plan. The fiduciary obligations contained in ERISA have generated substantial litigation against pension plan administrators where it appears that abuses of fiduciary obligations are taking place.

Provisions similar to those in the Ontario Act are contained in the federal PBSA,[7] the Nova Scotia *Pension Benefits Act* (the "Nova Scotia Act")[8] and the Manitoba *Pension Benefits Act,* (the "Manitoba Act").[9] The Alberta *Employment Pension Plans Act* (the "Alberta Act")[10] requires that anybody acting as an "administrator" of a pension plan stands "in a fiduciary capacity in relation to members, former members, and other members entitled to benefits." The Quebec *Supplemental Pension Plans Act* (the "Quebec Act")[11] also requires that a pension fund constitutes a "trust patrimony" that is appropriate to the payments and benefits to which the members and beneficiaries are entitled. The Ontario and Nova Scotia legislation go on to establish similar fiduciary liability for "agents" of the administrator and require everyone who employs such agents to be satisfied of the agents' suitability to perform their functions.[12]

As noted by the Ontario Divisional Court in the *Dominion Stores*[13] case, the fiduciary duty is the highest one known to law. Indeed, the court stated that such obligation is owed by the province's pension commission as well as the plan administrator.

In terms of protection for plan members, the serious fiduciary obligation imposed by statute is now one of the most basic protections available to those who are covered by pension plans.

However, one must be careful about the extent to which the fiduciary obligations in pension statutes apply. While courts have liberally applied such fiduciary standards,[14] pension regulators such as Ontario's former Pension Commission (now the Financial Services Commission) have made a distinction between situations where parties such as employers or unions act in their collective bargaining or employment law capacities as opposed to situations where they act as fiduciaries.[15]

Administration of Pension Plans

Pension statutes now contain the concept of an *administrator* of a pension plan, which is the body ultimately responsible for the pension fund. Whether the administrator is the employer in a single employer plan, a board of trustees in a multi-employer plan or other possibilities such as a pension committee or an insurance company, such person is ultimately responsible for the operation of the pension plan and is faced with all of the fiduciary obligations.[16] Most single employer plans can be administered either by the employer or by a "pension committee." Ontario and Nova Scotia require such pension committees to have at least one or more representatives of the plan members. The federal PBSA *requires* employers of 50 or more members to establish a pension committee where a majority of the members so request. Such pension committees must include at least one representative of the plan members and one representative of the retired members under the federal legislation.[17] Similarly, the Ontario and Nova Scotia legislation require employee participation of at least one member on such a committee. Accordingly, the only method of avoiding employee representation of any kind in the administration of a pension plan involves the employer naming itself as the administrator without establishing a pension committee or retaining an insurance company to provide pension benefits under the plan that are guaranteed by the insurer. The legislation in Ontario, Nova Scotia and Alberta, however, is not clear as to how any employee representative is chosen or who that person may be. It is conceivable that an employer may choose to administer its pension plan by way of a pension committee and choose a senior executive as the representative of the employees. This may, however, represent a conflict of interest on the part of the employer contrary to the fiduciary obligations in the legislation.

The regulations under the federal PBSA differ from the various provincial jurisdictions in that a trade union representing employees may appoint employee representatives. Where there is a request for a pension committee, such request can be expressed by way of employee petition.

It should be noted that the regulations under the Ontario Act and the applicable Revenue Canada rules require pension funds to be administered by a government, an insurance company or a trust. Where a trust is used, the trustees must be one of:

1. A loan and trust company
2. Three or more individuals at least three of whom reside in Canada and at least one of whom is independent of any employer or
3. A corporate pension society.

Where a multi-employer pension plan (MEPP) is established pursuant to a collective agreement or trust agreement, the legislation in all of the various provinces appears to require at least 50% employee representation on the board of trustees. Alberta, however, only makes this applicable to MEPPs created under collective agreements. In *CUPE v. Ontario Hospital Association*,[18] the Pension Commission of Ontario concluded that any multi-employer plan "established" pursuant to a trust agreement, including a trust agreement with a trust company, must be governed by a board of trustees of whom at least 50% of the representatives are the plan members. The Commission interpreted the word *established* to mean maintained under a trust agreement, not just one that was created under such an agreement. The Hospitals of Ontario Pension Plan was administered as if it were a single employer plan, even though it had been established pursuant to a trust agreement. The Commission held that this was unacceptable and that Section 8(1)(e) of the Ontario Act is mandatory for all MEPPs created and maintained under trust agreements as well as collective agreements. Joint trusteeship was required regardless of the form of trust agreement that established the plan. The case was ultimately resolved between the parties, and the Hospitals of Ontario Pension Plan is now the largest jointly trusteed pension fund in Canada. Since that time, numerous other pension plans in Ontario have adopted a joint trusteeship model, including the pension plans for Ontario's unionized public servants (the OPSEU Pension Plan) and the pension plan for Ontario's community college teachers. The concept has also been applied with respect to public sector workers in other provinces including hospital and municipal workers in Manitoba and other western provinces.

Note that in a subsequent Ontario decision, a plan was held not to be a multi-employer plan where plans sponsored by a group of hospitals created by a religious order were held to be independent separate plans run by separate hospital corporations and not a multi-employer plan.[19]

Advisory Committees

Section 24 of the Ontario Act permits a majority of pension plan members to establish an "advisory committee." Similar provisions exist under the PBSA, the New Brunswick *Pension Benefits Act*[20] and the Nova

Scotia Act. These committees are generally powerless and only have the authority to monitor the pension plan, make recommendations to the administrator and "promote awareness and understanding of the pension plan." They also have the authority to examine records of the administrator and make extracts,[21] but this authority is really no different from the authority that any pension plan member has by virtue of access to information or disclosure provisions under pension legislation in most jurisdictions.[22] It remains to be seen whether the advisory committee system will be adopted in many workplaces and whether there will indeed be a demand for such committees. Ontario advisory committees cannot be appointed where there is a pension committee administering the pension plan, where at least one member must be appointed by the pension plan members and, in respect of multi-employer plans established under collective agreements, where at least 50% of the trustees must be representatives of the members. Further, the Ontario legislation does not indicate the necessary steps that must be followed by the majority of client members in establishing an advisory committee and makes no provision for votes or other methods of obtaining such committees.

Notice of Proposed Amendments

One of the major procedural concerns with respect to the operation of employer-controlled pension plans is the ability of the employer to make amendments that may adversely affect the employees. Certain amendments may not be permitted as a matter of trust law, such as amendments where an employer is seeking to amend the plan to give itself the surplus on plan wind-up, where such surplus previously was to be allocated to the employees, and then shortly thereafter winds up the plan.[23] The validity of such amendments may be successfully challenged in court. Further, as was evident in the *Dominion Stores* case, the failure to give employees notice of a pension plan amendment that adversely affects them represents a breach of the rules of natural justice and procedural fairness and, accordingly, decisions of the Pension Commission permitting such amendments to allow surplus withdrawals were struck down by the court.[24] This sequence of events resulted in changes to the Ontario Act that require notice of proposed plan amendments before they are approved by the Superintendent under the act, where such changes may adversely affect pension benefits, rights or obligations of members.

Section 26 of the Ontario Act requires notice of such changes to each member, former member or other affected person. The Superintendent of Financial Institutions (formerly the Superintendent of Pensions) may, however, dispense with the notice if he or she is of the opinion that the amendment is of a technical nature and will not substantially affect pension benefits, rights or obligations or if the amendment has been agreed to by a trade union that represents the members.[25]

There is no clear definition in the Ontario statute of what type of amendment adversely affects pension benefits, rights or obligations of plan beneficiaries. Clearly, changes in surplus ownership are changes of this nature. Further, in the unreported decision of the Superintendent of Pensions in the *Ontario Hospitals Association* case,[26] the Superintendent found that a pension plan amendment that removes a pension committee as plan administrator and replaces it with the employer as administrator is a change that adversely affects the rights of plan members, and notice should be given under Section 26.

The approach taken in jurisdictions other than the three provinces noted above requires notice of any plan amendments to be given to plan members after they have been made and approved by the provincial regulatory authority. Accordingly, the Alberta *Employment Pension Plans Regulation* (the "Alberta Regulation"),[27] the Manitoba *Pension Benefits Regulation* (the "Manitoba Regulation"),[28] Newfoundland *Pension Benefits Act* (the "Newfoundland Act")[29] and the Saskatchewan *Pension Benefits Act* (the "Saskatchewan Act")[30] require notice to be given of plan amendments after they are made. Similarly, the Ontario *Pension Benefits Regulation* (the "Ontario Regulation") under Regulation 39 contains an additional requirement of notice of amendments *after* they are approved, as well as notice of proposed amendments.[31]

Access to Information

One of the major reforms contained in the recent legislation is the availability of information to plan members, former members, trade unions and other interested parties such as former spouses asserting a claim under family law legislation.

Pursuant to general trust law principles, beneficiaries of a trust are entitled to an "accounting" and to information about the administration of the trust. However, in the past, access to information involving pension plans has been denied to employees by many employers that view their pension plans as confidential or restricted company information. Under the former Ontario Act, only very limited access was permitted in respect of the pension plan text and annual statements that had to be filed with the Pension Commission, as well as recent actuarial certificates. Further, the Commission was reluctant to permit employees to view its files if the employer failed to provide the information directly. It was the absence of information regarding activities of employers in handling pension funds and the failure of the Commission to give such information to the employees that particularly disturbed the Divisional Court in the *Dominion Stores* case.[32]

The Ontario Act now contains numerous provisions that provide much more complete disclosure of pension plan information to beneficiaries. Section 27 requires annual statements containing prescribed information. Section 40 of the Ontario Regulation contains a substantial list of items to be contained in the annual statements, all of which must be provided within six months of the fiscal year-end of the plan.

Section 28 of the Ontario Act creates an obligation to provide plan members with a statement on termination of employment (except in the case of multi-employer plans). The Ontario Regulation contains extensive provisions in terms of the contents of such notices whenever a plan member retires, terminates or becomes deceased in Sections 41 to 44.

The primary "access to information" provisions are those contained in Sections 29 and 30 of the Ontario Act, which give members and former members, their spouses, agents or trade unions the right to inspect certain prescribed documents. Section 45 of the Ontario Regulation sets out a list of different types of documents that must be provided within 30 days of receipt of a request of an administrator. Such documentation includes:

- Current and past pension plan texts
- Documents filed with the Commission
- Provisions of any document setting out the employer's responsibilities with respect to the plan
- Documents delegating administration of plan
- Information returns and reports filed with the Commission
- Copies of correspondence with the Commission other than personal information relating to a member or former member without the consent of that person
- Copies of any part of an agreement concerning the purchase or sale of a business or assets of a business that relates to the pension plan.

Note that Ontario's Section 29(5) only permits a member, former member, spouse or trade union to make an inspection of the employer records once per calendar year. There is no rational explanation for this limitation, and it probably can easily be circumvented by having another member seek the same information. There is a right to inspect these documents under Section 30 at the offices of the Commission, in addition to the right to obtain these from the employer.

The Nova Scotia Act contains, in Sections 35 and 36, similar provisions to those of Ontario in respect of access to information, and virtually all jurisdictions maintain requirements for annual statements and statements on termination. Specifically, one should consult the following sections of the legislation in the jurisdiction set out below, namely:

1. The federal PBSA Section 28 and the PBSA Regulation Section 22[33]

2. The Alberta Act Section 8 and the Alberta Regulation.[34]
3. The Manitoba Act Section 29 and the Manitoba Regulation.[35]
4. The Saskatchewan Act Section 13 and the Saskatchewan *Pension Benefits Regulation* (the "Saskatchewan Regulations")[36]
5. British Columbia *Pension Benefits Standards Act* (the "British Columbia Act") Section 10 and the British Columbia *Pension Benefits Standards Regulation* (the "British Columbia Regulation").[37]
6. New Brunswick Act Sections 23 to 28 and the New Brunswick *Pension Benefits Regulation* (the "New Brunswick Regulation").[38]
7. The Quebec Act Sections 26 and 110 to 115, and the Quebec *Regulation Respecting Supplemental Pension Plans* (the "Quebec Regulation").[39]

Another possible method of access to information regarding pension plans in the federal jurisdiction and in the provinces that have "freedom of information" statutes is to file requests under such legislation to obtain documents filed with the regulatory authorities. A recent decision of Ontario's Freedom of Information Commissioner indicates that the Pension Commission of Ontario, for example, must release texts of pension plan investment policies that have been filed to anyone making a request.

SUBSTANTIVE BENEFIT PROTECTIONS

Eligibility

One of the major criticisms of the pre-1980s pension statutes was the ability to exclude certain groups and classes of employees from pension plans by virtue of stringent eligibility provisions. Access to pension plans would often be restricted by age and service requirements that would not permit employees even to *join* a pension plan until they had reached a certain age and attained a certain level of years of service. Further, certain classes of employees such as part-time employees would be excluded from the pension plan, even though they were working side by side with full-time employees who were participants. Many of the age discrimination provisions have been remedied by way of human rights legislation. However, improved minimum standards legislation was required to deal with exclusion on the basis of service and employee class.

In respect of full-time employees, most jurisdictions have imposed a maximum eligibility period of 24 months.[40] Under the Quebec Act Section 34 it appears that a member can join if his or her employment is similar or identical to that of members already belonging to the class of employees for whom the plan is established. Such a member must meet certain criteria in the calendar year preceding his or her application; namely, the member must have either completed 700 hours of employment or earned 35% of the maximum pensionable earnings under the Quebec Pension Plan (QPP).

There are differing provisions in the various jurisdictions in respect of part-time employees. As can be seen from the above provisions, Quebec does not distinguish between full-time and part-time employees and simply applies the test of the percentage of the year's maximum pensionable earnings (YMPE) or 700 hours. Ontario applies the same test in respect of part-time employees who have met these tests in each of the two consecutive calendar years immediately preceding membership. Nova Scotia, Alberta, Saskatchewan, Prince Edward Island, British Columbia and New Brunswick and the federal PBSA only employ 35% of YMPE in each of the two consecutive calendar years prior to membership as a relevant criterion and do not include the 700-hours test. Manitoba employs the test of 25% of YMPE for the two consecutive 12-month periods preceding membership. YMPE is determined annually under the Canada Pension Plan (CPP) and is a factor related to the average industrial wage.

It should be noted that under much of the provincial legislation (such as Section 34 of the Ontario Act), a separate pension plan may be maintained for part-time employees so long as such benefits are "reasonably equivalent" to those contained in the full-time employee pension plan.

Vesting

One of the major elements of pension reform is the reduction of the 45 and 10 vesting rule, which was prevalent in the legislation of the 1960s. The requirement to have maintained ten years of employment or plan membership before earning a minimum right to a pension was incredibly onerous in view of the mobility of employees among employers. Further, the age 45 restriction might be contrary to the prohibitions against age discrimination now enshrined in Section 15(1) of the Canadian Charter of Rights and Freedoms.

Most jurisdictions have now moved to a two-year vesting rule with no age limitation. Accordingly, the federal PBSA, the Alberta Act and the Ontario Act, all of which became effective as of January 1, 1987 for vesting purposes, grant an employee a vested right to a pension upon reaching normal retirement age if he or she has at least two years of service after January 1, 1987. For Nova Scotia employees, the effective date was January 1, 1988, and for Quebec employees it was January 1, 1990. Manitoba maintained a five-year vesting rule as of January 1, 1985 but has amended it to two years of continuous service or five years of plan membership, part of which is in Manitoba, after January 1, 1990.[41] Alberta and British Columbia have now moved to a two-year

vesting as well. In New Brunswick, Section 35(2) maintains a five-year vesting rule, while the unproclaimed Prince Edward Island legislation requires three years of membership and five years of service to vest. Saskatchewan maintained a one-year vesting rule so long as age plus service or plan membership was equal to 45 or more in respect of service between January 1, 1969 and December 29, 1993. As of January 1, 1994, Saskatchewan moved to a two-year continuous service vesting rule.[42] Quebec, however, in its Bill 102 tabled in March 2000 is contemplating an immediate vesting requirement for all pension plans.

The more difficult area is in respect of service *prior* to the effective date of the legislation. Most jurisdictions have maintained the age 45 and ten years of continuous service provisions in respect of any combination of service before and after the effective date.[43]

Generally, it is the termination of employment that triggers termination of membership under a pension plan. However, members of multi-employer plans or part-time or laid-off employees cannot terminate membership unless there have been no contributions made for them to the fund on their behalf for a consecutive period of 24 months or such shorter period as may be specified in the pension plan.[44]

One further factor to bear in mind in respect of vesting requirements is the possibility of return of employee contributions in the case of contributory pension plans. The minimum vesting requirements pertain to the right to obtain a locked-in pension or to transfer the commuted value of such pension to a locked-in registered retirement savings plan (RRSP). Where an employee has not vested, such an employee is always entitled to a return of his or her own contributions with interest at the rate prescribed in the applicable legislation.

Value of the Pension

Some jurisdictions have provided minimum protection in respect of the value of a pension to be paid out, particularly for employees in contributory plans. This is accomplished by requiring that the employer pay a certain percentage of the benefits that have accrued after a particular date, being the effective date of the legislation. The most common rule is the 50% employer cost rule, which requires that employers pay for at least 50% of the benefit in a contributory plan, with employee contributions being applied to provide the balance.[45]

Where there are excess employee contributions as a result of applying the 50% employer cost rule, there are different consequences that result. For example, the Ontario Act[46] together with the legislation in Nova Scotia[47] and New Brunswick[48] requires that the money must be refunded to the member in a lump-sum together with interest at the prescribed rate. Other jurisdictions such as federally under PBSA[49] and Quebec[50] require that the money must be applied to provide additional pension benefits. Still other jurisdictions allow an option of a lump-sum transfer to the member, using the money to increase benefits to be transferred to locked-in RRSPs or transferred to another pension plan.[51] It should be noted that the 50% employer cost rule is not retroactive and only applies to pension accruals after the effective date of the above legislation.

Portability

Another major aspect of pension reform is the mandatory portability available to an employee whose employment is terminated and who is entitled to a vested pension. The commuted value of the pension benefit can be transferred to another pension fund if the other pension fund agrees to accept the payment or into a locked-in RRSP or deferred life annuity provided by an insurer that cannot commence until ten years before the normal retirement date. These portability vehicles must be *locked-in,* in that the money cannot be removed by the employee for his or her own use and the annuity must be generated ultimately upon reaching retirement age.[52]

In Quebec, portability rights are further restricted if the member is within ten years of normal retirement age or has become entitled to an unreduced early retirement pension.[53]

Note that portability rights appear to occur when employment is terminated. However, the practice in multi-employer situations requires termination of plan membership as opposed to termination with any one employer.

Portability rights do not apply to members who have terminated employment and qualify for an immediate pension,[54] and some of the legislation, such as Ontario, permits the Superintendent of Pensions to restrict portability rights where the solvency of the entire plan may be in jeopardy.

A recent development in a number of jurisdictions including Ontario, the Prairie provinces, British Columbia and New Brunswick is the establishment of a *life-income fund* (LIF). This concept was developed to avoid the difficulty encountered by many persons receiving portability transfers who were obliged to convert their locked-in RRSPs to annuities upon reaching age 71 because RRSP eligibility ceases at that age under the *Income Tax Act.* In the past such individuals were not able to transfer their locked-in RRSP to a registered retirement income fund (RRIF) the way other RRSP holders are permitted to do and thus avoid purchasing an annuity. The LIF permits such a transfer into a non-commutable RRIF subject to conditions imposed by the regulations or statutes under provincial law. It permits the holder of a locked-in RRSP resulting from a pension portability transfer to delay the purchase of a life

annuity to age 80. Alberta and Saskatchewan do not require an annuity purchase at all. The owner of a LIF can determine the amount of annual withdrawals subject to the prescribed minimum and maximum withdrawal limits. However, the funds in the LIF remain subject to the usual conditions under provincial legislation for locked-in RRSPs and pension benefits including the 60% survivor benefit upon purchase of an annuity and the provisions dealing with marriage breakdown.

Most recently, Ontario and some of the other provinces have moved to the concept of a new locked-in retirement income fund (LRIF) that permits pensioners to benefit from a more flexible payment schedule and no longer forces them to convert their retirement funds to life annuities at age 80. Further, Ontario has removed the locking-in requirements for small pensions or for amounts in excess of the maximum available under the *Income Tax Act.*[55]

Interest on Employee Contributions

For contributory pension plans, a major source of employee dissatisfaction in the past was the low interest rate attributed to member contributions that were being refunded, particularly in the case of a terminated employee who had not vested. Pension plans that were controlled by employers, and particularly those funded through insurance carriers, would pay extremely low interest rates that did not reflect market rates, or even the rates attributable on regular savings accounts at chartered banks.

Starting with the federal PBSA, pension legislation in the 1980s required that plans attribute either the average of the five-year personal fixed term chartered bank deposit rates (CANSIM) or the rate of return that can reasonably be attributed to the pension fund to the employee contributions.[56] The plan administrator makes an election as to which of these two approaches to take, and then the interest rate is thus set. This approach has been adopted by Alberta, British Columbia, Ontario, Nova Scotia and Quebec. Saskatchewan and New Brunswick permit regulations prescribing the interest rate. However, in its recent Bill 102 proposals, Quebec is contemplating paying interest at the plan earnings rate. Manitoba requires the plan to pay either the rate paid by any financial institution on classes of investments that have been approved for the plan by the Superintendent or a rate within 1% of the rate of return earned by the pension fund.

Joint and Survivor Pension

Recognition of the interest of a spouse in a pension and the concern that surviving spouses of pensioners receive some form of income support from the plan have resulted in most jurisdictions mandating a joint and survivor form of pension, subject to the ability of the member and the spouse to elect an optional form of pension, including the one that is only paid to the member for life or guaranteed for a specified period of time. The amount of the pension can be adjusted to the actuarial equivalent of the normal pension available in the plan for a single member.

The most popular form of joint and survivor pension requires that the spouse get at least 60% of the pension the member receives prior to his or her death. This is mandated unless another option is elected with written permission from a spouse. These rules represent the minimum standard in all provinces with the exception of Manitoba. Manitoba requires a joint and survivor pension of at least two-thirds of the initial amount on the death of either spouse with the option to waive the pension on the written agreement of the spouse.[57]

The definition of *spouse* in the various statutes must be carefully reviewed, particularly in instances where there are common law spouses (or as noted below same-sex spouses), or the potential of a competition between a legally married spouse and a common law spouse with whom the member is living. The definitions adopted in most jurisdictions, including Ontario, are similar to that adopted under the CPP, where the definition of *spouse* includes *either of* a man and a woman who:

(i) are married to each other, or
(ii) are not married to each other but,
    (a) have been living together in a conjugal relationship for a period of not less than three years, or
    (b) in a relationship of some permanence, if they are the natural or adoptive parents of a child.

The federal PBSA contains a one-year cohabitation period, while Alberta, New Brunswick, Nova Scotia and Quebec have maintained the same three-year requirement as Ontario.

Same-Sex Partners

As a result of certain major court decisions regarding extending survivor spousal benefits to conjugal partners of the same sex, some jurisdictions have moved to change their pension and other statutes to permit survivor pension entitlements and other pension-related entitlements to partners of the same sex in a manner similar to common law spouses. This was originally triggered by a challenge to the provisions under the *Income Tax Act* in the case of *Rosenberg v. The Queen*[58] where the Ontario Court of Appeal struck down the constitutionality of the prohibition against same-sex partners as contrary to the Canadian Charter of Rights and Freedoms. A subsequent decision of the Supreme Court of Canada pertaining to same-sex partners claiming support rights in case of the breakdown of their relation-

ship, and a successful challenge to the Ontario provincial requirements under the *Pension Benefits Act* requiring spouses to be of the opposite sex, has established, by judicial determination, survivor pension and other pension rights for partners of the same sex.

The legislative response has taken the form of various provinces and the federal government amending their statutes to permit the same-sex benefits, while other provinces have yet to take any legislative action.

Quebec was the first jurisdiction under its Bill 32 enacted in June 1999 to amend 28 statutes including the Quebec *Supplementary Pension Plans Act* so that the definition of *spouse* includes living in a conjugal relationship with an unmarried member of either sex for at least three years, or one year if they are the natural parents or adoptive parents of a child. British Columbia followed shortly thereafter in July of 1999. Ontario, as a result of a case brought by the Ontario Public Services Employees Union challenging the definition of *spouse* in the pension legislation, was required to make a change effective December 8, 1998, being the date of the court decision. Effective March 1, 2000 Ontario Bill 5 amended 67 statutes to add a new definition of *same-sex partner* to those statutes including the *Pension Benefits Act*. The *same-sex partner* definition follows along the lines of the definition of a common law spouse.

More recently the federal government introduced the *Modernization of Benefits and Obligations Act,* Bill C-23, to amend a substantial number of statutes, including the *Income Tax Act,* PBSA and the *Canada Pension Plans Act,* to provide for a definition of *same-sex partner* that is consistent with the definition of a *common law partner.* The changes to the *Income Tax Act* are significant in that they implement the *Rosenberg* decision and ensure that plans will be registered if they contain the *same-sex* definition. Even though other provinces have not, at this writing, amended their pension benefits statutes, virtually all of them will register a pension plan that includes same-sex partners within the definition of *spouse.*

Pre-Retirement Death Benefits

Another major area where pension plans were severely lacking in employee protection was that of benefits for the spouses or families of plan members who died after earning a vested pension but before reaching retirement age. Large numbers of plans did not make any provision for a death benefit other than perhaps the return of members' contributions in the case of contributory plans. In such case, the interest allocated was minimal. Accordingly, the pension reform legislation of the 1980s sought to provide protection to spouses of deceased plan members who have not reached retirement age. Even in these circumstances, the "reform" legislation outlined below only covers pension credits earned after the effective date of the legislation (after January 1, 1987) and not pension credits earned prior to that time. Quebec only covers credits accrued after 1989, while Manitoba covers those accrued after 1984.

The approach taken by PBSA varied depending on whether the member was eligible to retire at the time of death. If he or she was not eligible, then the spouse receives a commuted value of the pension accrued after 1986, as a statutory minimum. For members who were eligible, the spouse receives a lifetime pension equal to 60% of the pension that the member would have received had he or she retired at the time of death. However, the death benefit may be reduced, or totally nullified, by other benefits payable under a group life insurance plan or other benefit plan of the employer that is approved by the Superintendent. Further, the reduction of the benefit cannot reduce the value of the pension to less than the value of the member's contributions with interest.[59]

The Ontario approach under Section 48 is to provide payment of a benefit to a spouse (or a same-sex partner), where there is one, or to a beneficiary where the employee dies without a spouse. Where there is a spouse, he or she is put to an election between a lump-sum payment or the pension, immediate or deferred, payable to a spouse, which is equal to the commuted value of the deferred pension that would have been paid to the member. Where there is no spouse, the only option available to a designated beneficiary is that of the lump-sum payment equal to the commuted value of the pension. Where there is no spouse or beneficiary, the estate receives the commuted value. Where the pension plan provides for payment of pension benefits to dependent children, the commuted value of the payments may be deducted from the entitlement of the designated beneficiary. Further offsets are available where the employer provides an additional benefit, similar to the regime adopted under PBSA.

The Quebec Act adopts the Ontario approach, except in cases of members who die after normal retirement date but prior to commencement of pension, in which case the spouse must receive a pension equal to that the member would have received on the day before his or her death had the member retired.[60] The PBSA approach of transferring 60% of the pension that the member would have received to the spouse has been adopted by Alberta, Nova Scotia and New Brunswick.[61] Spouses are generally given the option of transferring the commuted value to another pension plan or locked-in RRSP in these jurisdictions. Manitoba maintains the rule that any member who dies before retirement and after completion of five years of continuous service must have a pension paid to a surviving spouse of at least the commuted value of the pension. Surviving spouses receive a life annuity, and other non-spouse beneficiaries receive a lump-sum. Surviving spouses are entitled to transfer the commuted value to a locked-in RRSP.[62]

Early Commutations—Shortened Life Expectancy and Financial Hardship

A recent trend in legislative amendments has been to permit, in some instances, the unlocking of locked-in funds, be they in pension plans or locked-in retirement arrangements (LIRAs).

Previously, all jurisdictions except New Brunswick had made it **permissible** for a pension plan to allow for the unlocking of pension entitlements in cases of plan members with a shortened life expectancy. None of the statutes were particularly clear on the meaning of a *shortened life expectancy*. This is still the norm today in most jurisdictions in Canada subject to the recent changes outlined below.

Ontario in its Bill 27, the *Pension Benefits Statute Law Amendment Act, 1999,* proposed unlocking pensions or deferred pensions if the member or former member suffers from a mental or physical disability that is likely to considerably shorten his or her life expectancy. The conditions for permitting a member to make an application for withdrawal of all of the pension are set out in the new Regulations to the Ontario Act. Regulation 144/00 sets out the essential conditions, effective March 2000, for unlocking such pensions. The conditions apply to locked-in retirement accounts, pensions and deferred pensions. In order to qualify, the member must have a certificate from a physician indicating that he or she is expected to live no longer than two years, and a consent executed by a spouse or, where applicable, same-sex partner.

The Ontario legislation also provided for the possibility of unlocking money in a LIRA (but **not** a pension plan) for individuals suffering from financial hardship. Again, the definition of the necessary conditions was left to a regulation. Ontario's Regulation 242/00 released April 25, 2000 sets out the conditions in respect of financial hardship applications. Essentially they require the withdrawal of an amount that shall be at least $500 or more from any life income fund, locked-in retirement account or locked-in retirement income fund. The application must be made to the Superintendent. Spousal consent (or consent of a spousal equivalent) is required where applicable. Anyone making such application must sign a statement acknowledging that the funds released under such a consent are not exempt from execution, seizure or attachment.

The circumstances of financial hardship that are required to obtain a successful application are:
1. Written demand in respect of the non-payment of rent or eviction from a principal residence
2. Default on a debt such as a mortgage secured

against the residence that would result in eviction

3. Incurring expenses for treatment of illness or physical disability or for renovation or alterations required to adapt the principal residence to an illness or disability.

In all such applications, the owners' total income before taxes for the 12-month period following the date of signing the application must be 66⅔% or less of the year's YMPE.

No other provinces have yet to move to the Ontario standards in respect of unlocking funds with the exception of Quebec and New Brunswick, which require medical certification and spousal consent for shortened life expectancy. Other provinces have released discussion papers at the time of this publication, but Ontario is the only one with specific legislative initiative.

Benefits on Total or Partial Plan Wind-Up

A level of employee protections benefiting persons primarily employed in Ontario and Nova Scotia is the creation of additional pension plan liabilities on plan wind-up. The laws of most jurisdictions on plan wind-up will vest even those who have not vested. However, the Ontario Act and the Nova Scotia Act contain additional provisions that permit a plan member on the wind-up of a plan to "grow into" certain benefits that he or she has not yet attained but would attain had he or she continued in service.[63] Section 74 of the Ontario Act states that any member whose age plus years of continuous employment or membership in the plan equals at least 55 is entitled to a pension in accordance with the terms of the plan beginning the earlier of:

(a) The normal retirement date under the plan; or

(b) The date under which the member would be entitled to an unreduced pension if the plan were not wound up and if the member's membership continued to that date.

The Ontario Court of Appeal in *Firestone Canada v. Pension Commission of Ontario*[64] held that the object of this section, when read in the context of the act as a whole, is to provide benefits to employees. The practical effect of these provisions is to protect employees affected by plant closures by accelerating the payment of their pensions and requiring additional contributions from employers to fund those pensions. Thus, employees who are thrown out of work on a plant shutdown do not have to wait until they reach the normal retirement age (usually age 65) to collect their pensions, but are deemed to continue in service and to collect pensions commencing at their earliest retirement date permissible under the plan.

Subsequent to the *Firestone* case there were further developments regarding events that would trigger "grown-in rights" on a plan wind-up. In *Stelco v. Super-*

intendent of Pensions,[65] a corporate reorganization resulting in the termination of 700 employees was held to authorize the Superintendent of Pensions to order a partial wind-up of a pension plan on the basis that a "significant" number of employees had been terminated. Both the Commission and the court upheld the finding that 700 employees represented a significant number even though it was less than 20% of the plan members. The same principles were upheld by the PCO and the courts in *Imperial Oil v. Superintendent of Pensions,*[66] where the Commission continued to adopt a broad definition of the *reorganization* of a business.

The grow-in concept has been applied in Nova Scotia by its courts in the case of *Hawker-Siddeley Canada v. Superintendent of Pensions,*[67] where the Superintendent ordered a partial wind-up as a result of a shutdown that reached backwards in time to cover employees who had been terminated earlier through an early retirement program. The effect of the *Hawker-Siddeley* case is to ensure that the Superintendent's statutory obligation to protect the interest of the plan members is interpreted broadly so as to permit partial wind-ups to be ordered in such circumstances where members would lose their "grow-in" rights in the absence of a partial wind-up order. In *Hawker-Siddeley,* an attempt to reduce the liabilities and avoid grow-in obligations so that the employer could attempt to obtain more of the plan's surplus was held to be a violation of the fiduciary obligations of the employer under the plan.

Even where the Superintendent has been reluctant to order a partial wind-up, courts and pension tribunals have required investigations where there is a reorganization, and partial wind-ups have been contemplated in cases of mass lay-offs.[68]

It is evident that the "downsizing" and "reorganizations" that have taken place across Canada in recent years will give rise to more and more cases of requests for partial wind-ups and providing "grow-in rights" to plan members who lose employment.

A further issue, unique to Ontario and Nova Scotia, is whether the partial wind-up triggers a right to surplus from members of a pension plan who are affected by the partial wind-up. This is based on the provisions in both statutes (for example, Ontario's Section 17(6)), which grants members on a partial wind-up the same rights as they would have on a full wind-up of a plan). The concept is currently being tested in Ontario in the case of *Monsanto v. Superintendent of Pensions,* where the Superintendent's order that surplus should be distributed on a partial-up was overturned by a majority panel of the Financial Services Tribunal.[69] The case is currently on appeal to Ontario's Divisional Court.

Quebec in its Bill 102 has provided a possible solution to the issue of protecting employees on any termination, be it a mass layoff or an individual one. Bill 102 proposes that any terminated employee is provided with a benefit of "indexation" of accrued pensions using the Consumer Price Index (CPI) to the date of normal retirement. However, such indexation benefits may be offset by early retirement enhancements that are provided to terminating employees under the plan, so that the employee receives only the greater of the two. As a result of providing such early termination benefits and requiring immediate vesting, Quebec's legislation proposes the abolition of partial wind-ups.

There is no doubt that the issue for protecting employees who have their employment terminated involuntarily due to corporate restructurings or other related business reasons will pose a challenge for regulators in the years to come.

ENDNOTES

1. *Pension Benefits Standards Act, 1985,* R.S.C. 1985, c. 32 (2nd Supp.) (PBSA).

2. *Cowan v. Scargill,* [1984] 2 All E.R. 750 (Ch.D.).

3. Ontario *Pension Benefits Act,* R.S.O. 1990, c. P.8 (the "Ontario Act").

4. *Ibid.,* s. 22(1).

5. *Ibid.,* s. 22(4).

6. *Employee Retirement Income Security Act,* 29 U.S.C.A. §1001 (1974) (ERISA).

7. PBSA, *supra* note 1, ss. 8(4), (6).

8. Nova Scotia *Pension Benefit Act,* R.S.N.S. 1989, c. 340 (the "Nova Scotia Act"), ss. 29(1), (3).

9. Manitoba *Pension Benefits Act,* R.S.M. 1987, c. P32 (the "Manitoba Act"), ss. 28.1(2), (5).

10. Alberta *Employment Pension Plans Act,* S.A. 1986, c. E-10.05 (the "Alberta Act"), s. 6(5).

11. Quebec *Supplemental Pension Plans Act,* R.S.Q. c. R-15.1 (the "Quebec Act"), s. 6.

12. Ontario Act, *supra* note 3, Sections 22(5) and (7); Nova Scotia Act, *supra* note 8, Sections 29(4) and (5).

13. *Collins v. Pension Commission of Ontario* (1986), 56 O.R. (2d) 274 (Div.Ct.).

14. See *Anova Inc. Employee Retirement Pension Plan v. Manufacturers Life* (1994), 121 D.L.R. (4th) 162 (O.C. (G.D.)).

15. *Imperial Oil Limited Retirement Plan v. Pension Commission of Ontario* (Fall-Winter, 1997), PCO Bulletin 6:4 (P.C.O.), at p. 68.

16. See Section 8 of the Ontario Act, *supra* note 3; Section 14 of the Nova Scotia Act, *supra* note 8; Section 7 of PBSA, *supra* note 1, among others.

17. See Subsections 7(3)(b), 7(5) and (6) of PBSA, *supra* note 1.

18. *CUPE v. Ontario Hospital Association* (November 1991), PCO Bulletin 2:3 (P.C.O.), at p. 16, aff'd (1992), 91 D.L.R. (4th) 436 (Ont. Div. Ct.).

19. *C.U.P.E., Local 1144 & 1590 v. Ontario (Superintendent of Pensions)* (1998), 20 C.C.P.B. 312 (Financial Services Tribunal).

20. New Brunswick *Pension Benefits Act,* S.N.B. 1987, c. P-5.1(the "New Brunswick Act").

21. See for example the Ontario Act, *supra* note 3, s. 24(5).

22. See Section 29 of the Ontario Act, *supra* note 3.

23. See *Reevie v. Montreal Trust Company* (1986), 53 O.R. (2d) 595 (C.A.) and *Schmidt v. Air Products* (1994), 115 D.L.R. (4th) 631 (S.C.C.).

24. *Collins, supra* note 13.

25. Ontario Act, *supra* note 3, s. 26(4); the New Brunswick Act, *supra* note 20, s. 24; the Nova Scotia Act, *supra* note 8, s. 32.

26. *Ontario Hospitals Association* (Unreported decision of the Superintendent of Pensions dated May 4, 1989), reversed on other grounds by the Pension Commission of Ontario, *supra* note 18.

27. Alberta *Employment Pension Plans Regulation,* Alta. Reg. 364/86 (the "Alberta Regulation"), s.10(2).

28. Manitoba *Pension Benefits Regulation,* Man Reg. 188/87R (the "Manitoba Regulation"), s.23(7).

29. Newfoundland *Pension Benefits Act,* 1997, S.N. 1996, c. P-4.01 (the "Newfoundland Act"), s. 25(3).

30. Saskatchewan *Pension Benefits Act,* 1992, S.S. 1992, c. P-6.001, (the "Saskatchewan Act"), s. 17(1).

31. Ontario *Pension Benefits Regulations,* Regulation 909, (the "Ontario Regulation"), s. 39.

32. *Collins, supra* note 13.

33. *Pension Benefits Standards Regulation,* 1985, SOR/87-19 (the "PBSA Regulation").

34. Alberta Act, *supra* note 10, s.8; Alberta Regulation, *supra* note 27.

35. Manitoba Act, *supra* note 9, s. 29; Manitoba Regulation, *supra* note 28, s. 23.

36. Saskatchewan Act, *supra* note 30, s. 13; Saskatchewan *Pension Benefits Regulations,* 1993 R.R.S., c. P-6.001, Reg.1 (the "Saskatchewan Regulation"), ss.11-21.

37. British Columbia *Pension Benefits Standards Act,* R.S.B.C. 1996, c. 352 (the "British Columbia Act"); *Pension Benefits Standards Regulation,* B.C. Reg. 433/93 (the "British Columbia Regulation"), ss. 9-18.

38. New Brunswick Act, *supra* note 20, ss. 23 to 28; New Brunswick *Pension Benefits Regulation,* N.B. Reg. 91-195 (the "New Brunswick Regulation"), ss. 13-17.

39. Quebec Act, *supra* note 11, ss. 26 and 110 to 115; *Regulation Respecting Supplemental Pension Plans,* Q.C. 1158-90 (the "Quebec Regulation"), ss. 57-60.

40. PBSA, *supra* note 1, s. 14(1)(a); Alberta Act, *supra* note 10, s. 22; Manitoba Act, *supra* note 9, s.21; Nova Scotia Act, *supra* note 8, s. 37; Ontario Act, *supra* note 3, s. 31; Saskatchewan Act, *supra* note 30, s. 26; Prince Edward Island *Pension Benefits Act,* S.P.E.I. 1990, c. 41 not proclaimed in force (the "Prince Edward Island Act"), s. 37; New Brunswick Act, *supra* note 20, s. 29; British Columbia Act, *supra* note 37, s. 25.

41. Manitoba Act, *supra* note 9, ss. 39 and 40.

42. Saskatchewan Act, *supra* note 30, ss. 27 and 29.

43. PBSA, *supra* note 1, s. 17(3); Alberta Act, *supra* note 10, s. 23(1); Manitoba Act, *supra* note 9, s. 21(1); Nova Scotia Act, *supra* note 8, s. 42; Ontario Act, *supra* note 3, s. 37 (2); Quebec Act, *supra* note 11, s. 295; Only Newfoundland maintains the old age 45 and ten years of service rule, see Newfoundland Act, *supra* note 29, s. 17(1)(a).

44. Ontario Act, *supra* note 3, s. 39.

45. Such rules are effective under PBSA, *supra* note 1, s. 21(2); Ontario Act, *supra* note 3, s. 39(3); Alberta Act, *supra*

note 10, s. 29 (1); Manitoba Act, *supra* note 9, s. 21(11); Quebec Act, *supra* note 11, s. 60; Saskatchewan Act, *supra* note 30, s. 31; Nova Scotia Act, *supra* note 8, s. 47 (3); New Brunswick Act, *supra* note 20, s. 55(1)(3).

46. Ontario Act, *supra* note 3, s. 39(4).

47. Nova Scotia Act, *supra* note 8, s. 47.

48. New Brunswick Act, *supra* note 20, s. 55(2).

49. PBSA, *supra* note 1, s. 21(2).

50. Quebec Act, *supra* note 11, ss. 83 and 84.

51. Alberta Act, *supra* note 10, s. 29(2); Manitoba Act, *supra* note 9, s. 21(11); Saskatchewan Act, *supra* note 30, s. 31.

52. Legislation permitting this type of portability includes the Ontario Act, *supra* note 3, s. 42; PBSA, *supra* note 1, s. 26; Alberta Act, *supra* note 10, s. 30; Nova Scotia Act, *supra* note 8, s. 50; New Brunswick Act, *supra* note 20, s. 36(1); Manitoba Act, *supra* note 9, s. 21; Prince Edward Island Act, *supra* note 40, s. 49; Saskatchewan Act, *supra* note 30, s. 32.

53. Quebec Act, *supra* note 11, ss. 98 and 99.

54. Ontario Act, *supra* note 3, s. 42(3).

55. Ontario Regulation 144/00 effective March 2000.

56. PBSA, *supra* note 1, s. 19(2).

57. Manitoba Act, *supra* note 9, s. 23.

58. *Rosenberg v. The Queen* (1998), 158 D.L.R. (4th) 664 (O.C.A.).

59. PBSA, *supra* note 1, s. 23.

60. Quebec Act, *supra* note 11, ss. 86 and 88.

61. Alberta Act, *supra* note 10, s. 31; Nova Scotia Act, *supra* note 8, s. 56; New Brunswick Act, *supra* note 20, s. 43.

62. Manitoba Act, *supra* note 9, s. 21.

63. Ontario Act, *supra* note 3, s. 74 and the Nova Scotia Act, *supra* note 8, s. 78.

64. *Firestone Canada v. Pension Commission of Ontario* (1990), 1 O.R. (3d) 122 (C.A.).

65. *Stelco v. Superintendent of Pensions* (August 1993), PCO Bulletin 4:1 (P.C.O.), at p. 40, aff'd (1994), 115 D.L.R. (4th) 437(Ont. Div. Ct.).

66. *Imperial Oil v. Superintendent of Pensions (Ontario)* (1995), 12 C.C.P.B. 267 (P.C.O.), aff'd [1997] O.J. No. 1961 (G.D.), leave to appeal refused [1997] O.J. No. 2840 (C.A.).

67. *Hawker-Siddeley Canada v. Superintendent of Pensions* (1994), 113 D.L.R. (4th) 424 (N.S.C.A.).

68. See *Maynard v. Ontario (Superintendent of Pensions),* [2000] O.J. No. 881 (S.C.J.).

69. Reasons for Decision released April 14, 2000.

CHAPTER 3

Single Employer Pension Plans (SEPPs)

by Patrick Longhurst

INTRODUCTION AND SELECTED STATISTICS

In this chapter, we will be examining the specific characteristics of single employer pension plans, which may not necessarily apply to multi-employer pension plans (MEPPs). As the name suggests, the dominant feature is that the plan has been sponsored by one employer for the benefit of one or more classes of its employees. In the balance of this section, we will be reviewing the latest statistics covering this type of pension plan.

When analyzing pension plans in Canada, it is important to remember that statistics given by number of plans are not the same as those by number of participants. For example, of the 15,308 pension plans covered in Statistics Canada's publication, *Pension Plans in Canada* 1997,[1] 52.9% are defined contribution plans and 45.1% are defined benefit plans. However, only 11.2% of the participants belong to defined contribution plans. All the statistics we provide below are given by both number of plans and number of participants.

As stated above, at the beginning of 1997, 5,115,290 Canadian workers participated in 15,308 employer-sponsored pension plans. That total was comprised of 1,246 public sector plans with 2,419,022 members, and 14,062 private sector plans with 2,696,268 members. All numbers that follow include both public and private sector members.

The plans were divided this way: 8,818 were contributory and 6,490 were non-contributory. Since the vast majority of public sector plans are contributory, the distribution of members was 3,718,603 in contributory and 1,396,687 in non-contributory plans.

A breakdown of membership by number of members is shown in Table IV-3-I.

Table IV-3-I illustrates the great diversity of pension plans in Canada. Since 1986 the number of plans with less than ten members has declined from 11,200 to 5,383. Membership in other categories has steadily increased. Overall, the average number of members per plan is approximately 330.

An analysis of the types of plans available is presented in Table IV-3-II.

The large number of members in final/best average plans reflects the high proportion of public sector plans that fall into this category.

The required employee contribution rates in contributory plans are shown in Table IV-3-III.

More than 90% (92.8%) of all pension plans have a normal retirement age of 65, with an additional 6.1% having a normal retirement age of 60.

Thirty percent of all defined benefit plans provided for the automatic escalation of pensions in pay. Eighty-three percent of the members in these plans were in the public sector.

Constituting Documents of Single Employer Plans

Most plans established by corporations for their employees that are not multi-employer plans tend to follow one of two traditional formats:

1. Pension plan text and trust agreement or
2. Insurance policy.

For plans of any significant size, the most common approach is for the board of directors of the employer

Table IV-3-I

Class of Employees	Plans		Members	
1-9	5,383	35.2%	17,236	0.3%
10-99	6,518	42.6	243,489	4.8
100-499	2,416	15.8	528,285	10.3
500-999	457	3.0	315,394	6.2
1,000-9,999	477	3.1	1,228,360	24.0
10,000-29,999	38	0.2	700,082	13.7
30,000+	19	0.1	2,082,444	40.7
Total	15,308	100.0%	5,115,290	100.0%

Table IV-3-II

Type of Plan	Plans		Members	
Defined contribution	8,103	52.9%	574,769	11.2%
Defined benefit				
Final/best average	3,586	23.4	3,174,332	62.1
Career average	2,119	13.8	390,555	7.6
Flat benefit	1,196	7.8	889,020	17.4
Total defined benefit	6,901	45.1	4,453,907	87.1
Other plans	304	2.0	86,614	1.7
Total plans	15,308	100.0%	5,115,290	100.0%

Table IV-3-III

Employee Contribution Rates As a Percentage of Wages	Plans		Members	
Less than 3%	909	10.3%	135,620	3.7%
3% to 4%	2,014	22.8	279,922	7.5
5% to 6.99%	3,893	44.1%	1,087,295	29.2
7%+	391	4.5%	1,862,761	50.1
Flat dollar	340	3.9	36,123	1.0
Other	1,271	14.4	316,882	8.5
Total	8,818	100.0%	3,718,603	100.0%

to pass a resolution declaring a pension plan text to be in existence. The plan text is prepared, usually in consultation with the consulting actuaries and legal counsel, setting out the rules of the plan. Simultaneously, a trust agreement is entered into with a third-party custodian, usually a trust company (but sometimes an insurance carrier or a company affiliated with an insurance company), to hold the assets of the trust for the purposes of the pension plan. Most plans also adopt a written *investment policy,* which is mandatory in the provinces of Ontario and Quebec, for all plans, and in Nova Scotia, Newfoundland and federally regulated plans for defined benefit plans only. Investment policy statements are discussed in Chapter 9 of this section. A pension plan may enter into subsidiary documents such as investment counsel agreements, reciprocal agreements with other pension plans, and supplementary documents regarding pension plan assets and investments. However, the primary documents upon which the pension trust is established are the plan text and the trust agreement. Any amendments to the pension plan text generally take the form of resolutions of the corporate board of directors, unless a pension committee is established and has an independent right to amend the plan. Any changes to trust agreements must generally be negotiated with the custodian.

The insured approach generally involves establishing the pension plan by way of an insurance contract between the employer and an insurance company. The contract usually requires the insurance company to administer the plan, hold the assets and invest them. Further, the insurer is to purchase annuities for pensions as retirements take place. The rules of the plan are set out directly in the insurance contract. This approach tends to be more common with smaller plans where employers are willing to pay premiums for the insurer to administer the entire operation and purchase annuities through the insurance company. Although a formal trust is not created, it may still be argued that these monies are being held in trust for the employees by the insurer and, in any event, the fiduciary obligations existing under provincial pension benefits legislation (see Chapter 2 of this section on minimum standards) are still applicable.

In some instances, employers have established corporations known as *pension societies* to hold the assets of the plan, or have created a single employer trust agreement whereby the employer or its designates are the trustees of the fund. The pension committee or the trustees then adopt the pension plan text, rather than the employer's board of directors. Thus, the constituting documents in these circumstances comprise a trust agreement establishing the fund and a subordinate pension plan text. There may be a further agreement with a custodian such as a trust company to hold the assets.

In collective bargaining situations, another document that is important for the constitution of a pension plan is the collective agreement. In many instances, unions and employers negotiate extensive pension agreements within collective agreements that set out all the relevant provisions of the pension plan text. Some collective agreements contain *letters of understanding,* which stipulate the nature of the pension benefits and how the plan is to be administered. Often there is a joint employer-employee committee having certain obligations under the plan. Some pension matters may further be the subject matter of grievance arbitration if there is any dispute. Where collective agreements incorporate a pension plan or benefit package by reference and specifically permit grievances pertaining to pension issues, then the disputes are likely to be settled by arbitration.[2]

Even where there is an explicit agreement that pensions are not arbitrable, there may be an argument that such agreements are unlawful, given the provisions in labour relations statutes that require every collective agreement to provide for a final and binding settlement by arbitration *of all differences* between parties arising from the interpretation, application, administration or alleged violation of a collective agreement.[3]

The case law is unclear with respect to which document governs if there is a contradiction between the pension plan text and the trust agreement. For example, some of the pension fund surplus cases have held the wording of a trust agreement to prevail where it conflicts with the plan text itself.[4] It would appear that the approach many courts may use in these types of cases, particularly where plan beneficiaries are asserting a right against the employer that drafted the documentation, is that any inconsistency ought to be resolved in favour of the employees in accordance with the *contra proferentum* rule of contract interpretation where documents are interpreted against the interests of the person who prepared them, if there is ambiguous wording.

A final matter to be concerned with in the documents constituting a pension plan is that of representations contained in pension plan booklets given to employees (see Chapter 12 in Section I for a full discussion of this topic.). Particularly in situations where a booklet is given and the supporting pension plan text is *not* offered to the employees, it may be argued that the employer is "estopped" from relying on the plan text or trust agreement when it has made explicit representations to the employees to the contrary in its employee booklets. This is alluded to in the *Dominion Stores* case,[5] where the court makes reference to representations to employees that the pension fund would only be used for their benefit. Similarly, in the case of *Madott v. Chrysler Canada*[6] the court determined that an employer could not rely on "secret documents" to deprive an employee of his or her share of a performance bonus on the basis that the documents setting out the bonus plans were never provided to the employees and representations to the contrary were made to the employee by the employer.

The case law on booklets has been further advanced by the decision of the Supreme Court of Canada in *Schmidt v. Air Products,*[7] where statements and booklets were held *not* to be relevant unless there can be some evidence that the employees relied on these statements to their detriment. More importantly, the court determined that it would be inappropriate for employees to rely on booklets on pension surplus matters, which were issued decades earlier without updating, and in the context of a predecessor pension plan.

Statutory Requirements

The contents of pension plans, of course, vary with the type of plan. In addition, it is necessary that the plan text conform to the minimum standards contained in pension benefits legislation. However, three of the provinces have gone further with their legislation and, indeed, mandated certain matters that must be addressed in the "documents that create and support a pension plan." The prototype for this legislation is Section 10(1) of Ontario's *Pension Benefits Act,* which provides as follows:

The documents that create and support a pension plan shall set out the following information:

1. The method of appointment and the details of appointment of the administrator of the pension plan
2. The conditions for membership in the pension plan
3. The benefit and rights that are to accrue upon termination of employment, termination of membership, retirement or death
4. The normal retirement date under the pension plan
5. The requirements for entitlement under the pension plan to any pension benefit or ancillary benefit
6. The contributions or the method of calculating the contributions required by the pension plan
7. The method of determining benefits payable under the pension plan
8. The method of calculating interest to be credited to contributions under the pension plan
9. The mechanism for payment of the cost of administration of the pension plan and pension fund
10. The mechanism for establishing and maintaining the pension fund
11. The treatment of surplus during the continuation of the pension plan and on the wind-up of the pension plan
12. The obligation of the administrator to provide members with information and documents required to be disclosed under this Act and the regulations
13. The method of allocation of the assets of the pension plan on wind-up
14. Particulars of any predecessor pension plan under which members of the pension plan may be entitled to pension benefits
15. Any other prescribed information related to the pension plan or pension fund or both.[8]

Nova Scotia,[9] Alberta,[10] British Columbia,[11] New Brunswick,[12] Saskatchewan,[13] Quebec,[14] Newfoundland[15] and Prince Edward Island[16] have adopted similar requirements for registered pension plans in their respective provinces.

FUNDING AND SOLVENCY RULES

In preparing a valuation of a pension plan, the actuary is normally striving to compare some measure of the value of the benefits that have been earned in the plan (the *liabilities*) against some value for the investments held in the fund (the *assets*). The purpose of the valuation will dictate the assumptions and methods used by the actuary. For example, a valuation performed to indicate the long-term funding position of the plan may be very different from one to demonstrate solvency or to establish a value for a sale or acquisition. The assumptions fall into three categories: economic, personnel and demographic. The methods relate to the funding method and the asset valuation method.

Economic Assumptions

These relate to such key areas as the anticipated future rate of inflation, expected cost-of-living salary increases and the expected rates of return on various asset categories.

Personnel Assumptions

These relate to areas that can reasonably be influenced by the personnel policies of the plan sponsor. These include merit and promotion salary increases, termination rates, probability of retirement at various ages and new entrant rates if applicable.

Demographic Assumptions

These include those items that are generally applicable to Canadians as a whole, although they may be influenced by the nature of the employment. These include mortality rates, disability rates and the probability of being married.

Funding Methods

These vary depending on the need to pre-fund for certain benefits that will be earned in the future. The *unit credit method* simply calculates the value of the pensions earned to date of the valuation. The more common *projected unit credit method* includes allowance for salary increases up to retirement in final/best average plans. The *entry age normal* and *aggregate funding* methods try to provide the sponsor with a more level percentage of annual cost that should not vary as the average age of the membership changes. Generally speaking, the funding method will influence the emergence of liabilities over time. Ultimately, the cost of the pension plan will be the same regardless of the funding method used.

The Asset Valuation Method

This will dictate the value of the investments to be used. Clearly, the most simple value to adopt would be the market or book value of the investments. However, market value can be highly volatile, and book value can be very insensitive to the actual performance of the assets. For this reason, other asset valuation methods have been developed that will smooth the values from year to year and provide a more logical pattern of funding.

In the absence of any legislation, the actuary would use his or her best judgment to establish the assumptions and methods bearing in mind:

- The purpose of the calculations
- The professional guidelines of the Canadian Institute of Actuaries
- The objectives of the sponsor.

In this chapter, we will be examining two distinct types of valuations, those calculated on a "going concern" and those calculated on a "solvency" basis. A *going concern* valuation means a valuation of assets and liabilities of a pension plan using methods and actuarial assumptions considered by the actuary who valued the plan to be in accordance with generally accepted actuarial principles and practices for the valuation of a continuing pension plan.

Generally speaking, the actuary will use demographic and personnel assumptions that are realistic in the circumstances. The provincial pension regulators will likely express concern over the use of an out-of-date mortality table since, given ongoing improvements in life expectancy, this would understate the liabilities.

The critical issue for the economic assumptions is that they be internally consistent. To this end, the regulatory authorities have developed guidelines for the expected relationships between long-term rates of investment return and salary increases. Deviations from these guidelines would have to be justified.

The main concern on asset valuation methods is that the value used must bear some ongoing relationship to the market value.

Finally, the funding method must be on the list of methods acceptable to the regulatory authorities. Also, the benefits promised, and *only* the benefits promised, can be valued. If the plan is a final/best average type, then salary increases must be projected.

On the other hand, solvency valuations define the liabilities of the pension plan, determined as if the plan had been wound up.

On wind-up, all members will be immediately vested, so there is no need for termination assumption. Members will be assumed to commence their pension payments at the age that will place the maximum liability on the plan. No future allowance for salary increases will be made. The unit credit funding method must be used. An asset valuation method close to market value is appropriate.

In reality, there are only three assumptions that have any relevance:

- The rate of interest
- The rate of mortality
- The level of expenses.

Once the valuation has been completed, the second fundamental decision is how to deal with the resulting surplus or deficit. For an ongoing funding valuation, any funding deficit or *unfunded liability* must be amortized over a period of years, normally not exceeding 15. A funding surplus can be carried forward, applied to meet the cost of future benefit improvements or, under certain circumstances, used to reduce the sponsor's current service obligation. In the event that a solvency deficit is revealed, the situation becomes more critical, since a solvency liability should normally be the base line for the level of plan assets.

As you might expect, there is little uniformity between the provinces in the way the treatment of funding deficits or solvency deficiencies is handled. The rules are complex, and the explicit legislation should be reviewed in a specific case. However, the following provides a basic overview.

Historically, there were two major items, the *initial unfunded liability* and the *experience deficiency*. An *initial unfunded liability* represented the funding deficiency arising from:

- A new plan
- A plan amendment
- A change in actuarial assumptions or methods.

An *experience deficiency* occurred when the overall experience under the plan was less favourable than would have been anticipated under the ongoing actuarial assumptions. Typically, experience deficiencies had to be amortized over five years and initial unfunded liabilities over 15 years.

As other provinces and the federal jurisdiction have implemented pension reform, they have moved away from the historical approach to a system of dual valuations, ongoing and solvency. The unfunded liability on an ongoing basis, known variously as:

- The *going concern unfunded liability*
- The *initial unfunded liability*
- The *unfunded actuarial liability*

incorporates both the initial unfunded liability and any experience deficiencies.

The *solvency deficiency* represents the excess plan termination liabilities over the market value of assets plus the present value of certain previously established series of special payments. This deficiency must normally be amortized over five years. Once the solvency payments have been established, they can be taken into account in establishing the payments required to amortize the ongoing unfunded liability.

The other aspect of ongoing funding is the *current service contribution*. This generally represents the value of the benefits being earned in the year following the valuation date. The sponsor's contribution rate may be expressed as a percentage of covered payroll, as a percentage of required employee contributions or as a flat dollar amount, depending on the type of plan involved.

There are also rules that vary by province governing the timing of:
- Remitting employee contributions
- Paying required employer current service contributions
- Paying required employer special payments.

THE FUTURE

The future of single employer pension plans will be dependent on a number of external forces:
- Demographic trends
- Economic conditions
- Legislative environment.

Demographic Trends

It is well known that the population of Canada is aging and will continue to do so. Population projections contained in the most recent actuarial report on the Canada Pension Plan are as shown in Table IV-3-IV. The implications of these trends for sponsors of defined benefit pension plans are that:
- Required levels of current service contributions will increase as a percentage of payroll.
- Liabilities for retired members will become an increasing percentage of total assets and will be very sensitive to future requirements for indexation.
- Any future pension plan designs must be attractive to employees over age 50, since it will be essential to retain this group.

Economic Conditions

Conditions in Canada in recent years have favoured the defined contribution approach to pension planning. Inflation rates have been low, and rates of return on most asset classes have been consistently high. In an environment with high rates of inflation and low or negative rates of return, the defined benefit approach immediately becomes more attractive, particularly if the plan contains benefit guarantees based on final average earnings.

In the world of pensions, decisions are typically taken based on a very short-term view of the economy. Hence, we can expect that the pension pendulum will continue to swing backwards and forwards between defined benefit and defined contribution approaches as the economy goes through its regular cycles.

Legislative Environment

As Canada's population continues to age, the political pressure that Canada's retired voters can exert on the various levels of government will grow. This will bring not only the design of social security programs but also the direction of private pension legislation increasingly under the political microscope.

Already, the round of provincial legislation that started with the restatement of the Ontario and Alberta Acts in 1987 has had a significant effect on plan design. Some employers have found administrative compliance to be so onerous that this in itself has caused sponsors to switch from defined benefit to defined contribution plans. Present and future legislation requiring some measure of indexation of pensions may continue this trend.

At the same time, the updated rules governing maximum registered retirement savings plan (RRSP) contributions have caused employers to question the tax-effectiveness of their pension plans. Employers have sought to find some compromise between the inflexible

---

Table IV-3-IV

POPULATION AGING PROJECTION

Age Group	1996 (in millions)	2000 (in millions)	2025 (in millions)
20-34	5,253	5,059	5,702
35-49	5,378	5,832	6,137
50-64	3,100	3,634	6,014
Total	13,731	14,525	17,855
Over 65	2,748	2,950	5,726
Population over 65 as a percent of total workers	20.01%	20.31%	32.07%

approach of a mandatory defined benefit plan and the unstructured nature of an RRSP. This has led to a new era of flexibility with hybrid plans, two-tier plans and multiple options all becoming more common.

CONCLUSION

What of the future? It appears that the federal and provincial governments have no desire to increase government spending in the area of pensions and, indeed, it is a high priority to reduce the annual cost of the Guaranteed Income Supplement. While past efforts to move away from the universality of Old Age Security have proved unsuccessful, the federal government has taken a first step toward reform with the tax "clawback," and further changes can be expected. Debate continues over whether employers and employees will be prepared to pay the increasing Canada/Quebec Pension Plan (CPP/QPP) contributions or if cutbacks will be required.

Pension legislation has gone about as far as it can go, with the two key areas left to explore being:
- Refunds of surplus/contribution holidays
- Inflation protection.

The NDP government in Ontario was expected to take the lead in introducing legislated inflation protection and further limiting the use of surplus funds. However, under the current PC government, the trend is more toward the removal of red tape and the streamlining of legislation through self-regulation.

Overall pension plan design will continue to oscillate between defined benefit and defined contribution as the economy changes. However, the preponderance of older employees will likely lead to a greater emphasis on security. Ultimately, the solution will be found in more flexible combination plans that contain increased employee options. These will be discussed in Chapter 14.

A possible alternative to this scenario is one in which the government becomes so concerned about coverage that it introduces a second tier to the CPP/QPP. As in the United Kingdom, employers could gain an exemption from the second tier if their own plan meets certain minimum requirements. These requirements would include automatic indexing, immediate vesting and guaranteed portability.

Ultimately, the private and public pension systems combined will have to provide a typical Canadian with income replacement of 80-100% of pre-retirement take-home pay. Currently the CPP and OAS together will provide a replacement of 40% of the average industrial wage. Regardless of formula or plan design, the private sector will have to provide the other 40-60%. There is certain to be a trend for the government to play a larger watchdog role over these programs.

ENDNOTES

1. Statistics Canada, "Pension Plans in Canada" (1997) Catalogue No. 74-401-xib.

2. D. Brown and D. Beatty, *Canadian Labour Arbitration,* Third Edition (Aurora, Ontario: Canada Law Book Inc., 1988), at pp. 4-9 to 4-11.

3. George Adams, *Canadian Labour Law,* Second Edition (Aurora, Ont.: Canada Law Book Inc., 2000), at p. 2-102.

4. *Heilig v. Dominion Securities* (1986), 55 O.R. (2d) 783, rev'd on other grounds (1989), 67 O.R. (2d) 577 (C.A.); and *Reevie v. Montreal Trust Company* (1986), 53 O.R. (2d) 595 (C.A.), leave to appeal to SCC refused (1986), 56 O.R. (2d) 192 (Note).

5. *Collins v. Pension Commission of Ontario* (1986), 56 O.R. (2d) 274 (Div. Ct.).

6. *Madott v. Chrysler Canada,* [1989] O.J. No. 912 (G.D.).

7. *Schmidt v. Air Products* (1994), 115 D.L.R. (4th) 631 (S.C.C.).

8. Ontario *Pension Benefits Act,* R.S.O. 1990, c.P.8, s. 10(1).

9. Nova Scotia *Pension Benefit Act,* R.S.N.S. 1989, c.340, s. 16.

10. Alberta *Employment Pension Plans Act,* S.A. 1986, c. E-10.05, s. 21.

11. British Columbia *Pension Benefits Standards Act,* R.S.B.C. 1986, c. 352, s. 24.

12. New Brunswick *Pension Benefits Act,* S.N.B. 1987, c. P-51, s. 10(4).

13. Saskatchewan *Pension Benefits Act,* 1992, S.S. 1992, c. P-6.001, s. 25.

14. Quebec *Supplemental Pension Plans Act,* R.S.Q. 1990, R-15.1, s.14.

15. Newfoundland *Pension Benefits Act,* 1997, S.N. 1996, c. P-4.01, s.22.

16. Prince Edward Island *Pension Benefits Act,* S.P.E.I. 1990, c. 41, s.15. Not proclaimed in force as of May 1, 2000.

CHAPTER 4

Pension Plan Surpluses

by Mark Zigler and Ari N. Kaplan

INTRODUCTION— THE SURPLUS DEBATE

No aspect of pension plan administration seems to have generated more debate and litigation in the past 15 years than the area of surplus. On the one hand, advocates of employee entitlement to plan surplus claim that excess assets in a pension fund are a form of "deferred wages," i.e., that implicit in the employment contract is that the employee's total compensation package is simply divided between immediate salary and plan contributions. On the other hand, employers claim ownership of surplus on the basis that an employee defined benefit plan stipulates nothing more than a promised benefit at retirement, and that pension surplus is merely the result of overpayments and overfunding to those types of plans. Despite numerous studies, task forces and extensive academic commentary, the issue has not been resolved conclusively by either the legislature or the courts, possibly, as noted by one judge, "because of the uncertain impact of an unqualified acceptance of either view."[1]

The tension respecting legal ownership of surplus reached a climax in the early 1990s. First, during this time there was a great deal of public attention to this issue, in part because some of the cases involve high-profile companies (Dominion Stores, Ontario Hydro, the National Hockey League, Gainers, among others). Second, the mass layoffs, plant shutdowns and corporate restructuring of the early 1990s saw literally tens of thousands of employees lose their employment. The premature termination of many pension plans in connection with corporate reorganization resulted in a frequent contest over ownership of surplus plan assets between groups of terminated employees, on the one hand, and the employer/plan sponsor (or its creditors), on the other.

In disposing of the debate, it appears that two trends have emerged in recent years, namely:

1. *The judicial approach.* Courts have tended to deal with surplus matters on a contract and trust law analysis, based almost totally on the wording of the constating documents of the pension plan and trust and
2. *The legislative approach.* Pension benefits legislation either ignores the subject matter of pension surplus altogether (due to perhaps the political controversy involved) or, alternatively, attempts to force employers and their current and former employees to reach agreement on distributing surplus as a precondition to the provincial pension regulator consenting to the release of such surplus.

The judicial approach to determining surplus ownership is best highlighted in two landmark decisions, namely, that of the Supreme Court of Canada in *Schmidt v. Air Products of Canada Ltd.*[2] and that of the Ontario courts in the case of *Bathgate v. National Hockey League Pension Society.*[3] The different legislative approaches are illustrated by some provinces such as Ontario, whose *Pension Benefits Act* is emblematic of the approach requiring surplus disputes to be resolved by way of agreement between the parties. On the other hand, Quebec and British Columbia attempt to require arbitration as a last resort to resolving surplus disputes. The federal *Pension Benefits Standards Act* (Canada)

(PBSA) has followed Ontario's lead in this area by providing for negotiated settlements, but also permits arbitration in the event of dispute. Other provinces have yet to fully address the issue, leaving the decision making process unclear.

Before outlining in detail the different judicial and legislative frameworks to resolving the surplus debate, however, it is best to briefly explain what exactly is *pension plan surplus* and how it can arise.

THE NATURE OF PENSION SURPLUS

What Is Surplus?

Legislation offers little guidance in defining the parameters of pension plan surplus. For example, the Ontario *Pension Benefits Act* provides that:

> "surplus" means the excess of the value of the assets of a pension fund related to a pension plan over the value of the liabilities under the pension plan, both calculated in the prescribed manner.[4]

In other words, according to the legislation, plan surplus is simply the assets of a pension fund minus its liabilities, the latter being the present value of all accrued pension benefits promised under the plan. The federal jurisdiction, as well as Quebec, Alberta, Manitoba, British Columbia, New Brunswick and Nova Scotia, has adopted similar definitions.

The converse of plan *surplus* is a plan *deficit,* which occurs when the present value of all promised and statutory benefits under the plan exceed the assets of the pension fund.

Generally, there are two methods by which surplus can be valued, namely, the "going-concern" basis and the "solvency" basis (also sometimes referred to as the *wind-up* or *termination* basis). A going-concern surplus exists on any particular date when an ongoing pension plan is fully funded and discloses that the actuarial value of the assets exceeds the actuarial liability for the accrued benefits. The going-concern surplus at any particular time is an estimated amount, is rarely perfect, and depends on the actuarial asset and liability valuation methods and assumptions used by the plan actuaries.

On the other hand, the existence of surplus on plan termination is more easily identifiable. If on a particular date a pension plan were to be terminated, and there are assets remaining in the pension fund after the valuation of all promised and other statutory benefits, then the plan has a solvency surplus. In other words, a solvency surplus is a snapshot of the plan's funded status if it were to be terminated on a particular date.

How and Why Does Surplus Arise?

In a typical plan actuarial valuation, a solvency surplus may be either lower or greater than a going-concern surplus, depending, for example, on the method of assessing assets under each type of valuation, whether ongoing projected salary increases need to be taken into account, and whether the pension legislation in a particular jurisdiction imposes additional liabilities to the plan on termination.

Not surprisingly, a surplus can only be ascertained with certainty once all obligations under a pension plan are actually paid out to beneficiaries.

Any or all of the following factors in isolation or in combination with each other may contribute to the accumulation of surplus in a pension fund:

- Actual investment returns experienced by the fund are often higher than the actuarially calculated expected investment return on assets. This is because actuaries have historically tended to calculate fund growth according to conservative actuarial assumptions. Actuarial guidelines exist in most jurisdictions with respect to acceptable actuarial assumptions to be observed in connection with the funding of pension plans in accordance with the standards of the Canadian Institute of Actuaries.

- A corollary of the first factor is that inflation may cause a pension fund to experience large investment gains in excess of actuarial assumptions. Where inflation is an operating factor, the failure of the plan sponsor to improve pension benefits in accordance with increasing inflation rates (and correspondingly, increase plan liabilities) will also contribute to the accumulation of surplus.

- Surplus is created not only by an increase in the value of assets but by a reduction of plan liabilities. Such reduction can occur where mass layoffs of employees are involved, particularly if those employees are not vested.

- Surplus can be created almost instantaneously where actuaries change their assumptions in midstream. Sometimes these changes are made in response to actual experience, for example, to reflect increased employee turnover rates or expected salary changes, but other times they are made in response to the plan sponsor's objectives of being more or less conservative in calculating plan investment fund growth.

- Surplus may be shown to exist in a plan where the employer uses plan funds to purchase annuities for members. Because of the competitive nature of the annuity business, attractive interest rates may be offered. Because these interest rates will be higher than the conservative ones assumed by the plan, it will require less money to purchase these annuities than to provide the benefits out of the plan.

- Surplus may also arise as a result of a sale of business or partial termination of a plan.

The identification of the foregoing factors suggests

that it is improper to characterize surplus in plans as a windfall since surplus can be artificially created by a change in economic circumstances that can convert a surplus into a deficit.

When Does Surplus Arise?

As stated, above, integral and interrelated to the issues respecting how surplus arises is the problem of quantifying pension surplus. This is because until a pension plan is terminated and wound up, no one really knows how much surplus is in the plan. In this respect, it is difficult to precisely describe what exactly is surplus, or how much surplus exists at a given time, without asking the question *when* is surplus. To illustrate, the Ontario *Pension Benefits Act* and administrative policy guidelines set out by the Ontario pensions regulator, the Financial Services Commission of Ontario (FSCO), stipulate that in cases of proposed asset withdrawal from ongoing plans, a surplus cushion must remain in the fund. Where this is the case, available going-concern surplus will be less than the net actuarial, or wind-up surplus.

This differential treatment recognizes the reality that the amount of the surplus in a plan may vary from day to day. An actuarial determination of what is surplus can only come close to being precise when the plan is being wound up. Indeed, the Ontario Court of Appeal noted this distinction in the *Re Reevie and Montreal Trust Company* case where it stated:

> While the plan continues to operate, a surplus will simply afford a cushion against years during which the fund performs poorly, or, it may lead to the reduction of future contributions. If the plan is discontinued, other considerations will arise.[5]

JUDICIAL PRINCIPLES RESPECTING PENSION SURPLUS

As can be seen, legal issues respecting surplus arise in numerous contexts. Each gives rise to contentious legal issues, which are usually broadly divided between employer and employee interests (although often employee groups have interests adverse to one another depending upon whether the employees are active or retired, unionized or salaried). Typical surplus issues arise when a pension plan is:

1. In the process of being fully or partially terminated
2. Ongoing, and there is an application to withdraw surplus and
3. Ongoing, and the employer/plan sponsor is attempting to reduce its required contributions by applying previously existing surpluses (a.k.a. actuarial gains) to the current service cost. This is commonly known as "contribution holidays."

As will be explained, different approaches to the treatment and ownership of surplus exist in each of the foregoing situations.

While it is important to appreciate the circumstances under which surplus arises, these factors generally have not been persuasive in court decisions in determining who is entitled to use the surplus, and when.

The General Approach of the Courts

The matter of surplus ownership and the right to withdraw surplus, on either an ongoing or plan wind-up basis, or even the right to take contribution holidays, was the subject of contentious litigation across Canada from the mid-late 1980s until the Supreme Court of Canada resolved many of these issues in 1994. The general approach the courts have taken in these instances is to preclude any employer from obtaining any surplus out of a defined benefit pension plan unless the relevant plan documentation or trust agreements clearly provide the employer with the right to obtain the surplus. The courts have not looked at policy questions or arguments traditionally raised by employees and employers regarding surplus ownership but, instead, have stuck virtually exclusively to the strict wording of the documents.

Much of the debate in the courts has centred on whether a particular pension plan should be interpreted as a contract or a trust. The usual result of applying principles of contract law to the interpretation of a pension plan text is that the employer would be lawfully permitted to amend the plan's terms to provide for a surplus refund to itself. Alternatively, an irrevocable trust for the exclusive benefit of the plan membership would normally prohibit such an amendment. Courts in Alberta and Ontario, particularly, were inclined to adopt the trust analysis wherever possible, while the British Columbia courts tended to adopt a more contractual analysis.

As courts tended to take differing views on these cases, it remained for the Supreme Court of Canada to finally resolve some of the questions pertaining to surplus ownership. In *Schmidt v. Air Products* the Supreme Court put to rest many of the outstanding issues, and confirmed much of the previous case law in Ontario and Alberta in both the areas of surplus and contribution holidays.

Trust Law or Contract Law?

The Supreme Court in *Schmidt* stated that the language and structure of pension plan documentation is determinative of the issue of surplus ownership. The framework for determining surplus ownership begins with a review of the historical and current pension plan documentation in order to determine whether the pension funds are impressed with a trust, in which case the general principles of trust law apply or, alternatively, whether the funds are governed by contracts, in which case contract law will be applied. As the court stated:

> In the absence of provincial legislation providing otherwise, the courts must determine competing claims to pension surplus by a careful analysis of the pension plan and the funding structures created under it. The first step is to determine whether the pension fund is impressed with a trust. This is a determination which must be made according to ordinary principles of trust law. A trust will exist whenever there has been an express or implied declaration of trust and an alienation of trust property to a trustee to be held for specified beneficiaries.
>
> If the pension fund, or any part of it, is not subject to a trust, then any issues relating to outstanding pension benefits or to surplus entitlement must be resolved by applying the principles which pertain to the interpretation of contracts to the pension plan.
>
> If, however, the fund is impressed with a trust, different considerations apply. The trust is not a trust for a purpose, but a classic trust. It is governed by equity and, to the extent that applicable equitable principles conflict with plan provisions, equity must prevail.[6]

A pension fund is impressed with a trust whenever there has been an express or implied declaration of trust and an alienation of trust property to a trustee to be held for specified beneficiaries. This element of the *Schmidt* framework of analysis is perhaps the most important in determining surplus ownership. This is because when a pension plan is impressed with a trust, general principles of trust law restrict the right of the plan sponsor, usually the employer, to amend the plan in a manner that adversely affects the interests of plan members. As will be seen below, these restrictions include limitations on the right to amend a plan to provide that all surplus will revert to the employer on plan wind-up.

However, where there is no demonstrated intention to create a trust, then a court must resolve any issues relating to surplus entitlement according to principles relating to the interpretation of contracts. If contract law is applicable, then a general amending power may assist an employer to amend a plan so as to allow for surplus reversion to the company on plan wind-up.

All Plan-Related Documentation Is Relevant

In determining whether or not a pension fund is impressed with a trust, the court in *Schmidt* did not limit its examination to the most recent plan text, nor for that matter, to the plan texts themselves. Instead, the analysis requires an inquiry into the language contained in:

- Predecessor versions of the plan from its inception, including successor plans
- Plan funding instruments, such as trust agreements and insurance contracts and
- Employee booklets and other communications to plan members.

Where the words *trust* or *trustee* appear in the documentation, this will obviously assist in ensuring the application of trust principles. In *La Have Equipment Ltd. v. Nova Scotia (Supt. of Pensions)*[7] and *Bull Moose Tube Ltd. v. Ontario (Supt. of Pensions)*,[8] the courts held that funding of a pension plan by way of an insurance contract is not necessarily inconsistent with the intention to create a pension trust. In those cases, while the plans were funded by contract, there had nevertheless been an express declaration by the employer that the insurance policy itself would be held "in trust" for the benefit of the employees. Similar arguments were successfully made in Quebec in *Le Syndicat national des Salariés des outils Simonds c. Eljer Manufacturing Canada Inc.*[9] where the pension plan, although analyzed as a contract, could not be amended to provide surplus reversion to the employer.

Contrast these cases with *Howitt v. Howden Group Canada Ltd.*,[10] where the Ontario Court of Appeal rejected arguments by a group of employees that prior amendments to the pension plan that referred to "the assets of the trust fund" were sufficient to create a trust. While the court recognized that "although the exclusive benefit and distribution clauses on which the [employees] rely in this case are consistent with the existence of a trust, these clauses cannot, of themselves, satisfy the evidentiary requirement that the employer intended to create a trust." The court concluded that references to the term *trust fund,* which appeared in prior versions of the plan texts, were "isolated references" and, accordingly, the plan should be interpreted pursuant to contract law principles.

In *C.U.P.E., Local 185 v. Etobicoke (City),*[1] the subject plan was initially funded by insurance contracts, and the majority held that reference to the "trust fund" meant that "it was a trust for the *limited purpose* only of providing a mechanism to pay the defined benefits" and was not sufficient evidence of the parties' intention to create a trust.

Conflicts Between Competing Plan Documents

Since the documentation that creates a pension scheme is not limited to the pension plan text, it is intuitive that there may be inconsistencies in the documentation pertaining to surplus entitlement. The most common source of conflict between competing plan documents is where the plan text supports the conclusion that plan surplus will revert to the employer and the trust agreement prohibits such reversion. This was precisely the issue in *Lear Siegler Industries Ltd. v. Canada Trust Co.*[12] where the matter of surplus ownership on plan termination was litigated between the employer and the plan beneficiaries. Although the plan provided that on termination surplus would revert to the employer, the trust agreement stipulated that no part of the trust fund could be used for any purpose other than the exclusive benefit of plan members and beneficiaries. The court resolved the conflict against the employer, holding that "as there is an apparent conflict between the trust agreement and the pension plan, the trust agreement should prevail."

It is important to note that in *Lear Siegler* the trust agreement provided that the pension plan "shall form part of the trust agreement to the same extent as if all of its provisions were fully set forth therein." Accordingly, one should be hesitant to distil a general principle from the case. Conflicts between competing plan documentation must be resolved on a case-by-case basis.

Employer Can Reserve the Right to Revoke or Amend the Trust

Under a pension trust, an employer/plan sponsor cannot revoke the trust and require the return of the trust property unless there is an explicit reservation of that right. As the Supreme Court in *Schmidt* stated:

. . . However, an employer may explicitly limit the operation of the trust so that it does not apply to surplus.

The employer, as a settlor of the trust, may reserve a power to revoke the trust. In order to be effective, that power must be clearly reserved at the time the trust is created. A power to revoke the trust or any part of it cannot be implied from a general unlimited power of amendment.[13]

What the Supreme Court in *Schmidt* is saying is that the existence of a broad power of amendment in a plan text is insufficient to permit an employer/plan sponsor to unilaterally revoke a trust in favour of plan beneficiaries and appropriate part or all of the surplus to itself. Rather, the power to revoke a trust by way of amendment must be express in the plan text. One of the few cases in which the employer was found to have reserved an express power to revoke the pension trust in the plan documentation is *Ferro Canadian Employees' Pension Plan.*[14]

Nevertheless, an employer generally cannot amend a pension trust to provide payment of surplus funds to itself if the plan documents previously provided that contributions by the employer were irrevocable and that employees would be entitled to surplus if the plan were wound up.

External Representations to Employees May Be Binding

The Supreme Court in *Schmidt* also dealt to some degree with the issue of representations made in employee booklets to plan members regarding ownership of the pension fund assets. The Supreme Court reached the conclusion in that case that, although the employee booklets might appear to be misleading, there was no evidence that the employees ever relied on them, or that most of the employees had even read it. Accordingly, the content of the booklets provided little assistance to the court in determining the surplus ownership issue. This is to be contrasted with the approach taken by the Ontario Divisional Court in *Collins v. Pension Commission of Ontario* (the *Dominion Stores* case),[15] where the representations made in an employee booklet regarding use of plan assets gave rise to a reasonable belief that the company had no right to claim any part of the fund.

Employees Who Are No Longer Beneficiaries Under a Pension Trust

Another surplus issue that can arise is with respect to the surplus entitlement of former employees who are transferred out of a pension plan several years preceding the wind-up of that plan. In *Reichhold v. Wong,*[16] the court dismissed a motion by a group of former participants to a company pension plan to intervene in a court application to approve a surplus sharing agreement negotiated between the company on one hand and the active employees and pensioners under the plan, on the other. The former group was transferred out of the plan eight years earlier in conjunction with the divestment of one of the company's divisions, and the accrued pension benefits and corresponding assets relating to these employees, including a pro-rata share of surplus, were transferred to a successor employer's pension plan. The court observed that there was no dispute regarding whether the transferred amount was properly calculated, and held that since the former employees were no longer beneficiaries under the pension plan, accordingly, they had no further legal entitlement to any of the remaining assets of the plan. On this basis, and relying partially on *Schmidt,* the court concluded that "there is no contractual or trust law basis for any alleged right of [the transferred employees] to participate in the surplus proceeds."

It should be noted that *Reichhold* was a case in which a properly calculated pro-rata share of surplus corresponding to the former employees was transferred out of the plan. Accordingly, it remains open for debate whether former employees transferred from a plan without a corresponding distribution of surplus have any future right to claim surplus on wind-up of that plan.

Employer Fiduciary Obligations Re: Surplus

In *Reichhold,* the intervening employee group unsuccessfully argued that their former employer owed them a fiduciary obligation to include them in the surplus sharing agreement negotiated with the current plan beneficiaries. In rejecting this argument, the court determined that an employer owes no fiduciary duty to former plan beneficiaries relating to the use of surplus, where all the assets and liabilities relating to those persons have been transferred properly and legally to a successor plan.

What the court in *Reichhold* was not explicitly asked to do was decide the extent to which an employer that is also a plan administrator owes fiduciary duties to current plan beneficiaries in dealing with plan surplus.

Generally, a pension plan administrator (whether it be the employer or a board of trustees) owes fiduciary obligations to plan members since the plan administrator is responsible for the management of the pension fund, the collection of contributions and the payment of benefits. While these duties are practically self-evident given the nature of the relationship of the administrator to the fund, they are nevertheless codified in most provincial pension benefits legislation. For example, Section 22 of the Ontario *Pension Benefits Act* describes a plan administrator's duty of care, diligence and skill in the administration of a pension fund that a person of ordinary prudence would exercise in dealing with the property of another person.

In addition, an employer, whether or not it is the plan administrator, can also be said to owe fiduciary obligations to plan members when not acting solely in an administrative capacity. As was stated by the court in *Anova Inc. Employee Retirement Pension Plan (Administrator of) v. Manufacturers Life Insurance Co.:*

> An amendment of the Plan which violates the fiduciary duties owed to the members of the Plan is not sustainable.[17]

In that case, the plan sponsor in order to facilitate the sale of the company amended its employee pension plan (which included shareholders of the company) to utilize plan surplus by providing benefit enhancements only to the shareholder-employees. Despite the fact that the amendments granting the enhanced benefits were approved by the Pension Commission of Ontario (now the Financial Services Commission of Ontario), the court nevertheless found that the amendments were a breach of the fiduciary duties as well as the duty to act fairly toward the remaining employees.

Anova can be contrasted with the decision of the Pension Commission of Ontario in *Re Imperial Oil Ltd. Retirement Plan (1988)*[18] in which the Commission distinguished the nature of the duties owed by a plan sponsor to employees when it acts as an employer and its standard of care when acting as plan administrator. In this case, the plan sponsor was found not to owe a fiduciary duty to certain terminated employees since it was acting as employer, and not as administrator, when it amended its plan to limit the eligibility requirements to receive an early retirement pension.

It is important to note that *Imperial Oil* was not a case about the use of surplus but, rather, pertained to the ability of a plan sponsor to limit the eligibility of certain members to early retirement benefits. Presumably, the reasoning in *Anova,* and not *Imperial Oil,* would more likely apply to amendments by the plan sponsor respecting the improper use of surplus, including the diversion of surplus to itself, when such funds are held in trust irrevocably for the benefit of plan members.

The English courts have also developed jurisprudence regarding employers found to be liable for the improper use of surplus. *Re Courage Group Pension Scheme*[19] involved the purchase of a group of companies by H, a large holding company. H then resold some of the subsidiaries while attempting to retain the surplus that had accumulated in the employee pension plans. H attempted to achieve this by substituting itself for the original employer in the plan documents and amending the documentation to give itself a reversionary interest in the surplus. The court held that this was not a proper amendment of the document and the company could not act contrary to the purposes of the trust. The company could not act in bad faith or for an improper motive, namely, the seizure of the surplus for itself over the initial plan beneficiaries. In the subsequent English case of *Mettoy Pension Trustees Limited v. Idwal Evans et al.,*[20] the English Chancery Division again determined that trustees having a discretion to deal with surplus must act in the best interest of the plan beneficiaries.

Surplus in Ongoing Plans and Employer Contribution Holidays

As the Supreme Court stated in *Schmidt:*
> . . . The trust will in most cases extend to an ongoing or actual surplus as well as to that part of the pension fund needed to provide employee benefits. . . .[21]

The Supreme Court in *Schmidt* recognized that surplus in a pension trust extends to ongoing plans. Nevertheless, the Court also determined that the utilization by the employer of plan surplus to fund ongoing employer contribution requirements did not necessarily violate the terms of an irrevocable trust for the exclusive benefit of employees. The Supreme Court stated:
> The right to take a contribution holiday can be excluded either explicitly or implicitly in circumstances where a plan mandates a formula for calculating employer contributions which removes

actuarial discretion. Contribution holidays may also be permitted by the terms of the plan. When the plan is silent on the issue, the right to take a contribution holiday is not objectionable so long as actuaries continue to accept the application of existing surplus to current service costs as standard practice. These principles apply whether or not the pension fund is subject to a trust. Because no money is withdrawn from the fund by the employer, the taking of a contribution holiday represents neither an encroachment upon the trust nor a reduction of accrued benefits. These general considerations are, of course, subject to applicable legislation.[22]

The Supreme Court also held that, when permission to take contribution holidays is not explicitly given in the plan, it may be implied from the wording of the employer's contribution obligation:

> When permission is not explicitly given in the plan, it may be implied from the wording of the employer's contribution obligation. Any provision which places the responsibility for the calculation of the amount needed to fund promised benefits in the hands of an actuary should be taken to incorporate accepted actuarial practice as to how that calculation will be made. That practice currently includes the application of calculated surplus funds to determination of overall current service costs.
>
> . . .
>
> . . . whenever the contribution requirement simply refers to actuarial calculations, the presumption can only be that it also authorizes the use of standard actuarial practices.[23]

Generally, the funding of employer contribution obligations from ongoing plan surplus is considered acceptable and standard actuarial practice. As a result, a provision in a plan text that provides, in its employer funding formula, that the employer's annual contribution is not based on a set-out formula but, rather, is based on an amount to be calculated by an actuary, would likely be upheld by a court as permitting an employer contribution holiday.

The Supreme Court in *Schmidt* made it clear that the right to take contribution holidays was not an automatic one, rather, "an employer's right to take a contribution holiday must . . . be determined on a case-by-case basis" and "must be decided on the basis of the applicable plan provisions." Accordingly, contribution holiday litigation and analysis has been generally based on a comparative approach, i.e., contrasting the terms of the subject plan against the language in other cases that were previously decided. For examples of court decisions upholding the employer's right to take contribution holidays based on the language in the historical plan texts, reference should be made to *Askin v. Ontario Hospitals Association*[24] and *Maurer v. McMaster University*.[25] In *Schmidt*, as well, the Supreme Court upheld the employer contribution holidays.

For cases where the courts have concluded that the plan language did not support the taking of contribution holidays, reference should be made to *C.U.P.E., Local 1000 v. Ontario Hydro; Hockin v. Bank of British Columbia; Chateauneuf v. T.S.C.O. of Canada Ltd.;* and *Trent University Faculty Association v. Trent University*.[26]

Pension Surplus in the Collective Bargaining Context

The principles in *Schmidt* lend themselves to a trust analysis of most pension plans unless they are established through an insurance contract. In the collective bargaining context, where the bargaining and terms of employment lead to a contractual arrangement that may spawn a pension trust, the interaction between contract and trust law is often difficult to define. While pensions arise from the employee-employer relationship and from employment contracts, trust funds may be irrevocably committed towards particular purposes and the ability of an employer to reclaim them may be limited if not impossible.

Further, collective bargaining generally involves active employees, while pensioners and deferred vested employees may have had their assets contributed to the trust long before the current collective bargaining agreement was in place. It is uncertain whether a union can necessarily adversely affect trust assets on behalf of retired individuals.

The relationship between the law of trusts and the collective bargaining context was examined to some degree by the Honourable Mr. Justice Adams in *Bathgate v. National Hockey League Pension Society*. In his decision, Justice Adams examines the ability of the union to negotiate changes to pension plans and collective bargaining that may have an effect on surplus or other elements of a pension trust. It is clear from his reasoning that a balance must be drawn between the interests of former plan members and those of the current membership. Where assets have been irrevocably committed to the retired members, as was the case in the NHL situation, surplus arising from those assets are not available for the current group. However, Justice Adams found that pension benefits for active employees could be subject to a "properly authorized and reasonably balanced collective bargaining change to an otherwise irrevocable pension commitment."

While this is not a very clearly defined concept and certainly leaves much room for debate as to the limits of the union's negotiating authority on pensions, it ensures that a rigid application of the law of trusts should not stand in the way of collective bargaining negotiations in certain circumstances.

Further, Justice Adams queries whether the duty of fair representation owed by unions to their members extends to retirees and, moreover, whether a union has any obligation at all to such people. This issue was canvassed in the Supreme Court of Canada decision in *Dayco v. CAW*, where Justice LaForest writing for the majority noted that:

> In these circumstances, Canadian retirees may well find themselves in possession of a right without a remedy. The grievance procedure may be foreclosed, as described above. Retirees may not be entitled to bring a claim against the union for unfair representation, as such rights in Ontario appear to be limited to current members of the bargaining unit: see s.68 of the Act. Finally, Ontario's *Rights of Labour Act*, R.S.O. 1980, c. 456, s. 3(3), and like provisions in other jurisdictions, may foreclose the possibility of a court action by the retirees: see Adams, op. cit., at pp. 704-9. This problem does not arise in this case, as the union here did pursue a grievance on behalf of the retired workers. But in another case it seems to me that such a remedial vacuum, arising because the retirees are not party to the arbitration procedures guaranteed by the Act, may possibly be justification for allowing a court action to proceed. . . .[27]

The foregoing comments in *Dayco* were applied by the Manitoba Court of Appeal in *Bohemier v. Centra Gas Manitoba Inc.*[28] in which the court upheld the right of a group of pensioners to proceed with a court action against a union as well as their former employer. In that case, the employer and union bargained upon the disposition of a pension surplus and agreed to provide the employer with a contribution holiday. Retired employees did not benefit from this agreement and sued the employer, the union and the trustee of the pension fund. The union and the company took the position that the retirees' dispute was required to be arbitrated under the collective agreement and that if the union was not willing to pursue a grievance on the retirees' behalf, the plaintiffs should initiate a complaint to the labour relations board of an unfair labour practice. The Court of Appeal dismissed the claim against the plan trustees since they had limited responsibilities vis-à-vis the members. However, the court reinstated the action against the employer and the union on the basis that the retirees were not parties to the collective agreement and, accordingly, the matter was not arbitrable. Moreover, since the union would not proceed with a grievance on the retirees' behalf anyway, they were "frozen out of the grievance process." Referencing *Dayco*, the court observed:

> I do not see how [the retirees] could be bound by an agreement which works to their detriment and which was executed by parties that have no authority to represent their interests. The union cannot claim to be acting on behalf of persons other than employees as defined by the *[Labour Relations] Act* and by the description of the bargaining unit in the collective agreement.[29]

Bohemier implicitly affirms the principle set out in *Bathgate v. NHL Pension Society* that negotiated changes to a pension plan can be validly affected by a union and employer. At the same time, however, the case also illustrates the need for parties to the collective bargaining process to be sensitive to the multiplicity of stakeholder interests in the administration of pension plans.

Conclusions Regarding the Judicial Approach to Surplus Issues

The Supreme Court in *Schmidt* essentially settled much of the law in the approach to be taken on surplus cases by setting out a principled framework of analysis on surplus use and ownership issues. However, there still are questions and issues left unsettled. First, since surplus and contribution holiday disputes must be settled case-by-case, the cases still leave sufficient room for matters of interpretation of each pension plan. No doubt there will be plan texts that lend themselves to differing analysis. The fact that the *Schmidt* case itself involved two pension plans that were amalgamated, one of which was an irrevocable trust and the other an insurance contract, leaves a degree of confusion in attempting to reconcile situations where such plans have been merged.

Another unresolved issue that flows from *Schmidt* is that of the nature of "contingent" versus "crystallized" rights to surplus. This has proven to be particularly relevant and timely in Ontario on the issue of whether there is a requirement under Ontario's legislation that surplus be distributed when a pension plan is partially, but not wholly, terminated. In *Monsanto Canada Inc. v. Superintendent of Financial Services*,[30] the Court of Appeal upheld the decision of the Divisional Court to overturn the decision of the Financial Services Tribunal that found that Section 70(6) of the *Pension Benefits Act* (Ontario) did not require that surplus relating to a partial plan wind-up be distributed to plan beneficiaries affected by the wind-up. The Tribunal interpreted *Schmidt* to mean that surplus, which crystallizes on wind-up, is nevertheless still a contingent right on a partial wind-up since the plan as a whole is still ongoing. Accordingly, despite Section 70(6) of the legislation, which grants plan members "rights and benefits that are not less than the rights and benefits they would have on a full wind-up of the pension plan," the Tribunal determined that no surplus need be distributed until there is a full plan wind-up.

The Divisional Court overturned this decision and

adopted the position of the dissent at the Tribunal, which held that Section 70(6) requires that the affected employees were to be treated as if there was a full wind-up of the Plan on the effective date of the partial wind-up. The Court of Appeal agreed with the Divisional Court concerning the proper interpretation of Section 70(6) and held that the Tribunal is to be accorded significant deference but its interpretation of the section "is not just incorrect. It is clearly wrong. It is an interpretation which the subsection cannot reasonably bear."

What is most notable about the Supreme Court of Canada decision in *Schmidt,* as well as the comments of the court in *Bathgate v. NHL Pension Society,* is the call for a legislated solution to the surplus ownership problem. Nevertheless, most provinces have tended not to solve the substantive ownership matters by legislation, and instead the legislative approaches have tended to prefer statutory mechanisms for resolution of surplus ownership questions. Recent amendments to the federal *Pension Benefits Standards Act* (Canada) have not clarified matters either but have continued the trend towards negotiated or arbitrated solutions.

THE LEGISLATIVE APPROACHES TO SURPLUS

Introduction

Pension benefits legislation in Canada generally does not purport to deal with substantive surplus ownership issues. However, Ontario, Quebec, British Columbia, Manitoba and the federal jurisdiction have now, through amendments to the statutes or regulations, asserted some jurisdiction in this area. Other jurisdictions regulate minimum plan provisions required to deal with procedural steps required in the event of the attempt to withdraw surplus from a plan, either on a going-concern basis or on a plan wind-up basis. All jurisdictions have provisions with respect to the circumstances where contribution holidays may be taken given the solvency position of the plan. If, in addition, the plan documents do not preclude contribution holidays, the courts have upheld the validity of the regulations in the pension legislation.[31]

As Ontario, Quebec and other jurisdictions have adopted special approaches to surplus issues and, indeed, provided a forum for litigation of the disputes, they view the approaches in these two provinces separate from the others, to the extent that there is a preference toward having surplus issues adjudicated at the level of administrative tribunals, with some limited appellate jurisdiction in the courts. This approach may prove to be the wave of the future with respect to many surplus cases.

Minimum Statutory Requirements

There is a minimum requirement in most pension legislation that any registered single employer pension plan must deal with the matter of surplus ownership, both when the plan is ongoing and on plan termination. For example, Subsection 10(1)11 of the Ontario *Pension Benefits Act* provides that the documents that create and support a pension plan must set out,

The treatment of surplus during the continuation of the pension plan and on the wind up of the pension plan.[32]

Alberta, Newfoundland, Nova Scotia, Manitoba and Saskatchewan are other provinces that require as a condition of plan registration that information on the treatment of surplus be set out in the plan text. Indeed, Section 79(4) of the Ontario statute explicitly attributes surplus to employees on plan wind-up if the pension plan does not expressly declare surplus ownership in an employer. Similar provisions are contained in the New Brunswick and Nova Scotia pension benefits statutes.[33]

Withdrawal of Surplus—Generally

Most of the provinces (Prince Edward Island is the only exception) contain specific provisions in their legislation that prohibit an employer from receiving any payment of surplus unless the plan explicitly permits such a reversion.

The question of whether amendments permitting reversions to an employer on the wind-up of a plan are permissible is generally decided by the courts and, in the aftermath of the *Schmidt* case, such amendments are not likely to be valid in the case of a pension trust unless the employer reserved the right to make such amendment from the inception of the plan and trust.

For the most part, once the applicable pension regulatory authority is satisfied that surplus is properly calculated, the primary impact of the surplus provisions in pension benefits legislation is procedural in nature. Most of the procedures pertain to providing notice to all of the plan members of any withdrawals whether on an ongoing or a wind-up basis. For example, Sections 78(2) and (3) of the Ontario legislation contains an extensive code requiring 30 days' notice to members, former members, trade unions and pensioners. Subsections 25(1) and 28(5) of the Regulations prescribe that such notices must contain certain information, including:

• The review date of the actuarial report
• The amount of surplus in the plan
• Surplus attributable to employee and employer contributions in respect of ongoing plans
• The amount of surplus withdrawal requested
• Contractual authority for the withdrawal

- Location where documents in support of the application can be reviewed by plan members.[34]

Similar provisions are to be found in the federal PBSA and the legislation in Alberta, British Columbia, Manitoba, New Brunswick, Newfoundland and Nova Scotia.

Much of the concern with notice to members arose because of the failure to give any notice in the *Dominion Stores* case,[35] where the failure to give any notice was found by the court to be a breach of the administrative law duty of fairness. Thus, pension reform legislation in the above jurisdictions now contains a code that attempts to remedy the notice difficulties.

Withdrawals From Ongoing Pension Plans

One substantive area that pension legislation attempts to regulate is that of applications by employers to withdraw surpluses from ongoing plans. Quebec prohibits such withdrawals altogether, and Ontario prohibits ongoing withdrawals by the employer unless the unanimous consent of all plan members and former members can be obtained.[36] As a result of controversies in the 1990s over inflation protection or lack thereof in many plans, many jurisdictions shied away from permitting surplus withdrawals from ongoing plans. This trend appears to be reversing, however. Amendments to the British Columbia and Alberta legislation, as well as the federal PBSA, now permit withdrawals from an ongoing plan following the consent of two-thirds of the members and former members of the plan in connection with an employer proposal.

A review of the legislation and jurisdictions where such withdrawals are permitted does indicate that many statutes require the employer seeking to remove surplus from an ongoing plan to leave a cushion to cover the possibility of poor plan performance in future years. Alberta, Nova Scotia and Ontario, as well as the federal PBSA, maintain requirements for the greater of two years' normal employer costs to be left in the plan as well as a cushion of 25% of plan liabilities calculated on a solvency valuation basis. Alberta, however, uses a plan termination basis for purposes of calculating the cushion. Further, in cases of contributory plans, Nova Scotia and Ontario require surplus attributable to employee contributions to be left in the plan, although there is no clear formula for this calculation. In the Ontario case of *Otis Canada v. Superintendent of Pensions for Ontario,*[37] the court suggested that there may be a right to surplus for employees on plan wind-up in respect of their own contributions where there is a contributory plan. However, the fact that there can be surplus attributable to employee contributions is not necessarily determinative of the ownership of such surplus.

Section 10 of the Ontario *Pension Benefits Regulation* (the "Ontario Regulation") maintains very stringent requirements for payment of surplus out of a continuing plan to an employer. Apart from the unanimous consent of all members, other conditions include:

- A former member's contributions to the plan and the interest on the contributions will not be used to provide more than 50% of the commuted value of the benefit.
- Any allocations of surplus to employees must include the option of receiving surplus in the form of inflation adjustments to existing benefits, either through indexing with a formula tied to the Consumer Price Index or a fixed annual percentage or dollar amount.
- The plan must state or provide a mechanism regarding surplus entitlement for surplus payments that may exist after the payment in question.

Different Legislative Approaches to Surplus Withdrawal

The Ontario Approach

Because of the unanimity requirement and other stringent conditions, Section 10 of the Ontario Regulation is seldom used to permit surplus withdrawals from ongoing plans. Instead, pension stakeholders usually turn to the full wind-up procedures to access surplus.

As of December 19, 1991, the Ontario government promulgated what is now Section 8 of the Ontario Regulation. This provision is now in effect until December 31, 2000, although it has been extended a number of times since its introduction in 1991. Section 8 of the Regulation has come to be known as the *surplus sharing regulation.* It prohibits any payment to be made from a pension plan surplus on wind-up unless payment is made for the benefit of members, former members or persons other than the employer who are entitled to payments in the plans; or the payment is made to an employer with the written agreement of,

(i) The employer

(ii) The collective bargaining agent of the employees or, if there is no collective bargaining agent, at least two-thirds of the active members of the plan, and

(iii) Such number of former members and other persons as are entitled to payments under the plan on wind-up as the Commission considers appropriate in the circumstances.[38]

The effect of the above regulation is to either require payment of all of the surplus to employees on the wind-up of pension plan or to have the employer reach an agreement with its members and former members. The Financial Services Commission of Ontario has published various guidelines with respect to procedures and interpretations of the surplus sharing regulation for the benefit of the involved parties. In particular, there are various regulatory administrative practices that ought to be reviewed in dealing with these issues, particularly:

- Administrative Practice S900-508 entitled Surplus (effective July 1998)
- Administrative Practice S900-900 entitled Allocation of Surplus Distribution to Members and Former Members on Plan Wind-Up (PCO Bulletin, Spring 1994)
- Surplus Remaining in Wound-Up Plans (PCO Bulletin, August 1993).

Unfortunately, Section 8 of the Ontario Regulation does not contain any provision to resolve a dispute in the event that a surplus sharing agreement cannot be reached with the employer by the requisite number of plan members and former members. Further, the Superintendent of Financial Services is wary of situations where plan members are not represented by legal counsel and an attempt is made to obtain their consent. Although in many cases it may be preferable to have these issues dealt with by the regulator, Section 8 of the Ontario Regulation does not in any way oust the jurisdiction of the courts to deal with surplus ownership issues. Further, some practitioners have a concern about whether a determination of surplus sharing under the new regulation will oust the ability of any individual employee to go to court and challenge the jurisdiction of the Commission. Such a situation is unlikely, given that all plan members must receive notice of any surplus sharing agreement before it is approved by the Commission under its guidelines. Further, there is a right of appeal of Financial Services Tribunal decisions to the courts. However, this concern has led many, out of an overabundance of caution, to shy away from surplus sharing agreements without the blessing of a court.

The Superintendent and Tribunal have taken the position that its jurisdiction to deal with surplus ownership issues arises from Section 79(3) of the Ontario PBA whereby it must satisfy itself, among other things, that the pension plan provides for payment of surplus to the employer on wind-up. This permits an enquiry into the question of who owns the pension surplus.[39]

Despite the uncertainties that still exist in some quarters, Ontario's surplus sharing regulation has met with some success. However, the absence of a dispute resolution mechanism in the legislation (if there is no agreement, there is no way to resolve the dispute) has also limited the impact of the regulation. Until the Ontario legislature deals explicitly with the surplus issue in the statute, as was suggested by the Supreme Court in *Schmidt,* the Ontario Regulations will continue to have only limited success in resolving these disputes.

The Quebec Approach

The Quebec *Supplemental Pension Plans Act* prohibits any surplus withdrawal from an ongoing pension plan.[40] As of January 1, 1993, the Quebec government lifted its moratorium on surplus payments to an employer on plan wind-up. However, payment of surplus to an employer can only occur in Quebec as a result of an agreement between the employer and the plan members or, alternatively, through the decision of an arbitrator.

Once the Quebec Superintendent has determined that a plan termination date has been set and the plan wound up with respect to its basic benefits, the employer must send a draft agreement concerning surplus distribution to the pension committee. The legislation and its regulations require that surplus be allocated among employees on the basis of the commuted value of their benefits, and the agreement must state how their proportion of surplus is calculated. The pension committee is then obligated to forward the agreement to the plan members and beneficiaries and to publish notice in a local newspaper. Further, there must be a filing with the Superintendent. Surplus sharing agreements under this provision are binding unless 30% or more of the members and their beneficiaries oppose the agreement. Where such opposition arises, the issue will then be decided by mandatory final and binding arbitration.[41]

The arbitrator is appointed pursuant to a Quebec government-regulated process, and the plan members are to select their representatives for the arbitration. The arbitrator is to apply a standard of equity in resolving the dispute, and may look at such factors as:

- The origins of the surplus
- The history of the plan
- Prior surplus usage and
- Information given to members and beneficiaries.

The decision of an arbitrator is final and binding and may not be appealed under Section 243.14 of the Quebec legislation. The arbitrator has jurisdiction to award the costs of the parties out of the surplus.

The British Columbia Approach

The British Columbia *Pension Benefits Standards Act* requires that every pension plan provide for the allocation of surplus on wind-up to either the members, the employer or any combination thereof. Employers will not receive a refund of surplus assets unless the plan provides for the payment.[42]

If a pension plan does not clearly provide for payment or transfer of surplus assets to the employer, then the legislation provides for a negotiated solution whereby the employer may present a proposal to plan members for the withdrawal of surplus assets from either an ongoing or a terminating plan. Surplus assets may be withdrawn under the proposal if at least two-thirds of the members, former members and prescribed beneficiaries (including surviving spouses) consent to the proposal, followed by consent of the Superintendent.

Section 62 of the legislation further requires that every pension plan contain a provision for final and conclusive settlement by arbitration or any other method agreed to by the parties with respect to allocation of surplus assets on the winding-up of a pension plan or the taking of contribution holidays. If the plan does not contain such a provision, it is deemed to require that the matter be resolved by a single arbitrator. Failure to appoint an arbitrator will result in the Superintendent appointing such an arbitrator. The costs of the arbitrator must be paid by the parties of the arbitration, subject to the provisions of the plan. To date, there has been little or no experience with these arbitration provisions and the ability of employers to make amendments to attempt to give themselves surplus on plan wind-up. The arbitration provisions have recently been modified so that an arbitrator is no longer exempt from applying legal principles to the settlement of a dispute over use of surplus assets.

The Federal Approach

As of April 1, 1999, the following approaches are available for the withdrawal of surplus by an employer under the *Pension Benefits Standards Act, 1985*:

1. Surplus may be refunded to an employer if the employer establishes that it has an entitlement to the surplus under the plan.
2. Surplus may be refunded to an employer if at least two-thirds of the active members and two-thirds of the former members and any other persons in a prescribed class consent to the refund. If more than one-half but fewer than two-thirds of the persons in each of these categories agrees to the proposal, the employer may, or if the pension plan is terminated, shall submit the proposal to arbitration.
3. An employer must submit its claim to arbitration within 18 months after termination of the plan if: the employer has not established a claim to the surplus, the plan is being terminated, and the employer company is winding up or is in the process of being liquidated.[43]

The arbitrator is chosen either consensually or by the Superintendent if the parties cannot agree on an arbitrator within the prescribed time. Under the regulations, where the surplus distribution is to be decided by arbitration, the arbitration must include a procedure by which union members can make representations to the executive of their union. An arbitrator's decision is final and binding on the parties and on any other person affected by it.

ENDNOTES

1. See Justice George Adams in *Bathgate v. NHL Pension Society* (1992), 11 O.R. (3d) 449 (G.D.) at p. 497 aff'd (1994), 16 O.R. (3d) 761 (C.A.), application for leave to appeal dismissed (1994), 19 O.R. (3d) I (S.C.C.).
2. *Schmidt v. Air Products of Canada Ltd.* (1994), 115 D.L.R. (4th) 631 (S.C.C.).
3. *Bathgate v. National Hockey League Pension Society, supra* note 1.
4. Ontario *Pension Benefits Act,* R.S.O. 1990, c. P.8 (the "Ontario PBA"), s.1.
5. *Re Reevie and Montreal Trust Company* (1986), 53 O.R. (2d) 595 (C.A.) at p. 600.
6. *Supra* note 2, at p. 666.
7. *La Have Equipment Ltd. v. Nova Scotia (Supt. of Pensions)* (1994), 7 C.C.E.L. (2d) 245 (N.S.C.A.).
8. *Bull Moose Tube Ltd. v. Ontario (Supt. of Pensions)* (1994), 3 C.C.P.B. 187 (O.C.(G.D.)).
9. *Le Syndicat national des Salariés des outils Simonds v. Eljer Manufacturing Canada Inc.* (1995), 7 C.C.P.B. 257 (C.A.).
10. *Howitt v. Howden Group Canada Ltd.* (1999), 170 D.L.R. (4th) 423 (O.C.A.).
11. *C.U.P.E., Local 185 v. Etobicoke (City)* (1998), 17 C.C.P.B. 278 (O.Div.Ct.).
12. *Lear Siegler Industries Ltd. v. Canada Trust Co.* (1988), 66 O.R. (2d) 342 (H.C.).
13. *Supra* note 2, at p. 666.
14. *Ferro Canadian Employees' Pension Plan* (1995), 15 C.C.P.B. 12 (P.C.O.).
15. *Collins v. Pension Commission of Ontario* (1986), 56 O.R. (2d) 274 (Div. Ct.).
16. *Reichhold v. Wong* (2000), 47 O.R. (3d) 400 (S.C.C.).
17. *Anova Inc. Employee Retirement Pension Plan (Administrator of) v. Manufacturers Life Insurance Co.* (1994), 121 D.L.R. (4th) 162 (O.C.(G.D.)) at p. 179.
18. *Imperial Oil Ltd. Retirement Plan (1988)* (Fall-Winter 1997), PCO Bulletin 6:4 (P.C.O.) at p. 68.
19. *Re Courage Group Pension Scheme,* [1987] 1 All. E.R. 528 (Ch.D.).
20. *Mettoy Pension Trustees Limited v. Idwal Evans et al.,* [1991] 2 Ch. D., 513.
21. *Schmidt, supra* note 2, at p. 666.
22. *Ibid.,* at pp. 666-7.
23. *Ibid.,* at p. 664.
24. *Askin v. Ontario Hospitals Association* (1991), 2 O.R. (3d) 641 (C.A.).
25. *Mauer v. McMaster University* (1991), 82 D.L.R. (4th) 6 (O.C. (G.D.)), varied 125 D.L.R. (4th) 45 (O.C.A.).
26. *C.U.P.E., Local 1000 v. Ontario Hydro* (1989), 58 D.L.R. (4th) 552 (O.C.A.); *Hockin v. Bank of British Columbia* (1995), 123 D.L.R. (4th) 538 (B.C.C.A.); *Chateauneuf v. T.S.C.O. of Canada Ltd.* (1995), 124 D.L.R. (4th) 308 (Que. C.A.); and *Trent University Faculty Association v. Trent University* (1997), 150 D.L.R. (4th) 1 (O.C.A).

27. *Dayco v. CAW* (1993), 102 D.L.R. (4th) 609 (S.C.C.) at p. 659.

28. *Bohemier v. Centra Gas Manitoba Inc.* (1999), 170 D.L.R. (4th) 310 (M.C.A.).

29. *Ibid.,* at p. 321.

30. *Monsanto Canada Inc. v. Ontario (Superintendent of Financial Services)* (2002), 220 D.L.R. (4th) 385 (O.C.A.), (2001), 198 D.L.R. (4th) 109 (Ont. Div. Ct.), reversing (2000), 23 C.C.P.B. 148 (F.S. Trib.). Application for leave to appeal to the Supreme Court of Canada was granted on June 5, 2003 (Court File No. 29586).

31. See *Askin v. Ontario Hospitals Association* (1991), 2 O.R. (3d) 641 (C.A.); and *Schmidt, supra* note 2.

32. Ontario PBA, *supra* note 4, s. 10(1)11.

33. New Brunswick *Pension Benefits Act,* S.N.B. 1987, c. P-5.1, s. 59; Nova Scotia *Pension Benefit Act,* R.S.N.S. 1989, c. 340, s. 84.

34. Ontario PBA, *supra* note 4, ss. 25(1) and 28(5).

35. *Collins v. PCO, supra* note 15.

36. Ontario *Pension Benefits Regulation,* R.R.O. 1990, Reg. 909 (the "Ontario Regulation"), s. 10.

37. *Otis Canada v. Superintendent of Pensions for Ontario* (1991), 2 O.R. (3d) 737 (G.D.).

38. Ontario Regulation, *supra* note 36, s. 8.

39. *Cluett Peabody v. Superintendent of Pensions* (July 1991), PCO Bulletin, 2:2 (P.C.O.), at p. 15, and *Re: Arrowhead Metals v. Royal Trust Company* (June 1992), PCO Bulletin, 3:1 (P.C.O.), at p. 15.

40. Quebec *Supplemental Pension Plans Act,* R.S.Q. c. R-15.1, s. 283.

41. *Ibid.,* s. 230.7.

42. British Columbia *Pension Benefits Standards Act,* R.S.B.C. 1996, c. 352, s. 61.

43. *Pension Benefits Standards Act, 1985,* R.S.C. 1985, c. 32 (2nd Supp.), s. 9.2.

CHAPTER 5

Plan Wind-Up and Deficits

by Susan Rowland and Daniel Kingwell

OVERVIEW

The end of a pension plan is alternatively known as a "wind-up," a "termination" or a "discontinuance." In each case, the accrual of benefits comes to an end, and there is a disposal of all plan assets and liabilities.[1] A variety of issues may arise on plan wind-up that relate to the benefits and liabilities of interested parties.

Either the sponsor employer or the pension regulator (usually known as the Superintendent) may wind up a pension plan. In either case, the wind-up is governed by the terms of the pension plan, contractual obligations, trust or fiduciary duties, and by legislation. The applicable legislation will depend on, among other things, the existence of a collective agreement and the solvency of the employer. However, regardless of whether the plan is dissolved by the employer or the regulator, the same legislated minimum pension standards will apply.

WIND-UP DEFINED

In Canadian pension legislation, a *wind-up* refers to the distribution of assets on plan termination and the payment of liabilities to plan members. A plan is only finally wound up when both the plan sponsor and the regulator have fulfilled all obligations with respect to the plan. However, a *partial wind-up* only affects a distinct subgroup of members. In Canada, affected members have the same rights under both a full and partial wind-up, with the exception that immediate surplus distribution is prohibited in Quebec. In Ontario, in the first case to address the issue of surplus distribution on a partial wind-up, the Financial Services Tribunal ruled that the Ontario legislation did not entitle members affected by a wind-up to immediate distribution of part of the surplus in their plan.[2] The Tribunal noted that the

right of the members affected by the partial wind-up with respect to surpluses is only the right to participate in a surplus distribution, if and when the plan is fully wound up.

On appeal, the Divisional Court set aside the decision of the Tribunal and held that the affected employees were to be treated as if there was a full wind-up of the Plan on the effective date of the partial wind-up, including the right to have distributed that portion of the surplus that relates to the part of the pension plan being wound up. The Court of Appeal held that the Divisional Court was correct to overturn the Tribunal's decision because it was not just unreasonable but "clearly wrong."[3]

WHEN A WIND-UP MAY OCCUR

A wind-up may be initiated either by the sponsor employer or by the regulator. Some situations in which a full or partial wind-up may occur include:

a. Upon expiry of the pension plan
b. Where there are no remaining plan members
c. In the case of a multi-employer plan, where one employer leaves the plan
d. Where a sponsor becomes insolvent
e. Where benefits are no longer accruing
f. Where contributions cease or
g. Where a solvent employer decides, unilaterally, or with the consent of a bargaining agent, to wind up a plan in whole or in part.

Wind-Up by the Employer

It is usually the employer, and not the regulator, that initiates a plan wind-up. Employer-initiated plan wind-ups commonly occur in the case of the sale, merger or reorganization of the business. The wind-up is governed primarily by the terms of the plan itself. As a result, in the event of a wind-up, all interested parties should carefully examine the plan documents. To avoid disputes, a plan should provide clear rules for plan wind-up. The plan should address the issue of employer-initiated wind-up (how, when and by whom), and the manner of asset distribution and payment of liabilities. Provisions should allow for plan wind-up but may not permit the plan to be temporarily suspended.

Employee Rights

Where there is a collective agreement, this may restrict an employer that wishes to wind up a plan.[4] In a non-unionized workplace, the employer must still abide by obligations in the employment relationship that may restrict wind-up.

Trust or Contract?

Procedure on employer-initiated wind-up will also depend on whether the plan is a trust or a contract. If a pension plan is structured as a trust, then it may not be wound up unilaterally by the sponsor, unless it is clearly granted this power in the trust agreement, or unless the trust provides for an amendment power that is broad enough in scope to allow the introduction of a plan wind-up provision.[5] Where the employer retains the power of amendment or wind-up, the wind-up must still abide by the terms of the trust, and any action inconsistent with the trust duties may terminate the trust.[6] The courts have held that the merger of two pension plan trusts as part of the merger of two companies will not trigger the plans' termination provisions.[7] However, the courts will not likely allow a merger of plans where the sole motivation is to withdraw surplus.

Where a pension trust contains express wind-up provisions, the employer may only terminate it in accordance with this provision, subject to variation by court order.[8] If there is no express wind-up provision, then the pension trust may be terminated in two circumstances. First, if all plan beneficiaries are identifiable, and are adults of sound mind, they may all agree to wind up the trust.[9] Otherwise, the courts may order the wind-up of the trust or otherwise vary the trust for the benefit of the beneficiaries, though this power of the court must be exercised in accordance with applicable legislation.

Federal Legislation

Some legislation prohibits or restricts pension wind-up provisions. Bankruptcy law in Canada prevents the disposal of plan assets attributable to employer contributions upon bankruptcy. Other legislation requires that a pension plan contain certain standard provisions and will impose the provision if necessary. Since 1992, to be registered under the *Income Tax Act*, a plan

must contain a provision for allocation of surplus to the employer or plan beneficiaries upon wind-up. Federally, all members of a pension plan, and their spouses, must be given written notice of their plan benefits within 30 days of wind-up. Federal law also provides for a mandatory division of assets on wind-up to employer and employees.

Provincial Legislation

Provincially, there are a variety of mandatory plan wind-up terms imposed by pension standards legislation. Some legislation requires clarification of the calculation of benefits owing to beneficiaries, the procedure for dividing defined benefit plan assets in case of an asset shortfall and the method of allocating surplus. It may be mandatory for a multi-employer plan to state the effect of withdrawal of one employer sponsor. Plans may also be required to determine the method of payment of wind-up expenses and employee portability rights.

Wind-Up by the Regulator

Revocation of Registration

A pension plan may alternatively be wound up by the pension regulatory authority. This may be accomplished by several means. First, the regulator may issue a *revocation of registration*, which will trigger a plan wind-up. The regulator in every provincial jurisdiction has the power to revoke plan registration in case of non-compliance with pension standards legislation. Most legislation further states that revocation constitutes a termination of the plan.

Wind-Up Declaration

The regulator in every jurisdiction may alternatively issue a *wind-up declaration*, by which it effects a wind-up in whole or in part. Legislation dictates the grounds for a declaration and may include: cessation or suspension of employer contributions; discontinuance of business operations; insolvency; bankruptcy; non-compliance with pension standards legislation; and sale of business to a successor employer that does not provide a pension plan. Other reasons outlined in the legislation include the occurrence of a "prescribed event," a decrease in or suspension of members and, in Ontario, a risk that the liability of the provincial Guarantee Fund will substantially increase unless the plan is wound up.

Multi-Employer Plans

In the case of a multi-employer plan, the withdrawal of one employer is not grounds in itself for a wind-up order, unless the plan so provides. As an exception, Alberta requires a wind-up order in specific circumstances involving unionized employees. However, most pension authorities will exercise explicit or discretionary authority to order a partial wind-up to protect the interests of beneficiaries where an employer withdraws, specifically where there is a significant reduction of members or of employer contributions.

Appointment of an Administrator

With the possible exception of Manitoba, in all jurisdictions a regulator may appoint an administrator or trustee where the plan sponsor fails to wind up a plan in certain circumstances. Federally, this is done where the sponsor is bankrupt or fails to act in the best interests of the members, and the appointed administrator may distribute the assets in accordance with the legislation.

WIND-UP PROCEDURE

Wind-Up by the Employer

In the case of a voluntary wind-up by an employer, in most jurisdictions, the plan administrator or the employer must first establish a *wind-up date* and give notice of the date in accordance with the legislation. The notice requirements vary among the jurisdictions and may depend on whether the plan is contributory or noncontributory.

The employer is required to give *notice* to certain parties on plan wind-up. The parties vary among jurisdictions and may include the pension regulator, plan members and former members, trade unions whose members are affected, the plan administrator, the insurer and others with an interest in the plan. In Ontario, notice may be given by advertisement in some cases, and the employer is not required to give notice on partial wind-up to unaffected plan members. In most jurisdictions, notice must be given within a specified time. The contents of the notice are often prescribed as well, usually including information on the wind-up process and the rights of members therein.

A significant issue on plan wind-up is the distribution of *surplus*. In every province, surplus must be distributed on plan wind-up. For a detailed discussion of surplus issues, refer to Chapter 4 in this section dealing with the distribution of surplus.

Wind-Up by the Regulator

In case of a wind-up by *revocation of plan registration,* the regulator in most jurisdictions must specify a date of revocation in its notice. Revocation may not be automatic: Federally and in Newfoundland, the regulator must explain the details of non-compliance to the plan administrator and provide an opportunity to comply. The legislation in every jurisdiction except for Quebec provides procedures for objecting to or appealing the decision to revoke registration.

In every jurisdiction except Saskatchewan, a *wind-up*

declaration will specify the effective date of wind-up. In Saskatchewan, the plan is wound up when all objections and appeals have been exhausted. The legislation in most jurisdictions provides procedures for objections and appeals from a wind-up declaration.

In a revocation of registration, the regulator must first give *notice* to certain parties, possibly including the plan administrator, the employer and other interested parties. Federally, the administrator is given time to comply with the legislation, failing which an effective date of revocation is established. In other jurisdictions, the notice simply gives reasons for revocation—possibly noting the specific provision breached—and a date for revocation. The administrator may be given an opportunity to request reconsideration. Notice is similarly required in the case of a declaration of plan wind-up. In every jurisdiction, notice of a declaration must include the date of plan wind-up.

In most jurisdictions, the legislation specifies a procedure of *objection* to (or *appeal* of) a regulator-induced wind-up. The administrator will usually be given an opportunity to object to the regulatory decision. Following this, there will usually be a hearing or reconsideration. An appeal will then usually lie to a superior court. The legislation establishes time limits at each stage.

All Wind-Ups

In every case where a plan is wound up, either by the employer or by the regulator, the administrator may be required to file a variety of reports with the regulator, and possibly with Revenue Canada. At minimum, a *wind-up report* must always be filed. This report must be prepared by an actuary or other designated person and filed within a specified time period. The prescribed contents of the report may describe the nature and value of plan benefits, the method of determining, allocating and prioritizing plan benefits, and other information relating to the wind-up. Regulator approval of the report will usually be required before plan assets may be distributed. The regulator may refuse approval where the report fails to comply with legislated, plan or actuarial standards, or fails to protect the interests of plan members.

In every case of plan wind-up, members are entitled to *notice* of their entitlement under the plan. Others may also have a right to notice of entitlement, including former members and others entitled to benefits or refunds under the plan. The notice must be given in a timely manner and must set out the person's benefits and options in the wind-up process. Further, legislation may require other contents of the notice, including: an explanation of any new plan amendments; time limits on election of options; details of surplus allocation or benefit reduction, if applicable; and other information on benefits and wind-up procedure.

MEMBERS' BENEFITS ON WIND-UP

On wind-up, benefits are payable to plan members in accordance with the governing provisions of the plan and the legislation. Benefits may include cash refunds, immediate or deferred annuities, or transfers to registered retirement savings plans (RRSPs), registered retirement income funds (RRIFs) or another registered pension plan.

Common Legislated Minimum Standards

There is relative uniformity among jurisdictions on some aspects of benefits on wind-up. In most jurisdictions, legislation requires a pension plan to *list benefits* available to members on wind-up. Every jurisdiction requires that the proposed method of *asset allocation* on wind-up must receive regulatory approval prior to distribution. All legislation requires that members have the same *rights on partial wind-up* as in a full wind-up. Further, every province requires *automatic vesting of benefits* at the date of termination, entitling the members to a deferred pension, even if they would not have been so entitled had the plan continued.

Notably, in Ontario and Nova Scotia, legislation provides that members who have reached "factor 55" (see below) are entitled to count any applicable notice of termination period toward pensionable service, so long as they continue to contribute, if contributions are required.

Grow-In Benefits

In Nova Scotia and Ontario, members of defined benefit plans may be entitled to "grow-in" benefits on plan termination. In these two provinces, members who meet the so-called rule of 55, that is, whose age plus years of service or membership equals 55 or more on the effective date of plan wind-up, are entitled to receive the following:

- A pension in accordance with the terms of the pension plan if, under the pension plan, the member is eligible for immediate payment of the pension plan
- A pension in accordance with the terms of the pension plan to commence at the earlier of the plan's normal retirement date or the date the member would be entitled to an actuarially unreduced pension under the pension plan if the plan were not wound up and if the member's membership continued to that date or
- An actuarially reduced pension in the amount payable under the pension plan and commencing on the date the member would be entitled to a reduced pension under the pension plan if the plan were not wound up and if membership had continued to that date.

This provision gives rise to certain ambiguities. Specifically, when is a member entitled to a "pension in accordance with the terms of the pension plan"? The Ontario Court of Appeal[10] has ruled that this provision is designed to protect vulnerable employees affected by plant closure by accelerating the payment of their pensions. Therefore, the court held that the calculation of members' pensions under the "grow-in" provision is to be made as if the member would have been able to continue in employment until the retirement age of the pension plan, while the amount of the benefit is determined by years of credited service at the effective date of the wind-up. In other words, a member who has met the "rule of 55" is entitled to "grow in" to his or her benefits, and the amount of the member's pension will be calculated as though the member had continued to acquire credited service to the date he or she would have been entitled to retire.

Bridging Benefits

In Ontario and Nova Scotia, members who meet the "rule of 55" are entitled to any benefits they would have been entitled to receive under the plan had no wind-up occurred. Specifically, the member in these provinces will be entitled to any "bridging benefits" he or she would have received under the plan had it not been wound up and had membership continued to that date, if the member has completed at least ten years of employment or membership.

The 50% Rule

While all jurisdictions apply some form of the so-called 50% rule, the substance of the rule can be quite different. The 50% rule applies where a defined benefit plan is wound up. In essence, the 50% rule compares a member's contributions, including interest, from a *set date* to the date of wind-up, against the total benefit credit accrued in that period. Where the contributions exceed 50% of the credit, the member is entitled to certain benefits based on this excess.

Each jurisdiction applies the 50% rule in a somewhat different way. First, the manner in which the member may benefit from the excess will vary. In every case, the legislation recognizes that the member should not have been required to contribute more than 50% of the credit and, therefore, seeks to reimburse or reward the member. Thus, the benefit will be based on the amount of the excess and may be one of, or a choice among, the following options: a lump-sum cash refund, an increased pension or a transfer to another retirement savings vehicle (such as an RRSP or another pension plan). Second, the *set date* for calculation of the 50% rule varies between jurisdictions. In Ontario, the date is January 1, 1987. In Nova Scotia, however, the date is January 1, 1988. In Manitoba, there is no set date. In some provinces, the pension plan may vary the date. Third, the percentage may not always be 50%. In New Brunswick, 50% is the default, though the pension plan may vary this figure.

Transfer Rights

Members may also be entitled to transfer rights upon plan wind-up. That is, they may be allowed to transfer the accrued credit under the pension plan to another pension plan or retirement savings vehicle. In some jurisdictions, any member or former member who is not already receiving pension benefits may be given transfer rights. In Ontario, this may extend to beneficiaries as well. In other jurisdictions, only members or former members who are not eligible for early retirement under the terms of the pension plan or relevant legislation may exercise transfer rights—those who are entitled to receive their pension immediately must do so.

Protection of Interests of Members

The regulator must ensure that the interests of the members are protected in case of a wind-up. Where there are insufficient assets to pay all benefits owing on wind-up, the regulator will be especially vigilant. Legislation prescribes the payment priorities and reduction of benefits in the case of such an asset shortfall.

DEFICIT ON PLAN WIND-UP

Legislated Plan Provisions

In some cases, on wind-up of a defined benefit plan, there may be an asset shortfall. In some jurisdictions, a defined benefit plan is required to have provisions setting priorities in case of insufficient assets. Some legislation also sets out default provisions for prioritizing benefits in such cases—these rules are usually set out in the Regulations. Specifically, the legislation may place a low priority on "additional" benefits or benefits arising from recent retroactive amendments to the pension plan. Note that in Ontario, provisions dealing with reduction in benefits are subject to the application of the Pension Benefits Guarantee Fund, which is discussed below.

Benefits may also include a right to any plan surplus on wind-up, though this is a contentious issue that is to be determined with reference to the plan terms and the relevant legislation. As discussed above, all members and beneficiaries are entitled to notice of any benefits—including surplus—owing on plan wind-up.

Regulator Approval Required

Before the employer may claim any pension assets on wind-up, it must first provide all pension benefits payable under the plan and pension legislation. The employer must outline the scheme for provision of benefits in its wind-up report. No assets can be distributed until the report is approved by the regulator, with certain exceptions that may include payments to continue benefits commencing prior to wind-up, refunds of employee contributions, and various pre-approved payments.

Employer Liability for Deficit

Where there is a shortfall of assets on plan wind-up, the initial liability to fund the deficit falls on the employer. In every jurisdiction, the employer must pay into the fund all liabilities to the date of wind-up. Some jurisdictions further require payment of all amounts accrued to that date but not yet due to be paid. With the possible exceptions of Ontario and Quebec, the employer need not cover any unamortized unfunded liability, experience deficiencies and solvency deficiencies.

In Ontario, the existence of the Pension Benefits Guarantee Fund imposes special rules on employer liability on wind-up. Ontario employers on wind-up are required to pay, first, all liabilities due to date; second, all liabilities accrued but unpaid to date; and, third, an amount to ensure that the fund has sufficient assets to meet benefits potentially payable under the Guarantee Fund, vested benefits accrued with respect to employment in Ontario, and vested benefits accrued with respect to employment in Ontario under the 50% rule and under factor 55. Employers are required to meet these obligations by annual payments to be completed no later than five years after the wind-up date.

Time Limit to Fund Liability

Some jurisdictions establish a time limit for the employer to fund liability upon plan wind-up. This is generally within 30 days after the wind-up date, though the regulator may order otherwise in some jurisdictions.

Insolvent Employer

Where the employer is insolvent or otherwise unable or unwilling to meet its pension liabilities on wind-up, Canadian jurisdictions have gone to varying lengths to protect unpaid accrued benefits from other creditors upon wind-up. At minimum, most jurisdictions provide that unpaid accrued benefits are subject to a statutory trust, for the benefit of plan members and beneficiaries. Protected benefits will usually include all employee contributions and any employer contributions accrued to the wind-up date but not yet due. While the goal of the statutory trust is to protect the funds from other creditors, members will still lose out to any claims by secured creditors and creditors with preferred claims.

Statutory Lien or Charge

A stronger device for protecting benefits from other

creditors is the statutory lien or charge. In New Brunswick, Newfoundland, Nova Scotia and Ontario, legislation gives the plan administrator a lien or charge—both examples of secured interests—for the amount held in the statutory trust. The lien and charge are ahead of all unsecured claims and any secured claim that subsequently arises, and will lose out only to any previous secured claim. In this way, the lien and charge strengthen the trust and provide members with further protection.

Ontario Pension Benefits Guarantee Fund

Ontario offers a third level of protection for pension benefits on plan wind-up. The Pension Benefits Guarantee Fund was established in 1980 to guarantee payment of certain pension benefits in case of a full or partial wind-up. This plan is unique to Ontario—no other province offers similar protection. In Ontario, where the Superintendent of Financial Services declares that the Fund applies to a plan, the Fund guarantees payment of the following benefits:

a. Any pensions in respect of employment in Ontario
b. Where the member meets certain age and service requirements, all deferred pension benefits in respect of employment in Ontario accrued to plan members who terminated employment or plan membership prior to 1988, and a percentage of same for work on or after 1988
c. A percentage of deferred pension benefits in respect of employment in Ontario accrued to plan members who terminated employment or plan membership in or after 1988 and who meet certain service and age requirements
d. All additional voluntary contributions and the minimum value of required contributions, with interest, made by members while employed in Ontario
e. Certain benefits owing to spouses and survivors and
f. Bridging benefits owing to members.

However, the Fund does not guarantee the following benefits:

a. Payments for any plan established within three years of the wind-up
b. Benefit increases made within three years of the wind-up
c. Any benefits exceeding $1,000 per month
d. Benefits under a multi-employer plan or
e. Benefits under a defined benefit plan where employer's contributions are established by a collective agreement.

The Fund may apply if all of the following circumstances are met, subject to the Superintendent's discretion:

a. The pension is registered in Ontario or in a designated province.
b. The legislation does not exempt the plan from Fund protection.
c. There is a full or partial plan wind-up and
d. The Superintendent believes that the plan has failed to meet the legislative funding requirements.

The Superintendent's declaration that the Fund applies is subject to a hearing and appeal procedure before the Financial Services Tribunal, and there is a further right of appeal to Divisional Court. Absent any appeal, upon declaration the Commission must pay into the plan to ensure that all guaranteed benefits can be paid, plus a percentage portion of other benefits owing on wind-up. The Fund's liability, however, can never exceed its assets. For enforcement purposes, the Superintendent has a lien and charge on the employer's assets to the extent of Fund payments plus interest.

Employers that contribute to defined benefit plans are required to make annual payments into the Fund. Annual assessments are based on the number of members in the plan and any liability of the plan—based on a reasonable estimate by the employer—to a maximum of $4 million per year. There is a penalty for late filing.

Liability of Other Parties

Where an employer cannot or will not fund the plan deficit on wind-up, there may remain a shortfall (even after the application of the Pension Benefits Guarantee Fund in Ontario). Members may have to look elsewhere for funding of the full amount of the deficit. In such a case, members may seek to hold other parties liable for the balance.

In some cases, members may be able to hold the *plan administrator,* and its *agents, officers* and *directors* personally liable for the shortfall. The administrator of a plan is held to a high standard of care with respect to the funds of a pension plan. The Ontario pension standards legislation, for example, dictates that the administrator must "exercise the care, diligence and skill in the administration and investment of the pension fund that a person of ordinary prudence would exercise in dealing with the property of another person." Where the administrator delegates its duties to an agent, officer or director, this person will be held to the same standard of care.[11] If the shortfall on plan wind-up is the result of conduct falling below this standard of care, the administrator or its agents may be held personally liable to the members for the amount of the lost benefits. Further, they may be subject to prosecution for an offence under the governing pension standards legislation.

The *plan trustee* may be held liable for the shortfall, even where the deficit is the result of a failure of the employer to make contributions and not the direct result of any action of the trustee.[12] This will arise where the trustee has assumed a fiduciary duty with respect to the plan members, in other words, an overarching obligation to watch out for the interests of the plan members. The trustee's liability, however, will depend on the governing pension standards legislation, the terms of the trust agreement and the extent to which he or she has assumed responsibilities for the trust fund. Similarly, a *fund custodian* who is not a trustee may still be held liable for fund shortfall if found to be a fiduciary.[13]

In the case where the employer is bankrupt, the *trustee in bankruptcy* may also expressly or inadvertently assume the responsibility of covering any plan funding deficit. In one case,[14] a trustee in bankruptcy continued to manage the business of a bankrupt employer, paying the employees and deducting and remitting employee contributions under the defined benefit pension plan. Despite the clear statements by the trustee in bankruptcy at the outset that it was not assuming the liability of the former employer with respect to the funding of the pension plan, the Ontario Court of Appeal nonetheless held the trustee in bankruptcy liable to the members for the shortfall.

Members should also be aware that the *actuary* of the plan may be held liable if a shortfall is the result of his or her negligence in provision of services to the plan.[15] And an *auditor* of the plan may be liable for any shortfall arising as a result of negligent work or work that fails to meet the minimum auditing standards as set out in the relevant pension legislation.

ENDNOTES

1. For ease of discussion, this chapter will generally refer to all of these situations as a "wind-up," unless stated otherwise.

2. *Monsanto Canada Inc. v. Ontario (Superintendent of Financial Services)* (2000), 23 C.C.P.B. 148 (F.S. Trib.).

3. *Monsanto Canada Inc. v. Ontario (Superintendent of Financial Services)* (2002), 220 D.L.R. (4th) 385 (O.C.A.) at paragraph 60, aff'g (2001), 198 D.L.R. (4th) 109 (Ont. Div. Ct.). Application for leave to appeal to the Supreme Court of Canada was granted on June 5, 2003 (Court File No. 29586).

4. *Drohan v. Sangamo Co. (No. 2)* (1975), 11 O.R. (2d) 65, 65 D.L.R. (3d) 15 at 41-52 (Ont. H.C.).

5. *Reevie v. Montreal Trust Co. of Can.* (1986), 53 O.R. (2d) 595 (Ont. C.A.), leave to appeal to Supreme Court of Canada refused (1986), 56 O.R. (2d) (note) (S.C.C.).

6. *Heilig Ltd. v. Dominion Securities Pitfield Ltd.* (1986), 55 O.R. (2d) 783 (Ont. H.C.).

7. *Ibid.*

8. *International Brotherhood of Boilermakers v. Yarrows Ltd.* (1963), 39 D.L.R. (2d) 470 (B.C. S.C.).

9. This known as "The Rule in *Saunders v. Vautier*" (1841), 4 Beav. 115, aff'd 41 E.R. 482.

10. *Firestone Canada Inc. v. Ontario (Pension Commission)* (1990), 78 D.L.R. (4th) 52, 1 O.R. (3d) 122 (C.A.).

11. See, for example, *R. v. Blair* (1992), 7 O.R. (3d) 693 (Prov. Div.), rev'd on appeal (1995), 9 C.C.P.B. 1 (G.D.).

12. *Froese v. Montreal Trust Company of Canada et al.* (1996), 11 C.C.P.B. 233 (B.C. C.A.).

13. *Toronto (Metropolitan) Pension Plan (Trustees of) v. Aetna Life Assurance Co. of Canada* (1992), 98 D.L.R. (4th) 582 (O.C. (G.D.)).

14. *Re St. Mary's Paper Inc.* (1994), 4 C.C.P.B. 233 (Ont. C.A.).

15. *Wynne v. William M. Mercer Ltd.* (1995), 11 C.C.P.B. 1 (B.C. C.A.).

CHAPTER 6

Special Provisions Relating
to Multi-Employer Plans

by Mark Zigler

INTRODUCTION

Multi-employer pension plans (MEPPs) are now recognized as a major portion of the pension plan community in Canada. They thrive in both the private and public sectors, and provide benefits through both defined benefits and defined contribution plans. Some of Canada's biggest pension plans are MEPPs, and MEPPs represent a substantial percentage of Canada's pension plans. They are now as diverse as the Canadian population, and participation in MEPPs appears to be a growing phenomenon, while more traditional, single employer defined benefit plans are declining in numbers.

MEPPs provide their own special challenges for the trustees who traditionally govern MEPPs, plan members, employers and regulators. Unlike the traditional single employer, defined benefit pension plan, there is no employer guaranteeing the benefits in a MEPP (subject to certain exceptions that are negotiated), and therefore the governance and funding of a plan becomes much more important for the purposes of protecting the security of benefits. On the other hand, the insolvency of any one employer does not usually affect MEPP members. As a general matter, MEPPs are governed by boards of trustees, with trade unions and employees generally appointing at least one-half of the board members. Thus there is a greater stake in MEPP governance for the employees and generally a greater commitment as well.

The unique characteristics of MEPPs have been recognized in pension legislation and in many of the tribunal and court decisions, which are reviewed in this chapter.

MEPPs were not always the major players they are today. It is important to explore the reasons for their development and growth in order to understand the requirements of pension legislation and of the regulators that have developed in respect of MEPPs.

Origins and Characteristics of MEPPs

Employee benefits can be expensive to provide. Many small employers cannot afford either the cost of the benefits themselves or the administrative costs associated with providing them. Thus, employees in some industries were, historically, virtually excluded from the prospect of ever enjoying employer-sponsored pension benefits.

Where the nature of an industry is such that persons employed in it typically work for a succession of employers without establishing any sort of permanent employer-employee relationship, the employees may never work for one employer long enough to qualify for benefits. In addition, to the extent that small businesses prevail in these industries, as they do, for example, in the construction, entertainment, garment and maritime industries, the cost of providing benefits may be prohibitive to a single, small employer. In any event, there is little economic incentive for an employer to provide benefits—the employees are not going to work for the employer permanently, nor is the provision of benefits during the short-term likely to affect productivity significantly. Nevertheless, the employees are still likely to view benefits as desirable, if not necessary. It is in this context that multi-employer pension and benefit plans have traditionally developed in the private sector.

The development of MEPPs, governed by a board of trustees appointed entirely or substantially by unions, has become an attractive proposition to employees. MEPPs have traditionally expanded in private sector industries where there has been collective bargaining on an industry-wide basis, such as the construction, food and trucking industries, or in situations where unions have been successful in convincing employers to participate in MEPPs as a cost-control mechanism.

In recent years, public sector unions have taken the initiative to expand the MEPP concept. In many of the large public and "quasi-public sector" areas, the growth of MEPPs has occurred where large employers, such as governments and their agencies, hospitals and health care agencies, municipalities, public utilities and school boards, have sought to control their pension risks and costs by sharing the risk with unions and their members. This has resulted in the "joint trusteeship" of a number of significant public pension plans that are discussed in Section V.

Definition of *MEPP*

A *multi-employer pension plan,* or *any multi-employer benefit plan* for that matter, is one to which two or more, usually unrelated, employers contribute, with the result that service with all participating employers is aggregated in determining the individual employee's benefit entitlements. This will be our working definition of *MEPP.* The various statutory definitions will be considered in the second part of this chapter.

Role of Trade Unions and Collective Bargaining

The primary hallmark of MEPPs tends to be sponsorship either totally or jointly by one or more trade unions representing employees of several employers. Thus the genesis for any MEPP ultimately is that of collective bargaining. As was noted by the court in *Bathgate v. NHL Pension Society,*[1] it is bargaining in employment relations that gives rise to the trust obligations in pension plans and thus "labour relations reality" must be recognized in applying trust law principles to pension benefit plans.

Not all MEPPs arise solely out of a traditional collective bargaining relationship. Some MEPPs in the public sector have been established pursuant to statute. The *Ontario Municipal Employees Retirement System Act,*[2] the *Teachers Pension Act*[3] and the *Manitoba Municipal Act*[4] in respect of the Manitoba Municipal Employees Pension Plan are good examples of statutorily established MEPPs. Similar statutory MEPPs covering teachers and other public sector employees exist in the other provinces as well.

The vast majority of MEPPs that have been established without government initiatives (i.e., legislation) have tended to operate in the *private sector* (although plans like the Hospitals of Ontario Pension Plan and the Health-Care Employees Pension Plan in Manitoba are exceptions) and in *industries characterized by a high degree of craft unionism.* Thus a MEPP is typically established where employees of a particular craft or industry are in a collective bargaining relationship with the union that traditionally represents the craft. Whenever that craft union negotiates a collective agreement with an employer, it will stipulate a clause requiring the employer to contribute a certain amount per hour or a percentage of wages into the industry pension fund, payable on a monthly basis.

An employer that participates in a MEPP is typically obliged, pursuant to its collective agreement with the union, to contribute a defined amount per hour worked or a defined percentage of payroll applicable to eligible employees into the pension fund. The amount of the employer's contribution is thus finite and fixed in the absence of a specific agreement to the contrary. It cannot generally be changed during the life of the collective agreement or other applicable period without amending that agreement, and even on expiry of the agreement it can only be amended through the negotiating process. In other words, the employer's obligation to contribute to the pension plan begins and ends with its obligation under the contract; in no event can the employer be called upon to contribute any amount in excess of that calculated in accordance with the formula in that agreement. Conversely, should the plan be over-funded, the employer is not relieved of its obligation to contribute or entitled to any surpluses. There may be circumstances where a MEPP can be structured so that employers will have additional liabilities or benefits in certain circumstances, but this would depend on the terms of the trust agreement, the collective agreement or other applicable contractual document.

Administration of MEPPs

A MEPP is typically administered by a board of trustees. This board of trustees will either be a joint one, in which case its members are nominated by both the employers and the union bound to the collective agreement(s), or it will be composed of union-appointed trustees only. Most frequently, however, there is equal representation of the union and the employers on the board. Provincial pension statutes generally require that at least half of the trustees are representatives of the employees.

The foregoing is simply descriptive of the traditional form of MEPP administration: How this form of administration is affected by recent statutory reform is addressed in the second part of this chapter. There may be non-traditional forms of MEPP administration and, subject to the minimum standards in the legislation, there is some flexibility in the type of arrangement entered into to establish the MEPP.

The actual day-to-day administration of MEPPs is carried out by trustees either hiring their own employees (self-administration) or contracting with an independent administration firm (contract administration).

Role of the Trust Agreement

Most private sector MEPPs are established pursuant to a formal written trust agreement, with a collective agreement often stipulating the defined contribution. This document usually contains a declaration of the purposes of the trust and authorizes the trustees to receive contributions and hold assets in order to fulfill those purposes. The trust agreement also contemplates the creation of a whole set of subsidiary documents that are necessary to carry out trust purposes. Principal among these is the plan text, which the trustees are empowered to establish in order to govern the distribution of benefits from the pension fund. Additionally, a trust agreement may recognize other types of documents or agreements that oblige an employer to make contributions to the plan. Most importantly, the trust agreement is the source of the trustees' authority to operate the pension fund, and in that regard it spells out the scope of their powers and duties.

After the initial power to establish the pension plan, one of the most important powers conferred on trustees is the power to amend that plan consistent with its purposes. This includes the power to effect plan improvements by increasing benefits. Sometimes the settlors of the trust, namely, the union and employers, reserve to themselves the power of amendment and the power to negotiate benefit changes.

A trust agreement may confer on the trustees the power to delegate administrative powers and responsibility for decision making to subcommittees of the trustees, or to their agents or other individuals. Typically, MEPP trustees will retain a number of professional advisors to assist them in determining major policy and investment issues. Additionally, the trust agreement will commonly address the following matters:

- The number of trustees and the method of the appointment
- The removal, resignation or replacement of trustees
- Requirements respecting frequency of meetings, quorum, audits, etc.
- The responsibilities of trustees and their protection by way of indemnities
- Provisions for the amendment and termination of the fund
- The basis for accepting contributions to the fund and the availability of delinquency procedures
- Procedures for breaking trustee deadlocks.

Differences Between Single Employer Pension Plans and MEPPs

The operation and regulation of single employer pension plans was described in the preceding chapter. From our discussions of MEPPs thus far, it should be clear that these plans differ fundamentally from single employer plans with respect to governance, funding and plan administration, although there are other significant differences as well.

MEPPs are typically administered by boards of trustees, comprised either of both union and management nominees or of union nominees only. In the case of most single employer pension plans, by contrast, the plan is normally administered by the employer alone with little, if any, employee input. The traditional role assumed by the union in MEPP administration is, if anything, strengthened by legislative initiatives since the 1980s pension reform legislation. These legislative initiatives are outlined in the second part of this chapter.

Most MEPPs are funded solely from negotiated contributions in collective agreements or other agreements or statutes. They seldom require any employee contributions, with the exception of the public sector plans. Because the contribution rate is set out in the contract, it is usually fixed and cannot be changed, without an amendment to the contract. The contribution level will remain constant during the term of the agreement (unless the agreement is amended or increases have been negotiated) and will bear no relation to fund performance. Single employer defined benefit plans are typically funded by employer (and sometimes employee) contributions. The employer is required to contribute enough money each year to fund the plan's liabilities in accordance with applicable legislation and actuarial requirements. The amount will be estimated by its actuaries and will depend on such things as fund performance. This amount will usually vary from year to year.

All gains or surplus generated by a MEPP will remain in the plan and be used to reduce liabilities or improve benefits. In a single employer plan, actuarial gains and surplus are sometimes used by the employer to reduce contributions, or the surplus may be withdrawn and returned to the employer if the pension documents and the applicable laws in the jurisdiction permit it.

Benefit formulas in MEPPs do not vary greatly from single employer plans and indeed a cross section of MEPPs will reflect the same types of benefit formulas that a cross section of single employer plans will have, including: final or average salary plans, flat benefit plans or defined contribution arrangements. Given sporadic employment among members in many MEPPs, the formulas for earning benefit credits may be more liberal or may allow for the ability to qualify for benefits over a longer period of time than most single employer pension plans. More importantly, the funding for MEPPs must differ significantly in that the traditional "guarantor" of a single employer is not present. Actuaries have generally developed more conservative funding methods for MEPPs as a result of the need to secure the benefits. Pension legislation has now responded in terms of funding methods available for MEPPs. Further, MEPPs are susceptible to benefit reductions in the event of serious funding difficulties, while most pension legislation prohibits reduction of accrued benefits in a single employer pension plan. Solvency funding is now fairly common in all jurisdictions, and there is a major debate about the extension of solvency funding to MEPPs. While solvency funding is normally the protection against the ultimate insolvency of the single employer, and thus not generally applicable to MEPPs, MEPPs are susceptible in some industries to major reductions in the work force that are common in declining industries or industries with volatile employment patterns, where future employment levels will not produce sufficient contributions to pay for both past and present benefits. This has required careful attention to funding for many MEPPs.

What is most evident is that MEPPs have now matured as accepted pension arrangements in Canada, and plan members, employers and government regulators are paying closer scrutiny to the activities of MEPPs and their trustees.

STATUTORY PROVISIONS AFFECTING MEPPS

The Early Legislative Initiatives

Early legislative initiatives involving pension plans in Canada prior to the major pension reform legislation in the 1980s generally ignored MEPPs. While MEPPs were covered by the minimum standards legislation that was enacted in the 1960s in many provinces and (federally pursuant to the 1965 *Pension Benefits Standards Act* [5]), the statutory provisions were very basic and did not deal with unique concerns that affected MEPPs. While occasional regulation changes may have been made from time to time that would have created different funding requirements for MEPPs, recognition of the characteristics of MEPPs simply did not exist in the statutes. However, commencing with the federal *Pension Benefits Standards Act, 1985,* [6] and particularly with Ontario's legislative initiatives that led to the 1987 Ontario legislation, [7] pension statutes recognized for the first time some of the fundamental differences between MEPPs and other pension plans.

The rest of this chapter focuses on the special provisions relating to MEPPs that are found in pension benefits legislation. However, it is important not to lose sight of the fact that there is also special attention given to MEPPs in other statutes, primarily the *Income Tax Act,* [8] and labour relations legislation.

Below we review the key aspects of pension benefits legislation as they pertain to MEPPs.

Definition of a *MEPP*

Federal legislation, [9] as well as legislation in Alberta, [10] New Brunswick, [11] Nova Scotia, [12] Ontario, [13] Prince Edward Island, [14] Quebec [15] and British Columbia [16] all now contain a definition of *MEPP*. The Ontario definition is typical:

[MEPP] means a pension plan established and maintained for employees of two or more employers who contribute or on whose behalf contributions are made to a pension fund by reason of agreement, statute or municipal by-law to provide a pension benefit that is determined by service with one or more employers, but does not include a pension plan where all the employers are affiliates within the meaning of the *Business Corporations Act.* [17]

The PBSA provision differs slightly in that it excludes a pension plan where more than 95% of the plan members are employed by participating employers that are affiliated companies within the meaning of the *Canada Business Corporations Act.* [18] This avoids having plans of multi-corporate divisions included within the definition of *MEPP*. Recently the Ontario Pension Commission found that related non-profit corporations also do not come within the definition of *MEPP* where a religious order operated several hospitals using separate corporations. [19]

Manitoba differs from other provinces in that it does not contain a definition of *MEPP* in its statute but rather covers MEPPs under the rubric "multi-unit pension plans." Manitoba's legislation defines a *multi-unit plan (MUPP)* as a pension plan "designated as a multi-unit plan" by the Superintendent. [20] The Superintendent may designate multi-unit plans where:

(a) The trustees have in writing, declared their intent that the pension plan should be regulated as a multi-unit plan; and

(b) The plan is in compliance with the provisions of the legislation and regulations. [21]

All multi-unit plans have a board of trustees and the number of trustees representing members of the plan may not be less than the numbers of trustees representing employers. [22] Unlike other situations, employees in a plan that is about to be designated a multi-unit plan have a right to opt out, and the employer liability is limited to the amount contractually required to be contributed to the plan. [23] While a jointly trusteed single employer plan could comply with the Manitoba *MUPP* definition, this applies to all MEPPs and contemplates trusteed plans with different funding rules than traditional single employer plans.

MEPP Governance

Current pension legislation takes a much more active role with respect to who may administer plans and defines certain permitted categories of administrators. In the legislation of Nova Scotia,[24] New Brunswick[25] and Ontario,[26] MEPPs established pursuant to collective agreements or trust agreements must be administered by a board of trustees consisting of representatives of whom at least one-half are selected by the employees (usually through their union). A similar requirement is imposed by Prince Edward Island's Subsection 13(1)(e).[27] However, the P.E.I. pension legislation has not been proclaimed in force at the time of writing. Again, the language of the Ontario Act is useful as an illustration:

8(1)   A pension plan is not eligible for registration unless it is administered by an administrator who is:

. . .

(e) if the pension plan is a multi-employer pension plan established pursuant to a collective agreement or a trust agreement, a board of trustees appointed pursuant to the pension plan or a trust agreement establishing the pension plan of whom at least one-half are representatives of members of the multi-employer pension plan, and a majority of such representatives of the members shall be Canadian citizens or landed immigrants.[28]

The provisions in New Brunswick, Nova Scotia and Prince Edward Island are identical to Ontario.

The Ontario pension regulator has provided a very broad definition of *trust agreement* so that a corporate trustee appointed under a trust agreement for what otherwise appears to be an employer-administered plan will come within the definition of *MEPP* where there are multiple employers and a common trust agreement.[29]

Alberta's legislation contains a requirement for the MEPP to be administered by a board of trustees "or other similar body."[30] In Alberta, as in Ontario, New Brunswick and Nova Scotia, it is explicitly required that the administrative body for a MEPP established pursuant to a collective agreement must be composed of at least 50% employee nominees.[31] The federal legislation contains no such requirement.

Both the federal and Newfoundland legislation make reference to MEPPs established under one or more collective agreements requiring a board of trustees "or other similar body" to be constituted in accordance with

the terms of the plan or collective agreements to manage the affairs of the plan as the administrator.[32]

The federal legislation also specifies the form of administration that MEPPs other than those established pursuant to collective agreements must have. It requires that such MEPPs must be administered by a pension committee,[33] at least one member of which must be an employee representative if the majority of the employees so request.[34] Because the administrators (i.e., trustees) of a MEPP are inherently representative of members' interests as a result of the appointment process, the legislation does not provide for the establishment of an employees' advisory committee with respect to MEPP administration. However, such committees may be available for other plans.[35] Quebec's legislation requires that all pension plans be administered by a pension committee including representatives of active and, in some cases, inactive employees and pensioners.[36]

The British Columbia legislation requires a board of trustees to administer a multi-employer plan if a MEPP is established or maintained by contributions required under a collective agreement.[37] The British Columbia legislation further requires that the number of trustees representing members of the plan must not be less than the number representing the employers.[38]

As noted above, Manitoba has a bit of a circular definition in that trustees must declare their intent to be a multi-unit plan. Any multi-unit plan must be governed by a board of trustees where the number representing members of the plan is not less than the numbers representing employers.[39]

Appointment of Trustees

Most legislation requiring that MEPPs, established pursuant to a collective agreement or trust agreement, must be administered by a board of trustees, provides that those trustees are to be appointed in accordance with the plan documents or trust agreement.[40] Alberta's legislation, on the other hand, is silent with respect to this issue. Nova Scotia's legislation is the most interventionist, requiring not only that trustees be appointed pursuant to plan documents, but that those documents specifically set out the powers and duties of the board of trustees.[41] Legislation in Prince Edward Island and Newfoundland also follows the Nova Scotia model.[42]

However, courts have ruled that there is nothing in the pension legislation or as a matter of common law that requires every union participating in a pension plan to have the right to appoint any trustees.[43]

Governance Standards

One recent area of development for pension plans in Canada, and MEPPs are no exception, is the development of governance standards on a "best practices" basis. The initiative has been taken by the federal Office of the Superintendent of Financial Institutions (OSFI) charged with administering the *Pension Benefits Standards Act* (PBSA). In May 1998, the Superintendent published guidelines for governance of federally regulated pension plans setting out certain principles of good governance for pension plans generally (the "Guidelines").[44]

The Guidelines set out certain principles of good governance for pension plans, including:
- Clearly stated objectives
- Independence of the governing body from the plan sponsor(s)
- Separation of governance from operations, clearly defined roles and responsibilities
- Accountability and internal controls
- Adequate knowledge and skill tests
- Due diligence in decisions and supervision of delegated work
- Controls for expenses and protection from conflicts of interest and
- Transparency and full disclosure.[45]

While the Guidelines are generally adaptable to all pension plans, there are specific discussions in the appendixes that pertain to MEPPs. Reproduced below is Appendix V from the Guideline dealing with "Special Governance Issues When Board of Trustees is the Administrator," particularly directed at MEPPs and other "negotiated pension plans." We have excerpted the entire section because it is relevant in setting standards for MEPPs.

Negotiated pension plans pose special governance concerns because they are often important issues in collective bargaining.

1. **Composition and Orientation of the Board**

   Boards of trustees should pay special attention to educating the board members and planning for an orderly succession. Ideally, the board should have representation of the various groups with an interest in the plan: employers, active members, retirees and other former members. If a group is not explicitly represented, the board should consider other ways to obtain its views, such as special notifications with opportunity to comment.

2. **Investments**

   The trustees should ensure that they are managing the funds to achieve the plan objectives. Considerations of solidarity with other unions or locals or promotion of employment in an industry have to be dealt with by trustees in a manner that is consistent with the plan's investment policies and their own fiduciary responsibilities relating to the pension plan. The fiduciary obligations of the board should set the standard against which all investment decisions are measured. (For further discussion, refer to OSFI's pension plan investment guideline).

3. **Obtaining Independent Objective Advice**

   The adversarial nature of collective bargaining connected to the operation of the plan must not hinder trustees from acting on independent and objective advice. For example, the union may have reasons to exaggerate or minimize wage increase forecasts, or the employer may wish to exaggerate or minimize the possibility of lay-offs. In setting benefits, it is difficult to evaluate projections of future contributions required to finance the benefits when these contributions are yet to be negotiated. The difficulty obtaining independent objective advice should alert trustees to the need for special caution, especially when granting benefit increases.

4. **Benefit Increases**

   Preserving equity among generations of members is a rational concern, especially for trustees of a negotiated contribution/defined benefit plan, and suggests that trustees should ensure that each generation pay for the benefits it receives, and not rely on contributions of the members who follow. To do this and simultaneously safeguard promised benefits, trustees should strive to avoid unfunded liabilities and to finance future cost of living improvements in advance. For example, retroactive benefit improvements, such as inflation protection, could be phased in gradually, as funds become available. The board may find actuarial scenario testing, with a realistic range of assumptions, a helpful tool when considering benefit adjustments.

5. **Compensation of Trustees**

   The board of trustees should establish a policy for compensating its members for their time and earnings lost while they work as trustees. In doing so, they should seek the opinion of independent advisors with expertise in compensation. The policy should be reviewed by legal counsel to ensure that it is consistent with trust law and the specifics of the plan. The board should consider disclosing to members the actual compensation and any honoria or repayment of expenses to trustees as well as the plan's policy in this regard.

6. **Collection of Data and Contributions**

   Trustees should consider refusing participation to a group of employees if their collective agreement does not provide the plan with adequate authority to collect contributions and data. They should establish a delinquency control program including procedures for the collection of unremitted contributions. Timely information is especially important for negotiated contribution plans, because occasions to influence negotiations for contributions are infrequent. The trustees should be comfortable with the systems in place for collecting data and should establish remedies to deal with non-compliance. For instance, at the recommendation of the trustees, the union and the employers should include in their collective agreements the employer's duty to provide data, and the plan administrator's right to verify this information or collect it at the employer's expense should the employer fail to provide it on time.[46]

While the OSFI Guidelines are only "guidelines" and are published in the context of federally regulated pension plans, they are a useful source of information to be applied across Canada. There will likely be a move in years to come by provincial regulators to move toward "best practices" guidelines along the same lines as OSFI.

Conflicts of Interest

It is generally recognized that the administrators of employee pension plans stand in a fiduciary capacity vis-à-vis the members of those plans.[47] Many of the duties imposed on fiduciaries at common law are now codified and explicitly imposed on plan administrators pursuant to pension benefits legislation. The one exception is the Alberta legislation, which does not codify the fiduciary standards, but instead merely states that plan administrators stand in a fiduciary capacity toward plan members.[48]

The Quebec legislation similarly provides that the pension committee acts in the capacity of *trustee* but also codifies to some extent the standard of care imposed as a result of that status.[49] One of the traditional fiduciary duties now statutorily codified is the obligation of the administrator to avoid any conflict between interest and duty.[50] Under the federal legislation, in addition to a prohibition on conflicts of interest, there is a requirement that the conflict be eliminated or that the person with the conflict resign from the administrative body.[51] Under the Quebec statute, the pension committee is required to maintain a register setting out potential conflicts of interest for the administrator and its delegates. This register is to be made available for inspection during regular office hours and is also to be disclosed to plan members at a mandatory annual general meeting.[52]

At common law, trustees and other fiduciaries were restricted in their ability to employ agents or advisors. As we have noted, it is typical for MEPP boards of trustees to engage many such advisors. The pension ben-

efits legislation in many of the jurisdictions, in fact, explicitly recognizes this power.[53] The administrator of a pension plan under the Quebec statute is also empowered to delegate functions in accordance with the plan.[54] Additionally, the legislation imposes upon the agents selected the same fiduciary duties imposed upon the administrator itself. Subsections 23(5) and (8) of the Ontario statute are illustrative of this approach:

(5) Where it is reasonable and prudent in the circumstances so to do, the administrator of a pension plan may employ one or more agents to carry out any act required to be done in the administration of the pension plan and in the administration and investment of the pension fund.

(8) An employee or agent of an administrator is also subject to the standards that apply to the administrator.[55]

As in the case with single employer plans, wherever the MEPP administrators select an agent, they are ultimately responsible for personally selecting a suitable candidate and for supervising his or her actions.[56]

Because it is often advantageous for MEPP trustees to enter into cost-sharing arrangements with either union or management, which are, of course, the parties appointing them, several statutes contain specific provisions exempting these arrangements from the conflict-of-interest prohibition. A good example is the following section of the regulation under the Nova Scotia statute:

Subsection 29(3) of the Act does not apply to an administrator of a multi-employer pension plan, or where the administrator is a pension committee or board of trustees, a member of the committee or board who enters into arrangements related to the administration of the pension plan or pension fund which,

(a) is in the interest of the members and former members of the pension plan,

(b) is protective of the rights of the members and former members of the pension plan,

(c) is expressly provided for in the documents that create and support the pension plan; and

(d) is disclosed to members and former members of the plan prior to entering into the arrangement.[57]

A similar provision is also contained in Section 49 of the Regulations under the Ontario Act.[58]

Disclosure of Information and Plan Amendments

One of the key objectives of pension reform in the 1990s was the securing of greater access to information and participatory rights for employees or other plan participants. Consequently, pension legislation contains many provisions requiring the disclosure of benefit statements, plan summaries, etc., to interested persons.

These matters were covered in a general way in Chapter 2 dealing with minimum statutory standards.

One of the most significant items that must now be disclosed to plan participants is any plan amendment. Much of the recent surplus litigation involves the employer/plan sponsor's unilateral amendment of pension plans to provide for reversion of surplus to itself. Under the legislation, plan members must now receive notice of amendments that may adversely affect their interest in Ontario,[59] New Brunswick[60] and Nova Scotia,[61] and be provided with an opportunity to make representations to the regulator with respect to those amendments. In the federal jurisdiction[62] and in Alberta,[63] the statute does not require that plan participants be provided with advance notice of amendments, although the common law duty of fairness may still require such notice in accordance with the decision of the Ontario Divisional Court in *Re Collins and the Pension Commission of Ontario.*[64]

The requirement for advance notice of amendments may be dispensed with in Ontario upon the order of the Superintendent of Pensions in certain situations. One of the situations in which such notice may be dispensed with is where the amendment occurs with respect to a MEPP established pursuant to a collective agreement.[65] Undoubtedly, the rationale for this exception is that notice to the participants is not required since their interests are being looked after by the board of trustees, at least half of whom must have been appointed by the union. In New Brunswick,[66] Nova Scotia[67] and Prince Edward Island,[68] the requirement for notice of amendments may be dispensed with where a union that represents the employees agrees to the amendment. Effectively, this provision will eliminate most MEPPs from the notice requirements.

With respect to particular types of amendments, MEPPs are also treated differently from SEPPs. Although the legislation generally invalidates any amendment purporting to reduce accrued benefits, this provision does not apply to MEPPs in some jurisdictions.[69] This distinction in the treatment of MEPPs recognizes that, unlike defined benefit single employer plans, they also possess the characteristics of defined contribution plans, and their ability to provide benefits is dependent entirely on the amount of contributions received pursuant to the collective agreement and the investment performance of the fund.

Portability

As noted earlier, one of the key objectives when the very first pension benefits legislation was introduced in Ontario in 1965 was to increase the portability of pension benefits. However, no portability provisions were contained in the early legislation. When the pension reform legislation was being revised in the mid-1980s, one of the key objectives was increasing the portability of benefits. These portability provisions are described in Chapter 2 on minimum statutory standards. Essentially, they confer on a plan participant the right to require the plan administrator to pay an amount equal to the commuted value of the participants' deferred pension to another retirement savings vehicle, another plan, an annuity or an RRSP or LIRA. The participants' rights to demand this action on the part of the administrator crystallize upon the participants' termination of employment or a cessation of membership in the plan. These portability provisions are obviously not suitable for MEPP participants without some modification, since MEPP members frequently terminate their employment without terminating their participation in the MEPP. Further, MEPP members may often terminate their membership in the plan but, because they are covered by a reciprocal agreement with another MEPP, will still earn pension credits. In order to accommodate these unique factors, the Ontario legislation contains a section setting out in some detail when a MEPP participant is deemed to have terminated employment or membership in the plan for the purpose of triggering portability rights under the act. This section provides:

38(1) A person who is,

(a) a member of a multi-employer pension plan;

. . .

is entitled to terminate his or her membership in the pension plan if no contributions are paid or are required to be paid to the pension fund by or on behalf of the member for twenty-four consecutive months or for such shorter period of time as is specified in the pension plan.

(2) For the purpose of determining benefits under this Act, a person mentioned in subsection (1) who terminates his or her membership in a pension plan shall be deemed to have terminated his or her employment.

(3) Subsections (1) and (2) do not apply if contributions are not paid or are not required to be paid because the person has become a member of another pension plan and there is a reciprocal transfer agreement respecting the two pension plans.

(4) For the purpose of determining entitlement to a deferred pension a member of a multi-employer pension plan who terminates employment where the participating employer or an employer on whose behalf contributions are made under the pension plan shall be deemed not to have terminated employment until the member terminates membership in the pension plan.

(5) Where a member of a multi-employer pension plan is represented by a trade union, which, . . . ceases to represent the member, and

the member joins a different pension plan, the member is entitled to terminate membership in the first plan.

(6) Subsection (5) does not apply where there is a reciprocal agreement respecting the two pension plans.[70]

The special measures taken to adapt the portability principle to MEPPs offer the best example of how the new legislative provisions have been carefully tailored to take account of the unique features of these plans and the labour relations realities of the industries in which they thrive.

It should be noted that the Ontario standards for termination of MEPP membership are not uniform across Canada. For example, Saskatchewan, Alberta and British Columbia do not allow a plan to compel a person's termination of membership until the completion of two consecutive plan years in which the member has completed less than a total of 350 hours of employment.

Funding and Solvency Requirements

MEPPs differ substantially from single employer defined benefit pension plans when it comes to funding. On the one hand, more than one employer contributes to the plan and, accordingly, the insolvency of an employer will not bring an end to the plan as is the case with a single employer plan. Further, no one employer acts as a guarantor of the plan as is the case in a single employer plan. On the other hand, the employers contribute a fixed contribution determined under a collective agreement, and such contributions cannot be easily increased or decreased quickly. MEPPs have a statutory ability to reduce benefits (unlike single employer plans) in most jurisdictions precisely because there is no single employer acting as a guarantor.

As a result, actuaries often tend to be more conservative in terms of their assumptions and funding methods for a MEPP. Much of the success of MEPPs is predicated on the fact that they are conservatively funded.

The negotiated contribution aspect of MEPPs has resulted in slightly different funding rules for MEPPs than those traditionally applicable to single employer plans. In some jurisdictions the rules that pertain to funding for single employer plans (15-year amortization period for unfunded liabilities on a going-concern basis and five years on a solvency basis) tend not to apply to MEPPs.[71]

The triennial actuarial valuations for MEPPs in most jurisdictions require the actuary to demonstrate the sufficiency of the contributions required by the agreement or agreements to provide the benefits set out in the plan, without consideration for any provision for reduction of benefits.[72] Where the contributions are not sufficient to provide the benefits under the plan the actuary must propose "options available to the administrator of the plan" that will have the result that the required contributions will be sufficient to provide benefits.

In these circumstances the actuary must propose options in a report filed within 30 days after submitting the actuarial valuation, and the trustees must take such action that will result in the plan meeting the funding requirements within 90 days.[73]

The section in the Ontario Regulations is deliberately vague (as are comparable sections in some other provincial pension regulations) so that there is flexibility in MEPPs making adjustments where there is an unfunded liability. The strict five-year funding rule that has been applied for single employer plans does not apply in Ontario precisely because there is no concern that the MEPP employers will all go bankrupt, which is the primary driving force behind solvency funding in single employer plans. In addition, there is no government guarantee fund for MEPPs. MEPPs have the ability to reduce benefits if necessary, and sometimes this is one of the options proposed by the actuary in an unfunded liability situation, particularly where there is no room for increased contributions.

Other provinces have adopted a five-year solvency funding requirement for MEPPs in the same manner as single employer plans without regard for the difference in the nature of the types of plans.[74]

It appears that the entire issue of solvency funding for MEPPs will be a contentious one in the years to come, particularly in a low interest rate environment for pension plans. At the moment, there is no consistent practice for regulators nor is there likely to be one until the basic principles of solvency funding for MEPPs are agreed upon.

Suspended Pensions

Another recent area of contention, particularly in British Columbia, is that of pensions that are suspended when a retiree returns to work in the industry. There is little dispute about the ability to suspend pensions if the retiree returns to work with a participating employer in a MEPP. However, the matter becomes more complicated in situations where the person returns to work in the industry while receiving a pension but does not work for a participating employer. Most commonly in the construction industry, this often involves an individual returning to work for a non-union employer. In the 1998 case of *Sheet Metal Workers Local 280 Pension Plan v. Sheet Metal Workers Local 280,* a judge of the British Columbia Supreme Court, Trial Division, determined that the British Columbia *Pension Benefits Act* and Regulations prohibit a union pension plan from suspending the pensions of former members who commence new employment with a non-union employer.[75] This is particularly of concern because the individuals in question took enhanced early retirement benefits. However, the matter was subsequently addressed in amendments to the British Columbia legislation in Bill B-58 passed May 11, 1999. The statute now permits a MEPP to suspend the pension of a person on a subsidized early retirement who has returned to work in the same trade and industry with a non-participating employer.[76]

Termination of Bargaining Rights

A particular provision of interest in the Ontario legislation deals with the situation where a group of members in a MEPP are represented by a trade union and such union ceases to represent the members who become members of a different pension plan sponsored by a different union. The administrator of a predecessor pension plan is required to transfer to the administrator of a successor plan all assets and liabilities attributable to such members and the new plan is required to accept the assets and liabilities.[77] This provision will have some bearing in cases where there is a change in bargaining agents or when the members of a union choose to join a successor union. Note, however, that in some instances this may trigger a partial wind-up of the plan.[78] Further, such changes in union affiliation do not require a transfer of retirees to the new plan.[79]

ENDNOTES

1. *Bathgate v. NHL Pension Society* (1992), 11 O.R. (3d) 449 (G. D.); aff'd (1994), 16 O.R. (3d) 761 (C.A.); application for leave to appeal dismissed (1994), 19 O.R. (3d) i (S.C.C.).

2. Ontario *Municipal Employees Retirement Systems Act.* R.S.O. 1990, c. O.29.

3. *Teachers Pension Act.* R.S.O. 1990, c. T.1.

4. Manitoba *Municipal Act.* S.M. 1996, c. 58, c. M225.

5. *Pension Benefits Standards Act.* R.S.C. 1970, c. P.8.

6. *Pension Benefits Standards Act,* 1985. R.S.C. 1985, c. 32 (2nd Supp.).

7. *Pension Benefits Act,* 1987, S. O. 1987, c. 35.

8. *Income Tax Act.* R.S.C. 1985, c. 1 (5th Supp.).

9. *Supra* note 6, s. 2(1).

10. *Employment Pension Plans Act,* S.A. 1986, c. E.-10.05, s. 1(u).

11. *Pension Benefits Act,* S.N.B. 1987, c. P-5.1, s. 1.

12. *Pension Benefits Act,* R.S.N.S. 1989, c. 340, s. 2(w).

13. *Pension Benefits Act,* R.S.O. 1990, c. P.8, s. 1.

14. *Pension Benefits Act,* S.P.E.l. 1990, c. 41 s. 1(1). Not proclaimed in force as of June 1, 2000.

15. *Supplemental Pension Plans Act,* R.S.Q. c. R-15.1, s. 11.

16. *Pension Benefits Standards Act,* R.S.B.C. 1996, c. 352, s. 1(1).

17. *Supra* note 13.

18. *Supra* note 6.

19. *C.U.P.E., Locals 1144 & 1590 v. Ontario (Superintendent of Pensions)* (1998), 20 C.C.P.B. 312 (Financial Services Tribunal).

20. *Pension Benefits Act,* R.S.M. 1987, c. P32, s. 26.1(1).

21. *Ibid.,* s. 26.1(2).

22. *Ibid.,* s. 26.1(4).

23. *Ibid.,* s. 26.1(10).

24. *Supra* note 12, s. 14(e).

25. *Supra* note 11, s. 9(1)(e).

26. *Supra* note 13, s. 8(1)(e).

27. *Supra* note 14, s. 13(1)(e).

28. *Supra* note 13, s. 8(1)(e).

29. *C.U.P.E. v. Ontario Hospital Assn.* (November 1991), PCO Bulletin, 2:3 (P.C.O.), at p. 16, aff'd (1992), 91 D.L.R., (4th) 436 (O.C.(G.D.)).

30. *Supra* note 10, s. 5(1).

31. *Supra* note 10, s. 5(2).

32. *Pension Benefits Standards Act, supra* note 6, s. 7(1)(a); *Pension Benefits Act,* 1997, S.N. 1996, c. P-4.01, s. 13(1).

33. *Supra* note 6, s. 7(1)(b).

34. *Supra* note 6, s. 7(2).

35. *Pension Benefits Act, supra* note 13, s. 24(6)(b); *Pension Benefits Act, supra* note 11, s. 21(1).

36. *Supra* note 15, s. 147.

37. *Supra* note 16, s. 7(1).

38. *Supra* note 16, s. 7.2.

39. *Supra* note 20, s. 26.1(2)(a) and 26.1(4).

40. See *Pension Benefits Standards Act, supra* note 6, s. 7(1); *Pension Benefits Act, supra* note 11, s. 9(1)(e); *Pension Benefits Act, supra* note 13, s. 8(1)(e).

41. *Supra* note 12, s. 16(2).

42. *Pension Benefits Act, supra* note 14, s. 15(2); *Pension Benefits Act,* 1997, *supra* note 32, s. 13(3).

43. *Manitoba Health Organizations Inc. v. Healthcare Employers Pension Plan—Manitoba (Trustees of)*, [1998] 9 W.W.R. 364 (Man. Q.B.).

44. Office of the Superintendent of Financial Institutions, "Guideline for Governance of Federally Regulated Pension Plans"(May 1, 1998).

45. *Ibid.,* at pp. 2-3.

46. *Ibid.,* at pp. 20-21.

47. *Reevie v. Montreal Trust Company* (1986), 53 O.R. (2d) 595 (C.A.).

48. *Supra* note 10, s. 6(5).

49. *Supra* note 15, sections 150 and 151.

50. Ontario *Pension Benefits Act, supra* note 13, subsection 22(4); Nova Scotia *Pension Benefits Act, supra* note 12, subsection 29(3); New Brunswick *Pension Benefits Act, supra* note 11, subsection 17(3); and Prince Edward Island *Pension Benefits Act, supra* note 14, subsection 23(3).

51. *Supra* note 6, ss. 8(6),(7).

52. *Supra* note 15, s. 159.

53. Ontario *Pension Benefits Act, supra* note 13, subsection 22(5); Nova Scotia *Pension Benefits Act, supra* note 12, subsection 29(4); New Brunswick *Pension Benefits Act, supra* note 11, subsection 18(1); Prince Edward Island *Pension Benefits Act, supra* note 14, subsection 28(4).

54. *Supra* note 15, s. 152.

55. *Supra* note 13, s. 23(5)(8).

56. Ontario *Pension Benefits Act, supra* note 13, subsection 23(7); Nova Scotia *Pension Benefits Act, supra* note 12, subsection 29(5); New Brunswick *Pension Benefits Act, supra* note 11, subsection 18(2); Prince Edward Island *Pension Benefits Act, supra* note 14, subsection 28(5).

57. N.S. Reg. 269/87, s. 41.

58. R.R.O. 1990, Reg. 909, s. 49.

59.   *Supra* note 13, s. 26.

60.   *Supra* note 11, s. 24.

61.   *Supra* note 12, s. 32.

62.   *Supra* note 6, s. 28 (1)(a).

63.   *Supra* note 10, s. 8 (1)(a).

64.   *Re Collins* and *the Pension Commission of Ontario* (1986), 56 O.R. (2d) 274 (Div. Ct.).

65.   *Supra* note 13, s. 26(4)(c).

66.   *Supra* note 11, s. 24(4).

67.   *Supra* note 12. s. 32(4).

68.   *Supra* note 14, s. 32.

69.   Ontario *Pension Benefits Act, supra* note 13, subsection 14(2); Nova Scotia *Pension Benefits Act, supra* note 12, subsection 20(2); Prince Edward Island *Pension Benefits Act, supra* note 14, section 19.

70.   *Supra* note 13, s. 38.

71.   See specifically sections 6 and 7 of R.R.O. 1990, Regulation 909, under the Ontario *Pension Benefits Act* and section 6 of Nova Scotia Regulation 269/87.

72.   See for example Ontario Regulation 6(4)(a).

73.   See Ontario Regulation section 6(4)(b) and 6(5).

74.   See particularly British Columbia Regulation 433/93, s. 5; Quebec *Supplemental Pension Plans Act, supra* note 15, s. 137; and Manitoba Regulation 81/99, s. 4(3).

75.   *Sheet Metal Workers Local 280 Pension Plan v. Sheet Metal Workers Local 280* (1998), 17 C. C. P. B. 209 (B.C.S.C.).

76.   *Supra* note 16, s. 74(2).

77.   *Supra* note 13, s. 80(8)(9).

78.   *CEP v. Superintendent of Pensions* (1999), PCO Bulletin, 8:2 (P.C.O.), at p. 69.

79.   *Ibid.,* at p. 75.

CHAPTER 7

Taxation of Pension Benefits

by Andrew J. Hatnay

INTRODUCTION

As a general rule, employees are taxed on all income and benefits received from their employer. Obviously, both employees and employers are interested in opportunities to minimize the effect of taxation on employee benefits. As part of the social policy objective of ensuring adequate income for retirees, the *Income Tax Act* (Canada) (ITA)[1] contains a tax regime that confers tax advantages to plans in order to encourage employers and employees to work together to provide for employees' retirement and to promote fairness among taxpayers.

Retirement Savings Reform

In June of 1990, significant changes to ITA were proclaimed. Supporting regulations were added January 15, 1992, generally applicable after 1989. The changes provided a dramatic overhaul of the income tax regime with respect to retirement savings.

The stated objectives of the tax reform were:
- To integrate limits for tax-assisted retirement savings, applicable to all retirement savings vehicles, including registered pension plans (RPPs), registered retirement savings plans (RRSPs) and deferred profit-sharing plans (DPSPs)
- To codify the administrative rules set out in the Information Circular 72-13R8,[2] so as to apply them clearly and uniformly and

- To implement stringent anti-avoidance rules, so that no tax assistance would be available above the new integrated limits.

Registered Pension Plans (RPPs)

A registered pension plan (RPP) is granted numerous tax advantages in ITA. First, employer contributions to an RPP are not considered taxable benefits to employees and are not required to be included in an employee's taxable income under Section 6(1)(a)(i) of ITA.

Second, permissible employer and employee contributions to an RPP are tax-deductible. Section 8(1)(m) of ITA defines *permissible employee contributions,* while Section 20(1)(q) delineates allowable *employer contributions.*

Third, by way of Section 149(1)(o) of ITA, the earnings of an RPP trust are tax-exempt. This confers a dual advantage on an RPP: Pre-tax contributions can be invested, and investment returns can be re-invested without tax. This preferential treatment allows the trust fund to grow at a greatly accelerated rate.

In addition to registration under various provincial pension statutes, pension plans must also be registered with Revenue Canada (now called the Canada Customs and Revenue Agency, hereinafter referred to as the Revenue Agency). Registration with the Revenue Agency is required in order to ensure that contributions to the pension plan are deductible to the employer and, in the case of a contributory pension plan, to the employee as well. Further registration ensures that the investment income of the pension fund remains exempt from tax.

REGISTRATION OF PENSION PLANS

Generally, a pension plan is not eligible for registration with the Revenue Agency unless three broad requirements are fulfilled:

1. The plan administrator applies for registration in the prescribed manner according to the *Income Tax Act*.
2. The plan complies with the prescribed conditions for registration as set out in the *Income Tax Act* and related Regulations.
3. An application for registration under the applicable provincial pension statute has also been made.

The registration of the plan will not be effective earlier than January 1 of the calendar year in which the application for registration was made. Accordingly, it is important for a plan sponsor seeking to register a plan to be aware that if registration is not completed within a calendar year, the effective date of the plan will not likely be January 1 of that year. This in turn may lead to adverse tax consequences. Typically, the documents required to register a pension plan are:

- A plan text
- A trust agreement or other document governing the fund of the pension plan and
- A Revenue Agency application Form T510, known as the Application for Registration of a Pension Plan.

Once the documents have been submitted to the Revenue Agency, the plan is deemed to be a registered pension plan; however, until final registration has occurred the deemed plan may not accept direct transfers from any other registered plans nor may it participate in any tax-free rollovers provided under the *Income Tax Act*.

Once these documents have been examined to the satisfaction of the Revenue Agency, the pension plan will be a registered pension plan. The Revenue Agency then typically conducts an in-depth analysis of the plan text to ensure that it complies with the provisions of the *Income Tax Act* and will notify the plan sponsor to make changes to the plan text that it believes are not in compliance with ITA. If the plan sponsor does not amend the plan to bring the plan into compliance in a timely manner, or cannot persuade the Revenue Agency that the requested amendment is not necessary, the Revenue Agency can proceed to deregister the pension plan. Deregistration of a pension plan for failing to provide amendments to bring a plan in compliance with ITA is relatively rare; however, a request for amendments by the Revenue Agency must be reviewed and addressed with diligence to avoid revocation of registration of the plan. If a plan is deregistered, it will be considered a retirement compensation arrangement, described in greater detail below.

SPECIFIC REGISTRATION REQUIREMENTS

The rules relating to the registration of pension plans are largely codified in the *Income Tax Act* and the related Regulations. The more significant of the prescribed registration requirements are as follows.

The plan's primary purpose must be to provide periodic payments to individuals after retirement and until death in relation to their service as an employee. Generally, the only contributions that may be paid into a pension plan are those that are:

- By a member of the plan in accordance with the terms of the plan
- Eligible contributions, as defined in the *Income Tax Act*, by the employer under a defined benefit provision of the plan with respect to its employees or former employees and
- By the employer with respect to its employees or former employees in accordance with a money purchase provision of the plan as registered.

In addition, amounts transferred on a direct plan-to-plan basis from other registered vehicles, as well as other amounts that may be acceptable on a case-by-case basis to the Minister transferred to the plan from certain foreign pension plans, are also permissible contributions to a pension plan.

Employer contributions to a defined benefit pension plan are "eligible contributions" only if they are made on the recommendation of the plan actuary in whose opinion the contributions are required in order to ensure that the plan has sufficient assets to pay the promised benefits. Employee contributions to a defined benefit pension plan relating to current service are restricted to the lesser of:

- 9% of the employee's remuneration for the year from an employer that participates in the plan or
- $1,000 and 70% of the employee's pension credit for the year under the plan.[3]

The Regulations under the *Income Tax Act* prescribe the permissible benefits that may be paid from a registered pension plan. For a defined benefit plan, the benefits paid from the plan must also comply with certain restrictions applicable solely to defined benefit provisions, including the maximum amount of retirement benefits and rules relating to the guarantee period, early retirement, bridging benefits, post-retirement and pre-retirement survivor benefits. For money purchase pension plans, the benefits provided must comply with specific conditions relating to such items as bridging benefits and pre- and post-retirement survivor benefits. Further, benefits that the plan is required to provide pursuant to federal and provincial pension benefits standards legislation and payments to spouses or former spouses of members as required by provincial family laws are also permissible.

Generally, the permissible distributions from a pension plan include the following:

- Payment of benefits in accordance with the plan
- Direct transfers from a defined benefit plan to another defined benefit plan or a money purchase plan
- Refund of contributions made by a member of the plan or the employer provided that such refund is required to avoid revocation of registration of the plan
- Refund of contributions made by a member of a defined benefit plan, plus interest pursuant to an amendment to the plan that also reduces the future contributions that would otherwise be required to be made by the member
- Payment to a person of plan surplus under a defined benefit plan and
- Payment to the employer of money held under a money purchase plan.

The pension plan must also require that retirement benefits commence to be paid to the member not later than the end of the calendar year in which the member attains age 69.

The plan must provide that no right of a person under the plan is capable of being assigned or given as security, except for benefits assigned on marriage breakdown. This stipulation is interpreted by the Revenue Agency as applying only to a pension that is being accrued and not one that is in pay.

THE ADMINISTRATOR

According to the *Income Tax Act,* each registered pension plan must have a person or a group of persons who have "ultimate responsibility for the administration of the plan." The administrator must be a resident in Canada or, in the case of a pension committee, the majority of persons on the committee must be resident in Canada. Similar to the requirements under provincial pension statutes, the plan administrator is required to:

- Administer the plan in accordance with the terms of the plan as registered. The only exception to this is, where the plan fails to comply with the prescribed conditions for registration in the *Income Tax Act* or Regulations, the administrator may administer the plan as if it were amended to so comply.
- Inform the Minister in writing within 30 days after

becoming the administrator of the name and address of the administrator or the persons who constitute the body that is the administrator and
- Where there is any change in the foregoing information, inform the Minister in writing within 60 days of the change of the new information.[4]

The administrator must file an information return annually with the Revenue Agency known as an *Annual Information Return.* The administrator of a defined benefit pension plan is also required to file regular actuarial reports in order to qualify the employer's contributions to the plan as eligible contributions. However, the Revenue Agency has the power to demand an actuarial report at any time. The administrator of a plan is also responsible for past service pension adjustment reporting, as well as pension adjustment reporting, described in greater detail below.

FOREIGN PROPERTY RULE

Generally no tax is payable by the trust fund holding the funds of a registered pension plan. However, special taxes may be levied against the pension fund if, at the end of any month, the foreign property held by the trust exceeds 20% of the fair market value of all the property held by the trust at the time of the acquisition. The foreign property restriction has been recently changed as a result of the most recent federal budget and will increase to 30% by the end of the year 2000.[5]

PENSION ADJUSTMENT LIMITS

A key component of the income tax rules governing registered pension plans is the limitation on the amount of tax-sheltered retirement savings available under a registered pension plan. The concept is reflected in the requirements relating to the pension adjustment (PA). The PA is designed to measure the benefits that the individual member has earned in the preceding year under a registered pension plan (or under a deferred profit-sharing plan) and is the sum of all pension credits for the year. The pension credit of a member under a money purchase pension plan is generally equal to the total of all contributions made in the year by the member and by the employer on behalf of the member, plus any forfeited amounts and surplus amounts that are allocated to the member in the year.[6] For a defined benefit plan, the pension credit calculation is more complicated and is essentially determined by the following formula:

$$9 \times \text{individual entitlement minus } \$600\,[7]$$

The PA operates to limit the amount that an individual may contribute to a registered retirement savings plan (RRSP) for the calendar year by the amount of the PA for the preceding year. The employer is required to report the PA of each employee for the year by the end of February of the following year. Where an individual receives past service benefits under a defined benefit pension plan for service after 1989, the employer must calculate and report a past service pension adjustment (PSPA) in respect of that member as well. PSPAs are discussed in greater detail below. The *Income Tax Act* provides that a registered pension plan, other than a multi-employer plan, will be in a revocable situation where the pension adjustment for the year of a member of the plan in respect of a participating employer exceeds the lesser of the money purchase limit for the year, or 18% of the member's compensation from the employer for the year.[8]

Money purchase limit is defined in the *Income Tax Act* as a specified dollar amount, which is currently set at $15,500 for 2003.[9]

Retirement Compensation Arrangements

If an RPP does not qualify for registration or has its registered status revoked, it will be considered a *retirement compensation arrangement (RCA)* under ITA, which does not have the preferred tax status of an RPP. An RCA is a creature of ITA and contained in Sections 248(1) and 207.5 to 207.7. RCAs were added to ITA in 1986 and were designed to catch a variety of employer-funded schemes intended to provide income to an employee at some time in the future. An *RCA* is generally defined as a plan or arrangement under which an employer (and in some cases an employee) makes contributions to a custodian who holds the funds in trust with the intent of eventually distributing the funds to the employee on retirement or after some other termination of employment.[10] This definition clearly contemplates a pension plan. In contrast to employer contributions to an RPP, the contributions made by the employer to the custodian are taxable. The tax is equal to 50% of the amount of the contribution, which the employer must remit for deposit into a special RCA trust account. The 50% tax is refundable and is refunded to the employer as distributions from the RCA trust are paid to the employee. However, the investment earnings of the RCA are also subject to tax of 50%, which are similarly refundable as distributions are paid out to the employee. All distributions paid out of the RCA trust to the employee are subject to tax. The employee must report the amount received from the RCA trust on his or her income tax return.

Section 248(1) of ITA specifically exempts certain retirement arrangements from being considered an RCA. These exemptions include an RPP, DPSP, a salary-deferred arrangement and an employee trust.

Many supplemental retirement arrangements that are funded by an employer qualify as an RCA. Although the financial requirements are onerous, the main advantage of a funded RCA to provide supplemental benefits is security. The employee has security that the payments are protected from creditors in the event of the insolvency of the employer.

INTEGRATED CONTRIBUTION LIMIT

The cornerstone of the current tax regime relating to retirement savings is the *integrated contribution limit* that applies to RPPs, DPSPs and RRSPs. The limit is the maximum amount that can be contributed in total to tax-assisted retirement savings vehicles and is expressed as a percentage of *earned income,* subject to the annual *money purchase limit,* which is an absolute dollar limit. The money purchase limit is currently 18% of earnings. The dollar amount can vary from tax year to tax year, depending on government policy and the changes to ITA. Formerly $13,500, the money purchase limit has been increased to $15,500 for 2003.[11]

Limits for DPSPs

There are also limits applicable to each type of retirement savings vehicle. The maximum that can be contributed by an employer tax-free to a DPSP in one year is one-half the RRSP limit. Employees are prohibited from contributing to a DPSP.

Limits for RRSPs

The limit applicable to an RRSP in a tax year is the annual money purchase limit for the previous year.

THE PENSION ADJUSTMENT

General

All employers that sponsor an RPP or DPSP must calculate a "pension adjustment" (PA) for each plan member. Briefly, the *PA* is a figure, calculated annually, that seeks to represent the total benefits that a taxpayer accrued in a year in any tax-assisted retirement savings plan, including any RPP and DPSP. The PA operates to reduce the money purchase limit for those taxpayers that are members of employer-sponsored plans such as an RPP or DPSP. The PA is first calculated and then subtracted from the employee's money purchase limit. This ensures that limits for tax-assisted retirement savings are *comprehensive* and that taxpayers who are members of an employer-sponsored plan are not in a more advantageous position than self-employed taxpayers or those whose employers do not have such programs.

CALCULATING THE
PENSION ADJUSTMENT

The Revenue Agency has published a "Pension Adjustment Guide"[12] to assist plan administrators in performing calculations. The following is a summary of the Guide.

Each DPSP and each provision of an RPP produce a "pension credit" for the member. The pension credit is a measure of the value of the benefit earned or accrued during the calendar year. The method used to calculate pension credits depends on the type of plan and provision. A member's PA is the total of that member's pension credits from all plans in which the member's employer participates in the year, excluding RRSPs. The PA reduces the maximum amount that a member can deduct for contributions to an RRSP for the following year.

The first year in which PAs had to be calculated was 1990, and there are no PAs for earlier years. The first year that RRSP deduction room was reduced by PAs was 1991. An RRSP does not generate a pension credit or PA.

All employers that sponsor or participate in an RPP or DPSP must calculate a PA for each of their employees who participate in the plan. A union or employer association may also share responsibility for calculating a PA if the RPP is a specified multi-employer plan and the union or employer association receives multipurpose payments, a portion of which is then contributed to the RPP.

Since the PA has to be calculated according to the plan as it is registered, it is important that the administrator file any amendments to a plan within the 60-day filing requirement under the Regulations.

The employer should also ensure that the plan(s) in which it participates will not provide benefits that cause a member's PA to be higher than the specified limits; otherwise, the plan may be revocable. There are no limits for a specified multi-employer plan, unless the plan contains a money purchase provision. The limit in this case is found in Subsection 8510(7) of the Regulations.

Registered Pension Plans (RPPs)

An RPP can be regulated by provincial and federal pension legislation. An RPP, which may require or allow member contributions in addition to employer contributions, produces a retirement benefit that is generally paid out monthly. RPP pension credits are included for the year in the member's PA.

The determination of a PA depends on the nature of the benefit plan. The formula for calculation of a PA for a defined contribution provision differs from that for a defined benefit provision. Where a single plan contains both types of provisions, the plan will generate two respective PAs.

Calculating Pension Credits for DPSPs

To calculate pension credits for a DPSP, all employer contributions made in the year for the member, as well as contributions made by the end of February that re-late to the previous year as contributions for that year and any forfeited amount(s) and related earnings allocated in the year to the member, are included except for cash pay-outs to the member.

The legislative limits stipulate that an employer's contributions to one or more DPSPs for a year must not cause the employee's DPSP pension credit (or the total of the employee's DPSP pension credits) calculated by that employer to be more than *one-half* of the money purchase limit or 18% of the employee's actual earnings in the year, whichever amount is less.[13]

If two or more affiliated (i.e., non-arm's length) employers participate in the same DPSP or different DPSPs, each employer's contributions to the DPSP(s) for the year must not cause the total of the employee's DPSP pension credits calculated by all the employers to be more than one-half of the money purchase limit.

If the employee is also a member of another DPSP or an RPP in which the employer or a non-arm's length employer participates, each employer's contributions to the DPSP for a year must not cause the total of the employee's PAs reported by all the employers (the sum of all DPSP and RPP pension credits) to be more than the money purchase limit or 18% of the employee's total earnings from the employers, whichever amount is less.

Calculating Pension Credits for Single Employer RPPs

Money Purchase Provision

Pension credits include:
- All employer contributions relating to a year for the member (contributions made by the end of February that relate to the preceding year are treated as contributions for the preceding year)
- All member contributions relating to a year, excluding amounts transferred directly to the plan from an RRSP, RPP or DPSP
- Any forfeited amount, and related earnings, allocated in the year to the member, except for cash pay-outs of these amounts and
- Any surplus allocated to the member, whether it remains in the plan or is transferred out of the plan to another RPP or an RRSP.[14]

A surplus in a money purchase provision may arise if a defined benefit provision is converted to, or replaced by, a money purchase provision. The pension credit does not include certain contributions that were made in the year but are in respect of service for an earlier year(s).

Defined Benefit Provision

The calculation of the PA for a defined benefit provision is more complex. Essentially, a PA is calculated as a multiple of *benefit entitlement,* reduced by an *offset.*

Regulation 8302 defines the *benefit entitlement* by assessing the value of the accrual by using the following assumptions:

- The individual retires in the year.
- The individual's remuneration in the year is the same as in prior years.
- The individual's survivor and ancillary benefits maximize his or her pension benefits.
- The individual is fully vested and
- The value of cost-of-living adjustment is nil.

Note that under Regulation 8302(a), the accrual for a year is what can reasonably be considered to have accrued in respect of the year.

The *offset* for tax years prior to 1997 was $1,000. For 1997 and subsequent years, the offset is $600, thereby increasing the PA. The result is that PA is calculated as follows (note that a PA cannot be less than 0):

PA (prior to 1997) = [9 × benefit entitlement] − $1,000 (offset)

PA (since 1997) = [9 × benefit entitlement] − $600 (offset)[15]

Importantly, the values of both the benefit accrual and the PA for the year are limited by Subsections 147.1(8) and (9), which provide that an individual's PA for the year may not generally exceed:

- 18% of the individual's remuneration for the year or
- Money purchase limits for the year.

This reflects the comprehensive limits for tax assistance for retirement savings. If a pension plan adopts a benefit formula that generates a PA in excess of these limits, the registration of the pension plan may be revoked. Note, however, that since money purchase limits will increase in 2003 and 2004, but the PA for 1996 to 2003 will not change, some high earners will exceed the PA limit. The transitional provisions set out in Regulation 8509(12) stipulate that in these circumstances, the excessive PA will not render the RPP revocable.

Pension credits are calculated based on the benefit earned or accrued by the member in the RPP during the year. The full amount of the benefit accrued is used, even if the benefit is not yet vested. The first step to determine the pension credit is to calculate the benefit accrued during the year by doing the following:

- Calculate the annual amount of retirement pension that would be payable based on all years of service up to and including the year for which the PA is being calculated. Then subtract the annual amount of retirement pension that would have been payable based on all years of service up to, but not including, the year for which the PA is being calculated. Generally, you can use your plan's pension benefit formula, based on one year's service, to determine the benefit earned or
- If benefits are determined as a percentage of earnings, multiply the member's pensionable earnings for the year by the benefit rate or

- For flat benefit plans, take the flat benefit amount for the year.
- The final step is to apply the pension credit formula: (9 × BENEFIT EARNED) − $600 = PENSION CREDIT. If the calculation results in a negative amount, the pension credit is nil.[16]

Excluded Benefits

The following benefits are not included when calculating the accrued benefit:

- Bridging benefits (temporary benefits that terminate at a fixed date that was known before they started), even if paid
- Any indexing of earnings to reflect the increase in average wages and salaries between the year of earnings and the year in which benefits are determined
- Early retirement reduction, even if it applied to a member who has actually retired during the year
- Amounts resulting from the deferred commencement of a pension past age 65, when the increased pension is not more than the actuarial equivalent of the pension payable at age 65 or
- Cost-of-living adjustment made before the end of the year for a member whose pension starts in a year, if the increase is not more than the greater of 4% per annum and the increase in the Consumer Price Index between the date of retirement and the date of the increase.[17]

Calculating Pension Credits for Multi-Employer Plans (MEPs)

As discussed in Chapter 6 of this section, a multi-employer plan (MEP) may have several participating employers and a large membership.

Money Purchase Provision

The calculation of a pension credit is the same as the calculation for a money purchase provision of a single employer plan.

Defined Benefit Provision

The pension credit for a defined benefit provision is calculated in the same way as a defined benefit provision of a single employer plan, except for a member who:

- Worked for two or more employers in the year
- Worked part-time or less than the full year or
- Ended employment in the year.

The rules take account that an employer may not have all the information needed to calculate defined benefit pension credits, such as information about a member's employment in the year with other employers that also participate in the plan. In each of the three scenarios above, the pension credit formula is prorated for both the benefit earned and the PA offset by the portion of the year worked with each employer. Each employer has to calculate a pension credit as though the member had not worked for any other employer. The amount earned by the member is annualized, and the fraction of the year actually worked by the member is used to calculate the benefit earned. The same fraction is applied to the $600 offset in the pension credit formula.

REPORTING THE PENSION ADJUSTMENT (PA)

The PA is reported on the T4 Supplementary form filed on or before February 28 of each year. The employer is also responsible for reporting the pension adjustment when a member earns benefits while on a leave of absence or while absent from work because of a disability. The plan administrator of a MEP may choose to report on a T4A Supplementary the PAs related to the above periods of absence. However, the plan administrator must first apply for and receive written permission from the Registered Plans Division.

PAs for MEPPs

The PA for a multi-employer pension plan (MEPP) is determined in the same way as the PA for a defined contribution or defined benefit plan, with the exception that the offset for a MEPP must be prorated according to duration of service with the employer. For example, if an employee worked for only one-tenth of the year for Employer A, then the employee's offset with respect to Employer A will be one-tenth of $600.

THE COMPREHENSIVE LIMIT AND RRSP DEDUCTION ROOM

Unlike other tax-assisted retirement savings plans, contributions to RRSPs are not included in the calculation of the PA. Accordingly, a generous RPP or DPSP benefit will generate a significant PA that will limit the amount of tax-deductible contributions that can be made to an RRSP, while a person who does not belong to an RPP or a DPSP will not have a PA and can take advantage of the full RRSP tax deduction limit.

The limit on the amount that a taxpayer may contribute tax-free to an RRSP in a year is called *RRSP room*. Unused RRSP room in a year may be "carried forward" indefinitely and added to the RRSP limit in subsequent years. This is an important feature of the comprehensive limit.

A taxpayer's RRSP room for a year is calculated as follows:

- Any unused RRSP deductions carried forward, *plus*
- 18% of the individual's earned income in the prior year, up to the RRSP dollar maximum, *minus*
- The individual's PA for the prior year, if any, *minus*
- The past service pension adjustment (PSPA) for the year, if any.[18]

Accumulated RRSP room improves past service benefits in an RPP, as discussed below.

PAST SERVICE PENSION ADJUSTMENTS (PSPAs)

In addition to the benefit earned by a member for the current year (reflected in the member's PA), pension benefits may improve as a result of events related to past service. These "past service events" occur when, for periods of past service **after 1989**:

- Benefits are increased retroactively.
- An additional period of past service is credited to the member or
- There is a retroactive change to the way a member's benefits are determined.[19]

When any of these events occur, the value of the pension accrued is increased and gives rise to a past service pension adjustment (PSPA). A PSPA is equal to the additional **pension credits** that would have been included in the member's PA if the upgraded benefits or additional service had actually been provided in those previous years. Reporting the PSPA ensures that the overall limit on tax-assisted retirement savings is maintained. A PSPA is used to reduce the amount that a member can contribute to an RRSP in the current year (the year of the past service event) and perhaps following years. The plan administrator of a defined benefit RPP is responsible for calculating and reporting PSPAs when necessary. The Revenue Agency has published a "Past Service Pension Adjustment Guide"[20] to assist administrators in calculating PSPAs. The following is a summary of the Guide.

Past Service Events That Generate a PSPA

A PSPA is required to be calculated and reported, relating to post-1989 service where:

- A pension plan is amended to:
  - Retroactively increase the flat benefit or benefit rate
  - Credit additional years of past service to one or more members
  - Provide additional past service benefits for only certain members or
  - Retroactively change the way benefits are determined.
- Members purchase past service.
- Additional past service benefits are provided to a member who meets conditions for a higher benefit

(e.g., becoming a member of a senior executive plan).
- Benefits increase automatically according to plan provisions.
- The value of an annual, automatic indexing adjustment to pensions in pay changes.
- A defined benefit provision that recognizes past service is established.
- A member is credited with benefits for pensionable service with a previous employer.
- The plan is a specified multi-employer plan (SMEP), and **members** make a past service contribution (employer past service contributions are reflected in the PA of an employee).
- Benefits for a period of leave, reduced pay or disability are **retroactively** provided **after** April 30 of the year immediately following the year in which a member returns to work.
- The period of service during which the member was waiting to join the plan is automatically credited once the member joins.
- Past service benefits are being credited for time that the member worked outside Canada.[21]

Past Service Events That Do Not Generate a PSPA or That Generate a Nil PSPA

The following past service events do **not** give rise to a PSPA:
- An improvement to ancillary benefits
- Adjustments required as a result of increases in earnings under an earnings-related plan or
- An increase in a pension credit resulting from the indexation automatically factored into the maximum permissible lifetime retirement benefit.[22]

A past service event may result in a nil PSPA in certain situations, if the increase in benefits qualifies as an "excluded benefit." Depending on the situation, an *excluded benefit* is usually one that is equal to or less than increases in the Consumer Price Index, average wage or other wage measures.

Moreover, a past service event will result in a nil PSPA for a member if benefits under the plan are increased, but the member is not entitled to the increase retroactively because the member's past service benefits were capped by a legislative limit, or by an overriding limit in the plan or the limit continues to apply despite the past service event.

Section 8504 of the Regulations is an example of a legislative limit. It limits the amount of lifetime retirement benefits payable under a defined benefit provision in most plans. The terms of the plan may contain a different overriding limit that is even more restrictive than the legislative limits. Therefore, those members who were subject to such limits before the past service event will have a nil PSPA when benefits under the plan

increase. On the other hand, members who were unaffected by the limit will have a PSPA greater than nil, unless the PSPA is nil for other reasons described earlier in this section.

Benefits That Do Not Generate a PSPA

The following benefits do not generate a PSPA and, therefore, can be ignored for PSPA purposes:
- Bridging benefits, even if paid
- Any indexation of earnings to reflect the increase in average wages and salaries between the year the earnings were paid and the year in which benefits are determined
- Early retirement reduction, even if it applies for a member who retired during the year
- Pension deferral past age 65, when the increased pension is **not** more than the actuarial equivalent of the pension payable at age 65
- Cost-of-living adjustment made before the end of the year for a member whose pension starts in a year, when the increase does not exceed the greater of (a) 4% per annum and (b) the increase in the Consumer Price Index, between the date of retirement and the date of the increase
- Adjustments to a member's pension income that depend on whether the member is totally and permanently disabled when pension payments start and
- Additional benefits provided under a plan because a member has contributed more than 50% of the value of his or her pension (as required by most provincial pension legislation). This applies to all members if the plan covers members in a jurisdiction requiring such additional benefits.[23]

Possible Benefit Exclusions From PSPAs for All Plans, Except SMEPPs

The situations in which you may be able to exclude, in whole or in part, a benefit increase are:
- Cost-of-living increases to pensions in payment
- Cost-of-living increases before pension starts (in a deferral period)
- Flat benefit rate increases
- Flat benefit plan increases
- Pre-1992 agreements scheduling flat benefit rate increases
- Job category or rate-of-pay change resulting in benefit increase and
- Other benefit increases (subject to advance approval by the Minister of National Revenue).[24]

Special Rules for Specified Multi-Employer Plans (SMEPs)

The usual rules for determining PSPAs for benefit

upgrades do not apply to SMEPs, since SMEPs are treated as money purchase provisions for purposes of calculating pension credits. The member's annually reported PA reflects any past service benefit upgrades funded with contributions made by the **employer**.

When a **member** makes a contribution under a defined benefit provision of a SMEP for past service benefits, a past service event occurs. The PSPA will usually equal the member's past service contribution. This includes any contributions the member made that are conditional on certification of the PSPA. The PSPA must be certified by the Revenue Agency before the related benefit can be paid to the member.

A past service contribution does **not** include:
- Contributions included in the member's pension credit under the plan for the year or
- Tax-free transfers into the plan.

The Revenue Agency must certify all PSPAs from SMEPs, unless the less-than-$50 tolerance rule applies.

Reporting and Certification

A PSPA that is greater than nil must be reported to both the Revenue Agency and the employee. For a zero or nil PSPA, a PSPA need not be reported nor certified by the Revenue Agency. The additional benefit to the member can be paid immediately. There are two methods of reporting PSPAs depending on whether the Revenue Agency has to certify the PSPA.

PSPAs Less Than $50

If the calculated PSPA is less than $50, the PSPA need not be reported. This is currently an administrative rule that applies if:
- The original calculation of PSPA is less than $50 or
- The difference between an original PSPA and an amended PSPA is less than $50.

PSPAs Exempt From Certification

As mentioned above, a nil PSPA for a particular member does not need certification. Also, certification of a member's PSPA is not required if the past service event increases the benefits of all or most of the members of the plan and when all of the following conditions are met in either of the following situations.

When a defined benefit provision is established:
- There are at least ten active members under the provision.
- No more than 25% of the active members under the provision are specified active individuals.
- The member's PSPA is not more than $47,250.
- The member is not a specified active individual and
- If the member is not an active member, the member was neither a person connected with a participating employer nor a person who earned 2.5 times the

year's maximum pensionable earnings (YMPE) from the employment with the participating employers in any of the five years just before the year of the past service event.

After a defined benefit provision is established:
- There are at least ten active members under the provision.
- No more than 25% of the active members under the provision are specified active individuals.
- Benefits of all, or substantially all, of the active members are increased as a result of the past service event.
- The percentage increase in total benefits provided to any specified active individuals is not more than the percentage increase in the total benefits provided to other active members and
- Additional benefits provided to retired or terminated members are not more advantageous than additional benefits provided to active members.[25]

However, if the above conditions are substantially, but not entirely, met, employers can request that certification be waived for a past service event by sending a letter to the Registered Plans Division.

PSPAs Requiring Certification

All PSPAs that are greater than nil and that do not meet the conditions for exemption must be certified by the Revenue Agency. When a defined benefit provision is established, all PSPAs relating to specified active individuals must also be certified.

Generally, certification depends on whether the PSPA exceeds the member's unused RRSP deduction room at the end of the previous year by more than $8,000. The Revenue Agency must certify the PSPA before benefits relating to the past service event can be paid to the member. The sponsor can generally begin to make contributions to fund the additional benefits as soon as it has applied for certification. However, if the Revenue Agency denies certification, the contributions must cease immediately.

The certification formula is applied to the member's PSPA for the event and, if the total of this calculation is equal to or more than this PSPA, the PSPA will be certified.

Administrator's Responsibilities

The administrator's responsibilities include the following:
- Applying to register the plan (T510)
- Applying for approval of amendments to the plan within 60 days from the date the amendment is made (T920)
- Making sure that the plan is administered according to the terms of its registration or, where it fails to comply with the *Income Tax Act* and Regulations, to

administer the plan as if it had been amended to comply

- Filing actuarial reports with Revenue Canada, if necessary; filing annual information returns with Revenue Canada (T244)
- Dividing benefits among participating employers for pension adjustment (PA) purposes, if necessary
- Applying for past service pension adjustment (PSPA) certifications
- Reporting information to participating employers so they can report pension adjustments and past service pension adjustments, if necessary; and
- Under certain circumstances, reporting pension adjustments to Revenue Canada.

A plan that fails to comply with the conditions will not be registered, and an existing RPP that does not comply with a condition may have its registration revoked and thus be declared an RCA. The Revenue Agency can revoke the pension plan if, at any time after it has been registered by the Minister, it is not administered according to the terms of the plan or does not comply with the prescribed conditions in ITA for registering the plan.

THE PENSION ADJUSTMENT REVERSAL

What Is a Pension Adjustment Reversal (PAR)?

Under a defined benefit provision, a PAR is an amount that will restore lost registered retirement savings plan (RRSP) contribution room to an individual. This applies when the individual receives a termination benefit that is less than the individual's total pension adjustments (PAs) and past service pension adjustments (PSPAs). Under a deferred profit-sharing plan (DPSP) or a money purchase provision, an individual's PAR is the amount included in his or her pension credits but to which the individual ceases to have any rights at termination. An individual will only have a PAR under a DPSP or a money purchase provision if he or she is not fully vested at termination.

The PAR will restore individuals' RRSP contribution room in cases where their PAs and PSPAs are more than the benefits they received from the RPP or DPSP on termination. By restoring RRSP contribution room, PARs are designed to make the system for tax-assisted saving for retirement more fair and more effective for those who change jobs or move in and out of the work force.

Administrators of RPPs and trustees of DPSPs have to determine PARs for individuals who terminate from a plan provision in 1997 and later years. When an individual terminates from a provision, he or she is no longer entitled to benefits under the provision. An individual need not end employment, only stop participating in the provision. The date of termination is generally the date on which the termination benefit is paid from the provision. This can be a cash payment to the individual or a transfer to the individual's RRSP. For example, if an individual left employment in 1996 but did not receive his or her termination benefit until 1997, a PAR will have to be determined for the individual.

Usually, a plan administrator will have to report a PAR shortly after termination. A PAR will be added to an individual's RRSP contribution room for the year of termination. PARs for termination of membership in each quarter of the calendar year have to be filed on or before the 60th day after the end of the quarter.

The PAR is reported to the Revenue Agency so that the employee's RRSP contribution room can be increased.

A person is a member of a DPSP or benefit provision of an RPP as long as he or she has any rights to a benefit from the DPSP or benefit provision of the RPP. An individual who has rights to a benefit from the provision or plan because of another individual's participation in the provision or plan is not considered a member.

If an individual is entitled to benefits under an annuity contract to satisfy his or her entitlement to benefits under a provision or plan, he or she is still considered to be a member of the provision or plan. However, if the individual's entitlement to benefits is paid in cash, or is commuted and transferred to an RRSP or registered retirement income fund (RRIF) before the annuity is purchased, he or she is considered terminated from the provision or plan and a PAR needs to be calculated.

A special rule applies to an individual's rights to a surplus under a provision. If a person terminates membership except for any future surplus allocations or distributions, the Revenue Agency currently treats these individuals as though they have no entitlement to the surplus until it is actually allocated. This allows a PAR to be determined in cases where surplus ownership is in dispute or payment of surplus is delayed. If a PAR is calculated for an individual at termination, a future surplus can only be used to provide ancillary benefits for periods before 1990.

The Revenue Agency has published a "Pension Adjustment Reversal Guide"[26] to assist plan administrators in calculating PARs for their members. The following are the salient provisions of the Guide.

Rationale for the PAR

The PAR is designed to remedy problems inherent in the calculation of PAs. Prior to the PAR, the PA overestimated the actual pension credits accrued for individuals under the plan. The extent of the overestimation depended on the type of plan involved.

First, the so-called factor of 9 in the PA calculation for a defined benefit plan is problematic in the absence of a PAR. The PA for a defined benefit plan is calculated by multiplying the year's benefit entitlement by 9 (factor of 9), and then applying the offset ($600 in tax year 1999). The factor of 9 is designed to account for very generous ancillary benefits to the defined benefit plan, such as post-retirement indexation to inflation and early retirement incentives. However, many defined benefit plans do not provide such generous benefits. For those individuals, in the absence of a PAR, the factor of 9 unfairly reduces RRSP contribution room, and the actual value of the termination benefit paid from the plan could be less than the total PAs and PSPAs reported for the individual during plan membership.

Second, without the PAR, problems occur in case of termination of membership prior to vesting. When an individual terminates membership prior to vesting under an RPP, including a defined contribution plan, or under a DPSP, the individual loses the benefit of the plan. Though ITA provides a special rule for calculating the PA in the year of non-vested termination, this does not usually restore the total lost RRSP room.

The PAR is designed to reduce the above inequities by allowing individuals to recover the lost RRSP room when they terminate plan membership, particularly upon termination prior to retirement.

The PAR now acts to restore lost RRSP contribution room to plan members whose plan membership was terminated on or after January 1, 1997. PARs for individuals who terminated in 1997 were added to their RRSP deduction room in 1998. For those terminated after 1997, the PARs are added to their RRSP room in the year of termination.

Calculating a PAR for Deferred Profit-Sharing Plans (DPSPs)[27]

Termination Conditions for DPSPs

A PAR for an individual is calculated if he or she meets the following termination conditions:
- The termination occurs after 1996 and for a reason other than death.
- Instalment payments have not been made to the individual under the plan.

If an individual meets the termination conditions, the PAR is the total of all amounts that were included in his or her pension credits (PAs) up to the date of termination, but that he or she was not entitled to (not vested) at the time of termination. Investment earnings are disregarded.

Calculating a PAR for Registered Pension Plans (RPPs)[28]

Termination Conditions for RPPs

A PAR is calculated for an individual if he or she meets the following termination conditions:

- The termination occurs after 1996 and for a reason other than death.
- Retirement benefits have not been paid to the individual under the provision.

Money Purchase Provision

Under a money purchase provision, if an individual meets the termination conditions, the PAR is the total of all amounts that were included in the pension credits of the individual until the date of termination, but to which he or she was not entitled (not vested) at the time of termination. Investment earnings are disregarded.

Any amounts allocated after the person has terminated will be included in a pension credit at that time but will not affect the PAR that has already been calculated.

Defined Benefit Provision

If an individual meets the termination conditions, the PAR is determined according to the following formula:

$$A + B - C - D$$

A is the total of the terminated individual's pension credits under the provision. In the case of high-income earners, the maximum amount of a pension credit for a particular year included in amount A is the RRSP dollar limit for the following year. Amount A includes the individual's pension credits up to the date of termination even though these pension credits may not be reported until after the PAR is reported.

B is the total of the grossed-up amounts of PSPAs associated with any past service benefits provided to the individual under the provision before termination. It adds to the member's PAR the additional pension credits that are associated with the past service benefits. More specifically, the grossed-up amount is what the PSPA for the individual would have been if there had been no qualifying transfers to fund the past service benefits, and if any previous pension credits and PSPAs that may have applied to offset the PSPA amount were ignored.

C is the total specified distributions made for the individual under the provision on or before termination. A specified distribution is the part of an amount paid from the plan for the individual's post-1989 benefits. Certain amounts are not considered specified distributions. *C* **does not include** any part of an amount:
- That is a payment for pre-1990 benefits
- That is transferred to another defined benefit provision of an RPP (other than a SMEP)
- That is a payment of actuarial surplus
- That is a return of contributions, including interest, made as a result of an amendment under the plan

that also reduces or eliminates future member contributions

- That may reasonably be considered to be a payment of benefits provided for a period when the plan was a SMEP or
- That is related to past foreign service that did not generate a PSPA.

If a lump-sum payment partly relates to pensionable service before 1990 and partly to service after 1989, only the part of the payment that can reasonably be considered to relate to service after 1989 is included in amount C. If the benefit formula has not been amended during the period of the individual's service, prorating the payment, based on the post-1989 proportion of the total period of pensionable service, will normally be acceptable. However, if the rate of benefit accrual under the defined benefit provision has not been the same for all years of service, you have to consider this when you determine the post-1989 part of the payment.

D is the individual's PA transfer amount. This amount applies when the individual is credited with past service benefits under another defined benefit provision of an RPP for a period that was pensionable service under the former defined benefit provision. The PA transfer amount will apply, for example, where past service benefits are transferred between plans under a reciprocal or portability arrangement when an individual changes jobs. A PA transfer amount will also arise when an individual's benefits under the terminating provision are being replaced with benefits under another defined benefit provision of an RPP maintained by the same employer. In these two situations, the provisional PSPA associated with the past service benefits is determined in accordance with the modified PSPA rules. Under those rules, the PA value of benefits previously provided to the individual under the terminating provision is applied to offset the PSPA, resulting in either a nil PSPA or a substantially reduced PSPA. The PA transfer amount reduces the member's PAR by the PA value of those benefits, which is consistent with the fact that those benefits have not been lost, they have simply been replaced.

The administrator of the new plan gives this amount to the exporting plan administrator. The new plan administrator must advise the exporting plan administrator within 30 days of the transfer that there will be a PA transfer amount as a result of the past service benefits being recognized under the new plan. The new plan administrator has a total of 60 days from the date of the transfer to advise the exporting plan administrator of the actual PA transfer amount.

Timing of the PAR

A PAR is required to be calculated when an individual terminates membership in a DPSP or under a benefit provision of an RPP, and prior to the date on which retirement benefits commence payment. The following rules apply to determine when to calculate a PAR.

Membership Deemed Terminated on Final Payment From the Plan

Membership to a benefit provision of an RPP is deemed to terminate when the member receives a final payment from the plan. If the member transfers the commuted value of his or her pension benefits out of the plan in a year subsequent to the year employment was terminated, then the PAR will be calculated in the year of the transfer. There will only be a PAR for transfers occurring in or after 1997. Note that where an unvested member of a non-contributory plan terminates employment, the termination will trigger the PAR since the member will never be entitled to a plan payment.

Calculation on Termination of Plan Membership

A PAR is only calculated when an individual terminates plan membership. In the case of pension division on marriage breakdown, there is no PAR calculation on pension division. When plan membership is finally terminated, the PAR will be determined by adding the present value of the benefits previously allocated to the spouse to the member's allocation and subtracting this total from the actual benefits accrued during the member's period of service.

DPSPs and Defined Contribution RPPs

For DPSPs and defined contribution plans, PARs will only arise if the member is unvested at the time of membership termination. For a vested member of a defined contribution plan, no PAR is required because the member is entitled to the precise amount for which he or she has received a PA in the past.

Conversion From Defined Benefit to Defined Contribution Plan

A PAR is calculated upon the conversion of a defined benefit to a defined contribution plan for members who have terminated membership in and have no entitlement to benefits under the defined benefit plan. The PAR will be determined in the year that the benefits are paid out of the defined benefit plan.

Entitlement Under Multiple Plan Provisions

If a member is entitled to benefits under several defined benefit provisions of an RPP, and the granting of benefits under one defined benefit provision is dependent on entitlement to benefits under the other provisions, the PAR is not to be determined until membership ceases in all related provisions. Termination from such a related provision may occur prior to 1997.

A "specified distribution" made under one of the related provisions will reduce the individual's PAR under all of the related provisions unless the Revenue Agency waives this requirement. If the total PAR generated from all related provisions is less than it would have been if the related provisions were considered a single defined benefit provision, the Revenue Agency has indicated that it may waive the PAR reduction rule.

Defined Benefit Plan With a Defined Contribution Offset

For defined benefit plans with a defined contribution offset, in which the defined benefits are determined in relation to the benefits that can be purchased at retirement with the member defined contribution account, a PAR is to be determined only when the individual has also terminated membership in all the defined contribution offset provisions. A defined contribution "excess offset" will be calculated, which is, generally, the amount of investment income earned on the contributions in the offset provision after 1989. Since the benefits promised under the defined benefit provision take into account the investment returns in the defined contribution offset, no benefits are truly lost under the defined benefit provision when PAs are reported for this provision. When calculating the PAR on termination of membership in the defined benefit provision, the PAR will thus be reduced by the defined contribution excess offset amount.

Plan Wind-Up and Surplus

A PAR must be determined when a defined benefit plan winds up and benefits are commuted. This must be done even if the surplus ownership issue is not resolved. If surplus is then used to provide additional benefits resulting in the reporting of a PSPA, another PAR calculation will have to be performed because another termination is deemed to occur.

Member Elects Deferred Pension or Annuity on Termination of Employment

No PAR arises if a member terminates employment and elects to receive an immediate or deferred pension or purchases a deferred annuity since, in these instances, plan membership is deemed not to have terminated.

Termination of Membership on Death of Member

No PAR is calculated if termination of membership occurs because of a member's death since other specific tax rules apply upon the death of an individual.

Defined Benefit Provision of a SMEPP

No PAR is determined if individuals terminate from a defined benefit provision of a SMEPP. Pension credits are deemed to be zero during the time in which a plan is a SMEPP.

Effect on PSPA Calculations

As noted above, when benefits are provided on a past service basis after 1989 under a defined benefit provision, PSPAs must be reported by employers to reflect the increases in pension accruals for previous years. In this way, PSPAs decrease RRSP contribution room.

Prior to the introduction of the PAR, an individual was permitted to make a "qualifying transfer" of funds from an RRSP or another RPP to make room in the RRSP to absorb the associated PSPA. The PAR now limits the amount of the "qualifying transfer" to the part of the transfer that can be attributed to funding post-1989 benefits.

Prior to the PAR, special rules existed to determine PSPAs in certain situations. These rules effectively permitted an individual's PSPA to be offset by the PA value of benefits previously provided to the individual regarding past service. The introduction of the PAR removed the rationale for the offset. Under the PAR, a member who ceases entitlement to benefits under a defined benefit provision should have sufficient RRSP contribution room to absorb any PSPA related to a reinstatement or replacement of benefits.

However, the special rules continue to exist to offset PSPA in the following circumstances:
- Where an individual is credited with past service benefits from a defined benefit provision of an RPP with respect to a period of pensionable service of the individual under another defined benefit provision, if the period had previously ceased to be pensionable service under the other provision or will cease to be pensionable service under the other provision as a result of the provision of past service benefits, i.e., where termination from one plan will occur only if service in this plan is considered past service under another plan or defined benefit provision of the same plan
- Where termination occurred prior to 1997, and the benefits the individual has previously forfeited or cashed out under a defined benefit provision were subsequently reinstated under the provision
- Where termination occurred prior to 1997, and the benefits were provided under a defined benefit provision of a plan with respect to a period that was, but is no longer, pensionable service under another defined benefit provision.

Duty of Plan Administrators

Beginning in 1999, plan administrators must report

the PAR no later than 60 days after the end of the calendar year quarter in which termination occurred.

MAXIMUM PENSION RULE FOR DEFINED BENEFIT PLANS

The maximum pension rule applies to limit the yearly benefit accrual for individuals under a defined benefit plan. The rule dictates that the maximum pension that can be provided under a defined benefit provision is to be calculated as the lower of:

- 2% × member's years of service × member's highest average compensation or
- The defined benefit limit × years of service.

Up to the 1995 tax year, the defined benefit limit (in the calculation) was $1,722.22. Since 1996, this limit has increased to $1,722.22, *or one-ninth of the year's money purchase limit,* whichever is greater. Funding can be provided for this maximum pension benefit and permitted ancillary and indexation benefits, but not for excess benefits. Note that a SMEPP is exempt from maximum pension rule, even though it is by definition a defined benefit plan.

ENDNOTES

1. *Income Tax Act,* R.S.C. 1985, c.1 (5th Supplement), as am. (ITA).

2. Revenue Canada, Information Circular. IC72-13R8, "Employees' Pension Plans" (16 December,1988).

3. Income Tax Regulations, C.R.C., c.945 (the "Regulations"), s.8503(4).

4. ITA, *supra* note 1, s. 147.1(6)(7).

5. Finance Canada, "Budget 2000" (28 February 2000).

6. The Regulations, *supra* note 3, s.8301(4).

7. *Ibid.,* s.8301(6).

8. ITA, *supra* note 1, s.147.1(8).

9. *Ibid.,* s.147.1(1).

10. *Ibid.,* s.248(1).

11. Other recent and future annual money purchase limits are as follows: for 1990, $11,500; 1991, $11,500 and 1992, $12,500; 1993, $13,500; 1994, $14,500; 1995, $15,500; 1996 through 2002, $13,500; 2003, $15,500; 2004, $16,500; 2005, $18,000. For 2006, and subsequent years, the limit is calculated as the greater of (i) $18,000 x (the average wage for the year divided by the average wage for 2005), rounded to the nearest multiple of $10, or (ii) the money purchase limit for the preceding year. See ITA, *supra* note 1, s.147.1(1).

12. Revenue Canada, " Pension Adjustment Guide" (T4084(E), Revised 1998. Available at www.ccra-ardc.gc.ca.

13. *Ibid.,* at p. 9.

14. *Ibid.,* at p. 10.

15. *Ibid.,* at p. 11.

16. *Ibid.,* at p. 11.

17. *Ibid.,* at p. 11.

18. ITA *supra* note 1, s.146(1).

19. The Regulations *supra* note 3, s. 8300(1).

20. Revenue Canada, "Past Service Pension Adjustment Guide" (T4104(E)), Revised 1999. The Guide is available at www.ccra-adrc.gc.ca.

21. *Ibid.,* at p. 11.

22. *Ibid.,* at p. 12.

23. *Ibid.,* at p. 12.

24. *Ibid.,* at p. 14.

25. *Ibid.,* at p. 27.

26. Revenue Canada, "Pension Adjustment Reversal Guide" (RC4317). Available at www.ccra-adrc.gc.ca.

27. *Ibid.,* at p. 9.

28. *Ibid.,* at p. 10.

CHAPTER 8

Pension Fund Investments: The Fundamentals

by Gloria Lau

Although there are many investment vehicles that can be held by a pension fund, they can all be divided into two: equity and fixed income. This chapter will expand on each of these asset classes and will examine the advantages and disadvantages of each.

EQUITY

Equity is commonly known as *stock*. Corporations issue shares (i.e., equities) to increase their capital. In return for their purchase of shares, shareholders (also known as *stockholders*) own a portion of the corporation. Shareholders are like silent partners, as they neither participate in the day-to-day operation of the company, nor are they liable for any lawsuits involving the corporation.

Shareholders will experience an increase in the value of their stocks either through *capital appreciation* or by receiving a *dividend*.

Capital Appreciation

Capital appreciation occurs when the market price of a stock is greater than its purchase price. For example, if a stock was purchased at $35 and is currently trading at $40, it has appreciated by $5. So, why would the market price of a stock go up? The simplest explanation is that the corporation has increased its profit and hence increased its worth. Since shareholders own part of the corporation, their shares will also increase in value.

Another reason for the increase is driven by the economic concept of supply and demand. If there are more investors who are willing to buy stock in a corporation than there are shares available, then the price of the stock will increase. There may be increased demand for a given stock because the corporation's revenues have increased (as noted earlier), or it could be because of the anticipated growth of the company in the near future. The latter explains why some Internet stocks for companies that currently have negative earnings and are expected to experience exponential growth are trading at very high prices.

Dividend

When a company increases its earnings, it can either re-invest the profits in the company, enabling it to continue to grow and expand, or it can distribute some or all the profits to its investors as a dividend. The decision to declare a dividend, and the amount of the dividend, rests with the company's board of directors. The most popular types of dividends are:

1. A **stock dividend,** where the dividend is paid out in the form of shares of the company or
2. A **cash dividend,** where the dividend is paid out in cash to the investors.

When the dividend is paid out, the stock price will fall in proportion to the amount that is paid out per share.

Common Stock vs. Preferred Shares

There are two types of stocks: common and preferred. *Common stockholders* have voting rights. They can attend shareholder meetings and vote on the election of directors and other important corporate issues. If they cannot attend, they can still vote by proxy, which means that they can authorize another individual to vote on their behalf.

Preferred shareholders have the same ownership interest in the corporation as common stockholders, but they do not have the right to vote. In exchange for giving up their right to vote, they are given a preferred claim to any dividends declared by the corporation compared to common shareholders. The dividend payable on preferred shares is usually fixed and is also cumulative. Therefore, if the corporation chooses not to pay a dividend in a given period, when a dividend is next declared, preferred shareholders will receive both their past and present dividend entitlements before any monies or shares (depending on the type of dividend declared) are distributed to the common shareholders. If the company declares bankruptcy, preferred shareholders have a superior claim on the corporation's remaining assets as compared to common shareholders.

Equity Classified by Characteristics

There are many ways of grouping stocks. The following are common types of stock groups and a brief description of their characteristics.

- **Blue chip stocks** are high-grade stocks that have a long history of existence.
- **Cyclical stocks** are stocks that are greatly affected by the business cycle. The sales and earnings of these companies increase and decrease relative to the cycle.
- **Interest-sensitive stocks** are stocks whose prices are tied to changes in the interest rate. For example, bank stocks fall when the interest rate increases.
- **Defensive stocks** are the opposite of cyclical stocks. Their earnings and returns are not greatly affected by changes in market conditions. Examples of this type of stock are grocery stores and utilities.
- **Speculative stocks** have a high probability of experiencing a low rate of return and a low probability of experiencing high returns. Many junior gold mining stocks are considered speculative stocks.
- **Growth stocks** are defined as stocks that have posted a higher rate of return than similar stocks of the same risk category.
- **Value stocks** are stocks that are trading at below their worth. Managers buy these stocks because they believe that, when the market recognizes the corporation's potential, their value will increase.
- **Large cap stocks** are stocks with large market cap. In Canada, stocks with market cap of $1 billion and up are considered to be large cap stocks.
- **Mid-cap stocks** are stocks with market cap between $500 million and $1 billion.

- **Small cap stocks** are stocks with market cap of less than $500 million.[1]
- **Canadian stocks** are stocks of companies whose head offices are located in Canada. For example, as Alcan's head office is located Montreal, even though almost half of its sales are to companies outside of North America, and it is traded not only in Canada but also on the New York Stock Exchange, it is still considered a Canadian stock.
- Stocks can also be grouped by industry such as technology, resource stocks or geographic locations such as European or emerging market stocks.

These groups are not mutually exclusive, as a given stock can belong to more than one group. For example, BCE is a Canadian, large cap, blue chip stock.

Pension managers are allowed to invest in any stocks that fall within the plan's investment objectives and policies. The foreign property rule limits the amount of foreign property (including stocks and bonds) to 20%. However it will be raised to 25% in 2000 and 30% in 2001 and beyond.[2]

Why Do Managers Want to Put Stocks Into the Pension Fund?

The main reason for having stocks in the portfolio is growth. Out of all asset classes, in the long run, equity has the highest rate return. For example, the annual compounded rate of return from 1950 to 1999 for the U.S. Stock Total Return Index[3] was 14%, while the annual compounded rate of return for the TSE 300 Total Return Index[4] was 10.9%.

Risk of Equity

The sponsor of a plan must be willing to be patient. The long-term superior gain experienced by stocks is often associated with short-term cyclical influences. This implies that the value of the stocks can often be below the purchase price. Also, because companies can make mistakes in their business decisions and can even go bankrupt, investors run the risk of never recouping their losses, as was the case for those who invested in Bre-X.

FIXED INCOME BONDS

Another way for a corporation or agency to raise funds is to issue bonds. Bonds are a form of debt. The bondholder lends money to the bond issuer and, in return, the issuer agrees to repay the principal on the maturity date, and also to make periodic interest payments to the bondholder.

Fundamentals of Bonds

The following are a few terms that are often used when describing bonds.

- **Principal** (denomination) is the amount that the

bond issuer agrees to pay on the date of maturity. Another term is *face value*. It is important to note that the principal is not necessarily the market price of the bond.

- **Par, discount** and **premium** refer to how the current trading price of the bond relates to its face value. If the current price is the same as the face value, the bond is trading at par. If the current price is below par, the bond is trading at a discount, while if the current price is above par, the bond is trading at a premium.
- **Coupon payment** is the fixed amount of interest received by bondholders in a regular period. In general, the coupon payment is paid out on a semi-annual basis. However, holders of zero coupon bonds receive no periodic interest payments, but are instead paid the face value of the bond at its maturity, even when the bond is sold at a discounted value. For example, a zero coupon bond with face value of $1,000 may issue at $900.
- **Coupon rate** indicates the income investors will receive over the bond's life.
- **Term to maturity** is the remaining life of a bond. Take, for example, a bond issued in April 1998 with a term of ten years. In April 2000, it will be referred to as an eight-year bond. There are three segments of bond markets based on the maturity:
  - Money market instruments are short-term issues with maturities of one year or less.
  - Notes are intermediate-term with maturities from one to ten years.
  - Bonds are long-term with maturities of greater than ten years

Bond Rating

In Canada, there are two main agencies that independently rate different debt instruments, Dominion Bond Rating Services and Canadian Bond Rating Services. Debt rating is based on three factors: likelihood of default, nature of the obligation and protection of the obligation.

The following are the different rating categories, accompanied by a brief description of each:

- **AAA:** Bonds with the highest quality. Companies with this rating are generally large national and multi-national corporations that are essential to the Canadian economy.
- **AA:** Bonds with very good quality. Companies are still very good but the margin of assets may not be as large as the AAA companies.
- **A:** Bonds with good quality and positive long-term investment characteristics
- **BBB:** These are medium grade bonds. Bonds that are rated from the range of AAA to BBB are considered to be investment grade bonds. For all these

bonds, the protection of interest and principal are certain.
- **BB:** These bonds are lower medium grade and lean towards being speculative. The protection of interest and principal are not certain. Any bonds rated BB or below are considered speculative or high-yield bonds. These bonds will pay a higher coupon in order to compensate for their speculative nature. Pension managers often do not invest in high-yield bonds because of the conservative nature of their fund's policy.
- **B:** These bonds may have difficulty in paying interest and principal, especially in a recession.
- **CCC:** These are highly speculative bonds; there is a good chance that these bonds may have to default in the future.
- **CC:** These bonds have defaulted on either the interest or principal.
- **C:** Bonds with the lowest rating.

Why Do Managers Put Bonds Into Their Portfolios?

Bonds traditionally form a significant portion of a pension plan's portfolio. The plan is the bondholder and it is also the lender of the debt and therefore has the preferred right to claim the interest and principal, compared to the equity holder. This provides more security to the plan. In addition, the regular income stream from the interest payment also implies that the cash flow to the plan is more predictable. And the periodic re-investment of this income stream also allows the power of compounding to grow the plan's assets.

Risks of Bonds

In order for the power of compounding to occur, a bond's reinvested rate of return must be greater than the loss of purchase power due to inflation. Bonds also face other risks including:

- Default risk—issuer goes bankrupt or refuses to pay
- Interest rate risk—if interest rates increase, the bond price will decrease and
- Call risk—some bonds are callable bonds that the issuers have the right to retire. The issuer will pay the principal back but not the future interest payments. This usually occurs when the interest rate environment is low. For the bondholders, this implies future re-investment risk. However, in order to compensate for the possibility of calling the bonds, the coupon payment is generally higher.

OTHER FIXED INCOME PRODUCTS

There are other products that managers may purchase with pension plan assets.

Money Market Instruments

These are short-term debt securities, such as Treasury bills, issued by the government of Canada. These are highly liquid and virtually risk-free debts that are often regarded as a form of cash. Pension managers use money market instruments for payments to the plan participants or to purchase securities or bonds for the pension plan.

Guaranteed Investment Certificates (GICs)

These are deposit arrangements. The investor, for example a pension plan, will deposit money in the bank for a specified period and in return, on the maturity date, the bank will pay the investor back the deposited amount along with a preset amount of interest. GICs are different from bonds because they are not marketable securities, as there is not a market for buying or selling these instruments.

Pension managers use GICs because they help to match the cash flow of assets and liabilities and can also provide comfort to the contributors by reducing the volatility of the plan's assets (GICs are recorded at book value until maturity).

Mortgage-Backed Securities

These are bonds secured by mortgages. Although mortgages are non-marketable, if the mortgages are placed in a pool and the cash flow is redirected to the pass-through issued on this pool, the new pass-through securities may be traded in the secondary market, with a net effect of converting illiquid mortgages into liquid securities.

MUTUAL FUNDS

This investment vehicle has increased in popularity in recent years. Mutual funds are pools of asset that belong to many shareholders. These pools are used to acquire investment products, such as stocks or bonds. Mutual funds are used in many of the smaller group registered retirement savings plans (RRSPs) and also in defined contribution plans.

There are two major types of mutual funds: open-end and closed-end funds. Closed-end funds raise capital when they are first set up but cannot continue to sell additional shares. The shares of the closed-end fund can be transferred from one shareholder to another and can be sold at a discount or premium to the net asset value. Open-end funds can sell shares to new investors and redeem shares from unit holders on an ongoing basis. The net asset value is the share price, and it fluctuates with the value of the stocks and bonds within the portfolio.

Benefits of Mutual Funds

Liquidity: Mutual funds are easy and convenient to buy and sell. For most of the funds, investors can buy or sell on any business day.

Flexibility: After any major change in the investment policy of the plan, investors can easily change from one mutual fund to another.

Diversification: This is a risk reduction strategy. Mutual funds contain a range of securities, asset classes and/or geographic regions, which makes them less risky than holding one or two individual stocks.

Cost efficiencies: Through the economy of scale, transaction cost of equities is lower. Also, the plan does not need to employ custodial and recordkeeping services because such services are provided by the mutual fund itself.

OTHER INVESTMENT PRODUCTS

Index Funds

Many of the large pension plans have invested some of their assets in index funds. An index fund is a mix of securities that replicates the broad base group of securities or bonds, such as the TSE 300 or Scotia Bond index. This passive management style has some advantages:

- The management fee is lower.
- The portfolio is highly liquid: It is easy to sell the stocks or bonds into the market.
- In recent years, the index funds have experienced relatively strong performance.

Venture Capital and Private Placement

Venture capital involves investing in new or expanding businesses. This is a high-risk exercise and could enjoy high investment returns. A pension plan may invest in venture capital through limited partnership arrangements, or through the private placement of securities in a new company. Private placement can be for securities or for bonds. Most of the bonds issued through private placement are to large, institutional lenders.

INVESTMENT FUNDAMENTALS AND PLAN TRUSTEES

The reason for developing a pension fund is to provide employees with income when they retire. In order to achieve this goal, the plan must accumulate assets now to meet its future obligations. The plan is not simply a trading account where the investment manager can buy and sell different investment vehicles to increase the worth of the plan. One must establish an investment policy, evaluate the investment opportunities, implement portfolio management decisions and continue to monitor the plan's performance for changes.

The investment funding process begins with managers understanding the objectives and policies of the trustee. It is important for the trustee to possess the knowledge of investment fundamentals. This provides a strong base from which to communicate with the investment managers and to understand the factors that can influence the objectives of the plans as well as the long-term risks and rewards offered by different investment vehicles. This will result in better choices being made by investment managers, which will, in turn, add more value to the plan.

ENDNOTES

1. The criteria for large, small and mid-cap stocks are not rigid. It depends on the country and the market conditions, and also on the subjective opinions of fund managers.

2. Finance Canada, "Budget 2000" (28 February 2000).

3. Includes all common stocks on the NYSE, AMEX and NASDAQ markets, excluding REITs, ADRs, Referreds, Rights and Warrants.

4. Information for the period January 1950 to December 1955 was obtained from the Canadian Financial Markets Research Center, London, Ontario, Anthony DiMeo and Dexter Robinson, "99 Andex Chart for Canadian Investors" (Windsor, Ontario: Andex Associates Inc., 1999).

CHAPTER 9

Pension Fund Investments: Legal Aspects

by Michael Mazzuca and Roberto Tomassini

INTRODUCTION

Pension fund investments are regulated by both legislative and regulatory enactments by federal and provincial governments, as well as by principles and standards developed by the courts, which make up the "common law." The first part of this chapter reviews the statutory and regulatory regime applicable to pension fund investment, while the second part focuses on the common law duty of plan administrators with respect to investments.

THE STATUTORY AND REGULATORY REGIME IN CANADA

Investments of registered pension plans are required to meet the standards set by the relevant provincial or federal regulatory regimes. Plans falling under federal jurisdiction are required to comply with the *Pension Benefits Standards Act* (PBSA).[1] Several provinces, including Manitoba and Saskatchewan, follow the PBSA rules. Others combine the PBSA rules with specified provincial requirements (Alberta, British Columbia, Newfoundland and Nova Scotia). Prince Edward Island, the Northwest Territories, the Yukon and Nunavut are without standards of their own. Quebec and New Brunswick have their own investment rules. In addition, it must be noted that provisions in the *Income Tax Act* regulate foreign investment of all plans.

Effective in 1990, Ontario Regulation 909 (the "Ontario Regulations")[2] under the *Pension Benefits Act* (OPBA)[3] originally ushered in a new statutory standard

of pension fund investments with specific investment standards for pension plans registered in Ontario. However, the investment provisions under the Regulation were recently amended.[4] According to these amendments, effective March 3, 2000, the administrator of a pension plan may voluntarily adopt the federal investment regulations. Effective January 1, 2001, administrators of all pension plans registered in Ontario must ensure that their pension fund complies with the federal investment rules. If there are any pension fund investments that do not meet the requirements of the federal investment regulations on January 1, 2001, then the administrator must dispose of these investments by no later than January 1, 2005.

Each of the regulatory schemes of investment represents an attempt at resolving the tensions that have historically been at play in pension fund investment rules. Pension fund administrators have been subject to common law fiduciary obligations, including an obligation to invest pension assets prudently. In addition, there has been an evolution from the *legal list* restrictions on investments to much broader qualitative and quantitative investment. The legal list requirements governing pension investments had their origins in statutes governing permissible investments for life insurance companies. Financial scandals in the late 19th and early 20th centuries, compounded by the stock market collapse in 1929, induced governments in the United States and Canada to legislatively limit the types of investments in which life insurance companies could place their assets. These limits were both quantitative and qualitative.

Quantitative limits ensured that life insurance companies did not invest too great a proportion of their assets in any one type of investment. For example, limits were placed on the proportion of total assets that could be invested in equities and in real estate. Qualitative limits ensured that certain types of investments, especially equities, were quality and not speculative grade. Typically, for example, the qualitative standard would only permit investments in equities with prescribed dividend histories.

The legal list approach reached its zenith in the aftermath of the 1929 stock market crash. In 1948, the federal government amended the life insurance legislation by introducing the so-called basket clause. This permitted regulated companies to invest up to 3% of their ledger assets in loans and investments not otherwise permitted by the legislation. Real estate investment rules were also relaxed to permit investments in income producing properties. Liberalization of the legal list restrictions continued through successive reforms, and they are not generally considered to be overly restrictive today. The pension investment regulations of each jurisdiction must be considered with respect to the investments by plans governed by those jurisdictions. This chapter, however, will focus in some detail on the investment provisions of the federal legislation, since these are the dominant investment rules across the country. The investment rules of other jurisdictions will also be considered, but in less detail.

Statutory Standard of Care

Also at play in the pension plan investment sphere is the *prudent person standard,* which is discussed in detail in the second part of this chapter. The prudent person standard has always been a feature of the fiduciary obligations owed by fund administrators to plan beneficiaries. In the past, prudence was controlled, and to a certain extent overshadowed, by the legal list requirements. However, the courts did impose the prudence standard on pension fund trustees well before it was mandated by legislation. In *Cowan v. Scargill,* Sir Robert Megarry described the common law investment duties of pension fund trustees as follows:

Fourth, the standard required of the trustee in exercising his powers of investment is that he must take such care as an ordinary prudent man would take if he were minded to make an investment for the benefit of other people for whom he felt morally bound to provide.

That duty includes the duty to seek advice on matters which the trustee does not understand, such as the making of investments, and on receiving that advice to act with the same degree of prudence. The requirement is not discharged merely by showing that the trustee has acted in good faith

and with sincerity. Honesty and sincerity are not the same as prudence and reasonableness. Some of the most sincere people are the most unreasonable.

Accordingly, although the trustee who takes advice on investments is not bound to accept and act on that advice, he is not entitled to reject it merely because he sincerely disagrees with it unless in addition to being sincere he is acting as an ordinary prudent man would act.[5]

Most jurisdictions have imposed a statutory "prudent person" requirement for pension fund investments. The federal, British Columbia, New Brunswick, Nova Scotia, Ontario and Quebec pension laws require an administrator to exercise the care, diligence and skill in the investment of pension fund assets that a person of ordinary prudence would exercise in dealing with the property of another person.[6] These statutes also specifically make this same standard applicable to agents of pension fund administrators, such as investment managers and counsellors. With the exception of British Columbia, these statutes also require that the administrator and its agent use all relevant knowledge and skill they possess in their professional capacities in making investment decisions.[7]

For example, OPBA in Subsection 22(1) states:
The administrator of a pension plan shall exercise the care, diligence and skill in the administration and investment of the pension fund that a person of ordinary prudence would exercise in dealing with the property of another person.

Subsection 22(2) of OPBA further provides:
The administrator of a pension plan shall use in the administration of the pension plan and in the administration and investment of the pension fund all relevant knowledge and skill that the administrator possesses or, by reason of his or her profession, business or calling, ought to possess.

Thus, the objective prudence standard set out in Subsection 22(1) is amplified by the subjective standards of Subsection 22(2). Taken together, these subsections require not only that fund administrators act in accordance with an objective prudence standard, but that they employ as well all relevant skill and experience that they may have by reason of their business, profession or calling. The latter requirement implies, of course, that professional trustees will be held to a higher standard than lay trustees.

By virtue of Subsection 22(8) of OPBA, these standards are equally applicable to agents of pension fund administrators, including custodians and investment managers and counsellors. However, pursuant to Subsection 22(7), an administrator who employs an agent must personally select the agent and be satisfied that the agent is suitable to perform the act for which the agent is employed. In addition, the administrator must carry out prudent and reasonable supervision of the agent in the performance of its activities.

The Federal Regulations

The Regulations under PBSA (the "PBSA Regulation")[8] establish the investment rules for federally registered pension plans, as well as for pension plans registered in provinces that have by reference incorporated the federal standards and for pension plans registered in jurisdictions with no applicable pension legislation. Effective July 1, 1993, the PBSA Regulation was amended to adopt the prudent portfolio rule. Section 6 of the PBSA Regulation provides that every plan shall require that its funds be invested in accordance with the standards outlined in Schedule III to the PBSA Regulation, which sets out the permissible investments.

Schedule III was amended to adopt the prudent portfolio approach.[9] This has created some differences in the application of the PBSA rules to provincial plans. For example, Saskatchewan, Manitoba and Alberta require that the provincially registered plans comply with the federal investment rules as amended from time to time. British Columbia incorporates the PBSA Regulation as effective on July 1, 1993. Ontario adopts the federal investment rules as they read on December 31, 1999.

Quantity Restrictions

A pension fund is not permitted to invest more than 10% of the total book value of plan assets in any one company, including associated companies and affiliated corporations. There are specific exemptions to this general limitation. Fully insured funds held by a bank, trust company or other financial institution are not subject to the limit. In addition, the following funds are exempt:

- Mutual or pooled funds that themselves comply with the federal investment rules
- Unallocated general funds of life insurers
- An investment corporation, real estate corporation or resource corporation securities issued or fully guaranteed by the government of Canada, a province or territory
- A fund composed of fully government-guaranteed and mortgage-backed securities and
- A fund that replicates the composition of a widely recognized index of a broad class of securities traded at a public exchange.

The fund is also precluded from investing greater than 5% of the book value of the fund in any one property, 15% of the book value of the fund in resource properties and 25% of the book value of the fund in real estate and resource properties combined. Sections 11 through 13 of Schedule III of the PBSA Regulation prohibit an investment that would result in the acquisition of greater than 30% of the voting shares of a corporation. This limit does not apply to investments in real estate, resource or an investment corporation subject to certain specified conditions. These conditions provide that investments in a real estate corporation cannot exceed the 30% threshold unless the corporation undertakes to provide to the Superintendent copies of its annual financial statements, audited financial statements, lists and market value of assets, a list of officers, directors and shareholders and a certificate indicating that the corporation is complying with the undertaking. Other restrictions require an appraisal of any real property if requested by the Superintendent, a prohibition against lending to a related party of the plan and a prohibition against holding greater than 30% of the voting shares in another real estate corporation. Similar restrictions apply to resource and investment corporations.[10]

Related Party Transactions

For purposes of PBSA, *related party* means a person who is the plan administrator (including pension committee members); an officer, director or employee of the plan administrator; a person holding or investing assets of the plan (including officers, directors and employees of the holder or investor); an association or union representing members of the plan (including officers or employees of the association or union); a participating employer (including its officers, directors and employees); a member of the plan; and a person who owns, together with the spouse or child, more than 10% of the voting shares of the sponsoring corporate employer. Generally, a related party's spouse or child is also related. In addition, affiliated corporations and persons who have substantial ownership of the sponsoring employer are considered *related*.

The administrator is prohibited from, directly or indirectly, lending monies to a related party, investing in securities of a related party or entering into transactions with a related party on behalf of the plan. The same provisions apply to persons for the 12-month period after the date the person ceased to be a related party.

Transactions with related parties are permitted only if:

- The transaction is required for the operation of the plan and its terms and conditions are not less favourable than market conditions.
- The purchase of the securities of a related party is transacted at a public exchange or
- The value of the transaction is nominal or the transaction is immaterial to the plan.

Statement of Investment Policies and Procedures

The administrator of the pension plan must also have established a statement of investment policy. The contents of such statements must include policies and procedures in respect of the plan's portfolio of investments and loans, including:

- Categories of investments and loans, including derivatives, options and futures
- Diversification of the investment portfolio
- Asset mix and rate-of-return expectations
- Liquidity of investments
- The lending of cash or securities
- The retention or delegation of voting rights acquired through plan investments
- The method of, and the basis for, the valuation of investments that are not regularly traded at a public exchange and
- Related party transactions and the criteria used to establish whether a transaction is nominal or material.

The policy must consider all factors that may affect the funding and solvency of the plan and the ability of the plan to meet its financial obligations. The plan administrator must conduct an annual review of the policy. For defined benefit plans, a copy of the policy must be provided to the actuary. Further, any amendments to the policy must be submitted to the plan actuary and any pension committee that has been established. Administrators are not required to file the statement with the Office of the Superintendent of Financial Institutions (OSFI). However, an annual compliance form must be completed by the plan administrator and filed with OSFI.

Alberta Regulations

The Alberta *Employment Pension Plans Act*[11] incorporates the PBSA investment standards, as amended from time to time. A written statement of investment policies and procedures must have been established for the pension plan by no later than September 1, 1997. The contents of such statements are set out in Section 36.1 of the Alberta Regulations.[12]

Manitoba Regulations

The Manitoba *Pension Benefits Act*[13] provides that the investment rules for Manitoba are the same as those for the federal jurisdiction as described in PBSA.

New Brunswick Regulations

New Brunswick introduced its Regulations governing investments effective December 31, 1991. The rules parallel the approach in several other provinces in that a prudent person rule is adopted. Further, a statement of investment policies and goals must be prepared pursuant to Section 44.[14]

The Regulations impose quantity restrictions. Not more than 10% of the book value of plan assets can be invested in one person subject to prescribed exceptions. The exceptions cover fully insured deposits at financial institutions; segregated, mutual or pooled funds that comply with prescribed requirements; investment corporations subject to certain conditions and that comply with pension plan investment limits; and bonds or debentures issued by the federal, provincial or territorial government, the International Bank for Reconstruction and Development (established by the International Monetary Fund or under the Bretton Woods Agreements), the Inter-American Development Bank, the Caribbean Development Bank or the Asian Development Bank.

Securities lending is also restricted. It is permitted only when expressly authorized in the statement of investment policy. It must be secured by cash or readily marketable investments valued at least 105% of the loan and valued and maintained at or above this level weekly. Loans are permitted subject to certain restrictions.

Newfoundland Regulations

New rules under the Newfoundland *Pension Benefits Act*[15] were adopted effective January 1, 1997. Investments made previously must comply with the new rules by no later than January 1, 2000. The rules do also require an administrator to establish a written statement of investment policies and procedures similar to those required by other jurisdictions. The investment rules adopted by the Newfoundland Regulations are similar to those adopted in the federal jurisdiction.

Nova Scotia Regulations

Nova Scotia adopted a new investment Regulations effective January 31, 1996.[16] These Regulations do reflect the prudent portfolio approach and also require the adoption of a written statement of investment policies and procedures. The rules adopted under the Nova Scotia Regulations are similar to those adopted in the federal jurisdiction.

Saskatchewan Regulations

The Saskatchewan *Pension Benefits Act* adopts the PBSA investments standards as amended from time to time. Therefore, the current PBSA standards apply to Saskatchewan investments.[17]

Quebec Regulations

The Quebec *Supplemental Pension Plans Act* (QSPPA)[18] also adopts a "prudent person" approach. Pension plans are required to establish and adopt an investment policy. The contents of the investment policy are set out in Section 170. Investment policies must be formulated in accordance with the various quantitative and qualitative standards outlined in QSPPA. Section 172 provides that a maximum of 10% of the book value of the assets of the plan may be invested directly or indirectly in any one property or loan or group of loans. This limitation is subject to a number of exceptions found in Section 173. For example, the 10% limit rule does not apply to securities issued or guaranteed by the federal government or one of the provincial governments.

Section 175 provides that subject to certain limited exceptions, a plan shall not hold more than 30% of the voting shares in a legal person. Section 176 lists prohibited loan transactions. For example, no loan may be granted to a member of a pension committee or to a shareholder of an employer/plan administrator where the shareholder holds more than 10% of the capital stock of the employer. These investment rules came into effect January 1, 1990.

British Columbia Regulations

The British Columbia *Pension Benefits Standards Act*[19] generally took effect on January 1, 1993. The investment regulations made pursuant to the act were effective as of July 1, 1994. The Regulations adopt the federal PBSA rules under Schedule III as of July 1, 1993. An investment policy must have been prepared for existing plans by July 1, 1994 and is subject to annual review. Investments that do not conform with the investment rules must have been brought into conformity on the earlier of their maturity date, if any, or July 1, 1999.

Income Tax Act (Canada)

The *Income Tax Act* (ITA)[20] also regulates pension fund investments in a number of respects.

Foreign Property Limits

ITA limits the proportion of the cost amounts of pension fund property that may be invested in foreign property. The cost amount of property is roughly its book value. Foreign property holdings in excess of the maximum limits attract a monthly 1% penalty tax. The foreign property limit for 1994 and subsequent years is 20% of the book value of the total fund. Foreign property generally includes property located outside of Canada, shares and debt obligations of corporations that are not Canadian corporations, and interests in trusts and partnerships that are not located in Canada.

It should be noted that in its February 28, 2000 budget, the federal government announced its intention to increase the foreign property limits for registered pension plans and other deferred income plans. These limits would be increased from 20% to 25% for 2000 and to 30% after 2000.

Prohibited Investments

Similar to provincial pension standards legislation, Regulation 8514 under the ITA prohibits certain pension investments on conflict-of-interest grounds. Regulation 8514 prohibits pension fund investments in the capital stock or debt of:
- A participating employer
- A person connected with the employer who participates in the plan
- A member of the plan
- A person or partnership that controls, directly or indirectly, a person or partnership referred to above
- A person or partnership that does not deal at arm's length with a person or partnership referred to above.[21]

Regulation 8514 does, however, exempt certain investments from the category of excluded investments. These include publicly traded shares and debt instruments, insured mortgages and investments made prior to March 28, 1988.

THE COMMON LAW PRINCIPLES APPLICABLE TO PENSION FUND INVESTMENT: THE PRUDENT PERSON STANDARD

As discussed in the first part of this chapter, pension plan administrators and trustees are subject to both legislated restrictions and common law prudence standards when investing pension plan assets under their control. The first part of the chapter was primarily concerned with the legislative and regulatory schemes in place throughout Canadian jurisdictions that set the standards for investments. This part addresses the common law prudence standard obligations on pension fund investors. The focus of the prudent person standard in the pension investment context is on the process through which investment decisions are made, implemented and monitored, rather than on the performance of the actual investments.

The prudent person rule has its origins in the common law of trusts developed by common law courts over several hundreds of years. All provinces in Canada, save for Quebec, are governed by the trust law principles. In Quebec, the Civil Code codifies similar trust principles with respect to the fiduciary duties of trustees when investing the property of a trust.

Generally, the common law standard of care for a trustee is that which an ordinary prudent business person would exercise in conducting his or her own affairs.[22] That is, a pension plan fiduciary will not be liable for errors of judgment provided he or she exercises the same degree of caution with respect to investments as an ordinary prudent business person would while managing his or her own affairs.

The common law standard is a minimum standard applicable to all trustees. However, as noted above, in several Canadian jurisdictions, a more onerous standard of care is imposed under the applicable pension benefits legislation. The legislation requires the plan administrators or trustees to exercise the care, diligence and skill in the investment of pension funds that a person of ordinary prudence would exercise in dealing with the property *of another person*. This higher standard also has its roots in the common law and can be traced to the oft-quoted statement of Lord Justice Lindeley in the 1886 English case of *Re Whiteley:*

> The duty of a trustee is not to take such care only as a prudent man would take if he had only himself to consider, the duty rather is to take such care as an ordinary prudent man would take if you were minded to make an investment for the benefit of other people for whom he felt morally bound to provide.[23]

The later standard is more onerous because presumably people are more cautious and less speculative with the property of another entrusted to them than they might be with their own property.

There is little guidance from Canadian jurisprudence on the application of the prudent person rule in the context of pension plan investments. However, as noted elsewhere in this work, American case law developed under the *Employee Retirement Income Security Act of 1974* (ERISA)[24] does provide some guidance in this regard. In reviewing the American authorities one must bear in mind that U.S. case law is not binding on Canadian courts. Nonetheless, consideration and reliance on American authorities is commonplace when Canadian courts tread in uncharted waters, particularly as ERISA is based on common law.

The reader should also bear in mind that some Canadian jurisdictions impose a higher standard of care on pension plan administrators and trustees than the equivalent prudent person rule in ERISA. ERISA prudence standard is set out in Section 404, which states:

> a fiduciary shall discharge his duties with respect to a plan solely in the interest of the participants and the beneficiaries and with the care, skill, prudence and diligence under the circumstances then prevailing that a prudent man acting in a like capacity and familiar with such matters would use in the conduct of an enterprise of a like character and with like aims.[25]

The emphasis in this provision is on the standard of care and judgment that a prudent person exercises in the management of his or her own affairs, whereas, as noted above, in many Canadian jurisdictions the *Whiteley* standard has been adopted. Therefore, pension plan fiduciaries would be well advised to consider the standards as developed in U.S. case law as a minimum of what is expected of pension plan administrators and trustees with respect to pension plan investment in the Canadian context.

As discussed in Section I, Chapter 6, dealing with fiduciary duties in general, there is some authority to support the view that the standard of conduct expected of pension plan fiduciaries varies depending on the degree of knowledge and experience of the trustee or administrator whose conduct is being reviewed. Some courts have imposed a higher standard of care on professional trustees who are in a particular profession and hold themselves out to the world for employment as such, thereby representing themselves as reasonably competent to carry out the business they undertake in the course of such profession. In these circumstances, the court may impose upon professional trustees an obligation to show the care or diligence as is exercised in the ordinary and proper course, *and* such skill as is usual and requisite, in the business for which they receive payment.[26]

However, the leading judicial pronouncement on the issue in Canada by the Supreme Court of Canada contradicts this assertion. In *Fales v. Canada Permanent Trust Co.*[27] the Court stated:

> The weight of authority to the present has been against making a distinction between a widow, acting as trustee for her husband's estate, and trust company performing the same role. Receipt of fees has not served to ground, nor to increase exposure to, liability. Every trustee has been expected to act as the person of ordinary prudence would act. This standard, of course, may be relaxed or modified up to a point of the terms of a will and, in the present case, there can be no doubt that the co-trustees were given wide latitude. But however wide the discretionary powers contained in the will, a trustee's primary duty is preservation of the trust assets, and the enlargement of recognized powers does not relieve him of the duty of using ordinary skill and prudence, nor from the application of common sense.

This position may have been modified to some extent by the Supreme Court of Canada in *Hodgkinson v. Simms*[28] where the Supreme Court put particular emphasis on the specialization of knowledge and expertise of an investment counsellor to support the holding that investment advisors owed a fiduciary duty to their clients. It should be noted however that this case concerned the failure of an investment counsellor to disclose his interest in a real estate investment that he had recommended to the client. As such, the Supreme Court did not directly address the appropriate standard of care to be imposed on professional trustees or advisors when making investment decisions in the normal course.

In a similar vein, the Supreme Court, held in a more recent decision relating to the Quebec law of "mandatary," which is somewhat analogous to the common law of fiduciary, that a professional portfolio manager should be held to a higher or more stringent standard of care. This is particularly the case where the manager's client has very limited knowledge of investments.[29]

Procedural Prudence

The focus of the prudent person rule is not so much on what investment decisions are made but, rather, the process by which those decisions are arrived at.

> Prudence is a test of conduct not performance.... Neither the overall performance of the portfolio nor the performance of the individual investment should be viewed essential to the (prudence issue). Prudence should be measured principally by the process through which investment strategies and tactics are developed, adopted, implemented and monitored. Prudence is demonstrated by the process through which risk is managed rather than by the labelling of specific investments as either prudent or imprudent. It is the way in which they are used, and how decisions as to their use are made, that should be examined to determine whether the prudent standard has been met.[30]

If a trustee makes investment decisions after following a proper decision making process, he or she will not be in breach of his or her fiduciary duty and the prudence standard, even if the investment turns out to be unprofitable. Administrators and trustees must be concerned with adopting appropriate investigative methods when considering particular investment decisions and must be sensitive to the need to review investment decisions once they have been implemented. At a *minimum,* this requires plan fiduciaries to do the following in respect of any contemplated investment:

- Undertake a complete and impartial investigation of all of the advantages and disadvantages of a particular investment.
- Obtain sufficient information to make informed decisions about an investment.
- Retain qualified experts and consultants.
- Assess whether the investment is reasonably designed to further the purposes of the plan and in the context of the plan's overall investment portfolio.
- Compare the contemplated investment or transaction with other available options.
- Monitor the investment on a regular basis with reasonable diligence.
- If necessary, dispose of improper investments but only after advice from experts.

The Requirement to Obtain Sufficient Information

The key aspect of the prudent person rule in the context of investments is the obligation imposed on administrators and trustees to *undertake a thorough, complete and independent investigation prior to making any particular investment decision.*[31] Failure to conduct an appropriate investigation could result in a plan administrator or trustee falling astray of the prudence standard, particularly where it is determined that an adequate and thorough investigation would have revealed the investment was objectively imprudent.[32]

In *Brock v. Wells Fargo Bank, N.A.*[33] the U.S. Department of Labor was seeking an injunction against pension plan trustees who had approved a $4.5 million loan to a real estate developer to finance a particular project. Although the trustees obtained an appraisal of the property, the court found that the appraisal contained many deficiencies that were not rectified by the trustees through further investigation. In concluding that an injunction against the trustees was appropriate, the court stated:

> The evidence in this case strongly indicates that the trustees did not study this investment with the care required of pension-plan fiduciaries under ERISA. Although the testimony ... convinces this court that the trustees sincerely believed they were making an excellent investment in the best interest of the pension plan, it also seems clear that the trustees did not follow all of the appropriate methods to investigate and structure the investment. They did not properly appraise the property or adjust that appraisal to reflect problems that it overlooked, including a lack of water permits and other land-use approvals. They did not consider what they would do if the water permits were not issued or if water did not become available. They conducted no market surveys. They neglected to examine possible competition in the sale of the lots. They failed to identify the source of funds for development if the lots do not sell as quickly as hoped. They did not consider plans for the property in the event of default. They did not analyze what problems might arise in the event of default, including management difficulties or liability for unrelated business taxes. In short, no matter how successful an investment the loan might turn out to be, the trustees did not gather the information that a prudent investor would gather before making a $4.5 million payment.[34]

In *Metropolitan Toronto Pension Plan v. Aetna Life Assurance Co. of Canada*[35] the trustees of pension and benefits funds brought an action for breach of fiduciary duty against the Aetna Assurance Co., which undertook investment administration responsibility for various pension funds. The contract with the insurance company specifically provided that investments were to be in accordance with a guideline and schedule of acceptable loan investments. The insurance company submitted to the trustees for their consideration a mortgage loan that did not fall within the investment guidelines, and further the insurance company did not bring this fact to the trustees' attention.

The investment at issue was a mortgage loan on a seniors' building that due to flagrant mismanagement had deteriorated to a point that the entire building had to be gutted, and the occupancy dropped to zero despite waiting lists of seniors for positions in the building. In holding that the insurance company breached its fiduciary duty to the trustees, the court noted Aetna's failure to properly investigate the investment and monitor the state of the security. In particular, Aetna acted negligently in that:

- It failed to obtain and investigate corporate financial statements of the borrowers.
- It failed to obtain and examine the existing leases for the building.
- It failed to obtain and examine operating statements for the project. It failed to properly inspect the security when considering the loan.
- An inspection would have revealed serious deterioration in the physical condition of the building and a declining occupancy rate due to mismanagement.
- It failed to properly monitor and investigate the state of the building on a periodic basis.
- It failed to take legal action despite the deterioration of the security on the loan and arrears on the mortgage and taxes of over $230,000.

Although the case considered the duty of a professional investment counsel, the issues raised in this case apply equally to pension plan trustees, particularly where they undertake to make mortgage loans without professional advisors.

When evaluating fiduciary compliance with the prudence standard, courts are likely to be concerned with whether or not the trustees or administrators, at the time they engaged in the transactions, employed the appropriate methods to investigate the merits of the investment and to structure it accordingly.[36] This evaluation of the fiduciary's compliance with the prudence standard is mandatory notwithstanding that the administrator or trustee has complied with the explicit statutory restrictions on investments. In *Fink v. National Savings and Trust Company et al.,* the court held that pension employers' security could be in violation of their fiduciary duty as prescribed by the prudent person standard despite the fact that such an investment was in compliance with ERISA provisions regarding acquisition of employer security and exempt from the diversification requirements for plans holding employer securities.[37]

In *Whitfield v. Cohen,* the court found a pension plan administrator and trustee liable for breach of fiduciary duty for failure to abide by the prudent person standard with respect to investments. The administrator, on the advice of a co-administrator, transferred a substantial portion of the plan's assets to an investment management company without investigating and assessing the company's performance and the qualifications of its management. The court noted the following failures:

- Failure to make independent inquiries into the finances and review financial statements of the investment company
- Failure to inquire about the details of the company's investment policy
- Failure to investigate the location or specific value of secured properties
- Failure to inquire as to the experience of other pension plans that invested with the company
- Failure to obtain references or recommendations from other investors in the company
- Failure to consider alternate proposals from other investment management firms
- Failure to inquire as to the fees that would be charged by the investment company
- Failure to inquire as to the qualifications of the company's management personnel
- Failure to inquire whether the company or its key management individuals were registered in accordance with the applicable investment advisor legislation.[38]

Expert Advice

A trustee or administrator is not relieved of the obligations imposed by the prudent person rule and the fiduciary obligation to employ appropriate methods for investigating the merits of a contemplated investment merely because he or she lacks familiarity with investments.[39] Prudence is measured according to an *objective standard.* It considers how a prudent person familiar with the investments at issue and with similar capacity would act.

It is not uncommon in the pension plan context that the administrators and trustees responsible for making the investment decisions are not particularly experienced or knowledgeable in such matters. For union or jointly trusteed plans, union or employer executives or officials are often given the task of making plan investment decisions. It is these persons who must be particularly concerned about their exposure to liability for failing to comply with the prudence standards.

While the courts recognize that not all plan fiduciaries can be experts in all phases of investments and administration, this does not relieve someone who has assumed the office of the fiduciary obligations that attach to it. Rather, the non-professional trustee has an *affirmative duty to seek the advice and counsel of independent experts* where his or her own knowledge and experience is insufficient under the circumstances.[40]

In *Katsaros v. Cody* the union trustees of the Teamsters Local 282 Pension Trust Fund were subject to a claim of breach of fiduciary duty in respect of investment decisions, involving a loan for approximately $2 million to a bank. Ostensibly, the trustees fulfilled their fiduciary obligations to investigate the contemplated investment in that they received and reviewed extensive disclosure regarding the financial situation of the bank, and two of the trustees personally visited and viewed the real estate properties that were offered as security for the loan. On the basis of this investigation, the trustees entered into the transaction. However, two years after the loan had been completed, the bank was closed by federal and state regulatory officials and ceased making payments to the pension plan. Two plan beneficiaries and the Department of Labor brought an action against the trustees for breach of fiduciary duty.

The court accepted the evidence of the trustees' certified public accountant that neither he nor any of the fund staff had sufficient training to express an opinion as the soundness of the loan despite the disclosure of all relevant financial statements to the trustees. None of the trustees had an accounting or banking background, and they were therefore poorly equipped to analyze the figures presented to them to determine whether the borrower faced any serious financial problems. It was apparent that a person expert in banking and debt financing would have discovered, on reviewing the same financial information, that the bank simply did not have the resources to service the debt it was undertaking. Moreover, there were a number of accounting entries on the financial statements that would have prompted knowledgeable trustees to interrogate management as to the bank's financial position and ability to handle a loan of this nature.

Moreover, a further inquiry would have revealed that just prior to entering into the land transaction, the bank had been approached by the Federal Deposit Insurance Corporation urging the bank's board of directors to adopt a corrective plan to deal with the bank's undercapitalization, poor loan-to-deposit ratio, insufficient liquidity, high percentage of risky loans and improper lending practices. Moreover, a number of institutional lenders had refused to lend money to the bank to refinance its debt to a third party. In addition, one of the properties acting as collateral on the loan from the pension plan had been seized and sold for tax delinquencies on the day the loan agreement was signed.

The court in holding that the trustees failed to meet the prudence standards did not suggest that the trustees lacking in familiarity with the investments were required to make the appropriate inquiries on their own, but rather that they were under an affirmative duty to seek expert assistance.[41]

Selecting Expert Consultants

Where a trustee or administrator does not have the requisite knowledge and skill to make his or her own investment decisions, the trustee must not only *seek independent advice from an expert, but must make the necessary enquiries to determine whether the consultants or advisors chosen have the appropriate qualifications* in the subject area of the contemplated investment. The court in *Whitfield v. Cohen* stated that a pension plan trustee or administrator was required to:

Evaluate the consultant's qualifications including;
(a) His or her experience in the particular area of investment under consideration and with other pension plans
(b) His or her credentials
(c) Whether the consultant is registered with the applicable regulatory authorities
(d) An independent assessment of his or her qualifications by means of;
  (i) A widely enjoyed reputation in the business of investments;
  (ii) Client references; and/or
  (iii) The advice of a professional third party consultant.
(e) His or her record of past performance with investments of the type contemplated.[42]

Relying on Expert Advice

However, an independent appraisal from an expert will not satisfy a fiduciary's duty to act prudently, if the information provided to the consultants by the fiduciaries is inaccurate or based on erroneous assumptions. While administrators or trustees have a duty to seek independent advice where they lack the requisite education, experience and skill, *they must nevertheless make their own decisions based on that advice rather than rely wholly on the advice of others.*[43] As stated in *Donovan v. Cunningham*:

An independent appraisal is not a magic wand that fiduciaries may simply wave over a transaction to ensure that their responsibilities are fulfilled. It is a tool and, like all tools, is useful only if used properly. To use an independent appraisal properly, . . . fiduciaries need not become experts . . . they are entitled to rely on the expertise of others. However, as the source of the information upon which the expert's opinions are based, the fiduciaries are responsible for ensuring that the information is complete and up-to-date.[44]

Not only are the administrators and trustees required

to retain experts where they do not have sufficient knowledge and experience to evaluate an investment on their own, and are required to *ensure that any expert retained is appropriately qualified,* their fiduciary responsibility still requires them to *independently assess and review expert advice.* They cannot merely rely on such advice even when the expertise of the consultant is established.

> The mere retention of an expert cannot be permitted to act as a kind of talisman to protect the defendants against claims of failure to discharge their own fiduciary responsibilities. Expert advice must be considered as carefully as any other information that the trustees have available to them when making decisions to commit plan assets.[45]

Selecting Investment Managers

The principles discussed above with respect to retaining and consulting investment experts are equally applicable and particularly critical to the selection of investment managers. In the same way that plan fiduciaries cannot merely rely on the advice of a self-proclaimed expert and invoke this reliance as a shield against claims of breach of fiduciary duty, the fiduciaries may not simply appoint any individual as an investment manager and hide behind his or her decisions when imprudent investments are made. The fiduciary must also exercise prudence in selecting an investment manager. The liability of fiduciaries in cases where imprudent investments are made by investment managers will likely be assessed with regard to the investigation and procedures adopted by the fiduciaries for selecting the manager. In this regard consideration should be given to:

- The manager's ability to effectively manage the type of fund involved
- Whether the manager's organization and investment philosophies are consistent with the needs of the plan
- Whether the manager has performed well in managing similar investments for similar plans
- The manager's track record for meeting the stated objectives of plans he or she has managed
- The total assets under the control of the investment manager or his or her company
- The size of the investment manager's staff and the resources available to them
- How performance of investment portfolios is measured and reviewed
- Fees charged for asset management and reporting and how these compare with the industry average.[46]

Appendix IV—9-A at the end of this chapter sets out a checklist of suggested questions the trustees should consider asking a prospective investment manager/counsel.[47]

Considering Alternative Investments

The soundness of any investment decision will often turn upon the comparable alternatives a fiduciary might have adopted as opposed to the investment under scrutiny. Therefore, an essential aspect of procedural prudence in the investment context is the fiduciaries' consideration of or *failure to consider* other available investments opportunities when investment decisions are made.

In *Davidson v. Cook*[48] the union trustees of a health and welfare benefit fund were found to be in breach of their fiduciary duty in connection with a loan approved by the trustees to a corporation wholly owned by the union and incorporated for the purposes of holding a commercial property. The union-held corporation required financing for its purchase of a parcel of land and the construction of the building on the site. The corporation was unable to secure a loan from a commercial lender and turned to the trust fund for the financing required.

The court reasoned that the trustees' objective of benefiting the union with which it does not deal at arm's length is not in of itself a breach of the trustees' fiduciary obligation to perform their duties for the exclusive benefit of the participants of the trust fund. Rather, by virtue of the trustees' failure to *treat* the union's loan proposal at arm's length and *compare it to other available investments,* they breached their fiduciary obligations.

The prudence of measuring an investment decision against available comparative alternatives is perhaps most apparent where pension funds pursue "economically targeted," "ethical" or "socially responsible investment" policies. This issue is discussed in detail in Chapter 12 of this section.

Monitoring Investments

The duty to exercise the care, diligence and skill of a reasonably prudent person does not cease once the investment decision is made and implemented. The fiduciary has a continuing duty to *periodically monitor the investments* as well as monitor the performance of persons to whom they have delegated investment authority, including investment managers. Periodic review to ensure that investments continue to meet plan objectives and comply with legislative restrictions, and continue to be prudent, is an essential aspect of the fiduciary's role. Moreover, a fiduciary also has a duty to terminate an investment that is no longer suitable or appropriate for the plan.[49]

When investment decisions and administrative duties are delegated to third parties, such as investment managers, plan fiduciaries are not relieved of their duty to monitor the investment performance. In *Whitfield v. Co-*

hen[50] the pension plan trustees had delegated their investment powers to Penvest, an investment management company. The company invested plan funds in second mortgages, which resulted in a loss to the plan of approximately $640,000. For a three-year period, the trustees had no knowledge of the type of investments made by the investment company and received monthly statements setting out only the amount of principal invested and an unexplained interest calculation. Three years after the trustees had transferred the plan's assets to the investment company, they requested further information about the nature of the investments and their performance and realized for the first time that the plan was losing money on the investments made by Penvest.

With respect to the trustees' failure to monitor the performance of the plan's agents, the court stated:

> Nevertheless, [the trustee's] common law and ERISA responsibilities as a trustee did not end with the initial decision to invest Plan assets with Penvest.
>
> A fiduciary must ascertain within a reasonable time whether an agent to whom he has delegated a trust power is properly carrying out his responsibilities. . . . [The trustee] had a duty to monitor Penvest's performance with reasonable diligence and to withdraw the investment if it became clear or should have become clear that the investment was no longer proper for the Plan.[51]

The degree and nature of supervision required of fiduciaries varies depending on the context of each case. In particular, the degree of delegation of investment authority, the size of the fund, the expertise of the investment manager and the number of individuals to whom the investment authority is entrusted are facts to be considered when determining appropriate supervisory mechanisms. At a minimum, the fiduciary who delegates his or her authority with respect to the administration of plan assets should:

- Implement adequate procedures for the supervision of agents to whom fiduciary responsibilities have been delegated
- Conduct periodic performance evaluations
- Require periodic reports from investment managers that indicate the manager's progress in implementing the plan's investment strategy, and reports that establish that the financial position of the fund is sound.[52]

ENDNOTES

1. *Pension Benefits Standards Act,* 1985, R.S.C. 1985, c. 32 (2nd Supp.) (PBSA).

2. Ontario *Pension Benefits Regulation,* R.R.O. 1990, Reg. 909 (the "Ontario Regulation").

3. Ontario *Pension Benefits Act,* R.S.O. 1990, c. P.8 (OPBA).

4. Regulation to amend Reg. 909 of R.R.O. 1990, O. Reg. 144/00.

5. *Cowan v. Scargill,* [1984] 2 ALL ER 750 (Ch. D.) at p. 762.

6. PBSA, *supra* note 1, s. 8(4); British Columbia *Pension Benefits Standards Act,* R.S.B.C. 1996, c. 352 (the "British Columbia Act") s. 8(5); New Brunswick *Pension Benefits Act,* S.N.B. 1987, c. P-5.1 (the "New Brunswick Act") s. 17(1); Nova Scotia *Pension Benefit Act,* R.S.N.S. 1989, c. 340 (the "Nova Scotia Act") s. 29(1); Ontario Act, *supra* note 3, ss. 22(1), (5); and the Quebec *Supplemental Pension Plans Act,* R.S.Q. 1990, R-15.1 (the "Quebec Ac"), s. 151.

7. PBSA, *supra* note 1, s. 8(5); New Brunswick Act, *supra* note 6, s. 17(2); Nova Scotia Act, *supra* note 6, s. 29(2); Ontario Act, *supra* note 3, s. 22(2); and Quebec Act, *supra* note 6, Section 151.

8. *Pension Benefits Standards Regulation,* C.R.C. 1978, c. 1252 (the "PBSA Regulation").

9. PBSA Regulation, *supra* note 8, as amended by S.O.R. 93-299.

10. PBSA Regulation, *supra* note 8, ss. 13 and 14.

11. Alberta *Employment Pension Plans Act,* S.A. 1986, c. E-10.05.

12. Alberta *Employment Pension Plans Regulation,* Alta. Reg. 364/86.

13. Manitoba *Pension Benefits Act,* R.S.M. 1987, c. P32.

14. New Brunswick *Pension Benefits Regulation,* N.B. Reg. 91-195.

15. Newfoundland *Pension Benefits Act,* S.N. 1996, c. P-4.01.

16. Nova Scotia *Regulations Under the Pension Benefits Act,* N.S. Reg. 269/87 as amended by N.S. Reg. 19/96.

17. Saskatchewan *Pension Benefits Act,* 1992, S.S. 1992, c. P-6.001.

18. Quebec *Supplemental Pension Plans Act,* R.S.Q. 1990, R-15.1.

19. British Columbia *Pension Benefits Standards Act,* R.S.B.C. 1996, c. 352.

20. *Income Tax Act,* R.S.C. 1985, c. 1, (5th Supp.) (ITA).

21. ITA Regulation 8514, SOR/92-51.

22. *Fales v. Canada Permanent Trust Co.,* [1977] 2 S.C.R. 302.

23. *Re Whiteley* (1886), 33 Ch.d 347.

24. *Employee Retirement Income Security Act of 1974,* 29 U.S.C.A. §1001 (1974) (ERISA).

25. *Ibid.,* s. 404.

26. *Tonks v. Aetna Life Assurance Co.* (1992), 98 D.L.R. (4th) 582; *Ford v. Laidlaw Carriers, Inc.* (1993), 1 C.C.P.B. 97 (O.C.(G.D.)), rev'd in part (1994), 12 C.C.P.B. 179 (O.C.A.); *Bartlett v. Barclays Bank Trust Co. Ltd.,* [1980] 1 All. E.R. 139.

27. *Fales v. Canada Permanent Trust Co., supra* note 22 at p. 268.

28. *Hodgkinson v. Simms* (1994), 117 D.L.R. (4th) 161 (S.C.C.).

29. *Laflamme v. Prudential-Bache Commodities Canada Ltd.,* [2000] S.C.C. 26.

30. Bevis Longstreth, *Modern Investment Management and the Prudent Man Rule* (New York: Oxford University Press, 1986). The Pension Commission of Ontario, "Investment Re-

sponsibility: Prudence in Action"; P.C.O. Bulletin (May 1990, Volume 1, Issue 2).

31.   R. J. Albert and M. E. Brossman, "Legal Considerations Relating to the Investment of Plan Assets," in *Employee Benefit Issues: The Multiemployer Perspective* (Brookfield, WI: International Foundation of Employee Benefit Plans, Inc., 1994), p. 153.

32.   *Whitfield v. Cohen,* 782 F.Supp. 188 (S.D.N.Y. 1988).

33.   *Brock v. Wells Fargo Bank,* 7 EBC 1221 (N.D.Cal. 1986).

34.   *Ibid.,* at p. 1223.

35.   *Tonks v. Aetna Life Assurance Co., supra* note 26.

36.   *Fink v. National Savings and Trust Company et al.,* 772 F.2d 951 (D.C.Cir. 1985); *Donovan v. Mazzola,* 716 F.2d 1226 (9th Cir. 1983).

37.   *Fink v. National Savings and Trust Company, supra* note 36 at p. 955.

38.   *Whitfield v. Cohen, supra* note 32.

39.   *Katsaros v. Cody,* 744 F.2d 270 (2d Cir. 1984).

40.   Albert and Brossman, *supra* note 31. *Katsaros v. Cody, supra* note 39.

41.   *Katsaros v. Cody, supra* note 39, at p. 1784.

42.   *Whitfield v. Cohen, supra* note 32, at p. 193.

43.   *Ibid.,* at p. 194.

44.   *Donovan v. Cunningham,* 716 F.2d 1455 at 1474 (5th Cir. 1983).

45.   *Donovan v. Tricario,* 5 EBC 2057 at p. 2064 (S.D.Fla. 1984).

46.   Dona Campbell, "Investment Responsibility of Benefit Fund Trustees," [1993] 12 *Estates and Trust Journal* 307.

47.   Appendix adopted from a paper presented by Rory Judd Albert and Mark E. Brossman, *supra* note 31.

48.   *Davidson v.* Cook, 567 F.Supp. 225 (D. Virginia 1983).

49.   *Public Service Co. of Colorado v. Chase Manhattan Bank,* 577 F.Supp. 92 (S.D.N.Y.).

50.   *Whitfield v. Cohen, supra* note 32.

51.   *Whitfield v. Cohen, supra* note 32, at p. 196.

52.   Albert and Brossman, *supra* note 31.

APPENDIX IV—9-A

INVESTMENT COUNSEL SELECTION CHECKLIST

Suggested Questions to Be Asked of Potential Investment Counsel

☐ Description of the precise *services* the Investment Counsel is prepared to offer.

☐ History of the Investment Counsel's experience in the investment management business, including the total amount of *assets under its management.*

☐ A statement of the Investment Counsel's *investment approach* or philosophy, and whether it has any internal investment guidelines.

☐ The *number of accounts* under the Investment Counsel's management and their total current fair market value.

☐ Detailed schedule of proposed investment management *fees.*

☐ Description of the Investment Counsel's *current staffing,* details as to the names, general experience and educational qualifications of the individuals who would be primarily responsible for the plan's accounts.

☐ A statement as to whether members of the staff would be *available to meet* with the plan trustees on a regular basis.

☐ Description of *how investment policy is established* by the Investment Counsel and how it will be implemented with respect to the plan assets in question.

☐ A summary of *any investment policy* the Investment Counsel recommends for pension plan assets placed under its management.

☐ A tabulation of *time-weighted annual rates* of total investment return on the combined results of *all equity portfolios* under management for each of the previous five to ten years, and cumulatively for that period.

☐ A tabulation of *time-weighted annual rates* or total investment returns on the combined results of *all fixed income portfolios* under management for each of the previous five to ten years, and cumulatively for that period.

☐ A tabulation of *time-weighted annual rates* of total investment return on the combined results of *all portfolios* under management for each of the previous five to ten years, and cumulatively for that period.

☐ The dollar amount of the Investment Counsel's *fiduciary liability insurance* and *fidelity bond* that would be available to protect the interests of the plan and provide copies of the same for review by the plan's legal counsel.

☐ The existence of any current or past *litigation* involving claims against the Investment Counsel or any of its principals or investment professionals, and whether any of them have ever been held to be in violation of any Canadian or U.S. laws.

☐ Whether the Investment Counsel, or any of its principals, have ever undergone *bankruptcy,* liquidation, reorganization or similar proceedings; has had its registration or license revoked or activities restricted; has ever been sued by a client, the Ontario Securities Commission or the Securities and Exchange Commission (U.S.); or has ever been denied fiduciary liability or fidelity coverage.

☐ If the Investment Counsel is U.S.-based, is it *registered* with the Securities and Exchange Commission under the Investment Advisers Act of 1940 (U.S.), and the date of its initial registration.

☐ Whether the Investment Counsel is *registered* with the Ontario Securities Commission under the Ontario Securities Act, and the date of its initial registration.

☐ Whether the Investment Counsel is affiliated (or has any business relationship) with the broker-dealer it uses that could affect its investment decisions.

☐ *Financial information* relating to the Investment Counsel, including its most recent balance sheet.

☐ The Investment Counsel's policy with respect to the *voting of proxies*; A description of the Investment Counsel's *business structure,* principal owners and affiliates.

☐ The procedure to be employed by the Investment Counsel to ensure compliance with the *Income Tax Act* of Canada and the applicable pension benefits legislation in relation to prohibited transaction restrictions and whether the investments qualify under this legislation.

☐ *"Soft dollar"*practices if any of the Investment Counsel.

☐ Investment Counsel's familiarity and understanding of Canadian *legislation pertaining to investment of pension plan assets.*

CHAPTER 10

Pension Funds as Shareholders

by George P. Dzuro, Murray Gold, Arleen Huggins and Michael Mazzuca
with the assistance of Karen M. DeBortoli

SHAREHOLDER RIGHTS

Introduction

As a matter of corporate law, shareholders are entitled to vote on and participate in a number of issues that are critical to the proper governance of a corporation. They have these rights because the shareholders are the corporation's owners. The corporation's management is responsible and accountable to its shareholders for their actions since, in the final analysis, the shareholders bear the burdens or reap the benefits of management's activities.

Portfolio investors, such as pension plans, have often viewed themselves only as passive shareholders who express approval or disapproval of the management of a corporation by buying or selling its securities. Exercising a proxy vote and engaging management in constructive criticism may seem time-consuming and wasteful to the portfolio investor who can simply sell a security on bad news.

A number of changes in the pension industry have combined to change this view of institutional shareholders' interests in general and proxy voting. Today, the better legal view is that pension funds, and especially those of a certain size and illiquidity, have a fiduciary obligation to be actively concerned with how their investee companies are managed and must exercise their proxy votes. Voting a security does not preclude selling it; however, selling a security is not the alternative to voting it.

Some of the underlying changes in the pension industry that have contributed to this change of view are:

- **Increased Indexation**—More and more, institutional pension funds are investing in pooled funds that hold all of the stocks listed in a major market index. In Canada, the TSE 300 index is perhaps the most common. Once the decision to index has been made, the pension plan has also implicitly determined that it would not sell a security included in the index to protest against management. The only effective governance tools that the index investor retains are activist.
- **Asset Allocation**—Pension funds are also, to a greater degree than ever before, committed to the equity markets. Modern portfolio theory has shifted North American pension investment patterns significantly toward the equity markets since World War II. Not only are pension funds increasingly committed to all of the securities in an index for that part of their portfolio devoted to equities, but the portion of their portfolio invested in equities has increased considerably over the past 40 years.
- **Increased Size**—Pension funds have also grown considerably since World War II. One of the consequences of this growth, especially when combined with the increased exposure to equities, is that the largest pension funds hold significant interests in Canada's largest corporations. Although Canadian markets are generally liquid, selling significant blocks of shares may depress the share price and be costly to the institutional investor. Where possible, selling securities because of bad management is to be avoided, and ensuring that the investee company is well managed is to be preferred.

These factors all point to the conclusion that pension funds, as large long-term portfolio investors, have an interest in the good management of their investee companies. In the long run, good management is promoted and reinforced through vigilant shareholders, exercising their right to vote.

Pension legislation in Canada, as well as the policies of provincial regulators, also requires pension plans to exercise their proxy votes in a responsible way. The Ontario legislation and the policies of the Financial Services Commission of Ontario (FSCO) are all to this effect.

Section 22 of Ontario's *Pension Benefits Act* (PBA)[1] imposes on persons responsible for investing a pension fund the obligation to ". . . exercise the care, diligence and skill in the administration and investment of the pension fund that a person of ordinary prudence would exercise in dealing with the property of another person." Similar provisions exist in the legislation of other provinces.[2] While the administrator is permitted to delegate many aspects of fund investments, including proxy voting, the administrator is always required to personally select its delegate and to monitor the delegate's performance.[3]

With the exception of Prince Edward Island, all Canadian provincial jurisdictions require that pension plans adopt a statement of investment policies and procedures (SIP&P), also known as a statement of investment policies and goals (SIP&G).[4] These statements generally set a plan's asset allocation strategy and define those categories of assets in which the pension fund may be invested. Subsection 7.1(1) of the Regulations made under the federal *Pension Benefits Standards Act* requires, for example, that each SIP&P contain provisions respecting delegation of voting rights acquired through plan investments.[5]

Generally speaking, this requires that plan administrators have a proxy voting policy. In May 1990, the Pension Commission of Ontario published its "Compliance Assistance Guidelines," No. 3, which provided that such a policy:

. . . should set out the plan's policy on voting of securities carrying voting rights—specifically, whether the administrator will retain voting rights acquired through the plan's investments, or, if they are to be delegated, to whom. If the pension plan has a policy or policies on voting, these should be stated. The SIP&G should also describe the procedures to be followed to review proxy statements and solicitations and deciding how to vote securities.[6]

Accordingly, legislation in most Canadian jurisdictions requires the following in respect of proxy voting:

- That the SIP&P define whether voting rights will be exercised directly by the administrator, or delegated to investment counsel

- If a pension plan has specific policies with respect to how proxies ought to be voted, then these should also be explicit and included in the SIP&P.
- The SIP&P should describe the procedures to be followed in reviewing proxy statements and solicitations and deciding how to vote with respect to them.

Canadian legislation does not expressly state that pension plans are required to vote their proxies. In the United States, by contrast, the Department of Labor has published its position that ". . . the fiduciary act of managing plan assets that are shares of corporate stock includes the voting of proxies appurtenant to those shares of stock."[7] In other words, plan administrators' fiduciary obligations extend to the voting of proxies. According to the U.S Department of Labor, failure to vote a proxy is a breach of a plan administrator's fiduciary obligations.

While the U.S. position has not been expressly adopted by Canadian pension regulators, it is likely that it properly reflects a plan administrator's fiduciary obligations in Canada as well. Thus, fiduciary obligations have been defined and enforced in Canada at least as actively, if not more so, than in the United States. Because of its size and sophistication, many issues are addressed by U.S. regulators and U.S. courts long before they are formally addressed in Canada. This does not mean that Canadian law is any different from its U.S. counterpart, but only that the issues may take longer to be addressed and resolved than in the United States. Given the strength of fiduciary law in Canada, it is undoubtedly the case that Canadian regulators and courts would find, as have their U.S. counterparts, that plan administrators must exercise proxy votes as an aspect of their fiduciary obligations.

Typically, Canadian pension administrators delegate investment responsibilities to investment managers. For the purposes of the pension benefits legislation, these managers are "agents" of the plan administrator and subject to the same fiduciary obligations as the administrator itself, albeit only within the sphere of their delegated authority. As a rule, investment management agreements should expressly require that the investment managers vote proxies on behalf of the administrator. If an investment management agreement fails to delegate this responsibility to the investment manager, then, by implication, it may remain the responsibility of the plan administrator itself.

Where proxy voting is delegated to investment managers, the plan administrator must nevertheless monitor this activity. Proper monitoring requires that accurate records be maintained by the investment manager as to its proxy votes, and that the investment manager regularly report to the administrator with respect to its voting.

Proxy voting outside of North America is often more

complex than proxy voting in the United States and Canada. Where the cost of exercising the proxy vote outweighs any benefit from casting the vote, it is likely that the plan administrator's fiduciary obligations permit it to not vote those securities. As the U.S. Department of Labor has noted, however, the administrator's decision whether to vote should ". . . take into account the effect that the plan's vote, either by itself or together with other votes, is expected to have on the value of the plan's investment and whether this expected effect would out-weigh the cost of voting."[8]

As a practical matter, only the largest pension plans in Canada have adopted proxy voting guidelines. For the most part, these guidelines address corporate governance issues. Investment managers are generally directed to support a separation between the persons of chief executive officer and chairman of the board, to support independent directors, to limit stock options to senior management where these would have a significant dilution effect and to pursue other proper governance objectives. In some cases, plan administrators have also adopted socially responsible voting criteria. These are generally applied in a way that enhances, or at least does not detract, from shareholder value.

While proxy voting is the most common way in which institutional shareholders participate in corporate governance, it is by no means the only way, nor does the exercise of a proxy vote capture the entirety of an institutional shareholders' interests in corporate governance.

Disclosure obligations, for example, are critically important to all shareholders, and no less to institutional shareholders. All shareholders have a keen interest in knowing about the performance of their corporate investments, and in ensuring that the playing field with respect to corporate information is level. Otherwise, their investments may not be fully informed or, worse, the value of their holdings may be subject to manipulation by those with superior information. Not surprisingly, therefore, the law with respect to corporate disclosure has been of keen interest to institutional shareholders.

Where all else fails, all shareholders, including institutional shareholders, may have no choice but to commence legal action against the corporations in which they invest. They may want to hold the corporation's directors, or its officers, personally responsible for misdeeds. They may also want to access directors and officers errors and omissions insurance coverage where applicable. While this is a remedy of last resort, and still relatively uncommon in Canada, U.S. shareholders and institutional shareholders have been aggressively protecting their shareholder interests in the courts for some time.

This chapter reviews a number of issues of significant concern to institutional shareholders. It does not address the interests of all shareholders under all circumstances and is therefore no substitute for legal advice in particular cases. However, it does review some of the leading issues in this area and highlights some of the most important rights that institutional shareholders have vis-à-vis their investee corporations.

PENSION AND BENEFIT PLANS AS SHAREHOLDERS OF A CORPORATION

General

A corporation is an inanimate legal entity that is distinct in law from the persons who own it. It cannot do anything on its own. Human intervention is necessary to operate the corporation and its business. The persons who operate the business of a corporation are its directors, its officers and its shareholders. The aggregate activities of these three groups guide the behavior of a corporation. However, directors, officers and shareholders, each have their own spheres of activity.

Canadian companies in Canada are either governed by the companies legislation of the province in which they were incorporated,[9] or by the *Canada Business Corporations Act* (CBCA),[10] which governs federally incorporated companies. Such legislation delineates the spheres of activity that are exercisable by the directors, officers and shareholders. It is therefore necessary to appreciate the rights, obligations and remedies that the applicable corporation statute provides directors, officers and shareholders of a corporation.

Role of Shareholders

In corporate governance theory, the shareholders of a corporation own the corporation. The corporation is operated in the shareholders' best interests and on the shareholders' behalf. In practice, shareholders elect directors to manage the general business and affairs of a corporation, who in turn appoint officers to manage the day-to-day business of a corporation.

The term *shareholder* is only defined in the companies legislation of Manitoba, New Brunswick, Newfoundland, Prince Edward Island and Quebec.[11] Legislation in the remaining provinces, as well as CBCA, contains no definition of the term. Traditionally, shareholders were those persons who possessed share certificates issued by a corporation and whose names were registered on the share register maintained by a corporation. More recently, shares are generally registered in the name of securities depositories and other intermediaries that hold the shares for the benefit of the investor. While dividends and capital gains arising from the shares accrue to the "beneficial" shareholders, these shareholders are not necessarily registered on the share register of a corporation.

The rights, privileges, restrictions and conditions that

attach to shares can be found in the constating documents of a corporation.[12] These constating documents are generally part of the public record. Where a corporation has only one class of shares, all shares are equal and generally possess the following rights:

a. The right to vote at meetings of shareholders
b. The right to receive any dividend declared by the corporation and
c. The right to receive the remaining property of the corporation upon dissolution.[13]

However, where the constating documents so provide, the rights, privileges, restrictions and conditions attaching to different classes of shares of the same corporation can differ provided that the rights mentioned above must be attached to at least one class of shares, but both such rights are not required to be attached to any one class of shares.[14] In addition, the rights, privileges, restrictions and conditions that may be attached to any particular class of shares of a corporation, as set out in a corporation's constating documents, can include the following:

a. Cumulative, non-cumulative or partially cumulative dividends
b. Preference as to payment of dividends
c. Preference as to repayment of capital upon dissolution
d. Right to elect all or part of the board of directors
e. Right to convert into shares of another class
f. Redemption of shares at the option of the corporation or the shareholder
g. Purchase of shares by the corporation for cancellation and
h. Conditions, restrictions, limitations or prohibitions on the right to vote at shareholders' meeting.

Rights of Shareholders

Election and Removal of Directors

The most important right of shareholders who own voting shares is the right to elect directors to the board of directors of a corporation[15] and the right to remove directors from office.[16] The directors of a corporation have an obligation and duty to manage or supervise the management of the business and affairs of a corporation.[17]

Appointment of Auditors

To ensure that financial statements are prepared in accordance with generally accepted accounting principles, the voting shareholders have a right to appoint an auditor at each annual meeting of shareholders.[18]

The auditor is supposed to be the shareholders' representative or watchdog. He makes such examinations as are necessary in order to report to the share-

holders about the accuracy of the financial statements. An "unqualified" audit report from the auditor constitutes the auditor's opinion that the financial statements present fairly the financial position of the corporation as at its year-end and the results of its operations and changes of financial position in accordance with generally accepted accounting principles applied on a consistent basis.

If however the auditor issues a "qualified" report, it means that, in certain instances as specified by the auditor, an unqualified report could not be given. Shareholders should consider seeking an explanation from management at the annual meeting or from the auditor whenever they receive a "qualified" report.

In addition to providing that any director or officer, whether or not they are entitled to vote, may require a corporation's auditor or former auditor to attend a shareholders' meeting and answer questions, most provincial legislation provides that auditors have the right to receive notice of and attend any meeting that shareholders are entitled to attend. Auditors also have the right to speak on matters pertaining to their role as auditor.[19]

Approval of Fundamental Changes

There are certain changes affecting a corporation that are considered so fundamental that they cannot be approved by the directors or by the shareholders through an ordinary resolution. Instead, such changes must be approved by the shareholders by a special resolution. A *special resolution* is a resolution that is passed at a special meeting of shareholders of a corporation by a majority of not less than two-thirds of the votes cast. In addition, certain fundamental changes must be approved by each class and series of shares by not less than two-thirds of the shares of each class and series even if the class or series is ordinarily non-voting.

Fundamental changes that require approval by a special resolution of the shareholders include amendments to the corporation's constating documents,[20] an amalgamation (other than a short-form amalgamation),[21] the continuance of the corporation in another jurisdiction,[22] and the sale, lease or exchange of all or substantially all of the property of the corporation other than the ordinary course of its business.[23]

Shareholders who oppose certain fundamental changes may dissent and require the corporation to purchase their shares if the fundamental change occurs.[24] The theory underlying this shareholder dissent right is that a corporation is now fundamentally changed from the way in which it was when the shareholder decided to invest in it. Hence, the shareholder who opposes the change should be able to terminate his or her investment in such shares at their "fair value."

The notice of meeting of shareholders at which such

fundamental changes are to be considered must state that a dissenting shareholder is entitled to be paid the fair value of the shareholders' shares.

Shareholder Proposals

A proposal to amend the constating documents of a corporation may be initiated by any shareholder who is entitled to vote at an annual meeting of shareholders.[25] Such a shareholder is also permitted to submit to a corporation notice of a matter that the shareholder proposes to raise at a meeting of shareholders and to discuss the matter at the meeting.[26]

A shareholder proposal gives the shareholder a method of bringing a matter directly to the attention of other shareholders and of bypassing the board of directors of a corporation. Notice of the proposal and the statement in support of the proposal must be circulated in the management information circular sent to all shareholders unless:

a. If the matter is proposed to be raised at an annual meeting, the proposal is not submitted to the corporation at least 60 days before the anniversary date of the last annual meeting or

b. If the matter is proposed to be raised at a meeting other than an annual meeting, the proposal is not submitted to the corporation at least 60 days before such a meeting or

c. It clearly appears that the proposal is submitted by the shareholder to enforce a personal claim or redress a personal grievance against the corporation, or any of its directors, officers or shareholders, or for a purpose that is not related in any significant way to the business or affairs of the corporation or

d. The proposal was circulated in connection with a meeting of shareholders within two preceding years and not presented by the shareholder at the meeting, or was presented and was defeated.

A proposal may include a nomination for the election of directors if it is signed by the holders of not less than 5% of the shares in the aggregate, or 5% of the shares of any class or series of shares entitled to vote at the meeting.[27] New Brunswick's legislation requires that a proposal for the nomination of directors must be signed by 10% of shareholders.[28]

If a corporation refuses to circulate a shareholder's proposal, it must notify the shareholder of its decision and its reasons for the refusal. A shareholder may then apply to a court, and the court may restrain the holding of the shareholders' meeting or make another order as it thinks fit.

The power to call a meeting of shareholders is vested in the directors. Therefore, the directors need not call a special meeting of the shareholders to consider a proposal, but they must put a proposal before a special meeting of shareholders if one has been called and the proposal is one that qualifies for circulation to the shareholders. Legislation in Alberta, Manitoba, New Brunswick, Newfoundland, Ontario and Saskatchewan requires that directors call an annual meeting of shareholders not later than 18 months after the corporation comes into existence and subsequently not later than 15 months after holding the proceeding annual meeting.[29] As a result, a shareholder proposal must be considered at the next annual meeting at the latest. Shareholders may also requisition a meeting of shareholders.

As opposed to the requirements set out above, the British Columbia *Company Act* states that an annual meeting must be called no later than 15 months after incorporation, and that subsequent meetings be called no later than 13 months after the last meeting.[30] Nova Scotia's legislation requires that meetings be held once a calendar year, and not later than 15 months after the last meeting.[31] Finally, the Quebec *Companies Act* states that meetings are to be held as provided in the company by-laws. If the by-laws are silent, meetings are to be held on the fourth Wednesday in January each year.[32]

Requisition of Shareholders' Meetings

Under normal circumstances, the right to call shareholders' meeting is vested in the board of directors. However, in certain situations, shareholders have the right to requisition shareholders' meetings.

In Alberta, Manitoba, Newfoundland, Ontario and Saskatchewan, shareholders with at least 5% of the shares entitled to vote at meetings may require the directors to call a meeting.[33] Legislation in New Brunswick, Nova Scotia, and Quebec requires that the support of the holders of at least 10% of shares is required to requisition a meeting.[34] If the directors do not do so within 21 days following receipt of a shareholder's written requisition, any shareholder who made the original request may call the meeting in the usual way. However, the right to requisition a meeting is not absolute. The directors need not call a meeting of shareholders if a record date for a meeting has been fixed and notice of it has already been given, if the directors have already called a shareholders' meeting and have given notice of it, or if the matters to be discussed at the requisitioned meeting are of such a nature that the corporation would not be required to circulate a shareholder proposal.

The British Columbia *Company Act* provides that a meeting can be requisitioned by one or more shareholders holding at least 50% of all issued shares. The company must hold the meeting no later than four months after the date of the requisition.[35]

While the requisitioning and holding of a shareholders' meeting normally entails some expense, the corporation is obligated to reimburse a shareholder for the expenses incurred by it in requisitioning, calling and holding a shareholders' meeting unless the shareholder has not acted in good faith and in the interest of the shareholders of the corporation generally, or unless otherwise resolved.[36]

Voting by Proxy

Any shareholder entitled to vote at a meeting of shareholders has the right to appoint a person, who need not be a shareholder, to represent the shareholder and vote in the shareholder's stead, at the meeting, by executing a form of proxy.[37]

The management of a corporation that is a "reporting issuer" under applicable provincial securities legislation[38] is required, concurrently with giving notice of a meeting of shareholders, to send a form of proxy to each shareholder who is entitled to notice of the meeting.[39] When management solicits proxies, or for that matter when anyone solicits proxies, such form of proxy must be accompanied by an information circular.

The definition of *solicit* and *solicitation* is broadly cast to include efforts to have a shareholder withhold the giving of a proxy. For instance, a letter mailed from the United States to shareholders in Canada concerning the affairs of a company, which included a request to shareholders not to send in their proxy, was held to be a solicitation that required the distribution of a dissident information circular.[40] The definition of the terms *solicitation* and *solicit* do not purport to be exhaustive, but do include the following:

a. A request for a proxy whether or not accompanied by or included in a form of proxy
b. A request to execute or not to execute a form of proxy or to revoke a proxy
c. The sending of a form of proxy or other communication to a shareholder under circumstances reasonably calculated to result in the procurement, withholding or revocation of a proxy or
d. The sending of a form of proxy to a shareholder.

However, the following acts are deemed not to constitute the solicitation of proxies:

a. The sending of a form of proxy in response to an unsolicited request made by or on behalf of a shareholder
b. The performance of administrative acts or professional services on behalf of a person soliciting a proxy
c. The sending of materials by a registrant or custodian to the beneficial owner of such shares[41] or
d. A solicitation by a person in respect of shares of which the person is the beneficial owner.

The solicited form of proxy must provide a means whereby the person whose proxy is solicited is given the opportunity to specify that the shares registered in his or her name will be voted by the proxy holder either for or against each matter or group of related matters identified in the notice of meeting or a shareholder proposal, other than the appointment of an auditor, the remuneration of the auditor and the election of directors. On the questions of the appointment of an auditor, the remuneration of the auditor and the election of directors, the form of proxy must give a shareholder the opportunity to specify that the proxy holder shall vote his or her shares or withhold them from voting. A shareholder might wish to exercise his or her franchise on one or another matter coming before a meeting but might not be willing to support the nominees of management for the board of directors.

If the form of proxy is to confer authority to vote in respect of the appointment of an auditor or the election of a director, then a proposed nominee for the appointment or election must be named in either the form of proxy, the information circular or the shareholder proposal.

Management of a corporation that fails to comply, without reasonable cause, with the requirement of sending out a form of proxy along with the notice of a shareholders' meeting is guilty of an offence, as are the directors and officers who knowingly authorize, permit or acquiesce in such failure.[42]

Any person who solicits proxies in respect of a public company is required to send an information circular to each shareholder whose proxy is solicited, as well as to the corporation and its auditor.[43] In the case of a solicitation by management, the circular is referred to as a *management information circular* and, in all other cases, it is referred to as a *dissident's information circular*. The form of each circular is prescribed by statute.

The rationale for insisting on the dissemination of information is that a shareholder should not be called upon to give a proxy in favour of another unless he or she has been given all relevant information as to the matters in respect of which the proxy may be exercised.

Failure to comply with the requirements relating to the sending of an information circular constitutes an offence, and an offence is committed by a director or officer who, without reasonable cause, authorized, permitted or acquiesced in such offence.[44]

National Policy 41—Non-Registered Shareholders

National Policy Statement 41 adopted by the Ontario Securities Commission was instituted in 1988, primarily to ensure that non-registered shareholders have the same access to information and voting rights as do registered shareholders. The policy requires a public company to provide materials relating to meetings of its shareholders to financial intermediaries that hold securities on behalf of non-registered holders in sufficient time to allow the beneficial owners to receive the materials at least 25 days before the meeting.

A registrant or custodian who receives notice of shareholders' meeting, financial statements, information circulars and other material is required to forward such materials to the beneficial owners. Shares of a corporation not beneficially owned by the registrant may not be voted at a meeting of shareholders except in accordance with the written voting instructions received from the beneficial owner.

Rights of Dissent and Appraisal

A shareholder who dissents in connection with certain fundamental changes[45] is permitted to require a corporation to purchase his or shares at their "fair value."[46] A shareholder who dissents must offer to sell all of the shares of a class held by him or her to the corporation. Partial dissents are not permitted.

In order to dissent, the dissenting shareholder must send to the corporation a written objection to the resolution at or before a meeting of shareholders at which the matter in question is to be voted upon. If the shareholders adopt the resolution at the meeting, then the corporation must, within ten days, send to each shareholder who objected, a notice that the resolution was adopted, unless the shareholder voted for the resolution or has withdrawn his or her objection.

Within 20 days of receiving notice of the resolution, a dissenting shareholder must send to the corporation a written notice containing the dissenting shareholder's name and address, the number and class of shares in respect of which the dissenting shareholder dissents and a demand for payment of the fair value of such shares. Within 30 days of submitting the notice, a shareholder must send in the relevant share certificates to the corporation or its transfer agent. At the time the dissenting shareholder sends the notice requiring the corporation to purchase the shareholder's shares, the shareholder ceases to have any rights as a shareholder except the right to be paid the fair value of the shares, unless the dissenting shareholder withdraws the notice before the corporation makes an offer to pay the fair value for the shares or the directors revoke the resolution authorizing the change if the directors are authorized to do so. If the notice is withdrawn or the resolution is revoked, the shareholder's rights as a shareholder are reinstated as of the day on which the notice was sent.

The corporation is required to send a written offer to dissenting shareholders offering to pay an amount considered by the directors to be the fair value of the shares or notifying the shareholders that the corporation cannot lawfully pay for the shares. If a dissenting shareholder fails to accept the offer, then the issue of fair value is submitted to a court for determination. The court may appoint one or more appraisers to help it fix the fair value of the shares. The court may use whatever method or methods it considers appropriate for determining fair value in the circumstances.

Financial Statements

The principal indicator of the results of the management of a corporation and a corporation's financial condition is its financial statements. A corporation is required to keep financial statements and to present those financial statements to the shareholders at each annual meeting of shareholders. Such statements must be accompanied by a report of the corporation's auditor except where an auditor is not required to be appointed.

The financial statements of a corporation are prepared by, or more often under the supervision of, the directors and officers of the corporation in accordance with generally accepted accounting principles. A public company must also comply with the requirements of the applicable provincial securities legislation[47] relating to financial statements, including the preparation of interim comparative financial statements that must be mailed to every shareholder.

Generally, a public company will be required to provide shareholders with quarterly financial reports, which are not audited, but will typically be approved by the board of directors. The directors are required to approve the annual financial statements before they are circulated to shareholders. A public company is required to have an audit committee composed of not fewer than three directors of the corporation, the majority of whom are not officers or employees of the corporation. The role of the audit committee is to review the financial statements of the corporation and report thereon to the board of directors before such financial statements are approved.[48]

A public company must, either within a specified period before each annual shareholders' meeting or at the meeting itself, provide a copy of the financial statements, the auditor's report and any further information as is required to each shareholder.[49] Financial statements that are filed with the provincial securities administrators are considered part of the public record.

CORPORATE GOVERNANCE ISSUES

Structure of Corporate Governance

Institutional investors, with a long-term interest in corporate performance, have recently focused on a number of corporate governance issues. These are designed to reflect the interests of long-term shareholders and, in particular, to ensure that those interests are well represented in the corporate governance structure.

By and large, institutional shareholders protect these interests through the exercise of their proxy votes or through discussions with a corporation's board of directors. Often, these issues are specifically addressed in a pension plan's "proxy voting guidelines," which are often part and parcel of its statement of investment policies and procedures.

Some of the issues that have been of concern to the institutional investors and that have been raised by the Pension Investment Association of Canada (PIAC) in its *Corporate Governance Standards*[50] are discussed below.

The Board of Directors and Its Committees

The board of directors of a corporation is the entity that is ultimately responsible for oversight of all of the corporation's activities. The board is not responsible for day-to-day management of the corporation's business— that is the responsibility of management. But management is accountable to the shareholders for its performance, and the board of directors is the body that is responsible for representing shareholder interests in maintaining the accountability of management.

Because of the board's responsibility to oversee management, it is important that the board be independent of management and be capable of exercising effective oversight of management. In practical terms, institutional shareholders have supported the following initiatives with respect to the structure and composition of the board of directors, and of its committees:

- **Independent directors**—A corporation's board of directors may consist of persons who are entirely independent of the corporation, or of the corporation's own officers and employees. Of course, to the extent that the board consists of persons who are also management employees of the corporation, the board's independence and oversight capacity may be compromised. For this reason, institutional investors generally support initiatives to ensure that the majority of the members of the board of directors are persons who are independent of management, and whose only financial interest in the company is that of a shareholder. It is anticipated that the more independent the board is of management, the better able it will be to oversee management's activities and hold management accountable.
- **Separation of chair of the board and chief executive officer**—A corporation's chief executive officer (CEO) is its most senior management employee. The CEO is employed by the corporation, and is part of its management, with overall responsibility for the oversight of that management. Generally, a corporation's CEO is well versed in the affairs of the corporation and can make a valuable addition to the board of directors.

  The chair of the board of directors, on the other hand, is the leader or coordinator of a board of directors, which is responsible for the oversight of management, including the CEO. In the past, the CEO and the chair of the board were often the same person, giving this person a significant amount of power with respect to the corporation and effectively placing him or her in a conflict of interest.

  The chair of the board is responsible for oversight of management and, if the chair is also the CEO, is effectively responsible for supervising herself or himself. Accordingly, institutional investors have generally preferred to see the roles of chair of the board and CEO separated, so that the same person does not fulfill both functions.
- **Committees**—In general, boards of directors cannot function effectively without delegating important work to committees of the board with specific areas of responsibility. By organizing board members into committees, the board can do more work and be more effective than if it only meets as a single large group. Standing committees have performed useful oversight functions in the following areas:
  - Nominations to the board of directors
  - Oversight of the corporation's auditors
  - Oversight of management compensation.

  In general, institutional shareholders have supported the creation of the three committees to oversee each of these areas—a nominating committee, an audit committee and a compensation committee. They have advocated that the majority of the members of each of these committees be independent of management and, in particular, that the chair of each committee be independent of management.

  The independence of each of these committees is important, because of potential conflicts between management and the shareholders' interest in management oversight. For example, the composition of the board of directors itself, which is the responsibility of the nominating committee, must be independent of management. Otherwise, if management controls who sits on the board of directors, it may wield disproportionate influence over that board. Similarly, a corporation's auditors are responsible for conducting an independent audit of the corporation's financial statements. Financial statements are one of the most important ways in which management's performance is evaluated. Accordingly, the conduct of the audit, and the oversight of the audit, must be independent of management. Finally, management compensation is obviously an important responsibility for the board, which it must exercise completely independently of management. Quite clearly, management should not be in control of its own compensation.
- **Size of the board**—Boards of directors may benefit

from the participation of a number of persons with different backgrounds and expertise. On the other hand, boards in excess of a certain size may not be effective. In general, institutional investors advocate that boards be restricted to a reasonable size (between 12 and 15 members) and that individual board members restrict the number of other commitments so that they have sufficient time to devote to the requirements of the directorship.

Executive Compensation

In recent years, the level of management compensation has increased very substantially. At the same time, management compensation packages have been restructured and made to conform more closely to the interests of shareholders.

In general, institutional shareholders are concerned both with the structure of management compensation and with its overall levels. PIAC has summarized its criteria with respect to executive compensation as follows:

1. Shareholders' principal interest is in building long-term shareholder values. Compensation packages should induce management to become owners of enough stock that their interests coincide with the shareholders.
2. Compensation must be high enough to attract qualified management; to be competitive within its industry, but not structured to reward failure or mediocrity.
3. Executive compensation should motivate management to achieve its goal of increasing long-term share values. This requires a positive and significant correlation over a reasonable time period between pay and the enhancement of shareholder values.
4. Loans to purchase stock or options that obligate the executive beyond his or her ability to pay and could impose severe financial hardship if share prices fall should be avoided.
5. Unrestricted stock options, options priced below current market value or low interest loans are anathema to PIAC. Reducing the exercise price of options when the stock has under-performed the relative market is not acceptable.
6. Shareholders do not want to design pay packages, but they want directors serving on the compensation committee to be independent from management and capable of overseeing thorough, simple disclosure of all significant sources of executive compensation.[51]

Takeovers

In some cases, takeovers are initiated by outsiders or shareholder groups with a view to reorganizing a corporation on a more profitable basis. This may mean replacement of all or most of the incumbent management. In other cases, takeovers, or mergers, are initiated by friendly or hostile competitors, who wish to consolidate their own business with those of the acquired corporation. In this case as well, management at the acquired corporation may be ousted and replaced with management at the predatory corporation. In both of these cases, management may resist takeovers, notwithstanding that they may (or may not) be in the best interest of the shareholders.

As a rule, institutional investors oppose measures that may deter takeovers. Some of the anti-takeover techniques that have been used are the following:

- **Poison pills**—These types of arrangements provide shareholders with special rights to buy themselves shares at preferred prices in the event of a hostile takeover. This can make such a takeover very expensive, and such measures therefore have the effect of deterring them. This, in turn, may depress the market value of the corporation shares.
- **Crown jewel defences and going private transactions**—These techniques are also used to deter potential takeovers. In a "crown jewel defence" a corporation may sell important assets to a friendly third party. This will leave the takeover target without the assets that the acquirer seeks. In a "going private" transaction, a majority shareholder buys outstanding shares held by minority shareholders. Where the majority shareholder fixes the price of the minority shares in the absence of competition, minority shareholders may be disadvantaged.
- **Leveraged buyouts and locked-up arrangements**—In these cases, management, with a controlling ownership interest in the target company, may use the assets of the corporation or privileged information or relationships, to make a takeover bid and preclude competitive offers. Once again, this may deter competitive bidding and depress the price of the target corporation shares.

In each of these cases, institutional shareholders tend to oppose these arrangements, unless they can be satisfied that they are not in any way detrimental to the general shareholder interests. PIAC's position with respect to these measures is that it favours boards and directors that:

1. Submit major corporate changes to a committee of independent directors for review and approval.
2. Submit major corporate changes to a vote of

shareholders not controlled by management (without impediment).

3. Give shareholders ample time for review and enough information (usually audited financial statements) to make informed judgments.

4. Do not allow management to "short-track" a takeover bid by, for example:
   - Using the company's retained earnings or borrowing power to buy up large blocks of stock; or
   - Seeking out a friendly third party to buy large blocks of stock without extending the offer to other shareholders.[52]

Other Issues

A number of other issues have troubled institutional investors in recent years. In general, they concern techniques used either by management, or by controlling blocks of shareholders, to disadvantage minority shareholders. In this regard, while pension funds are large investors, they are diversified and are generally prevented by law from accumulating more than 10% of the corporation's voting securities. Thus, pension funds will not generally be controlling shareholders and must be vigilant that their interests are protected against them.

Some of the other issues of concern to institutional pension fund investors are the following:

- **Non-voting or unequal voting shares**—Shareholders will not have equal voting rights either where some shares are non-voting, or others carry more than one vote. The issuance of shares with more than one vote may advantage a particular group of shareholders having those shares, while the issuance of non-voting securities will deprive those shareholders of an essential right vis-à-vis the corporation. Pension funds tend to oppose measures that create unequal voting rights as between the shareholders.

- **Super majority provisions**—Corporations' constating documents may stipulate that certain measures require a "super majority" in order to pass. Such requirements may be applicable, for example, in respect of measures that would fundamentally change the corporation's business. On the other hand, they may prevent a majority of the corporation's shareholders from exercising their will. In general, institutional shareholders oppose super majority provisions where these are not required by law, especially where they require the votes of more than two-thirds of the outstanding shares.

- **Linked proposals**—These are proposals that are put before shareholders with two distinct aspects. They may tie together a positive and a negative proposal. In this way, shareholders are not given an opportu-

nity to vote on each element of a proposal but must vote on the "linked proposal." In general, institutional pension fund shareholders oppose linked proposals except where none of the linked elements are shareholder interests.

Ethical Issues

Ethical issues have been receiving increased attention from institutional pension plan investors. Because they are long-term investors, institutional shareholders tend to have a greater focus on the longer term reputations of their investee corporations, and in their relations with consumers, communities and workers. Over the longer term investment horizon of pension fund investments, many believe these issues are important to shareholder value. The issue of pension funds engaging in ethical investing is addressed in more detail in Chapter 12 of this section.

Ethical investment criteria generally address such issues as human rights, child labour, the environment, employment and labour issues, military issues, nuclear issues and animal rights and political contributions.

In general, they borrow from several sets of ethical principles that have been developed, often with the participation of large U.S.-based institutional investors. The CERES principles, for example, were developed out of an alliance between a number of large U.S. institutional investors and environmental groups in 1989. A number of large U.S.-based corporations and institutional investors have endorsed the CERES principles. For the most part, they address environmental, public health and employee health and safety issues.

Other sets of ethical criteria have been developed with respect to specific situations. The McBride principles, for example, address religious discrimination in the context of Northern Ireland. A number of major North American corporations have adopted them. Similarly, a statement of principles for South Africa articulates seven principles in regard to the status of racial minorities in South Africa.

In addition, organizations, such as the American Federation of Labor—Congress of Industrial Organizations (AFL-CIO) has published a set of ethical criteria covering a wide range of issues, including employment and labour relations issues.

In general, many of the ethical investment policies adopted by institutional pension funds are geared toward disclosure obligations, rather than outright prohibitions. Appropriate disclosure requirements may highlight the importance of ethical considerations for corporate management and minimize the possibility of reputation damaging cover-ups. On the other hand, disclosure obligations themselves do not tend to be expensive to implement nor to rigidly constrain corporate activity.

Corporate Disclosure

Operating in our public capital market is not, however, unqualified; it carries responsibilities, and one of the most fundamental is to provide full, true and plain disclosure on a timely basis.[53]

The Importance of Disclosure

Without meaningful information, investing in the stock market is like gambling at a slot machine. As investors, trustees and administrators of employee benefit plans want to know that the investment of fund assets is conducted on an informed basis, not on a speculative or disadvantaged basis.

Investors cannot and do not personally attend and investigate each corporation that they are targeting for investment. Instead, investors, including institutional pension funds, rely on information that is publicly disseminated by the corporation.

Statutory Disclosure

In Canada there are limited statutory disclosure requirements for public companies. In most Canadian jurisdictions, public disclosure is generally limited to a corporation's prospectus, its financial statements and event-triggered public disclosure of material changes in a corporation's business or affairs.

Securities regulation in Canada has traditionally focused on new offers of securities.[54] As a result, the emphasis has been on requiring complete disclosure in a corporation's prospectus. The prospectus must be filed before any distribution of a security.[55] In most cases, a prospectus is filed at the time of an initial public offering. It must provide full, true and plain disclosure of all material facts relating to the securities proposed to be distributed. A *material fact* is defined in the Ontario *Securities Act* and many other provincial acts as a "fact that significantly affects, or would reasonably be expected to have a significant effect on, the market price or value of the securities" that are the subject of the prospectus.[56] A prospectus must also be accompanied by the financial statements, reports or other documents that may be required.[57]

A public company must also make regular quarterly financial information available, including annual audited statements. There is also a requirement to make immediate disclosure of material changes in the affairs of the public company. Although this obligation is currently limited to "material changes," as discussed below, a corporation's continuous obligation to disclose has recently become a focus of much attention.

In reviewing the prospectus of a corporation, investors typically focus on a corporation's most recent financial statements. For example, the Ontario *Securities Act* requires that financial statements must be prepared in accordance with generally accepted accounting principles (GAAP) and audited and reported upon in accordance with generally accepted auditing standards (GAAS). While the legislation does provide the Ontario Securities Commission (OSC) with certain rule making powers with respect to the accounting and auditing standards to be applied in financial statements and auditor's reports filed with the OSC, it has not, to date, exercised these powers in any manner that overrides the standards set out in the Canadian Institute of Chartered Accountants' Handbook.[58]

Reliance upon financial statements to fulfill disclosure requirements is based on the premise that a corporation's auditors are independent of the corporation and provide a true and objective report of the corporation's financial position. Indeed, in most cases this is accurate. However, firms that conduct audits of a corporation are increasingly providing other services to that same corporation and, as noted by the chair of the OSC, potential for conflict of interest in certain circumstances is significant.[59] The effect of such conflicts upon the reliability of corporate disclosure has been an issue of growing concern to securities regulators in Canada and the United States.

If financial reporting is not full and fair, then the investing public may not have a realistic picture of a corporation's position. In today's volatile market, the ramifications of a corporation failing to meet its profit targets may be significant. The impetus to use "creative" accounting practices may be great. That is not to say that a corporation's auditors will contravene GAAP or GAAS in order to enhance its statements and shore prices but, then again, those principles and standards can be vague and subject to interpretation.

While this area is one of recent interest in relation to shareholder disclosure, other issues relating to the promptness of corporate disclosure, as well as its fullness and intelligibility, remain of concern to institutional investors.

Consequences of Failing to Disclose Accurate Information

Statutory Consequences

Unlike in the United States, investors in Canada do not have the same broad statutory rights of action against a corporation for misrepresentation. Any right to sue is limited to misrepresentations made in certain limited statutorily required documents. Most provincial securities statutes provide a statutory right to sue for misrepresentations made in prospectuses and/or take-over bid circulars, though they do not provide investors with a general right to sue for breach of a disclosure requirement.[60]

Many statutes also contain a general enforcement

provision similar to the following, which is found in the Ontario *Securities Act:*

(i) makes a statement in any application, release, report, preliminary prospectus, return, financial statement, information circular, take-over bid circular, issue or bid circular or other document required to be filed or furnished under Ontario securities law that, in a material respect and at the time and in light of the circumstances under which it is made, is misleading or untrue or does not state a fact that is required to be stated or that is necessary to make the statement not misleading; or

(ii) contravenes Ontario securities law.[61]

However, any oral statements and non-statutorily prescribed documents are not subject to such enforcement proceedings and, as stated above, are also not subject to any statutory right of action for misrepresentation.[62] As a result, any misrepresentations made in documents such as press releases, advertisements and other written material will not be subject to the statutory provisions. Also, and this is increasingly important, statements made by a corporation on its Web site are not subject to the statutory rights of action and/or enforcement proceedings.

Only British Columbia has attempted to expand the scope of statutory offences to include a general offence for misrepresentations. In British Columbia, the *Securities Act* now makes it an offence for a person, while engaging in "investor relations activities," or with the intention of affecting a trade in a security, to, among other things, make a statement that the person knows, or ought reasonably to have known, is a misrepresentation.[63] The term *investor relations activities* is defined as including any activities or oral or written communications, by or on behalf of an issuer or security holder of the issuer, that promote or reasonably could be expected to promote the purchase or sale of securities of the issuer, but does not include, among another things, the dissemination of information provided or records prepared in the ordinary course of the business of the issuer to promote the sale of products or services of the issuer or to raise public awareness of the issuer, that cannot reasonably be considered to promote the purchase or sale or securities of the issuer.[64] As a result, a wider scope of activities by issuing corporations in British Columbia may be subject to statutory enforcement proceedings.

Common Law Right of Action

Investors that have relied, to their detriment, upon public statements made by a corporation and that do not have a statutory right to sue may bring a civil lawsuit against the corporation based on fraudulent or neg-ligent misrepresentation. However, as the recent case of *Carom v. Bre-x Minerals*[65] demonstrates, these cases may be difficult to pursue since the plaintiff investor must be able to prove that he or she actually relied on the misrepresentation or mistake and suffered damages as a result of that reliance. Also, as discussed below, the case demonstrates that class actions may not be available to aggrieved investors in these circumstances.

Continuous Disclosure

For some years now, there has been recognition amongst Canada's securities regulators that the current disclosure regime may not provide sufficient protection for investors. As a result, in January 2000, the Canadian Securities Administrators (CSA) published for comment a Concept Proposal for an integrated disclosure system. The stated objective of the CSA is to foster fair and efficient markets in a changing market environment in a way that facilitates capital formation without compromising the protection of investors. The Concept Proposal states that through the Proposal the CSA seeks to:

• Facilitate prompt and flexible access by business to capital

• Enhance the ability of investors to make informed investment decisions using more useful and reliable information for securities issues and

• Achieve a better match of regulatory effort to existing prospective market conditions.[66]

The CSA acknowledges that the key to achieving the above objectives lies "in integrating and upgrading the quality of information made available on a continuous basis to all market participants."

The CSA Proposal would provide for deemed reliance by secondary market investors on continuous disclosures and public statements. In that regard, the Proposal would create a statutory liability for issuers, their directors, certain officers, promoters, insiders and experts for misrepresentations in publicly disseminated documents or public oral statements relating directly or indirectly to the business and affairs of the issuing corporation. Submissions will be received by the CSA regarding this Concept Proposal until June 1, 2000. Even if adopted, the Concept Proposal would, at least initially, be applicable on a voluntary basis and would not necessarily replace the current statutory regimes in place in each Canadian jurisdiction.

ENFORCEMENT OF SHAREHOLDERS' RIGHTS

Introduction

Directors and officers owe a fiduciary duty to the corporation they work for and not to its shareholders.

Accordingly, a basic question for shareholders is how they (especially minority shareholders) may obtain a remedy for breach of fiduciary duty.

Originally, under the common law, the corporation alone was considered the proper party to take legal action in respect of any wrongs done to it. Not only did courts consider that the corporation was prima facie the proper plaintiff in such an action but, where the alleged wrong was a transaction that could be made binding upon the corporation by a simple majority of shareholders, allowing a single shareholder to take legal action to stop the transaction was considered a violation of the principle of majority rule.[67]

Despite the general rule against allowing shareholders to sue directors and others for breach of fiduciary duty, there were two circumstances in which shareholders could commence such an action. The first was in cases where the transaction in issue was outside of the powers of the directors, while the second was where the transaction involved a fraud upon the company. Under either of these circumstances, individual shareholders could sue on behalf of the company. Unfortunately, while the shareholders bore the cost of maintaining such an action, any monies obtained if they won went directly to the company—the shareholders were supposed to be content with their moral victory.

The growth and influence of corporations and the dissatisfaction of shareholders with the remedies available to them for breach of fiduciary duty under the common law led to the creation of new legal avenues for addressing this issue. There are three of these avenues: derivative actions, oppression remedies and class actions.

Derivative Actions

A *derivative action* is an action brought either in the name of, or on behalf of, a corporation or any of its subsidiaries; an intervention in an action brought by or against the corporation or any of its subsidiaries; or an action by a shareholder or other complainant in order to assert or defend rights to which the corporation or subsidiary is entitled.

Availability of Derivative Actions

The ability to bring a derivative action has been limited by statute. For federally incorporated corporations, the CBCA[68] restricts the availability of derivative actions to "complainants," who can be any of the following:

a. A registered shareholder or beneficial owner, or a former registered holder or beneficial owner, of a security of a corporation or any of its affiliates

b. A director or an officer or a former director or officer of a corporation or any of its affiliates

c. The director or

d. Any other person who, in the discretion of the court, is a proper person to make an application under this part.[69]

Provincial corporation statutes in a number of jurisdictions contain provisions similar to those found in CBCA.[70]

While the first three categories of "complainant" set out above are self-explanatory, the last category has been subject to some judicial interpretation. As noted by the Alberta Court of Appeal in *First Edmonton Place v. 315888 Alberta Ltd.*:[71]

This is not so much a definition as a grant to the court of a broad power to do justice and equity in the circumstances of a particular case, where a person, who otherwise would not be a "complainant," ought to be permitted to bring an action . . . to right a wrong done to the corporation which would not otherwise be righted, or to obtain compensation himself or itself where his or its interests have suffered from oppression by the majority controlling the corporation or have been unfairly prejudiced or unfairly disregarded, and the applicant is a "security holder, creditor, director or officer."[72]

Even if an individual or group meets the definition of *complainant* contained in the applicable statute, a number of conditions precedent must be satisfied before a derivative action can be brought. CBCA contains three such conditions precedent,[73] as does provincial legislation in a number of jurisdictions.[74]

Reasonable Notice

The complainants must establish that they have given reasonable notice of their intention to bring a derivative action to the directors of the company before such an action can proceed. This requirement is usually met when the complainants send a letter to the directors stating the facts giving rise to the perceived problem and requesting that they take steps to address it. If, after a reasonable period of time has elapsed, no action has been taken by the directors, the complainants will be able to establish that the directors are unlikely to act to address the problem, and the first prerequisite will have been met.

Good Faith

After proving that the directors have been given notice of the complainants intending a derivative action, the complainants must prove that they are acting in good faith. The fact that the shareholders might profit from the success of their claim does not mean that they are not acting in good faith. As one court noted, what is important is that the fiduciaries are not able to profit from the breach of their duties, not that the shareholders may receive a windfall.[75]

Best Interests

One court has held that it is sufficient to establish that the complainants are acting in good faith and in the company's best interests for the matter to be allowed to proceed.[76] While the complainants do not need to prove the merits of their case at this stage, the court in *First Edmonton Place* stated that it would not allow a derivative action to proceed if it was clearly frivolous, vexatious or bound to be unsuccessful.[77]

Remedies

Courts can exercise broad remedial powers in a derivative action. For example, Section 240 of the CBCA provides that the court may "make any order it thinks fit," including:

a. An order authorizing the complainant or any other person to control the conduct of the action
b. An order giving directions for the conduct of the action
c. An order directing that any amount adjudged payable by a defendant in the action shall be paid, in whole or in part, directly to former and present security holders of the corporation or its subsidiary instead of to the corporation or its subsidiary and
d. An order requiring the corporation or its subsidiary to pay reasonable legal fees incurred by the complainant in connection with the action.[78]

As with the definition of *complainant,* numerous provincial statutes contain remedial provisions similar to those in the CBCA.[79]

Oppression Remedy

Unlike derivative actions, the oppression remedy is a **personal right** of shareholders, as the wrong that is addressed by this remedy is not one done to the corporation per se, but rather to the complainant.

Availability of Oppression Remedy

As is the case for derivative actions, an individual must still meet the statutory definition of *complainant* before being allowed to proceed with their claim. The CBCA contains the following list of grounds for the invocation of this remedy:

241. (1) A complainant may apply to a court for an order under this section.
(2) If, on an application under subsection (1), the court is satisfied that in respect of a corporation or any of its affiliates
a) any act or omission of the corporation or any of its affiliates effects a result,

b) the business or affairs of the corporation or any of its affiliates are or have been carried on or conducted in a manner; or
c) the powers of the directors of the corporation or any of its affiliates are or have been exercised in a manner

that is oppressive or unfairly prejudicial to or that unfairly disregards the interests of any security holder, creditor, director or officer, the court may make an order to rectify the matters complained of.[80]

Similar grounds are included in provincial corporations legislation.[81]

While the categories are not closed, there are three general classes of cases in which the oppression remedy is available. The first category involves cases where someone in control of the corporation treats its assets as his or her own to the detriment of the minority shareholders. An example of such a situation can be found in *Re National Building Maintenance,* where the director depleted the corporation's assets by making payments to himself, and then proceeded to redeem the minority shares based on the reduced value caused by his depletion.[82]

The second class involves cases where there is a falling-out among shareholders of a small, closely held corporation. To satisfy the court that they have been oppressed in this type of case, the complainant must establish that there was either a pre-existing partnership that was rolled into a corporation; the existence of restrictions on share transfers; or the existence of some sort of agreement or understanding between the parties that all members would be involved in the running of the business.[83]

The third category contains cases where a major reorganization or change in a corporation results in the oppression of minority shareholders. This situation typically arises when the board of a publicly traded corporation decides to take the corporation private, and minority shareholders are treated unfairly.

Remedies

The remedial powers given by statute to the courts for oppression are very broad and can be more sweeping than those available for derivative actions. A court can "make any interim or final order it thinks fit," including: an order to put the company into receivership; to amend the company's articles, by-laws or unanimous shareholder agreements; to direct an exchange of securities; to replace directors; or, to liquidate or dissolve the corporation.[84]

In one case, the Quebec Superior Court ordered that a company be put into receivership, appointed a receiver to run the company, suspended the powers of its directors, officers and managers and ordered the suspension of all contracts as part of its oppression remedy.[85]

Overlap Between Derivative Actions and the Oppression Remedy

There is an overlap between derivative actions and the oppression remedy. Although the two are fundamentally different in theory as derivative actions are filed on behalf of the corporation while the oppression remedy is personal, the oppression remedy makes actions and remedies available to individuals that used to be reserved to the corporation. When determining which action to commence, the general rule is that a derivative action should be filed if harm was done to the corporation that affects all shareholders, albeit indirectly, while an oppression action should be commenced if an action affects shareholders directly and has a differential impact on one shareholder or an identifiable group of them.

It is also noteworthy that some of the situations that give rise to the oppression remedy, as in the case of *Re National Building Maintenance*,[86] for example, where damages were caused to both the minority shareholders **and** the corporation. In such circumstances, at least one court has ordered that derivative and oppression actions could proceed simultaneously, as the first action addressed the injury done to the company, while the second addressed the injury to the shareholders.[87] However, when there is a choice between commencing a derivative or oppression action, it is generally easier to bring an oppression action, as it lacks the statutory prerequisites of the derivative remedy.

Class Proceedings

Class proceedings are a new and potentially potent procedural tool that may assist shareholders in their attempts to hold corporations, and others, legally accountable for their injuries.

However, the class action should be utilized strategically and with a view to the advantages and disadvantages that the procedure provides and the goals that can be realistically achieved.

A *class proceeding* is a civil action brought by one or more persons on behalf of a larger group having similar grievances or a civil action brought against one or more persons defending on behalf of a larger group similarly situated. A plaintiff class action is by far the most common form of class proceeding. Notwithstanding that class proceedings legislation has been enacted in the provinces of Ontario,[88] British Columbia[89] and Quebec,[90] only in Ontario is a class action available to both plaintiffs and defendants.[91] There is no federal class action legislation in Canada.

Class proceedings litigation is a procedural tool designed to:
a. Provide more efficient handling of potentially complex cases of mass wrong
b. Provide improved access to justice for those whose actions might not otherwise be asserted and
c. Inhibit misconduct by those who might be tempted to ignore their obligations to the public.[92]

To that end, the courts play an important role in overseeing class proceedings. The court exercises a continuing proactive role in the litigation from its commencement to its conclusion.[93] The degree to which they are supervised and managed by the court, as mandated by legislation, distinguishes class proceedings from traditional proceedings.

Availability of Class Proceedings

Class proceedings legislation does not alter the substantive law upon which a claim is based. A class action proceeding must disclose a cause of action. However, class proceedings litigation is a flexible tool that can be utilized in a wide breadth of arenas. In the context of enforcing shareholders' rights, it can be, and has been, used to pursue minority shareholders' claims, public offering misrepresentation, negligent and fraudulent misrepresentation as to the value of security, material nondisclosure and insider trading.

Obstacles to Class Proceedings

Certification. The statutory regimes in Canada governing class proceedings create particular rules which must be satisfied prior to a class action becoming "certified" to proceed. The purpose of the certification process is to screen out frivolous claims and to allow the court to determine whether the proposed asserted claims are the proper subject of a class proceeding, as opposed to another more appropriate procedure. In that respect, the court reviews each prospective class proceeding on a case-by-case basis.

Each of the provincial statutes concerning class proceedings contains criteria for the certification of classes and subclasses. In Ontario, the legislation requires, as a precondition to certification, that:
• The proceeding disclose a cause of action
• The proceeding disclose an identifiable class of two or more persons that would be represented by the representative plaintiff.
• The claims of the class members raise common issues.
• The class action is the preferable procedure for the resolution of the common issues.

- The representative plaintiff would fairly and accurately represent the interest of the class or subclass.
- The representative plaintiff demonstrates a willingness to pay or fund the expenses of the prosecution of the action.[94]

Notice. Class proceedings legislation also contain specific provisions concerning the notice that must be provided in respect of a class proceeding, including notice of certification, notice of the determination of common issues and notice for individual participation.

Thus in Ontario,[95] subject to the court exercising its discretion to dispense with notice, a representative party must notify other class members of the certification of a class proceeding and, as well, notify the class of the right to intervene and the right to opt out of the proceeding. Further, notice to class members may also be necessary where individual participation is required to determine individual issues.

Notification can be a cumbersome, time-consuming and expensive process, depending upon the size and composition of the class. While the plaintiff may have to pay all or part of the cost of notification, the court may make any order as to costs as it feels is appropriate, including an order apportioning the cost of notice among the parties.

Decertification. As the Canadian legislation provides for the court to control and direct the conduct of a class proceeding, a court can decertify a class proceeding if the certification criteria are no longer satisfied.[96]

Costs/Counsel Fees and Funding

Costs may be one of the most significant barriers to a class proceeding. The personal liability assumed by a representative plaintiff for a large cost award may serve as a strong deterrent to the commencement of the class action.

Notwithstanding the potentially onerous obligation for costs, the Ontario legislation adopts the standard "two-way" cost rule, which provides that the loser must pay the successful party's costs, subject to the court's inherent discretion to decide otherwise. Thus, if the class action is not successful, the representative plaintiff, and only the representative plaintiff, can be liable for the defendant's costs in respect to the common issues. Class members can only be liable for the defendant's costs with respect to the determination of their own individual claims.[97]

A representative plaintiff can apply for public funding from the Class Proceeding Fund. If granted, the funding only covers disbursements and indemnifies the representative plaintiff against any adverse cost award if the class action is unsuccessful. The funding does not cover legal fees. If the plaintiff's action is successful, the Fund recovers the amount paid to the plaintiff for disbursements and is also entitled to 10% of the plaintiff's award to replenish the Fund.[98]

In respect to legal fees, Ontario provides for a modified contingency fee arrangement whereby the court can apply a multiplier to the base legal fee to compensate a lawyer for undertaking the risk of a class proceeding where the lawyer is only to be paid in the event of success. However, any agreement in respect of counsel fees must be in writing and must be approved by the court to be enforceable.[99]

It is interesting to note that while costs are also awarded on the basis of the "two-way" scheme in Quebec, and only the representative plaintiff is liable to pay the defendant's costs if the action is unsuccessful, the Quebec legislation provides that a successful defendant can only be awarded costs based upon a specified reduced tariff. In Quebec, public funding is available through the Fonds D'aide au Recourse Collectif to cover both costs and disbursements and legal fees.[100]

The Quebec legislation also provides for contingency fee arrangements in respect to counsel fees, as approved by the court.[101]

In contrast to both Ontario and Quebec, British Columbia adopts the "no costs" rule, which provides that each party must bear their own legal costs regardless of success. The court does however still maintain the discretion to make a cost award in exceptional circumstances.[102] This will likely result in more class proceedings being brought in British Columbia than in other jurisdictions.

British Columbia's legislation also provides for contingency fees, as long as they are in writing and approved by the court.[103]

Recent Canadian Jurisprudence

A recent class action certification proceeding involving the enforcement of shareholders' rights is the case of *Rogers Broadcasting Limited v. Alexander.*[104]

This case concerned a counter-application by minority shareholders in Canadian Home Shopping Network (CHSN) Ltd. (CHSN) for certification of a class proceeding. The proposed class proceeding was in respect of an application for damages for oppressive conduct by the majority shareholder in causing the amalgamation of CHSN with an affiliate of the majority shareholder.

The proceeding began as an application brought by the plaintiff, Rogers Broadcasting Limited (Rogers), the successor to CHSN, to fix a fair value for the shares of the dissenting shareholders of CHSN. The respondent dissenting shareholders alleged that the going private transaction was effected in a manner that was oppressive and unfairly prejudicial to the minority.

Mr. Justice Montgomery held that the respondent dissenting shareholders' real objection was to the price being offered for their shares, and noted that there were a number of the minority shareholders who chose not to dissent and who made a conscious decision to either convert their shares or have their shares bought out for the price being offered.[105]

Accordingly, Mr. Justice Montgomery failed to find oppression as a common issue and refused to certify the class action.

Mr. Justice Montgomery further noted that had he found some common issues, he would have held that the preferable way to proceed with the dissenting claims was by way of a valuation of the shares pursuant to Section 190(15) of the CBCA.[106]

Maxwell v. MLG Ventures Ltd.,[107] another decision of the Ontario Court (General Division) [now the Ontario Superior Court of Justice], involved the certification of a class action by former shareholders who had sold shares based upon alleged misrepresentations in an offering circular issued by MLG Ventures Ltd. (Ventures).

The representative plaintiff claimed breaches of Sections 131 and 134 of the *Securities Act,* on behalf of all of the shareholders who tendered shares in response to the offer in the circular to purchase for cash all the outstanding shares of Maple Leaf Gardens Limited (MLGL).

In granting certification, Mr. Justice Ground found that there was an identifiable class of two or more persons and that the claim raised a common issue in that the same offer, which allegedly failed to disclose certain material facts relating to the business and financial position of MLGL and appraisals of the shares of MLGL by Venture, was made to all members of the class.

The court further held that a class action was the preferable procedure for advancing the claim as a number of the shareholders who tendered their shares pursuant to the offering circular were holders of a small number of shares and it would not be economic for them to commence individual actions for damages based upon misrepresentation.

Finally, the court determined that the representative plaintiff would fairly and adequately represent the interests of the class.

In a subsequent motion, the plaintiff sought leave of the court to amend the Statement of Claim in the certified class action, to allege, inter alia, that the defendant chairman and chief executive officer of MLGL breached a number of fiduciary duties owed to the plaintiff class.

Mr. Justice Ground however refused leave to amend to plead breach of fiduciary duty as such an amendment would "fundamentally change the nature of the action originally certified and would require a reconsideration by the court of all of the issues examined on the original application to certify the action."

The court further held that such an action should be separately constituted and might proceed as an oppression action under the Ontario *Business Corporations Act* (OBCA). Perhaps the most recent notable Canadian class action decision involving shareholders is that of *Carom v. Bre-X Minerals Ltd.*,[108] a certification decision of Mr. Justice Winkler of the Ontario Court (General Division) [now the Ontario Superior Court of Justice] heard in May 1999.

The Bre-X litigation raised a number of issues about the duties and responsibilities of Bre-X, its engineers and financial industry service providers toward shareholders and, as well, further clarified the judicial attitude toward class action proceedings.

In the certification application, Mr. Justice Winkler was called upon to determine whether, and to what extent, a class proceeding should be certified in Ontario on behalf of a representative group of shareholders of Bre-X, an Alberta mining corporation. Eight intended class proceedings were commenced by representative shareholder plaintiffs involving three types of claims.

The court determined that the representative plaintiff's actions did satisfy a number of the certification criteria, namely, that the pleadings did disclose a cause of action and that there was an identifiable class of two or more persons. However, the court made mixed rulings in respect of the test of common issues, the preferable procedure and the appropriateness of representative plaintiffs in each of the three types of claims.

Claims against Bre-X and its directors and officers. The plaintiff shareholders alleged that Bre-X, and related entities, conspired to increase the price of Bre-X shares for their own benefit, by misrepresenting that Bre-X had discovered gold in the Indonesian jungle. The shareholders advanced claims against Bre-X, and related entities, for conspiracy, fraudulent misrepresentation, negligent misrepresentation and breach of the *Competition Act.*

After a discussion of the Ontario *Class Proceedings Act* as it related to "common issues," Mr. Justice Winkler determined that, subject to amending the definition of the class, the class action as against Bre-X could proceed in respect to certain specified "common issues."

The court found that the claim for aggravated damages, however, was individual in nature and could not proceed as a common issue. Similarly, the court found that the claim in negligent misrepresentation did not present a common issue, as the determination of negligent misrepresentation would require an individual inquiry concerning the characterization of each individual representation, the plaintiffs' perceptions of the representations and the circumstances in which they were made.

The court found that in respect to the specified common issues, a class proceeding would be the preferable procedure for resolution and that the representative plaintiff could fairly and accurately represent the interests of the class. In the result, the claims of conspiracy, fraudulent misrepresentation and breach of the *Competition Act* were certified.

It is interesting to note that the issue of negligent and fraudulent misrepresentation was dealt with indirectly in a prior related motion brought by the representative plaintiff to amend Bre-X's Statement of Claim to include a claim for "fraud on the market." In that decision, Mr. Justice Winkler found that such a doctrine had no application in Canadian law.

"Fraud on the market" is an American-based doctrine arising from the application of Section 10(b) of the *U.S. Securities Exchange Act of 1934,* which is based upon the theory that:

> ... in an open and developed securities market, the price of a company's stock is determined by the company and its business ... Misleading statements will therefore defraud purchasers of stock even if the purchasers do not directly rely on the misstatements. ... The causal connection between the plaintiffs' purchase of stock in such a case is no less significant than in the case of direct reliance on misrepresentations.[109]

In the United States, the "fraud on the market" doctrine has been considered integral and a companion to the class proceedings rules. The "fraud on the market" doctrine enables a representative plaintiff to overcome the need for individual investors to establish individual knowledge of or reliance upon a misrepresentation, as the fact of a misleading statement is rebuttably presumed to affect the market price of the stock and to provide the investor who paid the affected price with a legal claim.

In rejecting the "fraud on the market" doctrine in Ontario, Mr. Justice Winkler stated:

i) The "fraud on the market" doctrine had evolved in the United States as an outgrowth of the *Securities Exchange Act* and within the limitations stipulated by that statute. Securities legislation in Canada does not establish a cause of action for misrepresentation and therefore does not establish the context for a "fraud on the market" approach;

ii) The plaintiffs' claim based upon a breach of the *Competition Act,* not being specific securities legislation, did not provide the statutory framework within which the "fraud on the market" doctrine could be developed;

iii) While class actions in the United States depend upon the "predominance of common issues" test, this test is not decisive in Canada. The Ontario *Class Proceedings Act* may be used where a class action is the preferable procedure for the resolution of common issues, and can be utilized even where the common issues do not predominate over individual issues.

Claims against the engineers. The Bre-X shareholders also advanced claims in negligence, negligent misrepresentation and on the basis of breaches of the *Competition Act* against the engineering companies that analyzed the gold resources.

In the decision, Mr. Justice Winkler held that as the essence of the claims against the engineers was negligence and negligent misrepresentation, it would be necessary to determine whether a duty of care was owed by the defendant engineers to the plaintiffs, which issue would have to be determined on an individual basis.

The court also found that, even if such common issues were present, a class action would not be the preferable procedure for dealing with those claims given their substance and complexity.

Similarly, the court found that, although the breach of the *Competition Act* could be said to be a common issue, the class action was not the preferable procedure for its determination as the resolution of that common issue involved mixed fact and law.

Finally, the court found that the representative plaintiff in the action against the engineers could not adequately and fairly represent the class as the trading activity of the plaintiff was idiosyncratic and the proposed plaintiff had a conflict of interest given his involvement, as a proposed representative plaintiff, in two interrelated actions.

In the result, the court held that the claims of negligence, negligent misrepresentation and breach of the *Competition Act,* as against the engineer defendants, should not be certified.

Claims against the brokers. The third class of claims advanced were against a number of brokerage firms and the financial analysts employed by them, who were alleged to have promoted Bre-X stock.

The claims were advanced on the basis of negligence, negligent misrepresentation, fraudulent misrepresentation and breach of the *Competition Act.*

Mr. Justice Winkler found that the theory of the plaintiffs' claims in negligence could be reduced to misrepresentation or, alternatively, a breach of the duty to warn. Mr. Justice Winkler found these claims to be individual rather than common in nature as they involved an analysis of the relationship between the broker and each investor.

Although the court found that there were common issues to be found in the claims for negligent misrepresentation, fraudulent misrepresentation and breach of the *Competition Act,* it determined that a class action proceeding was not the preferable procedure for resolving them as individual trials would be necessary to determine the essential elements of reliance, causation and damages. Further, the representative plaintiffs were found not to satisfy the conditions necessary to represent the class.

Conclusion

Although Bre-X arose in the context of an alleged fraud upon shareholders, the certification decision will have a significant impact on disputes between investors and investees that have at their root any type of misrepresentation.

The difficulty of course is that given Mr. Justice Winkler's ruling on the unavailability of "fraud on the market" doctrine in Canada, certification applications will likely not be successful where the shareholder plaintiffs are relying upon claims of negligence or negligent misrepresentation, which have as an essential element the individual's specific knowledge of and reliance upon the misstatements.

Such claims usually arise in the circumstance of secondary market trading and are customarily brought against analysts, brokerage companies or others, based upon oral statements made to individual clients. The complexity arising from the need to prove individual reliance, causation and damages seems to be a major impediment to certification even where common issues are identified. A Canadian shareholder does not have a statutory right to claim damages for false or misleading statements made during secondary market trades. A plaintiff would therefore be left to rely upon an individual claim based on tort, breach of contract, oppression or breach of statutes such as the *Competition Act*. In the primary market, where shares are sold pursuant to an offering prospectus or offering circular, reliance is deemed by statute in Ontario,[110] and such class actions would appear to be more easily certified.

ENDNOTES

1. *Pension Benefits Act,* R.S.O. 1990, c. P.8 as am (OPBA).

2. See *Employment Pension Plans Act,* S.A. 1986, c. E-10.05 as am (EPPA), s. 41; *Pension Benefits Standards Act,* R.S.B.C. 1996, c. 352 as am, s. 44 (BCPBSA); *Pension Benefits Act,* R.S.M. 1987, c. P32 as am, s. 28.1 (MPBA); *Pension Benefits Act,* S.N.B. 1987, c. P-5.1 as am (NBPBA), ss. 17 and 18; *Pension Benefits Act,* R.S.N.S. 1989, c. 340 as am, ss. 29(1)-29(2) (NSPBA); *Pension Benefits Act,* S.P.E.I., 1990, c.41 as am, ss. 28(1) and 28(2) (PEIPBA); *Supplemental Pension Plans Act,* R.S.Q. c. R-15.1 as am, s. 151 (SPPA).

3. See BCPBSA, *supra* note 2, ss. 9(7)-9(9); MPBA, *supra* note 2, ss. 28.1(6)-28.1(8); NBPBA, *supra* note 2, s. 18; NSPBA, *supra* note 2, ss. 29(4)-29(8); OPBA, *supra* note 1, ss. 22(5), 22(7) and 22(8); PEIPBA, *supra* note 2, ss. 28(4)-28(6) and 28(8); SPPA, *supra* note 2, ss. 152-155.

4. See *Employment Pension Plans Regulation,* Alta. Reg. 364/86 as am (the "EPPA Regulation"), s. 36.1; *Pension Benefits Standards Regulation,* B.C. Reg. 433/93 as am, (the "BCPBSA Regulation"), s. 38(3); *Pension Benefits Regulation,*

Man. Reg. 188/87R as am, (the "MPBA Regulation") (Note: Manitoba's legislation states that the investment policies of provincially registered pension plans are to be in accordance with the Federal *Pension Benefits Standards Act,* which requires the adoption of a SIP&P, s. 16(3); *Pension Benefits Regulation,* N.B. Reg. 91-195 as am (the "NBPBA Regulation"), s. 44(3); *Pension Benefits Act Regulations,* Nfld. Reg. 114/96, as am (the "NPBA Regulation"), s. 39(6); *Pension Benefits Regulation,* N.S. Reg. 269/87 as am, (the "NSPBA Regulation"), Sch. 1, s. 1(4); SPPA, *supra* note 2, ss. 69-170; *Pension Benefits Regulations, 1993,* R.R.S. c. P-6.001, Reg. 1 (the "SPBA Regulation"), s. 38 (Note: while Saskatchewan's legislation does not explicitly refer to either a SIP&P or a SIP&G, it states that the investment policies of provincially registered pension plans are to be in accordance with the federal *Pension Benefits Standards Act,* which requires the adoption of a SIP&P).

5. *Pension Benefits Standards Act,* R.S.C. 1985, c. 32, 2d Supp. as am (PBSA).

6. Financial Services Commission of Ontario, *Guide To Completing a SIP&G,* Compliance Assistance Guideline #3, May 1990, Index No. S700-100.

7. Pension and Welfare Benefits Administration, Department of Labor, *Interpretive Bulletin Relating to the Retirement Income Security Act of 1974,* 29 CFR §2509.942 (1994).

8. *Ibid.*

9. See *Business Corporations Act,* R.S.A. 1980, c. B.16 as am *(ABCA); Company Act,* R.S.B.C. 1996, c. 62 as am (BCCA); *The Corporations Act,* R.S.M. 1987, c. C225 as am (MCA); *Business Corporations Act,* S.N.B. 1981, c. B-9.1 as am (NBBCA); *Corporations Act,* R.S.N. 1990, c. C-36 as am (NCA); *Companies Act,* R.S.N.S. 1981 c. 81 as am (NCSA); *Business Corporations Act,* R.S.O. 1990, c. B.16 as am (OBCA); *Companies Act,* R.S.P.E.I. 1988, c. C-14 as am (PEICA); *Companies Act,* R.S.Q. c. C-38 as (QCA); *Business Corporations Act,* R.S.S. 1978, c. B-10 as am (SBCA).

10. *Canada Business Corporations Act* R.S.C. 1985, c. C-44 as am (CBCA).

11. See MCA, *supra* note 9, s. 1(1); NBBCA, *supra* note 9, s. 1(1); NCA, *supra* note 9, s. 2(dd); PEICA, *supra* note 9, s. 1(h); QCA, *supra* note 9, Part I s. 3(4); Part II s. 124(5) (Joint-Stock Companies).

12. For instance, the articles of incorporation, articles of amendment, articles of amalgamation and articles of arrangement.

13. See ABCA, *supra* note 9, s. 24(3); BCCA, *supra* note 9, s. 22(2); MCA, *supra* note 9, s. 24(4); NBBCA, *supra* note 9, s. 22(2); NCA, *supra* note 9, s. 47; OBCA, *supra* note 9, s. 22(3); PEICA, *supra* note 9, s. 13(4) (each share is equal and is subject to the designation, preferences, privileges and voting power restrictions or qualifications granted or imposed in respect of any class of share); QCA, *supra* note 9, Part IA, s. 123.40 (Companies Incorporated by the Filing of Articles); SBCA, *supra* note 9, s. 24(3).

14. See ABCA, *supra* note 9, s. 24(4); MCA, *supra* note 9, s. 24(3); NBBCA, *supra* note 9, s. 22(3); NCA, *supra* note 9, s. 48; NSCA, *supra* note 9, Sch. 1, s. 68; OBCA, *supra* note 9, s. 22(4); PEICA, *supra* note 9, s. 13(4); QCA, *supra* note 9, Part I s. 48, Part IA s. 123.40 (Companies Incorporated by the Filing of Articles), Part II ss. 146(2)-146(5) (Joint-Stock Companies).

15. See ABCA, *supra* note 9, s. 101(3); BCCA, *supra* note

9, s. 110(2); MCA, *supra* note 9, s. 101(2); NBBCA, *supra* note 9, ss. 65(1)-65(4); NCA, *supra* note 9, s. 175(3); NSCA, *supra* note 9, Sch. 1 s. 116; OBCA, *supra* note 9, s. 119(4); PEICA, *supra* note 9, ss. 24-25; QCA, *supra* note 9, Part I ss. 88-89, Part II, ss. 181-182, SBCA, *supra* note 9, ss. 101(3) and 101(8).

16. See ABCA, *supra* note 9, s. 104; BCCA, *supra* note 9, s. 130(3); MCA, *supra* note 9, s. 104(1); NBBCA, *supra* note 9, s. 67; NCA, *supra* note 9, s. 179; NSCA, *supra* note 9, Sch 1 s. 117; OBCA, *supra* note 9, s. 122; QCA, *supra* note 9, Part IA s. 123.77; SBCA, *supra* note 9, s. 104.

17. Subject to any unanimous shareholders' agreement. See ABCA, *supra* note 9, s. 117; BCCA, *supra* note 9, s. 118; MCA, *supra* note 9, s. 117; NBBCA, *supra* note 9, s. 79; NCA, *supra* note 9, s. 203; OBCA, *supra* note 9, s. 115(1).

18. See ABCA, *supra* note 9, s. 156; BCCA, *supra* note 9, s. 178; MCA, *supra* note 9, s. 156; NBBCA, *supra* note 9, s. 105(1); NCA, *supra* note 9, s. 265; NSCA, *supra* note 9, ss. 117(1) and 117(2); OBCA, *supra* note 9, s. 149; QCA, *supra* note 9, Part I s. 113, Part IA s. 123.97, Part II s. 206; SBCA, *supra* note 9, s. 156.

19. See ABCA, *supra* note 9, s. 164; BCCA, *supra* note 9, ss. 193 and 198; MCA, *supra* note 9, ss. 162(1)-162(2); NBBCA, *supra* note 9, ss. 109(1)-109(2); NCA, *supra* note 9, ss. 271-272; NSCA, *supra* note 9, ss. 117(8) and 119(1)-119(2); OBCA, *supra* note 9, s. 151(1); SBCA, *supra* note 9, s. 164.

20. See ABCA, *supra* note 9, s. 167(1); MCA, *supra* note 9, s. 167; NBBCA, *supra* note 9, s. 113(1); NCA, *supra* note 9, s. 279; NSCA, *supra* note 9, s. 19; OBCA, *supra* note 9, s. 168; QCA, *supra* note 9, Part IA s. 123.103; SBCA, *supra* note 9, s. 167(1).

21. See ABCA, *supra* note 9, s. 177; BCCA, *supra* note 9, ss. 248-250; MCA, *supra* note 9, ss. 177-178; NBBCA, *supra* note 9, ss. 122-123; NCA, *supra* note 9, ss. 19(j) and 134(4); OBCA, *supra* note 9, ss. 175-176; PEICA, *supra* note 9, s. 77(3); QCA, *supra* note 9, Part I ss. 18(3)-18(4), Part IA ss. 123.125-123.130; SBCA, *supra* note 9, ss. 177(1), 177(5) and 178.

22. See MCA, *supra* note 9, s. 182; NBBCA, *supra* note 9, s. 126(3); NCA, *supra* note 9, s. 299; OBCA, *supra* note 9, s. 181; PEICA, *supra* note 9, s. 86(2); SBCA, *supra* note 9, ss. 182(4)-182(5).

23. See ABCA, *supra* note 9, s. 183; MCA, *supra* note 9, s. 183(3); NBBCA, *supra* note 9, s. 130; NCA, *supra* note 9, s. 303; OBCA, *supra* note 9, s. 184(3); SBCA, *supra* note 9, ss. 183(2)-182(4).

24. See ABCA, *supra* note 9, s. 184; BCCA, *supra* note 9, s. 222; MCA, *supra* note 9, s. 184; NCA, *supra* note 9, s. 304; NSCA, *supra* note 9, Sch. 3, s. 2; OBCA, *supra* note 9, s. 185(1); SBCA, *supra* note 9, s. 184.

25. See ABCA, *supra* note 9, s. 13(1); MCA, *supra* note 9, s. 131(2); NBBCA, *supra* note 9, s. 89(1); NCA, *supra* note 9, s. 224; NSCA, *supra* note 9, Sch. 3 s. 9(1); OBCA, *supra* note 9, s. 169(1); SBCA, *supra* note 9, s. 131(1)(a).

26. See ABCA, *supra* note 9, s. 131(2); MCA, *supra* note 9, s. 131(1); NBBCA, *supra* note 9, s. 89(1)(a); NCA, *supra* note 9, s. 224; NSCA, *supra* note 9, Sch. 3 ss. 9(1)(a)-9(1)(b); OBCA, *supra* note 9, s. 99; SBCA, *supra* note 9, s. 131(1)(b).

27. See ABCA, *supra* note 9, s. 131(4); MCA, *supra* note 9, s. 131(4); NCA, *supra* note 9, s. 226; NSCA, *supra* note 9, Sch. 3 s. 9(4); OBCA, *supra* note 9, s. 99(4); SBCA, *supra* note 9, s. 131(4).

28. NBBCA, *supra* note 9, s. 89(4).

29. ABCA, *supra* note 9, s. 127; MCA, *supra* note 9, s. 127; NBBCA, *supra* note 9, s. 85(l); NCA, *supra* note 9, s. 217; OBCA, *supra* note 9, s. 94; SBCA, *supra* note 9, s. 127(a).

30. BCCA, *supra* note 9, s. 124.

31. NSCA, *supra* note 9, s. 83(1).

32. QCA, *supra* note 9, Part I s. 98, Part II s. 191.

33. See ABCA, *supra* note 9, s. 137; MCA, *supra* note 9, s. 137; NCA, *supra* note 9, s. 241; OBCA, *supra* note 9, s. 105; SBCA, *supra* note 9, s. 137(l).

34. See NBBCA, *supra* note 9, s. 96; NSCA, *supra* note 9, Sch. 3 s. 8; QCA, *supra* note 9, Part I s. 99, Part II s. 192.

35. BCCA, *supra* note 9, s. 147.

36. See ABCA, *supra* note 9, s. 137(6); MCA, *supra* note 9, s. 137(6); NBBCA, *supra* note 9, s. 96(5); NCA, *supra* note 9, s. 241(6); OBCA, *supra* note 9, s. 105(6); SBCA, *supra* note 9, s. 137(6).

37. See ABCA, *supra* note 9, s. 142(1); BCCA, *supra* note 9, s. 151 (1); MCA, *supra* note 9, s. 142(1); NBBCA, *supra* note 9, ss. 9(1)-9(2); NCA, *supra* note 9, s. 247; NSCA, *supra* note 9, ss. 85B(1)-85B(2); OBCA, *supra* note 9, s. 110; QCA, *supra* note 9, Part I s. 103, Part II s. 196; SBCA, *supra* note 9, s. 142.

38. The term *reporting issuer* is defined in the *Securities Act,* R.S.O. 1990, c. S.5 as am (OSA), s. 1(1) to mean a corporation that either:
(a) has filed a prospectus and obtained a receipt or has filed an securities exchange take-over bid circular; or
(b) the shares of which are listed and posted for trading on any stock exchange in Ontario recognized by the Ontario Securities Commission; or
(c) is offering its shares to the public as contemplated by OBCA; or
(d) whose existence continues following the exchange of shares of a company by or for the account of such company with another company or the holders of the securities of that other company in connection with a statutory amalgamation or arrangement or a statutory procedure under which one company takes title to the assets of the other company that in turn loses its existence by operation of law, or under which the existing companies merge into a new company, where one of the amalgamating or merged companies or the continuing company has been a reporting issuer for at least twelve (12) months.
See also *Securities Act,* S.A. 1981, c. S-6.1 as am, s. 1(1) (ASA); *Securities Act,* R.S.B.C. 1996, c. 418 as am, s. 1(1) (BCSA); *Securities Act,* R.S.M. 1987, c. S-50 as am, s. 80(1) (MCA); *Securities Act,* R.S.N. 1996, c. S- 13 as am, s. 2(1)(oo) (NSA); *Securities Act,* R. S.N. S. 1989, c. 418 as am, s. 2(1)(ao) (NSSA); *Securities Act,* R.S.Q. c. V-1.1 as am, s. 5 (QSA); *Securities Act,* S.S. 1988, c. S-42.2 as am, s. 2(1)(qq) (SSA). Such a company is, in general terms, usually referred to as a "public company" and that reference will continue to be used in this chapter.

39. See ABCA, *supra* note 9, s. 143(1); BCCA, *supra* note 9, s. 153(1); MCA, *supra* note 9, s. 143(1); NCA, *supra* note 9, s. 250; NSCA, *supra* note 9, s. 85D(1); OBCA, *supra* note 9, s. 111; SBCA, *supra* note 9, s. 143(1).

40. *Brown v. Duby* (1980), 111 D.L.R. (3rd) 418 (Ont. H.C.).

41. See ASA, *supra* note 38, s. 79; MSA, *supra* note 38, s. 79,

NCA, *supra* note 38, s. 255; NSSA, *supra* note 38, s. 55, OSA, *supra* note 38, s. 49; SSA, *supra* note 38, s. 55.

42. See ABCA, *supra* note 9, ss. 143(2)-143(4); BCCA, *supra* note 9, s. 151(2); MCA, *supra* note 9, s. 143(3); OBCA, *supra* note 9, s. 258(1)(c); SBCA, *supra* note 9, ss. 143(2)-143(4).

43. See ABCA, *supra* note 9, s. 144(1); BCCA, *supra* note 9, s. 154; MCA, *supra* note 9, ss. 144(1)-144(2); NCA, *supra* note 9, s. 251; NSCA, *supra* note 9, s. 85D(2); OBCA, *supra* note 9, s. 112(l); SBCA, *supra* note 9, s. 144.

44. See ABCA, *supra* note 9, ss. 143(4)-143(5); BCCA, *supra* note 9, s. 154(1); MCA, *supra* note 9, ss. 144(3)-144(4); OBCA, *supra* note 9, s. 258(1)(d); SBCA, *supra* note 9, ss. 143(3)-143(4).

45. See ABCA, *supra* note 9, s. 184; BCCA, *supra* note 9, s. 207; MCA, *supra* note 9, s. 184; NCA, *supra* note 9, s. 304; NSCA, *supra* note 9, Sch. 3 s. 2(1)(2); OBCA, *supra* note 9, s. 185(1); SBCA, *supra* note 9, s. 184(1).

46. See ABCA, *supra* note 9, s. 184(3); BCCA, *supra* note 9, s. 207(3); MCA, *supra* note 9, s. 184(3); NCA, *supra* note 9, s. 307; NSCA, *supra* note 9, Sch. 3 s. 2(4); OBCA, *supra* note 9, s. 185; SBCA, *supra* note 9, s. 184(3).

47. See ASA, *supra* note 38; BCSA, *supra* note 38; MSA, *supra* note 38; *Security Frauds Prevention Act,* R.S.N.B. 1973, c. S-6 as am (SFPA); NSA, *supra* note 38; NSSA, *supra* note 38; OSA, *supra* note 38; Securities Act R.S.P.E.I. 1988, c. S-3 as am (PEISA); QSA, *supra* note 38; SSA, *supra* note 38.

48. See ABCA, *supra* note 9, s. 165; BCCA, *supra* note 9, s. 187; MCA, *supra* note 9, s. 165; NCA, *supra* note 9, s. 276; OBCA, *supra* note 9, s. 158; SBCA, *supra* note 9, s. 165.

49. See ABCA, *supra* note 9, s. 153; BCCA, *supra* note 9, s. 172; MCA, *supra* note 9, s. 153(1); NBBCA, *supra* note 9, s. 100; NCA, *supra* note 9, s. 258(1); NSCA, *supra* note 9, s. 121(1); OBCA, *supra* note 9, s. 154(3); PEICA, *supra* note 9, s. 79; QCA, *supra* note 9, Part I s. 98(2), Part II, ss. 191(2)-191(3); SBCA, *supra* note 9, s. 149(1).

50. Pension Investment Association of Canada, *Corporate Governance Standards,* June 1998. For more information, visit www.piacweb.org.

51. *Ibid.*

52. *Ibid.*

53. David A. Brown, Q.C., Chair, Ontario Securities Commission, *Public Accounting at a Crossroads,* speech delivered to the Business Leaders Luncheon, the Institute of Chartered Accountants of Ontario, June 8, 1999.

54. Canadian Securities Administrators, *Concept Proposal for an Integrated Disclosure System,* January 2000, Part II.

55. See ASA, *supra* note 38, s. 81(1); BCSA, *supra* note 38, s. 61(1); MSA, *supra* note 38, s. 37(1); SFPA, *supra* note 47, s. 13(3); NSA, *supra* note 38, s. 54; NSSA, *supra* note 38, s. 58(1); OSA, *supra* note 38, s. 53(1); PEISA, *supra* note 47, s. 8(1); QSA, *supra* note 38, s. 11; SSA, *supra* note 38, s. 58.

56. See ASA, *supra* note 38, s. 1(1); BCSA, *supra* note 38, s. 1(1); NSA, *supra* note 38, s. 2(1)(x); NSSA, *supra* note 38, s. 2(1)(w); OSA, *supra* note 38, s. 1(1); PEISA, *supra* note 47, s. 8.1; QSA, *supra* note 38, s. 13; SSA, *supra* note 38, s. 61.

57. See ASA, *supra* note 38, s. 84; BCSA, *supra* note 38, s. 61; MSA, *supra* note 38, ss. 41-43; SFPA, *supra* note 47, s. 13(3); NSA, *supra* note 38, s. 57; NSSA, *supra* note 38, s. 61; OSA,

supra note 38, s. 56(2); PEISA, *supra* note 47, s. 8.1; QSA, *supra* note 38, s. 13; SSA, *supra* note 38, s. 61.

58. Brown, *supra* note 53, p. 4.

59. Brown, *supra* note 53, p. 7. See also David A. Brown, Q.C., *Towards an Open Market Place—Say No to Performance Enhancers,* speech delivered to the Investment Counsel Association of Canada, September 14, 1999.

60. See ASA, *supra* note 38, ss. 168-169; BCSA, *supra* note 38, ss. 131-132; MSA, *supra* note 38, s. 97; NSA, *supra* note 38, ss. 130-131; NSSA, *supra* note 38, ss. 137 and 139; OSA, *supra* note 38, ss. 130-131; *Securities Act Regulation,* R.R.O. 1990, Reg. 1015 Part IV; PEISA, *supra* note 47, s. 16; QSA, *supra* note 38, ss. 196-197; SA, *supra* note 38, ss. 137 and 139.

61. OSA, *supra* note 38, s. 122. See also ASA, *supra* note 38, s. 161; BCSA, *supra* note 38, s. 155; MSA, *supra* note 38, s. 136; SFPA, *supra* note 47, s. 41; NSA, *supra* note 38, s. 122; PEISA, *supra* note 47, s. 28(1); QSA, *supra* note 38, s. 195; SSA, *supra* note 38, s. 131.

62. David McIntyre, *Web site and Electronic Communications Policies and Practices for Canadian Companies,* Latest Issues in Public Disclosure, December 1999.

63. BCSA, *supra* note 38, s. 50(1).

64. BCSA, *supra* note 38, s. 1.

65. *Carom v. Bre-X Minerals* (1998), 20 C.P.C. (4th) 187 (O.C.J.).

66. Canadian Securities Administrators, "Concept Proposal for an Integrated Disclosure System."

67. See: *Foss v. Harbottle* (1943), 2 Hare 461 (Ch.); *Mozley v. Alston* (1847), 1 Ph. 790 (L.C.); *Edwards v. Halliwell* [1950] 2 All E.R. 1064 (C.A.).

68. *Supra* note 10.

69. *Supra* note 10, s. 238.

70. See ABCA, *supra* note 9, s. 231(b); MCA, *supra* note 9, s. 231; NBBCA, *supra* note 9, s. 163; NCA, *supra* note 9, s. 368(b); NSCA, *supra* note 9, Sch. 3 s. 7(5)(b); OBCA, *supra* note 9, s. 245; SBCA, *supra* note 9, s. 231(b).

71. *First Edmonton Place Ltd. v. 315888 Alberta Ltd.* (1988), 40 D.L.R. 28 (Alta. Q.B.); aff'd (1989), 45 B.L.R. 110 (C.A.).

72. *Ibid.* at p. 62 (Q.B.).

73. *Supra* note 10, s. 239.

74. See, for example, OBCA, *supra* note 9, s. 246(2).

75. *Abbey Glen Property Corp. v. Strumborg et al.,* [1976] 2 W.W.R. 1 (Alta. S.C.T.D.); aff'd (1978), 85 D.L.R. (3d) 35 (S.C.A.D.).

76. *Marc Jay Investments Inc. v. Levy* (1974), 5 O.R. (2d) 235 (H.C.J.).

77. *Supra* note 71.

78. *Supra* note 10, s. 240.

79. See ABCA, *supra* note 9, s. 233; MCA, *supra* note 9, s. 233; NBBCA, *supra* note 9, s. 165; NCA, *supra* note 9, s. 370; NSCA, *supra* note 9, Sch. 3 s. 4(3); OBCA, *supra* note 9, s. 247; SBCA, *supra* note 9, s. 233.

80. *Supra* note 10, s. 241(1) and (2).

81. See, for example, OBCA, *supra* note 9, s. 248(2).

82. *Re National Building Maintenance Ltd.,* [1971] 1 W.W.R. 8 (B.C.S.C.); aff'd, [1972] 5 W.W.R. 410 (C.A.).

83. See the discussion in *Diligenti v. RWMD Operations Kelowna Ltd.* (1976), 1 B.C.L.R. 36 (S.C.).

84. See CBCA, *supra* note 10, s. 241(3). See also ABCA, *supra* note 9, s. 234(3); MCA, *supra* note 9, s. 234(3); NBBCA, *supra* note 9, s. 166(3); NCA, *supra* ra note 9, s. 371(3); NSCA, *supra* note 9, Sch. 3 s. 5(3); OBCA, *supra* note 9, s. 248(3); SBCA, *supra* note 9, s. 234(3).

85. *Inversiones Montforte S.A. v. Javelin International Ltd.* (1982), 17 B.L.R. 230 (Qué. S.C.).

86. *Re National Building Maintenance, supra* note 82.

87. *Acapulco Holdings Ltd. v. Jegen,* [1997] 4 W.W.R. 601 (Alta. C.A.).

88. See Ontario's *Class Proceedings Act.* S.O. 1992, c.6 (OCPA), which came into force on January 1, 1993.

89. See British *Columbia's Class Proceedings Act,* S.B.C. 1995, c.21 *(BCCPA),* which came into force on August 1, 1995.

90. See: Quebec's *Act Respecting the Class Action,* L.Q. 1978, c.8 *(ARCA),* which came into force on January 19,1979.

91. See OCPA, *supra* note 88, ss. 1-4; BCCPA, *supra* note 89, s. 103; ARCA, *supra* note 90, art. 999.

92. See *Bendall v. McGhan Medical Corp.* (1993), 106 D.L.R. (4th) 339 (Ont. Gen.Div.) at 345; Ontario Law Reform Commission *Report on Class Actions* (Vols. I-III), Ministry of the Attorney General, 1982; and Attorney General's Advisory Committee on Class Action Reform Report, 1990.

93. See *Smith v. Canadian Tire Acceptance Ltd.* (1995), 22 O.R. (3d) 433 (Gen. Div.) at 443.

94. OCPA, *supra* note 88, ss. 5-6. See also BCCPA, *supra* note 89, ss. 4-7; ARCA, *supra* note 90, arts. 1003 and 1022. For a review of prima facie case within the context of the Quebec leg-islation, see: *Le Comite regional des usagers des transports en common de Quebec v. Quebec Urban Community Transit Commission,* [1981] 1 S.C.R. 424.

95. See OCPA, *supra* note 88, ss. 17-22; BCCPA, *supra* note 89, ss. 19-24; ARCA, *supra* note 90, arts. 1005, 1006, 1030 and 1046.

96. See OCPA, *supra* note 88, s. 10; BCCPA, *supra* note 89, s. 10; ARCA, *supra* note 90, art. 1026.

97. See OCPA, *supra* note 88, ss. 31-33.

98. See Ontario's *Law Society Amendment Act* (Class Proceeding Funding), S.O. 1992, c.7 and O.Reg.771/92 and *The Law Society Act* am. O.Reg.535/95.

99. See OCPA, *supra* note 88, s. 33.

100. See ARCA, *supra* note 90, arts. 1035(2) and 1050.1.

101. *Ibid.*

102. See BCCPA, *supra* note 89, s. 37.

103. *Ibid.,* s. 38.

104. *Rogers Broadcasting Limited v. Alexander* (1994), 25 C.P.C. (3d) 159 (O.C.(G.D.)).

105. *Ibid.,* at pp. 162-163.

106. *Ibid.,* at p. 163.

107. *Maxwell v. MLG Ventures Ltd.,* [1995] O.J. No. 1136 (G.D.).

108. *Carom v. Bre-X Minerals Ltd.* (1999), 44 O.R. (3d) 173 (G.D.).

109. *Basic Inc. v. Levinson,* 485 U.S. 224 (1988) at pp. 241-242.

110. See OSA, *supra* note 38, ss. 130-131.

CHAPTER 11

Pension Plan Investments and Fiduciary Duties: The Quebec (Civil Law) Perspective

by Michel Benoit

INTRODUCTION

The regulation of pension fund investments in Canada has changed significantly over the past ten years. Indeed, most jurisdictions prior to 1985 prescribed in detail the types of investments that were permitted for pension funds. Investments were subject not only to *quantitative rules* (for example, a maximum of 10% of the fund assets could be invested in any one investment, and no more than 30% of the voting shares of a corporation could be held) but also to *qualitative standards* (for example, investments in preferred shares of a corporation were permitted, provided they had earned a prescribed rate of return over a specific period of time).

By the mid-1980s, it became readily apparent that a detailed regulatory approach to investments had some serious flaws. The investment community had become very sophisticated and had "outgrown" the standards with which pension fund managers were required to comply. As a result, the regulations were constantly being amended to keep up with new forms of investment, and certain types of investments were required to be structured in a very complex and costly manner to meet the technical requirements of the legislation. This situation was considered by the investment community as inappropriate and unwarranted.

Another consequence of the detailed approach to pension fund investment regulation was that pension plan administrators were relying on the prescribed investment standards to determine whether they had met their obligation of investing assets in a prudent manner. In other words, authorized or prescribed investments were considered to be "sound" investments.

Between 1985 and 1990, most Canadian jurisdictions reformed their pension legislation by imposing new and more generous benefit standards on pension plans. On this occasion, the regulators chose also to change significantly their approach to the regulation of investments. While most of the quantitative rules remained, the qualitative standards were replaced by the requirement to adopt an investment policy. The burden of determining whether a particular investment was appropriate was therefore shifted from the regulator to the fund administrator.

This chapter will examine how this was accomplished in Quebec, Canada's only civil law jurisdiction. Of particular interest will be the interaction between the *Supplemental Pension Plans Act* (SPPA) that came into effect on January 1, 1990, and Quebec's new *Civil Code* that came into effect January 1, 1994.

ADMINISTRATION OF PROPERTY OF OTHERS UNDER THE CIVIL CODE

The *Civil Code of Quebec* (the "Code") contains the rules that must be applied in the absence of any specific statutory provisions or other contractual arrangements to the contrary.

While in many respects SPPA has rules that supersede those of the Code, it is nevertheless necessary to briefly consider the rules of the Code on the administration of property of others as they may provide a guide to plan administrators seeking comfort in respect of investment decisions. Article 1299 of the Code provides as follows:

Any person who is charged with the administration of property or a patrimony that is not his own assumes the office of administrator of the property of others. The rules of this Title apply to every administration unless another form of administration applies under the law or the constituting act, or due to circumstances.[1]

Thus, the administrator of a pension plan and any person with whom the administrator will have contracted for the investment of the assets will be considered as an administrator of the property of others under the Code.

The Code rules on the administration of property of others will be different depending on the kind of administration entrusted to the administrator.

If the administrator is charged with the *simple* administration of the property, Article 1301 of the Code requires that the administrator:

Perform all the acts necessary for the preservation of the property or useful for the maintenance of the use for which the property is ordinarily destined.[2]

Article 1304 also requires that such an administrator: Invest the sums of money under his administration in accordance with the rules of this Title relating to presumed sound investments.[3]

An example of *simple* administration would be a deposit or safekeeping arrangement with a financial institution in respect of the pension fund assets.

On the other hand, a person charged with the *full* administration of the property must, under Article 1306:

Preserve the property and make it productive, increase the patrimony or appropriate it to a purpose, where the interest of the beneficiary or the pursuit of the purpose of the trust requires it.[4]

The administrator of an uninsured plan is deemed under SPPA to hold the assets of the plan as a trustee. Under Article 1278 of the Code, such an administrator is thus considered to have the full administration of the assets. He or she will therefore not be required to invest the assets in accordance with the rules of the Code on presumed sound investments that are set out in Articles 1339 to 1344 of the Code and that are reproduced in Appendix IV-11-A at the end of this chapter. It is, however, noteworthy that Article 1343 of the Code provides that:

An administrator who acts in accordance with this section is presumed to act prudently.[5]

This provision does not appear to be limited to the administrator charged with *simple* administration but could also apply to the administrator charged with full administration.

As will be seen later, SPPA does not impose qualitative standards on the investment of pension fund assets. The requirement to invest in accordance with the plan's investment policy is not, however, necessarily incompatible with the rules of the Code on presumed sound investments. It is, therefore, quite possible that an administrator could decide to invest the assets in accordance with these rules. In such a case, the administrator could benefit from the presumption of prudence of Article 1343 of the Code.

Clearly, however, most plan administrators will consider the rules of the Code on presumed sound investments to be unnecessarily restrictive and inappropriate for a modern portfolio approach that is the current standard applied to determine whether a trustee has discharged his or her fiduciary obligations in respect of the investment of the pension fund assets.

THE TRUST UNDER THE CIVIL CODE

Among the most noteworthy features of the Code are the rules found in Articles 1260 to 1298 on the trust. Prior to the coming into force of the Code, the trust was not a recognized institution of the Quebec Civil Law except for wills and gifts. The Code now recognizes specifically the possibility of creating a separate and autonomous patrimony for a number of purposes, including the investment of monies and providing retirement for employees.

Article 1260 of the Code provides that:

A trust results from an act whereby a person, the settlor, transfer property from his patrimony to another patrimony constituted by him which he appropriates to a particular purpose and which a trustee undertakes, by his acceptance, to hold and administer.[6]

In addition, Article 1262 states that the trust patrimony:

Constitutes a patrimony by appropriation, autonomous and distinct from that of the settlor, trustee or beneficiary and in which none of them has any real right.[7]

Finally, Article 1262 states that a trust may be established by:

Contract, whether by onerous title or gratuitously, by will, or, in certain cases, by operation of law.

As can be seen, a trust under the Code is somewhat different from a common law trust that is based on the division of ownership of the trust assets between the trustee who has legal ownership and the beneficiaries of the trust who have beneficial ownership. The Code does not recognize such a division of ownership, which explains why the trust is considered to be a separate and *autonomous* patrimony.

Article 1278 of the Code provides that the trustee has: The control and exclusive administration of the trust patrimony, and the titles relating to the property of which it is composed are drawn up in his name; he has the exercise of all the rights pertaining to the patrimony and may take any proper measure to secure its appropriation.

A trustee acts as the administrator of the property of others charged will full administration.[8]

The importance of the rules of the Code on the trust lies not only in the fact that it is now possible to establish a trust for any number of purposes, but also in the fact that the beneficiaries of the trust are provided with recourses they may exercise directly against the trustee. In this connection, Articles 1290 and 1291 are of particular interest.

Art. 1290. The settlor, the beneficiary or any other interested person may, notwithstanding any stipulation to the contrary, take action against the trustee to compel him to perform his obligations or to perform any act which is necessary in the interest of the trust, to enjoin him to abstain from any action harmful to the trust or to have him removed.

He may also impugn any acts performed by the trustee in fraud of the trust patrimony or the rights of the beneficiary.

Art. 1291. The court may authorize the settlor, the beneficiary or any other interested person to take legal action in the place and stead of the trustee when, without sufficient reason, he or she refuses or neglects to act or is prevented from acting.[9]

Because SPPA clearly provides that the fund of an uninsured plan is a trust patrimony entrusted to the administration of a pension committee that is required to act as a trustee, the rules of the Code on trust will be applicable and will have the effect of complementing SPPA rules on the administration of the plan fund. The combined rules of the Code and of SPPA, therefore, provide a complete set of standards that must be complied with by the plan administrator who is clearly answerable to the plan members.

SUPPLEMENTAL PENSION PLANS ACT

SPPA has significantly changed the rules governing the administration of pension plans in Quebec by requiring that all plans be administered by a pension committee that acts as trustee of the pension fund. In this capacity, the committee is required to exercise prudence, diligence and skill and act with honesty and loyalty in the best interest of the members and beneficiaries of the plan.

Because the administration of a pension plan and its fund requires, in most cases, a significant amount of time and expertise, SPPA authorizes the pension committee to delegate all or part of its powers to any third party; in such case, the person or body exercising the delegated powers assumes the same responsibilities and incurs the same liability that the committee would have assumed or incurred had it exercised the delegated powers itself.

It should also be noted that under Section 154 of SPPA, the pension committee is accountable for the care with which it selected the delegatee and gave him or her instructions. If the delegation was not authorized, the committee will be accountable for all acts of the delegatee.

With respect to the administration of the pension fund, Section 168 of SPPA provides that:

Only the pension committee, the person or body to whom or which that power has been delegated or, if the pension plan so provides, the members of the plan may decide how the assets of the plan are to be invested.[10]

Moreover, Section 170 of SPPA requires that the pension committee adopt an investment policy as follows:

Unless the Régie authorizes, on the conditions it fixes, that the investment policy be simplified, the policy must set out

(1) the expected rate or return;

(2) the degree of risk involved in the investment portfolio particularly in regard to price fluctuations;

(3) liquidity requirements;

(4) the proportion of assets that may be invested in debt securities and equity securities, respectively;

(5) the permitted categories and sub-categories of investments;

(6) investment portfolio diversification measures conducive to an overall reduction of the degree of risk;

(7) rules and a time schedule applicable to the valuation of the investment portfolio and to the monitoring of the management of the investment portfolio and those applicable to the review of the investment policy;

Unless they are already set out in the plan, the policy must also include

(1) rules regarding the solvency of borrowers and the security required for granting loans out of the assets, in particular the lending of securities and hypothecary loans;

(2) rules applicable to the exercise of the voting rights attached to the securities forming part of the assets;

(3) the basis for the valuation of investments that are not traded on an organized market;

(4) rules applicable to the use of futures contracts, options, share purchase warrants or share rights or other financial instruments;

(5) rules regarding the loans that may be raised by the pension committee.[11]

Finally, Section 171 requires that all investments of the plan fund be made in the name of the pension fund or for its account.

Most pension committees have, for obvious reasons, contracted with professional investment managers for the investment of the assets or delegated to the sponsoring employer the necessary authority to do so. The scope of such contract varies according to the size of the pension fund. For smaller funds, the authority over all of the investments will generally be conferred on one manager that is often a financial institution such as a trust or insurance company that will invest the assets in one or more pooled funds sponsored by the manager.

For larger funds, the situation is more complex. Usually, more than one manager is retained, and authority is given to each manager over a selected portion of the pension fund, such as U.S. equities, Canadian equities, fixed income securities, etc. In addition, authority over specific types of investment is often exercised by "in-house personnel" in situations involving private placements, real estate investments and/or other investments that are out of the ordinary course.

Contracts entered into with investment managers, while requiring strict compliance with the plan's investment policy, provide that the actual investment decisions will be made by the managers and not by the "client" (pension committee or sponsoring employer). Because the authority given to the manager is not unfettered—he or she must at all times comply with the plan's investment policy—it has been suggested that it is unclear whether these contracts constitute a delegation of authority under SPPA or whether they should be considered simply as contracts for services.

The better view is that the pension fund investment management contract necessarily involves the delegation of authority. Moreover, the combined effects of SPPA and the provisions of the Quebec *Civil Code* on the administration of the property of others and trusts will result in the investment manager assuming significant liability.

As already mentioned, Section 153 of SPPA provides that anyone acting in a delegated capacity assumes the same responsibility as the pension committee would have assumed in exercising the same powers. This responsibility extends to the liability under Sections 180 and 181 of SPPA for investments made contrary to law, which, arguably would include investments made contrary to the plan's investment policy.

180. Every person who makes an investment otherwise than according to law is, by that sole fact and without further proof of wrongdoing, liable for any resulting loss.

The members of the pension committee who approved such an investment are, by that sole fact and without further proof of wrongdoing, solely liable for any resulting loss.

However, such persons incur no liability under this section if they acted within their powers and on the recommendation of persons whose profession gives credence to their opinion.

181. Any investment made in contravention with the law may be annulled by judicial action on the application of the Régie or any interested person. The court may order any person who is liable under section 180 to pay to the pension fund *an amount equal to the resulting loss or to the sums so invested.*[12]

Liability under these provisions is therefore considerable, especially when one considers that the exculpatory provision of Section 180 would *not* readily be available to the investment manager.

Finally, it should be noted that SPPA, while no longer prescribing specific qualitative standards for the investment of assets, has nevertheless maintained a number of quantitative rules and prohibitions, the most noteworthy of which are the following:

1. No more than 10% of the book value of the assets of the pension fund may be invested directly or indirectly in any one property or in one or more loans to a natural person or, in any form whatever, in any one person, corporation, association, partnership or trust.[13] Section 173 of SPPA provides, however, that the 10% limit does not apply to:

(a) Securities issued or guaranteed by the government of Canada or of a province.

(b) Units of a mutual fund, provided the investments of the fund comply with SPPA and its rules are comparable to those prescribed under the *Securities Act;* this latter requirement does not have to be met if all the units of the fund are held by pension funds. This allows mutual funds of the "master trust" type (i.e., where the units are all held by pension funds sponsored by the same employer or related group of employers) to operate without regard to the rules of the *Securities Act* applicable to mutual funds.

(c) Deposits with a financial institution insured by the Quebec Deposit Insurance Board or its Canadian equivalent but only up to the insured amount, which is currently set at $60,000 CDN.

(d) Deposits made under a management contract with an insurer authorized to carry on business in Canada. Two conditions must be met, however, in order that such deposits be exempted from the 10% limit:

(i) The insurer must guarantee the capital and a minimum rate of interest and the rules for the calculation of the premiums for the purchase of a pension are specified under the contract.

(ii) For defined contribution plans, the insurer binds himself directly toward each member of the plan and the contract gives each member the right to transfer to another recognized pension plan the sums deposited in his name that exceed the coverage provided by the Canadian Life and Health Insurance Compensation Corporation (CompCorp) that is comparable to the protection offered by the Quebec Deposit Insurance Board and its Canadian equivalent.[14]

It is noteworthy that this latter condition results from the liquidation of Cooperants Mutual Life Insurance Society, a Quebec insurance company that had issued a number of investment contracts held by pension funds. Creditors of the insurance company had contested the priority status of these contracts under the *Winding-Up Act* by arguing that they did not constitute annuity contracts and could therefore not be considered as policies.

The Quebec Court of Appeal[15] ruled against the creditors and held that, while the contracts were clearly made for investment purposes, each contained an undertaking by the insurance company to purchase an annuity at the request of the contract holder. This was sufficient to qualify these contracts as annuity contracts and, consequently, as policies under the *Winding-Up Act*.

The relative state of uncertainty, however, that resulted from this litigation prompted an amendment to SPPA designed to afford each member of a defined contribution plan the opportunity of limiting his or her exposure to loss by transferring to another plan amounts in excess of the coverage afforded by CompCorp.

2. Not more than 30% of the voting rights attached to the shares of any one corporation may be held by the pension fund unless such shares are those of a tax exempt pension fund investment corporation that invests the assets of the pension fund in real estate, natural resources (mining, oil and gas) or other types of permitted investments.[16]

3. Assets of the pension fund may not be invested in securities of a corporation to which a loan out of such assets is prohibited unless such securities are publicly traded on an organized market.[17]

4. Assets of the pension fund may not be loaned to:

(a) the administrator of the plan or any delegatee of authority including directors, officers or employees of the administrator or delegatee;

(b) a union representing members of the plan nor to its officers, directors or employees;

(c) the spouse or child of a person referred to in (a) and (b);

(d) where the employer is a corporation and administrator of all or part of the plan

(i) to a shareholder holding more than 10% of the issued shares or to his spouse or child,

(ii) to a shareholder or his spouse or child if together they hold more than 10% of the issued shares;

(e) where the employer administers all or part of the plan, to any corporation more than 10% of the shares of which are held by the employer;

(f) a corporation, other than the employer, more than 10% of whose shares are held by a person referred to in (a), (b), (c) or (d);

(g) a corporation, other than the employer, more than 50% of whose shares are held by a group made up exclusively of the persons referred to in (a), (b) or (d), of the employer administering all or part of the plan or of a spouse or child of any of them;

(h) a corporation, other than the employer, controlled by a person referred to in (a), (b), (c) or (d), or by the employer administering all or part of the plan or by a group made up exclusively of such persons;[18]

SPPA provides, however, that, notwithstanding the above prohibitions, a loan out of the assets of the plan may be made to a member of the plan or his or her spouse or child, to the employer or to a parent or subsidiary if any one of them is the employer. Such loans may not, in the aggregate, exceed 10% of the book value of the assets of the plan.[19]

In addition, any such loan must be secured in the manner provided for under the SPPA Regulation.

CONCLUSION

The investment of pension assets in the civil law jurisdiction of Quebec is, therefore, mainly governed by the statutory provisions of SPPA. However, it is clear that certain provisions of the Code will also govern, particularly with respect to the recourses the beneficiaries of the pension plan may exercise against those acting as trustees either by reason of the fact that they are members of the plan's pension committee or because they have received delegated authority over the investment of the pension fund. The absence of judicial precedent on the application of the rules of the Code and those of SPPA on the investment of pension fund assets make it difficult to determine whether or not the standards that will be applicable in a civil law jurisdiction will be more stringent than those that would be applicable in a common law jurisdiction. Judicial pronouncements on these questions should therefore be closely monitored.

ENDNOTES

1. *Code Civil du Québec,* L.Q. 1991, c.64, Article 1299.
2. *Ibid.,* Article 1301.
3. *Ibid.,* Article 1304.
4. *Ibid.,* Article 1306.
5. *Ibid.,* Article 1343.
6. *Ibid.,* Article 1260
7. *Ibid.,* Article 1262.
8. *Ibid.,* Article 1278.
9. *Ibid.,* Articles 1290 and 1291.
10. *Supplemental Pension Plans Act,* R.S.Q. 1990, R-15.1, s.168.
11. *Ibid.,* s.170.
12. *Ibid.,* Sections 180 and 181.
13. *Ibid.,* Section 172.
14. *Ibid.,* s.173.
15. *In the matter of the Winding-up of Cooperants Mutual Life Insurance Society,* [1993] R.J.Q. No. 2070 (C.A.).
16. *Supplemental Pension Plans Act, supra* note 10, s. 175.
17. *Ibid.,* Section 174.
18. *Ibid.,* s. 176.
19. *Ibid.,* s. 177.

APPENDIX IV-11-A

EXTRACTS FROM THE CIVIL CODE OF QUEBEC,

SECTION V

PRESUMED SOUND INVESTMENTS

Art. 1339. Investments in the following are presumed sound:

(1) titles of ownership in an immovable;

(2) bonds or other evidences of indebtedness issued or guaranteed by Quebec, Canada or a province of Canada, the United States of America or any of its member states, the International Bank for Reconstruction and Development, a municipality or a school board in Canada, or a fabrique in Quebec;

(3) bonds or other evidences of indebtedness issued by a legal person which operates a public service in Canada and which is entitled to impose a tariff for such service;

(4) bonds or other evidences of indebtedness secured by an undertaking, towards a trustee, of Quebec, Canada or a province of Canada, to pay sufficient subsidies to meet the interest and the capital on the maturity of each;

(5) bonds or other evidences of indebtedness of a company in the following cases:

    (a) they are secured by a hypothec ranking first on an immovable, or by securities presumed to be sound investments;

    (b) they are secured by a hypothec ranking first on equipment and the company has regularly serviced the interest on its borrowings during the last ten financial years;

    (c) they are issued by a company whose common or preferred shares are presumed sound investments;

(6) bonds or other evidences of indebtedness issued by a loan society incorporated by a statute of Quebec or authorized to do business in Quebec under the *Loan and Investment Societies Act,* provided it has been specially approved by the government and its ordinary operations in Quebec consist in making loans to municipalities or school boards and to fabriques or loans secured by hypothec ranking first on immovables situated in Quebec;

(7) debts secured by hypothec on immovables in Quebec;

    (a) payment of the capital and interest is guaranteed or secured by Quebec, Canada or a province of Canada;

    (b) if the amount of the debt is not more than seventy-five per cent of the value of the immovable property securing payment of the debt after deduction of the other debts secured by the same immovable and ranking equally with or before the debt;

    (c) if the amount of the debt that exceeds seventy-five per cent of the value of the immovable by which it is secured, after deduction of the other debts secured by the same immovable and ranking equally with or before the debt, is guaranteed or secured by Quebec, Canada or a province of Canada, the Central Mortgage and Housing Corporation, the Société d'habitation du Québec or a hypothec insurance policy issued by a company holding a permit under the Act respecting insurance;

(8) fully paid preferred shares issued by a company whose common shares are presumed sound investments or which, during the last five financial years, has distributed the stipulated dividend on all its preferred shares;

(9) common shares issued by a company that for three years has been meeting the timely disclosure requirements defined in the *Securities Act* to such extent as they are listed by a stock exchange recognized for that purpose by the government on the recommendation of the Commission des valeurs mobilieres, and when the market capitalization of the company, not considering preferred shares or blocks of shares of ten per cent or more, is higher than the amount so fixed by the government;

(10) shares of a mutual fund and units of an unincorporated mutual fund or of a private trust, provided that sixty per cent of its portfolio consists of presumed sound investments, in the following cases:

    (a) the shares or units meet the requirements of subparagraph a of paragraph 11 of section 3 of the *Securities Act;*

    (b) the company, the fund or the trust has been fulfilling the timely disclosure requirements defined by that Act for three years.

Art. 1340. The administrator decides on the investments to make according to the yield and the anticipated capital gain; so far as possible, he works toward a diversified portfolio producing fixed income and variable revenues in the proportion suggested by the prevailing economic conditions.

He may not, however, acquire more than five per cent of the shares of the same company nor acquire shares, bonds or other evidences of indebtedness of a legal person or limited partnership which has failed to pay the prescribed dividends on its shares or interest on its bonds or other securities, nor grant a loan to that legal person or partnership.

Art. 1341. An administrator may deposit the sums of money entrusted to him in or with a bank, a savings and credit union or any other financial institution, if the deposit is repayable on demand or on thirty days' notice.

He may also deposit the sums of money for a longer term if repayment of the deposit is fully guaranteed by the Régie de l'assurance-depxopts du Québec; otherwise, he may not do so except with the authorization of the court and on the conditions it determines.

Art. 1342. An administrator may maintain the existing investments upon his taking office even if they are not presumed sound investments.

The administrator may also hold securities which, following the reorganization, winding-up or amalgamation of a legal person, replace securities he held.

Art. 1343. An administrator who acts in accordance with this section is presumed to act prudently.

An administrator who makes an investment he is not authorized to make is, by that very fact and without further proof of fault, liable for any loss resulting from it.

Art. 1344. Investments made in the course of administration shall be made in the name of the administrator acting in that quality.

Such investments may also be made in the name of the beneficiary, if it is also indicated that they are made by the administrator acting in that quality.

CHAPTER 12

Pension Funds and
Socially Responsible Investing

by Roberto Tomassini

INTRODUCTION

In this chapter we provide an overview of various legal issues relating to socially responsible investment (SRI) as it applies to pension fund investment. As no definitive legal analysis on this issue is possible, this chapter will canvass the legal landscape by providing a synopsis of relevant authorities that can hopefully assist plan administrators, trustees and their advisors in the decision making process regarding the adoption of an SRI policy for their pension funds.

DEFINING *SOCIALLY RESPONSIBLE INVESTING (SRI)*

The *SRI* label is intended to capture a number of related concepts, including *ethical investing* and *economically targeted investing.*

Ethical investing encompasses investment policies that seek to support a political or moral position that is not directly related to the financial interests of the fund or the beneficiaries. A good example is an investment policy that prohibits investment in so-called sin industries such as tobacco or alcohol manufacturing.

Perhaps more relevant to pension fund administrators and, in particular, trustees of multi-employer plans (MEPPs) with joint union and employer representation, is the issue of *economically targeted investments.* Unlike "ethical investing,"these policies are intended to financially benefit the fund or its beneficiaries, but not necessarily by seeking to maximize returns on investments. The financial benefit is usually indirect or, in some cases, unrelated to the purpose of the fund. The most common example is a policy that directs fund investments toward a particular industry that may generate more employment opportunities for fund beneficiaries or stabilize the industry covered by the MEPP.

In this chapter, we use the concept of *socially responsible investing* to include both ethical and economically targeted investing policies, and any investment policy that seeks to promote a social, political or economic goal, not directly related to maximizing the returns on a fund's investment.

THE LEGAL ISSUE

The primary legal issue arising from SRI for pension funds is whether SRI is inconsistent with the fiduciary duties owed to the plan beneficiaries by plan trustees and administrators with respect to the investment of trust assets.

While on an individual level investors are free to select where their investment dollars will be directed, and their decisions may be dictated entirely by social, political or ethical concerns, the issue of social investing becomes somewhat more complicated where the monies being invested are pension monies. Of course, pension plans are made up of a collection of individuals who are unlikely to share the same political or moral objectives as each other, or as the trustees or administrators who are making the investment decisions. Trustees are entrusted with investing pension monies on behalf of **all** plan members. The ultimate goal is to provide these members with adequate and secure retirement income. The legal question is whether SRI is inconsistent with this ultimate purpose of a pension fund trust and the trustees' fiduciary obligation to fulfil this purpose.

THE REGULATORY ENVIRONMENT

While provincial pension benefits legislation in Canada imposes general fiduciary standards of conduct on plan administrators and their advisors with respect to pension fund investments, there are no statutory or regulatory prohibitions regarding the implementation of SRI or related investment policies. Provincial and federal pension legislation is silent on this issue.

However, in Ontario, while the Pension Commission of Ontario (now the Financial Services Commission, hereinafter referred to as the "Commission") has not adopted a comprehensive policy with respect to this issue, in its February 1992 Bulletin, the Commission did address the issue of "ethical" investing of pension funds in the Q&A section of its Bulletin. The Bulletin stated:

Q. Is it imprudent for a pension fund to take the position that it will make only "ethical investments"?

A. No. "Ethical" investing is permitted, but the SIP&G must state this position and set out the criteria for investments. The members of the plan should be notified of this position.[1] (emphasis added).

This is a startlingly bold statement. What is surprising is that the Commission is not just stating that ethical investing does not in and of itself violate the Ontario *Pension Benefits Act* (PBA) prudence standards, but rather that a fund that excludes from its investment portfolio **any** investments that are not deemed to be "ethical" by the trustees would still be prudent, as long as the disclosure requirements are met. Perhaps implicit in this response is that the investment policy of the fund must otherwise comply with the prudence requirements of PBA and that ethical investing is not, per se, imprudent.

Pension plan trustees ought to be cautious in relying fully on this kind of policy statement by the regulators, primarily because such statements are not law, and therefore not binding on anyone, including the regulators themselves. Ultimately, the policy statement could not be used as a complete defence if the trustees' investment decisions are subject to legal challenge. Nonetheless, the statement is a strong indication that at least one pension regulator does not view ethical investing as imprudent in and of itself.

In its "Best Practices Guideline,"[2] the Office of the Superintendent of Financial Institutions (OSFI) cautions trustees of federally registered plans against SRI policies. OSFI states:

The trustees should ensure that they are managing the funds to achieve the plan objectives. Considerations of solidarity with other unions or locals or promotion of employment in an industry **have to be dealt with by trustees in a manner that is consistent with the plan's investment policies and their own fiduciary responsibilities relating to the pension plan.** The fiduciary obligations of the board should set the standard against which all investment decisions are measured.[3] (emphasis added)

Again, the message from the regulator is that, while SRI policies are not per se imprudent, their adoption cannot otherwise compromise their fiduciary obligations to the plan. SRI policies, like all other investment policies, must be measured against the prudence standards applicable to all plan investment decisions.

While not specifically directed at SRI, the Ontario PBA does contain investment regulations of general application. Of particular interest are the regulations regarding the establishment by pension funds of a written Statement of Investment Policies and Goals (SIP&G). Subsection 67(2) of the Ontario PBA Regulations reads as follows:

In the establishment and application of the written Statement of Investment Policies and Goals, the selecting of investments shall be made with consideration given to the overall context of the investment portfolio without undue risk of loss or impairment and with a reasonable expectation of fair return or appreciation given the nature of the investment."[4]

This is an acceptance by the regulators of the modern prudent portfolio approach that makes clear that particular investments will not be judged in isolation, but rather in the context of the pension fund's investment portfolio as a whole. Therefore, trustees are unlikely to be vulnerable to fiduciary liability if one investment in the entire portfolio does not perform well, provided the investment forms part of an overall prudent portfolio.

In contrast to the regulatory silence on SRI in Canada, the U.S. Department of Labor has formally adopted a regulatory policy with respect to *economically targeted investments* by pension funds under the *Employee Retirement Income Security Act of 1974* (ERISA) in an Interpretive Bulletin issued on June 17, 1994.[5] As ERISA imposes similar fiduciary standards on plan trustees as Canadian pension legislation, and the common law of trusts, these regulatory policies can be instructive for the Canadian pension fund trustee, even though they are not legally binding. While the Bulletin only addresses economically targeted investments, which may be somewhat narrower in scope than SRI, the Guidelines are equally applicable.

The Bulletin sets forth the following broad principles:

a. ERISA does not exclude the consideration of collateral benefits in a fiduciary's evaluation of a particular investment opportunity.

b. Arrangements designed to bring areas of investment opportunity that provide collateral benefits to the attention of plan fiduciaries will not in and of themselves violate ERISA fiduciary standards, where the arrangements do not restrict the exercise of the fiduciaries' discretion.

c. Plan fiduciaries can be influenced by collateral factors that are not related to the plan's expected investment return only if, commensurate with risk and rate of return, such returns are equal or superior to alternative available investments.

d. Fiduciaries who are willing to accept reduced returns or greater risks to secure collateral benefits are in violation of ERISA.

In issuing this Bulletin, the Department of Labor noted that the Bulletin was, in part, intended to clarify misperceptions within the investment community that economically targeted investments are incompatible with ERISA's fiduciary obligations. This is clearly not the case in the regulator's view.

JURISPRUDENCE ON SOCIALLY RESPONSIBLE INVESTING

In the absence of specific Canadian statutory or regulatory standards, we must consider common law principles developed by courts in the areas of trust and fiduciary law to assess the legal implications of an SRI policy in the pension context.

There is no binding Canadian judicial authority that directly deals with the issue of whether engaging in SRI infringes a pension fund trustee's duties to fund beneficiaries. We review below relevant case law from other jurisdictions that may assist in determining how a Canadian court is likely to respond to this issue. We start the analysis, however, by reviewing the general basic trust principles applicable to trust fund investments.

The starting point for this analysis is the common law obligation imposed on all trustees to act **prudently** and in the **exclusive interest of the plan beneficiaries (the duty of loyalty)** in carrying out the purposes of the trust for which they are responsible.[6]

Applying these principles to the duties of a pension fund trustee with respect to investments, the obligation has been described as follows:

> The standard required of the trustee in exercising his powers of investment is that he must take such care as an ordinary prudent man would take if he were minded to make an investment for the benefit of other people for whom he felt morally bound to provide. . . . That duty includes the duty to seek advice on matters which the trustee does not understand such as the making of investments, and on receiving that advice to act with the same degree of prudence.[7]

This standard is codified in the pension legislation in most jurisdictions in Canada, including the Ontario PBA, which reads as follows:

> 22(1) The administrator of a pension plan shall exercise the care, diligence and skill in the administration and investment of a pension fund that a person of ordinary prudence would exercise in dealing with the property of another person.[8]

The legal authorities summarized below consider whether these duties can be discharged where the trustees engage in SRI policies.

Cowan v. Scargill

The leading judicial authority applying these principles to pension fund investment policies that can be broadly characterized as SRI suggests that the interests of the plan members means **their financial best interests,** except in very limited circumstances. Given that the purpose of a pension fund is to provide retirement income, the obligation of trustees is first and foremost to maximize investment returns.

In the English case of *Cowan v. Scargill,*[9] the union-appointed trustees of a jointly trusteed pension fund established for the employees of the National Coal Board refused to approve an annual investment plan for the pension fund unless restrictive screens were incorporated. The union trustees wanted to prohibit all foreign investments, as well as any investment in companies that operated in sectors that were in competition with the coal industry, such as oil companies. The court concluded that the union trustees breached their fiduciary duty to the plan beneficiaries by refusing to approve the investment plan because it did not include the restrictive screens proposed by the union trustees.

In this judgment, the court considered a wide range of issues relating to the trustees' duties with regard to the investment of pension funds. The salient points are as follows:

a. The same legal principles that courts have applied to investment of trust funds in general are equally applicable to pension funds, subject to any differences in the provisions of the pension plans themselves.

This is significant because traditional trust principles with respect to trust fund investments are very conservative, normally placing sole importance on pecuniary factors.

b. In using their investment powers, pension fund trustees have a duty to exercise those powers in the best interests of present and future beneficiaries of the trust, holding the scales impartially between different classes of beneficiaries.

This was particularly significant in this case because, while the court recognized that the investment restrictions advocated by the union trustees may benefit its active union members engaged in the coal industry, there is a significant class of beneficiaries, namely deferred pensioners, retirees and member beneficiaries, who would gain little or no advantage from the union's policies.

c. In considering what investments to make, the trustees are required to put aside their own personal interests and views. The trustees may have strongly held social or political views, which must be foregone if investments of a type that conflict with these views would be more beneficial to the beneficiaries under the pension plan than other investments. The court went so far as to say that trustees may even have to act dishonourably if the interests of their beneficiaries require it.

d. The court held that in most cases, the best interest of the plan beneficiaries means their best financial interest. This was qualified however by adding that in certain trusts that have adult beneficiaries with strict views of certain social or moral issues, financial considerations need not be paramount provided that the beneficiaries agree. For that group, the non-financial rewards might be preferable to financial benefits that result from an unacceptable activity. In the case of pension fund investments, however, the trustees must satisfy a heavy burden of proof. They must show that non-financial considerations and policies will lead to direct benefit for the plan beneficiaries and not just the general public.

While the principles advanced by the court in the *Cowan* decision appear to prohibit any type of SRI policies for pension fund trusts, some factors should be borne in mind when assessing the implications of this decision. The union trustees in this case were seeking to impose a blanket restrictive policy that significantly impacted upon the potential for investment diversification when they sought to screen out all foreign investments and investments in entire industries. Most importantly, however, they sought to do so without any regard or even consideration as to the impact this policy would have on the financial well-being of the fund. The court's decision may have been very different if the trustees had proposed an investment screening policy that they could demonstrate would not impact negatively on the investment performance of the fund, given the availability of comparable competitive investments.

In fact, the judge who decided the *Cowan* case, the Right Honourable Sir Robert Megarry, in a subsequent discussion of the case,[10] suggests the result may have been different if the union trustees had not expressed their policy as an absolute prohibition on foreign investments or investments in competing industries, but rather formulated the policy as a preference for domestic and non-oil investments where other factors were equal between competing investment choices.

Secondly, the decision may have been different, if rather than seeking to benefit one class of beneficiaries who happened to be active employees in the coal industry, the trustees imposed social or ethical screens that did not confer any special advantage on one class of beneficiaries that was potentially detrimental to other classes of beneficiaries. For instance, if the trustees' proposal was to prefer investments in coal industry companies where rate of return and risk were comparable to oil industry investments, the impact of the economically targeted investment would be neutral to the non-union beneficiaries of the pension trust. In these circumstances, a court is unlikely to conclude that the trustees' fiduciary duties are compromised by the investment policy.

Withers v. Teachers' Retirement System of The City of New York

In contrast to the *Cowan* decision, at least one American court has upheld a decision by pension fund trustees to make economically targeted investments where the policy could be justified on the basis that it was necessary to ensure the viability of the plan as a whole. In *Withers v. Teachers' Retirement System of the City of New York,*[11] the court upheld the purchase by the New York Teachers' Pension Plan of nearly $1 billion of New York City bonds when the city was in the midst of a financial crisis. Due to the pending bankruptcy of the city, the bonds did not have high value. However, the city was the major contributor to the pension plan.

Continuation of city contributions, which the trustees believed would cease if the city went bankrupt, was the principal motivating factor in the trustees' decision, based on the belief that their obligation was to safeguard the interests of all their members. The court held that this otherwise imprudent investment was consistent with the fiduciary responsibilities of the trustees, given the need to preserve a stream of contributions to the fund.

While the *Teachers* case is a good example of a court endorsing trustees' investment decision that are not motivated to maximize returns, the decision is not likely to be widely applied given the unique circumstances in this case. The decision may have been different if the investment was not made to save the city from bankruptcy, but rather, for example, to encourage the hiring of more teachers.

Both the *Cowan* case and the *Teachers* case are more primarily directed at economically targeted investments by pension funds, rather than SRI in the broad sense. This issue is more directly addressed in the *City of Baltimore* case.

The Board of Trustees v. City of Baltimore

The *City of Baltimore*[12] case involved a number of challenges to ordinances passed by the City of Baltimore requiring that three Baltimore City employee pension plans divest their holdings in companies doing business in South Africa. The ordinance stipulated that the divestiture was to be implemented within a two-year period. However, the trustees retained the discretion to suspend divestiture during the two-year period if the trustees concluded that the continued divestiture under the ordinance would be inconsistent with generally accepted investment standards for pension fund fiduciaries, or would cause financial losses to the fund.

The trustees of the plans challenged the ordinance on a number of grounds. The primary argument of interest for our purposes was the trustees' claim that the ordinance was unconstitutional because it altered its contractual obligations to its beneficiaries that incorporated the common law duties of prudence and loyalty.

At trial, the court concluded, based on the financial evidence presented, that it can not be concluded that the ordinance would impair the performance of the pension funds, largely because the existing evidence was inconclusive. The court made a number of evidentiary conclusions on the impact that the ordinance would have on the performance of the pension fund that are worth analyzing in a little more detail.

The court recognized that the ordinance prohibited investment in 120 of the 500 companies on the Standard and Poor's 500 Index (the S&P 500) and that these companies represented approximately 40% of the market capitalization of the S&P 500. Thus, the ordinance would require the pension fund portfolio to have more investments in relatively smaller companies whose stock prices tend to be more volatile. Notwithstanding this fact, the court found that the trust was not necessarily disadvantaged, reasoning that in the long run, such stocks perform as well or better than the stocks of larger companies.

The trustees also attempted to show that the investment restrictions would adversely affect their money managers' active style, which had proved to be very successful for the pension fund. The court acknowledged that by eliminating some potential investments in certain sectors, the ordinance would affect this active style but nonetheless concluded that any interference would be insignificant, as replacement stocks could be found for each sector, even though the "South Africa Free" investments would replace larger companies.

The trustees also attempted to argue that the restrictions would diminish the quality of the pension plan's portfolio by requiring their money managers to forego their first choice of investments. The court, while acknowledging that this might be the case, stated that it was not axiomatic that the managers' second choice is inferior to the first. The court reasoned that all money managers ordinarily invest in a limited number of companies with which they are familiar, the restrictions would merely require money managers to do additional research in order to locate adequate replacement stocks, which is not necessarily a bad thing, and could prove to benefit the pension fund.

The court also recognized that the ordinance would require divestiture of 47% of the pension fund's equity portfolio and 10% of its fixed income portfolio, and that this would create a one-time cost of approximately $750,000. In addition, because the "South Africa Free" companies were smaller in size, this would result in a larger volume of trading, which would add to the pension fund's costs in terms of broker's commissions fixed at approximately $300,000. The costs of divestiture represented about ⅟₁₆th of 1% of the fund's total value. The court also calculated that the ongoing costs of divestiture was $1.2 million per year or ⅟₁₀th of 1% of the fund's total value. The court concluded that the imposition of these costs on the trust fund to implement the ethical screens mandated by the ordinances was not inconsistent with the trustees' duties of prudence and loyalty, as the costs were *de minimis*.

While the court recognized that the ordinance would exclude a not insignificant segment of the investment universe, the city provided evidence, accepted by the court, that demonstrated that, under the divestiture program, economically competitive substitute investments remained available.

The court concluded that the ordinance did not alter or impair the trustees' duties of prudence. It noted that the divestiture program was to occur gradually over a two-year period and that the ordinance expressly empowered the trustees to suspend the program at any time for up to 90 days if they found that the divestiture became imprudent.

Finally, the trustees contended that the ordinance altered their duty of prudence by mandating considerations of social factors unrelated to investment performance. The Court of Appeal disagreed with this assertion. The court recited from a highly respected American authority on the law of trusts, who rejected the proposition that trustees are only bound to attempt to secure the maximum return on fund investments.

> Trustees in deciding whether to invest in, or to retain, the securities of a corporation may properly consider the social performance of the corporation. They may decline to invest in, or to retain, the securities of corporations whose activities, or some of them, are contrary to fundamental and generally accepted ethical principles. They may consider such matters as pollution, race discrimination, fair employment, and consumer responsibility.[13]

An analogy is drawn between the situation of the trustees and that of a corporation's board of directors. Corporate boards often conclude that charitable contributions are in the corporation's best interests on the belief that a corporation, with a proper sense of social obligation, is more likely to be successful in the long run than those that are solely driven by obtaining maximum amount of profits.

The Court of Appeal concludes that these views are consistent with the position that a trustee's duty is not necessarily to maximize the return on investments but rather to "secure a **just** or **reasonable**" return while avoiding undue risk.

Thus, if, as in this case, social investment yields economically competitive returns at a comparable level of risk, the investment should not be deemed imprudent.

. . . Moreover, given the vast power that pension trust funds exert in American society, it would be unwise to bar trustees from considering the social consequences of investment decisions in any case in which it would cost even a penny more to do so. **Consequently we conclude that if, as in this case, the cost of investing in accordance with social consideration is** *de minimis,* **the duty of prudence is not violated.**[14] (emphasis added)

In summary, the *City of Baltimore* decision advances several important principles on the issue of SRI, which we reformulate as follows:

a. It is perhaps critical when considering the implementation of an SRI policy that trustees retain the discretion to withdraw from the policy if it appears that to continue with it is clearly imprudent. The policy should not bind the trustees to one irreversible course of action.

b. Eliminating through screens otherwise prudent investments is not necessarily inconsistent with a trustee's duties to fund beneficiaries, provided prudent alternative investments are available with comparable risk and return profiles.

c. Considering non-financial factors is not, in and of itself, inconsistent with a trustee's duty of prudence and loyalty. This statement is in direct conflict with the central principle espoused by the English court in the *Cowan* decision.

d. Bearing a cost to implement an SRI policy is not imprudent where the cost is insignificant relative to the size of the fund.

Martin v. The City of Edinburgh District Council

The *City of Baltimore* case should be contrasted with the Scottish decision in *Martin v. The City of Edinburgh District Council,*[15] which also considered the legal implications of a "South Africa Free" investment policy. This case was concerned with the investment of public and charitable funds held by the City of Edinburgh District Council in trust. The City Council had decided to express its abhorrence of apartheid in South Africa by instructing the Council's investment advisors to report on any Council trust fund holdings in South African

companies and to propose alternative investments in substitution thereof. The court was asked to determine whether or not this investment decision was contrary to the fiduciary duties of the trustees.

While the court did not conclude that the investment policy in and of itself breached the trustees' duties to the beneficiaries, it did take issue with the process employed by the trustees in arriving at this decision. Primarily, the court was concerned that the trustees did not seek the advice of professional advisors as to whether or not it was in the interests of the trust and their beneficiaries to divest in South Africa. This, in the court's view, constituted a breach of the trust principle that a trustee is required to apply his or her mind to the best interests of the beneficiaries before any exercise of discretion. The court concluded:

Accordingly I conclude that the pursuer has proved a breach of trust by the Council in pursuing a policy of disinvesting in South Africa without considering expressly whether it was in the best interests of the beneficiaries and without obtaining professional advice on this matter.[16]

It is often said, that the standard of prudence against which trustees' actions are measured is more concerned with the process invoked by the trustees at arriving at their decisions, rather than the substantive merits of any particular decision. The Commission in Ontario has explicitly stated that the standard of prudence should be measured principally by the process through which investment strategies and tactics are developed, adopted, implemented and monitored.[17] The *Martin* case is a good example of this principle. Trustees must consider and analyze investment decisions closely with the best interests of plan members in mind and obtain the necessary advice to make an informed decision.

In assessing whether pension fund trustees have satisfied these procedural prudence requirements with respect to investments, a court will likely consider the following factors, which apply to all investment decisions by trustees, including SRI policies:

- Did the trustees employ proper methods to investigate, evaluate and structure the investment?
- Did the trustees exercise independent judgment when making investment decisions?
- Did the trustees conduct an impartial study of the advantages and disadvantages of the investment policies and/or the particular transaction under consideration?
- Did the trustees exercise due diligence in researching all aspects of the investment policy or transaction?
- Did the trustees retain qualified experts and consultants as appropriate in the circumstances and
- Did the trustees rely on complete and up-to-date information in reaching their decision?

Harries v. Church Commissioners

Under scrutiny in the English case of *Harries v. Church Commissioners*[18] was the duty of the trustees of a charitable trust with respect to its investment decisions, and whether or not the trustees would breach their fiduciary duties in taking into account non-financial considerations when making investment decisions. The case involved an application brought by the Bishop of Oxford and other clergy members against the Church Commissioners Board of Governors responsible for investing Church of England assets to fulfil its religious/charitable purposes. The applicants alleged that the Commissioners breached their duty by solely taking into account financial considerations when investing trust property and are required to give weight to the underlying purpose for which they hold their assets, being the promotion of the Christian faith through the Church of England. The applicants claimed that the Commissioners should not exercise their investment functions in a manner that would be incompatible with that purpose even if it involved the risk of financial loss.

The court starts with the basic principle that trustees should be primarily concerned with furthering the purposes of the trust for which they have accepted the office of trustee. All the powers vested in them must be exercised for these purposes.

The second primary principle enunciated by the court is that where property is held in trust for investment purposes, prima facie, the purposes of the trust will be best served by the trustees seeking to obtain therefrom the maximum return, whether by way of income or capital growth, which is consistent with commercial prudence.

> In most cases this *prima facie* position will govern the trustees conduct. In most cases the best interests of the charity require that the trustees' choice of investments should be made solely on the basis of well established investment criteria, having taken expert advice where appropriate and having due regard to such matters as the need to diversify, the need to balance income against capital growth, and the need to balance risk against return.[19]

The court recognized that in some cases there is an exception to this general principle, but these are comparatively rare. It notes that where a trust is established for a particular aim or purpose, and the investment clearly conflicts with the aim or purpose, even though it is the most prudent investment financially, it may be contrary to the terms of the trust to proceed with such an investment. The court cites the example of a cancer research charities holding tobacco shares, or trustees of temperance charities owning brewery and distillery shares. In those circumstances, where trustees are satisfied that investing in a company engaged in a particular type of business would conflict with the very objects of their trust is seeking to achieve, then they are duty bound not to so invest.

In other circumstances, where trustees would be entitled, or even required, to take in to account non-financial factors, is where the trust document itself requires it. This is an obvious, but rather important point. Trustees are required to fulfil the terms of their trust, which are commonly expressed in trust instruments. **If the subject trust explicitly required the trustees to consider social or ethical factors when making investment decisions, there would be little, if any, risk of the trustees being in violation their fiduciary duties if they adopted an SRI policy consistent with the terms of the trust. In such circumstances, the trustees would be in breach of trust if they did not adopt an SRI policy.**

The court in *Harries* notes, however, that while the general rule is that trustees cannot properly use assets held as an investment for other non-investment purposes, the trustees are not prohibited from accommodating views of those who consider that on moral grounds a particular investment would be in conflict with the object of the charity, so long as the trustees are satisfied that the course does not involve a risk of significant financial detriment.

Also of interest in this case was the court's review of the Commissioners' existing investment policy. What follows are some relevant passages from the policy:

> The primary aim in the management of our assets is to produce the best total return, that is capital and income growth combined. While financial responsibilities must remain of primary importance (given our position as trustees), as responsible investors we also continue to take proper account of social, ethical and environmental issues. . . . As regards our stock exchange holdings this means that we do not invest in companies whose main business is armaments, gambling, alcohol, tobacco and newspapers.
>
> . . . We do not invest in any South African company nor in any other company where more than a small part of their business is in South Africa. Where we do invest in a company with a small stake in South Africa we try to ensure that it follows enlightened, social and employment policies, so far as possible within the system of apartheid of which we have repeatedly expressed our abhorrence.
>
> . . . On the property side, either we shall continue to seek out development possibilities so as to discharge our duties as trustees, we are conscious of the effect of our actions upon local communities and their perceptions of the Church as a whole. We shall therefore continue to ensure that environmental considerations are properly taken into account when development schemes arise. . . .[20]

In reviewing the investment policy, the court noted that the Commissioners did in fact have "an ethical investment policy" and stated that there was nothing in the statement that was inconsistent with the general principles enunciated in the case. In this regard, the court noted that the Commissioners have demonstrated that they have felt able to exclude certain items from their investments for ethical purposes because there has remained open to the Commissioners an adequate width of alternative investments.

LEGAL COMMENTARY

While there are very few judicial authorities on the issue of SRI and pension fund fiduciary obligations, a significant body of legal literature exists, primarily American, on the topic. Legal commentators on the issue are quite polarized in their views. Some commentators hold quite strongly that any consideration of non-financial factors by plan trustees is contrary to their legal duties.[21] Other commentators argue strenuously that SRI by fund trustees is perfectly consistent with these duties.[22]

Rather than engage in an exhaustive review of all the legal literature, we summarize below the opinions expressed by two of the legal commentators whose views are most representative of the majority of legal commentators whose views fall closer to the middle of the spectrum in the polarized debate on the issue.

Marie O'Brien Hylton, an associate professor of law at DePaul University,[23] advances the position that pension funds can maximize income by following programs of ethical investing and therefore may fulfil their fiduciary responsibilities to the beneficiaries of the fund, but the scope of SRI must remain quite limited. Professor Hylton examines socially responsible investment in the context of ERISA and common law fiduciary duties of a trustee and primarily whether social investing objectives violate the duty of a pension fund fiduciary to act exclusively in the interests of the beneficiaries in the administration and investment of a pension fund. She notes that some commentators argue vigorously that SRI practitioners violate the duties of loyalty and prudence whenever a trustee favours a social cause over the beneficiaries' financial gain, while SRI supporters insist that socially responsible investing involves no financial sacrifice and therefore no breach of the duties of loyalty or prudence. Alternatively, they argue that small sacrifices in exchange for the satisfaction of ethical investing are permitted under ERISA.

Professor Hylton concludes that socially responsible investing is legally permissible for pension fund fiduciaries **only** as an incidental feature of otherwise traditional investment considerations. This means that screens that operate in such a way as to exclude large numbers of companies or even entire industries probably run afoul of prudence rules. In addition, funds that make positive investment choices based solely on social and political criteria, such as the existence of equal employment opportunity programs or unionized work force, are also likely to violate the fiduciary standards of ERISA. She concludes:

> The reality is that if SRI is permitted under any circumstances, as it is, it may only be practised without fear of liability when the screens, whether positive or negative, have a *de minimis* effect on the performance of an investment portfolio.[24]

Thus, in Professor Hylton's view, ERISA and fiduciary law permits pension fund trustees to engage in socially responsible investing where competing investments are equal, or nearly equal, with respect to traditional concerns of expected rate of return, risk, diversification and security of plan assets. What is problematic is determining how wide the gap must be between the reasonable rate of return on the SRI investment and market return may be before fiduciary standards are offended.

Professor Hylton, like several other commentators, recommends obtaining consent of the participants through disclosure and some form of opting out mechanism "as the only sensible mechanism available to avoid pension plan disputes."

Ian Lanoff, who was the Administrator, Office of Pension and Welfare Benefits Programs, at the U.S. Department of Labor, discussed the Department's view of social investment of pension plan assets in July of 1980.[25] Lanoff echoes the sentiments of many other commentators on the issue, in advancing the view that **investment performance may not properly be sacrificed** by plan fiduciaries in order to advance social or ethical objectives. However, such investments are not impermissible under ERISA solely because they have social utility. He states:

> If the socially beneficial investment meets objective investments criteria which are appropriate to the goals of the portfolio, it may be considered in the same manner as other investments which meets these criteria.

In other words, what the pension plan fiduciary needs to determine about an investment is not, first, whether it is socially good or bad, but how the proposed investment would serve the plans participants and beneficiaries. The stability of a company's labor relations, the political situation in a country in which the investment is located or with which a company does business, and the effect that the public view of the company's social commitment may have on the profitability of the company are all factors which may properly enter into the valuation of an investment.

If, after evaluating other factors, two investments appear to be equally desirable, then social judgments are permissible in determining which to select. The point is that social judgments may not properly be substituted for any factors which would otherwise be considered in a given case.[26]

Lanoff, however, also expresses a concern with respect to the requirement under ERISA for investment diversification. Where socially responsible investments requires ruling out certain investments completely, then pension fund fiduciaries run the risk of violating ERISA. In Lanoff's view, the fiduciary standards codified in ERISA lead to the inescapable conclusion that any plan that, for so-called social purposes, excludes investment possibilities without consideration of their economic and financial merit, is showing insufficient care for and disloyalty to individuals covered by the plans.

Lanoff concludes by suggesting that pension funds interested in social investing would be well advised to forsake a policy of exclusion and instead pursue a policy of inclusion. The more promising approach is to broaden the number and types of investment vehicles money managers will examine for investment purposes.

Lanoff presents as a model an agreement between United Auto Workers Union (the "UAW") and Chrysler that was approved by the Department of Labor relating to the question of social investment. The UAW and Chrysler established a joint investment committee that was to bring to the attention of those responsible for trust fund investments opportunities with social benefit features that might otherwise not have been considered. Under this model, the committee recommendations to the trustees were not binding, leaving plan fiduciaries free to reject those recommendations that failed to measure up economically under ERISA fiduciary standards. The parties anticipated that the committee would be able to identify for plan fiduciaries investment opportunities that are economically competitive with other investment opportunities that may not contain similar socially beneficial features.

In conclusion, Lanoff states:

Plan officials may wish to act on the basis of the perceived social benefit features of investments. This will be possible where they examine a broad range of investments and have found selections having those socially desirable features among a broad class of otherwise suitable and equally desirable investment opportunities meeting the economic objectives of the plan.[27]

SUMMARY AND CONCLUSION

It should be fairly obvious from this survey that a definitive answer to the legal question posed is unlikely given the current state of Canadian jurisprudence and legislation. At a fundamental level, some of the legal authorities from foreign jurisdictions are directly in conflict. On the one hand, the English court in *Cowan* suggests that consideration by trustees of non-economic factors in making investment decisions is contrary to the trustees' duties of prudence and loyalty. However the American courts, particularly in the *City of Baltimore* case, hold that such considerations are perfectly compatible with the trustees' duties.

Close analysis of the existing authorities does, however, reveal some common ground accepted by all authorities that may provide some practical guidance to trustees in considering the adoption of SRI policies.

First and foremost, the legal authorities reviewed above establish the principle that SRI is not in and of itself inconsistent with a trustee's duties to plan beneficiaries. That is, consideration of social, ethical and environmental factors in making investment decisions does not constitute a prima facie violation of a trustee's duty of prudence and loyalty. This basic principle is supported by the American jurisprudence and the English court decision in *Harries* and by virtually all legal commentators reviewed. Moreover, the policy statements by Ontario, OSFI and American regulators lend further support and credence to this proposition.

It is, however, important to recognize the limits of this principle. Ignoring for the moment the *City of Baltimore* case, the preponderance of authority suggests that trustees cannot sacrifice financial benefits for beneficiaries based on social or ethical beliefs held by the trustees, unless this is mandated by the trust documents themselves. Fiduciaries who are willing to accept reduced rates of return or greater risk to secure collateral benefits are likely to violate their fiduciary obligations. This may require, as stated by the court in *Cowan,* that trustees set aside social or ethical values where investments that conflict with these views would be more beneficial to the pension plan than other investments.

It is not, however, inconsistent with this principle for trustees to formulate investment preferences based on SRI values, where investment options are comparable, or similarly attractive based on traditional investment considerations. That is, where collateral social factors and benefits are neutral in their impact on financial return or risk, there is likely no infringement of fiduciary standards. In other words, SRI investments have to be prudent on traditional standards. As suggested in some of the legal authorities reviewed above, a prudent financial evaluation of any particular investment or investment policy may include, and may require, consideration of many social factors such as labour stability, environmental performance and other social or ethical values, where the trustees believe on reliable advice and information that such factors are properly considered in assessing the likely investment performance and/or risk associated with particular investments, or an investment portfolio.

The *City of Baltimore* case goes one step further in recognizing that ethical investment policies may have additional cost components, such as increased broker commissions associated with a higher volume of trading in smaller company stocks. The court accepts that such costs are consistent with a trustee's fiduciary duty where the costs are insignificant relative to the size of the fund. This proposition stands out because it implicitly accepts that financial returns can be compromised in favour of social factors, where the compromise is *de minimis*. This remains a grey area that, on its face, appears to conflict with the basic premise accepted by most authorities that financial benefits cannot be sacrificed for non-financial or collateral benefits. In straying into this grey area, trustees are best advised to adhere strictly to the cost parameters approved in the *City of Baltimore* case as a guide to what a court may find as an acceptable cost for SRI implementation.

At the end of the day, there is an irreducible risk associated with SRI of exposure to fiduciary liability for trustees implementing such policies. This, however, is also true of virtually all investment activity engaged in by pension fund trustees. The risks associated with SRI are perhaps enhanced because of the absence of clear legislative or judicial guidance on the issue, and the politically sensitive nature of SRI policies.

Ultimate protection for trustees from these risks would be provided by a trust document that specifically directs the trustee to engage in SRI or incorporates SRI values as one of the purposes the trust is intended to serve.

Absent such explicit authority in the trust documents, a trustee's decision to implement an SRI policy will ultimately be judged in accordance with the same standards and factors as courts would apply in reviewing all trust investment decisions. These factors primarily relate to the procedures adopted by the trustees in reaching investment decisions. Did the trustees employ proper methods to investigate, evaluate and structure investments? Did the trustees conduct an impartial study of the advantages and disadvantages in the investment policies? Did the trustees exercise due diligence in researching all aspects of the investment policy? Were qualified experts and consultants retained by the trustees to provide appropriate advice? Did the trustees consider and rely upon complete and up-to-date information in reaching their decision?

In applying these standards of procedural prudence to trustees in the SRI context, a court is likely to examine whether trustees considered the impact of SRI screening policies, for example, on the financial performance of the fund and whether alternative investments available provide a comparable investment portfolio with similar risk and rate-of-return characteristics. Did the trustees rely on credible and complete information in concluding that social and environmental performance of targeted companies bears a correlation with long-term financial viability of those companies and is therefore a proper factor to consider when assessing the prudence of investing or not investing in these companies?

In addition to the normal procedural prudence mechanisms applicable to all investment decisions by pension fund trustees, fiduciary liability risks may be further reduced in the SRI context through disclosure mechanisms as suggested by the Ontario Commission's policy statement and Professor Hylton in her analysis of the issue. It would be prudent for trustees who adopt SRI policy to specifically incorporate the policy in the fund's investment policy statement, specifically setting out the criteria to be met for investments under the SRI policy. Furthermore, disclosure of the SRI policy to plan beneficiaries, and perhaps the development of a mechanism to allow beneficiaries to provide input or comment on the social and ethical criteria incorporated in the SRI policy, may provide further liability protection to the trustees.

ENDNOTES

1. Pension Commission of Ontario, *PCO Bulletin* (February 1992) Vol. 2, Iss. 4, at p. 11.

2. Office of the Superintendent of Financial Institutions, "Guideline for Governance of Federally Regulated Pension Plans" (1 May 1998).

3. *Ibid.*, at p. 20.

4. R.R.O. 1990, Regulation 909, s. 67(2). The New Brunswick legislation contains an identical provision: N.B.Reg. 91-195, s.44 (4). The Quebec *Supplemental Pension Plans Act*, R.S.Q. 1990, R-15.1, s.170, adopts a similar "portfolio" approach in its investment guidelines. See also Office of the Superintendent of Financial Institutions, "Guideline for the Development of Investment Policies and Procedures for Federally Regulated Pension Plans" (April 2000).

5. U.S. Department of Labor, Interpretive Bulletin 94-1, "Economically Targeted Investments" (17 June 1994).

6. Donovan Waters, *The Law of Trusts in Canada*, 2d ed. (Toronto: Carswell, 1984) at p. 749.

7. *Cowan v. Scargill*, [1984] 2 All E.R. 750 (Ch. D).

8. *Pension Benefits Act* R.S.O. 1990, c. P.8, s.22(1).

9. *Supra* note 7.

10. Sir Robert Megarry, "Investing Pension Funds: The Mineworkers Case," in T.G. Youdan, ed. *Equity, Fiduciaries and Trusts* (Toronto: Carswell, 1989) at pp. 149-159.

11. *Withers v. Teachers' Retirement System of the City of New York*, 447 F. Supp. 1248 (S.D.N.Y. 1978) aff'd, 595 F.2d 1210 (2d Cir. 1979).

12. *The Board of Trustees v. City of Baltimore*, 562 A.2d 720 (M.D. 1989).

13. A.W. Scott, *The Law of Trusts*, 3rd ed. (Boston: Little,

Brown and Company, 1967) as cited in *Board of Trustees v. City of Baltimore supra* note 12, at p. 736.

14. *Board of Trustees v. City of Baltimore,* supra note 12, at p. 737.

15. *Martin v. The City of Edinburgh District Council,* [1988] S.C.L.R. 90 (O.H.).

16. *Ibid.,* at p. 96.

17. Pension Commission of Ontario, *PCO Bulletin* (May 1990) Vol. I, Iss. 2, at p. 12.

18. *Harries v. Church Commissioners,* [1993] 2 All E.R. 301 (Ch. D.).

19. *Ibid.,* at p. 304.

20. *Ibid.,* at pp. 306-307.

21. See Posner and Langbein, "Social Investing and the Law of Trusts," [1980] Vol. 79:72 *Michigan Law Review,* where the authors conclude: "... *a trustee who sacrifices the beneficiary's financial well-being for any other object breaches both his duty of loyalty to the beneficiary and his duty of prudence in investment.*"

22. See, for example, Adams, Edward, "A Charitable Corporate Giving Justification For The Socially Responsible Investment Of Pension Funds: A Populist Argument For The Public Use of Private Wealth" [1994] 80 *Iowa Law Review* 211. Professor Adams is a professor of law and director of the Centre for Law and Business Studies at the University of Minnesota Law School. Professor Adams develops the argument advanced by Professor Scott, and cited with approval in the *City of Baltimore* case drawing an analogy between the fiduciary duties owed by trustees to beneficiaries of a pension trust and the fiduciary duties owed by a director of a corporation to its shareholders. While directors of a business corporation owe fiduciary duties to its shareholders to conduct business so as to secure a profit, it is settled law that they should also recognize that the corporation operates as part of a community in that, within proper limits, they may make gifts of money of the corporation for charitable purposes, although this may, at least in the short term, diminish the profits of the corporation. Therefore, argues Professor Adams, by necessary implication, courts should allow pension fund fiduciaries to use reasonable social screens in making investment decisions, just as directors of corporations may make reasonable charitable contributions. As in *Baltimore,* courts should recognize that a trustee's use of reasonable socially responsible screens does not violate the duty of loyalty, because any infringement upon that duty is *de minimis*.

23. Hylton, Marie O'Brien, "Socially Responsible Investing: Doing Good Versus Doing Well in an Inefficient Market" [1992] 42:1 *American University Law Review.*

24. *Ibid.,* at p. 43.

25. Lanoff, Ian, "The Social Investments of Private Pension Plan Assets: May It Be Done Lawfully Under ERISA?" (July 1980) Vol. 31 No.7, *Labour Law Journal,* 387.

26. *Ibid.,* at pp. 390-391.

27. *Ibid.,* at p. 393.

CHAPTER 13

Pension Plans and the Challenge of Family Law

by Karen M. DeBortoli

INTRODUCTION

The issue of how to divide pension assets on marriage breakdown[1] is confusing and uncertain. It was not even clear whether pensions were actually matrimonial assets subject to division until the Supreme Court of Canada held, in *Clarke v. Clarke,*[2] that pensions are subject to division on marriage breakdown unless specifically excluded from division by statute. Following this decision, all provinces except Prince Edward Island have amended their legislation to specifically list pensions as divisible property, or to define *property* and/or *assets* in such a manner as to include pensions.

Clarke did not completely determine the status of pensions on marriage breakdown, and issues of the categorization, valuation and division of pension plan assets continue to pose problems. As pension plans provide essential retirement security for their members and, as after the matrimonial home, pensions are among the most valuable assets possessed by many individuals, there is a need for the clarification of the status of pension assets on marriage breakdown. The Canadian Institute of Actuaries (the "CIA") task force on the issue of pension division noted:

> The greater the degree of uncertainty underlying a pension division, the greater the chance of favouring one spouse at the expense of the other. The highest degree of equity will be achieved if as many of the unknown factors as possible are eliminated.[3]

Much of the uncertainty surrounding the division of pension assets on marriage breakdown stems from the fact that it involves the intersection of two very different branches of the law: pension and family law. The conflicting aims and methods of these two branches have resulted in a system for pension valuation and division that varies considerably from jurisdiction to jurisdiction and, as is the case with federal legislation, even within jurisdictions. The resulting confusion frequently creates judicial orders that are incomprehensible, unenforceable or inequitable.

The Supreme Court had the opportunity to address these issues and provide guidance in this area in its recent decision in the Ontario case of *Best v. Best,*[4] which dealt with the appropriate method of valuing and dividing a pension plan. However, while the majority found that the pro-rata method (which will be discussed in this chapter) better reflected the nature of a defined benefit pension, this determination was restricted to "the limited issues involved in this particular appeal"[5] and suggested that the issue would be best resolved through amendments to provincial family legislation.

This chapter addresses pension division in circumstances where the spouses do not have a written separation agreement addressing the pension division issue. In all provinces, an agreement to divide pension assets (unless otherwise prohibited) overrides statutory mandated pension splitting. While these agreements may take many forms, we have provided various sample provisions dealing with pension division in Appendix IV-13-A to this chapter. This agreement is for illustration purposes only, and each individual should receive appropriate advice to tailor such an agreement to his or her own circumstances.

This chapter provides an analysis of the terminology and issues surrounding pension valuation and division, an overview of the relevant provincial and federal legislation, and a discussion of ongoing and developing issues relating to the division of pension assets on marriage breakdown.

TYPES OF PENSION PLANS

Pension plans are designed to be either contributory or non-contributory. In a contributory pension plan, both the plan members and their employer make contributions, while in a non-contributory pension plan, contributions are made by the employer alone.

Apart from their basic design, individual plans vary widely in terms of how they are set up and what benefits they provide. The most common are the defined benefit and defined contribution plans, although a wide variety of hybrid plans can exist between these two extremes.

Defined Benefit Plans

In a defined benefit plan, the benefit to which a plan member will be entitled at retirement is prescribed by a formula that takes into account factors such as earnings and years of service. The following three formulas are the most commonly used.

Final Average Earnings Formula:
Annual benefit = (X% of average earnings over the best Y# of years) × total years of pensionable service

Career Average Earnings Formula:
Annual benefit = X% of annual earnings while a participant in the plan

Flat Benefit Formula:
Annual benefit = ($Z annual pension benefit) × (total years pensionable service)[6]

Defined Contribution Plans

In a defined contribution plan, also known as a *money purchase plan,* contributions are made to an investment pool, which contains an account in each plan member's name to which their contributions are credited. No valuation formula is used to determine the amount of the member's benefit, which is instead determined by the pool's investment performance. When the member retires, the money in his or her account is used to purchase an annuity or other similar financial vehicle for the member.

DIVORCE LAW AND PROPERTY DIVISION

Family law involves the interplay of many factors that are absent from other aspects of legal practice. Resolving a marital dispute involves handling personal relationships, often including the presence of children, which are characterised by a powerful emotional dynamic. The need to formulate solutions for custody,

support and property division that are prospective rather than retrospective further complicates matters. As noted by Julian Payne, the primary objectives of a sound divorce law are (i) to facilitate the legal termination of marriages that have irretrievably broken down with a minimum of hurt, hostility, humiliation and hardship; (ii) to promote an equitable disposition of the economic consequences of the marriage breakdown; and (iii) to ensure that reasonable arrangements are made for the upbringing of the children of divorcing parents.[7]

Another aspect of the family law is the economic component of property division. As noted in the case of *Fisher v. Fisher:*[8]

A distribution of matrimonial property upon dissolution of the marital relationship involves an attempt to reduce the economic interdependence of the spouses by severing the economic ties which, during the continuance of the marital relationship, served in part to bind the parties together. For this reason, the court should give due consideration to the objective of leaving the parties as free as possible to manage their economic affairs after the break-up of the marriage, without hindrance of economic ties that arise out of a marriage, which no longer exists.[9]

In most marriages, only one party has a pension. This is because the marriage was a traditional one, in which roles were divided between the "breadwinner," usually the husband, and the "homemaker," usually the wife. Alternatively, even in marriages where both spouses worked outside the home, only one had an employer that provided a pension plan for its employees. Therefore, aside from any private retirement arrangements such as registered retirement savings plans (RRSPs), one pension plan was intended to ensure a secure and comfortable retirement for both spouses. Despite this intention, notions of which spouse "owns" the pension may inform the parties' views on how a pension should be divided. The division of pension assets on marriage breakdown should accordingly be governed by an awareness of these issues.

There are three steps to effecting a division of property on marriage breakdown. The first is to determine which assets are subject to division and which are not. Personal dynamics aside, this determination is made by the relevant provincial statute, the terms of which may vary considerably from province to province. Despite this variation, two main models exist. The first is the *net gains division model,* which only divides assets acquired during the marriage. Matrimonial property legislation in Alberta, Manitoba, New Brunswick, Newfoundland and Quebec subscribes to this model. The second is the *asset division model,* which divides all matrimonial assets equally but permits the unequal division of other assets. The legislation in British Columbia, Nova Scotia, Ontario, Prince Edward Island and Saskatchewan follows this model, although it is important to note that the Nova Scotia *Matrimonial Property Act* is the only statute that includes property acquired before *or* during marriage under the definition of *matrimonial asset.*[10]

The asset division model provides lawyers and judges with more flexibility than the net gains division model when dividing property and facilitates a more equitable agreement between the parties. An example of this flexibility is found in Nova Scotia's *Matrimonial Property Act.*[11] Although the default method is the equalization of matrimonial assets, Section 13 allows the court to order an unequal division if it considers that an equal division would be unfair or unconscionable in light of any of the following factors:

a. The unreasonable impoverishment by either spouse of the matrimonial assets

b. The amount of the debts and liabilities of each spouse and the circumstances in which they were incurred

c. A marriage contract or separation agreement between the spouses

d. The length of time that the spouses have cohabited with each other during their marriage

e. The date and manner of acquisition of the assets

f. The effect of the assumption by one spouse of any housekeeping, child care or other domestic responsibilities for the family on the ability of the other spouse to acquire, manage, maintain, operate or improve a business asset

g. The contribution by one spouse to the education or career potential of the other spouse

h. The needs of a child who has not attained the age of majority

i. The contribution made by each spouse to the marriage and to the welfare of the family, including any contribution made as a homemaker or parent

j. Whether the value of the assets substantially appreciated during the marriage

k. The proceeds of an insurance policy, or an award of damages in tort, intended to represent compensation for physical injuries or the cost of future maintenance of the injured spouse

l. The value to either spouse of any pension or other benefit that, by reason of the termination of the marriage relationship, the party will lose the chance of acquiring

m. All taxation consequences of the division of matrimonial assets.[12]

PENSION VALUATION[13]

Once all the assets have been classified, they must then be valued. Pension valuation involves the use of calculations in order to arrive at an amount that represents the present value of a stream of pension payments to be received in the future and based on the factors stipulated in the plan. This is the amount that will be divided between the parties on marriage breakdown. There are two stages in the process of pension valuation. The first is to establish the valuation date, which determines the portion of the pension that is considered to be a divisible matrimonial asset. The standard procedure is to use the date of marriage and the date of separation, although the parties are free to specify a different valuation date in an agreement. It should, however, be noted that the courts have the discretion to substitute their own choice of date where they consider it appropriate.

The next stage involves a calculation of the value of the portion of the pension that is a matrimonial asset. While the vast majority of matrimonial assets, such as the matrimonial home, automobiles, jewellery and furniture, have a readily ascertainable market value, the value of a pension is difficult to determine. As the courts have noted, the problem lies in the fact that the right to receive a pension is a *future* as opposed to a *present* right, and is as such contingent on the occurrence of future events.[14]

The valuation problems associated with pensions are exacerbated by the differing compositions of the plans themselves. In terms of defined benefit plans, as most formulas, especially those of final and career average earnings plans, are based on information that may not be known at separation, determining the value of the portion of the pension that is a matrimonial asset involves making economic assumptions. It is relatively easy to determine the value of the portion of a defined contribution plan that is a matrimonial asset, as all benefits that accrue in a given year are credited to that year.

In its 1995 *Report on Pensions as Family Law: Valuation and Division,*[15] the Ontario Law Reform Commission (the "OLRC") provided the following guiding principles to be used when valuing pensions:

• Family property should be divided fairly and equally with due regard being given to the unique nature of pension assets.

• The overall regime for dealing with pensions should be flexible enough to accommodate the different needs and circumstances of the parties involved.

• Given the overall purpose of pensions, from both an individual and societal perspective, is to provide income security on retirement, the regime should encourage the payment of pension benefits at retirement to both parties.

• Costs to both parties should be minimized and the need for recourse to the courts reduced.

• To the greatest extent possible, the process for pension division at source should be streamlined and should not place an undue financial burden on pension plan administrators.[16]

The courts have used a variety of methods to ascribe a value to the portion of the pension that is a matrimonial asset on marriage breakdown, each of which uses different assumptions about the pension when making calculations. Courts generally choose which valuation method to use on a case-by-case basis, with the particular facts of each case dictating the method chosen. The Saskatchewan Court of Queen's Bench provided additional guidance regarding the choice of method in *Harrop v. Harrop.*[17]

In *Harrop v. Harrop,* the court held that when the time left to retirement is five years or less, the fairest method of pension valuation is the retirement method because the value of the asset is near its maximum, most of the contributions were made during the marriage, the probability that the assumptions made would actually occur is the greatest, and the division is the fairest. When more than five years remain to retirement, however, the court found that the fairest method would be the termination method since the value of the asset is near its actual value, only contributions made during the marriage are used in the calculation, and there is no need to make assumptions about the future that might or might not occur.[18]

Termination Method

The *termination method* is defined by the CIA as *an unprojected accrued valuation method.* "No increase in accrued benefits shall be reflected, except to the extent such increases are provided to deferred vested pension plan members."[19] This method also excludes plan improvements and unvested unreduced early retirement benefits from its calculations.

There have been two different approaches to the termination method. The first is the "strict termination method," which calculates the pension's value as if the member spouse terminated employment on the valuation date. The present value of the pension is then calculated based on the benefit accrued to the valuation date. This approach, while adopted in *Rickett v. Rickett,*[20] has been rejected in subsequent cases.[21]

The second approach to the termination method calls for no speculation to be made as to the plan member's future earnings. The calculation of the pension's value is instead based on the pension accrued for service prior to the valuation date and frozen at its value on the valuation date, thus avoiding unnecessary speculation.[22]

Retirement Method

The *retirement method* is a projected accrued valuation method that makes salary projections where ap-

propriate. It calculates the present value of the member spouse's anticipated future pension benefits, including any ancillary benefits, based on projected retirement salary levels. Unlike the termination method, it includes unvested unreduced early retirement benefits and plan improvements when calculating the value of the divisible portion of the pension.

There are also two approaches to this method, the first of which is the *speculative retirement method.* This method assumes that the plan member continues to be employed until retirement and attempts to estimate the member's future entitlement by speculating on future increases in the Consumer Price Index (CPI) and assuming that the member's pension will increase to reflect these increases, and possibly by considering future promotions.[23] The second method is the *real interest method* which, rather than speculating on future CPI increases, reflects indexing by choosing a low-discount rate to represent the "real" rate of interest.[24] The real interest method also assumes that the accrued pension prior to the valuation date is frozen at the amount applicable at the valuation date.

While it can produce a more reliable result than the termination method, the retirement method does not guarantee an accurate valuation of the portion of the member's pension that was earned during the marriage, as its calculations are based on economic projections. The Manitoba Court of Appeal noted in *George v. George*[25] that assessing the present value of the husband's future pension benefits without taking into account the probability or otherwise of the salary in his last years of employment could lead to an unrealistic determination of the pension's value to the owner.[26]

"Hybrid" Method

Some literature mentions the existence of a "hybrid" approach to pension valuation, although this term does not exist in the CIA *Standard of Practice.* A hybrid approach was used in *Haley v. Haley,*[27] where the court chose an approach that was midway between the termination and retirement methods due to the length of the marriage and the economic disadvantage that the wife suffered as a result of it.

Value-Added and Pro-Rata Approaches

Under the *value-added approach,* the pension's value at the date of marriage is deducted from that of the valuation date, with the difference constituting the value of the pension earned during the marriage. It is this amount that is divided between the spouses.

The *pro-rata method* was described by the Ontario Court of Appeal in *Best* as follows:

Under the pro-rata approach the accrued pension to the date of separation is also calculated. The value attributable to the years of marriage is then determined by pro-rating this pension value on the ratio of either: a) the benefits accrued during the marriage to the total accrued benefits (pro-rata on benefits), or b) the years worked during the marriage to the total of years worked by the pension holder (pro-rata on service).[28]

There has been considerable discussion as to which of these methods is preferable. In its 1995 report, the OLRC stated that the pro-rata on service approach was preferable, as it was more straightforward than the value-added approach.[29] The value-added approach has also been criticized as unfair to member spouses with many years of pensionable service prior to marriage, especially in a second or short (less than ten years) marriage.

The unfairness can become acute in cases of final or best average defined benefit plans, as the majority of the pension's value may have accumulated during the marriage, although the proportion of the length of the marriage to the length of pensionable service is quite small. This was the case in *Best*, where the parties were married for 12 of the husband's 32 years of pensionable service. The court had to value the portion of the husband's pension that was a matrimonial asset, an exercise that was further complicated by the absence of statutory guidance. At trial and on appeal, the value-added approach was chosen. The use of this method resulted in the classification of over 80% of the pension's value as net family property, while the use of the pro-rata approach would have classified only 36% as a family asset, a difference of over $100,000. The court stated that "even if the 'pro-rated' method was inherently equitable, it was not consistent with the equalization of family property contemplated by s. 5 of the *Family Law Act*."[30] It is important to note that the decision in *Best* did not state that the value-added method was the only appropriate method of pension valuation, just that it was "not inconsistent"[31] with Ontario's legislation.

In its treatment of the matter in *Best*, Mr. Justice Major, writing for the majority of the Supreme Court of Canada, made the following statement on the issue:

> . . . I believe that the termination *pro rata* method produces a fairer valuation of defined benefit pensions for equalization purposes than the termination value-added method. The *pro rata* method is not without flaws, nor will it inevitably be preferable to the value-added method. Although cases may arise where other considerations will tilt the balance in favour of a different valuation method, the nature of defined benefit pension [*sic*] indicates that, as a general rule, the *pro rata* method is preferable.[32]

Although the preceding statement suggests that it is still possible to use the value-added method to divide a pension, a number of courts have cited the Supreme Court's decision in *Best* as authority for the proposition that pensions must be divided on a pro-rata basis.[33]

PENSION DIVISION

Once the matrimonial assets have been ascertained and valued, the final step is to divide them. In *Marsham v. Marsham*,[34] it was held that after the non-member spouse's equalization entitlement has been determined, the court has discretion as to how the entitlement will be satisfied. A number of forms of division are available, and the method chosen depends on the nature of the asset to be divided. Four major methods of pension division have emerged in Canada.

1. The imposition of a trust on the spouse who is the nominal owner of the pension requiring his or her payment of a portion of it to the other spouse
2. The division and payment of the benefits at source, when payable, in proportion to the amount earned during the marriage
3. The payment of one-half of the value of the pension from the plan to the other spouse's registered retirement vehicle and
4. A valuation of the pension earned during the marriage and an accounting for that value in the distribution of other property.[35]

Trust-Type Arrangements

In this method of pension division, once the non-member's share has been ascertained, the member spouse is declared the trustee of the non-member's share of the pension. When pension payments commence, the member spouse will then pay the non-member his or her share of the benefit. If the member spouse dies prior to retirement, the non-member's benefit entitlement is lost; therefore this is also known as the "if-and-when" division method.

While this method was used by the Supreme Court in *Clarke*, the leading case on trust-type arrangements is *Rutherford v. Rutherford*.[36] At the conclusion of their 29-year marriage, Mrs. Rutherford was awarded a one-half interest of the pension as a tenant-in-common, which was changed on appeal to a one-half interest in the portion of the pension that was a matrimonial asset. The determination of what was a matrimonial asset was made using what is now known as the "*Rutherford* formula"— one-half times the number of months of married cohabitation during which pension contributions were made, divided by the total number of months during which pension contributions were or will be made, times the pension benefits payable.[37] In order to protect the wife's interest, the husband was made a trustee of her share of the pension, and ordered ". . . to do the things necessary to protect her interest."[38] Payments were ordered to commence on the earliest date at which the husband could retire with an unreduced pension. If, however, he elected to continue working for as long as possible, either the wife could elect to wait to receive her share of the pension, or she could require her husband to pay her compensation equal to her share of the pension until his retirement.

"If-and-when" division was rejected by the trial judge in *Best*. On appeal, this decision was upheld as it was within the trial judge's discretion and, as these orders are not expressly provided for in Ontario legislation. In *Mailhot v. Mailhot,*[39] the court held that this method should only be used in cases where not all of the pension is a family asset, or where the pension should not be divided equally.[40]

There are many problems with the "if-and-when" method of division. The first is that it results in complicated orders that can be difficult to enforce if, for example, the member spouse moves to another jurisdiction. A second problem is that the trust created by this type of arrangement is difficult to administer as it may remain purely executory for decades and, once executed, may have to be continued after the death of one of the spouses. The final problem is that it fails to create a clean break between the parties, thus putting it at odds with family law's goal of promoting a full and final settlement. Forcing the parties to remain in long-term contact with each other can be emotionally wrenching in many cases and is not advisable in cases where there has been abuse.

Division at Source

Most pension benefits legislation allows for the at-source division of pension assets. This means that, after receiving all the necessary documentation, the plan administrator will divide the member's pension into two separate pensions, one for the member and one for the non-member. When the member spouse retires, both parties will receive their pensions directly from the plan. This method of division is also known as a "deferred benefit split."

This method is easier to set up and administer than the "if-and-when" method; it allows the parties to make a clean break and also makes it easier for non-member spouses to enforce their rights. As they have a pension in their name, the non-members have the right to bring a claim against the plan in the event that they do not receive their share of the pension.

Lump-Sum Transfers

In a lump-sum transfer, once the pension's value is calculated and the non-member's share is determined, a lump-sum payment of the non-member's share is made to him or her. This is done either by having the plan administrator make a payment directly into an RRSP, annuity or other locked-in retirement vehicle (in which case the non-member will have access to the funds once the eligibility requirements for the vehicle have been met), or by having the member spouse pay the non-member an amount equal to the non-member's share of the benefit.

This method assigns a present value to an asset whose actual value may only be known when the member spouse retires. As such, it can result in the non-member spouse receiving an amount that will end up being less than his or her share is actually worth when the former spouse retires. Although it is easy for the plan administrator to make a lump-sum payment, requiring the member spouse to pay the non-member a lump-sum equivalent to his or her share of the pension can impose a significant financial burden. Unless the member spouse is quite wealthy, he or she will not possess sufficient assets to satisfy the non-member's share of the pension. Such was the case in *Best,* where the husband was ordered to pay his former wife $268,000 over a period time with interest. These payments were secured by having the husband make her the beneficiary of a life insurance policy for the amount owing.

Asset Trade-Offs

The use of an asset trade-off enables the member spouse to keep his or her entire pension by transferring to the non-member spouse an asset, or combination of assets, the value of which equals that of the pension. In the majority of asset trade-off cases, the pension is valued using the termination method. While asset trade-offs provide the parties with a clean break, it is not a viable option for all couples, as it requires that there be a sufficiently large pool of assets available to satisfy the trade-off. In the remainder of cases, completing a trade-off will leave the member spouse cash and/or asset poor.

The Problem of Double Dipping

Double dipping is what occurs when the payee spouse is the beneficiary of double recovery from one asset.[41] As noted by Professor James McLeod in his annotation to *Shadbolt v. Shadbolt*:[42]

"Double dipping" is the term used to describe the effect of a court awarding support from a payor's pension income in cases where the capital value of the pension was included in the matrimonial property accounting. In such cases, a person receives his or her share of a spouse's future pension income as part of the family capital and then receives another share of the spouse's pension as support when the pension is in pay.[43]

As noted by the Supreme Court of Canada in *Best,*[44] cases and commentators are divided on the issue of whether, once equalized as property, a pension can also be treated as income from which the member can make spousal support payments to the non-member spouse.

In both *Veres v. Veres*[45] and *Butt v. Butt,*[46] it was found that, following an equalization of property, the court should not then also try to equalize income through an award of support. However, an opposite view was taken by the Ontario Court of Appeal in *Linton v. Linton.*[47] In that case, the calculation of the equalization payment to be made to the wife took the husband's pension into account. The Court of Appeal found that any element of double dipping was "insignificant in its quantum,"[48] and that the adverse effects of double dipping were avoided by taking the equalization payment into account before determining the quantum of spousal support. Similarly, in *Nantais v. Nantais,*[49] the court found that the equalization of the husband's pension did not disentitle the wife to support from her husband's pension income.

The Supreme Court of Canada had an opportunity to provide some guidance on the issue of double dipping in the case of *Strang v. Strang.*[50] However, the Supreme Court found that the issue of double dipping did not arise in that case, as the method used to evaluate the husband's pension did not accurately assess the pension's worth and did not amount to a true division of the pension's value as future property. Under such circumstances, the Supreme Court found that it was not unjust to find that the post-retirement income from the husband's pension provided him with the means to pay spousal support.

Following *Strang,* there appeared to be a sense that, while it should be avoided if at all possible, there may be cases in which double dipping is justified.[51] As noted by Mr. Justice Bastarache in *Lemoine v. Lemoine:*[52]

> . . . there now seems to be an acknowledgment that the law of divorce is not property driven, but based on equitable resource distribution, and that "double-dipping" is but one of the fairness issues that must be dealt with.[53]

The Supreme Court will have the opportunity to comment on the current approach to double dipping when it revisits the issue in the upcoming case of *Boston v. Boston.*[54] Until either guidance is provided by the Supreme Court, or until pension and family legislation is amended to specifically address the issue of double dipping, the most prudent course for lawyers is to be aware of its existence and to take whatever steps are possible to address the issue.

OVERVIEW OF CANADIAN PENSION AND FAMILY LEGISLATION

Alberta

Section 7 of the *Matrimonial Property Act*[55] (MPA) allows the court to distribute between the spouses "all property owned by both spouses and by each of them" on marriage breakdown. Property that is acquired before the marriage is excluded from distribution by virtue of Section 7(2)(c). Section 7(4) states that the court will divide property equally on marriage breakdown unless it is unjust or inequitable to do so. Section 37 allows spouses to opt out of the mandatory division provisions contained in the MPA by concluding their own written agreement.

Section 59 of the *Employment Pension Plans Act*[56] (EPPA) states that pension benefits and locked-in funds cannot be alienated, assigned, charged or anticipated, and are exempt for execution, seizure and attachment. However, Section 60 provides that any plan member's benefit entitlement is subject to an order under the MPA or a similar order enforceable in Alberta from a court outside the province that affects the member. Section 61 states that the plan administrator can require that the non-member spouse provide evidence of his or her entitlement, either by affidavit, declaration or certificate.

Bill 30, the *Employment Pension Plans Amendment Act,*[57] which received Royal Assent on May 19, 1999, added a new section, Section 3.1, to EPPA dealing with the division of pension of benefits on marriage breakdown. The triggering event for division is now the receipt by the plan administrator of a Matrimonial Property Order or Agreement under the MPA. The benefit to be divided can only cover the portion of the total pension earned during the marriage, and the member's benefit can be reduced by no more than 50% of that value. The formula will be set out in the Regulation. Optional ancillary contributions and additional voluntary contributions are not subject to these limitations and may be distributed as decided by the court or the couple. The locking-in rules set out in EPPA also apply to the non-member spouse. Finally, plan administrators are protected against further claims by either spouse once the administrator has complied with the order or agreement.

The government of Alberta issued an *Employment Pensions Bulletin*[58] which, although it has no legal authority, contains a statement of the government's policy on the division of pension benefits on marriage breakdown. It states that the terms of any court order made under the MPA must expressly provide for the transfer of pension benefits and that its terms must be strictly complied with and cannot be varied without a subsequent court order. In terms of the splitting of a defined contribution plan that is not yet in pay, the policy provides that the funds in these plans are eligible for immediate transfer to a locked-in vehicle, subject only to investment liquidity and the plan's contractual requirements. An immediate transfer should not be made if the plan member's benefit has not fully vested or if the benefit ultimately payable to the member may be significantly less than the amount accrued at the time of transfer. Due to problems related to the valuation, the Bulletin states that no transfer should be made from a defined benefit plan until the member spouse has ceased accruing benefits. Finally, the Bulletin authorizes at-source division for pensions in pay.

British Columbia

Section 58(2) of the *Family Relations Act*[59] (FRA) defines *family assets* as "property owned by one or both spouses or a minor child of either spouse for a family purpose." Section 58(3)(d) specifically lists the right of a spouse under a pension plan as a family asset but does not limit this to the portion of the pension acquired during the marriage. The FRA is currently the only family law statute in Canada to contain specific provisions for the division of pensions as distinct from other matrimonial assets. Section 72 of Part 6 of the FRA allows for at-source division in specified cases by designating the non-member spouse as a "limited member" of the pension plan. His or her portion is then paid directly from the plan, and the non-member spouse has a limited right of enforcement against the plan. Section 73 permits a lump-sum payment to the non-member spouse in the case of a defined benefit plan where the benefits are not in pay. In the case of benefits not yet in pay from a defined benefit plan, Section 74 provides for either lump-sum or at-source payments to the non-member spouse. Section 76 covers matured pensions and provides for at-source division. Parties are allowed to opt out of the terms of the FRA by concluding a written agreement by virtue of Section 80.

Section 63(3)(b) of the *Pension Benefits Standards Act*[60] (PBSA) provides that the prohibition against the alienation of pension benefits contained in Section 63(1) does not apply to separation agreements, orders for separation or dissolution of marriage, declaratory judgments under Section 57 of the FRA, orders declaring a marriage void, or divisions of pension benefit entitlement under Part 6 of the FRA. This provision is reinforced by Section 64, which states that an individual's benefit entitlement under the plan is subject to any entitlement arising under a separation agreement or order made under the FRA or any entitlement arising under Part 6 of the FRA. Section 65 provides that plan administrators may require evidence in support of a claim of entitlement, by way of affidavit, certificate, declaration or another method.

Manitoba

Asset is defined in Section 1 of the *Marital Property Act*[61] (MPA) as "any real or personal property or equitable interest therein," and Section 1(2)(d) specifically lists rights under a pension or superannuation scheme

or plan as family assets. By virtue of Section 4(1), assets acquired before marriage, or the contemplation thereof, or after separation are not family assets. Section 13 provides that spouses have a right to an accounting and to an equalization of assets upon marriage breakdown. However, Section 14(1) permits an unequal division if the court considers that equalization would be "grossly unfair or unconscionable." On the subject of asset valuation, Section 15(3) provides that if the fair market value of an asset cannot be determined, the value will be determined "on such other basis or by such other means as is appropriate." Finally, Section 5(1) allows spouses to dispose of assets by concluding a spousal agreement instead of through reliance on the terms of the MPA.

Section 31(2) of the *Pension Benefits Act*[62] (PBA) allows the division and alienation of pension credits that were acquired during the period of cohabitation. Section 31(3) restricts the application of the preceding section to spouses or parties to a common law relationship that began living separate and apart after December 31, 1983. In order for the provisions to apply to a common law couple, the parties must execute a written declaration, filed with the plan administrator, identifying themselves, stating the date that their common law relationship began, and specifying that they wish to follow the pension division terms of the PBA. By virtue of Section 31(6) couples can opt out of the terms of the statute after receiving independent legal advice and a statement from the plan administrator showing either the commuted value of the member spouse's benefit or the amount of the payments under the plan to which each party would be entitled to under the terms of the statute. They must then sign a declaration that they are opting out and file it with the plan administrator. Section 31(4) permits either an at-source division or a lump-sum transfer to a pension plan or other locked-in retirement vehicle.

New Brunswick

Section 1 of the *Marital Property Act*[63] (MPA) defines *marital property* as that which was acquired during cohabitation or in contemplation of marriage.

Section 1(1) of the *Pension Benefits Act*[64] (PBA) defines *spouse* as including both married and common law parties. Although a scheme for pension division is set out in Section 44, Section 44(11) states that if a court order made under the MPA, a separation agreement, or a contract concluded by the spouses specifies how the pension is to be divided, those provisions, not those in the PBA, will operate. Section 44(16) states that only benefits accrued during the period of cohabitation can be divided, and the maximum percentage of the pension that can be transferred to the non-member spouse is set by Section 44(6) at 50%. Section 44(5) provides that the commuted value of the member spouse's pension benefit will be calculated as of the date of marriage breakdown. The commuted value for benefits that are not from deferred pensions will be determined, pursuant to Section 44(8), as if the member spouse had terminated employment on the date of marriage breakdown. The non-member spouse can select a lump-sum transfer to a pension plan or prescribed retirement savings arrangement, or the purchase of a deferred life annuity. If the non-member spouse fails to give instructions regarding the handling of his or her share to the pension plan administrator, Sections 43(3) and (11) state that the non-member is deemed to have selected a deferred life annuity. Once the pension has been divided, Section 45(10) provides that the non-member has no further rights against the plan. Section 45 provides that plan administrators are not liable for any payments where a marriage contract, separation agreement or court order provides for payment to the non-member spouse of a sum equal to the amount owing in relation to a pension or benefit.

Sections 27 to 34 of the *Pension Benefits Regulation*[65] contain criteria and formulas to be used in order to determine the commuted value of various plan types under a variety of circumstances.

Newfoundland

The *Family Law Act*[66] (FLA) defines *matrimonial assets* as the real and personal property acquired by either or both spouses during the marriage, subject to a number of listed exceptions, none of which cover pensions. Although Section 21(1) codifies the presumption that matrimonial assets will be divided equally, Section 22 allows the court to order an unequal division if it feels that an equal division would be "grossly unjust or unconscionable" with regard to all the factors to be considered under that section. Section 33 provides that assets may be divided according to the terms of a written agreement concluded by the parties.

Part VI of the *Pension Benefits Act*[67] (PBA) deals with pension division on marriage breakdown. Section 47 provides that the pensions are to be divided in accordance with the terms of the PBA, a court order or a separation agreement. Section 48(1) states that in the case of a defined contribution plan that is not yet in pay, the non-member spouse is entitled to have a lump-sum transfer of his or her portion of the pension to his or her credit. In the case of a defined benefit plan, Section 48(2) states that where the member spouse is not eligible to receive an unreduced pension the non-member is entitled to have a portion of the pension transferred directly to the non-member's credit. The process for division of a hybrid plan is set out in Section 48(3). If the member is entitled to receive an unreduced pension, the non-member is entitled to receive a separate pension

from the plan. Section 48(4) stipulates that payments to the non-member spouse will continue until the earlier of the death of the member spouse or the termination of the plan. Pursuant to Section 49, a non-member spouse can be designated a "limited member" in the plan, which allows the non-member to receive his or her share of the pension directly from the plan, and gives him or her certain rights enforceable against the plan. Section 51 states that where no election is made by the non-member spouse, he or she is deemed to have elected to receive a separate pension from the plan. Section 52 allows the non-member spouse to revoke an election of a separate pension in favour of a lump-sum transfer, provided the pension is not yet in pay. By virtue of Section 53, plan administrators can refuse to divide a pension if they feel that the order or agreement regarding division is unclear or incomplete, or they have been given notice that the member spouse is objecting to the terms of division. In the event of a conflict between this statute and the FLA, Section 56 stipulates that the latter prevails.

Section 30 of Regulation 114/96[68] contains calculations used to determine the non-member's share in a matured or unmatured defined contribution plan or an unmatured defined benefit plan. Section 31(1) of the Regulation allows for division at source.

Nova Scotia

Matrimonial assets are defined in Section 4(1) of the *Matrimonial Property Act*[69] (MPA) as comprised of the matrimonial home and all other real or personal property acquired by either or both spouses before or during the marriage, subject to a number of listed exceptions (none of which covers pensions). While Section 12 provides for presumptive equal division, Section 13 allows the court to order an unequal division of matrimonial assets, or the division of an asset that is not matrimonial, if it is satisfied that equal division would be "unfair or unconscionable" taking into account the enumerated factors.

Section 61 of the *Pension Benefits Act*[70] (PBA) states that a plan member's spouse can apply to the court to have the pension divided on marriage breakdown, and that the court may order that the non-member spouse may receive not more than one-half of the pension benefits earned during the marriage. This is at odds with Section 4(1) of the MPA, which states that all assets acquired before or during the marriage are subject to division. As Section 61(6) states that nothing in the PBA precludes a division of assets pursuant to Section 13 of the MPA, it is possible to divide a pension unequally. Section 61(4) provides that the non-member is entitled to receive his or her share of the pension on the member's normal retirement date or the date that the member actually retires, whichever is earlier, and that the member's death does not affect the non-member's entitlement.

Ontario

Section 4(1) of the *Family Law Act*[71] (FLA) defines *property* as "any interest, present or future, vested or contingent, in real or personal property." Section 4(1)(c) states that a spouse's interest in a pension plan, including contributions made by someone other than the spouse, is divisible property under the statute. Although spouses are entitled to an equalization of assets under Section 5(1), Section 5(6) provides that the court may order an unequal division if it considers that equalization would be "unconscionable" in light of the factors listed.

By virtue of Section 51(5) of the *Pension Benefits Act*[72] (PBA) a non-member spouse who has given the plan administrator a copy of a domestic contract or order under the FLA has the same entitlement as the member spouse once the member retires or terminates. This constitutes an implied authorization of at-source division. Section 51(1) mandates that no contract or order can authorize payments of a pension benefit to the non-member before the member retires or begins receipt of pension payments, whichever is earlier. This effectively prevents lump-sum payments. Section 51(2) states that no contract, agreement or order can award the non-member spouse more than 50% of the total pension benefit, which is at odds with Section 5(6) of the FLA.

Prince Edward Island

Although the convoluted definition of *family assets* contained in Section 3 of the *Family Law Reform Act*[73] (FLRA) neither specifically includes nor excludes pensions within its ambit, following *Clarke* it is clear that pensions are family assets. While Section 4(1) states that spouses are entitled to have assets divided equally on marriage breakdown, Section 4(5) permits unequal division where it would be "inequitable," with regard to the factors listed in the section, to equalize family assets.

Pursuant to Section 60(3) of the *Pension Benefits Act* (PBA), a court may order that the non-member spouse receive up to 50% of the portion of the pension that was earned during the marriage or a common law relationship of more than three years. Section 60(4) provides that the non-member spouse is entitled to receive payments once the member spouse retires or begins to receive pension payments, and allows the non-member to request a lump-sum transfer of his or her share of the member's pension to an annuity, pension or other locked-in retirement vehicle. Section 60(5) provides that the non-member's only right under the plan is to have a division of the benefits accrued during cohabitation. Section 60(6) states that nothing in the PBA precludes the making of an order for division under the FLRA.

Quebec

Section 107 of the *Civil Code of Quebec* (CCQ) provides for the establishment of a family patrimony that includes all benefits earned during the marriage under a retirement plan.[74] The value of this patrimony will then be divided equally on divorce.

Section 107 of the *Supplementary Pension Plans Act*[75] (SPPA) states that after a written application is made to the pension committee in the event of separation, divorce or annulment, a pension will be divided in accordance with the terms of either CCQ or a court order. The maximum amount that the non-member spouse can receive is set at 50% by Section 110. Following an application, Section 108 requires that both parties be given a statement of the member's benefits accrued under the plan. Section 109 states that, except as provided by regulation, the non-member's share must be used to purchase a life pension.

Part V of the *Supplemental Pension Plans Regulations*[76] provides specifics as to what must be included in the statement of benefits and prescribes formulas for determining the value of the capital benefits accumulated during the marriage in a variety of circumstances.

Saskatchewan

Matrimonial property is defined in Section 2(1) of the *Matrimonial Property Act*[77] (MPA) as "any real or personal property, regardless of its source, kind or nature, that, at the time an application is made pursuant to this Act is owned, or in which an interest is held, by one or both spouses or both spouses and a third person." Section 21(1) of the MPA mandates equal division, while Section 21(2) allows the court to make any order it considers fair if an equal division would be "unfair and inequitable."

Part VI of the *Pension Benefits Act*[78] (PBA) deals with pension division on marriage breakdown. Section 46(1) requires that the plan administrator divide the pension or other benefit in accordance with the terms of an order or agreement made under the MPA. Section 46(3) states that this division cannot reduce the member's share by more than 50%. The value of the pension to be divided is to be calculated by the plan administrator in accordance with the terms of Section 47. Section 48(1) provides that payment of the non-member's share may be accomplished either through a lump-sum transfer to a prescribed RRSP or at-source division. Section 49 stipulates that the plan administrator must give written notice to the member of the receipt of an order or agreement requiring division (except in cases where both spouses file jointly with the administrator) and must wait 30 days before dividing the pension, to allow the member to object to the terms of division. Pursuant to Section 49(3), there are only three grounds on which the member may file an objection, and the member must furnish evidence to establish the validity of any objection. The grounds for objection are:

1. The order/agreement has been varied or is of no force or effect.
2. The terms of the agreement have been or are being satisfied by other means and
3. Proceedings have been commenced in a court of competent jurisdiction to review/appeal the order or to challenge the terms of the agreement.

Federal Private Sector

Pensions for federal private sector employees are governed by the terms of the *Pension Benefits Standards Act*[79] (PBSA). Section 25(4) provides that, notwithstanding anything in the terms of the PBSA or provincial property law, a plan member can assign all or part of his or her pension benefits to a spouse on divorce, annulment or separation. The non-member spouse will be deemed to be a member of the plan following such an assignment. Section 25(5) states that, following the receipt of a request to divide a pension in accordance with the terms of a court order or agreement and a copy of the document, a plan administrator is to determine the non-member's share of the pension and to administer it in accordance with the terms of the order or agreement. Although Section 25(2) states that "*subject to this section,* pension benefits, pension benefit credits and any other benefits under a pension plan" (emphasis added) are to be divided in accordance with applicable provincial property law, the decision in *Cattran v. Cattran*[80] suggests that provincial legislation will always govern. In its ruling, the Nova Scotia Supreme Court stated that it is the terms of the relevant provincial pension legislation that should be applied in valuing and dividing the pension on marriage breakdown, not the PBSA. This decision casts doubt on the continuing relevance of the division terms of the PBSA.

Federal Public Sector

Federal public sector employees are governed by the terms of the *Pension Benefits Division Act*[81] (PBDA), which apply to parties who are either married or have cohabited for at least one year. Section 4 states that a plan member or the spouse or former spouse of a plan member can make a written application to the Minister to divide the pension benefits if the parties have lived separate and apart for at least one year, or there has been either a written agreement or court order requiring pension division. Supporting documentation must be attached to the application. Section 5 requires that the Minister send notice of an application for division, along with supporting documentation, to each interested party, i.e., the plan member, the spouse and former spouse(s), if any. These parties will be deemed to have

received the information 30 days after it was sent. An interested party may object to the proposed division pursuant to Section 6 on the grounds that the order or agreement is of no force or effect, its terms are being satisfied by other means or, if it is being appealed, and if evidence is provided in support of the objection. Pursuant to Section 7(3) the Minister may refuse to divide a pension on a number of grounds, including that, per Subsection (e), the Minister is satisfied that it would not be just to do so. Section 8 states that division is to be effected by transferring 50% of the value accrued during the period subject to division to the spouse, if the plan is a retirement compensation arrangement, or to a pension plan registered under the *Income Tax Act* if the plan permits, or to an RRSP of the prescribed kind or to a financial institution for the purchase of a deferred life annuity.

Connolly v. Connolly[82] has illustrated potential problems with this statute, at least in Nova Scotia. The court failed to follow the Supreme Court's position that specific legislation overrides general legislation in the event of a conflict[83] and used Sections 13(d) and (e) of the MPA to permit the unequal division of the husband's Canadian Armed Forces pension. As Section 4(1) of the MPA defines *matrimonial assets* as those earned before or during marriage, and as Section 4 of the PBDA allows a former spouse to apply for pension division, giving the MPA primacy can pose problems for pension division in second marriages. If a second spouse receives 50% of the value of the pension earned up to the valuation date, there will be no assets to satisfy a later application by a former spouse under Section 4 of the PBDA.

ONGOING ISSUES

Law Reform

There is presently much uncertainty surrounding the issue of pension division on marriage breakdown. The development of a nationally acceptable standard for pension valuation and division in this area would eliminate much of the current confusion. There have been proposals for reform from various quarters. In June 1998, the CIA issued a draft report on the division of pension assets on marriage breakdown. The report recommended that a "deferred settlement method" be adopted that divides pension benefits, not their value. The determination of which benefits were acquired during the marriage is made by dividing the years of marriage by the total years of pensionable service to obtain a percentage, which is then divided equally between the spouses.[84] In Ontario, the OLRC recommended that "valuation regulations" be attached to the FLA that would prescribe a method for valuing defined benefits plans based on the CIA's *Standard of Practice.*[85] Finally, the Nova Scotia Law Reform Commission recommended the adoption of a *Domestic Property Division Act* that would provide a specific mechanism for dividing pension entitlements on marriage breakdown.[86] There is therefore the possibility that the future will see alterations to the procedures by which pensions are currently divided on marriage breakdown in Canada.

Same-Sex Relationships

The increasing recognition that same-sex partners should be entitled to the same rights as heterosexual partners has implications for the division of pension assets.

The federal government has proposed changes to the *Public Service Superannuation Act*[87] (PSSA) that would extend survivor benefits to same-sex partners. Section 25(4) of Bill C-78, the *Public Sector Pension Investment Board Act,*[88] provides that when a person establishes that he or she has been cohabiting "in a relationship of a conjugal nature" with a public sector pension plan member for at least one year immediately before the plan member's death, the person will be considered the member's survivor for the purposes of the PSSA.[89] In addition, on April 11, 2000, the House of Commons passed the federal Bill C-23, the *Modernization of Benefits and Obligations Act,* which will amend the provisions of numerous federal statutes so that they apply to same-sex partners.

In *Rosenberg v. Canada (Attorney General),*[90] the Ontario Court of Appeal held that the definition of *spouse* in the provisions of the *Income Tax Act* relating to pension plan registration was discriminatory as it related to members of the opposite sex only. The court read the words *same-sex* into the definition to remedy the discrimination. In *M. v. H.,*[91] the court held that both heterosexual and same-sex relationships of more than three years give rise to a support obligation, and accordingly found that a partner in a ten-year lesbian relationship was entitled to spousal support. This decision was upheld by the Supreme Court,[92] which found that the Ontario FLA drew a distinction between heterosexual and same-sex cohabiting couples by specifically according rights to the former that were denied by omission to the latter. This denial was found to violate the Charter, so the court severed Section 29 of the FLA, with a six-month suspended declaration of invalidity. In the aftermath of this decision, Ontario enacted *An Act to amend certain statutes because of the Supreme Court of Canada decision in M. v. H.,*[93] which amended numerous statutes so that their provisions applied to same-sex and heterosexual partners.

The increasing rights afforded to same-sex couples as evidenced by Bill C-78 and the *Rosenberg* and *M. v. H.* decisions raise the possibility that same-sex spouses will soon be able to apply for the division of their pension assets when their relationships terminate.

ENDNOTES

1. The term *marriage breakdown* is used throughout this chapter to refer to the termination of any relationship of economic interdependence, whether, marital or common law.

2. *Clarke v. Clarke* (1990), 1 N.S.R. (2d) 1, [1990] 2 S.C.R. 795, 113 N.R. 321, 63 D.L.R. (4th) 1, 275 A.P.R. 1 (S.C.C.).

3. Canadian Institute of Actuaries Task Force on the Division of Pension Benefits Upon Marriage Breakdown, *Draft Report on the Division of Pension Benefits Upon Marriage Breakdown* (Ottawa: Canadian Institute of Actuaries, 1998) at p. 2.

4. *Best v. Best* (1993), 1 C.C.P.B. 8, 50 R.F.L. (3d) 120 (O.C. (G.D.)); (1997), 15 C.C.P.B. 170 (O.C.A.); varied (1999), 174 D.L.R. (4th) 235 (S.C.C.).

5. *Ibid.,* at p. 244 (S.C.C.).

6. Financial Services Commission of Ontario. *Understanding Your Pension Plan: A Guide for Members of Employer Sponsored Pension Plans.* February 10, 1999. Available at www.fsco.gov.on.ca/Pensions.

7. Julian D. Payne, *Payne on Divorce,* 4th ed. (Scarborough: Carswell Inc., 1996) at p. 2.

8. *Fisher v. Fisher* (1982), 31 R.F.L. (2d) 274, [1983] 2 W.W.R. 602, 21 Sask. R. 235 (Sask. Q.B.).

9. *Ibid.,* at p. 282 (R.F.L.).

10. *Matrimonial Property Act,* R.S.N.S. 1989, c. 275, s. 4(1).

11. R.S.N.S. 1989, c. 275 as am. 1995-96 c. 13 s. 83.

12. *Ibid.,* s. 13.

13. For a more detailed analysis of the various valuation methods, see *Bascello v. Bascello* (1995), 26 O.R. (3d) 342 (O.C. (G.D.)).

14. *Hauptman v. Hauptman,* [1982] 2 W.W.R. 62 at 69, 32 B.C.L.R. 119 (S.C.).

15. Ontario Law Reform Commission, *Report on Pensions as Family Law: Valuation and Division* (Ontario: Government of Ontario, 1995).

16. *Ibid.,* at p. 2.

17. *Harrop v. Harrop* (1991), 37 R.F.L. (3d) 433 (Sask. Q.B.).

18. James G. McLeod and Alfred A. Mamo, *Matrimonial Property Law in Canada,* Release No. 4 (Scarborough: Carswell Inc., 1993) at S-30-31.

19. Canadian Institute of Actuaries, *Standard of Practice for the Computation of Capitalised Value of Pension Entitlements on Marriage Breakdown for Purposes of Lump-Sum Equalisation Payments* (September 1, 1993), 2.

20. *Rickett v. Rickett* (1990), 25 R.F.L. (3d) 188, 72 O.R. (2d) 321, 67 D.L.R. (4th) 103 (H.C.); additional reasons (1990), 71 D.L.R. (4th) 734 (H.C.).

21. See, for example, *Dick v. Dick* (1993), 46 R.F.L. (3d) 219 (O.C. (G.D.)); *Halman v. Halman* (1993), 1 C.C.P.B. 268 (O.C.(G.D.)).

22. J. B. Patterson, *Pension Division and Valuation: Family Lawyers' Guide* (Aurora: Canada Law Book, 1991) at p. 180.

23. *Ibid.,* at p. 117.

24. *Supra* note 22 at pp. 167-168.

25. *George v. George* (1983), 35 R.F.L. (2d) 225 (Man C.A.).

26. *Ibid.,* at p. 241.

27. *Haley v. Haley,* [1996] 4 W.W.R. 564 (Sask. Q.B.).

28. *Supra* note 4, at pp. 180-81 (O.C.A.).

29. *Supra* note 17.

30. *Supra* note 4, at p. 8 (O.C.J.).

31. *Supra* note 4 at p. 184 (O.C.A.).

32. *Supra* note 4, at p. 275 (S.C.C.).

33. See *MacMillan v. MacMillan,* [2000] O.J. No. 104 (S.C.J.); *Holzer v. Holzer,* [1999] S.J. No. 571 (Q.B.); *Pisiak v. Pisiak,* [1999] S.J. No. 511 (Q.B., Family Law Division).

34. *Marsham v. Marsham* (1987), 4 R.F.L. (3d) 1 (Ont. H.C.).

35. *Supra* note 18 at A-29.

36. *Rutherford v. Rutherford* (1981), 23 R.F.L. (2d) 337 (B.C.C.A.).

37. *Supra* note 34, at p. 19.

38. *Supra* note 36, at p. 352.

39. *Mailhot v. Mailhot* (1988), 18 R.F.L. (3d) 1 (B.C.C.A.).

40. *Ibid.,* at p. 7.

41. *Vennels v. Vennels* (1994), 45 R.F.L. (3d) 165 (B.C.S.C.).

42. *Shadbolt v. Shadbolt* (1997), 32 R.F.L. (4th) 253 (O.C. (G.D.)).

43. *Ibid.,* at p. 253.

44. *Supra* note 4, at p. 284 (S.C.C.).

45. *Veres v. Veres* (1987), 9 R.F.L. (3d) 447 (Ont. H.C.).

46. *Butt v. Butt* (1989), 22 R.F.L. (3d) 415 (Ont. H.C.).

47. *Linton v. Linton* (1990), 30 R.F.L. (3d) 1 (Ont. C.A.).

48. *Ibid.,* at p. 36.

49. *Nantais v. Nantais* (1995), 26 O.R. (3d) 453 (G. D.).

50. *Strang v. Strang,* [1992] 2 S.C.R. 112.

51. See *Hutchinson v. Hutchinson,* [1998] O.J. No. 3027 (G.D.).

52. *Lemoine v. Lemoine* (1997), 185 N.B.R. (2d) 173 (C.A.).

53. *Ibid.,* at para. 28.

54. *Boston v. Boston,* [1999] O.J. No. 4140 (C.A.); leave to appeal granted, S.C.C. Bulletin of Proceedings, March 16, 2000, No. 27682.

55. *Matrimonial Property Act,* S.A. 1998, c. M-9.

56. *Employment Pension Plans Act,* S.A. 1998, c. E-10.05.

57. *Employment Pension Plans Amendment Act,* S.A. 1999, c. 21 (awaiting proclamation).

58. *Employment Pensions Bulletin,* Vol. 11, No. 1, January 31, 1997.

59. *Family Relations Act,* R.S.B.C. 1996, c. 128.

60. *Pension Benefits Standards Act,* R.S.B.C. 1996, c. 352.

61. *Marital Property Act,* R.S.M. 1987, c. M45.

62. *Pension Benefits Act,* R.S.M. 1987, c. P32 as am.

63. *Marital Property Act,* S.N.B. 1980, c. M-1.1.

64. *Pension Benefits Act,* S.N.B. 1987, c. P-5.1.

65. *Pension Benefits Regulation,* N.B. Reg. 91-195, am. by N.B. Regs. 93-144; 94-78; 95-8; 97-92; 97-124.

66. *Family Law Act,* R.S.N. 1990, c. F-2.

67. *Pension Benefits Act,* S.N. 1996, c. P-4.01.

68. *Pension Benefits Act Regulations,* 114/96 (Dec. 27) s. 26-35.

69. *Supra* note 9.

70. *Pension Benefits Act,* R.S.N.S. 1989, c. 340 as am. 1992, c. 27, 1993, c. 35.

71. *Family Law Act,* R.S.O. 1990, c. F.3.

72. *Pension Benefits Act,* R.S.O. 1990, c. P.8.

73. *Family Law Reform Act,* R.S.P.E.I. 1988, c. F-3.

74. *Civil Code of Quebec,* S.Q. 1989, c. 38.

75. *Supplementary Pension Plans Act,* R.S.Q. 1990, R-15.1, as am.

76. *Supplementary Pension Plans Regulations,* O.C. 1158-90, as am; 1159-90; 568-91; 1895-93; 658-94; 1465-95; 1681-97; 577-98.

77. *Matrimonial Property Act,* S.S. 1997, c. M-6.11.

78. *Pension Benefits Act,* S.S. 1992, c. P-6.001.

79. *Pension Benefits Standards Act,* R.S.C. 1985, c. 32 (2nd Supp.).

80. *Cattran v. Cattran* (1993), 45 R.F.L. (3d) 213, 119 N.S.R. (2d) 409, 330 A.P.R. 409 (N.S.T.D.).

81. *Pension Benefits Divisions Act,* S.C. 1992, c. 46 Sch. II.

82. *Connolly v. Connolly* (1998), Doc. 1201-43141 (N.S.S.C.), (1998), Doc. 149384 (N.S.C.A.).

83. See *Multiple Access Ltd. v. McCutcheon,* [1982] 2 S.C.R. 161, 138 D.L.R. (3d) 1, 44 N.R. 181, 18 B.L.R. 138 (S.C.C.).

84. Canadian Institute of Actuaries, Task Force on the Division of Pension Benefits Upon Marriage Breakdown, *Draft Report on the Division of Pension Benefits Upon Marriage Breakdown* (Ottawa: Canadian Institute of Actuaries, 1998).

85. *Supra* note 19.

86. Law Reform Commission of Nova Scotia, *Recommendations for Reform* www.chebucto.ns.ca/Law/LRC/recommend7MP2.html (accessed March 2, 1999).

87. *Public Service Superannuation Act,* R.S.C. 1985, c. P-36.

88. www.parl.gc.ca/36/1/paribus/chambus/house/bills/government/C-78/C-78_ 1/90070bE.html (accessed May 25, 1999).

89. *Ibid.*

90. *Rosenberg v. Canada (Attorney General)* (1998), D.T.C. 6286, 108 O.A.C. 338, 51 C.R.R. (2d) 1, 38 O.R. (3d) 577, 4 Admin. L.R. (3d) 165, 37 C.C.E.L. (2d) 259, 18 C.C.P.B. 1, C.E.B. & P.G.R. 8340 (headnote only) (O.C.A.).

91. *M. v. H.* (1996), 17 R.F.L. (4th) 365, 132 D.L.R. (4th) 538, 27 O.R. (3d) 593, 35 C.R.R. (2d) 123 (O.C. (G.D.)); additional reasons at (1996), 1 C.P.C. (4th) 167, 137 D.L.R. (4th) 569, 8 O.T.C. 171, (G.D.); affd (1996), 31 O.R. (3d) 417, 25 R.F.L. (4th) 116, 142 D.L.R. (4th) 1, 96 O.A.C. 173, 40 C.R.R. (2d) 240 (C.A.), leave to appeal to S.C.C. allowed (1997), 100 O.A.C. 159 (note), 215 N.R. 400 (note), 43 C.R.R. (2d) 187 (note), 43 C.R.R. (2d) 376 (note) (S.C.C.).

92. *M. v. H.* (1999), 171 D.L.R. (4th) 577 (S.C.C.).

93. *An Act to amend certain statutes because of the Supreme Court of Canada decision in M. v. H.,* S.O. 1999, c. 6.

APPENDIX IV-13-A

EXAMPLES OF SEPARATION AGREEMENT CLAUSES
ON PENSIONS AND EMPLOYMENT BENEFITS

Based on material provided by B. Lynn Reierson of Reierson Family Legal Services, Halifax, Nova Scotia

1. Waiver of Pension

The parties acknowledge that this Agreement constitutes, among other things, a division of assets and takes into account the pension entitlement of both spouses, and both the spouses agree that each shall continue to be the sole owner of his or her pension contributions and rights pursuant thereto, and the parties hereby release any claim which he or she may otherwise have had with respect to the other's pension pursuant to [relevant sections of provincial family and pension legislation], the *Pension Benefits Division Act* (Canada), the *Pension Benefits Standards Act* (Canada) or to any other similar legislation in [relevant province] or any other jurisdiction, whether provincial or federal.

2. Indemnity Where any Waiver of Pension

If any pension rights or benefits of either spouse vests in the other by the operation of any law or statute whatsoever, the spouse receiving or to receive the right or benefit will renounce the same to the other, or, if renunciation is not possible or permitted, agrees to hold the rights or benefits in trust for the other spouse or the designated beneficiary of the other spouse, and to pay and transfer that right or benefit to the other spouse or the designated beneficiary thereof when received, provided that such transfer shall be made with no unfavourable income tax consequences to the transferor, and in respect thereof, the transferee hereby indemnifies and saves harmless the transferor therefrom.

OR

2. No Waiver But No At-Source Division to Protect The Survivor Pension

(a) The parties agree that if the future divorce of the parties does not affect the _____'s eligibility to obtain a survivor pension from [name of employer], the parties agree that neither of them will apply for a division of the pension pursuant to [name of legislation]. Instead, the parties agree that the _____ shall, commencing in the month of _____ and each month thereafter, pay to the _____ an amount equivalent to half of h__ gross monthly pension, as non-reviewable spousal support, such payments to be due one business day after the _____ receives h__ pension payment, and to be taxed to the _____ and tax deductible to the _____ pursuant to the *Income Tax Act*. With respect to these payments, the parties further confirm:

    (i) The _____ is a trustee for the _____'s share of the pension and shall not act or omit to act in any way which might affect the _____'s prior consent;

    (ii) The _____ shall promptly pass along to the _____ any communication h__ receives from the plan administrator or any communications h__ has with the plan administrator where those communications in any way have an impact or the potential to impact on the _____'s share of the pension;

    (iii) The _____'s share of the pension shall include one-half of the gross amount of any increases in the pension payments which may occur from time to time, provided that such increases shall also be treated as non-reviewable spousal support, taxable to the _____ and tax deductible to the _____ pursuant to the *Income Tax Act.*

(b) If the future divorce of the parties would make the _____ ineligible for a survivor's pension from [name of employer], then the parties shall divide the [name of employer] pension pursuant to the terms of the [name of legislation] and commencing in [month] and in each month thereafter until the legislative division is processed, the _____ shall pay over half of the gross amount of h__ gross [name of employer] pension to the _____ as temporary spousal support which shall be taxed to the _____ and tax deductible to the _____. Further, the parties agree that if upon the processing of the division, the _____ receives payments related to the months in which the _____ was paying temporary spousal support pursuant to this paragraph, the _____ shall immediately pay over the double recovery the _____ may receive.

OR

2. Federal GAPDA

The parties acknowledge that the _____ is entitled to a one-half share of the _____'s pension through h__ employment with [name of employer] from [start date] until [end date], which pension is now being paid to the husband in the monthly amount of $_____. The parties agree and acknowledge that commencing _____, the sum of $_____ shall be paid to the _____ and that _____ shall make application to the _____ to have this sum paid directly to the _____ through provision of [name of provincial garnishment, attachment and diversion legislation]. It is acknowledged that this pension division shall take the form of a support order resulting in a payment taxable in the hands of the _____ for which the _____ shall receive a tax deduction.

OR

2. Division of Pension

The parties agree that the _____'s pension through h__ employment with [name of employer] shall be divided at source such that the pension benefits accumulated between [start date] and [end date], the date of separation, shall be equally divided according to the provisions of [name of relevant legislation] and the parties acknowledge that they will consent to an order to this effect.

OR

2. Pension in Pay

It is acknowledged that the _____ is presently receiving a monthly pension in the amount of $_____ [net of income tax/from which no income tax has been withheld] from h__ employment with [name of employer]. Until the division of the pension described in paragraph __ has come into effect, the _____ shall pay to the _____ one-half of this amount, or $_____, within 48 hours of receiving the same (**OR** the sum of $_____, representing one-half of the sum received by the _____ less an adjustment for income tax in the amount of $_____). It is acknowledged that this payment represents an asset division and is <u>not</u> to be claimed as maintenance by the receiving spouse nor deducted by the paying spouse.

OR

2. Pension May Go Into Pay

It is acknowledged that the _____ is expected to retire from h__ employment with [name of employer] on [date]. Should _____ begin receiving pension payments prior to the division of h__ pension as contemplated in clause __, then the _____ agrees that h__ will withhold one-half of the net (after-tax) value of the pension in trust for the _____. This amount will be paid to the _____ within forty-eight (48) hours of its receipt by the _____ until such time as the pension division has been effected. It is acknowledged that this payment represents an asset division and is not to be claimed as maintenance by the receiving spouse nor deducted by the paying spouse.

3. Provision of Information

The plan holder shall deliver to the _____ copies of all communication between h__ and the plan administrator with respect to h__ pension entitlement, benefits and rights within seven (7) days after the receipt of such communication for the purpose of facilitating the implementation of this Agreement.

4. Consents
(a) The plan holder hereby authorises the _____ or h__ solicitor to view any information relating to the pension, severance and any benefits deriving thereunder.
(b) The plan holder shall execute whatever agreements, authorizations, directions or further assurances as may be needed in order to give effect to this Agreement
(c) The plan holder agrees to comply forthwith but in no case later than one (1) week after this Agreement comes into effect, for a division of the pension pursuant to [name of relevant legislation].

5. Direction of Court

Either party shall be at liberty to apply to a court of competent jurisdiction for an order for further direction or security should difficulties occur with respect to the interpretation or administration or implementation of the pension provisions herein.

6. Waiver of Rights by New Common-Law Spouses

Until the _____'s pension is divided or the _____'s share thereof is paid to h__, the _____ shall have any party with whom h__ co-habits in a common-law relationship execute a release to the _____ of any claim which would affect h__ share of the pension as agreed to herein. Where such a release is not provided, or where it is provided but the _____'s common-law spouse or the pension plan administrator fails to honour the release, the _____'s estate shall indemnify the _____ for any losses suffered in relation to the breach of this clause, including without limiting the foregoing, legal costs on a solicitor-client basis.

7. Tax Adjustments

Note: **Use this clause when the non-member spouse receives their share of the pension directly instead of through division. It is not needed if the non-member's share is secured by calling it support.**

The _____ shall indemnify the [non-member spouse] from the tax liability attributable to h__ share of the pension. Each year there shall be an accounting to determine the _____'s obligations under this paragraph, which will occur at a mutually convenient time not later than ten (10) day s after the _____ has presented h__ Notice of Assessment for the relevant tax year. The amount will be determined by calculating the _____'s tax liability if the _____'s share of the pension had not been claimed by h__ as taxable income. The difference between h__ actual tax and the amount that would have been payable is the amount owing to the _____. If the spouses cannot do these calculations, they are to equally share the cost of obtaining assistance from a mutually agreed upon third party.

Optional Addition:

The _____ may withhold __% of the sum otherwise due to the _____ each month for h__ share of the pension from the payments made to h__ to be applied to the tax due to the _____ from the _____.

8. Member Spouse Working Past Normal Retirement Date

Where the _____ elects to work past h__ normal retirement date, [he/she] shall, on h__ normal retirement date, begin paying to the _____ the amount equivalent to what [he/she] would have received if the _____ had elected to retire on h__ normal retirement date. "Normal retirement date" for the purposes of this paragraph is such age or period of service as the _____'s employer and/or pension plan applies to the _____ from time to time. Any expenses incurred to calculate the amount payable to the _____ shall be paid by the [member spouse].

9. Elimination of Overpayments

The spouses acknowledge that, even after an application for division of the pension is made, a period of time may pass before the division is accomplished and by virtue of this the pension plan administrator may adjust contributions and make a retroactive payment to the _____, which would result in h__ receiving payments from both the administrator and the _____ for the same time periods. The _____ will continue to pay the _____'s share to h__ after he/she has applied for a division and before he/she receives direct payment from the administrator (the "adjustment period") provided that the _____ expressly agrees to:

(i) Notify the _____ promptly when he/she receives pension benefits directly;

(ii) Co-operate with the _____ to calculate any overpayments he/she may have received during the adjustment period; and

(iii) Permit the _____ to deduct from the support he/she would otherwise be liable to pay the amount of such overpayment, commencing with the first date on which support is payable to him/her after any overpayment has been calculated

OR

(iii) Share the cost of any necessary professional assistance required to calculate the overpayment should the spouses be unable to calculate it without professional assistance (including, without limiting the generality of the foregoing, the costs of each spouse having legal counsel and the cost of accountants and/or actuaries). If the spouses cannot agree upon the appropriate adjustments of the _____'s support with reference to the adjustment period (either with or without professional assistance), then either spouse may apply to the court for a resolution of the issue, and the court shall determine how the costs of the application shall be borne.

CHAPTER 14

Flexible Pension Plans

by Judy Gerwing

INTRODUCTION

Since 1990 a remarkable change has taken place in the Canadian pension world. Plans that had previously seemed perfectly adequate were suddenly the source of great concern. Members were asking to leave plans that provided non-contributory pension benefits. When people do not want something for nothing, there must be a problem! The key change to this situation was the introduction of a new, integrated system of tax-sheltered contribution maximums and, most significantly, the introduction of pension adjustments (PAs).

The new system was purported to be fair to all working Canadians by providing a maximum annual eligible registered retirement savings plan (RRSP) contribution of 18% of earnings, subject to a dollar maximum. This maximum RRSP contribution room is reduced by a "pension adjustment" that represents the deemed value of any registered pension plan (RPP) or deferred profit-sharing plan (DPSP) benefit earned in the prior calendar year.

For a defined contribution RPP, the PA simply equals the actual contributions made by the member and the employer in the calendar year. For a defined benefit RPP, an imputed value had to be developed, representing the value of the pension benefit earned in the given year. The PA formula developed was "nine times the benefit entitlement less $1,000," subsequently amended to "nine times the benefit entitlement less $600."

As an example, suppose that in 1998 an individual was earning $60,000 and had earned a defined benefit of $1,000 for the year. In 1999 his RRSP contribution room will be calculated as:

	i)	18% of 1998 earnings = $10,800
less	ii)	the PA = 9 × $1,000 − $600 = $8,400
plus	iii)	unused carried forward room from previous years.

The key issue is that the member's RRSP room has been reduced by $8,400 on account of benefit entitlement earned in the defined benefit plan. Unfortunately the "nine times" factor used in the PA formula is indiscriminate in regard to:

- The member's age
- The normal retirement age
- The normal form of pension payment
- Other ancillary features
- Whether the plan is flat dollar, career average or final average.

The "nine times" factor may grossly overstate the deemed value of the pension benefit for a young member in a plan with few to no ancillary benefits. This is particularly true if the member terminates his or her plan membership after only a short period of service.

In 1999, pension adjustment reversals (PARs) were introduced as an attempt to correct the effect of inappropriate PAs. However, the PA rules are still perceived as inequitable, and this is one of the main reasons that many young people no longer wish to belong to a defined benefit RPP. The wisdom of this choice can be demonstrated mathematically. The advantages of obtaining annual tax deductions on 18% of earnings and tax-exempt investment earnings outweigh the hard-to-quantify value of a defined benefit.

The second key issue in pension reform involves the dollar maximums previously referred to. The government originally intended to increase the dollar maximum RRSP contribution to $15,500 by 1995 and index the maximum thereafter. At the same time the maximum benefit payable from a defined benefit plan of $1,722.22 per year of service, which had been frozen since 1976, was also to be indexed after 1994. This made sense on the basis of a coming together of the maximums at an earnings level of $86,111 in 1994. Eighteen percent of $86,111 is $15,500; 2% of $86,111 is $1,722.22. The federal government believed that this would create a "level playing field" between defined benefit and defined contribution plans. Unfortunately, this fine ideal has yet to be achieved in practise.

In the 1996 federal budget the $1,722 maximum was frozen until 2004, only to be indexed starting in 2005. In addition, the increase in the defined contribution maximum to $15,500 was delayed and will not be indexed until after 2004. These changes to the original system have tilted the "level playing field" and magnified a clear advantage for defined contribution RPPs, especially for the younger employee. Many higher paid members of defined benefit plans have zero RRSP contribution room.

The stalling of pension reform, in combination with other issues, suggests that the traditional defined benefit RPP is not the retirement benefit solution that it used to be.

FRONT-END FLEX PLANS

In a typical contributory defined benefit pension plan, the member contributions make up a part of the overall funding of the benefits but are not "ear-marked" in any way for the purchase of any specific ancillary or base benefit.

Flexible plans differ in that the flex contributions made by the member are designated for the purchase of enhanced ancillary features. These features can include the following, and are subject to Revenue Canada guidelines:

- Post-retirement spousal benefits
- Unreduced early retirement pensions
- Bridge benefits payable until age 65
- Contractual indexing of pensions in payment or during deferral.

In a front-end flex plan the member makes a commitment up front as to the enhancement he or she would like to receive in return for a fixed additional contribution. Some flexibility is permitted to the members in switching enhancements closer to retirement on the basis of actuarial value.

For example, a front-end plan might provide a defined benefit of:

- 1% of final average earnings per year of service with minimal ancillary benefits on a non-contributory basis

- Plus a 60% joint and survivor normal form for a 2% employee contribution
- Plus pre- and post-retirement indexing for an additional 2% employee contribution.

While these plans were clearly tax-effective, the typical members often felt they were being asked to make a decision about an event that was too far into the future. For this reason, consultants developed a second generation back-end flexible pension plan.

BACK-END FLEX PLANS

In a back-end flexible pension plan, the member contributes to the RPP, and his or her contributions accumulate with interest until termination or retirement, at which time the member selects the enhancements he or she wants from a menu of choices. This approach provides the advantages of greater flexibility, coupled with no additional liability for the sponsor.

Both types of flex plans are important because they provide a direct response to the difficulties caused by the "nine times rule" built into the PA for defined benefit RPPs. Since the "nine times rule" is based entirely on the dollars of accrual and not on the nature of the plan features, allowing members to buy their own enhancements is very tax-effective:

- The PA is not affected.
- The member flex contributions are tax-deductible.
- The member has the chance to customize his or her pension benefits.

This approach can potentially provide the answer for young members, reducing their need to leave defined benefit plans. It is certainly of great advantage to highly-paid members.

A key challenge for these plans has been to meet regulatory requirements. Revenue Canada released rules covering flexible pension plans in a *Newsletter* dated November 1996.[1] These rules included the "use it or lose it" conditions that required that any contributions in excess of those required to provide the enhanced ancillary benefits must be lost by the member.

Debates continue within the Canadian Association of Pension Supervisory Authorities (CAPSA) as to the status of the flexible pension contribution (called *optional ancillary contributions* in the Revenue Canada Newsletter). The following issues were studied in a CAPSA Task Force report released in April 1999.[2]

1. How should optional ancillary contributions be classified?
2. How should the Revenue Canada forfeiture rule be dealt with?
3. Should the 50% employer funding rule apply to optional ancillary contributions?
4. Should optional ancillary contributions be locked in?

5. How should optional ancillary contributions be invested?
6. What basis should be used to convert optional ancillary contributions into ancillary benefits?
7. What basis should be used when members elect to transfer ancillary benefits?

Both British Columbia and Quebec have passed or proposed legislation on flexible pension plans. The federal pension regulator issued a policy paper in July 1999.[3]

VARIATIONS ON A THEME

Because of the regulatory delays around acceptance of these plans, some variations have been developed that more clearly address the issues of the nature of the contributions and their treatment under the 50% rule.

While some of these variations actually provide results that are superior to the basic back-end flex plan, the key challenge has been to find a satisfactory approach to administering and communicating these plans.

It appears that the best approach is to provide some type of interactive software that enables plan members to test the adequacy of their contributions. We expect that these innovative approaches to flexible pensions will continue to be explored.

ENDNOTES

1. Revenue Canada Registered Plans Division, *Newsletter* No. 96-3, "Flexible Pension Plans" (25 November 1996).
2. Canadian Association of Pension Supervisory Authorities, *Communiqué*, "Flexible Pension Plans" (30 April 1999).
3. Office of the Superintendent of Financial Institutions, "Flexible Pension Plans" (13 July 1999).

CHAPTER 1

Introduction

by Murray Gold

Since the early 1990s a number of major public sector pension plans in Canada have become jointly trusteed. Prior to joint trusteeship, these plans were sponsored by public and broader public sector employers and employer associations, which were ultimately responsible for their funding. Employees and trade unions generally participated in plan governance, if at all, through collective bargaining or participation on advisory committees. Their influence was limited. Since joint trusteeship, however, sponsorship has become a joint employer/member responsibility, and the ongoing responsibility for the administration of the plan and the investment of the fund has been assumed by a board of trustees constituted by an equal number of appointees from the employer and trade union sponsors.

Joint governance has taken a number of different forms, several of which are explored in the next chapter. Before examining the different models for joint trusteeship, however, it is important to understand the context in which the term *governance* is used and also to recognize that it operates at two different levels.

The context of the current interest in governance, and joint governance, is shaped by at least the following factors:

- **Regulatory model**—The regulatory model governing pension plans in Canada has changed. Until recently, pension regulators undertook to ensure that pension plan texts complied with applicable law and reviewed actuarial funding reports to ensure that plans were properly funded. By the year 2000, however, this attitude had changed. Partly because of resource limitations, regulators have stepped away from direct oversight, toward a less direct form of regulation. The current regulatory approach is to promulgate "best practices" standards, which then require that pension plan administrators and their agents assume full responsibility for compliance and funding. Under this approach, the withdrawal of regulatory supervision implies a greater emphasis on governance at the plan level.

- **Standing Senate Committee on Banking, Trade and Commerce**—In November 1998, the Senate Banking Committee (the "Banking Committee") released its "Report on the Governance Practices of Institutional Investors."[1] The Banking Committee had been interested in corporate governance issues for sometime, but its November 1998 report also contained a number of recommendations concerning the governance of institutional investors, including pension funds and mutual funds. While the Banking Committee is not in a position to enact legislation with respect to governance, it is a widely regarded public forum in which these issues have been raised and discussed. The Banking Committee has indicated that it intends to continue reviewing the governance of institutional investors and may, at some point, consider recommendations for legislative change. It can also reasonably be anticipated that the recommendations of the Banking Committee will have some effect on the "best practices" standards promulgated by regulatory authorities.

- **Funding deficiencies/surpluses**—Both funding deficiencies and surpluses in public sector plans require careful governance. In the early 1990s, deficiencies in major public sector plans had a significant impact on the public accounts of governments. They came under significant pressure to ensure that their pension liabilities were appropriately funded, and this, in turn, necessitated the restructuring of public sector plans and also generally required increased contribution levels. By the late 1990s, many public sector plans were in surplus, necessitating decisions about how surpluses would be used in the contexts of public sector labour relations and government finances. The existence of significant deficiencies and surpluses has necessitated mechanisms to adequately understand and manage them.

- **Contributory plans**—For the most part, employees in public and broader public sector plans are significant contributors to them. Because they do contribute so significantly to their plans, and consider their plans to be part of their overall salary and wage arrangement, employees and trade unions have demanded greater participation in the governance of their plans.

Against this background, significant changes have taken place with respect to the governance of pension plans in the public and broader public sectors. Having said that, it is important to recognize the two different levels of governance that these discussions have considered.

First, governance exists at the sponsor level. Here, fundamental governance decisions must be made concerning, for example, whether or not to establish a pension plan, how to design the benefits structure of governance arrangements and how to keep them up to date and relevant to the needs of the employer and employees. Important funding decisions are also made at the sponsor level, although, as we will see, funding issues also arise at the second level of governance, i.e., the implementation or operational level.

Once a plan is established, its ongoing administration and investment involves a second "implementation" level of governance. On the administration side, processes and procedures need to be adopted and monitored with respect to the maintenance of pension data, full and accurate communications about pension benefits, regulatory compliance and the provision of benefits to those who are entitled to them. On the investment side, important decisions need to be made and monitored concerning such issues as asset mix, selection of investment advisors and custodians and proxy voting.

There are important differences between the "sponsorship" and "implementation" aspects of pension plan governance that need to be understood when the governance of a pension arrangement, as a whole is considered.

Sponsorship decisions have historically been taken primarily by the employer. Employees have generally had an impact on decisions to establish pension plans, or

to change their design, only through collective bargaining. They have rarely had any impact on pension funding, although, occasionally, collective agreements do address contribution requirements. In the absence of "joint governance," employees have generally had little or no impact on pension plan governance structures.

Implementation decisions, on the other hand, are typically taken by a board of trustees (of a trusteed plan, typically a multi-employer plan or a jointly trusteed plan), or by a board of directors or pension committee of a corporate plan sponsor. In making implementation-level decisions, whether they be in relation to the administration of the plan or the investment of the fund, the implementation-level decision makers are bound by statutory and common law fiduciary obligations. They obligate administrators to place the interests of plan members above their own interests, to avoid conflicts of interest and to apply all their knowledge, skills and abilities to the decisions at hand.

Many governance discussions focus on the "implementation" level of governance and do not consider its "sponsorship" aspects. For instance, in its May 1, 1998 "Guideline for Governance of Federally Regulated Pension Plans," the federal Office of the Superintendent of Financial Institutions (OSFI) wrote:

A plan "sponsor" may establish, amend and terminate a pension plan, subject to contractual agreements, plan provisions and relevant legislation. The objectives of the plan are defined by the plan sponsor through plan documentation. While it is recognized that the plan sponsor plays a dual role in the pension plan it sponsors, the focus of this paper is the sponsor's actions as a plan fiduciary administrator, rather than as a sponsoring employer or union. [2]

An exclusive focus on implementation issues, however, may result in an incomplete approach to governance. While it is important to devote attention to appropriate processes and procedures for the investment of pension fund assets, and the administration of pension plan liabilities, it is equally important to attend to the fundamental issues of plan design and funding. While the regulators are requiring an increasingly demanding form of implementation-level governance, an important "governance deficit" remains in regard to such sponsorship-level issues as plan design, plan amendment and funding.

This dichotomy might well reflect the regulatory priority of ensuring that benefits promises, once made, are kept and a corresponding regulatory disinterest in the nature of the promises that are made in the first place. However, the regulatory focus on the implementation level does not provide a full answer to the governance question and does not well reflect the governance interests of employers and plan participants themselves.

While plan members are doubtlessly concerned that their plans be able to deliver the benefits that have been promised, they are also concerned about the adequacy of their retirement incomes, the suitability of their plan design for their early retirement and other requirements, and the equitable treatment of gains and losses that arise in their plans. The current regulatory focus on implementation-level issues addresses only some of these concerns.

The jointly trusteed model of plan governance is one way of enhancing the stature and the role of the plan administrator. A jointly governed plan is managed by a board that consists, in equal measure, of persons appointed by the employer sponsor on the one hand and by the plan members or their bargaining agent on the other. Joint trusteeship also enhances the stature of the administrator because members tend to have more confidence in a governance structure that includes them or their representatives. Joint governance strengthens plan administration, because it introduces a dynamic tension at the administrative level. Given the different backgrounds of board members, a jointly governed board is not likely to fall under a single powerful influence. Joint boards typically act unanimously, in accordance with their fiduciary obligations, in the best interest of plan members. However, such boards contain their own mechanisms to balance out differences of opinion or the assertion of improper influences. The natural balance on a jointly governed board between sponsor and plan member appointees provides a mechanism to ensure that nobody is in a position to control the board or to move it in an improper way.

The balance of this section examines the jointly trusteed model, in the public and broader public sector, and the issues that must be addressed in order for it to be established. In principle, joint governance involves a different allocation of funding responsibilities than the typical single employer model. In a single plan sponsor environment, the plan sponsor is solely responsible for the governance of the plan, but it is also exclusively responsible for any funding deficiencies. In a jointly governed model, governance of the plan is shared, but so, typically, is the funding risk. We will examine different ways in which access to gains and responsibility for losses can be shared between the parties. As well, the jointly governed model raises a unique set of governance issues, because of the participation of lay trustees in the governance of a pension plan. Some of the funding and governance aspects of the jointly trusteed model are also examined in this section.

ENDNOTES

1. Standing Senate Committee on Banking, Trade and Commerce, "Report on the Governance Practices of Institutional Investors" (November 1998).

2. Office of the Superintendent of Financial Institutions, "Guideline for Governance of Federally Regulated Pension Plans" (May 1, 1998) at p. 3.

CHAPTER 2

Jointly Trusteed Public Sector Plans:
Funding Issues

by Murray Gold

THE SINGLE EMPLOYER MODEL

Pension legislation in a number of provinces sets out minimum funding requirements applicable to pension plans.[1] For single employer-sponsored plans, the general requirements are straightforward. Plans must be actuarially valued in specified periods.[2] Valuations may be made and filed more frequently than legislation requires, but the frequency of these extra valuations is in the discretion of the plan administrator. Most provinces require that unfunded going-concern liabilities disclosed by a valuation be amortized over 15 years[3] and are the responsibility of the employer sponsor. Similarly, solvency deficiencies are the employer sponsor's responsibility and must be amortized over five years.[4] On the other hand, where a plan has no unfunded liabilities and no solvency deficiency, actuarial gains may be used by the employer sponsor in a variety of ways, including to reduce current service costs.[5] These minimum standards thus prescribe that single employer plan sponsors are responsible for unfunded liabilities and solvency deficiencies, but are entitled to the benefit of actuarial gains. An additional set of rules govern plan surpluses.[6]

THE MULTI-EMPLOYER MODEL

In jointly trusteed arrangements, the funding arrangements are different. Multi-employer plans (MEPs) that are jointly trusteed, for example, are governed by different legislative provisions.[7] While these rules generally apply without additional plan funding rules in the private sector, they are generally supplemented by important plan funding rules in the public and broader public sectors.

Under common legislative and regulatory rules, fixed contribution rates for both members and employers are collectively bargained, and are imposed on the parties by collective agreements. As with single employer plans, MEP administrators must file actuarial reports at specified intervals; however, such reports are subject to somewhat different requirements. Most provinces require actuaries to perform supplementary tests for MEPs to ensure that the contributions required by the collective agreement are sufficient to provide for the benefits set out in the plan without consideration of any provision for reduction of benefits set out in the plan.[8] In addition, where such contributions are not sufficient to fund the promised benefits, the actuary is required to propose options that will result in the required contributions being sufficient to provide the benefits under the plan.[9] The actuary is required to submit a report setting out such options to the administrator and file a copy of the report with the Commission. The administrator is required to act on the basis of the report and to take such actions needed to have the plan meet its funding requirements.[10] In the context of a deficiency, a MEP (unlike its single employer counterpart) may be amended to reduce accrued benefits.

The funding regime prescribed by the *Pension Benefits Act* (PBA) Regulations for jointly governed MEPs is therefore very much along a defined contribution model. Contributions are fixed through collective bargaining, and there is no statutory obligation on the employer to make any additional special payments in the event of a deficiency. Rather, deficiencies must be identified by the MEPs' actuaries, who are also responsible for proposing options that will eliminate them. The administrator is responsible for adopting an appropriate course of action, which may include the reduction of accrued benefits. In essence, PBA's minimum funding requirements for jointly governed MEPs prescribe a defined contribution model with no defined benefit guarantees of accrued benefits.

More sophisticated funding models, with plan provisions that guarantee the funding of accrued liabilities, have been developed for jointly governed single and multi-employer plans in the public and broader public sectors.

FUNDING ARRANGEMENTS IN THE PUBLIC AND BROADER PUBLIC SECTORS

The funding issues of deficiencies, gains and surpluses have been dealt with in somewhat different ways by different plans in the public and broader public sectors. In some cases, the plans are MEPs, while in other cases they are not, and this of course affects the applicable statutory background to the funding issues. As well, some of the plans are multi-bargaining unit and multi-union plans, while the members of other plans all belong to one trade union. This is also important, because it affects the ability of the parties to collectively bargain over pension issues. While collective bargaining is a practical and often desirable form in which to resolve pension issues as between an employer and a single trade union, collective bargaining may become unwieldy if it takes place across a number of different bargaining tables with a number of different trade unions. The governance of these plans and the funding arrangements with respect to them are all influenced by whether they are single employer or MEPs, and whether there is one or more collective bargaining agents representing plan members.

Ontario Teachers' Pension Plan

The Ontario Teachers' Pension Plan (OTPP) is an example of a MEP in which all the members are represented by a single agent for purposes of pension bargaining.[11] The largest employer, for pension purposes, is the province of Ontario, however, and it behaves with respect to the OTPP as would any single employer plan sponsor. The single bargaining agent for the plan members is the Ontario Teachers' Federation (OTF). For practical purposes, the governance of the OTPP is therefore essentially single employer, although it is a MEP. Thus, the OTPP is governed by a board, having a maximum of nine members. Each of Ontario and the OTF appoint four members, and the ninth member, the chair, is selected by Ontario and the OTF together.

The OTF and Ontario retain significant roles with respect to the plan as well. In particular, the OTF and Ontario (collectively referred to as the *partners*) are responsible for making decisions and taking actions with respect to funding deficiencies or actuarial gains. However, the partners have agreed on certain parameters with respect to the funding of deficiencies and the application of gains. These parameters require that any contribution rate increase required to fund a deficiency would be equally shared between Ontario and the members. Ontario and the members also share responsibility for liquidating solvency deficiencies, although the members are permitted to pay their share of the liability over a longer period than Ontario, given the members' lesser ability to pay. Actuarial gains must first be applied to eliminate any unamortized balances of any solvency deficiencies. Additional gains may be used to fund a contingency reserve, reduce contribution rates or improve benefits, as may be agreed by the partners.

In the event that the partners cannot agree on the contributions necessary to fund a deficiency, or on the application of actuarial gains after solvency deficiencies have been paid, then the parties undertake a mediation and arbitration process, culminating in final and binding arbitration.

Significantly, however, the partners to the OTPP— the OTF and the province of Ontario—are not collective bargaining parties and do not bargain with respect to other terms and conditions of employment. Accordingly, pension governance is quite separate from employment-based collective bargaining.

Accordingly, under the OTPP joint governance model, funding decisions remain with the partners, who operate under the constraints of agreed parameters and refer any disputes to final and binding arbitration. The agreed parameters ensure that the plan is fully funded, and that funding deficiencies are remedied by contribution rate increases, rather than benefit reductions.

OPSEU Pension Trust

The OPSEU Pension Trust (OPT or OPSEU Plan) presents a slightly different funding model. It is sponsored by the Ontario Public Service Employees' Union (OPSEU) and the province of Ontario.[12] While three other trade unions also have members in the OPSEU Plan, they do not participate in plan governance as their memberships are quite small. Accordingly, like the OTPP, the governance of the OPSEU Plan's funding arrangements is based on a single employer and single bargaining unit model. Each of OPSEU and Ontario appoint five persons to a board of trustees, which is responsible for administering the OPSEU Plan and investing its assets.

In the event of a going-concern or solvency deficiency in the OPT, Ontario and the members are required to increase their contributions so as to fund the deficiency. Like the OTPP, the OPT's defined benefit structure is thus protected through a shared obligation on both sponsors to increase their contributions as required.

Unlike the OTPP, however, the OPSEU Plan provides that gains are to be split into two pools, half of which are to be used at the direction of the trade union for the benefit of the members, and the other half of which may be used for the benefit of Ontario. OPSEU and Ontario are also free to collectively bargain for something other than a 50/50 split of any gains. Thus, the allocation and use of gains is more closely tied to the collective bargaining process under the OPT arrangement than under the OTPP. As well, the OPT funding arrangement, which divides gains into pools, involves less negotiation between the sponsors than the OTPP arrangements, which treat the gains as forming a single pool.

Colleges of Applied Arts and Technology Plan (the CAAT Plan)

Similar funding arrangements exist with respect to the Colleges of Applied Arts and Technology Pension Plan.[13] Like the OTPP, the CAAT Plan is a MEP and thus operates against a different regulatory background from the OPSEU Plan.

The principal difference between the funding arrangements governing the CAAT Plan and those governing the OTPP and the OPSEU Plan is that the CAAT Plan requires the accumulation of a contingency reserve at the rate of .4% of liabilities per year to a maximum of 2% of liabilities. Going concern or solvency deficiencies are dealt with first by exhausting this contingency reserve. Once it is exhausted, however, deficiencies must be paid by equal percentage increases of both member and employer contributions, much like the OTPP and the OPSEU Plan. Gains under the CAAT Plan are applied first to eliminate any going concern unfunded liability, then to eliminate solvency deficiencies and finally to create a contingency reserve up to 2% of liabilities. Additional gains above the level required to fully fund the contingency reserve may be used to increase benefits with respect to the period prior January 1, 1992, and are then subject to negotiation between the sponsors of the CAAT Plan. Accordingly, the CAAT Plan contains strong direction to improve pre-January 1, 1992 benefits, and then leaves the disposition of additional gains to negotiation between the sponsors.

As for the other plans, the CAAT Plan protects its defined benefit structure through a shared obligation to fund deficiencies. Agreed parameters control the use and application of gains until certain contingency reserve and benefit improvement thresholds have been reached, after which the sponsors bargain over additional gains.

Hospitals of Ontario Pension Plan (HOOPP)

HOOPP has funding arrangements that are quite distinct from those governing the other plans. This may be because HOOPP is not only a MEP, it is also a multi-bargaining unit plan.[14] Four different trade unions represent members of HOOPP. The principal distinguishing characteristic of the HOOPP funding model is that responsibility for funding deficiencies and gains is vested in the plan administrator, a board of trustees appointed by the Ontario Hospital Association (OHA) and the participating trade unions. This contrasts with the OTPP, OPT and CAAT Plans, all of which confer responsibility for funding deficiencies and gains on the sponsoring parties.

The HOOPP mechanism for dealing with gains and losses is somewhat complicated. At each valuation, the plan's actuary is required to determine the total annual cost of the plan, including any amortization payments associated with any unfunded liabilities. All things being equal, an increase in unfunded liabilities will increase the total annual cost for the plan. This increase is dealt with through increased contributions, the cost of which is allocated to the parties pursuant to an agreed-upon formula. Essentially, employer contributions are permitted to range between 120% and 150% of member contributions. This range is referred to as the *employer contribution corridor*. If new unfunded liabilities increase the plan's total annual cost, and the employers are at the low end of the contribution corridor, then employer contribution rates will increase to pay the additional cost. On the other hand, if the employers' contribution rates are already at the upper end of the contribution corridor, then the burden of any increased cost falls on the members. Depending upon the size of the increased funding requirement, and the existing level of employer contributions, the burden of amortizing any unfunded liability will fall on either the employers or the members or on some combination of both. Interestingly, however, the allocation of these contribution rate increases is governed by the HOOPP documents and is, therefore, fairly mechanical.

Gains in HOOPP are also generally applied against amortization payments associated with going-concern and solvency deficiencies, unless the board of trustees determines otherwise. Surpluses, on the other hand, are not dealt with mechanically. The board of trustees administering HOOPP is responsible for determining what portion of the surplus is used to improve benefits or reduce the fund's annual cost. Although the plan documents encourage the administrator to use surpluses in excess of 10% of actuarial liabilities to improve benefits, there is no requirement that the administrator act in this way. Accordingly, the application of surpluses is very much at the discretion of the plan administrator. This distinguishes HOOPP from the OTPP, the OPT and the CAAT plans, all of which reserve stronger roles for the plan sponsors in determining surplus applications.

British Columbia Pension Plans

In British Columbia, the *Public Sector Pension Plans Act* (PSPPA)[15] governs four public sector plans in British Columbia—the College Pension Plan, the Municipal Pension Plan, the Public Service Pension Plan and the Teachers' Pension Plan.

PSPPA enacted the following.

Establishment of British Columbia Pension Corporation (BCPC)

In British Columbia, the public sector plans are not self-administered, but rather are administered by the BCPC. BCPC is governed by a Pension Management Board, having at least eight directors, two of whom are from each of the boards governing the four public sector plans that it administers. So, for example, the board governing the College Pension Plan appoints two directors to the Pension Management Board of the BCPC, as do the boards of the Municipal Pension Plan, the Public Service Pension Plan and the Teachers' Pension Plan. As noted below, a joint governance agreement currently applies to the College Pension Plan, so that its board appoints two directors to the BCPC Board as a matter of right. For the other plans, however, the appointments to the BCPC Board are technically made by the "trustee" of each of these plans, on the recommendation of their respective boards. The BCPC has a chief executive officer, whose responsibilities are also set out in the statute.

British Columbia Investment Management Corporation (the "Investment Corporation")

Similarly, the British Columbia legislation requires that the public sector plans invest their assets through the Investment Corporation, although it does contemplate that the plans can withdraw some or all of their assets and invest them independently. Like the BCPC, the Investment Corporation is also managed by a board of directors with representation from the various public sector plans. However, in the case of the Investment Corporation, its board consists of one director from each of the public sector boards, one director appointed by the Deputy Minister of Finance and Corporate Relations and two directors appointed by "other clients" of the Investment Corporation. As with the BCPC, the College Board, by virtue of its joint governance, is entitled to appoint one director to the Investment Management Board as of right, while the appointments from the Municipal Board, Public Service Board and Teachers' Board are made by the trustees of those boards, on the recommendations of those boards. The day-to-day duties of the Investment Corporation are carried out by a chief investment officer, whose duties and responsibilities are set out in the statute.

The Four Plans

The provisions of British Columbia's four public sector plans are set out in schedules to the PSPPA. Each schedule establishes a board to govern the plan and provides for the persons who will sit on that board. In the case of the Municipal Plan, for example, the board consists of 13 persons, four of whom are appointed by the government and two of whom are appointed by the Union of British Columbia Municipalities. Six members are appointed by the Municipal Employees Pension Committee (representing plan members) and one person (the 13th) is appointed by the government and appointed as chair of the board. The chair of the board is the "trustee" of the pension fund and the person ultimately responsible for making appointments to the boards of the Investment Corporation and the BCPC. The board of the Municipal Pension Plan is responsible for the administration of the plan and for dealing with appeals from persons who wish to challenge decisions of the BCPC. While the board is empowered to make recommendations with respect to plan design, these rules must ultimately be adopted by the Treasury Board. Similar provisions govern the Public Service Pension Plan and the Teachers' Pension Plan.

Funding

Under the applicable schedules of the PSPPA, the Municipal Pension Plan, the Public Service Pension Plan and the Teachers' Pension Plan remain government-sponsored plans. However, unlike private sector plans, they are not required to amortize the unfunded liabilities in existence as of the effective date of the PSPPA. Rather, they are required to amortize any increase in the existing unfunded liability over 15 years, while also making contributions necessary to meet the normal cost of the plan and to hold the initial unfunded actuarial liability constant as a percentage of payroll. In the event of a surplus, the legislation entitles the employers to reduce their contributions in an amount sufficient to amortize the identified surplus over a period of at least 15 years. Different rules apply with respect to the College Pension Plan, as noted below.

Joint Trusteeship

The schedules to the PSPPA governing the Municipal Pension Plan, the Public Service Pension Plan and the Teachers' Pension Plan contemplate that the "partners" to the plans may negotiate joint management agreements dealing with, among other things, the sharing of gains and liabilities for deficiencies, the method for amending the plan and the resolution of disputes. Provisions governing the type of joint trusteeship arrangements that may be negotiated are set out in Part II to the applicable schedules.

Joint Trusteeship of the College Pension Plan

As noted, the College Pension Plan has been negotiated as a jointly trusteed plan. It is governed by a board of ten trustees, four of whom are appointed by the government, four by two unions representing members, and one retiree and one non-union member, both of whom are appointed by the employer and employer parties. Decisions by the board must be made by a majority of at least 80% of the voting members on the board. The board is generally responsible for the administration of the plan and the investment of the fund, although it is required to utilize the services of the BCPC for plan administration and the services of the Investment Corporation. The board will have some flexibility to move some or all of its assets away from the Investment Corporation one year after the first valuation of the plan if it considers that "alternative funds management services are in the best financial interest of the plan members."

Any actuarial gains in the College Pension Plan must first be applied to offset previous actuarial losses and outstanding unfunded liabilities and may then be used for any of the following purposes, subject to the requirements of the *Pension Benefits Standards Act:*

    a. Increase the reserve established for stabilizing contribution rates

    b. Transfer a portion of the gain to an account within the pension fund established to provide for indexing of benefits for retired plan members

    c. Share equally in any reduction or elimination of employer and plan member contributions for a period of time

    d. Make changes to the benefit provisions as set out in Section 15 regarding amendments to the plan rules.

Finally, the board does have a certain amount of authority to amend the technical rules of the plan without approval of the sponsoring parties. It may also amend the plan where the amendment does not result in contribution rate increases and does not create, or increase, an unfunded liability. Otherwise, it would appear that benefit improvements must be agreed between the government and the union partners.

Alberta

In Alberta, discussion papers have been published with respect to the province's five largest pension plans administered by the Alberta government—the Public Service Pension Plan (the "PSPP"), the Local Authorities Pension Plan (the "LAPP"), the Public Service Management Pension Plan (the "PSMPP"), the Universities Academic Pension Plan (the "UAPP") and the Special Forces Pension Plan (the "SFPP"). In 1991, the Alberta government identified a significant unfunded liability in these five plans, whose assets were, at the time, accounted for collectively in a "pension account" held in the province's General Revenue Fund. In order to eliminate the collective unfunded liability, the province introduced contribution surcharges for itself and for contributing employers and employees.

In 1993, Alberta introduced its *Public Sector Pension Plans Act* (PSPPA).[16] Highlights of that legislation were as follows.

Segregation of Fund Assets

The assets of the various pension funds administered by the Alberta government were segregated into separate pension plan funds. The Provincial Treasurer retained the mandate to invest these funds for the benefit of plan members.

Boards of Trustees

Boards of trustees were created with respect to each of the plans, with prescribed responsibilities. The boards were responsible for adjusting member and employer contribution rates to fully fund going-concern and solvency requirements. The provincial government, on the other hand, retained the authority to amend the plans' benefit provisions. Schedules governing the LAPP and the UAPP contained a series of process requirements anticipating the joint trusteeship of those plans. The schedule governing the Management Employees Pension Board also contemplated joint governance discussions, as did the schedule governing the PSPP.

Subsequent to the government's passage of PSPPA, discussions ensued with respect to joint trusteeship. In principle, the government of Alberta has committed itself to "privatizing" those plans of which it is not a direct sponsor. In the case of the LAPP, for example, the Alberta government has pledged to withdraw from plan governance, leaving the participating employers in the municipal, health and education sectors to govern LAPP together with the sponsoring trade unions and employee groups. Discussions in this regard have been underway since 1993.

ENDNOTES

1. See *Employment Pension Plans Act,* S.A. 1986, c. E.10.05 as am, s. 38 (EPPA); *Pension Benefits Standards Act,* R.S.B.C. 1996, c. 352 as am, s. 41 (BCPBSA); *Pension Benefits Act,* R.S.M. 1987, c. P.32 as am, s. 41 (MPBA); *Pension Benefits Act,* 1997, S.N. 1996, c. P-4.01 as am, s. 35 (NPBA), and *Pension Benefit Act Regulation,* Nfld. Reg. 114/965 as am, s. 12; *Pension Benefits Act,* R.S.N.S. 1989, c. 340 as am. ss. 62-67 (NSPBA); *Pension Benefits Regulation,* R.R.O. 1990, Reg. 909 as am, ss. 14-17 (Regulation 909); *Pension Benefits Act,* S.P.E.I. 1990, c. 41 as am, ss. 61-66 (PEIPBA); *Supplemental Pension Plans Act,* R.S.Q. c. R.15.1 as am, ss. 120-125 (the "SPPA").

2. See EPPA, *supra* note 1, s. 7(3); *Employment Pension Plans Regulation,* Alta. Reg. 364/86 as am, ss. 8(2) and 8(5) (EPPA Regulation); BCPBSA, *supra* note 1, s. 9(3); *Pension Benefits Standards Act Regulation,* B.C. Reg. 433/93 as am, s. 4 (BCPBSA Regulation); *Pension Benefits Regulation,* Man. Reg. 188/87 R as am, s. 3(3) (the "MPBA Regulation"); *Pension Benefits Regulation,* N.B. Reg. 91-195 as am, ss. 8 and 9 (NBPBA Regulation); *Pension Benefits Regulations,* Nfld. Reg. 114/96 as am, s. 5(3) (the "NPBA Regulation"); *Pension Benefits Regulation,* N.S. Reg. 269/87 as am, s. 11 (the "NSPBA Regulation"); Regulation 909, *supra* note 1, s. 14 (note: actuarial valuations must, however, be prepared annually where there are solvency concerns pursuant to Section 14(3), or where the plan is a "qualifying plan" for solvency funding purposes (Sections 5.1-5.4)); SPPA, *supra* note 1, s. 118; *Pension Benefits Act,* 1992, S.S. 1992, c. P-6.001 as am, s. 11(4)(b) (SPBA).

3. See EPPA Regulation, *supra* note 2, s. 34(3)(b); BCPBSA Regulation, *supra* note 2, s. 35(3)(b); MPBA Regulation, *supra* note 2, s. 4(3)(b); NPBA Regulation, *supra* note 2, s. 12(3)(c); NSPBA Regulation, *supra* note 2, s. 5(1)(b); Regulation 909, *supra* note 1, s. 5(1)(b); *Pension Benefits Regulation,* R.R.S., c. P-6.001, Reg. 1 as am, s. 36(3)(b) (SPBA Regulation). Note: s. 137(2) of SPPA, *supra* note 1 requires that going-concern liabilities be funded over five years.

4. See EPPA Regulation, *supra* note 2, s. 34(3)(c); BCPBSA Regulation, *supra* note 2, s. 35(3)(c); MPBA Regulation, *supra* note 2, s. 4(3)(c); NPBA Regulation, *supra* note 2, s. 12(3)(d); NSPBA Regulation, *supra* note 2, s. 5(1)(c); Regulation 909, *supra* note 1, s. (1)(e) (note: modified rules exist with respect to solvency deficiencies arising prior to November 26, 1992); SPBA Regulation, *supra* note 2, s. 36(3)(c).

5. See EPPA Regulation, *supra* note 2, s. 34(9); BCPBSA Regulation, *supra* note 2, s. 35(7); MPBA Regulation, *supra* note 2, s. 4(18); NPBA Regulation, *supra* note 2, s. 13; NSPBA Regulation, *supra* note 2, s. 7; Regulation 909, *supra* note 2, s.7(3); SPBA Regulation, *supra* note 2, s. 36(7). This, of course, is subject to any contrary terms in the plan's constating documents. See also *Schmidt v. Air Products* (1994), 115 D.L.R. (4th) 631 (S.C.C.); *Maurer v. McMaster University* (1991), 82 D.L.R. (4th) 6 (O.C.(G.D.)); *Hockin v. Bank of British Columbia* (1995), 123 D.L.R. (4th) 538 (B.C.C.A.); *Chateauneuf v. TSCO of Canada Ltd.* (1995), 124 D.L.R. (4th) 308 (Que. C.A.); *Trent University Faculty Association v. Trent University* (1992), 99 D.L.R. (4th) 451 (Ont. Div. Ct.); *Askin v. Ontario Hospital Association* (1991), 2 O.R. (3d) 641 (C.A.).

6. See EPPA, *supra* note 1, s. 58; EPPA Regulation, *supra* note 2, s. 39; BCPBSA Regulation, *supra* note 2, s. 42; MPBA, *supra* note 1, s. 26(2.1); NBPBA, *supra* note 1, s. 59; NBPBA Regulation, *supra* note 2, ss. 47 and 48; NPBA, *supra* note 1, s. 57; NPBA Regulation, *supra* note 2, ss. 19-22; NSPBA, *supra* note 1, ss. 83-86; NSPBA Regulation, *supra* note 2, ss. 24 and 25; *Pension Benefits Act,* R.S.O. 1990, c. P.8 as am, s. 79 (OPBA); Regulation 909, *supra* note 1 ss. 8, 10 and 10.1; SPBA Regulation, *supra* note 3, s. 41.

7. See EPPA, *supra* note 1, ss. 7(3)(c), 7(3)(d) and 38(4); EPPA Regulation, *supra* note 2, ss. 34(11) and 34(16)-34(18.2); BCPBSA, *supra* note 1, s. 9(3)(c); BCPBSA Regulation, *supra* note 2, ss. 35(9), 35(15) and 35(16); MPBA Regulation, *supra* note 2, ss. 4(8)-4(11) and 4(20); NPBA Regulation, *supra* note 2, s. 7; NSPBA Regulation, *supra* note 2, ss. 4(5), 6 and 14(1)(2); Regulation 909, *supra* note 2 s. 6; SPBA Regulation, *supra* note 3, ss. 10(1)(j) and 36(8).

8. See BCPBA Regulation, *supra* note 2, s. 35(15); MPBA Regulation, *supra* note 2, s. 4(8)(a); NPBA Regulation, *supra* note 2, s. 7(1)(a); NSPBA Regulation, *supra* note 2, s. 6(4)(a); Regulation 909, *supra* note 1, s. 6(4).

9. See BCPBA Regulation, *supra* note 2, s. 35(16); MPBA Regulation, *supra* note 2, ss. 4(9)-4(11); NPBA Regulation, *supra* note 2, s. 7(1)(b); NSPBA Regulation, *supra* note 2, s. 6(4)(b); Regulation 909, *supra* note 1, s. 6(4)(b).

10. See BCPBA Regulation, *supra* note 2, s. 35(16); MPBA Regulation, *supra* note 2, ss. 4(8)(b) and 4(9)-4(11); NPBA Regulation, *supra* note 2, ss. 7(2)-7(4); NSPBA Regulation, *supra* note 2, ss. 6(5)-6(7); Regulation 909, *supra* note 1, s. 6(5)(c).

11. See *Teachers Pension Act,* R.S.O. 1990, c. T-1, and a Partners Agreement between Her Majesty the Queen in Right of the Province of Ontario as represented by the Minister of Education and Training and the Ontario Teachers Federation represented by its Executive, July 15, 1991.

12. See Ontario Public Service Employees' Union Pension Act, 1994, S.O. 1994, c. 17; Sponsorship Agreement between Ontario and OPSEU, April 18, 1994.

13. See the Colleges of Applied Arts and Technology Pension Plan, consolidated to August 31, 1996.

14. See Hospitals of Ontario Pension Plan.

15. British Columbia *Public Sector Pension Plans Act,* S.B.C. 1999, c. 44.

16. *Public Sector Pension Plans Act,* S.A. 1993, c. P-30.7.

CHAPTER 3

Jointly Trusteed Public Sector Pension Plans: Governance Issues

by Murray Gold

Jointly governed plans share the same governance challenges as any other pension plan. Their administrative and investment objectives are similar to single employer plans, and their governance and management arrangements must therefore deal with the same issues as any other pension plan.

However, at least three features distinguish the jointly governed arrangement from the single employer model. First, they are generally, if not always, bound up much more closely with the collective bargaining process than single employer plans. In the private sector multi-employer model, the trade union and employer sponsors of the multi-employer plan (MEP) will collectively bargain with respect to contributions. Bargaining over pensions will be bound up with collective bargaining generally and will take place in the same forum and will involve the same persons generally as collective bargaining. In the public and broader public sectors, there are varying degrees of relation between the collective bargaining process and pension funding. Generally, the application of surpluses is dealt with between collective bargaining parties. There are some exceptions to this, particularly where collective bargaining is dysfunctional because a number of different trade unions represent plan members, as in the HOOPP case. However, in each of the other public and broader public sector plans described in Chapter 2 of this section, collective bargaining is the forum for determining surplus utilization.

Second, persons appointed to a board of trustees by a trade union tend to have a perspective on pension plan governance that is distinct from persons appointed by employer plan sponsors. In part, this is due to the member-service orientation of trade unions. It is part of a trade union representative's everyday experience to receive questions and complaints from the union's members and to seek to resolve members' issues and problems. Accordingly, trade union appointees are often sensitive to the quality of service delivered by the pension plan, including the quality of its communications, the timeliness of its services and the accuracy of its data. These priorities are shared by employer appointees with responsibilities in the human resources or labour relations areas. Persons appointed by employer sponsors, on the other hand, often have a financial background. More than their trade union appointee counterparts, employer sponsor appointees tend to be interested in the asset or investment side of the plan. The trade union appointee focus on the liability and administrative side of the plan is actually quite complementary to the employer sponsor appointee focus on the asset and investment side of the equation. Together, the two perspectives may make for a well-rounded board of trustees, with a good overall sense of plan governance. Nevertheless, reconciling these two different starting points is another distinguishing feature of multi-employer governance.

Third, jointly governed boards often include some or a number of lay persons. The administration of a corporate plan may be the responsibility of a board of directors, or a committee of the board, all of whose members have backgrounds in financial matters to one degree or another. In jointly trusteed arrangements, the composition of a board of trustees tends to be less uniform. In general, there is a greater tendency towards lay trustees in the jointly governed environment than in the corporate environment. This is also a distinctive aspect of governance, since the complexity of pension matters can be especially challenging for lay trustees, who may also bring fresh perspectives to bear on governance.

Given these distinctive factors, it may be useful to review the application of trust and fiduciary principles to jointly governed pension plans.

DUTIES OF A BOARD OF TRUSTEES

Boards of trustees of a jointly trusteed arrangement are typically the administrators of the plan for purposes of provincial pension legislation.[1] The legislation has adopted a "buck stops here" approach to governance, under which the plan administrator is the ultimate authority that may be held accountable for the administration of the plan and the investment of the fund.

In administering the plan and investing the fund, plan administrators are held to a fiduciary standard of care, which has two branches. The administrator is required to exercise the care, diligence and skill that a person of ordinary prudence would exercise in dealing with the property of another person and then, in addition, the plan administrator is required to use all relevant knowledge and skill that the administrator possesses or, by reason of the administrator's profession, business or calling, ought to possess. Section 22 of the Ontario *Pension Benefits Act* provides as follows:

22(1) The administrator of a pension plan shall exercise the care, diligence and skill in the administration and investment of the pension fund that a person of ordinary prudence would exercise in dealing with the property of another person.

(2) The administrator of a pension plan shall use in the administration of the pension plan and in the administration and investment of the pension fund all relevant knowledge and skill that the administrator possesses, or, by reasons of the administrator's profession, business or calling, ought to possess.[2]

Section 22(3) explicitly provides that both of these standards are applicable to individual members of a board of trustees. Similar legislative provisions exist in other provinces.[3]

In addition to legislating the standard of care applicable to pension plan trustees, provincial legislation such as the Ontario *Pension Benefits Act* specifically addresses the issue of conflict of interest:

22(4) An administrator or, if the administrator is a pension committee or a board of trustees, a member of the committee or board that is the administrator of a pension plan shall not knowingly permit the administrator's interest to conflict with the administrator's duties and powers in respect of the pension fund.[4]

Jointly governed plans, like most other plans, are typically constituted as trusts, so that the law of trusts also informs the nature of the duties and obligations of the plan administrator. This is because, for common law purposes, a plan administrator is also the "trustee" of the plan. Courts have held that pension trusts are essentially similar to other trusts,[5] and that the common law of trusts applies to pension trust funds in much the same way as it applies to other trust funds, except, of course, to the extent that PBA or other legislation stipulates higher or different standards with respect to a pension trust.

In this regard, it is useful to emphasize the high standards stipulated by PBA for a pension trustee, by contrasting them with the common law trust standards. The common law of trusts, typically applicable to testamentary trusts and a variety of *inter vivos* trusts, requires a trustee to act as a "man of ordinary prudence in managing his own affairs."[6] Further, the common law of trusts does not traditionally impose a higher standard of care on the professional trustee than on a lay trustee.[7] Both principles are well illustrated in the case of *Fales v. Canada Permanent Trust Company*. That case involved a testamentary trust that held shares in a private company in which the testator had been one of a few active shareholders. The testator appointed his wife and the Canada Permanent Trust Company as executors, and directed them to sell the shares, but permitted them to postpone the disposition. In the *Fales* case, the trust company did not dispose of the shares, and did not, in the court's findings, meet its standard of care in the administration of the estate. The court discussed the applicable common law principles as follows:

Traditionally, the standard of care and diligence required of a trustee in administering a trust is that of a man of ordinary prudence in managing his own affairs (*Learoyd and Carter v. Whiteley et al.* (1887), 12 App. Cas. 727 at p. 733; *Underhill's Law of Trusts and Trustees,* 12th ed., art. 49; *Restatement of the Law on Trusts,* 2nd ed., para 174) and traditionally the standard has applied equally to professional and non-professional trustees. The standard has been of general application and objective though, at times, rigorous. There has been discussion of the question whether a corporation which holds itself out, expressly or impliedly, as possessing greater competence and ability than the man of ordinary prudence should not be held to a higher standard of conduct than the individual trustee. It has been said by some that a higher standard of diligence and knowledge is expected from paid trustees: *Underhill's Law of Trusts and Trustees,* art. 49, relying upon *obiter* of Harnman, J., in *Re Waterman's Will*

Trusts: Lloyds Bank, Ltd. v. Sutton, [1952] 2 All E.R. 1054 at p. 1055, and upon *dicta* found in *National Trustees Co. of Australasia v. General Finance Co. of Australasia,* [1905] A.C. 373 (P.C.), a case which did not turn upon the imposition of a greater or lesser duty but upon the relief to which a corporate trustee might be entitled under the counterpart of section 98 of the *Trustee Act* of British Columbia, to which I have earlier referred.

In the case at bar the trial Judge held that the law required a higher standard of care from a trustee who charged a fee for his professional services than from one who acted gratuitously. Mr. Justice Bull, delivering the judgement of the Court of Appeal, was not prepared to find, and held it unnecessary to find that a professional trustee, by virtue of that character and consequential expertise, had a greater duty to a *cestui que* trust than a lay trustee.

The weight of authority to the present, save in the granting of relief under remedial legislation such as section 98 of the *Trustee Act,* has been against making a distinction between a widow, acting as trustee of her husband's estate, and a trust company performing the same role. Receipt of fees has not served to ground, nor to increase exposure to, liability. Every trustee has been expected to act as the person of ordinary prudence would act.[8]

Significantly, legislation has altered both of these standards for pension trust purposes, requiring that plan administrators use the care, diligence and skill that a person of ordinary prudence would exercise in dealing *with the property of another person,* rather than the *Fales* test, which required trustees to act as though they were dealing with their own property. In general, the sense of obligation and prudence is higher when dealing with another's property, than with one's own, so that the legislative standard is generally thought to be higher than the common law standard.[9] As well, the legislation expressly mandates a higher standard of obligation on those having specialized knowledge than the *Fales* case suggests. Whereas *Fales* recites the then-established law that professional trustees and lay trustees are held to the same standard of care, and declines to comment further on that proposition in the context of that particular case, legislative provisions expressly provide that plan administrators are required to apply the knowledge or skill not only that they do have, but that they ought to have as a result of their profession, business or calling. Accordingly, the legislative standard of care is set at a high level and imposes onerous obligations on plan administrators, including jointly trusteed boards.

Provincial pension legislation has also modified the common law with respect to conflicts of interest. This is an important body of law for all pension plans, since the employer sponsor of a pension plan always has a structural conflict of interest if the employer also acts as plan administrator. It is also an important body of law for jointly governed arrangements, because persons appointed to a jointly governed board often have interests relating to the party that appoints them. It is not unusual, for example, to see persons with labour relations responsibilities for employers appointed to joint boards of trustees, nor is it unusual to see trade union representatives with collective bargaining responsibility on those same boards. To a certain extent, there may be an inbuilt conflict of interest in these situations, where the interests of the employer or trade union sponsor conflict with the trustees' fiduciary interests.

Such a structural conflict must, however, be approached in the context of the legislation, and of its provisions regarding the permissible administrators of a pension fund. Section 8 of the Ontario *Pension Benefits Act* sets out permissible pension plan administrators and stipulates that a pension plan is not eligible for registration unless it is administered by one of the entities listed in that section, including the employer. Legislation in New Brunswick, Nova Scotia and Prince Edward Island contains similar provisions.[10]

In the case of a multi-employer pension plan established pursuant to a collective agreement or a trust agreement, however, some provincial legislation requires that such plans be administered by a board of trustees at least one-half of whom are representatives of members of a multi-employer pension plan.[11]

The legislative provisions governing who may administer a pension plan are important to understanding the legislative conflicts-of-interest regime, for two reasons. In the first place, legislation expressly permits employers to administer their single employer-sponsored plans. There is, however, in this case, a strong structural conflict between the interests of the employer and those of the beneficiaries that the trustees are required to protect. For example, employer sponsors may have different funding priorities than the members, or may be inclined to interpret plan provisions or implement administrative procedures that are contrary to the members' interests. As a matter of practice, these conflicts are mediated through actuaries and dealt with by plan administrators, but they are, nevertheless, conflicts. The legislative provisions against conflicts of interest must be interpreted in the context of this permissible structural conflict of interest.

By the same token, in some jurisdictions, multi-employer plans established pursuant to a trust agreement or a collective agreement *must* be administered by a joint board of trustees. Section 8(1)(e) of the Ontario *Pension Benefits Act,* for example, presumes, as was commonly the case at the time it was drafted, that one-half of the multi-employer plan board's members will be appointed by an employer or employer association, and that the other half would be appointed by a trade union or trade union organization. Once again, it appears that Section 8 expressly contemplates such a structural conflict.

Although the rule against conflicts is susceptible to a number of different interpretations, two particular approaches recommend themselves. As discussed above, a plan administrator may not "knowingly permit" its interests to conflict with its duties. Does this mean that, if a member of a board of trustees knows of the conflict, then the trustee may not take any decision with respect to it? Or does it mean that a trustee may know of a conflict, but may not permit the conflicting interest to affect the trustee's decision in respect of the pension plan? In other words, does provincial legislation prohibit any known conflicts, or does it prohibit a trustee, on a more subjective level, from permitting a known conflict to influence the trustee's decision?

While an outright prohibition of known conflicts may be attractive from an ethical point of view, it may also result in a high level of dysfunctionality if trustees are regularly precluded from decision making because of relatively immaterial conflicts. For those provinces whose legislation specifies the entities that can administer pension plans, which expressly permits basic structural conflicts, it is unlikely that the conflicts provisions are intended to be construed as a strict prohibition against any known conflicts.

An important case dealing with conflicts of interest is the U.K. decision of *Cowan v. Scargill*.[12] In *Cowan,* the union trustees of a jointly trusteed pension plan set up for the benefit of mine workers refused to approve an investment policy unless it prohibited foreign investment and any investment in industries that competed with coal. The union trustees were motivated by a desire to protect mine worker employment, not to obtain the highest reasonable rate of return for the pension plan. The court rejected the union trustees' position, and held that they could only have regard for the best financial interests of the pension plan, and had to set aside their own personal interests and views:

> In considering what investments to make trustees must put on one side their own personal interests and views. Trustees may have strongly held social or political views. They may be firmly opposed to any investment in South Africa or other countries, or they may object to any form of investment in companies concerned with alcohol, tobacco, armaments or many other things. In the conduct of their own affairs, of course, they are free to abstain from making any such investments. Yet under a trust, if the investments of this type would be more beneficial to the beneficiaries than other investments, the trustees must not refrain from making the investment by reason of the views that

they hold. . . . trustees may even have to act dishonourably (though not illegally) if the interests of said beneficiaries require it.[13]

Cowan provides a good illustration of the less strict approach to conflicts. On a strict approach, the trustees of the Mine Workers Plan might not have been able to adopt an investment policy at all, because of their patent interest in the health of the coal industry and the British economy generally. They would be conflicted in formulating the policy, because their interests in the coal industry might have conflicted with their fiduciary obligations. On a strict view of conflicts, these trustees would all have had to step aside and delegate the investment policymaking process to others.

The court did not, however, adopt this approach. Rather, it simply required that the trustees set aside their personal views, and not act upon them. In other words, the trustees of the Mine Workers Plan could not *knowingly permit* their interests in the health of the coal mining industry to conflict with their duties as trustees. They had to disregard their personal interests and views and make the investment policy decisions exclusively in the best financial interests of the plan's beneficiaries. The fact that certain of the trustees had a known conflict, however, did not disqualify them from the decision making.

U.S. decisions under the *Employee Retirement Income Security Act of 1974* (ERISA) are generally to the same effect. U.S. courts have explicitly approved of trustees "wearing two hats"—in other words, being both a trustee and representative of an employee or employer organization.[14]

Some U.S. courts have distinguished between conflicts that are minor and others that are so great "that it is virtually impossible for the fiduciary to discharge the duties with an eye single to the beneficiaries." In *Newton v. Van Otterloo,*[15] the court proposed the following three-pronged test for assessing breach-of-fiduciary obligation in relation to conflicts of interest:[16]

(1) whether the conflict of interest is so great that it is virtually impossible for the fiduciary to discharge the duties with an eye single to the beneficiaries, and

(2) if not, whether the fiduciary engaged in an intensive and independent investigation of options to ensure that the action taken was in the beneficiaries' best interest, and

(3) the extent to which the use of the trust's assets track the best interest of another party.

These cases are particularly useful because they refer to another technique whereby fiduciaries may protect themselves against allegations of conflict of interest. This is by obtaining expert advice, and acting upon it. In cases of potential conflict, third-party advice provides an independent basis upon which to justify the decision and to protect trustees from allegations of conflict. The duty to make independent investigation may rise to its highest standard where a trustee has dual loyalties.[17]

These decisions indicate that U.S. courts do not adopt a absolute prohibition against any conflicts of interest. To the contrary, they have explicitly accepted that pension plan trustees may wear two hats, and have also articulated tests with respect to conflicts of interest that distinguish between strong and weak conflicts, and contemplate reliance on third-party advice in the event of strong conflicts.

As noted above, most pension legislation adopts a "buck stops here" approach to plan governance. This is best reflected by provisions such as Section 19 of the Ontario *Pension Benefits Act:*

19(1) The administrator of a pension plan shall ensure that the pension plan and the pension fund are administered in accordance with this Act and the regulations.

(2) Subsection (1) applies whether or not the pension plan is amended to comply with this Act and the regulations.

(3) The administrator of a pension plan shall ensure that the pension plan and the pension fund are administered in accordance with,

(a) the filed documents in respect of which the Superintendent has issued an acknowledgement of application for registration or a certificate of registration, whichever is issued later; and

(b) the filed documents in respect of an application for registration of an amendment to the pension plan, if the application complies with this Act and the regulations and the amendment is not void under this Act.

(4) Subsection (3) does not apply to enable the administrator to administer the pension plan contrary to this Act and the regulations.[18]

Thus, Section 19 makes the administrator responsible for all aspects of the plan's compliance with PBA and its regulations, and all filed plan documents. Coupled with the administrator's fiduciary and conflict obligations, set out in Section 22, these provisions provide a simple but overarching obligation on the plan administrator to take responsibility for the proper administration of the plan and investment of the fund.

While both PBA and the common law of trusts require that a plan administrator and trustee take responsibility for the administration of the plan and the investment of the fund, neither precludes the administrator/trustee from delegating certain functions, or from relying on professional advice. Indeed, the applicable law requires plan administrators to do both. An important question in the governance of all pension plans, particularly jointly trusteed plans, is the extent to which lay trustees may rely on expert advice, or delegate technical matters, and the extent to which they are obligated to educate themselves about administrative and investment matters, and make administrative and investment decisions themselves. Put succinctly, to what extent does Section 19 of PBA, coupled with the fiduciary and conflict obligations imposed on administrators by the law of trusts and under Section 22, compel administrators to educate themselves to the point where they are making material decisions, and to what extent are trustees permitted to delegate decisions to experts, or rely upon their advice, in the administration of a plan and the management of a fund?

DELEGATION AND EXPERT ADVICE

Administrators of contemporary pension plans tend to rely heavily on expert advice, and also to delegate substantial decision making, on both the liability and asset sides, to employees and agents. To a great extent, this is a function of the size and complexity of contemporary pension trusts, and the general evolution of business practices.

Jointly governed plans are no different in these respects from corporate plans. However, unlike corporate plans, jointly governed plans tend not to rely on internal corporate resources for pension plan management and pension fund investment to nearly the same extent as may be the case in single employer plans. Rather, jointly governed arrangements will tend to rely more heavily on independent professional advisors, agents and employees. In general, reliance on independent expertise and independent agents and employees is an advantage, since it implies an ability to select freely from among third-party experts and agents. Jointly governed arrangements are typically not under any obligation to use the services of a corporate sponsor for plan administration or investment services.

Since the beginning of the 19th century, the common law has permitted trustees to delegate at least some of their functions. Prior to that time, equity prohibited trustees from delegating any of their duties whatsoever, on the theory that trustees had assumed personal responsibility for the administration of the trust and could not shift such responsibility onto anybody else. The demands of the commercial world steadily eroded this view, however, so that the common law restrictions on delegation in contemporary times are much weaker.[19]

Still, the common law retains some concerns over trustee delegation and continues to prefer that trustees execute the most important functions of their office personally. In this regard, courts have clearly been cognizant of common business practice and have been more inclined to permit delegation where it conforms to such practices. Delegation of functions that are commonly retained by trustees, however, risks censure by the courts. Courts have also refused to permit trustees to delegate duties that, on a fair construction of the trust's documentation, were intended by the settlor to be exercised personally by the particular trustee. This rule, however, is unlikely to be of particular application to pension trusts. Finally, accordingly to Waters, the courts have tended to insist that trustees make "policy" decisions personally. Waters defines *policy decisions* as follows:

> A policy decision is one which, if dispositive, determines how much and what time a beneficiary takes; if administrative, it directly affects the likelihood of the trust's object or purpose being achieved.[20]

Against this common law background, however, provincial legislatures enacted provisions similar to Sections 22(5), (7) and (8) of the Ontario *Pension Benefits Act*, which provide as follows:

22(5) Where it is reasonable and prudent in the circumstances so to do, the administrator of a pension plan may employ one or more agents to carry out any act required to be done in the administration of the pension plan and in the administration and investment of the pension fund.

(7) An administrator of a pension plan who employs an agent shall personally select the agent and be satisfied of the agent's suitability to perform the act for which the agent is employed, and the administrator shall carry out such supervision of the agent as is prudent and reasonable.

(8) An employee or agent of an administrator is also subject to the standards that apply to the administrator under subsections (1), (2) and (4).[21]

These provisions generally permit plan administrators to delegate "where it is reasonable and prudent in the circumstances so to do." This provides a broad statutory umbrella for the delegation of virtually any function, provided that such delegation is reasonable and prudent. By the same token, however, Section 22(7) requires that a pension plan administrator personally select the agent to which functions are being delegated, and further imposes upon the administrator an obligation to supervise and monitor the agent. Further, the agent is specifically made a fiduciary, and required to act in accordance with both branches of the standard of care stipulated in Sections 22(1) and (2), and to comply as well with the conflicts-of-interest rule contained in provincial legislation.

In the context of pension trusts, provincial legislation appears to have codified a relatively liberal rule with respect to delegation. No delegations are prohibited outright, even of "policy" decisions. Responsibilities are not divided into delegable and non-delegable functions. To the contrary, the wide drafting of Section 22(5) implies that virtually any function may be delegated, where such delegation is in the best interest of the beneficiaries.

Indeed, sections such as Ontario's Section 22(5) invite a functional approach to delegation. Is a function better performed by the trustees or by a delegate? Do the trustees have the expertise to perform the function, or is the expertise found in an employee or a professional agent? Are the trustees organized in such a way as to be responsive to the timeliness of required decision making, or is it necessary, in the context of financial and commercial decision making, to delegate time-sensitive decisions to persons or bodies that may be more responsive? If a given function requires a high level of expertise that the trustees do not have, or requires a level of responsiveness that the trustees are not able to administer, then it would seem reasonable and prudent to delegate that function to an agent or employee with expertise and the ability to respond in a timely way.

On the other hand, delegation is not without risk. Agents have their own interests and conflicting priorities. Agents and employees can be costly, and their costs, if not properly monitored, may tend to deplete the fund. Most important, the use of agents and employees does not relieve trustees of fiduciary responsibility; it merely shifts the trustees' responsibility away from performance of the actual function, to selecting and monitoring the agent. Accordingly, the use of agents and employees implies a trustee obligation to establish proper selection and supervision processes. The more complex the function performed by the agent or employee, the more difficult the supervision may be.

Especially as concerns policy decisions, administrators will often have a choice when it comes to delegation. In some circumstances, it may be appropriate for them to select an appropriate agent, delegate the decision to the agent and supervise the agent's performance. In other cases, however, it may be more appropriate for the trustees to seek independent expert advice and retain responsibility and authority for the decisions themselves.

The soliciting and taking of independent expert advice is almost always a positive indicator that trustees are fulfilling their fiduciary responsibilities. In this regard, U.S. courts have articulated an obligation of "independent inquiry" that is generally taken to require trustees to undertake the fullest investigation (including commissioning, receiving and considering expert advice) prior to making a decision. In this regard, however, U.S. courts have held that trustees cannot act upon expert advice without reflection. Although courts have stipulated that trustees need not become experts themselves in the subject matter of an expert report, they are responsible for reviewing the report, and considering the assumptions and information upon which it is based, and are also responsible for independently reviewing the report to determine that it is an appropriate basis upon which to base their actions. The mere receipt of an expert report will not exonerate trustees who act on the basis of its conclusions.[22]

To date, courts have not had the opportunity to comment as to when it is appropriate for pension administrators to rely on expert advice and retain responsibility and authority for important decisions themselves, and when it is appropriate for trustees to select an expert agent, delegate the decision to the expert and supervise the expert in an appropriate way. PBA does not offer much guidance in regard to this issue either, as it permits delegation of any function. The wide drafting of PBA's delegation provisions suggests, however, that a functional approach to this issue is appropriate. Functions that are better performed by agents and employees should be delegated, subject to proper selection and supervision processes. On the other hand, where the best interests of plan members are best served by the trustees retaining responsibility for informed decisions, then delegation may not be appropriate.

CONCLUSION

The regulatory environment for pension plans is changing. This will imply a lesser degree of oversight by an informed authority with respect to pension plan administration. In turn, this will renew the focus on appropriate plan governance. The removal of a regulatory authority as a "check" or a "balance" on a plan administrator suggests that other checks and balances should be examined.

Jointly governed plans provide one way of introducing checks and balances into the pension plan governance process. Joint governance, under which a pension plan is governed by a board appointed equally by the employer sponsor and the members or their trade union, creates an internal balance, and may give confidence to the membership that the plan is being appropriately governed.

Jointly governed plans generally imply a sharing of the risks and rewards of pension funding. As reviewed in Chapter 2, there are a number of models under which gains and losses are shared in the private, public and broader public sectors, all of which provide useful precedents for this type of arrangement. PBA also well accommodates joint governance in its current form, by establishing a fiduciary, conflicts and delegation regime that is well suited to jointly governed boards.

ENDNOTES

1. See *Employment Pension Plans Act*, S.A. 1986, c. E.10.05 as am, s. 5 (EPPA); *Pension Benefits Act*, S.N.B. 1987, c. P-5.1 as am, s. 9(1)(e) (NBPBA); *Pension Benefits Act*, R.S.O. 1990, c. P.8 as am, s. 8(1)(e) (OPBA). See also *CUPE v. Ontario Hospital Association* (1992), 91 D.L.R. (4th) 436 (Ont. Div. Ct.).

2. OPBA, *supra* note 1, s. 22.

3. See EPPA, *supra* note 1, s. 41; *Pension Benefits Standards Act*, R.S.B.C. 1996, c. 352 as am, s. 44 (BCPBSA); *Pension Benefits Act*, R.S.M. 1987, c. P32 as am, s. 28.1 (MPBA); NBPBA, *supra* note 1, ss. 17 and 18; *Pension Benefits Act*, R.S.N.S. 1989, c. 340 as am, ss. 29(1)-29(2) (NSPBA); *Pension Benefits Act*, S.P.E.I., 1990, c.41 as am, ss. 28(1) and 28(2) (PEIPBA); *Supplemental Pension Plans Act*, R.S.Q. c. R-15.1 as am, s. 151 (SPPA).

4. OPBA, *supra* note 1, s. 22(4). See also BCPBSA, *supra* note 3, s. 9(5); MPBA, *supra* note 3, s. 28.1(5); NBPBA, *supra* note 1, s. 17(3); NSPBA, *supra* note 3, s. 29(3); PEIPBA, *supra* note 3, s. 28(3); SPPA, *supra* note 3, s. 158.

5. See *Schmidt v. Air Products Canada Ltd.*, [1994] 2 S.C.R. 611 at p. 654; *Cowan v. Scargill*, [1984] 2 All E.R. 750 (Ch. D.).

6. *Fales v. Canada Permanent Trust Company* (1976), 70 D.L.R. (2d) 257 (S.C.C.), at p. 268.

7. *Fales, supra* note 6 at p. 268.

8. *Fales, supra* note 6 at p. 268.

9. Dona Campbell, "Investment Responsibility of Benefit Fund Trustees," (1993) 12 *Estates and Trusts Journal* 309 at p. 311.

10. See NBPBA, *supra* note 1, s. 9; NSPBA, *supra* note 3, s. 14; PEIPBA, *supra* note 3, s. 13.

11. See EPPA, *supra* note 1, s. 5; BCPBSA, *supra* note 3, s. 7; NBPBA, *supra* note 1, s. 9(1)(e); *Pension Benefits Act*, 1997, S.N. 1996, c. P-4.01 as am, s. 13 (NPBA); NSPBA, *supra* note 3, s. 14(1)(e); OPBA, *supra* note 1, s. 8(1)(e); PEIPBA, *supra* note 3, s. 14(1)(e).

12. *Cowan v. Scargill, supra* note 5.

13. *Cowan v. Scargill, supra* note 5 at p. 754.

14. *Evans v. Bexley*, 6 EBC 1418 (11th Cir., 1985).

15. *Newton v. Van Otterloo*, 13 EBC 1532 (Dis. Indiana, 1991).

16. *Struble v. New Jersey Brewery Employees' Welfare Fund*, 5 EBC 1676 (3rd Cir., 1984).

17. *Donovan v. Bierworth*, 3 EBC 1417 (2d Cir. 1982).

18. OPBA, *supra* note 1, s. 19. See also EPPA, *supra* note 1, s. 6; BCPBSA, *supra* note 3, s. 8; NBPBA, *supra* note 1, s. 14; NSPBA, *supra* note 3, s. 26; PEIPBA, *supra* note 3, s. 25; *Pension Benefits Act*, 1992, S.S. 1992, c. P-6.001 as am, s. 11.

19. D.W. Waters, *Law of Trusts in Canada*, 2nd Edition, (Toronto: The Carswell Company Ltd., 1984) p. 696.

20. Waters, *supra* note 19, p. 707.

21. OPBA, *supra* note 1, ss. 22(5), 22(7) and 22(8). See also BCPBSA, *supra* note 3, ss. 9(7)-9(9); MPBA, *supra* note 3, ss. 28.1(6)-28.1(8); NBPBA, *supra* note 1, s. 18; NSPBA, *supra* note 3, ss. 29(4)-29(8); PEIPBA, *supra* note 3, ss. 28(4)-28(6) and 28(8); SPPA, *supra* note 3, ss. 152-155.

22. See *Whitfield v. Cohen*, 782 F.Supp. 188 (S.D.N.Y.) at p. 193; *Wagner v. Van Cleeff* (1991), 5 O.R. (3d) 477 (Div. Ct.); *Linsley v. Kirstiuk* (1986), 28 D.L.R. (4th) 495 (B.C.S.C.).

CHAPTER 1

The Shift From Defined Benefit to Employee-Directed Defined Contribution Plans

by Raymond Koskie, Roberto Tomassini and Frank Aiello

INTRODUCTION

The primary focus of Section VI is an examination of the potential fiduciary responsibility of plan sponsors, administrators and plan advisors, in the context of non-regulated retirement benefit plans in Canada. By *non-regulated retirement schemes* we refer to the *money purchase arrangements* or *defined contribution plans* including group registered retirement savings plans (group RRSPs) (also referred to as *individual account plans,* particularly in the United States) that are, generally speaking, not subject to provincial or federal pension legislation.

The need for such an examination is twofold:

- In recent years, there has been a proliferation of non-regulated retirement arrangements, of the defined contribution variety, and a consequent decline in highly regulated defined benefit plans.
- Concern over security of retirement monies invested in these retirement vehicles is acute due to the high-profile collapse of a large financial institution that was once secure across North America. In Canada, the collapse of the Confederation Life Insurance Company (Confed) was a watershed event. It has prompted some serious examination by plan sponsors and their advisors of their responsibility and potential liability when maintaining non-regulated plans.

THE CHANGING RETIREMENT MARKET

During the period between 1983 and 1993, the percentage of employed individuals in Canada contributing to RRSPs (non-regulated, individual account retirement arrangements) almost doubled from 18% to 35%.[1] From 1987 to 1997, RRSP contributions increased by 138%.[2] On the other hand, the number of registered, highly regulated pension plans dropped 28% between 1988 and 1998.[3] Contributions to registered pension plans (RPPs) amounted to $19.6 billion in 1997. Total RRSP contributions in 1997 were just over $27 billion.[4]

Since 1995, RRSP contributions have surpassed RPPs, making RRSPs the most important form of retirement savings for Canadians in terms of both contributors and contributions.[5]

Even among RPPs, defined contribution plans comprised almost 53% of all RPPs in Canada. However, these plans only accounted for 12.5% of all RPP members in Canada. While the proportion covered by defined contribution plans continues to be relatively low, their numbers have increased steadily. Between 1996 and 1998, the number of defined contribution plan members grew by close to 20%.[6]

Although defined benefit plans are still predominant for larger employers, the shift to defined contribution plans and group RRSPs is significant. In particular, many employers with small numbers of employees are shifting to group RRSPs.

There is some empirical evidence supporting the belief that many employers are converting their defined benefit plans to defined contribution plans. Statistics Canada in its 1996 data on plan terminations indicated that there have been a significant number of conversions from defined benefit to defined contribution plans.[7]

A small survey in 1994 of 223 plans found that of the new money purchase plans put in place in the last five years, 40% were the result of a conversion of an existing defined benefit plan to a defined contribution plan.[8] In addition, many employers that administer a registered pension plan for their employees are also offering group RRSPs in addition to the registered plans. One survey of 242 organizations found that almost 50% of them provided a group RRSP for their employees.[9]

What's Wrong With Defined Benefit Plans?

The shift in the retirement scheme market is attributable to several factors:

- Most commentators suggest that the primary catalyst is the onerous legislative and regulatory requirements for defined benefit and other RPPs in Canada under both federal and provincial pension legislation, as well as income tax legislation. In stark contrast, group RRSPs fall outside the scope of both federal and provincial pension legislation.

- RPPs, of the defined benefit type, require plan sponsors to guarantee the pension benefits that may lead to additional payments and costs not originally contemplated when the plan was established.

- On the flip side, disputes over surplus ownership due to conservative actuarial assumption, or better than expected earnings experience, are now commonplace in Canada, and costly. Moreover, Canadian courts have been inclined to apply traditional trust law principles in awarding surplus ownership to employees.

- The risk of acquiring significant unfunded liabilities in a defined benefit plan also complicates mergers and acquisitions, therefore, making businesses less attractive to potential purchasers and investors, and making it more expensive for potential buyers to conduct due diligence searches for target companies.

- Not to be overlooked is the increasing popularity of mutual funds and the desire of many employees to manage their own retirement savings. Greater control means employees can structure their investment portfolio to reflect their personal circumstances and needs using their own risk-return profile.

The Allure of Money Purchase Plans

Money purchase or individual account retirement schemes, particularly the non-registered variety such as group RRSPs, hold the allure of:

- An unregulated, or less regulated, environment
- Much reduced administrative costs
- Eliminating the need to consult actuaries and
- The possibility of avoiding the fiduciary liability traps that exists with defined benefit plans.

However, plan sponsors and their advisors in Canada are best advised to be sensitive to potential fiduciary liabilities that the common law may impose in connection with the administration of group RRSPs and other non-regulated retirement plans, particularly where the defined contribution scheme includes the ability for employees to select investment options from a range of available options. Because of the many and varied investment options available to choose from, sponsors and their advisors must be sensitive to the balance between offering employees a sufficiently broad range of investments and the risk of potential liability for being negligent and exposing employees to highly speculative investment alternatives. This, of course, underscores the need for professional and competent advisors for plan sponsors and, in particular, investment expertise.

MORE LITIGATION?

The shift to money purchase arrangements, particularly non-regulated individual account schemes such as group RRSPs, is likely to engender more disputes and litigation, and consequently even greater scrutiny of the conduct of sponsors and their advisors in relation to plan administration and investments. In the defined benefit regime, the benefit payable to a member is calculated by a fixed formula, which leaves little or no room for dispute between the participant and the sponsor. Moreover, the employer bears the risk of poor investment performance or inaccurate actuarial assumptions.

However, the uncertainty of benefit levels in money purchase arrangements may increase the likelihood of such disputes where members are dissatisfied with the level of their benefits. These disputes will most likely focus on:

- Poor investment performance
- Investment losses
- Poor selection and monitoring of fund carriers and trustees and
- Insufficient or improper communication with participants regarding the risks associated with any investment.

Sponsors' fiduciary responsibilities, and the role of

their advisors, may become even more significant in this new retirement benefits market.

Editor's note: This section was originally presented as a booklet for the Investment Management Consultants Association, "Investment Fiduciary Responsibilities in the 1990's: A Practical Guide for Sponsors and Investment Advisors of Individual Account Retirement Plans" (October, 1996). It has been modified and updated for this book.

ENDNOTES

1. Statistics Canada, "Canada's Retirement Income Programs: A Statistical Overview" (1996) Catalogue No. 74-507-XPB.

2. Statistics Canada, "Pension Plans in Canada" (1997) Catalogue No. 74-401-XPB, at p. 10.

3. *Ibid.,* at p. 36.

4. *Ibid.,* at p. 11.

5. *Ibid.*

6. *Ibid.,* at p. 35.

7. Statistics Canada, "Retirement Savings Through RPPs and RRSPs 1991 to 1993" (1996) Catalogue No. 75-001-XPE.

8. University of Western Ontario and The Financial Executive Institute of Canada, "Survey of Pension Plans in Canada" 10th ed. (1994).

9. KPMG, "1995/1996 Annual Salary Survey, General Employment Practices Report" (1995), pp. 53-54.

CHAPTER 2

The Regulatory Environment: Does One Exist?

by Raymond Koskie, Roberto Tomassini and Frank Aiello

PENSION LEGISLATION IN CANADA

Generally speaking, whether a retirement plan is subject to pension legislation in Canada is determined by who is responsible for making the contributions to fund the retirement scheme. In Ontario, for example, pension plans that are not subject to the onerous regulations and administrative requirements of the *Pension Benefits Act* (PBA) include:

- An employee's *profit-sharing plan* or a *deferred profit-sharing plan (DPSP)* as those terms are defined by the *Income Tax Act* (ITA)
- A plan to provide a *retiring allowance* as defined by the ITA and
- A plan under which all benefits are provided by members' contributions.[1]

Therefore, defined contribution plans funded, in whole or in part, by employer contributions are still subject to the legislative requirements of provincial and federal pension legislation. The federal legislation has a similar exclusion, with one minor variation in that it includes supplemental pension plans whose membership eligibility is contingent upon mandatory membership in another pension plan and the supplemental plan is an integral part of the other plan.[2]

GROUP REGISTERED RETIREMENT SAVINGS PLANS (GROUP RRSPs)

Pension Legislation

Group RRSPs largely fall outside the scope of the legislative environment. In fact, even where employer contributions are made on behalf of participants in group RRSPs, the ITA deems the contributions to be employment income and therefore employee contributions when remitted to the RRSP. Therefore, they are not included within the meaning of *pension plans* contained in most pension legislation in Canada that is similar to the definition referred to above in the Ontario PBA. In fact, in some provinces, such as British Columbia and Saskatchewan, pension regulations specifically exclude RRSPs from the definition of *pension plan* and, therefore, explicitly remove these types of plans from the scope of their pension legislation.[3]

The one exception to the general rule across Canada that group RRSPs are not governed by pension benefits legislation was in the province of New Brunswick. In 1997, the Superintendent of Pensions for New Brunswick determined that group RRSPs did in fact meet the definition of a *pension plan* under the New Brunswick pension statute, where an employer made contributions to the plan on behalf of its employees. The Superintendent's position was that the federal ITA could not shield a group RRSP from the requirements of provincial pension legislation, unless the requirements of the New Brunswick *Pension Benefits Act* prevented compliance with the ITA. In the case of group RRSPs, this was clearly not the case.

As such, the Superintendent ordered the Saint John Shipbuilding company to register its group RRSP plan. Upon refusal to comply, the Superintendent ruled that the company was in violation of the New Brunswick PBA.[4] The decision was in fact affirmed by the New Brunswick Labour and Employment Board.[5]

No other pension regulator has followed this decision and interpreted its pension legislation to include group RRSPs. The decision is unlikely to have a significant impact on the regulation of RRSPs. In fact, following the decision of the New Brunswick Labour and Employment Board in the *Saint John Shipbuilding* case, the New Brunswick government amended the *Pension Benefits Regulations* to specifically exempt group RRSPs from the application of the New Brunswick PBA.[6]

The Income Tax Act (ITA)

Although these retirement schemes are not subject to provincial or federal pension legislation, they are registered under the federal ITA. The ITA does prescribe some restrictions concerning fund investment to avoid tax penalties to the annuitant. The ITA requires that RRSPs must invest in "qualified investments" only. *Qualified investments* are defined in the ITA and include:
- Shares of public corporations
- Units of mutual fund trusts
- Interest in a trust or share capital stock of a corporation that is a "registered investment"
- Guaranteed investment certificates (GICs).[7]

The ITA also imposes foreign content rules on group RRSPs, limiting the amount of funds invested in foreign property to 20% of the total cost for tax purposes of the RRSP properties. This limit was increased to 30% by the federal government in its 2000 budget.[8]

RPP vs. Group RRSP: Regulatory Requirements

Unlike provincial RPPs, there are no legislated requirements on the sponsors of group RRSPs to file annual information returns and financial statements. There are no requirements to prepare and file periodic actuarial reports. Group RRSP sponsors do not pay any insurance fund fees. There are no "super-vesting" or other wind-up liabilities applicable to group RRSPs. As well, the group RRSP administrator enjoys relatively less onerous investment guidelines or requirements to prepare detailed investment policies, as imposed on registered plan administrators.

Perhaps most significant is the absence of legislatively imposed standards of conduct and duty of care on plan sponsors, administrators and their professional consultants. Provincial and federal pension legislation generally imposes fiduciary standards of conduct on these persons for RPPs. Typically, the legislation requires these players to:

Exercise the care, diligence and skill in the administration and investment of the pension fund that a person of ordinary prudence would exercise in dealing with the property of another person.[9]

While the non-regulated environment may attract many employers seeking to avoid the costs and statutory liability associated with RPPs, they may encounter unknown fiduciary pitfalls as group RRSP sponsors imposed on them by courts pursuant to common law principles. The application of fiduciary principles to group RRSP sponsors is discussed in detail in Chapter 3 in this section.

The lack of legislated requirements associated with these plans means little guidance for sponsors and advisors on avoiding such pitfalls. Legal advisors in Canada look to fiduciary common law principles and attempt to apply them to the non-regulated retirement regime when advising sponsors.

U.S. LEGISLATION

The Canadian regulatory environment stands in stark contrast with the American legislative framework for similar retirement arrangements under the *Employee Retirement Income Security Act of 1974* (ERISA).[10] Plan sponsors and other traditional plan fiduciaries are, generally speaking, subject to the same fiduciary requirements as plan sponsors, administrators and advisors under Section 4.04 of ERISA. However, the American Congress has recognized that, where effective control over retirement fund investment remains with the employees, traditional fiduciaries may be exempt from ERISA fiduciary standards and liabilities by virtue of the Section 404(c) "safe harbour" provision.

The section contemplates exemption from fiduciary liability for administrators or sponsors of individual account plans where the plan permits a participant or beneficiary to exercise control over his or her account and a loss results from the exercise by the participant of that control.

Detailed regulations set the standards to be met by sponsors wishing to take advantage of the 404(c) safe harbour. These regulations deal primarily with the conditions that must exist in order for a participant to have effective control over the assets. The regulations deal with the factors associated with the participant's opportunity to give investment instructions, the availability of adequate investment alternatives to make that control meaningful and the requirement that the participant be provided with sufficient information, or an opportunity to obtain such information, to make informed decisions regarding the investment options.[11]

Presently, no similar requirements exist in Canada for individual account plans. However, as in the area of pension regulation generally, Canadian sponsors and advisors often look to, and are guided by, the American regulatory experience. Moreover, the increase of group RRSPs will inevitably lead to a call for more regulation, which may mirror, in many respects, the American legislative scheme. In fact, in 1989 a report of an Ontario Task Force recommended that employer-sponsored group RRSPs, if not supplementary to a substantial pension plan, be covered by provincial pension legislation.[12]

CANADIAN SECURITIES LEGISLATION

Defined contribution and group RRSPs largely fall outside of the scope of Canadian securities legislation. Some commentators have called for legislative or regulatory extension of securities law and policy to these types of retirement plans, particularly where they incorporate employee-directed investment features.[13] The argument focuses on the vulnerability of individuals dependent on these types of plans for retirement savings. It is argued that this combination of vulnerability and dependence demands the protective devices of securities legislation with respect to information disclosure and investor education. Moreover, given the vast pools of monies in these plans that are not subject to regulatory scrutiny, a strong potential is created for abuses such as self-dealing, fraud and negligence.[14]

The current problem is that to the extent that these plans offer investment choices to the participants to direct their contributions to pooled funds or mutual funds offered by insurance companies, trust companies and banks, they may be exempt from the registration and prospectus requirements of securities legislation. The Ontario legislation, for example, exempts the largest providers of these types of plans—licensed insurance companies, registered trust companies and banks—from registration requirements, except in respect of mutual funds.

The exemption from registration deprives plan participants of significant protections offered to other investors, such as unit holders of publicly traded mutual funds. For example, in Ontario unit holders in a registered vehicle would benefit from the following protections:

- They must receive a prospectus by the end of the second business day after their first purchase of units of a mutual fund.
- The prospectus is required to contain full, true and plain disclosure of all material facts relating to the fund.
- They have the opportunity to rescind the purchase two days after receiving the prospectus.
- Unit holders receive annual and semi-annual financial statements of the fund.
- Purchases are made through a dealer who is registered under the legislation and has a statutory mandate to know and service the needs and objectives of each investor.

- The dealer has to meet standards of knowledge and expertise, and integrity, to become registered.
- There is public notice of any material change in the fund that may influence the unit holder's investment decision.

Accordingly, the absence of a regulatory regime applicable to employee-directed defined contribution plans, in both the pension law and securities law regime, renders the participants vulnerable to the actions of their employer/sponsors and their advisors. The participant is dependent on the employer's ability to offer a selection of funds that are appropriately diversified, and appropriately monitored, and to make adequate information available to members so that they can make informed choices. There is, however, no statutory regime in place that ensures that the sponsor and its advisors perform these obligations in accordance with a standard that is commensurate with the importance of the funds to the participant's financial security in retirement.

As discussed in the next chapter, the absence or paucity of statutory restrictions applicable to defined contribution plans does not mean that participants are entirely without legal protection. Where there are gaps in the statutory regime, the common law fills the void. The next chapter discusses the application of the common law in the context of defined contribution plans.

ENDNOTES

1. Ontario *Pension Benefits Act,* R.S.O. 1990, c. P.8, s. 1.
2. *Pension Benefits Standards Act,* 1985, R.S.C. 1985, c.32, subsections 4(2)(3).
3. British Columbia *Pension Benefits Standards Regulation,* B.C. Reg. 433/93, s.2(2); Saskatchewan *Pension Benefits Regulations,* S.P.B. Reg. 1993, c. P-6.001, as am. by Sask. Reg. 60/97, s. 3(2).
4. In the Matter of Saint John Shipbuilding Ltd.—Hourly Employees Group Retirement Savings Program (unreported decision of the Superintendent of Pensions, March 6, 1997).
5. *Re Saint John Shipbuilding Ltd. v. The Superintendent of Pensions and International Brotherhood of Electrical Workers, Local 2282* (unreported decision of the New Brunswick Labour and Employment Board, PA-003-97, released on January 19, 1999).
6. New Brunswick *Pension Benefits Regulation,* N.B. Reg. 91-195, as am. by N.B. Reg. 99-9, s.2.1.
7. *Income Tax Act,* R.S.C. 1985, c. 1 (5th Supp.), as am, s. 146(g).
8. Finance Canada, "Budget 2000" (28 February 2000).
9. *Supra* note 1, s. 22.
10. *Employee Retirement Income Security Act of 1974,* 29 U.S.C.A. §1001 (1974).
11. Pension and Welfare Benefits Administration, Department of Labor, Rules and Regulations for Fiduciary Responsibility: ERISA Section 404(c) plans, 29 CFR §2550.404c-1 (1992). Available at www.dol.gov/dol/allcfr/PWBA.

12. Report of the Task Force on Inflation Protection for Employment Pension Plans (Ontario: January 1988) at pp. 224-228.

13. See for example G. Stromberg, *Regulatory Strategies for the Mid-90's: Recommendation for Regulating Investment Funds in Canada, January 1995* (Queen's Printer for Ontario, 1995) at pp. 33-42; and Priscilla Healy, "Unstacking the Deck: The Application of Securities Law to Money Purchase Plans" (Canadian Bar Association-Ontario, 1997 Institute of Continuing Legal Education, *Money Purchase Plans: Transferring Risk or Risky Business?*, Royal York Hotel, Toronto, 30 January, 1997).

14. Priscilla Healy, "Unstacking the Deck: The Application of Securities Law to Money Purchase Plans," *supra,* at p. 2.

CHAPTER 3

Fiduciary Duties in Defined Contribution Plans

by Raymond Koskie, Roberto Tomassini and Frank Aiello

In addition to any legislated standards, and in the absence of other standards, retirement plan sponsors and their advisor are subject to judicially developed standards of conduct at common law. A legal duty, standards of care and liability to plan participants, may flow from:
- Express or implied terms of the contractual arrangements with their clients
- Negligence, including negligent misrepresentation and
- Breach of fiduciary duty.

We will focus below on potential fiduciary liabilities imposed by the common law on plan sponsors and their advisors in the non-regulated retirement scheme market.

WHAT AND WHO IS A FIDUCIARY?

The term *fiduciary* comes from the Latin *fiducia,* meaning trust or confidence. In law, a person in whom trust or confidence is reposed is termed a *fiduciary* and is impressed with a duty of loyalty to those placing their trust in him or her.[1]

Whether particular persons or institutions can be labeled with the term *fiduciary* depends on whether or not their behaviour, in law, constitutes the reposing of trust or confidence in them. In the context of group registered retirement savings plans (group RRSPs), a court would consider whether or not the participants reasonably placed their trust and confidence in the sponsors and their consultants in a manner that should attract liability where they breached the confidence or trust.

Where fiduciary duties and responsibilities are visited upon individuals, the common law imposes upon the fiduciary a standard of conduct that is the highest known to law. The duty of the fiduciary is to act exclusively and in the best interests of those to whom the duty is owed and, at a minimum, to carry out his or her responsibilities with a degree of diligence in the execution of his or her office that a person of ordinary prudence would exercise in the management of his or her own affairs.[2]

These fiduciary duties may attach to a person or relationship in one of three ways:
- Legislation may explicitly impose fiduciary duties on individuals who may or may not have a fiduciary character at common law.
- Where a person occupies a role or office that has been recognized at common law as fiduciary, such as a trustee
- The common law may impose upon some persons, in some circumstances, fiduciary duties even where those person do not belong to a recognized category of fiduciaries.

As noted in Chapter 2, there are no specific legislated standards of conduct imposed upon sponsors or advisors in connection with non-registered retirement vehicles such as group RRSPs. For registered pension plans (RPPs), almost every jurisdiction in Canada now has legislative provisions explicitly imposing upon sponsors, administrators, agents and professional advisors fiduciary-like standards of conduct.[3]

For defined contribution plans that are registered and subject to provincial or federal pension legislation, this statutorily imposed duty applies to plan administrators and their advisors. However, the substantive provisions of pension legislation in Canada is primarily concerned with the administration of defined benefit plans. There are few provisions that assist sponsors and advisors of registered defined contribution plans in fulfilling their fiduciary duties.

As noted in Chapter 2, for non-registered defined contribution plans, such as group RRSPs, legislated standards of conduct do not apply. Absent legislative imposition of these duties, the common law may impress the sponsors and advisors of non-registered retirement vehicles with the fiduciary label.

There are presently no judicial authorities in Canada that deal directly with the issue of whether or not a sponsor of a group RRSP owes to its employees a fiduciary duty with respect to the administration of the plan. However, it should be noted that in one case the sponsor of a group RRSP and deferred profit-sharing plan (DPSP) was held liable for damages where it made a representation to employees that their entitlements would be calculated in a manner that was contrary to the plan terms.[4] Liability in that case was based on contractual principles and, therefore, no consideration was given to the sponsor's potential fiduciary duties.

IS THERE AN AGENCY RELATIONSHIP?

An agency relationship is one of those relationships such as trustee and beneficiary, partners, directors and shareholders, recognized at common law as the type of relationship to which the fiduciary label attaches. Generally speaking, where one individual undertakes to act on behalf of another who consents to that individual so acting, then an agency relationship arises. Where an agency is created, fiduciary duties are imposed upon the agent, which broadly speaking, refers to the duty of utmost good faith and fidelity owed to the agent's principal.

Agency law may be significant in the group RRSP context because the sponsor acts as the agent of the employees for the purposes of the plan. The agency relationship is imposed by Revenue Canada as a condition of registration.[5] The agency relationship is typically a term of the contract or trust document between the sponsor and the investment carrier. The appointment of the sponsor as the employees' agent is usually found in the application for participation in the plan completed by each employee.

The extent of the sponsor's fiduciary duties to its employees depends in part upon the scope of the agency relationship established. A sponsor may legitimately argue that it is simply a facilitator and only undertakes to deduct member contributions from their pay and forward them to the administrator, and perhaps fulfil other minor administrative roles, such as forwarding investment statements to the employees. Where a sponsor assumes a limited role in the operation of the plan, it may be difficult for aggrieved participants to establish that their trust or confidence reposed in the sponsor would attract fiduciary obligations.

Therefore, the scope of the sponsor's agency role is important when considering whether or not the sponsor has fiduciary obligations as an agent. The scope of the agency may be explicitly defined in the plan documents or in express contracts between employer and employee. However, often the scope of the agency is not made explicit and is, therefore, determined only with regard to the circumstances of a particular relationship. In this regard, it is necessary to consider the role and responsibilities assumed by the sponsor.

Where the sponsor:

- Is exclusively responsible for selecting the investment vehicles, investment options, insurance carriers, trustees
- Unilaterally negotiates the terms of the plan and contract with third-party providers
- Undertakes to provide the participants with information regarding the plan and the investment alternatives
- Prepared the application forms to be completed by the participants and
- Actively encouraged members to participate in the plan

then the scope of the agency and, hence, the fiduciary duty of the sponsor may be unrestricted.

One of the central features of the agent's duty is the obligation to disclose "all material information upon which the principal may make informed decisions regarding agency matters." The nature of this duty has been described by one Canadian appellate court as follows:

In my opinion, the trial judge's interpretation of the obligation owed to a principal by its agent is too restrictive. The duty of disclosure is not confined to those instances where the agent has gained an advantage in the transaction or where the information might affect the value of the property, or where a conflict of interest exists. The agent certainly has a duty of full disclosure in such circumstances; they are commonly occurring circumstances that require full disclosure by the agent. However, they are not exhaustive.

The obligation of the agent to make full disclosure extends beyond these three categories and include "everything known to him respecting the subject matter of the contract which would be likely to influence the conduct of his principals" or, everything which ". . . would be likely to operate upon the principal's judgement." In such cases, the agent's failure to inform the principal would be material non-disclosure.[6]

In *Metropolitan Toronto Pension Plan v. Aetna Life Assurance Co. of Canada,*[7] the trustees of a pension and benefits plan brought an action for breach of fiduciary duty against Aetna, which undertook investment administration responsibilities for the trustees. The contract with Aetna specifically provided that investments were to be in accordance with a guideline and schedule of acceptable loan investments. The insurance company submitted to the trustees for their consideration a mortgage loan that did not fall within the investment guidelines and did not bring this fact to the trustees' attention.

The investment at issue was a mortgage loan on a seniors' building that, due to flagrant mismanagement, had deteriorated to a point that the entire building had to be gutted, and the occupancy dropped to zero despite waiting lists of seniors for positions in the building. In holding that the insurance company breached its fiduciary duty to the trustees, the court noted that Aetna failed to properly investigate the investment and monitor the state of the security. In addition, the court also found that Aetna, acting as agent for the trustees, failed in its duty to disclose the fact that the investment was not in compliance with the prescribed guidelines and the full extent of the building's deterioration and the vacancy problem.

The agency characterization and the disclosure obligation raises a number of potential areas of responsibility and liabilities for sponsors in the administration of non-registered pension plans. For example, where an employer offers as an investment option guaranteed investment certificates (GICs) with one particular institution, and the sponsor or its advisors become aware of financial difficulties being suffered by that institution, the agency relationship arguably requires the sponsor and/or its advisor to disclose the fact to the plan participants, as it is clearly information that is material to their decision to remain or participate further in the plan.

In Canada, GICs with life insurance companies have the benefit of limited insurance coverage by an industry established compensation fund. The extent of the coverage is up to $60,000. Over and above this amount, the annuitant faces a risk of loss. Based on agency law, and the duty of disclosure alone, participants who suffer a loss may bring breach-of-fiduciary-duty actions against their employer for failure to provide information that is material to their ability to assess the risks associated with their investments.

As it may be the a plan advisor or custodian who has or may be the source of the material information regarding plan investments, they bear a special burden to advise the sponsors of such information and should be sensitive to their client's obligation to communicate such information to the participants.

IS THERE AN IMPLIED FIDUCIARY DUTY AT COMMON LAW?

Apart from the legally recognized categories such as trustees and agents, the common law will impose fiduciary duties upon certain individuals due to the nature of the relationship. As noted by the Supreme Court of Canada:

It is the nature of the relationship, not the specific category of the actors involved that gives rise to the fiduciary duty. The categories of fiduciary, like those of negligence, should not be considered closed.[8]

Fiduciary relationships have generally been held to exist

whenever any person acquires a power of any type on condition that he also receives with it a duty to utilize the power in the best interests of another and the recipient of that power uses the power.[9]

The elements of fiduciary relationships have been considered in a number of Supreme Court of Canada decisions, including *International Corona Resources Limited v. LAC Minerals Limited,*[10] *Frame v. Smith*[11] and most recently in *Hodgkinson v. Simms.*[12] In summary, these cases hold that to establish that an individual owes a fiduciary obligation to another as a result of the nature of the relationship, a court must be satisfied that:

- One party had the scope for the exercise of some discretion or power.
- That party could unilaterally exercise the power or discretion in a way that affected the other's legal or financial interests.
- The other party was vulnerable to being harmed by an improper exercise of this discretion or power and
- The other party actually relied on the holder of the discretion or power with respect to that exercise of discretion or power.

With respect to the first of these requirements, it may not be difficult to establish in most cases that the sponsor of a group RRSP has the scope for the exercise of some discretion and that the sponsor exercises the discretion in ways that can significantly impact upon the participants' legal and financial interests. Sponsors normally retain the discretion and power as follows:

- With respect to the investment options available to the participants
- The terms of the investment vehicles selected
- The choice of the administrator or trustees responsible for these funds
- The ability to unilaterally terminate the group RRSP and
- The exclusive power to replace existing administrators and trustees.

Participants usually play no role in establishing the terms of the plan, yet are subject to and are at the mercy of these sponsors' discretionary powers.

Similarly, for typical group RRSP arrangements it is not difficult to establish that the participants are vulnerable to being harmed by the improper exercise of the sponsors' discretion. A poor choice of administrators or investment options or investment vehicles can clearly have negative repercussions for the participants. As well, an inappropriate decision to terminate or not terminate a particular contract with a particular provider could have material adverse effects on plan members.

The final element necessary to establish a fiduciary relationship is that the participants actually relied on the sponsors when making investment decisions. This is perhaps the most problematic aspect in determining whether or not a sponsor is a fiduciary, and it largely depends upon the facts of each particular case. Typically, however, sponsors actively encourage their employees to participate in their group RRSP arrangements. In fact, in some circumstances participation may be mandatory. Where the sponsors are sophisticated and have extensive resources to select investment options, negotiate terms of the investment contracts and monitor the stability of those investments, it may be easier to establish reliance.

Also significant in this regard are the steps that a sponsor takes to caution or warn participants that the risk of loss is theirs, and that they should undertake to analyze the prudence of any investment they make, which may include obtaining independent advisors. Generally, a court may ask whether, in the circumstances of the particular case, the sponsor knew, or ought to have known, that its employees would reasonably rely on the company to safeguard their interest vis-à-vis their investment in the retirement savings arrangement.

The issue of reliance may also turn upon the particular terms of the investment options made available to the employees. Where employees are free to withdraw funds from certain investment options without restriction and have a broad range of diverse investment options available, then the argument in favour of employee reliance carries less weight. In these circumstances, it would be harder to establish that the participants' reliance on the sponsor led to the loss if it can be established that the loss would have been avoided if the participant had exercised an option to withdraw or transfer funds out of the impugned investment.

ARE ADVISORS EXPOSED TO FIDUCIARY LIABILITY?

As is the case with sponsors, there is no Canadian judicial precedent regarding the fiduciary responsibilities or liabilities of advisors, such as investment consultants, with respect to services provided in connection with group RRSP administration and investment. There is, however, a fairly developed jurisprudence regarding fiduciary duties of professional advisors in general, which may guide the consultant in the non-regulated pension field.

The most significant Canadian judicial pronouncement is the fairly recent Supreme Court of Canada decision in *Hodgkinson v. Simms*.[13] This decision deals with fiduciary responsibilities in general and, in particular, in the professional advisor context.

In the *Simms* case, Hodgkinson retained the services of Simms, a chartered accountant who held himself out as an expert in real estate tax shelters. In particular, he professed a particular competence with respect to investments in multi-unit residential buildings (MURBs) for tax planning and sheltering purposes. Hodgkinson put himself in Simms' hands with respect to his tax planning and investment needs. In the course of their relationship, Simms recommended four MURB projects to Hodgkinson in which he invested. However, Simms did not disclose that he had a financial relationship with the developers of the projects and gained personally through commissions when Hodgkinson invested.

As a result of the dramatic decline of the real estate market in the early 1980s, Hodgkinson lost substantially all of the monies invested in these tax shelters. Hodgkinson relied entirely on Simms' advice and invested on Simms' recommendations.

Distilling the judicial principles that would assist in determining whether or not a particular relationship was a fiduciary one, the court stated:

> In these cases, the question to ask is whether, given all the surrounding circumstances, one party could reasonably have expected that the other party would act in the former's best interests with respect to the subject matter at issue. Discretion, influence, vulnerability and trust were mentioned as non-exhaustive examples of evidential factors to be considered in making this determination.
>
> Thus, outside the established categories, what is required is evidence of a mutual understanding that one party has relinquished its own self interest and agreed to act solely on behalf of the other party.[14]

The Supreme Court noted that, in the advisory context, there must be something more than the simple undertaking by one party to provide information to the other and execute orders for the other before the relationship can be characterized as fiduciary. The court sets as an example the everyday transactions that occur between a bank and its customers on a debtor-creditor basis. It is where the advisory relationship takes on elements of trust, confidentiality and with increased complexity and importance of the subject matter that it may be reasonable for the recipient of the advice to expect that the advisors are obligated to exercise their special skills in that other party's best interests.

The court noted that the elements of trust and confidence in a relationship involving a professional advisor are often self-evident where the advisor is regulated as part of a professional body with rules and codes of conduct. In such cases, the professional is required to act in the best interest of his or her clients and disclose any conflict of interest that the professional may have. Such is the case with chartered accountants such as Simms.

The court also noted that reliance was an essential element necessary before fiduciary obligations and liabilities would be imposed on a professional advisor. The court cautioned, however, that reliance in the context of a professional advisor relationship does not require a wholesale substitution of decision making power from the investor to the advisor.

What a court must do is look to see if the decision is effectively that of the advisor, given the overriding influence the advisor has over his or her client. This determination involves a close examination of the facts of each specific case.

In the *Simms* case, Hodgkinson had no experience in dealing with large real estate tax shelters and developed a relationship with Simms where it was obvious to both that Simms had assumed responsibility for Hodgkinson's choice and effectively chose the investment for him. This reliance and dependence was actively cultivated by Simms, who held himself out as an expert in the particular area and strongly influenced the investor to follow his recommendations.

In conclusion, the court held that a fiduciary obligation clearly existed between these two parties, that the duty was breached by Simms' decision not to disclose a pecuniary interest with the developers.

On the issue of damages, the court repeated a test developed by common law courts in the fiduciary context. The victim is entitled to be compensated for all losses where the party can show that, but for the relevant breach of duty, it would not have entered into a given contract. The court rejected the argument that the victim of the breach should not be compensated where the loss is caused primarily by market fluctuations.

> From a policy perspective it is simply unjust to place the risk of market fluctuations on a plaintiff who would not have entered into a given transaction but for the defendant's wrongful conduct.[15]

The Court noted that this punitive principle is supported on policy grounds insofar as there is a need to put special pressure on those in positions of trust or power over others in situations of vulnerability from abusing the trust and confidence reposed in them. As such, the Court had no difficulty in resorting to a measure of damages that places the exigencies of the marketplace on the fiduciaries. The Court confirmed that the investor must be compensated for the entire loss suffered as a result of the investment.

While the relationship between investment consultants and other plan advisors, vis-à-vis their clients is not per se fiduciary, because of the special expertise they possess and the extent to which investors depend on their services, a court may be inclined to impose upon them a high standard in providing advice. As is often the case, the relationship between the investment consultant and other advisors with the client displays elements of trust, confidence and reliance on the skill and knowledge of the consultant. As the Court stated in *Simms,* it is these elements that attract fiduciary obligations, from which professional advisors are certainly not immune.

An accurate summation of the fiduciary principle applicable to the independent professional advisory relationship was enunciated by an Ontario court in the decision of *Varcoe v. Sterling.*[16]

> The relationship of the broker and client is elevated to a fiduciary level when the client reposes trust and confidence in the broker and relies on the broker's advice in making business decisions. When the broker seeks or accepts the client's trust and confidence and undertakes to advise, the broker must do so fully, honestly and in good faith. . . . It is the trust and reliance placed by the client which gives to the broker the power and in some cases, discretion, to make a business decision for the client. Because the client has reposed that trust and confidence and has given over that power to the broker, the law imposes a duty on the broker to honour that trust and respond accordingly.[17]

The Supreme Court of Canada in *Simms* approved this passage as an accurate statement of fiduciary law in the context of independent professional advisors, whether the advisors are accountants, stockbrokers, bankers or investment counsel.

These principles have been applied in jurisdictions across Canada to hold investment consultants, advisors and brokers liable for breach of duties as fiduciaries.[18]

In contrast with *Simms* and many other Canadian authorities imposing fiduciary duties on professional advisors, a decision of the British Columbia Court of Appeal suggests that professional advisors in the pension plan context will not always be held liable as a fiduciary for their negligence. In *Wynne v. William M. Mercer Ltd.,*[19] Mercer, the plan actuary, had negligently provided a plan valuation to the plan trustees that disclosed, erroneously, a surplus of over $11 million in the plan. Although Mercer discovered the error shortly after providing the valuation, it failed to disclose the error for two years on the belief that the error would be corrected in the next valuation. As a result of the error, and in reliance on the mistaken belief that there was an excess of surplus in the plan, the trustees of the multi-employer pension plan increased benefits.

There is no question in this case that Mercer's valuation was provided negligently and without proper exercise of due skill and care. The trial court awarded approximately $500,000 to compensate the plan for the consequences of the negligent valuation by Mercer. However, the trustees argued that they were entitled to a greater award on the basis that Mercer was a fiduciary and its negligence was tantamount to a breach of fiduciary duty when it failed to disclose the error in a timely fashion.

The Court of Appeal disagreed. It found that, although Merccr had been negligent, it refused to hold that Mercer stood in a fiduciary relationship to the trustees or breached any alleged fiduciary duty. In reaching this conclusion, the Court of Appeal reasoned that, even if Mercer was a fiduciary, it had not placed its own interest ahead of its duty to provide actuarial services to the trustees in accordance with their contract.

More importantly, the court suggested that it would be impossible for the trustees to successfully advance a breach-of-fiduciary-duty argument because it would be necessary to establish that they were wholly reliant on their professional advisors. Such an admission by the trustees, stated the Court of Appeal, would place the trustees themselves in a breach of their duties because of the trust law principle that prohibits trustees from delegating their responsibilities in their entirety. Although pension plan trustees can employ and rely on professional advisors, they cannot delegate ultimate responsibility for carrying out the duties of their office.

Although the *Mercer* case is somewhat contradictory, and perhaps inconsistent with the Supreme Court of Canada decision on the fiduciary duties of professional advisors, it highlights that the question of whether or not advisors can be held to fiduciary standards remains an open one in Canada.

WHAT ARE THE COMMON LAW FIDUCIARY DUTIES?

Where fiduciary duties and responsibilities are visited upon an individual, the common law imposes upon the fiduciary a standard of conduct that is the highest known to law. The duty of the fiduciary is to act exclusively and in the best interests of those to whom the duty is owed, and at a minimum to carry out his or her responsibilities with a degree of diligence in the execution of his or her office that a person of ordinary prudence would exercise in the management of his or her own affairs.[20] If a fiduciary possesses special investment knowledge or skills by reason of his or her profession or business, a court could impose an even higher standard of care.

As noted above, one of the central features of this duty is the obligation to disclose "all material information upon which the principal may make informed decisions regarding agency matters."

In addition to the duty of disclosure, Canadian and U.S. law and jurisprudence has developed a number of duties applicable to pension plan fiduciaries that are likely applicable in the defined contribution plan context. The following is a summary of those duties that defined contribution plan sponsors and their advisors should consider when establishing and maintaining these plans:

- *The Sole Interest Rule:* A fiduciary must discharge his or her duties with respect to a plan solely in the interest of the participants and beneficiaries.
- *The Standard of Care Rule:* A fiduciary must be active in carrying out his or her duties and perform them with complete integrity.
- *The Exclusive Purpose Rule:* A fiduciary must act for the exclusive purpose of providing benefits to participants and their beneficiaries and defraying reasonable expenses of administrating the plan.
- *The No Delegation Rule:* The fiduciary must carry out his or her duties personally as a result of the trust and confidence reposed in him or her. However, as an exception to this rule, a fiduciary is permitted to select agents to perform certain tasks where it would be regarded as prudent for a person in the ordinary course of business to delegate the performance of these duties. In these circumstances, the fiduciary is responsible for overall supervision of agents.
- *The Even-Handed Rule:* The fiduciary must act impartially between the participants.
- *The Plan Document Rule:* A fiduciary must discharge his or her duties in accordance with the plan documents and investment policy statements.
- *The Prudence Rule:* At a minimum a fiduciary must conduct himself or herself with the care, skill, prudence and diligence under the circumstances then prevailing that a prudent person acting in a like capacity and familiar with such matters would use in the conduct of an enterprise of a like character and with like aims. This is a prudent expert standard.
- *The Diversification Rule:* A fiduciary must protect plan assets by, among other things, efficiently diversifying the investments to minimize the risk of large losses, unless under the circumstances it is clearly prudent not to do so.

QUEBEC LAW

The foregoing discussion has examined the common law principle of fiduciary duty, which is applicable in all

Canadian jurisdictions except Quebec. Quebec is the only Canadian jurisdiction subject to a *civil* law, as opposed to *common* law, system. Sponsors and advisors of group RRSPs in Quebec must consider the provisions of the new *Civil Code of Quebec* (the "Code"),[22] which contains the rules that must be applied in the absence of any specific statutory provisions or other contractual arrangements to the contrary.

The Code codifies many of the common law principles of fiduciary duty and trust law discussed above. Please review Chapter 11 of Section IV for a detailed discussion of the Code provisions applicable to registered and unregistered pension plans.

The Supreme Court of Canada recently pronounced on the application of the predecessor Code in the context of an investment advisor/portfolio manager relationship with a client.[23] The *Laflamme* case is significant as the Supreme Court analyzed and applied principles very similar to common law fiduciary principles to hold a portfolio manager liable to his client for losses sustained by the client as a result of the portfolio manager's breach of duty.

In *Laflamme*, 60-year-old Armand Laflamme and his brother sold their business, the proceeds of which provided Armand Laflamme with $2.2 million, which he hoped would provide him with retirement income. Having very little investment or portfolio management experience, Laflamme hired an expert, Jules Roy, to manage his portfolio and transferred the proceeds of his business sale to Roy's company (initially Burns Fry).

Despite advising Roy that the portfolio assets were intended to secure a retirement income, Roy invested a significant portion of the fund in very speculative stocks and, without instruction to do so, Roy managed the portfolio on margin. Within the first year, Roy's investments subjected Laflamme to losses of approximately $200,000. Within two years, the value of the portfolio dropped significantly, with continued losses sustained as a result of drops in share prices.

In holding Roy liable for Laflamme's losses, the Superior Court of Quebec noted the following "gross" faults committed by Roy:

1. Failure to be properly knowledgeable about his client's situation
2. Failure to act in accordance with the client's objectives
3. Failure to adequately inform the client concerning the nature, return on and risks of the investments
4. Failure to comply with the client's specific instructions
5. Failure to deal with his client in good faith and in accordance with good practice
6. Extremely large numbers of transactions for the purpose of increasing commissions

7. Failure by the defendant company to exercise proper supervision
8. Clear conflict of interest with Roy's supervisor, who received a 50% share of the defendant's commissions.[24]

In confirming the liability finding of the lower court, the Supreme Court of Canada analyzes the "rules of mandate" under the Code, which governs the legal relationships between the client and the securities dealer or portfolio manager. The Supreme Court notes that, much like the common law of agency, the standard of care imposed on a "mandatary" varies depending on the scope of the mandate. Where the scope of the mandate is narrow, as in the case where the dealer merely executes specific transactions as instructed by the client, the standard of conduct imposed is lower than is the case where, as in the *Laflamme* case, the client appoints the dealer to manage a portfolio and delegates to the dealer his decision making authority.

In the latter case, the Supreme Court notes:

. . . the mandate between a manager and his client is imbued with the concept of trust, since the client places his trust in the manager—the mandatary—to manage his affairs. . . . This spirit of trust is reflected in the weight of the obligations that rest on the manager, which will be heavier where the mandator is vulnerable, lacks specialized knowledge, is dependent on the mandatary, and where the mandate is important. The corresponding requirements of fair dealing, good faith and diligence on the part of the manager in relation to his client will thus be more stringent.[25]

Most notable about this passage is the similarity in language and concepts—trust, vulnerability, dependence, fair dealing, good faith, diligence—used to describe an advisor's duty under the Code and the fiduciary principles applied by the courts in common law jurisdictions in similar contexts. Likewise, the content of the mandatary duty bears very close resemblance to the fiduciary duties discussed above.

One of the most fundamental of these obligations is that the manager exercise reasonable skills and all the care of a prudent administrator. The conduct is not that of the best of managers, nor the worst. Rather, it is the conduct of a reasonably prudent and diligent manager performing similar functions in an analogous situation. . . . He must also deal in good faith, honestly and fairly with his clients. . . . The mandate also imposes an obligation for the manager to inform his client and in certain circumstances, a duty to advise him.[26]

The Supreme Court also noted that the content of this duty will be more stringent where the advisor has specialized knowledge and the client is relatively unsophisticated.[27]

Applying these duties in the *Laflamme* case, the Supreme Court easily found Roy to be liable holding that he

- Failed to comply with the conduct required of a prudent and diligent manager
- Failed to construct an organized and diversified portfolio
- Carried out transactions that were inconsistent with the client's general instructions
- Acquired speculative securities and failed to have regard to his client's investment objectives and
- Failed to deal fairly and honestly with his client— particularly where Roy failed to comply with Laflamme's direct instructions concerning amounts to be invested in the stock market and the immediate cessation of transactions on margin.[28]

As a result, the Supreme Court held Roy and his firm liable to Laflamme for $924,372 in damages representing the loss sustained and the profit of which Laflamme was deprived.

The *Laflamme* decision evidences the Supreme Court's inclination to interpret and apply the Quebec Code in a manner that is consistent with fiduciary principles, to protect the interests of beneficiaries who are vulnerable to the discretionary exercise of power by parties in whom the beneficiary has reposed trust and confidence. The courts are likely to be particularly sensitive to cases where an individual's retirement income security may be compromised as a result of inappropriate conduct by specialized advisors.

APPLYING THE JUDICIAL PRINCIPLES

Attempting to apply these principles to the context of sponsors and advisors associated with an individual account or group RRSPs schemes, three different relationships need to be examined:

- Does the advisor owe a fiduciary duty to the plan sponsor?
- Does the sponsor owe a fiduciary duty to the participants?
- Does the advisor owe a fiduciary duty to the participants?

The answers to these questions largely turn on the factual circumstances in each case.

Where a sponsor contracts with an advisor, such as an investment consultant, and selects and establishes investment alternatives for its employees but, where the consultant has little or no contact or direct relationship with the employees, it is unlikely that a Canadian court will find that the employees repose their trust and confidence in the advice of the consultant in a way that would attract the fiduciary label. Unlike the direct relationship that existed in the *Simms* and *Laflamme* cases between the advisor and the client, the consultant who remains largely anonymous to plan participants is not in a position to cultivate a relationship of reliance and trust with them, nor would such reliance in these circumstances be reasonable.

Most often, the employees repose their trust and confidence and their reliance on their employer that establishes the plan and makes the decisions regarding the investment options and the trustees and carriers for the various investment vehicles and, in most instances, actively encourages members to participate in the retirement schemes. That is not to say that, if these employees were to suffer a loss as a result of the investment selections available, they would not also bring an action against the investment consultants and other service providers associated with the plan, notwithstanding the absence of a direct relationship with them.

The likelihood of success against the consultant or advisor is stronger where the consultant plays a more active role in communicating with plan members regarding the various investment alternatives, particularly where those communications may be construed as investment advice. However, where the sponsor and its advisors fail to educate plan participants on prudent investment, they may also expose themselves to liability.

Where the participants are successful against the sponsors, the sponsors that reposed their trust and confidence in their investment consultants or custodians may very well seek indemnity from them.

ENDNOTES

1. D. Waters, *Law of Trusts in Canada,* 2nd ed.(Toronto: Carswell, 1984) at p. 33.

2. *Learoyd v. Whiteley* (1887), 12 App. Cas. 727 (H.L.) at p. 733.

3. For example, see Section 22 of the Ontario *Pension Benefits Act,* R.S.O. 1990, c. P.8.

4. *Ford v. Laidlaw Carriers Inc.* (1993), 1 C.C.P.B. 97 (O.C. G.D.), rev'd in part (1994), 12 C.C.P.B. 179 (O.C.A.), leave to appeal refused (1995), 191 N.R. 400 (note) (S.C.C.).

5. Revenue Canada, Information Circular IC-72-22R9, "Registered Retirement Savings Plans" (17 June 1996), at p. 5.

6. *Ocean City Realty Ltd. v. A & M Holdings Limited* (1987), 36 D.L.R. (4th) 94 (B.C.C.A.) at p. 98.

7. *Metropolitan Toronto Pension Plan v. Aetna Life Assurance Co. of Canada* (1992), 98 D.L.R. (4th) 582 (O.C.(G.D.)).

8. *Guerin v. The Queen,* [1984] 2 S.C.R. 335 at p. 341.

9. J.C. Shepherd, *The Law of Fiduciaries,* (Toronto: Carswell, 1981) at p. 96.

10. *International Corona Resources Limited v. LAC Minerals Limited,* [1989] 2 S.C.R. 574.

11. *Frame v. Smith,* [1987] 2 S.C.R. 99.

12. *Hodgkinson v. Simms* (1994), 117 D.L.R. (4th) 161 (S.C.C.).

13. *Ibid.*

14. *Ibid.,* at pp. 176-77.

15. *Ibid.*, at p. 207.

16. *Varcoe v. Sterling* (1992), 7 O.R. (3d) 204 (G.D.) at p. 236, aff'd (1992), 10 O.R. (3d) 574 (C.A.).

17. *Ibid.*, at p. 236.

18. *Maxmilian v. M. Rash & Co.* (1987), 62 O.R. (2d) 206 (G.D.); *Blair v. Merrill Lynch* (1987), 53 Alta. L.R. (2d) 352 (Q.B.); *Burns v. Kelly Peters and Associates Ltd.*, [1987] 6 W.W.R. 1 (B.C.C.A.); *Franklin v. Richardson Greenshields of Canada Limited* (1989), 75 Sask. R. 63 (C.A.).

19. *Wynne v. William M. Mercer Ltd.* (1995), 131 D.L.R. (4th) 256 (B.C.C.A.).

20. *Learoyd v. Whiteley* (1887), 12 App. Cas. 727 (H.L.) at p. 733.

21. *Ocean City Realty Ltd. v. A & M Holdings Limited, supra* note 6 at p. 98.

22. *Civil Code of Quebec,* S.Q. 1991, c.64.

23. *Laflamme v. Prudential-Bache Commodities Canada Ltd.,* [2000] S.C.C. 26.

24. *Ibid.*, at p. 12.

25. *Ibid.*, at pp. 18-19.

26. *Ibid.*, at p. 19.

27. *Ibid.*, at p. 21.

28. *Ibid.*, at p. 22.

CHAPTER 4

Avoiding Fiduciary Pitfalls
for Sponsors and Plan Advisors

by Raymond Koskie, Roberto Tomassini and Frank Aiello

The analysis in the last two chapters in this section should alert defined contribution plan sponsors and their advisors that they face potential fiduciary responsibility in the administration of these plans. However, there are some obvious precautions that can be taken to protect against liability. As there is no Canadian jurisprudence or legislation imposing standards on Canadian sponsors and advisors, this discussion inevitably draws upon the *Employee Retirement Income Security Act of 1974* (ERISA) statutory and regulatory imposed requirements.

COMMUNICATION OF
INFORMATION TO EMPLOYEES

With the growth of participant-directed individual account pension plans, more employees are directing the investment of their pension plan assets and assuming more responsibility for ensuring the adequacy of their retirement income. At the same time, there is increasing concern that many participants may not have a sufficient understanding of investment principles and strategies to make their own informed investment decisions. Canadian pension regulators believe that most financial institutions that administer defined contributions plans do a good job educating members about investments but recognize the need for regulatory intervention to ensure plan members have adequate information to make their investment decisions.[1] However, there continues to be a concern about the lack of employer programs to educate employees about invest-

ment principles, financial planning and retirement. The lack of such programs is no doubt a result of the concern employers and investment advisors have about their fiduciary responsibility in providing "investment advice." The fact that there is an absence of Canadian legislation in this area adds to this concern. Effective employee education reduces the sponsors' potential liability by reducing the likelihood that employees will be dissatisfied with their retirement benefits.

Canadian lawmakers, plan sponsors and advisors often look to, and are guided by, their U.S. counterparts and, in particular, fiduciary standards imposed under ERISA,[2] to explore this void in the Canadian legislative framework. The ERISA 404(c) Regulation[3] outlines the informational requirements that must be met by individual account plan sponsors in order to take advantage of the Section 404(c) fiduciary liability exemption. Interpretive Bulletin IB 96-1, entitled "Participant Investment Education" (the "Interpretive Bulletin") issued by the Department of Labor (DOL)[4] seeks to clarify the distinction between investment *education* and investment *advice,* upon which hinges the determination of fiduciary obligations and availability of the so-called safe harbour provisions under ERISA for plan sponsors and advisors. The Regulation and Interpretive Bulletin are designed primarily to ensure that the employees have sufficient information to make informed decisions regarding the available investment alternatives.

Providing employees with investment information can be a double-edged sword in the Canadian context. Where the employee communications take on a character of investment advice, they may attract the fiduciary liability that sponsors and consultants seek to avoid. The appearance of being the investment advisor for the employees may cultivate, or at least appear to cultivate, the kind of reliance, trust and confidence the Supreme Court of Canada has said will attract fiduciary responsibilities.

On the other hand, failure to inform and educate members at all could also lead to fiduciary liability. Where a number of investment options are available to participants, the absence of any information to them regarding the nature of the investment and its risk and return characteristics may induce members to believe that all options are equally as good and lead members to rely on and trust their employer to make good selections. An employer-selected investment option, particularly where the participants are told the selection was made on the advice of an investment consultant, without more information, is, from the members' perspective, a stamp of approval. This is particularly true where the employer is a large, sophisticated consumer of financial products, and the employees are not.

ERISA Regulation

For Canadian sponsors, and their advisors, the ERISA Regulation can be used as a guide to the type of informational requirements that should be met. To summarize the most salient provisions, the Regulation requires:

- A description of investment alternatives, including a description of the general investment objectives and risk-return characteristics of each option. A description of the type of assets and the diversification of assets is also prudent.
- An explanation of how members may give investment instructions and to whom
- An explanation of the terms attaching to each investment, especially restrictions on transfers and withdrawals
- A description of administrative fees and expenses payable by the member
- Statements or reports regarding past and/or current investment performance for each option
- Notice that the employer is seeking exemption from fiduciary liability. In the Canadian context, a warning to employees that the sponsor is not guaranteeing the investments and will not be liable for the employees' choices.

The DOL Interpretive Bulletin

The Interpretive Bulletin can also provide further guidance for sponsors and their advisors as to the type of informational requirements that should be met to avoid exposure to fiduciary liability.

Overview

The general thrust of the Interpretive Bulletin is that employees must have sufficient information to make informed decisions regarding available investment alternatives. Whether or not the nature of the information given will trigger a fiduciary obligation for the plan sponsor or investment consultant is a function of how closely the information addresses the individual's own circumstances, or if the information makes specific investment recommendations.

The Interpretive Bulletin provides guidance to those who may have been reluctant to provide extensive education regarding investment plans to employees because of concern about fiduciary exposure. This reluctance is due to uncertainty regarding the extent to which the provision of investment-related information may be considered "investment advice," thereby imposing a fiduciary obligation. The Interpretive Bulletin identifies four categories of investment information and materials, which constitute the "safe harbours," that will not constitute "investment advice" under ERISA's definition of *fiduciary* and therefore provide an exemption from fiduciary liability. These so-called safe harbours apply to sponsors and investment consultants who provide investment information within four specific categories: *plan information, general financial and investment information, asset allocation models,* and *interactive investment materials,* reviewed below.

Plan Information

This is a fairly general category that evades the application of a fiduciary obligation on the basis that the information and materials it includes relate to the plan and plan participation in general, without reference to the appropriateness of any discrete investment option for a particular participant or beneficiary.

This category includes information and materials that inform about benefits of plan participation, including the benefits of increasing plan contributions, the impact of pre-retirement withdrawals on retirement income and a description of the terms of or the operation of the plan.

Information regarding investment alternatives under the plan, including descriptions of investment objectives and philosophies, risk and return characteristics, historical return information, or related prospectuses, and information relating to generic asset class (e.g., equities, bonds or cash) of the investment alternatives are also included within this first general category of investment education.

General Financial and Investment Information

The Interpretive Bulletin simply provides a list of

information and materials that fall within this second broad category of investment education, including:

- General financial and investment concepts, such as risk and return, diversification, dollar cost averaging, compounded return and tax-deferred investment
- Historic differences in rates of return between different asset classes (e.g., equities, bonds, cash) based on standard market indexes
- Effects of inflation
- Estimating future retirement income needs
- Determining investment time horizons
- Assessing risk tolerance.

Asset Allocation Models

Asset allocation models, in forms such as pie charts, graphs or case studies, that provide models of hypothetical individuals with different time horizons and risk profiles constitute the third category of investment education. The designation of these models as safe harbours, like their counterpart in the fourth category, requires the satisfaction of a number of common conditions that will be outlined below.

Interactive Investment Materials

The provision of questionnaires, worksheets, software and other such materials that provide a participant or beneficiary the means to estimate future retirement income needs and assess the impact of different asset allocations on retirement income will not constitute investment advice. However, as noted in the description of the third category, the *educational,* as opposed to *advisory* status of this fourth category, also depends on the satisfaction of several conditions.

In order to escape the imposition of a fiduciary obligation, information or materials provided under the third or fourth categories must satisfy the following conditions:

- They must be based on "generally accepted investment theories that take into account the historic returns of different asset classes" over defined periods of time.
- They must be accompanied by a description of "all material facts and assumptions" that may affect a participant's or beneficiary's assessment of the model or materials.
- To the extent that any specific investment alternative available under the plan is identified, there must be an accompanying statement indicating that other investment alternatives having similar risk and return characteristics may be available under the plan and identifying where information on those investment alternatives may be obtained.
- They must include a statement reminding partici-

pants and beneficiaries that they must consider their own individual situations in applying models and interactive materials, such as other assets, income and investments.

There is one other condition, which applies only to the category of interactive investment material. When plan sponsors, fiduciaries or investment consultants provide interactive investment materials, they must ensure that there is an "objective correlation between the asset allocations generated by the materials and the information and data supplied by the participant or beneficiary."

What Is "Investment Advice"?

Under ERISA, a person is considered a fiduciary with respect to an employee benefit plan to the extent the person:

renders investment advice for a fee or other compensation, direct or indirect, with respect to any moneys or other property of such plan, or has any authority to do so . . .[5]

The DOL cautions that a person will be considered to be rendering "investment advice" if he or she advises as to the value of securities or other property, or makes recommendations as to the advisability of investing in, purchasing, or selling securities or other property. If the person, directly or indirectly,

has discretionary authority or control with respect to purchasing or selling securities or other property; or,

renders advice on a regular basis . . . pursuant to a mutual agreement, arrangement or understanding . . . with the participant or beneficiary that the advice will serve as a primary basis for . . . investment decisions, etc. with respect to plan assets and that such person will render individualized advice based on the particular needs of the participant or beneficiary,[6]

then such person will be considered to be giving "investment advice."

There can be little doubt that Canadian courts have adopted, and will continue to adopt, a similar approach under common law.

Selecting and Monitoring Educators and Advisors

Persons, such as plan sponsors, when designating and monitoring people to provide investment education or materials, are obliged to act prudently and in the sole interest of plan participants. Applying this standard, the sponsor should not be liable for losses incurred by the participants with respect to the actions of a third party selected by the participant to provide investment education or investment advice.

Additional Investment Information

The DOL also recommends that plan participants need to be informed about the impact on retirement savings of pre-retirement withdrawals and other fundamental principles regarding plan participation and contribution levels. According to a recent study, this is an infrequently discussed topic that could have serious impact on the employee's retirement income. The DOL encourages sponsors, fiduciaries and investment consultants to emphasize that participants should:

- Participate in available plans as soon as they are eligible
- Make the maximum contribution possible to the plan
- If they change employment, refrain from withdrawing their retirement savings and opt instead to directly transfer or roll over their plan account into another retirement vehicle.

In addition, there are considerations peculiar to the Canadian context, which should be included in participant communication. The first relates to contribution limits imposed on individual registered retirement savings plans (RRSPs) by Canadian tax legislation. Each individual is limited in his or her ability to make tax-deductible contributions to RRSPs, which is determined on an annual basis with reference to factors such as the employee's income, contributions from prior years, whether the employee participates in other retirement schemes, and carry forward or carry back provisions in the *Income Tax Act* (ITA). Where sponsors are not regulating contributions to ensure contribution limits are not exceeded, they must be sure to advise participants that contribution limits exist, and that the participants bear the responsibility for ensuring the limits are not exceeded.

Second, particular investments may be protected by insurance schemes or compensation funds. The Canadian insurance industry has its own compensation fund that protects investments with participating institutions up to $60,000 in the event of insolvency. A sponsor should communicate this feature of each investment option where applicable or direct participants to the appropriate authority to inquire about possible investment protections and their limitations.

MONITORING AND CONTROL OF INVESTMENTS

The philosophy of the ERISA Regulation is that sponsors may avoid fiduciary responsibility where the plan gives effective and meaningful control over investment decisions to their employees. Having the power to select one's investments is meaningless if an adequate range of investment alternatives is not available. Therefore, ERISA stipulates that sponsors seeking fiduciary exemption must provide an opportunity to members to select from a broad range of investment alternatives. ERISA goes further by stipulating that the options must provide members with an opportunity to materially affect their potential return and the degree of risk, and an opportunity to diversify so as to minimize the risk of large losses. At a minimum, ERISA requires that sponsors provide at least three categories of investment.

No similar legislated requirements are imposed on Canadian sponsors. However, sponsors and their investment consultants are well advised to similarly offer a sufficient range of options that would allow risk diversification. In light of the collapse of Confed, sponsors that continue to place all plan funds in guaranteed investment certificates (GICs) (for example) with one institution on the belief the institution is secure do so at their peril, particularly where plan participants are not warned of the risk associated with the lack of diversification.

Closely connected to the range of investments offered to participants is the method by which investments or carriers are selected and monitored by sponsors and their consultants. The U.S. law on the fiduciary obligation of pension plan administrators to prudently select and monitor investments, investment managers and consultants, and their other agents is well developed. Canadian legal advisors for pension plan sponsors often cite U.S. cases under ERISA such as *Whitfield v. Cohen*[7] and *Brock v. Wells Fargo Bank*[8] for the principle that fiduciaries owe a duty to undertake a thorough, complete and independent investigation prior to making any investment decisions, and the duty to monitor those decisions periodically afterwards.

These principles have been specifically adopted by Canadian courts, in various fiduciary contexts[9] and are likely to be applied to sponsors of group RRSP plans if a court is inclined to characterize them as fiduciaries. While there are many factors a court may consider in determining whether a sponsor has prudently made and monitored investment decisions, a few may be particularly important in the context of individual account plans and the Canadian investment experience.

In selecting investment options and product providers, sponsors and their advisors must assess the options through an objective selection process with regard to each potential selection as a whole. For example, undue weight given to the highest return available, with no consideration for the stability of the carrier or the term of the investments, could get sponsors into trouble. As well, wholesale reliance on professional advisors or credit and bond rating agencies may also be insufficient to fulfil a sponsor's duties. As stated in the oft-quoted passage from *Donovan v. Cunningham*:

> An independent appraisal is not a magic wand
> that fiduciaries may simply waive over a trans-

action to ensure that their responsibilities are fulfilled. It is a tool and, like all tools, is useful only if used properly, . . . fiduciaries need not become experts . . . they are entitled to rely on the expertise of others. However, as the source of the information upon which the expert's opinions are based, the fiduciaries are responsible for ensuring the information is complete and up-to-date.[10]

In the Confed situation, despite the general awareness that the company was in trouble as a result of its overexposure in real estate investments, some sponsors did not act to reduce their plan exposure in the company. They relied almost entirely on the continued good ratings given to Confed by credible bond and credit rating agencies. Although not legally tested, this kind of reliance on independent experts may constitute a breach of the sponsor's duties to its participants to independently select and monitor investment choices, particularly when it can be established that there was good cause for concern.

THE USE OF INVESTMENT POLICY STATEMENTS IN MANAGING PLAN ASSETS

Since ERISA requires that "care, skill, prudence and diligence" be applied in the investment decision making process, it is presumptuous to think that this requirement can be met without succinctly written directives.[11]

The establishment of written investment policies and goals for registered pension plans (RPPs) is generally required by Canadian legislation governing these plans. Investment policy statements are intended to protect not only plan participants, but also their sponsors and professional advisors. Logically then, individual account plans should adopt investment policy statements as well.

The need for a written investment policy is essential to achieving a mutual understanding between the supervising fiduciaries and the investment professionals serving the plans. The absence of this understanding is the most significant cause of not attaining investment objectives.

Essentially, the investment policy statement becomes the overall game plan from which all investment strategies and their implementation evolve. The policy, and evolving strategies of the plan, must respond to the objectives of the plan sponsor and participants, as well as economic realities. The statement becomes the steppingstone for the individual policy guidelines for the plan's investment manager(s).

Design of the Investment Policy Statement

A well-designed investment policy statement should be established for every investing entity, individual or institutional client and should contain the following elements, among others.

Statement of purpose: Provides background information relating to the plan and the sponsor, including; name and type of plan; the purpose for which it was established; and participant demographics. Factors relating to the sponsor that may have an impact on the plan's variability may be included, such as the sponsor's industry, profitability and sensitivity to the economic and business cycle. In addition, specific needs or characteristics of the plan should be included, such as the source(s) of contributions.

Statement of responsibilities: Identifies the parties associated with the plan and the functions, responsibilities and activities of each with respect to the management of plan assets. Parties include, without limitation:

- **Fiduciaries** who are ultimately responsible for the plan, the appropriateness of its investment policy and implementation. They may include the board of trustees, administrative committee or investment policy committee.
- **Investment manager(s)** with responsibility for day-to-day investment management of assets, including specific security selection and the timing of purchases and sales
- **Master custodian** with responsibility for safekeeping securities, collection and disbursements, and periodic accounting statements
- **Investment consultant** with responsibility for assisting the sponsor in developing investment policy and objectives and for monitoring performance of the plan and its investment managers.

Investment objectives: Describe the sponsor's return expectations, sensitivity to risk and time horizon. Investment objectives and goals should be realistic and appropriate, given the plan's needs.

Investment goals: Specific numeric targets by which we measure whether or not objectives have been met. They may be expressed as an absolute return target, relative to a market index, or a minimum required dollar amount or income yield.

Investment guidelines: The framework within which investments are made. These guidelines may contain language pertaining to issues such as proxy voting, liquidity needs, trading and execution guidelines or social responsibility in investing.

Asset mix guidelines: Identify asset classes approved for investment with the maximum and minimum range for each asset category. The asset mix policy and acceptable minimum and maximum ranges established by the trustees represent a long-term view. As such, rapid and significant market movements may cause the plan's actual asset mix to fall outside the policy range, but any divergence should be of a short-term nature.

Limitations and restrictions: Such as quality ratings, diversification, and selection criteria and restricted investments.

Investment performance review and evaluation: Establishes the basis for measuring and evaluating plan manager performance. Measurement will include the performance results for the individual investment managers, the total performance and the asset class performance all against appropriate benchmarks on a quarterly basis.

Communications: An integral part of the management process. This section addresses the need for regular and continued communications between the plan fiduciaries and investment managers by establishing the reporting requirements and the frequency of review meetings. Communications with the investment consultant may be addressed in this section as well.

Comment

The depth or brevity of the investment policy statement will vary from plan to plan. The language should provide meaningful guidance in the management of plan assets but not be overly restrictive given changing economic, business and investment market conditions. This statement should be reviewed at least once each year and confirmed or amended to reflect any change in circumstances. This provides an opportunity for plan fiduciaries to review with a fresh eye the plan structure, manager line-up and investment portfolio.

OSFI'S "BEST PRACTICE" GUIDELINES

As a further development, the Office of the Superintendent of Financial Institutions (OSFI) has published "best practice" guidelines for the administration of federally regulated pension plans.[12] Included in the Guidelines are specific recommendations regarding financial education for members of defined contributions plans. Although the Guidelines are only recommendations and do not have the force of law, OSFI has indicated that it expects plan administrators will comply. Further, it is anticipated that these Guidelines will influence how fiduciary obligations are interpreted by the courts in the future.

OSFI's Disclosure Guideline

On March 6, 1998, OSFI published its Disclosure Guideline, which sets out recommendations regarding the disclosure of relevant financial information to plan members.[13] In the Disclosure Guideline, OSFI recommends that the administrators of defined contributions plans provide an enrolment package to new members, which would include educational materials. The document sets out an extensive list of information that should be provided to new plan members including discussions on:

- The impact of compounding
- Fundamental long-term risk and return of different asset classes
- The impact of different asset mixes on long-term risk and return expectations
- Benefits of diversification of securities
- Benefits of tax deferral
- Detailed investment options including a description of each fund's objectives, how the fund is invested, the risks associated with the fund, and who is the fund manager
- Risk tolerance assessment guidelines and strategies to help members decide their own risk tolerance
- Examples of how individuals in specific circumstances might invest.

The Disclosure Guideline also recommends that the administrator of the defined contributions plan provide ongoing communication to members regarding the performance of their investment options and the other investment options available.

There are also specific recommendations directed at investment managers that propose that the manager provide a written report to be available to all plan members, outlining

- The relationship between fund assets and the plan's investment objectives
- Performance goals set by the plan and whether portfolio managers have met those goals
- Comparison of pension fund's performance with relevant benchmarks
- Impact of interest and exchange rates on the plan's performance, as well as a discussion of trends likely to affect the fund
- Comparative analysis of changes in the asset mix from year to year
- Discussion of the use of derivatives.

CHECKLIST

To assist sponsors and their advisors, we have provided as appendixes to this chapter two checklists setting out the type of information that should be disclosed to participants and the items that should be included in an investment policy statement for group RRSPs and other defined contribution plans.

ENDNOTES

1. Canadian Association of Pension Supervisory Authorities (CAPSA), "Pension Regulators Discuss Disclosure of Investment Information to Members of Defined-Contribution Pension Plans" (released April 6, 2000). This release notes that CAPSA is developing basic investment disclosure principles for defined contribution plans.

2. *Employee Retirement Income Security Act of 1974*, 29 U.S.C.A. §1001 (1974) (ERISA).

3. Pension and Welfare Benefits Administration, Department of Labor, Rules and Regulations for Fiduciary Responsibility: ERISA Section 404(c) plans, 29 CFR §2550.404(c)-1 (1992). Available at www.dol.gov/dol/allcfr/PWPA.

4. Pension and Welfare Benefits Administration, Department of Labor, Interpretive Bulletin Relating to Participant Investment Education, 29 CFR §2509.96-1. Available at www.Dol.gov/dol/allcfr/PWBA.

5. ERISA, *supra* note 2, Subsection 3(21)(A)(ii).

6. Interpretive Bulletin 96-1, *supra* note 4, at p. 3.

7. *Whitfield v. Cohen*, 782 F.Supp. 188 (S.D.N.Y. 1988).

8. *Brock v. Wells Fargo Bank*, 7 EBC 1221 (N.D.Cal. 1986).

9. *Metropolitan Toronto Pension Plan v. Aetna Life Assurance Co. of Canada* (1992), 98 D.L.R. (4th) 582 (O.C. (G.D.)); *Fales v. Canada Permanent Trust Co.* (1976), 70 D.L.R. (3d) 257 (S.C.C.).

10. *Donovan v. Cunningham*, 716 F.2d 1455 (U.S.C.A. 5th Cir. 1983) at p. 1474.

11. Investment Management Consultants Association, *The Investment Policy Statement* (1982), at p. 105.

12. Office of the Superintendent of Financial Institutions, "Guideline for Governance of Federally Regulated Pension Plans" (1 May 1998).

13. Office of the Superintendent of Financial Institutions, "Disclosure of Information to Pension Plan Members and Former Members" (6 March 1998).

APPENDIX VI-4-A

INFORMATION TO BE PROVIDED TO PLAN BENEFICIARIES
BY PLAN SPONSORS: CHECKLIST

Included

☐   Benefits of Plan Participants

☐   Alternatives to Plan Participants

☐   Cost of Plan Participation

☐   Investment Planning Questionnaire

☐   Future Benefit Calculation Tools

☐   Investment Planning and Forecasting Tools

☐   Understanding of Capital Markets History

☐   Asset Allocation and Policy Mix Education

☐   Understanding of Investment Alternatives

☐   Risk/Return Profile of Various Investment Alternatives

☐   Recommended Investment Proposals

The inclusion of recommended investment proposals obviously increases the potential for fiduciary liability by the plan sponsor and should therefore be issued with discretion.

APPENDIX VI-4-B

INVESTMENT POLICY STATEMENT CHECKLIST

As a minimum, investment policy statements should address each of the following elements:

Included

☐   Background information on the fund

☐   Identification of fiduciaries

☐   Organizational structure

☐   Cash flow requirements

☐   Lines of authority and delegation

☐   Diversification of the portfolio

☐   Active/passive strategies

☐   Definition of assets

☐   Performance objectives

☐   Guidelines

☐   Brokerage

☐   Voting of proxies

☐   Trusteeship/custodianship

The statement related to each investment manager would include background information; future fund and cash flow projection; investment objectives; policies related to the voting of proxies; portfolio guidelines; reporting requirement; and review, evaluation and modification methodologies.

CHAPTER 1

Savings Plans

by Judy Gerwing

INTRODUCTION

Savings plans constitute a whole class of programs under which the employee and/or the employer make contributions to accumulate assets that are payable at specified times under certain conditions. Many types of savings plans involve the use of after tax funds and are not covered in this chapter. Others constitute registered pension plans and have already been discussed in Section IV. The specific plans to be covered in this chapter are registered retirement savings plans (RRSPs) and profit-sharing plans. This latter category may be subdivided into deferred profit-sharing plans (DPSPs) and employees' profit-sharing plans (EPSPs).

A *registered retirement savings plan* is essentially a vehicle for employee contributions only. Where employer contributions are paid into an RRSP, they are treated for tax purposes as additional employee contributions and the employee's T4 earnings are increased by the amount of the employer contributions. All contributions made are immediately vested and are tax-deductible by the employee within certain limits. Investment income is also tax-sheltered.

Since January 1, 1991 only employers may contribute to a DPSP. These contributions are tax-deductible for the employer within certain limits and do not confer an immediate taxable benefit upon the employee. Investment income is tax-sheltered. Employer contributions must vest 100% with the employee after 24 months of plan membership.

Both employees and employers may contribute to EPSPs; however, the employees' contributions are not tax-deductible, and the employers' contributions create an immediate taxable benefit for the employee. Employers' contributions are tax-deductible and may vest immediately or over a period of years. There is no mandatory minimum vesting period. All realized investment income is taxable to the employee.

In the balance of this chapter we will provide more specific details on:
- Plan design
- Registration requirements
- Contribution limits
- Tax treatment
- Pay-out options
- Investment restrictions.

PLAN DESIGN

Registered Retirement Savings Plans

There are no design features to an RRSP. It is purely a vehicle for accumulating employee contributions on a tax-sheltered basis. The RRSP may be issued on an individual or a group basis. The major advantages to the group RRSP are the immediate tax deductibility of payroll contributions by the employee and the generally lower level of investment management fees and expenses. RRSPs may be "locked-in" in two senses:
- They may be used as a vehicle to accept the transfer of a commuted value from a registered pension plan. In this case the money is "locked-in" under the provisions of the applicable pension benefits act.
- A group RRSP may be "locked-in" in the sense that "as a condition of employment" the employee agrees to participate in the group RRSP and agrees that no contributions will be removed while the employee remains employed by the sponsor. In the normal way, an RRSP can be collapsed at any time.

Profit-Sharing Plans

Revenue Canada Information Circular 77-1R4,[1] which is reproduced as Appendix VII-1-B to this chapter, defines the principal features of *profit-sharing plans* as follows.

The plans involve an arrangement whereby an employer may share profits with all or a designated group of employees of the employer's business or from the business of the employer and one or more corporations with which the employer does not deal at arm's length.

The amounts payable by the employer normally are computed with reference to profits (e.g., 5% of *profits* as defined in the plan), but under some circumstances may be computed on another basis as long as they are paid out of profits. The payments made by the employer must be made to a trustee in trust for the benefit of the employees.

There must be a complete allocation by the trustee within specified time limits, either contingently or absolutely, of:

a. All amounts received under the plan from an employer and
b. All income received, capital gains made, and capital losses sustained by the trust.

For a DPSP, the major design features include the contribution formula, the vesting rules and the rules for applying to forfeitures arising from non-vested terminations. The maximum vesting requirement is two years of membership. Forfeitures may be applied to reduce subsequent employer contributions, reallocated to remaining plan members or refunded to the employer.

The critical issue is, of course, the formula to be used to determine the employer's contribution. Contributions may be "by reference to profits," in which case they must be a percentage of profits for the year. Alternatively, contributions can be "out of profits," in which case greater flexibility is available, and undistributed profits of prior years may be incorporated. Formulas could include:

a. A percentage of salary
b. A percentage of employee's contributions to a group RRSP or
c. A fixed dollar amount.

There is no minimum annual contribution. For an EPSP, the employer's contributions must be "by reference to profits" or, if the employer files the appropriate election, "out of profits."

If the "out of profits" method is used, the employer is obligated to make a minimum contribution, such as $100 per member, in any year in which there is a profit. If the "by reference to profits" method is used, contributions could be:

• A percentage of members' salaries (minimum 1%)

• An amount equal to members' contributions (minimum 1%) or
• A fixed dollar amount (minimum of $100 per member). The employer must select the vesting rules and also decide whether or not employee contributions are permitted.

REGISTRATION OF PLANS

Registered Retirement Savings Plans

Information Circular 72-22R9[2] outlines the requirements for the registration of a registered retirement savings plan. These are set out in full in Appendix VII-1-A.

RRSPs are generally issued by banks, insurance and trust companies, but may also be issued by other approved companies such as investment dealers. A specimen of any proposed plan and the application form must be submitted to Revenue Canada for approval at least a month before it is issued. There are particular terms the RRSP *cannot* include, such as paying general benefits before maturity (with two specific exceptions) or paying premiums after maturity. There are also terms that *must* be included, such as a maturity date before the end of the 69th year of the annuitant and prohibiting the assignment of retirement income.

A group RRSP is essentially a collection of individual RRSPs under a single trust or contract for which the association or employer acts as agent. Property or investments held by the trust must be identifiable for each individual plan.

Deferred Profit-Sharing Plans

The following documents are needed to apply for the registration of a DPSP:

1. Form T2214, with which the trustee of the plan and the employer apply for registration of the plan as a DPSP
2. A certified copy of the resolution of the directors authorizing the application to be made
3. A copy of the trust agreement and plan text constituting the plan.

When accepted, the effective date of registration of the plan will be the later of the date mailed or the date specified in the application.

A specimen plan, including a statement of permitted variables with the plan documents, may be submitted for pre-approval. If the plan conforms to an approved specimen plan (subject to variables), the application should certify that it conforms to a specimen plan and give details about permitted variables.

There are also several statutory conditions the DPSP must meet and certain Revenue Canada requirements (see Appendix VII-1-B). For instance, a DPSP must prohibit investment of its funds in bonds or debentures of the contributing employer and ensure that no one related to the employer, a specified shareholder or partner may become a beneficiary under the plan. Revenue Canada requires the plan to spell out a realistic formula for the employer to calculate contributions. For instance, there is a difference between "out of profits" and "by reference to profits," though either is acceptable.

Employees' Profit-Sharing Plans

Unlike RRSPs and DPSPs, EPSPs are not registered. An EPSP is an arrangement to make payments calculated "by reference to profits"—usually a certain percentage—to some or all employees.

An employer must apply to Revenue Canada to have the arrangement qualify as an EPSP.

The plan may permit employee contributions either as a requirement or on a voluntary basis. The plan must provide that there be a complete allocation by the trustee to the employees each year, either contingently or absolutely, of:
- All amounts received from the employer
- All realized investment earnings (including net capital gains or losses) and
- Any forfeited amounts.

CONTRIBUTION LIMITS

The 2003 federal budget increased the limit for RRSP contributions. For 2003, the maximum employee contributions to a registered retirement savings plan are defined to be 18% of 2003 earned income less any pension adjustments (PAs) to a dollar maximum of $14,500 in 2003.

Maximum contributions in subsequent years will similarly be based on 18% of the previous year's earned income less the PA. The RRSP dollar limit will be $15,500 for 2004 and $16,500 for 2005.

At the present time there is a rollover provision that allows unused RRSP contribution room to be carried forward for an indefinite number of years.

The maximum employer DPSP contribution in a year is equal to half the maximum contribution that may be made to a money purchase pension plan. One-half of that limit is $6,750 in 1999. The money purchase dollar limit will increase by $1,000 per year starting in 2002 to $15,500 in 2003, and indexed thereafter. This contribution forms part of the current year's PA. Employee contributions to a DPSP are prohibited.

There are no maximum contributions to an EPSP, since any employer's contributions are reported as other income by the trustee and are taxable in the employee hands and any employee contribution is not tax-deductible.

THE RRSP OVER-CONTRIBUTION ALLOWANCE

1. *Over-contribution* means contributions in excess of taxpayer's deductible contribution room. They are not deductible in the current year.
2. The first $2,000 of a cumulative over-contribution is not subject to penalty tax.
3. Any contribution over $2,000 attracts a penalty tax of 1% per month of the excess.
4. An over-contribution can be removed without negative tax results within a specified time after making the over-contribution.
5. An over-contribution can be deducted in future years if sufficient RRSP contribution room is available.
6. If not removed under rule 4 or deducted under rule 5, the over-contribution will be taxed on withdrawal.

TAX TREATMENT

Registered Retirement Savings

As previously stated, employee contributions to RRSPs are tax-deductible within certain limits.

A trust governed by an RRSP is generally exempt from taxation except if the trust:
(a) Borrowed money for a use other than to carry on a business.
(b) Carried on a business in the taxation year.
(c) If, at the end of any month in a taxation year, the trust holds foreign property (other than property that was not a qualified investment at the end of the month), and if the cost amount of all foreign property held exceeds the total of:
  i. 20% of the cost amount of all property held at the end of any month; and
  ii. The lesser of three times the small business investment limited partnership amount, and the small business investment amount of the trust for the month and 20% of the cost amount of all property held at the end of the month;
tax is payable by the trust equal to 1% of the lesser of the excess described above and the cost amount of all foreign property.
(d) Held investments acquired after, at the end of any month in the year that were qualified when acquired but that had become nonqualified investments while held by the trust.
(e) Was governed by a plan that became an "amended plan" under subsection 146(12) of

the *Income Tax Act* and, as a consequence, is deemed not to be an RRSP.

(f) Is taxable on its income for each year after the year of death of the last annuitant when the last annuitant under an RRSP has died, and all the funds were not paid out of the trust in the taxation year.

(g) Has entered an agreement described in subsection 206.1 to acquire shares at a price that may differ from the fair market value at the time the shares may be acquired.

(h) Has acquired a property that is not a qualified investment.

(i) Held prescribed properties at the end of the month of which the aggregate of the fair market value, at the time of acquisition, exceeded 50% of the aggregate of the fair market value at the time of acquisition of all properties held.

Any tax payable by a trust is payable with the annual return that must be filed on behalf of the trust.

Deferred Profit-Sharing Plan

Normally no tax is payable by a trust governed by a DPSP. However, tax is payable in the following circumstances:

(a) Tax is payable on the taxable income of a trust for a taxation year during any part of which the trust was governed by a revoked plan.

(b) If, in a taxation year, the trust acquires a non-qualified investment, tax is payable equal to the fair market value of such investment at the time it was acquired. A refund of the tax can be claimed if the trust disposes of a property that, when acquired, was a non-qualified investment. The refund is equal to either the amount of the tax imposed as a result of the acquisition of the property, or the proceeds of disposition, whichever is less.

(c) If a trust owns property, which was a qualified investment when acquired and which later becomes a non-qualified investment, tax is payable equal to 1% of the fair market value at the time of acquisition of such property for each month throughout which the non-qualified investment was held.

(d) If in a taxation year, trust property is used as security for a loan, tax is payable equal to the fair market value of the property as of the date it is so used. A refund of the tax can be claimed, if such property ceases to be so used. The refund is equal to the tax imposed when the property was used minus any net loss sustained by the trust because of such use.

(e) If, at the end of any month in a taxation year, the trust holds foreign property (other than property that was not a qualified investment at the end of the month), and if the cost amount of all foreign property held exceeds the total of:

(i) 20% of the cost amount of all property held at the end of any month and

(ii) the lesser of three times the small business investment limited partnership amount, or the small business investment amount of the trust for the month and 20% of the cost amount of all property held at the end of the month;

tax is payable by the trust equal to 1% of the lesser of the excess described above and the cost amount of all foreign property.

(f) The trust is liable to pay a tax if an agreement is entered into for the acquisition of shares at a price that may differ from the fair market value on the date of purchase. The tax payable is equal to the total of all amounts each of which is the amount, if any, by which

(i) the dividend paid on the shares at any time when the trust is a party to the agreement exceeds

(ii) the amount, if any, of the dividend received by the trust.

(g) If, the trust disposes of property to a taxpayer at a price that is less than the fair market value at the time of the transaction, or acquires property from a taxpayer at a price that is more than the fair market value at the time of the transaction, tax is payable by the trust for the calendar year in which the transaction occurs equal to 50% of the difference between the fair market value and the sale or purchase price. The registration of a DPSP becomes revocable if forfeited amounts are not reallocated or paid to participating employers.

If, in a taxation year, a trust is covered by a revoked plan, tax is payable by that trust as described in paragraphs (a), (b), (d) and (g).

If (b) or (d) above apply, tax is payable by the trust within ten days of the day on which the trust acquires the non-qualified investment or uses the property as security, whichever applies. Otherwise, any tax payable by a trust, even if it is calculated on a monthly basis as in (c), (e) and (f), above, is payable with the annual return that must be filed on behalf of the trust.

If a tax has been paid as required by Subsection 199(1) on initial non-qualified investments, the trust can apply for a refund under Subsection 199(2) of such tax that has not previously been refunded when it disposes of those investments.

Employees' Profit-Sharing Plans

No tax is payable under Part I of the *Income Tax Act* by a trust on its taxable income for a period during which the trust was governed by an EPSP.

Amounts to Be Included in Income of a Beneficiary

Generally speaking, under an EPSP, amounts are required to be included in the income of an officer or employee who is a beneficiary, hereafter referred to as a *member,* when they are allocated to the member's account, either contingently or absolutely, and amounts are not required to be included in income of a beneficiary when received.

Allocation of Amounts to Members

All amounts allocated to a member are required to be included in the member's income as ordinary income except:

a. Amounts contributed to the EPSP by the member
b. A capital gain made by the trust
c. A dividend received by the trust from a taxable Canadian corporation
d. Interest received by the trust.

Special rules apply to allocations of certain capital gains, dividends and interest excluded under b, c and d above and of foreign non-business income that is not excluded from ordinary income by a, b, c or d. Generally speaking, such types of income when allocated to a member are treated as if received directly by the member. The special rules are dealt with below.

Allocation of Capital Gains and Losses

Any capital gain or any capital loss of a trust governed by an EPSP for a taxation year allocated to a member is deemed to be a capital gain or loss as the case may be of the member for the taxation year in which the gain or loss was so allocated.

Allocation of Taxable Dividends and Interest, Received by the Trust From Taxable Canadian Corporations

Where in a taxation year a trust governed by an EPSP receives taxable dividends from taxable Canadian corporations and the trustee allocates such dividends to a member, that member shall be deemed to have received such dividends equal to the amount so allocated. The grossed-up amount of such dividends must be included in the member's income for the year, and the member is entitled to a dividend tax credit on such amount. Interest received by the trust and allocated to a member in a taxation year shall be deemed to have been received by the member in that year. These amounts are not reported as a taxable benefit by the employer. The member pays the tax on April 30 when he or she files the annual tax return.

Allocation of Foreign Non-Business Income

Foreign non-business income of a trust governed by an EPSP for a taxation year must be allocated each year by the trustee to the members of the plan. The amount so allocated to a member is ordinary income if the amount was allocated. The member is entitled to a foreign tax credit based on a pro-rata portion of the tax paid by the trust to the governments of the foreign country and political subdivisions thereof on the foreign non-business income received by the trust from that country. Reference should be made to the precise wording of Subsection 144(8.1) of the *Income Tax Act*.

Payments Out of a Plan

As stated above, amounts received from an EPSP trust are, generally speaking, not required to be included in the income of a beneficiary when received. However, in certain circumstances, some part of the amounts received may have to be included in income. The most common situation is where property allocated to a beneficiary has appreciated in value while so allocated and the beneficiary elects to receive payment in money. Instruction regarding the determination of amounts, if any, to be included in income in various circumstances is contained in Interpretation Bulletin IT-379.[3]

Forfeitures and Refunds of Tax

Amounts allocated to a member are required to be included in the member's income for the year of allocation regardless of whether the allocation was contingent or absolute. Thus, where an amount, such as an employer's contribution, is allocated to a member contingent on the member continuing in employment for a period of years, the member must include this amount in income even though, if employment is terminated before the number of years specified in the plan has expired, the member will not receive the amount. Subsection 144(9) of the *Income Tax Act* provides that where, by virtue of a contingent allocation, an amount has been included in a member's income for a particular taxation year or a previous year, and where the member ceases to be a beneficiary under the plan in the year and has not received and is not entitled to receive the amount, the member may deduct, in computing the person's income for the year, the total of all amounts that were contingently allocated and subsequently forfeited upon termination from the plan.

PAY-OUT OPTIONS

Registered Retirement Savings Plans

Under an RRSP, payments can be in the form of:
- A lump-sum refund
- The purchase of an annuity certain or an annuity payable for life
- The transfer into a registered retirement income plan (RRIF)
- The transfer into a registered pension plan.

Regardless of the option selected, the RRSP must mature before the end of the year in which the individual attains 69 years of age.

If the RRSP is *locked-in,* then the payment options are limited by the provisions of the applicable provincial pension legislation.

Deferred Profit-Sharing Plans

Payments under a DPSP may be made as a lump-sum, an annuity certain or a life annuity, or a transfer into a registered retirement savings plan. Like an RRSP, the payments will normally be taxable to the individual in the year they are received.

Employees' Profit-Sharing Plans

Payments made under an EPSP will normally not be taxable in the hands of the individual.

INVESTMENT OPTIONS

Registered Retirement Savings Plans

Qualified investments for RRSPs are set out in Subsection 146(1) of the *Income Tax Act* and Section 4900 of the Regulations. All investments of a trust governed by an RRSP must be registered in the name of the trustee, not in the name of the annuitant.

Deferred Profit-Sharing Plans

Section 204 of the *Income Tax Act* defines a *qualified investment* for a trust governed by a DPSP or a revoked plan as an investment listed in that paragraph and in Section 4900 of the *Income Tax Regulations,* while Section 204 defines a *non-qualified investment.* Subsections 198(6) and (7) of the act provide that amounts paid by such a trust to acquire interests in life insurance policies shall be deemed not to be the acquisition of a non-qualified investment. In the event that interest acquired in life insurance policies is not deemed to be qualified investments, Subsection 198(8) of the act provides rules for determining when such non-qualified investments have been disposed of and the process of disposition.

Employee Profit-Sharing Plans

There are no investment restrictions for EPSPs.

ENDNOTES

1. Revenue Canada, Information Circular IC77-1R4, "Deferred Profit Sharing Plans" (30 December 1992).
2. Revenue Canada, Information Circular IC72-22R9, "Registered Retirement Savings Plan" (17 June 1996).
3. Revenue Canada, Interpretation Bulletin IT-379R, "Employee Profit Sharing Plans—Allocation to Beneficiaries" (29 September 1999).

APPENDIX VII-1-A

INFORMATION CIRCULAR 72-22R9
JUNE 17, 1996
REGISTERED RETIREMENT SAVINGS PLANS

This circular cancels and replaces Information Circular 72-22R8 dated March 18, 1991.

1.   This circular interprets certain provisions of the *Income Tax Act* (the "Act") that apply to registered retirement savings plans (RRSPs) and outlines the Department's rules for companies that issue RRSPs. Additional information is available in the publications listed in paragraph 44 below.

2.   This circular has five parts:

Part I—Approval (paragraphs 3-20)

Part II—Registration (paragraphs 21-27)

Part III—Annuities (paragraphs 28-32)

Part IV—Receipts (paragraphs 33-40)

Part V—General (paragraphs 41-45)

PART I—APPROVAL

Authority—(Section 146 of the *Income Tax Act*)

3.   The following can issue RRSPs:

   (a)   companies that are licensed to carry on an annuities business in Canada (e.g., insurance companies);

   (b)   Canadian trust companies;

   (c)   corporations that have been approved by the Governor in Council to sell investment contracts for RRSPs; and

   (d)   a depositary defined in section 146 of the Act as:

      (i)   a member or a person eligible to become a member of the Canadian Payments Association; or

      (ii)   a credit union that is a shareholder or member of a central corporate body for purposes of the *Canadian Payments Association Act*.

This circular provides comments directly to you, the issuer of a retirement saving plan (RSP), concerning the administration of the plan.

4.   The term "annuitant" as used in this circular is defined in subsection 146(1) of the Act. The annuitant is the individual for whom the RSP provides the retirement income. If the annuitant dies after the plan has matured, the annuitant's spouse may become the annuitant.

We have to approve an RSP specimen plan before any contracts can be registered and sold under that plan. Contributions can only be deducted in respect of registered plans. Therefore, an RSP should not be sold until we have given approval.

5.   The following documents make up a specimen plan.

   (a)   For an RSP issued by a company described in 3(a) above the following documents are required:

      (i)   a copy of the complete contract (policy, application form, schedules, and any riders or locking-in addenda);

    (ii)   a copy of the endorsement needed to qualify the contract for registration as an RRSP, unless the contract itself is a self-contained RSP; and

    (iii) a copy of the annuitant's application form requesting that the contract be registered as an RRSP, if not contained in the policy application or RSP endorsement.

(b)   For an RSP issued by other than an insurance company the following documents are required:

    (i)   a copy of the declaration of trust or text of the arrangement, and any applicable locking-in addenda;

    (ii)   a copy of the application form; and

    (iii) if requested, confirmation from the Canadian Payments Association of the depositary's status as referred to above in 3(d)(i).

Plan text

6.   The RSP must **not** provide for any of the following:

(a)   The RSP cannot provide for the payment of any benefit **before** maturity except:

    (i)   a refund of premiums in a lump sum; and

    (ii)   a payment to the annuitant.

(b)   The RSP cannot provide for the payment of any benefit **after** maturity except:

    (i)   retirement income to the annuitant;

    (ii)   full or partial commutation of retirement income under the plan to the annuitant; and

    (iii) commutation referred to in 7(c) below.

(c)   The RSP cannot provide for a payment to the annuitant of a retirement income except by:

    (i)   equal annual or more frequent periodic payments until there is a payment in full or partial commutation of the retirement income; and

    (ii)   when the commutation is partial, equal annual or more frequent periodic payments afterwards.

(d)   The RSP cannot provide for periodic payments in a year under an annuity after the death of the first annuitant that total more than the payments under the annuity in a year before the death.

(e)   The RSP cannot provide for the payment of any premium after maturity.

7.   The RSP **must** provide for the following:

(a)   maturity no later than the end of the year in which the annuitant reaches 69 years of age (see Note);

(b)   payment of an amount to a taxpayer to reduce the amount of tax the taxpayer would otherwise have to pay because of over-contributions by the taxpayer; and

(c)   the commutation of each annuity payable that would otherwise become payable to a person other than an annuitant under the plan.

Note

The March 1996 federal budget announced the proposed change in the maturation limit from age 71 to 69. No retirement savings plan will be registered after 1996 unless it complies with the revised requirements. For more details, or for information regarding the budget's impact on existing plans, you can contact the Registered Plans Division at the address in 11 below. You can also call (613) 954-0419 (English) or (613) 954-0930 (French).

8. The RSP **must** include provisions that do the following:

(a) The annuitant or a person with whom the annuitant was not dealing at arm's length cannot receive an advantage that is conditional on the existence of the plan, other than:

  (i) a benefit;

  (ii) amounts included in a deceased annuitant's income or included in the income of an RRSP trust for years that the trust has lost its exempt status due to the death of the last annuitant;

  (iii) the payment or allocation of any amount to the plan by the issuer;

  (iv) an advantage from life insurance in effect on December 31,1981; or

  (v) an advantage obtained from administrative or investment services provided for the plan.

(b) The RSP must prohibit all or any part of the retirement income from being assigned.

(c) For a depositary, the RSP must clearly state that:

  (i) the depositary cannot use the property held under the plan to offset any debt or obligation owing to the depositary; and

  (ii) the property held under the plan cannot be pledged assigned, or in any way alienated as security for a loan or for any purpose other than to provide the annuitant with a retirement income starting at maturity.

Where an advantage, for example a gift, that is prohibited under paragraph 8(a) above, is extended to an RRSP annuitant, you may be assessed a penalty under subsection 146(13.1) of the Act. For more information on the application of subsection 146(13.1) please refer to IT-415 Deregistration of Registered Retirement Savings Plans.

Note

The terms of the RSP can be more restrictive than those required by the Act (e.g., additional restrictions on the maturity date, withdrawals before maturity, or commutation), as long as the restrictions are clearly stated in the plan text.

Application form

9. A specimen plan consists of an application form and the specimen text. The application form has to request the following information:

(a) the annuitant's name, address, social insurance number, and date of birth;

(b) the contributor's name and social insurance number, if other than the annuitant;

(c) the annuitant's signature (the contributor who is not the annuitant does not sign the application form);

(d) the contract number (account, certificate or identifying number);

(e) the issuer's name;

(f) the signature of an authorized officer of the issuer accepting the application.

The application form has to include a clause in which the annuitant requests the issuer to apply for registration of the plan as an RRSPs under section 146 of the Act. If the specimen plan is for a particular employer, association, or other organization, the application form has to include a clause in which the annuitant authorizes the applicable organization to act as the annuitant's agent.

10. Do not use the word "registered" or the full acronym RRSP when referring to the name of the plan in the application form or specimen documents. This is because only the individual arrangements issued in the approved form are registered, and not the specimen itself. (See Part II, Registration.)

11. Submit your draft of the proposed RSP to:

Registered Plans Division
Revenue Canada
700 Industrial Avenue
Ottawa ON K1A 0L8

Group RSPs

12. An association, employer, or other organization can sponsor a group RSP. A group RSP is essentially a collection of individual RRSPs for the employees or members of the applicable organization. Individuals belonging to the organization or their spouses are eligible to participate. The organization can act as agent for the annuitant for certain purposes, such as receiving contributions to the RSP. If applicable, the text of the RSP contract and its application form should clearly show that the annuitant has authorized the organization to act as his or her agent and for what purpose.

13. When the organization acts as agent for the annuitant the plan has to state that the ultimate responsibility for the administration of each plan remains with you, as issuer. You have to deal directly with the Department concerning all RSP matters and reporting requirements unless we have your written authorization to deal with another person. The organization may not make changes to the approved specimen plan.

Agency agreement

14. You may have an agreement with an agent, such as an investment broker, that allows the agent to provide you with certain administrative and investment functions. It is not necessary to submit the agency agreement with the specimen plan. If you appoint the agent as custodian of the securities, and the securities are registered in the agent's name, then the agency agreement, the identity of the trustee, and the contract or identification number of the RRSP that governs the trust should be clearly disclosed in the security registration form.

15. The specimen plan must contain a clause stating that the ultimate responsibility for the administration of each plan remains with you, as issuer. The agent cannot make changes to the approved specimen plan.

Locked-in RRSPs

16. As issuer, you may set up an RSP specifically for locked-in registered pension plan funds. If a locking-in addendum or supplementary agreement is used together with an existing specimen plan, separate accounts have to be kept for the locked-in and non-locked-in portions.

Notification of acceptance

17. We will notify you when the RSP can be accepted for registration as an RRSP, and will request a final printed copy of the documents that constitute the specimen plan.

Amendments or revisions

18. We should approve all amendments or revisions to the specimen plan before the amendments are put into effect. Your submission to us should identify the nature of each change. If you amend the specimen plan to accommodate the transfer of locked-in registered pension plan funds, you have to include a copy of the locking-in addendum or supplementary agreement.

Change of issuer

19.   The terms of your specimen plan may allow you to resign as the issuer and appoint a successor issuer. This is generally considered to be an amendment to the specimen plan. To process the change, we need a letter telling us that the issuer has changed, and giving the effective date of the change. We also need confirmation from you or from the successor issuer that each annuitant who has a contract conforming to the specimen plan has been informed of the change. The successor issuer should send any amendments to the specimen plan resulting from the change to us for approval at the address in 11 above.

Termination of the inactive specimen plan

20.   You should advise us when you are no longer selling individual plans under the specimen plan. Also notify us when there are no longer any outstanding individual plans that conform to the specimen plan so that we can close our files.

PART II—REGISTRATION

21.   The address to register RSPs is:

Registered Plans Division
Revenue Canada
700 Industrial Avenue
Ottawa ON K1A 0L8

22.   To register RSPs for new annuitants, you have to:

(a)   provide us with a list of the plans and include:

(i)   the name, address, and social insurance number of each annuitant; and

(ii)   contract numbers you have assigned for each arrangement (contract, account, certificate, or identifying number); and

(b)   identify:

(i)   the name of the specimen plan and the number assigned by us to the specimen plan; and

(ii)   the calendar year or the period, such as the first 60 days of the calendar year, in which the plans listed were set up.

23.   You can submit lists on a quarterly or other basis, but not later than 60 days after the end of the calendar year for which you want the plans to be registered. Include with each list a separate Form T550, Application for Registration of Retirement Savings Plans or covering letter for each specimen plan with the signature of an authorized officer of the issuer who:

(a)   affirms that:

(i)   the annuitants of the plans listed have requested registration of their plans;

(ii)   the contracts or arrangements listed comply with the provisions of section 146 of the Act; and

(iii)   the plans conform in all respects with the specimen plan approved by us and identified on the list; and

(b)   states:

(i)   the number of contracts or arrangements listed for each specimen plan, including the assigned number; and

(ii)   the number of pages of the list.

Please do not submit lists as an attachment to Form T3R-G, Registered Retirement Savings Plan Group Information Return.

24.   Each plan can be registered only once. Use a separate notice for corrections such as names or social insurance numbers.

25.   You cannot list a plan for registration until you receive a contribution, as the plan doesn't exist until the payment is received.

Locked-in registered pension funds

26.   For all jurisdictions in Canada that have pension legislation, the term locking-in generally means that benefits cannot be cashed out either before or after maturity. Transfer to a registered retirement income fund may generally be made if it is a locked-in fund. When a locked-in RRSP matures, the total value of the plan must be used to purchase a life annuity contract.

27.   The federal *Pension Benefits Standards Act, 1985* (PBSA) or the equivalent provincial law allows the transfer of locked-in registered pensions to an RRSP provided the RRSP meets the federal or provincial RRSP conditions for locked-in pension funds. The PBSA governs the Northwest Territories and Yukon, as well as federally regulated industries.

PART III—ANNUITIES

Retirement income

28.   Generally, the Act defines retirement income in subsection 146(1) to include a life annuity with or without a guaranteed term, or a fixed-term annuity that provides benefits up to and including the age of 90. The guaranteed term for a life annuity cannot be more than 90 minus:

(a)   the annuitant's age in whole years at the maturity of the plan; or

(b)   if the annuitant's spouse is younger than the annuitant and the annuitant so elects, the spouse's age in whole years at the maturity of the plan.

Notice of purchase of annuity

29.   When you, as the issuer, arrange for the purchase of an annuity with the RRSP funds, you should complete Form T2037, Notice of Purchase of Annuity with Plan Funds, and give a copy to the issuer of the annuity. When you directly provide the annuity, however, Form T2037 is not necessary.

30.   To find out what forms an annuitant should use when directly transferring to or from an RRSP or when purchasing an annuity, please refer to Information Circular 79-8, Forms To Use To Directly Transfer Funds To Or Between Plans, Or To Purchase An Annuity, as well as the latest version of the RRSP and Other Registered Plans For Retirement guide.

31.   The commuted RRSP annuity can be used to purchase another life annuity for the annuitant. The annuity can be for the life of the annuitant (or the lives jointly of the annuitant and the annuitant's spouse), with or without a guaranteed term, or it can be a fixed-term annuity providing benefits up to and including the age of 90. The guaranteed term in years for a life annuity cannot be more than 90 minus:

(a)   the annuitant's age at the time of the acquisition; or

(b)   the age of the annuitant's spouse at the time of acquisition.

32.   A trust governed by an RRSP or another authorized entity can acquire an annuity contract (as described by the definition "retirement income" in subsection 146(1) of the Act) prior to the date of maturity of the RRSP and defer the commencement of the payments until the plan's maturity date. We consider the deferred life annuity contract to be an investment of the RRSP funds and not a method of providing an immediate retirement income. The annuity contract has to be owned by the trust or other entity.

PART IV—RECEIPTS

33.   Each year you should issue a receipt to the annuitant for contributions made by the annuitant, or for property received as a result of a transfer of a commuted RRSP annuity. If the annuitant's spouse contributed to the plan, you should instead give the receipt to the spouse. The receipt cannot be more than 8½ inches wide and should state that it is a receipt for an RRSP. In addition to giving instructions to submit the receipt with the contributor's income tax return, the receipt has to include the following:

(a)   the name of the issuer of the RRSP;

(b)   the signature of an authorized official (we will accept a facsimile signature as long as the receipts are numbered serially and a copy is kept at the issuer's head office);

(c)   the contract or arrangement number;

(d)   the name, address, and social insurance number of the annuitant;

(e)   the name and social insurance number of the contributor if other than the annuitant;

(f)   the total amount of premiums paid;

(g)   the dates of payment of premiums (the receipt may show the amount received in the initial 60 days of the year and the amount received during the remainder of the year); and

(h)   whether the contributions (premiums) were in whole or in part in kind, using the following text:

Contributions were in whole or in part in kind.

☐ (check)

You should advise the annuitant to submit an explanation of any contribution in kind with his or her income tax return.

34.   You may issue a receipt for each premium payment or for more than one payment. You may issue receipts for more than one payment twice a year. The first receipt is for payments made in the initial 60 days of the calendar year, and the second receipt is for payments made in the balance of the calendar year.

35.   If you only issue one receipt for a fiscal period ending 60 days after the end of a calendar year, the receipt should identify the total payments you received prior to January 1, and the total payments received in the 60-day period on or after January 1. If only a part of a premium payment is for an RRSP, the receipt should indicate the amount that qualifies as an RRSP contribution for income tax purposes. A duplicate receipt should be clearly identified as a copy for the annuitant's records.

Instant receipts

36.   An instant receipt is one which is provided to the contributor at the time the contribution is made. All enquiries and matters concerning instant receipts should be directed to:

T1 Programs Division
Revenue Canada
Ottawa ON K1A 0L8

You can issue instant receipts for premiums as long as the receipts are not issued for any rollover or direct transfer of property. The instant receipts should contain the same information requested in 33 above, and should be typewritten, produced on a cheque printer, or computer-generated. We recommend sending a draft of the receipt specimen to the T1 Programs Division.

37.   You can issue instant receipts without a contract number, but you should give the annuitant the contract number at a later date. Issue duplicate and amended receipts with a contract number as well as a reference to the original receipt number.

38.   Please clearly indicate on the receipt if the contributor's spouse is the annuitant.

39. You should retrieve an instant receipt if it was issued in error, or if the receipt became invalid due to a stop payment or a non-sufficient funds (NSF) cheque. If all copies of an invalid receipt are not returned, we ask that you inform us as follows including the annuitant's name, social insurance number, and the receipt number:

    (a) for contributors served by the Ottawa, Toronto, Mississauga, Scarborough, or North York tax services offices, inform the Assistant Director of Client Assistance at the appropriate office;

    (b) For all others, inform the Assistant Director of Enquiries and Adjustments at the taxation centre that serves the annuitant.

40. If you cannot account for any unissued instant receipts, you have to provide the T1 Programs Division with any missing receipt numbers.

PART V—GENERAL

41. A taxpayer who contributes to an RRSP any time during the year or no later than 60 days after the end of the year is eligible to deduct RRSP contributions from income, as long as the taxpayer or the taxpayer's spouse is the annuitant. The taxpayer can deduct all or part of the contributions (other than certain rollovers and other exempted amounts) made no later than 60 days after the end of the year from his or her income for that year. These deductions are subject to the limitations in the Act.

42. A trust governed at any time in the year by an RRSP has to file an income tax return.

43. For detailed information on reporting and deduction requirements, taxation of a trust, and foreign property issues, please refer to the following publications: T4RSP and T4RIF Guide, IT-320, Registered Retirement Savings Plans—Qualified Investments, and IT 412, Foreign Property of Registered Plans.

44. The following publications have RRSP information. They are available at any Revenue Canada tax services office:

    RRSP and other Registered Plans for Retirement Guide
    T4RSP and T4RIF Guide
    IT-124 Contributions to Registered Retirement Savings Plans
    IT-307 Spousal Registered Retirement Savings Plans
    IT-320 Registered Retirement Savings Plans—Qualified Investments
    IT-408 Life Insurance Policies as Investments of Registered Retirement Savings Plans
        and Deferred Profit Sharing Plans
    IT-412 Foreign Property of Registered Plans
    IT-415 Deregistration of Registered Retirement Savings Plans
    IT-500 Registered Retirement Savings Plans (maturing after June 29,1978)—
        Death of Annuitant after June 29, 1978
    IC 74-1 Form T2037, Notice of Purchase of Annuity with "Plan" Funds
    IC 76-12 Applicable Rate of Part XIII Tax on Amounts Paid or Credited to Persons in Treaty Countries
    IC 77-16 Non-Resident Income Tax
    IC 78-14 Guidelines for Trust Companies and Other Persons Responsible for filing
    T3R-IND, T3R-G,
    T3RIF-IND, T3RIF-G, T3H-IND, T3H-G, T3D, T3P, T3S, T3RI and T3F Returns
    IC 79-8 Forms to be Used for Direct Transfer of Funds to or Between Plans or for the Purchase of an Annuity

Personal information

45. Information that we obtain for taxation purposes is strictly confidential. Only the taxpayer or a person the taxpayer or the law authorizes has access to this information. The *Privacy Act* and the *Access to Information Act* reinforce this protection.

APPENDIX VII-1-B

INFORMATION CIRCULAR 77-1R4
DECEMBER 30, 1992
DEFERRED PROFIT SHARING PLANS

This circular cancels and replaces Information Circular 77-1R3, dated December 12, 1983. This revised circular deals only with deferred profit sharing plans. The circular includes comments on changes to the *Income Tax Act* resulting from pension reform. The circular incorporates comments formerly in Interpretation Bulletin IT-354, which will be cancelled.

An election by an employer under subsection 144(10) of the *Income Tax Act* to have a certain type of arrangement qualify as an employees profit sharing plan was previously filed at the address noted in paragraph 7 below. The election should now be filed at the taxation centre serving the employer. If you have any questions concerning the filing of an election, please call your local district office.

1.   This circular explains the provisions of the *Income Tax Act* and the administrative rules that deal with registering deferred profit sharing plans (DPSPs). It also provides general information on reporting requirements for DPSPs and revoked plans. You can find more information in the publications listed in paragraph 58.

2.   The circular is divided into three parts:

Part I: Registration

(paragraphs 4 to 38)

Part II: Transfers

(paragraphs 39 to 42)

Part III: Reporting Requirements and Taxation of the Trust

(paragraphs 43 to 57)

Authority

3.   Sections 147 and 198 to 207.2 of the *Income Tax Act* contain most of the provisions about DPSPs.

PART I—REGISTRATION

Principal Features of Deferred Profit Sharing Plans

4.   A DPSP involves an arrangement where an employer may share with either all or a designated group of employees of the employer the profits from the employer's business, or from the business of the employer and one or more corporations with which the employer does not deal at arm's length.

5.   The amounts payable by the employer are normally calculated by reference to profits (e.g., 5% of profits as defined in the plan), but can calculated on another basis as long as they are paid out of profits. The payments made by the employer must be made to a trustee in trust for the benefit of the employees or former employees of the employer, as provided under subsection 147(1).

6.   There must be a complete allocation by the trustee within specified time limits, either contingently or absolutely, of:

(a)   all amounts received under the plan from an employer, or transferred to the plan on behalf of a member; and

(b)   all income received, capital gains made, and capital losses sustained by the trust.

Acceptance and Registration

7.   Section 1501 of the *Income Tax Regulations* lists the documents needed to apply for registration of a DPSP, and also sets out the manner in which you should make the application. However, we have designed Form T2214 to serve as the letter otherwise required from the trustee and the employer. Forward the application by registered mail to the following address:

> Registered Plans Division
> Revenue Canada, Taxation
> Ottawa, Ontario
> K1A 0L8.

8.   The following documents constitute a proper application:

(a)   Form T2214, with which the trustee and the employer apply for registration of the plan as a DPSP;

(b)   if the employer is a corporation, a certified copy of the resolution of the directors authorizing the application to be made; and

(c)   a copy of the trust agreement and plan text (these can be combined in one document) constituting the plan or, if the plan conforms to an approved specimen plan (subject to variables), certification of Form T2214 by the company that secured approval of the specimen plan to which the plan conforms (see 12 and 14 below).

9.   When accepted, the effective date of registration of the plan will be either the date of postal registration of a proper application, or a later date as requested in the application or specified in the plan. Normally, we will accept applications submitted by ordinary mail if the application is otherwise acceptable. In such cases, however, the effective date of registration will be at the discretion of the Department, and we cannot give assurance that it will be earlier than the date we receive the application at our Head Office in Ottawa. We cannot give retroactive registration of a plan, regardless of the circumstances. If the application is incomplete, we may restrict the effective date of registration to the date you submit the missing documents. If the text of the plan or trust agreement has to be amended to meet our requirements, registration will normally be effective on the date we would otherwise have accepted the original complete submission.

10.   On the initial registration of a plan that permits participation by more than one employer, we need an application from each employer participating in the plan at the time registration is requested. Once the plan is registered, however, we do not need an application from employers who later join the plan. Such subsequent participation should be properly authorized by a resolution of the directors if the employer is a corporation, must be permitted by the terms of the plan, and can be effective from the beginning of the employer's current fiscal period. You must notify us at the address in 7 above that an additional employer is participating in the plan. The notification must:

—quote the registration number of the plan;

—state the effective date of participation; and

—if the employer is a corporation, provide a copy of the company's resolution authorizing participation.

The subsequent participation by an employer will only be permitted if the DPSP has been amended to meet the conditions for registration (see 17, 18, and 19 below) that apply on the effective date of that employer's participation.

Specimen Plans

11.   A trust company, insurance company, or consultant who wants to simplify the marketing and registration under section 147 of profit sharing plans can submit for approval in principle a package consisting of a plan text and trust agreement, as well as a statement of limited variables to be permitted within such documents.

Submission should be made to the address shown in 7 above. Once approved, we will assign the specimen plan a number for identification purposes, and we will advise the applicant of our acceptance, the identification number, and the variables that we will permit.

12.   When a plan conforms to an approved specimen plan, you do not need to submit a plan text or trust agreement with each application. The application should merely certify that it conforms to an identified specimen plan, and should provide details about permitted variables, if there are any.

13.   It is intended that there should be few variables, because otherwise the purpose of the specimen plan is defeated. Examples of permissible variables are the vesting schedule, administration fee schedule, retirement age, and designated investment funds.

14.   Applications for the registration of plans conforming to a specimen plan should still be submitted individually, and the effective date of registration will be in accordance with 9 above.

15.   If a plan that conformed to a specimen plan at the time of application is later amended so that it no longer conforms, you should submit a complete amended text and trust agreement to the address shown in 7 above.

16.   Correspondence to the Department about an approved specimen plan (but not about a specific registered plan) must identify the specimen plan by its assigned identification number. Correspondence, returns, or other submissions regarding a registered plan, whether or not it conforms to a specimen plan, must identify that plan by its registration number.

Statutory Conditions for Registration

17.   The following specific statutory requirements are numbered to correspond with subsection 147(2):

(a)   The plan must provide that all payments made under the plan to a trustee for the benefit of beneficiaries be allocated by the trustee (in the year in which they are received by the trustee) to the individual beneficiary for whom the amounts were so paid.

(a.1) The plan must stipulate that no contributions can be made to the plan other than the employer's contribution made according to the terms of the plan for the benefit of the employer's employees who are beneficiaries under the plan, or an amount transferred to the plan in accordance with subsection 147(19).

(b)   The plan must not permit loans to be made to an employee or other beneficiary.

(c)   The plan must provide that no part of the trust funds under the plan can be invested in notes, bonds, debentures, or similar obligations of an employer making payments under the plan, or of a corporation with which that employer does not deal at arm's length.

(d)   The plan must provide that no part of the trust funds can be invested in shares of a corporation with at least 50% of its property consisting of the property described in (c) above.

(e)   The plan must stipulate that no right or interest of an employee who is a beneficiary under the plan is capable, either in whole or in part, of surrender or assignment.

(f)   The plan must stipulate that each of the trustees under the plan is a resident of Canada.

(g)   The plan must provide that, if a corporation licensed or otherwise authorized under the laws of Canada or a province to carry on in Canada the business of offering to the public its services as trustee is not a trustee under the plan, there must be at least three trustees who are individuals.

(h) The plan must provide that all income received, capital gains made, and capital losses sustained by the trust be allocated to beneficiaries under the plan within 90 days after the end of the trust year, unless they have been allocated in previous years.

(i) The plan must provide that all amounts allocated or reallocated to a beneficiary vest irrevocably in that beneficiary:

    (i) in the case of an amount allocated or reallocated before 1991, not later than five years after the end of the year in which the amounts are so allocated or reallocated, unless the beneficiary has ceased before that time to be an employee of an employer who has participated in the plan; and

    (ii) in the case of any other amount, no later than the later of either the time of allocation or reallocation, or the day on which the beneficiary completes a period of 24 consecutive months as a beneficiary under the plan, or under any other DPSP for which the plan can reasonably be considered to have been substituted.

(i.1) The plan must require that each forfeited amount and earnings that can be reasonably attributed to the forfeited amount be paid to participating employers or be reallocated to beneficiaries on or before the later of December 31, 1991, and December 31 of the year immediately following the calendar year in which the amount is forfeited, or such later time the Minister permits in writing.

(j) The plan must provide that the trustee inform, in writing, all new beneficiaries of their rights under the plan.

(k) The plan must provide that all amounts vested in each employee who is a beneficiary become payable to the employee or, in the event of the employee's death, to a beneficiary designated by the employee or to the employee's estate, not later than 90 days after the earliest of:

    (i) the death of the employee;

    (ii) the day on which the employee ceases to be employed by a contributing employer;

    (iii) the day on which the employee becomes 71 years old;

        and

    (iv) the termination or winding up of the plan.

If the employee elects and if permitted by the plan, all or any part of amounts payable to the employee:

—can be paid in equal annual or more frequent instalments over a period of not more than 10 years from the day on which the amount becomes payable; or

—can be used to purchase an annuity from a person licensed or otherwise authorized under the laws of Canada or a province to carry on in Canada an annuities business.

If an annuity is purchased, it must begin on or before the 71st birthday and, if it has a guaranteed term, such a term must not be more than 15 years. (A DPSP may permit members to withdraw all or a portion of their vested interest in the plan while continuing in employment.)

(k.1) If the plan is registered after March 1983, the plan must require that no benefit or loan, other than:

    (i) a benefit the amount of which has to be included when calculating the beneficiary's income;

    (ii) an amount referred to in paragraph 147(10)(a) or (b);

    (iii) a benefit derived from an allocation or reallocation referred to in subsection 147(2); or

    (iv) the benefit derived from the provision of administrative or investment services for the plan;

that is conditional in any way on the existence of the plan, can be extended to a beneficiary or to a person with whom the beneficiary was not dealing at arm's length.

(k.2) If the plan is registered after March 1983, the plan must provide that no individual can become a beneficiary under the plan who is:

    (i)   a person related to the employer;

    (ii)   a person who is, or is related to, a specified shareholder of the employer or of a corporation related to the employer;

    (iii) if the employer is a partnership, a person related to a member of the partnership; or

    (iv) if the employer is a trust, a person who is, or is related to, a beneficiary under the trust.

(l)   The plan must comply with the *Income Tax Regulations.*

Note: DPSPs registered before January 1, 1991, are subject to revocation if they are not amended to comply with (a.1), (i), and (i.1) above with effect from January 1, 1991.

18.   Plans registered after 1990 must include terms that are adequate to ensure the contribution limits outlined in subsection 147(5.1) will be satisfied for each calendar year (see 25 and 26 below). DPSPs registered before 1991 are subject to the limits in subsection 147(5.1) and become revocable if the limits are violated after 1990 (see 37(g) below). We expect all plans registered before 1991 to be amended so that they can be operated in compliance with subsection 147(5.1).

Departmental Requirements

19.   A plan must also meet the following administrative rules:

(a)   For non-public corporate employers, at least one of the trustees must be independent of the operations of the company, and must not be a shareholder.

(b)   The plan must not provide for divesting because of dismissal for cause or union membership.

(c)   The trustee(s) must have sufficient authority to ensure that the plan is implemented and operated and that the payment of benefits to the beneficiaries is made.

(d)   If the plan or trust agreement empowers the trustees to borrow monies against the assets of the trust, such borrowing must be only to facilitate the payments of benefits under the plan without forcing a distress sale of long-term investments. The borrowing must also be on a short-term basis (see 51(d) below).

(e)   The plan must provide that employee contributions made before 1991 and amounts transferred to the plan on behalf of the beneficiary from another DPSP are fully vested in the beneficiary. The Act does not allow employee contributions, other than a direct transfer from another DPSP, after 1990.

Employer Contributions

20.   Effective after 1990, a plan can permit contributions to be made at the employer's discretion, or to be contingent on a prerequisite such as employee performance, without requiring the employer to make a minimum contribution. The text must clearly provide, however, that contributions will be subject to the maximum contribution limits noted in 26 below.

21.   Contributions can be made "by reference to profits" or "out of profits." If "by reference to profits," the contribution is expressed as a percentage of profits for the year. If "out of profits," the contribution can be expressed in various ways, and profits can be defined either as profits of the year or as undistributed profits of the year and previous years.

22.   An employer whose contributions are determined by referring to profits can base such contributions on its own profits for the year or on the combined profits for the year of it and corporations with which it does not deal at arm's length. An employer, however, can only contribute to a plan on behalf of its own employees.

23.   When an employer does not make any contributions to a DPSP in a calendar year, the other provisions of the plan must continue to operate, and the trustee must continue the administrative duties for the plan.

24.   No deduction can be made in calculating the income of an employer for a taxation year for a contribution to a DPSP for a beneficiary who is described in 17(k.2) above (see also 46 below).

Contribution Limits

25.   Contributions to a DPSP on behalf of a beneficiary and forfeited amounts that have been reallocated to a beneficiary are included in the beneficiary's pension credit for a year. A forfeited amount is an amount to which a beneficiary under the plan has ceased to have any rights, other than the portion of that amount that is payable to another person because of the beneficiary's death. The Employers' Pension Adjustment Calculation Guide, available at the district office, provides details on how to calculate pension credits and the pension adjustment.

26.   The plan must include terms that ensure the following limits will be satisfied for each calendar year (see also the notes below):

    (a)   the total of a beneficiary's pension credits for the year regarding an employer under DPSPs cannot be more than one of the following amounts, whichever is less:

        (i)   one-half (½) of the money purchase limit for the year; and

        (ii)   18% of the beneficiary's compensation for the year from the employer;

    (b)   the total pension credits of a beneficiary under DPSPs for a year regarding an employer and regarding any other non-arm's length employers cannot be more than one-half (½) of the money purchase limit for the year; and

    (c)   the total of the beneficiary's pension adjustments for the year regarding an employer and regarding any other non-arm's length employers cannot be more than one of the following amounts, whichever is less:

        (i)   the money purchase limit for the year; and

        (ii)   18% of the beneficiary's total compensation for the year from the employers.

Notes:

    (A)   Refer to the current version of the Employers' Pension Adjustment Calculation Guide for the money purchase limit.

    (B)   For the purposes of the above limits, compensation includes total salary, wages, and other amounts from the beneficiary's employment with the employer that have to be included in calculating the beneficiary's income for the year. In (c) above, but not in (a), compensation includes amounts prescribed by Regulation 8507 for periods when a beneficiary's remuneration is less than normal because of periods of disability, leaves of absence, or similar causes. If the beneficiary is not a resident of Canada for a period in the year, compensation in (a) and (c) above does not include remuneration for that period that does not relate to duties performed in Canada or that is exempt from tax in Canada under a tax treaty with another country, except to the extent that is acceptable to the Minister.

    (C)   In the year a beneficiary terminates employment, compensation can be based on the beneficiary's compensation for the year of termination, or on the beneficiary's compensation for the immediately preceding year, if it is more.

    (D)   A forfeited amount that is reallocated and paid out to the beneficiary in the year of reallocation does not have to be included in the calculation of the beneficiary's pension credit. An amount that is transferred to another DPSP, registered pension plan (RPP), or registered retirement savings plan (RRSP) is not considered to have been paid out.

(E)   A beneficiary's pension credit under a DPSP is nil for the year the beneficiary terminates employment, if the beneficiary loses all entitlement to benefits under the DPSP because of terminating employment, and if no amounts other than a repayment of the beneficiary's contributions plus earnings have or will be paid to the beneficiary from the DPSP.

(F)   For the purposes of calculating a beneficiary's pension credit under a DPSP, contributions made in the first two months of the calendar year but applying to the previous year will be considered as having been made in the previous year.

27.   The employer must determine whether a DPSP contribution or reallocation of a forfeited amount will cause the limits in subsection 147(5.1) to be exceeded before making the contribution or reallocation. Particular caution must be exercised with the timing of contributions, and if more than one plan exists or more than one related employer is contributing on behalf of the same individual.

28.   If the limits are not respected for a calendar year, registration of the DPSP is revocable. The employer is denied a deduction for contributions made in the year, except as expressly permitted in writing by the Minister. Amounts withdrawn from the plan by the employer do not reduce the amount of the original contribution and are appropriations which must be included in the employer's income (see 45 below).

Allocations to Beneficiaries

29.   Capital gains made and capital losses sustained must be allocated to beneficiaries under the DPSP on or before the day that is 90 days after the end of the year in which they were made or sustained, as indicated in 17(h) above. The plan can provide for the allocation of unrealized gains and losses, as long as this basis is used consistently from year to year.

30.   All capital losses sustained (or accrued) must be allocated to beneficiaries under the plan, regardless of whether or not such losses are more than the capital gains realized (or accrued) in that particular year. These capital losses are not deductible by the beneficiary. They may, however, ultimately reduce the taxable amount received by the beneficiary from the DPSP.

31.   A DPSP can provide for different methods of allocating different sources of income. For example, the plan can provide that investment income is to be allocated to beneficiaries based on the balances in their accounts at the beginning of the year, whereas proceeds of a life insurance policy on a member are to be allocated solely to the deceased member's account. If the plan is silent about the method of allocation of the various sources of income, we do not object to an allocation of each source on any reasonable basis.

32.   Amounts allocated or reallocated to a beneficiary that remain not vested at the time the beneficiary ceases to be employed can, depending on the provisions of the plan, be paid out to the beneficiary or be forfeited by the beneficiary. In addition, the plan can provide for vesting of amounts allocated or reallocated to a beneficiary either at the time the beneficiary ceases to be employed, or at any time after the beneficiary ceases employment, subject to the vesting schedule in 17(i) above. Amounts which vest after the beneficiary ceases employment are not subject to the requirement described in 17(k) above.

33.   If a non-vested amount is paid to the beneficiary or if vesting continues after employment ceases, the beneficiary will not be considered to have lost all entitlement to benefits (i.e., Note E to paragraph 26 above does not apply). Therefore, any contribution or reallocation made on behalf of the beneficiary in the year of termination of employment must be included in the beneficiary's DPSP pension credit for that year. Contributions and reallocations of forfeited amounts, however, cannot continue on behalf of a beneficiary after the calendar year in which the beneficiary's employment ceases (except for contributions made in the first two months of the following calendar year that relate to the year of termination).

Amendments or Revisions

34.   All amendments or revisions to the DPSP, together with a copy of the authorizing resolution or by-law, if any, and advice of any change in the corporate identity of any employer participating in the plan or any change of trustees, should be submitted promptly to Revenue Canada, Taxation at the address noted in 7 above. The submission should identify the nature of the changes. Failing to submit amendments may prejudice the registered status of the plan.

35.   A DPSP that is amended or revised retains its registered status unless advice of revocation of registration is given to a trustee under the plan and to the participating employer. Such revocation may be retroactive if the amendments are not in accordance with the law or departmental requirements.

Termination of a DPSP

36.   If an employer terminates a DPSP or terminates participation in such a plan, the following information should be submitted to Revenue Canada, Taxation after all funds have been distributed:

    (a)   if the employer is a corporation, a copy of the board resolution terminating the plan or participation in it;

    (b)   the effective date of termination, if it is not included in the resolution; and

    (c)   a statement from the trustees setting out the date and manner the assets of the fund were distributed.

Note: All the amounts vested in an employee become payable to the employee not later than 90 days after the plan terminates or winds up. This information is to be sent to the address noted in 7 above, and is in addition to the final return that has to be filed by the DPSP trustee when the trust ceases to exist (see 55 below).

Revocation of Registration

37.   The Minister can revoke a DPSP's registration if the following situations arise:

    (a)   the plan has been revised or amended in such a way that, following the revisions or amendments, the plan no longer complies with the registration requirements for a DPSP;

    (b)   any provision of the plan has not been complied with;

    (c)   if on any day after June 30, 1982, a benefit or loan is extended or continues to be extended because of the existence of a deferred profit sharing plan, and that benefit or loan would be prohibited if the plan met the requirement for registration contained in 17(k.1) above;

    (d)   an amount is transferred from the plan to another registered plan, and the transfer is not in accordance with 40 or 41 below;

    (e)   the plan does not comply with the conditions for registration outlined above in 17(a) to (k) and (l);

    (f)   if the plan was registered after March 1983, the plan does not comply with the requirements of 17(k.1) and (k.2) above;

    (h)   the limits described in 26 above are not satisfied for a calendar year; or

    (i)   an employer who participates in the plan failed to file an information return, as and when required, reporting the pension adjustment of a plan member.

If the Minister revokes the registration of a DPSP, the revocation will be effective as follows:

    —if (e) or (f) above apply, not before January 1, 1991;

    —if (g) above applies, at the end of the year for which the requirements are not satisfied;

    —if (h) above applies, any date after the information return had to be filed; and

    —in all other cases, the date of the infraction.

In any case, the Minister may revoke the registration on any later date. Notice of revocation and the effective date will be given by registered mail to the trustee of the plan and to an employer of employees who are beneficiaries under the plan.

Rules that Apply to a Revoked Plan

38. The following special rules apply to a revoked plan:

    (a) the revoked plan is considered not to be a DPSP, an employee profit sharing plan, or a retirement compensation arrangement;

    (b) the revoked plan cannot be accepted for registration under the Act until at least one year after the effective date of revocation;

    (c) the trust is taxable on its taxable income for a taxation year if the plan was a revoked plan for any part of that year;

    (d) the employer cannot deduct payments made to a trustee under the plan at a time when the plan is a revoked plan;

    (e) any amount received by a beneficiary under the plan will be included in the beneficiary's income as if the plan had been a deferred profit sharing plan;

    (f) the value of any funds or property appropriated to or for the benefit of a taxpayer who is an employer making payments to the plan, or a corporation with which such an employer does not deal at arm's length, other than payments for, or on account of, shares of the capital stock of the taxpayer purchased by the plan trust, will be income of the taxpayer in the year of appropriation (appropriations that are repaid within a year from the end of the year in which the appropriation was made and that are not part of a series of appropriations and repayments do not have to be included in income); and

    (g) if property of a revoked plan is disposed of to, or is acquired from, a taxpayer for a consideration other than the fair market value of the property at the time of the transaction, the difference between the consideration and the fair market value will be taxable, as provided in 48 below.

PART II—TRANSFERS

39. Registration of a DPSP is revocable if, after 1988, an amount is transferred from the plan to an RPP, an RRSP, or another DPSP unless the transfer is in accordance with subsection 147(19) (see 40 below) or a deduction is available under paragraph 60(j) or (j.2) to the individual on whose behalf the transfer is made (see 41 below). Specific transfer provisions do not need to be included in the DPSP in order to satisfy registration requirements. Amounts can be transferred into or from a DPSP if the Act permits the transfer and as long as the terms of the DPSP do not prevent the transfer.

40. An amount can be transferred from a DPSP to another registered plan if the amount is:

    —a lump-sum amount and not part of a series of periodic payments;

    —made on behalf of an individual employed or formerly employed by an employer who participated in the DPSP on behalf of the individual, or the individual's spouse who is entitled to benefits as a result of the individual's death ("spouse" for this purpose includes a common-law spouse as defined in subsection 146(1.1));

    —in full or partial satisfaction of the individual's entitlement to benefits under the plan;

    —an amount that would have been taxable if it was paid directly to the individual; and

    —transferred directly to an RPP for the individual's benefit, to an RRSP under which the individual is the annuitant, or to another DPSP, as long as the other DPSP can reasonably be expected to have at least five (5) beneficiaries throughout the calendar year in which the transfer is made.

Note: Contributions made by a beneficiary cannot be transferred. However, the earnings that are attributable to beneficiary contributions do qualify for a direct transfer.

You can use Form T2151, Record of Direct Transfer of a "Single Amount" (subsection 147(19) or section 147.3), to record the transfer. An amount that is transferred under subsection 147(19) is not to be included in the income of the person on whose behalf the transfer was made. Also, that person cannot deduct the amount transferred.

41.   An amount can also be transferred from a DPSP to another registered plan if the amount is included in the beneficiary's income and is deductible by the beneficiary on whose behalf the amount is transferred under paragraph 60(j) or (j.2).

—Deductions under paragraph 60(j) after 1989 are limited to DPSP benefits that flow through a testamentary trust, or a distribution of shares from a DPSP for which the beneficiary has elected under subsection 147(10.1).

—Paragraph 60(j.2) permits a maximum deduction of $6,000 a year from 1989 to 1994 for periodic DPSP payments that are transferred to a spousal RRSP.

You will find more information on transfers from DPSPs in the Pension and RRSP Tax Guide.

Transfers on Behalf of Non-Residents

42.   DPSP funds can be transferred on behalf of a non-resident person to an RPP or an RRSP in accordance with 40 above, or to a spousal RRSP where the amount would be deductible under paragraph 60(j.2) if the non-resident were a resident. In both cases, the DPSP trustee has to make the transfer directly to the receiving plan, using Form NRTA1, Authorization for Non-Resident Tax Exemption.

PART III—REPORTING REQUIREMENTS AND TAXATION OF THE TRUST

Reporting Payments and Other Amounts

43.   Once benefits become payable under the plan, the trustee has to secure an employer account number from the local district office for the purpose of reporting such payments.

44.   Every person making a payment under a DPSP or a revoked plan to a beneficiary shall, subject to 47(a) below, report such payments on the T4A Supplementary and T4A Summary forms.

45.   The amount or value of any funds or property appropriated in any manner whatever to or for the benefit of a taxpayer who is an employer making payments to the plan, or is a corporation with which such an employer does not deal at arm's length, other than payments for, or on account of, shares of the capital stock of the taxpayer purchased by the plan trust, shall be reported on the T4A Supplementary and T4A Summary forms as income of the recipient. This includes forfeited amounts paid under the terms of the plan to the employer. Appropriations that are repaid within a year from the end of the year in which the appropriation was made and that are not part of a series of appropriations and repayments do not have to be included in income.

46.   When an allocation of an amount contributed by an employer to the plan after December 1, 1982, or for taxation years starting after 1981, a reallocation of a forfeited amount, is made to an individual described in 17(k.2) above, the amount must be included in the individual's income under subsection 147(10.3). The amount should be reported on Form T4A in the year of allocation or reallocation. If the amount of the allocation or reallocation is paid out in the same year as the allocation or reallocation, the payment does not need to be reported again on Form T4A. When the payment is made in a year after the allocation or reallocation, that payment must be reported on Form T4A. The fact that an amount was taxable under subsection 147(10.3) does not exclude it from the taxing provisions of 147(10) on payout in a year after allocation or reallocation.

Determining Income from a DPSP

47.   Amounts received in a taxation year by a beneficiary (other than an employer) from a trust governed by a DPSP or revoked plan shall be included in calculating the beneficiary's income subject to the following exclusions and deductions:

   (a)   The following amounts do not have to be included in the beneficiary's income, and should not be reported on the T4A Supplementary and T4A Summary forms:

      (i)   the cost of an annuity described in 17(k) above purchased under the plan for the beneficiary;

      (ii)   amounts allocated to the beneficiary when the plan was an employees' profit sharing plan and excluded from income because of subsection 147(11);

      (iii)   amounts contributed to the plan by the beneficiary when the plan was a DPSP but excluded from income because of subsection 147(12);

      (iv)   an amount representing a deferred capital gain on shares transferred out of a DPSP for which the beneficiary has made an election under subsection 147(10.1); and

      (v)   amounts transferred directly to another registered plan as described in 40 above.

   (b)   The following are amounts which the beneficiary can deduct on his or her income tax return from the amount reported on the T4A Supplementary form if the beneficiary makes certain transfers or elections:

      (i)   a spouse who receives a payment from a DPSP through a testamentary trust on the death of an employee who was a beneficiary of the plan can deduct such amounts under paragraph 60(j) that are paid in the year, or within 60 days after the end of the year, as a contribution to an RPP or as a premium under an RRSP ("spouse" for this purpose includes common-law spouse as defined in subsection 146(1.1));

      (ii)   amounts paid in the year or within 60 days after the end of the year as a contribution to an RPP or as a premium under an RRSP representing the cost amount to the beneficiary of shares transferred out of a DPSP, as permitted by paragraph 60(j), if the beneficiary has made an election under subsection 147(10.1) concerning the shares; and

      (iii)   for the 1989 to 1994 taxation years, amounts representing periodic payments received from the DPSP, but not more than $6,000 in any one year, that are paid in the year the periodic payments are received or within 60 days after the end of the year as a premium under a spousal RRSP, as permitted by paragraph 60(j.2).

   (c)   If a payment is made to a beneficiary's heirs or estate, any succession duty paid under a provincial succession duty act that applies to that payment can be deducted when calculating the income of the recipient, as permitted by paragraph 60(m.1).

48.   A taxpayer is considered to have received a benefit from a DPSP if property of a trust governed by a DPSP or a revoked plan is disposed of to the taxpayer at a price that is less than the fair market value at the time of the transaction, or if property is acquired from the taxpayer at a price that is more than the fair market value at the time of the transaction.

The difference between the fair market value and the sale or purchase price must be reported on the T4A Supplementary and T4A Summary forms and included in the taxpayer's income for the calendar year in which the transaction occurs. Such a transaction also subjects the trust to a penalty tax (see 51(g) below).

49.   An amount reported on Form T4A in the name of an employer under the plan or a corporation with whom the employer does not deal at arm's length must be included in the income of the taxpayer named, unless the funds or property, or an amount equal to the value of the funds or property, was repaid to the trust within one year of the end of the taxation year, and as long as the repayment was not part of a series of appropriations and repayments.

Taxation Year of Trust

50.   The taxation year of a trust governed by a DPSP or a revoked plan is the calendar year or part-year during which the trust existed.

Tax Payable by a Trust

51.   A trust governed by a DPSP is exempt from tax except in the circumstances described below:

(a)   Tax is payable on the taxable income of a trust for a taxation year during any part of which the trust was governed by a revoked plan.

(b)   If, in a taxation year, the trust acquires a non-qualified investment, tax is payable equal to the fair market value of such investment at the time it was acquired. Such tax is payable within 10 days of the day on which the non-qualified investment is acquired. A refund of the tax can be claimed if the trust disposes of a property that, when acquired, was a non-qualified investment. The refund is equal to either the amount of the tax imposed as a result of the acquisition of the property, or the proceeds of disposition, whichever is less (non-qualified investments are dealt with in 56 below).

(c)   If a trust owns property acquired after August 24, 1972, which was a qualified investment when acquired and which later becomes a non-qualified investment, tax is payable equal to 1% of the fair market value at the time of acquisition of such property for each month throughout which the non-qualified investment was held.

(d)   If, in a taxation year, trust property is used as security for a loan, tax is payable equal to the fair market value of the property as of the date it is so used. Such tax is payable within 10 days of the day on which the property is used as security for a loan. A refund of the tax can be claimed, if such property ceases to be so used. The refund is equal to the tax imposed when the property was used minus and net loss sustained by the trust because of such use.

(e)   If, at the end of any month in a taxation year, the trust holds foreign property acquired after June 18, 1971 (other than property that was not a qualified investment at the end of the month), and if the cost amount of all foreign property held exceeds the total of:

(i)   10% of the cost amount of all property held at the end of any month in the 1989 and prior taxation years, 12% at the end of any month in 1990, 14% in 1991, 16% in 1992, 18% in 1993, and 20% in 1994 and following years; and

(ii)   the lesser of three times the small business investment amount of the trust for the month and 20% of the cost amount of all property held at the end of the month;

tax is payable by the trust equal to 1% of the lesser of the excess described above and the cost amount of all foreign property acquired after June 18, 1971.

(f)   The trust is liable to pay a tax if certain agreements are entered into for the acquisition of shares at a price that may differ from their fair market value on the date of purchase. The tax payable is equal to 1% for each month in a taxation year that an agreement described in section 206.1 is outstanding, calculated on:

(i)   the maximum purchase price of the shares for agreements entered into after December 11, 1979, and before July 14, 1990; and

(ii)   the fair market value of the shares at the time the agreement was entered into for agreements entered into after July 13, 1990.

(g)   If, after 1990, the trust disposes of property to a taxpayer at a price that is less than the fair market value at the time of the transaction, or acquires property from a taxpayer at a price that is more than the fair market value at the time of the transaction, tax is payable by the trust for the calendar year in which the transaction occurs equal to 50% of the difference between the fair market value and the sale or purchase price (this is in addition to the income inclusion by the taxpayer noted in 48 above).

(h) The trust is taxable on an excess amount created by contributions made by beneficiaries or gifts to the trust held at the end of any month. The excess amount for a DPSP trust at the end of a particular month is the total of all amounts each of which is:

(i) The total of all contributions made by a beneficiary after May 25, 1976, other than:

A. contributions that have been deducted by the beneficiary under paragraph 60(k);

B. transfers on behalf of the beneficiary under subsection 147(19); or

C. contributions (except those referred to in (A) and (B) above) made by the beneficiary in each calendar year before 1991 that are not more than $5,500; that have not been returned to the beneficiary before that time; or

(ii) the amount of any gifts received by the trust after May 25, 1976. A separate calculation under (i) above is required for each beneficiary whose contributions result in an excess amount in the trust in the year and tax at 1% of the excess amount at each month-end continues to be payable in later years until the excess contributions are returned to the beneficiary. (Any beneficiary contributions made after 1990, other than a direct transfer from another DPSP, are not only subject to this tax, but cause registration of the DPSP to become revocable.)

Note: For taxation years before 1991, the trust had to pay a tax equal to 50% of the forfeitures arising in the trust in the year, to the extent that such forfeitures were not reallocated in the year or 90 days after that to beneficiaries under the plan within the amounts specified in former paragraph 201(2)(b) or paid to the employer in the year and included in the employer's income. Effective in 1991, the registration of a DPSP becomes revocable if forfeited amounts are not reallocated or paid to participating employers in accordance with 17(i.1) above.

52. If, in a taxation year, a trust is governed by a revoked plan, tax is payable by that trust as described in paragraphs 51(a), (b), (d), and (g) above.

53. If 51(b) or (d) above apply, tax is payable by the trust within 10 days of the day on which the trust acquires the non-qualified investment or uses the property as security, whichever applies. Otherwise, any tax payable by a trust, even if it is calculated on a monthly basis as in 51(c), (e), (f), and (h) above, is payable with the annual return that must be filed on behalf of the trust (see 55 below).

54. If a tax has been paid as required by subsection 199(1) on initial non-qualified investments (certain investments held since December 21, 1966), the trust can apply for a refund under subsection 199(2) of such tax that has not previously been refunded when it disposes of those investments.

Annual Returns of Trust

55. Form T3D, Deferred Profit Sharing Plan or Revoked Plan Information Return and Income Tax Return, is to be completed by a trustee of a trust governed at any time in the year by a DPSP or a revoked plan. The return must be filed within 90 days of the end of the calendar year. If it later becomes necessary to submit additional or revised information, such information should be submitted by letter and not by filing an amended return.

Qualified and Non-Qualified Investments

56. Paragraph 204(e) defines a qualified investment for a trust governed by a DPSP or a revoked plan as investments listed in that paragraph and in section 4900 (section 1502 before 1981) of the Income Tax Regulations, while paragraph 204(d) defines a non-qualified investment.

57. Amounts paid by a trust governed by a DPSP or a revoked plan to acquire interests in life insurance policies are non-qualified investments unless the interest is in a policy described in subsections 198(6) and (6.1) or within the limits stated in subsection 198(7). Interests in life insurance policies falling under those subsections are deemed not to be acquisitions of non-qualified investments. Subsection 198(8) provides rules for determining when such investments have been disposed of and the proceeds of disposition. (Note: These investments are not qualified investments even though they are deemed not to be acquisitions of non-qualified investments.)

Other Publications

58.   You will find additional DPSP information in the current version of the following publications. They are available at your local district office:

Pension and RRSP Tax Guide
Employers' Pension Adjustment Calculation Guide
Employers' Guide to Payroll Deductions
Guide for Payers of Non-Resident Tax

IT-281	Elections on Single Payments from a Deferred Profit Sharing Plan
IT-363	Deferred Profit Sharing Plans—Deductibility of Contributions and Taxation of Amounts Received or Allocated
IT-408	Life Insurance Policies as Investments of RRSPs and DPSPs
IT-412	Foreign Property of Registered Plans
IC 77-16	Non-Resident Income Tax
IC 78-14	Guidelines for Trust Companies and Other Persons Responsible for Filing T3R-IND, T3R-G, T3RIF-IND, T3RIF-G, T3H-IND, T3H-G, T3D, T3P, T3S, T3RI and T3F Returns
IC 79-8	Forms to be Used for Direct Transfer of Funds to or Between Plans or for the Purchase of an Annuity

Personal Information Banks

59.   Information obtained by the Department for taxation purposes is strictly confidential. Only the taxpayer or persons authorized by the taxpayer or law have access to this information. The *Privacy Act* and the *Access to Information Act* reinforce this protection.

CHAPTER 2

Prepaid Legal Services:
Helping to Make the Law More Accessible

by Michael Mazzuca

INTRODUCTION

The expense of legal services may often place an overwhelming financial burden on an individual. A person may fail to assert his or her legal rights because of the anticipated legal costs and, similarly, an individual forced to defend a civil action or criminal charge may often risk personal financial ruin. The concept of prepaid legal services or legal costs insurance is an attempt to alleviate the financial burden of legal costs for the average individual.

Prepaid legal services is not a new idea. Legal expense insurance has been available in Europe for more than 50 years and in the United States since the early 1970s. In the United States, these plans had their origins through insurance and automobile club offerings. Legal services have been available as a result of membership in a group since about 1971.

The question most often asked is whether there is a *need* for these services. In 1974, a report was issued by the American Bar Association's Special Committee to Serve Legal Needs.[1] The ultimate conclusion in this report was that the vast majority of middle-income Americans were not receiving effective legal representation. The Canadian Bar Association's Special Committee on Prepaid Legal Services[2] came to a similar conclusion:

Historically, legal services always have been available to our citizens but in large measure until the last thirty years or so, only the business community and the wealthier segment of our population have availed themselves of these services. There have been exceptions, of course, such as automobile accident cases, workmen's compensation and the like, but until the introduction of free legal aid to indigent persons by the many Law Societies across Canada, the vast majority of our population never retained the services of a lawyer. In fact, that is still the situation today, even with the rapid expansion of free legal aid services in both criminal and civil matters, and in spite of the tremendous amount of publicity given to these plans. It is estimated that between 70% and 75% of our population have not retained the services of lawyers. The greater majority of these are in the middle income group. . . .

To make legal services more accessible and available to a large portion of our population, better systems of delivering these services are definitely needed. One such system is the prepaid legal services plan.

Not surprisingly, similar conclusions were reached by the Federation of Law Societies of Canada:[3]

Prepaid Legal Services Plans provide a valid answer to a need and an entitlement, especially in an era of high costs of legal services which are only likely to continue to escalate. . . . There is little doubt that proper and effective Prepaid Legal Services Plans can be of genuine benefit to their subscribers who, in exchange for a set premium of a relatively moderate amount, can have their professional fees covered when they require the services of a lawyer.

Canada's Charter of Rights alone, with its notion of equality before the law, has and will continue to generate a need for specialized legal services that are clearly not affordable to most Canadians.

THE BASIS OF PREPAID LEGAL SERVICE PLANS

Simply described, a prepaid legal service plan involves:

1. A prepaid sum of money, paid by:
   - An employer on behalf of bargaining unit employees as required by a collective agreement
   - An employer voluntarily for certain employees
   - An employee or employees directly, or through payroll deductions.
2. Which sums can be paid to:
   - A prepaid legal services trust fund
   - Insurance company or
   - Private entrepreneurial company.
3. The recipient of this money in turn provides certain described services to the employees and possibly their families.
4. The legal services are provided by:
   - The plan's in-house or staff lawyer and/or
   - Existing law firms.

GENERAL OBJECTIVES OF A LEGAL SERVICE PLAN

Availability of High-Quality Legal Services on a Personal and Individual Basis

In order to ensure that low- and middle-income persons receive the same quality of legal services as wealthier persons do, a prime objective of any plan should be to provide high-quality services by engaging lawyers of established ability and integrity. These participating lawyers must, as they would do for their regular clients, provide legal services on a personal and individual basis while preserving the confidential lawyer-client relationship.

Lower Cost

Any plan must provide the needed legal services at the lowest possible cost, which will be discussed later in greater detail.

Extent of Freedom of Choice of a Lawyer

There will always be certain members of a group who will desire an unrestricted choice of lawyer. Nevertheless, as will become evident in the discussion of open and closed panels, the extent to which a plan member can have freedom of choice of a lawyer will have an important effect on the plan's administrative costs. Plan designers will be required to strike a fair and equitable balance between these competing objectives.

Easier and Speedier Access to Lawyers

Consistent with the objective of providing legal services at a low cost is the objective of permitting plan members to have quick and simple access to these services. Experience has established that if persons have the advantage of consulting a lawyer at an early stage of a problem, this could avoid potentially lengthy and expensive litigation, thereby reducing the plan's overall costs. It is, therefore, essential that procedures for obtaining the services of a lawyer be as simple and convenient as possible, so as not to discourage members from using these services. In addition, such procedures should be communicated to the group members as soon as is practicable.

Providing a Broad Basis of Legal Services

A broad basis of legal services at the outset of a plan might be difficult to achieve because of cost factors. Nevertheless, this objective is one that should be satisfied as quickly as finances will permit.

CONSIDERATIONS IN DESIGNING A PREPAID LEGAL SERVICE PLAN

Enrolment in the Plan

Voluntary. Here, persons enrol usually in an insured plan on an individual rather than a group basis. This concept has resulted in persons enrolling who have immediate need for legal services—adverse selection—which obviously leads to a higher cost factor and with the further result that coverage is often more limited. This type of plan has met with only limited success in the United States.

Automatic. This concept involves a plan where coverage is automatically made available to all persons comprising the group. This arrangement is commonly known as the *true group* plan, which can be funded, for example, by employer contributions.

Eligibility for Benefits

An important decision to be made in designing a plan is to decide who will be covered for benefits. If the members of the group are already participants in other employee benefit plans, such as health and welfare, it might be convenient to determine eligibility on the same basis as in the other plan. If the plan extends benefits to both members and their dependants, then obviously the overall cost of the program will increase. The question to be resolved, therefore, is whether coverage should be on an individual or family basis.

Available Benefits and Exclusions

Particularly at the outset, it may be advisable to begin with a less comprehensive program and expand the benefits on a gradual basis. This avoids the embarrassment of having to reduce benefits due to lack of funds.

It is, of course, possible to avoid having to limit the benefits by providing that members of the group will pay a portion of the legal costs, and this can be established whether or not the plan is insured.

Available benefits will vary considerably. Most plans provide coverage for a variety of legal matters including:

- Divorce
- Landlord and tenant
- Legal separation
- Consumer credit and debt problems
- Adoption
- Wills
- Real estate transactions
- Estate matters
- Highway traffic and other minor offences.

Depending upon the sophistication of the group, certain plans will offer legal advice with respect to preparation of income tax returns and related matters. A common feature is to provide for consultations with the objective of identifying potential legal problems before they turn into costly and extensive litigation—"preventive law." Serious criminal offences are often excluded, as the plan sponsors are anxious to avoid public criticism over providing free or subsidized legal services to so-called criminals. In addition, actions against the trade union, contributing employers and the sponsoring insurance company are usually excluded as well.

In order to provide as broad a base of coverage as possible, consideration should be given to categorizing the available benefits. For example, the more important benefits might be covered fully by the plan, whereas a cost limit could be imposed in relation to lesser important matters, in which event members utilizing these particular services will be responsible for any excess costs.

Legal services can be categorized in three different ways:

- Develop a benefits schedule listing available services and provide complete coverage for those matters
- Consider the member to be entitled to a certain number of "bank hours" that can be expended on any matter, subject to possible exclusions
- Divide covered services into three activity categories—advice and consultation, office work, and legal representation—and set an hourly or dollar ceiling on the use of services in each category.

Sources of Funding: Employer and Employee Contributions

If a plan is funded wholly with regular negotiated employer contributions as with other employee benefit plans, employers will no doubt want to have some degree of control over the administration of the plan.

In voluntary enrolment legal service plans, the union may endorse a particular plan, usually from an insurance company, and members will pay the premiums individually if they desire to enrol. However, as indicated earlier, this type of plan is not popular, as people tend to enroll only when they have an immediate problem, resulting in high utilization and, therefore, higher costs.

All of these funding alternatives have potential income tax consequences that are discussed later.

Union Dues

Here, the contribution to the plan is deducted from the employee's weekly wage rather than having the employer contribute additional sums for the availability of this benefit. Funding through union dues will leave the union with complete control of the program, which, depending on the circumstances, may or may not be advisable. Some argue that union control of the plan results in a more realistic program of benefits. On the other hand, employer involvement can be important, particularly since employers tend to have more experience in such matters as financing, budgets, etc.

Existing Trust Funds

Certain health and welfare funds may have substantial reserves or surpluses, which can be utilized to fund an additional benefit, such as legal services.

PLAN ADMINISTRATION

The various alternatives are as follows.

Self-Administration

Proponents of this type of administration argue that they have better day-to-day control over both the cost and quality of the legal services. A professional administrator may be hired, who may or may not be a lawyer, and such person will be responsible for:

- Selection of plan lawyers (if closed panel)
- Eligibility for benefits
- Claims approval and payment
- Ensuring that participants receive benefits as and when prescribed by the plan
- Ensuring that the quality of legal services is of a high level.

In any event, if the plan is self-administered, it is often advisable to retain an independent consultant, as one would do in the case of any other self-administered employee benefit plan.

Third-Party Administration

An outside or contract benefit plan administrator may be retained to operate the program, including attending to such administrative details as selecting lawyers, processing claims, payment of legal fees, etc. However, special care should be exercised to ensure that the administrator is sufficiently qualified to oversee and monitor the quality of legal services. An alternative is to assign this function to an outside lawyer or law firm.

Insurance or Other Entrepreneurial Companies

In Canada, as in the United States and Europe, certain insurance and other entrepreneurial companies have marketed plans that are available to members of any group on an individual and voluntary basis, and usually require payment of a set monthly fee. In fact, such plans are extremely popular in both the United Kingdom and Germany.

There are a number of companies in Canada now offering these plans, and many companies offer incentives such as 24-hour legal advice lines where an individual may speak with a lawyer any time of the day. One major Canadian department store offered its credit cardholders optional membership in its own legal insurance plan. Indeed, the market has expanded to the point where some companies now even offer commercial legal expenses insurance.

As indicated earlier, these plans may be *voluntary enrolment* plans or *true group* plans. However, a union would have very little, if any, involvement in such plans, thus making it difficult to monitor the quality of the legal services being provided. On the other hand, such plans might be attractive to a union if it is not interested in the day-to-day plan administrative problems. In any event, the union or employer (if there is no collective bargaining agent representing the employees) should carefully review the actual wording of the insured plan to make certain that the plan will, in fact, deliver the legal services described in the promotional literature.

METHODS OF DELIVERY

As discussed earlier, a legal service program should be designed so as to ensure efficient delivery of legal services, which can be provided by the following methods.

Open or Closed Panels

A pure *open panel* program entitles a participant to select any lawyer he or she desires. In the United States, this type of plan has usually been sponsored either by a bar association or insurance company.

A *closed panel* is one that limits the number of lawyers participating in the program to a specially selected panel. This panel could consist of the members of one particular law firm having one or more offices in the geographic area being serviced. Alternatively, the closed panel could consist of a staff of salaried lawyers, or it may even be a group of individual lawyers from various law firms who have been chosen because they each specialize in a particular area of the law in which the participants of the plan may require the most services. Alternatively, the panel may be a combination of both a general practice firm and several other specialist lawyers.

In reality, there very rarely are true open or closed panels. For example, in an open panel program, usually the number of lawyers who ultimately provide these services narrows substantially because of the composition and geographic location of those within the group. If a majority of the group are of one ethnic origin, the tendency seems to be that those persons will choose lawyers who they feel will better understand and appreciate their particular problems.

On the other hand, in a closed panel program if the participants live, for example, in several cities throughout a province then, in order to accommodate all these persons, the so-called closed panel would no doubt have a greater degree of openness and permit these individuals to use lawyers in their own geographic area.

In the United States and Canada, there has been much debate with respect to the merits of *closed* versus *open* panels. Bar associations argue in favour of the open panel concept, as it is a carryover of the traditional method of providing legal services and enables participants to have complete freedom of choice of a lawyer. On the other hand, proponents of the closed panel system argue that any prohibition of this concept will infringe on the freedom to choose a plan that will best suit the needs of the participants.

U.S. studies indicate that the closed panel concept produces legal services at a much lower cost than the open panel format. It appears that in the United States larger law firms are chosen in the closed panel concept because they are able to provide a broader scope of services, as well as having more persons available to meet the needs of the group. Because these firms are able to spread their costs over a larger client base, they are able to maintain superior research facilities and more modern equipment and provide other essential support services that lawyers require.

The smaller, more individual law firms participating in open panel programs are faced with a greater overhead expense per client. These lawyers tend to allocate their efforts depending on the income yielding potential of each case, and they also attempt to reduce their costs by devoting less time to research and preparation, all to the detriment of the plan participants. On the other hand, in a closed panel program involving larger law firms, most of these problems would either not exist or be substantially less. It would also be difficult and costly to monitor and improve upon the legal services being delivered in an open panel system. Finally, because lawyers in a closed panel system provide services on a volume basis, this enables them to develop greater legal expertise than lawyers in an open panel who would receive work on a random basis.

Accordingly, because of lower costs, closed panel programs are able to provide their members with broader coverage, while still giving the participant some degree of freedom of choice of lawyer.

Employing Staff Lawyers

Employing staff lawyers to provide legal services to union members gives the union great control over costs, quality and accessibility of legal services.

A staff lawyer arrangement can be coupled with a closed or open panel arrangement. For example, a staff of lawyers can provide services for members living in a particular city, and arrangements can be made for members employed in remote areas to consult with specific lawyers or select a lawyer of their own choice. In either case, the plan would pay for all or part of the cost incurred, depending on the particular program.

From the foregoing, it is clear that there are many and different delivery mechanisms available for the provision of legal services. The specific method to be used by any particular group will, of course, depend on the needs of the members.

Often a plan may involve multiple methods of delivering legal services to its members. In fact, recently established plans in the construction industry demonstrate how a single plan may employ various modes for the delivery of services so as to best suit its members' needs. Members of one plan have the option of retaining services from staff lawyers employed directly by the plan or hiring their own lawyer. Should a member opt for the latter, then the plan sets maximum limits for which the member may be reimbursed. Should the member opt for a staff lawyer, then the complete services are covered under the plan. Thus, the plan provides the members with the ability of choosing their own counsel while ensuring that plan assets are not misused to obtain excessive services. Offering members such a combination of methods will likely also resolve any potential problems with provincial legal societies, as is exemplified below.

CANADIAN AUTO WORKERS' PREPAID LEGAL PLAN (CAW PLAN): AN EXAMPLE OF DELIVERY OF LEGAL SERVICES

The CAW was involved in a highly publicized confrontation with the Law Society of Upper Canada (the "Law Society") in relation to establishing the CAW plan. The dispute centered around the nature of the relationship between lawyers and the CAW plan. The Law Society demanded that members of the CAW plan have the freedom to choose any lawyer. On the other hand, the CAW argued that it could only control the cost and quality of legal services by requiring members to use either staff lawyers or lawyers who had entered into a contractual relationship with the CAW plan.

The dispute was resolved during April 1987; the CAW plan and the Law Society entered into an agreement covering the structure of the plan. More specifically, the agreement provides the framework within which the CAW plan can operate. It expressly provides that the CAW plan may deliver services through staff lawyers and cooperating lawyers. On the other hand, the Law Society's authority to regulate and discipline staff and cooperating lawyers is preserved, as is the traditional relationship of solicitor and client confidentiality.

In the agreement, the CAW plan acknowledges that its schedule of fees must be maintained at a level that enables legal services to be provided in a competent and professional manner. The agreement expresses the intention of the plan to continue providing a schedule of fees that meets these objectives.

In addition, the agreement provides for the following:

- In the event that the cooperating lawyer agreement (see discussion below) is terminated by either party without cause, the CAW plan agrees to provide details and reasons for the termination of such agreement at the request of the Law Society.
- In the event that a member does not select a lawyer of his or her own choice, the CAW plan agrees that the member will be referred to a lawyer in a professional and objective manner according to the member's legal needs.
- The CAW plan agrees to advise the Law Society as to its operation and to provide statistics relating to its usage.
- There is a mechanism for settling disputes between cooperating lawyers and members, which mechanism is contained in the cooperating lawyer agreement.

The CAW Plan and Delivery of Legal Services

By Staff Lawyers

Legal services are delivered through the CAW plan by staff lawyers, cooperating lawyers and non-cooperating lawyers.

There are approximately 25 staff lawyers working for the CAW plan. They are paid as salaried employees. Approximately 50% of the services provided by the CAW plan are delivered through staff lawyers. The plan has approximately 105,000 members.

Staff lawyers provide the full range of services covered by the plan. In addition, they will provide non-covered personal legal services to plan members at a standard rate.

The CAW plan does not use *paralegals*. These are persons who are not qualified to practice law but may be useful in assisting lawyers with the provision of legal services.

By Cooperating Lawyers

Cooperating lawyers are persons who have entered into a cooperating lawyer agreement with the CAW plan. These lawyers are placed on a referral list, and members of the plan are referred to them if they do not wish to be served by a staff lawyer. The CAW has a referral list or panel of approximately 1,000 lawyers.

The cooperating lawyer agreement governs the provision of "prepaid benefits" and "referral benefits." *Prepaid benefits* are those benefits for which the plan pays. These benefits are closely described in the fee schedule appended to the cooperating lawyer agreement. *Referral benefits* are also described in the fee schedule. These include a wide range of personal legal services and are paid for directly by the member. The cooperating lawyer must provide referral benefits to members at the same hourly rate as the CAW plan pays the lawyer for prepaid benefits.

The cooperating lawyer agreement also contains a mechanism for resolving disputes between a CAW plan member and a cooperating lawyer. The agreement entitles the CAW plan member to file a written complaint with the CAW plan director, who may resolve the dispute to the mutual satisfaction of both parties or render a written decision on the matter. Either party may appeal the director's decision to the administrative committee of the plan, whose decision shall be final and binding on both the member and the cooperating lawyer.

In addition to covering services, fees and the method for resolving disputes, the cooperating lawyer agreement also addresses the following matters:

- The cooperating lawyer must be a member in good standing of the Law Society of Upper Canada.
- The cooperating lawyer must comply with the laws governing the practise of law and must advise the CAW plan immediately if his or her right to practice law is suspended, revoked or expires.
- The cooperating lawyer is obliged to maintain errors and omissions or malpractice insurance satisfactory to the CAW plan.
- The cooperating lawyer is prohibited from promoting or publicizing his or her status as such.
- The CAW plan is obliged to maintain a panel of all cooperating lawyers and to refer members from those panels in accordance with geographical location.
- The CAW plan expressly declines any responsibility for payment of referral benefit legal services.
- The cooperating lawyer is obliged to provide prepaid and referral benefit legal services to CAW plan members who retain them in accordance with the CAW plan's fee schedule. Revisions to the fee schedule are prospective only and do not apply to cases already in progress.
- The CAW plan accepts responsibility for the payment of prepaid legal service fees only if it has issued a case number to the cooperating lawyer. Case numbers are only issued once a member's eligibility has been confirmed.
- For all referral benefits, cooperating lawyers must sign a written fee agreement or retainer with the CAW plan member prior to rendering services, a copy of which must be provided to the member. The cooperating lawyer agreement stipulates the form of such a fee agreement or retainer and requires that it provide that the lawyer agrees to charge the member in accordance with the fee schedule set by the plan.
- The cooperating lawyer is obliged to seek an award of costs in all cases in which it is appropriate to do so. Any costs received go to defray, first, the plan's obligations if the benefit is a prepaid benefit, or the member's obligations if it is a referral benefit. Any remaining monies are applied toward disbursements and, if any costs are left over, they are applied to the benefit of the lawyer.
- The cooperating lawyer is obliged to submit a signed Lawyer Activity and Summary Billing Report to the CAW plan for all prepaid benefits. For referral benefits, the accounts must be sent to the member with a copy of the CAW plan.
- The cooperating lawyer may not delegate the performance of legal services except with the written consent of the member.
- The CAW plan is expressly prohibited from interfering with or controlling the performance of the cooperating lawyer. The lawyer is stipulated to be an independent contractor, and the CAW plan is expressly stated not to be liable for any damages caused by any of his or her acts or omissions.
- The cooperating lawyers are prohibited from giving any gifts or gratuities to any employees in the CAW plan or any of its fiduciaries.
- It is expressly provided that the cooperating lawyer agreement does not restrict the lawyer in any of his or her professional activities or representation.
- The cooperating lawyer agreement may be terminated by either party, without cause, upon written notice to the other party. The agreement provides,

however, that legal services in progress shall continue, with the member's consent, notwithstanding the termination.

By Non-Cooperating Lawyers

Non-cooperating lawyers have no agreement with the CAW plan. They may bill the member over and above the CAW plan fee schedule.

CAW plan members who use non-cooperating lawyers must pay those lawyers directly. They may be reimbursed to the extent that the CAW plan fee schedule covers prepaid legal benefits.

The CAW plan has no contractual or other relationship with a non-cooperating lawyer and has no role in supervising the non-cooperating lawyer or resolving disputes between the non-cooperating lawyer and the CAW plan member.

THE COST OF A PREPAID LEGAL SERVICE PROGRAM

There are several factors to be considered in estimating the cost of the program.

The Numbers of Persons Intended to Be Covered

Is it intended that only the individual be covered or should all of his or her dependents be covered as well? Obviously, the larger the group, the less costly the program should be for each participant.

Geographic Area

If the program participants live in a concentrated area, this will lend itself to the less costly staff lawyer approach. On the other hand, if the participants both work and live long distances from each other, then consideration should be given to providing either multiple staff lawyer offices or a combination of open or closed panels as discussed earlier.

Start-Up Costs

As is the case with most employee benefit plans, start-up costs are usually high. One reason is because of a heavy anticipated demand for legal services at the beginning of the program, particularly in such areas as wills, consultations, traffic offences, etc. It is, therefore, advisable and, indeed, necessary to establish a comfortable reserve prior to making services available. It is further recommended that at the outset the available services should be limited, and thereafter the same can be steadily increased as the plan progresses and experience is gained in utilization of these services. By adopting a cautious approach, financial embarrassment in a self-insured plan will be avoided.

Projected Utilization of Services

In the United States, the prediction of utilization of prepaid legal service plans is still rather uncertain, although patterns have definitely emerged. For example, first year utilization will be approximately 10% of the membership. During the second year, as members become more familiar with the plan and fellow members tell of their hopeful satisfaction, utilization will probably increase to 12-15%. In the third year, it is anticipated that utilization will reach 18-25%. Although certain plans have reached a utilization level of 30% after three years, this seems to be the maximum.

Utilization will also increase with the aid of educational programs designed to inform members of the services available and to encourage them to use certain of the services. For example, members should be encouraged to consult with lawyers whenever they anticipate having a legal problem, so that they can avoid lengthy and costly court proceedings.

POSSIBLE LEGAL AND OTHER OBSTACLES IN ESTABLISHING PREPAID LEGAL SERVICE PLANS

Provincial Insurance Legislation

It is possible that group legal service plans will be considered as insurance and, therefore, subject to regulation by the provinces. If so, the provider of the services, such as a union, employer or trust fund, might be required to be licensed under the various provincial insurance acts. This would necessitate meeting certain onerous requirements, such as minimum capitalization, which would constitute obstacles in the development of prepaid legal service plans, particularly with respect to union or employer-sponsored plans.

Possible Conflict With Canons of Ethics of Provincial Law Societies and the *Competition Act* of Canada

Although to date none of the provincial law societies appear to have changed their codes of professional conduct to effectively prohibit closed panel legal service plans, the legal profession in many parts of Canada opposes this concept of legal services. Such opposition could result in the law societies running afoul of the *Competition Act*. Although this matter has not yet been finally determined, it has been intimated that an attempt to prohibit or discourage the establishment of closed panel legal service plans could be interpreted as improper limiting of competition, as the public would be denied the unimpeded right to obtain less expensive legal services.

In the United States, after many legal proceedings involving various state bar associations, the closed panel system has finally been accepted by the legal profession. The United States Supreme Court has steadfastly refused to condone or support any attempt by state bar associations to interfere with the fundamental right to obtain meaningful access to the courts.

ALTERNATIVE INCOME TAX STRUCTURES FOR A PREPAID LEGAL SERVICE PLAN

General Context for the Taxation of Employee Benefit Plans

In general, the value of any benefits received or enjoyed by an employee in respect of, in the course of, or by virtue of his or her employment, is included in the employee's income from employment (Section 6(1)(a)(i) of the *Income Tax Act* (the "Act")).

If the benefit is paid directly from the employer to the employee, then the employer is entitled to deduct the value of the benefit in the year it is paid, and the employee is taxable on the benefit in the same year.

Where benefits are delivered through plans administered at arm's length from the employer, the tax situation is somewhat more complex. (See Table VII-2-I.) There are two possible tax structures for such plans:
- The employee benefit plan (EBP) and
- The employee trust (ET).

Both terms are defined in Section 248 of the Act.

The intent behind both the EBP and the ET is to ensure that the employee pays tax on the benefit in the same year that the employer takes a deduction for the contribution. Both arrangements are designed to eliminate situations in which employers take immediate deductions for employee benefits, but employees do not pay tax in respect of them until some later time.

The EBP synchronizes the employer deduction and

Table VII—2-I

INCOME TAX CONSEQUENCES TO AN EMPLOYEE AND EMPLOYER UNDER AN "EMPLOYEE BENEFIT PLAN" AND "EMPLOYEE TRUST"

	Employee Benefit Plan		Employee Trust	
	Employer	Employee	Employee	Employer
Contributions by employer	Not deductible	Not included in income	Deductible	Included in income
Payments from the plan (a) To an employee	Deduction available unless payment is a return of employee contributions or a distribution of plan income	Taxable unless return of employee contributions, death benefit or related to non-resident status	No effect	Not included in income
(b) To the employer	Included in income to extent it exceeds previous non-deductible contributions	N/A	Included in income	N/A
Income of the plan	No effect	Included in income when distribution	No effect	Included in income as a result of allocation
Distribution of property to beneficiary	N/A	No consequences to plan—value included in income	N/A	Plan disposes of it **at fair market value**—income resulting must be allocated

the employee tax in the year that the benefit is received by the employee. In that year, the value of the benefit is taxable to the employee, and the employer is entitled to deduct any contributions made to provide that benefit. It is important to keep in mind that under an EBP arrangement the employer cannot deduct its contribution unless and until the employee receives a benefit, which could be of great inconvenience to employers.

An ET synchronizes the employer deduction and the employee tax in the year the employer makes the contribution. Under an ET, the employer takes an immediate tax deduction in the year it makes the contribution. The plan notionally allocates these contributions among all plan members, and they each pay tax as if they had received a share of the contributions in that year. When they eventually receive benefits under the plan, employees pay no tax.

Financing a prepaid plan through *union dues* is a third option that may be attractive from a tax perspective only if the dues that finance the plan are tax-deductible by the employee.

Detailed Examination of the Alternative Tax Structures

The EBP

The *EBP* is an arrangement under which:
- Contributions are made by an employer (or by a person with whom the employer does not deal at arm's length).
- Contributions are then given to a custodian.
- Thereafter payments are made for the benefit of employees or former employees, or for persons who do not deal at arm's length with such employees.

There is no particular formality required for an arrangement to constitute an EBP. The arrangement must involve a payment (other than a payment that would not be considered an employee benefit) by an employer to an intermediary and must provide that the payments be made to, or for the benefit of, an employee or former employee.

A second aspect of an EBP is that it must deliver *benefits* to employees. This term is very broadly interpreted and, if anything, the recent judicial trend is to expand it to include more and more payments.

The Supreme Court of Canada held in *Savage*[4] that the words *benefit of whatever kind* in paragraph 6(1)(a) of the Act are to be broadly interpreted. Similarly, in *Nowegijick*[5] the Supreme Court of Canada stated on page 25 that:

the words "in respect of" are, in my opinion words of the widest possible scope . . . the phrase "in respect of" is probably the widest of any expression intended to convey some connection between two related subject matters.

Thus, an arrangement to provide free personal legal services to employees by virtue of their employment relationship is almost certainly a *benefit*. It is likely that a plan financed by employer contributions, whether directly or indirectly, that gives rise to payments for the benefit of employees will be characterized as an EBP under the Act.

Tax Consequences to an Employee, Employer and Custodian Under an EBP

The Employee

The tax consequences of EBPs to employees depend upon the nature and financial structure of the plan. It can be employer funded, jointly funded by employers and employees, or financed by union dues.

Employees are not taxable on a current basis on employer contributions to an EBP.[6] An employee is taxable only when he or she receives an "amount" out of the plan.[7] The term *amount* is broadly defined to include "rights or things . . . or the value in terms of money of the right or thing" and likely includes the value of a benefit.[8] Such amounts are included in the employee's income in the year he or she receives the payment. Thus, the principal advantage of an EBP is that the employee defers any tax liability until such time as he or she actually receives payment out of the plan for his or her own benefit. The corresponding difficulty, as noted above, is that employers must delay their deductions until the employees actually receive their benefits.

Where an EBP is a contributory plan (that is, contributions into the plan are made both by the employer and the employee), the employee will not be permitted to deduct his or her contributions. Payments out of the plan will, however, only be taxable to the employee to the extent that they exceed his or her contributions into the plan. In effect, an employee is not taxable on payments that represent a return of his or her own contributions into the plan.

The custodian of the plan determines the portion of payments that represent a return of the employee's contributions at the time the payment is made from the plan.

The amount taxable to the employee is taxable as employment income, regardless of the nature of the income from which the payments have been made. Thus, the character of the income earned by the plan (for example, interest, dividends, capital gains, etc.) does not in any way influence the characterization of the income for tax purposes when it is paid out to the employee. All such income is taxable as employment source income.

The tax consequences to employees may depend upon the type of plan, i.e., an in-house or an independent legal counsel plan.

The Act taxes an employee on "the aggregate of all

amounts . . . received by him in the year out of or under an employee benefit plan. . . ."[9] The word *receive* has not been interpreted under this particular section, and there is no direct jurisprudence on the point. *Receive* has, however, been interpreted under Section 5 of the Act and means ". . . to get or to derive benefit from something, to enjoy its advantages without necessarily having it in one's hands."[10]

If, however, the plan is structured as an in-house plan, there may be a weak argument that employees would not be entitled to receive an *amount* from the plan and would not, in fact, receive anything other than the service provided. If that is the case, there is a possibility that the employee will not be taxable under paragraph 6(1)(g) of the Act for services provided through the plan.

In the event that the plan is structured so as to employ independent legal counsel, the tax consequences to employees are more clear-cut. Payments to legal counsel on account of services rendered to employees will be considered *benefits* received by the employee in the year that the service and account are rendered. They will be taxable on the value of the benefits in the year they are received.

The Employer

Where the plan is fully or partially funded by an employer, the employer's deduction for contributions into the plan is deferred until the employee actually receives a benefit out of the plan. Thus, the employer deduction is synchronized with the inclusion of benefits in the employee's income.

The formula for employer deductions in a multi-employer EBP may be problematic. The EBP is structured to accommodate single employer plans and to match the deduction of the single employer with the benefit received by its employees. In a multi-employer context, however, where an employee may be employed by any number of employers, the matching of employer deductions to employee benefits can be significantly more complex.

Finally, the employer's deduction is in any event restricted to payments made out of the capital of the plan from its contributions. The employer is not entitled to deductions for any payment made out of the income that is earned by the plan.

The Custodian

If a union acts as custodian of the plan, it should not be taxable on the contributions made into the plan and may not be taxable on the plan's net income because unions generally are non-taxable entities. If the custodian is a trust, it will be taxable on the plan's net income.

The ET

An *ET* is an arrangement under which:
- Payments are made by an employer to a trustee in trust for the sole benefit of employees or former employees.
- The right of the benefits vests in the beneficiaries at the time of each payment.
- The amount of the benefit does not depend on the beneficiary's position, performance or compensation as an employee.
- The trustee allocates annually to the beneficiaries the employer's contributions to the trust.
- The trustee elects in the trust tax return to be an ET.

The employee's right to the benefit must vest at the time of each payment, and the trustee must allocate annually the employer's contribution into the plan together with the income of the trust for the year and capital gains realized by the trust from a disposition of property. Thus, the employee's interest in an ET is a clearly vested interest, and the amount vested is determined on an annual basis.

Tax Consequences to an Employee, Employer and Custodian Under an ET

The Employee

An employee is taxable annually on any amounts allocated to him or her by the trustee for the year. An amount allocated to the employee (beneficiary) is taxable as employment source income, regardless of the nature of the income when received by the trustee.

The amount to be allocated to an employee during the year is the aggregate of:
- The employer's contributions for the year into the plan
- The net income of the trust for the year from investments
- Capital gains realized by the trust in the disposition of property.

The trust is entitled to deduct certain losses and expenses from the above amounts in calculating the amount to be allocated to employees.

The Employer

Employers may deduct their contributions to an ET immediately in the year they are made.

The Custodian

The custodian could be a trust, union, employer or any other person or entity different from the contributor. The custodian is required to allocate all of its income to the members of the plan. Accordingly, it should not have any taxable income and should not have to pay any tax.

Financing a Plan Through Union Dues

The third alternative tax structure is where a plan is funded in whole or in part through employee contributions incorporated into union dues. Here, two issues are to be considered, namely:

- Whether such contributions can be considered to be *union dues* for the purposes of the Act and therefore enabling the employee to deduct the same from his or her taxable income
- Whether provision of benefits by the plan to employees would constitute a return of contributions to them.

An employee can deduct an amount contributed as "annual dues to maintain membership in a trade union as defined by section 3 of the *Canada Labour Code.*"[11] A *trade union* means any organization of employees formed for the purpose of regulating relations between employers and employees. *Annual dues* means annual dues paid by a member to maintain membership in a trade union but does not include initiation fees and special assessments.

However, the Act expressly provides that an employee may not deduct union dues to the extent that they are, in effect, levied for a fund or plan for annuities, insurance or similar benefits.[12] Further, Interpretation Bulletin IT-103R provides that union dues are not deductible to the extent that they are, in effect, levied for any purpose directly related to the ordinary operating expenses of the trade union to which they were paid.[13]

Thus, the first question to be determined is whether the plan constitutes, in substance, an *insurance* plan or a plan that confers similar benefits. This will depend upon whether the plan is structured along insurance principles. Generally speaking, an *insurance contract* is one whereby, in exchange for a stipulated consideration, one party undertakes to compensate the other for the loss of a specified subject by specified perils. Thus, indemnification against loss is the key feature of an insurance contract. If the plan is structured so as to indemnify union members against losses incurred through future legal expenses incurred on account of specified events or transactions, then it is in substance equivalent to an insurance plan. In these circumstances, Revenue Canada would probably not view the employee's contributions as deductible expenses on account of *union dues* under Paragraph 8(1)(i).

Moreover, even if the plan is not an insurance type of plan, it would be difficult to construe the plan as a *normal operating expense* of the union. Accordingly, it is highly unlikely that union dues could be properly used to finance a prepaid legal services plan.

In the unlikely event that contributions into the plan are deductible through union dues, it may be possible to argue that legal services provided to the employee are not taxable under Paragraph 8(1)(i). This may give the employee a deduction for the dues for contributions into the plan and a tax-free receipt of benefits in the form of legal services.

Summary of the Three Alternative Tax Structures

An EBP

If the plan is structured as an EBP, employers will not be entitled to immediate deduction for their contributions. They can do so only when benefits are received by employees. Employees, on the other hand, pay no tax in respect of employer contributions. Rather, employees are taxed on the value of benefits received in the year they are received. Thus, for example, if an employee receives services worth $2,000 in a year, he or she will be liable for tax on that $2,000. Employees who receive no benefits in a year will pay no tax.

From an administrative point of view, an EBP may be extremely complex in a multi-employer context. The custodian of the plan will be responsible for allocating the amounts to be deducted by the various employers that have contributed toward each employee's benefit. This will likely require that the custodian keep track of the amounts that individual contributors have contributed in respect of particular employees, so that those employers may be credited with the tax deduction when the particular employee receives a benefit.

An ET

If the plan structure is an ET, then the custodian allocates all contributions among all the plan members equally. Each member pays some tax on the amount allocated to him or her, regardless of whether the member receives any benefits. Since the members have already paid tax in respect of the contributions, there is no tax payable by employees when they receive a benefit. Employers are entitled to deduct their contributions to an ET in the year they are made.

Union Dues

From a tax point of view, it is unlikely that union dues can be properly used to finance a plan. The plan is likely an insurance type plan and may not be treated as a normal union operating expense. Consequently, it is likely that any monies paid by members to the union on account of the plan would not be deductible by them. From a tax perspective, this is, therefore, the least attractive option, since it likely would mean employee financing with no tax assistance.

ENDNOTES

1. Curran and Spalding, *The Legal Needs of the Public,*

Preliminary Report of a National Survey by the Special Committee to Serve Legal Needs of the American Bar Association (American Bar Foundation, 1974).

2. R. Smethurst, Q.C., "Prepaid Legal Services" (1972), 20 Chitty's L.J. 303.

3. *Federation of Law Societies of Canada Committee on Prepaid Legal Services Report* (March 6, 1977), p. 2. See also Barreau du Quebec, Le Rapport du Commite sur l'Assurance Frais Juridique, 1976.

4. *Savage,* [1983] C.T.C. 393 (S.C.C.).

5. *Nowegijick,* [1983] C.T.C. 20 (S.C.C.).

6. Section 6(1)(a)(ii) of the *Income Tax Act,* R.S.C. 985, c.1 (5th Supp.).

7. *Ibid.,* Section 6(1)(g).

8. *Ibid.,* Section 248.

9. *Ibid.,* Section 6(1)(g).

10. *Morin* [1975] C.T.C. 106 (F.C.(T.D.). The court was considering an amount withheld from a taxpayer's salary on account of provincial income taxes. The court held that the amounts withheld at source were in fact amounts received by the taxpayer and on which he was taxable.

11. *Income Tax Act, supra* note 6, Section 8(1)(i)(iv).

12. *Ibid.,* Section 8(5).

13. Revenue Canada, Interpretation Bulletin IT-103R, "Dues Paid to a Union or to a Parity or Advisory Committee" (4 November 1988), paragraph 2.

CHAPTER 3

Training and Education Plans

by Peter Landry and Christopher May

INTRODUCTION

There is little doubt that training is an important business activity for the economic well-being of Canadian companies and their employees. For many, especially small employers and individuals, these costs are unaffordable and therefore avoided. This has serious consequences in an increasingly competitive global market. However, in certain unionized industries involving a large number of small employers, such as the construction industry, the concept of multi-employer *training trust funds (TTFs)* emerged to provide training and re-training to workers. Like other multi-employer trust fund benefits, training can be provided on a more economical and effective basis. Of course, the TTF concept is workable as between a single employer and its employees regardless of whether or not they are unionized. Although various forms of government assistance have been made available to TTFs in the past, governments in Canada have chosen to significantly reduce their investment in training during the 1990s.

TTFs in many cases have had to fill the vacuum; i.e., due to government reductions, a TTF providing training is an important benefit to both workers and their employers and is often the only economical option available to unemployed workers or companies seeking a skilled work force.

ESTABLISHING AND ADMINISTERING A TTF

Once a union, or a group of employees where there is no union, agrees to set up a single or multi-employer TTF, the following steps should be taken.

Contributions

The parties should negotiate how much the employer(s) and employees will contribute to the TTF. This is often done through a "check off" system of a certain amount per hours worked.

Trust Agreement

The parties, with the assistance of a lawyer, should then agree upon the contents of a trust agreement that, among other things, should:
- Establish a board of trustees, usually with equal representation from labour and management
- Establish the TTF's objectives, i.e., types of training to be provided, such as pre-apprenticeship, apprenticeship, upgrading, rehabilitation of injured workers, etc.
- Define the trustees' duties and responsibilities.

Budget

The trustees, together with their accountant and training director, should establish a 12-month budget for training and related activities such as curriculum development. Since the TTF may wish to obtain government financial assistance, it is recommended that this should take into account the fiscal period of government(s), which is usually the period ending March 31. However, like any other trust fund, accounting for the TTF's fiscal period must still be for the period ending December 31 as required by the *Income Tax Act.*[1]

Training Director and Staff

In order to implement, carry out and monitor the

training program, the trustees should consider hiring a competent and experienced training director and instructor(s).

Training Program

The training director should recommend to the trustees the details of the various types of needed training to be offered during a 12-month period. These details should include, among other things:
- Nature, details and objective of each training course
- Training period for each course
- Budgets
- Location of training
- Curriculum and training standards
- Provider of training, i.e., by the TTF itself or by another provider such as a college
- Equipment, tools and materials required for each course and the cost thereof
- Procedure for screening of potential trainees
- Testing procedures
- Certification to be given to successful trainees.

Selection of Administrator

As is the case with any other employee benefit plan trust fund, the trustees should hire a salaried administrator and staff or retain a third-party contract administrator to manage the day-to-day operations of the TTF, such as:
- Collection of contributions
- Short-term investment of TTF money
- Handling inquiries of potential and existing trainees
- Obtaining quotations for equipment, tools and materials
- Statistical reporting to governments where financial grants are provided to the TTF
- Determining the skills required by the industry.

BENEFITS PROVIDED BY A TTF

The benefits or, more specifically, training courses, that TTFs can provide are as follows.

Pre-Apprenticeship

Prior to trainees' becoming apprentices in a particular trade or craft, trustees may wish to provide pre-apprenticeship training. The purpose is to enable the trainee to become more familiar with an occupation at an earlier stage, thereby better preparing him or her for the formal apprenticeship training. As is the case with almost any type of training, pre-apprenticeship training normally includes both academic and practical instruction.

Apprenticeship

Increasingly TTFs are providing the "in-school" portion of apprenticeship in their own training facilities. Historically, apprenticeship training was provided by colleges of applied arts and technology that are funded by the federal Department of Human Resources Development and the various provincial ministries across Canada.

New Entry/Non-Apprentice Training

There are many areas of skills training where apprenticeship either does not exist or is not legislated. This type of training can be provided by TTFs both to encourage new workers in an industry and to upgrade the skills of those already employed.

Rehabilitation of Injured Workers

In addition to workers' compensation boards providing rehabilitation training, TTFs can provide the same, usually with some form of financial assistance from a provincial workers' compensation board. This will be discussed in further detail below.

TTFs are often able to offer training in response to particular employer demands much more quickly and effectively than it could be made available through the traditional public college system.

FUNDING OF TTF

Generally speaking, all funding for skills training by TTFs is derived from two sources: employees and employers.

As is the case with all employee benefit plan trust funds, all contributions are pooled in a common fund that provides the training benefits.

Funding by Employers

Contributions to TTFs are normally made by participating employers as provided for in a collective agreement. These contributions usually take the form of the employer paying a certain number of cents per hour worked or earned by each bargaining unit employee, or a percentage of wages.

Funding by Employees

Occasionally, a collective agreement may require employees to make additional contributions to a TTF.

Funding by Government

Formerly, the federal government provided certain financial assistance to TTFs as part of the Canadian Jobs Strategy Program. Further, various provinces also provided assistance. The training landscape changed significantly on January 1, 1996 with the coming into force of Canada's new *Employment Insurance (EI) Act,* replacing its forerunner the *Unemployment Insurance Act* and the *National Training Act.* The new EI Act represents a fundamental restructuring of the re-employment system in Canada with the withdrawal of the federal government from labour market development in recognition of provincial jurisdiction. The federal government no longer purchases training courses from the province or private or public institutions such as TTFs. Instead all such responsibility falls under the jurisdiction of each individual province and territory. Further, most funding is now linked directly to individuals who may use their funding to purchase training from the institution of their choice, including the TTF.

Most re-employment benefits are now considered taxable income to the trainee. It is therefore important that TTFs that have training centres seek certification as a *private educational institution* in Canada through the Minister of Human Resources Development for the purposes of Sections 118.5 and 118.6 of the *Income Tax Act.* This certification will allow them to issue tuition tax receipts for the eligible tuition fees paid by trainees who may then claim a tax credit on their income tax to offset the tax consequences of the training benefit.

The state of training in Canada is continuing to undergo substantial change due to the devolution of training to the provinces. Many programs that individuals and institutions relied upon to meet training and skills upgrading have either been terminated or are currently being reviewed or substantially changed. It is important to contact the relevant federal and provincial agencies to get up-to-date information. The federal Human Resources Development Canada's Sectoral and Occupational Studies Division is a good source. It produces the "Inventory of Provincial Sectoral and Occupational Initiatives," which is available on the Internet at www.hrdc-rhc.gc.ca/sector/publications/other.html. Some of the contacts responsible for provincial programs are shown in Appendix VII-3-A to this chapter.

INVESTMENTS

Since TTF trustees are required to provide continuous and ongoing training benefits, it would be unusual for these funds to accumulate large surpluses. In any event, the trustees should retain professional investment counsel to ensure competent fund management. Investment of TTFs is discussed in Chapter 6 of this section.

INCOME TAX CONSIDERATIONS

Employer Contributions

These amounts are generally deductible from an employer's income.

Employee Training Funds

Neither the value of the employer's contributions to a TTF nor the value of the training benefits is taxable to the employee.

The TTF

Trusts are, subject to certain exceptions, taxable entities to the extent that they earn any income and are unable to deduct expenditures required to earn the same. Accordingly, earning of interest or other income by a TTF may result in some tax consequences if proper planning measures are not undertaken. One training fund attempted to avoid paying property taxes by arguing that it was a seminary of learning maintained for educational purposes. The Ontario Divisional Court held that in order for this argument to succeed, the training fund must be a "separate institution" from the union.[2]

In order for a training fund to be a separate institution, it must be a true trust or a separate corporation.[3] This Ontario Divisional Court case highlights the need to incorporate a company to hold the land and buildings associated with the training centre.

Even if the training fund is a "separate institution," it will not be exempted from taxes if it does not meet the requirements that all of its profits be applied to educational purposes. Where excess money is diverted for other employee benefits, this requirement will not be met.[4] For a detailed explanation of the effect of the Canadian income tax system on employee benefit plan trust funds and participating employers and employees, see Chapter 8 of Section I.

THE GOODS AND SERVICES TAX (GST)[5]

The general rule with respect to the GST is that every recipient of a "taxable supply" made in Canada is, in respect of the supply, required to pay tax equal to 7% of the consideration for the supply. The term *taxable supply* is broadly defined as follows:

"Taxable supply" means a supply that is made in the course of a commercial activity.

For these purposes, it is important to note that the definition of a *taxable supply* excludes exempt supplies.

Exempt supplies are listed in Schedule V of the *Excise Tax Act.* Insofar as a TTF is concerned, reference is made to Part III of Schedule V, which defines certain educational services as *exempt supplies.* In particular, Section 6 of Part III provides that the following is an *exempt supply:*

6. A supply of
    (a) a service of instructing individuals in courses leading to, or for the purpose of

maintaining or upgrading, a professional or trade accreditation or designation recognized by a regulatory body, or

(b) a certificate, or a service of administering an examination, in respect of a course, or in respect of an accreditation or designation described in paragraph (a),

where the supply is made by a professional or trade association, government, vocational school, university or public college or by the regulatory body, except where the supplier has made an election under this section in prescribed form containing prescribed information.

Section 8 of Part III also defines the following service as an exempt supply:

8. A supply, other than a zero-rated supply, made by a school authority, vocational school, public college or university of a service of instructing individuals in, or administering examinations in respect of, courses leading to certificates, diplomas, licences or similar documents, or classes or ratings in respect of licences, that attest to the competence of individuals to practise or perform a trade or vocation where

(a) the document, class or rating is prescribed by federal or provincial regulation;

(b) the supplier is governed by federal or provincial legislation respecting vocational schools; or

(c) the supplier is a non-profit organization or a public institutions.

In order for the supply of courses by a TTF to be an *exempt supply* within the meaning of Section 6, Part III of Schedule V, the courses must lead to, or be for, the purpose of maintaining or upgrading, a trade accreditation or designation *recognized by a regulatory body*. The term *regulatory body* is defined in Section 1 of Part III of Schedule V as follows:

"Provincial regulatory body" means a body that is constituted or empowered by an Act of Parliament or of the legislature of a province to regulate the practice of a profession or trade by setting standards of knowledge and proficiency for practitioners of the profession or trade.

By way of example, in the province of Ontario, the legislation governing the trades is the *Trades Qualification and Apprenticeship Act* (TQAA)[6] or the *Apprenticeship and Certification Act* (ACA).[7] The acts provide for the appointment of a director of apprenticeship.

The director of apprenticeship or the Ministry of Training, Colleges and Universities act as *regulatory bodies* in Ontario for the purposes of Part III of Schedule V of the GST. If a TTF provides skills training that leads to a trade accreditation or designation recognized by the director of apprenticeship, or where such training is for the purpose of maintaining or upgrading such a trade accreditation or designation, then the supply of such training by TTFs may be an *exempt supply* within the meaning of Section 6 of Part III of Schedule V. It is important to note, however, that even if these courses do meet the definition of *exempt supply* in Section 6, that section still permits the TTF to elect to treat the courses as taxable supplies.

For similar reasons, courses offered by TTFs may be *exempt supplies* within the meaning of Section 8 of Part III of Schedule V. In order to comply with this section, the instruction provided by the TTFs must be in respect of courses leading to "certificates, diplomas or similar documents that are prescribed by provincial regulation. . . ."

A further condition for complying with Section 6 is that the courses must be offered by a "professional or trade association, government, vocational school, university or public college or the provincial regulatory body." Similarly, in complying with Section 8, the course must be offered by either "a school authority, vocational school, public college or university." Many TTFs are likely *vocational schools,* which are defined in Section 1 of Part III of Schedule V as follows:

"vocational school" means an organization that is established and operated primarily to provide students with correspondence courses, or instruction in courses, that develop or enhance students' occupational skills.

In summary, where training courses provided by TTFs are directed towards obtaining or upgrading a trade accreditation or designation recognized as above, or lead to certificates, diplomas or similar instruments prescribed by provincial regulation, these courses may not be taxable supplies. Accordingly, the GST may not be payable on employer contributions to TTFs. On the other hand, even if courses provided by TTFs meet the definition of an *exempt supply* in Section 6, the TTF may still elect to treat the provision of these courses as a taxable supply. In this case, contributions to the TTF would attract GST, but the TTF would be able to deduct its input tax credits from the GST it is required to remit to the government.

Treatment of training funds can vary. If the funds are paid into a trust and the funds are administered by the trust, rather than the industry association, it is likely that the contributions will be viewed as part of the employees' remuneration and, thus, will be outside the scope of the GST. For this to be the case, it should be evident that the employer does not acquire membership or rights to services or benefits in any other manner, by virtue of the contribution.

On the other hand, if the funds are given directly to

the industry association, rather than to a separate person, and the employer acquires rights or benefits by virtue of the contributions, or if the contribution is a requirement of membership by the employer and the industry association, the contributions will likely be viewed as payment for membership or consideration for supplies made to the employer by the association.

If the employer's contribution is in respect of services (i.e., training) provided to the employees, rather than membership provided to the employer, the payment will be outside the scope of the GST and will be regarded as part of the employees' remuneration, assuming that the contribution is pursuant to an employment contract (i.e., a collective agreement).

COMMUNICATION

In order that both employers and workers are aware of the training provided by a TTF, a Web page, a booklet or bulletin should be made available to interested groups such as government and Employment Insurance officials. This should set forth such training details as:
- Type of courses offered
- Times when these courses are available
- Locations of training courses
- Who is eligible for training/criteria.

CONCLUSION

Like most other employee benefits, skills training is often a combined effort of employers, unions or employees and government. TTFs provide the necessary skills training both to enable new workers to obtain employment in response to industry demand and to upgrade the skills of existing workers. Government sometimes makes grants available to TTFs that, in turn, are able to provide incremental training. Most often government grants or loans are made directly to the trainee as part of a government program such as Employment Insurance. Further, the *Income Tax Act* of Canada provides an incentive to establish this sort of an employee benefit plan trust fund, provided that the statutory conditions are met. TTFs can also apply for certification as a private educational institution, which allows them to issue a tuition tax receipt for the fees that a trainee may be required to pay for courses taken at the TTF's training centre.

ENDNOTES

1. *Income Tax Act,* R.S.C. 1985, c.1 (5th Supp.), ss. 104 (2), 249.

2. *Labourers' International Union of North America, Local 506 v. Ontario* (Regional Assessment Commissioner, Region No. 14), [1994] O.J. No. 784 (G.D.).

3. *Labourers' International Union of North America, Local 506, supra* note 2.

4. *Labourers' International Union of North America , Local 506,supra* note 2.

5. *Excise Tax Act,* R.S.C. 1985, c. E-15, Parts VIII and IX.

6. *Trade Qualification and Apprenticeship Act,* R.S.O. 1990, c. T. 17.

7. *Apprenticeship and Certification Act,* 1988 S.O. 1998, c. 22.

APPENDIX VII-3-A

SUMMARY OF PROVINCIAL AND TERRITORIAL GOVERNMENT TRAINING AND FINANCIAL ASSISTANCE CONTACTS

ALBERTA

Human Resources and Employment
324 Legislature Building
10800 - 97 Avenue
Edmonton Alberta
T5K 2B6
Phone: (780) 415-4800
Fax: (780) 422-9556
Web: www.gov.ab.ca/hre
Email: webeditor@lab.gov.ab.ca

Alberta Learning
#227, 10800–97 Avenue
Edmonton, AB
T5K 2B6
Phone: (780) 427-2025
Fax: (780) 427-5582
Web: www.learning.gov.ab.ca/
Email: comm.contact@edc.gov.ab.ca

BRITISH COLUMBIA

Ministry of Advanced Education, Training and Technology
PO Box 9885, Stn Prov Govt
Victoria, BC
V8W9T6
Phone: (250) 356-2156
Fax: (250) 356-6942
Web: www.aett.gov.bc.ca

MANITOBA

Ministry of Advanced Education and Skills Training
Room 168
Manitoba Legislative Building
450 Broadway
Winnipeg, MB
R3C 0V8
Phone: (204) 945 3720
Fax: (204) 945 1291
Web: www.edu.gov.mb.ca
Email: mbedu@minet.gov.mb.ca

NEWFOUNDLAND

Department of Human Resources and Employment
Labour Market Development
P.O. Box 8700
St. John's, Newfoundland
A1B 46J
Phone: (709) 729-2719
Fax: (709) 729-5560
Web: www.gov.nf.ca
Email: info@mail.gov.nf.ca

Department of Education
P.O. Box 8700
St. John's, NF
A1B 4J6
Phone: (709) 729-5097
Fax: (709) 729-5896
Web: www.gov.nf.ca/edu/
Email: webmaster@edu.gov.nf.ca

NEW BRUNSWICK

Department of Training & Employment Development
Province of New Brunswick
P.O. Box 6000
Fredericton, New Brunswick
E3B 5H1
Phone: (506) 453-2568
Fax: (504) 453-3038
Web: www.gov.nb.ca

NOVA SCOTIA

Department of Human Resources
One Government Place
1700 Granville Street
P.O. Box 943
Halifax, Nova Scotia
B3J 2V9
Phone: (902) 424-7660
Fax: (902) 424 0611
Web: www.gov.ns.ca/humr/

ONTARIO

Ministry of Training, Colleges and Universities
14th Floor, Mowat Block
900 Bay Street
Toronto, Ontario
M7A 1L2
Phone: 1-800-387-5514
Fax: (416) 325-6348
Web: www.edu.gov.on.ca
Email: info@edu.gov.on.ca

PRINCE EDWARD ISLAND

Department of Education
Second Floor, Sullivan Building
16 Fitzroy Street
P.O. Box 2000
Charlottetown, PEI
C1A 7N8
Phone: (902) 368-4600
Fax: (902) 368-4663
Web: www2.gov.pe.ca/educ/index.asp

QUEBEC

Ministère de L'Emploi et de la Solidarite
Ministère du Travail
200, chemin Sainte-Foy, 6e étage
Québec (Québec)
G1R 5S1
Phone: (418) 643-5297
Fax: (418) 644-0003
Web: www.gov.qc.ca
Email: ministre@travail.gouv.qc.ca

SASKATCHEWAN

Saskatchewan Post Secondary
Education and Skills Training
2220 College Avenue
Regina, Saskatchewan
S4P 1C6
Phone: (306) 787-1401
Fax: (306) 787-7182
Web: www.sask.gov.sk.ca

NORTHWEST TERRITORIES

Government of the Northwest Territories
Department of the Executive
Box 1320
Yellowknife NT X1A 2L9
Canada
Phone: (867) 669-2301
Fax: (867) 873-0169
Web: www.gov.nt.ca

YUKON

Government of Yukon
Box 2703
Whitehorse, Yukon
Y1A 2C6
Phone: (867) 667-5811
Fax: (867) 393-6254
Web: www.gov.yk.ca

Nunavut
Web: www.gov.nu.ca/eng/dept.html

Department of Human Resources
Bag 800
Iqaluit Nunavut
X0A 0H0
Phone: (867) 975-6200
Fax: (867) 975-6215

Education-Nunavut
Bag 800
Iqaluit Nunavut
X0A 0H0
Phone: (867) 975-5600
Fax: (867) 975-5605

CHAPTER 4

Vacation Pay Trust Funds

by Mark Zigler

INTRODUCTION

"Vacation pay trust funds" are a misnomer, as most of these trust funds are created for purposes of holding both vacation *and holiday pay* to which employees are entitled under collective agreements. These funds are used primarily in the construction industry, and in other industries where there are itinerant workers, who often work for one employer on a short-term basis, and then transfer to another employer. These workers do not ordinarily receive paid vacations or paid holidays, and vacation pay funds are intended to provide payment in lieu of such benefits. It is also in these industries that there is a high incidence of employer insolvencies. Vacation pay trust funds are also advantageous as they avoid certain difficulties under the *Employment Insurance Act*[1] in industries where there are many layoffs. The idea of vacation pay funds is becoming increasingly popular in industries with substantial labour mobility.

Some provinces have established legislative conditions and requirements, such as those under the Ontario *Employment Standards Act,*[2] that require registration and government approval of these funds. Otherwise, vacation pay funds are not *specifically* regulated, although the fact that they usually take the form of a multi-employer trust fund means that they are subject to the law of trusts. Fund trustees will also be subject to traditional fiduciary obligations. In addition, union-sponsored vacation pay trust in Ontario must file their financial statements with the Ministry of Labour, pursuant to Section 93(2) of the Ontario *Labour Relations Act, 1995.*[3]

STRUCTURE OF VACATION PAY FUNDS

Vacation pay funds generally exist pursuant to a collective agreement that requires each employer to make a monthly remittance of a percentage of an employer's wages to the fund. The most common percentage is 10% of wages, which covers 6% statutory holiday pay and 4% vacation pay. The purpose of the fund is to protect the member against loss of vacation pay or holiday pay because of an employer becoming insolvent or defaulting on payment. Vacation pay in most provinces, under minimum employment standards legislation, is generally paid when employees take an annual holiday. Statutory holiday pay is paid when employees, having attained a certain seniority, are off work on a statutory holiday and receive pay.

In industries such as construction, where there are no annual vacation periods (except in the province of Quebec), employees are typically not paid for statutory holidays and, pursuant to employment standards legislation, have no entitlement to a fixed vacation. They are, however, entitled to vacation pay.

Most funds are structured as trusts with an equal number of trustees appointed by labour and management. Some of the funds have trustees appointed only by the union. The board of trustees makes all decisions regarding management and administration of the fund. Like any other employee benefit fund, there may be a third-party administrator or an in-house administrator.

Vacation pay fund administrators must attend to the following items in the administration and day-to-day management of the fund:

- Collect and account for the contributions
- Monitor delinquencies
- Allocate the contributions to the individual members by employer
- Arrange payment of the annual or semi-annual distribution and any interim requests
- Maintain proper accounting records and
- Invest the monies.[4]

Most vacation pay funds require an account to be kept for each employee and have an annual or semi-annual pay-out. The trust agreements usually permit pay-outs on certain other occasions such as:

- Unemployment of the member
- The member enrolling in an educational training course
- The member leaving the union or the jurisdiction and
- Long-term illness.

Some funds also permit one discretionary pay-out per year, subject to the approval of the trustees.

Vacation pay trust funds are subject to general trustee legislation (such as the Trustee Acts of most provinces) that would limit investments to those normally permitted to trustees, subject to any further limitations contained in the trust agreement. Many trust agreements limit vacation pay fund investments to short-term vehicles, as the money is generally paid out, (subject to the maintaining of a contingency reserve) on an annual or semi-annual basis. There are often problems regarding delinquencies, and it is important to recover vacation pay trust fund money that is owing or there may be a sizable liability to the fund.

In the event that the money is not recoverable through collection procedures, including construction liens, the investment income earned by the fund is generally applied for such purposes. Interest earned by the fund is also used to pay all necessary administration costs and expenses of the fund, as well as trustee expenses. Some funds still retain an annual surplus after the payment of all expenses and outstanding claims. In such circumstances, many vacation pay trust agreements allocate the surplus to employees or trade unions. In some instances there may be allocations to an employer association, although this may have certain consequences for income tax purposes as noted below. In recent years, when interest rates have been low, many vacation pay trusts have encountered some financial difficulties, as the interest income has not been sufficient to fund the delinquency and administration costs.

One problem that often arises is that of vacation pay that is owing to beneficiaries who cannot be located. Such payments have to ultimately be paid over to provincial authorities, under employment standards legislation. Accordingly, it is incumbent on trustees to make every effort to locate beneficiaries.

REGULATION OF VACATION PAY TRUST FUNDS

In Ontario, vacation pay trust funds are regulated pursuant to the *Employment Standards Act.*[5] The act contains certain minimum standards for payment of vacation pay and also contains the following provision:

31. Agreements respecting vacation or vacation pay.—Any agreement between an employer and employee or employees or his, her or their agent respecting the method of providing funds for paying vacation pay, or payment in lieu of vacation, or of any arrangements for the taking of vacation, is subject to the approval of the Director.[6]

Given the authority of the Director of Employment Standards under Section 31, it is not possible to establish a vacation pay trust fund in Ontario without the Director of Employment Standards approving the trust agreement and other documentation. In the past, it was necessary to prepare an application to establish a vacation pay trust fund to the Ontario Ministry of Labour, but the Director of Employment Standards no longer requires this. Rather, a detailed trust agreement must be prepared and forwarded to the Director that sets out the terms upon which vacation pay is to be paid. In the absence of such regulatory approval, it is not possible to establish a vacation pay trust fund.

The following matters must be dealt with in the trust agreement:

- Method of appointing trustees
- Trustees' duties and responsibilities
- Method for proceeding regarding insolvencies
- Collection of monies
- Accounting for and auditing of trust funds
- Payments to members, the extent of distributions and basis for distribution and
- Distribution of earnings and surpluses.

Attached, as Appendix VII-4-A to this chapter is a draft trust agreement prepared by the Ontario Ministry of Labour. Although this agreement meets the requirements of the Director, we caution that there may be many additional provisions to be included in a trust agreement that are not found in the draft agreement. Most trust funds do not use the standard form but have their legal counsel prepare a trust agreement that is tailored to the needs of the particular trust.

Another method of regulation of vacation pay trust fund is the disclosure requirements under labour relations statutes such as Ontario's *Labour Relations Act, 1995.*[7] Section 93(2) of the act requires an annual filing with the Ministry of Labour of audited financial statements for all vacation pay trust funds, welfare benefit funds and pension funds that are jointly trusteed. Among the matters to be contained in such financial statement are:

- A description of the coverage provided by the fund
- The amount contributed by each employer
- The amount contributed by the member, if any
- Statement of assets
- Statement of liabilities, receipts and disbursements and
- Statements of salaries, fees and commissions charged to the fund or plan, to whom they are paid and in what amounts and for what purposes.

Another important matter with respect to vacation pay is the "deemed trust" contained in Section 15 of the *Employment Standards Act,*[8] whereby vacation pay is deemed to be held in trust for the employee whether or not it is in fact kept separate and apart by the employer. The deemed trust in the past ranked ahead of the interest of secured creditors.

However, as a result of the Supreme Court of Canada's decision in *British Columbia v. Henfrey Samson Belair Ltd.*[9] and the provisions of the *Bankruptcy and Insolvency Act,*[10] deemed trusts have been rendered virtually ineffective in most insolvency situations. For a discussion on this issue and the decision in *Henfrey Samson Belair Ltd.,* see Section VIII, Chapter 3.

TAXATION OF VACATION PAY TRUST FUNDS

Vacation pay is a taxable benefit to the employee. Although the vacation pay is generally remitted monthly by the employer to the fund, it is deemed to be income of which the employee is in receipt when earned. Under Section 153 of the *Income Tax Act,*[11] tax must be withheld by the employer for vacation pay accrued every pay period if it is payable into a trust fund. Accordingly, the vacation pay trust fund remittances are deemed to be included in income *when earned* and not when actually received during the pay-out period. Any distributions of interest to an employee would be taxable at the time of pay-out.

The vacation pay trust fund itself *may* be exempt from tax on its investment income if it meets the criteria set out in Subsection 149(1)(y) of the *Income Tax Act.*[12] Under this provision a trust is exempt from paying tax on its income if at any time after 1980 its income or property is *only* payable to employees or their legal representatives, or a labour organization, i.e., a trade union, and the sole purpose of the trust is to provide for the payment of vacation or holiday pay. Accordingly, if benefits can only be paid to members, or surplus paid to a union, then the trust is not taxable on any of its investment income. This is set out in greater detail in Revenue Canada Interpretation Bulletin IT-389R,[13] which is attached as Appendix VII-4-B to this chapter.

A much more difficult situation exists where employer organizations are made beneficiaries of a trust. In such circumstances, Section 149(1)(y) does not apply, and the trust is not exempt from tax on its net income. However, the trust, like any other trust, may deduct from its income certain expenditures, such as administration costs and payments to beneficiaries if they are made in the year in which the income is earned. Subsection 104(6)(b) of the *Income Tax Act*[14] permits deductions from the income of the trust of any amount that is *payable in the year* to a beneficiary, and was included in computing the income of the beneficiary for the year. Arguably, where employer associations are beneficiaries of the trust, together with unions, these amounts may be deducted from the income of the trust. However, this is not the standard situation contemplated by the *Income Tax Act* and, accordingly, careful tax planning must be undertaken if the trust fund is going to make payments to persons other than the individual employees or the union.

VACATION PAY TRUST FUNDS AND EMPLOYMENT INSURANCE

A contentious issue under the *Employment Insurance Act* is the treatment of pay-outs from vacation pay trust funds to persons who happen to be unemployed at the time of the pay-out and were thus collecting employment insurance. This is a fairly commonplace occurrence in the construction industry, where employees may be out of work for considerable periods of time during poor economic times but may be collecting vacation pay accrued from previous employment.

Under the former *Unemployment Insurance Act,*[15] the Supreme Court of Canada determined, in *Bryden v. Canada Employment and Immigration Commission,*[16] that vacation pay trust fund pay-outs were *savings,* as opposed to *earnings,* during the period of unemployment. Section 26(2) of the *Unemployment Insurance Act, 1971*[17] only permitted the inclusion of *earnings* during the week of unemployment to reduce unemployment insurance benefits.

The unemployment insurance regulations were revised in 1985 and appeared to allocate vacation pay payments from a trust fund to periods of unemployment rather to when the money was earned. However, the Federal Court of Appeal in *Vennari v. Canada Employment and Immigration Commission*[18] upheld the principle from *Bryden,* and noted that income tax and unemployment insurance premiums are paid on this money when it is initially remitted to the trust fund, and thus it becomes *savings* and cannot be *earnings* to be allocated to a later period of unemployment.

However, where vacation pay is not paid to a vacation pay trust fund, but rather held in trust by the employer, the payment of vacation pay does constitute earnings during a period of unemployment.[19]

ENDNOTES

1. *Employment Insurance Act,* S.C. 1996 c. 23.

2. *Employment Standards Act,* R.S.O. 1990, c. E.14, as am.

3. *Labour Relations Act,* 1995, S.O. 1995, c. 1, Sch. A.

4. Gordon Manion, "Vacation Pay Trust Funds—How Are the Trustees Managing Their Affairs Today," *Canadian Employee Benefits (1984),* Proceedings of the International Foundation of Employee Benefit Plans Canadian Conference.

5. *Supra* note 2.

6. *Supra* note 2, s. 31.

7. *Supra* note 3.

8. *Supra* note 2.

9. *British Columbia v. Henfrey Samson Belair Ltd.,* [1989] 2 S.C.R. 24, (1989), 59 D.L.R. (4th) 726, (1989), 97 N.R. 61, [1989] 5 W.W.R. 577, (1989), 38 B.C.L.R. (2d) 145, (1989), (1989), 34 E.T.R. 1, (1989), 2 T.C.T. 4263 (S.C.C.).

10. *Bankruptcy and Insolvency Act,* R.S.C. 1985, c. B-3, as am.

11. *Income Tax Act,* R.S.C. 1985, c.1 (5th Supp.) as am, s. 153(1).

12. *Ibid.,* s. 149(1)(y).

13. Revenue Canada, Interpretation Bulletin IT-389R, "Vacation Pay Trusts Established Under Collective Agreement" (30 August 1985).

14. *Supra* note 10.

15. *Unemployment Insurance Act,* S.C. 1970-71-72, c. 48.

16. *Bryden v. Canada Employment and Immigration Commission,* [1982] 1 S.C.R. 443, (1982), 133 D.L.R. (3d) 1, (1982), 41 N.R. 480, 82 C.L.L.C. para. 14,175 at 171 (S.C.C.).

17. *Supra* note 15.

18. *Vennari v. Canada Employment and Immigration Commission,* [1987] F.C.F. No. 211, (1987), 36 D.L.R. (4th) 614, (1987), 3 F.C. 129, (1987), 76 N.R. 147, 87 C.L.L.C. para. 14,018 at 12,139 (F.C.A.).

19. *Liberati v. Canada (Employment and Immigration Commission),* [1993] F.C.J. No. 987 (C.A.), leave to appeal to Supreme Court of Canada refused [1993] S.C.C.A. No. 495 (S.C.C.).

Appendix VII—4-A

VACATIONS WITH PAY TRUST FUND AGREEMENT
APPROVED BY THE ONTARIO MINISTRY OF LABOUR

BETWEEN:

_____
(Insert name of Employer Group)

—AND —

_____
(Insert name of Employee Group and/or Local No.)

—AND—

_____
(Administrator appointed by the Trustees)

Annual Income	1. *Annual income* shall mean all income earned on Trust Fund capital or capitalized income in any fiscal year less all items in Article 33 accrued due during such fiscal year.
Administrator's Responsibilities	2. Terms of Administration For the purposes of this application, *Administrator* means a duly qualified agency, corporation, entity or person to whom the Board of Trustees shall, in accordance with these terms of administration, delegate all powers necessary for the sound and efficient administration of the plan and to hold in trust for the employees all vacation pay due under the *Employment Standards Act*.
Administrator Appointed	3. The Board of Trustees shall appoint _____ _____ as the administrator, provided that the said administrator shall be bonded in an amount acceptable to the Board of Trustees, and he shall be subject to the termination, control, direction and guidance of the Board of Trustees.
Employee Defined	4. For the purposes of this application, *Employee* means _____ _____ or any person on whose behalf his employer makes contributions to the Trust Fund for paying vacations with pay.
Employer Defined	5. For the purposes of this application, *Employer* means those employers bound by the Collective Agreement dated _____between the employer and the union or any successor agreement which may be in force from time to time, *listed on Schedule "A"* attached hereto, or any person, firm, contractor or subcontractor bound by any Collective Agreement adopting in substance but not necessarily in form the terms and conditions of the said Collective Agreement between the parties, or responsible directly or indirectly for the employment of an employee.
Legislative Authority	6. For the purposes of this application, *Act* refers to Section 32 of *The Employment Standards Act,* as amended from time to time.
Trust Fund Defined	7. A *Trust Fund* is to be established consisting of all the contributions payable under the said Collective Agreement with respect to vacation with pay, together with all capital gain and income, including income upon income produced thereby from time to time.
	8. The Trust Fund shall be known as: _____ _____ (State Legal Name of Fund)
Trustee Defined	9. The *Board of Trustees* of the Trust Fund shall be the Board of Trustees appointed from time to time as the Board of Trustees of the _____ _____ _____

Trustee Responsibilities

10. The Board of Trustees shall administer the Trust Fund in accordance with the terms of the administration applicable herein to the Trustees and such other terms and provisions as shall be established by such Board of Trustees relating to meetings of the Board of Trustees, decisions of the Board of Trustees, and the winding up or termination of the Trust Fund.

Discretionary Powers of Trustees

11. (i) Subject to the terms of this agreement, the Board of Trustees is to have all discretionary powers to pass by resolution all matters pertaining to the collection and disbursement of the monies in the Trust Fund in accordance with the Act, Collective Agreement, or any type of participation agreement.

Grieved Employees

(ii) An employee aggrieved by a decision of the Board of Trustees shall have the right to appeal to the Director of Employment Standards, Ministry of Labour for Ontario, from the Board of Trustees' decision, . . .

Collection Problems

12. The collection, payment and distribution of deposited monies in the Trust Fund is to be administered in accordance with the contents of this application, subject to the following sentence, "Should a problem arise in the collection of the Vacation Pay money, the problem will be referred to the Board of Trustees and they shall resolve such problem in accordance with the Collective Agreement."

Contribution Remittance Deadline

13. (i) All employers must remit their monthly contributions to the Administrator no later than the 15th day of the month following the month in which the vacation pay was earned.

Late Contributions Demand

(ii) Any employer whose contributions have not been received by the 22nd day of the month following the month the vacation pay was earned, shall be issued a letter of demand of payment by the Administrator with a copy to the designated Trustees of the employers and the designated Trustees of the employees.

Idem

14. (i) If within 15 days of the letter of demand referred to in Article 13(ii), the employer has not brought his contributions up to date, the Board of Trustees shall take immediate action to collect all outstanding contributions in accordance with the Collective Agreement or in any manner deemed more expedient.

Failure to Collect

(ii) The Board of Trustees will not be held responsible for the failure to collect payment from any employer signatory to the Collective Agreement, but the Board of Trustees shall take any steps which may be available to them either in law or in equity or in bankruptcy as may be necessary or desirable to effect collection of such payment.

Costs of Collection

(iii) All costs incurred in the collection of said payment shall be charged to such defaulting participating employer and in the event that the Board of Trustees is unable to collect from the defaulting participating employer, then the costs shall be paid out of the income from the Trust Fund generated during the vacation year that the vacation was earned.

Acts and Omissions by Trustees	15. No member of the Board of Trustees acting hereunder shall be liable for any action taken or omitted by him in good faith, or for any act or omission of any agent or employee selected with reasonable care, by the Board of Trustees, nor for the acts or omissions of any member of the Board of Trustees, nor shall any member of the Board of Trustees be individually or personally liable for any of the obligations of the Board of Trustees as such or of the Trust Fund.
Trustees Not Agents or Signatories	16. The Board of Trustees shall not be considered to be the agent of the employers signatory to the Collective Agreement or of the Union or of the members of the said Union. The responsibility of the Board of Trustees is to assure the proper administration of the Trust Agreement including the collection and disbursement of all the money in connection with the Fund.
Claims Under Bankruptcy	17. (i) If a participating employer declares bankruptcy, the Administrator will, on behalf of the Board of Trustees, prepare and forward the necessary claim forms to the person appointed as the Trustee of the bankruptcy. The application shall be tendered to the Trustee of the bankrupt estate as a claim for monies held by the bankrupt employer in trust for any other person in accordance with section 67(1) of the *Bankruptcy and Insolvency Act* (Canada).
Bankruptcies Settlement	(ii) Subject to Article 33, any employee of a bankrupt employer who is a participant in the Trust Fund, will be reimbursed from the earnings of the Fund for any loss of vacation pay due him while working for the bankrupt participating employer in accordance with the following terms:

(a) All claims of the employees on the Fund due to a bankruptcy shall be limited to the amount earned by the Fund during the vacation year on which the claim was based plus the immediate preceding year or such further amounts agreed upon by the employer and employee representative trustees of the Fund, and payable at the end of the year in which the payout was due.

(b) Subject to clause (a) above, 100% of the claim if the retained earnings in the Fund are sufficient, or

(c) In proportion of the claim to retained earnings, if such earnings are not sufficient to satisfy in accordance with clause (b), or

(d) 100% of claim if recovery from the bankrupt estate is sufficient to pay on that basis or if the amount of the retained earnings of the Trust Fund for the period plus the amount recovered from the bankrupt estate is sufficient, or

(e) Any other scheme or system approved by the Director of Employment Standards.

Setting up of Trust Account	18. A separate trust account is to be kept in the name of the Trust Fund with a trust company or chartered bank selected by the Board of Trustees and is to be used for the deposit of employer contributions to the Trust Fund. The Board of Trustees is authorized to receive and commingle contributions from each of the participating employers.
Banking of Funds	19. All employer contributions will be banked by the Administrator after the employer remittances have been verified for accuracy. The employer must record the amount due and social insurance number of each employee on the monthly remittance sheet that is submitted to the Administrator.
Responsibility for Non-negotiable Cheques	20. The Administrator is authorized to accept non-certified cheques on the assumption that they will be accepted by the bank or trust company. If the cheque is not acceptable by the trust company or the bank, the Administrator or the Board of Trustees is not responsible or liable for said cheques. All vacation pay money being earned by the employee is a Trust Fund in the hands of the employer until the money is paid to the administrator.
Auditing of Fund	21. The Trust Fund is to be audited once a year, by an independent firm of auditors appointed by the Board of Trustees. Certified copies of the audit report are to be forwarded to the Director of Employment Standards, Ministry of Labour for Ontario, and to the Board of Trustees of the Trust Fund. Certified copies are to be forwarded to the Director of Employment Standards within six months of the closing date of the fiscal period for which the audit was performed. The Director may require, upon his demand, that an interim financial report be filed at any time.
Record-Keeping	22. The Administrator will keep a general ledger for the Trust Fund so that the auditor will be able to verify all contributions and disbursements on a month-to-month basis. The general ledger will also be used for the preparation of a report to be submitted to the Board of Trustees at each Board of Trustees meeting by the administrator.
Idem	23. The Administrator will set up an employee record showing the employee's name, social insurance number, address, and keep a continuous record of the total amount of money paid into the Trust Fund, by participating employers, for each employee, on a monthly basis, before the distribution of the vacation pay from the Trust Fund. These contributions will be accumulated for the period as stipulated in Article 24. The total amount of contributions made by each employer will be verified with the amount credited to each employee's account.

Pay-out Schedules

24. (i) Initial Regular Pay-out
During the month of _____, on or before the _____ day of said month, the Administrator will issue a cheque to each employee for whom contributions have been made. The cheque will include all vacation pay money received and recorded by the duly designated depositor for the _____ month period ending on the _____day of _____

(ii) Subsequent Regular Pay-outs
During each month of _____, subsequent to the initial regular pay-out, on or before the _____ day of said month(s), the Administrator will issue a cheque to each employee for whom contributions have been made. The cheque will include all vacation pay money received and recorded by the depositor since the previous regular pay-out, less any payments made to the employee in accordance with Article 25 hereof.

(iii) Fiscal periods
The first fiscal period of the Trust Fund shall comprise the _____ calendar months ending the _____ day of _____, _____. Subsequent fiscal periods shall comprise the 12 calendar month period ending the _____ day of _____ in each calendar year thereafter.

Time Off

(iv) Provisions must be made to permit employees to take a vacation within the 12 month period following the period in which the vacation was earned.

Additional Pay-out

25. In addition to the payments designated in Article 24, in the case of an annual payment, two other pay-outs may be made; in the case of semi-annual payments, one other payment may be made during any vacation year, providing the following conditions are complied with:
(a) The Union confirms in writing that the applicant is no longer a member or that the applicant is in daytime attendance at a trade school;
(b) The applicant is registered as unemployed with The Employment Insurance Commission, and requests in writing, payment from the Fund;
(c) The applicant has left the jurisdiction of the Collective Agreement.

Income Tax Deductions

26. The participating employer will deduct income tax on the vacation pay on the basis of the employee's wage scale at the time the contribution was calculated. Employers will show the vacation pay contributed and the deduction on the employee's T4 form.

Time of Pay-out

27. Any employee who is eligible for pay-out from the Fund shall be paid all accrued credits received and recorded to the date of his application, no later than ten (10) days following the date of the application. Any money due him and received after the date of the application will be sent to his last known address within sixty (60) days of the application made under Article 25.

Multiple Employers

28. If an employee is employed by a series of employers during a single fiscal period, subject to Article 25 hereof, no vacation pay will be paid until the regular pay-out date(s) in Article 24 hereof.

Unable to Locate Employee 29. If the Administrator is unable to locate any employee who is entitled to vacation pay money, he will forward annually, all money to which the employee is entitled under the *Employment Standards Act* to the Director of Employment Standards, together with a list showing:
(a) Name and address
(b) Social insurance no.
(c) Amount due
(d) Period covered
and in any fiscal year where all employees have been located and all such money paid out, the Administrator shall file a letter so certifying with the Director of Employment Standards.

Attendance at Board Meetings 30. The Administrator will attend such meetings as the Board of Trustees may call and notify the Board of Trustees in advance of the time, date and place of such meetings. The Administrator will keep and prepare the minutes and distribute them to the Trustees.

Administrator to Answer Enquiries 31. The Administrator will answer all enquiries from employers or employees with respect to the requirements and procedures of the Trust Fund, and forward copies of correspondence to a Trustee representative of the Union designated by the Union Trustees, and a Trustee representative of the employers signatory to the Collective Agreement designated by the Trustees of the employers signatory to the Collective Agreement.

Administrator to Arrange Printing 32. The Administrator will arrange for the printing and distribution of all forms required in the administration of the Trust Fund, annual reports, and similar material to eligible employees and contributing employers.

Distribution of Fund Earnings 33. The Board of Trustees may retain, employ and compensate trust companies, banks, agents, administrators, consultants, auditors, and legal counsel, who, in their discretion, are deemed proper and necessary. The income earned by the investment of the monies in the Trust Fund shall be applied firstly to the cost of administration, the printing and distribution of all forms in the operation of the Trust Fund and any liability under the *Income Tax Act* and, secondly, in accordance with Article 17(ii), any deficit caused by the bankruptcy of a contributing employer.

Idem 34. Subject to the rights of the employee including, without restricting the generality thereof, the employee rights pursuant to Article 17(ii), any balance remaining in the earnings of the Fund when all items in Article 33 are paid, may be set up as a reserve or distributed in a manner recommended by Trustees of both employer and employee and in accordance with the terms of the applicable Collective Agreement.

We agree to adhere to the terms of administration in the above application and the provisions therein.

DATED AT _____ in the Province of _____,
this _____ day of _____, 20___.

WITNESSED BY: SIGNATORIES:
                                            Representing Employers
                                    Signatory to the Collective Agreement

_____   _____
Employer   Signatory's Name

                                        _____
                                        Signature

_____   _____
Employer   Signatory's Name

                                        _____
                                        Signature

_____   _____
Employer   Signatory's Name

                                        _____
                                        Signature

                                    Representing the Union

_____   _____
Union   Signatory's Name

                                        _____
                                        Signature

_____   _____
Union   Signatory's Name

                                        _____
                                        Signature

_____   _____
Union   Signatory's Name

                                        _____
                                        Signature

                        _____
                        Administrator for (Name of the Fund)

The foregoing agreement respecting the method of providing funds for paying vacation pay or payment in lieu of vacation as contained in Articles 7, 13, 21, 24, 25, 27 and 29 is approved.

Dated this _____ day of _____, 20___.

                                    _____
                                    Director of Employment Standards

Note: Any amendment to the articles in this agreement will void the Director's approval.

Schedule "A"

(See Article 5)

Index

Appendix VII—4-B

INTERPRETATION BULLETIN IT-389R
AUGUST 30, 1985
VACATION PAY TRUSTS ESTABLISHED UNDER COLLECTIVE AGREEMENTS

Paragraph 149(1)(y) and (k) (also section 5 and paragraph 18(1)(a))

This bulletin cancels and replaces IT-389 dated August 15, 1977 since paragraph 149(1)(y) was made effective for the 1972 and subsequent taxation years.

1.   The Federal Government and all of the provinces and territories have passed legislation providing for the payment by employers of salaries or wages to employees (other than those excepted by the legislation) for periods while the employees are on vacation.

2.   Collective agreements between an employer (or an association of employers) and employees (or their labour organization) may require the employer to make periodic contributions to a trust on account of vacation credits earned by individuals. The amount of the contribution is determined by the agreement as revised from time to time but must meet any minimums established under the relevant legislation. Under the terms of a typical vacation pay plan the trustees manage the trust property and make payments at specified or determinable times to individual employees on account of vacation credits accumulated by them. None of the trust property, whether as to capital or income, may become payable to employees before the time determined under the plan for making payments to them.

3.   Paragraph 149(1)(y) applies to a trust established pursuant to the terms of a collective agreement between an employer or an association of employers and employees or their labour organization for the sole purpose of providing for the payment of vacation or holiday pay. No part of the property of the trust, after payment of its reasonable expenses, may be available after 1980 or be paid after December 11, 1979, to any person (other than a tax exempt labour organization as described in paragraph 149(1)(k)) otherwise than as a consequence of being an employee or an heir or a legal representative of the employee. As the sole purpose of such a plan must be the payment of vacation or holiday pay, amounts paid into the trust will normally be disbursed by the trustee no later than in the year following receipt.

4.   After 1979, a vacation pay trust that does not meet the requirements of paragraph 149(1)(y) falls within the employee benefit plan definition contained in Subsection 248(1). The tax result to the employer, employee and trustee of an employee benefit plan is explained in IT-502. Prior to 1980, such a trust was subject to the provisions of Subdivision k of Division B of Part I of the Act.

Tax Result to Qualifying Trust

5.   No tax is payable under Part I on the income of a trust that meets the conditions described in 3 above. However, pursuant to Subsection 204(1) of the Regulations, the vacation pay trust is still required to file a T3 Information Return and Income Tax Return each year and should indicate thereon that it is non-taxable under paragraph 149(1)(y).

Tax Result to Employer Under Qualifying Trust

6.   An employer who computed income on an accrual basis may claim a deduction for employees' vacation pay credits for the period in which the liability arose even though payment to the trust is not made until after the end of the period. Withholding on account of tax, Quebec or Canada Pension Plan contributions and unemployment insurance premiums is required at the time the payment is made to the trust as though the amounts had been paid directly to the employees. Whether it is the net amount after deductions which is paid into the trust, or the gross amount with the prescribed deduction being withheld from regular pay, is determined by the provisions of the plan. In either event the employer includes the gross vacation pay contributions made during the year in respect of each employee as an element of gross wages on forms T4 Summary and T4 Supplementary.

Tax Result to Employee

7.   An employer's contributions to the trust in respect of vacation credits of a particular employee are included in the employee's income in the year during which the contribution is made. Subsequent payments by the trust out of those contributions are received by the employee free of tax.

8.   Amounts received by an employee out of income of the trust are brought into income as vacation pay since they are received by virtue of the employment contract and no payments other than vacation pay may be made to an employee if the trust is to remain qualified under paragraph 149(1)(y). The source of the trust funds used to pay such amounts does not affect this characterization and the trust is required to withhold amounts on account of income tax and to file the related T4 information returns (rather than T3 Supplementary) in respect of the amounts paid. Such payments might be made where vacation pay is ordinarily met in part out of income earned by the trust or where the employer (through bankruptcy) fails to make contributions to the trust for employees' vacation credits earned.

Other Arrangements

9.   Where the collective agreement provides that the employer make contributions to an entity other than a trust, e.g., a custodian, the vacation pay plan is an employee benefit plan subject to the tax consequences outlined in IT-502.

10.   Where the employer pays vacation pay directly to employees, whether or not pursuant to a vacation pay plan under a collective agreement, such payments are included in gross compensation and, if deductible by the employer, are deductible in the year paid or earned by the employees. An employee includes such amounts in income from an office or employment in the taxation year in which they are received. As a component of gross compensation, vacation pay is subject to income tax withholding at source, Quebec or Canada Pension Plan contributions and unemployment insurance premiums and is reported in forms T4 Summary and T4 Supplementary as part of "Total Earnings."

CHAPTER 5

Employee Assistance Plans

by Peter O'Hara

INTRODUCTION

Over the last 50 years, the clinical labels that we apply to certain social illnesses have changed. *Alcoholism* and *drug addiction* are no longer the descriptives. Instead, the medical community and, indeed, the community at large now refer to these conditions collectively as *substance abuse.* On the surface this may seem insignificant. However, the underlying fact is that this change in terminology reflects a greater change in societal attitudes, both in terms of how these illnesses are perceived and of how we have come to deal with and treat them. Nowhere is this change more evident than in the evolution of the programs that address employee health and well-being.

Employee assistance plans (EAPs), also referred to as *workforce health programs* and, more recently, *wellness programs,* are not a new feature to the Canadian benefits scene. In fact, Bell Canada pioneered such a program for its employees over 50 years ago. Established in 1947, it focused on the treatment of drug and alcohol abuse, the predominant characteristic of EAPs through the 1950s and early 1960s.[1]

Those earlier programs also tended to be of the mandatory referral type. Employees had no choice but to participate. When they were found to be in need of assistance, the plan turned into an extension of the company's disciplinary process.

Over the last four decades, however, there have been some significant changes in the workplace. The 1960s ushered in an era of major social change. Women entered the work force in greater numbers than ever before. Eventually, by 1980, more than half of Canadian women (50.3%) were officially part of the labour force.[2] Immigration and multiculturalism in Canada have also had a considerable impact on this evolutionary process.

Another powerful influence on the evolution of EAPs has been organized labour. In the early 1970s, the Canadian Labour Congress became a strong advocate for the removal of the mandatory component in programs aimed at substance abuse. It was felt that the disciplinary process had become too entwined with the EAP. Workers lost confidence or did not utilize the programs for fear of reprisal. Therefore, the programs lost credibility.[3] As a result of their efforts (in part), plan sponsors moved away from the concept of mandatory referral. Furthermore, organized labour is now a strong proponent of EAPs for its members.

In addition to social reform, economic upheaval has effected the work environment. The 1970s was an unprecedented decade of inflation in North America. In the 1980s and 1990s trade barriers fell, markets went global and the technological revolution took hold of economies. These forces have created an extremely competitive marketplace in Canada and abroad.

As the workplace evolved, so too have employee benefit programs. Plan sponsors and benefit negotiators alike have broadened the scope of EAP services to meet the new challenges of the workplace. Plans now address a wider array of employee concerns, such as stress, finance, legal, family and marriage, as well as substance abuse. In the mid-1990s, one Addiction Research Foundation study noted, the focus of EAPs has shifted from drug and alcohol abuse to any of the conditions that affect employee well-being and performance.

As we head into the next century, the evolution continues. With the escalating cost of medicines, downloading of services and products by the public sector and an aging population, the rising cost of providing employee benefit programs is staggering. The emphasis has necessarily shifted to "preventative medicine." Nutrition, fitness and a generally healthy lifestyle help control the future usage of traditional benefits, such as prescription drugs and income replacement. A comprehensive EAP fits nicely into an employee wellness strategy and, by virtue of the statistical data, plan sponsors are beginning to see its virtues. In 1989, the Addiction Research Foundation sponsored a provincial survey in Ontario. The results of that study found that "in Ontario alone, EAPs are an integral part of 16.1% of all worksites with over 50 employees. That represents over 700,000 employees or 27.3% of all employees in that province."[4] More recently, Watson Wyatt Canada surveyed 305 companies of various sizes. Of those surveyed, 69% had an EAP program.[5] A similar survey by the Conference Board of Canada found that "over 80% of Canadian companies with 500 or more employees have Employee Assistance Programs or Employee and Family Assistance Programs (EAPs/EFAPs)."[6]

What began as a disciplinary procedure has become part of a growing health initiative.

STANDARD EAP FEATURES

On-site or in-house EAPs are usually espoused by sponsors large enough to administer programs through their occupational health and safety or human resources departments. In turn they may develop a complete support structure inhouse, or they may utilize some of the outside facilities that have been created to serve rising demands. As is the case with the implementation of any benefit plan, these decisions are driven by simple economics. Cost-effectiveness, along with the proper delivery of services, is paramount.

Conversely, *off-site* EAPs are the overwhelming choice of small-to-medium size plan sponsors. This approach has been encouraged by the advent of health care networks specializing in the delivery of many of the needed services. Health care networks provide smaller sponsors with access to a great number of services, without the overhead and expense associated with in-house operations.

The cornerstone of modern EAPs, whether of the internal or external variety, is confidentiality. Successful plans formalize and publish their related polices. Of equal importance, they demand rigid adherence to those polices on the part of the program staff. Otherwise, they have learned, employee confidence will quickly diminish, and the hard work and good intentions expended on the program will reap only ill will. Worse still, if the program has emerged from collective bargaining, a breach of confidentiality will result in severe and expensive

grievance procedures. Therefore, secrecy, in fanfare and in fact, is the primary ingredient for success.

PLAN DESIGN

Before implementing an EAP, certain other steps should be taken in order to ensure its success, both in terms of promoting a healthy work environment and of managing plan-related costs.

As with most other benefit plans, EAPs should be tailored to the eventual users. The peculiarities of the workplace, in terms of physical and mental stresses, need to be wedded, realistically, to management and, if applicable, to union principles and objectives. Employee profiles must be developed from socio-economic analyses and then merged with the workplace information to build a foundation of requirements. From there, the plan can be designed.

It has been argued that a third party, rather than an in-house person or group, is better able to determine the needs of a given organization. Perhaps employees tend to respond more openly to an outsider than to a fellow employee or company supervisor, but empirical evidence supports neither approach with any certainty. Rather, it may be concluded that each sponsor should perform an honest, critical analysis of its inherent resources and then choose the method for design.

Once the needs of plan beneficiaries have been assessed, policies and procedures should be established. Policies, outlined in a plan document, should clarify both the responsibilities of the employees/members and the obligations of the plan sponsor to the plan and to its beneficiaries.[7]

The following are some of the provisions that a comprehensive EAP plan document should include:

1. Mission statement/statement of objectives
2. Statement of confidentiality
3. Referral provisions
4. Explanation of services
5. Location of services (on-site/off-site)
6. Administrative structure
7. Key contacts (i.e., program coordinator, administrator)
8. Formula for periodic evaluation.

ADMINISTRATION

Once a plan document has been written, consideration should be given to establishing administration procedures.

Like health and welfare programs, EAPs are provided either through a group insurance arrangement or on a self-insured basis. In either case, a financial commitment is generally made by the sponsor/employer. Although some plans are partially funded by employee contributions, this tends to be the exception rather than the rule. Plans can be sponsored by a single employer or by a multi-employer health and welfare trust fund. In the case of a multi-employer trust fund, participating employers commit to a defined contribution.

Payment in respect of services can be made on a cost-plus basis or on an experience rated basis, where an insurance carrier is involved. In light of these possibilities, administrative procedure and delivery of services can significantly vary from plan to plan.

Group Insurance Arrangement

Where an EAP is provided under a group insurance policy, it is generally experience rated like other benefits. This means that cost is based on utilization, and a monthly premium is remitted by the employer/sponsor to the insurer. The premium is adjusted up or down each policy year, depending on whether utilization exceeds or consistently runs under anticipated levels. This type of arrangement can be administered by the insurance company, self-administered by a trust fund or administered by a third-party contract administrator. Insurers may also offer EAP services on a cost-plus basis. In this case there are no monthly premiums. Plan sponsors merely remit amounts sufficient to cover the cost of utilization on a monthly, quarterly or semi-annual basis. This arrangement commonly involves the usage of a health care network, with the insurance company operating as a conduit.

Self-Insured Arrangement

Self-insured EAPs do not use the services of an insurance carrier. The cost of services is directly paid by the employer(s), or the trust fund—in the case of multi-employer plans—generally on a cost-plus basis.

If the EAP is a single employer-sponsored plan, the employer is responsible for its administration and maintenance, either by utilizing existing in-house systems or through a third-party contract administrator. In the case of in-house delivery of EAP services, a committee can be created to oversee the daily business of the plan and to make recommendations for modifications, if necessary. EAP committees include representatives from the employer, the employees and, in some cases, an external consulting agency.

In the case of multi-employer plans, it is the trustees of the trust fund who are responsible for the administration and maintenance of the EAP. Generally, the trustees will secure the services of a third-party contract administrator to handle the day-to-day business of the EAP. However, self-administration, whereby the trust fund creates its own administrative services to manage the day-to-day business of the plan, has become more commonplace in the last ten years.

WHY AN EMPLOYEE ASSISTANCE PLAN?

The modern day philosophy that employers have adopted for implementing employee benefit plans stems from both a humanitarian concern, a concern for maintaining a competitive edge and, more recently, as a means of controlling costs. With the consistent erosion of government-sponsored benefits services over the last decade, employers have had to pick up the slack where employee benefits are concerned. In some cases this has been a voluntary process. However, major inroads have been made in this regard through the collective bargaining process. The second consideration for employers in today's job market is creating an attractive environment for prospective employees. Benefit plans, such as pension, health and welfare and EAPs, have become an integral part of an employee's total compensation package. Therefore, in order for employers to attract skilled and competent workers, benefit plans have become a necessary ingredient, alongside wages.

There is an increasing body of evidence, however, that suggests that EAPs, unlike other employee benefits, actually provide a return on the investment. This, in fact, is the very premise under which these plans were created some 45 years ago. The assumption back in the late 1940s, which still prevails, is that there is a direct link between employee well-being and productivity. This premise has been articulated in a number of studies, including a 1988 report that was prepared for the St. Boniface General Hospital, located in Winnipeg, Manitoba.[8] The report purported that:

... at least 10% of the labour force will experience some form of potentially debilitating emotional mental health or chemical dependency problem at some point in their work history.

The report went on to conclude that:

... evidence suggests that these problems also have an effect on work history and loss of money through absenteeism, sick time and reduced productivity.

The difficulty over the years has been measuring, precisely, the savings incurred through the implementation of an EAP. Until recently little emphasis was placed on assessment of the financial impact of these programs. It was generally agreed that there was a positive impact on productivity, but to what extent no one was sure.

Part of the difficulty in assessing the effectiveness of EAPs has been the lack of hard information, due primarily to the confidential nature by which they must necessarily be governed. Another stumbling block in this regard has been creating a consistent methodology by which to measure EAPs.

The determination of actual cost savings (if one is basing a decision on bottom-line rationale) ap-

Table VII- 5-I

SUMMARY OF COST-EFFECTIVENESS STUDY RESULTS

Organization	Number of Participants	Year of Study	Length of Study	Findings (Based on Employees Who Used EAP Services)
Illinois	402	1974	5 years	• 46% decrease in sick days • 63% decrease in off-the-job accidents • 81% decrease in on-the-job accidents
Philadelphia Fire Dept.	51	1975	1 year	• 2% decrease in injured days • 45% decrease in sick days
Philadelphia Police Dept.	170	1975	1 year	• 38% decrease in sick days • 62% decrease in injured days • $238,000 savings
United States Postal Service	15	1974	1 year	• 93% decrease in sick days
University of Michigan Medical Center	321	1987	1 year	• 30% decrease in sick days • $87,058 savings

pears to be less than fully documented. Experience tends to vary widely, ranging from as much as 10% productivity improvement in the first year and ratios of payback ranging from $2.00 for every dollar invested to $5.00 for every dollar invested thereafter.[9]

However, several studies have emerged that attempt to measure the cost-effectiveness of EAPs and wellness programs. One such study was included in a report prepared by an independent benefit consultant summarized in Table VII-5-I.[10] In 1978 Canada Life developed a health promotion program that was independently evaluated over a ten-year period. The program showed a return of $6.85 on each corporate dollar invested based on reduced employee turnover, greater productivity and decreased medical claims by participating employees. A review of worldwide wellness studies by Dr. Ray Shephard for the Canadian government found that workplace wellness programs have a return on investment of between $1.95 to $3.75 per employee, per dollar spent.[11]

TAXATION OF EMPLOYEE ASSISTANCE PLANS

As is the case with life and health insurance benefits, general taxation principles for EAPs are outlined in Section I, Chapter 8, which deals with Revenue Canada policy on taxation of employee benefits and the general system of taxation of income.

Section 6(1)(a)(iv) to the *Income Tax Act* expressly exempts from tax employees covered under an EAP, whereby the value of any contributions made by the employer for counseling services in respect of mental or physical health is not considered income for taxation purposes. Furthermore, as outlined in Section III, Chapter 3, Revenue Canada issued a release in December of 1989 indicating that certain "counselling benefits" will not be treated as taxable benefits.

Those counselling services are:

• In respect of an employee's physical or mental health
• Re-employment counselling for employees whose employment is being terminated
• Retirement counselling for employees age 50 or more or where the counselling is given in any two-year period that includes the employee's retirement date.[12]

This release clearly enfolds most services provided by EAPs. However, one of the more recent additions to EAP-based services is clearly excluded. Revenue Canada Information Bulletin IT-470R,[13] which deals primarily with fringe benefits, expressly excludes financial counselling services from the tax-exempt services noted above. Furthermore, a majority of employee benefits, particularly those provided through a trust, remain tax-exempt in the hands of beneficiaries.

ENDNOTES

1. "EAP Alert," *Benefits Canada* 17:6 (June 1993).
2. Labour Canada, *Women in the Workforce,* Part 1.

Women's Bureau, Labour Canada, (1993).Cat. No. L24-1068/81B.

3. Canadian Labour Congress, *Proceedings Annual Congress Conference,* Quebec City (Ottawa: Canadian Labour Congress, 1978).

4. MacDonald and Dooley, *Employee Assistance Programs (EAPs) 1989 Provincial Survey, Ontario Worksites With 50 or More Employees; The Nature and Extent of EAPs, Programs and Worksite Characteristics* (Addiction Research Foundation, 1989).

5. "Allies Against Disability," *Employee Health + Productivity* 5:8 (January 1998).

6. "Wrapping Up The Wellness Package," *Benefits Canada* 23:1 (January 1999).

7. *Ibid.*

8. Ken C. Sime, *Report on Employee Assistance Programs, A Report to the St. Boniface General Hospital,* Section II (May 1988).

9. *Ibid.,* at p. 2.

10. R. Csiernik, "Developing an Employee Assistance Program: Essential Aspects and Components," EAP Council of Hamilton-Wentworth (1991), at p. 17.

11. "Wrapping Up The Wellness Package," *supra* note 6.

12. Revenue Canada, Interpretation Bulletin Special Release IT-470RSR, "Employee Fringe Benefits" (11 December 1989).

13. Revenue Canada, Interpretation Bulletin IT-470R, "Employees' Fringe Benefits" (8 April 1988).

CHAPTER 6

Investments

by Michael Sandell

GENERAL

The investments of other benefit funds can be extremely varied; from employees' profit-sharing plans (EPSPs), whose investments can be as exotic as the employer wants, to vacation pay trusts, whose investments should be short-term and very conservative.

Most other benefit funds are governed by a trust document. This document, among other things, should set out the broad investment guidelines for the trust. If investment guidelines are not addressed, then the trust's investments are governed by the Trustee Act of the province of residence. For a more in-depth discussion of trust fund balances refer to Section III, Chapter 6.

However, these guidelines should be seen as a starting point only. A separate statement of investment policy and guidelines should accompany each trust document and should address such items as term of investment, credit quality and diversification.

Most trusts are not taxable. The exception to this rule relates to foreign content. In general, trusts can invest up to 30% of the book value of assets in foreign investments. Amounts in excess of this limit are taxed at the rate of 1% per month.

REGISTERED RETIREMENT SAVINGS PLANS

Registered retirement savings plans (RRSPs) are long-term in nature, providing funds for retirement that may be 30 years from now for some members. Short-term changes in interest rates and stock markets will not have a major impact on availability of assets to meet pension commitments. Consequently, investment strategy should focus on long-term factors. Such things as asset mix strategy, diversification guidelines and hiring an

investment manager are sufficiently complex and varied that they should only be accomplished with the guidance of a qualified investment consultant. The plan's administrator can suggest two or three consultants to be interviewed by the trustees.

Once a consultant is hired, the trustees should discuss tolerance for risk versus anticipated return and then formulate a set of investment guidelines for the RRSP.

OTHER SAVINGS PLANS

Deferred profit-sharing plans (DPSPs), employee profit-sharing plans (EPSPs) and employee stock option plans (ESOPs) are also long-term in nature. DPSPs and EPSPs have contributions that are tied to company profits. Investment guidelines should be set in conjunction with a qualified investment consultant. ESOP investments are quite often tied to the stock of the employer company. This is a good way of making employees aware of the financial status of the company. However, it also increases the employee's exposure to the fortunes of the company; not only is the employee's job tied to the company but so are his or her investments. ESOPs should only be undertaken with care and only after getting advice from an outside consultant.

OTHER BENEFIT FUNDS

Surpluses from other benefit funds, such as training and vacation pay trusts, should generally be invested in low-risk, short-term securities. This is because the liabilities of these plans are also short-term. Consequently, investment guidelines for these funds are generally similar to health and welfare trust funds. Please see Chapter 6 of Section III for a discussion of these guidelines.

CHAPTER 1

Meeting the Problem of Delinquencies in Multi-Employer Plans

by Ron Davis and Stephen Tatrallyay

DUTIES AND RESPONSIBILITIES OF TRUSTEES

One of the most basic duties of a fiduciary is to collect all monies due and owing to the trust.[1]

The collection of contributions due to the trust fund is one of the most important duties of the trustee. It is also one of the most difficult for trust funds with a large number of contributing employers. It is a fundamental rule that trustees are under a duty to the beneficiaries to make a reasonable effort to collect delinquent contributions.

A generous feeling toward the debtor is not a sufficient reason for ignoring the duty to collect delinquent accounts. Trustees have a duty to the trust fund and its beneficiaries that must transcend personal feelings.

From the trustees' viewpoint, collection should not be a matter of labour vs. management; it should be a matter of performing a fiduciary function.[2]

A trustee must take all reasonable and proper measures to obtain possession of the trust property if it is outstanding and to get in all debt and funds due to the trust estate.[3]

As is clear from the above quotations, collecting contributions due to a trust fund to provide employee benefits is one of the most important duties of trustees. It can be an extremely difficult task, given the large number of contributing employers and the fact that most contributions are the subject of reports submitted by the employers without the ability to verify *all* of the information. Nevertheless, a serious delinquency problem can impair the ability of any trust fund to deliver its benefits, deprive employees of proper coverage for health, insurance and retirement benefits, and unfairly punish employers that report accurately and pay on a timely basis. Accordingly, it is important that the handling of delinquencies be given special priority by trustees. The importance of collecting delinquent contributions was highlighted in the *Report of the Royal Commission on the Status of Pensions in Ontario,* 1980:

Some degree of contribution delinquency is to be expected in most multi-employer plans. Because the majority of employers involved are small and lack depth of financial resources, the slightest reduction in demand for their services may give rise to difficulties in meeting their financial commitments including payments due to the pension plan. In prolonged slack periods many participating employers may go out of business. *If the plan is not to suffer a loss, the trustees therefore must watch for delinquencies and make every effort to collect contributions due.* (Emphasis added.)[4]

Many boards of trustees have delinquency committees and have appointed special "delinquency control officers" who are responsible for monitoring employer payments and pursuing delinquencies. A critical factor for all trustees in fulfilling their obligations to plan beneficiaries is to develop a basis for dealing with delinquencies that will involve all the various approaches set out below.

Although there may be some uncertainty as to the extent of a trustee's responsibility concerning a delinquent employer, there can be no doubt as to the trustee's obligation to ensure that all reasonable efforts are made to collect unpaid contributions. Further, the trustees are obligated to promptly inform the union of any delinquent employers or possible inaccuracies in employer contribution reports, so that appropriate action can be taken quickly.

Generally speaking, collection proceedings can be instituted by the union under the collective agreement's grievance and arbitration procedure. Trustees, even though they are not party to the applicable collective agreement, may have powers granted to them under the collective agreement or trust agreement to pursue delinquencies or may be able to do so pursuant to applicable pension legislation in the case of pension fund trustees. The trustees can, of course, settle claims against delinquent employers or even decline to institute collection proceedings but, in either case, they must act prudently and in good faith.

Trustees must exercise independent judgment with respect to the timing and methods used for collections. If the trustees in a bona fide exercise of their discretion believe that an attempt to enforce a claim against a delinquent employer would make it impossible for such employer to pay it, and where a reasonable extension of time would more likely result in payment, the trustees may properly delay enforcement of the claim and seek a compromise. Once again, underlying this exercise of discretion is the principle that the trustees must act in good faith and in the best interests of the beneficiaries.

TO WHAT LIABILITY IS THE TRUSTEE EXPOSED?

A breach of trust occurs when the duties of trustees to act exactly within the terms of their obligations are not fulfilled. It is immaterial that there was no intention on the part of a trustee to depart from his or her duty. Notwithstanding this apparent strict liability, the courts have taken the position that, where a trustee has committed a "technical breach," he or she will not be liable to compensate the beneficiaries for any loss that has occurred as a result of such a breach of trust, provided that the trustee has acted with honesty and reasonable prudence.

A breach of trust may arise in several ways, including direct interference with the trust property for improper purposes, failure to exercise proper diligence in discharging a duty (i.e., failure to collect contributions) or the improper exercise of discretion granted to the trustee pursuant to the trust agreement.

A trustee is liable for a loss that arises through his or her own willful default. *Willful default* implies either a consciousness of negligence or a breach of duty or recklessness in the performance of a duty. A mere error in judgment does not in itself constitute a breach of trust, and a trustee is presumed to have dealt honestly and properly with the trust estate until the contrary is shown.

It is, therefore, strongly recommended that in order to avoid a breach of their fiduciary responsibilities, trustees should, in co-operation with their advisors, establish and implement collection procedures that are reasonable, diligent and systematic.

VARIOUS PROBLEMS AND REMEDIES RELATING TO DELINQUENCIES IN EMPLOYEE BENEFIT PLANS

Causes of Delinquency

Some common causes for delinquencies include:
1. Employer avoidance or deliberate evasion in making payments—including the employer refusing to pay because of dispute with the union over the terms of the collective agreement
2. Administrative problems of employers such as:
   • Inadequate bookkeeping
   • Clerical errors.
3. Employer financial problems—inability to pay due to:
   • Financial instability, insolvency or the like
   • Under-capitalized business
   • Mismanagement
   • Misappropriation of funds
   • Priorities of employer.
4. Communication problems—lack of information given to the employer regarding details of contractual obligations to contribute or misunderstanding about these obligations.

The Role of the Collective Agreement

In general, the collective agreement should set out the employer's obligations in clear and unambiguous terms, including the following:
1. Amounts to be paid and the basis of calculation
2. When contributions are payable
3. Specific employee classifications on whose behalf contributions are to be made
4. To whom funds are to be remitted.

The collective agreements should include provisions regarding the following issues for dealing with delinquencies:
1. The employer should be required to maintain for a defined period a complete set of employment records, including:
   • Employee's name, address, date of birth and social insurance number
   • Number of hours worked by the employee in each day and week
   • Employee's wage rate and gross net earnings

- Amount and description of deductions from the employee's wages
- Particulars of any allowances or other payments or benefits to which the employee is entitled.

2. The employer should give an authorization to the plan administrator and trustees for inspection, audit or examination of its books, ledgers, vouchers, payrolls and other records relevant to employer benefit plan contributions.

3. Both collective agreements and trust agreements should empower trustees to accelerate the payment of contributions on a weekly or bi-monthly basis where an employer has been delinquent.

4. In order to minimize losses in delinquent situations, consideration should be given to clauses in collective agreements requiring employers to post bonds or other forms of security to ensure payment of all contributions.

5. Collective agreements should contain provisions for payment by delinquent employers of reasonable interest on late contributions and legal and collection costs, including arbitration fees. Where damages cannot be readily ascertained, there should be a "liquidated damages" provision that should make the delinquent employer responsible for a percentage of the delinquent amount in respect of the trustees' collection costs.

6. The full and proper name of the employer should be described in the collective agreement in the event that it later becomes necessary to institute legal proceedings against a delinquent employer.

Consideration should be given to whether the business is being carried on by a corporation, partnership or individuals. Where there is any doubt, corporate searches can be done at the companies branch of the applicable provincial government or through any of the various computerized corporate search companies operating across Canada.

There is often a problem of businesses carried on by or through more than one corporation, individual, firm, syndicate or association, or any combination thereof, under common control or direction. Resort may be had to applicable "related employer" provisions under provincial labour legislation to bind all of the related companies.

The execution of the collective agreement is an important consideration. This should be undertaken by a duly authorized officer. The corporate seal, if applicable, should be affixed to the company signature.

The participation agreement is another important step. At the same time a collective agreement is signed, the employer, where applicable, should execute a participation agreement whereby it agrees to be bound by all of the terms and conditions of the trust agreement.

Employer Understanding of Obligations

The employer must understand its obligations under the collective agreement concerning employee benefit plans.

The union representative in the course of his or her continuous contact with the employer must remind the employer of its obligations, including submitting complete and accurate contribution report forms and the calculation of contributions.

Trustees or administrators should advise employers of changes in trust agreements or of procedural changes in administration of the trust fund.

Procedures to Avoid Delinquencies

Employee's Function (Self-Help)

Employees should be made aware of their entitlement to contributions by the employer and the way they are calculated so that employees can verify the correctness of the contributions by the employer on payroll slips. Also, the employees can compare the calculations with the employer's contribution reports, which can be obtained by the union representatives to be used in a spot check.

Employee participation may result in uncovering employer's bookkeeping errors or failure or refusal by the employer to contribute to the trust funds for all hours, particularly in respect of overtime hours.

Administrator's Function

The benefit plan administrator should:
1. Define procedures to be followed for making contributions to the fund and communicate these procedures to employers
2. Establish strict procedures to control delinquencies
3. Provide employer contribution reports, insist upon their use and strict compliance within time requirements and inform employers of consequences of non-payment
4. Upon receipt of report forms, the administrator should verify hours, contributions and calculations and compare this information with earlier report forms.
5. The administrator should periodically issue a member confirmation of contributions statement, so that the beneficiary will be aware of the amount of contributions received on his or her behalf over a relatively recent period of time. Where the member is of the view that insufficient contributions have been made,

then a complaint may be lodged with the administrator.

6. The administrator, with the co-operation of the union, should carry out periodic spot checks of both employer and employee records to ensure that contributions are made for the correct number of hours.

7. In the event of delinquency, the administrator should immediately notify the delinquent employer in accordance with defined procedure. If delinquency persists, then the administrator should notify the trustees and the union and consider instituting collection proceedings.

Union's Function

The union's roles with respect to delinquencies includes:

1. Alerting the administrator to any anticipated delinquency problems

2. Maintaining continuous contact with employers, urging compliance with timely payment obligations

3. In order to ensure accuracy of employer's contribution reports, union representatives should carry out spot checks of employees' records and compare those records with the completed employer report forms. The administrator should then be advised of any discrepancy, and the union representative should follow up to ensure correction of the reports.

Trustee's Function

Since trustees have a responsibility concerning delinquent employers, they should communicate to the administrator all available and relevant information to assist in alleviating this problem.

In addition to ensuring that the administrator and/or the union pursue delinquent employers, the trustees should apply lawful pressure through, for example, demand letters and warnings concerning legal proceedings against delinquent employers.

Alternative Procedures for Handling Delinquencies

Union's Function

Unions may take advantage of several mechanisms to address employer delinquencies. These include:

1. Process a grievance against employer and refer to arbitration pursuant to collective agreement, or where applicable, pursuant to existing labour legislation.

2. Commence court proceedings, including:
   - Summary proceedings—filing arbitration awards in court and enforcing them

   - Small claims court, including the possibility of garnishment proceedings against an employer prior to obtaining final judgment
   - Filing construction lien claims, where applicable, to the extent allowed under the governing provincial legislation
   - Filing claims with respect to public works and projects under applicable federal and provincial legislation
   - Resort to proceedings under provincial employment standards legislation for recovery of unpaid wages, including employer contributions to benefit plans. Most provinces have legislation whereby a defaulting employer may be summoned to appear before a justice of the peace or provincial judge and, in addition to the penalty imposed, may be ordered to pay the wages and benefit contributions owing.
   - Consider legal proceedings against directors of insolvent corporations who may be responsible for unpaid wages and benefit contributions under applicable provincial legislation.
   - Where there is a labour and materials payment bond on a project, making a claim against the bond.

3. In the event the employer becomes bankrupt, an appropriate claim should be filed with the trustee of the bankrupt estate for any unpaid wages, employee benefits, contributions, etc.

Trustees' Function

Although a collection agency may be retained, it is preferable to pursue other alternatives discussed above.

Consideration should be given to entering into a cost-sharing agreement with the union(s) participating in the trust fund that could provide for sharing of collection costs. Such cost-sharing agreements must be permitted by the trust documents and must ensure that any remuneration to the union is reasonable and determined by an independent third party, as there is concern over conflicts of interest. Legal advice should be obtained when entering into a cost-sharing agreement because of the conflict-of-interest concerns.

Trustees should retain legal counsel to advise generally with respect to individual cases and whether or not legal proceedings should be commenced, as well as advising with respect to chances of recovering unpaid contributions. Sometimes a letter of demand by a lawyer to the employer accelerates payment, thereby minimizing delay and expenses.

Settling or Compromising Claim

In certain circumstances, it may be unwise or uneconomical to pursue particular delinquent situations to their ultimate conclusion. Accordingly, the trustees may settle or compromise a particular claim but, in doing so, they must always balance the interests of the beneficiaries of the fund with the overall financial stability of the trust fund. Further, in settling or compromising a claim, consideration should be given to the question of costs and fees incurred, interest charges, audit costs, etc.

Consequences of Delinquencies

It must be remembered that as a result of serious delinquencies the following problems can result, namely:

1. Loss of employees' entitlement to benefits under a trust fund
2. Distortion of the financial position of the trust fund
3. Loss of revenue
4. Deterioration of relationships between:
   • Employer and employee
   • A member and the union
   • The delinquent employer and contributing employers
   • Employees obtaining benefits and employees unable to obtain benefits by reason of employer delinquency.

Accordingly, an appropriate delinquency control program should be a priority for all boards of trustees.

ENDNOTES

1. *Employee Benefit Issues—The Multiemployer Perspective* (Brookfield, WI: International Foundation of Employee Benefit Plans, Inc., 1989), p. 473.

2. *Trustees' Handbook* (Brookfield, WI: National Foundation of Health, Welfare and Pension Plans, Inc., 1970), pp. 31 and 132.

3. *Halsburys Laws of England,* 4th ed., vol. 48, para. 819.

4. *Report of the Royal Commission on the Status of Pensions in Ontario,* 1980, vol. 1, p. 229.

CHAPTER 2

Legal Enforcement Mechanisms for Delinquencies

by Ron Davis and Stephen Tatrallyay

ENFORCEMENT MEASURES

There are a number of enforcement measures available to trustees when there are delinquencies in employee benefit plan contributions. Many of these measures use the same methods and techniques as those under collective agreements, i.e., through grievance and arbitration proceedings. However, many cases can be resolved without resort to arbitration or resort to the courts where arbitration is not available. In the most difficult cases, arbitration or court proceedings are required. Even where arbitration proceedings take place, it is often necessary to resort to court proceedings in order to actually collect. In many instances there will be disputes between the trustees or the union to whom monies are owed and other creditors, including secured creditors such as banks, trust companies and mortgage holders. Enforcing delinquencies is not an easy matter but one in which trustees and trade unions must engage to protect the integrity of their trust funds.

Where there is an actual bankruptcy or insolvency, the trustees must make reasonable efforts to recover what they can. In many cases, it will become evident to the trustees that collection procedures are not likely to yield a result, and in such circumstances there is no point in wasting the trust fund resources on collection costs, legal fees, audit costs or other expenses. However, without making the effort the trustees will not be in a position to know whether there is a reasonable chance to recover.

OBTAINING THE EVIDENCE

Before a successful claim for a delinquency can be made, it is critical that the trustees or union involved take the necessary steps to quantify their claims and prove their case. Because the payment of contributions to a benefit fund is usually a function of hours worked or a percentage of payroll, trustees must rely on the employers' self-reporting to deal with any claims. Where there is a delinquency, it is often difficult to quantify the claim. Where there is a belief that an employer is deliberately underreporting the hours worked or the percentage of payroll, a very complicated information gathering exercise might be necessary.

Often it is the evidence of employees themselves that is required to prove the case. Most often, however, it is necessary to subpoena the employer's own books and records to prove the case, if one cannot otherwise get access to them. The further back in time one must go, the more difficult it is to prove claims. This is particularly true in instances where there is a mobile work force, such as in the construction industry, where it may be necessary to make claims under lien legislation on a jobsite-by-jobsite basis.

However, there are some basic information gathering tools that should be considered by any board of trustees, trade union or delinquency control officer. The type of information that is usually required to be kept includes:

- Copies of all remittance forms if they have been completed. It is not uncommon that the employer submits a remittance form with a cheque that ultimately is returned NSF and the employer has to be pursued for the delinquency. The remittance form constitutes an admission by the employer that the employees listed have worked for the hours listed and that the amount of money is, in fact, owing.

- Employer banks and bank account numbers on which previous remittance cheques have been remitted, or that are used by the employer for purposes of payroll or payment of other monies out of its general accounts. At some stage it may be necessary to send a sheriff or other officer to the employer's bank to enforce a judgment, and knowledge of bank accounts and account numbers is helpful.
- A corporate search for the proper legal name of the company should always be obtained.
- Pay stubs, pay records, income tax forms and other documents that are kept by employees are often helpful and provide firsthand evidence in cases where it is difficult to have the employer produce its payroll records, whether by means of subpoena or otherwise. In addition, many unions suggest that employees mark down in a notebook or on a calendar the number of hours they have worked each day and, for construction industry employees, the name of the jobsite. Accordingly, if employees are not paid, they can then produce their own record, made contemporaneously with the event, indicating how much money they are owed. The employee's own log can also keep track of overtime hours and other premiums.
- Finally, it is useful to create a "jobsite log" for union representatives who are concerned about an employer that is not remitting properly or on a timely basis. This is done by having a union representative or, in the construction industry, a working foreman or key employee keep a record of who is on the job each day and how many hours each employee has worked. Jobsite documents such as a jobsite log created at the time of the job can be invaluable in assisting counsel to determine who was working on a particular project. A sample jobsite log is contained as Appendix VIII-2-A at the conclusion of this chapter. These can be prepared on a weekly basis or at the conclusion of any particular construction job.

OBTAINING THE INITIAL AWARD OR JUDGMENT

In most cases, the first step in asserting a claim for any delinquency is to exercise arbitration rights under a collective agreement to prove the amount of the claim. This means resorting to the grievance and arbitration provisions of the applicable collective agreement[1] and proving, at an arbitration, the amount of the claim, together with any interest, costs and liquidated damages. This is then incorporated into an arbitration award.

It is critical that delinquency arbitrations proceed to a quick decision. Accordingly, if there is an expedited arbitration method available under the collective agreement or under applicable provincial labour legislation, it should be used. In Ontario, for example, Section 49 of the Ontario *Labour Relations Act* provides for a speedy arbitration provision in most instances, while Section 133 provides for an arbitration within two weeks of referral of the grievance to the Ontario Labour Relations Board in the construction industry.[2] These speedy arbitration mechanisms are only a first step in enforcing a judgment, although the mere bringing of the proceedings is in many cases sufficient to induce the employer to negotiate a settlement. Often, it is wise to have the settlement incorporated in the form of an arbitration award or an order of the applicable Labour Relations Board, as these can be filed in court in the event the employer is not complying with the settlement, particularly where time to pay is extended.

There are not many legal issues that arise in these arbitrations, but one must be wary of certain procedural and technical matters. Like any other arbitration, there is still an obligation to prove one's case and, accordingly, if the union has not gathered the necessary evidence through employee pay stubs, jobsite logs, remittances and NSF cheques, it may be necessary to subpoena the employer's books and records. This can be a time-consuming process. Some delinquency situations involve the right of the union or trustee to conduct an audit, and it is necessary to produce all of the evidence properly before the Arbitration Board in order to make one's case.

Another important matter to be proven is the existence of a valid collective agreement with the employer, and thus unions and trustees must be able to prove the source of their bargaining rights, particularly if these are in question. It is not sufficient to merely assert that one has bargaining rights without some documentary proof.

Numerous court decisions have made it clear that, where the union can prove that it has unemployed members out of work, in the construction industry, wages and damages will be awarded in respect of non-union employees employed by a delinquent employer.[3] In Ontario, the Labour Relations Board has further awarded benefits in respect of non-union employees, even where there are no union employees unemployed at the time of the grievance. In cases where an employer is consistently delinquent, a possible remedy is a form of "cease and desist" order such as that upheld by Ontario's Divisional Court in *Re Samuel Cooper and International Ladies Garment Workers' Union.*[4]

One area that requires some care is a claim for interest and retail sales tax (RST) where eligible on unpaid contributions. Trustees and unions should ask for RST and interest on outstanding amounts in the original grievance form or demand. There is an argument that under the federal *Interest Act* it is only possible to collect interest on outstanding delinquencies at realistic interest rates if the collective agreement or other applicable document expresses the interest liability, calculated on an *annual* basis (e.g., 12% annually, as opposed to 1% per month). If this is not so, then the *Interest Act* only permits interest at the rate of 5% per annum. However, this can also often be countered by the argument that arbitrators and labour boards have the jurisdiction to award interest on damages like any other court or tribunal. However, where the collective agreement has an excessive interest rate, labour boards have previously struck them down as was done by the Ontario Board in *Commercial Contracting Corporation,*[5] where a rate of 1% interest *per day,* compounded daily, was struck down and held to be unconscionable by the Board. Instead the Board awarded interest in accordance with its usual practice on outstanding awards, namely, using the Bank of Canada prime rate.

Where an arbitration award for delinquent amounts is obtained, most provincial labour legislation permits such award to be registered with the courts of the province and enforced as if it were a judgment of that court. A court judgment also attracts interest in accordance with the rate of interest of the applicable court, which is often tied to the Bank of Canada prime lending rate.

METHODS OF ENFORCEMENT OF ARBITRATION

Where an arbitration award is registered in the applicable court, the same methods that are available for debt collection generally in the province are available to the union or trustees having obtained the award. The precise rights that creditors have are dependent on the legislation of the particular province, and a review of all creditors' rights legislation in Canada is well beyond the scope of this book. However, below we review some of the basic creditors' remedies available in most provinces. It must be remembered, however, that these remedies often take second place to the claims of secured creditors such as mortgage holders, lien holders, or holders of debentures or other securities against the property of the employer (often a bank or other lender) so that the ability to exercise these remedies is often restricted.

Bank Seizures

Often a sheriff or local enforcement officer can seize bank accounts once a judgment is registered and the appropriate "writ" is obtained by the trustees or union. Generally it is necessary to tell the sheriff at which branch of which bank the employer maintains accounts, and the sheriff will then seize all accounts at that branch. If the union or trustees are aware that the employer is putting money into the bank regularly on a certain day of the week or day of the month, the sheriff can even be told to attend on that day and serve the seizure. The sheriff can only seize what is in the bank account the day that the seizure is made, so if this information is available it is important. The sheriff can usually be instructed not to seize a particular account, such as the payroll account.

Garnishment

If it is possible to satisfy the court where the judgment is registered that someone owes the employer money, the court in many provinces can issue a "Notice of Garnishment," which is then served on the person liable to pay, otherwise referred to as the "garnishee." Service of the notice requires the garnishee to pay the sheriff any monies that may be due and owing to the employer up to the amount of the outstanding judgment. Of course, it is necessary to obtain knowledge of who may owe the employer money.

Seizure of Equipment

Often sheriffs will, subject to obtaining a deposit, seize equipment of the employer. The equipment can then be auctioned off by the sheriff. However, most equipment is usually subject to some form of security interest, particularly automobiles and machinery, and accordingly it is necessary to make a search under the relevant provincial personal property security legislation to see that there are no prior claims. Most provinces have an exemption for " tools of the trade" such that equipment used by a debtor in his business may be exempt from seizure up to a certain dollar value.

Seizure of Land

If a Writ of Seizure and Sale or comparable document is obtained, this writ can be filed in the relevant registry offices where the employer owns any real estate and can be an impediment to the sale of any real property once it is registered. Sometimes it is also possible to have the sheriff sell the property if the debt has been outstanding for more than a minimum period under the applicable provincial registry legislation (often six months or more). As a practical matter, many employers do not hold land in the name of the same company as the employer and, accordingly, this type of remedy does not always prove to be useful.

Judgment Debtor Examination

Once a judgment is obtained, provincial legislation in most jurisdictions permits the creditor the right to conduct an examination of the debtor (i.e., the employer) or the personal representative of the employer in order to determine what assets the employer has or is likely to obtain. Judgment debtor examinations often turn up assets that the union or trustees do not know about. Failure to attend such an examination can result in the relevant employer or officer of the company being held in contempt of court.

Sharing the Wealth

It must be remembered that in most jurisdictions money recovered through creditors' relief legislation must be held by the sheriff for a period of time (usually 30 days) and shared among all creditors who have filed judgments with the sheriff during that period. Amounts are usually paid out on a pro-rata basis valued up to the size of the creditors' debts. Creditors are given a period to object to the proposed distribution and, if there are no objections, the sheriff then sends out the cheques. Claims by the federal and provincial governments have priority over all other claims, such that it is not at all uncommon to see claims for income tax, workers' compensation levies and the like being paid, notwithstanding that a garnishment or seizure was realized by some other creditor who is not receiving any funds at all.

CONSTRUCTION LIEN LEGISLATION

For workers in the construction industry, the statutes dealing with builders' liens provide a special priority in most provinces for wages and benefits. Some provinces only extend a priority to wages and, accordingly, lien legislation is not helpful in collecting benefit delinquencies, unless the benefits are in the nature of deductions from the pay cheque rather than employer contributions. Other provinces, such as Ontario, have gone as far as recognizing the existence of a "workers' trust fund" in the legislation and grant the trustees an independent status to lien for benefits and a special priority. Construction lien legislation generally involves the ability to lien the land and buildings on a construction project and thus obtain part of the money (i.e., the holdback) that is otherwise owing to the employer that has failed to pay the contributions. In most provinces, the standard holdback is 10% of the value of the contract. In addition there are other claims that may be made under the lien legislation, and additional monies that are owing to the contractor who is delinquent may be the subject of a lien over and above the 10% holdback.

Most provinces accord a special priority for "wages." The construction lien legislation in all provinces and territories, except Quebec, accord a special priority for wages ahead of other subcontractors and suppliers who could also be liening a project. However, the difficulty lies in the definition of *wages*. Ontario and Newfoundland have historically recognized that wages include "monetary supplementary benefits," and Ontario further defines a *workers' trust fund* to mean "any trust fund maintained in whole or in part on behalf of any worker on an improvement and into which any monetary supplementary benefit is payable. . . ."[6] Other provinces such as Saskatchewan accord a wage priority to include welfare benefits and holiday pay under both the Saskatchewan *Mechanics Lien Act*[7] and the Saskatchewan *Labour Standards Act.*[8] The Saskatchewan *Builder's Lien Act*[9] also has an expanded definition of *wages* that includes "all supplementary benefits whether provided for by statute, contract, or collective bargaining agreement."

The Court of Appeal in Nova Scotia has held that, notwithstanding that there is not a specific inclusion of workers' trust funds in wages in the Nova Scotia lien legislation, it should nevertheless be interpreted to include monetary supplementary benefits, and that monetary supplementary benefits should be accorded the same priority as wages.[10] However, courts in Alberta, in *Noren v. Tarsands Machine and Welding Company,*[11] determined that union dues deductions constitute *wages* under the Alberta *Builder's Lien Act*[12] but contributions by employers to health, welfare, insurance, pension and training funds are not wages when the employer's liability is to the union fund and not to the individual employee. A similar finding was made under the British Columbia *Mechanics Lien Act,*[13] where the B.C. Court of Appeal in *Cronkhite Supply Limited v. Workers' Compensation Board*[14] determined that payments made under a collective agreement to health, pension and other funds are not under the B.C. legislation. In *Cahoon v. West Oaks Holdings Ltd.,*[15] the British Columbia Court of Appeal reaffirmed its decision in *Cronkhite,* but adopted the Alberta court's approach to union dues, confirming that they were contained within the definition of *wages.* Recent revisions to the British Columbia legislation have added a much broader definition of *wages* that includes, among other things,

  (i) money required under a contract of employment to be paid, for an employee's benefit, to a fund, insurer or other person . . . , and
  (ii) money required to be paid under a collective agreement.[16]

In most jurisdictions, the priority may be limited to six weeks' wages or, in Ontario, to the extent of the amount of 40 days' wages with any other outstanding wages sharing equally with other creditors.

What is most critical, however, is the requirement to register a lien on the legal title to the property within a fixed time period of the last day worked by the workers. For example, in Ontario the time limit is 45 days. It is, therefore, critical that trustees act quickly if there is a delinquency, because the 45-day period may be virtually over by the time the contributions are due. It is necessary to gather information on the hours worked on a particular project as one can only lien a project for work done on *that* project and not for delinquencies that are attributable to other projects.

Some provincial lien statutes also have provision for claims under "trust fund" provisions. If there are any funds still owing to the defaulting contractor over and above the amounts for which liens have been registered, if there are monies available, a claim can be made under the trust fund provisions. However, as a general principle, lien claimants are entitled to a priority over simple trust claims,[17] and only when all lien claims are satisfied will any money be distributable to mere trust claimants. As a result, it is possible that trust claimants would not receive any payment at all. However, of late, courts in Ontario at least have begun to enforce the trust sections against the officers and directors, or others who have control of the delinquent payor pursuant to the provisions of Section 13 of the *Construction Lien Act*. In *Dietrich Steel Ltd. v. Shar-Dee Towers (1987) Ltd.*[18] and *Rudco Insulation v. Toronto Sanitary Inc.*,[19] the Ontario Court of Appeal has clearly indicated that using project funds for any purpose other than payment of suppliers of services and materials to the project will constitute a breach of trust for which anyone who knowingly participated may be held personally liable. In *Don Park Inc. v. S.E. Mechanical Engineering Ltd.*[20] the court went even further and upheld an award of personal liability against, not only the principals of the corporation that breached the trust, but also against their son, who was a principal of the general contractor that hired the defaulting corporation, on the grounds that he had sufficient involvement in and control of the defaulting corporation to also be held liable under Section 13. Therefore, this area may prove to be fertile ground for recovery of benefit claims in the future.

The importance of accurate factual communication among employees, unions, trustees and legal counsel cannot be overemphasized. Registration of a claim for lien against the wrong property or in an excessive amount that the claimant knew or ought to have known he or she was not entitled to can give rise to claims for damages and vitiate an otherwise valid lien claim.

In most provinces, a lien may be registered against the title to any land upon which members have worked, except land owned by the federal, provincial and municipal governments. Land owned by the federal government cannot be liened at all, although frequently federal government contracts require the general contractor to maintain a holdback in any case, and a claim made against such contractor will sometimes be successful. In Ontario, while a lien cannot be registered against lands owned by the provincial government, a separate proceeding is created in the legislation allowing for service of notice of such liens on the appropri-

ate government authority following which the lien binds the payments as if a lien had actually been registered. The provincial government is required to maintain holdback like all other owners of land in the province, and lien claimants are entitled to a charge against those holdbacks. Other similar procedures are created for lands that are railways, highways or municipal roadways.

As a practical matter, trustees or trade unions preparing information for legal counsel to register a claim for lien will have to gather some very basic data. Specifically, what is required in most instances is the following:

- Name of owner
- Name and address of general contractor
- Name and address of the employer
- Names, addresses and phone numbers of employees involved
- Hours worked by each employee on the jobsite in question and the last day worked by each employee
- Legal description of the jobsite or municipal address if no legal description is possible
- The amount owing for wages and benefits
- Copies of pay stubs, NSF cheques and employer report forms.

In many instances all of the above information is not immediately available, and some research or "leg work" will be required to uncover it. Often the names of owners and general contractors are not available without checking at the jobsite itself or obtaining the copy of the relevant building permit from the municipality. The building permit will also usually give a legal description. Data with respect to hours worked by employees and their last day worked can often only be obtained through employee interviews or expedited arbitration. Often the arbitration hearing will take place after the time limits for the lien have expired, so that the union or trustees must generate their own data through their own sources as soon as possible. Some lien statutes, such as that of Ontario, have provisions requiring disclosure of information by contractors and employers, and these should be resorted to wherever possible.

LABOUR AND MATERIAL PAYMENT BOND

With increasing frequency, owners and general contractors in the construction industry are requiring subcontractors to post what is known as a *labour and material payment bond*. They are almost always required now on jobs owned by the federal government and sometimes in private sector jobs, particularly where the payor has doubts about the subcontractor's ability to meet the payroll or pay suppliers. A *labour and material payment bond* is a contract of suretyship whereby the surety company undertakes to pay any labourer or supplier who was unpaid by the obligee, being the person liable to pay. On federal government projects, one bond is taken out by the general contractor and usually covers all labour performed on the site, but limits the contractor's liability to the amount the contractor would have been liable for if the relevant builders' lien legislation had applied to the project. On private sector projects, or where the bonds are taken out by subcontractors, they ordinarily apply only to labour performed directly for the subcontractor or trade providing the bond.

Under the terms of the Ontario *Construction Lien Act,* owners are required to advise trustees who are lien claimants of the existence of any labour and material payment bond. In such cases the bonding company is notified of the claim, and recourse may be had against the bonding company to require payment of the claim if the funds are not otherwise forthcoming.

It should be noted that bonds frequently have notice requirements setting out the form of notice required (usually registered mail), and the time limits both for giving notice and for starting an action to enforce payment. These time limits are often quite short, and it is, therefore, important to find out about the bond as soon as possible. Often a copy of the bond is posted on the jobsite itself and, if the union or trustees become aware of it, it is important to let legal counsel know that the bond exists and, if possible, get a copy of it. The time limits in the commonest form of bond require notice to be given within 120 days after the employees should have been paid, and an action to be commenced within a year after the contractor has completed all work. These are not, however, found in every bond, and that is why it is important to obtain a copy of the bond. The Supreme Court of Canada has ruled, in *Elance Steel Fabricating Co. v. Falk Brothers Industries Ltd.,*[21] that the courts have power to relieve against the failure to give notice in a timely fashion, in appropriate circumstances and where no prejudice has been caused to anyone as a result of the failure to give notice within the time limits set out in the bond.

RECOVERY UNDER PENSION LEGISLATION

A new possible source of recovery for pension contribution delinquencies independent of the rights under any collective agreement or similar contract may exist under provincial pension legislation. These new sources can be divided into:
- Rights of action for administrators (including statutory liens and charges on employer assets)
- Enforcement by government officials
- Enforcement through quasi-criminal proceedings.

Rights of Action for Administrators

The Ontario *Pension Benefits Act* (PBA) provides an independent right of action under Section 59 to the "administrator" (i.e., the trustees or other persons responsible for the plan) to commence proceedings in a court of competent jurisdiction to obtain payment of contributions due under a pension plan, the PBA or the Regulations.[22]

Enforcement by Government Officials

In Ontario, the Superintendent of Financial Institutions is empowered to make orders requiring employers to comply with plans pursuant to Section 87 of the PBA, subject to a right of appeal under Section 91. Other provinces' pension legislation contains similar provisions. In other jurisdictions, the Superintendent may obtain an order from a court on a few days' notice requiring employers to make delinquent contributions. Further, in Ontario the administrator must give notice to the Superintendent under Section 56 of contributions that are not paid when due, within 60 days after the date on which the administrator or its agent first became aware of the failure to pay the contribution. The obligation on administrators to give notice of delinquencies is also found in pension legislation in many other provinces.

Enforcement Through Quasi-Criminal Proceedings

Virtually all jurisdictions provide for criminal prosecutions of employers that fail to comply with provincial pension legislation, including making timely contributions. Almost all provinces also grant the criminal courts the power to order employers to make payment of contributions owing, if they find required contributions have not been made.

ACTIONS AGAINST THE DIRECTORS OF A CORPORATE EMPLOYER

Where the employer is a corporation that either becomes insolvent or otherwise does not meet its payroll or satisfy its obligations to remit pension and other contributions, it is open to the employees to sue the directors of the corporation personally under the applicable company law legislation.

Business Corporations Statutes

Section 131 of the Ontario *Business Corporations Act,*[23] which relates to those corporations incorporated under the laws of Ontario, provides that the directors of a corporate employer are personally liable to the employees for unpaid debts due to the employees for services rendered to the corporation, up to a monetary limit equivalent to six months' wages and 12 months' vacation pay.

A director is only liable for debts that accrued while he or she was a director and is also only liable if he or she is sued within six months of when the monies became due and owing or when he or she ceased to be a director, whichever is earlier. Directors subject to those limitations are "jointly and severally" liable, which means essentially that each director is liable for the full amount. If one director pays more than his or her share, that director is then entitled to turn around and claim over against the other directors for indemnity.

It is not uncommon for a corporation to carry on business in a province without having been incorporated there. For example, there is nothing to prevent a corporation incorporated under the laws of Canada from carrying on business in Ontario. A corporation incorporated in one province of Canada can also carry on business in another province with certain limitations. Most of the jurisdictions in Canada have legislative provisions similar to Ontario's, as does the federal government for federally incorporated companies. However, the technical provisions vary from jurisdiction to jurisdiction. For example, under the Canada *Business Corporations Act*,[24] unpaid employees have up to two years to sue directors. It is, therefore, important to know prior to starting an action of this sort what the incorporating jurisdiction is and what provisions its laws contain. This can be done by simply conducting a corporate search. The Quebec corporations legislation also permits actions against directors. However, the trend in some other jurisdictions has been to create liability for directors under the employment standards legislation as discussed later in this chapter.

Amounts Recoverable

The various business corporations statutes all contain provisions similar to Ontario's, which provides that the directors are liable for "all debts owing to employees of the corporation for services rendered to the corporation, not exceeding six months' wages and twelve months' vacation pay." Directors have occasionally seized upon these words to argue that they are only liable for wages (i.e., hourly pay) and vacation pay, and not for such matters as health and welfare contributions, pension contributions, union dues and the like. This argument has, however, been rejected by courts in Ontario and Quebec. The courts have interpreted the provision as meaning that what the directors are liable for is all *debts* to employees, as long as those debts were incurred for services rendered to the corporation. The debts are subject to a maximum limitation in that the directors cannot be held liable for any more than a monetary amount equal to six months' wages or 12 months' vacation pay. Thus directors may now be sued for such matters as the health and welfare contributions and pension contributions. The Supreme Court of Canada has said that one cannot collect damages for wrongful dismissal from a director[25] but upheld a Quebec Court of Appeal decision that held that severance pay requirements in a collective agreement may be recovered from directors if the employer does not pay.[26]

Directors' and Officers' Liability Under Employment Standards Legislation

Several provinces, including Alberta, Manitoba, Saskatchewan and Ontario, as well as the Northwest Territories, have included directors' and officers' liability for unpaid wages in their employment standards legislation. The definition of *wages* will depend on the statute of the particular province. As the Alberta legislation is relatively new, there does not appear yet to be any case law regarding the inclusion of contributions to benefit funds within the definition of *wages*. However, in other contexts, the Alberta courts have held that wages do not include contributions by employers to health and welfare funds.[27]

Manitoba has directors' liability under its *Employment Standards Act*[28] and a broad definition of *wages* under its *Construction Industry Wages Act*[29] for employees in that industry. Joint and several directors' and officers' liability applies up to a limit of six months' wages and all unpaid vacation pay. The Saskatchewan legislation also contains a directors' and officers' liability provision for six months' unpaid wages, with a broad definition of *wages* that includes vacation pay and benefits, as well as termination pay. Ontario's definition excludes termination pay and severance pay, as well as pay equity makeup contributions, but expressly includes vacation pay, and may include other monetary supplementary benefits, although it does not expressly say so one way or the other.[30] Unionized employees in Ontario must pursue their claims against directors and officers under the *Employment Standards Act* through the grievance and arbitration provisions, not through a claim to the Director of Employment Standards.

In *Rizzo v. Rizzo*[31] the Supreme Court of Canada held that a termination of employment resulting from a bankruptcy of the employer was a termination that triggered the liability for termination and severance pay under the Ontario *Employment Standards Act*. The *Employment Standards Act* was also amended to expressly provide that termination of employment included termination by operation of law, including bankruptcy, insolvency and receivership.[32]

WAGE EARNER PROTECTION PLAN

The trend in most jurisdictions in recent years has been to discontinue or repeal established wage earner protection funds that allowed claims for wages and benefits to be recovered from a government-administered fund that is then subrogated to the rights of the employees. There have been extensive proposals and discussions over the years to establish such a fund under the umbrella of federal bankruptcy reform, but no fund has ever been implemented.

In Ontario an Employee Wage Protection Program was introduced in October 1991, retroactive to October 1990, by the *Employment Standards Amendment Act*. However, the program was discontinued in 1997.[33] In Quebec, pursuant to the Construction Industry Decree under *An Act Respecting Labour Relations, Vocational Training and Manpower Management in the Construction Industry*,[34] compensation is provided to employees for unpaid wages, vacation pay and benefits normally paid by the employer. This fund covers not only loss of wages and other benefits where the loss is due to bankruptcy, but any case where unpaid amounts are owing to the employee.

ENDNOTES

1. In Ontario, the *Employment Standards Act* requires employees covered by a collective agreement to pursue their *Employment Standards Act* claims by grievance arbitration, including claims against directors.

2. Ontario *Labour Relations Act*, S.O. 1995, c.1, Sections 49 and 133.

3. *Re Blouin Drywall Contractors* (1975), 8 O.R. (2d) 103 (C.A.).

4. *Re Samuel Cooper and International Ladies Garment Workers' Union*, [1973] 2 O.R. 841 (Div.Ct.).

5. *Commercial Contracting Corporation*, [1990] O.L.R.B. Reports 399 April.

6. Ontario *Construction Lien Act*, R.S.O. 1990, c.30 s.1(1).

7. Saskatchewan *Mechanics Lien Act*, R.S.S. 1978, c. M-7.

8. Saskatchewan *Labour Standards Act*, R.S.S. 1978, c. L-1; *Re Kenroc Building Materials* (1982), 128 D.L.R. (3d) 189 (S.C.A.).

9. Saskatchewan *Builders Lien Act*, S.S. 1984-85-86, c. B-7.1.

10. *Dermot v. Cornwallis Realties Ltd.* (1989), 57 D.L.R. (4th) 147 (C.A.).

11. *Noren v. Tarsands Machine and Welding Company* (1982), 138 D.L.R. (3d) 335 (Alta. Q.B.).

12. Alberta *Builders' Lien Act*, R.S.A. 1980, c. B-12.

13. British Columbia *Mechanics Lien Act*, R.S.B.C. 1960, c.199, s.3.

14. *Cronkhite Supply Limited v. Workers' Compensation Board* (1979), 8 B.C.L.R. 54 (C.A.).

15. *Cahoon v. West Oaks Holdings Ltd.* (1993), 107 D.L.R. (4th) 289 (B.C.C.A.).

16. British Columbia *Builders Lien Act*, S.B.C. 1997, c.45, s.1(1) "wages" (e) and (f).

17. See, for example, Ontario *Construction Lien Act, supra* note 6, s.85.

18. *Dietrich Steel Ltd. v. Shar-Dee Towers (1987) Ltd. et al.* (1999), 42 O.R. (3d) 749 (C.A.).

19. *Rudco Insulation v. TSI Inc. et al.* (1998), 167 D.L.R. (4th) 121, 41 C.L.R. (2d) 1 (O.C.A.).

20. *Don Park Inc. v. S.E. Mechanical Engineering Ltd.* (1998), 43 C.L.R. (2d) 7 (O.C.A.) upholding (1997), 43 C.L.R. (2d) 1 (G.D.).

21. *Elance Steel Fabricating Co. v. Falk Brothers Industries Ltd.* (1989), 35 C.L.R. 225 (S.C.C.).

22. Ontario *Pension Benefits Act*, R.S.O. 1990, c.P.8, s. 59.

23. Ontario *Business Corporation Act*, R.S.O. 1990, c. B.16, s. 131.

24. Canada *Business Corporation Act*, R.S.C. 1985, c. C-44, s.119.

25. *Barrette v. Crabtree* (1993), 101 D.L.R. (4th) 66 (S.C.C.).

26. *Schwartz v. Scott*, [1993] 1 S.C.R. 1027.

27. See, for example, *Noren v. Tarsands Machine and Welding Company, supra* note 11.

28. Manitoba *Employment Standards Act*, R.S.M. 1987, c. E-110, as amended.

29. Manitoba *Construction Industry Wages Act*, R.S.M. 1987, c. C-190, as amended, s.1.

30. Ontario *Employment Standards Act*, R.S.O. 1990, c. E.14, as amended..

31. *Rizzo v. Rizzo*, [1998] 1 S.C.R. 27.

32. Section 57(2.1) of the Ontario *Employment Standards Act*, enacted by S.O. 1995, c. 1, s.74(1).

33. Ontario *Employment Standards Amendment Act*, S.O. 1991, c.16.

34. *An Act Respecting Labour Relations, Vocational Training and Manpower Management in the Construction Industry*, R.S.Q. c. R-20.

Appendix VIII—2-A

JOBSITE LOG
For Week Ending

NAME OF JOBSITE:

MUNICIPAL ADDRESS:

LEGAL DESCRIPTION
(FROM BUILDING PERMIT):

EMPLOYER:

GENERAL CONTRACTOR:

NAME OF PERSON KEEPING THIS LOG:

EMPLOYEES ON SITE:

Rate
NAME: (See Note) Mon. Tues. Wed. Thurs. Fri. Sat. Sun.   TOTAL

NOTE: INDICATE IF EMPLOYEES ARE ENTITLED TO PREMIUM
(e.g., Foreman, Night Work, High Work, etc.) or APPRENTICES.

_____

Signature

CHAPTER 3

Wage and Benefit Claims
in Employer Insolvencies

by Ron Davis and Stephen Tatrallyay

INTRODUCTION

The purpose of this chapter is to set out the effects of employer insolvencies on wage and benefit claims. Unfortunately, these claims are often adversely affected by insolvencies because of the different legal regimes that govern in such circumstances.

INSOLVENCY AND BANKRUPTCY

Many employers owe more money than they could possibly ever pay if everyone demanded payment at the same time. These employers rely on the "confidence" of their various creditors that payment will be made within the time granted the employer in their various credit arrangements. Anyone who does not demand cash on delivery, including employees, is a creditor of the employer. For example, employees give the employer credit for their weekly wages, monthly benefit contributions and yearly vacation pay.

Secured and Unsecured Creditors

Some larger creditors require that they be given "security" before they will grant an employer credit. This security, in effect, gives the creditor an interest in the property or other valuable rights of the employer that takes precedent over the employer's ownership of the property to the extent of the debt owed to the creditor. These creditors are called *secured creditors*. Often the agreement granting the creditor security provides the creditor a right to take over the employer's business, on default in payment, by appointing a "receiver" to run and/or sell the business until the debt can be paid.

Other creditors, including employees, are *unsecured*; that is, they only have the right to take legal proceedings to collect the debt owed to them (as set out in the previous chapter), and their claims can be satisfied only to the extent that the employer has assets available to pay them.

Insolvency

If an employer's business is not going well, there comes a point at which the creditors lose "confidence" in the employer's ability to pay the debts owed to them, usually because the employer is unable to meet liabilities as they become due. At this point creditors and the employer have a number of legal options that will have different consequences for employees' wage and benefit claims. The options are:

- A secured creditor can appoint a receiver/manager under the security agreement to operate the business with a view to selling it or liquidating it (receivership).
- The employer can ask a trustee licensed under the *Bankruptcy and Insolvency Act* (BIA)[1] to act as trustee and, if the trustee agrees, the employer can file for protection under the BIA while it tries to obtain the creditors' agreement to a debt restructuring proposal (BIA protection).
- Employers with larger debts (at least $5 million) can seek protection under the *Companies Creditors' Arrangement Act* (CCAA)[2] while they attempt to work out a restructuring of their debt with all their creditors and the employer continues to operate under the supervision of a court-appointed "monitor" (CCAA Restructuring).

- If the employer has not filed for protection, then creditors or the employer may file for "bankruptcy" in which the employers' assets are divided pursuant to the scheme of the BIA by a trustee in bankruptcy and, after the assets are distributed, the employer is absolved of further liability for the debts (bankruptcy).

RECEIVERSHIP

Statutory Trusts

A number of provincial statutes create "deemed trusts" for benefits such as vacation pay and contributions to pension plans. Clearly, a secured creditor's security interest in the property of the employer would not extend to property the employer was holding "in trust" for the employees. However, in the case of *Abraham v. Coopers & Lybrand Ltd.*, the Ontario Court of Appeal ruled that the deemed trust provisions in employment standards and pension legislation were subject to the claims of secured creditors under the *Bank Act*. The Court of Appeal ruled that because the *Bank Act* security was a "fixed charge" on the employer's assets, present and future, this meant the employer never had title to the assets, only a right of redemption to which a deemed trust did not apply.[3]

However, both provincial and federal legislation grant priority ranking to certain employee claims over the interests of secured creditors. For example, if a bank realizes on security under Section 427 of the federal *Bank Act,* employee claims for unpaid wages for the three-month period preceding bankruptcy have priority over the Section 427 security.[4]

In Ontario, vacation pay and certain unpaid pension contributions have priority over secured interests in inventory and accounts receivable registered under the *Personal Property Security Act*.[5] However, this provision has yet to be considered by a court in respect of its constitutional validity.

Receivers are open to lawsuits if they fail to make payment of the monies of the employer in accordance with the common law and applicable legislation. Receivers are also subject to such statutes as provincial construction lien legislation. Note: The trust provisions under these statutes do not take priority over the *Bankruptcy and Insolvency Act*.[6] As a practical matter, secured creditors can usually avoid the deemed trusts by petitioning the employer into bankruptcy.

Receivers as Successor/Related Employers

It is often to the secured creditor's benefit to have the debtor's business continue to operate. Often, the sale of a "going concern" is worth much more than the price available for the assets by themselves. This provides employees with an opportunity to negotiate payment of any outstanding wage and benefit claims along with the wages to be paid while the receiver manages the business, pending sale or liquidation.

In cases where the employees are unionized, the appointment of a receiver provides an opportunity to impose liability for payment of both past and present wages and benefits on a receiver. This can occur because the "successor employer" provisions in labour relations statutes bind the purchasers of a unionized business to any existing collective agreement as if they had been a party to the agreement. Thus, the successor employer may become liable for breaches of the collective agreement after the sale has occurred, including those that occurred prior to the sale.

Under labour relations legislation, both labour boards and courts have distinguished between privately or instrument-appointed receiver from one appointed by the courts.

In *Price Waterhouse Limited,*[7] the Ontario Labour Relations Board held that a privately appointed receiver-manager was not a successor employer because there was no sale of business as defined by the Ontario Act. However, the Board ruled that a receiver-manager must honour the existing collective agreement between the insolvent employer and the union since the employer's obligations under the collective agreement are not extinguished by the receiver-manager's appointment. In a subsequent case involving *Price Waterhouse Limited,*[8] the Ontario Board followed the rationale of the above decision but made a distinction between a privately appointed receiver and one appointed by the courts. The Board held that, in the former case, the receiver is merely the agent of the insolvent employer while, in the latter case, it is a principal in its own right. The next leading case dealing with this issue was *Maritime Life Assurance Company v. Chateau Gardens (Hanover) Inc. et al.*[9] The court ruled that the receiver appointed by the courts was a successor employer under Section 63 (now Section 69) of the Ontario *Labour Relations Act*[10] and was therefore bound by the insolvent employer's collective agreement. The British Columbia Labour Relations Board in *Caledonia Inns Ltd.*[11] has also held that a court-appointed receiver-manager was a successor employer under the B.C. *Labour Code.*

The Ontario Labour Board has extended successor employer liability not only to receivers, but also to managers of insolvent businesses. In *Hamilton Cargo Transit Limited,*[12] the Board held that a manager appointed by the receiver and the bank to operate and manage the insolvent employer's business until the completion of the sale of the business was a successor employer. Two of the key factors in this decision were that the manager was entitled to retain any profits earned and paid a monthly fee to the bank for use of the insolvent's assets.

Although a privately appointed receiver-manager may not constitute a successor employer under the Ontario statute, its manager may well be a successor employer in the event that the manager carries on the insolvent employer's business for its own benefit. In any event, whether the receiver-manager is a successor employer or the employer's agent, it is still liable for the ongoing debts incurred in carrying on the insolvent employer's business and must abide by the terms of the existing collective agreement.

In addition to requiring adherence to a collective agreement, the Board has also imposed other labour relations responsibilities on receivers. In *Price Waterhouse Limited,*[13] the Board held the receiver liable for breaching Section 64 (now Section 70) of Ontario's *Labour Relations Act,* which prohibits, among other things, an employer or a person acting on its behalf from interfering with the representation of employees by a trade union.[14] A receiver-manager, carrying on an insolvent employer's business, may also be in breach of the *Labour Relations Act* if it fails or refuses to hire union members contrary to the act, and a trade union may be certified as the bargaining agent for its employees.

Partly in reaction to these rulings, in the late 1980s and early 1990s it became somewhat commonplace for court-appointed receivers (and liquidators appointed under the federal *Winding-Up Act,*[15] which applies to banks, insurance and trust companies) to obtain ex parte orders from the courts that declared the receiver was not a successor employer. In *Canadian Union of Public Employees v. Deloitte Touche,*[16] the Ontario Board considered the following clause in a court order:

> The retention of any employee of the [insolvent employer] shall not constitute the Receiver as a "successor employer" to the [insolvent employer] or any of its affiliates or otherwise make the Receiver liable for obligations of the [insolvent employer].

After reviewing the cases discussed above, the Board held that

> this provision cannot be determinative in this case. It is the Board's exclusive jurisdiction to determine whether there has been a sale for labour relations purposes. The [receiver-manager] cannot be relieved of its statutory obligations under the Act by the above term of the Order.[17]

The Board then determined that despite the transitory role of the receiver in carrying on the nursing home until it could be sold, because it effectively had complete control over the business to which bargaining rights attached, it was therefore a successor employer and bound by the terms of the collective agreement. An application for judicial review was dismissed by the Ontario Divisional Court.

Therefore, a privately appointed receiver is treated as an agent of the employer, for labour relations purposes, while court-appointed receivers are capable of being declared successor employers under labour relations legislation and becoming liable for all outstanding amount owed to employees under the applicable collective agreements.

Purchasers of Business as Successor/Related Employers

Eventually, a secured creditor will want to sell the employer's business, whether in a going-concern or asset purchase. There is no question that the successor rights provision of the Ontario *Labour Relations Act* applies to the purchaser of the insolvent's business from a receiver or, for that matter, a trustee in bankruptcy. In *United Brotherhood of Carpenters and Joiners of America, Local 3054 and Cassin-Remco Ltd. et al.,*[18] the court held such a successor liable for the insolvent's pre-existing debt to its employees. The Board has also held that a purchaser must recognize rights and benefits that accrued to the employees under the predecessor's collective agreement with their union, including the right to keep their job if the successor continues to employ people in such jobs.[19]

There are related and successor employer provisions in employment standards legislation[20] on which employees may also rely to recover unpaid wages. In *550551 Ontario Ltd. v. Framingham,*[21] the Divisional Court upheld an order made by an employment standards officer that held companies related to a bankrupt employer liable for the latter's obligation for unpaid wages, vacation pay, and termination and severance pay to its employees. The court held the related companies liable on the basis that they were under common or related control and ownership. Also, because there was a close functional interdependence among the companies and the bankrupt, the court held that remedial social legislation, such as the *Employment Standards Act* "modified the strict application of watertight legal compartments."

Again, in response to such legislation, it has also become somewhat commonplace to see ex parte court orders that have provisions stating that such statutes do not apply to court-appointed receivers or liquidators. In another case, however, the courts applied a successor employer provision in pension legislation to hold a trustee in bankruptcy that continued to operate the business during the period of trusteeship liable as the "employer" for pension plan contributions and special payments to existing pension plans under the Ontario *Pension Benefits Act.*[22] Therefore, it is difficult to say that such ex parte court orders would bind a tribunal or court, where they have been given exclusive jurisdiction over the determination of whether or not the receiver is a successor employer.

BIA PROPOSALS
AND CCAA RESTRUCTURING

Court Ordered Stay of All Debt Collection

Debt restructuring is often the first choice when an employer is experiencing financial difficulties. Often this is done formally through proceedings in court under the *Bankruptcy and Insolvency Act* or the *Companies' Creditors Arrangement Act.* This legislation provides for a stay of all debt collection activity for a time in order to allow the employer and creditors time to try to restructure employer's debt or its operations into a viable operation. Employees are entitled to take an active part in such proceedings and, in many seemingly hopeless restructuring cases, the result is that the business and the jobs are saved.

Unless the employer is able to make appropriate repayment arrangements or is itself able to reorganize its affairs to satisfy its lenders, or if the business is simply abandoned, then it is likely that a professional receiver, a liquidator or a trustee in bankruptcy will be appointed. Such professionals will be selected in order to deal with the business undertaking in an orderly way. A monitor must be appointed by the court under CCAA. A *monitor* is a court-appointed officer who helps facilitate the restructuring process with the creditors.

The period of the stay under the BIA Protection provisions is limited to 30 days. The stay applies to both secured and unsecured creditors. Such a stay is automatically granted, provided a licensed trustee in bankruptcy has agreed to file the proposal under the BIA. Extensions of the stay may be sought from the court up to a maximum of six months. If a successful reorganization proposal is made, then the BIA requires that payment of wage claims under s. 136(1)(d) (up to $2,000 per employee for the six months prior to the bankruptcy proceeding) be made before a court can sanction a proposal.[23]

Under the CCAA Restructuring provisions the initial stay is also 30 days. However, there is no statutory maximum for the length of any extensions. Unlike the BIA, however, the stay is not automatic and requires court approval. The stay applies to both secured and unsecured creditors, as well.

Negotiating With Monitor/Employer About Continued Employment

As in the case of a receivership, during the period of the BIA Proposal or the CCAA Restructuring, the employees or their trade union are in a position to negotiate both ongoing payment of their wages and benefits, as well as the payment of any arrears or outstanding sums. The employer and the other creditors have an interest in the continued operation of the business, while restructuring efforts are ongoing. This interest may enable employees to bargain payment of some, if not all, of the amounts owing to them in return for continuing to provide their services to the enterprise.

Voting on Proposal

If a proposal is made, then, if a majority of the members of a class of creditors, representing two-thirds of the value of those creditors' claims, vote in favour of a proposal, then that proposal is binding on the creditors in those classes. Thus, formal restructuring has the advantage of binding all the creditors, if their class votes in favour of the plan or arrangement with the required majorities and the court subsequently approves.

LIQUIDATION

Liquidation by Receiver

As set out above, a receiver may be appointed by the employer's secured creditor under provisions in the security agreement allowing the creditor to "deem" the receiver to be the agent of the creditor and the insolvent company in order to facilitate the asset realization. However, when dealing with the ranking (or priorities) of the employer's creditors, it is the law governing the enforcement of the various legal rights that is important.

For example, a privately appointed receiver is confined to realizing on those assets that are covered by the security agreement, and any fiduciary duties owed are, by and large, to the appointing creditor. (Please note that there is a developing body of law that suggests a receiver may also owe fiduciary duties to the company, as well as others of the company's creditors, including its employees and government agencies, but a discussion of this issue is beyond the scope of this book.)

Receivers and Bankruptcy

A trustee, on the other hand, is licensed through the federal Superintendent of Bankruptcy and is obliged, in carrying out his or her duties, to comply with the *Bankruptcy and Insolvency Act.* A liquidator appointed under the federal *Winding-Up Act* to wind up a financial institution such as a trust or insurance company must similarly comply with the legislation governing the appointment. Both a trustee and a liquidator realize on those assets that are unsecured (i.e., not covered by a security agreement), and any fiduciary duties owed are to those whose interests the statute protects.

In a practical sense, where the employer has been "shored up" by a lender prior to a bankruptcy, there may be few, if any, assets that are not the subject of security agreements, and thus nothing to be realized.

Often, there are two systems of asset realization operating concurrently: a receivership and a bankruptcy. These two systems are possible because of the interpretation placed by the courts on certain key words in Subsection 136(1) of the *Bankruptcy and Insolvency Act*. This subsection reads as follows:

Subject to the rights of secured creditors, the proceeds realized from the property of a bankrupt shall be applied in priority of payments as follows . . .[24] (emphasis added).

Courts have held that, other than being required to value their security and give notice to the debtor under Section 244 of the *Bankruptcy and Insolvency Act,* secured creditors are not affected by bankruptcy proceedings, except to account to the trustee for any surplus over the amount of the secured debt. Therefore, only those assets of the insolvent company that remain after all security interests have been satisfied are distributed under this section.

Accordingly, it is necessary to consider the status of claims for employee benefits and pensions in both bankruptcy and receivership situations.

"Priority" in Bankruptcy

Any money held in trust by a bankrupt does not form part of the bankrupt's estate and therefore would not be available for distribution in the bankruptcy. Though their effectiveness against some types of secured creditors has been diminished recently by the decision of the Ontario Court of Appeal in *Abraham v. Coopers & Lybrand Ltd.* discussed above, in the past, "deemed trusts" created under provincial legislation for benefits such as pension contributions and vacation pay have been held to take priority over the rights of secured creditors.[25] Other provinces did not uphold such deemed trusts.[26]

Then, on April 23, 1989, the Supreme Court of Canada in *British Columbia v. Henfrey, Samson Belair Ltd.*[27] held that a statutory deemed trust created by provincial legislation in favour of the Crown for sales taxes was not effective in a bankruptcy. The court held that trust claims should be confined to a "trust arising under general principles of law." The reasoning of the Supreme Court of Canada in respect of refusing priority to statutory trusts or deemed trusts in a bankruptcy has been followed in numerous cases since then.[28]

Limits on Employees' Preferred Claims

The appropriate starting point for assessing employee claims against an employer in bankruptcy is the federal *Bankruptcy and Insolvency Act.* The BIA provides a preferred claim for employee wages. Although this employee claim is called a "preferred claim," in practice the scheme of distributions is as follows:

1. All secured claims must be paid in full.

2. Preferred claims will be paid in full in the following order:
   - Legal personal representative of the deceased bankrupt for reasonable funeral and testamentary expenses
   - The costs of administration of the bankruptcy
   - The levy payable under Section 147 of the act
   - Employee claims for unpaid wages.

The amount of the employee preferential claim (fourth ranking) for wages, salaries, commissions or compensation is up to $2,000 for the six months preceding the bankruptcy. The employee's preferred claim, like all other "preferred" claims in bankruptcy, is subject to the rights of secured creditors to sell the assets to pay the debt owed to them. The "preferred" creditors share what is left after the secured creditor is paid.

The employee wage claim has been held to include employee benefit contributions, including contributions to pension, health and welfare, and vacation pay trust funds.[29] On the other hand, the court has held that pension benefits do not fall within the priority scheme.[30] The employee's claim for wages in excess of $2,000 ranks as an unsecured claim under Section 136(3) of the *Bankruptcy and Insolvency Act.*[31]

Claims and Trust Claims in Bankruptcy

In the usual bankruptcy situation, the union and employees will only discover that the employer is bankrupt after the fact, when they are served with a *Notice of Assignment in Bankruptcy* or a *Notice of Proposal.* A *Notice of Assignment in Bankruptcy* is a document prepared by the trustee in bankruptcy and forwarded to all known creditors of the employer. Assuming that the employer has listed his or her employees and/or their union as creditors (which some employers oddly enough neglect to do), the trustee will serve the union with notice. The trustee also generally serves claimants with Form 61 under the *Bankruptcy and Insolvency Act.* This is a form entitled "Proof of Claim." This is not the correct form to use to make a trust claim against the estate of the bankrupt. This form should only be used if one is only making a claim for priority for wages under Section 136 of the *Bankruptcy and Insolvency Act.*

The correct form to be used to make a trust claim is Form 63 under the *Bankruptcy and Insolvency Act.* Such a claim must be sworn before a commissioner for oaths, unlike the normal proof of claim, and in addition demands payment of the trust claim within 15 days. However, given recent court decisions reviewed above, success on "deemed trust" in bankruptcy proceedings has become a very difficult prospect. In view of these decisions, it might be better to make a preferred claim for wages, inclusive of any delinquent contributions.

Another reason to be cautious about filing trust

claims is the procedure required to be followed, when one is filed. The trustee is required, within 15 days after receipt of the claim, to deliver the property or to reject the claim. Unfortunately, in the *Bankruptcy and Insolvency Act* there is no third alternative, such as taking a "wait and see" approach and seeing what monies the trustee can collect. Most trust proofs of claim are therefore immediately rejected by the trustee. Trust claimants are given an opportunity to appeal the rejection of claims to the local registrar in bankruptcy. While the appeal must be brought within 15 days, it does not have to be heard within 15 days. Agreements are frequently reached with trustees to adjourn such an appeal indefinitely, pending the collection and determination of assets by the trustee.

Bankruptcy Procedure

The proceeding in a bankruptcy is a fairly simple one. Within five days of its appointment, the trustee of the bankrupt estate calls the first meeting of the bankrupt's creditors. The meeting must be set within 15 days of the date of mailing of the notices. Any creditor who has delivered a proof of claim or a trust claim prior to that date is entitled to attend and vote at that meeting.

The meeting is chaired by the official receiver. Generally what happens is that the trustee makes a very short statement of the assets and liabilities he or she has to date been able to confirm, and inspectors are elected. The role of the inspector in the bankruptcy is to review and approve (or, of course, reject) all the actions of the trustee. As a general rule more than one inspector is selected, and they are frequently representatives of various creditors.

There is no obligation upon any creditor, including trust claimants, to attend the first meeting of creditors, and a creditor's claim is not prejudiced if he or she fails to attend. However, it is recommended that a representative of the union attend the first meeting if possible. On occasion, unions have had substantial success in recovering money in bankruptcies by having a union trustee appointed as an inspector. This seems to give the trustee in bankruptcy a bit more of an incentive to ensure that no stone is left unturned in finding the assets of the bankrupt and in dealing with the wage or trust claims of the employees. Naturally, if the trust claims for some reason cannot be demonstrated or, if there is no trust claim, the employees are primarily unsecured creditors and, to that extent, representation as an inspector is important.

The inspectors are expected to approve the accounts of the trustee. They also may give the trustee instructions from time to time as to the sale of assets, the pursuit of accounts payable and other similar matters.

The inspectors may also instruct the trustee to challenge the bankrupt's past dealings if it appears that the bankrupt has fraudulently gotten rid of some of his or her property by setting up a trust for some other person or by selling it in suspicious circumstances. Such conveyances may be set aside by the court, particularly where the court finds that the bankrupt intended to defeat the claims of creditors by getting rid of property while still retaining the benefit of it.

The trustee is required to collect all outstanding assets (again, noting that trust monies in the hands of persons liable to pay the bankrupt, such as construction lien trust monies, are not part of the assets). Frequently, the trustee will conduct an auction sale of equipment and other property owned by the bankrupt if this equipment is not subject to a security agreement for a loan made to the bankrupt.

Once all the assets are collected, the trustee circulates a "Scheme of Proposed Distribution" among secured and unsecured creditors that is subject to challenge. If the inspectors and trustee and the creditors are unable to reach an agreement on how to distribute the assets, they may apply to the court for directions. Once the assets have been collected and a distribution proposed and accomplished, the trustee may apply to the court for the assessment of his or her fees, and for the discharge of the trustee and of the bankrupt. The discharge may be opposed by any creditor. In some cases where unsecured creditors have been completely unsuccessful in obtaining any recovery and it appears that the bankrupt will be going back into business, the court will order that the bankrupt make future payments for the benefit of the unsecured creditors. Corporations, however, may not be discharged unless all creditors have been paid in full.

OTHER REMEDIES IN BANKRUPTCY

Statutory Directors' and Officers' Liability

The preceding chapter explained the provisions in various corporation and employment standards legislation that impose liability on officers and/or directors for debts to employees. Under the BIA Proposal and CCAA Restructuring, there is a stay on all debt collection activity, including collection from directors and officers. Part of the Proposal or Restructuring may include a compromise of the debts owed by the employer. To the extent that employees agree to compromise their claims in these proceedings, they will not then be able to claim the balance from the directors and officers at the end of the stay period.

However, if there is no Restructuring, then the employees will be free to seek payment of the claims from the directors and/or officers under these statutes, once they have determined whether or not they will receive any part of the money in a bankruptcy distribution.

ENDNOTES

1. *Bankruptcy and Insolvency Act,* R.S.C. 1985, c. B-3, as am.

2. *Companies' Creditors' Arrangement Act,* R.S.C. 1985, c. C-36.

3. *Abraham v. Canadian Admiral Corporation (Receiver of)* (1998), 39 O.R. 176 (C.A.), leave to appeal application dismissed [1998] S.C.C.A. No. 276 (S.C.C.).

4. *Bank Act,* S.C. 1991, c.46, s. 427.

5. Ontario *Personal Property Security Act,* R.S.O. 1990, c. P.10, Subsection 30(7).

6. *John M. Troup Limited v. Royal Bank of Canada,* [1962] S.C.R. 487.

7. *Price Waterhouse Limited,* [1979] O.L.R.B. Reports 1950 January.

8. *Price Waterhouse Limited,* [1983] O.L.R.B. Reports 944 June.

9. *Maritime Life Assurance Company v. Chateau Gardens (Hanover) Inc. et al.* (1983), 43 O.R. (2d) 754 (H.C.).

10. Ontario *Labour Relations Act,* 1995, S.O. 1995, c.1 Schedule A, s. 69.

11. *Caledonia Inns Ltd.,* 85 C.L.L.C. ¶14,306 (B.C.L.R.B.).

12. *Hamilton Cargo Transit Limited,* [1983] O.L.R.B. Reports 887 June.

13. *Price Waterhouse Limited,* [1983] O.L.R.B. Reports 944 June.

14. Ontario *Labour Relations Act, supra* note 10, s.70.

15. The *Winding-Up and Restructuring Act,* R.S.C. 1985, c. W-11.

16. *Canadian Union of Public Employees v. Deloitte Touche,* 93 C.L.L.C. ¶16,031 (O.L.R.B.).

17. *Ibid.,* at paragraph 20.

18. *United Brotherhood of Carpenters and Joiners of America, Local 3054 and Cassin-Remco Ltd. et al.* (1979), 105 D.L.R. (3d) 138 (Ont. H.C.).

19. *Emrick Plastics Inc.* [1982] O.L.R.B. Reports 1961 June.

20. See, for example, Sections 12 and 13 of Ontario's *Employment Standards Act,* R.S.O. 1990, c. E. 14.

21. *550551 Ontario Ltd. v. Framingham* (1991), 4 O.R. (3d) 571 (Div.Ct.).

22. *Re St. Mary's Paper Inc.* (1994), 26 C.B.R. (3d) 263 (O.C.A.).

23. S. 60(1.3) of the *Bankruptcy and Insolvency Act, supra* note 1.

24. *Bankruptcy and Insolvency Act, supra* note 1, s. 136(1).

25. *Re Phoenix Paper Products Ltd.* (1983), 44 O.R. (2d) 225 (Ont. C.A.).

26. *Robinson, Little & Co. Ltd. v. Manitoba Ministry of Labour* (1986), 61 C.B.R. 221 (Man. C.A.).

27. *British Columbia v. Henfrey, Samson Belair Ltd.* (1989), 59 D.L.R. (4th) 726 (S.C.C.).

28. *Husky Oil Operations v. M.N.R.* (1995), 35 C.B.R. (3d) 1 (S.C.C.); *Robinson, Little & Co. (Trustee of) v. Sask. (Min. of Lab.)* (1989), 63 D.L.R. (4th) 392 (S.C.A.); *Bassano Growers v. Diamond S. Produce Ltd. (Trustee of)* (1998), 216 A.R. 328 (C.A.).

29. See, *Re Canadian Display and Exhibit Co. Ltd.* (1968), 12 C.B.R. (N.S.) 180 (S.C.O. Registrar in Bankruptcy).

30. See, *Abraham v. Coopers & Lybrand Ltd.* (1993), 13 O.R. (3d) 649 (O.C.(G.D.)).

31. *Bankruptcy and Insolvency Act, supra* note 1, s. 136(3).

CHAPTER 1

Human Rights Issues
and Employee Benefit Plans

by Fiona Campbell

THE LEGISLATIVE FRAMEWORK

Canadians have human rights protections at both provincial and federal levels of government. At the federal level, the most important legislative enactments are the Canadian Charter of Rights and Freedoms (the "Charter") and the Canadian *Human Rights Act.* Provincially and territorially, human rights are legislatively safeguarded primarily by provincial human rights codes. Both federally and provincially, human rights may also be impacted by a variety of other statutes and regulations such as employment standards acts, workers' compensation acts, occupational health and safety acts, and pay equity legislation.

THE CHARTER

The Charter came into force on April 17, 1982 with the exception of the equality rights provision, Section 15, which came into force on April 17, 1985. Section 15 is most relevant for employment benefit purposes. Its equality rights provisions overlap with the protections afforded by federal and provincial human rights codes. However, there are important differences in the types of legal relationships that are governed by the Charter, on the one hand, and human rights legislation, on the other. Section 32(1) of the Charter states that it applies,

to the Parliament and government of Canada in respect of all matters within the authority of Parliament including all matters relating to the Yukon Territory and Northwest Territories; and to the legislature and government of each province in respect of all matters within the authority of the legislature of each province.[1]

From the outset, it was clear that the Charter applied to the legislation of federal and provincial governments. If such legislation contravenes the Charter, it can be struck down. Thus, the Charter can clearly be used to protect individual rights from government legislation that purports to infringe them. The Charter also applies to government action taken pursuant to statute or common law. The term *government* includes not only direct government actors such as the Governor General in Council, Ministers and public servants within government departments, but also Crown Corporations and public agencies that are outside the formal departmental structure. The test is whether the agency is subject to a "substantial degree of government control."[2]

Initially, some argued that the Charter also applied to protect individuals from each other. That is, not only were individuals' legal relations with the state governed by its provisions, but individuals' legal relations with non-governmental entities, such as corporations or other individuals, were also subject to the Charter. However, the Supreme Court of Canada resolved this debate by restricting the Charter's reach to legal relations between individuals and governments.[3]

The Charter may reach private legal relations indirectly when it can be applied to government legislation that regulates private activity. For example, the provisions of provincial human rights legislation are subject to Charter scrutiny.[4] However, for the most part, private persons who are discriminated against in the workplace by private employers do not have recourse to the Charter. Rather, in a private employment context, it is necessary to rely on human rights and employment standards legislation and turn to the appropriate tribunals to redress discrimination.

Substantively, Section 15 of the Charter expressly prohibits discrimination based on "race, national or ethnic origin, colour, religion, sex, age or mental or physical disability." Other "analogous" grounds of discrimination may also be prohibited under Section 15, but the courts have defined those potential additional grounds narrowly. In order to determine whether a ground is analogous to those listed in Section 15, it is necessary to consider the nature and situation of the group at issue and the social, political and legal history of the treatment of that group in Canadian society. The ground will only be considered analogous if it can be shown that differential treatment premised on the ground has the potential to bring into play human dignity. The recognition of the ground as analogous must advance the purpose of Section 15 of the Charter.[5]

The human rights protections in Section 15 are subject to Section 1 of the Charter. Section 1 provides as follows:

> The Canadian Charter of Rights and Freedoms guarantees the rights and freedoms set out in it subject only to such reasonable limits prescribed by law as can be demonstrably justified in a free and democratic society.

Thus, even if there has been a violation of Section 15 of the Charter, it is necessary to consider whether Section 1 of the Charter is applicable. In *R. v. Oakes,*[6] the Supreme Court of Canada set out four criteria that must be satisfied under Section 1:

1. The law must have an objective that is sufficiently important to warrant limiting a right under the Charter.
2. The law must be rationally connected to the objective.
3. The law must impair the right that is at issue no more than is necessary to accomplish the objective and
4. The law must not have a disproportionate effect on the persons to whom it applies.[7]

HUMAN RIGHTS CODES

While Canadian human rights legislation is older than the Charter, it is still in its infancy. It was only in 1962 that Ontario gathered a rather eclectic mixture of anti-discrimination laws, which were directed toward specific practices and grounds of discrimination, and created the Ontario *Human Rights Code,* which was administered by the Ontario Human Rights Commission, created one year earlier. By 1975, all Canadian provinces had also established human rights commissions to administer their respective human rights codes. A commission was established at the federal level, under the Canadian *Human Rights Act,* in 1977.

Human rights legislation is expressly designed to regulate in the sphere of private relations. Unlike the Charter, its application is not restricted to government actions. Rather, it governs the conduct of private persons, including corporations, trade unions and individuals.

Although human rights legislation applies to private relations, it may also be used to challenge governments and their legislation. The Supreme Court of Canada has held that human rights legislation has a quasi-constitutional status and can be used to override other pieces of legislation. In *The Winnipeg School Division v. Craton,* Mr. Justice McIntyre writing for a unanimous Supreme Court stated:

> [H]uman rights legislation is public and fundamental law of general application. If there is a conflict between this fundamental law and other specific legislation, unless an exception is created, the human rights legislation must govern.[8]

The Supreme Court of Canada reiterated the special status of human rights legislation in *Ontario Human Rights Commission and O'Malley v. Simpson-Sears,*[9] indicating that such legislation must be liberally interpreted to give effect to its broad purposes, and that "[l]egislation of this type is of a special nature, not quite constitutional but certainly more than the ordinary."

The courts have also held that private parties may not contract out of human rights codes provisions. This notion was first articulated by the Supreme Court of Canada in *Ontario Human Rights Commission v. Etobicoke,*[10] where an employer argued that the union had voluntarily agreed in the collective agreement to mandatory retirement age of 60 for firefighters and was therefore precluded from relying on the Code. This argument was rejected on the basis that public statutes constituted public policy that could not be waived or varied by private contract.

DISCRIMINATION

A number of different types of discrimination have been recognized in the legislation and the case law. The most commonly known form is *direct discrimination.* Discrimination is difficult to define. However, an example of *direct discrimination* would be an employer refusing to hire someone because he or she is black. Another less obvious example is a situation in which an employer does not actually say that he is firing an employee because she is pregnant, but there is sufficient evidence from which a conclusion can be drawn that the employee's pregnancy was one of the factors that led to her dismissal.

The second type is *constructive discrimination,* also commonly referred to as *indirect* or *adverse effect discrimination.* The concept of constructive discrimination was first formally recognized by the Supreme Court of Canada in the *Simpson-Sears* case. Constructive discrimination is well illustrated by the facts of the *Simpson-Sears* case where the complainant was required to work periodically on Friday evenings and Saturdays as a condition of her employment. Her religion required a strict observance of the Sabbath from sundown Friday to sundown Saturday. Simpson-Sears refused to give the complainant a full-time position because she was unable to work on Saturdays. The Supreme Court of Canada held that the actions of Simpson-Sears constituted discrimination even though Simpson-Sears had legitimate business reasons for requiring employees to work on Saturday. Thus, constructive discrimination was defined by the court as follows:

It [constructive discrimination] arises when an employer for genuine business reasons adopts a rule or standard which is on its face neutral, and which will apply equally to all employees, but which has a discriminatory effect upon a prohibited ground on one employee or group of employees in that it imposes, because of some special characteristic of the employee or group, obligations, penalties or restrictive conditions not imposed on other members of the work force.[11]

It was also in the *Simpson-Sears* case that the Supreme Court of Canada recognized the concept of the duty of accommodation short of undue hardship. That is, the court stated that if it can be established that there is a seemingly neutral rule that has an adverse impact on a person or group that is protected by the Code, the onus shifts to the employer to show that reasonable measures have been taken to accommodate the employee or group, short of undue hardship. The concepts of constructive discrimination and the resulting duty to accommodate have been codified in some provincial human rights codes. For example, Section 11 of the Ontario Code provides as follows:

(1) A right of a person under Part I is infringed where a requirement, qualification or factor exists that is not discrimination on a prohibited ground but that results in the exclusion, restriction or preference of a group of persons who are identified by a prohibited ground of discrimination and of whom the person is a member, except where,

(a) the requirement, qualification or factor is reasonable and *bona fide* in the circumstances; or

(b) it is declared in this Act, other than in section 17, that to discriminate because of such ground is not an infringement of a right.

(2) The Commission, a Board of Inquiry or a court shall not find that a requirement, qualifica-

tion or factor is reasonable and *bona fide* in the circumstances unless it is satisfied that the needs of the group of which the person is a member cannot be accommodated without undue hardship on the person responsible for accommodating those needs, considering the cost, outside sources of funding, if any, and health and safety requirements, if any.[12]

Another type of discrimination is systemic discrimination. The following definition of *systemic discrimination* was adopted by the Supreme Court of Canada in the case of *Canadian National Railway Co. v. Canada (Canadian Human Rights Commission):*[13]

Discrimination . . . means practices or attitudes that have, whether by design or impact, the effect of limiting an individual's or a group's right to the opportunities available because of attributed rather than actual characteristics. It is not a question of whether this discrimination is motivated by an intentional desire to obstruct someone's potential, or whether it is the accidental by-product of innocently motivated practices or systems. If the barrier is affecting certain groups in a disproportionately negative way, it is a signal that the practices that lead to this adverse impact may be discriminatory. This is why it is important to look at the results of the system.

The facts of the *Canadian National* case also provide a good illustration of systemic discrimination. In that case, the evidence showed that many of the male employees believed that women simply could not do the heavier jobs and were not afraid to share these opinions with the female employees. In addition, there was testimony that women who applied to C.N. were channeled into secretarial positions in which there was little chance for advancement. Another problem was that qualifications such as welding that were unrelated to the job were required for entry level positions and had the effect of excluding women.

DISCRIMINATION AND EMPLOYEE BENEFITS

Although employers are generally not required to provide employee benefits, once an employer has made employee benefits part of the compensation package, the benefits must be provided to all employees in a nondiscriminatory manner. As Mr. Justice Dickson stated in *Brooks v. Canada Safeway Ltd.,* a case involving sex/ pregnancy discrimination:

Increasingly, employee benefit plans have become part of the terms and conditions of employment. Once an employer decides to provide an employee benefit package, exclusions from such schemes may not be made in a discriminatory fashion. Selective compensation of this nature would clearly amount to sex discrimination. Benefits available through employment must be disbursed in a non-discriminatory manner.[14]

To date, many of the discrimination cases that have arisen in the employee benefits area relate to three issues. First, courts and tribunals have examined whether employee benefit plans can provide different coverage to pregnant women. Second, there have been a number of recent cases that have considered discrimination arguments in the context of the provision of benefits to disabled employees. The third issue dealt with in the case law is whether there is an obligation to cover same-sex spouses under employee benefit plans on the same basis as opposite-sex spouses. More recently, there have also been some cases concerning age discrimination in the employee benefits area.

Sex and Pregnancy Discrimination

Most of the cases in this area involve allegations that pregnant women or women who have recently given birth are subject to discriminatory treatment under disability benefit policies.

The Supreme Court of Canada dealt with this issue in 1989 in *Brooks v. Canada Safeway Ltd. Brooks* involved the validity of Canada Safeway's employee disability benefit plan, insofar as it excluded pregnant women from coverage during a 17-week period commencing 11 weeks before the anticipated birth date and ending six weeks after the birth. Even if pregnant employees were disabled for non-pregnancy-related reasons, they could not receive benefits under the plan for that 17-week period. Instead, the employees were required to rely upon the much less generous pregnancy benefit provisions pursuant to the *Unemployment Insurance Act* (now the *Employment Insurance Act*).

This provision was challenged by three women employees who were denied benefits in accordance with the plan. The employer argued that pregnancy is not a sickness or an accident and, therefore, it need not treat pregnant employees the same as employees who are unable to work because of sickness or an accident. The Supreme Court of Canada rejected this argument and held that, while pregnancy is not properly characterised as sickness or an accident, it is a valid health-related reason for absence from work and should not have been excluded from the employer's plan. The Supreme Court found that the defect in the Safeway plan was not only its exclusion of non-pregnancy-related illnesses and accidents during the period prior to birth when maternity leave was generally available but, "it is enough that the plan excludes compensation for pregnancy."

There have been a number of subsequent human rights decisions that have clarified and expanded upon *Brooks*. In *Alberta Hospital Association v. Parcels*,[15] a complaint was made by a nurse under the Alberta *Individual's Rights Protection Act* about a provision in the collective agreement that obliged an employee going on maternity leave to pre-pay 100% of the premiums for benefits in order to ensure the availability of those benefits during her maternity leave. Employees taking regular sick leave were only required to pay 25% of the premiums during their leave. The Alberta Court of Queen's Bench held that this requirement was directly discriminatory, at least with respect to the portion of maternity leave that is health related.

> For that part of the maternity leave that is health-related, the sub-article is clearly directly discriminatory as it does not treat maternity leaves in the same manner as other health-related leaves, for example, leaves for illness or accident.

In *Stagg v. Intercontinental Packers Limited*,[16] a Saskatchewan Board of Inquiry decided that the denial of weekly and long-term sickness benefits to persons on pregnancy leave violated Section 16(1) of the Saskatchewan *Human Rights Code*. In that case, the complainant became pregnant after two years with the employer and, when complications arose, she was given medical advice to stay home from work. She received weekly sick benefits for several weeks, but these were terminated when the employer made the assumption that she had commenced maternity leave. Under the company's benefit plan, women on maternity leave were not eligible for weekly sick benefits. After receiving no benefits for a month, Ms. Stagg applied for and received the maximum 15-week payment for unemployment insurance maternity leave benefits.

The Board of Inquiry determined that the employer's weekly benefit plan's exclusion of women on maternity leave from receiving benefits solely on the basis of their pregnancy was discriminatory. The Board also found that, because of the employer's actions, Ms. Stagg did not apply for long-term disability benefits, which would otherwise have been available to her until two weeks after childbirth, and awarded her damages with interest for this amount.

In *Ontario Secondary School Teachers' Federation, District 34 v. Essex County Board of Education*,[17] the Ontario Divisional Court held that an arbitration board erred by failing to find that an employer had discriminated on the basis of pregnancy in refusing a woman access to the sick leave plan under the collective agreement for that period after childbirth that was related to the recovery of her health. Although the employee was on maternity leave pursuant to the *Employment Standards Act*, the court held that the arbitration board erred in that it did not interpret sick leave provisions consistently with the *Human Rights Code*. The sick leave plan included physical disability, and the court found that the term could include pregnancy-related conditions.

The Ontario Divisional Court also dealt with a similar issue recently in *Ontario Cancer Treatment & Research Foundation v. Ontario Human Rights Commission.*[18] There, an oncologist, Dr. Crook, filed a human rights complaint when she was denied the use of sick leave benefits during a period after she had given birth. Dr. Crook chose not to take maternity leave, but rather used vacation days for the period immediately after the birth. She then made a request for sick leave benefits when she was unable to return to work for medical reasons, including a stress-related condition, which had commenced before the birth, and postpartum depression. The employer denied her the sick benefits because she was considered to be on maternity leave, and the employer did not provide benefits to employees who were on an unpaid leave of absence. The complaint was upheld before the Board of Inquiry. Although Dr. Crook then settled her case with the employer, the employer appealed the Board's order that it apply the terms of the sick leave plan so as not to exclude women oncologists from benefits for the period after birth that they are unable to work for health-related reasons.

The Divisional Court agreed with the decision of the Board of Inquiry and found that denying a woman access to the use of sick leave around the time of childbirth when she is unable to work for health-related reasons, including the recovery from normal childbirth, amounts to discrimination on the basis of pregnancy. The court also held that Section 25(2) of the Code was not applicable in that case. Section 25(2) protects "an employee superannuation or pension plan or fund or a contract of group insurance between an insurer and an employer" that complies with the provisions of the *Employment Standards Act* and its regulations. The *Employment Standards Act* and the regulations permit discrimination against pregnant women by denying access to disability plans during maternity leave. However, the court found that Section 25(2) did not apply in the case before it because the employer's sick leave plan was self-funded and was not a group insurance contract.

Although Section 25(2) of the Code was found not to be applicable on the facts of Dr. Crook's case, the court's reasoning indicates that Section 25(2) would likely provide a defense in the case of group insurance contracts.

In another decision on a different but related issue, *Anderson v. Saskatchewan Teachers' Superannuation Commission,*[19] the Saskatchewan Court of Appeal dealt with the impact of maternity leave on pension entitlement. The case involved two women who had been teachers in Saskatchewan for 28 years who became pregnant during the 1950s and early 1960s, before maternity leave was available. Therefore, they were forced to resign from their employment in order to take pregnancy leave and later were rehired. In 1990, they applied to the Superannuation Commission to purchase one year of contributory service for the period of maternity leave. The Saskatchewan *Teachers' Superannuation Act* provided that, in order to purchase the credit, the teachers must have been granted leave by the Board of Education. Their requests were denied because they had resigned rather than take a leave. The Saskatchewan Court of Appeal held that this was not discrimination on the basis of sex or pregnancy as male teachers and adoptive parents who took parental leave prior to board-approved leaves being instituted were also denied the option to buy back lost pension benefits.

Discrimination on the Basis of Disability

Many of the cases in this area have arisen in the labour arbitration context and have considered whether employers must continue to make benefit contributions for employees who are on disability leave. Another issue that often arises at the same time is whether employees on disability benefits continue to accrue service and/or seniority.

Recently, the Ontario Court of Appeal considered these issues in *O.N.A. v. Orillia Soldiers Memorial Hospital.*[20] That case involved a policy grievance of a scheme under a collective agreement where, after certain periods, nurses on unpaid leave of absence due to disability did not accumulate seniority or service and were required to pay 100% of premiums to their benefit plans. With respect to the benefit plan premiums, the court found that the provision in the collective agreement was not directly discriminatory. The relevant comparator group was other employees who were not working, and the disabled employees who were not working were treated more generously than the other employees in this group. If the provision amounted to adverse effect discrimination, the court found that requiring work in exchange for compensation was a bona fide occupational requirement. There was no way to accommodate the needs of the group so that they could perform the work. The court applied the same reasoning to service accrual, which was used to fix employee compensation levels. However, the court held that provision in the collective agreement regarding the accrual of seniority was discriminatory. The court found that seniority was not directly related to compensation and accrued only through the passage of time but directly affected the ability of employees to access, remain in and thrive in the workplace.

The Supreme Court of Canada dealt with a somewhat different disability-related question in *Battlefords and District Co-operative Ltd. v. Gibbs.*[21] The issue in that case was whether the provisions of a disability insurance policy amounted to discrimination under Section 16 of the Saskatchewan *Human Rights Code.* Under the policy, disabled employees who were off work were entitled to benefits. However, if the disability in question was mental illness, the policy provided that the benefit would terminate after two years, unless the person with the mental disability was in an institution. The Court held that the purpose of the insurance plan was to insure employees against the income-related consequences of disability. Therefore, the appropriate comparator group was those receiving disability benefits generally. In the circumstances, the Court found that the differential treatment of employees with mental disabilities was discriminatory. In a partial dissent, Madame Justice McLachlin expressed concerns about the "purpose test" formulated by the majority in that it only functions if the purpose is formulated broadly with reference to the need, which the plan seeks to address. However, if the purpose is defined in terms of specified injuries or target groups, the result may be to condone the exclusion of many valid claims.

Discrimination on the Basis of Sexual Orientation

In the past decade, the courts and tribunals have dealt with numerous cases in which employees have been denied requests to have their benefits extended to their same-sex spouses. The issue typically arose because of definitions of the term *spouse* in private benefit plans, collective agreements or legislation that exclude same-sex spouses. In the past, there has been considerable confusion as to whether benefits must be provided to same-sex spouses and the legal consequences if such benefits are not provided. However, as a result of the recent decisions of the Supreme Court of Canada in *M. v. H.*[22] and the Ontario Court of Appeal in *Rosenberg v. Canada (Attorney General),*[23] the law has become much clearer. As a result of these cases, legislation has been passed and introduced in many Canadian jurisdictions replacing opposite-sex definitions of *spouse* with definitions that include same-sex spouses. There are, however, some remaining areas of uncertainty.

Charter Cases

There has been rapid development in the approach of the courts toward same-sex benefits and discrimination on the basis of sexual orientation under the Charter in the past several years. As sexual orientation is not listed as a ground in Section 15 of the Charter, the first step was for the courts to recognize it as an analogous ground under Section 15. The Supreme Court of Canada did so in 1995 in *Egan v. Canada.*[24] *Egan* involved a challenge to the opposite-sex definition of *spouse* under the *Old Age Security Act,* as a result of which Egan's same-sex spouse did not qualify for a spousal allowance that is available to the opposite-sex

spouse of pensioners if the couple's income falls below a certain level. There, the court held that sexual orientation is ". . . a deeply personal characteristic that is either unchangeable or changeable only at unacceptable personal costs" and that gays, lesbians and bisexuals, ". . . whether as individuals or couples, form an identifiable minority who have suffered and continue to suffer serious social, political and economic disadvantage. . . ."[25]

In *Egan,* the majority of the Court also held that the denial of benefits to same-sex spouses amounted to a violation of Section 15 of the Charter by discriminating on the basis of sexual orientation. However, a differently constituted majority held that the violation of Section 15 could be justified under Section 1 of the Charter.

In *Rosenberg,* the Ontario Court of Appeal considered a challenge to the opposite-sex definition of *spouse* in the *Income Tax Act.* This prevented the Canadian Union of Public Employees from registering a pension plan that provided survivor benefits to same-sex spouses with Revenue Canada. In accordance with *Egan,* the court held that the definition of *spouse* in Section 252(4) of the *Income Tax Act* violated Section 15 of the Charter. The court went on to find that the infringement of Section 15 was not justified under Section 1 of the Charter. The court relied on a decision of the Supreme Court of Canada in *Vriend v. Alberta,*[26] which was released after *Egan,* and took a different approach than *Egan* to the analysis of Section 1 of the Charter. The court ordered that the definition of *spouse* in Section 252(4) of the *Income Tax Act* must be read to include same-sex spouses. The federal government decided not to seek leave to appeal *Rosenberg* to the Supreme Court of Canada.

The effect of *Rosenberg* is that pension plans that provide survivor benefits to same-sex spouses may now be registered with Revenue Canada. However, Revenue Canada has taken the position that it will not register amendments to pension plans that provide same-sex benefits retroactively for the period before April 23, 1998, the date of the *Rosenberg* decision. Revenue Canada has stated that it will consider claims for same-sex benefits that arose prior to April 23, 1998 on a case-by-case basis.

Relying on *Rosenberg,* in *O.P.S.E.U. Pension Plan Trust Fund (Trustees of) v. Ontario (Management Board of Cabinet),*[27] the Ontario Court (General Division) held that the opposite-sex definition of *spouse* in the Ontario *Pension Benefits Act* was contrary to Section 15 of the Charter and was not justified by Section 1. As a result, the court ordered that the definition of *spouse* in the *Pension Benefits Act* must be read to include same-sex spouses. This means that pension plans in Ontario are required to provide survivor benefits to same-sex spouses as a minimum standard pursuant to the *Pension Benefits Act.* The Financial Services Commission of

Ontario recently released a policy in the wake of the *OPSEU Pension Trust* case effective December 8, 1998.[28] The policy states that pension plans are not required to be amended to provide same-sex benefits, although it is good practice to do so. However, the policy further states that pension plan administrators must provide same-sex benefits as pension plans are required to be administered in accordance with the *Pension Benefits Act.*

The most recent case in which the constitutionality of an opposite-sex definition of *spouse* was at issue was *M. v. H.,* where the Supreme Court of Canada considered the support obligations of same-sex spouses under the Ontario *Family Law Act.* The Court held that the opposite-sex definition of *spouse* in Section 29 of the *Family Law Act* was contrary to Section 15 of the Charter and was not justified under Section 1 of the Charter. The Court severed Section 29 of the *Family Law Act,* with a six-month suspended declaration of invalidity. Although the case did not deal directly with same-sex benefits, it has provided an impetus to Parliament and the legislatures across the country to amend the definition of *spouse* in various statutes to include same-sex spouses.

Human Rights Cases

In the early-to-mid 1990s, many human rights complaints regarding the denial of same-sex benefits were upheld by tribunals and the courts. During this period, in *Leshner v. Ontario,*[29] an Ontario Board of Inquiry held that Section 25(2) of the Ontario *Human Rights Code* provided a defense to complaints regarding the denial of survivor benefits to same-sex spouses under pension plans. Section 25(2) permits discrimination on the basis of marital status and thus allows pension plans to provide different benefits to single members than to married members. The Board of Inquiry reasoned that since the Code contains an opposite-sex definition of *spouse,* the complainant was single for the purposes of the Code, and Section 25(2) provided a full defense. However, the Board went on to find that the definition of *spouse* in the Code was contrary to Section 15 of the Charter and that the definition of *spouse* should be read to include same-sex spouses. Therefore, the Board held that the denial of same-sex survivor benefits was contrary to the Code as modified by the Charter. The Board of Inquiry's approach in *Leshner* was later approved by the Ontario Divisional Court in *Ontario Blue Cross v. Ontario (Human Rights Comm.).*[30]

The major stumbling block at that time, particularly with respect to pension plans, was that Revenue Canada was not willing to register pension plans that provided survivor benefits to same-sex spouses. Therefore, the issue in many cases was whether the court or tribunal should order pension plans to provide survivor benefits to same-sex spouses in arrangements outside of the registered pension plan. In some cases, such as *Leshner,* tribunals ordered respondents to set up "off-side" arrangements and, in other cases, they did not.[31]

Having regard to the decision of the Ontario Court of Appeal in *Rosenberg,* pension plans providing same-sex benefits may be registered with Revenue Canada, and it is no longer necessary for tribunals to consider the issues surrounding whether employers should be ordered to set up off-side pension plans as a remedy. In most Canadian jurisdictions, this means that tribunals are likely to uphold human rights complaints regarding same-sex benefits and simply order benefit or pension plans to provide benefits to same-sex spouses.

However, in Ontario, the Human Rights Commission has taken the position that it cannot refer same-sex benefits complaints to Boards of Inquiry because of the decision of the Supreme Court of Canada in *Cooper v. Canada (Human Rights Commission).*[32] In that case, the Court held that human rights commissions do not have the power to apply the Charter to the provisions of their own legislation. As noted above, in *Leshner,* the Board of Inquiry held that Section 25(2) of the Code provided a full defense to same-sex benefits complaints and only upheld the complaint when the Charter was applied to modify the definition of *spouse* in the Code. This approach was approved by the Ontario Divisional Court in *Ontario Blue Cross v. Ontario (Human Rights Comm.)* and is therefore binding on the Commission. As the Ontario Commission no longer has the power to apply the Charter to its enabling legislation, it was left with the conclusion that Section 25(2) of the Code provides a defense to same-sex benefits complaints. However, as a result of the *M.v.H.* decision, the Ontario *Human Rights Code* was amended by Bill 5 to recognize "same-sex partner status" as a prohibited ground of discrimination.[33]

Legislative Initiatives

A number of Canadian jurisdictions have now passed or introduced legislation to amend definitions of *spouse* to include same-sex spouses.

On June 16, 1999, the Quebec government gave Royal Assent to Bill 32, *An Act to amend various legislative provisions concerning de facto spouses.*[34] Bill 32 amends 28 statutes and 11 regulations in Quebec to recognize same-sex spouses. Most significantly for these purposes, Bill 32 amends the provisions of the *Supplemental Pensions Plan Act* with respect to death benefits and division of pensions upon separation. Employers must comply with these requirements within 90 days.

In British Columbia legislation recognizing same-sex spousal relationships has been passed. Bill 58, the *Pension Benefits Standards Amendment Act, 1999*[35] amends the definition of *spouse* in the *Pension Benefits Stan-*

dards Act to include same-sex spouses. However, under the bill, a married spouse will have priority over a common law spouse for two years after the married spouses began living separate and apart.

Federally, Bill C-78, the *Public Sector Pension Investment Board Act,* was assented to September 14, 1999. Bill C-78 amends the definition of *spouse* in various federal public sector pension plans to include same-sex spouses. The federal government also amended several other statutes with Bill C-23, which introduced the concept of *common law partner* to confer "spousal" benefits, rights, and responsibilities to same-sex partners who have cohabited for at least one year.[36]

Age Discrimination

The Supreme Court of Canada recently **considered** the issue of age discrimination in the benefits area in *Law v. Canada (Minister of Employment and Immigration).*[37] In that case a 30-year-old woman challenged the provisions of the Canada Pension Plan that gradually reduce survivor pensions for able-bodied spouses between the ages of 35 and 45 so that the threshold to receive benefits is age 35. The Court held that these provisions did not violate Section 15 of the Charter even though they clearly result in differential treatment based on age. The Court found that the differential treatment of younger people in these circumstances did not reflect or promote the notion that they were less worthy of concern or respect nor did it violate their human dignity. Another factor taken into account by the Court was that Parliament's intent in providing limited survivor benefits to those under 45 appears to have been to allocate funds to older spouses whose ability to overcome need was the weakest.

ENDNOTES

1. *Constitution Act,* 1982, R.S.C. 1985, Appendix II, No. 44, Part I, s.32(1).
2. *Douglas/Channel Faculty Assn. v. Douglas College,* [1991] 2 S.C.R. 570.
3. *Retail, Wholesale and Department Store Union, Local 580 v. Dolphin Delivery Ltd.,* [1986] 2 S.C.R. 573.
4. *Vriend v. Alberta,* [1998] 1 S.C.R. 493 and *Re Blainey* (1986), 54 O.R. (2d) 513 (C.A.) leave to appeal to S.C.C. refused (1986), 58 O.R. (2d) 274 (S.C.C.).
5. *Law v. Canada (Minister of Employment and Immigration)* (1999), 170 D.L.R. (4th) 1 (S.C.C.).
6. *R. v. Oaks,* [1986] 1 S.C.R. 103.
7. Hog, Peter W. *Constitutional Law of Canada* (Looseleaf Edition) (Toronto: Carswell, 1992).
8. *The Winnipeg School Division v. Craton* (1985), 21 D.L.R. (4th) 1 at (S.C.C.) at p. 26.
9. *Ontario Human Rights Commission and O'Malley v. Simpson-Sears,* [1985] 2 S.C.R 53.

10. *Ontario Human Rights Commission v. Etobicoke* (1982), 132 D.L.R. (3d) 14 (S.C.C.).
11. *Ontario Human Rights Commission v. Simpson-Sears Ltd., supra* note 9.
12. Ontario *Human Rights Code,* R.S.O. 1990, c. H.19, as am.
13. *Canadian National Railway Co. v. Canada (Canadian Human Rights Commission)* (1987), 8 C.H.R.R. D/4210 (S.C.C.).
14. *Brooks v. Canada Safeway Ltd.* (1989), 59 D.L.R. (4th) 321 (S.C.C.) at pp. 336-7.
15. *Alberta Hospital Association v. Parcels* (1992), 90 D.L.R. (4th) 703 (Alta. Q.B.).
16. *Stagg v. Intercontinental Packers Limited* (1992), 92 C.L.L.C. ¶16, 236 (Sask. Bd. Inq.).
17. *Ontario Secondary School Teachers' Federation, District 34 v. Essex County Board of Education* (1996), 136 D.L.R. (4th) 34 (Ont.Div.Ct.).
18. *Ontario Cancer Treatment & Research Foundation v. Ontario Human Rights Commission* (1998), 38 O.R. (3d) 72 (Div.Ct.).
19. *Anderson v. Saskatchewan Teachers' Superannuation Commission* (1995), 130 D.L.R. (4th) 602 (Sask.C.A.).
20. *O.N.A. v. Orillia Soldiers Memorial Hospital* (1999), 169 D.L.R. (4th) 489 (O.C.A.), application for leave to appeal to the Supreme Court of Canada dismissed [1999] S.C.C.A. No. 118.
21. *Battlefords and District Co-operative Ltd.,* [1996] 3 S.C.R. 566.
22. *M. v. H.* (1999), 171 D.L.R. (4th) 577 (S.C.C.).
23. *Rosenberg v. Canada (Attorney General)* (1998), 38 O.R. (3d) 577 (C.A.).
24. *Egan v. Canada* (1995), 124 D.L.R. (4th) 609 (S.C.C.).
25. *Ibid.,* at paragraph 5.
26. *Vriend v. Alberta, supra* note 4.
27. *O.P.S.E.U. Pension Plan Trust Fund (Trustees of) v. Ontario (Management Board of Cabinet)* (1998), 20 C.C.P.B. (O.C.(G.D.)).
28. Financial Services Commission of Ontario, Bulletin 7/1, dated April 1999.
29. *Leshner v. Ontario* (1992), 16 C.H.R.R. D/184 (Ont.Bd.Inq.).
30. *Ontario Blue Cross v. Ontario (Human Rights Comm.)* (1994), 21 C.H.R.R. D/342 (Ont.Div.Ct.).
31. See for example *Dwyer v. Toronto (Metro) (No. 3)* (1996), 27 C.H.R.R. D/108 (Ont. Bd. Inq.) and *Laessoe v. Air Canada* (1996), 27 C.H.R.R. D/1 (C.H.R.T.).
32. *Cooper v. Canada (Human Rights Commission)* (1997), 140 D.L.R. (4th) 193 (S.C.C.).
33. *An Act to amend certain Statutes because of the Supreme Court of Canada decision in M. v. H.,* S.O. 1999, c.6, s. 28.
34. *An Act to amend various legislative provisions concerning de facto spouses,* S.Q. 1999, c. 14.
35. *Pension Benefits Standards Amendment Act, 1999,* S.B.C. 1999, c. 29.
36. *Public Sector Pension Investment Board Act,* S.C. 1999, c. 34.
37. *Law, supra* note 5.

A Selected Employee Benefits Glossary

A

Accidental Death and Dismemberment Benefits—A lump-sum payment is assured if the insured dies as the result of an accident, within a specified period. Usually the same sum is paid on the accidental loss of both limbs, hand and foot, or the sight of both eyes.

Accountability—An obligation to periodically disclose appropriate information in adequate detail and consistent form to all involved parties in a benefit plan.

Accrual of Benefits—In the case of a *defined benefit pension plan,* the process of accumulating pension credits for years of credited service, expressed in the form of an annual benefit to begin payment at normal retirement age. In the case of a *defined contribution plan,* the process of accumulating funds in the individual employee's pension account.

Accrued Future Service Benefit—That portion of a participant's retirement benefit that relates to his or her period of credited service after the effective date of the plan and before a specified current date.

Accrued Pension—Amount of pension credited to a plan member according to service, earnings, etc., up to a given time.

Active Management—A style of investment management that seeks to attain above-average risk-adjusted performance.

Active Participant—An individual who is a participant and for whom at any time during the taxable year benefits are accrued under the plan on his or her behalf, or for whom the employer is obligated to contribute to or under the plan on his or her behalf or for whom the employer would have been obligated to contribute to or under the plan on his or her behalf if any contributions were made to or under the plan.

Actuarial Accrued Liability—
—The actuarial accrued liability of a pension plan at any time is the excess of the present value, as of the date of valuation, of total prospective benefits of the plan (plus administrative expenses if included in the normal cost) over the present value of future normal cost accruals, determined by the actuarial cost method in use.
—That portion, as determined by a particular actuarial cost method, of the actuarial present value of pension plan benefits and expenses that is not provided for by future normal costs. The presentation of an actuarial accrued liability should be accompanied by reference to the actuarial cost method used.

Actuarial Assumptions—In an actuarial valuation, a set of estimates of future developments affecting the cost of benefits to be provided under a pension plan (e.g., mortality, salary increases, investment return, employee turnover, retirement ages).

Actuarial Cost Method—
—System for determining either the contributions to be made under a retirement plan or the level of benefits when the contributions are fixed. In addition to forecasts of mortality, interest and expenses,

some of the methods involve estimates as to future labour turnover, salary scales and retirement rates. The methods of prime importance are those such as the entry age method, attained age method and unit credit method.

—A recognized technique for establishing the amount and incidence of the actuarial cost of pension plan benefits, or benefits and expenses, and the related actuarial liabilities.

Actuarial Equivalent—

—If the present value of two series of payments is equal, taking into account a given interest rate and mortality according to a given table, the two series are said to be *actuarially equivalent.* For example, under a given set of actuarial assumptions, a lifetime monthly benefit of $67.60 beginning at age 60 can be said to be the actuarial equivalent of $100 a month beginning at age 65. The actual benefit amounts are different, but the present value of the two benefits, considering mortality and interest, is the same.

—A benefit having the same present value as the benefit it replaces.

—Of equal actuarial present value.

Actuarial Gain or Loss—The effects on actuarial costs of deviations or differences between the past events predicted by actuarial assumptions and the events that actually occurred. An *actuarial gain* results when the actual experience under the plan is more favourable than the actuary's estimate, while an *actuarial loss* reflects an unexpectedly adverse deviation.

Actuarial Present Value—The value of an amount or series of amounts payable or receivable at various times, determined as of a given date by the application of a particular set of actuarial assumptions.

Actuarial Reduction—The reduction in the normal retirement benefit that offsets a cost increase to the plan when a participant retires ahead of schedule.

Actuarial Report—An actuary's report to the company recommending how much to contribute yearly to the pension fund to fund promised benefits.

Actuarial Valuation—Examination of a pension plan by an actuary to assess the solvency of the plan and determine the level of contributions required to maintain its solvency.

Actuarial Value of Assets—The value of cash, investments and other property belonging to a pension plan, as used by the actuary for the purpose of an actuarial valuation. The statement of actuarial assumptions should set forth the particular procedures used in determining this value.

Actuary—A professionally trained specialist in the pension and insurance fields who deals scientifically with the financial, social and demographic implications and consequences, present and future, of contingent events called *risks.* Full professional recognition requires membership in the Canadian Institute of Actuaries.

Ad Hoc Adjustment—Amount added to a pension after retirement, on an irregular basis and not as a result of a prior commitment or contract. To be distinguished from *indexing.*

Additional Voluntary Contributions—Contributions to a pension plan, made voluntarily by an employee in addition to those required for specific plan benefits. Extra benefits are purchased by the additional contributions, but no additional cost is borne by the employer.

Administrative Services Only—Plans that do not require the underwriting services of the insurer. Instead, the only services required are administrative services, in particular, claim paying services. There is no premium to be paid and no premium tax. The client may open a bank account and direct the bank to accept cheques written against the account by authorized individuals of the insurance company or administrator.

Administrator—The person designated as such by statute or the instrument under which the plan is operated, or the individual or company responsible for administering a group benefit plan.

Adverse Selection—The tendency of an individual to recognize his or her health status in selecting the option under a retirement system or insurance plan that tends to be most favourable to him or her (and more costly to the plan). In insurance usage, a person with an impaired health status or with expected medical care needs applies for insurance coverage financially favourable to himself or herself and detrimental to the insurance company. Also known as *anti-selection.*

Agency/Agent—A relationship in which one person acts for or represents another by the latter's authority.

Amendment—

—(General) An addition, deletion or change in the legal document.

—(Employee Benefit Plans) A change in the terms of an existing plan or the initiation of a new plan. A plan amendment may increase benefits, including those attributed to years of service already rendered.

—(Insurance) A formal document changing the provisions of an insurance policy signed jointly by the insurance company officer and the policyholder or his or her authorized representative.

Amortization—Paying off an interest-bearing liability by gradual reduction through a series of instalments as opposed to paying it off by one lump-sum payment. A technique for gradually extinguishing a liability, deferred charge or capital expenditure over a period of time. Includes such practices as depreciation, depletion, write-off of intangibles, prepaid expenses and deferred charges (e.g., mortgages are amortized by periodically retiring part of the face amount). The liquidation of a debt on an instalment basis.

Ancillary Benefits—Benefits in addition to regular pension and survivor benefits, such as bridging and enriched early retirement benefits.

Annual Statement—The yearly report, provided by insurers to provincial and federal authorities, showing assets and liabilities, receipts and disbursements, and other financial data.

Annualize—To express a rate of return for a period greater than one year or less than one year in terms of 12 months.

Annuitant—A person entitled to receive payments under an annuity.

Annuity—In pension terminology, periodic payments (usually monthly) provided by the terms of a contract for the lifetime of an individual (the annuitant); may be a fixed or varying amount and may continue for a period after the annuitant's death.

Annuity Contract—A contract in which an insurance company unconditionally undertakes a legal obligation to provide specified pension benefits to specific individuals in return for fixed consideration or premium. An annuity contract is irrevocable and involves the transfer of significant risk from the employer to the insurance company. Annuity contracts are also called *allocated contracts*.

Annuity Rate—Price charged by an issuer of annuities to provide a dollar of annuity (usually per month) under specified conditions to an individual based on the person's age, interest rates, etc.

Appraisal—An estimation of quantity, quality or value. The process through which conclusions of property value are obtained; also refers to the report setting forth the estimate and conclusion of value reached by correlation, unless a single technique is used.

Approved Plan—A pension, deferred profit-sharing or stock bonus plan that meets the requirements of the applicable Revenue Canada regulations. Such approval qualifies the plan for a favourable tax treatment. Approval of a pension plan does not indicate any judgment regarding the plan's actuarial soundness.

Arbitration/Arbitrator—The submitting of a matter in

dispute to the judgment of a specified number of disinterested persons called *arbitrators,* whose decision, called an *award,* is binding upon the parties.

Asset Allocation Models—The modern portfolio theory application area that addresses the problem of the amount of assets to be allocated among various investment alternatives.

Asset Mix—The percentage investment in different types of securities such as stocks, bonds and money market.

Audit—Any systematic investigation of procedures or operations for the purpose of determining conformity with prescribed criteria.

Audit Trail—The availability of a manual or machine-readable means for tracing the status and contents of an individual transaction record backward or forward and between output, processing and source.

B

Balance Sheet—A condensed financial statement showing the nature and amount of an employee benefit plan's assets, liabilities and capital on a given date.

Balanced Funds—Investment companies that diversify their portfolio holdings over a wide list of common stocks, bonds and/or preferred issues.

Bankers Acceptance—Short-term loan to a bank, backed by a trade receivable.

Bankruptcy—A condition characterized by the inability to repay debts in full because the liabilities (amounts owed) exceed the assets. Legally, a *bankrupt* is an individual or corporate debtor that is judged insolvent by a court.

Basis Point—One-hundredth of a percent. There are 100 basis points in 1%.

Benchmark—An investment target used to evaluate an investment manager's rate of return.

Beneficiary—
—Person named by the participant in an insurance policy or pension plan to receive any benefits provided by the plan if the participant dies.
—A person designated by a participant, or by the terms of an employee benefit plan, who is or may become entitled to a benefit thereunder.

Benefit—The rights of the participant or beneficiary to either cash or services after meeting the eligibility requirements of the pension or other benefit plans. *Pension benefits* usually refer to monthly payments payable on retirement or disability.

Benefit Booklet—A booklet for the employee that contains a general explanation of benefits and related provisions of the health plan.

Benefit Formula—Provision in a pension plan for calculating a member's defined benefit according to years of service, earnings (career or final average), a fixed dollar amount, etc.

Benefit Fund—The monies set aside by the plan sponsor with a trustee or insurance company for the payment of benefits.

Best Earnings Formula—A defined benefit formula that applies the unit of benefit credited for each year of service to the member's average earnings for a specified period of higher earnings (e.g., best five of the last ten years of service).

Bond—
—An obligation of an insurer to protect the insured against financial loss caused by the acts of another.
—A certificate of debt (i.e., an IOU or promissory note) issued by such entities as corporations, municipalities and the government and its agencies, that represents a part of a loan to the issuer, bears a stated interest rate and matures on a stated future date. A bondholder is a creditor of the issuer and not part owner as is a stockholder. Short-term bonds, issued for five years or less, are often called *notes.*
—A long-term loan, with some type of guarantee attached, and the usually semi-annual interest payments.

Breach of Fiduciary Duty—A fiduciary's violation of a duty owed to an employee benefit plan or a participant or beneficiary in such a plan.

Breach of Trust—Violation of a duty of a trustee to a beneficiary.

Bridge Benefit—A supplemental pension benefit payable from the date of early retirement until the age of entitlement for government pensions.

Bridging Supplement—A supplemental benefit payable in addition to regular benefits under a pension plan to an employee who retires before becoming eligible for government benefits, but ceasing when OAS or CPP/QPP benefits are payable (or offset by those benefits).

Broker—
—An insurance solicitor, licensed by a province, who places business with a variety of insurance companies and who represents the buyers of insurance rather than the companies even though he or she is paid commissions by the companies.
—An agent who handles the public's orders to buy and sell securities, commodities or other property. For this service, a commission is charged that, de-pending upon the firm dealt with and the amount of the transaction, may or may not be negotiated.

Building Lien—A builder's charge or encumbrance upon property. *See also* Mechanics Lien.

By-Laws—The rules adopted by the members or by the board of directors of a corporation or other organization for its government. By-laws must not be contrary to the laws of the land and affect only the members of the given corporation or organization; they do not apply to third parties.

C

Canada Pension Plan/Quebec Pension Plan—The two major social security programs in Canada. The provisions of these two government-administered plans are virtually identical. Both are funded by employee and employer contributions on a partial pay-as-you-go basis. The Quebec Pension Plan operates in the province of Quebec; the Canada Pension Plan operates in the rest of Canada.

Canadian Association of Pension Supervisory Authorities—Consists of senior government officials (provincial and federal) responsible for the administration of pension legislation in each jurisdiction.

The Canadian Institute of Actuaries (the "CIA")—The professional regulatory body that regulates the actuarial profession in Canada, and is responsible for ensuring that the appropriate level of education, skill and expertise exists among its membership, and requires that actuaries, to be recognized and practice as such, comply with the CIA's prescribed criteria for qualification and Rules of Professional Conduct.

Capitation—A fixed pre-determined amount paid to a provider of medical or dental services for each person served, without regard to the actual number or nature of services provided to each person in a set period of time.

Career Average Formula—A defined benefit formula that applies the unit of benefit to earnings of the member in each year of service, and not to final or final average earnings.

Carry Forward—The portion of an RRSP deduction entitlement unused in a particular year may be carried forward for the following seven years. The amount carried forward is in addition to the regular RRSP contribution for that current year.

Cash Equivalents—Short-term investments held in lieu of cash and readily converted into cash within a short time span (e.g., CDs, commercial paper, Treasury bills).

Cash Withdrawal—A return of personal pension contributions to a member whose employment is terminated.

CERES Principles—A ten-point environmental reporting and accountability code previously called the Valdez Principles and now named after the U.S. Coalition for Environmentally Responsible Economies (CERES). The ten principles are intended to expand the concept of socially responsible action with an emphasis on environmental issues.

Certificate of Deposit—A written certification by a bank or a trust company that a fixed dollar amount has been deposited with it for a fixed period of time at a pre-determined rate of interest.

Certified Employee Benefit Specialist—A designation granted jointly by the International Foundation of Employee Benefit Plans and Dalhousie University of Halifax to individuals who complete ten college level courses and examinations in the areas of design and operation of employee benefit plans and who pledge to a code of ethical standards and continuing education.

Change-in-Classification Card—From time to time an employee will change his or her insurance classification and, in that case a change-in-classification card is filled out in order that the coverage can be changed and the appropriate charge made thereafter. This may happen because of a change in salary or because of a change in position, etc.

Change-of-Dependants Card—When a single employee marries or when a married employee becomes single because of the death or divorce of a spouse without children, a change-of-dependants card is filled out to advise the insurance company of this change in status.

Children's Benefits—The dependent child of a person receiving a CPP/QPP disability pension is eligible to receive a fixed monthly children's benefit. A person is a dependent child if he or she is under the age of 18 and is the natural or adopted child, or is a child in the care and control, of the contributor in receipt of the disability pension; or alternatively, if he or she is between the ages of 18 and 25 and is in full-time attendance at a recognized educational institution.

Claim Cost Control—Efforts made by an insurer both inside and outside its own organization to restrain and direct claim payments so that health insurance premium dollars are used as efficiently as possible.

Claim Reserves—Must be held by an insurance company to cover the liability that has been incurred by reason of carrying the risk to a certain point of time. Even though the risk may be discontinued at that point, claims may still be due under the terms of the contract, and other claims may not be reported until after the actual date of termination of the contract. The claim reserve must be sufficient to meet all such claims that are properly payable even though they may not be reported at the precise time of cancellation.

Claims Charged—Denotes amount of claim dollars actually charged to a group policy. If pooling or claim averaging is used to stabilize a group's experience during a single contract period, the claim expense "charged" to the group's premium in that single year may be more or less than the group's actual incurred claims.

Claims Experience—The frequency with which insured employees file claims to receive benefits. One of the primary factors used in calculating insurance premiums.

Claims Fluctuation Reserve—Insurance companies attempt to set premium rates at such a level that after deducting claims incurred and the company's retention, the balance is likely to be positive, leaving available a cash amount that, after reserves have been set up, may be refunded to the policyholder. The reserve is held to the credit of the policyholder and may be used to cover any negative results that may occur in future experience, depending on the terms of the policy.

Claims Incurred—This is the total of claims paid for the period plus changes in the reserves held for incurred but unreported, unsettled or continuing claims. It represents the estimate of the total liability created in the policy year by the plan of benefits in effect for that policy year.

Claims Incurred but Unpaid—Incurred claims that have not been paid as of some specified date (may include both reported and unreported claims).

Claims Procedure—Each employee benefit plan should provide a claims procedure, which must be explained to plan participants and beneficiaries. The denial of a claim made under the claims procedure should be in writing, with an explanation of the reasons for the denial.

Closed Panel—The provision of legal services to plan members by a limited group of lawyers, whose fees are based on a pre-determined schedule. The term also applies to a limited number of physicians or dentists who provide medical or dental services to plan members.

Coinsurance—A policy provision, frequently found in major medical insurance, by which the insured person and the insurer share the hospital and medical expenses resulting from an illness or injury in a specified ratio (e.g., 80%:20%), after the deductible is met. Also called *percentage participation clause*.

Collective Bargaining—The process of good faith negotiation between employer and employee representatives concerning issues of mutual interest.

Collective Bargaining Agreement or Contract—Formal agreement over wages, hours and conditions of employment entered into between an employer or group of employers and one or more unions representing employees of the employers.

Commercial Paper—Short-term loan to a corporation.

Commingled Closed-End Real Estate Funds—A pooling of multiple investors' capital. Rather than constantly taking in new subscribers, however, these funds set a pre-determined minimum and maximum subscription level. Once this has been achieved, the fund is closed to all new subscribers.

Commingled Funds—The collective investment of the assets of a number of small pension funds, allowing for broader and more efficient investing.

Commingled Open-End Real Estate Funds—Allows the investor to purchase units in a pool of assets. Participants buy and sell at a unit price based on appraised value of total assets. Participants can leave and enter at any time. Properties continually are added to the fund.

Commission—The broker's basic fee for purchasing or selling securities or property as an agent. This fee may or may not be negotiated.

Common Law—A body of law derived from judicial decisions, as opposed to legislatively enacted statutes and administrative regulations.

Commuted Value—Amount of an immediate lump-sum payment estimated to be equal in value to a future series of payments.

Compound Interest—Interest credited to the investor at a specified rate and on specified dates and added to the principal for the purpose of subsequent interest calculations.

Compulsory Retirement—Provision in a pension plan, collective agreement or employer's rules requiring that an employee must retire at a certain age or under other specified conditions.

Consultant—A person or firm specializing in the design, sale and service of employee benefit plans, usually representing the policyholder in placing insurance coverage with an insurer. Compensation is provided either by commissions from the insurer or by the policyholder on a fee-for-service basis, or a combination thereof.

Consumer Price Index—The name given in the United States and Canada to the series of numbers whose ratios measure the relative prices at various times of a selected group of goods and services that typify those bought by urban families.

Contingency Reserve—A reserve established to share among all policyholders the cost to the insurer of unpredictable, catastrophic losses.

Continuous Service—Period during which an employee is continuously employed by the same employer; may be defined in a pension plan (or by law) so as to include certain periods of absence and service with an associated or predecessor employer. To be distinguished from *credited service*.

Contract—A promissory agreement between two or more persons that creates, modifies or destroys a legal relation. In general, it must have the following elements: creates an obligation, competent parties, subject matter, legal consideration, mutuality of agreement, mutuality of obligation, must not be so vague or uncertain that terms are not ascertainable, and generally must be in writing signed by both parties.

Contract Holder—The group, entity or person to whom a group annuity contract is issued – in jointly administered plans, the trustees.

Contribution—A payment made into a fund by an employer and/or employee.

Contribution Holiday—Usually used in reference to pension plans, is the practice of using actuarial surplus to fund current service costs in place of contributions.

Contribution Integration—Provision for reducing the required contributions to a pension plan by contributions prescribed in the Canada Pension Plan (or QPP). To be distinguished from treatment of contributions in step-rate integration.

Contribution Rate—
—As to an employee—a factor, such as a percentage of compensation, used in determining the amounts of payments to be made by the employee under a contributory pension plan.
—As to an employer—a factor, calculated in an actuarial valuation, to be used in determining the employer's annual normal cost contribution under a pension plan. An employer's contribution rate may be either a percentage to be applied to the total compensation paid to covered employees for a particular year, or an amount in dollars to be applied to the total number of covered employees at a particular date.

Contributory Plan—A pension plan that requires the employee to make contributions by payroll deduction in order to qualify for benefits under the plan.

Conversion—Privilege given to participants to convert to individual policies on termination of group coverage without evidence of insurability.

Copayments—Payments made by consumers, in addition

to deductibles and coinsurance, to discourage inappropriate utilization and to help finance health benefit plans. *See also* Coinsurance.

Corporate Governance—The legal and practical system for the exercise and control of power in the conduct of the business of a corporation. Includes relationships among the shareholders, board of directors and committees, and the executive officers.

Corporate Trustee—A trust company or the trust department of a bank.

Cost/Benefit Analysis—A comparison of the cost of an action with the economic benefits it produces through elimination of other direct and indirect costs.

Cost-of-Living Adjustment—An across-the-board increase (or decrease) in wages or pension benefits according to the rise (or fall) in the cost of living as measured by some index, often the Consumer Price Index.

Cost Sharing—Arrangements whereby unions, employers' organizations and employee benefit plans share certain costs of administering an employee benefit plan.

Covered Service—Period of employment during which an employee is a participant in an employee benefit plan.

Credit Splitting—A provision in a pension plan or legislation entitling a spouse, on divorce or breakup, to a share of pension credits earned by the other during the marriage or thereafter.

Credited Service—A period of employment before or after the effective date of the plan that is recognized as service for one or more plan purposes, such as determination of benefit amounts. entitlement to benefits and/or vesting.

Current Service—Period of service of an employee after becoming a member of a pension plan. *Current service cost* usually refers to the cost of benefits credited to members of a plan in a given year.

Custodial Arrangement—Simple warehousing of securities by a bank or a trust company for purposes of safekeeping. The bank or trust company may collect income and do simple reporting on the value of the assets.

Custodian—The organization (usually a bank or trust company) that holds in custody and safekeeping the securities and other assets of a trust fund.

D

Death Benefit—The payment made to designated beneficiaries upon the death of a participating employee.

Debenture—A long-term loan with, usually, semi-annual interest payments.

Deed—A written instrument, signed, sealed and delivered according to the applicable law, containing some transfer, bargain or contract with respect to property; the common term for an instrument transferring the ownership of real property.

Deferred Compensation Plan—Arrangement by which compensation to employees for past or current service is postponed until some future date. Pension and profit-sharing plans are tax-favoured deferred compensation plans.

Deferred Profit-Sharing Plan—Type of profit-sharing plan defined in the *Income Tax Act,* often used as a defined contribution pension plan. Employee contributions are not deductible from income for tax purposes.

Deferred Vested Pension (Annuity)—A specified pension determined at the time of termination of employment or termination of a plan but not payable until some later date, usually normal retirement age.

Defined Benefit Plan—A plan that defines the pension to be provided (based on service, average earnings, etc.) but not the total contributions. If a plan is contributory, the rate of employee contributions may be specified, with the employer paying the balance of cost. To be distinguished from *Defined Contribution Plan.*

Defined Contribution (Money Purchase) Plan—A plan that defines contributions to be made by employer and possibly employees, but not the benefit formula. Accumulated contributions and interest are used to purchase an annuity for the member. To be distinguished from *Defined Benefit Plan.*

Delinquent Contributions—Failure by a participating employer to make promised payments to a multi-employer benefit fund.

Demographic Projection—An estimate of the future size and composition of the population, based on past and current census data and assumptions as to birth and death rates, immigration, etc.

Dental Capitation Plan—Particular types of dental services are provided by a closed panel of dentists for a fixed per capita fee.

Dependants—Generally the spouse and children of a covered individual, as defined in a contract. Under some contracts, parents or other members of the family may be dependants.

Dependent Child's Benefit—Under the Canada Pension Plan (or QPP), a monthly amount payable to each dependent child of a disability pensioner or deceased contributor.

Deposit Administration—A contract with an insurance company to administer a pension plan, but with the employer responsible for solvency until funds are used to purchase annuities, usually at the time of retirement.

Directed Commissions—Those commissions charged by a broker for executing securities transactions that are placed by the investment manager with a particular broker, or brokers, resulting from instructions received from the client of the manager.

Disability—A physical or mental condition that makes an insured person incapable of performing one or more duties of his or her occupation.

Disability Benefit—Periodic payments, usually monthly, payable to participants under some retirement plans if such participants are eligible for the benefits and become totally and permanently disabled prior to the normal retirement date.

Disability Income Insurance—These plans pay a periodic cash amount, for example, 70% of normal earnings. Short-term plans begin benefits the first day off work, or soon after, and continue payments for a limited number of weeks. Long-term plans normally start benefits three to six months after the onset of disability and continue payments for a stated term or to a stipulated age.

Diversification—The spreading of risk by buying several different investments.

Diversification Duration—
—Weighted average term to maturity of cash flows of an investment.
—A measure of volatility (risk).

Division of Pension Credits—Also known as *credit splitting,* a provision in the Canada Pension Plan (and QPP) whereby one spouse, on dissolution of marriage, may obtain an equal division of pension credits earned by one or both partners during the period of marriage.

Dollar-Weighted Rate of Return—
—This method of calculating rate of return is affected by the amount and the timing of cash flows during a given time period. This rate is an effective measure of the fund's rate of growth, giving full weight to the impact of cash flows on fund assets. The dollar-weighted rate also is referred to as the *internal, discounted cash flow* or the *real rate of return.*
—Assesses what happened to all money available to a given fund during a given period. As such, it is the best way of assessing the actual condition of the fund at any point, but it may not accurately reflect

the skill of the investment manager, since he or she has no control over cash flows (deposits, etc.) as to either timing or amount. Compare with *time-weighted rate of return.*

Drop-Out Months—Under the Canada Pension Plan, certain low earnings months that are not counted in calculating average contributory earnings on which the contributor's pension is based.

E

Early Retirement—Provision in a pension plan for retirement earlier than the normal pension age. The amount of pension credited under the plan formula may be reduced according to the member's attained age; or an unreduced pension may be payable if a specified service condition (e.g., 30 years) has been met.

Earnings—A person's money income from employment or self-employment; usually excludes such forms of income as rents or bond interest. In some pension plans certain bonuses, sick pay, etc., may be excluded in calculating benefits.

Earnings-Related Plan—Any plan with a benefit formula based on earnings (as opposed to a *flat benefit plan*). Includes career average and final average plans.

Economically Targeted Investing (ETI)—Investing the plan's money in an investment vehicle that directly affects the employment environment of the industries in which the participants of the plan are employed, or bolsters the economy by creating jobs or affordable housing, for example. *See also* Socially Responsible Investments.

Eligibility Date—A period of time, usually 31 days, when potential members of a group life or health insurance plan can enroll without evidence of insurability.

Eligibility Requirements—
—Conditions that an employee must satisfy to participate in a plan.
—Conditions that an employee must satisfy to obtain a benefit.

Employee Assistance Program (EAP)—An employment-based health service program designed to assist in the identification and resolution of a broad range of employee personal concerns that may affect job performance. These programs deal with situations such as substance abuse, marital problems, family troubles, stress and domestic violence, as well as health education and disease prevention. The assistance may be provided within the organization or by referral to outside resources.

Employees Profit-Sharing Plan—A plan, defined in the

Income Tax Act, under which employer contributions must be declared as income by the employee, and employee contributions are not deductible. Benefit payments out of the fund are generally tax-free.

Entry Age Normal—A costing method used in arriving at a level premium cost for a group. It bases costs on the average career of employees from an assumed average age of entry into the plan to normal retirement age.

Equities—Refers to ownership of property, usually in the form of common stocks, as distinguished from fixed income-bearing securities, such as bonds or mortgages.

Errors and Omissions Insurance—Liability insurance for employee benefit plans, trustees, administrators and professionals, in the event of an error or omission committed in the administration of an employee benefit plan.

Excess Earnings—Earnings from investments of a pension fund in excess of an assumed or expected rate of return.

Experience—Refers to the premium/claim history of a given risk. The larger the risk, the more valid the ratio of claims to premiums. Generally, used to calculate renewal rates.

Experience Deficiency—An unfunded liability, revealed by an actuarial review of a pension plan, resulting from a difference between actual experience (investment earnings, salary levels, etc.) and assumptions made at the time of a previous valuation.

Experience-Rated Premium Rates—Premium rates for a group coverage that are based, wholly or partially, on the past claims experience of the group to which they will apply.

Experience Rating—The process of determining the premium rate for a group risk wholly or partially on the basis of that risk experience.

Experience Refund—The amount of premium returned by an insurer to a group policyholder when the financial experience of the particular group (or the experience refund class to which the group belongs) has been more favourable than anticipated in the premiums collected from the group.

Extended Medical Expense—This term refers to a medical plan that has a deductible and/or reimburses covered expenses at some percentage less than 100%. These plans are in addition to the provincial medical coverage. This is sometimes referred to as *major medical.*

F

Fiduciary—
—Indicates the relationship of trust and confidence where one person (the *fiduciary*) holds or controls property for the benefit of another person. For example, the relationship between a trustee and the beneficiaries of an employee benefit plan trust fund.

—One who acts in a capacity of trust and who is therefore accountable for whatever actions may be construed by the courts as breaching that trust. Fiduciaries must discharge their duties solely in the interests of the participants and beneficiaries of an employee benefit plan. In addition, a fiduciary must act exclusively for the purpose of providing benefits to participants and beneficiaries and defraying reasonable expenses of the plan.

Fiduciary Liability Insurance—A form of errors and omissions insurance.

Fifty Percent Rule—Each jurisdiction in Canada has some variation on the 50% Rule. The rule applies where a defined benefit plan is wound up. In essence, the "50% rule" compares a member's contributions, including interest, from a *set date* to the date of wind-up, against the total benefit credit accrued in that period. Where the contributions exceed 50% of the credit, the member is entitled to certain benefits based on this excess.

Final Average (Earnings) Formula—A defined benefit formula that applies the unit of benefit credited for each year of service to the member's average earnings for a specified number of years just before retirement.

Final Earnings Formula—A defined benefit formula that applies the unit of benefit credited for each year of service to the member's final salary rate or annual earnings immediately before retirement.

Final Pay Plan—Term commonly used for any pension plan whose benefits are based on earnings in a member's last years of service.

Fixed Annuity—An annuity contract in which the insurance company makes fixed (or guaranteed) dollar payments to the annuitant for the term of the contract (usually until the annuitant dies).

Flat Benefit Formula—A defined benefit formula that specifies a dollar amount of pension to be credited for each year of service. Term should be distinguished from *Flat Rate Pension.*

Flat Rate Pension—A defined benefit expressed as a dollar amount of monthly pension, not related to service or earnings, but paid on retirement after meeting certain qualifying conditions.

Foreign Property Rule—The limit imposed on pension fund investments in foreign assets set by the *Income Tax Act* expressed as a percentage of total plan assets.

The limit was increased from 20% to 30% in the February 2000 federal budget.

Fully Funded—Term describing a plan that, at a given time, has sufficient assets to provide for all pensions and other benefits in respect of service up to that date.

Fund—Used as a verb, *fund* means to pay over to a funding agency (to fund future pension and other benefits). Used as a noun, *fund* refers to assets accumulated for the purpose of paying benefits as they become due.

Fund Earnings—Earnings that return to a benefit trust fund for reinvestment or payment of benefits.

Funded Ratio—Ratio of the assets of a pension plan to its liabilities.

Funding—Systematic payments into a fund that, with investment earnings, are expected to provide for all pensions and other benefits as they become payable.

Future Service—Describes the service from the date of entry into the plan or from the date of calculation to normal retirement date.

Future Service Benefits—Benefits accruing for service after the effective date of coverage under the plan.

G

Garnishment—A court order to an employer to withhold all or part of an employee's wages and send the money to the court or to a person who has won a lawsuit against the employee

Generally Accepted Accounting Principles (GAAP)—Uniform minimum standards of and guidelines to financial accounting and reporting, which govern form and content of financial statements. GAAP encompass principles necessary to define accepted accounting practice at a particular time and include detailed procedures as well as broad guidelines.

Going-Concern Basis—Refers to the assumption, when making an actuarial valuation, that the pension plan will continue in operation indefinitely.

Grace Period—A specified period after a premium payment is due, in which the policyholder may make such payment, and during which the protection of the policy continues.

Group Annuity—A contract under which an insurance company agrees to provide retirement pensions to members of a group.

Grow-In—A benefit conferred upon members of plans registered in Nova Scotia and Ontario whose age plus years of service equal at least 55 when their plan winds up. The grow-in right allows the member to "grow into" certain benefits that the member would have at-

tained had he or she continued in service had the plan not been terminated.

Guaranteed Annuity—An annuity that will be paid for the lifetime of a person, but in any event for a minimum period; e.g., if annuity is guaranteed for five years and the annuitant dies after three years, payments will be continued to a beneficiary or the estate for two years.

Guaranteed Income Supplement—A monthly payment under the federal *Old Age Security Act* to needy recipients of the OAS pension, based on a guaranteed minimum income amount.

Guaranteed Investment Contract—An investment contract entered into with an insurance company that guarantees the repayment of principal and a compound interest return. Terms of the contract and maturities vary from company to company and, over time, within the same company.

H

Hour Bank—
—A method of banking or crediting the hours worked by a worker to his or her individual account and then drawing out the required hours at each determination date, to establish or maintain the worker's eligibility for health insurance benefits.
—A variation of the system puts only the hours (or some portion of the hours) worked in excess of those required to maintain current eligibility in the hour bank account. Hour bank provisions usually specify the maximum number of hours that can be held in the account.

I

Immediate Annuity—An annuity under which income payments begin one annuity period (e.g., one month or one year) after the annuity is purchased.

Immediate Vesting—That form of vesting under which rights to vested benefits are acquired by a participant, commencing immediately upon his or her entry into the plan.

Income (Personal)—Generally, all monies received by or credited to a person; may be defined to include receipt of certain goods or services, as well as non-earned income (interest, rents, etc.). For purposes of income tax and government support programs, some forms of income may be excluded; or certain deductions may be allowed in computing net income.

Income Supplement—A regular payment made to a person, usually on the basis of need or other special circumstances, in addition to other income such as earnings or pensions.

Income Test—Method by which the income of a person or family is taken into account in determining eligibility for (or amount of) a payment under a government program.

Indemnity—A benefit paid by an insurer for a loss insured under a policy.

Indexing—Provision for periodically adjusting a benefit amount (usually after retirement) according to a formula based on a recognized index of price or wage levels, e.g., the Consumer Price Index.

Individual Account Plan—A defined contribution plan that allows participants to choose from a broad range of investment options how their own accounts will be invested.

Individual Annuity—Annuity purchased for an individual and held in trust by the employer until the person's retirement. Plan may be referred to as a *pension trust.*

Individual Pension Plan—A personalized, employer-sponsored registered pension plan that provides a guaranteed lifetime pension. When used with an RRSP, the plan can boost tax-sheltered retirement savings. The plan can be structured in either defined benefit or defined contribution format; it is used primarily for executives.

Injunction—A judicial process by which a party is required to do a particular thing or to refrain from doing a particular thing. Imposed when the complaining party will suffer irreparable injury as a result of unlawful actions by the other party.

Institutional Investor—An organization the primary purpose of which is to invest its own assets or those held in trust by it for others. Includes pension funds, investment companies, universities and banks.

Insured Pension Plan—A plan in which all benefits are purchased from and guaranteed by an insurance company as contributions are received.

Integrated Contribution Limit—The cornerstone of the current tax regime relating to retirement savings is the *integrated contribution limit* that applies to RPPs, DPSPs and RRSPs. The limit is the maximum amount that can be contributed in total to tax-assisted retirement savings vehicles and is expressed as a percentage of *earned income,* subject to the annual *money purchase limit,* which is an absolute dollar limit.

Integration—Provision in a pension plan that relates plan contributions and/or benefits to those of a government pension program, e.g., Canada Pension Plan. Not to be confused with *Level Income Option.*

Investment Consultant—An individual or firm that provides investment advice for a fixed fee, a fee based upon a percentage of assets or a fee derived from brokerage commission. Such advice generally includes analyzing portfolio constraints, setting performance objectives, counselling on allocation of assets, educating the investment manager, and selecting and monitoring services. It may or may not include performance measurement services.

Investment Earnings—Investment income on contributions, which is not normally subject to income tax for employee benefit plans but that may be taxable in certain circumstances.

Investment Policy—A document describing how contributions to an employee benefit plan are utilized from the time they are received until benefits are paid. This document should include, among other things, the goals and objectives of the plan and identify the nature of the plan's liabilities. The written policy should state investment guidelines covering such matters as investment portfolio diversification, including the aggregate and individual investment limits, asset mix policy and rate-of-return expectations, categories and subcategories of investments, and loans that may be made, lending of cash or securities, retention or delegation of voting rights acquired through investments, a conflict-of-interest policy in respect of investments, etc.

Investment Return (Yield)—Earnings of a pension fund including interest on fixed income securities (bonds, mortgages, etc.), dividends, capital gains, etc.

J

Joint Administration—Provision for a union-management committee or board of trustees to assume supervisory functions relating to administration of an employee benefit plan.

Joint and Survivor Annuity—A pension payable until the death of both the retired employee and his or her spouse. Required in all Canadian jurisdictions to be provided as an option at the time of retirement. Some pension plans provide for a level amount of pension. Some jurisdictions allow a reduction in the pension when either one of the couple dies, whereas others allow a reduction only on the death of the retired employee. Some jurisdictions allow both forms of reduction.

Joint Beneficiary—Person or persons legally entitled to share in the proceeds of an insurance policy.

L

Lapsed Policy—A group master contract that has automatically expired, as provided by its terms, due to non-payment of premium.

Level Income Option—Also referred to as a *notched option:* provision for employee, at time of retirement, to elect an increased pension, subject to a reduction by a specified amount when the retiree becomes eligible for pension under a government program.

Level Premium—A premium that remains unchanged throughout the life of a policy. In a level premium plan, reserves accumulate in the early years of the policy because the actual cost of coverage is less than the premium charged.

Level Premium Funding—Funding method in which equal annual payments, per employee or a percentage of payroll, are contributed to a pension fund over the estimated working life of employees in a pension plan to fund all benefits under the plan. To be distinguished from *single premium funding.*

Lien—A lien created under a statute to assist workers and suppliers in collecting overdue wages, employee benefit plan contributions, money due on account of the supply of materials and services. The real property of the owner in relation to which the services and materials were provided becomes subject to a lien in the event of non-payment. Provincial and federal laws vary as to procedures and the degree of protection accorded.

Life Annuity—A series of payments under which payments, once begun, continue throughout the remaining lifetime of the annuitant. Under this form of annuity, there is no further benefit payment of any kind after the death of the annuitant.

Life Expectancy—Number of years a person of given sex and age is expected to live, based on statistics of mortality.

Liquidity—
—An actuarial concept that prescribes that sufficient cash, or cash-like securities, be available at times of disbursement for retirement, disability or separation.
—The ease at which an investment can be sold.

Loading—An amount added to the estimated cost of a pension plan to provide for expenses of a variable or minor nature; e.g., special retirement pensions, trustee fees.

Locking-In—Requirement under legislation that pension contributions made after a certain date cannot be withdrawn or otherwise forfeited if the employee on termination of employment has attained a certain age or has completed a certain period of service or plan membership.

Long-Term Disability—Income protection in the event of time lost due to sickness or accident of a long-term nature. Generally, monthly payments commence after a specified waiting period and continue while the employee remains disabled—usually up to age 65.

Loss-of-Income Benefits—Payments made to an insured person to help replace income lost through inability to work because of an insured disability.

M

Mandatory Pension Plan—An employment pension plan that employers are required by law to establish and maintain for their employees.

Market Value—The price an investor will pay for each share of common stock at any given time. Market value is determined by the laws of supply and demand.

Master Trust—A pooling of directed and/or discretionary trusts (a *discretionary trust* is one in which the bank is trustee and also has investment responsibility for all or part of the assets). The "pure" definition is pooling of one sponsor's assets that include multiple managers and multiple plans under one trust agreement.

Matching Contributions—Made by an employer to a plan on an employee's behalf when the employee makes elective or nonelective contributions.

Maximum Pension Rule for Defined Benefit Plans—The maximum pension rule applies to limit the yearly benefit accrual for individuals under a defined benefit plan. The rule dictates that the maximum pension that can be provided under a defined benefit provision is to be calculated as the lower of 2% × member's years of service × member's highest average compensation, or the defined benefit limit × years of service.

Means Test—Method by which a person's assets as well as income are taken into account in determining eligibility for or amount of payment under a government program.

Mechanic's Lien—A lien created under statute to assist labourers and suppliers in collecting their accounts and wages. It subjects the real property of the owner to a lien in the event of non-payment for contracted improvements. Provincial laws vary as to procedures and the degree of protection accorded. *See also* Building Lien.

Money Market—Short-term investments such as Treasury bills and commercial paper.

Money Purchase Plan—A type of defined contribution plan. Considered the reverse of a *Defined Benefit Plan.* The cost in a money purchase plan is fixed, and the pension benefit is variable. The contribution to the plan is normally expressed as a percentage of salary with the employer making an equal matching contribution (subject to statutory limitations).

Contributions are accumulated with interest and are used to purchase an annuity from an insurer when pension age is reached.

Mortality Table—A table showing expected rates of death at various ages for people born in various periods. Used by actuaries to arrive at mortality assumptions when estimating the cost of pensions for a group. Term *unisex* is used when mortality estimates for males and females are combined in a single table.

Mortgage-Backed Security—A loan to a financial institution. The interest and principal payments are tied to mortgages held as collateral.

Multi-Employer Plan—A plan, established through collective bargaining or by statute, that covers employees of two or more financially unrelated employers. A common fund is used for accumulating contributions and paying benefits. An employee's service with any of the contributing employers counts toward benefit eligibility unless a *break in service* (as defined by the plan) cancels credits earned before the break.

N

Needs Test—Method of assessing a person's or family's expenditure requirements (shelter, food, fuel, etc.) in relation to other income or means, to determine amount of income support to be provided under a government program (e.g., in most provincial family benefit programs).

Net Replacement Ratio—Measurement of adequacy of retirement income by relating it to income immediately before retirement, taking into account income taxes, tax credits, etc.

Non-Contributory—A term used to describe when employees do not contribute to an employee benefit plan and the employer pays the entire cost.

Normal Cost—Amount of annual contribution required to pay for the current service cost of a pension plan. Term usually refers to a level premium, based on a "normal" age assumption (e.g., entry age normal).

Normal Form of Benefit—Amount and other features of the annuity (pension) payable on retirement unless the plan member elects an optional form of benefit.

Normal Pension—Amount of pension, according to the benefit formula, to which an employee is or would be entitled on reaching normal retirement age, based on earnings and/or service.

Normal Retirement—A termination of employment involving the payment of a regular formula retirement allowance without reduction because of age or service and with special qualification such as disability.

O

Offset—Generally, the amount of one type of benefit used to reduce the amount of another benefit payable to a person, e.g., a disability pension where disability insurance benefits are provided by the same employer.

Offset Integration—Provision in a pension plan for directly reducing a plan benefit by all or a portion of pensions payable to the individual from a government program.

Old Age Security—Federal government program providing a universal, flat rate pension to all residents age 65 and over, regardless of need; also provides income-tested supplements.

Optional Form of Benefit—Form of annuity that a plan member may elect on retirement, differing from the normal form of benefit in amount and other conditions but of actuarially equivalent value.

Orphan Benefits—The child of a deceased contributor who met the minimum contribution eligibility requirements is entitled to monthly orphan benefits under CPP/QPP. Like the children's benefit, the orphan's benefit is paid until the child reaches the age of 18 or, alternatively, if the person is between the ages of 18 and 25, so long as he or she is in full-time attendance at a recognized educational institution.

P

Participant-Directed Plan—A plan under which participants determine the investment of their account balance.

Participating Annuity—A form of annuity in which the contractual amount of regular payments may be increased to reflect investment returns that are higher than originally assumed.

Participation Agreement—A written agreement between the trustees of a benefit plan and each participating employer that establishes the employer's contractual obligation to contribute to the plan fund.

Passive Management—A style of investment management that seeks to attain average risk-adjusted performance.

Past Service—Period of service of an employee before becoming a member of a pension plan. Term may be used to define certain benefits that differ from those for current service (future service).

Past Service Benefit—Credit toward a pension, provided by the employer, for all or part of a participant's years of service with the company before the adoption or amendment of a pension plan, or before the employee's entry into the plan.

Past Service Pension Adjustments (PSPAs)—In addition to the benefit earned by a member for the current year (reflected in the member's PA), pension benefits may improve as a result of events related to past service. These "past service events" occur when, for periods of past service, benefits are increased retroactively; an additional period of past service is credited to the member; or there is a retroactive change to the way a member's benefits are determined. When any of these events occur, the value of the pension accrued is increased and gives rise to a past service pension adjustment (PSPA). A PSPA is equal to the additional **pension credits** that would have been included in the member's PA if the upgraded benefits or additional service had actually been provided in those previous years.

Pay-as-You-Go Plan—Term used for benefits that are not funded except as and when they are paid to individuals; i.e., payment is made from current revenue or other sources outside the plan as such.

Pension Adjustment (PA)—The value of pension benefits accruing to a plan member during a year as defined in the *Income Tax Act*. The PA is subtracted from the member's comprehensive retirement contribution limit (18% of pay, subject to specified dollar limits) to determine the maximum RRSP contribution allowed for the following year.

Pension Adjustment Reversal (PAR)—Under a defined benefit provision, a PAR is an amount that will restore lost registered retirement savings plan (RRSP) contribution room to an individual. This applies when the individual receives a termination benefit that is less than the individual's total pension adjustments (PAs) and past service pension adjustments (PSPAs). Under a deferred profit-sharing plan (DPSP) or a money purchase provision, an individual's PAR is the amount included in his or her pension credits but to which the individual ceases to have any rights at termination.

Pension Benefit Formula—The basis for determining payments to which participants may be entitled under a pension plan. Pension benefit formulas usually refer to the employee's service or compensation or both.

Pension Plan—A plan organized and administered to provide a regular income for the lifetime of retired members; other benefits that may be provided include payments on permanent disability, death, etc.

Pensionable Earnings—Defined portion of an individual's total earnings, used in calculating pension entitlement (e.g., excluding certain bonuses).

Plan Document (Text)—This document sets forth the benefits available under an employee benefit plan and the eligibility requirements. This document is often separate from the trust agreement in order to allow plan modifications without frequent trust agreement amendments.

Plan Liabilities—Include normal costs, accrued liability, past service liabilities and experience losses. Plan liabilities are to be determined under the funding method used generally to determine costs under the plan. Experience gains and any decreases in plan benefits that reduce plan liabilities are also subject to this rule. Plan costs must be determined on the basis of actuarial assumptions that, in the aggregate, are reasonable.

Plan Participant—Any employee or former employee of an employer, member or former member of an employee organization, sole proprietor or partner in a partnership who is or may become eligible to receive a benefit of any type from an employee benefit plan, or whose beneficiaries may be eligible to receive any such benefit.

Plan Sponsor—The party that establishes and maintains the plan, which is (1) the employer, in the case of an employee benefit plan maintained by a single employer; (2) the employee organization, in the case of a plan maintained by an employee organization; or (3) the association, committee, joint board of trustees or other similar group of representatives of the parties involved, in the case of a plan maintained by one or more employers and one or more employee organizations.

Plan Termination—Discontinuance of an employment pension plan, voluntary or involuntary (e.g., as in bankruptcy); wind-up procedure regulated by pension benefits legislation.

Portability—Any provision for retaining pension rights when changing from one employer to another. Vested rights are non-forfeitable.

Postponed (Late) Retirement—Retirement of a member later than the time prescribed for normal retirement.

Preferred Share—A share whose dividend is paid before common share dividends.

Premium Refund—Premium returned to a policyholder (usually because of favourable experience; i.e., an experience rating refund).

Premium Tax—An assessment levied by a provincial government on the net premium income collected in a particular province by an insurer.

Present Value—Amount of money that, if invested today at a given rate of compound interest, would provide a defined benefit commencing at a specified future date.

Priorities (Plan Termination)—A set of rules, in an employment pension plan or legislation, under which the assets of a plan that is discontinued are allocated among members and beneficiaries to provide as far as possible for all accrued benefits.

Private Health Services Plan— Defined in Section 248 of the *Income Tax Act;* essentially refers to a contract of insurance in respect of hospital expenses, medical expenses or any combination of such expenses, or a medical care insurance plan or hospital care insurance plan or any combination of such plans.

Proof of Loss—Documentary evidence required by an insurer to prove a valid claim exists. In group life insurance, it usually consists of a completed claim form and proof of death (death certificate or acceptable substitute); in group medical care insurance, it usually consists of a completed claim form and itemized medical bills.

Provisionally Funded—In pension benefits legislation, term used to describe a pension plan that is not fully funded but is "solvent"; i.e., current service costs are being met year by year, and special payments are being made to amortize all unfunded liabilities.

Proxy—A written authorization given by a shareholder to someone else to vote his or her shares at a stockholders' annual or special meeting called to elect directors or for some other corporate purpose.

Prudent Person Rule—A common law standard applicable to the administration and investment of trust funds. Briefly stated:

> All that can be required of a trustee in the administration and investment of trust funds is that he conduct himself faithfully and exercise sound discretion. He is to observe how men of prudence, discretion and intelligence manage their own affairs, or those of others, not in regard to speculation, but in regard to the permanent disposition of their funds, considering the probable income as well as the probable safety of the capital to be invested.

Public Sector Plan—An employment pension plan offered by an employer in the public sector, covering civil servants, teachers, municipal employees, etc.

Q

Qualification Period—The period of time between the beginning of a disability and the start of a policy's benefits.

R

Reciprocal Agreement—An agreement between two or more employee benefit plans, under which service with any signatory plan will be recognized for purposes such as (1) satisfying minimum service requirements for plan participation; (2) fulfilling minimum service requirements for benefit entitlement; (3) preventing a break in continuous service; or (4) accumulating benefit credits. The two principal types are the *pro rata agreement,* under which each plan pays its appropriate share of pension benefits, and the *money-follows-the-man agreement,* under which employer contributions are remitted to the participant's home or terminal fund, which then pays the full retirement benefit.

Registered Pension Plan—An employment pension plan accepted for registration for tax purposes under the *Income Tax Act,* and/or for registration under applicable federal or provincial pension benefits legislation.

Registered Retirement Income Fund (RRIF)—Governed by Section 146.3 of the *Income Tax Act,* it is an arrangement between an authorized person or corporation (the "carrier") and an individual, under which the carrier accepts property from an RRSP (or another RRIF) of which the individual is the annuitant and undertakes to pay to the annuitant (or his or her spouse, as the successor annuitant; or his or her estate in lump-sum, in prescribed circumstances) an annual amount determined by a prescribed formula whereby the assets of the fund will have been paid or distributed in total in the year the annuitant reaches 90 years of age.

Registered Retirement Savings Plan (RRSP)—A contractual arrangement registered under Section 146 of the *Income Tax Act* between an individual and an insurer, trust company or corporation authorized (as prescribed in Section 146(1)(j)) to accept payments (contributions) from an individual (the "annuitant") or his or her spouse for the purpose of providing a retirement income for that individual or his or her spouse by, upon maturation of the plan, purchase of a prescribed form of annuity or transfer of the plan assets to a registered retirement income fund (RRIF). Subject to prescribed maximums, such contributions made by a resident of Canada having (Part I) earned income are deductible for income tax purposes.

Reinsurance—The acceptance by one or more insurers, called *reinsurers,* of a portion of the risk underwritten by another insurer that has contracted for the entire coverage.

Reserves—In group insurance, reserves are normally two types: (1) claim reserves and (2) special (or contingency) reserves. *Claim reserves* are for claims that have occurred but not yet been reported or that are unsettled or continuing (open) in nature. *Special reserves* are used to accomplish specific goals. They include premium stabilization reserves, rate reduction reserves, special risk reserves, retired life insurance reserves, etc.

Residual—The remaining part of a debenture after all interest payments have been stripped from it.

Retention—That portion of the premium retained by the insurer for expenses, contingencies and profits or contribution to surplus.

Retirement—Withdrawal from the active work force because of age; may also be used in the sense of permanent withdrawal from the labour force for any reason, including disability.

Retirement Compensation Arrangement—A funded supplementary pension arrangement that provides retirement benefits, but is not a registered pension plan.

Retirement Income—Income from pensions and other sources to which a retired person is entitled. Term may include both private and public pension payments, income from personal savings, government income supplements and imputed income (e.g., free health insurance premiums).

Rider—An amendment that modifies the terms of the group contract or certificates of insurance. It may increase or decrease benefits, waive a condition or coverage, or in any way amend the original contract.

Risk—The possibility of losing money on an investment. The volatility of rates of return.

S

Safe Harbour Rules—Regulations that describes certain acts or behaviours that will not be illegal under a specific law, even though they might otherwise be illegal. Typically this refers to federal regulations that specify conduct exempt from the fraud and abuse laws.

Securities Lending—A practice whereby owners of securities either directly or indirectly lend their securities to primarily brokerage firms for a fee, and against which either cash, securities or a letter of credit is pledged to protect the lender. Securities are borrowed to cover fails of deliveries or short sales, provide proper denominations and enable brokerage firms to engage in arbitrage trading activities.

Security—Any note, stock, Treasury stock, bond, debenture, evidence of indebtedness, certificate of interest or participation in any profit-sharing agreement, collateral trust certificate, pre-organization certificate or subscription, transferable share, investment contract, voting trust certificate, certificate of deposit for security, fractional undivided interest in oil, gas or other mineral rights or, in general, any interest or instrument commonly known as a security, or any certificate of interest or participation in, temporary or interim certificate for, receipt for, guarantee of, or warrant or right to subscribe to or purchase any of the foregoing.

Segregated Fund—Assets of a pension plan held by an insurance company for investment management only; funds are segregated from assets of the insurance company, and principal and interest are not guaranteed.

Self-Directed Investment—Any plan in which plan participants control the investment of their accounts.

Self-Insurance (Self-Funding)—A fully non-insured or self-insured plan is one in which no insurance company or service plan collects premiums and assumes risk. In a sense, the employer is acting as an insurance company—paying claims with the money ordinarily earmarked for premiums. Regardless of the specific self-funding technique a firm chooses, it will need to either buy its administrative services (ASO) outside the company or develop them in-house. Hence, self-funded arrangements are referenced as ASO or self-administered.

Single Employer Plan—A pension plan maintained by one employer. Also, the term may be used to describe a plan maintained by related parties such as a parent and its subsidiaries.

Socially Responsible Investments—Generally considered to include those investments that (1) carry a lesser rate of return and/or, (2) have a lower credit rating and quality and/or (3) have less liquidity or marketability than other forms of investment or specific investments readily available in the marketplace, but that will (1) create employment opportunities for plan participants and/or (2) have a greater social or moral quality.

Also includes "socially sensitive" investments that otherwise are equal to other investments when compared by traditional financial analysis, but have favourable non-economic characteristics. Socially responsible investments are known as *divergent, target* and *political investments.*

Social Security—Term used to refer to a system of government programs providing for income security of individuals, especially the aged, disabled, etc. In Canada, the term as applied to the elderly usually includes Old Age Security, income supplements (federal and provincial), the Canada and Quebec Pension Plans; may include other income support programs.

Soft Dollars—The portion of a plan's commissions expense incurred in the buying and selling of securities that is allocated through a directed brokerage arrangement for the purpose of acquiring goods or services for the benefit of the plan. In many soft dollar arrangements, the payment scheme is effected through a brokerage affiliate of the consultant.

Solvency—In a pension plan, the ability of the plan to meet its present and future obligations; the adequacy of provisions for funding.

Split Funding—The use of two or more funding agencies for the same pension plan. In some cases, part of the contributions to the plan is paid to a life insurance company and the remainder is invested through a corporate trustee, generally in equities.

Spouse's Benefit—Payments to the surviving spouse of a deceased employee, usually in the form of a series of payments upon meeting certain requirements and usually terminating with the survivor's remarriage or death. Refer to *Joint and Survivor Annuity*.

Stock—Common stock or share. A part ownership of a company.

Stop-Loss Insurance—Contract established between a self-insured group and an insurance carrier providing carrier coverage if claims exceed a specified dollar amount over a set period of time.

Straight Life Annuity—An annuity that is payable only during the lifetime of the annuitant; i.e., it is not guaranteed to be paid for a minimum period and no part of it is payable to another person after the annuitant's death.

Strip—An interest payment that has been separated from the original debenture.

Subrogation—The acquiring by the insurer of the insured's rights against third parties for the indemnification of a loss to the extent that the insurer pays the loss.

Supplemental Benefits—Benefits provided by a pension plan in addition to regular retirement benefits. Supplemental benefits vary according to the terms of a plan and include such items as the payment of benefits in the event of terminations, death, disability or early retirement.

Surplus—The excess of the value of the assets of a pension fund related to a pension plan over the value of the liabilities under the pension plan, both calculated in the prescribed manner. The assets of a pension fund minus its liabilities, the latter being the present value of all accrued pension benefits promised under the plan.

Surviving Spouse's Pension—A monthly benefit payable under a pension plan to the surviving spouse of a deceased employee or pensioner; usually refers to a benefit other than payments under a guaranteed annuity or joint and survivor annuity.

Suspended Pensions—Refers to the suspension of a re-

tiree pension when the individual returns to work with the same employer, or with respect to MEPPs in some provinces, within the same industry.

T

Tax Credit—Provision for a reduction of income tax payable (not a deduction from taxable income) by an amount of other taxes payable or a portion of housing or other expenses of the taxpayer; e.g., Ontario tax credits. Tax credit is said to be "refundable" if it is payable to a person with no taxable income.

Tax Deferral—Provision in the *Income Tax Act* whereby certain pension and similar contributions are tax deductible and employer contributions and investment income are not included in a member's current taxable income; but benefit payments are considered income for tax purposes in the year in which they are received.

Treasury Bill—Short-term loan to a government.

Trust—A legal entity that is created when a person or organization transfers assets to a trustee for the benefit of designated persons.

Trust Agreement (Trust Deed)—An agreement that spells out the methods of receipt, investment and disbursement of funds under an employee benefit plan. It contains provisions for investment powers of trustees; irrevocability and non-diversion of trust assets; payment of legal, trustee and other fees relative to the plan; clauses pertaining to the liability of trustees; periodic reports to the employer or union by the trustees; records and accounts to be maintained by the trustees; conditions for removal, resignation or replacement of trustees; benefit payments under the plan; and the rights and duties of the trustees and/or parties in the case of amendment or termination of the plan. The plan agreement is often separate from the trust.

Trust Fund—A fund whose assets are managed by a trustee or a board of trustees for the benefit of another party or parties. Restrictions as to what the trustee may invest the assets of the trust fund in are usually found in the trust instrument and applicable provincial and federal laws.

Trustee—
—A person, bank or trust company designated in a trust agreement as having responsibility for holding and investing plan contributions (and possibly having responsibility over other financial aspects of the plan).
—One who acts in a capacity of trust as a fiduciary and to whom property has been conveyed for the benefit of another party.

Trusteed Pension Plan—An employment pension plan

whose funds are held and invested by trustees, and the plan sponsor is responsible for making sufficient contributions to maintain the plan's solvency. Benefits are not insured except to the extent annuities are purchased.

U

Underwriter—Anyone who undertakes to provide future payments (e.g., pensions, disability benefits, etc.) in certain specified circumstances, in return for premiums paid by or on behalf of those who may become entitled to benefits; usually refers to an insurance company.

Unfunded Liability (Unfunded Actuarial Liability)—Generally, any amount by which the assets of a pension plan are less than its liabilities. An initial unfunded liability exists when benefits are created in respect of prior service, e.g., and not provided for in current service contributions.

Unit Benefit Formula—Any defined benefit formula providing a benefit credit expressed as a percentage of a member's earnings for each year of service (to be distinguished from *Flat Benefit Formula*).

Unit Credit Actuarial Cost Method—
—A method of computing pension benefits based on certain units, such as percentage of salary and years of service.
—An acceptable actuarial cost method under which the plan's normal cost for a year is the present value of the benefit credited to all participants for service in that year, and the accrued liability is the present value at the plan's inception of the units of benefits credited to participants for service before the plan's inception. This method is also known as the *accrued benefit cost method*.

Utilization—The extent to which a given group uses a specified service in a specific period of time. Usually expressed as the number of services used per year per 100 or per 1,000 persons eligible for the service, but utilization rates may be expressed in other types of ratios.

V

Vesting—The right of an employee, on termination of employment, to part or all of his or her accrued pension; usually requires locking-in of employee's contributions. Vesting is usually in the form of a deferred annuity commencing at retirement age. Vesting is said to be *contingent* or *conditional* if employee has the option of cash withdrawal. *Statutory* vesting occurs when employee meets the age and/or service conditions set out in pension benefits legislation and applies to benefits accrued after a specified date.

Voluntary Additional Contributions—*See* Additional Voluntary Contributions.

W

Waiver of Premium—A provision that under certain conditions a person's insurance will be kept in full force by the insurer without further payment of premiums. It is used most often in the event of permanent and total disability.

Welfare Fund or Plan—When employer and/or employee contributions for medical or hospital care benefits, dental, accident, disability, death, etc., are placed in a trust fund that is administered by a board of trustees.

Wellness Programs—A broad range of employer- or union-sponsored facilities and activities designed to promote safety and good health among employees. The purpose is to increase worker morale and reduce the costs of accidents and ill health such as absenteeism, lower productivity and health care costs. May include physical fitness programs, smoking cessation, health risk appraisals, diet information and weight loss, stress management and high blood pressure screening.

Wind-Up—The termination or discontinuance of a pension plan. The wind-up of a pension plan stops the accrual of benefits and requires a disposal of all plan assets and liabilities.

Y

Year's Maximum Pensionable Earnings (YMPE)—The maximum amount of annual earnings, prior to reduction of the amount of the year's basic exemption, upon which benefits and contributions for purposes of the Canada Pension Plan and the Quebec Pension Plan are based. The YMPE has been subject to yearly adjustments and is targeted, at some future time, to equal the average wage of industrial workers in Canada.

Yield—The rate of return on a fixed income investment if held to maturity. The yield of a fixed income investment is inversely proportional to its price.

Yield Curve—Interest rates available for each maturity from one day out to 30 years.

Index—Subject

Editor's note: Legal cases cited in this book are listed in a separate index following this one.

Q

R

Registered pension plans
administrator, 255
foreign property rule, 255
integrated contribution limit, 256
pension adjustment limits, 255-256
specific registration requirements, 254-255
tax advantages, 253-254
see also Pension adjustment (PA)

Registered retirement savings plans (RRSPs)
contribution limits, 389
defined, 118
design, 387-388
investment of assets, 392, 455
over-contribution allowance, 389
pay-out options, 392
registration, 118, 388-389
tax treatment, 389-390
see also Flexible pension plans, Savings plans

S

Savings plans
plan design, 387-388
see also Deferred profit-sharing plans (DPSPs),
Employee profit-sharing plans (EPSPs),
Registered retirement savings plans (RRSPs)

Shift from defined benefit to employee-directed defined contribution plans
allure of money purchase plans, 364
areas for potential litigation, 364-365
changing retirement market, 363-364
problems with defined benefit plans, 364
see also Communication of information to employees

Single employer pension plans
constituting documents, 215-217
funding and solvency rules, 218-220
legislative environment, 220-221
number of plans, 215
role of collective agreement, 151
statutory requirements, 217-218
see also Multi-employer pension plans

Socially responsible investing
definition, 316
legal commentary, 323-324
legal issue, 316-318
regulatory environment, 317-318
relevant jurisprudence, 318-323

Supplemental Pension Plans Act see Quebec civil law
perspective on pension plan investments and
fiduciary duties

T

Taxation of employee benefits
changes in tax policy, 37-38
exemptions, 37
general tax system pertaining to employee benefits,
xxiv-xxvi
multi-employer trusts as vehicles for delivering
tax-exempt benefits, 37-38
Ontario retail sales tax, 38
Quebec retail sales tax, 38
see also Income Tax Act, Tax status of life and health
insurance benefits, Tax status of pension benefits

Tax status of life and health insurance benefits
counselling services, 167
general taxation principles, 164
group sickness or accident plans, 165
group term life insurance, 167
health and welfare trust funds, 168
medical expense credit, 168
miscellaneous benefits, 167
private health service benefits, 165-166
Quebec regulations, 166
recent trends, 164-165
retail sales and goods and services taxes, 169-170
see also Taxation of employee benefits

Tax status of pension benefits
maximum pension rule for defined benefit plans, 266
retirement savings reform, 253
see also Pension adjustment (PA), Registered
pension plans (RPPs), Taxation of employee
benefits

Training trust funds (TTFs)
benefits provided, 428
communication, 431
concept, 427
establishing and administering, 427-428
funding, 428-429
goods and services tax (GST), 429-431
income tax considerations, 429
investment of plan assets, 429, 455
Retirement savings reform, 253

Trustee duties and responsibilities
checklist, xxxiii
conduct at trustee meetings, xxxii
explained, xxix-xxxii
legal aspects of trustee attendance at educational
programs, 42-46
liability for breach of trust, xxxii, 45-46
minimizing expenses, xxxii
reports trustees should obtain, xxxiii-xxxiv
see also Delinquencies in multi-employer plans,
Benefit trust administration, Fiduciary duties

Trustee fiduciary liability insurance
Canadian market, 58
coverage, 58-60
need for, 57
right to purchase, 57-58

U

Unemployment insurance *see* Employment insurance (EI)
Unions
role in employee benefits, 3

V

Vacation pay trust funds
employment insurance issues, 436-437
investment of plan assets, 455
regulation of, 435-436
structure, 434-435
taxation, 436

W

Workers' compensation
administration, 93
comprehensive scheme of prescribed benefits, 95
coverage, 93-94
death and survivor benefits, 97-99, 116
definition of *employee,* 95
definition of *employer,* 94-95
description of program, 115
history, 92-93
maximum earnings and taxation of benefits, 95
permanent partial disability, 96
premiums/funding, 93-94
rehabilitative services/return to work, 99-100
special benefits for the handicapped, 100-101
temporary total disability benefits, 95-96
waiting periods, 97

Index—Legal Cases

Editor's note: For readers' convenience, legal cases referred to in this book are indexed separately. Parentheses around a number in an entry indicate an endnote reference; e.g., 161(4) refers to endnote 4 on page 161.

C

D

J

Re James et al. v. Town of Richmond Hill, 162(33), 185-186, 188(40, 41, 42)
John M. Troup Limited v. Royal Bank of Canada, 477(6)

K

Katsaros v. Cody, 30(50), 280, 283(39, 40, 41)
Keech v. Sandford, 24, 29(8)
Keeprite, 163(80)
Re Kenroc Building Materials, 469(8)

L

Labotts Ontario Breweries Ltd., 152, 162(6)
Labourers' International Union of North America, Local 506 v. Ontario, 431(2, 3, 4)
Lac Minerals Ltd. v. International Corona Resources Ltd., 30(34, 41)
Laessoe v. Air Canada, 486(31)
Laflamme v. Prudential-Bache Commodities Canada Ltd., 282(29), 376-377, 378(23, 24, 25, 26, 27, 28)
La Have Equipment Ltd. v. Nova Scotia (Supt. of Pensions), 225, 233(7)
Laskin v. Bache and Company, 29(3)
Law v. Canada (Minister of Employment and Immigration), 80, 82(16), 486(5, 37)
Learoyd v. Whiteley, 29(11), 47(14), 357, 377(2), 378(20)
Lear Siegler Industries Ltd. v. Canada Trust Co., 226, 233(12, 13)
Le Comite regional des usagers des transports en common de Quebec v. Quebec Urban Community Transit Commission, 307(94)
Lehune v. Kelowna (City), 73(24)
Lemoine v. Lemoine, 333, 339(52, 53)
Lennox Industries v. The Queen, 47(28)
Leshner v. Ontario, 485, 486(29)
Le Syndicat national des Salaries des outils Simonds v. Eljer Manufacturing Canada Inc., 233(9)
Lever Pond's, 162(21)
Libbey St. Clair Inc., 162(27)
Liberati v. Canada (Employment and Immigration Commission), 437(19)
Linsley v. Kirstiuk, 362(22)
Linton v. Linton, 333, 339(47, 48)
Lufkin Rule Co. of Canada Ltd., 162(21)

M

MacMillan v. MacMillan, 339(33)
Madott v. Chrysler Canada, 73(18), 217, 221(6)
Mailot v. Mailot, 332, 339(39, 40)

Manitoba Health Organizations Inc. v. Healthcare Employers Pension Plan—Manitoba (Trustees of), 251(43)
Manuga v. Prudential Assurance Co. Ltd., 73(21)
Marc Jay Investments Inc. v. Levy, 306(76, 77, 78)
Maritime Life Assurance Co. v. Chateau Gardens (Hanover) Inc. et al., 472, 477(9)
Marsham v. Marsham, 339(34)
Martin v. The City of Edinburgh District Council, 321, 326(15, 16)
Maurer v. McMaster University, 228, 233(25), 355(5)
Maxmilian v. M. Rash & Co., 378(18)
Maxwell v. MLG Ventures Ltd., 302, 307(107)
Maynard v. Ontario (Superintendent of Pensions), 74(28), 214(68)
McGann v. H. & H. Music Company, 187, 188(50, 51)
McKnight v. Southern Life Insurance Company, 73(16)
McLaughlin v. Falconbridge Ltd., 36(10)
McNeese v. Health Plan Marketing Inc., 30(52)
Metropolitan Toronto Pension Plan v. Aetna Life Assurance Co. of Canada, 30(19, 20), 278-279, 372, 377(7), 385(9)
Metropolitan Toronto Police Services Board v. Ontario Municipal Employees Retirement Board, 30(24)
Mettoy Pension Trustees Limited v. Idwal Evans et al., 227, 233(20)
Meyer v. Allstate Insurance, 163(102)
Meyer v. M. N. R., 165, 170(3)
Mississauga Transit, 158, 163(75)
Molson's Brewery, 161(4)
Monsanto v. Superintendent of Pensions, 212, 229, 233(30), 241(2, 3)
Morin, 426(10)
Mozley v. Alston, 306(67)
M. v. H., 78, 82(10), 338, 339(91, 92), 484, 486(22)

N

Nantais v. Nantais, 333, 339(49)
Re National Building Maintenance, 299, 300, 306(82), 307(86)
National Trustees Co. of Australasia v. General Finance Co. of Australasia, 358
Newton v. Van Otterloo, 359-360, 362(15)
Nichols v. Trustees of Asbestos Workers Pension Plan, 30(51)
Noren v. Tarsands Machine and Welding Company, 465, 469(11, 27)
North Central Plywoods, 153, 162(25, 26)
Nowegijick, 423, 426(5)

O

P

Q

R

S